D1517266

陈向东 / 编著

GMAT®

逻辑推理

分类思维训练及试题解析

浙江教育出版社·杭州

图书在版编目(CIP)数据

GMAT逻辑推理：分类思维训练及试题解析 / 陈向东
编著. 一杭州：浙江教育出版社，2015.10（2016.10重印）
ISBN 978-7-5536-3077-9

Ⅰ.①G… Ⅱ.①陈… Ⅲ.①逻辑推理—研究生—入
学考试—自学参考资料 Ⅳ.①B812

中国版本图书馆CIP数据核字（2015）第123162号

GMAT 逻辑推理：分类思维训练及试题解析
GMAT LUOJI TUILI: FENLEI SIWEI XUNLIAN JI SHITI JIEXI

编　　著	陈向东
责任编辑	孔令宇
美术编辑	韩　波
封面设计	大愚设计
责任校对	刘文芳
责任印务	时小娟

出版发行	浙江教育出版社
	（杭州市天目山路40号　　邮编：310013）
印　　刷	三河市龙大印装有限公司
开　　本	880mm×1230mm　1/16
成品尺寸	210mm×275mm
印　　张	33.25
字　　数	812 000
版　　次	2015年10月第1版
印　　次	2016年10月第2次印刷
标准书号	ISBN 978-7-5536-3077-9
定　　价	59.00元
联系电话	0571 - 85170300 - 80928
电子邮箱	dywh@xdf.cn
网　　址	www.zjeph.com

前　言

《GRE GMAT LSAT逻辑推理》是我编著的第一本书，但出乎意料的是，这本书一经出版不仅受到GMAT考生的热捧，一印再印，GMAT考生几乎人手一册，而且中国MBA考试试题以及市面上许多逻辑应试书籍大量"照搬"、"引用"或者"改编"这本书的内容，报考清华大学、北京大学、长江商学院等MBA的考生中，相当多的朋友凭借这本书取得了逻辑部分考试的高分。这本书的盗版据推测至少有5万之多。2005年中秋节，正在哈佛商学院学习的我应邀参加了哈佛大学肯尼迪政府学院中国学生会组织的中秋节联欢会。正在肯尼迪政府学院学习的中国60余名高官也出席了由美国华商会赞助的这次联欢会，并且谈话中经常不经意地论及他们所学的哈佛案例或者正在迅猛崛起的中国的改革。我越发感觉到在美国学习的中国学生或旅美的炎黄子孙的自信以及作为中国人的自豪与骄傲。

由于ETS在投资优先决策、战略导向以及实施能力等方面不再能够很好地满足GMAC（Graduate Management Admission Council）的要求，GMAC决定：自2006年1月1日起，ACT公司将替代ETS接管GMAT考试的研发工作，而由Pearson VUE负责该考试的实施。GMAT考试贯彻其一向的切实和可靠的风格，由Pearson VUE提供的GMAT成绩可以与由ETS提供的成绩进行直接比较，GMAT成绩在五年之内仍旧有效。因此，尽管GMAT考试的承包商发生了变化，但其难度、可信度在五年之内应具有可比性，其考试内核与实质不应该会有较大的变化。

做点事情的责任感促使我"忙中偷闲"来修改本书。本次修订我将书名改为《GMAT逻辑推理——分类思维训练及试题解析》，采纳了许多读者来信中的建议，整合了过去几年GMAT考试的考点和精华，对现在GMAT机考中黑体句子作用题做了重点讲解。同时，我参考了大量的相关文献与著作，对未来几年GMAT的发展趋势做出了预测。由于时间与本人水平所限，恳请广大读者能多提宝贵意见，意见可发送邮件至：better365@gmail.com。

在全球化的竞争中，商学院教育全球化的竞争正在影响着整个世界。而竞争的微观表现主要有最优质学生的竞争、最资深教授的竞争、最无边界制度创新设计的竞争等。哈佛商学院2005财政年度的收入达到了3.3亿美元，捐助资金达到了21亿美元，科研经费达到了7700万美元，而毫无疑问，全球现在是互相联结的，已经不存在"纵容"我们可以苟安一隅的纯粹孤岛。在当今的全球竞逐与机会中，我们如何能够占据一席之地？我相信大家准备GMAT考试并去追逐自己的梦想本身就是对这个问题最好的回答和诠释。世界上最稀缺的可能是时间。阅读一本书的时间成本要远远大于购买一本书的成本。我真心希望这本书能够帮助你节省稀缺的时间，增强你真正的自信，取得你的伟大成功！

陈向东

第一版前言

申请美国大学研究生院所要求的三大标准化考试——GRE、GMAT和LSAT中，很重要的一部分就是逻辑推理题，而逻辑推理题历来是中国考生最头痛的部分，因为它不仅仅考查考生的阅读能力，而且还考查考生进行论证、评价论述以及形成或评价行动方案的能力，因此正确解题有时需要反复推敲，甚至得反复重读段落。本书作为国内目前第一本全面讲解GRE、GMAT和LSAT逻辑推理题的书，写作动力主要源于以下几个事实：

■ GMAT和GRE改为计算机化考试之后，逻辑推理题难度有所增加，其重要性也有所提高。如GRE机考后，一般每个section的前5道题决定考试难度，第1道题一般为中等难度的题目，后面每一道题的难度将依赖于前一道题。而逻辑section的前2~3道题一般为逻辑推理题，逻辑推理题的解题正确与否直接影响到后面将会遇到的题目的难度，并且逻辑section在机考现场最易影响整个GRE考试的心理状态。逻辑推理题在LSAT中的重要地位更是不言而喻，总共四个section中有两个section都是逻辑推理题。

■ 在GMAT考试中，逻辑推理题作为Critical Reasoning出现，在GRE与LSAT中，作为Logical Reasoning出现。尽管这三类考试的逻辑部分在出题背景、问题目的类型及时间和阅读要求方面有些差异，但整个逻辑推理的思维却无任何差异。

■ 很多考完GRE、GMAT或LSAT的考生都有这样的体会：逻辑推理题的出题思路比较固定，考题的局限性很强，因此按照问题目的类型的不同进行分类思维训练，不仅能把握一类题的命题规律，而且能更快更好地培养解答逻辑推理题的感觉，从而节省我们宝贵的时间。

成就本书的几个原因决定了本书的基本内容。本书具有以下几个特点：

■ **精选试题**：本书精选逻辑推理重点题难题。

■ **中文翻译**：大多中国考生最终还是亏在阅读，要么读不懂，要么误读。因此本书对所有题目全部附上中文参考译文，以有助考生正确分析、了解段落的语法结构，从而准确深刻地理解段落以从根本上提高推理和解题能力，节省考生查阅字典及其他工具书的宝贵时间。

■ **分类讲解**：本书使用分类思维训练的方法，依据问题目的的不同类型及中国考生的思维特点，将逻辑推理题分为假设、支持、反对、评价、归纳、解释和逻辑应用与技法七大类，进行分类讲解，并对书中试题给予解析，必将激发考生的逻辑推理能力，为夺得逻辑高分打下坚实的基础。

■ **趋势预测**：不仅对逻辑推理题的变化趋势给出分析，而且对机考之后才出现的划线句子考题给予讲解。

尽管本书从构思、选题到最终成书历时一年多，几易其稿，但由于笔者才疏学浅，恐仍有纰漏之处，尚祈同行和读者不吝指正。如果您对本书有什么好的建议，可发E-mail至我的信箱：xiangdongbooks@sina.com

陈向东

使 用 说 明

1. 逻辑部分决定考试心理状态，而阅读是一切逻辑推理题成功解题的基础，也是考试中决定心理状态的关键因素。本书的每道逻辑推理题均给出中文翻译，并且在中文翻译的正确答案下加上下划线，以方便读者查对答案，试题的解析部分放在练习的后面，请读者在解完题后再参阅解析部分。

2. 第二篇各章试题精练部分最好限时训练，建议每次做20道逻辑推理题，可控制在32分钟完成。请读者在平常训练时注重限时训练，唯有此才能真正有效、迅速地培养考试现场的感觉，从而迅速找到解题方向。阅读本书第三篇时更要强调时间意识，并且GMAT考生的最佳使用时间为考试前30天左右。还要强调的是：The intuition in deciding which answer is right and the pace of solving Logical or Critical Reasoning problems are very important and essential for our success，而intuition 与 pace的培养要靠平时科学、系统的限时训练。

3. 读者应把阅读本书的重点放在把握每类题型的解题思路上，而不仅仅是哪一个选项为正确答案，同时应仔细体会其他四个选项为什么不对。在参阅每题的翻译及解析之前，最好自己限时解题，再对照翻译及解析体会自己的思维及题目的推理特点。因限于篇幅，本书略去部分试题解析，请读者自己去体会其解题思路。读者在阅读完每章之后，应该自己再总结一下，加深理解同类逻辑推理题的推理特点，掌握每一类题的命题规律及解题方略，以达到去芜存菁，举一反三，触类旁通而准确解题的效果。

目　　录

第　一　篇
总　论

第　一　章

GMAT、GRE与LSAT逻辑推理题比较

　　申请美国大学研究生院所要求的三大标准化考试——GRE、GMAT和LSAT中，很重要的一部分就是逻辑推理。在GRE与LSAT考试中，逻辑推理作为Logical Reasoning出现；在GMAT考试中，作为Critical Reasoning出现，尽管这三类考试的逻辑部分在出题背景、问题目的类型及阅读要求方面有些差异，但整个逻辑推理的思维却无任何差异。尽管自2002年10月开始，美国教育考试服务中心（Educational Testing Service, ETS）将原GRE考试中包含逻辑推理（Logical Reasoning）的Analytical Section取消，替换为分析性写作（Analytical Writing），但GRE曾经考查的逻辑推理（Logical Reasoning）题目却具有更加重要的参考价值。考生关注的三类考试的逻辑问题（这里，GRE考试的结构与内容为2002年10月之前的数据）分布情况如下表所示：

Summary of Logic Question Distributions

	Numbers of Logic Sections	Minutes Per Section	Questions Per Section	Arrangement of Questions
GRE Computer Adaptive Test	1	60	35	21-25 Analytical Reasoning; 10-14 Logical Reasoning
LAST	3	35	24–26	One section Analytical Reasoning; two sections Logical Reasoning
GMAT Computer Adaptive Test	1 (Part of combined verbal score)	75	41	Approximately 14 Critical Reasoning Questions (same as Logical Reasoning) interspersed with other verbal questions

　　下面来看三道分别来自于GRE、GMAT与LSAT的逻辑推理题：

GRE SAMPLE

A recent study of an insurance company's underwriters indicated that those who worked in pleasant physical surroundings were 25 percent more productive than their peers in unpleasant physical surroundings. Objective criteria for

译文： 最近对一家保险公司的保险商的一项研究表明，处于令人舒适的工作环境中的雇员比处于不大舒适的工作环境中的同事的效率要高25%。评价工作业绩的

evaluating job performance included caseload and complexity of cases. This shows that improving workers' environments increases those workers' productivity.

Which of the following, if true, most seriously weakens the conclusion above?

(A) On average, less-productive employees spend no fewer hours per day at their workstations than do their more-productive peers.

(B) Unpleasant surroundings give employees less motivation to work hard than more pleasant surroundings do.

(C) The more-productive employees are generally rewarded with pleasant office space.

(D) More-productive employees do not work any more hours than their less-productive peers.

(E) Peer pressure discourages employees in crowded, unpleasant surroundings from making phone calls to their own family members during work time.

客观标准包括工作量与案例的复杂程度。这表明，改善工人的工作环境能够提高他们的效率。

以下哪一项，如果正确，最能削弱以上结论？

(A) 平均而言，生产效率低的雇员并不比他们工作效率高的同事在工作场所花费的时间少。

(B) 令人不适的工作环境，相对于令人舒适的工作环境来说，更不能激励雇员卖力工作。

(C) 效率较高的雇员通常被回报以令人舒适的工作环境。

(D) 效率较高的雇员并不比效率较低的同事工作时间长。

(E) 同行的压力使得在拥挤、令人不适的环境里工作的雇员不能在工作时间给家人打电话。

解析： 段落推理是由一项研究的结果："处于令人舒适的工作环境中的雇员比处于不大舒适的工作环境中的同事的效率要高25%"，就得出结论："改善工人的工作环境能提高他们的效率"。但此研究结果中涉及的效率高与工作环境好二者之间谁导致谁并不知道，就由此研究得出结论说"工作环境好导致效率高"。本题是典型的Weaken，重点在于Weaken结论，那么选项(C)表明，效率高导致了工作环境好，与推理的结论明显冲突。因此(C)正确。(A)、(D)讲述的是效率低的雇员与效率高的雇员的相同点，不可能起到Weaken作用；(B)起到部分支持作用；(E)涉及新概念making phone calls，因此为无关选项。

GMAT SAMPLE

A researcher discovered that people who have low levels of immune-system activity tend to score much lower on tests of mental health than do people with normal or high immune-system activity. The researcher concluded from this experiment that the immune system protects against mental illness as well as against physical disease.

The researcher's conclusion would be most seriously weakened if it were true that

(A) there was a one-year delay between the completion of a pilot study for the experiment and the initiation of the experiment itself.

(B) people's levels of immune-system activity are not affected by their use of medications.

(C) a few people with high immune-system activity had scores on the test of mental health that were similar to the scores of people who had normal immune-system activity.

译文： 一个研究人员发现免疫系统活性水平较低的人在心理健康测试中得到的分数比免疫系统活性水平正常或较高的人低。该研究人员从这个试验中得出结论，免疫系统既能抵御肉体上的疾病也能抵御心理疾病。

以下哪个如果正确，研究人员的结论将得到最有力的削弱？

(A) 在针对试验的试验性研究的完成与开始试验本身之间有一年的间隔时间。

(B) 人们的免疫系统活性水平没有受到他们服用的药物的影响。

(C) 免疫系统活性高的一些人在心理测试方面的得分与免疫系统活性正常的人的得分相似。

(D) 与免疫系统活性正常或高的人相比，免疫系统活性低的人更易得过滤性毒

(D) people who have low immune-system activity tend to contract more viral infections than do people with normal or high immune-system activity.

(E) high levels of stress first cause mental illness and then cause decreased immune-system activity in normal individuals.

菌引起的感染。

(E) 高度压力首先导致心理疾病，然后导致正常人的免疫系统活性的降低。

解析： 本题为反对题型。段落推理为：该研究人员从免疫系统活性水平低与心理健康的低分数的联系中得出结论，免疫系统活性实际上可以抑制心理疾病。很明显，在我们只知道免疫系统活性水平低与心理健康测试得分低这两类事情存在，并不知道是前者导致后者，还是后者导致前者，就得出结论说免疫系统活性实际上可以抑制心理疾病时，就可能会犯错误。如果高度压力导致心理疾病进而导致免疫系统活性降低，正如(E)所说，则会把上段落推理因果倒置，因此，削弱了上面研究人员的结论。所以(E)正确。(A)中的"间隔时间"与上述结论无关；(B)对上面推理也起不到作用；(C)说的是共同点，因此不可能削弱上面结论；(D)与"心理健康测试"无关。

LSAT SAMPLE

Doctors in Britain have long suspected that patients who wear tinted eyeglasses are abnormally prone to depression and hypochondria. Psychological tests given there to hospital patients admitted for physical complaints like heart pain and digestive distress confirmed such a relationship. Perhaps people whose relationship to the world is psychologically painful choose such glasses to reduce visual stimulation, which is perceived as irritating. At any rate, it can be concluded that when such glasses are worn, it is because the wearer has a tendency to be depressed or hypochondriacal.

The argument assumes which one of the following?

(A) Depression is not caused in some cases by an organic condition of the body.

(B) Wearers do not think of the tinted glasses as a means of distancing themselves from other people.

(C) Depression can have many causes, including actual conditions about which it is reasonable for anyone to be depressed.

(D) For hypochondriacs wearing tinted glasses, the glasses serve as a visual signal to others that the wearer's health is delicate.

(E) The tinted glasses do not dim light to the eye enough to depress the wearer's mood substantially.

译文： 长时间以来，英国的医生认为戴墨镜的病人更易于消沉并患上忧郁症。对因诸如心脏疼痛和消化不良等身体不适而住院的病人进行的心理测试证实了这一联系。或许觉得周围的一切使得心理上痛苦的人选择这样的墨镜去减少视觉刺激，视觉刺激被认为是令人易发怒的。不管怎么说，人们可以得出结论，如果人们戴上这样的墨镜，这是因为戴墨镜者有消沉或患有忧郁症的倾向。

上述论述做了下面哪一个假设？

(A) 消沉在某些情况下不是由身体的有机条件造成的。

(B) 戴墨镜者认为墨镜不是一种把自己与别人疏远开来的方法。

(C) 消沉有很多原因，包括任何人消沉都合乎情理的真实条件。

(D) 对于戴墨镜的忧郁症患者来说，眼镜可以作为让别人看来戴镜者的健康不佳的视觉信号。

(E) 墨镜没有把光线变得如此暗淡以致使戴镜者的心情急剧消沉。

解析： 本题为假设，重点看前提与结论。因此读题重点放在段落最后一句。通过读段落最后一句，我们发现，存在现象A_1——戴墨镜与现象A_2——这些戴墨镜者易压抑消沉，我们并不知道是A_1导致A_2，还是A_2导致A_1，段落就得出结论说是A_2导致A_1，那么必然要基于的假设是A_1没有导致A_2。这样，(E)就

3

切中要害。其他选项中(A)最易误选，但(A)只能是支持选项，我们可以在(A)中加入not来判定。当(A)中加入not后，只表明消沉在某些情况下是由身体的有机条件决定的，而我们只要得知，消沉在某些情况下不是由身体状况决定的，上面推理结论仍然可以正确，因此(A)支持了上面结论。(B)与"压抑消沉"无关；(C)只是一个解释性说明；(D)无论离前提还是离结论都较远。

通过对上面三道GRE、GMAT、LSAT逻辑推理题的分析，我们可以看出这三种考试在逻辑推理部分的考查类型、问题目的类型、答案选择和思维模式都大致相同。有所不同的是，这三类考试逻辑部分题量与时间要求不大相同。GRE机考约11～14道逻辑推理题，每题平均2分钟；GMAT机考约14道，每题平均1分40秒；而LSAT每个Section 24～26道题，35分钟完成，每题平均不到1分半钟。LSAT的阅读量明显大于笔试的GRE与GMAT，但GRE、GMAT机考之后逻辑推理题有所变长，其中有2～3道题与LSAT相当。这也是为什么笔者精选GRE、GMAT、LSAT考题以供想在逻辑推理题上有所提高的读者使用的初衷。

第 二 章

逻辑推理题考查内容及问题目的类型

逻辑推理题主要考查以下推理能力：1）进行论证的能力；2）评价论述的能力；3）形成或评价行动方案的能力。按照美国ETS命题人员的说法，逻辑推理题主要考查考生在以下三个方面能否进行有效推理的能力。

一、论点构建（Argument construction）

这一方面的问题主要让你去识别或找到：

（一）论述的基本结构（The basic structure of an argument）

（二）正确得到的结论（Properly drawn conclusion）

（三）基于的假设（Underlying assumption）

（四）被强有力支持的解释性假说（Well-supported explanatory hypotheses）

（五）结构上相似的论点的平行结构（Parallels between structurally similar arguments）

二、论点评价（Argument evaluation）

这一方面的问题主要让你在分析既定的论点基础之上去识别：

（一）加强或削弱既定论点的因素（Factors that would strengthen, or weaken, the given argument）

（二）在进行论述时所犯的推理错误（Reasoning errors committed in making that argument）

（三）进行论述所使用的方法（The method by which the argument proceeds）

三、形成并且评价行动方案（Formulating and evaluating a plan of action）

这方面的问题主要让你去识别：

（一）不同行动方案的相对合适性、有效性或效率（The relative appropriateness, effectiveness, or efficiency of different plans of action）

（二）加强或削弱拟议行动方案成功可能的因素（Factors that would strengthen, or weaken, the prospects of success for a proposed plan of action）

（三）拟议行动计划所基于的假设（Assumptions underlying a proposed plan of action）

根据逻辑推理题的考查内容，我们认为熟悉逻辑推理的主要题型对你大有裨益，下面是我们在考试中将遇到的十一类逻辑推理题。

（一）假设（Assumption）：

这类考题主要考查我们识别根据什么前提得出论点的能力，这类题目往往用以下方式：

The conclusion above depends on which of the following assumptions?

The author of the passage above makes which of the following assumptions?

The author of the passage above presupposes that...

The statement above assumes which of the following?

（二）支持（Support）：

这类考题主要考查我们识别一种附加事实信息支持论点的能力，这类题往往用如下措词：

Which of the following, if true, would constitute the strongest evidence in support of the claim made above?

Which of the following, if true, does NOT support the claim that...

（三）反对（Weaken）：

这类考题主要考查我们识别一种附加事实信息反对论点的能力，这类题主要用以下措词：

Which of the following, if true, would additionally weaken the traditional opinion that...

The persuasiveness of the claim made above is most weakened by...

（四）评价（Evaluation）：

这类考题主要考查我们评价论点的能力，这类题往往用以下方式：

Which of the following would be most important to know in evaluating the accuracy of the argument above?

Knowledge of which of the following would be LEAST useful in evaluating the claims made in the passage above?

（五）推断（Inference）：

这类考题主要考查我们通过作者明确的表述看出其含义的能力，这类题可能用如下措词：

It can be inferred from the passage above that the author believes that...

Which of the following is implied by the passage above?

From the information above, which of the following can be most reasonably inferred about...

（六）结论（Conclusion）：

这类考题主要考查我们根据文章中的论据能提出什么合乎逻辑的主张的能力，这类题往往用这些方式：

If the statements above are true, which of the following conclusions can be properly drawn?

Choose the most logical completion for the following paragraph.

Which of the following would provide the most logical conclusion for the preceding paragraph?

The statements in the passage, if true, best support which of the following conclusions?

（七）中心思想：

这类题主要考查我们理解文章要点的能力，这类题往往用如下措词：

The statement cited above conveys which of the following propositions?

The passage above emphasizes which of the following points?

The author in the passage above argues that...

Which of the following expresses the point the author of the passage above makes?

（八）解释（Explain）：

这类考题主要考查我们解释某个现象、结果或缓解某种矛盾的能力，这类题的问法如下：

Which of the following hypotheses, if true, would help resolve the apparent paradox introduced above?

If all of the statements above are correct, an explanation of their apparent contradiction is provided by...

Which of the following, if true, provides the most logical completion of the passage below?

（九）应用：

这类考题主要考查我们将一个论点的指导性原则用于另一论点的能力，这类题可能用如下措词：

Which of the following parallels the method of argumentation above?

The argument above is most like which of the following?

Which of the following suffers from a flaw that, in its logical aspects, is most like the difficulty described above?

Which of the following identifies a flaw in the speaker's reasoning?

（十）技法：

这类考题主要考查我们识别论点的结构方法或技法的能力，这类题可能用如下措词：

The author's point is made primarily by...

The labor negotiator minimizes his differences with management by...

The passage above criticizes the authorities by...

（十一）划线句子作用：

这类考题主要考查我们论点构建中的某句话对结论或前提是否起作用或起什么作用的能力。

逻辑推理考题由段落（图表）、问题、五个选项构成，做题思维的第一重点是明晰问题目的。根据上面所列出的问题目的类型，结合GRE、GMAT和LSAT中各类问法的考查频率，针对中国考生的思维特点，作者将考题分为**假设、支持、反对、评价、归纳（包括推断、结论、中心思想等）、解释、逻辑应用与技法（包括Flaw、应用、技法、划线句子作用等）七大类**。当然，我们读完本书后将会发现，在很多情况下，假设、支持、反对与评价都是让你从下面的五个选项中选择一个答案，放到上面的段落中，以达到问题目的的要求。这四类考题在解题思维方法上的共性都是"自下而上"，并且段落所面临的推理只是有待评价的推理；有时，假设题的解题思路与推断题的解题思路完全一样；有时，完成段落题有两个答案方向，一种答案方向是对段落推理的解释（可归入解释题型），另一种答案方向是从段落推理中得出的结论（可归入归纳题型）。因此，我们不应仅仅拘泥于上述七种分类，在对待问题目的的类型上，"运用之妙，存乎一心"，切不可胶柱鼓瑟，生硬地对号入座，这一点会在本书后面详细论述。

第 三 章

逻辑推理题四大出题原则及三大解题步骤

一、四大出题原则

（一）不需专业背景知识原则

逻辑推理题都是基于一个段落（或图表），所涉及的内容像阅读理解的文章一样，涉及研究生在学术研究、日常研读或日常生活中阅读的材料，这些材料可以涉及任何主题——艺术、社会学、历史、哲学、政府、体育、广告等等。虽然涉及内容包罗万象，读懂文章、回答问题，无需任何学科、专业的特定知识，并且不能借助自己熟悉的专业知识来考察，而应着重从逻辑推理的角度来思维。尽管逻辑应用与技法类型的考题有些涉及逻辑学的部分专用术语，但并不需专门的逻辑学专业的知识，否则将违反ETS许诺的公平性原则：对任何一个考生都是公平的。当然，作为一名大学生，一些common sense 必不可少，如供求规律、数学里的比例、交集等。我的建议是：不要因你所读到的问题的主题是你不熟悉的而感到畏惧。即使主题是你从未读到的或听到的，你回答问题所需的一切信息均已包容在段落之中。

（二）Which of the following 原则

逻辑推理题的大多数问题有which of the following，要求你根据段落里所给信息及逻辑推理，从下面五个选项中选出一个选项，从而实现问题目的。有时，或许这个选项并不是专业知识背景下或常识中的最佳选项，但只要是五个选项中最能实现问题目的的选项就可以了。逻辑推理题中一般不会出现两个或两个以上选项同时实现问题目的，让考生挑选一个最好的选项。实际上，在问题目的中的most在绝大多数情况下无意义，也就是说，五个选项中，只有一个对，其他四个必然不对。不过，在有些情况下，问题目的中的best有意义。请认真体会以下两个例子：

The skulls and pelvic bones of some species of dinosaur share characteristics with the skulls and pelvic bones of all modern birds. Even though not all dinosaurs have these characteristics, there are scientists who claim that all animals that do have these characteristics are dinosaurs.

If the statements above and the claim of the scientists are true, which of the following must also be true?

(A) Birds share more characteristics with dinosaurs than they do with other animals.

(B) Some ancient dinosaurs were indistinguishable from modern birds.

(C) All animals whose skulls share the characteristics of those of modern birds also have pelvic bones that are similar to those of modern birds.

(D) Modern birds are dinosaurs.

(E) All dinosaurs are birds.

译文：一些恐龙的头盖骨和骨盆骨与所有现代鸟类的头盖骨和骨盆骨有许多相同特征。虽然不是所有的恐龙都有这些特征，但一些科学家声称，所有具有这些特征的动物都是恐龙。

如果上面的陈述和科学家的声明都是正确的，下列哪一项也一定正确？

(A) 鸟类与恐龙的相似之处要多于鸟类与其他动物的相似之处。

(B) 一些古代恐龙与现代鸟类是没有区别的。

(C) 所有动物，如果它们的头盖骨和现代鸟类的头盖骨具有相同特征，那么它们的骨盆骨也一定和现代鸟类的骨盆骨具有相同特征。

(D) 现代鸟类是恐龙。

(E) 所有的恐龙都是鸟类。

解析：科学家根据陈述："一些恐龙的头盖骨与骨盆骨与所有现代鸟类的头盖骨和骨盆骨有许多相同特征"，就得出结论："所有具有这些特征的动物是恐龙"。根据逻辑推理，我们发现(D)正确。显然，若根据常识，(D)必错无疑，但就逻辑推理而言，归纳的段落所面临的推理是必定成立的推理，所以(D)可从上面段落中推出来且与上面段落吻合，所以(D)正确。(A)做了一个无关比较，无关比较必然不对，且"the animals"是新概念；(B)中的"indistinguishable"不可能从上面段落中得到；(C)中的"all animals"把讨论范围扩大，犯了递推的错误；(E)中的all明显也是把段落中的"some"范围扩大化，因此也必然不对。

The ice on the front windshield of the car had formed when moisture condensed during the night. The ice melted quickly after the car was warmed up the next morning because the defrosting vent, which blows only on the front windshield, was turned on full force.

Which of the following, if true, most seriously jeopardizes the validity of the explanation for the speed with which the ice melted?

(A) The side windows had no ice condensation on them.

(B) Even though no attempt was made to defrost the back window, the ice there melted at the same rate as did the ice on the front windshield.

(C) The speed at which ice on a window melts increases as the temperature of the air blown on the window increases.

(D) The warm air from the defrosting vent for the front windshield cools rapidly as it dissipates throughout the rest of the car.

(E) The defrosting vent operates efficiently even when the heater, which blows warm air toward the feet or faces of the driver and passengers, is on.

译文：水汽会在夜晚凝结，在汽车的前挡风玻璃上形成冰。第二天早上汽车逐渐发动起来以后，因为除霜口调到最大，而除霜口只吹向前挡风玻璃，因此（在前挡风玻璃上的）冰很快就融化了。

以下哪一选项，如果是正确的，最严重地威胁到这种关于冰融化速度的解释？

(A) 两边的玻璃没有冰凝结在上面。

(B) 尽管没有采取任何措施对后窗进行解冻，但那儿的冰同前挡风玻璃上的冰的融化速度一样快。

(C) 冰在一块窗上融化的速度随着吹向这块窗的空气温度的升高而加快。

(D) 从除霜口吹向前挡风玻璃的热空气，当它扩散到汽车内其他部分时迅速地冷却。

(E) 即使当把热空气吹向司机和乘客的脚和脸部的暖气打开时，除霜口仍可以很有效率地工作。

解析：挡风玻璃上的冰融化的速度取决于从除霜口全力吹向前挡风玻璃的空气。如果如(B)所说，没有采取措施对后窗进行解冻，而后窗的冰同前挡风玻璃上的冰融化得一样快，那么就削弱了该解释，因此，(B)是正确答案。在没有其他信息的条件下，(A)中所提到的在边窗上没有冰的凝结同该解释的有效性无关；选项(C)可以支持该解释，因为从解冻风口吹出的空气是热的；(D)和(E)都不能提出一个理由去怀疑是从风口吹出的空气导致了冰的融化，因此都没有威胁到该解释的有效性。从这个例子我们可以看出，五个选项中只有(B)可以实现问题目的，而其他四个选项都不可能实现问题的目的，即只有一个选项是正确的。

（三）if true原则

if true在许多考题中出现，紧接在Which of the following之后，有时表述为if practicable, if accepted, if feasible, if correct, if established等。这使得选项在即使违反常识或专业知识的情况下，我们也不能质疑其正确性。应牢记的是：在五个选项内容本身无可质疑的情况下，通过考察推理能否成立，有无缺陷，去实现问题目的。段落或选项中所表述的信息、观点或事实是否正确并不是我们所关注的问题。

Pandas are rapidly disappearing from the wild. Therefore, in order to preserve the species, existing pandas should be captured and placed in zoos around the world.

Which of the following statements, if true, casts most doubt on the conclusion drawn above?

(A) When in captivity, pandas typically produce more young than they do in their native habitat.

(B) Newborn pandas in zoos are not likely to die from infectious diseases, whereas newborn pandas in the wild are likely to die from these diseases.

(C) Sufficient quantities of bamboo, the panda's only food, cannot be made available outside the panda's native habitat.

(D) Many zoos are eager to increase their stock of rare and exotic animals, but there are not enough pandas for all the zoos that want one.

(E) Pandas in zoos have as many offspring that survive to adulthood as do pandas in the wild.

译文：野生大熊猫正在迅速减少。因此，为了保护该物种，应把现存熊猫捕捉起来并放到世界各地的动物园里去。

下面哪个，如果正确，对上述结论提出了最严重的质疑？

(A) 大熊猫在关起来时通常会比在天生栖身地时生下更多的小熊猫。

(B) 在动物园中刚生下来的熊猫不容易死于传染病，但是野生的熊猫很可能死于这些疾病。

(C) 在熊猫的栖息地以外，很难弄到足够数量的竹子，这是熊猫唯一的食物。

(D) 许多动物园急于增加收藏稀有的珍奇的动物，但是大熊猫的数量不够所有想得到一只的动物园分配。

(E) 动物园里的大熊猫和野生的大熊猫后代中能够活到成年的熊猫的数量相当。

解析：本题推理为达到一个目的而提出一种解决方法，即为了保护熊猫，应把他们放到动物园里。反对大多反对A，即方法A不可行或无意义。(A)、(B)起到支持作用；(D)动物园的希望与为了保护熊猫而提出的方法无关；(E)无关选项，虽然动物园里与野生环境中的熊猫有相同数量的后代，但仅仅由数量并不能说明问题。例如野生环境中有50只熊猫，有10只存活，动物园中有500只熊猫，也有10只存活，虽然存活数量相同，但基数不一样，结论则大相径庭。如果熊猫唯一的食物竹子不能在天然栖息地之外得到，正如(C)所说，那么也就反对了上面所提出的方法：把这些熊猫放到动物园里。但有的读者根据常识认为，大熊猫作为国宝，如果用飞机把熊猫的天然栖息地的竹子运过去就行了，因此(C)不正确。这样是思维所犯的错误就是没有理解"if true原则"的含义，"if true原则"限定了(C)选项的本身意思不能受到质疑。请读者认真体会if true的意思。

（四）五中选二的原则（The rule of 2 out of 5）

逻辑推理题编写的一个基本原则是五个选项中的一个选项必须比其他的四个好。然而，正确选项的设计不能比其他四个选项明显地好以致问题的难度变得太小。这个原则使逻辑推理题的命题人员陷入了左右为难的境地。如果一个问题让你去驳斥一个论证，那么一个选项必须能对段落的内在逻辑构成反对。这个选项将是"credited response"。另外四个选项——迷惑选项distractors一定在某些方面不完美，但他们不能一目了然，使问题变得ridiculously easy。从某种意义上讲，Preparing workable distractors is actually more difficult than writing the credited response。因此，通常五个选项中只有两个选项值得考虑（两者中仅仅有一个是对的）。另外三个选项，尽管有时与推理主题有点关联，但它们都忽略了论点的推理结构。牢记：**Usually only two of the answer choices have any real merit (one being the correct choice)**。

总之，The rule of 2 out of 5使得五个选项中只有一个难以排除，其他三个选项在很多情况下可能与问题目的无关，所以怎么样迅速排除三个选项是提高解题速度的关键。我在与ETS负责命题的官员谈话时明显觉察到：编制逻辑推理题的最大痛苦与挑战不在于如何编制出一个正确答案，而在于如何编制出一个非常像正确答案但又绝对不是正确答案的选项。实际上，有时五个选项中四个选项都编得极为荒谬，错得极为明显，只要阅读水平没问题，正确答案便跃然纸上。读者应在本书的大量归类讲解与训练中，培养挑选正确选项的感觉，进而找出错误选项的错误特征。请看下面这个例子：

Over the past fifteen years, the largely urbanized Northeastern United States has shown more and more the influence of the Southwestern portion of the country. Once, very few people in New York City could be found sporting cowboy boots and Stetson hats, and no major radio station boasted twenty-four-hour-a-day programming of country and western music. The latest development is the rapid proliferation of restaurants serving chili, nachos, burritos, and other Tex-Mex dishes.

The passage above makes which of the following assumptions?

(A) The lifestyle of people in the Northeast has been enriched by the influence of the Southwestern states.

(B) Most residents of the Southwestern states regularly eat at Tex-Mex restaurants.

(C) Over the last fifteen years, residents of the Southwestern United States have increasingly adopted lifestyles similar to those of the Northeast.

(D) Tex-Mex dishes are an element of the regional cuisine of the Southwestern states.

(E) People in the Northeastern United States eat out more frequently than they did fifteen years ago.

解析：本题的正确答案是(D)。The author claims that the Northeast has absorbed elements of the culture of the Southwest and provides three examples. A tacit assumption (one which is not proved) of the argument is that a certain mode of dress, a kind of music, and a type of cuisine are found in the Southwest. (D) articulates this assumption.

Three of the remaining choices are really just "flak." They lack any real plausibility after a reasonably careful reading. These are (A), (C), and (E).

(A) goes beyond the scope of the initial statement. The author simply states that certain cultural elements of the Southwest have been transplanted to the Northeast, but no value judgment is contained in the paragraph about that process

(C) reverses the causal linkage described by the initial statement. According to the author, the Southwest has influenced the Northeast—not vice versa

(E) goes beyond the scope of the initial statement. Nothing in the argument suggests that people in the Northeast are eating out more frequently than they did fifteen years ago—only that there are more Tex-Mex restaurants in the region than there were fifteen years ago

对大多数人而言，(B)最易误选。It at least has the merit of being fairly closely connected to the argument in the initial statement. It might be true that people in the Southwest regularly patronize the Tex-Mex restaurants. That, however, is not necessarily an assumption of the argument. All that is required for the argument is that there exist in the Southwest such restaurants—not that residents of that area patronize those restaurants with any frequency.

由上例可以看出，五个选项中的(A)、(C)和(E)的编写都非常荒谬，错得较为明显。"五中选二"的两个选项为(B)、(D)，也就是说这五个选项中只有(B)、(D)值得考虑。(B)易误选。而正确答案只有一个，即(D)。

二、三大解题步骤

（一）读问题，明晰问题目的，从而迅速确定解题方向。

先读问题而非段落似乎有违常理，但这样可以事先了解题目类型。只有知道了问题目的类型，阅读段落才能更具有针对性。另外，问题目的本身变化不多，往往一眼就可以看出题型。**注意：警惕选项中出现的not, unless, except, least等词，许多人由于漏看了这些"小词"而与正确答案无缘。**

（二）读段落，根据不同的问题目的确定不同的解题重点。

如问题属于"假设、支持、反对、评价"类，读段落时重在找出论点的前提与结论。边读边思考：从前提中能否推出结论？结论成立还需要哪些假设？

如问题属于"归纳"类，读段落时要注重其逻辑层次结构及去向，边读边琢磨：作者想要说明什么？

如问题属于"逻辑应用与技法"类，读段落时分清前提与结论。边读边考虑：段落推理犯了哪种逻辑错误？结论的成立还需要哪些假设？假设的合理性如何等？

如问题属于"解释"类，读段落时要格外关注要解释的对象以及解释对象的特点。边读边斟酌：怎么样才能找一个与要解释的内容直接相关的答案？

（三）找答案，注意有些题型可调整看选项的顺序。

读完问题与段落之后，寻读五个选项，选出正确答案。有时，阅读选项时要放慢速度，有时甚至应反复掂量。当然，若费时过多，猜测并非下策。而像假设的某类题型（后有详述）以及Except题型，可以调整看选项顺序。

第 四 章

逻辑推理题三大思维总则

一、读题"摄影洗相式"

试题作为对知识水平的测试，应尽可能避免许多客观因素的影响，任何人接受测试都应享有充分的被公平对待的权利，并且保证无地域、国别、种族、性别、文化背景、专业之间的差异。如果我们持着乐观积极的人生观，那么做每一道逻辑推理题就如同欣赏一道道不同的风景。与我们在平常日子里欣赏风景不同的是，试卷里欣赏什么样的风景，重点是什么，是命题人员预先设定好的，你必须根据命题人员所设定的问题目的去读段落，按照不同的问题目的锁定不同的读题重点，且思维应在题目之内。你的眼睛就如摄影机的镜头摄入设定的风景，然后整个思维的过程犹如洗相片的过程，尽可能Copy原来的风景且不至于失真。

二、答案不需要充分性

任何一确定事物的发生都依赖于许多条件或许多原因，但现实生活中，我们很难找到某一确定事物发生的所有条件或所有原因，因此当问题目的让我们去寻求一个支持或反对段落推理的答案时，我们的目标是去寻求一个使结论成立的可能性增大或减少的答案，而绝非一定要去寻求一个使结论必然成立或必然错误的答案。GRE中有这样一道考题：Luis正好看到两只渡鸦，因此，Luis看到的下一只鸟也是渡鸦。让我们寻求一个支持上面论述的选项，正确答案是渡鸦成群飞。有的考生认为这个答案不正确，因为Luis看到的两只渡鸦可能是成群飞的渡鸦中最后的两只。这种思维错误主要在对答案并不需要充分性没有清楚的认识。就这道题而言，渡鸦成群飞这个条件确实使得上面论述的结论"Luis看到的下一只鸟也是渡鸦"的可能性增大，因此它是正确答案。但即使这个条件找到了，我们也并不保证结论就一定正确，我们对于支持题型，仅仅是找一个使结论成立可能性增大的选项而已。

三、不能有段落之外信息的进一步推理

由于命制试题的无需专业背景知识原则，所以在解读逻辑推理时，思维一定在题目之内，不能有段落之外信息的进一步推导，尤其是加上自己的专业背景知识进行递进推理。另外，不能有段落之外信息的进一步推导原则还涉及东西方的思维差异。西方人思维推理相对简单但严谨，推理仅局限于一个逻辑层面。如果推理涉及两个逻辑层面，转了两个弯，美国人就认为上升到了哲学的高度，而不再是逻辑推理了。也正由于东西方的思维差异，中国考生在逻辑推理部分最易犯的错误，就是总对考题进行段落之外信息的进一步推理。看到某一选项，马上就联系专业或生活知识进行推理，尤其是"如果……那么就……所以……"的递进推理。切记：所有的逻辑思维只在一个层面上进行，并且只能在段落所给出的信息的基础上进行推理。请看下面这个例子：

Popular culture in the United States has become Europeanized to an extent unimaginable twenty-five years ago. Not many people then drank wine with meals, and no one drank imported mineral water. No idea would have been more astonishing than that Americans would pay to watch soccer games. Such thoughts arise because of a report that the

译文：美国大众文化的欧洲化已经达到了25年前无法想象的程度。那时没有多少人在用餐的时候喝葡萄酒，也没有人饮用进口的矿泉水，最令人诧异的是，美国人竟然会花钱去看英式足球比赛。这种观点的提出源于一份报告，该报告指出美国

American Association of State Highway and Transportation Officials has just adopted a proposal to develop the country's first comprehensive interstate system of routes for bicycles.

Which of the following inferences is best supported by the passage?

(A) Long-distance bicycle routes are used in Europe.

(B) Drinking imported mineral water is a greater luxury than drinking imported wine.

(C) United States culture has benefited from exposure to foreign ideas.

(D) Most Europeans make regular use of bicycles.

(E) The influence of the United States on European culture has assumed unprecedented proportions in the last twenty-five years.

州际高速公路与运输官员协会刚刚采纳了一项提议，准备开发美国的第一条综合性的州际自行车道路系统。

该段文字最好地支持了下面哪一项推论?

(A) 欧洲使用长距离自行车道路。

(B) 饮用进口矿泉水比饮用进口葡萄酒更加奢侈。

(C) 美国文化对外国观念的开放性使之受益匪浅。

(D) 大多数的欧洲人经常使用自行车。

(E) 在过去25年中，美国对欧洲文化的影响达到了前所未有的程度。

解析：本段落的结论是第一句话 "Popular culture in the United States has become Europeanized..."；原因（或前提）是最后一句话 "Such thoughts arise because of a report..."。即上面段落的推理可以简化为：因为美国准备开发州际自行车道路系统，所以美国的大众文化欧洲化了。现在让我们找出一个被上面段落所支持的一个推论，很明显，本题要让我们找一个使上面推理的结论成立的一个必要条件。(A)说明欧洲使用long-distance自行车道路系统，再加上美国准备开发interstate自行车道路系统，必然能得到"美国文化欧洲化"的结论。所以(A)是结论成立的必要条件。如果对(A)取非，欧洲没有使用long-distance自行车道路系统，那么"美国文化欧洲化"这个结论必然不对。另外，我们注意到，long-distance与interstate是同义词，所以(A)正确。(D)最易误选，选(D)的人犯了递进推理的错误，认为如果欧洲人经常使用自行车，那么就必然有自行车道路系统，而自行车道路系统中必然有长距离自行车线路系统，但是递推的这两步在段落之中并没有涉及，因此(D)不正确；(B)中涉及的是imported mineral water和imported wine的比较，而上文中根本没有这个比较，因此也不对；(C)中的benefit涉及段落中没有的新的价值判断；(E)说明美国对欧洲文化的影响，和上面段落探讨的"欧洲对美国文化的影响"相违背，必不正确。

由上例可以看出，逻辑推理题的正确答案必须是其本身含义加上段落之中的信息来实现问题目的，决不能对选项的意思进行递进推理。换而言之，思维只能在段落之内，不能有段落之外信息的进一步推导。

第 五 章

逻辑推理题两大推理模式

逻辑推理题是阅读理解和逻辑推理的杂交品。逻辑推理题由段落（图表）、问题目的以及五个选项组成。一般而言，段落陈述论点，论点一般由论据（或前提）和结论组成。论点的结构与解答逻辑推理题关系密切。在整个逻辑推理题中，假设、支持、反对、评价多是围绕论点与论据设置问题。因此，在解答逻辑题时，应带有目的去读段落，这目的就是论据（或前提）和结论。而两者比较，结论比论据（或前提）更重要。

由于一个论点的结论可以出现在段落中的任何一个地方，所以命题人员通常会使用一些引导词告诉你结论的位置。下面是一些经常用来引导结论的常用语：

therefore

thus

so

hence

concluding

consequently

as a result

it follows that

it can be inferred that

in conclusion

which proves that

which shows that

which means that

which suggests that

与结论相同，命题人员也往往用一些过渡性的语言来指示一个前提：

because

for

since

as

in as much as由于，因为

in so far as就…而论

in view of

论据（前提）与结论之间的关联便是推理。不过有时候，你可能需要剖析论点以便找到结论。这时，你一定要有意识地问自己，"What is the author trying to prove here?"一般地，作者设法要证明的便是结论。由于论点经常围绕着结论而组织，因此，在分析论点时找到结论是非常重要的一步。

如果我们把先发生的记作A，后发生的记作B，那么，逻辑推理题的两大推理模式为：

一、"B，A"模式

逻辑推理题中有很大一部分题目是由一个survey, record, data, study, experiment或phenomena等而得出一个结论，但这个结论往往是对survey, record, data, study, experiment, phenomena等内容做出了一种解释。按照先发生的记作A，后发生的记作B的原则，我们把survey, record, data, study, experiment, phenomena等记作B，而把由此而得出的解释性结论记作A。当由B得到解释性结论A时，推理所做的hidden premise多为A是唯一的原因。换句话说，当一个推理是从一个已知的、已经发生的事实，已经存在的现象或一个研究的发现中得出一个解释性的结论时，一般暗含除了这个解释性的结论以外没有别的因素可以解释B。此类推理模式典型的引导词有demonstrate, show, result, due to, attribute to, reason, hypothesize, the explanation is, be responsible for等。这里的A为conclusion。

另外，当推理是为达到一个目的而提出一个方法或建议的时候，推理成立暗含的假设为这个方法或建议是唯一或最具关键性的能够实现目的的方法或建议。由于只有先实施了某一方法之后才可能达到某一目的，因此，按照"先发生的为A，后发生的为B"的原则，我们把目的记作B，把方法或建议记作A，这里的A为conclusion。

二、"A，B"模式

（一）当推理是由某个原因而试图得到某个结果时，推理成立的hidden premise是这个原因能够得到这个结果。由于原因一般发生在前，结果一般发生在后，因此我们把原因记作A，结果叫做B，这里的B为conclusion（注意because, since, for等原因引导词）。

（二）当推理是由某一条件而试图得到一个结论时，推理成立的hidden premise是该条件确能得到此结论。我们把条件叫A，结论叫B（注意if, when, as long as引导条件）。

（三）当推理是由某一方法而试图达到某一目的时，推理成立的hidden premise是该方法确能实现此目的。我们把方法叫A，目的叫B。注意这时并不表明A是唯一的，只表明A是可行的（注意 by 引导方法，to的不定式，in this way等引导目的）。

（四）当推理由一个事实现象、研究的结论而试图类推（由此及彼）或外推（由过去及将来）或不完全归纳推理（由某类的部分对象推至该类的全部对象）时，推理成立的 hidden premise是此与彼、过去与将来、某类的部分对象与该类的全部对象在所有属性上没有差异。我们按照"先发生记作A，后发生记作B"的原则，把事实、现象、研究的结论记作A，而把类推、外推或不完全归纳推理记作B。请注意此类推理与"B，A"模式的根本差异：尽管两个推理都是由一个事实、现象、研究出发，但"B，A"模式的A是对B的一个解释，说明A是导致B的原因，且暗含A是唯一的，所以A为结论；而"A，B"的B是类推、外推或进行的不完全归纳推理，且这里B是结论。

就假设（assumption）、支持（support）、反对（weaken）、评价（evaluate）这四类题型来说，把握上面两大推理模式尤为重要。因为无论是"A，B"还是"B，A"模式，绝大多数论证都依赖于hidden premise。在日常生活中，这通常不是因为说话人有意通过隐含信息去欺骗听众（尽管有时是真的）。**Rather, the reason most arguments rely on hidden premises is for economy of communication.** If you think that you and your listener enjoy a common view, for instance, that actions that hurt others are immoral, then there is no need for you to articulate that premise. Your argument will have its persuasive appeal even though it rests upon a suppressed premise. The role of suppressed premises is highlighted when two parties in discussion agree implicit premises of an argument but disagree about the conclusion.

请看以下例子：

Mary: Rembrandt is the greatest painter of all times. His dramatic yet highly realistic representations give us an accurate picture of the people of his time.

Alan: No, VanGogh is the greatest painter of all times. His impassioned use of color and authoritative brushstrokes let us feel the anguish through which he interpreted the world.

解析：上述对话的双方不大可能很容易解决他们之间的分歧，因为他们每人都做了另一方不大赞同的一系列implicit premises。按照Mary 的观点，评价一个画家主要看his ability to depict people or events in a highly accurate and realistic manner，然而按照Alan的观点，评价一个画家主要看his ability to communicate emotion。因此，尽管二者在the explicit premise 方面可能没有分歧，但在画家风格的重要因素方面，二者却有显著的差异。**注意：Many GRE or GMAT or LSAT items ask you to uncover implicit or hidden premises. Sometimes, a careful reading of the stimulus material will allow you to anticipate one or more implicit premise, particularly if the argument is relatively simple.**

由于假设、支持、反对、评价都是让我们从下面寻求一个选项放到上面段落中对段落推理起到评价作用，因此段落是由一个"有待评价的推理"组成的，又加上段落推理的成立还有赖于一些hidden premises，因此根据不同的问题目的而对hidden premise 起到一定的作用是解题的关键。下图表达了这四类题的主要解题侧重点：

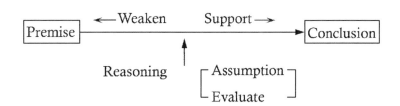

Premise（前题），Conclusion（结论），Reasoning（推理过程，前提到结论的思维变迁）。假设、支持、反对、评价这四类题所面临的是一个"待评价的推理"，也就是从前提到结论的这个推理是否能成立我们是不知道的，需要对它进行评价。根据不同的问题目的，确定不同的解题方向：问支持，就找一个选项说它可能对；问反对，就找一个选项说它不一定对；问假设，则考虑使结论成立需要什么，哪一个是使其成立的一个必要条件。

① 如何正确理解weaken, support

　1) 支持（support）：将答案放在论据（前提）和结论之间，对段落推理或者结论有支持作用就可以，所以既可非充分又可非必要。

　2) 驳斥（weaken）：将答案放在论据（前提）和结论之间，对段落推理或者结论有驳斥作用就可以，所以也是既可非充分又可非必要。

② Weaken, Support读题

　1) 对于由原因推出结果之类的推理，重点是找出原因和结果两句话，如果没有任何原因指示词，那么重点在结论，紧靠结论因果词（therefore, thus）前面的往往就是原因。

　2) 对to的不定式要读出（往往表示为对一个目的提出一个方法）

　3) 对any, all, none, everyone, each, no, in general, on the whole等词需注意，因可能会为范围差异。

　4) 对only, solely加以注意。

　5) 对动词的程度修饰词加以注意。

注意：When we talk about premises, we often say that a conclusion "rests" on its premises or that the premises "support" the conclusion. The logical function of a premise is analogous to that of the foundation of a building. For this reason, premises play an extremely important role in the attack and defense of an argument. If a key premise can be shown to be false, then the argument, like a building with a weakened foundation, will collapse. Some GRE or GMAT or LSAT questions ask you to find an idea that weakens an argument. Others ask you to find one that strengthens an argument. The correct answer to both types of questions is often a hidden premise. In the case of a question that asks for an attack on the argument, the correct choice will be a statement that an implicit assumption is false, while in the case of a question that asks for a defense of an argument, the correct choice will be a statement that an implicit assumption is true. **从某种意义上讲，假设、支持、反对、评价这四种题型中60%的题与段落推理所做的隐含假设（前提）有关，这也是为什么笔者把假设放在第二篇第一章进行讲解的原因。**

为了帮助大家熟悉一些基本命题知识和本书所使用的一些符号，特给出以下归纳：

- **基本命题及其常用表达法：**
  1. 若A→B为原命题，则B→A为逆命题

     $\overline{A}→\overline{B}$为否命题

     $\overline{B}→\overline{A}$为逆否命题

     原命题和逆否命题为等价命题，逆命题和否命题为等价命题
  2. unless:=if not 即not A unless B 表达为A→B

     A unless B 表达为$\overline{A}$→B

     if: A if B 表达为B→A

     Only if: A only if B 表达为A→B

     if only: A if only B 表达为B→A

     if and only if: A if and only if B 表达为A↔B

     A is necessary to B, precondition: B→A

     Whenever, whoever, wherever=if

- **或命题和与命题**

  或命题：B_1 or B_2 表达为B_1+B_2

  与命题：B_1 and B_2 表达为$B_1 B_2$

  A→B_1+B_2的逆否命题为$\overline{B_1}\overline{B_2}→\overline{A}$

  A→$B_1 B_2$的逆否命题为$\overline{B_1}+\overline{B_2}→\overline{A}$

  B_1+B_2→A的逆否命题为$\overline{A}→\overline{B_1}\overline{B_2}$

  $B_1 B_2$→A的逆否命题为$\overline{A}→\overline{B_1}+\overline{B_2}$

- **如何理解充分条件和必要条件**
  1. 充分：所谓充分条件就是仅有这条件就足以带来结果，无需考虑别的条件了。它是谁成立，谁一定也成立，比如A→B，如果A成立，那么一定有B，则A是B的充分条件。
  2. 必要：所谓必要条件就是没有这个条件，结论一定不对。比如B→A成立，那么A是B成立的必要条件。

第 二 篇
逻辑推理题分类思维训练

第 一 章

假 设

在本书第一篇中已经提过，假设、支持、反对、评价这四种题型在整个逻辑推理题中占了相当大的比重，而支持、反对与评价这三种题型的答案方向多是针对段落推理的hidden premise，再加上归纳题型的推理题有时就是hidden premise，所以假设在逻辑推理中占有非常重要的位置。

就"B，A"模式而言，若B→A，那么我们就说：A是推理成立的必要条件；就"A，B"模式而言，若B→A，我们也可以说，A是推理成立的必要条件。下面我们给出假设的定义：

● 假设是使推理成立的一个必要条件。

● 若一个推理在没有某一条件时，这个推理就必然不成立，那么这个条件就是段落推理的一个假设。若A是B的一个必要条件，那么$\overline{A}→\overline{B}$。

● Assumption 有时也可用required premise, hidden premise, presupposition来表示。

根据本书第一篇第四章中的"答案不需要充分性"的思维总则，由于假设仅仅是推理成立的一个必要条件，所以我们找到了推理的一个假设，并不能够肯定段落推理必然成立。我们只有找到了推理成立的所有必要条件，才能够得出一个确定性的结论，推理才能够成立。不过，在考试时，我们只需要找到一个使推理成立的必要条件，尽管不能保证推理一定正确，但由于答案不需要充分性，所以就做对了"假设"的题目。请读者用心体会下面一题的推理。

1. "On the whole," Ms. Dennis remarked, "engineering students are lazier now than they used to be. I know because fewer and fewer of my students regularly do the work they are assigned."

The conclusion drawn above depends on which of the following assumptions?

(A) Engineering students are working less because, in a booming market, they are spending more and more time investigating different job opportunities.

(B) Whether or not students do the work they are assigned is a good indication of how lazy they are.

(C) Engineering students should work harder than students in less demanding fields.

译文： "总体而言"，丹尼斯女士说，工程学的学生比以往懒惰了。我知道这一点是因为我的学生中能定期完成布置的作业的人越来越少了。

以上得出的结论依下面哪个假设？

(A) 在繁荣的市场情况下，工程学的学生做的作业少了，因为他们把越来越多的时间花在调查不同的工作机会上面了。

(B) 学生做不做布置的作业很好地显示出了他们的勤奋程度。

(C) 工程学的学生应该比其他要求稍低的专业的学生更努力学习。

(D) Ms. Dennis' students are doing less work because Ms. Dennis is not as effective a teacher as she once was.

(E) Laziness is something most people do not outgrow.

(D) 丹尼斯女士的学生做的作业比以往少了，因为她作为老师所做的工作不像以前那样有效了。

(E) 绝大多数人都不能克服懒惰的毛病。

上面的推理是由一个事实"越来越少的丹尼斯女士的学生做布置给他们的工作"，就类推出"工程学的学生更懒了"，这是一个典型的类比推理（由此及彼）。注意：类比推理是根据两个对象在一系列属性上是相同的，而且知道其中的一个对象还具有另一种属性，由此推出另一个对象也具有这一属性的推理。类比推理的客观依据是，现实中的事物的各个属性并不是孤立存在的，而是互相联系互相制约的。如两个对象在一系列属性上是相似的，那它们完全可能在另外的属性上也是相似的。类比推理的结论是或然的，即尽管其前提是真实的，也不能保证结论的真实性。这是因为，A和B毕竟是两个对象，它们尽管在一系列属性上是相同的，但仍存在着差异性，这种差异性有时就表现为A对象具有某属性，而B对象不具有某属性。如何提高类比推理的结论的可靠性呢？第一，前提中确认的相同属性愈多，那么结论的可靠程度也就愈大；第二，前提中确认的相同属性愈是本质的，相同属性与要推出的属性之间愈是相关的，那么结论的可靠程度也就愈大。

我们把上题推理的事实记作A，类推的结论记作B，那么我们发现，A对象与B对象属性并不完全一样，A与B之间有差异，即A对象与B对象的属性并不完全一样，A与B之间有明显的跳跃：做工作做得少就必然懒吗？因此段落推理成立需要依赖选项(B)这个假设 "whether or not students do the work they are assigned is a good indication of how lazy they are"，并且选项(B)把A与B之间的一个跳跃连了起来，所以(B)正确。(A)只是解释了工程系的学生为什么工作少了，但与"工程系学生是否懒了"没有直接关系。当然我们可以加入not来判断。根据假设的定义，若某条件是推理成立所做的假设，那么没有这个条件，推理必不成立。而(A)加入not以后，对段落推理不起任何作用，推理仍然可以成立，所以(A)必然不是一个假设；同理(D)也只是解释了丹尼斯女士的学生为什么工作做得少了，而与"工程系的学生是否懒了"无关；(C)是一个无关的新比较，与上述推理无关，所以也不正确；(E)好像是一个真理，但与上述推理无关。注意：逻辑推理题是要我们找一个与段落推理有关并对段落推理起到某种作用的选项，而并不是一个真理。

但是，即使我们找到了(B)这个假设，上面的推理还仍然有缺陷，因为(A)中的 "Ms. Dennis' students"与(B)中的"engineering students"不是同一对象，因此上述推理的缺陷是：The argument assumes that Ms. Dennis' students are representative of engineering students in general，因为段落推理所隐含的假设是没有证实的。

我们从这个题可以看出，本题推理的成立依赖两个假设，即①Whether or not students do the work they are assigned is a good indication of how lazy they are 和②Ms. Dennis' students are representative of engineering students in general. 在这两个假设的共同作用下，本题推理必然成立。但由于"答案不需要充分性"，我们只需要找出(B)，就是找到了一个假设，所以(B)就是正确答案，但正是由于我们仅仅只是找到了推理成立的一个假设，所以我们说假设题型（包括支持、反对、评价）的段落推理是"有待评价的推理"。

由于假设是推理成立的必要条件，所以不论段落推理是"B，A"模式，还是"A，B"模式，假设题型的思维主要以三种方式出现：A与B之间有本质联系；A可行或A有意义；除了A以外没别的因素影响B。

一、A与B之间有本质联系

若我们所面临的段落推理的A与B之间有明显的跳跃，A的讨论对象与B的讨论对象之间有差异，那么，这个段落推理成立所隐含的一个假设是A的讨论对象与B的讨论对象是有本质联系的或本质上是相关的或本质上是相同的。请体会如下推理：

Theft is an action that hurts another person. Therefore, theft is immoral.

我们发现A的探讨对象是"an action that hurts another person"，而B的探讨对象是"immoral"，它们之间有差异，因此这个推理需要用"A与B之间是有本质联系"即"Actions that hurt others are immoral"这一假设。根据假设的定义之一：若没有这个假设，则段落推理必然不成立。所以，我们可以在一个选项中加入not，若段落推理必不成立，则这个选项必为假设。若在某选项中加入not，放到段落中，推理仍然成立，则这个选项绝对不是假设。当我们把上面推理的A与B之间用"not"断开，则上面推理必不成立，所以"Actions that hurt others are immoral"是推理成立的一个假设。

2. Unlike other forms of narrative art, a play, to be successful, must give pleasure to its immediate audience by reflecting the concerns and values of that audience. A novel can achieve success over months or even years, but a play must be a hit or perish. Successful drama of the Restoration period, therefore, is a good index to the typical tastes and attitudes of its time.
The author of the passage above assumes that
(A) plays written for Restoration audiences do not appeal to modern audiences.
(B) plays are superior to novels as a form of narrative art.
(C) Restoration audiences were representative of the whole population of their time.
(D) playgoers and novel readers are typically distinct and exclusive groups.
(E) Restoration drama achieved popular success at the expense of critical success.

译文：和其他形式的叙述艺术不同，戏剧要想成功，必须通过反映其直接观众的关注点和价值观来给观众带来乐趣。小说可在几个月甚至在几年内才成名，但戏剧必须是一举成名，否则便会销声匿迹。因此，复辟时期获得成功的戏剧是那个时代典型品味和态度的反映。
上文的作者假定：
(A) 复辟时期的戏剧不合现代观众的口味。
(B) 戏剧作为一种叙述艺术要比小说更高级。
(C) 复辟时期的观众是那个时代整个人口的代表。
(D) 去剧院的人和看小说的人是两个不同的独立群体。
(E) 复辟时期的戏剧牺牲了评论界的赞誉，在大众间取得了成功。

解析：本题第一句话可看作是推理的一个大前提："成功的戏剧必定反映其直接观众的关注点和价值观。"第三句话的前半部分"复辟时代一些戏剧获得了成功"可以看作一个小前提，因此推理的隐含结论应为"复辟时代成功的戏剧反映了其直接观众的关注点与价值观"。但本段落推理的结论是"复辟时代成功的戏剧反映了其时代的品味与态度"。很明显这两者——"immediate audience"与"its time"之间有差异，因此应把这二者连起来。若"复辟时代的观众是那个时代整个人口的代表"，如(C)所说，那么就是一个很好的假设，所以(C)正确。(A)与"its time"无关；(B)中涉及新比较必然不对；(D)、(E)均与上述推理无关。

3. A small dose of widely used tranquilizer allows people to lie during lie detector tests without being discovered. The stress responses that lie detector tests measure can be inhibited by the drug without noticeable side effects. One of the implications of this fact is that the drug can also be effective in reducing stress in everyday situations.
An assumption of the passage is that
(A) tranquilizers are always an effective treatment for stress.
(B) the inhibition of stress responses increases subjective stress.

译文：小剂量地广泛使用镇定剂可以使人在测谎仪检测中撒谎而不被发现。药物可以抑制测谎仪所检测的压力反应，而不会产生明显的负作用。这一事实的一个推论是，该药物也可以有效地缓解日常情况下的压力。
文中的一项假设前提是：
(A) 镇定剂总能有效地治疗压力。
(B) 对紧张反应的抑制增加了主观压力。

(C) stress as measured by a lie detector is similar to everyday stress.

(D) persons who lie during a lie detector test always display signs of stress.

(E) it is not desirable to reduce stress in everyday situations.

(C) 测谎仪测量的压力与日常生活的压力相类似。

(D) 在测谎仪检测中撒谎的人总会表现出压力。

(E) 不必减少日常情况下的压力。

解析：本题是由一个事实"镇静剂能抑制测谎仪检测的压力反应"，而得出one of the implications of the fact："镇静药也能缓解日常情况下的压力"。虽然本题是由一个事实来进行推理，但是它是把这样一个事实类推至"日常生活情况下的压力"，我们把这个事实称为A，类推（由此及彼）称为B，那么一般推理暗含的假设为测谎仪测量的压力与日常生活中的压力类似，而(C)刚好与之吻合，把A与B之间的跳跃连了起来，所以(C)正确。(A)易误选，但(A)只能是一个支持，支持关键就在always上，我们可以取非验证。如果镇静药在减轻压力方面并不总是有效的，但只要在减轻日常情况下的压力与测谎仪下的压力方面有效，上述推理的结论"镇静剂也能缓减日常情况下的压力"仍然成立，所以(A)必然不是假设。但是当把(A)中的always去掉之后，(A)便可以作为一个假设。(B)、(D)、(E)中均出现了段落推理中没有出现的新概念，因此都不正确。

下面再给出几个例子，请大家自己用心体会"A与B之间有本质联系"作为假设的推理模式：

4. Even though most universities retain the royalties from faculty members' inventions, the faculty members retain the royalties from books and articles they write. Therefore, faculty members should retain the royalties from the educational computer software they develop.

The conclusion above would be more reasonably drawn if which of the following were inserted into the argument as an additional premise?

(A) Royalties from inventions are higher than royalties from educational software programs.

(B) Faculty members are more likely to produce educational software programs than inventions.

(C) Inventions bring more prestige to universities than do books and articles.

(D) In the experience of most universities, educational software programs are more marketable than are books and articles.

(E) In terms of the criteria used to award royalties, educational software programs are more nearly comparable to books and articles than to inventions.

译文：尽管大多数大学拥有教职员工发明的专利权，但教职员工拥有他们著书或文章的版税。因此，教职员工应该拥有他们编制的教学计算机软件的版税。

如果将以下哪一项作为一项补充的前提插入以上论述，会更合理地得出该结论？

(A) 发明的专利权收入比教学计算机软件的版税收入高。

(B) 比起发明来，教职员工更愿意编制教学软件程序。

(C) 发明会给大学带来比书和文章更多的声誉。

(D) 根据大多数大学的经验，教学软件程序比书和文章更易销售。

(E) 根据用来抽取版税的标准来看，教学软件程序与书和文章相比比与发明相比有更大的可比性。

解析：该短文得出结论，在考虑教职员工工作成就的版税时，软件应当同书和文章一样对待，而不是同发明一样对待。该结论要求一个补充的前提，说明软件在相关方面，与书和文章比比与发明比有更大的可比性。选项(E)提供了这种前提，并因此成为正确答案。选项(A)、(B)、(C)和(D)，相反地，每一项都描述了软件和发明之间［选项(A)和(B)］，或发明与书和文章之间［选项(C)］，或软件与书和文章之间［选项(D)］的区别，但是都没有在发明软件与书和文章之间建立起要求的联系。

5. When limitations were in effect on nuclear-arms testing, people tended to save more of their money, but when nuclear-arms testing increased, people tended to spend more of their money. The perceived threat of nuclear catastrophe, therefore, decreases the willingness of people to postpone consumption for the sake of saving money.

The argument above assumes that

(A) the perceived threat of nuclear catastrophe has increased over the years.

(B) most people supported the development of nuclear arms.

(C) people's perception of the threat of nuclear catastrophe depends on the amount of nuclear-arms testing being done.

(D) the people who saved the most money when nuclear-arms testing was limited were the ones who supported such limitations.

(E) there are more consumer goods available when nuclear-arms testing increases.

译文： 当关于核武器试验的限制生效时，人们倾向于储蓄更多的钱；但当核武器试验次数增加时，人们倾向于花更多的钱。因此，可以感知到的核灾难的威胁降低了人们为了存钱而推迟消费的意愿。

以上论述假设

(A) 可感知到的核灾难的威胁随时间而增长。

(B) 大多数人支持发展核武器。

(C) 人们对于核灾难的感知依赖于已完成的核武器试验的次数。

(D) 限制核武器试验时存了最多钱的那些人就是那些支持这种限制的人。

(E) 当核武器试验次数增加时，有更多的消费品供应。

解析： 基于观测到的武器试验和人们存钱的倾向之间的相关性，该论述得出结论，认为在威胁的感知和不存钱的倾向之间存在因果关系。(C)假设威胁的感知和完成的试验次数之间的联系是正确的，除非(C)成立，否则这种关系不能成立。该结论并不依赖于感知的威胁随时间而增长或多少人支持发展核武器。因此，并没有假设(A)或(B)。更进一步，该论述同支持武器限制的人或消费品的供应无关，因此，没有假设(D)和(E)。

6. If the airspace around centrally located airports were restricted to commercial airliners and only those private planes equipped with radar, most of the private-plane traffic would be forced to use outlying airfields. Such a reduction in the amount of private-plane traffic would reduce the risk of midair collision around the centrally located airports.

The conclusion drawn in the first sentence depends on which of the following assumptions?

(A) Outlying airfields would be as convenient as centrally located airports for most pilots of private planes.

(B) Most outlying airfields are not equipped to handle commercial-airline traffic.

(C) Most private planes that use centrally located airports are not equipped with radar.

(D) Commercial airliners are at greater risk of becoming involved in midair collisions than are private planes.

(E) A reduction in the risk of midair collision would eventually lead to increases in commercial-airline traffic.

译文： 如果将中心位置的机场附近的空域仅限于商用客机和那些装备了雷达的私人飞机使用，私人飞机流量的绝大部分将被迫使用偏远的机场。这种私人飞机流量的减少将降低在中心位置的机场附近发生空中撞机的危险。

在第一句中得出的结论依赖于以下哪一假设？

(A) 对于大多数私人飞机的飞行员来说，使用偏远的机场同中心位置的机场一样方便。

(B) 大多数偏远的机场没有装备处理商业客机流量的设备。

(C) 大多数使用中心位置机场的私人飞机没有装备雷达。

(D) 商业客机比私人飞机有更大的空中相撞的危险。

(E) 空中撞机危险的减少将最终导致商业客机流量增加。

解析： 第一句话得出结论，禁止没有装备雷达的私人飞机使用中心位置的机场将迫使大多数私人飞机不在这些机场起降。除非如选项(C)所说，大多数使用这些机场的私人飞机是没有装备雷达的，否则该结论不能成立。因此第一句话的结论假设了选项(C)，(C)是正确答案。该结论不需要假设偏远的机场对私人飞机很方便［选项(A)］，因为该项限制使没有装备雷达的飞机别无选择。该结论仅关心对雷达的要求对私人飞机流量有什么样的影响，因此，选项(B)，只与商业客机有关和选项(D)和(E)，只与空中撞机的危险有关，不一定需要它们为假设。

7. Traditionally, decision-making by managers that is reasoned step-by-step has been considered preferable to intuitive decision-making. However, a recent study found that top managers used intuition significantly more than did most middle or lower-level managers. This confirms the alternative view that intuition is actually more effective than careful, methodical reasoning.

The conclusion above is based on which of the following assumptions?

(A) Methodical, step-by-step reasoning is inappropriate for making many real-life management decisions.

(B) Top managers have the ability to use either intuitive reasoning or methodical, step-by-step reasoning in making decisions.

(C) The decisions made by middle and lower-level managers can be made as easily by using methodical reasoning as by using intuitive reasoning.

(D) Top managers use intuitive reasoning in making the majority of their decisions.

(E) Top managers are more effective at decision-making than middle or lower-level managers.

译文： 传统上，认为由经理们一步一步理性的分析做出决策要优于直觉做出的决策。然而，最近的一项研究发现高级经理使用直觉比大多数中级或低级经理多得多。这确证了一项替代观点，即直觉实际上比仔细的、有条不紊的理性分析更有效。

以上结论基于以下哪一项假设？

(A) 有条不紊的，一步一步的理性分析在做出许多真实生活中的管理决策时不适用。

(B) 高级经理既有能力使用直觉判断，也有能力使用有条不紊的、一步一步的理性分析来做出决策。

(C) 使用有计划的分析和使用直觉判断一样可以轻松地做出中级和低级经理做出的决策。

(D) 高级经理使用直觉判断做出他们的大部分决策。

(E) 高级经理比中级或低级经理在做决策方面更有效。

解析： 如果高级经理不是更有效的决策者，那么他们比低层的经理更经常地使用直觉这个事实就不能支持直觉更有效这一结论，因为该论述必须假设(E)，选项(E)是正确答案。就低效率的方法不适用而言，短文没有假设(A)，但支持它。由于该论述没有考虑高级经理不会使用两种方法中的一种的可能性，选项(B)不合适。由于使用哪种方法容易不是要讨论的问题，选项(C)不合适。该论述与各级经理使用直觉做少数决策没有矛盾，因此，选项(D)不合适。

二、A可行或A有意义

无论段落推理是"A，B"模式还是"B，A"模式，若假定"A可行或A有意义"，那么这个假定就是段落推理成立的必要条件。因为若A根本就不可行或A没有实际意义，那么段落推理必然不成立，所以这个假定是个假设。请读者体会这个例子：为了精减老师的数目，某学校决定把最无效的老师去掉。本题推理为"为达到一个目的而提出一个方法"，属于"B，A"模式，这个推理若想成立，那么依赖的假设是"这个学校能够决定老师是否有效"，即"A可行"。若这个学校不能决定老师是否有效，那么这个学校就不可能辨别出最无效的老师，因此也不可能达到目的"精减老师的数目"。所以"A可行或A有意义"是推理成立的一个很好的假设。

8. A famous singer recently won a lawsuit against an advertising firm for using another singer in a commercial to evoke the famous singer's well-known rendition of a certain song. As a result of the lawsuit, advertising firms will stop using imitators in commercials. Therefore, advertising costs will rise, since famous singers' services cost more than those of their imitators.

The conclusion above is based on which of the following assumptions?

(A) Most people are unable to distinguish a famous singer's rendition of a song from a good imitator's rendition of the same song.

(B) Commercials using famous singers are usually more effective than commercials using imitators of famous singers.

(C) The original versions of some well-known songs are unavailable for use in commercials.

(D) Advertising firms will continue to use imitators to mimic the physical mannerisms of famous singers.

(E) The advertising industry will use well-known renditions of songs in commercials.

译文： 一个著名的歌手获得了一场诉讼的胜利，控告一个广告公司在一则广告里使用了由另一名歌手对一首众所周知由该著名歌手演唱的歌曲进行的翻唱版本。这场诉讼的结果，广告公司将停止在广告中使用模仿者的版本。因此，由于著名歌手的演唱费用比他们的模仿者要高，因此广告费用将上升。

以上结论基于以下哪一项假设？

(A) 大多数人无法将一个著名歌手某一首歌的版本同一个好的模仿者对同一首歌的演唱区分开来。

(B) 使用著名歌手做广告通常比使用著名歌手的模仿者做广告更有效果。

(C) 一些广为人知的歌曲的原版不能在广告中使用。

(D) 广告公司将继续使用模仿者来模仿著名歌手的形体动作。

(E) 广告业将在广告中使用歌曲的广为人知的版本。

解析： 本题读题重点为段落最后一句话，且A为著名歌手的演唱费用比他们的模仿者要高，B为广告费用上升。如果没有假设选项(E)，即A无意义，那么演唱歌曲的广为人知的版本的著名歌手的演唱费用不会影响广告费用。然而，因为著名歌手演唱费用相对较高，预计广告费用会上升，因此假设了(E)，(E)是正确答案。(E)为典型的原因A有意义的答案。选项(A)与该论述无关，因为不管怎么说，著名歌手的演唱费用比模仿者的高。该论述讨论广告费用，而不是广告效果，因此，没有假设选项(B)。该论述假设某些歌曲的广为人知的版本是可以使用的，但没有要求任何版本都不能使用〔选项(C)〕。由于该论述指出广告公司将停止使用模仿者，没有假设选项(D)。

9. In recent years many cabinetmakers have been winning acclaim as artists. But since furniture must be useful, cabinetmakers must exercise their craft with an eye to the practical utility of their product. For this reason, cabinetmaking is not art.

Which of the following is an assumption that supports drawing the conclusion above from the reason given for that conclusion?

(A) Some furniture is made to be placed in museums, where it will not be used by anyone.

(B) Some cabinetmakers are more concerned than others with the practical utility of the products they produce.

(C) Cabinetmakers should be more concerned with the practical utility of their products than they currently are.

译文： 最近几年，许多精细木工赢得了很多赞扬，被称为艺术家。但由于家具必须实用，精细木工在施展他们的精湛手艺时，必须同时注意他们产品的实用价值。为此，精细木工不是艺术。

以下哪一项是支持从为该结论给出的原因中可以得出该结论的假设？

(A) 一些家具制作出来是为了陈放在博物馆里，在那儿它不会被任何人使用。

(B) 一些精细木工比其他人更关注他们制作的产品的实用价值。

(C) 精细木工应比他们现在更加关注他们的产品的实用价值。

(D) An object is not an art object if its maker pays attention to the object's practical utility.

(E) Artists are not concerned with the monetary value of their products.

(D) 一个物品，如果它的制作者注意到它的实用价值，就不是艺术品。

(E) 艺术家们不关心他们作品的货币价值。

解析： 该论述得出结论，因为精细木工要考虑他们产品的实用价值，因此精细木工不是一门艺术。如果一个物品，假定它的制作者注意到该物品的实用价值就不是一件艺术品是正确的，如选项(D)所说，该结论就得到了支持，因此，选项(D)是最佳答案。该论述只关注精细木工是否必须考虑他们的产品的实用价值，既与它们的货币价值［选项(E)］无关，也与它们实际上发生了什么事［选项(A)］无关。该论述也与精细木工考虑家具的实用价值的精确程度无关，因此，选项(B)和(C)都不合适。

我们知道，若A是B的一个必要条件，可表示为B→A，那么其逆否命题为$\overline{A}$→$\overline{B}$且与原命题等价。换句话说，由于假设是推理成立的必要条件，所以对于"A，B"模式或"B，A"模式而言，若我们能得出$\overline{A}$→$\overline{B}$，那么我们就可以得出A是推理成立的必要条件，即$\overline{A}$→$\overline{B}$是段落推理成立所依赖的一个假设。

10. The best argument for the tenure system that protects professional employment in universities is that it allows veteran faculty to hire people smarter than they are and yet remain secure in the knowledge that unless they themselves are caught in an act of moral turpitude—a concept that in the present climate almost defies definition—the younger faculty cannot turn around and fire them. This is not true in industry.

Which of the following assumptions is most likely to have been made by the author of the argument above?

(A) Industry should follow the example of universities and protect the jobs of managers by instituting a tenure system.

(B) If no tenure system existed, veteran faculty would be reluctant to hire new faculty who might threaten the veteran faculty's own jobs.

(C) The traditional argument that the tenure system protects scholars in universities from being dismissed for holding unconventional or unpopular beliefs is no longer persuasive.

(D) If a stronger consensus concerning what constitutes moral turpitude existed, the tenure system in universities would be expendable.

(E) Veteran faculty will usually hire and promote new faculty whose scholarship is more up-to-date than their own.

译文： 长期聘用制度保住了大学里专职人员的工作，其最好的理由是这种制度允许老资格的教职员工雇用比他们更聪明的教员，而同时仍能保持其稳定位置，除非他们自己卷入道德卑鄙——一个在目前环境下几乎无法定义的概念——的行为中，否则那些年轻的甭想能反过来把他们解雇掉。然而这一制度在工业上并不存在。

进行上述论证的作者最可能进行了下面哪个假设？

(A) 工业不应走大学的路子，用长期聘用制度来保护经理的位子。

(B) 如果长期聘用制度不存在，老教工可因新教工可能威胁他们自己的工作而不愿招聘新教员。

(C) 长期聘用制度保护大学里的学者不因持不寻常的或不受欢迎的想法而被解雇这一传统观点已不再有说服力。

(D) 如果人们一致同意什么可称为道德卑鄙，那么大学里的长期聘用制度将寿终正寝。

(E) 老教工通常能雇用和提升那些学识比他们更能跟得上时代的新教工。

解析： 笔者曾拿这道题让一美国考生做，那位美国考生读完题目，看完选项，就把(B)选了出来，他认为(B)就是段落的第一句话换了一种说法，此题的关键在于读题。当我们把题目读懂后，发现"长期聘用制度"发生在前，"老资格的教员愿意雇用比他们年轻的教员"发生在后，所以前者为A，后者为B，从A能得到B吗？我们需要做一假设。(B)选项指出若没有tenure system ($\overline{A}$)，那么就没有老资格教员愿意去雇用新教员(B̄)，即Ā→B̄，而其逆否命题为B→A，说明A是B的一个必要条件，所以(B)是一个无因就无果（即A可行或A有意义）的假设，因此(B)正确。(D)易误选，但对(D)取非，发现段落推理仍然可以成立，所以(D)不正确。

11. The percentage of people between the ages of 18 and 24 living with their parents increased from 48 percent in 1980 to 53 percent in 1986. It can be concluded that in 1986 it was harder for people in this age group to afford to live by themselves.

The conclusion drawn in the passage above depends on which of the following assumptions?

(A) People in this age group who could not afford to live by themselves preferred living with people their own age to living with their parents.

(B) There are people in this age group who, if they could have afforded to do so, would have chosen to live by themselves, rather than with their parents.

(C) People in this age group who lived with their parents did not make any financial contribution toward housing expenses.

(D) The number of rental housing units suitable for single people dropped between 1980 and 1986.

(E) There are people in this age group who although they lied with their parents at the time of survey, had previously lived alone.

译文： 1980年，年龄在18岁到24岁之间，与父母生活在一起的人占该年龄段人口的比例为48%，而1986年，这一比例上升至53%。可以说，在1986年，这一年龄段的人更加难于负担独立生活。

上文得出的结论是基于下列哪项假设？

(A) 这一年龄段中不能自立的人更愿意和同龄人生活在一起，而不是和父母。

(B) 这一年龄段中有些人，只要他们能独立生活，就会选择独立，而不再和父母生活在一起。

(C) 这一年龄段中与父母生活在一起的人，不分担房费支出。

(D) 在1980年到1986年间，适合单人租用的住房数目减少了。

(E) 这一年龄段中有些人尽管在调查时和父母住在一起，而在此之前是独立生活的。

解析： 本题由"与父母共住的18岁～24岁的人的比例上升"这一事实，得出一个解释性结论"这一年龄段的人更难以负担独立生活"，属于典型的"B，A"型的假设。解题思路要么是"除了他们更难以负担独立生活以外，没有别的原因导致他们与父母共住"，要么是"无因就无果"。(B)说明若无A就无B，所以是一个很好的假设。

由于假设是段落推理的必要条件，找到了段落推理的一个假设，那么其推理成立的可能性就必然增大，这个假设对段落推理起到了支持作用，所以假设必然是支持，因此在支持题型中也有部分考题用"无因就无果"或"A可行或A有意义"的选项来作为正确答案。请看以下几个例子：

12. The population of peregrine falcons declined rapidly during the 1950's and 1960's and reached an all-time low in the early 1970's. The decline was attributed by scientists to the widespread use of the pesticide DDT in rural areas.

Which of the following, if true, gives the strongest support to the scientists' claim?

(A) DDT was not generally in use in areas devoted to heavy industry.

译文： 20世纪五六十年代，游隼（一种肉食鸟）的数量快速下降并在70年代初期达到了历史的最低点。科学家们认为下降的原因是在农村地区大量地使用了杀虫剂DDT。

下列哪项，如果正确，最能支持科学家的声明？

(A) DDT在重工业区并不常用。

(B) In the time since the use of DDT was banned in 1972, the population of peregrine falcons has been steadily increasing.

(C) Peregrine falcons, like other birds of prey, abandon eggs that have fallen out of the nest, even if the eggs remain intact.

(D) Starlings, house sparrows, and blue jays-birds the peregrine falcon preys on were not adversely affected by DDT in their habitats.

(E) Other birds of prey, such as the osprey, the bald eagle, and the brown pelican, are found in the same areas as is the peregrine falcon.

(B) 自从1972年禁止使用DDT后，游隼的数量开始稳步增加。

(C) 像其他肉食鸟一样，如果游隼的蛋掉出了窝，即使没有摔坏，它也不要了。

(D) 琼鸟、麻雀和蓝树鸟都是游隼的猎物，它们在栖息地没有受到DDT负面影响。

(E) 在游隼栖息地区也发现了其他肉食鸟，如白鹭、秃鹰和棕色鹈鹕。

解析：本题由"游隼数量快速下降"这一事实，得出一个解释性的结论"DDT是原因"，属于典型的"B，A"题型的支持，如果自从1972年DDT被禁用以后，游隼数量稳步增加，正如(B)所说，相当于"没有DDT，就没有游隼数量的下降"，即无因就无果。所以(B)是上述推理成立的一个假设，而假设本身就是支持，所以(B)正确。

13. The town of Stavanger, Norway, was quiet and peaceful until the early 1960's, when Stavanger became Norway's center for offshore oil exploration. Between then and now, violent crime and vandalism in Stavanger have greatly increased. Clearly, these social problems are among the results of Stavanger's oil boom.

Which of the following, if it occurred between the early 1960's and now, gives the strongest support to the argument above?

(A) The people of Stavanger rarely regret that their town was chosen to be Norway's center for offshore oil exploration.

(B) Norwegian sociologists expressed grave concern about the increase in violent crime and vandalism in Stavanger.

(C) Violent crime and vandalism have remained low in Norwegian towns that had no oil boom.

(D) Nonviolent crime, drug addiction, and divorce in Stavanger increased approximately as much as violent crime and vandalism did.

(E) The oil boom necessitated the building of wider roads for the increased traffic in Stavanger.

译文：挪威的Stanvanger城在20世纪60年代以前一直是安静平和的，但在60年代初，Stanvanger城成了挪威远洋石油开发的中心。从那时至今，Stanvanger城的犯罪和蓄意破坏的现象不断增多。显然，这些社会问题是Stanvanger城石油兴盛的一个产物。

下列哪项，如果发生在60年代初至今的这段时间内，最能支持上述观点？

(A) Stanvanger城的人很少对Stanvanger城被选为挪威的远洋石油开发中心表示遗憾。

(B) 挪威的社会学家对Stanvanger城日益增多的暴力犯罪和蓄意破坏现象很担忧。

(C) 暴力犯罪和蓄意破坏现象在挪威没有发生石油兴盛的城市，仍然很少发生。

(D) 在Stanvanger城，非暴力犯罪、吸毒、离婚等现象像暴力犯罪以及蓄意破坏一样在增多。

(E) 石油的快速发展要求修建更宽的公路以缓解Stanvanger城的交通紧张。

解析：本题是由一个事实"犯罪与蓄意破坏现象增多"而得出一个解释性结论，"石油兴盛是原因"，属于典型的"B，A"题型。(C)通过指出没有石油兴盛的城市($\overline{A}$)，就很少发生这种现象($\overline{B}$)，即$\overline{A} \rightarrow \overline{B}$，所以(C)是一个"无因就无果"（即A可行或有意义）的假设，而假设可以作为一个很好的支持。

所以(C)是正确答案。请注意，这道题是GRE1992年2月考题，但在GRE1998年11月中重考，只不过重考时是把(C)放入段落中，然后问段落论述所使用的推理方法。

14. In a physical education class, 20 students were tested on archery target shooting. These students were then given a two-day training course in archery technique. The students were tested again and showed a 30 percent increase in accuracy. This result proves that the course was effective in increasing people's target-shooting accuracy.

Which of the following, if true, gives the strongest support to the argument above?

(A) The students were all excellent athletes, and excellent athletes tend to be good at target shooting.

(B) The first testing session functioned as a practice session for the second testing session.

(C) The accuracy with which people can shoot arrows is strongly related to the sharpness of their vision.

(D) A similar group of students who were also tested on archery target shooting but were not given the course did not show an increase in accuracy.

(E) Excellence in archery target shooting is an accomplishment achieved by relatively few of the people who take up the sport.

译文：在一次体育课上，20名学生进行了箭靶射击测试。随后这些学生上了两天的射箭技能培训课，这些学生又重新进行了测试，他们的准确率提高了30%。该结果表明，培训课对于提高人们的射靶准确率是十分有效的。

下列哪个选项，如果正确，最能支持以上论述？

(A) 这些学生都是出色的田径运动员，出色的田径运动员一般都善于射靶。

(B) 第一次测试是作为第二次测试的演习阶段。

(C) 人们射箭的准确性和他们的视觉敏锐度有很大关系。

(D) 另一组学生，也进行了箭靶射击测试，但没有进行培训，他们的准确度没有提高。

(E) 只有少数从事射箭运动的人才能掌握精湛的射靶技艺。

解析：本题也是由一个试验"上了两天的培训课准确率提高了30%"，而得出一个解释性结论"培训课有效"，属于典型的"B，A"题型。(D)通过指出没有培训($\overline{A}$)，就没有准确度的提高($\overline{B}$)，即 $\overline{A}\rightarrow\overline{B}$，所以(D)是一个"无因就无果"（即A可行或A有意义）的假设，而假设可作为一个很好的支持。所以(D)是正确答案。

三、除了A以外没有别的因素影响B

在第一篇第五章中已指出，当段落推理是由一个survey、 record、 data、study或experiment等而得出结论，并且这个结论是对survey、 record、 data、study或 experiment等内容做出一种解释，即当由B得出解释性结论A时，推理成立所做的hidden premise多为"A是唯一的原因"。因此寻求这类题的假设的思维方向可以是"A与B之间有本质联系"和"A可行或A有意义（或$\overline{A}\rightarrow\overline{B}$）"，但在更多的情况下是"除了A以外没有别的因素影响B"。当推理是对要达到的一个目的而提出一个方法或建议时，假设的思路也大致如此。

15. Statistics over four consecutive years showed that four percent more automobile accidents happened in California during the week following the switch to daylight saving time and during the week following the switch back to standard time than occurred the week before each event. These

译文：连续四年里的统计数字显示，在加州转入夏令时的一星期里和转回正常时间制的一星期里发生的机动车事故要比转换时制的前一星期多4%。这些数字显示这些时制转换给加州司机的机敏度造成了

statistics show that these time changes adversely affect the alertness of California drivers.

The conclusion in the argument above is based on which of the following assumptions?

(A) Drivers in California as well as those in the rest of the United States have similar driving patterns.

(B) The observed increases in accident rates are due almost entirely to an increase in the number of minor accidents.

(C) Four years is not a sufficiently long period of time over which to judge the phenomenon described.

(D) There are no other factors such as school vacations or holiday celebrations that cause accident rates to rise during these weeks.

(E) A time change at any other time of year would not produce a similar increase in accident rates.

负面影响。

上面论证中得出的结论依据于下面哪个假设？

(A) 加州的司机与美国其他地区的司机有着类似的驾驶方式。

(B) 观察到的事故率升高几乎完全是由于较小的事故的增加而引起的。

(C) 四年的时间对判断上述现象不足够长。

(D) 没有其他的因素——如学校假期或节日庆祝——引起事故发生率在这几星期内增加。

(E) 在一年的其他时间的时制转换不会引起类似的事故率上升。

解析：本题由一个statistics "转入夏令时与转回正常时间的一周中事故多了"，而得出解释性的结论 "时制转换是原因"，属于典型的 "B，A" 型假设，思路要么为A可行或有意义（无因就无果），要么为除了A以外没有其他原因了。(D)指出没有其他引起事故发生增加的因素，所以符合了第二种思路，因此(D)正确。(A)讨论的 "the rest of the United States" 为新概念；(B)的 "minor accidents" 也为新概念；(C)起到了反对作用；(E)主要错在 "similar" 这个词，所以其部分地反对了上述推理。

16. Prolonged and unseasonable frosts produce frost rings in deciduous trees, which grow in moderate climates. Frost rings do not appear in any of the fossilized deciduous trees that have been found in Antarctica. Hence, it is unlikely that such frosts occurred in Antarctica at the time the fossilized trees lived.

Which of the following is an assumption on which the argument depends?

(A) There are fossilized nondeciduous trees from Antarctica that bear frost rings.

(B) Deciduous trees are more likely to bear frost rings than are other tree varieties.

(C) The process of fossilization does not completely obscure frost rings in deciduous trees.

(D) Present-day deciduous trees are more sensitive to changes in temperature than were the deciduous trees of ancient Antarctica.

(E) Prolonged and unseasonable frosts that might have occurred in Antarctica when the now-fossilized trees were still living did not always produce frost rings in deciduous trees.

译文：延长的不合季节的霜冻会在生长在温带的落叶树上产生霜冻年轮。在南极洲发现的落叶树的化石中没有一个有霜冻年轮。因此，在南极洲，当这些已形成化石的树木生长的时候，不大可能发生这种霜冻的现象。

以上论述依据下面哪个假设？

(A) 南极洲的一些形成化石的非落叶性树木上有霜冻年轮。

(B) 落叶树比其他树种更容易产生霜冻年轮。

(C) 形成化石的过程不会使落叶树中的霜冻年轮完全模糊。

(D) 现在的落叶树比古代南极洲的落叶树对温度的变化更敏感。

(E) 在现已成为化石的树木还生存着的时期，在南极洲发生的延长的不合季节的霜冻不总是在落叶树上产生霜冻年轮。

解析：本题推理也是由一个事实"霜冻年轮没有出现在落叶树的化石中"，而得出一个解释性结论："那时的南极洲的落叶树上没有霜冻"，属于典型的"B，A"型假设，思路应为"没有别的原因来导致B"。如果形成化石的过程使得落叶树中的霜冻年轮完全模糊，那么也就从另外一个角度解释了为什么"霜冻年轮没有出现在落叶树的化石中"，因此上面的解释性结论必然不对。所以(C)是一个使结论成立的必需条件，因此(C)是正确答案。(A)、(B)、(C)均为无关选项；(E)易误选，但(E)中的"not always"表明了(E)起到了部分支持作用。

17. From a certain farming region, trucks can carry vegetables to market in New Mexico in two days for a total cost of $300. A train will carry the vegetables there in four days for $200. If reducing time in transit is more important to the owner of the vegetables than is reducing the shipping bill, he or she will send the vegetables by truck.

Which of the following is an assumption made in the passage above?

(A) Vegetables can be sold more profitably when shipped by train than by truck.

(B) Other than speed and cost, there are no significant differences between truck and train transportation from the farming region to New Mexico.

(C) The time required to ship vegetables by train from the farming region to New Mexico could be reduced to two days if the price for this service were raised.

(D) Most owners of vegetables in the region are more concerned with shipping costs than with the time involved in shipping vegetables to market.

(E) Transportation of vegetables by truck is worth at least $200 per day to owners of the vegetables in the farming region.

译文：用卡车能把蔬菜在2天内从某一农场运到新墨西哥的市场上，总费用是300美元。而用火车运输蔬菜则需4天，总费用是200美元。如果减少运输时间比减少运输费用对于蔬菜主人更重要的话，那么他或她会用卡车运蔬菜。

下面哪个是上面段落所做的一个假设？

(A) 用火车运的蔬菜比用卡车运的蔬菜在出售时获利更多。

(B) 除了速度和费用以外，用火车和卡车来进行从农场到新墨西哥的运输之间没有什么差别。

(C) 如果运费提高的话，用火车把蔬菜从农场运到新墨西哥的时间可以减少到2天。

(D) 该地区的蔬菜主人更关心的是运输成本而不是把蔬菜运往市场花费的时间。

(E) 用卡车运输蔬菜对该农业区的蔬菜主人而言每天至少值200美元。

解析：本题由一个数据事实而进行推理："若时间比费用更重要，则用卡车运输。"那么这个推理暗含的假设是："时间和费用"是最主要的考虑因素或唯一的因素"。而选项(B)恰好表明"除了时间和费用以外没有别的原因影响选择"，即典型的"除了隐含的假设A以外没有别的因素影响B"，所以(B)正确。

请读者认真思考下面这道考题的思路与上面一题的相同之处（解析思路与17题完全一样，这里略去解析）：

18. An acre of average farmland produces only about 400 pounds of grain amaranth, as against 2,400 pounds per acre, or six times as much, for wheat. It follows that whenever the grain-amaranth price is projected to be more than six times the projected price of wheat, farmers wishing to maximize profits will grow grain amaranth rather than wheat.

译文：平均每英亩土地仅能生产400磅amaranth，却能产出2400磅的小麦，或者说是amaranth产量的6倍。于是，只要当amaranth的价格预计比小麦的价格高出6倍以上时，希望利润最大化的农民就会种植amaranth而非小麦。

The argument above is based on which of the following assumptions?

(A) An acre's worth of grain amaranth is no more expensive to grow and bring to market than an acre's worth of wheat.

(B) There is no crop that produces a higher yield in terms of pounds harvested per acre than wheat.

(C) By choosing which crops to grow, farmers can exert a significant influence on the prices of those crops.

(D) Farmers are no less motivated by the desire to maximize profits than are other occupational groups.

(E) Prices of grain crops can change faster than farmers can change the acreage devoted to various grain crops.

以上论证依据下列哪个假设?

(A) 比起一英亩小麦来讲,种植一英亩的amaranth并把它拿到市场上去销售所花费的成本并不高。

(B) 小麦是所有粮食中每亩产量最高的。

(C) 通过选择耕种哪种粮食,农场主对这些粮食的价格施加了显著的影响。

(D) 农民与其他职业的人一样,希望使利润最大化。

(E) 谷物的价格变化很快,农民不能改变种植不同谷物的面积来适应这种变化。

下面再给出几个例子,请大家用心体会"除了A以外没别的因素影响B"作为假设的推理模式:

19. To prevent some conflicts of interest, Congress could prohibit high-level government officials from accepting positions as lobbyists for three years after such officials leave government service. One such official concluded, however, that such a prohibition would be unfortunate because it would prevent high-level government officials from earning a livelihood for three years.

The official's conclusion logically depends on which of the following assumptions?

(A) Laws should not restrict the behavior of former government officials.

(B) Lobbyists are typically people who have previously been high-level government officials.

(C) Low-level government officials do not often become lobbyists when they leave government service.

(D) High-level government officials who leave government service are capable of earning a livelihood only as lobbyists.

(E) High-level government officials who leave government service are currently permitted to act as lobbyists for only three years.

译文:为防止利益冲突,国会可以禁止政府高层官员在离开政府部门后三年内接受院外游说集团提供的职位。然而,一个这种类型的官员得出这样的结论,认为这种禁止是不幸的,因为它将阻止高层政府官员在这三年里谋求生计。

这个官员的结论,从逻辑上讲,依赖于以下哪一项假设?

(A) 法律不应限制前政府官员的行为。

(B) 院外游说集团主要是那些以前曾担任过政府高层官员的人。

(C) 当政府低层官员离开政府部门后,他们一般不会成为院外游说集团成员。

(D) 离开政府部门的政府高层官员只能靠做院外游说集团成员来谋生。

(E) 目前只允许离开政府部门的政府高层官员为院外游说集团工作三年。

解析: 段落推理为:该官员争辩说禁止政府高层官员在三年内接受院外游说集团提供的职位将阻止这些官员们在这段时期内谋生。这个推理暗自将这些官员通过院外游说之外的工作来谋生的可能性排除了。因此,表述出了这种暗含的假设的选项(D)是正确答案。该官员的争论不依赖于假设(A)、(B)、(C)或(E);因为如果一些对政府官员行为的限制是令人向往的(A),或如果院外游说集团成员主要不是前政府高层官员(B),或如果前政府低层官员也经常成为院外游说集团成员(C),或如果前政府高层官员可以不限制时间地为院外游说集团工作(E),并不能使该论述不成立。

20. A researcher discovered that people who have low levels of immune-system activity tend to score much lower on tests of mental health than do people with normal or high immune-system activity. The researcher concluded from this experiment that the immune system protects against mental illness as well as against physical disease.

The researcher's conclusion depends on which of the following assumptions?

(A) High immune-system activity protects against mental illness better than normal immune-system activity does.

(B) Mental illness is similar to physical disease in its effects on body system.

(C) People with high immune-system activity cannot develop mental illness.

(D) Mental illness does not cause people's immune-system activity to decrease.

(E) Psychological treatment of mental illness is not as effective as is medical treatment.

译文：一个研究人员发现免疫系统活性水平较低的人在心理健康测试中得到的分数比免疫系统活性水平正常或较高的人低。该研究人员从这个试验中得出结论，免疫系统既能抵御肉体上的疾病也能抵御心理疾病。

该研究人员的结论依赖于以下哪一项假设？

(A) 较高的免疫系统活性水平比正常的免疫系统活性水平能更好地抵御心理疾病。

(B) 心理疾病在对身体系统的影响上与肉体疾病相似。

(C) 免疫系统活性水平高的人不会得心理疾病。

(D) 心理疾病不会使人们的免疫系统活性水平降低。

(E) 对心理疾病的心理治疗没有药物治疗有效。

解析：该研究人员从免疫系统活性水平低与心理健康的低分数的联系中得出结论，免疫系统活性实际上可以抑制心理疾病。如果，与(D)相反，心理疾病可抑制免疫系统的活性，提到的那种联系就不支持该研究人员的结论，因此必须有(D)这个假设。即使免疫系统活性水平高能增加抵御能力不成立，与(A)所述相反，或免疫系统活性水平高能预防心理疾病不成立，与(C)所述相反，正常的免疫系统活性水平仍可以抵御心理疾病。因此，没有假设(A)或(C)。该结论不依赖于心理和肉体疾病的相似之处，因此没有假设(B)。也不依赖于治疗手段的区别，因此没有假设(E)。

21. The program to control the entry of illegal drugs into the country was a failure in 1987. If the program had been successful, the wholesale price of most illegal drugs would not have dropped substantially in 1987.

The argument in the passage depends on which of the following assumptions?

(A) The supply of illegal drugs dropped substantially in 1987.

(B) The price paid for most illegal drugs by the average consumer did not drop substantially in 1987.

(C) Domestic production of illegal drugs increased at a higher rate than did the entry of such drugs into the country.

(D) The wholesale price of a few illegal drugs increased substantially in 1987.

(E) A drop in demand for most illegal drugs in 1987 was not the sole cause of the drop in their wholesale price.

译文：1987年的控制违法药物进入该国的计划是个失败。如果该计划成功了，1987年大多数违法药物的批发价将不会大幅下降。

该短文中的论述依赖于以下哪一项假设？

(A) 1987年违法药物的供给大幅下降。

(B) 1987年一般顾客对大多数违法药物支付的价钱没有大幅下降。

(C) 国内生产的违法药物以比这种药物进入该国更高的速度增加。

(D) 1987年一些违法药物的批发价大幅上升。

(E) 1987年对大多数违法药物的需求下降不是它们的批发价下降的唯一原因。

解析： 要合理地从违法药物批发价的下降得出该计划失败这个结论，唯一必须正确的选项是(E)，正确答案。如果是由需求下降引起的价格下降，就没有理由怀疑有任何由进入该国的药物增加而引起的供给增加。其他选项由于对该争论没有影响，因此是错误的。违法药物的供给不一定下降〔选项(A)〕，零售价可以下降〔选项(B)〕，违法药物进入该国的速度可以上升到比国内生产更快的水平上〔选项(C)〕，违法药物不一定必须经历价格大幅上升的过程〔选项(D)〕。

四、总结

由于在考试时，不可能迅速判断假设究竟属于哪一类，所以在平时练习假设题型时，要训练迅速读出段落推理的论点与已存在的前提的能力，然后根据其关系做出判断。

若为"B，A"模式，则假设思路多为"除了A以外没有别的因素影响B"（在90%的情况下如此），那么假设答案中大多有否定概念的出现，并且是针对主句谓语的否定概念（注意不是定语从句中的否定概念）。否定概念的主要标志词有never, not, no, neither...nor, unlikely, something remains the same, something remains unchanged（相当于没有某物的变化因素）。当然，并不是所有这类考题都有否定概念，有时即使有否定概念的选项也不一定就是假设，有时你还会发现五个选项中都有否定概念。但是，当你看选项时先用否定概念来定位选项，只不过是调整了看选项顺序，又增加了选对选项的速度，何乐而不为呢？若段落为"A，B"模式，假设答案方向极不确定，但当推理属于类比推理时，符合"A与B之间有本质联系"思路的选项必为正确答案。如果段落推理中的A与B很难定位，则主要是寻找段落推理的核心关键词，且用此核心关键词来定位选项。

总之，在实战中，针对假设题型，首先应能寻找出段落推理的论点与已存在的前提，并利用A与B中的核心关键词来定位选项；其次用上面的三种思维方向去判断该选项是否为正确答案；最后，当只剩下两个选项而不知谁为假设时，则通过对选项加入not的方法来判断推理是否成立。若加入not，段落推理必不成立，则其必为假设；若加入not，段落推理仍可成立，则绝对不是假设。注意：这种方法对假设的难题非常有效，因为命题人员加大假设题难度无一例外地是在加大阅读的前提下设计出一个支持选项，而这时的易混淆支持选项必然不是段落推理成立的必要条件，所以可用加入not的方法去掉这个易误选的支持答案。

五、试题精练及解析

1. The sense of delayed gratification, of working now for later pleasure, has helped shape the economic behavior of our society. However, that sense is no longer nurtured as consistently in our children as it once was. For example, it used to take a bit of patience to put together the toys that children got in cereal boxes; now the toys come from the boxes whole.

Which of the following is an assumption of the passage above?

(A) The toys in cereal boxes have changed partly because the economic conditions of our society have improved.

(B) The influence of promotion gimmicks on the economic behavior of our society has increased over the years.

(C) The toys that used to come in cereal boxes were put together by the same children who played with them.

(D) Part of the pleasure of any toy lies in putting the toy together before playing with it.

(E) Today's children do not expect a single toy to provide pleasure for a long period of time.

现在工作为了以后享受的延迟满足的观念帮助塑造了现代社会的经济行为。然而，这种观念不再像从前那样不断地在孩子身上加以培养了。例如，过去孩子们需要花许多耐心才可把从麦片盒子里得来的玩具组装起来，而现在玩具从盒子里出来就是完整的。

下面哪一句是上文的假设？

(A) 由于社会的经济状况改善了，所以麦片盒子里的玩具有了部分的改动。

(B) 促销这一花招对社会经济行为的影响逐年增加了。

(C) 麦片盒子里的玩具是拿它玩的孩子组装的。

(D) 玩具的部分乐趣在于玩之前先把它组装起来。

(E) 现在的孩子不指望一件玩具能给他们提供很长时间的乐趣。

2. The greatest chance for the existence of extraterrestrial life is on a planet beyond our solar system. The Milky Way galaxy alone contains 100 billion other suns, many of which could be accompanied by planets similar enough to Earth to make them suitable abodes of life.

The statement above assumes which of the following?

(A) Living creatures on another planet would probably have the same appearance as those on Earth.

(B) Life cannot exist on other planets in our solar system.

(C) If the appropriate physical conditions exist, life is an inevitable consequence.

(D) More than one of the suns in the galaxy is accompanied by an Earth-like planet.

(E) It is likely that life on another planet would require conditions similar to those on Earth.

地球以外的生命最大可能是存在于太阳系以外的某个行星。银河系本身包括1000亿个其他的类似太阳的恒星，其中很多都可能有行星相随，这些行星与地球的相似程度足以使其成为生命的所在地。

上面的陈述是以下面哪句为假设的?

(A) 另一星球上的生物可能具有和地球上的生物相同的外貌。

(B) 在太阳系的其他行星上不可能存在生命。

(C) 如果存在适合的物理条件，生命的出现是不可避免的。

(D) 银河系中不止一个类似太阳的恒星伴随有类似于地球的行星。

(E) 另一行星上的生命很可能需要与地球相类似的生存条件。

3. Some people assert that prosecutors should be allowed to introduce illegally obtained evidence in criminal trials if the judge and jury can be persuaded that the arresting officer was not aware of violating or did not intend to violate the law while seizing the evidence. This proposed "good-faith exception" would weaken everyone's constitutional protection, lead to less careful police practices, and promote lying by law enforcement officers in court.

The argument above for maintaining the prohibition against illegally obtained evidence assumes that

(A) defendants in criminal cases should enjoy greater protection from the law than other citizens do.

(B) law enforcement authorities need to be encouraged to pursue criminals assiduously.

(C) the legal system will usually find ways to ensure that real crimes do not go unprosecuted.

(D) the prohibition now deters some unlawful searches and seizures.

(E) courts should consider the motives of law enforcement officers in deciding whether evidence brought forward by the officers is admissible in a trial.

有些人坚持认为，在刑事审判中应该允许起诉人使用非法获得的证据只要法官和陪审团被说服而相信执行警员在获得证据时并没意识到违法或并不想有意违法。这种被建议的"善意的例外"将会削弱宪法对每个人的保护，导致警察行为的不谨慎，鼓励执法官员在法庭上说谎。

上述的禁止非法获得证据的论证假设:

(A) 刑事犯罪的被告应比其他公民享有更多的法律保护权。

(B) 应鼓励执法机关更努力地搜捕罪犯。

(C) 立法制度通常能找到确保真正的罪犯被起诉的方法。

(D) 如今禁令阻止了一些非法搜查和拘留。

(E) 法庭应考虑执法官在决定警官提出的证据是否能拿到法庭上时的动机。

4. The world's annual food production slightly exceeds the amount of food required to provide a minimally adequate diet for the world's population. To predict that insufficient food production will cause a hunger crisis in the future is nonsense.

世界粮食年产量略高于世界人口最低限度吃饱所需的食物总量。预言未来因粮食产量不足而引起饥荒纯属无稽之谈。导致任何饥荒的不是生产问题，而是分配问题。

Any hunger crisis will result from a distribution problem rather than a production problem.

The statement above assumes which of the following?

(A) The world's food requirements are greater than they will be in the future.

(B) A shortfall in the world's food production can be prevented by a better distribution system.

(C) The world's food production will continue to be sufficient to meet or exceed needs.

(D) The distribution of the world's existing food supply will be improved in the future.

(E) The world hunger crisis will not exist in the future.

5. Some United States psychologists have concluded that one specific set of parental behaviors toward children always signifies acceptance and a second set always signifies rejection, for there is remarkable agreement among investigators about the maternal behaviors designated as indicative of these parental attitudes.

The conclusion of the psychologists mentioned above logically depends on the assumption that

(A) most maternal behaviors have been interpreted as conveying either acceptance or rejection.

(B) the maternal behaviors indicating acceptance or rejection are exhibited by fathers as well.

(C) the behaviors of fathers toward children have been studied as carefully as have the behaviors of mothers.

(D) acceptance and rejection are the easiest to recognize of all parental behaviors.

(E) parental attitudes are best conveyed through behaviors that the parents have consciously agreed on.

6. Some geologists argue that if oil is as common in unsampled areas of the world as it is in those already sampled, our current estimate of reserves that exist underground must be multiplied by a factor of 10,000. From this we can conclude that we can meet the oil needs of the entire world for at least five centuries, even assuming that future consumption grows at an accelerating rate.

To reach the stated conclusion, the author must assume which of the following?

(A) It is possible to recover the oil contained in unexplored areas of the world.

(B) The consumption rate for oil will not grow rapidly.

以上的论述做了下面哪个假设？

(A) 全世界目前的粮食需求比将来的要大。

(B) 更好的分配系统能预防世界粮食产量的亏空。

(C) 世界粮食产量将继续与需求量持平或超过需求量。

(D) 现存的粮食供应的分配在将来将得以改进。

(E) 未来不会出现世界性的饥荒。

一些美国心理学家得出结论认为：父母对儿童采取的行为一种是总表示接受，一种是总表示拒绝。心理学家得出这样的结论是因为研究者高度同意母亲的行为能表明这些父母的态度。

上面提及的心理学家所得的结论依据于这样的假设，即

(A) 大多数父母行为都被解释为要么表达接受，要么表达拒绝。

(B) 父亲也表现出与母亲相同的代表接受或拒绝的行为。

(C) 父亲对孩子行为的研究与母亲对孩子行为的研究一样认真。

(D) 接受和拒绝是父母行为中最容易识别的。

(E) 父母的态度最能通过他们取得一致意见的那些行为传递出来。

有些地理学家认为如果世界上未抽样地区的石油与已抽样地区的石油一样普遍，那么我们现在对地下石油贮备的估算，必须要乘以万倍了。由此我们可以得出结论，即使假定未来的石油消费加速增长，我们至少可以再满足5个世纪整个世界的石油需求。

为了得出上述结论，作者必须假设下面哪个？

(A) 人们有可能在未开发地区再发现石油。

(B) 石油的消费速度不会迅速增长。

(C) 在至少500年内，石油仍将是重要的

(C) Oil will remain an important energy source for at least 500 years.

(D) The world will achieve and maintain zero population growth.

(E) New technology will make oil discovery and drilling more feasible than ever before.

7. Last year, support for the social and behavioral sciences represented only about three percent of the government's total budget for research funds in the United States. Thus, the particularly sharp reductions imposed on such programs this year seem dictated not by financial constraints but by social philosophy.

Which of the following is an assumption on which the conclusion of the passage above is based?

(A) The government funds allocated for research in the social and behavioral sciences are not sufficient for the work that needs to be done.

(B) The social and behavioral sciences are as valuable as the physical and biological sciences.

(C) The current reductions will stop research in the social and behavioral sciences.

(D) Government funding is the primary source of research money in the United States.

(E) Three percent is an insignificant portion of the government's total budget for research funds.

8. It has been hypothesized that much of the matter in the universe is "dark," i. e., unseen. Studies have shown that galaxies in many galaxy clusters are moving faster with respect to one another than they would if visible stars constituted all their mass. The studies suggest that the galaxies are moving under the gravitational influence of unseen mass in considerable quantity.

Which of the following is an assumption underlying the passage above?

(A) Measurements of the speed of moving galaxies are extremely unreliable.

(B) The workings of gravitational forces are not particularly well understood.

(C) The aggregate mass of visible stars in the galaxies mentioned above can be estimated with some confidence.

(D) The general composition of unseen matter in the universe has been determined.

能量来源。

(D) 世界人口将实现并保持零增长。

(E) 新技术将使石油的发现和钻井比以前更可行。

去年，美国政府研究基金的总预算里只有3%是扶持社会和行为学科的。因此，今年这些项目上资金的骤减，与其说是经济压力的原因，不如说是社会观念的原因。

下面哪一个是上文的结论所依据的假设？

(A) 分配给社会行为学科的研究资金不足以完成必需的工作。

(B) 社会行为学科与物理学、生物学具有同等价值。

(C) 目前资金的缩减将中止社会行为学科的研究。

(D) 在美国，政府拨款是研究工作所需资金的首要来源。

(E) 3%是政府用于科研工作的总体预算中微不足道的一部分。

宇宙中的大多数物质都被假定是"暗的"，即见不到的。研究已经表明，如果很多星系群中的星系组成物质是可见的恒星，相对于其他星系的移动速度就会快得多。这一研究表明星系在相当大量的不可见物质的引力作用下运动。

下面哪个是上文依据的假设？

(A) 运动星系速度的测量是极不可靠的。

(B) 重力的作用形式没有被特别好地理解。

(C) 对于上述星系中可见恒星的总的质量的估计是有一定把握的。

(D) 宇宙中不可见物质的大体组成已经被确定了。

(E) Without exception, the galaxies mentioned above move toward one another.

9. In March 300 college students turned out in Washington to protest against proposed cuts in student loan funds. Another 350,000 collegians flocked to Florida's sun-drenched beaches during March for "spring break." Since the Florida sun-seekers were more numerous, they were more representative of today's students than those who protested in Washington, and therefore Congress need not heed the appeals of the protesting students.

The argument above makes which of the following assumptions?

(A) The students who vacationed in Florida did not oppose the cutting of student loan funds by Congress.

(B) The students who vacationed in Florida were not in agreement with the opinion of the majority of United States citizens about the proposed cut in loan funds.

(C) The students who protested in Washington were more seriously concerned about their education than were the students who vacationed in Florida.

(D) The students who neither protested in Washington in March nor vacationed in Florida in March are indifferent to governmental policies on education.

(E) The best way to influence congressional opinion about a political issue is to communicate with one's elected representative in Washington.

10. Some doomsayers are warning that long-range warming or cooling trends in weather patterns will drastically reduce grain production. More optimistic reports, however, point out that, even if such drifts in average temperature do occur, we should expect little change in grain production because there is little evidence that changes in rainfall patterns will occur. Moreover, for most crops, climate-induced yield trends will be masked by both the year-to-year fluctuation of yields and by the enhancement of yields because of technological factors.

Which of the following is an assumption on which the more optimistic reports mentioned in the passage are based?

(A) Long-range changes in weather patterns cannot be accurately predicted.

(B) The growing of grain is so highly dependent on technological factors that improvements in yield are unlikely, regardless of climatic conditions.

(E) 上面提到的星系都毫无例外地向彼此移动。

3月，300名大学学生在华盛顿抗议削减学生贷款基金的提案。另外有35万大学生在3月期间涌向佛罗里达的阳光海滩度"春假"。因为在佛罗里达的晒太阳的人数更多一些，所以他们比在华盛顿抗议的学生更能代表当今的学生，因此国会无需注意抗议学生的呼吁。

上面的论证进行了下面哪个假定？

(A) 在佛罗里达度假的学生没有反对国会削减学生贷款基金。

(B) 在佛罗里达度假的学生在削减学生贷款基金提议问题上与大多数美国公民意见不一致。

(C) 在华盛顿抗议的学生比在佛罗里达度假的学生更关心其学业。

(D) 既没去华盛顿抗议、也没有去佛罗里达度假的学生对政府的教育政策漠不关心。

(E) 影响议会关于某政治问题的观点的最好方法是在华盛顿与其选举出来的代表交流。

有些末日论者警告说天气形势长期转暖或转冷的趋势都将大量减少谷物产量。但是比较乐观的报告指出，即使平均气温的这种变化真的发生，我们可以预期谷物产量不会有太大变化，因为几乎没有迹象表明降雨量的改变。此外，对大多数庄稼来说，气候导致的产量变化将被年产量的波动和科技因素引起的产量增加而掩盖。

下面的哪个是上文提到的较乐观报告所基于的假设？

(A) 天气形势长期的变化无法被准确地预测。

(B) 谷物的生产高度依赖于科技因素，以至于不论气候条件如何，产量提高的可能性都不大。

(C) Trends in rainfall patterns are more difficult to isolate than are trends in temperature.

(D) Long-range warming or cooling trends are more damaging to grain production if they are accompanied by changes in rainfall patterns than if they are not.

(E) Long-range cooling trends are potentially more destructive to grain production than are long-range warming trends.

(C) 降雨量的变化趋势比温度变化趋势更难孤立地去考虑。

(D) 长期的转暖或转冷趋势如果伴随有降雨形势的变化，其对谷物产量的破坏比没有降雨形势的变化时更大。

(E) 长期转冷趋势比长期转暖趋势对谷物产量的潜在破坏更严重。

11. A child watching television experiences a procession of sights and sounds that flash from the screen just long enough for the eyes and ears to take them in. Unlike the pages of a book, which can be read as slowly or as quickly as the child wishes, television images appear with a relentless velocity that stunts rather than enhances the child's powers of imagination.

The view expressed above is based on an assumption. Of the following, which can best serve as that assumption?

(A) When allowed to choose a form of entertainment, children will prefer reading to watching television.

(B) A child's imagination cannot be properly stimulated unless the child has access both to television and to books.

(C) A child's imagination can develop more fully when the child is able to control the pace of its entertainment.

(D) Children should be taught to read as soon as they are able to understand what they see on television.

(E) A child's reaction to different forms of sensory stimuli cannot be predicted, since every child is different.

看电视的儿童经历的是一种图像和声音的过程，这种过程可以在屏幕上闪现的时间仅仅可以使眼睛和耳朵能够接受。不像书页，儿童可以以自己想要的速度来读，电视图像出现的速度如此机械而无情，它阻碍了而不是提高了儿童的想象力。

上述观点基于一个假设。下面哪一个最能作为那个假设？

(A) 当被允许选择一种娱乐时，儿童会更喜欢读书而不是看电视。

(B) 儿童除非可以接触电视和书，否则其想象力不会得到适当的激发。

(C) 当儿童可以控制娱乐的速度时，他的想象力能得到更完全的发展。

(D) 儿童刚刚能够理解他们在电视上所看到的，就应教他们读书。

(E) 由于每个孩子都是不同的，因此孩子对不同感官刺激的反应是不可预测的。

12. No botanist lives long enough to study the complete life cycle of an individual California redwood tree. Nevertheless, by observing many trees at different stages, botanists can piece together the evolution of a single tree. Exactly the same principle applies in astronomy to the study of the life-story of globular clusters, huge spherical aggregations of about a million stars all swarming about each other.

Which of the following is an assumption made in the passage above?

(A) The methods of scientists in one field generally carry over to other fields even if the subject matter is vastly different.

(B) Observations of the life cycle of a single individual have little value in scientific studies.

没有一个植物学家的寿命足以研究一棵加州红松的一个完整生命周期。然而，通过观察处于不同阶段的许多棵树，植物学家能够拼凑出一棵树的成长过程。完全相同的规则适用于天文学中对星群的发展过程的研究——一些大约有100万的恒星聚集在一起的群团。

下面的哪个是上文所做的假设？

(A) 一个领域中科学家所用的方法通常适用于其他领域，即使这些领域的主题大不相同。

(B) 在科学研究中，对某一个体的生命周期的观察价值甚微。

(C) Globular clusters at different stages of development are accessible to astronomers for observation and study.

(D) There are globular clusters that have not so far been detected by astronomers.

(E) Redwoods and globular clusters must both be studied intensively now, while they still exist in sufficient numbers.

13. In any negotiations between a party with limited aims and an opposing party with unlimited aims, the party with limited aims is bound to lose. This is so because the scope of a negotiating party's aims determines the energy and the perseverance that will be brought to the negotiations by that party.

Which of the following is an assumption implicit in the passage above?

(A) The intensity with which parties conduct negotiations affects the outcome of those negotiations.

(B) Negotiations almost always pit against one another parties whose aims differ in scope.

(C) The outcome of negotiations cannot be correctly predicted in advance.

(D) A negotiator who has exceptionally high aims needs exceptional perseverance in order to avoid losing.

(E) Negotiating parties are typically not aware of the scope of each other's aims until the outcome is no longer in doubt.

14. One of the world's most celebrated paintings, *The Man with the Golden Helmet*, long attributed to Rembrandt, is not a Rembrandt after all. So say several art experts, who base their conclusion on an analysis of stylistic features, especially details both of shading and of brushwork. In order to ascertain who really painted the well-known masterpiece, the experts have begun a series of sophisticated new tests, including one that involves the activation of neutrons. These tests yield patterns for any painter that are as distinctive as a good set of fingerprints.

Which of the following is an assumption on which the conclusion of the art experts depends?

(A) *The Man with the Golden Helmet* was not painted during Rembrandt's lifetime.

(B) If even *The Man with the Golden Helmet* is of questionable attribution, then any supposedly authentic Rembrandt has

---

(C) 天文学家可以对球状聚群的不同发展阶段进行观察和研究。

(D) 目前有尚未被天文学家发现的球状聚群。

(E) 红松和球状聚群必须在现在被集中地研究，现在它们的数量还很充足。

在有着有限目的的一方与有着无限目的的对立方之间的任何谈判中，带有有限目的的一方都必定要输。其原因是，谈判一方目的的大小决定了该方带到谈判中的能量与坚持程度。

下面哪个是上文暗含的假设？

(A) 谈判双方进行谈判的强度影响谈判的结果。

(B) 谈判总是使目的大小不同的双方互相竞争。

(C) 无法提前准确地预测谈判的结果。

(D) 有着非常高的目标的谈判者必须非常坚持以避免失败。

(E) 谈判的双方通常不知各自目标的大小，直到谈判的结果出现。

世界上最著名的油画之一《戴着金色钢盔的人》一直被认为是伦勃朗的作品，但其实根本不是伦勃朗所作。几位专家如是说，他们的结论是基于对作品风格特点，尤其是对比度和笔工的细节的分析。为了确认到底是谁画了这部众所周知的杰作，专家们展开了一系列的复杂的新测试，包括一项激活中子的试验。这些试验对任何画家产生的结果就像指纹一样有独特特点。

下面哪个是艺术品专家得出该结论所依据的假设？

(A) 《戴金色钢盔的人》不是在伦勃朗的在世期间创作的。

(B) 如果连《戴金色钢盔的人》的作者归属都有疑问，那么任何被认为是伦勃

now become suspect.

(C) The painting known as *The Man with the Golden Helmet* is a copy of a Rembrandt original.

(D) The original ascription of *The Man with the Golden Helmet* to Rembrandt was a deliberate fraud.

(E) There are significant consistencies among authentic Rembrandts in certain matters of style.

朗的真品的作品现在都变得可疑了。

(C) 名为《戴金色钢盔的人》这幅画是伦勃朗原作的一个临摹。

(D) 最初将《戴金色钢盔的人》归于伦勃朗之作是一个故意的骗局。

(E) 在伦勃朗的真品中，其风格的某些方面上有明显的一致性。

15. In 1985 a consumer agency concluded that Xylo brand bicycles are safer to ride than are Zenon brand bicycles. The agency based the conclusion on the ratio of the number of rider injuries to the number of riding hours for each brand of bicycle from 1981 through 1984. Yet for identically designed bicycles manufactured since 1985, the number of rider injuries has been twice as great among riders of Xylos as among riders of Zenons. Therefore, the agency's conclusion would have been different for the period since 1985.

Which of the following is an assumption that, if true, supports the claim that the agency's conclusion would have been different for the period since 1985?

(A) For the period since 1985, the number of riding hours for Zenons totaled at least half the number of riding hours for Xylos.

(B) Of all the bicycles ridden in the period since 1985, the percentage of Xylos ridden was twice the percentage of Zenons ridden.

(C) Prior to 1985, Zenon owners were more likely than Xylo owners to report the injuries they sustained while riding their bicycles.

(D) In 1985 the agency had miscalculated the ratio for Xylos, for Zenons, or for both.

(E) Soon after the agency had issued its report, consumer demand for Xylos increased more rapidly than did consumer demand for Zenons.

在1985年，某消费者机构得出结论，Xylo牌的自行车比Zenon牌自行车骑起来更安全。这一机构所得结论的依据是在1981年到1984年这两种品牌的自行车各自骑车者受伤数与自行车行驶小时数之比。但是对于在1985年生产的同样设计的自行车，骑Xylo牌自行车的人受伤数是骑Zenon牌自行车受伤人数的2倍。因此，自1985年以来的时间里，该机构得出的结论已经有所变化。

下面哪个，如果正确，是支持该机构的结论自1985年后将不同于这一观点的假设？

(A) 自1985年以来的时间里，骑Zenon牌自行车的小时总数至少是骑Xylo牌自行车总数的一半。

(B) 自1985年以来的时间里所有被骑的自行车中，Xylo牌自行车所占百分比是Zenon牌自行车百分比的2倍。

(C) 1985年以前，Zenon牌自行车车主比Xylo牌自行车车主更可能报告他们在骑车过程中受到的损伤。

(D) 在1985年，该机构计算的Xylo牌自行车的比例是错误的，或将Zenon牌自行车比例算错，或将二者的比例均计算错误。

(E) 该机构发布报告后不久，消费者对Xylo牌自行车的需求量比对Zenon牌自行车的需求量上升得更快。

16. In the 1960's, long-term studies of primate behavior often used as subjects tamarins, small monkeys that were thought ideal because they require only small cages, breed frequently, and grow quickly. Field studies were not used because they were costly and difficult. Tamarins were kept caged in male-female pairs, because otherwise, serious fights erupted

在20世纪60年代，对灵长类动物行为的长期研究经常用被认为很理想的小猴子即小绢猴作为实验对象，因为它们只需用小笼子养，且繁殖频繁，长得又快。实地研究很少进行，因为那很费钱也很困难。雄雌小绢猴被成对地关在同一笼中，因为

between unrelated females. On the basis of the fact that breeding occurred, tamarins were viewed as monogamous.

The view taken by the researchers concerning the monogamy of tamarins depended on a questionable assumption. Which of the following could have served as that assumption?

(A) The suppression of fighting between related females serves to protect their common genetic inheritance.

(B) Adult male tamarins contribute to the care of tamarin infants.

(C) The social system of tamarins requires monogamous pairing.

(D) Male tamarin monkeys do not display aggressive behavior in the wild.

(E) The way the tamarins were kept in cages did not affect their mating behavior.

17. Board member: As a longtime member of the college's board of trustees, I believe that the board has functioned well in the past because each of its members has had a broad range of experience and interests. Thus, if in the future any members are elected primarily to press for a particular policy, such as reducing tuition, the board will function less well.

In drawing the conclusion above, the board member must have been making which of the following assumptions?

(A) The college will suffer financially if the board reduces tuition.

(B) The college will not be able to operate if and when the board functions less well than it does currently.

(C) The board functions well because its members are primarily interested in particular academic policies rather than in financial policies such as the level of tuition.

(D) In order to be elected as a member of the board, one must have a broad range of experience and interests.

(E) Each of the people who would be elected to the board primarily to press for a particular policy lacks a broad range of experience or interests.

18. Although part of the ivory available on world markets was taken from wild elephants that were killed illegally, some ivory is derived from sources that nearly all nations define as legal, such as elephants that have died natural deaths. The world's few remaining wild elephant herds, therefore, are not endangered when those buying ivory at wholesale make a

如果不这样，在不相关的雌性小绢猴之间会爆发出严重的争斗。根据有繁殖发生这一事实，小绢猴被视为是单一配偶制的。

研究者们关于小绢猴单一配偶制的观点基于一个有疑问的假设。下面哪个可以作为那个假设？

(A) 制止雌性间的争斗能保护其共同的基因遗传。

(B) 成年雄小绢猴负责幼儿的抚养。

(C) 小绢猴的社会制度要求单一的配偶搭配。

(D) 雄小绢猴在野外不显示出好斗的行为。

(E) 将小绢猴笼养的方式不影响它们的交配行为。

委员会成员：作为一名长期的大学信托委员会的成员，我认为在过去的时间里该委员会运作得很好，因为它的每一个成员都有丰富的经历和兴趣。因此，如果将来有些成员被选举主要为了坚持要求某一政策，如减少学费，那么这个委员会就不再会起那么好的作用。

该委员会成员在得出上述结论的时候，进行了下面的哪个假设？

(A) 如果委员会减少学费，大学将在经济上受损失。

(B) 如果并且当委员会运行得不如现在好的时候，大学将无法运作。

(C) 委员会之所以起了很好的作用，是因为它的成员的主要兴趣在于某一学术政策而非经济政策，例如学费水平。

(D) 一个要被选为委员会的成员，必须有广泛的经历和兴趣。

(E) 每一个被选入委员会并且主要坚持要求制定某一政策的人都缺乏丰富的经历和兴趣。

虽然世界市场上供应的一部分象牙来自被非法捕杀的野生大象，但还有一部分是来自几乎所有国家都认为合法的渠道，如自然死亡的大象。因此，当人们在批发市场上尽力限制自己只购买这种合法的象牙时，世界上仅存的少量野生象群便不会

serious effort to limit their purchases to such legal ivory.

The argument above depends on the assumption that

(A) wholesale buyers attempting to limit their purchases to legal ivory can reliably distinguish legal from illegal ivory.

(B) the demand for products made from legal ivory will continue to grow in the near future.

(C) there are currently fewer wholesale sources of legal ivory in the world than there are of illegal ivory.

(D) wholesale buyers of ivory products are generally unaware of the reasons for the dwindling world supply of ivory.

(E) a continued supply of legal ivory is ensured because elephants reproduce in captivity.

受到威胁。

以上的论证依据了这样的假设，即

(A) 试图将购买限于合法象牙的批发商能够可靠地区分合法与非法象牙。

(B) 在不久的将来，对于合法象牙产品的需求会持续增长。

(C) 目前世界上合法象牙的批发来源远远少于非法象牙的批发来源。

(D) 象牙的批发商总是意识不到世界象牙供应减少的原因。

(E) 持续地提供合法象牙可以得到保证，因为大象在被关着时可以繁殖。

19. Riothamus, a fifth-century king of the Britons, was betrayed by an associate, fought bravely against the Goths but was defeated, and disappeared mysteriously. Riothamus' activities, and only those of Riothamus, match almost exactly those attributed to King Arthur. Therefore, Riothamus must be the historical model for the legendary King Arthur.

The argument above requires at least one additional premise. Which of the following could be such a required premise?

(A) Modern historians have documented the activities of Riothamus better than those of any other fifth-century king.

(B) The stories told about King Arthur are not strictly fictitious but are based on a historical person and historical events.

(C) Riothamus' associates were the authors of the original legends about King Arthur.

(D) Legends about the fifth century usually embellish and romanticize the actual conditions of the lives of fifth-century nobility.

(E) Posterity usually remembers legends better than it remembers the actual historical events on which they are based.

Riothamus，这位5世纪的不列颠国王和哥特人勇敢作战，但被副将所出卖而失败，最后神秘地消失了。Riothamus的行为，并且也只有他的行为与亚瑟王的那些几乎完全吻合。因此，Riothamus一定是传奇中亚瑟王的历史原型。

以上论述至少还需要一个前提，以下哪个能够成为一个这样的前提？

(A) 现代历史学家考证了Riothamus的行为比5世纪任何国王的行为都更卓越。

(B) 亚瑟王的故事并不是完全虚构的，而是有历史人物和历史事件作基础的。

(C) Riothamus的副将是最初的亚瑟王传说的作者。

(D) 关于5世纪的传说通常润饰了5世纪贵族生活的真实情况，增加了它的浪漫色彩。

(E) 后人对历史事件的记忆总是不如对建立在这些真实事件上的传说的记忆准确持久。

20. Tinea is a skin infection caused by certain fungi. A significant fraction of the people who contract tinea have outbreaks of its symptoms again and again. This proves that, for each of these individuals, the original case of tinea was, in fact, never completely cured.

The argument above assumes that a person who has outbreaks of tinea symptoms again and again

Tinea是由某种真菌引起的皮肤感染。很大一部分患了tinea的人反复表现出其症状。这证明，对患者中的每个人而言，实际上tinea病从一开始就没有被彻底治愈。

以上论述假设，一个反复出现tinea症状的人：

(A) can never be completely cured of tinea.

(B) does not understand what causes tinea.

(C) did not get medical treatment for the original case of tinea.

(D) did not take steps to avoid contracting tinea.

(E) has not been repeatedly infected with tinea.

21. Inspection system X and inspection system Y, though based on different principles, each detect all product flaws, but they each also erroneously reject three percent of flawless products. Since false rejections are very costly, money will be saved by installing both systems, instead of either one or the other, and rejecting only products found flawed by both.

The argument above requires which of the following assumptions?

(A) The three percent of flawless products that system X rejects are not all the same products, piece for piece, that system Y erroneously rejects.

(B) It is less costly to accept a flawed product than to reject a flawless one.

(C) In their price range, systems X and Y are the least error-prone inspection systems on the market.

(D) Whichever system performs the second inspection needs to inspect only products not rejected by the first system.

(E) Any way of detecting flaws, other than by using either system X or system Y, requires complete disassembly of the products.

22. Fragments of charred antelope bone have recently been found at a million-year-old settlement of Homo erectus, an early human species. This discovery demonstrates that humans were making controlled use of fire to cook meat at a very early stage of their development.

The argument above makes which of the following assumptions?

(A) Every human species since Homo erectus has made controlled use of fire.

(B) Homo erectus could not have eaten antelope meat unless the meat had been cooked.

(C) Early human settlements can be identified by the presence of charred antelope bones.

(D) The diet of Homo erectus consisted in large part of antelope meat.

(A) 他的癣永远也不能被彻底治愈。

(B) 不明白癣的病因。

(C) 在最初得癣时没有采取药物治疗。

(D) 没有采取措施避免患上癣。

(E) 不是反复患上tinea的。

检测系统X和检测系统Y尽管依据的原理不同，但都能检测出所有的产品缺陷，而它们也都会错误地淘汰3%无瑕疵产品。由于错误淘汰的成本很高，所以通过同时安装两套系统，而不是其中的一套或另一套，并且只淘汰两套系统都认为有瑕疵的产品就可以省钱。

以上论述需要下面哪一项假设？

(A) 系统X错误淘汰的3%无瑕疵的产品与系统Y错误淘汰的3%无瑕疵产品不完全相同。

(B) 接受一个次品所造成的损失比淘汰一个无瑕疵产品所造成的损失大。

(C) 在同等价格范围的产品中，X系统和Y系统是市场上最少出错的检测系统。

(D) 不论采用哪一系统，第二次检测只需要对第一次没被淘汰的产品进行检验。

(E) 除了采用X系统或Y系统，其他的检验疵点的方法都需要把产品全部拆开。

最近在百万年以前的智人遗址——智人是一种早期人种——发现了烧焦的羚羊骨头碎片。这项发现表明人类在其发展的很早时期便开始使用火来烧肉了。

以上论述做了下面哪个假设？

(A) 智人以后的每个人种都掌握了用火。

(B) 智人不吃羚羊肉，除非做熟了。

(C) 通过烧焦的羚羊骨骼的存在可以确认早期人类部落的存在。

(D) 构成智人的食物的较大一部分是羚羊肉。

(E) The antelope bones were charred in a fire controlled by humans.

23. Although many brands of gasoline are sold on Haibei island, gasoline companies there get all of the refined gasoline they sell from Haibei seaport's only storage tank, which is always refilled with the same quality of gasoline. Therefore, the brands of gasoline for sale on Haibei may be different in name and price, but they are identical in quality.

The conclusion drawn above depends on which of the following assumptions?

(A) Consumers are usually unaware of variations in the quality of the gasoline they buy unless those variations are announced by the gasoline companies.

(B) When tankers make gasoline delivery at Haibei's seaport, the storage tank an Hailed always receives the same quantity of gasoline as that in the preceding delivery.

(C) There is a wide variation in the price at which the different brands of gasoline on Haibei are sold.

(D) If any gasoline company on Haibei alters the quality of its gasoline before sale, the other gasoline companies also use methods before sale that result in the same change in the quality of their gasoline.

(E) The gasoline storage tank on Haibei's large enough to meet the needs of all of Haibei's different gasoline companies.

24. Until 1984 only aspirin and acetaminophen shared the lucrative nonprescription pain-reliever market. In 1984, however, ibuprofen was expected to account for fifteen percent of all nonprescription pain-reliever sales. On that basis business experts predicted for 1984 a corresponding fifteen percent decrease in the combined sales of aspirin and acetaminophen.

The prediction mentioned in the last sentence above was based on which of the following assumptions?

(A) Most consumers would prefer ibuprofen to both aspirin and acetaminophen.

(B) Aspirin, acetaminophen, and ibuprofen all relieve headache pain and muscular aches, but aspirin and ibuprofen can also cause stomach irritation.

(C) Before 1984 ibuprofen was available only as a prescription medicine.

(E) 羚羊的骨头是被人类控制的火烧焦的。

虽然在Haibei岛上有多种品牌的汽油出售，但当地的汽油公司销售的精炼汽油都是从Haibei港口唯一的储油罐中得来的，该油罐总是补充同一质量的汽油。因此，在Haibei岛销售的汽油也许品牌和价格不同，但实际上质量是相同的。

以上得出的结论依据下列哪个假设？

(A) 消费者总意识不到他们所购买的汽油质量的变化，除非汽油公司宣布质量的改变。

(B) 当汽油从Haibei的海港上被运走时，Haibei唯一的储油罐总是被注入和以前质量一样的汽油。

(C) Haibei出售的不一样品牌的汽油，价格有很大差异。

(D) 如果Haibei哪家汽油公司在出售汽油之前改变了汽油的质量，其他公司也会采用相应的手段使汽油在售出以前和这家公司的汽油质量一样。

(E) Haibei的汽油储藏罐非常大，能满足Haibei不同汽油公司的所有需求。

直到1984年，只有阿斯匹林和退热净占据利润丰厚的非处方止痛药市场。然而在1984年，布洛芬预计占非处方止痛药销售份额的15%。在这个基础上，商业专家预测在1984年，阿斯匹林和退热净的总销售量相应下降了15%。

以上最后一句提到的预测依据下面哪个假设？

(A) 大多数消费者倾向使用布洛芬而不是阿斯匹林或退热净。

(B) 阿斯匹林、退热净和布洛芬都能减轻头痛和肌肉疼痛，但阿斯匹林和布洛芬会引起胃肠不适。

(C) 1984年以前，布洛芬只能遵医嘱才能食用。

(D) The companies that manufacture and sell aspirin and acetaminophen would not also manufacture and sell ibuprofen.

(E) The introduction of ibuprofen would not increase total sales of nonprescription pain relievers.

(D) 生产和出售阿斯匹林和退热净的公司不生产出售布洛芬。

(E) 布洛芬的加入并没增加非处方止痛药的市场的总销售量。

25. FilmPro sells millions of videocassettes directly to consumers at $25 apiece for a $10 profit on each. However, FilmPro is losing money because people are buying illegally copied versions of its $25 videocassettes at far cheaper prices. So far, one million illegally copied cassettes have been sold for $5 each. Illegal copying, therefore, has cost the company at least $10 million in potential profits.

Which of the following is an assumption that, if true, would allow the conclusion above to be properly drawn?

(A) The price of the illegally copied videocassettes never goes below$5 apiece.

(B) At least one million more cassettes would have been purchased from FilmPro for$25 apiece if the illegally copied cassettes had not been available.

(C) FilmPro refunds money to customers dissatisfied with the original cassettes.

(D) The illegally copied tapes are of such high quality that it is virtually impossible to differentiate between them and the originals.

(E) FilmPro never sells discontinued videocassettes at less than $25 apiece.

FilmPro直接向顾客销售几百万盘录像带，每盘售价25美元，利润为10美元。然而，由于人们以低得多的价格购买非法盗版的录像带，FilmPro出现了亏损。到现在为止，已经有100万盘盗版录像带以5美元一盘出售了。因此，盗版行为已使公司至少失去了1000万美元的潜在利润。

下面哪个，如果正确，是恰当得出以上结论的假设？

(A) 盗版录像带的单价不会再低于5美元。

(B) 如果没有盗版录像带，FilmPro至少会以25美元的价格卖出100万盘录像带。

(C) 该公司给对原版录像带不满意的顾客退款。

(D) 非法盗版的录像带质量很好，以至于很难分清哪些是盗版，哪些是原版。

(E) 该公司开始以低于25美元的价格出售绝版录像带。

26. X-ray examination of a recently discovered painting — judged by some authorities to be a self-portrait by Vincent van Gogh — revealed an underimage of a woman's face. Either van Gogh or another painter covered the first painting with the portrait now seen on the surface of the canvas. Because the face of the woman in the underimage also appears on canvases van Gogh is known to have painted, the surface painting must be an authentic self-portrait by van Gogh.

The conclusion above is properly drawn if which of the following is assumed?

(A) If a canvas already bears a painted image produced by an artist, a second artist who uses the canvas to produce a new painting tends to be influenced by the style of the first artist.

(B) Many painted canvases that can be reliably attributed to van Gogh contain underimages of subjects that appear on

一项对一幅刚发现的画——某些权威判断是梵高的自画像——的X光检验发现在其下面有一幅妇女的面部像的底影。或是梵高，或是别的画家用现在看到的帆布表面的画像覆盖了第一幅画。因为底影中的妇女的脸也出现在已知的由梵高画的画中，所以表面上的画一定是梵高的自画像。

先假设下面哪个能适当得出以上结论？

(A) 如果画布上已经有了一位画家的一部作品，第二个用这块画布创作新作品的画家会受到第一个画家画风的影响。

(B) 许多已经被确认为是梵高的表面画都包含有底影，而这底影至少出现在已知的由梵高画的另外一幅帆布画中。

at least one other canvas that van Gogh is known to have painted.

(C) Any painted canvas incorrectly attributed to van Gogh would not contain an underimage of a subject that appears in authentic paintings by that artist.

(D) A painted canvas cannot be reliably attributed to an artist unless the authenticity of any underimage that painting might contain can be reliably attributed to the artist.

(E) A painted canvas cannot be reliably attributed to a particular artist unless a reliable X-ray examination of the painting is performed.

(C) 所有被误认为是梵高的画都没有曾在其真品中出现过的某对象的底影。

(D) 如果一幅油画的底影不能断定是某位画家的真品，那么也无法判定这幅画出自那位画家之手。

(E) 一幅画只有经X光检测才能确定是哪位画家的作品。

27. To provide extra revenue for improving city bus service, the mayor of Greenville proposed a fare increase. The director of the bus service, however, pointed out that the previous bus fare increase had resulted in so many regular riders abandoning the bus system altogether that revenues from bus service had decreased. Another fare increase, the director argued, would only lead to another revenue drop.

The director's argument depends on which of the following assumptions?

(A) The previous fare increase was the same amount as the proposed fare increase.

(B) Fare increases do not necessarily lead to lower revenues from city bus service.

(C) A decrease in fares would result in increased ridership and increased revenues from bus service.

(D) The fare increase would make Greenville's bus service much more expensive than bus services in other comparable cities.

(E) Some of the people currently using the bus have the option of not traveling by bus.

为提供额外收入改善城市公交服务，Greenville的市长建议提高车费。公交服务公司的领导却指出，前一次提高公交车费导致很多通常乘公交车的人放弃了公交系统服务，以致该服务公司的总收入降低。这名领导争辩道，再次提高车费只会导致另一次收入下降。

该名领导的论述基于下面哪个假设？

(A) 以前车票价格提高的数量和这次建议的一样。

(B) 抬高车费不一定引起城市公共汽车服务业的收入减少。

(C) 降低车费可以吸引更多的乘客，从而提高了公共汽车服务业的收入。

(D) 抬高车费，Greenville的公共汽车服务会比同等城市的公共汽车服务昂贵。

(E) 目前乘坐公共汽车的人可以选择不坐公共汽车。

28. Springtown's fire department wants the town council to buy it another ladder truck. These trucks are useful in fighting fires in high-rise buildings. The town council argues, however, that Springtown has only two high-rise buildings, and it already owns enough ladder trucks to fight any fires there. So, they say, Springtown does not need another ladder truck.

The town council's argument assumes that

(A) Springtown cannot afford to buy another ladder truck.

(B) Springtown's high-rise buildings all meet or exceed current fire safety standards.

Springtown的消防部门想让镇议会再为它购置一辆悬梯卡车。这种卡车在扑灭高层建筑的火灾时很有用。然而镇议会争辩道，Springtown只有两座高层建筑，它拥有的悬梯卡车已经足够用来抢救那里的任何火灾。因此，他们说，Springtown不需要另买一辆悬梯卡车。

镇议会的论述假设：

(A) Springtown买不起另一辆消防悬梯卡车。

(B) Springtown现有的高层建筑都达到或

(C) the number of high-rise buildings in Springtown is likely to grow.

(D) at least one of Springtown's ladder trucks is not due to be permanently removed from service in the immediate future.

(E) it is possible to fight fires successfully in high-rise buildings without using ladder trucks.

超过了安全防火标准。

(C) Springtown的高层建筑数量有增多的趋势。

(D) Springtown在不久的将来，至少能有一辆悬梯卡车不会被永久性撤除。

(E) 没有悬梯卡车也能扑灭高层建筑的火灾。

29. Bracken, a poisonous weed, is spreading and damaging much pastureland in the Northern Hemisphere. One potentially inexpensive and self-sustaining countermeasure is to introduce natural enemies of the plant; therefore, some scientists have proposed to control bracken by a release of bracken-eating moths native to the Southern Hemisphere into bracken-infested areas in the Northern Hemisphere.

If the scientists' proposal for controlling bracken is adopted, which of the following is a necessary condition for its success?

(A) That bracken in the Northern Hemisphere grows in approximately the same climates and soil conditions in which it grows in the Southern Hemisphere.

(B) That the released moths will feed on weeds other than bracken that are native to the Northern Hemisphere.

(C) That the livestock that will return to pastures now lost to bracken will develop immunities to the diseases caused by bracken.

(D) That the released moths will survive in sufficient numbers to build a population large enough to reduce bracken and retard its growth.

(E) That traditional methods of control, such as burning, cutting, and chemical spraying, will not become less expensive or labor-intensive than they are now.

Bracken，一种有毒的野草，正在北半球蔓延并毁坏了许多牧场。一种潜在的费用低廉而且可以自我维持的对付办法是引入这种植物的天敌；因此，一些科学家建议通过把产于南半球的吃bracken的飞蛾放养到受bracken影响的北半球地区来控制bracken的生长。

如果科学家控制bracken的建议被采纳，下面哪个是其成功所必要的条件？

(A) 南北半球的Bracken生长的地区必须拥有相同的气候和土壤条件。

(B) 释放的飞蛾以野草为食，但不吃原产于北半球的bracken。

(C) 要回到现在遍地都是bracken的牧场的家畜要对bracken引起的疾病有免疫力。

(D) 放养的飞蛾存活数量形成的群体足够减少bracken并抑制它的生长。

(E) 一些传统的控制办法如火烧、刀割、喷化学药品等并不比现在的方法少花钱、少用劳动力。

30. Although the ratio of physicians to total population is about the same in the United States and Canada, the United States has 33 percent more surgeons per capita. Clearly, this is the reason people in the United States undergo 40 percent more operations per capita than do Canadians.

The explanation given above rests on an assumption that

(A) patients in the United States do not have a greater need for surgery than do patients in Canada.

(B) the population of the United States is not larger than that of Canada.

虽然美国和加拿大内科医生占人口总数的比例大致相同，但美国人均拥有的外科医生比加拿大多33%。显然，正是由于这个原因，在美国平均每人做的手术比加拿大人多40%。

上面解释依据的假设是：

(A) 美国的患者对手术的需要不如加拿大的患者多。

(B) 美国人口不比加拿大人口多。

(C) United States patients sometimes travel to Canada for certain kinds of surgery.

(D) general practitioners in the United States do not as a rule examine a patient who is a candidate for surgery before sending the patient to a surgeon.

(E) there are no unnecessary surgical operations performed in Canada.

(C) 美国患者有时去加拿大做某种手术。

(D) 美国的普通医生在直接把患者交给外科医生之前，原则上不给要做手术的患者做检查。

(E) 在加拿大所有的外科手术都是必需的。

31. A random sample of shoppers responded to the questions contained in a marketing survey. Six months later, another random sample of shoppers responded to exactly the same questions, except that the questions were now arranged in a different order. The pattern of responses to many individual questions was greatly different, thus demonstrating that a question will sometimes elicit different responses depending only on what question precedes it.

The argument above depends on which of the following assumptions?

(A) The reordering of the questions did not put each question in a different sequential position from its position six months previously.

(B) Shoppers who respond to a marketing survey do not generally remember six months later what responses they gave.

(C) There was no motive for the second survey except that of discovering whether the ordering of the questions mattered.

(D) The survey was not composed of questions to which shoppers would give different responses at different times of the year.

(E) The first sample of shoppers did not have any individuals in common with the survey sample of six months later.

一个随机抽取的顾客群样本回答了一项市场调查中的问题。6个月之后，另一个随机抽取的顾客群样本回答了相同的问题，只是问题排列顺序调换了一下。两组样本对许多单个问题的回答方式有很大不同，这表明有时某个问题只因它前面的问题就会导致不同的回答。

以上论述依据下面哪个假设？

(A) 对问题的重新排序并没有使6个月前每个问题的前后顺序都发生改变。

(B) 回答市场调查问题的顾客6个月后通常记不住当初他们的回答。

(C) 第二次调查的目的就是为了发现问题的排列顺序是否很重要。

(D) 调查不包含顾客在一年中不同时间会给出不同回答的问题。

(E) 第一个样本中的顾客和6个月后第二次调查样本的顾客没有任何相同的人。

32. Ounce for ounce, blends of different artificial sweeteners match any individual artificial sweetener in sweetening power. When used to sweeten food, blends greatly decrease the likelihood that consumers will exceed acceptable daily intakes for individual sweeteners. Blends should therefore be used, rather than single sweeteners alone, since blends are clearly more healthful, yet equally effective.

The argument above depends on which of the following assumptions?

(A) When ingested together, different artificial sweeteners in the blends do not interact in a way that makes them harmful to human health.

就盎斯而言，不同人工增甜剂的混合物在增甜效果上与单一人工增甜剂一样。当用来使食物变甜时，混和物大大降低了饮食者对单一增甜剂的日摄入量超过可接受水平的可能性。因此，应使用混和物而非单一的人工增甜剂，因为混和物明显地更健康，并且同样有效。

以上论证依据下面哪个假设？

(A) 当一起消化时，混和物中不同人工增甜剂不会相互作用以至于对健康有害。

(B) Different artificial sweeteners, when used together in food, do not contribute a more desirable flavor to the food than would any one of them by itself.

(C) The acceptable daily intake for any given artificial sweetener is a conservative figure that could probably be greatly exceeded at little or no risk.

(D) Consumers who substitute artificial sweeteners for sugar in their diets generally keep track of their daily intake of different sweeteners.

(E) The ill effects on health produced by the intake of excessive quantities of any single artificial sweetener cannot be reversed by reducing intake later.

33. During a single hour, an automatic camera photographed 100 vehicles that were speeding on a one-way road, and police a mile farther down the road photographed 49 vehicles that were speeding. Since every vehicle that passed the automatic camera also passed the police during the hour, the police photographed fewer than half of the vehicles that were speeding when passing them.

Which of the following is an assumption on which the reasoning in the argument above depends?

(A) Fewer than half of the vehicles that were speeding when they passed the police were already speeding when they passed the automatic camera.

(B) Drivers who are not exceeding the speed limit are less likely than drivers who are speeding to reduce their driving speed when they see a marked police car.

(C) Most of the vehicles that were speeding when they passed the automatic camera were still speeding when they passed the police.

(D) More than 100 vehicles passed the automatic camera during the hour in which the automatic camera photographed 100 speeding vehicles.

(E) Not more than 100 vehicles drove past the police during the hour in which the police photographed 49 speeding vehicles.

34. A thorough search of Edgar Allan Poe's correspondence has turned up not a single letter in which he mentions his reputed morphine addiction. On the basis of this evidence it is safe to say that Poe's reputation for having been a morphine addict is undeserved and that reports of his supposed addiction are untrue.

(B) 把不同种的人工增甜剂混合加入食品时，不会比它们中的任一个单独使用给食品带来更好的味道。

(C) 原来规定对人工增甜剂可以接受的摄入量是个保守的数字，超过这一标准，基本没有危险。

(D) 在饮食中用人工增甜剂代替糖的消费者一般保持不同增甜剂的每日摄入量。

(E) 进食一种人工增甜剂过多对健康造成的损害是以后减少摄入量所无法弥补的。

在一小时内，一部自动摄像机拍摄到在一条单行线上有100辆超速的汽车，而一英里以外的警察只拍下了49辆。由于在这一小时中，每部经过了自动摄像机的汽车也都从警察身边通过，所以警察拍下了经过他们的不到一半的超速汽车。

以上论述中的推理依据了下面哪个假设？

(A) 经过警察时超速的汽车中，不到一半在经过自动摄像机时已经超速。

(B) 如果司机没有超速驾驶，当他看到警车时会比超速驾驶的司机减速的可能性更小。

(C) 大部分在经过自动摄像机时超速的车辆在经过警察时仍然保持超速状态。

(D) 在自动摄像机拍下100辆超速汽车的这个小时内，有更多的车经过自动摄像机。

(E) 在警察拍下了49辆超速汽车的这个小时内，经过他的汽车总数不超过100辆。

一项对Edgar Allan Poe的信件的精确研究发现，他没有在任何一封信中提到过他因之出名的吗啡瘾。在这个证据的基础上，可以讲poe得到"吗啡上瘾者"的名声是不恰当的，那些关于他的吗啡瘾的报道也是不真实的。

Which of the following is assumed by the argument above?

(A) Reports claiming that Poe was addicted to morphine did not begin to circulate until after his death.

(B) None of the reports of Poe's supposed morphine addiction can be traced to individuals who actually knew Poe.

(C) Poe's income from writing would not have been sufficient to support a morphine addiction.

(D) Poe would have been unable to carry on an extensive correspondence while under the influence of morphine.

(E) Fear of the consequences would not have prevented Poe from indicating in his correspondence that he was addicted to morphine.

上文的论述做了下列哪一个假设？

(A) 有关Poe对吗啡上瘾的报道直到Poe死后才广为流传。

(B) 没有一项有关Poe对吗啡上瘾的报道是由真正认识Poe的人所提供的。

(C) Poe的稿费不足以支付其吸食吗啡的费用。

(D) 在吗啡的影响下，Poe不可能写这么多的信件。

(E) Poe不会因害怕后果而不在其信中提及对吗啡的嗜好。

35. Excluding purchases by businesses, the average amount spent on a factory-new car has risen 30 percent in the last five years. In the average household budget, the proportion spent on car purchases has remained unchanged in that period. Therefore the average household budget must have increased by 30 percent over the last five years.

Which of the following is an assumption on which the argument relies?

(A) The average number of factory-new cars purchased per household has remained unchanged over the last five years.

(B) The average amount spent per car by businesses buying factory-new cars has risen 30 percent in the last five years.

(C) The proportion of the average household budget spent on all car-related expenses has remained unchanged over the last five years.

(D) The proportion of the average household budget spent on food and housing has remained unchanged over the last five years.

(E) The total amount spent nationwide on factory-new cars has increased by 30 percent over the last five years.

除了企业购买外，过去五年中购买一辆新的刚刚出厂的汽车平均开支的金额增长了30%。在同样的时期中，购买汽车的开支占家庭平均预算的比例并未发生变化。因此在过去的五年中家庭平均预算一定也增加了30%。

以上论述依据下面哪个假设？

(A) 在过去五年中，平均每个家庭购买新的刚出厂的汽车的数量没有变化。

(B) 在过去五年中，企业平均在每辆新车上的花费增长了30%。

(C) 在过去五年中，家庭平均花在和汽车有关的方面的费用没有变。

(D) 在过去五年中，家庭平均花在食物和住房上的开支没有变。

(E) 在过去五年中，全国花费在新的刚出厂的汽车上的费用增长了30%。

36. Armtech, a temporary-employment agency, previously gave its employees 2.5 paid vacation days after each 700 hours worked. Armtech's new policy is to give its employees 5.0 paid vacation days after each 1,200 hours worked. Therefore, this new policy is more generous to Armtech employees in giving them more vacation days per hour worked than the old policy did.

Which of the following is an assumption on which the argument depends?

一个临时雇佣机构Armtech以前在它的雇员每工作700小时后，给他们两天半的有偿假期。Armtech的新政策则是在其雇员每工作1200小时后给他们五天的有偿假期。所以，这项新政策对雇员更加慷慨了，它使雇员平均每小时工作得到的假期比以往更多了。

这一论述依据下面哪个假设？

(A) Most current Armtech employees approve of the company's new vacation policy.

(B) A few Armtech employees leave the company before having worked 700 hours.

(C) Most Armtech employees were not aware that the company planned to change its vacation policy until after it had already done so.

(D) A significant portion of Armtech employees stay with the company long enough to work for 1,200 hours.

(E) Armtech's new vacation policy closely matches the vacation policies of competing temporary employment agencies.

(A) 目前绝大部分的工人赞同公司的新政策。

(B) 一些工人在没工作到700小时就离开了公司。

(C) 大多数工人在公司的政策改变之前从来没意识到公司计划改变政策。

(D) 相当一部分雇员能够工作长达1200小时。

(E) Armtech的新政策和其他与之竞争的临时雇佣公司一致。

37. Editorial：

Critics of nuclear power complain about the allegedly serious harm that might result from continued operation of existing nuclear power plants. But such concerns do not justify closing these plants; after all, their operation has caused no more harm than that caused by pollution generated by coal and oil-burning power plants, the most important other sources of energy.

Which of the following is an assumption on which the argument depends?

(A) Existing nuclear power plants should be closed only if it can be conclusively demonstrated that their continued operation is likely to cause harm more serious than the harm their operation has already caused.

(B) Closing existing nuclear power plants would require greatly increased reliance on coal and oil-burning power plants.

(C) The harm that has resulted from operation of existing coal and oil-burning power plants has been significant.

(D) The harm that a nuclear power plant is likely to cause as it continues to operate can be reliably predicted from the past history of nuclear power plants.

(E) The only harm that has resulted from operation of existing coal and oil-burning power plants has resulted from the pollution generated by these plants.

社论：

对核能持批评态度的人抱怨继续经营现有的核电厂可能会导致严重的危害。但是这样的抱怨并不能证明关闭这些核电厂是合理的；毕竟，它们的经营导致的危害还不及燃煤和燃油发电厂——最重要的其他电力来源——产生的污染所导致的危害大。

以上论述依据下面哪个假设？

(A) 仅当能证实核电厂的继续运行会比现在运行已造成的危害大时，现有的核电厂才应该被关闭。

(B) 关闭核电厂会大量增加对燃煤发电厂和燃油发电厂的依靠性。

(C) 到目前为止，现有燃油和燃煤发电厂的运营产生的危害已相当大。

(D) 继续运行核电厂可能产生的危害能根据它们以前产生的危害可靠地预测。

(E) 现有的燃煤和燃油发电厂的运营产生的唯一危害是它们产生的污染。

38. Fossils of the coral Acrocora palmata that date from the last period when glaciers grew and consequently spread from the polar regions are found at ocean depths far greater than those at which A. palmata can now survive. Therefore, although the fossilized A. palmata appears indistinguishable

上一个冰川形成并从极地扩散时期的珊瑚Acrocora palmata化石在比它现在生长的地方深得多的海底被发现了，因此，尽管它与现在生长的Acrocora palmata看起来没多大区别，但能在深水中生长说明它们

from A. palmata now living, it must have differed in important respects to have been able to live in deep water.

The argument depends on the assumption that

(A) no fossils of the coral A. palmata have been found that date from periods when glaciers were not spreading from the polar regions.

(B) geological disturbances since the last period during which glaciers spread have caused no major downward shift in the location of A. palmata fossils.

(C) A. palmata now live in shallow waters in most of the same geographical regions as those in which deep-lying A. palmata fossils have been found.

(D) A. patlmata fossils have been found that date from each of the periods during which glaciers are known to have spread from the polar region.

(E) A. palmata can live at greater depths where the ocean temperature is colder than they can where the ocean temperature is warmer.

39. Census data for Prenland show that unmarried Prenlandic men in their thirties outnumber unmarried Prenlandic women in that age group by about ten to one. Most of these men do wish to marry. Clearly, however, unless many of them marry women who are not Prenlandic, all but a minority will remain unmarried.

The argument makes which of the following assumptions?

(A) Emigration from Prenland is more common among women than among men.

(B) A greater proportion of Prenlandic women in their thirties than of Prenlandic men of the same age would prefer to remain unmarried.

(C) It is unlikely that many of these unmarried Prenlandic men will marry women more than a few years older than themselves.

(D) Prenland has a high rate of divorce.

(E) Most of the unmarried Prenlandic men are unwilling to marry women who are not Prenlandic.

40. Although the prevailing supposition has been that it is too hot for microorganisms to survive deep below the Earth's surface, some scientists argue that there are living communities of microorganisms there that have been cut off from surface life for millions of years. These scientists base their argument on the discovery of living microorganisms in

之间在重要的方面有很大的不同。

上述论证依据下面哪个假设？

(A) 还未发现冰川未从极地扩散之前时期的珊瑚Acrocora palmata的化石。

(B) 冰川扩散时代的地理变动并未使Acrocora palmata化石下沉。

(C) 今天的palmata大都生活在与那些在较深处发现的palmata化石具有相同地理区域的较浅位置。

(D) 已发现了冰川从极地扩散的各个时期的Acrocora palmata化石。

(E) Acrocora palmata能够在更深、比它们现处较暖温度更冷的水中生存。

Prenland的人口普查数据表明，当地30多岁未婚男性的人数是当地30多岁的未婚女性人数的10倍，这些男性都想结婚，但是很显然，除非他们多数与Prenland以外的妇女结婚，否则除去一小部分外，大多数还是会独身。

以上论述依据下面哪个假设？

(A) 女性比男性更易离开Prenland。

(B) 30多岁的女性比同年龄的男性更趋向于独身。

(C) Prenland的男性不大可能和比他们大几岁的女性结婚。

(D) Prenland的离婚率很高。

(E) 绝大部分未婚的Prenland的男性不愿意和外地女性结婚。

虽然普遍的猜想认为地表以下深层的地方太热以致微生物不可能存活，一些科学家还是争辩说地表深处存在着与地表生物隔绝了数百万年的活的微生物群体。他们观点的根据是从1.74英里深的钻洞里取出的样本物质中发现了活着的微生物。

samples of material that were taken from holes drilled as deep as 1.74 miles.

The scientists' argument depends on which of the following assumptions?

(A) The microorganisms brought up were of a species that is related to those previously known to science.

(B) No holes have been drilled into the Earth's surface to a distance deeper than 1.74 miles.

(C) The microorganisms did not come from surface soil that came into contact with the drilling equipment.

(D) The stratum from which the samples came has been below the surface of the Earth ever since the Earth came into existence.

(E) The temperature at the bottom of the holes drilled was not significantly hotter than that of the hottest spots on the Earth's surface.

41. Automobile exhaust is a serious pollution problem in Riverside, and instituting tolls at Riverside's bridges would reduce the total number of miles traveled by automobiles. Nevertheless, overall pollution levels would not decrease because there would be long lines at the toll booths, and automobiles expel more exhaust per minute while idling than in any other driving situation.

The argument above depends on which of the following assumptions?

(A) Any reduction in automobile exhaust resulting from a reduction in the miles traveled by cars would be matched or surpassed by the additional exhaust resulting from toll lines.

(B) Cars in Riverside spend more time, on average, idling than they do in other driving situations.

(C) Increasing automobile exhaust at the bridges will not significantly affect air pollution because few drivers use the bridges in Riverside frequently.

(D) Reducing automobile exhaust is not the most effective way of reducing air pollution.

(E) The inconvenience of idling in the long toll lines at Riverside's bridges will cause most drivers to change their driving routes, not the amount of driving that they do.

42. One state adds a 7 percent sales tax to the price of most products purchased within its jurisdiction. This tax, therefore,

科学家的论述依据下面哪个假设？

(A) 这些取出来的微生物与先前科学家所熟知的物种有联系。

(B) 地表以下钻的洞没有再比1.74英里深的。

(C) 这些微生物并不是来自于钻机接触到的地表土壤中。

(D) 得到试样的地层是自从地球形成时就一直在地表以下。

(E) 所钻洞的底部温度并不比地表温度高多少。

汽车尾气是Riverside一项严重的污染问题，对Riverside的桥梁征收通行费能够减少汽车行驶的总里程。然而，总的污染水平并没有减少，这是因为收费站处将有许多汽车排起长队，而汽车在开着发动机不行驶的状态下，每分钟所排出的尾气比在其他任何行驶状态下排出的尾气都多。

以上的观点是建立在下列哪个假设的基础上的？

(A) 减少汽车行驶里程可以减小污染量，但在收费站停留时排出的尾气所造成的污染的增加量和减少量持平，甚至会超过减少量。

(B) 平均而言，Riverside的汽车处于开着发动机而不行驶的状态下的时间比处于其他行驶状态下的时间长。

(C) 大桥处汽车尾气的增加量不会显著影响空气污染，这是因为在Riverside没有多少汽车司机经常通过大桥。

(D) 减少汽车尾气不是减少空气污染的最有效办法。

(E) 由于在收费站排长队很不方便，Riverside的许多司机就改变路线，其行车里程也就随之变化。

某州针对在其境内购买的大多数产品的价格增收了7%的销售税。从而，这项税

if viewed as tax on income, has the reverse effect of the federal income tax: the lower the income, the higher the annual percentage rate at which the income is taxed.

The conclusion above would be properly drawn if which of the following were assumed as a premise?

(A) The amount of money citizens spend on products subject to the state tax tends to be equal across income levels.

(B) The federal income tax favors citizens with high incomes, whereas the state sales tax favors citizens with low incomes.

(C) Citizens with low annual incomes can afford to pay a relatively higher percentage of their incomes in state sales tax, since their federal income tax is relatively low.

(D) The lower a state's sales tax, the more it will tend to redistribute income from the more affluent citizens to the rest of society.

(E) Citizens who fail to earn federally taxable income are also exempt from the state sales tax.

43. The interview is an essential part of a successful hiring program because, with it, job applicants who have personalities that are unsuited to the requirements of the job will be eliminated from consideration.

The argument above logically depends on which of the following assumptions?

(A) A hiring program will be successful if it includes interviews.

(B) The interview is a more important part of a successful hiring program than is the development of a job description.

(C) Interviewers can accurately identify applicants whose personalities are unsuited to the requirements of the job.

(D) The only purpose of an interview is to evaluate whether job applicants' personalities are suited to the requirements of the job.

(E) The fit of job applicants' personalities to the requirements of the job was once the most important factor in making hiring decisions.

44. A recent report determined that although only three percent of drivers on Maryland highways equipped their vehicles with radar detectors, thirty-three percent of all vehicles ticketed for exceeding the speed limit were equipped with them. Clearly, drivers who equip their vehicles with radar detectors are more

收如果被视为一种收入税，其与联邦收入税的效果是相反的：收入越低，每年收入被征税的比率越高。

下面哪个说法被假定为前提时，可以适当地得出以上的结论？

(A) 不同收入水平的人在该州税法适用的产品上所花费的钱都是一样的。

(B) 联邦收入税对高收入的人有利，而该州的销售税对低收入的人有利。

(C) 年收入较低的人可能把他们的收入中相对较高的比例用来支付州的销售税，因为他们的联邦收入税相对要低。

(D) 一个州的销售税越低，它越倾向于把较富的人的收入再分配到社会其他人那里。

(E) 挣不到联邦应税收入的人也不用交纳州的销售税。

面试是成功的招聘程序中必要的一部分，因为有了面试以后，性格不符合工作需要的求职者可以不予考虑。

以上的论证在逻辑上依据下面哪个假设？

(A) 如果一项招聘程序包括面试，它就会是成功的。

(B) 一项成功的招聘程序中，面试比求职信的情况更重要。

(C) 面试可准确识别出性格不符合工作需要的求职者。

(D) 面试的唯一目的是评价求职者的性格是否符合工作需要。

(E) 在做出招聘决定时，求职者的性格符合工作需要曾经是最重要的因素。

一份最近的报告确定，尽管只有3%的在马里兰州的高速公路上驾驶的司机为其汽车装备了雷达探查器，因超速而被开罚单的汽车上却有33%以上装备了雷达探查器。显然，在车上装备了雷达探查器的

likely to exceed the speed limit regularly than are drivers who do not.

The conclusion drawn above depends on which of the following assumptions?

(A) Drivers who equip their vehicles with radar detectors are less likely to be ticketed for exceeding the speed limit than are drivers who do not.

(B) Drivers who are ticketed for exceeding the speed limit are more likely to exceed the speed limit regularly than are drivers who are not ticketed.

(C) The number of vehicles that were ticketed for exceeding the speed limit was greater than the number of vehicles that were equipped with radar detectors.

(D) Many of the vehicles that were ticketed for exceeding the speed limit were ticketed more than once in the time period covered by the report.

(E) Drivers on Maryland highways exceeded the speed limit more often than did drivers on other state highways not covered in the report.

45. Researchers have found that when very overweight people, who tend to have relatively low metabolic rates, lose weight primarily through dieting, their metabolisms generally remain unchanged. They will thus burn significantly fewer calories at the new weight than do people whose weight is normally at that level. Such newly thin persons will, therefore, ultimately regain weight until their body size again matches their metabolic rate.

The conclusion of the argument above depends on which of the following assumptions?

(A) Relatively few very overweight people who have dieted down to a new weight tend to continue to consume substantially fewer calories than do people whose normal weight is at that level.

(B) The metabolisms of people who are usually not overweight are much more able to vary than the metabolisms of people who have been very overweight.

(C) The amount of calories that a person usually burns in a day is determined more by the amount that is consumed that day than by the current weight of the individual.

(D) Researchers have not yet determined whether the metabolic rates of formerly very overweight individuals can be accelerated by means of chemical agents.

(E) Because of the constancy of their metabolic rates, people

司机比没有这么做的司机更有可能经常超速。

以上得出的结论依据下面哪个假设?

(A) 在车上装备了雷达探查器的司机比没有这么做的司机因超速而被开罚单的可能性更小。

(B) 因超速而被开罚单的司机比超速而未被开罚单的司机更可能经常超速。

(C) 因超速而被开罚单的汽车数量大于装备了雷达探查器的汽车数量。

(D) 在该报告涉及的时期内,许多因超速而被开罚单的汽车不止一次被开罚单了。

(E) 在马里兰州的高速公路上驾驶的司机比在这份报告没有涉及的其他州的高速公路上驾驶的司机更经常地超速。

研究人员们发现当过度超重的人——他们的新陈代谢速度相对较低——主要通过节食减肥时,他们的新陈代谢通常没有变化。这样一来,在新的体重下,他们比其他体重正常处于那一水平的人消耗明显更少的卡路里。所以,这些刚刚瘦下来的人最终还会胖起来,直至他们的身体重量与其新陈代谢速度再次匹配。

以上论证所得的结论依据下面哪个假设?

(A) 相对于在那一水平体重正常的人来讲,通过节食把体重降低到一个新重量的过度超重的人很少会坚持吃进明显更少的卡路里。

(B) 没有超重的人的新陈代谢比过度超重的人的新陈代谢更能够变化。

(C) 一个人每天通常吃进的卡路里数量更多地是由他当天进食的数量决定,而不是由他目前的体重决定。

(D) 研究人员们尚未确定以前过度超重的人的新陈代谢速度是否可以通过化学物质的方法来加快。

(E) 因为新陈代谢速度是稳定的,那些处于他们的正常体重的人增肥和减肥都

who are at their usual weight normally have as much difficulty gaining weight as they do losing it.

46. Previous studies have indicated that eating chocolate increases the likelihood of getting heart disease. However, a new, more reliable study has indicated that eating chocolate does not increase the likelihood of getting heart disease. When the results of the new study become known, consumption of chocolate will undoubtedly increase.

Which of the following is an assumption on which the conclusion above is based?

(A) Most people who eat a great deal of chocolate will not get heart disease.

(B) Although they believe that eating chocolate increases the likelihood of getting heart disease, some people still eat as much chocolate as they want.

(C) People who have heard that eating chocolate increases the likelihood of getting heart disease do not believe it.

(D) There are people who currently eat as much chocolate as they want because they have not heard that eating chocolate increases the likelihood of getting heart disease.

(E) There are people who currently limit their consumption of chocolate only because they believe that eating chocolate increases the likelihood of getting heart disease.

47. Exports of United States wood pulp will rise considerably during this year. The reason for the rise is that the falling value of the dollar will make it cheaper for paper manufacturers in Japan and Western Europe to buy American wood pulp than to get it from any other source.

Which of the following is an assumption made in drawing the conclusion above?

(A) Factory output of paper products in Japan and Western Europe will increase sharply during this year.

(B) The quality of the wood pulp produced in the United States would be adequate for the purposes of Japanese and Western European paper manufacturers.

(C) Paper manufacturers in Japan and Western Europe would prefer to use wood pulp produced in the United States if cost were not a factor.

(D) Demand for paper products made in Japan and Western Europe will not increase sharply during this year.

(E) Production of wood pulp by United States companies will not increase sharply during this year.

非常困难。

以往的研究已经表明，吃巧克力增加了患心脏病的可能性。但是，一项新的更值得信赖的研究表明，吃巧克力不会增加患心脏病的可能性。当这项新的研究结果公布的时候，巧克力的消费量会毫无疑问地增加。

下面哪个是以上结论所依据的假设？

(A) 大多数吃很多巧克力的人不会患心脏病。

(B) 虽然有些人相信吃巧克力增加了患心脏病的可能性，他们吃的巧克力数量还是凭自己喜好。

(C) 听说吃巧克力增加了患心脏病的可能性的人并不相信这种说法。

(D) 有些人现在还是凭自己喜好吃巧克力，因为他们还没有听说吃巧克力增加了患心脏病的可能性。

(E) 有些人目前控制了他们消费的巧克力数量，仅仅因为他们相信吃巧克力增加了患心脏病的可能性。

美国纸浆的出口量今年会显著上升，出口量上升的原因在于美元的贬值使得日本和西欧的造纸商从美国购买纸浆比从其他渠道购买便宜。

下面哪个是为得出以上结论所做的假设？

(A) 日本和西欧的工厂出产的纸制品今年会急剧增加。

(B) 美国生产的纸浆质量足以满足日本和西欧造纸商的生产目的。

(C) 如果成本不成为影响因素，日本和西欧的造纸商会倾向于使用美国生产的纸浆。

(D) 对日本和西欧生产的纸制品的需求今年不会急剧增加。

(E) 美国公司的纸浆产量今年不会急剧增加。

48. A company's personnel director surveyed employees about their satisfaction with the company's system for awarding employee performance ratings. The survey data indicated that employees who received high ratings were very satisfied with the system. The personnel director concluded from these data that the company's best-performing employees liked the system.

The personnel director's conclusion assumes which of the following?

(A) No other performance rating system is as good as the current system.

(B) The company's best-performing employees received high ratings.

(C) Employees who received low ratings were dissatisfied with the system.

(D) Employees who receive high ratings from a performance-rating system will like that system.

(E) The company's best-performing employees were motivated to perform well by the knowledge that they would receive performance ratings.

一家公司的人事主管调查了员工们对公司的奖励员工绩效等级体系的满意度。调查数据显示得到较高等级的员工们对该体系非常满意。这位人事主管从这些数据中得出结论认为，公司中表现最好的员工们喜欢这个体系。

该人事主管的结论假定了下面哪种说法？

(A) 其他的绩效等级体系都比不上既有的体系。

(B) 该公司的表现最好的员工们得到了高的等级。

(C) 得到低等级的员工们对该体系不满意。

(D) 从一种绩效等级体系中得到高等级的员工们会喜欢这个体系。

(E) 该公司的表现最好的员工们受到激励去好好工作，因为他们知道他们会得到绩效等级。

49. The wild mouflon sheep of the island of Corsica are direct descendants of sheep that escaped from domestication on the island 8,000 years ago. They therefore provide archaeologists with a picture of what some early domesticated sheep looked like, before the deliberate selective breeding that produced modern domesticated sheep began.

The argument above makes which of the following assumptions?

(A) The domesticated sheep of 8,000 years ago were quite dissimilar from the wild sheep of the time.

(B) There are no other existing breeds of sheep that escaped from domestication at about the same time as the forebears of the mouflon.

(C) Modern domesticated sheep are direct descendants of sheep that were wild 8,000 years ago.

(D) Mouflon sheep are more similar to their forebears of 8,000 years ago than modern domesticated sheep are to theirs.

(E) The climate of Corsica has not changed at all in the last 8,000 years.

科西嘉岛上的野生摩弗伦绵羊是8000年前该岛逃过家庭驯养的绵羊的直接后代。因此它们为考古学家们提供了在刻意选种产生现代绵羊开始之前早期驯养的绵羊的模样。

以上的论证得到了下面哪个假设？

(A) 8000年前的驯养绵羊与现在的野生绵羊非常不同。

(B) 同时逃过家庭驯养的绵羊品种中，不存在其他的作为摩弗伦羊的祖先。

(C) 现代的驯养绵羊是8000年前野生绵羊的直接后代。

(D) 摩弗伦绵羊与它们8000年前的祖先之间的相似之处比它们与现代驯养绵羊之间的相似之处多。

(E) 在过去8000年中，科西嘉岛的气候一点也没有变化。

50. Within 20 years it will probably be possible to identify the genetic susceptibility an individual may have toward any particular disease. Eventually, effective strategies will be discovered to counteract each such susceptibility. Once these effective strategies are found, therefore, the people who follow them will never get sick.

The argument above is based on which of the following assumptions?

(A) For every disease there is only one strategy that can prevent its occurrence.

(B) In the future, genetics will be the only medical specialty of any importance.

(C) All human sicknesses are in part the result of individuals' genetic susceptibilities.

(D) All humans are genetically susceptible to some diseases.

(E) People will follow medical advice when they are convinced that it is effective.

51. Although computers can enhance people's ability to communicate, computer games are a cause of underdeveloped communication skills in children. After-school hours spent playing computer games are hours not spent talking with people. Therefore, children who spend all their spare time playing these games have less experience in interpersonal communication than other children have.

The argument depends on which of the following assumptions?

(A) Passive activities such as watching television and listening to music do not hinder the development of communication skills in children.

(B) Most children have other opportunities, in addition to after-school hours, in which they can choose whether to play computer games or to interact with other people.

(C) Children who do not spend all of their after-school hours playing computer games spend at least some of that time talking with other people.

(D) Formal instruction contributes little or nothing to children's acquisition of communication skills.

(E) The mental skills developed through playing computer games do not contribute significantly to children's intellectual development.

52. How do the airlines expect to prevent commercial plane crashes? Studies have shown that pilot error contributes to

在20年内，识别针对某个人可能有的对某种疾病的基因敏感性或许是可以做到的。结果是，可以找出有效的措施来抵制每种这样的敏感性。所以，一旦找到了这样的措施，按这些措施做的人就再也不会生病了。

以上的论证依据下面哪个假设？

(A) 对每种疾病来讲只有一种阻止其发生的措施。

(B) 在将来，基因学是唯一的有重要意义的医学专业。

(C) 所有的人类疾病部分意义上都是个人基因敏感性的结果。

(D) 所有人在基因上对某些疾病都是敏感的。

(E) 当确信某种医疗建议时，人们会按建议去做。

虽然计算机可以增进人们交流的手段，计算机游戏却是儿童交流技巧发展水平低的一个原因。课后花在玩计算机游戏上的时间也就是没有花在与其他人交谈上面的时间。所以，把所有闲暇时间都用来玩这些游戏的儿童比其他儿童有更少的人际交流经验。

这个结论依据下面哪个假设？

(A) 看电视、听音乐等被动活动没有阻碍儿童交流技巧的发展。

(B) 除了课后时间，大多数儿童有其他机会来进行选择是玩电脑游戏还是与其他人交际。

(C) 没有把他们所有课后时间都用于玩电脑游戏的儿童至少会花费一部分时间来与别人交谈。

(D) 正式的教育对儿童交流技巧的获得很少或者讲没有贡献。

(E) 通过玩电脑游戏而发展的心理技巧不能显著地对儿童的智力发展产生作用。

航空公司是怎样来防止商业飞机坠毁的呢？研究表明，在所有这样的坠毁事故

two-thirds of all such crashes. To address this problem, the airlines have upgraded their training programs by increasing the hours of classroom instruction and emphasizing communication skills in the cockpit. But it is unrealistic to expect such measures to compensate for pilots' lack of actual flying time. Therefore, the airlines should rethink their training approach to reducing commercial crashes.

Which one of the following is an assumption upon which the argument depends?

(A) Training programs can eliminate pilot errors.

(B) Commercial pilots routinely undergo additional training throughout their careers.

(C) The number of airline crashes will decrease if pilot training programs focus on increasing actual flying time.

(D) Lack of actual flying time is an important contributor to pilot error in commercial plane crashes.

(E) Communication skills are not important to pilot training programs.

53. Current legislation that requires designated sections for smokers and nonsmokers on the premises of privately owned businesses is an intrusion into the private sector that cannot be justified. The fact that studies indicate that nonsmokers might be harmed by inhaling the smoke from others' cigarettes is not the main issue. Rather, the main issue concerns the government's violation of the right of private businesses to determine their own policies and rules.

Which one of the following is a principle that, if accepted, could enable the conclusion to be properly drawn?

(A) Government intrusion into the policies and rules of private businesses is justified only when individuals might be harmed.

(B) The right of individuals to breathe safe air supersedes the right of businesses to be free from government intrusion.

(C) The right of businesses to self-determination overrides whatever right or duty the government may have to protect the individual.

(D) It is the duty of private businesses to protect employees from harm in the workplace.

(E) Where the rights of businesses and the duty of government conflict, the main issue is finding a successful compromise.

中，有2/3的事故归因于飞行员的失误。为了正视这个问题，航空公司通过增加课堂教育时间和强调飞行员在座舱里的通讯技巧来升级它们的训练方案，但是期望这些措施能补偿飞行员实际飞行时间的缺乏是不现实的。因此，航空公司应当重新考虑它们的通过训练来减少商业飞机坠毁的方法。

下面哪一点，是上述论述依赖的假设？

(A) 训练计划能消除飞行员的失误。

(B) 商业飞行员在他们的整个职业生涯中，要经历附加的日常训练。

(C) 如果飞行员训练计划能着重增加飞行员的实际飞行时间，那么航空公司的飞机坠毁数量就会下降。

(D) 缺乏实际飞行经验是飞行员在商业飞机坠毁事故中失误的主要原因。

(E) 通讯技巧对飞行员训练计划不重要。

目前，要求私营企业为抽烟者和不抽烟者设立不同的办公区的法规是一种对私营部门进行侵犯的不合理法规。研究指出的不抽烟者可能会由于吸入其他抽烟者的烟味而受害的事实并不是主要的问题。相反主要的问题是政府侵犯了私营企业决定它们自己的政策和法规的权利。

下面哪条原则，如果能被接受，能合理地推出上述结论？

(A) 仅当个人可能会被伤害时，政府侵犯私营企业的政策和法规的行为才是正当的。

(B) 个人呼吸安全空气的权利高于企业不受政府侵犯的权利。

(C) 企业的独自裁决权高于政府必须保护个人的一切权利和义务。

(D) 保护雇员在工作场所不受伤害是私营企业的义务。

(E) 当企业权利与政府的职责发生冲突时，最主要的问题是找到一个成功的折衷办法。

54. The brains of identical twins are genetically identical. When only one of a pair of identical twins is a schizophrenic, certain areas of the affected twin's brain are smaller than corresponding areas in the brain of the unaffected twin. No such differences are found when neither twin is schizophrenic. Therefore, this discovery provides definitive evidence that schizophrenia is caused by damage to the physical structure of the brain.

Which one of the following is an assumption required by the argument?

(A) The brain of a person suffering from schizophrenia is smaller than the brain of anyone not suffering from schizophrenia.

(B) The relative smallness of certain parts of the brains of schizophrenics is not the result of schizophrenia or of medications used in its treatment.

(C) The brain of a person with an identical twin is no smaller, on average, than the brain of a person who is not a twin.

(D) When a pair of identical twins both suffer from schizophrenia, their brains are the same size.

(E) People who have an identical twin are no more likely to suffer from schizophrenia than those who do not.

55. Fire ants from Brazil now infest the southern United States. Unlike queen fire ants in Brazil, two queens in the United States share a nest. Ants from these nests are more aggressive than those from single-queen nests. By destroying virtually all insects in the nest area, these aggressive ants gain sole access to food sources, and the ant population skyrockets. Since certain predator insects in Brazil limit the fire-ant population there, importing such predator insects into the United States would be of overall benefit to the environment by stopping the increase of the fire-ant population in the United States.

Each of the following is an assumption made in the argument EXCEPT:

(A) The imported insects would not prove more damaging to the environment in the United States than are the fire ants themselves.

(B) The predator insects from Brazil could survive in the ecological environment found in the United States.

(C) The especially aggressive fire ants from the two-queen nests would not be able to destroy the Brazilian predator insects.

同卵双生子的大脑在遗传上是完全相同的。当一对同卵双生子中的一个人患上精神分裂症时，受感染的那个人的大脑中的某个区域比没受感染的那个人的大脑中的相应区域小。当双胞胎中的两个人都没有精神分裂症时，两人就没有这样的差异。因此，这个发现为精神分裂症是由大脑的物质结构受损而引起的理论提供了确定的证据。

下面哪一点是上述论述需要的假设？

(A) 患有精神分裂症的人的大脑比任何不患精神分裂症的人的大脑小。

(B) 精神分裂症患者的大脑的某些区域相对较小不是精神分裂症或治疗它的过程中使用的医药的结果。

(C) 同卵双生子中一个人的大脑平均来说不比非同卵双生子的人的大脑小。

(D) 当一对同卵双生子都患有精神分裂症时，他们大脑的大小是一样的。

(E) 拥有同卵双生子的人患精神分裂症的可能性和那些不拥有同卵双生子的人患精神分裂症的可能性是一样的。

来自巴西的火蚁现在正大批出没于美国的南部地区。不像巴西的火蚁王后，在美国两个火蚁王后分享一个窝。来自这些窝的火蚁比来自单一王后的窝里的火蚁更具侵略性。通过摧毁几乎所有在它们的窝所属区域出现的昆虫，这些具有侵略性的火蚁就独自霸占食物资源，于是这些火蚁的数量猛烈地增长。既然在巴西有某些捕食火蚁的昆虫能限制那儿火蚁数量的增加，那么向美国进口这些捕食火蚁的昆虫来抑制该地区火蚁数量的增加将从总体上对那儿的环境有益。

下面除了哪一点之外，都是上述论述中所做的假设？

(A) 进口的昆虫对美国环境造成的危害不会比火蚁自身对环境造成的危害大。

(B) 来自巴西的那些捕食火蚁的昆虫在美国的生态环境中也能存活。

(C) 那些来自双王后的窝的特别具有侵略性的火蚁不会消灭巴西的那些捕食火蚁的昆虫。

(D) The predator insects would stop the increase of the ant population before the ants spread to states that are farther north.

(E) The rate of increase of the fire-ant population would not exceed the rate at which the predator insects could kill the ants.

56. The workers at Bell Manufacturing will shortly go on strike unless the management increases their wages. As Bell's president is well aware, however, in order to increase the workers' wages, Bell would have to sell off some of its subsidiaries. So, some of Bell's subsidiaries will be sold.

The conclusion above is properly drawn if which one of the following is assumed?

(A) Bell Manufacturing will begin to suffer increased losses.

(B) Bell's management will refuse to increase its workers' wages.

(C) The workers at Bell Manufacturing will not be going on strike.

(D) Bell's president has the authority to offer the workers their desired wage increase.

(E) Bell's workers will not accept a package of improved benefits in place of their desired wage increase.

57. One sure way you can tell how quickly a new idea, for example, the idea of "privatization," is taking hold among the population is to monitor how fast the word or words expressing that particular idea are passing into common usage. Professional opinions of whether or not words can indeed be said to have passed into common usage are available from dictionary editors, who are vitally concerned with this question.

The method described above for determining how quickly a new idea is taking hold relies on which one of the following assumptions?

(A) Dictionary editors are not professionally interested in words that are only rarely used.

(B) Dictionary editors have exact numerical criteria for telling when a word has passed into common usage.

(C) For a new idea to take hold, dictionary editors have to include the relevant word or words in their dictionaries.

(D) As a word passes into common usage, its meaning does not undergo any severe distortions in the process.

(D) 那些捕食火蚁的昆虫会在火蚁延伸到比较靠北的州之前抑制住火蚁数量的增加。

(E) 火蚁的数量增加的比率不会超过那些捕食火蚁的昆虫杀死火蚁的比率。

Bell制造业的工人很快就要举行罢工，除非管理部门给他们涨工资。因为Bell的总裁很清楚，为给工人涨工资，Bell必须卖掉它的一些子公司。所以Bell的某些子公司将会被出售。

如果假设下面哪一项，就可以合理地推出上面的结论？

(A) Bell制造业将会开始蒙受更多的损失。

(B) Bell的管理部门将会拒绝给它的工人们涨工资。

(C) 在Bell制造业工作的工人将不会举行罢工。

(D) Bell的总裁有权力来满足给他的工人们要求的工资增长。

(E) Bell的工人不会接受以一系列改善的福利来代替他们渴望的工资增加。

要断定一个新的概念，例如"私人化"这个概念能多快在公众中占据一席之地的一个确信的办法是观察代表这个概念的单词或短语多快能变成一种习惯用法。关于短语是否确实已被认为变成了一种习惯用法可以从字典编辑那里得到专业意见，他们对这个问题非常地关心。

上面描述的断定一个新的概念能多快被公众接受的办法依赖于下面哪个假设？

(A) 字典编辑从职业上讲对那些很少使用的短语并不感兴趣。

(B) 字典编辑有确切的数量标准来断定一个单词是在什么时候转变成了一种习惯用法。

(C) 一个新的概念要被接受，字典编辑就必须在他们的字典里收录相关的单词或短语。

(D) 当一个单词转变成一种习惯用法时，它的意思在转变的过程中不会经受任

(E) Words denoting new ideas tend to be used before the ideas denoted are understood.

58. Scientists attempting to replicate certain controversial results reported by a group of experienced researchers failed to get the same results as those reported. The conclusion drawn from this by the scientists who conducted the replication experiments was that the originally reported results had been due to faulty measurements.

The argument of the scientists who conducted the replication experiments assumes that

(A) the original experiments had not been described in sufficient detail to make an exact replication possible.

(B) the fact that the originally reported results aroused controversy made it highly likely that they were in error.

(C) the theoretical principles called into question by the originally reported results were themselves based on weak evidence.

(D) the replication experiments were not so likely as the original experiments to be marred by faulty measurements.

(E) the researchers who originally reported the controversial results had themselves observed those results only once.

59. Since Mayor Drabble always repays her political debts as soon as possible, she will almost certainly appoint Lee to be the new head of the arts commission. Lee has wanted that job for a long time, and Drabble owes Lee a lot for his support in the last election.

Which one of the following is an assumption on which the argument depends?

(A) Mayor Drabble has no political debt that is both of longer standing than the one she owes to Lee and could as suitable be repaid by an appointment to be the new head of the arts commission.

(B) There is no one to whom Mayor Drabble owes a greater political debt for support in the last election than the political debt she owes to Lee.

(C) Lee is the only person to whom Mayor Drabble owes a political debt who would be willing to accept an appointment from her as the new head of the arts commission.

(D) Whether Lee is qualified to head the arts commission is irrelevant to Mayor Drabble's decision.

何严重的歪曲。

(E) 那些表示新概念的单词倾向于在它所表示的概念被理解之前被使用。

那些企图重复被一群有经验的科学家报道的某些有争议的实验结果的科学家没有得到与那些报道相一致的结果。进行重复试验的科学家由此得出结论认为起初报道的结果是由于错误的测量引起的。

进行重复试验的科学家的论述假设认为……

(A) 最初的实验被描述得不够详尽，使得完全重复这样的试验变得不大可能。

(B) 最初报道的实验结果引起了争议的事实使得这些结果很有可能是错的。

(C) 受最初报道的试验结果质疑的理论原则本身就基于不充分的证据。

(D) 那些重复实验不可能像原始实验那样被错误的测量所损害。

(E) 那些最初报道有争议的结果的研究者们自己也仅观察到这些结果一次。

因为Drabble市长通常都会尽快地偿还她在政治上的债务，所以她一定会委任Lee为艺术委员会的新领导。Lee很长一段时间以来都想得到那个工作，并且Drabble因在上次选举中得到了Lee的支持而欠他很多。

下面哪一项是上面论述依赖的一个假设？

(A) Drabble市长没有比欠Lee的时间更长，并且比委任Lee作为艺术委员会的领导更合适的方式偿还政治上的债务。

(B) Drabble市长在上次选举中因得到别人的支持而欠的债中，欠Lee的债最多。

(C) Lee是仅有的一个Drabble市长欠他政治债的人，并且他愿意接受Drabble市长委任他为艺术委员会的新领导。

(D) Lee是否有资格领导艺术委员会与Drabble市长的决定无关。

(E) The only way that Mayor Drabble can adequately repay her political debt to Lee is by appointing him to head the arts commission.

60. The number of hospital emergency room visits by heroin users grew by more than 25 percent during the 1980s. Clearly, then, the use of heroin rose in that decade.

The author's conclusion is properly drawn if which one of the following is assumed?

(A) Those who seek medical care because of heroin use usually do so in the later stages of addiction.

(B) Many heroin users visit hospital emergency rooms repeatedly.

(C) The number of visits to hospital emergency rooms by heroin users is proportional to the incidence of heroin usage.

(D) The methods of using heroin have changed since 1980, and the new methods are less hazardous.

(E) Users of heroin identify themselves as such when they come to hospital emergency rooms.

61. When permits for the discharge of chemicals into a waterway are issued, they are issued in terms of the number of pounds of each chemical that can be discharged into the waterway per day. These figures, calculated separately for each chemical for which a permit is issued, are based on an estimate of the effect of the dilution of the chemical by the amount of water flowing through the waterway. The waterway is therefore protected against being adversely affected by chemicals discharged under the permits.

The argument depends on the assumption that

(A) relatively harmless chemicals do not interact with each other in the water to form harmful compounds.

(B) there is a swift flow of water in the waterway that ensures rapid dispersion of chemicals discharged.

(C) there are no chemicals for which discharge into waterways is entirely prohibited.

(D) those who receive the permits do not always discharge the entire quantity of chemicals that the permits allow.

(E) the danger of chemical pollution of waterways is to be

(E) Drabble市长能充分地偿还她欠Lee的政治债的唯一办法是委任他领导艺术委员会。

在20世纪80年代期间，海洛因服用者就诊医院急诊室的次数的增加比率超过了25%。因此很明显，在那个10年中海洛因的服用在增加。

如果假设下面哪一项，作者的结论可被合理地推出？

(A) 那些因服用海洛因而寻求医学治疗的人通常在上瘾的后期阶段接受治疗。

(B) 许多海洛因服用者经常就诊医院急诊室。

(C) 海洛因服用者就诊医院急诊室的次数与海洛因被吸食的发生率成比例。

(D) 自从1980年，服用海洛因的方法已经改变，新的方法降低了服用海洛因的危险性。

(E) 当海洛因服用者到医院急诊室就诊时，他们承认自己是因服海洛因而到急诊室来的。

当颁发向河道内排放化学物质的许可证时，它们是以每天可向河道中排放多少磅每种化学物质的形式来颁发的。通过对每种化学物质单独计算来颁发许可证，这些许可证所需的数据是基于对流过河道的水量对排放到河道内的化学物质的稀释效果的估计。因此河道在许可证的保护之下，可以免受排放到它里面的化学物质对它产生不良的影响。

上面论述依赖的假设是……

(A) 相对无害的化学物质在水中不相互反应形成有害的化合物。

(B) 河道内的水流动得很快，能确保排放到河道的化学物质被快速地散开。

(C) 没有完全禁止向河道内排放化学物质。

(D) 那些持有许可证的人通常不会向河道内排放达到许可证所允许的最大量的化学物质。

(E) 化学物质对河道污染所带来的危险只

evaluated in terms of human health only and not in terms of the health of both human beings and wildlife.

应用它是否危及人类健康的观点来评价，而不应以它是否危及人类和野生动植物的观点来评价。

62. Claim: Country X's government lowered tariff barriers because doing so served the interests of powerful foreign companies.

Principle: In order for a change to be explained by the advantage some person or group gained from it, it must be shown how the interests of the person or group played a role in bringing about the change.

Which one of the following, if true, can most logically serve as a premise for an argument that uses the principle to counter the claim?

(A) Foreign companies did benefit when Country X lowered tariff barriers, but consumers in Country X benefited just as much.

(B) In the period since tariff barriers were lowered, price competition among importers has severely limited importers' profits from selling foreign companies' products in Country X.

(C) It was impossible to predict how Country X's economic reforms, which included lowering tariff barriers, would affect the economy in the short term.

(D) Many of the foreign companies that benefited from Country X's lowering tariff barriers compete fiercely among themselves both in Country X and in other markets.

(E) Although foreign companies benefited when Country X lowered tariff barriers, there is no other evidence that these foreign companies induced the change.

声明：X国降低了关税，因为这样做符合有实力的外国公司的利益。

原则：为了使一个变革被一些人或团体从中获得的利益所解释，就必须表明这些人或团体的利益在造成这场变革中起了什么样的作用。

下面哪一项，如果正确，能最有逻辑地作为上面论述中使用原则来反对声明的一个前提？

(A) 当X国降低关税时，外国公司确实获益，但是X国消费者也同样获益。

(B) 在关税降低以后的那段时间内，进口商之间的价格竞争已严重地限制了进口商在X国销售外国公司产品的所得利润。

(C) 要预测X国导致降低关税的经济改变在短期内会怎样影响该国的经济是不可能的。

(D) 许多从X国降低关税中获益的外国公司相互之间在X国内和其他市场上竞争相当激烈。

(E) 尽管当X国降低关税时，外国公司获益，但是没有其他证据表明是这些外国公司引起了这场变革。

63. No computer will ever be able to do everything that some human minds can do, for there are some problems that cannot be solved by following any set of mechanically applicable rules. Yet computers can only solve problems by following some set of mechanically applicable rules.

Which one of the following is an assumption on which the argument depends?

(A) At least one problem solvable by following some set of mechanically applicable rules is not solvable by any human mind.

没有计算机能做人类大脑所能做的一切事情，因为有一些问题不能通过遵循任何一套可被机械地应用的原则来解决。然而，计算机仅能通过遵循一些可被机械地应用的原则来解决问题。

下面哪一项是上述论述依赖的一个假设？

(A) 至少有一个通过遵循一些可被机械地应用的原则而解决的问题不能被任何人的大脑所解决。

(B) At least one problem not solvable by following any set of mechanically applicable rules is solvable by at least one human mind.

(C) At least one problem solvable by following some set of mechanically applicable rules is solvable by every human mind.

(D) Every problem that is solvable by following more than one set of mechanically applicable rules is solvable by almost every human mind.

(E) Every problem that is solvable by following at least one set of mechanically applicable rules is solvable by at least one human mind.

64. Proponents of organic farming claim that using chemical fertilizers and pesticides in farming is harmful to local wildlife. To produce the same amount of food, however, more land must be under cultivation when organic farming techniques are used than when chemicals are used. Therefore, organic farming leaves less land available as habitat for local wildlife.

Which one of the following is an assumption on which the author's argument depends?

(A) Chemical fertilizers and pesticides pose no health threat to wildlife.

(B) Wildlife living near farms where chemicals are used will not ingest any food or water containing those chemicals.

(C) The only disadvantage to using chemicals in farming is their potential effect on wildlife.

(D) The same crops are grown on organic farms as on farms where chemicals are used.

(E) Land cultivated by organic farming methods no longer constitutes a habitat for wildlife.

65. More than a year ago, the city announced that police would crack down on illegally parked cars and that resources would be diverted from writing speeding tickets to ticketing illegally parked cars. But no crackdown has taken place. The police chief claims that resources have had to be diverted from writing speeding tickets to combating the city's staggering drug problem. Yet the police are still writing as many speeding tickets as ever. Therefore, the excuse about resources being tied up in fighting drug-related crime simply is not true.

(B) 至少有一个不能通过遵循任何一套可被机械地应用的原则而解决的问题至少能被一个人的大脑所解决。

(C) 至少有一个能通过遵循一些可被机械地应用的原则而得到解决的问题能被每个人的大脑所解决。

(D) 每一个能通过遵循多套可被机械地应用的原则而得到解决的问题几乎都能被每一个人的大脑所解决。

(E) 每一个能通过遵循至少一套可被机械地应用的原则而得到解决的问题都能至少被一个人的大脑所解决。

有机农业的提议者声称在耕作中使用化肥和杀虫剂对当地的野生动物有害。然而,当使用有机农业技术时,要生产相同数量的食物,就要比使用化学物质时耕种更多的土地。因此,有机农业减少了当地野生动物可用的生活领地。

下面哪一项是作者论述依赖的假设?

(A) 化肥和杀虫剂不会给野生动物的健康造成威胁。

(B) 生活在使用化学物质的农场附近的野生动物不会摄取任何含有那些化学物质的食物或水。

(C) 在农业中使用化学物质的唯一缺点是它们对野生动物有潜在的影响。

(D) 在有机农场上种植的庄稼与使用化学物质的农场上种植的庄稼是一样的。

(E) 用有机农业方法耕作的土地不再成为野生动物的栖息地。

一年多以前,市政当局宣布警察将对非法停车进行严厉打击,将从写超速处罚单的人员中抽出更多资源以对非法停车开单处罚,但是并没有产生任何效果。警察局局长声称,必须从写超速处罚单的警察中抽出一部人来打击本市非常严重的毒品问题。然而,警察们一如既往地写了许多超速处罚单。因此,人力被困在打击与毒品有关的犯罪中的说法很显然是不正确的。

The conclusion in the passage depends on the assumption that

(A) every member of the police force is qualified to work on combating the city's drug problem.

(B) drug-related crime is not as serious a problem for the city as the police chief claims it is.

(C) writing speeding tickets should be as important a priority for the city as combating drug-related crime.

(D) the police could be cracking down on illegally parked cars and combating the drug problem without having to reduce writing speeding tickets.

(E) the police cannot continue writing as many speeding tickets as ever while diverting resources to combating drug-related crime.

短文中的结论基于下面那个假设?

(A) 每个警察都有资格从事处理本市的毒品问题。

(B) 与毒品有关的犯罪并不像警察局长声称的那样严重。

(C) 对这个城市来说,写超速处罚单与打击毒品犯罪一样的重要。

(D) 警察可以在处罚非法停车和打击毒品的犯罪的同时,并不减少超速处罚单的数量。

(E) 如果警察当局把人力都转移到了打击毒品犯罪的活动上,警察将不能写那么多的超速罚款单。

66. Scientific research that involves international collaboration has produced papers of greater influence, as measured by the number of times a paper is cited in subsequent papers, than has research without any collaboration. Papers that result from international collaboration are cited an average of seven times, whereas papers with single authors are cited only three times on average. This difference shows that research projects conducted by international research teams are of greater importance than those conducted by single researchers.

Which one of the following is an assumption on which the argument depends?

(A) Prolific writers can inflate the number of citations they receive by citing themselves in subsequent papers.

(B) It is possible to ascertain whether or not a paper is the product of international collaboration by determining the number of citations it has received.

(C) The number of citations a paper receives is a measure of the importance of the research it reports.

(D) The collaborative efforts of scientists who are citizens of the same country do not produce papers that are as important as papers that are produced by international collaboration.

(E) International research teams tend to be more generously funded than are single researchers.

涉及国际合作的科学研究所发表的论文比没有合作的研究所发表的论文具有更大的影响力。如果一篇论文影响力的大小通过随后发表的文章对该论文的引用次数来衡量。国际合作研究发表的论文平均被引用7次,而单独作者所发表的论文却仅被引用3次。这个差异表明国际合作研究项目比单个研究人员进行的研究项目具有更大的重要性。

上面的论述基于下面哪一个假设?

(A) 多产的作家可以在随后发表的论文中通过自我引述来提高他们的论文的引用次数。

(B) 可以通过一篇论文被引用的次数来确定该论文是否是国际合作研究的成果。

(C) 一篇论文被引用的次数是其所报道的研究项目的重要性的评价标准。

(D) 由同一国家的科学家合作发表的论文的重要性抵不上国际合作所发表的论文的重要性。

(E) 与单一研究者相比,国际研究小组更易得到丰厚的资助。

67. The seventeenth-century physicist Sir Isaac Newton is remembered chiefly for his treatises on motion and gravity. But Newton also conducted experiments secretly for many years based on the arcane theories of alchemy, trying unsuccessfully to transmute common metals into

17世纪的物理学家伊萨克·牛顿爵士主要因他在运动和地球引力方面的论文而受到纪念。但是牛顿也基于神秘的炼丹术理论秘密地做了许多年的试验,企图使普通金属变成金子,并制出返老还童的长生不

gold and produce rejuvenating elixirs. If the alchemists of the seventeenth century had published the results of their experiments, chemistry in the eighteenth century would have been more advanced than it actually was.

Which one of the following assumptions would allow the conclusion concerning eighteenth-century chemistry to be properly drawn?

(A) Scientific progress is retarded by the reluctance of historians to acknowledge the failures of some of the great scientists.

(B) Advances in science are hastened when reports of experiments, whether successful or not, are available for review by other scientists.

(C) Newton's work on motion and gravity would not have gained wide acceptance if the results of his work in alchemy had also been made public.

(D) Increasing specialization within the sciences makes it difficult for scientists in one field to understand the principles of other fields.

(E) The seventeenth-century alchemists could have achieved their goals only if their experiments had been subjected to public scrutiny.

68. When a group of children who have been watching television programs that include acts of violence is sent to play with a group of children who have been watching programs that do not include acts of violence, the children who have been watching violent programs commit a much greater number of violent acts in their play than do the children who have been watching nonviolent programs. Therefore, children at play can be prevented from committing violent acts by not being allowed to watch violence on television.

The argument in the passage assumes which one of the following?

(A) Television has a harmful effect on society.

(B) Parents are responsible for the acts of their children.

(C) Violent actions and passive observation of violent actions are not related.

(D) There are no other differences between the two groups of children that might account for the difference in violent behavior.

(E) Children who are treated violently will respond with violence.

老药, 这些尝试都以失败告终。如果17世纪的炼丹家发表了他们的试验结果, 那么18世纪的化学将会比它实际上更为先进。

下面哪一个假设可以合理的推出关于18世纪化学的结论?

(A) 科学的进步因历史学家不愿承认一些伟大的科学家的失败而受阻。

(B) 不管试验成功与否, 有关这些试验的报道若能被其他科学家所借鉴, 将会促进科学的进步。

(C) 如果牛顿在炼丹术方面的工作结果也被公布于众的话, 那么他在运动和地球引力方面的工作将不会得到普遍的接受。

(D) 科学日趋专业化, 使得一个领域的科学家很难理解其他领域内的原理。

(E) 如果17世纪的炼丹家让他们的试验结果接受公众审查的话, 他们将有可能达到他们的目标。

当一群观看包括暴力活动内容的电视节目的孩子送去与观看不包括暴力活动内容的电视节目的孩子一块玩耍时, 发现那些观看暴力节目的孩子诉诸暴力行为的次数比那些观看非暴力节目的孩子要高得多。因此, 不让孩子们观看暴力节目能防止他们在玩耍时表现出暴力行为。

文中的论述依赖于下面哪条假设?

(A) 电视对社会有不良的影响。

(B) 父母应对他们的孩子的行动负责。

(C) 暴力行为与被动地观看暴力表演没有关系。

(D) 两群孩子之间并没有其他的不同来解释他们在暴力行为方面的差异。

(E) 被施予暴力的孩子会以暴力相抗。

69. The public is well aware that high blood cholesterol levels raise the risk of stroke caused by blood clots. But a recent report concludes that people with low blood cholesterol levels are at increased risk of the other lethal type of stroke-cerebral hemorrhage, caused when a brain artery bursts.The report suggests that because blood cholesterol plays a vital role in maintaining cell membranes, low blood cholesterol weakens artery walls, making them prone to rupture. The conclusion thus supports a long-standing contention by Japanese researchers that Western diets better protect against cerebral hemorrhage than do non-Western diets.

The argument is based on which one of the following assumptions?

(A) Western diets are healthier than non-Western diets.

(B) Western diets result in higher blood cholesterol levels than do non-Western diets.

(C) High blood cholesterol levels preclude the weakening of artery walls.

(D) Cerebral hemorrhages are more dangerous than strokes caused by blood clots.

(E) People who have low blood pressure are at increased risk of cerebral hemorrhage.

众所周知，高的血液胆固醇水平会增加由血液凝结而引起的中风的危险性。但是，最近的一篇报告指出，血液胆固醇水平低使人患其他致命类型的中风（即脑溢血，由大脑的动脉血管破裂而引起）的危险性在增大。报告建议，因为血液胆固醇在维持细胞膜的韧性方面起着非常重要的作用，所以低的血液胆固醇会削弱动脉血管壁的强度，从而使它们易于破裂。由此，上述结论证实了日本研究者长期争论的问题，即西方饮食比非西方饮食能更好地防止脑溢血。

上述论述基于下面哪条假设？

(A) 西方饮食比非西方饮食更有益于健康。

(B) 与非西方饮食相比，西方饮食易使人产生较高的血液胆固醇。

(C) 高的血液胆固醇水平能消除动脉血管的衰弱。

(D) 脑溢血比血液凝结引起的中风更危险。

(E) 血压低的人患脑溢血的危险性在增大。

70. The more television children watch, the less competent they are in mathematical knowledge. More than a third of children in the United States watch television for more than five hours a day; in South Korea the figure is only 7 percent. But whereas less than 15 percent of children in the United States understand advanced measurement and geometric concepts, 40 percent of South Korean children are competent in these areas. Therefore, if United States children are to do well in mathematics, they must watch less television.

Which one of the following is an assumption upon which the argument depends?

(A) Children in the United States are less interested in advanced measurement and geometric concepts than are South Korean children.

(B) South Korean children are more disciplined about doing schoolwork than are children in the United States.

(C) Children who want to do well in advanced measurement and geometry will watch less television.

(D) A child's ability in advanced measurement and geometry increases if he or she watches less than one hour of television a day.

孩子们看的电视越多，他们的数学知识就越贫乏。美国有超过1/3的孩子每天看电视的时间在5小时以上，在韩国仅有7%的孩子这样做。但是鉴于在美国只有不到15%的孩子懂得高等测量与几何学概念，而在韩国却有40%的孩子在该领域有这个能力。所以，如果美国孩子要在数学上表现出色的话，他们就必须少看电视。

下面哪一个是上述论证所依赖的假设？

(A) 美国孩子对高等测量和几何学概念的兴趣比韩国的孩子小。

(B) 韩国的孩子在功课方面的训练比美国孩子多。

(C) 想在高等测量与几何学上取得好成绩的孩子会少看电视。

(D) 如果一个孩子每天看电视的时间不超过1小时，那么他在高等测量与数学方面的能力就会提高。

(E) The instruction in advanced measurement and geometric concepts available to children in the United States is not substantially worse than that available to South Korean children.

71. Light utility trucks have become popular among consumers who buy them primarily for the trucks rugged appearance. Yet although, these trucks are tough-looking, they are exempt from the government's car-safety standards that dictate minimum roof strength and minimum resistance to impact. Therefore, if involved in a serious high-impact accident, a driver of one of these trucks is more likely to be injured than is a driver of a car that is subject to these government standards.

The argument depends on the assumption that

(A) the government has established safety standards for the construction of light utility trucks.

(B) people who buy automobiles solely for their appearance are more likely than other people to drive recklessly.

(C) light utility trucks are more likely than other kinds of vehicles to be involved in accidents that result in injuries.

(D) the trucks' rugged appearance is deceptive in that their engines are not especially powerful.

(E) light utility trucks are less likely to meet the car-safety standards than are cars that are subject to the standards.

72. Medical research findings are customarily not made public prior to their publication in a medical journal that has had them reviewed by a panel of experts in a process called peer review. It is claimed that this practice delays public access to potentially beneficial information that, in extreme instances, could save lives. Yet prepublication peer review is the only way to prevent erroneous and therefore potentially harmful information from reaching a public that is ill equipped to evaluate medical claims on its own. Therefore, waiting until a medical journal has published the research findings that have passed peer review is the price that must be paid to protect the public from making decisions based on possibly substandard research.

The argument assumes that

(A) unless medical research findings are brought to peer review by a medical journal, peer review will not occur.

（E）美国孩子在高等测量与几何学概念方面所能接受的教育并不比韩国孩子的差很多。

轻型实用卡车已越来越受消费者的欢迎，他们购买这种卡车主要是因为它们具有结实的外表。然而尽管这类卡车看起来制作结实，但是它们并不需要达到政府的汽车安全标准，该标准规定了车顶的最低强度和汽车最低抗冲击能力。因此，如果这类卡车遇上了一起非常严重的高速碰撞事故，这类卡车的司机就很有可能比那些符合政府标准的汽车司机更易受伤害。

上述论述依赖于假设……

（A）政府已经制定了制造轻型实用汽车的安全标准。

（B）那些买车时只在乎汽车外表的人很有可能比其他的人开车粗心。

（C）轻型实用卡车比其他类型的车辆更易卷入致使伤残的事故。

（D）卡车坚固的外表具有欺骗性，因为他们的发动机不是特别地强劲有力。

（E）轻型实用卡车达到汽车安全标准的可能性不如那些符合标准的汽车大。

医学研究发现在医学杂志上发表之前通常并不公布于众，它们首先得被专家小组以所谓的评委审阅的方式审查通过后才能发表。据称，这种做法延迟了公众接触潜在的有益信息。这种信息，在极特殊的情况下，可以挽救生命。然而，发表前的评委审阅是仅有的可以防止错误的方式，并从而使自身缺乏评价医学声明的公众免受了潜在有害信息的袭击。因此，为了防止公众基于不合标准的研究而做出的选择，我们就必须等待，直到研究结果被评委审阅通过，并在药学杂志上发表为止。

上面论述假设……

（A）除非医学研究结果被医学杂志送给评委评阅，否则评委评阅不会发生。

(B) anyone who does not serve on a medical review panel does not have the necessary knowledge and expertise to evaluate medical research findings.

(C) the general public does not have access to the medical journals in which research findings are published.

(D) all medical research findings are subjected to prepublication peer review.

(E) peer review panels are sometimes subject to political and professional pressures that can make their judgments less than impartial.

(B) 不在医学评委小组工作的人不具有评价医学研究结果的必要知识和专业技能。

(C) 普通群众没有接触那些发表医学研究结果的期刊的机会。

(D) 所有医学研究结果都要接受发表前的评委评阅。

(E) 评委小组有时会迫于政治上或职业上的压力而做出不太公正的审判。

73. In Malsenia sales of classical records are soaring. The buyers responsible for this boom are quite new to classical music and were drawn to it either by classical scores from television commercials or by theme tunes introducing major sports events on television.Audiences at classical concerts, however, are continually shrinking in Malsenia. It can be concluded from this that the new Malsenian Converts to classical music, having initially experienced this music as recorded music, are most comfortable with classical music as recorded music and really have no desire to hear live performances.

The argument assumes which one of the following?

(A) To sell well in Malsenia, a classical record must include at least one piece familiar from television.

(B) At least some of the new Malsenian buyers of classical records have available to them the coupon of attending classical concerts.

(C) The number of classical concerts performed in Malsenia has not decreased in response to smaller audiences.

(D) The classical records available in Malsenia are for the most part not recordings of actual public concerts.

(E) Classical concerts in Malsenia are not limited to music that is really available on recordings.

在Malsenia，古典唱片的销量急剧增加。这次销售强劲的买者是音乐方面的新手，他们要么被来自于电视广告的古典乐谱所吸引，要么被电视上引入的重大体育盛事的主题曲所吸引 。然而，Malsenia的古典音乐会上的观众却持续下降。我们可以从这个事实得出结论：Malsenia的古典音乐的新入道者由于最初欣赏古典音乐是通过唱片音乐的方式，所以很满意作为唱片音乐的古典音乐，并且实际上也没有听取现场表演的欲望。

上述论述做了下面哪一个假设？

(A) 一古典唱片要想在Malsenia畅销，那么它至少包括一首来自电视的耳熟能详的音乐。

(B) 在Malsenia古典唱片的新购买者中，至少有一部分人能得到参加古典音乐会的赠券。

(C) 在Malsenia上演的古典音乐会的数量并没有由于更少的观众而减少。

(D) 在Malsenia可以得到的古典唱片绝大部分都不是真实公共音乐会的录音。

(E) 在Malsenia，古典音乐会并不局限于唱片上可以听到的音乐。

参考答案：

1. C	2. E	3. D	4. C	5. B
6. A	7. E	8. C	9. A	10. D
11. C	12. C	13. A	14. E	15. A
16. E	17. E	18. A	19. B	20. E
21. A	22. E	23. D	24. E	25. B

26. C	27. E	28. D	29. D	30. A
31. D	32. A	33. C	34. E	35. A
36. D	37. D	38. B	39. C	40. C
41. A	42. A	43. C	44. B	45. A
46. E	47. B	48. B	49. D	50. C
51. C	52. D	53. C	54. B	55. D
56. C	57. D	58. D	59. A	60. C
61. A	62. E	63. B	64. E	65. E
66. C	67. B	68. D	69. B	70. E
71. E	72. A	73. C		

2. 解析：本题根据银河系中有许多恒星，这些恒星的行星具有与地球相似的环境从而得出了某个行星上可能存在生命的结论。要寻找结论所依赖的假设，就要从得出这个结论的比较入手。本题是从其他行星与地球环境相似，推出其他行星上有生命存在。由此很容易推出，本题的结论是以其他行星上生命的存在需要与地球相似的环境条件为前提，即(E)正确；(A)和(B)与题中内容无关；(C)与题中的假设无关，且"inevitable"为段落中所没有的绝对化语言，与段落中的"the greatest chance"不一致；(D)与题中结论无关。

4. 解析：本题的结论是"将来不会发生饥荒，导致任何饥荒的不是产量问题，而是分配问题"；结论的前提是"目前世界粮食年产量略高于世界人口基本上吃饱所需的食物总量"。本题显然是通过目前与将来的对比进行了类比推理，然后根据今天的情况来确定将来的情况，因此将来关于粮食产量的情况应和今天具有相似性，也就是说将来世界食物的产量也会满足或超过人们的需要。由此分析可知(C)是正确答案；(A)易被误选，将来世界对粮食的需求量比目前的小，但是如果食物产量降低了更多，那么将来的粮食产量将不能满足所需要，必定会发生饥荒，因此(A)不正确；(B)和(D)为无关选项；(E)只是重申了结论，不可能作为一个假设。

10. 解析：本题属于"无因就无果类型"的假设。本题的结论是"作物产量没有变化"，结论成立的前提是"在天气长期变暖或变冷的过程中，降雨形势没有发生变化"。很显然，如果前提条件不能满足，那么结论就很难成立。也就是说，如果在天气长期变暖或变冷的过程中伴随着降雨形势的变化，那么作物产量就会变化。由此分析可知本题结论显然是假定长期的变暖或变冷天气过程中伴随降雨形势的变化将比不伴随降雨形势的变化对农作物的产量影响大，即$\overline{A}\to\overline{B}$。由此分析可知(D)为正确答案；(A)、(B)、(C)和(E)都是无关选项。

11. 解析：本题属于对比推理，读题重点在最后一句话，结合"Unlike the pages of a book…"，我们知道原因A为"电视图像以儿童不希望的速度出现"，结果B为"阻碍了儿童的想象力"。而(C)选项说明，当儿童能够控制娱乐速度时($\overline{A}$)，其想象力不会被阻碍($\overline{B}$)。所以(C)是一个符合典型的$\overline{A}\to\overline{B}$思路的假设答案，所以(C)正确；(B)易误选，(B)虽然描述的是一个真理，但与上面的推理无关，因为本题讨论的并不是想象力能否得到适当的激发，所以(B)不正确；(A)、(D)、(E)均与本题推理无关，因此也都不能作为假设。

25. 解析：段落推理为"因为100万盘盗版录像带以5美元一盘出售，所以FilmPro损失了1000万美元的潜在利润"，那么这个推理成立暗含的假设是：正版带也能以每盘25美元，利润10美元卖出100万盘。所以(B)为正确答案；(A)、(C)、(D)均与推理无直接关系；(E)易误选，但"discontinued"段落中没有涉及，所以也不正确。

31. 解析：本题推理是由一个事实"相同的问题在6个月后以不同的顺序向另一随机取样的顾客提问得到不同的回答"，得出一个解释性的结论，"不同的顺序是原因"，属于典型的"B、A"题型，其隐含假设是除了A以外没有别的原因导致B。由于(D)指出调查不包含顾客的因素，所以(D)可以作为一个假设，因此(D)为正确答案；(A)与推理无关；(B)易误选，但由于6个月前后抽样的顾客都是随机的，所以不存在购物者完全相同的问题；(C)的"motive"为新概念；(E)说明不了任何问题且与推理无关，所以不对。

32. **解析**：本题是由一个事实而得出一个结论："Blends should be used"，并且又对得出的这一结论进行了解释"since blends are clearly more healthful, yet equally effective"。一般地，当原因放在结论之后表示强调原因的重要性或唯一性。所以上述推理成立所依赖的假设应为"除了A以外没有别的原因影响B"，若混合物一块消化时，不会相互作用以至于对健康有害，如(A)所说，就是一个很好的假设。可以对(A)进行取非验证，即若混合物一起消化会产生负作用，那么上面的"Blends should be used"必然不对，所以(A)必定正确。

33. **解析**：本题推理是由一个事实"自动摄像机拍下100辆超速的汽车，而警察只拍下了49辆"，得出了一个解释性的结论"警察拍下了不到一半的超速的汽车，其推理做了一个假设：没有别的原因导致警察拍下了不到一半的超速的汽车"。若大部分在经过自动摄像机时超速的车辆在经过警察时没有超速，那么就表明警察拍得少主要是由于车不超速了，即上面推理必不成立。所以(C)是一个很好的假设；(A)说明不了任何问题；(B)是一个新的无关比较；(D)、(E)都是无关选项。

34. **解析**：本题推理是由一个事实"Poe的信件中未提到吗啡瘾"，而得出一个解释性的结论"Poe没有吗啡瘾"，属于典型的"B、A"模式，其隐含的假设是："除了A之外无别的因素影响B"。我们可以用否定概念来定位选项，不过本题5个选项均有否定词，所以应该用A或B中的关键词来定位。当我们用B的关键词"correspondence"来定位选项时，发现(D)、(E)也有这个词。如果由于担心后果而使Poe没有在信中提到他的吗啡瘾，如(E)所说，那么就排除了其他可能，所以(E)是一个假设。(D)对上述推理起到了支持作用。

35. **解析**：在解答本题时一定要注意数量关系的变化，我们可以借助简单的数学公式加以推导，设一个家庭开始时在每辆汽车上的花费为x，平均购买汽车数为n，家庭预算为y；在变化后这三项数值分别为x′、n′、y′。则根据本题中的描述，我们很容易得出三个等式，即①：x′=1.3x，②：y′=1.3y，③：nx/y=n′x′/y′。把①、②式同时代入③式，得出n=n′，即每个家庭在这5年当中，平均购买汽车的数量不变。由此分析可知，要使本题的结论成立，那它一定是以(A)选项所描述的内容为assumption。

36. **解析**：要寻找一个结论所依赖的假设，就要找使这个结论成立所需的必要条件。只有在雇员能享受到更多的有偿假期时，才能说明新政策比以前的政策更慷慨。而在新政策中，雇员能享受到更多的有偿假期的必要条件是他们得工作长达1200小时，由此分析可知绝大多数雇员能够工作长达1200小时是本题结论所依赖的假设，所以(D)为正确答案；(A)、(B)、(C)、(E)都不可能做为假设。

37. **解析**：寻找本题结论的假设，就是要找一个使不应当关闭核电站这个结论成立的必要条件。由题可知，本题结论成立的必要条件，就是一个能对核能批评家的态度构成反对或削弱的条件。根据以上分析可知，5个选项中只有(D)选项的内容能对核能批评家的态度构成反对，其推理如下：目前核电厂的经营产生的危害不及燃煤或燃油发电厂，而继续运行核电厂可能产生的危害又能根据它们以前的危害可靠地推出，也就是说继续运行现有的核电厂不可能会导致严重的危害，所以(D)为正确答案；(B)容易误选，因为它起到很好的支持作用，但它并不是结论成立的必要条件，因为即使违反(B)关闭核电站不大量增加对煤炭和燃油发电站的依赖，本题的推理仍然成立，所以(B)不对，(B)中的"greatly"去掉之后，则可以作为一个假设；(C)也是起到支持作用，但它也不是本题结论成立所需的必要条件，因此，也为错误选项。

38. **解析**：本题仅根据冰川形成期的Acrocora palmata珊瑚化石的位置比它们现在生长的地方深，就做出了冰川形成期的Acrocora palmata珊瑚与今天的Acrocora palmata珊瑚在许多重要的方面有很大不同的结论。要使结论成立，就要对结论的前提中所提及的"深"做进一步的限制。本题的5个选项中，只有(B)表明化石的位置较深不是由他因引起的，从而就可合理地推出冰川时期paclmata珊瑚实际生活的区域与它们的化石形成的区域基本上一致，这样才能使本题论证中的结论合理地推出，由此分析可知(B)为正确答案；(A)为无关选项；(C)、(D)和(E)都不能从本题的论证中合理地推出。

39. 解析：本题仅根据未婚男性比同龄未婚女性多得多，就得出了大多数男的要想摆脱单身局面，就必须娶preplanned以外的女性为妻的结论，因此很显然本题是以30多岁的男性只会娶30多岁的女性为前提，也就是说30多岁的男性不会和20多岁的女性或40多岁的女性结婚是本题结论所依赖的假设。由以上分析可知，(C)为正确答案；选项与本题论述所列举的事实相反，(A)、(D)和(E)都不能从本题的论述中合理地推出。

40. 解析：本题根据从地表以下1.74英里深的地方取得的样品中存在活着的微生物，得出了在地层深处存在活着的微生物的结论，属于典型的"B，A"模式。要想使本题的结论成立，就必须寻找一个原因来解释或加强样品确实取自地层深处，即排除他因。由此分析可知(C)为正确答案；(E)是较易误选的选项，从表面上看它似乎能对普遍的猜想构成反对，从而对本题的结论构成支持。但是要知道，地表以下温度太高是一个既定的事实，那些科学家的实验只是为了证实地层深处存在微生物的可能性，而不是要证实微生物一定要在和地面表层温度相一致的温度区间内才能存活，因此(E)为错误选项。

42. 解析：转化为数学去思维可很容易得出(A)为答案，并可对(A)进行取非验证。

43. 解析：典型的"A可行或A有意义"思路。

44. 解析：本题段落前半部分可以提炼为"有雷达探测器的司机比没有雷达探测器的司机更易得罚单"，后半部分可提炼为"有雷达探测器的司机比没有雷达探测器的司机更经常超速"。(B)把这两部分的跳跃"更易得罚单"与"更经常超速"连了起来，因此可以作为一个假设；(A)正好与段落信息相违背。

45. 解析：burn v. 消耗 consume v. 吃进

47. 解析：本题为重点题目，属于典型的"B，A"型的假设，答案思路应为"除了A以外没有别的原因可以影响B"，因此应用否定概念去定位选项。(B)说明没有质量不合乎目的的情况，可以作为一个很好的假设，属于没有否定词的否定答案，可以对(B)取非验证。

49. 解析：本题要关注三个关键词："the wild mouflon sheep"、"early domesticated sheep"与"modern domesticated sheep"。(D)涉及这三个关键词，指出"mouflon sheep"相比较于"modern domesticated sheep"而言，与早期驯养的绵羊更相似，从而做了一个很好的假设，如果"mouflon sheep"还没有"modern domesticated sheep"提供的信息多，那么考古学家完全可以通过家庭驯养羊去研究早期驯羊的模样，则上面结论不成立。所以(D)正确；(C)易误选，但(C)只涉及关键词"modern domesticated sheep"，而没有说明"mouflon sheep"怎么样，所以必然不对。

50. 解析：(C)中的"all human sickness"与段落中的"any particular disease"相对应，并把段落中的A与B连了起来，因此(C)实现了问题目的；(D)易误选，但(D)中的"all human"与段落里的"the people who follow them"不对应，且为绝对化概念，必错。注意：一般在假设选项中出现only、solely, in part, partly可以忽略，在取非判定时尤其如此，但在段落中出现这四个词要格外关注。

51. 解析：本题推理为对比推理。因为计算机游戏导致儿童交流技巧发展水平低，所以把所有闲暇都用来玩游戏的孩子比其他儿童有更少的人际交流经验。论据当中并未涉及其他儿童，而论点中涉及儿童时，一定要对论据中未涉及的对象做一个假设。(C)指出其他儿童至少花费了一部分时间交流，且(C)中的"spend at least some of..."与段落中的all相对应，所以做了一个很好的假设，因此(C)正确；(A)易误选，但(A)要想成为一个假设，结论（论点）必须变为"玩游戏阻碍人际交流的发展"，所以(A)为无关选项。

52. 解析：航空公司通过采用增加课堂教育时间和强调飞行员通讯技巧的训练方案来防止商业飞机的坠毁。本题的结论为这些措施不能补偿飞行员实际飞行时间的缺乏，也就是说实际飞行时间的缺乏是飞行员在商业飞机坠毁事故中失误的最主要的原因。所以(D)为正确选项；(A)是不对的，因为训练计划只能减少飞行员的失误，并不能消除飞行员的失误；(B)与本题的结论无太大的关系；(C)是本题的迷惑选项，它虽然在某种程度上也具正确性，但是它没有指明是缺乏实际飞行时间还是缺乏课堂教育及通讯技巧是造成飞机坠毁的主要原因，因此从(C)得不出本题的结论；(E)本身就具有逻辑错误，对飞行员训练计划不主要的东西不一定就不重要，很难想象没有通讯技巧的飞行员能安全地驾驶一架飞机。

53. **解析：** 本题的逻辑关系比较简单，由题中的论述可知，政府侵犯私营企业决定它们自己的政策和法规的权利的问题要比抽烟者可能会因吸收其他抽烟者的烟味而受害的问题更严重，由此可推知企业的独自裁决权高于政府必须保护个人的一切权利和义务是本题的结论成立的前提条件。所以(C)是正确答案；(A)和(B)对本题的结论构成反对；(D)和(E)与本题的结论无关。

54. **解析：** 本题的证据是精神分裂患者的大脑中的某些区域比正常人的小，结论是精神分裂症是由大脑的物质结构受损引起。因此要使证据支持结论，只要说明精神分裂症患者大脑中的某些区域较小不是由除了精神分裂症以外的其他原因引起的就可以了。由以上分析可知(B)排除了他因，是本题的辩论所依赖的假设，为正确答案；(A)认为患精神分裂症者的大脑较小是由精神分裂症引起的，对本题的结论构成了反对；选项(C)、(D)和(E)既不能作为本题结论成立的前提，也不能从本题的论述中合理地推出。

55. **解析：** 本题不好直接找答案，因此最好用排除法。由本题的论述可以推知要想从巴西引进的昆虫能对美国南部地区的环境有益，首先得保证这种昆虫在该地区能够存活，其次是这种昆虫给这个地区的环境带来的益处要大于害处；要想使这种昆虫抑制住火蚁数量的增加，首先就要求是这种昆虫吃掉了火蚁，而不是火蚁吃掉了这种昆虫，其次要求这种昆虫杀死火蚁的比率要超过火蚁数量增加的比率。根据此分析可知(A)、(B)、(C)、(E)选项都是上题论述依赖的假设；(D)选项的 "the ant population" 为模糊概念，可能包括 "fire ants"，也可能没包括 "fire ants"，所以(D)为无关选项，因此(D)选项不是本段落论述依赖的假设。

56. **解析：** 本题的结论是Bell的某些子公司将会被出售，该结论是给工人涨工资的必要条件，而给工人涨工资又是工人不举行罢工的必要条件，因此Bell的某些子公司将被出售是工人不举行罢工的必要条件，也即工人不举行罢工，那么必要条件 "Bell的某些子公司被出售" 必定发生，由此分析可知(C)是正确答案。其余四个选项既不能推出结论，也不能从结论中推出，都是错误选项。

57. **解析：** 由题义可知，代表某个新概念的单词或短语在转变为习惯用法时，若单词的意思发生了较大的改变，那么这些单词将不能再表达它们以前所表达的新概念。因此本题的结论成立的必要条件是当一个单词变成一种习惯用法时，它的意思在转变过程中不会经受任何严重的改变，即(D)是正确答案；(E)提及了新内容，既不能支持结论，也不能从短文中合理地推出，因此是错误选项；(A)、(C)、(D)三选项都与段落中论述的内容相反，均为错误选项。

58. **解析：** 从段落中我们可以很容易地看出，进行重复试验的科学家一定是在认为他们进行重复实验所用的测量方法是正确的前提下认为以前的测量方法有误，以致他们得不到一致的结果。因此(D)是正确答案；(B)具有一定的迷惑性，但是一定要把题读清楚了，在进行重复试验的科学家看来以前的结果有误并不是起因于这些结果有争议的事实，而是起因于得到这些结果所用的测量方法不正确。(A)、(C)和(E)三选项均不能从段落中合理地推出。

59. **解析：** 根据题中段落的论述可知Drabble市长现有的一个偿还政治债务的方法是委任某人为艺术委员会的领导，Lee是Drabble的债权人之一，并且Drabble通常会尽快偿还她在政治上的债务，所以要使Drabble委任Lee为艺术委员会的首领，那一定是没有其他债务的偿还会比委任Lee为艺术委员会首领更及时、更合适，所以很明显(A)是正确的答案；(D)选项与短文的论述无关；(B)、(C)和(E)选项都不能从段落中推出。

60. **解析：** 本题应该注意的是：不是每一个服用了海洛因的人都到急诊室去就诊，因此要从急诊室这10年里海洛因服用者就诊的次数的增加，推出服用海洛因的整体人数都在增加，就必须指出到急诊室就诊的海洛因服用者与服用海洛因的总的人数之间的特定关系。在5个选项中只有(C)指出了这种特定关系，因此，正确选项为(C)；其余四个选项都不是本题结论所依赖的假设。

61. 解析：因为保护河道的许可证的发放是基于对每种化学物质的最高允许排放量的计算，因此要确保河道内的水在许可证的保护之下，还必须确保那些根据许可证的要求排放到河道内的水中的化学物质相互之间不会发生形成有害物质的反应。由此分析可知(A)为正确答案；而(B)、(C)、(D)和(E)均为无关选项。

62. 解析：声明中用外国有实力的公司的利益来解释X国降低关税的原因，而原则表明要用有实力的外国公司的利益来解释X国降低关税的原因，声明中还必须表明有实力的外国公司的利益在降低关税中起了什么作用。也就是说外国有实力的公司的利益在X国降低关税中的作用是用前者来解释后者的必要条件。由此分析可知，原则反对声明的一个前提是声明中没有表明是这些外国公司引起了这场变革，即(E)为正确答案。

63. 解析：由本题的论述可推知，有一些能被人类大脑解决的问题不能被计算机解决，这是因为这些问题不能通过遵循任何一套可被机械地应用的原则来解决。由此我们可以推出有一些不能通过遵循任何一套可被机械地应用的原则的问题可被人类大脑所解决，因此(B)是正确的；其余四个选项均不能从本题的论述中推出，所以都是错误选项。

64. 解析：本题的结论是，有机农业因占用了更多的土地而使野生动物生活的领地减少，而只有在野生动物的生活范围不涉及有机农业的土地时，上述结论才能成立。因此(E)中的陈述："用有机农业方法耕作的土地不再含有野生动物的栖息地"是作者论述依赖的假设，其余几个选项都是明显错误的。

65. 解析：作者根据警察们写的超速罚款单的数量不变，而做出人力被困在打击与毒品有关的犯罪中的说法不正确的结论。该命题的逆否命题是：如果人力资源被困在了打击与毒品有关的犯罪中的说法是正确的，警察们将不能写那么多数量的超速罚款单。因此(E)是正确答案；选项(A)、(B)、(C)和(D)均不能从本题的论述中合理地推出。

66. 解析：本题根据国际研究发表的论文被引用的次数较多，做出了国际研究项目的重要性较强的结论，因此作者结论所依赖的假设很明显就是一篇论文被引用的次数是它所报道的研究项目的重要性的标准，也即(C)是正确答案；(A)、(B)、(D)和(E)四选项均不能从本题的论证中推出。

67. 解析：本题的结论是18世纪的化学将会比它实际上更为先进，结论成立的前提是如果17世纪的炼丹家发表了他们的试验结果。17世纪的炼丹家只有发表了他们的试验结果，别的科学家才有借鉴这些试验结果的可能，尽管这些结果可能是错误的。由此我们可以推出，不管17世纪的炼丹家的试验成功与否，有关这些试验的报道若能被其他科学家借鉴，将会促进科学的进步，即(B)选项为正确答案。(A)、(C)、(D)和(E)均不能从本题的论证中推出。

68. 解析：(D)通过排除他因的方法证实了孩子们诉诸暴力行动的次数仅与他们观看的电视节目有关的论断，从而进一步支持了不让孩子们观看暴力节目能防止他们在玩耍时表现出暴力行为的结论，因此(D)是文中的论证所依赖的假设；(C)选项对本题的结论构成了反对；(A)、(B)和(E)选项都不能从短文中合理地推出。

69. 解析：由本题段落中的论述可知，高的血液胆固醇水平能防止脑溢血，西方饮食比非西方饮食能更好地防止脑溢血。因此我们很容易推出西方饮食比非西方饮食容易使人产生高的血液胆固醇水平是本题的结论所依赖的假设，亦即(B)是正确答案；(C)是本题提及的低的血液胆固醇水平会削弱动脉血管的强度的否命题，原命题正确，否命题不一定正确，因此(C)不是本题的结论依赖的假设；选项(A)、(D)和(E)都不能从本题的论述中推出，因此都是错误的选项。

70. 解析：要使孩子们看的电视越多，他们的数学知识就越贫乏的结论成立，就要排除其他因素对孩子们的数学能力的影响。美国孩子比韩国孩子看的电视多，因此美国孩子的数学能力比韩国孩子的差。但是若美国孩子在数学方面所能接受到的教育比韩国孩子差时，就很难得出美国孩子数学能力差是由于他们看电视较多的结论，因此(E)是本题的论证所依赖的假设；(A)和(B)两选项都对本题的结论构成了反对；(C)和(D)都不能从本题的论证中合理地推出。

71. 解析：本题的结论是轻型实用卡车因没有受政府的汽车安全标准的制约而使得它们的司机比那些受标准制约的汽车司机容易受伤害。由此结论我们很容易推出轻型实用卡车达到汽车安全标准的可能性不如那些受标准制约的汽车的大，即(E)是正确答案；本题的(C)是比较容易误选的选项，这里应当注意的是，从文中我们只能推出，轻型实用卡车卷入事故时，这类卡车的司机比其他卡车的司机更易受伤害，而推不出轻型实用卡车比其他类型的汽车更易卷入导致伤残的事故。

72. 解析：本题读题重点是最后一句话，为典型的"就目的提方法"类型的假设。目的是：为了防止公众基于不合标准的研究而做出选择，必须要等到研究结果被评委会审阅读过。其隐含假设为评委评阅发生的必要条件为医学杂志送交评委评阅，而(A)选项正好符合这个思路，所以(A)是假设。我们可以对(A)取非验证。若评委评阅不一定非要经过医学杂志的媒介，那么可通过其他途径来使得评委评阅，然后尽早公布于众，因此结论必不正确，所以(A)正确。

73. 解析：上述推理为：观众减少的事实是由于新入道者不去听音乐会，属于事实得出原因类型，即"B，A"模式。此类假设在很多情况下为"没有他因"。(C)通过指出演出的经典音乐会的数量没有下降，做了一个很好的假设；(A)易误选，误选犯的错误是递进推理；而(B)、(D)、(E)均为无关选项。

第 二 章

支 持

这类考题的特点是在段落中给出一个推理或论证，但或者由于前提的条件不够充分，不足以推出其结论；或者由于论证的论据不够全面，不足以得出其结论，因此需用某一选项去补充其前提或论据，使推理或论证成立的可能性增大。但由于"答案不需要充分性"的原则，所以只要某一选项放在段落推理的论据（前提）或结论之间，对段落推理成立或结论正确有支持作用，使段落推理成立、结论正确的可能性增大，那么这个选项就是支持的正确答案。所以支持的答案既可以是段落推理成立或结论正确的一个充分条件，也可以是一个必要条件（这时等同于假设，因为假设答案必将可以支持推理），可以是非充分条件，也可以是非必要条件。

由于支持可以直接支持结论正确（不像假设是找一个使结论成立的必要条件），所以不论是"A，B"模式或"B，A"模式，支持题型主要以四种方式出现：A与B之间有联系（不一定是本质联系）；A可行或有意义；除了A以外没有别的因素影响B（与假设思路相同，多针对"B，A"模式）；直接支持B。

下面我们先来看几道支持考题：

1. The average life expectancy for the United States population as a whole is 73.9 years, but children born in Hawaii will live an average of 77 years, and those born in Louisiana, 71.7 years. If a newlywed couple from Louisiana were to begin their family in Hawaii, therefore, their children would be expected to live longer than would be the case if the family remained in Louisiana.

Which of the following statements, if true, would most significantly strengthen the conclusion drawn in the passage?

(A) As population density increases in Hawaii, life expectancy figures for that state are likely to be revised downward.

(B) Environmental factors tending to favor longevity are abundant in Hawaii and less numerous in Louisiana.

(C) Twenty-five percent of all Louisianians who move to Hawaii live longer than 77 years.

(D) Over the last decade, average life expectancy has risen at a higher rate for Louisianians than for Hawaiians.

(E) Studies show that the average life expectancy for Hawaiians who move permanently to Louisiana is roughly equal to that of Hawaiians who remain in Hawaii.

译文： 对于美国人口总体来说平均的期望寿命是73.9岁，但是在夏威夷出生的小孩将平均活到77岁，而那些在路易斯安那出生的人将平均活到71.7岁。如果一对从路易斯安那来的新婚夫妇在夏威夷开始他们的家庭生活，那么，他们的孩子预期将比他们留在路易斯安那的情况下活得更长。

以下哪一论述，如果是正确的，将最显著地加强短文中得出的结论？

(A) 随着夏威夷人口密度的增加，该州的寿命预期数据可能要向下修正。

(B) 有利于长寿的环境因素在夏威夷有很多，而在路易斯安那州比较少。

(C) 所有的迁移到夏威夷去的路易斯安那人中，有25%的人活过了77岁。

(D) 过去10年中，路易斯安那人的平均寿命预期比夏威夷人上升的速度更快。

(E) 研究表明，那些永久地迁移到路易斯安那州的夏威夷人的平均寿命预期同那些留在夏威夷的夏威夷人大致相同。

解析：支持重点支持结论，即支持"孩子的寿命变长"。若(B)是对的，它提到的具有更丰富的促进长寿的环境因素可能至少部分地解释在夏威夷寿命预期更高，在夏威夷出生的孩子从出生就从这些因素中获益。因而，那些在夏威夷生下小孩的路易斯安那人提高了他们的孩子活得更长的可能性。因此，(B)是正确答案；如果夏威夷的寿命预期将要下降，如选项(A)所言，将会削弱而不是加强该结论；选项(C)和(E)，在缺乏其他相关信息的情况下，同该结论没有关系；因而，(C)和(E)不合适。选项(D)是无关选项，因为它提到的关于增长速度的信息可能已经融入了短文中引用的统计数据中。

2. Insurance Company X is considering issuing a new policy to cover services required by elderly people who suffer from diseases that afflict the elderly. Premiums for the policy must be low enough to attract customers. Therefore, Company X is concerned that the income from the policies would not be sufficient to pay for the claims that would be made.

Which of the following strategies would be most likely to minimize Company X's losses on the policies?

(A) Attracting middle-aged customers unlikely to submit claims for benefits for many years.

(B) Insuring only those individuals who did not suffer any serious diseases as children.

(C) Including a greater number of services in the policy than are included in other policies of lower cost.

(D) Insuring only those individuals who were rejected by other companies for similar policies.

(E) Insuring only those individuals who are wealthy enough to pay for the medical services.

译文：保险公司X正在考虑发行一种新的保单，为那些身患困扰老年人疾病的老年人提供他们要求的服务。该保单的保险费必须足够低廉以吸引顾客。因此，X公司将为从保单中得到的收入不足以支付将要产生的索赔而忧虑。

以下哪一种策略将最有可能将X公司在该保单上的损失降低到最小？

(A) 吸引那些将在未来很多年里都不可能提出要求从该保单中获益的中年顾客。

(B) 仅向那些在幼年时没有得过任何严重疾病的个人提供保险。

(C) 在该项保单中提供比其他成本更低的保单中数量更多的服务。

(D) 仅向那些被其他保险公司在类似保险项目中拒绝的个人提供保险。

(E) 仅向那些足够富有，可以支付医疗服务费用的个人提供保险。

解析：本题让我们寻找一个选项以使得X公司在该保单上的损失降至最低，实际上是寻找一个支持选项。如果保险公司向尽可能多的属于低风险群的人们提供保险，它就可以提高收入与要求偿付保险金的比例，从而使损失最小化。因为选项(A)中描述的策略向保单持有人这个群体中增加了一个低风险群，(A)是正确答案；选项(B)是无关选项，因为在幼儿时期的疾病和影响老年人的疾病之间没有建立任何联系；选项(C)不合适，因为增加提供服务的数量不可能使损失最小化；选项(D)不合适，因为这会增加产生对该保单的索赔要求的可能性。因为保单持有人需书面要求按保单提供相应的服务，而不需要他们自己为这些服务付费，选项(E)是无关选项。

3. Company Alpha buys free-travel coupons from people who are awarded the coupons by Bravo Airlines for flying frequently on Bravo airplanes. The coupons are sold to people who pay less for the coupons than they would pay by purchasing tickets from Bravo. This marketing of coupons results in lost revenue for Bravo.

To discourage the buying and selling of free-travel coupons, it would be best for Bravo Airlines to restrict the

(A) number of coupons that a person can be awarded in a particular year.

译文：艾尔法公司从那些由于经常乘坐布拉沃航空公司的飞机而得到布拉沃公司奖励票券的人们那里买来了一些免费旅行票券，将这些票券以低于从布拉沃公司购买的机票价的价格向人们出售。这种票券的市场交易导致了布拉沃公司的收入损失。

为抑制这种免费旅行票券的买卖行为，对布拉沃航空公司来说最好是限制

(A) 某一年里一个人被奖励的票券的数量。

(B) use of the coupons to those who were awarded the coupons and members of their immediate families.

(C) days that the coupons can be used to Monday through Friday.

(D) amount of time that the coupons can be used after they are issued.

(E) number of routes on which travelers can use the coupons.

(B) 票券的使用仅限于那些被奖励了票券的人和他们的直系家庭成员。

(C) 票券的使用时间为星期一至星期五。

(D) 票券发行后可以被使用的时间的长短。

(E) 旅行者使用票券旅行的路线的数量。

解析：把票券的使用范围限制在那些被奖励了票券的人员的直系家庭成员里，如(B)所说，将使票券对其他人没有任何价值，因此不可能出现对这些票券的市场交易行为。然而，这些票券仍然可以使那些被布拉沃航空公司奖励了票券的人享受免费旅行，因此，奖励票券仍然是一个强烈地刺激人们经常乘坐布拉沃航空公司飞机的诱因，因此，(B)是正确答案；选项(A)，相反地，对减少票券的再出售价格毫无作用；选项(C)、(D)和(E)都不仅没有阻止艾尔法销售票券同布拉沃公司自己的机票销售竞争，而且暗自降低了票券对那些被奖励了票券的人的使用价值。

4. A recent spate of launching and operating mishaps with television satellites led to a corresponding surge in claims against companies underwriting satellite insurance. As a result, insurance premiums shot up, making satellites more expensive to launch and operate. This, in turn, has added to the pressure to squeeze more performance out of currently operating satellites.

Which of the following, if true, taken together with the information above, best supports the conclusion that the cost of television satellites will continue to increase?

(A) Since the risk to insurers of satellites is spread over relatively few units, insurance premiums are necessarily very high.

(B) When satellites reach orbit and then fail, the causes of failure are generally impossible to pinpoint with confidence.

(C) The greater the performance demands placed on satellites, the more frequently those satellites break down.

(D) Most satellites are produced in such small numbers that no economies of scale can be realized.

(E) Since many satellites are built by unwieldy international consortia, inefficiencies are inevitable.

译文：最近关于电视卫星发射和运营中发生的大量事故导致相应的对承担卫星保险公司提出索赔的大幅增加，结果保险费迅速上升，使得发射和运营卫星更加昂贵。反过来，这又增加了从目前仍在运营的卫星榨取更多工作负荷的压力。

以下哪一项，如果是正确的，同以上信息综合在一起，能最好地支持电视卫星成本将继续增加这个结论？

(A) 由于对卫星提供的保险风险仅由为数很少的单位承担，保险费必须非常高。

(B) 若卫星到达轨道后无法工作，通常来说不可能很有把握地指出它无法工作的原因。

(C) 要求安装在卫星上的工作能力越大，卫星就越经常出现故障。

(D) 大多数卫星生产的数量很少，因此不可能实现规模经济。

(E) 由于很多卫星是由庞大的国际财团建造的，无效率是不可能避免的。

解析：根据短文，卫星事故导致保险索赔大量增加，依次地，提高了保险费。更高的保险费使得卫星更昂贵，导致对卫星工作能力增加的需求。如果(C)是正确的，对工作能力的更大需求会通过增加事故的次数导致成本的进一步上升，因此推动保险费进一步上升，因此，(C)是正确答案；选项(A)、(D)和(E)都描述了与成本相关的因素，但没有理由相信，短文中所描述的情形会导致由这些因素引起的成本上升；相似地，不可能有指出它无法工作的原因，如(B)提到的，与卫星成本维持稳定没有矛盾。

5. Affirmative action is good business. So asserted the National Association of Manufacturers while urging retention of an executive order requiring some federal contractors to set numerical goals for hiring minorities and women. "Diversity in work force participation has produced new ideas in management, product development, and marketing," the association claimed.

The association's argument as it is presented in the passage above would be most strengthened if which of the following were true?

(A) The percentage of minority and women workers in business has increased more slowly than many minority and women's groups would prefer.

(B) Those businesses with the highest percentages of minority and women workers are those that have been the most innovative and profitable.

(C) Disposable income has been rising as fast among minorities and women as among the population as a whole.

(D) The biggest growth in sales in the manufacturing sector has come in industries that market the most innovative products.

(E) Recent improvements in management practices have allowed many manufacturers to experience enormous gains in worker productivity.

译文："肯定性行动"是一宗好买卖。全国制造商协会在努力促使保留一项要求一些联邦政府采购供应商设立可用数字表示的雇用少数民族和妇女的目标的行政命令时宣称。"劳动力的多元化可能在管理、产品的发展和市场营销方面产生出新的想法"。该协会这样宣称。

以下哪一项如果是正确的，将最有力地加强该协会以上短文中所述的论述？

(A) 工商业中少数民族和妇女工人比例的上升比很多少数民族和妇女组织预期的慢。

(B) 那些少数民族和妇女工人比例最高的企业也是最有创新能力和利润率最高的企业。

(C) 可支配收入在少数民族和妇女中与在全体人中上升得一样快。

(D) 制造业中销售增长最快的是那些销售最有创新能力的产品的行业。

(E) 最近的在管理实践中的改进使制造商们从工人的生产率提高中得到巨大的收益。

解析：如果，如(B)所说，那些少数民族的妇女工人比例最高的企业是最赚钱的，有理由相信，因为它增加了妇女和少数民族在劳动力中的参与水平，因此，"肯定性行动"方案会有很好的收益。因此，(B)是正确答案；选项(A)指出少数民族和妇女组织有理由支持"肯定性行动"方案，但它没有指出"肯定性行动"方案会有很好的收益。因为没有指出在可支配收入上的改善，如(C)提到的，是由于"肯定性行动"方案，(C)没有加强对"肯定性行动"方案的论述；选项(D)指出销售增长而(E)指出管理的改进，但都没有努力说明这些获益是由于"肯定性行动"方案。

6. If the airspace around centrally located airports were restricted to commercial airliners and only those private planes equipped with radar, most of the private-plane traffic would be forced to use outlying airfields. Such a reduction in the amount of private-plane traffic would reduce the risk of midair collision around the centrally located airports.

Which of the following, if true, would most strengthen the conclusion drawn in the second sentence?

(A) Commercial airliners are already required by law to be equipped with extremely sophisticated radar systems.

(B) Centrally located airports are experiencing overcrowded

译文：如果将中心位置机场附近的空域仅限于商用客机和那些装备了雷达的私人飞机使用，私人飞机流量的绝大部分将被迫使用偏远的机场。这种私人飞机流量的减少将降低在中心位置的机场附近发生空中撞机的危险。

以下哪一项，如果是正确的，将最有力地加强第二句话得出的结论？

(A) 法律已经要求商业客机装备非常复杂的雷达系统。

(B) 中心位置机场附近的空域非常拥挤，

airspace primarily because of sharp increases in commercial-airline traffic.

(C) Many pilots of private planes would rather buy radar equipment than be excluded from centrally located airports.

(D) The number of midair collisions that occur near centrally located airports has decreased in recent years.

(E) Private planes not equipped with radar systems cause a disproportionately large number of midair collisions around centrally located airports.

主要是因为商业客机流量的急剧增加。

(C) 许多私人客机的飞行员宁愿购买雷达设备，也不愿被排除在中心位置的机场之外。

(D) 在中心位置的机场附近发生的空中撞机的数量最近几年已经下降了。

(E) 没有装备雷达系统的私人飞机在中心位置的机场附近造成了异乎寻常的大量空中撞机事件。

解析：第二句话得到结论，第一句话中描述的减少将降低中心位置的机场附近的空中撞机的危险，根据(E)，这种减少将把那种造成很多空中撞机事件的飞机清理出去，因此，(E)是正确答案；选项(B)和(C)关心的是这种拟议中的限制是否会减少飞机流量，而不是这种相应的减少是否降低空中撞机的危险的问题；因为(A)没有提到私人飞机流量的减少是否降低空中撞机的危险的问题，(A)不合适；空中撞机事件数量的最近下降与拟议中的减少是否会进一步减少撞机事件无关，因此(D)不合适。

通过体会以上例题，下面我们按照支持的考查方向来看一些考题：

一、A与B之间有联系

7. Bats emit sounds and generally use the echoes of these sounds highly efficiently to detect, locate, and catch their prey. However, it is claimed that the characteristic efficiency of this process is reduced by moths able to hear the sounds emitted by insect-eating bats.

Which of the following statements, if true, best supports the claim above?

(A) Those moths that cannot hear the sounds emitted by insect-eating bats live longer on the average than those that can hear such sounds when both kinds of moth are in an environment continuously free of such bats.

(B) Those moth species that cannot hear the sounds emitted by insect-eating bats are among the species of insects that are most likely to be caught by such bats.

(C) When a moth changes its speed or direction of flight, there is a change in the sound pattern generated by the moth's wing movements.

(D) Moth species that can hear the sounds emitted by insect-eating bats are less likely to be caught by such bats than are moth species that cannot hear these sounds.

(E) Moths that are capable of hearing the sounds emitted by insect-eating bats differ in their abilities to use evasive action to escape capture by such bats.

译文：蝙蝠发射声波并通常非常高效地利用声波的反射来发现、予以定位并捕捉其猎物。然而，据说该过程特有的效率因蛾子能够听到蝙蝠发出的声波而减低。

下面的哪个说法，如果正确，最能支持上面说法？

(A) 听不见食昆虫的蝙蝠发射声波的蛾子与听得见该声波的蛾子如果都生活在持续没有该类蝙蝠的环境中，听不见的蛾子平均而言比听得见的蛾子的寿命长。

(B) 听不见食昆虫的蝙蝠发射声波的蛾子是最易被这种蝙蝠捉住的昆虫之一。

(C) 当蛾子改变其飞行的速度和方向时，其翅膀运动所产生的声波波形也改变。

(D) 能听见食昆虫的蝙蝠产生的声波的蛾子比听不到的蛾子被这种蝙蝠捕捉到的可能性更小。

(E) 听得到食昆虫的蝙蝠发射声波的蛾子，在其采取躲避行动来逃脱该种蝙蝠捕捉的能力上各不相同。

解析：本题读题重点在"However"之后的部分，"...by moths able to hear the sounds emitted by insect-eating bats"表示原因，段落推理关系为：因为蛾子能听见蝙蝠发出的声音，所以蝙蝠抓昆虫的效率降低。若听得见蝙蝠发出声音的蛾子更不大可能被蝙蝠抓住，如(D)所说，那么就把原因A中的关键词"听得见声音的蛾子"与B中的"蝙蝠抓昆虫的效率降低"连了起来，所以(D)为正确答案；(B)易误选，但(B)只说明听不见蝙蝠发出声音的蛾子是最容易被抓住的"insect"，而不是"moth"，另外(B)也并未表明听得见蝙蝠发出声音的蛾子是否容易被抓住，所以(B)说明不了任何问题；(A)中的"live"与段落推理无关；(C)中的"the sound pattern generated by the moth's wing movements"明显属于"偷换概念"；(E)中的"differ"只表明不同，但究竟谁不容易被抓住我们并不知道，所以(E)为无关选项。

8. Two decades after the Emerald River Dam was built, none of the eight fish species native to the Emerald River was still reproducing adequately in the river below the dam. Since the dam reduced the annual range of water temperature in the river below the dam from 50 degrees to 6 degrees, scientists have hypothesized that sharply rising water temperatures must be involved in signaling the native species to begin the reproductive cycle.

Which of the following statements, if true, would most strengthen the scientists' hypothesis?

(A) The native fish species were still able to reproduce only in side streams of the river below the dam where the annual temperature range remains approximately 50 degrees.

(B) Before the dam was built, the Emerald River annually overflowed its banks, creating backwaters that were critical breeding areas for the native species of fish.

(C) The lowest recorded temperature of the Emerald River before the dam was built was 34 degrees, whereas the lowest recorded temperature of the river after the dam was built has been 43 degrees.

(D) Nonnative species of fish, introduced into the Emerald River after the dam was built, have begun competing with the declining native fish species for food and space.

(E) Five of the fish species native to the Emerald River are not native to any other river in North America.

译文：Emerald河大坝建成20年后，Emerald河土产的8种鱼中没有一种仍能在大坝的下游充分繁殖。由于该坝将大坝下游的河水温度每年的变化范围由50度降到了6度，科学家们提出一个假想，认为迅速升高的河水温度在提示土产鱼开始繁殖周期方面起了一定作用。

以下哪一项论述，如果是正确的，将最有力地加强科学家们的假想？

(A) 土产的8种鱼仍能但只能在大坝下游的支流中繁殖，在那里每年温度的变化范围保持在大约50度。

(B) 在大坝修建以前，Emerald河每年都要漫出河岸，从而产生出土产鱼类最主要繁殖区域的回流水。

(C) 该坝修建以前Emerald河有记录的最低温度是34度，而大坝建成之后的有记录的最低温度是43度。

(D) 非土产的鱼类，在大坝建成之后引入Emerald河，开始同日益减少的土产鱼类争夺食物和空间。

(E) Emerald河土产的五种鱼在北美其他任何河流中都不算是土产的。

解析：要说明该假说是可靠的，证明Emerald河流域中温度差别较大的河水中生长的鱼没有失去它们的繁殖能力就很重要，选项(A)说明这些鱼仍能繁殖，因此是正确答案；选项(B)通过提出一个完全不同的假说削弱了该假说；选项(C)试图支持温度变化减小了的说法，但没有证明这是正确的解释；由于(D)谈到土产鱼类开始减少后的一种发展，同关心这种减少的最初原因的该假说无关；选项(E)强调了该问题的严重性，但没有说明是什么原因造成的。

二、A可行或A有意义

9. In recent years shrimp harvests of commercial fishermen in the South Atlantic have declined dramatically in total weight.

译文：近年来，以营利性为目的的渔民在南大西洋的河虾捕获量在总重量上急

The decline is due primarily to competition from a growing number of recreational fishermen, who are able to net young shrimp in the estuaries where they mature.

Which of the following regulatory actions would be most likely to help increase the shrimp harvests of commercial fishermen?

(A) Requiring commercial fishermen to fish in estuaries.

(B) Limiting the total number of excursions per season for commercial fishermen.

(C) Requiring recreational fishermen to use large-mesh nets in their fishing.

(D) Putting an upper limit on the size of the shrimp recreational fishermen are allowed to catch.

(E) Allowing recreational fishermen to move out of estuaries into the South Atlantic.

剧下降。这个下降主要是由于日益增多的以娱乐性为目的的渔民的竞争，他们能够在河虾成熟的河湾处捕捉到小的河虾。

下面哪一个管制规则将最可能有助于增加以营利性为目的的渔民的河虾捕获量？

(A) 要求以营利性为目的的渔民在河湾处钓鱼。

(B) 限制以营利性为目的的渔民每季郊游的总次数。

(C) 要求以娱乐性为目的的渔民在钓鱼时使用大网眼的网。

(D) 对以娱乐性为目的的渔民被准许捕获的鱼的大小规定一个上限。

(E) 允许以娱乐性为目的的渔民移出河湾进入南大西洋。

解析：本题问题目的是让我们去寻求选项以增加commercial fishermen的河虾捕获量，因此，方法只能从消除commercial fishermen的河虾捕获量下降的原因入手，而这个原因是由于recreational fishermen在河虾成熟的海湾处捕捉到young shrimp。(C)指出要求recreational fishermen使用大网眼的网，这样就可以使小河虾仍然在河中生长繁殖，从而消灭了这个原因，实现了问题目的，所以(C)正确；(A)、(B)、(E)可很容易排除；(D)易误选，但(D)中"upper"的意思与我们的问题目的刚好相反，若把"upper"改为"lower"就对了。

10. Toughened hiring standards have not been the primary cause of the present staffing shortage in public schools. The shortage of teachers is primarily caused by the fact that in recent years teachers have not experienced any improvements in working conditions and their salaries have not kept pace with salaries in other professions.

Which of the following, if true, would most support the claims above?

(A) Many teachers already in the profession would not have been hired under the new hiring standards.

(B) Today more teachers are entering the profession with a higher educational level than in the past.

(C) Some teachers have cited higher standards for hiring as a reason for the current staffing shortage.

(D) Many teachers have cited low pay and lack of professional freedom as reasons for their leaving the profession.

(E) Many prospective teachers have cited the new hiring standards as a reason for not entering the profession.

译文：日益苛刻的雇用标准并不是目前公立学校师资缺乏的主要原因，教师的缺乏主要是由于最近几年教师们的工作条件没有任何改善和他们薪水的提高跟不上其他职业薪水的提高。

以下哪一项，如果是正确的，将最能支持以上所述观点？

(A) 如果按照新的雇用标准，很多现在已经是教师的人就不会被雇用。

(B) 现在更多的进入这个职业的教师拥有比以前更高的教育水平。

(C) 一些教师认为更高的雇用标准是当前师资缺乏的一个原因。

(D) 许多教师认为工资低和缺乏职业自由是他们离开这个职业的原因。

(E) 许多未来的教师认为新的雇用标准是他们不进入这个职业的原因。

解析: 短文排除了一种对于缺乏教师的解释——由于更苛刻的雇用标准——并提出了一种替代的解释——教师缺乏是由于工资低和工作条件不佳,选项(D)通过指出对于许多前教师来说,低工资和工作环境差是他们放弃这项职业的原因,为后面这种解释提供了支持性的证据,因此,(D)是正确答案;选项(A)、(C)和(E)提供了证据显示新的雇用标准和师资缺乏有关,从而支持了短文反对的一种解释;选项(B)描述新雇用标准的一种可能的结果,但它没有提供证据来支持关于师资缺乏的一种解释优于另一种解释。

11. A cost-effective solution to the problem of airport congestion is to provide high-speed ground transportation between major cities lying 200 to 500 miles apart. The successful implementation of this plan would cost far less than expanding existing airports and would also reduce the number of airplanes clogging both airports and airways.

Which of the following, if true, could proponents of the plan above most appropriately cite as a piece of evidence for the soundness of their plan?

(A) An effective high-speed ground-transportation system would require major repairs to many highways and mass-transit improvements.

(B) One-half of all departing flights in the nation's busiest airport head for a destination in a major city 225 miles away.

(C) The majority of travelers departing from rural airports are flying to destinations in cities over 600 miles away.

(D) Many new airports are being built in areas that are presently served by high-speed ground-transportation systems.

(E) A large proportion of air travelers are vacationers who are taking long-distance flights.

译文: 一个解决机场拥挤问题的节省成本的方案是在间距200到500英里的大城市之间提供高速地面交通。成功地实施这项计划的花费远远少于扩建现有机场,并且能减少阻塞在机场和空中的飞机的数量。

以上计划的支持者们为了论证该计划的正确性,最适于将以下哪一项,如果是正确的,作为一项论据?

(A) 一个有效的高速地面交通系统要求对许多高速公路进行大修,并改善主干道。

(B) 在全国最忙的机场,一半的离港班机是飞往一个225英里以外的大城市。

(C) 从乡村地区机场出来的旅行者,大多数飞往600英里以外的城市。

(D) 在目前由高速地面交通系统提供服务的地区,修建了很多新机场。

(E) 乘坐飞机旅行的人中很大一部分是乘坐长途航班的度假者。

解析: 该计划提出解决机场拥挤的问题,高速地面交通是比扩建机场更便宜的一个方案,选项(B)指出在实施该计划的城市中有足够的空中客流量,对此地面交通可以将其取代,因此,(B)是正确答案,没有其他选项可以被拿来作为适当的证据;选项(A)和(D)都提供了反对该计划的证据,(A)通过强调提供高速地面交通可能的成本,(D)通过表明仅靠该替代方案自身不能解决机场拥挤问题;选项(C)和(E)说拟议中的系统实际上对很多旅行者不能提供替代方案。

12. If there is an oil-supply disruption resulting in higher international oil prices, domestic oil prices in open-market countries such as the United States will rise as well, whether such countries import all or none of their oil.

If the statement above concerning oil-supply disruptions is true, which of the following policies in an open-market nation is most likely to reduce the long-term economic impact on that nation of sharp and unexpected increases in international

译文: 如果石油供应出现波动导致国际油价上涨,在开放市场国家,如美国,国内油价也会上升,不管这些国家的石油是全部进口还是完全不进口。

如果以上关于石油供应波动的论述是正确的,在开放市场国家中,下面哪一种政策最有可能减少由于未预料到的国际油价剧烈上涨而对该国经济的长期影响?

oil prices?

(A) Maintaining the quantity of oil imported at constant yearly levels.

(B) Increasing the number of oil tankers in its fleet.

(C) Suspending diplomatic relations with major oil-producing nations.

(D) Decreasing oil consumption through conservation.

(E) Decreasing domestic production of oil.

(A) 把每年进口的石油数量保持在一个恒定的水平上。

(B) 增加该国舰船中油轮的数量。

(C) 暂停同主要石油生产国的外交关系。

(D) 通过节能措施减少石油消耗量。

(E) 减少国内的石油生产。

解析：如果关于石油供应波动的论述是正确的，当石油供应波动导致国际油价上涨时，开放市场国家中国内油价也会上涨。在开放市场国家里，减少消耗的石油量能够减少这种上涨对经济的影响。选项(D)给出了一个减少石油消耗的办法，并因此成为正确答案。其他选项没有合适的。选项(A)和(E)实际上描述了增加国际油价上涨造成的长期影响的政策，文中没有提到经济影响和油轮数量﹝选项(B)﹞或外交关系﹝选项(C)﹞之间的关系。

13. Male bowerbirds construct elaborately decorated nests, or bowers. Basing their judgment on the fact that different local populations of bowerbirds of the same species build bowers that exhibit different building and decorative styles, researchers have concluded that the bowerbirds' building styles are a culturally acquired, rather than a genetically transmitted, trait.

Which of the following, if true, would most strengthen the conclusion drawn by the researchers?

(A) There are more common characteristics than there are differences among the bower-building styles of the local bowerbird population that has been studied most extensively.

(B) Young male bowerbirds are inept at bower-building and apparently spend years watching their elders before becoming accomplished in the local bower style.

(C) The bowers of one species of bowerbird lack the towers and ornamentation characteristic of the bowers of most other species of bowerbird.

(D) Bowerbirds are found only in New Guinea and Australia, where local populations of the birds apparently seldom have contact with one another.

(E) It is well known that the song dialects of some songbirds are learned rather than transmitted genetically.

译文：雄性的园丁鸟能构筑精心装饰的鸟巢，或称为凉棚。基于他们对于本地同种园丁鸟不同群落构筑凉棚的构筑和装饰风格不同这一事实的判断，研究者们得出结论，园丁鸟构筑鸟巢的风格是一个后天习得的，而不是基因遗传的特征。

以下哪一项，如果是正确的，将最有力地加强研究者们得出的结论？

(A) 经过最广泛研究的本地园丁鸟群落的凉棚构筑风格中，共同的特征多于它们之间的区别。

(B) 年幼的雄性园丁鸟不会构筑凉棚，在能以本地凉棚风格构筑凉棚之前很明显地花了好几年时间观看比它们年纪大的鸟构筑凉棚。

(C) 一种园丁鸟的凉棚缺少大多数其他种类园丁鸟构筑凉棚的塔形和装饰特征。

(D) 只在新圭亚那和澳大利亚发现有园丁鸟，而在那里本地鸟类显然很少互相接触。

(E) 公众周知，一些鸣禽的鸣唱的方法是后天习得的，而不是基因遗传的。

解析：选项(B)中的信息说年轻的园丁鸟慢慢地掌握了构筑凉棚的方式，这表明这种技巧是他们必须学习才能得来，而不是完全基因遗传得来的。选项(B)也指出了一种后天修习传播的一种方式，即通过观看年长的鸟的技术。因此，(B)支持了该结论，是正确答案；构筑方式的相似超过差异﹝选项(A)﹞和本地鸟群很少接触﹝选项(D)﹞都与构筑方式的差异是后天习得的或通过遗传传递的没有矛盾；园丁鸟种类之间的差异［选项(C)］不是要讨论的问题；最后，选项(E)确认了鸟类学习技巧的可能性，但并不能证明构筑凉棚的方式是习得的。

三、除了A以外没有别的因素影响B

14. The average age and racing experience of the drivers at the Indianapolis 500 automobile race increased each year between 1965 and 1980' The reason for the increase is that high-speed racing drivers were living longer than their predecessors. Race-car safety features that reduced the severity of crashes of the kind that formerly took drivers' lives were primarily responsible for the increase in the average age of the Indianapolis 500 competitors.

Which of the following, if true, would be most likely to be part of the evidence used to show that safety features on the cars that protected drivers in major crashes were responsible for the increase in the average age of drivers at the Indianapolis race?

(A) Younger drivers at high-speed racetracks were involved in major accidents at a slightly higher rate than were older drivers between 1965 and 1980.

(B) Major accidents on high-speed racetracks occurred at about the same frequency in the years after 1965 as in the years before 1965.

(C) The average age of drivers attempting to qualify for the Indianapolis 500 decreased slightly between 1965 and 1980.

(D) Accidents on highways in the United States occurred at about the same frequency in the years after 1965 as in the years before 1965.

(E) Other safety features, involving the condition of the racetrack and the uniforms worn by the drivers while driving, were adopted at Indianapolis between 1965 and 1980.

译文：自1965年到1980年，Indianapolis 500赛车比赛中赛车手的平均年龄和赛车经历逐年增长。这一增长原因是高速赛车手比他们的前辈活得长了。赛车的安全性能减少了以前能夺走驾驶者生命的冲撞的严重性，它们是Indianapolis 500赛车比赛中车手平均年龄增长的根本原因。

下面的哪个，如果正确，最可能成为证明汽车安全性能在重大撞车中保护了车手，是赛车中赛车手平均年龄增长的原因？

(A) 在1965年到1980年间，快速车道上发生重大事故的年轻车手略多于年长的车手。

(B) 1985年之前和之后，发生在高速赛车道上的重大事故发生频率相同。

(C) 在1965年到1980年，试图取得资格参赛Indianapolis 500的车手的平均年龄有轻微下降。

(D) 1965年之前和之后，在美国高速公路上事故发生的频率相同。

(E) 在1965年到1980年间，其他的安全措施，包括车道的状况及车手驾车所穿的衣服，也在Indianapolis中被采纳。

解析：本题推理是由一个事实"Indianapolis 500赛车手平均年龄与赛车经验增长"，而得出一个解释结论说"Safety features是原因"，属于典型的"B，A"模式，假设答案多为"除了A之外没有别的因素影响B"，而假设答案就是支持。(B)中的"the same frequency"属于否定概念，表示没有事故发生率的变化，即否定了有别的原因影响B，因此(B)为正确答案；(A)是一个无关比较；(C)与推理无关；(D)讨论的是"United states"，与我们讨论的"Indianapolis"出现了范围差异；(E)指出other safety features的采纳使用，指出了别的因素的存在，所以(E)对段落推理起到了反对作用。

15. Medical personnel who served in heavy combat in a recent war—even those who escaped physical injury—now have lower incomes and higher divorce rates, and score lower

译文：最近一次战争里在重战区中执行任务的医疗人员，即使是那些身体未受伤害的，现在比在该战争不太激烈的战斗

on psychological profiles measuring general happiness, than medical personnel who served in less stressful settings during that war. This evidence demonstrates that exposure to heavy-combat situations produces serious adverse effects, even among those who suffered no physical harm.

Which of the following, if true, most strengthens the conclusion drawn above?

(A) The medical personnel who served in heavy combat had completed significantly less schooling prior to military service than had other medical personnel.

(B) The medical personnel who served in heavy combat tended to be younger at the time of their entry into military service than were other medical personnel.

(C) Parents of medical personnel who served in heavy combat show no significant difference in incomes, divorce rates, or general happiness from parents of other medical personnel.

(D) Income levels, divorce rates, and levels of general happiness are the same for the medical personnel who served in heavy combat as they are for construction workers.

(E) Medical personnel who served in heavy combat in an earlier war show no significant difference in incomes, divorce rates, or general happiness from other medical personnel who served in that war.

中执行任务的医疗人员收入低而离婚率高，在衡量整体幸福程度的心理状况测验中得分也较低。这一证据表明即使是那些激烈的战争环境下没有受到身体创伤的人，也会受到负面影响。

下面哪个，如果正确，最强有力地支持了以上得出的结论?

(A) 重战区的医疗人员和其他战区的医疗人员相比，服役前所接受的学校教育明显比较少。

(B) 重战区的医疗人员比其他战区的医疗人员刚入伍时年轻。

(C) 重战区医疗人员的父母和其他战区医疗人员的父母，在收入、离婚率和整体幸福程度方面没有什么显著差别。

(D) 那些在重战区服务的医疗人员和建筑工人在收入、离婚率和整体幸福程度等方面非常相似。

(E) 早期战争中的重战区服务的医疗人员在收入、离婚率和整体幸福程度等方面，和其他在该战争中服役的医疗人员没有表现出太大差别。

解析：本题推理是由一个事实而得出一个解释性结论，其隐含的假设是除了激烈的战争环境之外没有别的因素影响B。(C)指出这两类人的父母没有显著差异，实际上指出没有遗传因素影响B，所以(C)是一个假设，而假设可以作为一个支持，因此(C)正确；(A)、(B)、(D)与推理无关；(E)说明早期战争的两类人没有区别，从而对段落推理提出了质疑，起到了反对作用，所以(E)不可能是支持。

16. In tests for Pironoma, a serious disease, a false positive result indicates that people have Pironoma when, in fact, they do not; a false negative result indicates that people do not have pironoma when, in fact, they do. To detect pironoma most accurately, physicians should use the laboratory test that has the lowest proportion of false positive results.

Which of the following, if true, gives the most support to the recommendation above?

(A) The accepted treatment for Pironoma does not have damaging side effects.

(B) The laboratory test that has the lowest proportion of false positive results causes the same minor side effects as do the other laboratory tests used to detect Pironoma.

译文：在检测Pironoma 这种严重的疾病时，一个错误的阳性结果指出人们患Pironoma实际上他们没有；一个错误的阴性结果指出人们没有患Pironoma实际上他们患有。为更准确地检查Pironoma，医生应采用产生错误阳性结果比例最低的实验室测试手段。

以下哪一项，如果是正确的，为以上建议提供了最有力支持?

(A) Pironoma病人接受的治疗没有损害性的副作用。

(B) 产生错误的阳性结果比例最低的实验室测试与用来检测Pironoma的其他实验室

(C) In treating Pironoma patients, it is essential to begin treatment as early as possible, since even a week of delay can result in loss of life.

(D) The proportion of inconclusive test results is equal for all laboratory tests used to detect Pironoma.

(E) All laboratory tests to detect Pironoma have the same proportion of false negative results.

手段一样会产生同样微小的副作用。

(C) 在治疗Pironoma病人时，尽可能早地开始治疗非常重要，因为即使一周的耽误也会导致失去生命。

(D) 无法得出结论的测试结果比例对所有用来检测Pironoma的实验室测试手段都是一样的。

(E) 所有的检测Pironoma的实验室测试手段有相同的出现错误的阴性结果的比例。

解析：检测Pironoma最准确的测试办法应是产生错误结果最少的办法，如果所有的测试方法有相同的出现错误的阴性结果的比例，那么最准确的办法应是产生错误的阳性结果比例最低的办法，因此，(E)支持了该建议，是正确答案；选项(A)和(C)谈到Pironoma的治疗，与检测Pironoma的测试准确程度无关。选项(B)谈到检测Pironoma测试的负作用，与它们的准确程度无关。无法得出结论的测试结果比例对所有测试手段是一样的［选项(D)］，由于它没有指出哪种测试错误的结果最少，没有回答哪种测试更准确的问题。

四、直接支持B

17. The attitude that it is all right to do what harms no one but oneself is usually accompanied by a disregard for the actual interdependence of people. Destroying one's own life or health means not being available to help family members or the community, it means, instead, absorbing the limited resources of the community for food, health services, and education without contributing fully to the community.

Which of the following, if true, most strongly supports the view expressed above?

(A) The cost of avoidable accidents and illnesses raises health insurance rates for everyone.

(B) Harm to one person can result in an indirect benefit, such as the availability of work in health-related fields, to others.

(C) Life would be dull if it were necessary to abstain from all of the minor pleasures that entail some risk of harm to a person who indulges in them.

(D) The contribution a person makes to the community cannot be measured by that person's degree of health.

(E) The primary damage caused by the consumption of alcohol, tobacco, and unauthorized drugs is done to the person who uses those substances.

译文：那种认为只伤害自己而不伤害他人就行的态度，实际上是忽视了人们彼此间的相互依存关系。破坏自己的生活或健康就意味着不能帮助家庭成员或社会；相反，它意味着要耗费社会的食物、健康服务和教育方面的有限资源，却不能完全地回报于社会。

下面哪一条最能支持上面的观点？

(A) 本可避免的事故和疾病的费用提高了个人的健康保险费。

(B) 对某个人的伤害可能带来间接的益处，如在与健康相关的领域里给其他人提供工作机会。

(C) 戒绝所有可能对参加者造成伤害的娱乐，生活会变得乏味不堪。

(D) 人对社会做出的贡献不能由个人的健康程度衡量。

(E) 喝酒、吸烟、服非法的毒品，造成主要伤害的对象是那些消费这些物品的人。

解析：本题阅读有一定难度。段落的结论B为第一句话，第二句是对第一句话的进一步补充说明。注意到第一句话中的"interdependence of people"，如果本可避免的事故和疾病的费用提高了health insurance rates for everyone,正如(A)所说，那么就发现(A)不仅与段落第一句话对应，而且通过说明会增加每个人的健康保险费，直接支持了段落的第一句话即结论，即直接支持了B，所以(A)正确；(D)易误选，虽然(D)是一个真理，但我们不能由一个人的健康程度来评价一个人对社会的贡献，而且这个真理与段落推理没有直接关联，根本就不能回答问题目的；(B)、(C)、(E)均为无关选项。

18. Since the routine use of antibiotics can give rise to resistant bacteria capable of surviving antibiotic environments, the presence of resistant bacteria in people could be due to the human use of prescription antibiotics. Some scientists, however, believe that most resistant bacteria in people derive from human consumption of bacterially infected meat.

Which of the following statements, if true, would most significantly strengthen the hypothesis of the scientists?

(A) Antibiotics are routinely included in livestock feed so that livestock producers can increase the rate of growth of their animals.

(B) Most people who develop food poisoning from bacterially infected meat are treated with prescription antibiotics.

(C) The incidence of resistant bacteria in people has tended to be much higher in urban areas than in rural areas where meat is of comparable quality.

(D) People who have never taken prescription antibiotics are those least likely to develop resistant bacteria.

(E) Livestock producers claim that resistant bacteria in animals cannot be transmitted to people through infected meat.

译文：由于常规的抗生素的使用可以产生能在抗生素环境下存活的抗生菌，人体内存在抗生菌是由于人们使用处方抗生素，但是一些科学家相信人体内大多数抗生菌是由人们吃下的已经被细菌感染的肉类而来的。

以下哪一项论述，如果是正确的，将最显著地增强这些科学家的假想？

(A) 给牲畜喂的饲料中通常含有抗生素，这样畜牧业主可以提高他们牲畜的生长速度。

(B) 大多数吃了已经被细菌感染的肉类而食物中毒的人，是用处方抗生素来医治。

(C) 在城市人口中抗生菌的发现率比在肉类质量相仿的乡村地区高得多。

(D) 从来不使用处方抗生素的人是那些最不可能有抗生菌的人。

(E) 畜牧业主宣称动物中的抗生菌不能通过感染的肉类向人类传播。

解析：如果牲畜通常喂有抗生素，如选项(A)指出的，由于任何常规的抗生素使用会产生抗生菌，牲畜的肉可能含有抗生菌，因此选项(A)是正确答案；食物中毒的情况是如何治疗的［选项(B)］没有指明感染的细菌是否是抗生菌；选项(C)指出肉类的食用不是抗生菌高发现率的首要嫌疑；选项(D)有助于支持处方抗生素应为此负责这一相对立的假想；选项(E)指出畜牧业主宣称该假想是错误的，但没有提供基础来评价这一宣称的真实性。

19. Excavation of the ancient city of Kourion on the island of Cyprus revealed a pattern of debris and collapsed buildings typical of towns devastated by earthquakes. Archaeologists have hypothesized that the destruction was due to a major earthquake known to have occurred near the island in A.D. 365.

Which of the following, if true, most strongly supports the archaeologists' hypothesis?

(A) Bronze ceremonial drinking vessels that are often found in graves dating from years preceding and following A.D. 365 were also found in several graves near Kourion.

译文：Cyprus岛上Kourion古城的挖掘工作中挖出的废墟和倒塌的建筑物表明该城是一座典型的被地震毁灭的城镇。考古学家提出一种假说认为该城的毁灭是由于公元365年在该岛附近发生的一次大地震。

以下哪一项，如果是正确的，将最有力地支持考古学家的假说？

(A) 在Kourion附近的一些坟墓里发现了仪式用的青铜酒具，在时间确定为公元365年前后的坟墓中经常发现这些酒具。

(B) No coins minted after A.D. 365 were found in Kourion, but coins minted before that year were found in abundance.

(C) Most modern histories of Cyprus mention that an earthquake occurred near the island in A.D. 365.

(D) Several small statues carved in styles current in Cyprus in the century between A.D. 300 and 400 were found in Kourion.

(E) Stone inscriptions in a form of the Greek alphabet that was definitely used in Cyprus after A.D. 365 were found in Kourion.

(B) 在Kourion没有发现公元365年以后铸造的硬币，但公元365年以前铸造的有很多。

(C) 大多数Cyprus现代史提到公元365年在该岛附近发生了一次地震。

(D) Kourion发现了一些用公元300到400年之间这个世纪Cyprus流行的一种风格雕刻的小雕像。

(E) Kourion发现了用希腊字母的石刻，可以确定这种石刻在公元365年以后才在cyprus使用。

解析： 考古学家提出一种假说，认为Kourion是被已知于公元365年发生的一场地震摧毁的，由于选项(B)提供了证据表明公元365年是Kourion毁灭的时间，因此，B支持是公元365年的地震毁灭了Kourion这种假说，因此，(B)是正确答案；相比较而言，选项(A)、(D)和(E)都给出了关于在Kourion发现的或使用的文物的信息，但他们都没有特别指出公元365年是毁灭发生的时间，因此，(A)、(D)和(E)不合适；由于选项(C)支持了一项得到证实的观点，即公元365年发生了一场地震，因此(C)不合适。

20. Airline: Newly developed collision-avoidance systems, although not fully tested to discover potential malfunctions, must be installed immediately in passenger planes. Their mechanical warnings enable pilots to avoid crashes.

Pilots: Pilots will not fly in planes with collision-avoidance systems that are not fully tested. Malfunctioning systems could mislead pilots, causing crashes.

The pilots' objection is most strengthened if which of the following is true?

(A) It is always possible for mechanical devices to malfunction.

(B) Jet engines, although not fully tested when first put into use, have achieved exemplary performance and safety records.

(C) Although collision-avoidance systems will enable pilots to avoid some crashes, the likely malfunctions of the not-fully-tested systems will cause even more crashes.

(D) Many airline collisions are caused in part by the exhaustion of overworked pilots.

(E) Collision-avoidance systems, at this stage of development, appear to have worked better in passenger planes than in cargo planes during experimental flights made over a six-month period.

译文： 航空公司：最新开发的避免撞机系统，尽管没有进行完全的测试以发现潜在的功能失灵，但应该立即安装在客机上。它们的自动警报能使飞行员避免相撞。

飞行员：飞行员不能驾驶装有未经过完全测试的避免撞机系统的飞机，系统功能失灵会误导飞行员，造成撞机。

如果以下哪一项是正确的，将最有力地加强飞行员的反对意见？

(A) 机械装置总有可能失灵。

(B) 喷气发动机，尽管第一次投入使用时没有经过完全测试，但已经取得了优异的表现和安全记录。

(C) 尽管避免撞机系统可以使飞行员避免一些撞机事故，但未经完全测试的系统可能的失灵会导致更多的撞机事故发生。

(D) 许多飞机相撞事件是部分由于工作负担过重的飞行员的过度疲劳引起的。

(E) 发展到这个阶段的避免撞机系统在为期6个月的试验飞行过程中，在客机上比在货机上工作得更好。

解析： 选项(C)指出飞行员认为可能发生的事情有可能发生，因此，(C)是正确答案；选项(A)不合适，因为它没有提到飞行员，那些可能被误导的人最关心的功能失灵问题，(A)也没有将经过测试的和未经过完全测试的系统区分开来；选项(B)不合适，可以用来加强飞行员反对意见的关于使用未充分测试设备的例子只能是有负面结果的例子；但(B)提出一个正面结果的例子；选项(D)不合适，因为它提到的是需要解决是否应该立即安装该避免撞机系统的问题；选项(E)不合适，因为它没有提供任何证据说明任何功能失灵会误导飞行员造成撞机。

21. Many breakfast cereals are fortified with vitamin supplements. Some of these cereals provide 100 percent of the recommended daily requirement of vitamins. Nevertheless, a well-balanced breakfast, including a variety of foods, is a better source of those vitamins than are such fortified breakfast cereals alone.

Which of the following, if true, would most strongly support the position above?

(A) In many foods, the natural combination of vitamins with other nutrients makes those vitamins more usable by the body than are vitamins added in vitamin supplements.

(B) People who regularly eat cereals fortified with vitamin supplements sometimes neglect to eat the foods in which the vitamins occur naturally.

(C) Foods often must be fortified with vitamin supplements because naturally occurring vitamins are removed during processing.

(D) Unprocessed cereals are naturally high in several of the vitamins that are usually added to fortified breakfast cereals.

(E) Cereals containing vitamin supplements are no harder to digest than similar cereals without added vitamins.

译文： 许多早餐谷类食物中加有维生素添加剂，一些这样的谷类食物均提供了100%的每天维生素的建议摄取量。但是，一份比较均衡的早餐，包括各种食物，比起这种增强型早餐谷类食物自身，是一种更好的获取那些维生素的来源。

以下哪一项，如果是正确的，将最有力地支持以上观点？

(A) 在许多食物中，维生素与其他营养物质的自然组合使那些维生素比通过维生素添加剂增加的维生素能更好地被身体利用。

(B) 经常吃加有维生素添加剂的谷类食物的人有时忽视了吃一些含有自然维生素的食物。

(C) 食物经常必须添加一些维生素添加剂，因为自然状态的维生素在食物加工过程中被去除掉了。

(D) 未经过加工的谷类食物自然含有较高的经常添加到增加型早餐谷类食物中的多种维生素。

(E) 包含有维生素添加剂的谷类食物不比类似的没有添加维生素的谷类食物更难消化。

解析： 通过指出维生素出现在与其他营养物质的自然组合时，能够比那些以添加剂形式增加的维生素能更好地被身体利用，选项(A)提出了理由使人相信一份搭配均衡的早餐比起增强型的早餐谷类食物是一种更好的获取维生素的来源，(A)是正确答案；选项(B)不支持短文中提出的观点，尽管提出的观点，如果是正确的与提到的人们有关；选项(E)描述了增强型谷类食物和其他谷类食物的相似之处；选项(C)提出了一个向加工过的谷类食物添加添加剂的理由；选项(D)给出了关于未经过加工的谷类食物的信息，但都没有为提出的搭配均衡的早餐相对于增强型的谷类食物的优势增加支持。

五、总结

由于支持答案最终要对段落推理尤其是结论起作用，因此找到推理结论的核心关键词是最为重要的，特别是在问题目的中已清晰地告诉我们所要支持的内容的时候，我们可以用要支持的内容的核心关键词去定位选项。有时一些题目会让我们分析论据（前提）与结论的关系，因为这类题的正确答案是填补这种关系，以实现支持的目的。总之，解答支持题一定要抓住要支持的内容（大多数情况下是结论），然后用支持的内容的核心关键词去定位选项，进而进行判断。

六、试题精练及解析

1. Infection is the biggest threat to the life of a burn patient. The skin, the body's natural barrier against bacteria, is damaged or gone in the burned areas. The bacteria that are a threat are unpredictable in both variety and number. Moreover, those found affecting any one patient may change completely from one day to the next. The standard treatment, therefore, is the administration of broad-spectrum antibiotics.

Considering only the information given about burn patients in the passage above, which of the following is most likely to enhance the effectiveness of the standard treatment of a burn patient?

(A) Keeping the patient in an air-conditioned room until recovery is assured.

(B) Keeping the areas affected by burns as dry as possible.

(C) Continuously monitoring the patient's vital signs with electronic equipment.

(D) Feeding the patient a diet extra rich in calories.

(E) Keeping the patient in a maximally sterile environment.

2. For many people in the United States who are concerned about the cost of heating homes and businesses, wood has become an alternative energy source to coal, oil, and gas. Nevertheless, wood will never supply more than a modest fraction of our continuing energy needs.

Which of the following, if true, does NOT support the claim made in the last sentence in the passage above?

(A) There are many competing uses for a finite supply of wood, and suppliers give the lumber and paper industries a higher priority than they give individual consumers.

(B) Wood produces thick smoke in burning, and its extensive use in densely populated cities would violate federal antipollution guidelines.

(C) There are relatively narrow limits to how far wood can be trucked before it becomes more economical to burn the gasoline used for transportation instead of the wood.

(D) Most apartment dwellers do not have adequate storage space for the amount of wood necessary to supply energy for heating.

(E) Most commercial users of energy are located within range of a wood supply, and two-thirds of United States homes are located outside of metropolitan areas.

感染是对烧伤病人生命的最大威胁。皮肤是人体抵抗细菌的天然屏障，而在烧伤处皮肤已经遭到破坏或没有了。构成威胁的细菌的种类和数目都是无法预测的。而且，那些被发现危害病人的细菌在一两天内会发生彻底的变化。因此，最一般的治疗方法是服用广谱抗生素。

只考虑上文给出的关于烧伤病人的信息，下面哪个最可能提高对烧伤病人的一般治疗方法的效果？

(A) 在康复前让病人一直呆在一间有空调的房间里。

(B) 让烧伤部分尽可能保持干燥。

(C) 不停地用电子设备监测病人的主要指标。

(D) 让病人吃含热量多的食物。

(E) 让病人呆在无菌程度最好的环境里。

对许多关心家庭和办公取暖费用的美国人来说，木材已成为煤、石油、汽油的燃料的替代性来源了。然而，木材最多只能提供给我们将来能源需求中有限的一部分。

下面哪个，如果正确，不支持上文最后一句的观点？

(A) 对于供应量有限的木材有许多竞争性的用途，供应者把更多的优先权给了建筑木材业和造纸业而不是个人消费者。

(B) 木头在燃烧时要发出浓烟，因此木材在人口稠密城市的广泛使用将会破坏联邦政府反污染的方针。

(C) 在运输中燃烧汽油要比燃烧木头更经济之前，关于木材被运多远的限制相对较小。

(D) 大多数住公寓的人没有足够的地方来贮藏供热需用的木材。

(E) 大多数使用能源的商业用户都位于木材供应的范围之内，而2/3的美国家庭不在市区内。

3. Approximately 5,000 people who have been convicted of nonviolent crimes in the state have been given community-service sentences instead of prison sentences. These offenders perform services commensurate with their training and skills, from scrubbing floors to conducting research for the state. The community-service program, which began in 1979, has grown immensely as a result of drunken-driver legislation enacted a few months ago.

The introduction of the community-service program in 1979 was most probably prompted by which of the following, all of which occurred during the 1970's?

(A) A decrease in the number of violent crimes in the state.

(B) An increase in the number of crimes committed by employees of the state.

(C) A gradual decrease in the median age of judges in the state.

(D) The overcrowding of prisons in the state.

(E) The passage of drunken-driver legislation in other states.

某州大约5000名被判犯有非暴力罪行的罪犯没有去坐牢，而是去参加社区服务，这些人按照他们的技能为社区服务，包括从擦地板到做研究等不同工作。始于1979年的这种社区服务计划，由于几个月以前醉酒司机惩罚条例的实施而得以迅速发展。

下面各项均发生在70年代，其中哪个最可能促进了1979年社区服务项目的产生？
(A) 该州暴力犯罪的人数的减少。
(B) 该州犯法的职工的增多。
(C) 该州审判员平均年龄的逐渐降低。
(D) 该州监狱的拥挤不堪。
(E) 其他州通过了醉酒司机惩罚条例。

4. Researchers have discovered a new poison, bromethalin, that is lethal to all rats, even to those species that have become immune to other poisons, as well as to those rats that eat only the most minute quantities. Tests have demonstrated that rats will not learn to avoid bromethalin and that carcasses of rats killed by bromethalin pose no threat to the well-being of other animals.

Which of the following statements, if true, would support the researchers' claim that carcasses of rats killed by bromethalin will not pose a threat to other animals?

(A) Rats that consume bromethalin die immediately.

(B) Animals, prompted by curiosity, often examine carcasses that appear in their territory.

(C) Chemicals in the digestive tract of dead rats quickly break bromethalin down into a nontoxic substance.

(D) Traces of bromethalin remain in the rat's mouth and saliva after the rat eats the poison.

(E) Certain animals are scavengers and feed habitually on refuse and dead flesh.

研究人员发现了一种新的名为溴化钍的毒药，这种药对所有老鼠，甚至是对其他毒药有免疫力的鼠种以及只吃了极微量药的老鼠都是致命的。实验已经证实老鼠不会学会躲开溴化钍，而且由于食用溴化钍而死亡的老鼠尸体对其他健康的动物是无害的。

下面哪个，如果正确，能证明研究人员的观点，即被溴化钍杀死的老鼠尸体对其他动物无害？
(A) 吃了溴化钍的老鼠当即死去。
(B) 出于好奇，动物们经常查看出现在它们领地的尸体。
(C) 死老鼠消化道内的化学物质能迅速将溴化钍分解成无毒物质。
(D) 老鼠吃下溴化钍后，有微量残渣留在嘴中和唾液里。
(E) 有些老鼠是食腐动物，它们经常以垃圾和死尸为食。

5. Many geologists theorize that the trail of volcanic craters and cinder cones along the Snake River plain of southern Idaho was produced as the North American continent slid westward over a stationary "plume," a vertical channel through which molten rock rose intermittently from the

很多地理学家从理论上推理，Idaho州南部的Snake River平原上的一条火山口和火山锥的痕迹是北美大陆向西越过一个静止的"地幔热柱"时形成的。这个"地幔热柱"是个垂直的通道；通过它熔岩时断

Earth's core to burst through its crust.

Which of the following, if true, tends to support the geologists' theory of how the trail was produced?

(A) The largest craters and cinder cones are on the eastern margin of the trail.

(B) The most violent volcanic activity apparently occurred at the western margin of the trail.

(C) The craters and cinder cones are evenly spaced throughout the extent of the trail.

(D) The newest craters and cinder cones are on the eastern margin of the trail.

(E) The craters and cinder cones on the western margin of the trail generally took longer to form than did those on the eastern margin.

6. The plant called the scarlet gilia can have either red or white flowers. It had long been thought that hummingbirds, which forage by day, pollinate its red flowers and that hawkmoths, which forage at night, pollinate its white flowers. To try to show that this pattern of pollination by colors exists, scientists recently covered some scarlet gilia flowers only at night and others only by day: plants with red flowers covered at night became pollinated; plants with white flowers covered by day became pollinated.

Which of the following, if true, would be additional evidence to suggest that hummingbirds are attracted to the red flowers and hawkmoths to the white flowers of the scarlet gilia?

(A) Uncovered scarlet gilia flowers, whether red or white, became pollinated at approximately equal rates.

(B) Some red flowers of the scarlet gilia that remained uncovered at all times never became pollinated.

(C) White flowers of the scarlet gilia that were covered at night became pollinated with greater frequency than white flowers of the scarlet gilia that were left uncovered.

(D) Scarlet gilia plants with red flowers covered by day and scarlet gilia plants with white flowers covered at night remained unpollinated.

(E) In late August, when most of the hummingbirds had migrated but hawkmoths were still plentiful, red scarlet gilia plants produced fruit more frequently than they had earlier in the season.

7. The Wheat Farmers Alliance, a political action committee, attracts 70 percent of its contributors from an advertisement

时续地从地核通过地壳喷发出来。

下面哪个，如果正确，能支持地理学家关于痕迹是如何被产生的理论？

(A) 最大的火口和火山锥位于该痕迹的东部边缘地区。

(B) 最猛烈的火山活动很明显地发生在该痕迹的西部边缘地区。

(C) 火山口和火山锥在这个痕迹上是均匀分布的。

(D) 最新的火山口和火山锥都分布于这个痕迹的东部边缘。

(E) 该痕迹的西部边缘的火山口和火山锥的形成时间比东部的要长。

名为scarlet gilia的植物花朵为红色或白色。人们一直认为白天觅食的蜂鸟为它的红花授粉，而夜间觅食的天蛾为它的白花授粉。为了证明这种以颜色决定的授粉方式存在，科学家们最近将一部分scarlet gilia花只在白天遮住，而另一些scarlet gilia花只在夜晚遮住：结果开有红花在夜间被遮住的植物被授粉，而开有白花在白天被遮住的植物也被授粉。

下面哪个，如果正确，将是证明蜂鸟被红花吸引而蛾被白花吸引的又一证据？

(A) 未被遮住的scarlet gilia花，无论是红色的还是白色的，被授粉的比率大致相等。

(B) 有些没被遮住的scarlet gilia的红花一直未被授粉。

(C) 在夜间被遮住的白色scarlet gilia花授粉的频率大于未被遮住的白色scarlet gilia花。

(D) 白天被遮住的红色scarlet gilia和夜间被遮住的白色scarlet gilia花仍旧未被授粉。

(E) 在8月底，当大部分蜂鸟迁徙而蛾依然繁多之时，开红花的scarlet gilia植物比该季节早些时候更频繁地结果。

名为小麦农场主联盟的政治行动委员会，只凭放在9月、10月、11月的《农庄

requesting contributions placed only in the September, October, and November issues of the Grange Report, a monthly newsletter for wheat farmers. The president of the Wheat Farmers Alliance, to increase the number of contributors, decides to advertise in each of the monthly issues of the Grange Report. She expects that, as a result of the additional Grange Report advertisements, the number of contributors will be increased to at least double the present number.

Which of the following, if true, would most strongly support the president's expectation?

(A) The September, October, and November advertisements were noticed by fewer than one-third of those readers of the Grange Report who would be willing to contribute to the Wheat Farmers Alliance.

(B) Wheat farmers traditionally repay their bank loans in late summer after the winter wheat crop has been harvested and sold.

(C) The majority of the readers of the Grange Report with a great enough interest in the Wheat Farmers Alliance to contribute have already responded to the advertisements.

(D) Most of those who contribute to the Wheat Farmers Alliance in the course of a year do so in response to advertisements in the Grange Report.

(E) The total number of readers of the Grange Report is stable from year to year.

8. In the early 1970's, when art reached its current high levels of popularity and value, a rash of thefts of works by great artists occurred in major art museums around the world. But, after 1975, sophisticated new security systems were installed in every major museum. As a consequence, important thefts in major museums declined markedly.

Which of the following, if true, is strongest if offered as part of the evidence to show that improved security systems were responsible for the decline in thefts of important works from major museums?

(A) The typical art work stolen during both the 1970's and the 1980's was a small piece that could be concealed on the person of the thief.

(B) Premiums paid by major museums to insure their most important works of art increased considerably between 1975 and 1985.

(C) The prices paid to art thieves for stolen works were lower

报道》——一个小麦农场主月刊——上的呼吁捐款的广告吸引了70%的捐款者。小麦农场主联盟的主席为增加捐款者的人数，决定在《农庄报道》的每一期上登广告。她预计，增加在《农庄报道》上的广告的结果是捐献者至少会两倍于目前的人数。

下面哪个，如果正确，将最有力地支持该主席的预测？

(A) 9月、10月、11月的广告被少于《农庄报道》读者中愿意为小麦农场主联盟捐献的1/3的人注意到。

(B) 种小麦的农场主过去一直在夏末收割、出售完冬小麦后还银行贷款。

(C) 《农庄报道》的读者中，大部分对小麦农场主联盟有足够兴趣愿意捐款的人已经对广告做出了反应。

(D) 大多数在一年中捐款给小麦农场主联盟的人这样做是对《农庄报道》的广告做出的反应。

(E) 《农庄报道》各年的读者总数是稳定不变的。

20世纪70年代早期，当艺术达到了它现在这样的流行和价值水平时，全世界主要的博物馆中接二连三地出现了对大艺术家作品的盗窃之风。但在1975年之后，每家主要的博物馆中都安装上了先进的安全系统。结果，在主要博物馆中的重大盗窃显著下降。

下面哪个，如果正确，能成为最强有力的证据证明先进的安全系统使得主要博物馆中的重大盗窃减少？

(A) 典型的在70年代和80年代被窃的作品是一件小得能藏在窃贼身上的作品。

(B) 在1975年到1985年之间，主要博物馆为它们最重要的作品所付的保险金有了相当幅度的增加。

(C) 在80年代购买窃贼所盗窃的作品的价格比在70年代购买相当作品付给窃贼

during the 1980's than the prices paid to art thieves for comparable works during the 1970's.

(D) Thefts from private collections and smaller galleries of works by great artists increased sharply starting in the late 1970's.

(E) Art thefts in Europe, which has the largest number of works by great artists, outnumbered art thefts in the United States during the 1980's.

9. People often do not make decisions by using the basic economic principle of rationally weighing all possibilities and then making the choice that can be expected to maximize benefits and minimize harm. Routinely, people process information in ways that are irrational in this sense.

Any of the following, if true, would provide evidence in support of the assertions above EXCEPT:

(A) People tend to act on new information, independent of its perceived relative merit, rather than on information they already have.

(B) People prefer a major risk taken voluntarily to a minor one that has been forced on them, even if they know that the voluntarily taken risk is statistically more dangerous.

(C) People tend to take up potentially damaging habits even though they have clear evidence that their own peers as well as experts disapprove of such behavior.

(D) People avoid situations in which they could become involved in accidents involving large numbers of people more than they do situations where single-victim accidents are possible, even though they realize that an accident is more likely in the latter situations than in the former.

(E) People usually give more weight to a physician's opinion about the best treatment for a disease than they do to the opinion of a neighbor if they realize that the neighbor is not an expert in disease treatment.

10. Proportionally, more persons diagnosed as having the brain disorder schizophrenia were born in the winter months than at any other time of year. A recent study suggests that the cause may have been the nutrient-poor diets of some expectant mothers during the coldest months of the year, when it was hardest for people to get, or afford, a variety of fresh foods.

的钱要低。

(D) 从70年代晚期开始，私人收藏和小展馆中发生的大艺术家作品盗窃急剧上升。

(E) 在20世纪80年代，拥有最多的大艺术家作品的欧洲发生的艺术盗窃比美国发生的艺术盗窃要多。

人们通常不使用基本的经济原则来进行决策，该原则理性地衡量所有可能性，而后做出预计能够将利益最大化、并将损失最小化的选择。常规上讲，人们在这方面是以非理性的方式处理信息。

下面每个，如果正确，都将为支持上述推断提供论据，除了

(A) 人们倾向于依据其可看到的相对好处对新信息采取行动，而不是依据他们已有的信息。

(B) 人们更愿意选择一个他们主动选择的大的冒险，而不愿意选择一个强加于他们的小的冒险，即使他们知道主动采取的冒险从统计上讲更危险。

(C) 人们倾向于形成有潜在危害的习惯，即使他们有清楚的证据显示他们的同辈以及专家反对这种行为。

(D) 人们更避免卷入有很多人在内的事故境况中，而不那么避免可能发生单人受害的事故的境况，虽然他们能认识到在后一种情况下，发生事故的可能性更大。

(E) 人们通常对医生关于对某种疾病最佳治疗的意见给予更多的重视，而不对邻居的观点给予重视，如果他们意识到邻居不是疾病治疗的专家。

从比例上讲，被诊断患有大脑紊乱精神分裂的人中，出生在冬季月份的人比出生在一年中其他时间的人多。最近的一项研究显示，其原因可能是未来母亲在一年中最冷的几个月中的营养不良。在这一时期，人们最难买到或买得起多种新鲜食品。

Which of the following, if true, helps to support the conclusion presented above?

(A) Over the years the number of cases of schizophrenia has not shown a correlation with degree of economic distress.

(B) Most of the development of brain areas affected in schizophrenia occurs during the last month of the mother's pregnancy.

(C) Suicide rates are significantly higher in winter than in any other season.

(D) The nutrients in fresh foods have the same effects on the development of the brain as do the nutrients in preserved foods.

(E) A sizable proportion of the patients involved in the study have a history of schizophrenia in the family.

11. Any lender about to make a loan wishes to know the real rate of interest; i. e., the contractual rate of interest less the rate of inflation. But what rate of inflation to use, past or expected? Past inflation is the better choice, because we have specific firm figures for it so that the real rate of interest will also emerge as a specific figure.

Which of the following, if true, is the strongest point that an opponent of the position above might make in arguing that the rate of expected inflation is the proper figure to use?

(A) Since the contractual interest is future income to a prospective lender, it is more appropriate to adjust that income in terms of inflation expected for the future.

(B) Since estimating the rate of expected inflation presupposes careful economic analysis, lenders might derive coincidental benefits from doing such an estimate.

(C) The rate of expected inflation will differ little from the rate of past inflation when inflation is steady.

(D) No official rate of past inflation is computed for any period shorter than a month.

(E) The official rate of past inflation is a figure that depends on what commodities, in what proportions, determine the official price index.

12. Within the last fifty years, the majority of the United States work force has moved from the manufacturing to the service sector of the economy. This shift has occurred, not because of a decline in the production of goods, but because, with applications of new technology, more production of

下面哪个，如果正确，能帮助支持上述的结论？

(A) 几年以来，精神分裂症的发病率未显示出与经济萧条的程度有关。

(B) 大部分精神分裂症中染病的脑部区域是在母亲怀孕期的最后一个月发育的。

(C) 冬季的自杀率明显高于其他季节。

(D) 新鲜食品中的营养与冷藏食品中的营养对脑部发育产生的效果相同。

(E) 相当一部分被调查研究的病人有精神分裂症的家族病史。

任何将发放贷款的人都想知道真正的利率，也就是合同的利率减去通货膨胀率。但是用哪一个通货膨胀率呢？是过去的，还是预计的？过去的通货膨胀率是个更好一些的选择，因为我们有具体确定的数字，这样真正的利率也会以一个具体数字的形式出现。

下面哪个，如果正确，是反对上面观点的人会用来证明预计的通货膨胀率是适合使用的数字的最强有力的观点？

(A) 因为合同规定的利息是将贷款借给他人的未来收入，所以用预计未来的通货膨胀率计算该利息更恰当。

(B) 因为估算未来的通货膨胀率预先假定了认真的经济分析，贷款人可能会从这样的估算中得到偶然的好处。

(C) 在通货膨胀稳定的时候，预计通货膨胀率与过去通货膨胀率相差无几。

(D) 官方统计通货膨胀率的时间段不短于一个月。

(E) 官方统计的过去的通货膨胀率依赖于什么商品在多大程度上决定官方价格指数。

在过去的50年中，美国的大部分劳动力由其经济的制造业转移到了服务业。这种转移的产生不是因为物质生产的减少，而是因为应用了新技术后，更多的物质生产可以由相对较少的人来完成，因此，有

goods can now be achieved with relatively fewer people, and more people are therefore available to satisfy the increased demand for services.

Which of the following, if true, provides evidence to support the claim made above that more production of goods can now be achieved with relatively fewer people?

(A) Many manufacturing industries in the United States have lost a significant share of their domestic and foreign markets to foreign producers.

(B) Services accounted for half of all jobs in the late 1940's but today account for seventy percent of all jobs.

(C) Manufacturing output was one-third higher in 1980 than in 1970, while manufacturing employment grew only five percent during that period.

(D) Manufacturing industries, on average, pay a higher per-hour wage and use fewer part-time employees than do service industries.

(E) Living standards in states that have shifted to manufacturing economies within the last fifty years are closer to the national average now than in 1940.

13. A common defense of sport hunting is that it serves a vital wildlife-management function, without which countless animals would succumb to starvation and disease. This defense leads to the overly hasty conclusion that sport hunting produces a healthier population of animals.

Which of the following, if true, best supports the author's claim that sport hunting does not necessarily produce a healthier population of animals?

(A) For many economically depressed families, hunting helps keep food on the table.

(B) Wildlife species encroach on farm crops when other food supplies become scarce.

(C) Overpopulation of a species causes both strong and weak animals to suffer.

(D) Sport hunters tend to pursue the biggest and healthiest animals in a population.

(E) Many people have strong moral objections to killing a creature for any reason other than self-defense.

14. Scientists have found that inserting genes from a plant virus into the genes of a plant susceptible to that virus increases the plant's resistance to the virus. Because viral

更多的人来满足增长了的服务需求。

下面哪个，如果正确，支持上面提出的更多的物质生产可由相对较少的人来完成这一说法？

(A) 美国很多制造业失去了他们的很多国内外市场份额给外国生产者。

(B) 服务业在20世纪40年代占所有工作的1/2，而今天占所有工作的70%。

(C) 1980年的制造业产值比1970年高出1/3，而制造业的就业人数比那时只高出5%。

(D) 平均而言，制造业支付的小时工资高于服务业，并且它使用的兼职工人比服务业少。

(E) 在最近50年中转为制造经济的州的生活水平比1940年更加接近国家平均水平。

对狩猎运动一个普遍的辩护是认为它起到了重要的管理野生动物的作用，如果没有它，无数动物将遭受饥饿和疾病。该辩护导致一个太过草率的结论，即狩猎运动，产生了一个更健康的动物群体。

下面哪个，如果正确，最好地支持了作者的立场，即狩猎运动不一定能产生一个更健康的动物群体？

(A) 对许多经济窘迫的家庭来讲，狩猎可以保证餐桌上的食物。

(B) 野生动物在其他食物供应变得稀少时就会破坏庄稼。

(C) 某种动物数量过多，对于强、弱动物都会造成伤害。

(D) 狩猎运动员愿意追杀最大和最强健的动物。

(E) 对于自卫以外的任何残杀动物的理由，许多人都能提出强有力的道德上的反对意见。

科学家发现，将一种从植物病毒中提取的基因注射到一种易受该病毒感染的植物的基因中可提高该植物对这种病毒的抵

diseases account for a significant proportion of crop losses, such genetic alterations, even if carried out on only a modest scale, will significantly reduce crop losses.

Each of the following, if true, strengthens the conclusion above EXCEPT:

(A) In areas where two successive crops are raised per year, protecting the first crop from a virus will generally protect the second crop from that virus as well.

(B) By repeatedly attacking plants that are genetically altered to become virus-resistant, the virus often becomes less lethal to plants that are not genetically altered in that way.

(C) Plants that are genetically altered to become virus-resistant often pass virus-resistant genes on to their offspring.

(D) Plants that are made genetically resistant to one kind of virus often acquire resistance to related viral strains as well.

(E) Plants that are made genetically resistant to one kind of virus are then more susceptible to infection by unrelated viruses.

15. The dramatic rise in the number of homeless people in the 1980's cannot be attributed to the discharge of mentally ill persons from hospitals into "community care." even though it is true that provisions for such community care are for the most part nonexistent.

Which of the following, if true, best supports the claim above?

(A) The policy of discharging mentally ill persons from hospitals was based on the supposition that their illnesses couldbe controlled by newly developed drugs.

(B) Without supervision in a hospital setting those people whose mental illness can be controlled by medication might not actually take prescribed medication.

(C) Some community-care programs for mentally ill persons did exist in the 1980's, but those programs consisted primarily of outpatient clinics.

(D) The policy of discharging significant numbers of mentally ill persons from hospitals took effect in the 1960's.

(E) There have always been some people in large cities who have led a homeless existence.

抗力。由于病毒疾病引起的谷物损失占了很大的比重，这种基因转换，即使在一个最有限的范围内开展，也能显著减少谷物损失。

下面每个，如果正确，都能增强以上的结论，除了

(A) 在一些每年相继种植两种谷物的地区，如果保证第一种谷物不会感染一种病毒，另一种谷物通常也不会感染此病。

(B) 由于反复地侵入那些经过基因变异而成为抗体的植物，这些病毒对于那些没有发生基因变异的植物，不是那么致命了。

(C) 植物经历了基因变异，成为病毒的抗体以后，也会把这种抗体基因传给后代。

(D) 如果一种植物成为一种病毒的抗体，它也会获得对相关病毒的抵抗力。

(E) 如果一种植物成为一种病毒的抗体，它会更容易受不相关的病毒感染。

20世纪80年代无家可归人数的急剧增加不能归因于将精神病患者从医院推向"社区护理"，尽管大部分对这种社区护理的供给是确实不存在的。

下面哪个，如果正确，最能支持以上论述？

(A) 把精神病患者请出医院的政策依据于这样的假设，即一种新研制的药物可以使他们的病情得到控制。

(B) 没有医院的监督，那些病情可以由药物得到控制的患者可能不会真正遵医嘱进药。

(C) 20世纪80年代确实存在针对精神病人的社区护理计划，但主要是一些针对门诊病人的诊所组成。

(D) 在20世纪60年代就采取了把大量精神病人遭送出医院。

(E) 在大城市总是有一些人无家可归。

16. The first people to inhabit North America came from Asia. Scientists had hypothesized that these people traveled across a now-submerged landmass that connected the two continents until 14,000 years ago, depending for food only on the land animals they hunted as they traveled. Recent discoveries have led to the new hypothesis that the first people came by boat along the southern shore of the landmass, eating fish and sea mammals.

Which of the following, if true, most strongly supports the new hypothesis by casting doubt on the earlier hypothesis?

(A) The landmass connecting North America and Asia extended very far to the north.

(B) In Europe, maritime cultures primarily dependent on the sea for food developed no earlier than 10,000 years ago.

(C) People living in Asia at the time the two continents were connected hunted land animals for food.

(D) The landmass was so bitterly cold that its vegetation would have been too sparse to support land animals.

(E) Sophisticated and mature North American and Asian cultures that display great similarities to each other existed as far back as 8,000 years ago.

17. The presence of microorganisms that produce a toxin causes seawater to turn brownish red, a phenomenon known as a red tide. Sea otters do not feed in areas where clams, their main source of food, have become contaminated with this toxin. According to a proposed explanation of the otters' behavior, the otters sample the clams in a potential feeding area and can taste any toxin in them.

Which of the following, if true, would most strongly indicate that the hypothesis described in the last sentence of the passage is not correct?

(A) In some of the areas where red tides occur, neither clams nor sea otters are indigenous species.

(B) The presence of sea otters in a given area has a significant effect on which other marine organisms are to be found in that area.

(C) When seawater in an area unaffected by red tide is artificially dyed brownish red, sea otters do not feed on the clams in that area.

(D) If the clams in a given area are contaminated with toxins, sea otters move to other areas in search of food.

最早的居住在北美的人来自亚洲，科学家曾假设这些人是穿过一块现在已沉入海底的陆地过来的，直到1.4万年前那块陆地还连接着这两个大陆，人们在旅行时，靠捕猎到的陆地动物为食。最近的发现又引起了一个新的假说，即最初的这些人是乘船绕陆地的南海岸过来的，以鱼和海洋哺乳动物为食。

下面哪个，如果正确，通过对早先假设提出质疑而最强有力地支持了新的假设？

(A) 连接北美洲和亚洲的这块大陆向北延伸到很远。

(B) 在欧洲，由于靠海洋为生而产生的海洋文化在1万年前就开始发展起来了。

(C) 当两个大陆还相互连接着时，住在亚洲的人是靠打猎为生的。

(D) 这块陆地如此严寒，以至于那里的植物太稀少了，不足以喂养陆地动物。

(E) 发达、成熟的北美与亚洲文化表现出了巨大的共同点，而且这一共性可追溯到8000年以前。

一种微生物能产生一种毒素，它的存在会使海水变为棕红色，这种现象被称为赤潮。海獭的主要食物来源蛤被毒素污染时，它们就不会在那些地方觅食。根据一项关于海獭行为的解释，海獭在一个潜在的进食地内对蛤取样并可以尝出其中的任何毒素。

下面哪个，如果正确，最强有力地表明上文最后一句的假设是错误的？

(A) 在一些赤潮发生的地区，没有蛤，也没有水獭。

(B) 在特定地区水獭的出现对当地可找到的其他海洋生物有巨大的影响。

(C) 当未受赤潮影响的一片海水被人为染成棕红色时，海獭也不会吃在那些地方的蛤。

(D) 如果某个特定区域的蛤被毒素污染了，海獭就移到另外的区域寻找食物。

(E) Although very small amounts of the toxin produced during a red tide are not harmful, large doses can be fatal to animals the size of sea otters.

18. United States advertising agencies are increasingly using interviews at shopping malls, called "mall intercepts", to test for advertising effectiveness, product concept viability, and consumer buying habits. Critics of mall intercepts maintain that the shopping habits of mall shoppers are not representative of those of the larger population.

Which of the following, if true, would provide evidence that most supports the critics' claim about mall intercepts?

(A) Some mall shoppers patronize more than one store in any given shopping trip.

(B) Mall shoppers, on average, spend 50 percent more time shopping than shoppers at other locations do.

(C) In the course of any year, 95 percent of all households in the United States have at least one member who does some shopping at a mall.

(D) Mall shoppers who use public transportation to reach the mall tend to have lower incomes than mall shoppers who drive to the mall.

(E) Indoor malls often attract the customary numbers of shoppers even during inclement weather when outdoor malls are likely to lose business.

19. "Headhunters" are firms that, for a fee, undertake to recruit for their clients personnel who are greatly needed yet hard to find. The clients, in turn, require that they be off-limits to headhunters whose services they buy; i. e., headhunters cannot raid one client's staff on behalf of other clients.

Of the following, which would, if feasible, be the best strategy for a company to pursue if that company wanted both to use headhunters to fill a vacancy and, if successful in filling the vacancy, to reduce the risk of losing the newly hired employee to a competitor?

(A) Find out which headhunters recruit workers of the sort being sought and employ all those headhunters.

(B) Find out which headhunter has the highest success rate in recruiting for its clients and hire that firm.

(C) Find out how much the company's competitors currently pay staff of the sort being sought and offer to pay prospective employees higher salaries.

(E) 虽然，赤潮中产生的非常少量的毒素是无害的，大量的毒素对海獭这样大小的动物却可能是致命的。

美国的广告代理商正越来越多地使用被称为"商城拦截"的在商城的采访，以测试广告效果、产品概念可行性以及消费者的购买习惯。对商城拦截的批评者坚持认为商城消费者的购买习惯不能代表更广大的人群。

下面哪个，如果正确，提供了最能支持该批评者关于商城拦截的宣称的证据？

(A) 一些购物者在一次采购过程中会光顾几家商店。

(B) 平均而言，商城购物者比其他场所购物的人多花50%的时间购物。

(C) 每年，美国95%的家庭中至少会有一人在商城里买东西。

(D) 乘坐公交车来商城的购物者要比开车来的购物者收入低。

(E) 室内商城即使在恶劣的天气也能吸引像平常一样数量的顾客，而在此时，户外商场就会丧失生意。

"猎头"就是这样一种公司，它为了获取费用，为其每个客户招募那种非常需要却又很难找到的人才。反过来。客户要求为其服务的猎头公司将客户自己的公司列在"猎头"范围之外。也就是说，猎头公司不能为了其他客户的利益而去猎取他其中一个客户的员工。

如果一个公司既想利用猎头公司来弥补人员空缺，当空缺弥补后又想降低此新雇员被竞争对手挖走的风险，那么，下列哪个，如果可行，对公司来讲是最佳策略？

(A) 查出所有招募公司正在寻找的那类员工的猎头公司并将他们全部雇用。

(B) 查出哪家猎头公司为其客户进行招募成功率最高，然后雇用这家公司。

(C) 查出其他竞争对手支付给所需人才的薪水数额，然后支付给这位未来的雇

(D) Find out whether any of the company's competitors are seeking to recruit workers of the sort being sought and, if so, make sure not to hire the same headhunters that they hire.

(E) Find out which of the company's competitors are on the client lists of the headhunters who are being considered for the job.

员更高的薪水。

(D) 查出是否有其他公司正在寻找他所需的人才，如果有绝对不和那一家公司雇用同一家猎头公司。

(E) 针对正在考虑招募人才的工作，查出他想雇用的猎头公司的客户名单中有哪些竞争对手。

20. Jan: People should not go to the new exhibition of Thornton's paintings. Thornton will be given a portion of the admission proceeds and Thornton, a violent sociopath, should not be supported.

Kim: Your recommendation is inconsistent with your actions, because you read poems by poets who also were violent sociopaths.

Which of the following, if true, provides the strongest basis for Jan to counter Kim's argument?

(A) Thornton's portion of the exhibition's proceeds are being donated to a cause deemed worthy by Thornton.

(B) It is quite difficult, if not impossible, for Jan to discover the behavioral tendencies of the artists Jan reads.

(C) Kim does not use products made by companies whose hiring practices Kim finds abhorrent.

(D) The poets derived no benefit from Jan's reading their poems.

(E) The poets' violent behavior is better known to the public than is Thornton's violent behavior.

Jan：人们不应该去观看Thornton的绘画新展览。因为Thornton将得到一部分门票收入，而其作为一个恶名昭著的反社会者，不应该得到人们的支持。

Kim：你的言论与行为不相符合，因为你所读的一些诗的作者也是反社会者。

下面哪个，如果正确，为Jan反驳Kim的论述提供了最强有力的依据？

(A) Thornton所得的门票收入捐给了他认为有价值的事业。

(B) Jan也很难了解其所阅读的艺术家的行为习惯。

(C) 如果发现一公司招人的做法令人生厌，Kim不会使用其产品。

(D) Jan阅读诗作对诗人没有任何好处。

(E) 比起Thornton的狂热行为，公众更了解诗人们的狂热。

21. Government bans on the dumping of sludge anywhere in the ocean are based on the belief that the spread of sludge by ocean currents poses a danger to people. Since it is not clear that sludge dumped on the ocean bottom, far from coasts, would endanger people, the bans should be revised to apply only to coastal waters.

Each of the following, if true, supports the conclusion that the bans on ocean dumping should be revised EXCEPT:

(A) The slow-moving water near the ocean bottom mixes so slowly with water closer to the surface that sludge dumped on the ocean bottom would be decomposed by bacteria before currents could bring it to the surface.

(B) Many locations on the ocean bottom far from coasts are geologically stable, and unlikely to be disrupted by earthquakes or volcanic eruptions.

政府对在海洋中任何地点排放污物的禁令依据的是他们相信洋流导致污物扩散会对人类造成危害。由于还不清楚倾倒在海底——远离海岸的污物是否会产生危害，这项禁令应被修订以仅适用于海岸海水。

下面每个，如果正确，都能支持在海洋倾倒的禁令应被修改的结论，除了：

(A) 靠近海洋底部的流动很慢的水流，经过太长的时间才能与表层的海水相混合，以至于倒在深海的污物被带到水面时已经被细菌分解了。

(B) 远离沿岸的海底的许多地方在地质上非常稳定，不可能受地震和火山喷发的侵袭。

(C) Deep-sea marine plants and animals in the human food chain live at depths far above the ocean bottom.

(D) Dumping large amounts of sludge would have an unknown effect on organisms that live on the ocean bottom.

(E) The technology exists to lower sewage sludge to ocean-bottom dump sites without contaminating waters closer to the surface.

(C) 人们常吃的海洋动植物生活在远在海底之上的地方。

(D) 把大量污物倒入海洋会对生活在海底的有机物造成一种未知的影响。

(E) 存在一种技术可以把污物降到海底垃圾场却不会污染海面附近的水。

22. Counselor: Every year a popular newsmagazine publishes a list of United States colleges, ranking them according to an overall numerical score that is a composite of ratings according to several criteria. However, the overall scores generally should not be used by students as the basis for deciding to which colleges to apply.

Which of the following, if true, most helps to justify the counselor's recommendation?

(A) The vast majority of people who purchase the magazine in which the list appears are not college-bound students.

(B) Colleges that are ranked highest in the magazine's list use this fact in advertisements aimed at attracting students.

(C) The rankings seldom change from one year to the next.

(D) The significance that particular criteria have for any two students is likely to differ according to the students' differing needs.

(E) Some college students who are pleased with their schools considered the magazine's rankings before deciding which college to attend.

顾问：某畅销新闻杂志每年都要公布一个美国大学的排名，上面将美国的大学按照几项标准评判所得综合分数进行排名。然而，学生通常不应以这个综合得分作为决定申请哪些学校的依据。

下面哪个，如果正确，最有助于证明顾问的建议是正确的？

(A) 大多数购买登有这一排名的杂志的人并不是需上大学的学生。

(B) 这本杂志中排名最高的大学在广告中利用这个事实来吸引学生。

(C) 这类排名各年之间一般很少改变。

(D) 对任何两位学生来说，某些衡量标准的重要性会因他们的需求不同而不同。

(E) 一些对其所在大学表示满意的学生在选择学校之前参考了这一杂志排名。

23. A list of the fifteen operas most frequently performed in recent times includes no works by the nineteenth century German composer Richard Wagner. Although music producers tend to produce what audiences want, relative infrequency of performance probably does not indicate lack of popularity in Wagner's case, since Wagner's operas are notoriously expensive to perform on stage.

Which of the following, if true, most strongly support the conclusion of the argument above?

(A) The list of most frequently performed operas does not include operas produced by small amateur groups.

(B) Some opera companies are backed by patrons who are willing to commit large sums of money in order to enjoy lavish productions.

(C) All of the fifteen most frequently performed operas of

最近最经常上演的15部歌剧中没有19世纪德国作曲家理查德·瓦格纳的作品。虽然音乐制作人都希望制作听众想听的作品，但瓦格纳的作品没有被相对频繁地演出并不能表明他的作品不受欢迎，而是因为他的歌剧的舞台演出费用极其昂贵。

下面哪个，如果正确，最能支持上面的结论？

(A) 经常上演的歌剧中不包括小型业余作曲群体的作品。

(B) 演出公司经常得到一些为了能看豪华气派的歌剧而赞助的人的支持。

(C) 所有最近经常上演的歌剧至少是已流行了75年的作品。

recent times are works that have been popular for at least 75 years.

(D) More recordings have been produced recently of the works of Wagner than of the works of any other composer of opera.

(E) Operatic works of all kinds have been increasing in popularity in recent years.

(D) 近期瓦格纳的作品录音带出得比别人都多。

(E) 近年来各类歌剧作品受欢迎的程度不断提高。

24. During the nineteenth century, Britain's urban population increased as its rural population diminished. A historian theorizes that, rather than industrialization's being the cause, this change resulted from a series of migrations to urban areas, each occasioned by a depression in the agrarian economy. To test this hypothesis, the historian will compare economic data with population census data.

The historian's hypothesis would be most strongly supported if which of the following were found to be true?

(A) The periods of greatest growth in the industrial economy were associated with a relatively rapid decline in the rural population.

(B) The periods of greatest weakness in the agrarian economy were associated with relatively slow growth in the population as a whole.

(C) Periods when the agrarian economy was comparatively strong and the industrial economy comparatively weak were associated with a particularly rapid decline in the rural population.

(D) Periods when the agrarian and industrial economies were both strong were associated with particularly rapid growth in the urban population.

(E) The periods of greatest strength in the agrarian economy were associated with relatively slow growth in the urban population.

19世纪，英国城市人口增加而农村人口下降。一位历史学家推理说，这种变化并不是因为工业化，而是由于人口向城市地区的一系列迁移，每次迁移都伴随有农业经济的衰退。为证实这一假说，这位历史学家打算比较经济数据与人口普查数据。

下列哪个，如果被证实是正确的，将最有力地支持这位历史学家的假说？

(A) 在工业经济增长最快的时期，同时农村人口也相对减少。

(B) 当农业经济最萧条的时候，整个人口增长也减慢了。

(C) 当农业经济相对强劲，工业经济不景气的时候，农村人口会急剧下降。

(D) 当工、农经济都比较好时，城市人口增长较快。

(E) 当农业经济最强劲的时候，城市人口增长较慢。

25. Children whose biological parents both have Tic Syndrome Z (TSZ), which is characterized by the involuntary contraction of certain muscles, are about four times more likely to develop such contractions than are children whose biological parents do not have TSZ. It is likely, therefore, that predisposition to TSZ is an inherited trait.

Which of the following, if true, would most strengthen the conclusion above?

(A) Children whose parents have TSZ are more likely to develop TSZ if they are under unusual stress at school or at home than if they are not under such stress.

亲生父母双方都患有TSZ——一种表现为某些肌肉非自愿性收缩的病症——的孩子患病的可能是亲生父母都没有TSZ的孩子的4倍。所以，患TSZ的倾向可能是一项遗传特性。

下面哪一项，如果正确，能最强有力地支持上述结论？

(A) 父母患有TSZ的孩子们如果在学校或在家承受了不正常的压力，要比未承受这些压力的孩子更容易患TSZ。

(B) Children whose biological parents do not have TSZ are more likely to develop TSZ if they are raised by adoptive parents with TSZ than if they are raised by their biological parents.

(C) Children whose biological parents have TSZ are as likely to develop TSZ if they are raised by adoptive parents who do not have TSZ as if they are raised by their biological parents.

(D) Children whose biological parents have TSZ and who develop TSZ usually avoid developing a severe form of the syndrome if they seek treatment for TSZ shortly after developing the first signs of it.

(E) Children with TSZ whose biological parents do not have TSZ are less likely to have the syndrome diagnosed when symptoms first appear than are children with TSZ whose biological parents have TSZ.

26. Juries in criminal trials do not base verdicts on uncorroborated testimony given by any one witness. Rightly so, because it is usually prudent to be highly skeptical of unsubstantiated claims made by any one person. But then, to be consistent, juries should end an all-too-common practice: convicting defendants on the basis of an uncorroborated full confession.

Which of the following, if true, most strengthens the argument above?

(A) Juries often acquit in cases in which a defendant retracts a full confession made before trial.

(B) The process of jury selection is designed to screen out people who have a firm opinion about the defendant's guilt in advance of the trial.

(C) Defendants sometimes make full confessions when they did in fact do what they are accused of doing and have come to believe that the prosecutor has compelling proof of this.

(D) Highly suggestible people who are accused of wrongdoing sometimes become so unsure of their own recollection of the past that they can come to accept the accusations made against them.

(E) Many people believe that juries should not convict defendants who have not made a full confession.

27. In Bassaria a group of that country's most senior judges has criticized the uniform mandatory sentences recently introduced for certain specific crimes. The judges argue that

(B) 亲生父母未患有TSZ，但由患TSZ的养父母带大的孩子患TSZ的可能性比由自己的亲生父母带大的孩子患TSZ的可能性大。

(C) 亲生父母患TSZ的孩子无论是由亲生父母带大还是由未患TSZ的养父母带大，患TSZ的可能性是相同的。

(D) 亲生父母患有TSZ的孩子在患上TSZ后，如果他们在染上早期症状时就寻求治疗，就可以避免更严重的症状。

(E) 在出现最初的TSZ症状时，与亲生父母患TSZ的孩子相比，亲生父母未患有TSZ的孩子被诊断为TSZ的概率要小。

刑事案件中的陪审团不会依据任何证人所做的未经证实的证词而做出决定。这是十分正确的，因为对任何人所做的未经证实的指控保留高度怀疑是比较明智的。但为了一致，陪审团应该结束那种通行的做法，即依据未经完全证实的招供而给被告定罪。

下面哪个，如果正确，最能增强上述论点?

(A) 当被告推翻其在审判前的坦白的时候，陪审团通常宣判其无罪。

(B) 陪审员的选择过程被设计为选择在审判前那些认定被告有罪的人。

(C) 当被告确实做了其被指控的罪行时，他们会全部坦白，并且相信原告掌握了足够的证据。

(D) 那些易受暗示影响的人若被控有罪，有时会对其过去的经历不太肯定以至于承认所加之罪名。

(E) 许多人认为陪审团在被告完全坦白之前不应对其定罪。

Bassaria国的一群最高级法官已经批评了最近采用的对某些类型犯罪采取统一的强制判决的方法。这些法官论证道：这

such sentences, by depriving them of all discretion in setting sentences, make it impossible for them to consider either aggravating or extenuating circumstances and so make it impossible to achieve true justice —the fitting of the severity of the punishment to the gravity of the particular crime.

Which of the following, if true, provides the strongest evidence for the claim that in Bassaria the newly introduced mandatory sentences are not necessarily a change for the worse with respect to achieving true justice as defined in the argument?

(A) Before mandatory sentencing, judges in eastern Bassaria imposed strikingly different sentences from those in western Bassaria for equally grave instances of the same kind of offense.

(B) In Bassaria the frequency of crimes that have been made subject to mandatory sentences is lower now than it was just prior to the introduction of mandatory sentencing.

(C) The law introducing mandatory sentences was passed in the legislature of Bassaria by a large majority and is unlikely to be repealed in the foreseeable future.

(D) There used to be a wide difference between the minimum and the maximum sentences allowed by law in cases of crimes now subject to mandatory sentences.

(E) In Bassaria judges are appointed for life and are thus not easily influenced by political pressure groups.

28. A group of paintings made approximately 15,000 years ago in a cave in the Loire River valley in what is now France depicts a number of different animals. One of the animals depicted seems to resemble the chiru, a rare antelope of the Himalayas.

Which of the following, if true, best supports the hypothesis that in painting the animal that resembles a chiru the cave artist painted a chiru with which she or he was familiar?

(A) There are numerous representations of imaginary animals in cave paintings of similar age.

(B) Fossilized remains of a chiru, approximately 16,000 years old, have been found at the northern end of the valley.

(C) The cave that contains the depiction of an animal that resembles a chiru contains stylized representations of plant life.

(D) Older caves from the same region contain no representations of animals that resemble a chiru.

(E) The antlers of the animal in the painting are longer than those of the mature Himalayan chiru.

种判决，剥夺了他们在判决时所具有的判断力，使他们无法根据情况考虑加刑或减刑，因此不能达到真正的公正——惩罚的力度与犯罪的严重程度相符。

下面哪个，如果正确，为这一论证提供了强有力的证据，即在达到上文论述中所定义的真正的公正方面，Bassaria新采用的强制判决法不一定比以往方法更糟？

(A) 在采用强制性判决以前，Bassaria国东西两地的法官对同一种类型的，且严重程度相同的犯罪的判决差异很大。

(B) 现在的Bassaria，那些已统一判决的罪行犯罪率要比未统一判决前低。

(C) 引入统一判决制度是由Bassaria议会绝大多数票通过的，因此在将来是不太可能被撤销的。

(D) 现在引入统一判决的这些罪行中，原来的最高量刑与最低量刑之间有很大差别。

(E) Bassaria的法官们是终身制的，因此他们不易受政治压力的影响。

在现在的法国境内，Loire河谷的一个洞穴中有一组大约创作于1.5万年前的壁画，这些画描绘了不同种类的动物。其中描绘一种动物看上去很像Chiru，喜马拉雅山上的一种罕见的羚羊。

下列哪个，如果正确，最能支持以下假设，即在描绘像Chiru这种动物时，这位洞穴艺术家画的是他或她所熟悉的Chiru？

(A) 在同时期的洞穴作品中，有许多想象中的动物的代表作。

(B) 在山谷北端发现了大约有1.6万年历史的Chiru的化石残骸。

(C) 这座山洞不仅有像Chiru的动物的图画，还有赋予一定形式的植物图画。

(D) 本地区更古老的山洞里没有像Chiru这样的动物的图画。

(E) 画中动物的角比成年的喜马拉雅山的Chiru的角长。

29. Marine archaeologists recently discovered underwater in an ancient Mediterranean harbor several hundred ceramic objects, dating back approximately 4,000 years. Although any remnants of a ship's wooden frame would have long ago decayed, the quantity and variety of the ceramics discovered in the initial investigation led the archaeologists to hypothesize that they had discovered an approximately 4,000-year-old shipwreck.

Which of the following, if true, gives the strongest support to the archaeologists' hypothesis?

(A) Marine archaeologists have discovered a 3,000-year-old shipwreck in another ancient Mediterranean harbor.

(B) The rate at which wood decays when submerged in water varies greatly with the type of wood involved.

(C) Two confirmed shipwrecks, approximately 3,500 and 3,000 years old, respectively, have been discovered in the same harbor in which the ceramic objects were discovered.

(D) The ceramics discovered in the harbor are similar to ceramics found in several other ancient Mediterranean harbors.

(E) Bronze ship's fittings, approximately 4,000 years old, were discovered on the seabed among the ceramic objects.

海洋考古学家最近在一个古地中海港口的水下发现了几百件陶器，大概是4000年前留下的。尽管船只任何一点木制结构的残迹都早该腐烂了，在最初调查中发现的这些陶器的数量和多样性使得考古学家做出假设，认为他们发现了一艘约4000年前的沉船的残骸。

以下哪项，如果正确，对考古学家的假设提供了最大的支持？

(A) 海洋考古学家已经在另一个古地中海港口发现了一艘3000年前的船的残骸。

(B) 木头浸在水中时腐烂的速度受木头质地的影响很大。

(C) 在发现这些陶器的同一港口发现了两艘被探明的沉船的残骸，它们分别具有3500年和3000年的历史。

(D) 在该港口发现的陶器与在其他几个古地中海港口发现的陶器很相似。

(E) 在陶器之间的海床上，发现了铜制的船零件，大概有4000年左右历史。

30. The human craving for sweets was once beneficial: it attracted people to foods that were healthful (ripe fruit, for example) in preference to foods that were not healthful (unripe fruit, for example). However, now that sugar has been refined, it follows that a craving for sweets is no longer beneficial, because refined sugar is not healthful.

Which of the following, if true, would most strengthen the argument above?

(A) Some foods can be healthful when cooked even if they are not healthful when eaten raw.

(B) Some people who crave sweets are more likely to eat a piece of ripened fruit than they are to eat a piece of candy.

(C) People who crave sweets are more likely to eat a food that contains refined sugar than a naturally sweet food like ripe fruit.

(D) Prehistoric humans probably were not able to distinguish

人类对甜食的热衷曾一度是对人体有益的：因为喜欢甜食，人们更乐于去吃那些有益健康的食品（如成熟的水果），而不吃无益的食品（如不成熟的水果）。然而，现在的糖都经过了提炼，因此对甜食的热衷不再是有益的，因为精制的糖是不利健康的。

下列哪项，如果正确，将支持以上观点？

(A) 一些食物即使生吃时不利健康，但做熟了吃，就对健康有好处。

(B) 一些喜欢吃甜食的人更愿意吃成熟的水果，而不是糖块。

(C) 喜欢吃甜食的人会更愿意吃含有精炼糖的食品，而不是吃成熟的水果这类自然的甜食品。

(D) 史前期的人类可能不依靠味觉，就无法辨别出健康食品和非健康食品。

between healthful foods and unhealthful foods without relying on their sense of taste.

(E) Some unrefined foodstuffs are no more nutritious than their refined counterparts.

31. Psychological research indicates that college hockey and football players are more quickly moved to hostility and aggression than are college athletes in noncontact sports such as swimming. But the researchers, conclusion—that contact sports encourage and teach participants to be hostile and aggressive—is untenable. The football and hockey players were probably more hostile and aggressive to start with than the simmers.

Which of the following, if true, would most strengthen the conclusion drawn by the psychological researchers?

(A) The football and hockey players became more hostile and aggressive during the season and remained so during the off-season, whereas there was no increase in aggressiveness among the swimmers.

(B) The football and hockey players, but not the swimmers were aware at the start of the experiment that they were being tested for aggressiveness.

(C) The same psychological research indicated that the football and hockey players had a great respect for cooperation and team play, whereas the swimmers were most concerned with excelling as individual competitors.

(D) The research studies were designed to include no college athletes who participated in both contact and noncontact sports.

(E) Throughout the United States, more incidents of fan violence occur at baseball games than occur at hockey or football games.

32. Kale has more nutritional value than spinach. But since collard greens have more nutritional value than lettuce, it follows that kale has more nutritional value than lettuce.

Any of the following, if introduced into the argument as an additional premise, makes the argument above logically correct EXCEPT:

(A) Collard greens have more nutritional value than kale.

(B) Spinach has more nutritional value than lettuce.

(C) Spinach has more nutritional value than collard greens.

(E) 某些没有精炼过的食品不比其精炼后的产物更有营养。

　　心理学上的研究表明，大学里的曲棍球和橄榄球运动员比参加游泳等非对抗性运动的运动员更快地进入敌对和攻击状态。但是，这些研究人员的结论——对抗性运动鼓励和培养运动的参与者变得怀有敌意和具有攻击性——是站不住脚的。橄榄球和曲棍球队员可能天生就比游戏运动员更怀有敌意和具有攻击性。

　　下面哪个，如果正确，最能增强心理学研究人员们得出的结论？

(A) 橄榄球和曲棍球队员在赛季中变得更怀有敌意和具有攻击性，在赛季结束后会保持下去，而游泳运动员们的攻击性没有增加。

(B) 棒球和曲棍球队员，而不是游泳运动员，在实验开始的时候知道他们正在被检查攻击性。

(C) 同一次心理学研究发现橄榄球和曲棍球运动员非常重视协作和集体比赛，而游泳运动员最关心的是擅长个人竞争。

(D) 这次研究考察设计时没有包括同时参加对抗性和非对抗性运动的大学运动员。

(E) 全美国球迷的暴乱事件在棒球比赛中比在曲棍球或橄榄球比赛中多。

　　Kale比Spinach更有营养价值，但是由于collard green比lettuce更有营养价值，也就是说Kale比lettuce更有营养价值。

　　以下任一项，如果作为一个增加的前提引入上述论述中，可以使以上论述在逻辑上是正确的，除了

(A) collard greens比Kale 更有营养价值。

(B) Spinach比lettuce更有营养价值。

(C) Spinach比collard greens更有营养价值。

(D) Spinach and collard greens have the same nutritional value.

(E) Kale and collard greens have the same nutritional value.

33. The value of a product is determined by the ratio of its quality to its price. The higher the value of a product, the better will be its competitive position. Therefore, either increasing the quality or lowering the price of a given product will increase the likelihood that consumer will select that product rather than a competing one.

Which of the following, if true, would most strengthen the conclusion drawn above?

(A) It is possible to increase both the quality and the price of a product without changing its competitive position.

(B) For certain segments of the population of consumers, higher-priced brands of some product lines are preferred to the lower-priced brands.

(C) Competing products often try to appeal to different segments of the population of consumers.

(D) The competitive position of a product can be affected by such factors as advertising and brand loyalty.

(E) Consumers' perceptions of the quality of a product are based on the actual quality of the product.

34. Sales of telephones have increased dramatically over the last year. In order to take advantage of this increase, Mammoth Industries plans to expand production of its own model of telephone, while continuing its already very extensive advertising of this product.

Which of the following, if true, provides most support for the view that Mammoth Industries cannot increase its sales of telephones by adopting the plan outlined above?

(A) Although it sells all of the telephones that it produces, Mammoth Industries' share of all telephone sales has declined over the last year.

(B) Mammoth Industries' average inventory of telephones awaiting shipment to retailers has declined slightly over the last year.

(C) Advertising has made the brand name of Mammoth Industries' telephones widely known, but few consumers know that Mammoth industries owns this brand.

(D) Mammoth Industries' telephone is one of the three brands

(D) Spinach和collard greens有同样的营养价值。

(E) Kale和collard greens有同样的营养价值。

一种产品的价值由其质量与价格之间的比率决定。一种产品的价值越高，其会处于越好的竞争地位，所以对于既定产品而言或者通过提高质量，或者通过降低价格，都会提高消费者选择这种产品而不选择竞争性产品的概率。

下面哪个，如果正确，最能支持以上得出的结论？

(A) 可以同时提高一种产品的质量和价格而不改变产品的竞争地位。

(B) 对于消费者人群中特定的部分来讲，一些产品系列的较高价格的品牌比低价品牌更受青睐。

(C) 竞争性的产品常常试图吸引消费者人群中的不同部分。

(D) 一种产品的竞争地位可能受广告和品牌忠诚度等因素影响。

(E) 消费者对一种产品质量的了解是依据这种产品的实际质量。

过去10年间电话的销售量急剧上升，为了利用这一上升趋势，Mammoth企业计划扩大它自己的型号的电话生产，同时继续沿袭其已经非常广泛的对这种产品的广告宣传活动。

以下哪一项，如果是正确的，将最能支持如果Mammoth企业通过采取以上规划的计划，不能增加其电话销量的观点？

(A) 尽管它销售出去了它的所有生产出来的电话，但去年Mammoth企业占整个电话销售的份额下降了。

(B) Mammoth企业等待发运给零售商的电话平均存货量去年稍稍下降。

(C) 广告宣传已经使Mammoth企业生产的电话品牌广为人知，但很少有顾客知道Mammoth企业拥有这个品牌。

(D) Mammoth企业的电话是引起去年销量大量增长的三种品牌的电话之一。

of telephone that have together accounted for the bulk of the last year's increase in sales.

(E) Despite a slight decline in the retail price, sales of Mammoth Industries' telephones have fallen in the last year.

35. Useful protein drugs, such as insulin, must still be administered by the cumbersome procedure of injection under the skin. If proteins are taken orally, they are digested and cannot reach their target cells. Certain nonprotein drugs, however, contain chemical bonds that are not broken down by the digestive system. They can, thus, be taken orally.
The statements above most strongly support a claim that a research procedure that successfully accomplishes which of the following would be beneficial to users of protein drugs?

(A) Coating insulin with compounds that are broken down by target cells, but whose chemical bonds are resistant to digestion.

(B) Converting into protein compounds, by procedures that work in the laboratory, the nonprotein drugs that resist digestion.

(C) Removing permanently from the digestive system any substances that digest proteins.

(D) Determining, in a systematic way, what enzymes and bacteria are present in the normal digestive system and whether they tend to be broken down within the body.

(E) Determining the amount of time each nonprotein drug takes to reach its target cells.

36. There is a great deal of geographical variation in the frequency of many surgical procedures—up to tenfold variation per hundred thousand between different areas in the numbers of hysterectomies, prostatectomies, and tonsillectomies.
To support a conclusion that much of the variation is due to unnecessary surgical procedures, it would be most important to establish which of the following?

(A) A local board of review at each hospital examines the records of every operation to determine whether the surgical procedure was necessary.

(B) The variation is unrelated to factors (other than the surgical procedures themselves) that influence the incidence of diseases for which surgery might be considered.

(C) There are several categories of surgical procedure (other than hysterectomies, prostatectomies, and tonsillectomies) that are often performed unnecessarily.

(E) 尽管零售价稍稍下降，去年Mammoth企业的电话销量仍下降了。

有用的蛋白质药品，如胰岛素，仍然必须通过繁琐的皮下注射程序来予以实施。如果蛋白质被口服，它们就会被消化而不能到达目标细胞。但是，有些非蛋白质药物含有不会被消化系统分解的化学键。

以上的论述最强烈地支持了这样的论断，即一种成功实现下面哪个目标的研究计划可使蛋白质药品的使用者受益？

(A) 将胰岛素包上一种能被目标细胞分解、但其化学键不会被消化的混合物。

(B) 通过实验室里起作用的程序把不会被消化的非蛋白质药品转化为蛋白质化合物。

(C) 把消化系统里面消化蛋白质的任何物质永久清除掉。

(D) 以系统的方法来确定正常消化系统中存在什么酶和细菌，以及它们是否能在体内被分解。

(E) 确定每一种非蛋白质药品到达其目标细胞所需的时间。

许多外科手术施行频繁的地区差异很大——不同地区间每10万人中被实施子宫切除术、前列腺切除术和扁桃体切除术的人数量上有10倍的差异。

为了支持这种差异很大部分是由于不必要的外科手术这样的结论，最重要的是确定以下哪个？

(A) 每所医院中当地的调查委员会检查每次手术的记录，以确定外科手术是否是必要的。

(B) 这种差异与影响到可能要考虑使用手术来治疗疾病发生的因素（不是外科手术本身）无关。

(C) 有一些种类的外科手术（除了子宫切除术、前列腺切除术和扁桃体切除术）的施行是不必要的。

(D) For certain surgical procedures, it is difficult to determine after the operation whether the procedures were necessary or whether alternative treatment would have succeeded.

(E) With respect to how often they are performed unnecessarily, hysterectomies, prostatectomies, and tonsillectomies are representative of surgical procedures in general.

37. In Argonia the average rate drivers pay for car accident insurance is regulated to allow insurance companies to make a reasonable profit. Under the regulations, the rate any individual driver pays never depends on the actual distance driven by that driver each year. Therefore, Argonians who drive less than average partially subsidize the insurance of those who drive more than average.

The conclusion above would be properly drawn if it were also true that in Argonia

(A) the average accident insurance rate for all drivers rises whenever a substantial number of new drivers buy insurance.

(B) the average cost to insurance companies of insuring drivers who drive less than the annual average is less than the average cost of insuring drivers who drive more than the annual average.

(C) the lower the age of a driver, the higher the insurance rate paid by that driver.

(D) insurance company profits would rise substantially if drivers were classified in terms of the actual number of miles they drive each year.

(E) drivers who have caused insurance companies to pay costly claims generally pay insurance rates that are equal to or lower than those paid by other drivers.

38. Which of the following, if true, would provide most support for concluding from the survey results described above that the use of illegal drugs by people below the age of 20 is declining?

(A) Changes in the level of drug use by high school seniors are seldom matched by changes in the level of drug use by other people below the age of 20.

(B) In the past, high school seniors were consistently the population group most likely to use illegal drugs and most likely to use them heavily.

(C) The percentage of high school seniors who use illegal

(D) 对于某些外科手术来讲，手术之后很难确定手术是否必要或者其他的替代治疗是否有效。

(E) 关于外科手术有多么经常地被不必要地施行，子宫切除术、前列腺切除术和扁桃体切除术可以代表整体情况。

在Argonia,司机为汽车事故保险而支付的平均费用是被管制的，从而使保险公司能取得合理的利润，在这种管制之下，个别的司机支付的费用从来不是依赖于该司机每年行驶的距离。所以，驾驶距离少于平均水平的Argonia人部分补贴了那些驾驶距离多于平均水平的人支付的保险费用。

上面的结论可以被恰当地得到，如果在Argonia，这样的情况也是真实的：

(A) 无论何时，很多新司机购买保险时，所有司机平均要支付的事故保险费用也会上升。

(B) 对保险公司来讲，花在行驶距离少于平均水平的人身上的成本要小于花在行驶距离多于平均水平的人身上的成本。

(C) 司机年龄越低，该司机支付的保险费用越高。

(D) 如果根据每年行驶的距离对司机进行分类，保险公司的利润就会显著上升。

(E) 那些使保险公司为之付出昂贵的赔偿额的司机所支付的保险费用等于或低于其他司机支付的保险费用。

一项每年进行的全国性的调查表明，过去30年里高中的高年级学生们对非法药品的使用呈持续而明显的下降。

要想从上面描述的调查结果得出结论认为20岁以下的人对非法药物的使用正在下降，下面哪个，如果正确，能提供最多的支持?

(A) 高中的高年级学生们使用非法药品的水平的变化很少与20岁以下的其他人使用非法药品的水平的变化相符。

(B) 在过去，高中的高年级学生一直是最

drugs is consistently very similar to the percentage of all people below the age of 20 who use illegal drugs.

(D) The decline revealed by the surveys is the result of drug education programs specifically targeted at those below the age of 20.

(E) The number of those surveyed who admit to having sold illegal drugs has declined even faster than has the number who have used drugs.

可能使用非法药品和最可能大量使用非法药品的人群。

(C) 高中的高年级学生使用非法药品的比例与所有的20岁以下的使用非法药品的人的比例非常相似。

(D) 这项调查显示的下降趋势是特别针对20岁以下的人进行的药物教育计划的结果。

(E) 比起使用非法药品的人数，被调查者中承认出售过非法食品的人数下降得更快。

39. The level of lead contamination in United States rivers declined between 1975 and 1985. Federal regulations requiring a drop in industrial discharges of lead went into effect in 1975, but the major cause of the decline was a 75 percent drop in the use of leaded gasoline between 1975 and 1985.

Which of the following, if true, best supports the claim that the major cause of the decline in the level of lead contamination in United States rives was the decline in the use of leaded gasoline?

(A) The level of lead contamination in United States rivers fell sharply in both 1975 and 1983.

(B) Most of the decline in industrial discharges of lead occurred before 1976, but the largest decline in the level of river contamination occurred between 1980 and 1985.

(C) Levels of lead contamination in rivers fell sharply in 1975-1976 and rose very slightly over the next nine years.

(D) Levels of lead contamination rose in those rivers where there was reduced river flow due to drought.

(E) Although the use of leaded gasoline declined 75 percent between 1975 and 1985, 80 percent of the decline took place in 1985.

美国河流中的铅污染水平在1975～1985年间下降了。要求降低工业排放铅的联邦法令在1975年开始实施，但铅污染水平下降的主要原因是1975～1985年间，含铅汽油的使用量降低了75%。

下面哪个，如果正确，最能支持这种说法，即美国河流中铅污染水平下降的主要原因是含铅汽油使用量的降低？

(A) 在1975年和1983年，美国河流中的铅污染水平都大幅下降了。

(B) 大多数工业排放铅的数量降低发生在1976年之前，但河流中铅污染水平的最大程度的下降发生在1980～1985年间。

(C) 河流中铅污染水平在1975～1976年大幅下降了，在此后的9年内有轻微的上升。

(D) 铅污染水平在那些由于干旱而使流入的水减少的河中上升了。

(E) 虽然1975～1985年间含铅汽车的使用量降低了75%，80%的这种降低却发生在1985年。

40. Despite the approach of winter, oil prices to industrial customers are exceptionally low this year and likely to remain so. Therefore, unless the winter is especially severe, the price of natural gas to industrial customers is also likely to remain low.

Which of the following, if true, provides the most support for the conclusion above?

尽管冬天来临了，工业消费者使用的石油价格今年特别低，并且可能会保持下去。所以，除非冬天特别严寒，工业消费者使用的天然气价格也可能会保持在低水平。

下面哪个，如果正确，为上面的结论提供了最多的支持？

(A) Long-term weather forecasts predict a mild winter.

(B) The industrial users who consume most natural gas can quickly and cheaply switch to using oil instead.

(C) The largest sources of supply for both oil and natural gas are in subtropical regions unlikely to be affected by winter weather.

(D) The fuel requirements of industrial users of natural gas are not seriously affected by the weather.

(E) Oil distribution is more likely to be affected by severe winter weather than is the distribution of natural gas.

(A) 长期天气预报预测会有一个温和的冬季。

(B) 消费大多数天然气的工业用户可以很快和便宜地转换到石油这种替代品。

(C) 石油和天然气二者的最大供给来源地在亚热带地区，不大可能受冬季气候的影响。

(D) 天然气的工业用户的燃料需求量不会严重受气候影响。

(E) 石油销售比天然气销售更易受到恶劣气候的影响。

41. Residents of an apartment complex are considering two possible plans for collecting recyclable trash. Plan 1—Residents will deposit recyclable trash in municipal dumpsters located in the parking lot. The trash will be collected on the first and the fifteenth days of each month. Plan 2—Residents will be given individual containers for recyclable trash. The containers will be placed at the curb twice a week for trash collection.

Which of the following points raised at a meeting of the residents, if valid, would most favor one of the recycling plans over the other?

(A) Residents will be required to exercise care in separating recyclable trash from nonrecyclable trash.

(B) For trash recycling to be successful, residents must separate recyclable bottles and cans from recyclable paper products.

(C) Penalties will be levied against residents who fail to sort their trash correctly.

(D) Individual recycling containers will need to be made of a strong and durable material.

(E) Recyclable trash that is allowed to accumulate for two weeks will attract rodents.

一座公寓建筑里的居民正在考虑两种可能的收集可再循环的垃圾的计划。

计划1：居民们把可再循环的垃圾放置到停车场里的市政垃圾车里。垃圾会被在每个月的第1天和第15天收集。

计划2：向居民们各自发放装可再循环垃圾的容器。这些容器每周两次放在路边以方便收集垃圾。

下面是一次居民集会上提出的观点，其中哪个，如果正确，最能支持再循环计划中的一个而非另一个？

(A) 居民们会被要求小心地把可再循环的垃圾从不可再循环的垃圾中分离出来。

(B) 为了使垃圾再循环成功进行，居民们必须把可再循环的瓶瓶罐罐从可再生的纸制品中分离出来。

(C) 未能正确把垃圾分类的居民会被处以罚款。

(D) 个别的再循环容器需要以坚硬耐久的原料制造。

(E) 可以存放两周的可再循环垃圾会引来老鼠。

42. Human beings can see the spatial relations among objects by processing information conveyed by light. Scientists trying to build computers that can detect spatial relations by the same kind of process have so far designed and built stationary machines. However, these scientists will not achieve their goal until they produce such a machine that can move around in its environment.

通过处理由光传递的信息，人们可以看到物体之间的空间联系。试图建造可以通过相同处理程序来察觉空间联系的计算机的科学家们至今已经设计和建造了固定的机器。但是，只有在这些科学家们生产出可以在其所处环境中移动的机器以后，他们才会实现其目标。

Which of the following, if true, would best support the prediction above?

(A) Human beings are dependent on visual cues from motion in order to detect spatial relations.

(B) Human beings can often easily detect the spatial relations among objects, even when those objects are in motion.

(C) Detecting spatial relations among objects requires drawing inferences from the information conveyed by light.

(D) Although human beings can discern spatial relations through their sense of hearing, vision is usually the most important means of detecting spatial relations.

(E) Information about the spatial relations among objects can be obtained by noticing such things as shadows and the relative sizes of objects.

43. Most geologists believe oil results from chemical transformations of hydrocarbons derived from organisms buried under ancient seas. Suppose, instead, that oil actually results from bacterial action on other complex hydrocarbons that are trapped within the Earth. As is well known, the volume of these hydrocarbons exceeds that of buried organisms. Therefore, our oil reserves would be greater than most geologists believe.

Which of the following, if true, gives the strongest support to the argument above about our oil reserves?

(A) Most geologists think optimistically about the Earth's reserves of oil.

(B) Most geologists have performed accurate chemical analyses on previously discovered oil reserves.

(C) Ancient seas are buried within the Earth at many places where fossils are abundant.

(D) The only bacteria yet found in oil reserves could have leaked down drill holes from surface contaminants.

(E) Chemical transformations reduce the volume of buried hydrocarbons derived from organisms by roughly the same proportion as bacterial action reduces the volume of other complex hydrocarbons.

44. Woodsmoke contains dangerous toxins that cause changes in human cells. Because woodsmoke presents such a high

下面哪个，如果正确，最能支持以上的预言？

(A) 人们依靠有序运动得出的视觉暗示来发现空间联系。

(B) 人们往往可以轻易发现物体之间的空间联系，即使这些物体处于运动状态。

(C) 发现物体之间的空间联系需要对由光传递的信息进行推理。

(D) 虽然人们可以通过他们的听觉来识别空间联系，视觉通常是发现空间联系的最重要的方法。

(E) 物体间空间联系的信息可以通过注意阴影和物体的相对大小等事情而得到。

大多数地理学家相信，石油是埋在古代海洋下面的有机物所产生的碳氢化合物的化学转变物。与之不同，有人假设石油实际上产生于在地球内分离的其他复杂的碳氢化合物上面的细菌活动。众所周知，这些碳氢化合物的规模超过了被埋有机物的规模。所以，我们的石油储备要多于大多数地理学家所认为的。

下面哪个，如果正确，对以上关于我们的石油储备的论证提供了最强有力的支持？

(A) 大多数地理学家对地球的石油储备持乐观态度。

(B) 大多数地理学家已经对以往发现的石油储备进行了精确的化学分析。

(C) 古代的海洋在许多地方被埋到地球里了，那里的化石非常丰富。

(D) 已经在石油储备中发现的唯一细菌很可能是从地面污染物中通过钻孔渗透下来的。

(E) 化学变化减少了来自有机物的被埋碳氢化合物的规模，减少的比例与细菌活动对其他复杂碳氢化合物的规模的减少比例大致相同。

燃烧木头所形成的烟含有使人的细胞发生变化的毒素。因为燃烧木头所形成的

health risk, legislation is needed to regulate the use of open-air fires and wood-burning stoves.

Which of the following, if true, provides the most support for the argument above?

(A) The amount of dangerous toxins contained in woodsmoke is much less than the amount contained in an equal volume of automobile exhaust.

(B) Within the jurisdiction covered by the proposed legislation, most heating and cooking is done with oil or natural gas.

(C) Smoke produced by coal-burning stoves is significantly more toxic than smoke from woodburning stoves.

(D) No significant beneficial effect on air quality would result if open-air fires were banned within the jurisdiction covered by the proposed legislation.

(E) In valleys where wood is used as the primary heating fuel, the concentration of smoke results in poor air quality.

45. Today's low gasoline prices make consumers willing to indulge their preference for larger cars, which consume greater amounts of gasoline as fuel. So United States automakers are unwilling to pursue the development of new fuel-efficient technologies aggressively. The particular reluctance of the United States automobile industry to do so, however, could threaten the industry's future.

Which of the following, if true, would provide the most support for the claim above about the future of the United States automobile industry?

(A) A prototype fuel-efficient vehicle, built five years ago, achieves a very high 81 miles per gallon on the highway and 63 in the city, but its materials are relatively costly.

(B) Small cars sold by manufacturers in the United States are more fuel efficient now than before the sudden jump in oil prices in 1973.

(C) Automakers elsewhere in the world have slowed the introduction of fuel-efficient technologies but have pressed ahead with research and development of them in preparation for a predicted rise in world oil prices.

(D) There are many technological opportunities for reducing the waste of energy in cars and light trucks through weight, aerodynamic drag, and braking friction.

(E) The promotion of mass transit over automobiles as an alternative mode of transportation has encountered

烟对健康有很大的危险，因此需要立法来管理使用露天暖气炉和燃烧木材的火炉。

下面哪个，如果正确，为以上的论证提供了最多的支持？

(A) 燃烧木头所形成的烟中包含的毒素数量比相同容积的汽车废气中包含的毒素数量大得多。

(B) 在被提议的法案的管理权限中，大多数取暖和烹调是通过石油或天然气进行的。

(C) 燃煤火炉生出的烟比燃烧木材的火炉生出的烟更毒。

(D) 如果在提议的法案的管理权限中，露天暖气炉被禁止了，最终对空气质量不会有什么明显有益的效果。

(E) 在一些把木材作为主要取暖燃料的河谷，烟雾的集中导致了恶化的空气质量。

如今的低汽油价格使消费者们心甘情愿地青睐于更大的汽车，这些汽车会消耗更多的作为燃料的汽油。所以，美国的汽车制造商不愿意积极地寻求新的节能技术。但是，美国汽车工业的这种特别的消极态度会威胁到该工业的未来。

下面哪个，如果正确，给以上关于美国汽车工业的未来的说法提供了最多的支持？

(A) 5年前制造的一辆示范性的节能汽车，在高速公路上每加仑汽油的行驶里程可达到很高的81英里，在城市里可达到63英里，但它的原料相对昂贵。

(B) 美国的制造商现在出售的小汽车要比1973年石油价格突然上涨前节省燃料。

(C) 世界其他地区的汽车制造商已经减慢引入节能技术，但已经抢先进行节能技术的研究和开发以应付预计的世界石油价格的上涨。

(D) 通过重量空气动力牵引和制动摩擦等方面的改进，有很多技术上的机会来减少汽车和轻型卡车的能源浪费。

(E) 对公共汽车运输作为交通的替代手段的促进遭遇了消费者的抵制，因为公共运输很难解决旅程起点和终点分散过广的问题。

consumer resistance that is due in part to the failure of mass transit to accommodate the wide dispersal of points of origin and destinations for trips.

46. In Swartkans territory, archaeologists discovered charred bone fragments dating back 1 million years. Analysis of the fragments, which came from a variety of animals, showed that they had been heated to temperatures no higher than those produced in experimental campfires made from branches of white stinkwood, the most common tree around Swartkans. Which of the following, if true, would, together with the information above, provide the best basis for the claim that the charred bone fragments are evidence of the use of fire by early hominids?

(A) The white stinkwood tree is used for building material by the present-day inhabitants of Swartkans.

(B) Forest fires can heat wood to a range of temperatures that occur in campfires.

(C) The bone fragments were fitted together by the archaeologists to form the complete skeletons of several animals.

(D) Apart from the Swartkans discovery, there is reliable evidence that early hominids used fire as many as 500 thousand years ago.

(E) The bone fragments were found in several distinct layers of limestone that contained primitive cutting tools known to have been used by early hominids.

47. The pharmaceutical industry argues that because new drugs will not be developed unless heavy development costs can be recouped in later sales, the current 20 years of protection provided by patents should be extended in the case of newly developed drugs. However, in other industries new-product development continues despite high development costs, a fact that indicates that the extension is unnecessary. Which of the following, if true, most strongly supports the pharmaceutical industry's argument against the challenge made above?

(A) No industries other than the pharmaceutical industry have asked for an extension of the 20-year limit on patent protection.

(B) Clinical trials of new drugs, which occur after the patent is granted and before the new drug can be marketed, often now take as long as 10 years to complete.

在Sartkans境内，考古学家们发现了烧焦了的100万年前的骨头碎片。这些碎片来自不同的动物，对其分析表明，它们被加热到的温度不会超过实验中白臭木树枝燃烧形成的露营火所产生的温度。

下面哪个，如果正确，和以上的信息一起，为这种说法提供了最好的基础，即这些烧焦了的骨头碎片是早期原始人类使用火的证据？

(A) 白臭木被如今Swartkans的居民用来作为建筑材料。

(B) 森林大火可以把木头加热到露营火中发生的温度范围。

(C) 骨头碎片被考古学家们组合在一起以形成一些动物的完整的骨骼。

(D) 除了Swartkans的发现，有可信的证据证明早期的原始人类在50万年前使用了火。

(E) 这些骨头碎片被在一些不同的石灰层中发现，这些石灰石中含有原始的被认为是早期原始人类使用过的用来切割的工具。

制药行业争论道，因为只有当巨额的开发费用能在今后的销售中予以补偿，新药品才会被开发出来，目前专利权提供的20年的保护在新药品的情况下必须延长。但是，在其他行业中，尽管开发费用很高，新产品的开发在继续进行，这一事实表明延长专利权保护年限是没有必要的。

下面哪个，如果正确，最强有力地驳斥了以上的质疑而支持了医药行业的论点？

(A) 只有制药行业要求延长专利权保护的20年的限定。

(B) 新药品的临床试验——发生在专利权被授予后，新药品可以上市前——现在通常花10年的时间来完成。

(C) There are several industries in which the ratio of research and development costs to revenues is higher than it is in the pharmaceutical industry.

(D) An existing patent for a drug does not legally prevent pharmaceutical companies from bringing to market alternative drugs, provided they are sufficiently dissimilar to the patented drug.

(E) Much recent industrial innovation has occurred in products—for example, in the computer and electronics industries—for which patent protection is often very ineffective.

(C) 有些行业的研究和开发费用对收入的比率比制药行业的这一比率高。

(D) 既存的药品专利权不能在法律上阻止别的制药公司把替代性药品推向市场，只要这些替代性药品与专利药品有充分的不同之处。

(E) 最近的许多工业革新发生在专利权保护通常不十分有效的产品上——例如，在计算机和电子行业中的革新。

48. Passengers must exit airplanes swiftly after accidents, since gases released following accidents are toxic to humans and often explode soon after being released. In order to prevent passenger deaths from gas inhalation, safety officials recommend that passengers be provided with smoke hoods that prevent inhalation of the gases.

Which of the following, if true, constitutes the strongest reason not to require implementation of the safety officials' recommendation?

(A) Test evacuations showed that putting on the smoke hoods added considerably to the overall time it took passengers to leave the cabin.

(B) Some airlines are unwilling to buy the smoke hoods because they consider them to be prohibitively expensive.

(C) Although the smoke hoods protect passengers from the toxic gases, they can do nothing to prevent the gases from igniting.

(D) Some experienced flyers fail to pay attention to the safety instructions given on every commercial flight before takeoff.

(E) In many airplane accidents, passengers who were able to reach emergency exits were overcome by toxic gases before they could exit the airplane.

乘客们必须在事故发生以后迅速离开飞机，因为事故后释放的气体对人体有毒并且通常在释放以后很快爆炸。为了防止乘客因吸气而死亡，安全官员们建议向乘客们提供防烟兜帽以阻止气体的吸入。

下面哪个，如果正确，构成了不需执行安全官员们的建议的最有力的理由？

(A) 撤离试验表明，戴上防烟兜帽非常多地增加了乘客离开机舱的总时间。

(B) 一些航空公司不愿意购买防烟兜帽，因为他们认为防烟兜帽价格太昂贵了。

(C) 虽然防烟兜帽保护了乘客免受毒气之害，但它们对阻止气体燃烧无能为力。

(D) 一些有经验的飞行员没有注意每次商业飞行起飞前被提供给的安全建议。

(E) 在许多飞机事故中，不能到达紧急出口的乘客在离开飞机前就受制于有毒气体了。

49. Caterpillars off all species produce an identical hormone called "juvenile hormone" that maintains feeding behavior. Only when a caterpillar has grown to the right size for pupation to take place does a special enzyme halt the production of juvenile hormone. This enzyme can be synthesized and will, on being ingested by immature caterpillars, kill them by stopping them from feeding.

所有种类的毛虫都产生一种同样的称为"幼年荷尔蒙"的激素，这种激素维持了进食的行为。只有当毛虫生长到可以化蛹的大小时，一种特殊的酶才会阻止幼年荷尔蒙的产生，这种酶可以被合成，一旦被未成熟的毛虫吸收，就可以通过阻止毛虫进食而杀死它们。

Which of the following, if true, most strongly supports the view that it would not be advisable to try to eradicate agricultural pests that go through a caterpillar stage by spraying croplands with the enzyme mentioned above?

(A) Most species of caterpillar are subject to some natural predation.

(B) Many agricultural pests do not go through a caterpillar stage.

(C) Many agriculturally beneficial insects go through a caterpillar stage.

(D) Since caterpillars of different species emerge at different times, several sprayings would be necessary.

(E) Although the enzyme has been synthesized in the laboratory, no large-scale production facilities exist as yet.

50. Because postage rates are rising, Home Decorator magazine plans to maximize its profits by reducing by one half the number of issues it publishes each year. The quality of articles, the number of articles published per year, and the subscription price will not change. Market research shows that neither subscribers nor advertisers will be lost if the magazine's plan is instituted.

Which of the following, if true, provides the strongest evidence that the magazine's profits are likely to decline if the plan is instituted?

(A) With the new postage rates, a typical issue under the proposed plan would cost about one-third more to mail than a typical current issue would.

(B) The majority of the magazine's subscribers are less concerned about a possible reduction in the quantity of the magazine's articles than about a possible loss of the current high quality of its articles.

(C) Many of the magazine's long-time subscribers would continue their subscriptions even if the subscription price were increased.

(D) Most of the advertisers that purchase advertising space in the magazine will continue to spend the same amount on advertising per issue as they have in the past.

(E) Production costs for the magazine are expected to remain stable.

51. One variety of partially biodegradable plastic beverage container is manufactured from small bits of plastic bound

下面哪个，如果正确，最强有力地支持了这种观点，即通过向农田喷射上文提到的酶来灭除经历毛虫阶段的农业害虫是不可取的？

(A) 大多数种类的毛虫被一些自然捕食行为吃掉了。

(B) 许多农业害虫不经历毛虫阶段。

(C) 许多对农业有益的昆虫经历毛虫阶段。

(D) 因为不同种类的毛虫出现在不同时期，必须进行若干次喷射。

(E) 虽然这种酶已经在实验室中被合成出来了，大规模的生产设备尚不存在。

由于邮费不断上涨，家庭装饰杂志计划通过把其每年出版的期刊数量减半来最大化其利润。文章的质量、每年发表的文章数量以及订阅价格都不会变化。市场研究表明，如果该计划被予以实施，订阅者和广告商都不会受到损失。

下面哪个，如果正确，提供了最强有力的证据证明该计划的实施可能使该杂志的利润下降？

(A) 在新的邮费条件下，邮寄一期典型的提议计划的杂志耗费的成本比邮寄一期典型的目前的杂志高出约1/3。

(B) 该杂志的订阅者中大多数更关心目前文章的高质量可能下降，而较少关心杂志中文章数量的减少。

(C) 即使订阅价格提高了，许多该杂志的长期订阅者也会继续他们的订阅。

(D) 大多数在该杂志上购买广告篇幅的广告商会在每期杂志上花费和以前一样的资金。

(E) 杂志的生产成本预计会保持不变。

一种部分可被生物分解的塑料饮料罐是将很小的塑料用玉蜀黍淀粉等粘合剂粘

together by a degradable bonding agent such as cornstarch. Since only the bonding agent degrades, leaving the small bits of plastic, no less plastic refuse per container is produced when such containers are discarded than when comparable nonbiodegradable containers are discarded.

Which of the following, if true, most strengthens the argument above?

(A) Both partially biodegradable and nonbiodegradable plastic beverage containers can be crushed completely flat by refuse compactors.

(B) The partially biodegradable plastic beverage containers are made with more plastic than comparable nonbiodegradable ones in order to compensate for the weakening effect of the bounding agents.

(C) Many consumers are ecology-minded and prefer to buy a product sold in the partially biodegradable plastic beverage containers rather than in nonbiodegradable containers, even if the price is higher.

(D) The manufacturing process for the partially biodegradable plastic beverage containers results in less plastic waste than the manufacturing process for nonbiodegradable plastic beverage containers.

(E) Technological problems with recycling currently prevent the reuse as food or beverage containers of the plastic from either type of plastic beverage container.

52. Naturalist: For decades we have known that the tuatara, a New Zealand reptile, have been approaching extinction on the South Island. But since South Island tuatara were thought to be of the same species as North Island tuatara there was no need to protect them. But new research indicates that the South Island tuatara are a distinct species, found only in that location. Because it is now known that if the South Island tuatara are lost an entire species will thereby be lost, human beings are now obliged to prevent their extinction, even if it means killing many of their unendangered natural predators.

Which one of the following principles most helps to justify the naturalists' argumentation?

(A) In order to maximize the number of living things on Earth, steps should be taken to preserve all local populations of animals.

(B) When an animal is in danger of dying, there is an obligation to help save its life, if doing so would not interfere with the health or well-being of other animals or people.

在一起而制造出来的。因为只有粘合剂分解掉了，留下了细小的塑料，这些饮料罐被丢弃时每个罐子产生的塑料垃圾并不比类似的不可被生物分解的罐子被丢弃时产生的塑料垃圾少。

下面哪个，如果正确，最能加强以上的观点？

(A) 部分可被生物分解的和不可被生物分解的塑料饮料罐都能被垃圾压缩机完全压平。

(B) 为了弥补粘合剂的弱化效果，制造部分可以被生物分解的塑料饮料罐比制造不可被生物分解的塑料饮料罐需要更多的塑料。

(C) 许多消费者关心生态问题，他们宁愿购买装在可被生物分解的塑料饮料罐里的产品而不愿购买装在不可被生物分解的塑料饮料罐里面的产品，即使前者价格要高一些。

(D) 部分可被生物分解的塑料饮料罐的生产程序比不可被生物分解的塑料饮料罐的生产程序产生更少的塑料废物。

(E) 目前再循环技术上的问题阻止了任何一种类型的塑料饮料罐的塑料被重新做成食品罐或饮料罐来使用。

博物学家：几十年来，我们已经了解到大蜥蜴，一种新西兰的爬行动物，在南部岛屿已濒临灭绝。但是，因为南部岛屿大蜥蜴与北部岛屿大蜥蜴被认为是同一种类的生物，所以没有必要去保护它们。然而新的研究表明南部岛屿大蜥蜴是一种仅在那个地方发现的，与众不同的生物。因为人们现在知道如果南部岛屿大蜥蜴灭绝了，那么这个种类的大蜥蜴就会因此全部灭绝，所以人们不得不防止它们灭绝，即使这意味着要杀死许多以它们为食的没有灭绝危险的自然捕食者。

下面哪一条原则最有助于证明博物学家论述的合理性？

(A) 为了最大限度地增加地球上的生物数量，人们应当采取措施来保护所有当地的动物群体。

(B) 当一动物有死亡危险时，人们有义务

(C) The threat of local extinction imposes no obligation to try to prevent that extinction, whereas the threat of global extinction does impose such an obligation.

(D) Human activities that either intentionally or unintentionally threaten the survival of an animal species ought to be curtailed.

(E) Species that are found in only one circumscribed geographical region ought to be given more care and attention than are other species because they are more vulnerable to extinction.

53. If the public library shared by the adjacent towns of Redville and Glenwood were relocated from the library's current, overcrowded building in central Redville to a larger, available building in central Glenwood, the library would then be within walking distance of a larger number of library users. That is because there are many more people living in central Glenwood than in central Redville, and people generally will walk to the library only if it is located close to their homes.

Which one of the following, if true, most strengthens the argument?

(A) The public library was located between Glenwood and Redville before being moved to its current location in central Redville.

(B) The area covered by central Glenwood is approximately the same size as that covered by central Redville.

(C) The building that is available in Glenwood is smaller than an alternative building that is available in Redville.

(D) Many of the people who use the public library do not live in either Glenwood or Redville.

(E) The distance that people currently walk to get to the library is farther than what is generally considered walking distance.

54. For the writers who first gave feudalism its name, the existence of feudalism presupposed the existence of a noble class. Yet there cannot be a noble class, properly speaking, unless both the titles that indicate superior noble status and the inheritance of such titles are sanctioned by law. Although feudalism existed in Europe as early as the eighth century,

帮助挽救它的生命，即使这样做会妨碍到其他动物或人类的健康或幸福。

(C) 某一地区性的生物灭绝不会迫使人们去尽力防止它的灭绝，而全球性的生物灭绝则迫使人们努力去保护它。

(D) 应该控制故意和非故意的影响到动物生存的人类活动。

(E) 仅在某一个限定的地区发现的生物应该比其他种类的生物受到更多的关心和照顾，因为这类生物比其他生物易于灭绝。

如果把被两个相邻城镇（Redville和Glenwood）分享的公共图书馆从现在位于Redville中心的一所过分拥挤的建筑物搬迁到Glenwood市中心的一个更大的可利用的建筑物内，那么这个图书馆将在更多的图书馆读者的步行范围之内。这是因为Glenwood市中心的居住人口要比Redville市中心的多得多，并且只有当图书馆的位置离他们的家较近时，一般人们才会步行去图书馆。

下面哪一项，如果正确，最能加强上述论证?

(A) 公共图书馆在移往现在的位置——Redville市中心之前位于Glenwood和Redville之间。

(B) Glenwood市中心覆盖的区域面积与Redville市中心覆盖的区域面积几乎是一样的。

(C) Glenwood市的那个可利用的建筑物比Redville市的另一个可利用的建筑物小。

(D) 公共图书馆的许多读者既不住在Glenwood，也不住在Redville。

(E) 现在人们步行去图书馆所走的距离比普遍认为的步行距离远。

对那些最先给封建主义起名字的作家来说，封建主义的存在也就预先假定了贵族阶级的存在。然而正确地说来贵族阶级是不可能存在的，除非那些表明较高的贵族地位的头衔和这些头衔的继承权被法律所认可。尽管封建主义早在8世纪时就已

it was not until the twelfth century, when many feudal institutions were in decline, that the hereditary transfer of legally recognized titles of nobility first appeared.

The statements above, if true, most strongly support which one of the following claims?

(A) To say that feudalism by definition requires the existence of a nobility is to employ a definition that distorts history.

(B) Prior to the twelfth century, the institution of European feudalism functioned without the presence of a dominant class.

(C) The fact that a societal group has a distinct legal status is not in itself sufficient to allow that group to be properly considered a social class.

(D) The decline of feudalism in Europe was the only cause of the rise of a European nobility.

(E) The prior existence of feudal institutions is a prerequisite for the emergence of a nobility, as defined in the strictest sense of the term.

经存在，但是直到12世纪，当许多封建机构处于衰落时，法律上承认的世袭贵族头衔才第一次出现。

上面的陈述如果正确，最强有力地支持下面哪一个主张？

(A) 认为从封建主义定义上讲要求贵族阶级的存在就是在使用一个歪曲历史的定义。

(B) 12世纪之前，欧洲的封建制度机构是在没有统治阶级存在的情况下运行的。

(C) 某个社会团体具有与众不同的法律地位的事实本身并不足以说明这个团体可被合情合理地认为是一个社会阶层。

(D) 欧洲封建主义的衰退是欧洲贵族阶级出现的唯一原因。

(E) 按照贵族阶级这一词的最严格的定义来讲，先前的封建机构的存在是贵族阶级出现的先决条件。

55. A certain species of bird has two basic varieties, crested and noncrested. The birds, which generally live in flocks that contain only crested or only noncrested birds, tend to select mates of the same variety as themselves. However, if a bird that is raised in a flock in which all other members are crested is later moved to a mixed flock, then that bird—whether crested or noncrested—is likely to select a crested mate. This fact indicates that the birds' preference for crested or noncrested mates is learned rather than genetically determined.

Which one of the following, if true, provides the most support for the argument?

(A) Birds of other species also tend to show preferences for mates that have one or another specific physical feature.

(B) In general there are few behavioral differences between the crested and noncrested birds of the species.

(C) Both the crested and noncrested birds of the species tend to select mates that are similar to themselves in size and age.

(D) If a crested bird of the species is raised in captivity apart form other birds and is later moved to a mixed flock, that bird is likely to select a crested mate.

某种鸟有两种基本变种，有冠的和无冠的。那些生活在仅由有冠的鸟或仅由无冠的鸟组成的鸟群中的鸟倾向于选择一个和它们同一个变种的鸟作配偶。然而，如果一只生活在所有其他成员都是有冠的鸟群中的鸟后来移居到一个混杂的鸟群中，那么不管那只鸟是有冠的还是无冠的，都有可能选择一只有冠的鸟作配偶。这个事实说明一只鸟喜欢选择有冠的鸟还是无冠的鸟作配偶不是由遗传决定的，而是由后天习得的。

下面哪一项，如果正确，最能支持上述论证？

(A) 其他品种的鸟也倾向于喜欢那些具有一个或另一个明显身体特征的配偶。

(B) 一般来说，有冠变种的鸟和无冠变种的鸟在行为上几乎没有差别。

(C) 有冠变种的鸟和无冠变种的鸟都倾向于选择那些大小和年龄都与它们相似的鸟作配偶。

(D) 如果一只有冠的鸟被抓获后与其他的鸟分开来饲养，后来又把它放入一个

(E) If a bird of the species is raised in a flock that contains both crested and noncrested birds, that bird shows no preference for one variety or the other in its selection of a mate.

56. Advertisers are often criticized for their unscrupulous manipulation of people's tastes and wants. There is evidence, however, that some advertisers are motivated by moral as well as financial considerations. A particular publication decided to change its image from being a family newspaper to concentrating on sex and violence, thus appealing to a different readership. Some advertisers withdrew their advertisements from the publication, and this must have been because they morally disapproved of publishing salacious material.

Which one of the following, if true, would most strengthen the argument?

(A) The advertisers switched their advertisements to other family newspapers.
(B) Some advertisers switched from family newspapers to advertise in the changed publication.
(C) The advertisers expected their product sales to increase if they stayed with the changed publication, but to decrease if they withdrew.
(D) People who generally read family newspapers are not likely to buy newspapers that concentrate on sex and violence.
(E) It was expected that the changed publication would appeal principally to those in a different income group.

57. Despite improvements in treatment for asthma, the death rate from this disease has doubled during the past decade from its previous rate. Two possible explanations for this increase have been offered. First, the recording of deaths due to asthma has become more widespread and accurate in the past decade than it had been previously. Second, there has been an increase in urban pollution. However, since the rate of deaths due to asthma has increased dramatically even in cities with long-standing, comprehensive medical records and with little or no urban pollution, one must instead conclude that the cause of increased deaths is the use of bronchial inhalers by asthma sufferers to relieve their symptoms.

混杂的鸟群中，这只鸟有可能选择一个有冠的鸟作配偶。

(E) 如果那个品种的一只鸟被饲养在一群由有冠变种和无冠变种混杂而成的鸟群中，那么这只鸟在选择配偶时不会对某个变种的鸟有所偏好。

广告商经常因不择手段地操纵人们的喜好与需求而受指责。然而，有证据表明，有些广告商不仅出于财政上的考虑，而且受道德观念所驱使。有一刊物决定改变其形象，从以家庭内容为主，转向以性爱和暴力为主，以迎合不同的读者。有一些广告商就从该刊物上撤走了他们的广告，这一定是因为他们在道义上不赞成该刊物刊登猥亵的内容。

下面哪一点，如果正确，最能加强上面论述？

(A) 那些广告商们把他们的广告转向了其他家庭报刊。
(B) 有些广告商把它们的广告从家庭报转向了那家改变后的报刊。
(C) 如果那些广告商们继续在改变后的刊物上登广告，他们的产品销量就有望增加；如果他们撤走广告，他们的产品销量就会下降。
(D) 通常那些家庭报刊的读者不大可能会买以性爱和暴力为主的报纸。
(E) 人们期望这家改变后的刊物能主要迎合那些不同收入群体的读者。

尽管治疗哮喘病的手段有所提高，但是在过去的10年里，哮喘病的死亡率比以前提高了一倍。死亡率的升高有两个可能的原因。其一，在过去的10年里，对哮喘病死亡的记录与以前相比变得更为广泛和准确；其二，城市污染有所增加。然而，即使在很少或者没有污染、且具有长期综合医疗记录的城市里，哮喘病的死亡率也呈急剧增加之势，因此，一定可以得出相反的结论：死亡率的升高起因于哮喘病患者为减轻症状而使用支气管吸入器。

Each of the following, if true, provides support to the argument EXCEPT:

(A) Urban populations have doubled in the past decade.

(B) Records of asthma deaths are as accurate for the past twenty years as for the past ten years.

(C) Evidence suggests that bronchial inhalers make the lungs more sensitive to irritation by airborne pollen.

(D) By temporarily relieving the symptoms of asthma, inhalers encourage sufferers to avoid more beneficial measures.

(E) Ten years ago bronchial inhalers were not available as an asthma treatment.

58. In opposing the 1970 Clean Air Act, the United States automobile industry argued that meeting the act's standards for automobile emissions was neither economically feasible nor environmentally necessary. However, the catalytic converter, invented in 1967, enable automakers to meet the 1970 standards efficiently. Currently, automakers are lobbying against the government's attempt to pass legislation that would tighten restrictions on automobile emissions. The automakers contend that these new restrictions would be overly expensive and unnecessary to efforts to curb air pollution. Clearly, the automobile industry's position should not be heeded.

Which one of the following, if true, lends the most support to the automakers' current position?

(A) The more stringent the legislation restricting emissions becomes, the more difficult it becomes for automakers to provide the required technology economically.

(B) Emissions-restriction technology can often be engineered so as to avoid reducing the efficiency with which an automobile uses fuel.

(C) Not every new piece of legislation restricting emissions requires new automotive technology in order for automakers to comply with it.

(D) The more automobiles there are on the road, the more stringent emission restrictions must be to prevent increased overall air pollution.

(E) Unless forced to do so by the government, automakers rarely make changes in automotive technology that is not related to profitability.

下面每一项，如果正确，除了哪一项之外都可对上面论证构成支持？

(A) 城市人口在过去的10年中增加了一倍。

(B) 在过去20年中对哮喘病死亡的记录与过去10年中的一样准确。

(C) 有证据表明，支气管吸入器使肺对空中传播的花粉更易发生过敏反应。

(D) 只是暂时地解除哮喘病的症状，吸入器使患者错过了其他更有益治疗的机会。

(E) 10年以前，作为治疗哮喘病的支气管吸入器还没出现。

在反对1970年的静化空气法令时，美国汽车工业论述说，使汽车尾气合乎法令的标准不但在经济上不可行，而且从环境方面讲也不必要。然而，1967年发明的催化转化器，有效地使汽车制造商达到了1970年的标准。目前，汽车制造商正在通过游说反对政府打算通过加强汽车尾气限制的法令。汽车制造商争论说，要达到这些新的限制不但要使他们付出非常昂贵的代价，而且对抑制空气污染来说也不需要。很明显，不应关注汽车制造商的立场。

下面哪一点，如果正确，能对汽车制造商的现在立场构成最有力的支持？

(A) 限制汽车尾气的法令越苛刻，汽车制造商就越难比较经济地提供所需的技术。

(B) 尾气限制技术可常常被设计用来克服汽车在燃烧汽油时效率的降低。

(C) 对汽车制造商来说，并非每一条新的尾气限制法都要求新的汽车技术来遵从它。

(D) 为了能抑制总的空气污染的增加，路上的汽车越多，对汽车排放的尾气的限制就应越严格。

(E) 除非迫于政府方面的压力，汽车制造商很少做一些与自身利益无关的汽车技术改进。

59. A society's infant mortality rate is an accepted indicator of that society's general health status. Even though in some localities in the United States the rate is higher than in many developing countries, in the United States overall the rate has been steadily declining. This decline does not necessarily indicate, however, that babies in the United States are now, on the average, healthier at birth than they were in the past.

Which one of the following reasons, if true, most strongly supports the claim made above about the implications of the decline?

(A) The figure for infant mortality is compiled as an overall rate and thus masks deficiencies in particular localities.

(B) Low birth weight is a contributing factor in more than half of the infant deaths in the United States.

(C) The United States has been developing and has achieved extremely sophisticated technology for saving premature and low-birth-weight babies, most of whom require extended hospital stays.

(D) In eleven states of the United States, the infant mortality rate declined last year.

(E) Babies who do not receive adequate attention from a caregiver fail to thrive and so they gain weight slowly.

一个社会的婴儿死亡率是其整体健康状况的公认标志。尽管美国某些地区的婴儿死亡率比许多发展中国家高，但美国整体的该比率一直在下降，但是这种下降并不一定说明，平均说来，美国现在的婴儿在他们出生时比以前更健康了。

下面哪一点，如果正确，能最强有力地支持上面对婴儿死亡率下降所做的声明？

(A) 作为整体计算的婴儿死亡率数据掩饰了特殊地区的不足。

(B) 出生体重低是美国一半婴儿死亡的主要原因。

(C) 大多数早产和低出生体重的婴儿都需要在医院内住较长的时间，而美国在这方面已发展并具有非常精湛的技术。

(D) 在美国11个州内，去年的婴儿死亡率下降了。

(E) 那些不能从照看者那里得到充分关心的婴儿不能健康地成长，所以他们的体重增长较慢。

60. It is very difficult to prove today that a painting done two or three hundred years ago, especially one without a signature or with a questionably authentic signature, is indubitably the work of this or that particular artist. This fact gives the traditional attribution of a disputed painting special weight, since that attribution carries the presumption of historical continuity. Consequently, an art historian arguing for a deattribution will generally convince other art historians only if he or she can persuasively argue for a specific reattribution.

Which one of the following, if true, most strongly supports the position that the traditional attribution of a disputed painting should not have special weight?

(A) Art dealers have always been led by economic self-interest to attribute any unsigned paintings of merit to recognized masters rather than to obscure artists.

(B) When a painting is originally created, there are invariably at least some eyewitnesses who see the artist at work, and thus questions of correct attribution cannot arise at that time.

(C) There are not always clearly discernible differences between the occasional inferior work produced by a

今天，很难证明某一幅两三百年前的绘画毫无疑问的是这一个或那一个特定画家的作品，特别是在画上没有签名或当签名的真实性具有争议时尤其是这样。该事实使得有争议画的传统归属法显得极为重要，因为这种归属法以历史的连续性为前提。因此，仅当一个艺术历史家能强有力地证明某一幅画另有所属时，他才能广泛地说服其他艺术历史家该画不属于某一作家。

下面哪一点，如果正确的话，能最强有力地支持不应给予传统上归属有争议的绘画方法以太多份量的立场？

(A) 艺术商经常受自我经济利益的驱使，从而把任何未签名的绘画或作品归为一个知名的大家，而不是一个默默无闻的艺术家。

(B) 当一幅画起初被创作时，总有一些见证者，目击了艺术家的工作，因此，在当时正确地归属该作品是不成问题的。

(C) 在大师偶然的质量较差的作品与才能较低的画家的佳作之间并不一定总是

master and the very best work produced by a lesser talent.

(D) Attribution can shape perception inasmuch as certain features that would count as marks of greatness in a master's work would be counted as signs of inferior artistry if a work were attributed to a minor artist.

(E) Even though some masters had specialists assist them with certain detail work, such as depicting lace, the resulting works are properly attributed to the masters alone.

61. Psychologists today recognize childhood as a separate stage of life which can only be understood in its own terms, and they wonder why the Western world took so long to see the folly of regarding children simply as small, inadequately socialized adults. Most psychologists, however, persist in regarding people 70 to 90 years old as though they were 35 years old who just happen to have white hair and extra leisure time. But old age is as fundamentally different from young adulthood and middle age as childhood is—a fact attested to by the organization of modern social and economic life. Surely it is time, therefore, to acknowledge that serious research into the unique psychology of advanced age has become indispensable.

Which one of the following principles, if established, would provide the strongest backing for the argument?

(A) Whenever current psychological practice conflicts with traditional attitudes toward people, those traditional attitudes should be changed to bring them in line with current psychological practice.

(B) Whenever two groups of people are so related to each other that any member of the second group must previously have been a member of the first, people in the first group should not be regarded simply as deviant members of the second group.

(C) Whenever most practitioners of a given discipline approach a particular problem in the same way, that uniformity is good evidence that all similar problems should also be approached in that way.

(D) Whenever a society's economic life is so organized that two distinct times of life are treated as being fundamentally different from one another, each time of life can be understood only in terms of its own distinct psychology.

有明显的差异。

(D) 归属可影响人们的观念，因于某一个在大师的作品里被认为是优点的特征，当该作品被归属为一个较次的画家时，该特征就会被认为是较差的艺术手法的迹象。

(E) 即使有专家帮助一些大师们完成某些零活，例如描画饰边，最终的作品也只应当归属大师。

今天的心理学家认为儿童时代是人生一个单独的驿站，并且只能以它自身的方式去理解，他们想知道为什么这么长时间以来西方国家荒谬地把儿童看作是小的、未充分社会化的成年人。然而，大多数的心理学家把那些70岁到90岁的老年人看作是好像刚开始出现白发和有额外的闲暇时间的35岁的人。但是老年人与儿童一样与年轻的成年人和中年人大相径庭，这一事实已被现代社会与经济生活体制所证实。因此，确实应该承认对老年人独特的心理进行认真的研究是必不可少的。

下面哪一原理，如果正确的话，最能强有力地支持上述论断？

(A) 当现行心理学实践与人们的传统态度相抵触时，那些传统的态度应该改变，以使它们能与现行的心理学实践相一致。

(B) 当两组人以这种方式相互联系，即第二组中的任一成员都必须曾是第一组的成员，那么第一组人不应该被简单地认为是第二组成员的脱离分子。

(C) 当某一特定领域的大多数开业者用同一种方法来解决某一特定问题时，这种一致性就是所有类似的问题都应当以那种方法来解决的很好的见证。

(D) 当一个社会的经济生活以这种方式来组织，即两个明显不同时代的生活相互之间被认为是根本不同的，那么每个时代的生活都应以它自己独特的心理学方式来理解。

(E) Whenever psychologists agree that a single psychology is inadequate for two distant age groups, they should be prepared to show that there are greater differences between the two age groups than there are between individuals in the same age group.

62. Defendants who can afford expensive private defense lawyers have a lower conviction rate than those who rely on court-appointed public defenders. This explains why criminals who commit lucrative crimes like embezzlement or insider trading are more successful at avoiding conviction than are street criminals.

The explanation offered above would be more persuasive if which one of the following were true?

(A) Many street crimes, such as drug dealing, are extremely lucrative and those committing them can afford expensive private lawyers.

(B) Most prosecutors are not competent to handle cases involving highly technical financial evidence and have more success in prosecuting cases of robbery or simple assault.

(C) The number of criminals convicted of street crimes is far greater than the number of criminals convicted of embezzlement or insider trading.

(D) The percentage of defendants who actually committed the crimes of which they are accused is no greater for publicly defended than for privately defended defendants.

(E) Juries, out of sympathy for the victims of crimes, are much more likely to convict defendants accused of violent crimes than they are to convict defendants accused of "victimless" crimes or crimes against property.

（E）当心理学家认为用单一的心理学来研究两组年龄差距较大的人是不够的时，他们就应着手揭示两个不同年龄组成员之间的差异要比同一年龄组的不同成员之间的大。

能支付起昂贵的私人辩护律师费用的被告被定罪的比率要小于那些依靠法庭任命公共辩护者的被告。这解释了为什么犯了诸如侵吞公款罪或内幕交易罪的罪犯，相对于街头罪犯来说，更易成功地逃避定罪。

如果下面哪一个正确，上面所提供的解释将更具说服力？

（A）许多诸如药品交易的街头犯罪获利颇丰，并且犯这种罪的人能支付起昂贵的私人律师的费用。

（B）绝大多数检察官不能胜任去处理涉及高度技术化的金融事实的案件，但在起诉抢劫或简单强暴案件方面取得的成功较多。

（C）被因街头犯罪而被定罪的罪犯的数量要远远大于因盗用公款或内幕交易而被判罪的罪犯的数量。

（D）被公共指定律师辩护的被告中，真正犯了他们被指控的罪的被告所占的比例不大于请私人辩护律师的被告中真正犯了罪的人的比例。

（E）陪审团出于对犯罪者的同情，更可能去宣判那些被指控暴力犯罪的被告有罪，而不大可能宣判那些被指控内幕交易或侵吞财产的被告有罪。

参考答案：

1. E	2. E	3. D	4. C	5. D
6. D	7. A	8. D	9. E	10. B
11. A	12. C	13. D	14. E	15. D
16. D	17. C	18. B	19. A	20. D
21. D	22. D	23. D	24. E	25. C
26. D	27. A	28. B	29. E	30. C
31. A	32. A	33. E	34. E	35. A
36. B	37. B	38. C	39. B	40. B
41. E	42. A	43. E	44. E	45. C
46. E	47. B	48. A	49. C	50. D

2. **解析**：本题的结论是：在将来的能源需求中，木材只能占有限的一部分。(E)选项的"多数消耗能源的商业用户位于木材的供应范围之内"，表明木材有可能成为其能源的主要来源，反对了本题的结论，(E)中的最后一句话"2/3的美国家庭位于大都市之外"与文中的最后一句话没有任何关系，起不到支持作用。综上所述(E)为正确答案；(A)表明个人消费者在有限的木材供应中能得到的份额相当少，起到了支持作用；(B)木材燃烧产生的浓烟限制了木材的使用范围，起支持作用；(C)说明当燃烧石油比燃烧木材更经济时，木材被使用的范围将受限制，支持了文中最后一句话的观点；(D)说明贮藏木材需要的较大的空间限制了木材在居民中的广泛使用，所以(D)也起支持作用。

6. **解析**：本题的结论是：蜂鸟只在白天为红花授粉而天蛾只在夜间为白花授粉。(D)蜂鸟在白天觅食，白天被遮住的红色花朵未被授粉，从另一方面说明了红色花朵不会吸引在夜间觅食的天蛾，也就是说红花只吸引白天觅食的蜂鸟。同理，夜间被遮住的白色花朵未被授粉说明了白花只吸引夜间觅食的天蛾，由以上分析可知(D)正确；(A)与本题的结论无关；(B)说明红花不吸引蜂鸟和天蛾，反驳了结论；(C)引入了新的比较，因此(C)不对；(E)提出了与结论无关的新概念。

9. **解析**：本题的结论是：人们通常不用理性的方式来处理信息。(E)选项表明人们在某种疾病的治疗上通常是信赖医生而不是他们那些不是医疗专家的邻居，这说明人们对待疾病的态度是理性的，也就是说，(E)对本题的结论构成了反对，因此(E)正确；(A)、(B)、(C)和(D)四个选项，人们都以非理性的方式来处理问题，因此都对本题的结论构成了支持。

10. **解析**：本题是由一个事实"大脑精神分裂症患者出生于冬季的人比其他时间的人多"，而提出一个解释性的原因"冬季营养不良是原因"。(B)选项指出大部分精神分裂症的脑部区位（记为B）是在母亲怀孕期最后一个月长成的（记作A），把A与B连了起来，所以(B)起到了支持作用，说明确实是因为冬天营养不良的饮食；(A)中的"economic distress"；(C)中的"suicide rates"均与上面推理无关；(D)与(E)都从某种程度上起到了反对作用，说明未必是营养不良的饮食的原因。

12. **解析**：本题支持的内容非常明确，已在问题目的中清晰列出，即让我们找一个选项说明确实"更多的物质生产可由相对较少的人完成"，读完问题目的马上可以理解答案内容。(C)说明1980年比1970年高出1/3，而就业人数只高出5%，实现了问题目的，所以(C)正确；(B)易误选，但(B)并不能表明"更多的物质生产可由相对较少的人完成"；(A)、(D)、(E)均无法实现问题目的。

13. **解析**：本题问题目的非常清晰，我们可以用问题目的中的关键词："Sports hunting"来定位选项，涉及这一关键词的只有(D)，又根据要支持的内容：关键词是否产生了一个更为healthy的动物群体，发现也只有(D)说明了这一点，所以(D)正确。(A)、(B)、(C)、(E)均不能在一个逻辑层面上对问题目的起到支持作用，所以不对。

15. **解析**：本题让我们寻求一个选项支持"20世纪80年代无家可归人数的急剧增加不能归因于将精神病人从医院推向社区护理"。若这一政策在20世纪60年代已实施了，那么无家可归人数的增加应从60年代就开始了，所以现在80年代无家可归人数的剧增必定是由其他原因导致的，所以(D)支持了段落论述，因此(D)正确；(A)易误选，但由于这只是这项政策所基于的假设，这个假设是否成立我们并不知道，所以起不到任何作用；(B)起到了反对作用；(C)、(E)与推理无关。

16. **解析**：两种假说只能有一种正确。因此能对第一种假说质疑的选项就能给第二种假说提供支持，质疑第一种假说就是怀疑人们当时不可能从那块陆地上到达北美。(D)指出那块土地如此寒冷，以至于那里的植物很稀少，不足以喂养陆地动物就质疑了第一种假说中的"人们在那块陆地上旅行时，靠捕猎到的陆地动物为食"。没有动物，横穿大陆的人就无以生存，横穿那块现已沉到海下的大陆就成为一种美丽的童话，因此(D)为本题的正确答案；(A)为无关选项；(B)易被误选，选(B)的人会认为

(B)对第二种假说构成了支持，但应注意两种观点所争执的是发生在1.4万年前的事，因此1万年前海洋文化的开始削弱了人们乘船到达北美的假说；(C)对第一种假说构成了支持；(E)与两种假说的结论无关。

18. **解析**：本题问题目的是支持该批评者关于"商城拦截"的宣称，因此读题重点应为最后一句话："...the shopping habits of mall shoppers are not representative of those of the larger population"，可用关键词"mall shopper"来定位选项。若商城购物者比其他场所购物的人多花50%的时间购物，如(B)所说，那么就表明商城购物者确实与其他人不一样，不能够作为广大消费者购物习惯的代表，起到了支持作用，所以(B)正确；(A)的"some"不能去说明一般情况，所以起不到任何作用；(C)、(E)与段落推理无关；(D)做了一个与段落推理无关的比较。

22. **解析**：要解答本题，就是要找一个选项说明基于总分的排名不应当被学生们用作申请学校的标准的结论是正确的，(D)选项表明总分所依赖的particular criteria对不同的学生来说，可能会因为他们需求的不同而具有不同的重要性，也就是说学生们应根据他们各自的需要而不是根据总分来选择学校，所以(D)是正确答案；(B)是易被误选的选项，但是要注意的是，广告的内容不一定都不正确，学校的排名高是既定的事实，而不是被学校给吹捧出来的，也就是说排名高的学校用此做广告并不能说明总分不应该作为申请学校的标准。(A)、(C)和(E)都是无关选项。

23. **解析**：本题论述的结论是：造成查理·瓦格纳作品演出不频繁的原因不是因为他的作品不受欢迎而是因为他的作品的舞台演出费用极其昂贵。由此结论可知，瓦格纳的作品是本题论述的重点，因此要对本题的结论构成支持，就要以瓦格纳的作品为出发点来说明他的作品是受欢迎的。本题的5个选项中，只有(D)涉及了瓦格纳的作品，且间接说明了他的作品广受欢迎。因此(D)为正确答案。

24. **解析**：这位历史学家认为农业经济衰退时期的农村人口向城市迁移是造成英国城市人口上升而农村人口下降的原因。(E)选项所表明的农业经济强劲时，城市人口增长相对缓慢，支持了农业经济衰退时的农村人口向城市迁移是城市人口上升的原因，因此(E)为正确答案；(A)工业人口增长与农村人口之间毫无关系；(B)和(C)与上述支持的推理相反；(D)同样无法对上面的推理做出支持。

25. **解析**：要支持本题"predisposition to TSZ is an inherited trait"的结论，就是要排除他因，说明患TSZ病不是由后天的环境因素造成的。(C)说明亲生父母患有TSZ的孩子不管由谁抚养，得TSZ病的可能性是一样的，所以(C)选项排除了环境因素，对结论构成了支持，为正确答案；(A)、(B)均说明了孩子们患有TSZ起因于环境因素，所以均起到了反对作用；(D)和(E)都与本题的推理无关。

26. **解析**：本题根据"对未经证实的证词持怀疑态度"是正确的，做出了"陪审团不应根据未经完全证实的招供而给被告定罪"的结论，要对本题的结论构成支持，就要找一个能说明an uncorroborated full confession可能并不正确的选项。(D)选项表明highly suggestible people易被误导而承认他们没有做过的事情，所以能最强有力地支持上面的"应该停止根据未经证实的招供而给被告定罪"的结论；(A)易误选，但是(A)并没说明陪审团为什么会acquit，因此(A)不能支持结论；(C)不能说明为什么不能停止由uncorroborated full confession而给被告定罪；(B)和(E)都是无关选项。

27. **解析**：正确解答本题的关键是对"the fitting of the severity of the punishment to the gravity of the particular crime"的把握。要找一个满足本题要求的选项，很显然就是找一个选项能说明采用"the uniform mandatory sentences recently introduced"比以前法官们的传统做法更有可能达到公正的判决。(A)选项表明Bassaria不同地区的法官对同一类型且严重程度也相同的犯罪的判决的显著差异就很有力地说明了法官们以前所具有的判决力是不可能达到真正的平等，而相比之下"the uniform mandatory sentences"有可能更为公正，所以(A)为正确答案；(D)易被误选，但要注意的是过去在最强判决和最弱判决之间有很大不同的案件现在属于统一强制判决的论述仅仅说明了强制判决可能妨碍真正的公正，所以(D)支持的是上面的段落，而不是问题中所提出的结论。

28. **解析**：要支持这个洞穴艺术家画的是他或她所熟悉的Chiru，就需要找一个选项表明在这个艺术家生活的那个时代，那个地方存在Chiru这种动物。从(B)选项所陈述的内容，我们很容易推出Chiru这种动物至少在1.6万年之前已经在那个地方出现，比这个艺术家创作壁画的时代早一千多年。由此分析可知(B)是正确答案。(A)和(D)对本题问题的假设构成了反对；(C)中的"植物"与本文无关；(E)引入了与本文推理无关的新的比较，因此(A)、(C)、(D)、(E)均为错误选项。

32. 解析：问题要求找出一项增加的前提不能使该论述在逻辑上是正确的。将选项(A)加入到短文给出的信息中，按照营养价值的顺序有可能有出现这样的蔬菜排列：collard greens, lettuce, kale, spinach，因为这个顺序同该论述的结论矛盾，(A)存在使该论述的结论成为错误的可能性，(A)因此是正确答案；相比较而言，(B)、(C)、(D)和(E)中的任何一个，加到短文中去时，由于Kale的营养价值比Spinach高，并且Collard greens的营养价值比lettuce高，使得该结论——kale比lettuce更有营养价值——在逻辑上顺理成章。

33. 解析：本题实际上就是在考单词。(E)选项中的the actual quality=value，与段落的第一句话"The value of product is determined by the ratio of its quality to its price"结合，可以很好地支持上述结论；(A)符合常识，似为真理，但与上面段落推理无关，所以不能支持段落推理的结论；(B)起到部分反对作用；(D)指出"广告与品牌忠实程度"这些其他原因可影响产品的竞争地位，所以反对了上面的结论，因此(D)也不正确。

34. 解析：选项(E)指出尽管广告宣传很猛烈，但Mammoth企业已经不能赶上该行业销量增加的趋势了，因此生产更多的相同型号的电话不可能使Mammoth销量增加，(E)是正确答案；如果Mammoth已经卖出了它生产的所有电话，即使它失去了一些市场份额，如(A)所说，仍可能通过生产更多的电话来增加销量；选项(D)指出Mammoth的销量在增加；如果存货的减少是由于向零售商交付了更多的电话，对(B)也是类似的；只要顾客认识Mammoth企业的电话的品牌，如(C)所说，他们是否将品牌与Mammoth联系起来可能并不重要。

41. 解析：由本题问题目的可知，我们要寻找的答案应能支持一方驳斥另一方，所以应找带有不同点的选项。对话里两个方案的不同点主要在时间与地点上。(E)说到了时间方面的影响，所以为正确答案；而(A)、(B)、(C)、(D)与"时间"、"地点"均无关，因此都不正确。

42. 解析：支持重点读两句话，即"只有生产出可以在其所处环境中移动的机器，科学家才能察觉空间联系。"(A)中的"on visual cues from motion"与段落的"by the same kind of process"相对应，并且把前提A与结论B连了起来，因此可以对结论起到支持作用；(B)中的运动对象并非段落里的"机器"，所以为无关选项；(D)易误选，虽然(D)陈述的可能是一种事实，但与"移动的机器"无关，所以不可能正确。

45. 解析：本题读题重点是"unwilling to pursue the development of new fuel-efficient technologies"与"threaten the industry's future"。本题问题目的非常清晰，让我们支持关于美国汽车工业"future"的宣称，(C)与"future"有关，并可以很好地实现问题目的；(A)、(D)、(E)均为无关选项；(B)易误选，但(B)仅讨论的是小汽车，而段落推理讨论的是汽车业，所以也说明不了任何问题。

47. 解析：本题让我们支持一方驳斥另一方，应利用双方的争论焦点来定位选项。很明显，段落的质疑与医药行业的论点之争主要在于有无必要延长专利权保护年限，因此答案应与时间有关。若新药品的临床试验需要10年时间完成，且试验是在专利权授予之后与新药品上市获得收入以前，如(B)所说，那么对巨额开发费用的补偿只有10年时间，补偿的时间变得更短了，因此需要延长专利时间，所以支持了医药行业观点而反对了上述质疑。(D)易误选，但(D)与时间无关；(A)、(E)都是无关选项；(C)为一无关比较。

50. 解析：读题重点是第一句话里的"...plans to maximize its profits by reducing by one half the number of issues it published each year"，本题属于"就目的提方法"类型的支持，但让支持的内容是杂志利润会下降，所以实质上是让反对上面的那句话，所以重点反对方法A。(D)表明广告商在每期杂志上花的钱不变，那么期数变少了，总广告收入必然下降，因此，杂志的总利润将下降。所以(D)正确；(A)、(B)、(E)均起到了与问题目的相反的作用；(C)是一个无关选项。

51. **解析**：本题难点在于读题，注意段落中since后面的"only"以及"no less than"为"不少于"的意思。如果制造partially biodegradable plastic beverage产生的塑料并不少于comparable nonbiodegradable containers丢弃时产生的塑料，正如(B)所说，那么结论"no less plastic refuse...are discarded"，可以得到很好地支持，所以(B)正确；(A)指出了两者的共性，但与"能否产生塑料"无关；(C)与"refuse"无关；(D)颠倒了两者关系，起到了反对作用；(E)与(A)一样，指出了两者共性，但并不能支持为什么有上述结论，因此(E)不正确。

   注：biodegradable *adj.*可被生物分解的，可由细菌分解降落的 refuse *n.*废物，废料，垃圾

52. **解析**：当人们认为南部岛屿大蜥蜴与北部岛屿大蜥蜴是同一物种时，南部岛屿大蜥蜴的濒临灭绝没有受到人们的重视；但是一旦发现南部岛屿大蜥蜴与北部岛屿大蜥蜴不同时，人们就被迫采取措施来保持它。这也就是说当南部岛屿大蜥蜴的灭绝能带来该物种的全球性灭绝时，人们就必须尽力采取措施来保护它，很明显(C)为正确答案；(E)有一定的迷惑性，但是应当注意(E)所讨论的内容与博物学家谈论的内容不符，博物学家是在谈论某一濒临灭绝的生物应该被保护，而(E)则谈论的是仅在一个地方发现的生物应该受到更多的关心和照顾，因此(E)虽然具有一定的正确性，但与(C)相比，就差远了；(A)、(B)和(D)都犯了一刀切的毛病，都是片面性或绝对化的方法，显然都不能证明博物学家的论述。

53. **解析**：段落推理的结论"迁移后的图书馆将在更多的图书馆的使用者的步行范围之内"，前提是"Glenwood中心住着更多的人"。而(B)通过指出Glenwood中心所占面积与Redville中心所占面积基本相同，再加上推理前提"Glenwood中心住着更多的人"，就可以得出Glenwood中心人口密度大，那么在人们步行范围之内人数必然更多，从而支持了推理的结论；选项(A)论述的是搬迁至Redville之前的情况，是个无关选项；(C)、(D)和(E)也均为无关选项。

54. **解析**：读明白问题永远是最重要的。本题问题目的中的support实际上不同于前面的support，它要求我们在段落论述正确的前提下，用段落的信息去支持五个选项中的一个选项，因此本题应属于"归纳"题型。这一点我们将在本篇第五章还有论述。本题的结论是只有法律认可那些预示较高地位的贵族头衔和这些头衔的继承权时，noble class才有可能存在。Feudalism在欧洲起源于8世纪，但是当时法律上并没有对such titles和inheritance of such titles认可。因此，认为Feudalism by definition需要nobility的存在很明显是在使用一个歪曲历史的定义，所以选项(A)是正确选项；(E)为段落原命题的逆命题；(D)毫无根据地把先前发生的事物当作是随后出现的事物的必要条件；(B)和(C)都不能从段落的结论中合理地推出。因此(B)、(C)、(D)和(E)都是错误选项。

55. **解析**：要决定一只鸟在选择配偶时的行为是由遗传决定的，还是后天习得的，就要看它们生活的环境对他们选择配偶有多大的影响。(E)表明了一只生活在由两种变种组成的鸟群中的鸟在选择配偶时不会对某一个变种的鸟有所偏好就表明了是这只鸟生活的环境而不是它的遗传特性决定它在择偶时的行为，所以(E)能对本题的结论形成最有力的支持；(D)反对本题的结论；(A)、(B)和(C)均为无关选项。

56. **解析**：本题的5个选项中，(A)、(B)、(D)和(E)4个选项都不能从本题的论述中合理地推出。(C)选项的内容表明那些广告商即使在蒙受经济损失的情况下，依然撤走了他们的广告，这就充分证明了他们此举不是出于财政上的考虑，而是在道义上不赞成该刊物刊登猥亵的内容。因此(C)是正确答案。

57. **解析**：选项(A)是明显不能支持上述论述的选项。在其他条件不变的前提下，城市人口在过去10年中增加了一倍，也只能使死于哮喘病的人增加一倍，而不能使哮喘病的死亡率增加一倍，因此本题的正确选项为(A)。(B)、(C)、(D)和(E)选项经有细分析后可发现它们都可以支持段落的论证。

58. **解析**：根据汽车制造商要达到新的限制，他们就得付出非常昂贵的代价的论述可知，限制汽车尾气的法令越苛刻，他们为此付出的代价就越高，因此(A)选项是正确答案；(D)选项对汽车制造商的立场构成了反对；(B)、(C)、(E)三选项均不能从本题的论述中推出。

59. 解析：婴儿死亡率的高低由两个重要因素决定：第一是婴儿出生时的健康状况；第二是婴儿接受的后天护理的好坏，因此若美国在对婴儿，特别是容易死亡的早产以及低出生婴儿护理方面的技术比以前大为提高时，能确保它的婴儿死亡率下降，但并不一定能说明美国现在的婴儿在他们出生时比以前更健康了。由此分析可知，(C)是正确答案，(A)、(B)、(D)和(E)均与本题的答案无关。

60. 解析：根据题中的论述可知，传统归属法有其内在的弊病。一旦一幅未签名的画被归属于某人时，别的艺术历史家就很难说服别人这幅画不是那个人的作品。而艺术商们又经常受自我利益所驱使，他们会把任何未签名的绘画归为一个知名的大师的作品，而用传统归属法又很难证明这些画不属于那些大师们。因此传统归属法的有效性就得到了极大的削弱，所以(A)最能支持不应给予传统归属有争议绘画方法以太多份量的立场；(B)、(C)、(D)和(E)均为无关选项。

61. 解析：心理学家的见解是：儿童和老年人是两个与众不同的群体，对他们的心理只能以各自独特的方式去研究。因此很明显选项(D)所描述的原理对本题的论证构成了最强有力的支持。其余的4个选项均不能从本题的论证中推出。

62. 解析：本题为支持段落里所提供的解释，因此，可以用段落里解释的关键词 "Defendants who can afford expensive private defense lawyer" 与 "those who rely on court-appointed public defenders" 来定位可以很快发现选项(D)涉及双方且与解释相吻合；(A)部分反对；(B)用它因作为反对；(C)无关选项；(E)也是用他因作为反对。

第 三 章

反 对

反对题型的解题思路与支持题型的解题思路基本一样，只不过是其答案对段落推理的作用刚好相反。只要将某选项放入 A 与 B 之间，使段落推理成立或结论正确的可能性降低，这个选项就是正确答案，所以反对答案既可以是段落推理不成立的必要条件，也可以是充分条件，还可以是既非充分又非必要条件，其答案方向与支持的答案方向一样，主要有四个方面：A 与 B 之间没有联系或有差异，A 不可行或 A 没有意义；除了 A 以外有别的因素影响 B；直接说 B 不正确。下面我们先来看几个反对题，体会其解题的基本思维点。

1. A conservation group in the United States is trying to change the long-standing image of bats as frightening creatures. The group contends that bats are feared and persecuted solely because they are shy animals that are active only at night.

Which of the following, if true, would cast the most serious doubt on the accuracy of the group's contention?

(A) Bats are steadily losing natural roosting places such as caves and hollow trees and are thus turning to more developed areas for roosting.

(B) Bats are the chief consumers of nocturnal insects and thus can help make their hunting territory more pleasant for humans.

(C) Bats are regarded as frightening creatures not only in the United States but also in Europe, Africa, and South America.

(D) Raccoons and owls are shy and active only at night; yet they are not generally feared and persecuted.

(E) People know more about the behavior of other greatly feared animal species, such as lions, alligators, and snakes, than they do about the behavior of bats.

译文：美国的一个动物保护组织正努力改变长期以来把蝙蝠看作一种令人恐怖的动物的印象。该组织争论说蝙蝠让人害怕和烦乱仅仅因为它们见人就躲避，且仅在夜间活动。

以下哪一选项，如果是正确的，将对该组织的争论的准确性提出最严重的质疑？

(A) 蝙蝠逐渐失去了它们天然的栖息之处，如洞穴和中空的树，因此逐渐到人口更密集的地区寻找栖息之处。

(B) 蝙蝠是夜间昆虫的主要捕食者，因此，使它们捕食范围内的地区更适于人类生活。

(C) 不仅在美国，而且在欧洲，非洲和南美洲，蝙蝠都被视为令人恐怖的动物。

(D) 浣熊和猫头鹰也见人就躲避，且只在夜间活动；然而它们一般来说并不让人害怕和烦乱。

(E) 人们对其他的非常令人害怕的动物种类，如狮子，短吻鳄和蛇的行为的了解多于对蝙蝠的行为的了解。

解析：读题重点放在最后一句话的 "solely because they are shy animals..."。该组织的论述指出见人就躲避并且在夜间活动的动物因此让人害怕和烦乱，选项(D)指出浣熊和猫头鹰也见人就躲避并且也在夜间活动，但是它们既不让人害怕也不令人烦乱。因此，(D)是正确答案。尽管蝙蝠出没范围的扩大可以解释提出人们对蝙蝠的恐惧这个问题的重要性，选项(A)没有指出产生这种恐惧的根本原因。选项(B)和(E)，尽管与人们对蝙蝠的恐惧的理性分析有关，但不影响对该组织论述准确性的评判；除美国之外，蝙蝠也让人害怕，如(C)所述，同该组织对在美国出现的对于蝙蝠的恐惧的解释并不矛盾。

2. Some who favor putting governmental enterprises into private hands suggest that conservation objectives would in general be better served if private environmental groups were put in charge of operating and financing the national park system, which is now run by the government.

Which of the following, assuming that it is a realistic possibility, argues most strongly against the suggestion above?

(A) Those seeking to abolish all restrictions on exploiting the natural resources of the parks might join the private environmental groups as members and eventually take over their leadership.

(B) Private environmental groups might not always agree on the best ways to achieve conservation objectives.

(C) If they wished to extend the park system, the private environmental groups might have to seek contributions from major donors and the general public.

(D) There might be competition among private environmental groups for control of certain park areas.

(E) Some endangered species, such as the California condor, might die out despite the best efforts of the private environmental groups, even if those groups are not hampered by insufficient resources.

译文： 一些赞成将政府企业转变为私人经营的人指出，如果由私人的环境组织来负责经营国家公园系统并掌管它的财务，该系统现由政府经营，总的来说，环境保护的目标会得到更好的实现。

以下哪一项，假设它是现实可能的，最强烈地反对以上提出的建议？

(A) 那些寻求废除对公园内自然资源开发做出的所有限制的人，可能作为成员加入这些私人环境组织，并最终取得对它们的领导权。

(B) 私人环境组织不一定总是采取那些实现环境保护目标的最好办法。

(C) 如果他们希望扩张该公司系统，私人环境组织可能不得不从大的捐献人和公众那里寻求捐款。

(D) 在私人环境组织之间为了控制某些公园区域会产生竞争。

(E) 尽管私人环境组织做出了最大努力，即使这些组织，没有受到资源不足的阻碍，一些濒危种群，如加州秃鹰，仍可能会灭绝。

解析： 如果那些寻求废除关于对公园内自然资源开发做出的限制的人获取了一个负责经营该公园系统的组织的领导权，环境保护目标不会得到更好的实现。选项(A)指出提议的政策会导致这样一种情况，因此是正确答案。

3. The fewer restrictions there are on the advertising of legal services, the more lawyers there are who advertise their services, and the lawyers who advertise a specific service usually charge less for that service than lawyers who do not advertise. Therefore, if the state removes any of its current restrictions, such as the one against advertisements that do not specify fee arrangements, overall consumer legal costs will be lower than if the state retains its current restrictions.

Which of the following, if true, would most seriously weaken the argument concerning overall consumer legal costs?

(A) The state has recently removed some other restrictions that had limited the advertising of legal services.

(B) The state is unlikely to remove all of the restrictions that apply solely to the advertising of legal services.

(C) Lawyers who do not advertise generally provide legal services of the same quality as those provided by lawyers who do advertise.

译文： 对法律服务进行广告宣传的限制越少，为他们的服务进行广告宣传的律师就越多，并且为某项服务进行广告宣传的律师对该项服务的收费比没有进行广告宣传的律师低。因此，如果这个州取消这些限制中的任何一项，例如禁止那些没有标明收费标准的广告，那么总的消费者在法律事务中的花费将低于该州保留目前的限制的情况。

以下哪一项，如果是正确的，将最严重地削弱关于总的消费者在法律事务中的花费的论述？

(A) 该州最近取消了一些其他的对法律服务进行广告宣传的限制。

(B) 该州不可能取消所有的仅适用于对法律服务进行广告宣传的限制。

(C) 那些不进行广告宣传的律师和那些进

(D) Most lawyers who now specify fee arrangements in their advertisements would continue to do so even if the specification were not required.

(E) Most lawyers who advertise specific services do not lower their fees for those services when they begin to advertise.

行广告宣传的律师提供相同质量的法律服务。

(D) 大多数现在在他们的广告宣传中标明了收费标准的律师，即使不要求这种标明，他们也会继续这样做。

(E) 大多数为某些服务进行广告宣传的律师并没有在他们开始进行广告宣传时，降低他们对那些服务的收费。

解析：如果(E)是正确的，那些在限制取消后开始进行广告宣传的律师可能都是那些在开始广告宣传时没有降低收费的律师，在这种情况下消费者在法律事务中的花费没有减少，因此，(E)削弱了该论述，是正确答案。由于(A)没有把最近限制的取消同消费者在法律事务中的费用联系起来，仅靠(A)自身没有削弱该论述。由于该论述同哪些限制实际上保留下来无关，而仅关注哪些限制将要被取消，(B)没有削弱该论述。选项(C)和(D)同评价该论述无关，该论述考虑从费用的角度分析，不考虑法律服务的质量或律师的广告内容。

4. Opponents of laws that require automobile drivers and passengers to wear seat belts argue that in a free society people have the right to take risks as long as the people do not harm others as a result of taking the risks. As a result, they conclude that it should be each person's decision whether or not to wear a seat belt.

Which of the following, if true, most seriously weakens the conclusion drawn above?

(A) Many new cars are built with seat belts that automatically fasten when someone sits in the front seat.

(B) Automobile insurance rates for all automobile owners are higher because of the need to pay for the increased injuries or deaths of people not wearing seat belts.

(C) Passengers in airplanes are required to wear seat belts during takeoffs and landings.

(D) The rate of automobile fatalities in states that do not have mandatory seat-belt laws is greater than the rate of fatalities in states that do have such laws.

(E) In automobile accidents, a greater number of passengers who do not wear seat belts are injured than are passengers who do wear seat belts.

译文：有项法律要求汽车司机和乘客系上安全带。该项法律的反对者们争辩说，在一个自由社会，人们有权去冒险，只要冒险的结果没有伤害到其他人。因此，他们得出结论，是否系上安全带应由每个人自己决定。

以下哪一选项，如果是正确的，将最严重地削弱上文得出的结论？

(A) 很多新车配有当人坐上前排座位就自动拴好的安全带。

(B) 因为需要为日益增多的因没有系安全带造成的人们的伤亡支付保险金，所以对所有汽车车主收取的汽车保险费率越来越高。

(C) 在起飞和降落时飞机乘客也被要求系上安全带。

(D) 没有强制系安全带法律的州的汽车事故死亡率比有这种法律的州的汽车事故死亡率高。

(E) 在汽车交通事故中，没有系安全带的乘客受伤的人数比系安全带的乘客受伤的人数多。

解析：段落推理为：人们有权力冒受伤的风险，只要他们不因此伤害其他人。如果能够证明，如(B)表明，这个决定的确伤害了其他人，这个原则不能使个人有决定是否系上安全带的权力是合理的，因此，(B)是正确答案。该论述隐含地承认了个人不系安全带承担了风险，因此，(D)和(E)都只是简单地确认了这种承认，而没有削弱该结论。选项(C)引用了一个同争论中的问题相似的要求，但它的存在本身同争论中的问题的合理性没有关系。选项(A)指出该法律在一些情况下可能无关紧要，但它没有评论该项法律的合理性问题。

5. The average life expectancy for the United States population as a whole is 73.9 years, but children born in Hawaii will live an average of 77 years, and those born in Louisiana, 71.7 years. If a newlywed couple from Louisiana were to begin their family in Hawaii, therefore, their children would be expected to live longer than would be the case if the family remained in Louisiana.

Which of the following, if true, would most seriously weaken the conclusion drawn in the passage?

(A) Insurance company statisticians do not believe that moving to Hawaii will significantly lengthen the average Louisianan's life.

(B) The governor of Louisiana has falsely alleged that statistics for his state are inaccurate.

(C) The longevity ascribed to Hawaii's current population is attributable mostly to genetically determined factors.

(D) Thirty percent of all Louisianans can expect to live longer than 77 years.

(E) Most of the Hawaiian Islands have levels of air pollution well below the national average for the United States.

译文：对于美国人口总体来说平均寿命是73.9岁，但是在夏威夷出生的小孩将平均活到77岁，而那些在路易斯安那出生的人平均活到71.7岁。如果一对从路易斯安那来的新婚夫妇在夏威夷开始他们的家庭生活，那么，他们的孩子预期将比他们留在路易斯安那的情况下活得更长。

以下哪一个选项，如果是正确的，将最严重地削弱短文中得出的结论？

(A) 保险公司统计人员不相信迁移到夏威夷会显著地延长路易斯安那人的寿命。

(B) 路易斯安那州州长错误地宣称关于该州的统计数据是不准确的。

(C) 归属于夏威夷现居民的长寿很大程度上归因于基因决定的因素。

(D) 预计所有路易斯安那人的30%能够活过77岁。

(E) 大部分夏威夷岛屿的空气污染水平远远低于美国的全国平均水平。

解析：本题为"B，A"类型，即由一个事实得出一种结论，削弱结论多为"除了A之外还有别的因素影响B"。并且此题在很多情况下也可以用"要么环境，要么遗传"来思维。选项(C)指出夏威夷人口中相当一部分是因遗传因素先天决定的长寿。由于路易斯安那人不一定有这种先天的因素，并且由于路易斯安那人的孩子将从他们的父母那里获得他们的遗传特征，而不是从他们的出生地。选项(C)提出了一个理由来怀疑原路易斯安那人的在夏威夷出生的孩子将有更长的预期寿命，因此，(C)是正确答案。

因为该结论关注那些在夏威夷出生的人，而不是一般的路易斯安那人，(A)没有削弱该结论。因为州长的宣称是错误的〔选项(B)〕，它不能影响该结论。选项(D)不能削弱该结论，因为它同给出的信息和关于寿命的结论并不矛盾。通过指出夏威夷的环境是一个非常健康的环境，选项(E)支持该结论。

6. The price the government pays for standard weapons purchased from military contractors is determined by a pricing method called "historical costing." Historical costing allows contractors to protect their profits by adding a percentage increase, based on the current rate of inflation, to the previous year's contractual price.

Which of the following statements, if true, is the best basis for a criticism of historical costing as an economically sound pricing method for military contracts?

(A) The government might continue to pay for past inefficient use of funds.

译文：政府为从军火商那里购买的标准武器支付的价格是由一种叫"历史成本法"的定价方法决定的。历史成本法允许军火商基于当前的通货膨胀率，在上一年合同价格上增加一个百分比，以此来保护他们的利润。

以下哪一项陈述，如果是正确的，可以成为批评将历史成本法作为军火合同定价办法在经济上的合理性的最好基础？

(A) 政府可能会继续为过去的无效率的资金使用而进行支付。

(B) The rate of inflation has varied considerably over the past twenty years.

(C) The contractual price will be greatly affected by the cost of materials used for the products.

(D) Many taxpayers question the amount of money the government spends on military contracts.

(E) The pricing method based on historical costing might not encourage the development of innovative weapons.

(B) 在过去二十年中，通货膨胀率发生了很大变化。

(C) 合同价格会受到生产这些产品用的原料成本的很大影响。

(D) 很多纳税人质问政府花费在军火合同上的钱的数量。

(E) 在历史成本基础上的定价方法可能不会促进改进型武器的发展。

解析：如果最初购买武器的合同价中包含了资金的无效使用，那么由于历史成本法只是向最初价格上增加，它就把这些无效率保留了下来。一种经济上合理的定价方法至少应该允许降低价格的可能性，例如将这种无效率去除掉，因此，(A)是正确答案。

因为历史成本对通货膨胀作出反应，(B)和(C)都与历史成本的经济合理性不矛盾——(B)因为它提到通货膨胀率而(C)因为它提到受通货膨胀影响的成本。选项(D)尤其没有为质疑历史成本的经济合理性提供任何理由。历史成本仅适用于标准武器，而不是(E)中提到的改进型武器。

通过对上面几个例题的理解，我们根据反对题型的答案方向来分析一下：

一、A与B之间没有联系或有差异

这种类型的反对主要看A与B之间有无差异，并用A、B双方关键词来定位选项。

7. It is important to teach students to use computers effectively. Therefore, students should be taught computer programming in school.

Which of the following, if true, most weakens the argument above?

(A) Only people who use computers effectively are skilled at computer programming.

(B) Only people skilled at computer programming use computers effectively.

(C) Some people who use computers effectively cannot write computer programs.

(D) Some schools teach computer programming more effectively than others.

(E) Most people who are able to program computers use computers effectively.

译文：教学生有效地使用计算机是很重要的。因此，学校应给学生开设计算机程序设计课。

下面哪个，如果正确，最能削弱上面的论证？

(A) 只有有效使用计算机的人才擅长程序设计。

(B) 只有精通程序设计的人才能有效地使用计算机。

(C) 一些能有效使用计算机的人并不会编计算机程序。

(D) 有些学校教授的编程课比其他学校更有效率。

(E) 绝大多数能编程的人能有效使用计算机。

解析：本题的推理是为达到一个目的"让学生有效使用计算机"而提出一种方法"让学生学习computer programming"，我们发现B与A的核心关键词之间有差异。(C)刚好断开了A与B的联系，指出了A与B之间没有联系，所以起到了反对作用，因此(C)为正确答案。(A)把A与B联系了起来，但(A)是个无关选项；(B)与(E)都是很好的支持选项；(D)是一个新比较，且与上述推理无关，所以(D)不正确。

8. A research study reports that a particular educational program has improved the prospects for success in later schooling for those children aged three to five who were subjects of the study. It follows, then, that introducing similar programs for all children aged three to five will improve their chances for success in later schooling.

Which of the following, if true, would most weaken the argument above?

(A) The parents of preschool children in the United States are attracted to educational fads and do not have a clear idea of what sorts of early education programs might benefit their children.

(B) The cognitive abilities of children are constantly changing between ages three and five.

(C) The researchers unwittingly included a substantial number of children who had been previously exposed to another educational enrichment program.

(D) Many parents erroneously presume that early formal instruction takes up time that children could better spend exploring their worlds independently.

(E) It would require extraordinary public expense to establish such educational enrichment programs on a national basis.

译文：一份研究报告指出，为接受研究的3-5岁的孩子准备的一个特殊教育方案提高了他们在今后学校教育中获得成功的可能。因此，对所有孩子实行类似的教育方案会提高他们在以后学校教育中取得成功的机会。

下面哪个，如果正确，最能削弱上面的论点？

(A) 在美国，学龄前儿童的父母被教育的流行风尚所吸引了，他们并不清楚孩子接受什么样的早期教育才是有利的。

(B) 儿童在3-5岁时的认知能力是不断变化的。

(C) 调查人员并未意识到他们把以前曾受过另一种教育培养训练的一大批孩子包括了进来。

(D) 很多父母错误地认为早期正规教育将占用孩子们本来可以更好地独立探索世界的时间。

(E) 在国家的基础上建立这样的教育培训项目需要特别的公共支出。

解析：本题推理是一个research的结果类推至all children，属于"A，B"模式，其暗含假设是A与B的探讨对象本质属性一样，要反对应反对隐含假设。(C)指出研究人员无意识地包括了相当多的以前接受过的教育启智项目的孩子，因此，作为这个研究人员测试对象的孩子是特别（或不具有代表性）的，他们的成功性增大完全有可能是另外教育启智项目的结果，所以(C)为正确答案。(B)中的"cognitive abilities"与段落推理无关。

9. The recent decline in the value of the dollar was triggered by a prediction of slower economic growth in the coming year. But that prediction would not have adversely affected the dollar had it not been for the government's huge budget deficit, which must therefore be decreased to prevent future currency declines.

Which of the following, if true, would most seriously weaken the conclusion about how to prevent future currency declines?

(A) The government has made little attempt to reduce the budget deficit.

(B) The budget deficit has not caused a slowdown in economic growth.

(C) The value of the dollar declined several times in the year prior to the recent prediction of slower economic growth.

译文：由于预测明年经济增长速度会放慢，引起了最近美元币值的下跌。但是如果没有政府的巨额预算赤字，该预测就不会对美元有负面影响，因此必须降低该赤字来防止将来的货币贬值。

以下哪一项，如果是正确的，将最严重地削弱关于如何防止将来货币贬值的结论？

(A) 政府几乎没有做过努力来预算赤字。

(B) 预算赤字没有造成经济增长速度的减缓。

(C) 这一年在最近的经济增长放缓的预测之前，美元的币值已下跌了好几次。

(D) Before there was a large budget deficit, predictions of slower economic growth frequently caused declines in the dollar's value.

(E) When there is a large budget deficit, other events in addition to predictions of slower economic growth sometimes trigger declines in currency value.

(D) 在没有巨额预算赤字时，更慢的经济增长的预测经常导致美元的贬值。

(E) 当存在巨额预算赤字时，除了经济增长放缓的预测之外的其他事件有时也引起了币值的下跌。

解析： 该论述假设一个特定的预测只有在伴随有巨额预算赤字时才会引起货币贬值，由于选项(D)指出这项预测在没有巨额预算赤字时也能引起货币贬值，选项(D)是正确答案。

一种方法没有充分地执行并不代表该方法是无效的。因此，选项(A)不合适。由于没有提到经济增长放缓的发生，什么引起的这次放缓是无关的，因此，选项(B)不合适。由于(C)支持预算赤字是货币贬值的潜在原因，(C)不合适。选项(E)不合适，因为它支持必须减少预算赤字的论述。

10. The imposition of quotas limiting imported steel will not help the big American steel mills. In fact, the quotas will help "mini-mills" flourish in the United States. Those small domestic mills will take more business from the big American steel mills than would have been taken by the foreign steel mills in the absence of quotas.

Which of the following, if true, would cast the most serious doubt on the claim made in the last sentence above?

(A) Quality rather than price is a major factor in determining the type of steel to be used for a particular application.

(B) Foreign steel mills have long produced grades of steel comparable in quality to the steel produced by the big American mills.

(C) American quotas on imported goods have often induced other countries to impose similar quotas on American goods.

(D) Domestic "mini-mills" consistently produce better grades of steel than do the big American mills.

(E) Domestic "mini-mills" produce low-volume, specialized types of steels that are not produced by the big American steel mills.

译文： 对进口钢材施加配额限制将不会有助于美国的大型钢铁厂。实际上，配额有助于"小型厂"在美国的繁荣发展，那些国内的小型厂将从美国大型钢铁厂那里抢走比在没有配额时外国钢铁厂抢走的更多的生意。

以下哪一项，如果是正确的，将对以上最后一句所作的宣称提出最严重的质疑？

(A) 在决定用于某种特殊用途时的钢铁种类时，质量而不是价格是一个主要因素。

(B) 外国钢铁厂长时间以来生产的钢铁等级与美国大型钢铁厂生产的钢铁质量相当。

(C) 美国对进口商品的配额经常引起其他国家对美国商品施加类似的配额。

(D) 国内"小型厂"生产的钢铁等级，一贯来说比美国大型厂生产的好。

(E) 国内"小型厂"生产规模较小，生产美国大型钢铁厂不生产的特种钢。

解析： 如果，像选项(E)指出的一样，大型和小型厂生产不同类型的钢材，小型厂销量的增加不一定导致大型厂销量的减少，因此，选项(E)对于该宣称提出了最严重的质疑，是正确答案。

选项(A)没有提供足够的关于外国和国内钢厂生产的钢铁的相对质量的信息来质疑该宣称。相似地，选项(B)没有提供关于美国小型厂的足够信息。选项(C)没有提供关于外国施加配额的可能后果的足够信息来质疑该宣称。选项(D)倾向于支持该宣称，因为更好的钢应该比差质量的钢销量大。

有时我们会见到A或B中有always, only, solely, any 等绝对化语言，在大多数情况下，这种推理的反对重点就放在这些词上，通过说明这些绝对化的语言实现不了，就可以起到削弱的作用。

11. Sometime during the 1950's, rock music permanently ousted jazz from the music scene. This is evident from the behavior of youths of that time. In crowded nightclubs they would applaud rock acts enthusiastically. But when a jazz act began, they went outside and got refreshments. They came back in only when the jazz set was finished.

Which of the following statements, if true, is a valid objection to the conclusion drawn above?

(A) Jazz is the most important musical contribution of the United States to world culture.

(B) Although some young people who attended nightclubs in the 1950's did try to listen to jazz, they eventually became bored with it.

(C) Since the 1960's, rock music has not only provided youths with recreation but has, as well, become a rallying point for making social statements.

(D) Although by 1960 jazz performances were less popular, there has since been a revival of interest in jazz among middle-class professionals.

(E) Jazz steadily increased in popularity between the 1930's and the 1950's.

译文：20世纪50年代的某个时期，摇滚乐永久性地把爵士乐逐出了乐坛。这一点从那时年轻人的行为能明显地看出来。在拥挤的夜总会，他们热烈地为摇滚乐欢呼。但当爵士乐表演开始时，他们就出去喝饮料，只有爵士乐表演结束时他们才回来。

下面的哪个陈述，如果正确，对上面结论构成有效的反驳？

(A) 爵士乐是美国对世界文化在音乐方面最重要的贡献。

(B) 虽然有些50年代去夜总会的年轻人确实也试图听爵士乐，但他们最终对之感到厌倦。

(C) 自20世纪60年代以来，摇滚乐不仅给年轻人带来娱乐，还成为表达对社会意见的一种集聚点。

(D) 虽然到1960年爵士乐不那么流行了，然而在中产阶级行业人员中有一股对爵士乐兴趣的复兴潮流。

(E) 爵士乐在20世纪30年代到50年代之间的流行程度稳步上升了。

解析：本题让我们反驳上述结论，而段落推理的结论显然是第一句话，并且第一句话的"permanently"相当于绝对化语言，但它从后面陈述的原因推不出来。若1960年中产阶级行业人员有一股对爵士乐兴趣的复兴潮流，如(D)所说，那么就与上面"permanently"相冲突。(A)讨论的"贡献"，(C)讨论的摇滚乐的"作用"，(E)讨论的"20世纪30年代到50年代之间怎么样"均与段落推理无关。(B)最多起到部分支持作用。

二、A不可行或A无意义

这种类型的反对应该用A中的关键词来定位选项，找一个能说明A不可行或A无意义的选项。

12. The Supreme Court is no longer able to keep pace with the tremendous number of cases it agrees to decide. The Court schedules and hears 160 hours of oral argument each year, and 108 hours of next year's term will be taken up by cases left over from this year. Certainly the Court cannot be asked to increase its already burdensome hours. The most reasonable long-range solution to this problem is to allow the Court to decide many cases without hearing oral argument; in this way the Court might eventually increase dramatically the number of cases it decides each year.

Which of the following, if true, could best be used to argue against the feasibility of the solution suggested above?

译文：最高法院再也来不及处理那些它同意审理的数目庞大的案件了。最高法院每年计划听取160个小时口头申诉，然而明年有108个小时被今年剩下的案子占去了。当然不能要求最高法院再增加本已令它难以负荷的时间了，解决这个问题的最合理的长远办法便是让法院不用听取许多案件的口头申诉而直接做出裁决。通过这种办法，最高法院便会大大地增加它每年处理的案件数目。

下面哪个，如果正确，最能反驳上面提出的解决办法的可行性？

(A) The time the Court spends hearing oral argument is only a small part of the total time it spends deciding a case.

(B) The Court cannot legitimately avoid hearing oral argument in any case left over from last year.

(C) Most authorities agree that 160 hours of oral argument is the maximum number that the Court can handle per year.

(D) Even now the Court decides a small number of cases without hearing oral argument.

(E) In many cases, the delay of a hearing for a full year can be extremely expensive to the parties involved.

(A) 最高法院每年花在听取口头申诉上的时间只是它审理案件所需时间的一小部分。

(B) 最高法院不能在程序上避免听取去年留下案件的口头申诉。

(C) 大多数权威人士都认为160个小时的口头申诉是法院每年能处理的最大数目。

(D) 即使现在，最高法院对一小部分案件没有听取口头申诉就做出了裁决。

(E) 在很多案件里，把听取口头申诉拖延一整年对当事人来说所需费用是极其高昂的。

解析：本题问题目的清晰，让我们反对上述推理中的the feasibility of the solution，因此读题重点应放在段落最后一个句子上，且最后一个句子明显是提出一个方法"to allow the court to decide many cases without hearing oral argument"，而达到目的（in this way为引导目的的关键词）"法院能eventually increase dramatically..."（请注意dramatically），反对重点反对the solution即方法。若法院用于听取口头辩论的时间仅仅占裁决一个案件所花费时间的很少一部分，如(A)所说，那么即使裁决案例时不听取口头辩论，也不可能"dramatically"增加每年裁决的案件数目。所以(A)选项通过对段落推理所提出的方法A的质疑，而起到了反对作用。因此(A)正确。(D)易误选，但若在听取口头辩论时每年裁决10个案例，而不听取口头辩论每年裁决30个案件（尽管也很少），但是有了一个"dramatically"的增加，所以(D)不可能起到反对作用。(B)中的"last year"与本题推理无关；(E)中的"expensive"与推理的"increase dramatically"也无关。

13. If athletes want better performances, they should train at high altitudes. At higher altitudes, the body has more red blood cells per unit volume of blood than at sea level. The red blood cells transport oxygen, which will improve performance if available in greater amounts. The blood of an athlete who trains at high altitudes will transport more oxygen per unit volume of blood, improving the athlete's performance.

Which of the following, if true, would be most damaging to the argument above, provided that the athlete's heart rate is the same at high and low altitudes?

(A) Scientists have found that an athlete's heart requires a period of time to adjust to working at high altitudes.

(B) Scientists have found that the body's total volume of blood declines by as much as 25 percent at high altitudes.

(C) Middle-distance runners who train at high altitudes sometimes lose races to middle-distance runners who train at sea level.

(D) The performances of athletes in competitions at all altitudes have improved markedly during the past twenty years.

译文：如果运动员想有更出色的表现，他们应该在高海拔地区训练。在高海拔地区，身体中每单位体积的血液里含有的红血球数量比在海平面上多。红血球运输氧气，而氧气供应充足便能提高竞技水平，在高海拔地区训练的运动员每单位体积的血液能运载更多的氧气，这样便会有更出色的表现。

如果运动员的心跳速率在高地时和在低地时相同，下面哪个，如果正确，对上面的论点打击性最大？

(A) 科学家发现运动员的心脏需要一段时间调整，才能适应在高海拔地区的训练。

(B) 科学家发现在高海拔地区人体内的血液总量降低了25%。

(C) 在高原训练的中距离跑运动员有时会败给在海拔为零的平地上训练的运动员。

(D) 在过去20年，运动员在所有高海拔地

(E) At altitudes above 5,500 feet, middle-distance runners often better their sea-level running times by several seconds.

区进行的比赛中成绩都明显提高了。

(E) 在海拔5,500米以上的高地，中距离跑运动员的速度要比在海拔为零的平地上快几秒钟。

解析：本题推理可提炼为两句话："因为每单位血液中红血球多，所以高海拔训练好"。一般地，当段落推理由单位或比例而得出一个结论时，推理成立暗含假设为"总量或数量没有发生变化"。反对主要是反对假设。(B)通过指出血液总量下降而反对了假设，所以(B)正确。(A)中的"require a period of time"与推理并无直接关系。有人认为若如(A)所说，高海拔训练需适应一段时间，那就相当于指出了高海拔训练的缺点，所以起到了反对作用。但究竟高海拔训练带来的最终收益我们并不知道，完全有可能最终收益大于训练适应成本，所以(A)为无关选项；(C)中的"sometimes"说明不了任何问题；(D)中的"at all altitudes"把范围扩大；(E)中指出了一个"5000英尺"的特例，也并不能对上面描述的一般现象构成反对。

14. As a practical matter, the copper available for industrial use should not be thought of as limited by the quantity of copper deposits, known or unknown. The transmutation of one chemical element into another is a modern reality, through the methods of nuclear physics. Therefore, the quantity of a natural resource such as copper cannot be calculated even in principle, because copper can be made from other metals.

Which of the following, if true, is the strongest argument against the argument above?

(A) Although it is possible that additional deposits of copper will be found, geological considerations strongly indicate that they will not amount to more than a fifty-year supply.

(B) The production of copper from other metals in industrial quantities would be prohibitively expensive in energy and materials.

(C) Synthetic materials have been discovered that can serve as practical substitutes for copper in most of its uses.

(D) It will be impractical, in the foreseeable future, to mine any deposits of metal that may exist on the Moon or on other planets.

(E) Methods for estimating the amount of copper available in currently known deposits have become very sophisticated and have proved quite accurate.

译文：实际上，工业可用的铜不应受已知的或未知的铜矿贮量所限制。通过核物理上的一些方法把一种化学元素转变成另一种在现代已成为现实。因此像铜这样的自然资源的数量即使在大体上也是无法计算的，因为铜可以由其他金属制成。

下面哪个，如果正确，将对上文论点做出最强有力的驳斥？

(A) 尽管可能找到其他的铜矿，但地质考察已强有力地显示出它们最多只能支撑50年。

(B) 工业用铜如用其他金属炼制，耗费的能源和材料将过分地昂贵。

(C) 人们发现了一些能在铜的大部分应用中替代铜的合成物质。

(D) 在可以预见的将来，去开采在月球上或其他星球上存在的金属是不现实的。

(E) 估算已知铜矿中可利用铜的数量的方法已经变得十分先进和精确。

解析：反对主要反对原因，尤其是当段落推理把"because-clause"放在后面时，往往表示强调这个原因，因此读题重点应放在段落最后一句话。当我们用原因中的关键词copper来定位选项时，发现五个选项均有copper（但这仅仅是一个个案，不能反对一般，大多数题目涉及关键词的选项只有2个或3个）。(B)中的"prohibitively expensive"具有否定意思，所以(B)是一个很好的反对。

15. The excessive number of safety regulations that the federal government has placed on industry poses more serious hardships for big businesses than for small ones. Since large companies do everything on a more massive scale, they must alter more complex operations and spend much more money to meet governmental requirements.

Which of the following, if true, would most weaken the argument above?

(A) Small companies are less likely than large companies to have the capital reserves for improvements.

(B) The operations of small companies frequently rely on the same technologies as the operations of large companies.

(C) Safety regulation codes are uniform, established without reference to size of company.

(D) Large companies typically have more of their profits invested in other businesses than do small companies.

(E) Large companies are in general more likely than small companies to diversify their markets and products.

译文： 联邦政府对产业所规定的数量过多的安全管制规则对大企业造成的严重困难要多于小企业。因为大企业做任何事情都是基于更大的规模，所以他们必须调整更加复杂的操作并且花费更多的钱去达到政府的要求。

以下哪一个，如果正确，将最削弱以上论述？

(A) 小企业比大企业更不大可能有用于改进的资金储备。

(B) 小企业的操作通常与大企业的操作依赖相同的技术。

(C) 安全管制规则不论企业大小都一样。

(D) 大企业通常会比小企业把更多的利润投资于别的产业。

(E) 总体上讲，大企业比小企业更有可能把市场与产品多元化。

解析： 本题推理可提炼为："规则对大企业更加不利，因为大企业大、复杂、花钱多"，当段落把原因放在后半部分，大多是强调原因，因此这类题的反对应着重反对原因。通过对比推理，我们可以把上述推理表示为："规则对小企业更有利，因为小企业花钱少"。若小企业根本不可能有用以改进的储备资金，如(A)所说，那么小企业若必须符合政府安全管制规则，小企业就必定破产，而大企业虽然花钱多，但它毕竟还能够有钱来改进而继续生存，所以(A)直接驳了原因，因此(A)正确；(B)中的"the same technologies"起到了支持作用，并且，"technology"与"operation"不能等价；(C)只能表明规则对大企业与小企业来讲都是公正的，但与上面段落推理的结论"serious hardships"无关；(D)、(E)明显都是做的无关比较，且与"serious hardships"无直接关系，所以(D)、(E)都不正确。

16. Since the Airline Deregulation Act of 1978, major airline companies in the United States have cut their employee ranks by more than 3,000 persons. Thus, although deregulated competition has afforded consumers dramatically lower fares, the economy of the United States has been harmed by deregulation of the airlines.

The argument above would be most seriously weakened if it were true that

(A) a poll of people in the United States expressed exceptionally strong support for airline deregulation.

(B) fewer passengers now travel on commercial airlines than traveled on them in 1978, with the consequence that fewer employees are needed to operate the airlines than were needed in 1978.

(C) airlines now fly a more restricted regular schedule of routes than they did in 1978, with the consequence that

译文： 自从1978年的航空公司管制法通过以来，美国主要的航空公司已经裁减了3000多人。因此尽管放松管制带来的竞争帮消费者大大减低了票价，但美国的经济也受到对航空公司放松管制的破坏。

以上的论述会被最严重地削弱，如果

(A) 美国很多人表达了对解除航空公司管制的强烈支持。

(B) 现在乘坐商业航班的人数要比1978年的人数减少了，结果是运行航班所需的雇员也比1978年少了。

(C) 现在的航班定期飞行的路线比1978年更加少了。因此航空业比1978年以前更加集中了，竞争也更激烈了。

the industry is more highly concentrated and competitive than it was before 1978.

(D) several major airlines now enjoy significantly higher profits and levels of employment than they did in the years preceding the Deregulation Act.

(E) smaller carriers of passengers have thrived as a result of deregulation and now provide more new jobs than the major airlines have eliminated since 1978.

(D) 几家主要的航空公司现在的利润和雇佣水平都比放松管制法通过以前要高了。

(E) 小型的旅客承运商因为该放松管制法案的实施而繁荣起来，现在他们提供的新工作比1978年以来主要航空公司取消的岗位要多。

解析：本题的推理为"因为major airline companies削减了3000多名雇员，所以美国的经济受到了损害"，因此答案应与"人数"有关，或与"经济"有关。不妨做逆向思维，上述推理要想成立的一个隐含假设是"小的航空公司没有增加雇员或增加雇员少于3000人"。反对多反对隐含假设。(E)指出小企业由于放松管制提供了3000多人的就业机会，就直接驳斥了推理中A的可行性，所以(E)为正确答案；(D)中的"several"为个案，并且有可能(D)中所说内容已经包括在原因之中了，所以对段落推理起不到任何作用；(A)的民意调查与推理无关；(B)、(C)均做了无关比较，所以都不可能是正确答案。

请体会第17题的推理模式——A′，not A→B：

17. Some soil scientists have asserted that decaying matter on the forest floor is a far greater source of the acidity in mountain lakes than is the acid rain that falls on these lakes. Therefore, they contend, reducing acid rain will not significantly reduce the acidity levels of mountain lakes.

Which of the following statements, if true, most seriously weakens the argument above?

(A) It is natural for mountain lakes to have acidity levels higher than those of other lakes.

(B) The harmful effects of increased acidity levels in lakes have been greatly underestimated.

(C) Acid rain is found in urban and heavily industrialized regions of the country.

(D) There is much disagreement among soil scientists about the causes of acid rain.

(E) While plant life remains, acid rain significantly increases the amount of decaying organic matter in natural environments.

译文：有些土壤学家声称森林地面的腐烂物比降在湖中的酸雨更会增加高山湖水酸性。因此，他们认为减少酸雨并不一定能明显地降低高山湖泊的酸性水平。

下面哪个论述，如果正确，最严重地削弱了上面的论点？

(A) 高山湖泊的酸性比其他湖泊高是很正常的事。

(B) 人们严重低估了湖水酸性升高的危害。

(C) 能在城市和重工业地区发现酸雨。

(D) 土壤学家对酸雨的成因意见分歧很大。

(E) 如果有植物生命存在，酸雨会显著增加自然环境中腐烂的有机物的数量。

解析：若我们用A′表示森林里的腐烂物质，用A代表酸雨，用B表示山中湖泊酸性增加，那么段落推理可表示为"A′，not A→B"。当段落推理说不是某一原因导致某一结果时，反对大多为"就是这个原因导致了某一结果"，因此应用A中的关键词来定位选项。"A′，not A→B"推理模式的反对思路有二：①就是A导致了B；②A导致了A′。(E)通过指出A导致了A′，起到了反对作用，所以(E)为正确答案；(A)、(B)、(C)、(D)均为无关选项。

三、除了A以外还有别的因素影响B

这种类型的反对主要针对"B，A"推理模式，并且反对主要是反对这种推理模式的隐含假设（假设的反面是反对）。请体会以下两个题目。

18. Earthquakes, volcanic eruptions, and unusual weather have caused many more natural disasters adversely affecting people in the past decade than in previous decades. We can conclude that the planet Earth as a natural environment has become more inhospitable and dangerous, and we should employ the weather and earth sciences to look for causes of this trend.

The conclusion drawn above is most seriously weakened if which of the following is true?

(A) The weather and earth sciences have provided better early warning systems for natural disasters in the past decade than in previous decades.

(B) International relief efforts for victims of natural disasters have been better organized in the past decade than in previous decades.

(C) There are records of major earthquakes, volcanic eruptions, droughts, landslides, and floods occurring in the distant past, as well as in the recent past.

(D) Population pressures and poverty have forced increasing numbers of people to live in areas prone to natural disasters.

(E) There have been no changes in the past decade in people's land-use practices that could have affected the climate.

译文： 地震、火山喷发和异常的天气在最近十年里造成的对人们产生不利影响的自然灾害要比前数十年多得多。我们可以得出结论，作为一种自然环境，地球变得愈加不友善和危险了，我们应该利用气象学和地球学来探寻这种趋向的原因。

下面哪一个，如果正确，将最严重地削弱上述所得结论？

(A) 气象学和地球学在近十年里提供的针对自然灾害的早期预警系统比前数十年要好。

(B) 在近十年里，对受自然灾害的灾民进行的国际救援行动要比前数十年组织得好。

(C) 发生在近十年和前数十年的主要地震、火山爆发、干旱、山崩和洪水均有记录。

(D) 人口压力和贫困迫使越来越多的人住在易受自然灾害影响的地区。

(E) 过去十年里，可能影响气候的土地使用情况并没改变。

解析： 本题是由一个事实而得出结论"地球变得不友好和危险是原因"，属于典型的"B，A"模式，所以反对思路主要是反对段落推理的隐含假设，即用"除了A以外有别的因素影响B"；(D)指出了"population pressures and poverty"这个因素可能影响B，所以(D)正确；由于段落推理的最后一句话是个suggestion，所以(A)只与suggestion有关，但与结论A还有一定的距离，所以(A)不对；(B)与推理无关；(E)排除了其他因素影响B的可能，所以可以作为一个假设；(C)易误选，但(C)是一个无关选项，若(C)在"records"之前加入"the same"，则(C)就变为一个假设。

19. A common misconception is that university hospitals are better than community or private hospitals. In fact, university hospitals have a lower survival rate for patients than do other hospitals. From this it seems clear that the quality of care at university hospitals is lower than that at other hospitals.

Which of the following, if true, most forcefully undermines the argument of the passage above?

(A) Many doctors divide their working hours between a university and a community or private hospital.

译文： 一个常见的误解认为大学的附属医院比社区医院或私人医院要好。实际上，大学的附属医院救活率比其他医院都小。从这点可以清楚地看到大学附属医院的治疗水平比其他医院都低。

下面哪个，如果正确，最强有力地削弱了上文的论证？

(A) 很多医生既在大学工作，又在私人医院工作。

(B) Doctors at university hospitals often earn less than doctors at private hospitals.

(C) University and community hospitals often cannot afford the elaborate facilities of private hospitals.

(D) The emphasis at many university hospitals is on pure research rather than on the treatment and care of patients.

(E) The patients who seek help at university hospitals are usually more seriously ill than those at private or community hospitals.

(B) 在大学附属医院工作的医生赚的钱比私人医院的医生少。

(C) 大学附属医院和社区医院买不起私人医院里的精密设备。

(D) 大学附属医院的重点是纯科学研究，而不是治疗和照顾病人。

(E) 寻求大学附属医院帮助的病人病情通常比在私人或社区医院的病人重。

解析： 本题推理是由一个事实"大学医院里的病人救活率低"而得出一个解释性结论"治疗质量低是原因"，属于"B，A"模式，反对大多用"除了A以外还有别的因素影响B"的思路。(E)指出了一个其他因素，所以(E)正确；(A)、(B)、(C)、(D)均为无关选项。

四、直接反对B

这种类型的反对的问题目的一般已明确告诉B，只要我们用B中的关键词来定位选项，并且选项与B刚好相违背即为正确答案。

20. Public education suffers from what can be diagnosed as the sickness of an overgoverned society. This sickness denies many parents control over the kind of education their children receive. The power once held by parents has gravitated to professional educators. The sickness has been aggravated by increasing centralization and bureaucratization of schools.

Which of the following, if true, would weaken the claim that there is continuing erosion of parents' control over their children's education?

(A) As a result of community pressure, growing numbers of school administrators follow recommendations made by parents.

(B) The number of professional educators has risen sharply over the last decade even though the number of students has declined.

(C) Parents' organizations that lobby for changes in school curriculums are generally ineffectual.

(D) More members of school boards are appointed by school administrators than are elected by the public.

(E) The use of state-wide curriculum programs increased in the Untied States during the past two decades.

译文： 公共教育正在遭受社会管理过度这种疾病的侵袭。这种疾病剥夺了许多家长对孩子接受教育类型的控制权。父母们曾经拥有的这种权利被转移到专职教育人员那里了。而且这种病症随着学校集权化和官僚化而变得日趋严重。

下面哪个，如果正确，会削弱以上关于家长对孩子教育控制减弱这种观点？

(A) 由于社会压力，越来越多的学校管理者听从了家长提出的建议。

(B) 尽管过去十年里学生的数目减少了，但是专职教育人员的数目却大大增加了。

(C) 游说更改学校课程设置的家长组织通常是白费力气。

(D) 大多数学校理事会的成员是由学校管理者任命的，而不是公众选举的。

(E) 在过去20年里，州范围内统一使用的课程方案增加了。

解析： 本题问题目的清晰，可直接用问题目的中的核心关键词"parents"去定位选项，发现(A)、(C)中有"parents"而(C)为支持选项，所以(A)正确。注意：本题若加大难度，可把问题目的中的"the claim"的内容去掉，让大家自己寻求反对内容。这时，若我们用A′表示professional educators，用A表示

parents，用B表示控制孩子的教育，那么段落推理模式为"A′，not A→B"，因此若用"A导致A′"的思路定位选项，发现(A)完全吻合，所以(A)为正确答案。

五、总结

真正在考试现场，我们会发现很难判断考题属于哪一类，但不管是哪一类，反对都最终对推理或结论起作用，所以找到结论非常重要，并且选项应与结论有关；在很多情况下，结论的成立依赖于前提（或假设），所以对于强调原因类型的题目，应把解题重点放在A上，从而迅速正确地解题。下面我们再看一些例题，请大家自己体会属于哪一种类型。

21. During the Second World War, about 375,000 civilians died in the United States and about 408,000 members of the United States armed forces died overseas. On the basis of those figures, it can be concluded that it was not much more dangerous to be overseas in the armed forces during the Second World War than it was to stay at home as a civilian.
Which of the following would reveal most clearly the absurdity of the conclusion drawn above?

(A) Counting deaths among members of the armed forces who served in the United States in addition to deaths among members of the armed forces serving overseas.

(B) Expressing the difference between the numbers of deaths among civilians and members of the armed forces as a percentage of the total number of deaths.

(C) Separating deaths caused by accidents during service in the armed forces from deaths caused by combat injuries.

(D) Comparing death rates per thousand members of each group rather than comparing total numbers of deaths.

(E) Comparing deaths caused by accidents in the United States to deaths caused by combat in the armed forces.

译文：在第二次世界大战中，大约有37.5万名平民在美国本土死亡而有大约40.8万名美国军人在海外死亡。基于这些数字可以得出结论，在第二次世界大战中作为军人派驻海外并不比作为平民留在本土危险很多。

以下哪一项最能清楚地揭示出以上得出的结论的荒谬？

(A) 除了派驻海外的军人死亡数外，将在美国本土死亡的军人数量计算出来。

(B) 把平民的死亡人数和军人死亡人数之间的差别用占全部死亡人数的百分比表达出来。

(C) 把在军队中服役期内由事故引起的死亡从由战斗中受伤而导致的死亡中区分出来。

(D) 比较一下每一种类中每千人的死亡率而不是比较总的死亡人数。

(E) 把在美国由事故造成的死亡人数同军队里在战斗中的死亡人数进行比较。

解析：从两组人中死亡人数接近而得出结论认为在两组人中相对的死亡危险是接近的，这是荒谬的，因为在这里一组人的人数要少的多。选项(D)通过指出需要比较两组的死亡率（这种比较将揭示出人数少的一组有更高的死亡率）从而揭露了这种荒谬。因此，(D)是正确答案；由于该结论承认了平民死亡人数和军人死亡人数的差别，将这种差别表现为百分比，如(B)所述，偏离了主题；选项(A)不合适，因为它只是向被比较的两组人中增加了第三组；因为死亡的原因同本题无关，(C)和(E)是无关选项。

22. A proposed ordinance requires the installation in new homes of sprinklers automatically triggered by the presence of a fire. However, a home builder argued that because more than ninety percent of residential fires are extinguished by a household member, residential sprinklers would only marginally decrease property damage caused by residential fires.

译文：一项拟议中的法令要求在新的住宅中安装一旦出现火情就自动触发的喷水装置，然而，一个住宅建筑商争辩说，因为超过90%的居室火灾是由住户中的人扑灭的，因此居室中的喷水装置只能稍微减轻由居室火灾引起的财产损失。

Which of the following, if true, would most seriously weaken the home builder's argument?

(A) Most individuals have no formal training in how to extinguish fires.

(B) Since new homes are only a tiny percentage of available housing in the city, the new ordinance would be extremely narrow in scope.

(C) The installation of smoke detectors in new residences costs significantly less than the installation of sprinklers.

(D) In the city where the ordinance was proposed, the average time required by the fire department to respond to a fire was less than the national average.

(E) The largest proportion of property damage that results from residential fires is caused by fires that start when no household member is present.

以下哪一项，如果是正确的，将最严重地削弱该住宅建筑商的论述?

(A) 绝大多数人没有受过如何扑灭火灾的正规训练。

(B) 由于新的住宅在城市中可以使用的房屋中只占很小的一部分，这种新的法令在适用范围上将非常狭小。

(C) 在新住宅中安装烟雾探测器将比安装喷水装置的成本低很多。

(D) 在这个拟议该法令的城市，消防部门要求的对火灾做出反应的平均时间低于全国平均水平。

(E) 由居室火灾引起的财产损失中，最大的一部分是由住户中无人在家时发生的火灾造成的。

解析：该住宅建筑商从关于绝大部分居室火灾的证据得出关于喷水装置在防止财产损失方面的有效性的结论，但这个论证是错误的，因为存在一种可能性，即大部分财产损失是由住宅建筑商的证据中排除的少量火灾引起的。如果(E)是正确的，这种可能性就会实现。因此，(E)是正确答案；因为建筑商的论述既与安装喷水装置的成本无关，也与消防部门的表现与其他地方的比较无关，选项(C)和(D)是无关选项；住宅建筑商引述的证据指出为了灭火正规训练［选项(A)］不是必需的；选项(B)支持建筑商的安装喷水装置只有有限效果的观点。

23. With the emergence of biotechnology companies, it was feared that they would impose silence about proprietary results on their in-house researchers and their academic consultants. This constraint, in turn, would slow the development of biological science and engineering.

Which of the following, if true, would tend to weaken most seriously the prediction of scientific secrecy described above?

(A) Biotechnological research funded by industry has reached some conclusions that are of major scientific importance.

(B) When the results of scientific research are kept secret, independent researchers are unable to build on those results.

(C) Since the research priorities of biotechnology companies are not the same as those of academic institutions, the financial support of research by such companies distorts the research agenda.

(D) To enhance the companies' standing in the scientific community, the biotechnology companies encourage employees to publish their results, especially results that are important.

译文：随着生物技术公司的出现，人们害怕这些公司对它们的专职研究员和他们的学术顾问的专利化成果施加沉默。这种抑制，依次地将会减缓生物科学和工程的发展。

以下哪一项，如果是正确的，将有助于最严重地削弱以上描述的关于科学保密的预测?

(A) 由实业界资助的生物技术研究已经取得了一些具有重大科学意义的结果。

(B) 当科学研究的结果作为秘密保存起来时，独立的研究人员无法利用这些结果做进一步发展。

(C) 由于生物技术公司研究的优先次序与学术机构的不同，对这些公司的研究工作提供经济资助扭曲了研究的正常次序。

(D) 为提高公司在科学界的地位，生物技术公司鼓励员工将他们的成果，特别是重要的成果公开发表。

(E) Biotechnology companies devote some of their research resources to problems that are of fundamental scientific importance and that are not expected to produce immediate practical applications.

(E) 生物技术公司将一部分研究资源投入到具有基础性科学意义和并不能期望立即产生实际应用的问题的研究上。

解析：选项(D)通过说明生物技术公司有很强的动机鼓励他们的研究人员公开发表他们的成果，削弱了关于保密的预测，因此，(D)是正确答案。(A)或(B)或(E)都没有提出任何理由来判断该预测是否能实现。选项(A)和(B)支持一个论述，这个论述是如果关于保密的预测实现了，将减缓生物科学和工程的发展；选项(E)提到生物技术公司将一部分资源投入到没有立即现实收益的基础研究，它只是与该论述不矛盾而已，并不能削弱该预测；(C)中指出的研究的正常次序的扭曲与科学保密问题无关。

24. Shelby Industries manufactures and sells the same gauges as Jones Industries. Employee wages account for forty percent of the cost of manufacturing gauges at both Shelby Industries and Jones Industries. Shelby Industries is seeking a competitive advantage over Jones Industries. Therefore, to promote this end, Shelby Industries should lower employee wages.

Which of the following, if true, would most weaken the argument above?

(A) Because they make a small number of precision instruments, gauge manufacturers cannot receive volume discounts on raw materials.

(B) Lowering wages would reduce the quality of employee work, and this reduced quality would lead to lowered sales.

(C) Jones Industries has taken away twenty percent of Shelby Industries' business over the last year.

(D) Shelby Industries pays its employees, on average, ten percent more than does Jones Industries.

(E) Many people who work for manufacturing plants live in areas in which the manufacturing plant they work for is the only industry.

译文：Shelby企业生产和销售与Jones企业一样的仪表。Shelby企业和Jones企业中员工的工资都占了生产仪表成本的40%。Shelby企业正在寻求强于Jones企业的竞争优势。因此，为促使达到这个目的，Shelby企业应该降低员工的工资。

以下哪一项，如果是正确的，将最能削弱以上论述？

(A) 因为他们生产少量的精密仪器，仪表制造商们不能在原材料上获得批量折扣。

(B) 工资降低会降低员工工作质量，这种质量降低将导致销量的下降。

(C) Jones企业去年抢走了Shelby企业20%的生意。

(D) Shelby企业付给它的员工的工资，平均来说，比Jones企业高10%。

(E) 许多为制造业工厂工作的人居住的地区附近，他们工作的制造工厂是唯一的企业。

解析：本题读题重点为最后一句话，属于"就目的提方法"的"B，A"推理模式，反对思路要么为A不可行或无意义；或者除A之外还有别的因素影响B。根据选项(B)，降低工资的效果是充分降低质量从而降低销量，这是一个很好的理由来怀疑工资减少会给Shelby企业带来任何竞争优势。因此，(B)是正确答案。一些其他选项提供了支持，而不是反对降低工资的很好的理由。选项(A)暗示不可能降低原材料成本；选项(D)指出Shelby企业的工资相对较高；选项(E)指出如果Shelby企业降低工资，它不会失去很多工人；选项(C)给出了一个理由让Shelby企业去关注它的竞争地位，但没有给出削减工资将不会改善这种地位的理由。

25. Red blood cells in which the malarial-fever parasite resides are eliminated from a person's body after 120 days. Because the parasite cannot travel to a new generation of red blood cells, any fever that develops in a person more than 120

译文：疟疾热寄生虫的血红细胞在120天后被排除出人体，因为这种寄生虫无法移到新一代的血红细胞内。在一个人迁移到一个没有疟疾的地区120天后，发

days after that person has moved to a malaria-free region is not due to the malarial parasite.

Which of the following, if true, most seriously weakens the conclusion above?

(A) The fever caused by the malarial parasite may resemble the fever caused by flu viruses.

(B) The anopheles mosquito, which is the principal insect carrier of the malarial parasite, has been eradicated in many parts of the world.

(C) Many malarial symptoms other than the fever, which can be suppressed with antimalarial medication, can reappear within 120 days after the medication is discontinued.

(D) In some cases, the parasite that causes malarial fever travels to cells of the spleen, which are less frequently eliminated from a person's body than are red blood cells.

(E) In any region infested with malaria-carrying mosquitoes, there are individuals who appear to be immune to malaria.

生在这个人身上的任何发烧情况都不是由疟疾热寄生虫引起的。

以下哪一项，如果是正确的，将最严重地削弱以上结论？

(A) 疟疾寄生虫引起的发烧可能同流感病毒引起的发烧相似。

(B) 主要的疟疾寄生虫携带者是疟蚊，在世界上很多地区已经被消灭了。

(C) 除发烧外的很多疟疾的其他症状，能被抗疟疾药物抑制，但在停用药物后120天内会重新出现。

(D) 在某些情况下，引起疟疾热的寄生虫可以移动到脾细胞中，而脾细胞被清除出人体的频率比血红细胞的频率低。

(E) 在任何携带疟疾的蚊子大量存在的地区，有一些人对疟疾有免疫能力。

解析：该短文得出结论，因为疟疾寄生虫不能在血红细胞中寄居超过120天，在传染发生120天之后，那些疟疾寄生虫就不能引起发热了。然而，根据(D)，人体内有一个地方该寄生虫可以在传染之后寄居超过120天，因此，(D)削弱了该结论并成为正确答案；选项(A)仅指出疟疾热的症状与其他疾病的症状相似，选项(C)仅指出别的疟疾热症状的存在，选项(E)仅指出了对疟疾免疫的可能性，但这三个选项均与在什么条件下会出现疟疾热的问题无关；选项(B)确认了有没有疟疾的地区存在，但同该结论没有其他关系。

26. The number of people diagnosed as having a certain intestinal disease has dropped significantly in a rural county this year, as compared to last year, health officials attribute this decrease entirely to improved sanitary conditions at water-treatment plants, which made for cleaner water this year and thus reduced the incidence of the disease.

Which of the following, if true, would most seriously weaken the health officials' explanation for the lower incidence of the disease?

(A) Many new water-treatment plants have been built in the last five years in the rural county.

(B) Bottled spring water has not been consumed in significantly different quantities by people diagnosed as having the intestinal disease, as compared to people who did not contract the disease.

(C) Because of a new diagnostic technique, many people who until this year would have been diagnosed as having the intestinal disease are now correctly diagnosed as suffering from intestinal ulcers.

译文：在某乡村，同去年相比，诊断为患上某种肠道疾病的人数大大下降。卫生部门的官员把这种下降完全归功于水处理厂卫生条件的改善，从而今年产出更清洁的水，并因此减少了该种疾病的发生。

以下哪一项，如果是正确的，将最严重地削弱该卫生部门官员对于该疾病发生率降低的解释？

(A) 在该乡村，过去的5年中，修建了许多新的水处理厂。

(B) 同没有患上该病的人相比，那些被诊断为患上该肠道疾病的人消费瓶装矿泉水的数量没有很大不同。

(C) 由于一项新诊断技术，很多直到今年还会被诊断为患上该肠道疾病的人现在能被正确地诊断为患肠溃疡。

(D) Because of medical advances this year, far fewer people who contract the intestinal disease will develop severe cases of the disease.

(E) The water in the rural county was brought up to the sanitary standards of the water in neighboring counties ten years ago.

(D) 由于今年的医疗进步，患上该肠道疾病的人中少得多的人病情会进一步恶化。

(E) 该乡村的水质10年前就已达到邻县的卫生标准。

解析：该卫生部门官员的解释做了一个假设，被诊断为患上该病的人数的减少准确地反映了该病实际发生的减少，通过指出这一点是错误的，(C)削弱了该官员的解释，因此是正确答案；由于(A)支持卫生条件已经改善的观点，它有助于支持该官员的解释；(B)同样如此，(B)排除了这一因素，这个因素本可以将那些患病的和没有患病的区分开来，因此也排除了一种替代解释；诊断出来的病情的严重程度的减少（选项D）与该官员的解释无关；由于邻县他们自己的卫生标准可能并不充分，E并没削弱该官员的解释。

27. Most archaeologists have held that people first reached the Americas less than 20,000 years ago by crossing a land bridge into North America. But recent discoveries of human shelters in South America dating from 32,000 years ago have led researchers to speculate that people arrived in South America first, after voyaging across the Pacific, and then spread northward.

Which of the following, if it were discovered, would be pertinent evidence against the speculation above?

(A) A rock shelter near Pittsburgh, Pennsylvania, contains evidence of use by human beings 19,000 years ago.

(B) Some North American sites of human habitation predate any sites found in South America.

(C) The climate is warmer at the 32,000-year-old South American site than at the oldest known North American site.

(D) The site in South America that was occupied 32,000 years ago was continuously occupied until 6,000 years ago.

(E) The last Ice Age, between 11,500 and 20,000 years ago, considerably lowered worldwide sea levels.

译文：很多考古学家曾有这样的观点，在不到2万年以前，人类通过一个陆地桥进入北美大陆到达美国。但最近在南美发现的测定时间为3.2万年以前的人类遗址，使研究者们猜想人类先坐船横穿太平洋到达南美洲，然后向北扩展。

以下哪一项，如果被发现，将成为反对以上猜想的恰当证据？

(A) 宾州匹兹堡附近一个石头作的遗址发现有被1.9万年前的人类使用过的证据。

(B) 一些北美的人类遗址比任何在南美发现的遗址时间要早。

(C) 这个有3.2万年历史的南美遗址比发现的最古老的北美遗址所在的气候更加温暖。

(D) 南美的遗址在3.2万年以前有人居住后，一直有人居位，直到6000年前。

(E) 上一个冰纪，在1.15万年到2万年以前，使世界海平面大大下降了。

解析：该研究者猜想人们首先到达南美，这个猜想后面的推理是没有比在南美发现的人类遗址之前更早的北美遗址的证据。如果发现，如(B)所述，一些北美遗址比南美遗址更古老，该猜想后面的推理就无法成立，因此，(B)是正确答案；(A)和(E)中提到的事实都发生在短文讨论的事物之后的时间段，因此没有与该猜想产生矛盾；尽管(C)和(D)描述了关于南美遗址的发现，但(C)中提到的相对气候和(D)中提到的居住的时间长短，都没有提供反对该猜想的证据。

28. Since the mayor's publicity campaign for Greenville's bus service began six months ago, morning automobile traffic into the midtown area of the city has decreased seven percent.

译文：自从6个月前开始的市长公开呼吁乘坐Greenville's公共汽车的宣传活动以来，早上进入该城市中心地区的汽车流

During the same period, there has been an equivalent rise in the number of persons riding buses into the midtown area. Obviously, the mayor's publicity campaign has convinced many people to leave their cars at home and ride the bus to work.

Which of the following, if true, casts the most serious doubt on the conclusion drawn above?

(A) Fares for all bus routes in Greenville have risen an average of five percent during the past six months.

(B) The mayor of Greenville rides the bus to City Hall in the city's midtown area.

(C) Road reconstruction has greatly reduced the number of lanes available to commuters in major streets leading to the midtown area during the past six months.

(D) The number of buses entering the midtown area of Greenville during the morning hours is exactly the same now as it was one year ago.

(E) Surveys show that longtime bus riders are no more satisfied with the Greenville bus service than they were before the mayor's publicity campaign began.

量减少了7%。同一段时间里，搭乘公共汽车进入市中心地区的人数有相等数量的增加。显然，市长的公开宣传活动说服很多人将汽车留在家里，搭乘公共汽车去上班。

以下哪一项，如果是正确的，对以上得出的结论提出了最严重的质疑？

(A) Greenville所有路线公共汽车的车费在过去的6个月里平均上涨了5%。

(B) Greenville市长经常乘坐公共汽车去位于城市中心地区的市政厅。

(C) 在过去的6个月里，由于道路翻修，使通往中心地区主要街道的通勤车可以使用的车道大大减少。

(D) 现在早上进入Greenville市中心地区的公共汽车数量与一年前完全相同。

(E) 调查显示，长期乘坐公共汽车的乘客对Greenville公共汽车现在的服务不比市长公开宣传活动以前更满意。

解析：短文得出结论，市长公开宣传活动说服人们乘公共汽车去上班而不是开车去，并且它把早上汽车流量的减少和进入市中心地区公共汽车乘客的增加引为证据。但(C)中描述的道路翻修为这个证据提出一个替代性的解释。因此(C)是正确答案；选项(A)排除了更低的票价作为乘客增加的一种可能的解释，因此它支持而不是质疑该结论；同样地(D)和(E)都排除了一种可能的解释：(D)中公共汽车数量未变和(E)中长期的公共汽车乘客的态度表明乘客的增加不能用服务改善来解释；(B)中提到的，市长乘坐公共汽车，可能有助于公开宣传活动的效果，但同评价该宣传活动是否使乘客增加无关。

29. Most consumers do not get much use out of the sports equipment they purchase. For example, seventeen percent of the adults in the United States own jogging shoes, but only forty-five percent of the owners jog more than once a year, and only seventeen percent jog more than once a week.

Which of the following, if true, casts most doubt on the claim that most consumers get little use out of the sports equipment they purchase?

(A) Joggers are most susceptible to sports injuries during the first six months in which they jog.

(B) Joggers often exaggerate the frequency with which they jog in surveys designed to elicit such information.

(C) Many consumers purchase jogging shoes for use in activities other than jogging.

(D) Consumers who take up jogging often purchase an athletic shoe that can be used in other sports.

译文：大多数顾客不经常使用他们购买的运动器材。例如，美国17%的成年人有慢跑鞋但是有慢跑鞋的人中只有45%的人一年的慢跑次数多于一次，只有17%的人每周慢跑次数多于一次。

以下哪一项，如果是正确的，对于大多数顾客很少使用他们购买的运动器材的宣称提出了最严重的质疑？

(A) 慢跑者在他们慢跑最初6个月里最容易在运动中受伤。

(B) 在得出以上信息的这项调查中，慢跑者经常夸大他们从事慢跑活动的频率。

(C) 许多顾客购买慢跑鞋是为参加慢跑以外的活动。

(D) 参加慢跑活动的顾客经常购买一双田径鞋，可以在其他运动中使用。

(E) Joggers who jog more than once a week are often active participants in other sports as well.

(E) 每周慢跑次数多于一次的慢跑者通常也是其他运动项目的积极参与者。

解析： 大多数顾客很少使用他们购买的运动器材的宣称从慢跑鞋不经常用来慢跑得到了支持，这种推理忽视了慢跑鞋用于其他目的的可能性，因此，选项(C)是正确答案；因为受伤的慢跑者更不可能使用他们的慢跑鞋，选项(A)不合适；如果(B)是正确的，慢跑者使用慢跑鞋的次数比该研究引述的更少，因此，(B)不合适；因为在(D)和(E)中分别提到的顾客和慢跑者最有可能是那些经常使用运动器材和那些论述中承认其存在的人。

30. A drug that is highly effective in treating many types of infection can, at present, be obtained only from the bark of the Ibora, a tree that is quite rare in the wild. It takes the bark of 5,000 trees to make one kilogram of the drug. It follows, therefore, that continued production of the drug must inevitably lead to the Ibora's extinction.

Which of the following, if true, most seriously weakens the argument above?

(A) The drug made from Ibora bark is dispensed to doctors from a central authority.
(B) The drug made from Ibora bark is expensive to produce.
(C) The leaves of the Ibora are used in a number of medical products.
(D) The Ibora can be propagated from cuttings and grown under cultivation.
(E) The Ibora generally grows in largely inaccessible places.

译文： 一种治疗许多感染非常有效的药物目前只能从Ibora的树皮中获得，这种树野生状态下非常稀少，而制造一公斤该药物要用5000棵树的树皮。因此，也就是说，继续生产该药物必然会不可避免地导致Ibora的灭绝。

以下哪一项，如果是正确的，将最严重地削弱以上论述？

(A) 用Ibora树皮制造的药物由中央当局发放给医生。
(B) 用Ibora树皮来制造该药物，生产起来很昂贵。
(C) 许多医药制品都使用了Ibora的树叶。
(D) Ibora可以通过插条繁殖，在人工种养下生长。
(E) Ibora通常生长在人们不可能到达的地方。

解析： 如果人类可以成功地种植Ibora，就可能在不威胁Ibora生存的情况下继续生产该药物，因此，选项(D)是正确答案；如果生产继续，生产出来以后分配该药物的方法〔选项(A)〕不可能仅凭此得到Ibora继续生存的结果；药物的价格〔选项(B)〕也不可能；如果Ibora的树叶也有用处〔选项(C)〕，那么Ibora灭绝的危险增强了而不是减弱了；最后，如果Ibora大部分生长在人类无法到达的地方〔选项(E)〕，这与该药物的生产是否能继续的问题有关，但与如果生产继续下去将发生什么无关。

31. A group of children of various ages was read stories in which people caused harm, some of those people doing so intentionally, and some accidentally. When asked about appropriate punishments for those who had caused harm, the younger children, unlike the older ones, assigned punishments that did not vary according to whether the harm was done intentionally or accidentally. Younger children, then, do not regard people's intentions as relevant to punishment.

Which of the following, if true, would most seriously weaken the conclusion above?

译文： 向一群不同年龄的小孩讲述人们做坏事的故事，其中有一些人是故意做的坏事而一些人是无意的。当被问及对那些做坏事的人如何进行惩罚时，年纪小一些的孩子，与年纪大一些的孩子不同，提出的惩罚方式没有因这种坏事是有意做的还是无意做的而不同，那么年纪小一些的孩子不认为人们的意愿与惩罚方式有联系。

以下哪一项，如果是正确的，将最严重地削弱以上结论？

(A) In interpreting these stories, the listeners had to draw on a relatively mature sense of human psychology in order to tell whether harm was produced intentionally or accidentally.

(B) In these stories, the severity of the harm produced was clearly stated.

(C) Younger children are as likely to produce harm unintentionally as are older children.

(D) The older children assigned punishment in a way that closely resembled the way adults had assigned punishment in a similar experiment.

(E) The younger children assigned punishments that varied according to the severity of the harm done by the agents in the stories.

(A) 在理解这些故事时，听者必须借助于一些人类心理中相对成熟的心智来区分坏事是有意造成的还是无意造成的。

(B) 这些故事中清楚地指明了所做坏事的严重程度。

(C) 年纪小一些的孩子们和年纪大一些的孩子们一样容易无意中做坏事。

(D) 年纪大一些的孩子提出的惩罚方式与成人们在类似试验中提出的惩罚方式非常相似。

(E) 年纪小一些的孩子提出的惩罚方式根据故事中的人做的坏事的严重程度不同而不同。

解析：选项(A)为正确答案，指出年纪小一些的孩子可能不能区分故事中的坏事是否是有意造成的。因此，即使年纪小一些的孩子确实认为人们的意愿是相关因素，他们在这里也可能不能够应用这项标准，因此，(A)削弱了对于该结论的支持；选项(B)和(E)通过指出另一个因素——坏事的严重程度，要么可能［选项(B)］要么实际上［选项(E)］促使年纪小一些的孩子在提出的惩罚方式上的变化来支持该结论。选项(C)和选项(D)都不影响该结论，该结论关注孩子们如何认识其他人的行为，不是孩子们自己的行为［选项(C)］。年纪大一些的孩子和成年人提出的方案的相似性［选项(D)］没有回答为什么年纪小一些的孩子提出的方案会不同这一问题。

32. The program to control the entry of illegal drugs into the country was a failure in 1987. If the program had been successful, the wholesale price of most illegal drugs would not have dropped substantially in 1987.

The argument in the passage would be most seriously weakened if it were true that

(A) in 1987 smugglers of illegal drugs, as a group, had significantly more funds at their disposal than did the country's customs agents.

(B) domestic production of illegal drugs increased substantially in 1987.

(C) the author's statements were made in order to embarrass the officials responsible for the drug-control program.

(D) in 1987 illegal drugs entered the country by a different set of routes than they did in 1986.

(E) the country's citizens spent substantially more money on illegal drugs in 1987 than they did in 1986.

译文：1987年的控制违法药物进入该国的计划是个失败。如果该计划成功了，1987年大多数违法药物的批发价将不会大幅下降。

如果以下哪一项是正确的，将最严重地削弱短文中的论述？

(A) 1987年，违法药物的走私者，作为一个组织比该国海关部门控制了多得多的资金。

(B) 1987年违法药物的国内生产显著增加。

(C) 作者发出这些言论只是为使负责药物控制计划的官员们感到尴尬。

(D) 1987年进入该国的违法药物是经过一组与1986年不同的路线进入该国的。

(E) 该国公民1987年花在违法药物上的钱比1986年多得多。

解析：如果国内生产的违法药物显著增加，总供给就可能在没有更多违法药物进入该国和该计划没有任何失败的情况下上升（从而价格下降）。因此，选项(B)是正确答案；其他选项没有削弱该论述。走私者有更多的钱［选项(A)］说明他们可能有能力避开控制。该作者的意图［选项(C)］与该论述表达的推理是否有说服力无关；路线的改变［选项(D)］可能会增加该计划失败的可能性；花费钱的数量的增加［选项(E)］在给定的价格水平降低的情况下，也提供了该计划的确失败的证据。

33. When hypnotized subjects are told that they are deaf and are then asked whether they can hear the hypnotist, they reply, "No." Some theorists try to explain this result by arguing that the selves of hypnotized subjects are dissociated into separate parts, and that the part that is deaf is dissociated from the part that replies.

Which of the following challenges indicates the most serious weakness in the attempted explanation described above?

(A) Why does the part that replies not answer, "Yes"?

(B) Why are the observed facts in need of any special explanation?

(C) Why do the subjects appear to accept the hypnotist's suggestion that they are deaf?

(D) Why do hypnotized subjects all respond the same way in the situation described?

(E) Why are the separate parts of the self the same for all subjects?

译文：当告诉被催眠的受试人说他们是聋子，然后问他们是否能听到催眠师说的话，他们回答说"听不到"。一些理论家通过证明，被催眠的受试人的自身被分隔为单独的各部分，并且聋的部分与回答的部分是分隔开的，来试图解释这个结果。

以下哪一项质问将指出以上所描述的尝试性的解释的最严重的弱点？

(A) 为什么回答的那部分不回答"听到了"？

(B) 为什么观测到的事实需要特殊的解释？

(C) 为什么受试人看上去接受了催眠师提出的他们是聋子的暗示？

(D) 为什么被催眠的受试人在描述的情形下都以同样的方式做出了回应？

(E) 为什么所有受试人自身分开的部分是相同的？

解析：由于该问题引出了回答，可以推测出听到了该问题，但不能推测出是被聋的部分听到的。因此，该解释明显的弱点是没有指出为什么负责回答的部分好像它就是那个聋的部分一样做出回答，选项(A)指出了这个问题，是正确答案；选项(B)没有询问这个解释本身，而是把是否需要一种解释放在第一位；选项(C)和(D)提出与描述的事实有关的问题，但没有提到对于这些事实做出的解释；选项(E)提出了一个由该尝试性的解释引起的问题，但没有质问该解释是否充分。

六、试题精练及解析

1. Many researchers believe that the presence of RNA in brain cells is the biochemical basis of memory; that is, the presence of RNA enables us to remember. Because certain chemicals are known to inhibit the synthesis of RNA in the body, we can test this hypothesis. Animals that have learned particular responses can be injected with an RNA inhibitor and then tested for memory of the learned responses.

Which of the following test results would most seriously weaken the case for RNA as the basis of memory?

(A) After an injection of RNA inhibitor, a wide range of behaviors in addition to the learned responses were affected.

很多研究者认为脑细胞中的RNA是记忆的生物化学基础，也就是说，RNA的存在使我们能够进行记忆。由于已知某些化学物质能阻碍体内RNA的合成，我们可以用此来检验上面的假设。先给已学会某种反应的动物注射一种RNA抑制剂，然后再检测其对学过的反应的记忆。

下面哪个检测结果最严重地削弱了RNA是记忆基础的说法？

(A) 注射过RNA抑制剂后，除了学过的反应在内，很大范围内的行为都受到了影响。

(B) After an injection of RNA inhibitor, animals that had not consistently been giving the learned responses were able to give them consistently.

(C) After injections of RNA inhibitor, some animals lost memory of the learned responses totally but others lost it only partially.

(D) After a small injection of RNA inhibitor, animals responded well, but as the size of the injection increased, they gave fewer of the learned responses.

(E) After an injection of RNA inhibitor, animals could not learn a new response.

2. It was long thought that a now-rare disease of the joints, alkaptonuria, was epidemic in Egypt 2,500 years ago. Evidence came from the high proportion of mummies from that period showing symptoms of the disease. Recently, however, chemical analyses of skeletons have led scientists to propose that the joint damage was actually caused by chemicals used by Egyptian embalmers.

Which of the following, if true, would additionally weaken the traditional view that alkaptonuria afflicted many Egyptians 2,500 years ago?

(A) X-rays of the mummies showed shadows that clearly suggested joint damage, and recent inspection of the skeletons has confirmed that hypothesis.

(B) Although alkaptonuria is a disease that can be inherited, it did not appear in the descendants of the Egyptian population in which the symptoms were found.

(C) Egyptian embalming methods were highly secret, and scientists are still not certain of the nature of some of the chemicals that were used.

(D) Possible evidence of alkaptonuria has been pointed out in pictures representing the human figure found on artifacts left by other Middle Eastern cultures of that period.

(E) Some mummies of that period show no evidence of joint damage at all.

3. Psychological maladjustment in children is caused by the stress of the birthing process as is proved by the discovery of a positive relationship between the duration of the mother's labor and the amount of time the child spent crying in the first month of life.

（B）注射过RNA抑制剂后，那些原来不能连续做出学过的反应的动物能连贯地做出反应。

（C）注射过RNA抑制剂后，一部分动物丧失了全部学过的反应的记忆，而另一部分则部分丧失了对此的记忆。

（D）注射过少量RNA抑制剂后，动物能做出良好的反应，但随着注射量的增加，它们的反应便越来越少了。

（E）注射过RNA抑制剂后，动物不能再学会另一种新反应了。

很久以来，人们一直认为一种现在很罕见的关节病——alkaptonuria——2500年前在埃及很流行。证据来源于相当高比率的木乃伊上表现出这种疾病的症状。然而，最近对头盖骨的化学分析已经使科学家们得出一个推论：关节损害实际上是由埃及香料师所使用的化学试剂造成的。

下面哪个，如果正确，会进一步削弱那种传统的认为2500年前alkaptonuria折磨了许多埃及人的看法？

（A）木乃伊的X射线显示出了清晰表明关节痛的阴影，而最近对头盖骨的考察已经证明了该假设。

（B）尽管alkaptonuria这种疾病是可遗传的，但是有此类症状的埃及人的后代并没患这种疾病。

（C）埃及人防止尸体腐烂的方法是高度保密的，科学家仍不能确定一些他们使用的化学试剂的性质。

（D）alkaptonuria这种疾病的证据已经在一些人体轮廓的图片上找到了，这些图片是在那个时期其他中东文化遗留的古迹中发现的。

（E）那个时期的一些木乃伊根本没有显示出关节损害的迹象。

儿童心理失调是由婴儿在分娩过程中受到的压力而导致的。这一点已得到了证实——人们发现母亲分娩的时间和婴儿出生后第一个月中啼哭的时间有正比的关系。

Which of the following, if true, LEAST damages the author's assertion?

(A) There is no relationship between the amount of time spent crying and psychological maladjustment.

(B) Behavior indicative of psychological maladjustment does not appear until the third month of a child's life.

(C) From the infant's point of view, a hurried labor is more stressful than a gradual, slow delivery.

(D) The estimates of the duration of labor were based on obstetricians' estimates of the time of the onset of labor.

(E) The infants who have experienced the greatest stress during birth are often too weak to cry for extended periods of time.

下面哪个，如果正确，最不能破坏作者的宣称？

(A) 哭的时间和心理失调之间毫无关系。

(B) 婴儿心理失调的行为迹象到其长到三个月大时才会显现出来。

(C) 从婴儿角度看，在很快的分娩中受到的压力要大于缓慢的分娩。

(D) 分娩时间的估算依据于产科医生对分娩前阵痛时间的估算。

(E) 那些在出生时经受了很大压力的婴儿经常由于太虚弱而在出生后无力哭喊。

4. Found in caves with the bones of australopithecines, which are thought by some to be ancient ancestors of the human species, were great collections of animal bones. From the frequencies of types of bones, it can be seen that many bones represented only parts of animals that must have died elsewhere. The australopithecines thus must have been mighty hunters, to have brought home so much meat.

Which of the following, if true, most seriously weakens the conclusion drawn above?

(A) The australopithecines sometimes moved from cave to cave for shelter and did not remain in one cave for a lifetime.

(B) The australopithecine bones found in the caves were those of adult males, adult females, and juveniles.

(C) Evidence of the use of fire was absent from the caves in which the collections of bones were found.

(D) Marks on the bones, including the bones of the australopithecines, are consistent with teeth marks of large catlike animals of the period.

(E) The bones in the cave did not include bones of an elephantlike animal that existed in the area at the time of the australopithecines.

在有australopithecine人——有人认为其是人类的祖先——遗骨的洞穴中发现了很多动物遗骨。从各种骨头出现的频率看，许多动物是死在别处后，只有身体的某些部分被带回了洞穴中。所以，能带回这么多猎物，australopithecine人一定是很英勇的猎人。

下面哪个，如果正确，最严重地削弱了上文结论？

(A) australopithecine人有时在洞穴之间搬来搬去以寻找庇护，他们一生不只呆在一个洞穴中。

(B) 在洞穴中发现的australopithecine人的遗骨是成年男女和少年人的。

(C) 在发现聚集了动物遗骨的洞穴中没有用火的证据。

(D) 包括australopithecine人遗骨在内的所有骨头上的印迹都是那个时代的一种大型猫样动物的牙印。

(E) 洞穴中的遗骨不包括与australopithecine人同时期的一种大象类动物的骨头。

5. The ratio of divorces to marriages has increased since 1940. Therefore, there must be a greater proportion of children living with only one natural parent than there was in 1940.

Which of the following, if true, most strongly weakens the inference drawn above?

(A) The number of marriages entered into by women twenty-five to thirty-five years old has decreased since 1940.

从1940年以来，离婚结婚的比例增大了，因此，现在生活在单亲家庭中的儿童比例也一定比1940年时要大了。

下面哪个，如果正确，最强有力地削弱了以上得出的推断？

(A) 自1940年以来，妇女在25～35岁间结婚的人数减少了。

(B) When there is a divorce, children are often given the option of deciding which parent they will live with.

(C) Since 1940 the average number of children in a family has remained approximately steady and has not been subject to wide fluctuations.

(D) Before 1940 relatively few children whose parents had both died were adopted into single-parent families.

(E) The proportion of children who must be raised by one parent because the other has died has decreased since 1940 as a result of medical advances.

(B) 离婚时，孩子通常有权选择跟哪位家长生活在一起。

(C) 1940年以来，家庭中孩子的数目大致保持稳定，并且没有大幅度的波动。

(D) 1940年以前，父母双亡后被单亲家庭收养的孩子是比较少的。

(E) 由于医学的进步，1940年以来，由于父母中一位去世而由另一位家长抚养的孩子比例减小了。

6. Noting that the number of crimes committed in a certain city had decreased in 1982 by 5.2 percent in comparison with 1981, the police chief of the city said, "We see here the result of the innovative police program put into effect in the city at the beginning of 1982."

Which of the following, if true, most seriously weakens the conclusion drawn by the police chief?

(A) Several cities that have recently increased spending for police programs experienced no decrease in crime in 1982, as compared with 1981.

(B) The number of crimes committed in the city is estimated, by the same method each year, from the number of crimes reported.

(C) The number of crimes committed in the suburban areas surrounding the city rose by about 5 percent in 1982 over the figure for 1981 and were nearly equal in number to those in the city in 1982.

(D) The number of crimes committed in the city in 1982 was 10 percent higher than the number committed in 1972.

(E) The size of the age group most likely to commit crimes decreased considerably in the city in 1982, as against 1981, because of a declining birth rate.

注意到某城市1982年的犯罪率与1981年相比下降了5.2%，该城市的警察局长说，"我们现在看到了1982年年初开始在该城实施的革新警察计划的结果了"。

下面哪个，如果正确，最严重地削弱了警长得出的结论？

(A) 若干最近增加用在警察计划上的开销的城市1982年犯罪率并未比1981年有所下降。

(B) 该城市通过报告犯罪数目估计实际犯罪数目，每年使用的估计方法是一样的。

(C) 在环绕城市的郊区发生的犯罪数目在1982年比1981年高出5%，并且总数目与1982年城市内的犯罪数目基本相同。

(D) 1982年城市的犯罪数比1972年的数目高10%。

(E) 城市内最易犯罪年龄段的人数在1982年比1981年有相当的减少，原因是出生率的降低。

7. Our words are meaningless and cannot be distinguished from their opposites, as can be proved by an example. People think that they know the difference between the meanings of "bald" and "having hair." Suppose an average person twenty-one years of age has N hairs on his or her head. We say that that person is not bald but has hair. But surely one hair less would make no difference, and a person with N-1 hairs on his or her head would be said to have hair. Suppose we kept on, with one hair less each time. The result would be the same. But what would be the difference between someone who

我们的词汇是无意义的并且无法与其反义词区分开来，举一个例子可以证明这一点。人们认为他们知道"秃头"与"有头发"之间的区别。假设一个21岁的普通人头上有N根头发。我们说这个人不是秃头而是有头发的。但是少一根头发当然不会有什么分别，有N-1根头发的人会被说成有头发。假设我们继续，每次减少一根头发，结果将是相同的。但是有一根头发的人和没有头发的人的区别是什么呢？我

had one hair and someone who had none? We call them both bald. Nowhere can we make a distinction between "bald" and "having hair."

Which of the following statements best counters the argument above?

(A) The word "bald" can be translated into other languages.

(B) A word can have more than one meaning.

(C) A word such as "cat" can be applied to several animals that differ in some respects.

(D) Words can lack precision without being meaningless.

(E) People cannot think clearly without using words.

8. In a recent study, sedentary middle-aged men who drink more than two cups of coffee a day were found more likely than other sedentary middle-aged men to have a high blood level of cholesterol, which is a factor increasing risk of heart disease. Cholesterol can reach the blood from food and drink but is not contained in coffee.

Which of the following, if true, most seriously weakens a conclusion from the study that for sedentary middle-aged men coffee increases the risk of heart attack?

(A) A sedentary style of life increases levels of cholesterol in the blood.

(B) Coffee contains caffeine, which acts as a stimulant that increases heart rate.

(C) The men studied drank their coffee without milk or cream, which contain cholesterol.

(D) In both groups, the men were likely to be overweight, and excess weight is a factor that increases risk of heart diseases.

(E) The men who drank more than two cups of coffee a day also ate more foods high in cholesterol.

9. The Occupational Safety and Health Administration (OSHA) was established to protect workers from accidents and unsafe conditions on the job. There has actually been an increase in the number of job-related accidents under OSHA. This demonstrates the agency's ineffectiveness.

Which of the following, if true, concerning the period during which the increase occurred, most seriously weakens the argument above?

(A) A number of job categories, excluded from the jurisdiction of OSHA in the legislation originally establishing the agency, have continued to be outside OSHA's jurisdiction.

们把他们都称之为秃头。我们没有能区分"秃头"和"有头发"的地方。

下面的哪个陈述最能反驳上面结论?

(A) "秃头"一词可以翻译为其他语言。

(B) 一个词可以有不止一个意思。

(C) 像"猫"这样的词可以被用于在某些方面不同的几种动物上面。

(D) 词汇可以缺乏准确却不至于无意义。

(E) 人们不用词汇就无法清楚地进行思考。

最近的一项研究发现,每天喝两杯以上咖啡的从事久坐工作的中年男子比其他从事久坐工作的中年男子更可能血液胆固醇含量高,而胆固醇是患心脏病可能性增加的一个因素。胆固醇能够由饮食进入血液,但咖啡中不含该物。

下面哪个,如果正确,最严重地削弱了该研究的一个结论:咖啡增加从事久坐工作的中年男子得心脏病的危险?

(A) 久坐的生活方式增加血液中的胆固醇含量。

(B) 咖啡里含有咖啡因,而咖啡因刺激心跳加速。

(C) 被观察者喝的咖啡中没有加含有胆固醇的奶或奶油。

(D) 在两组人之中的男人可能有些超重,而多余的体重又是增加心脏病的可能的因素。

(E) 每日喝两杯以上咖啡的男人还吃更多胆固醇含量高的食物。

职业安全与健康署(缩写OSHA)的成立是为了保护工人免遭事故及远离工作中的危险条件。在存在OSHA的情况下,与工作相关的事故数量实际上有所增加。这显示了该机构的无能。

下面哪个关于事故增加发生期间的陈述,如果正确,将最严重地削弱以上的论证?

(A) 很多种工作在OSHA最初成立时的立法中被排出在其管辖范围之外,现在继续处于其管辖范围之外。

(B) OSHA has been assigned a greater number of kinds of workplace activities to monitor.

(C) There has been an increase in the total number of people at work, and the ratio of work-related deaths and injuries to size of work force has fallen in OSHA-supervised occupations.

(D) Regulations issued by OSHA have met with political criticism from elected officials and the mass media.

(E) The increase in job-related accidents has occurred mainly in a single job category, whereas the number of job-related accidents has remained approximately constant in other categories.

10. Being an only child has little to do with a child's social development. A recent study that followed thirty only children and thirty-five first-born children to the age of three found that the two groups of children behaved very similarly to each other toward their peers, their parents, and other adults.

Which of the following, if true, most weakens the conclusion drawn above?

(A) The groups being compared did not contain the same number of children.

(B) More time was spent observing the interactions of children with their mothers than with their fathers.

(C) Most of the researchers involved in the study were persons who had no brothers or sisters.

(D) The first-born children were, on the average, nearly three when their parents had the second children.

(E) The "other adults" described in the study consisted mainly of members of the research team.

11. Geographers and historians have traditionally held the view that Antarctica was first sighted around 1820, but some sixteenth-century European maps show a body that resembles the polar landmass, even though explorers of the period never saw it. Some scholars, therefore, argue that the continent must have been discovered and mapped by the ancients, whose maps are known to have served as models for the European cartographers.

Which of the following, if true, is most damaging to the inference drawn by the scholars?

(A) The question of who first sighted Antarctica in modern times is still much debated, and no one has been able to present conclusive evidence.

(B) OSHA被分配到更多种类的工作场所去进行监督。

(C) 工作的工人总数有所增加，而在OSHA监管的职业中，与工作相关的死伤数与劳动力数量之比有所下降。

(D) OSHA发布的规章制度遭到当选的官员和大众媒体的政治批评。

(E) 与工作相关的事故上升主要是在一种工作里，而在其他种类的工作中，与工作相关的事故数量大致保持不变。

是否是独生子与孩子的社会能力发展几乎毫无关系。最近对30名独生孩子与35名第一胎的孩子一直到3岁的跟踪研究发现，这两组的孩子对其同代人、其家长及其他大人的行为非常相似。

下面哪个，如果正确，最能削弱上述结论？

(A) 进行对比的两组孩子人数不同。

(B) 花在观察孩子与母亲的接触上的时间多于花在观察孩子与父亲接触上的时间。

(C) 大部分参与研究的研究者没有兄弟姐妹。

(D) 一般而言，第一胎的孩子在接近3岁的时候，他们的父母有了第二个孩子。

(E) 研究中描述的"其他大人"主要是研究组中的成员。

地理学家和历史学家过去一直持有的观点认为南极第一次是在1820年左右被发现的，但是有些16世纪欧洲地图上显示着与极地相似的一片地域，虽然那时的探险家从未见到过它。因此有些学者争论说该大陆是被古代人发现并画到地图上，而大家知道这些古人的地图曾为欧洲制地图者起到了模型的作用。

下面哪个，如果正确，最能削弱上面学者所得的推论？

(A) 谁最先发现南极的问题在现代依然很有争议，没有人能给出结论性的论据。

(B) Between 3,000 and 9,000 years ago, the world was warmer than it is now, and the polar landmass was presumably smaller.

(C) There are only a few sixteenth-century global maps that show a continental landmass at the South Pole.

(D) Most attributions of surprising accomplishments to ancient civilizations or even extraterrestrials are eventually discredited or rejected as preposterous.

(E) Ancient philosophers believed that there had to be a large landmass at the South Pole to balance the northern continents and make the world symmetrical.

(B) 在3000到9000年以前，地球比现在更温暖，极地可能比现在要小。

(C) 只有几张16世纪的世界地图显示出了南极大陆。

(D) 将难以理解的成就归功于古代文明甚至外星力量，最终大多不被人相信，或者被认为是荒谬的而被抛弃。

(E) 古代的哲学家认为在南极应该会有一大块地域来与北极大陆相平衡并使地球对称。

12. Persons imprisoned for violent street crimes often commit the same crimes again after being released. Persons imprisoned for white-collar crimes such as receiving bribes or embezzlement, however, typically do not, after being released, repeat the crimes for which they have been imprisoned. It is fair to conclude that imprisonment, while it often fails to change the behavior of violent street criminals, does succeed in making white-collar criminals unwilling to repeat their crimes.

Which of the following, if true, would most seriously weaken the conclusion stated above?

(A) Statistics show that persons convicted of committing white-collar crimes rarely have a prison record.

(B) The percentage of those who commit white-collar crimes and are imprisoned for doing so is lower than the percentage of those who commit violent street crimes and are imprisoned for doing so.

(C) White-collar criminals whose prison sentences are shortened return to criminal activities at a slightly higher rate than white-collar criminals who serve their full sentences.

(D) Persons released from prison after white-collar crimes are seldom given high positions or access to other people's money.

(E) Persons who commit violent street crimes seldom commit white-collar crimes, and vice versa.

由于街头暴力犯罪而坐牢的人在被释放出来后经常再次犯同样的罪行。但是因诸如受贿或侵吞公款一类的白领犯罪而坐牢的人在被释放之后一般不再犯同样的罪了。所以，可以公正地得出结论，坐牢虽然经常不能改变街头暴力罪犯的行为，却能够成功地使白领罪犯不愿再次犯罪。

下面哪个，如果正确，将最严重地削弱上述结论？

(A) 统计数字显示被证实有白领犯罪的人很少有过坐牢的记录。

(B) 进行白领犯罪并因此坐牢的人数的百分比低于进行街头暴力犯罪并因此坐牢的人数的百分比。

(C) 刑期被减短了的白领罪犯再犯的比率要高于服满刑期的白领罪犯。

(D) 白领犯罪之后被从监狱释放的人很少再被给予高职，或被允许接触他人钱财。

(E) 进行街头暴力犯罪的人很少进行白领犯罪，反之亦然。

13. According to a 1980 survey, ten percent of all United States citizens over the age of sixteen are functionally illiterate. Therefore, if the projection that there will be 250 million United States citizens over sixteen in the year 2000

根据1980年的一项调查，所有超过16岁的美国公民中有10%是功能性文盲。因此，如果在2000年16岁以上美国公民将达2.5亿人的设想是正确的，我们可以预计，

is correct, we project that 25 million of these citizens will be functionally illiterate.

Which of the following, if true, would most weaken the conclusion drawn by the author of the passage above?

(A) The percentage of high school graduates who do not go on to college has grown steadily over the past two decades.

(B) From 1975 to 1980 there was a three-percent decrease in the rate of functional illiteracy among United States citizens over the age of sixteen.

(C) Many United States citizens included in the 1980 survey would also be included in a survey conducted in the year 2000.

(D) Surveys that are improperly designed usually provide inaccurate results.

(E) In 1980 sixty-five percent of all United States citizens were over the age of sixteen.

14. On the basis of figures it compiles, a citizens' group argues that congressional members of Party X authorize the spending of more taxpayer dollars than do congressional members of Party Y. The group's figures are based on an analysis of the number of spending bills for which members of Congress vote.

The figures of the citizens' group will be unreliable as a gauge of which party in Congress spends more taxpayer dollars if which of the following is true?

(A) The group weighs all votes for spending bills equally, no matter how much taxpayer money is involved in each bill.

(B) The group counts votes for all spending bills, including bills concerning the salaries of members of Congress.

(C) Most spending bills that are introduced in Congress are passed by Congress.

(D) Most spending bills that members of Party X vote for are written and sponsored by members of Party X.

(E) All spending bills, before being voted on by Congress, must be approved by committees in which members of both parties participate.

15. How does a building contractor most readily prove compliance with the building codes governing new construction? By using those established technologies that the

这些公民中有2500万人会是功能性文盲。

下面哪个，如果正确，将最严重地削弱上文作者得出的结论？

(A) 在过去的20年中，不上大学的高中毕业生比例稳步上升。

(B) 从1975年到1980年，美国16岁以上公民功能性文盲的比率减少了3%。

(C) 在1980年接受调查的很多美国公民在2000年进行的一项调查中也将被包括在内。

(D) 设计不适当的调查通常提供不准确的结果。

(E) 1980年，美国的所有公民中有65%的人超过16岁。

根据其汇编的数字，某公民团体认为X党的议员比Y党的议员批准花费纳税人更多的钱。这一团体的数字是基于对国会成员投票通过的支出议案的数目的分析得出的。

如果下面哪个正确，该公民团体用来衡量国会中哪一党花费更多纳税人的钱的数字将会不可靠？

(A) 该团体把对所有支出议案的投票视为等同，不论每项议案涉及的钱数是多少。

(B) 该团体计入为所有支出议案投的票，包括关于国会议员的工资的议案。

(C) 大部分提交到国会的支出议案得到国会的通过。

(D) 大多X党投票支持的支出议案是由X党成员起草、发起的。

(E) 所有支出议案在国会投票之间，必须被由两党议员均参加的委员会批准。

房屋承建商如何最容易地证明其遵循了监管新建筑的建筑规则呢?通过在制定技术指标时使用规则制定者认为适当的确

authors of the codes had in mind when setting specifications. This, unfortunately, means that there will never be any significant technological innovation within the industry.

Which of the following, if true, casts the most serious doubt on the conclusion above?

(A) Among the authors of codes governing new construction are people who were formerly building contractors.

(B) The authors of codes governing new construction are under pressure to set rigorous specifications.

(C) What are now regarded as established technologies were once so innovative that the authors of the codes then applicable could not have foreseen them.

(D) Noncompliance with the codes governing new construction can prove extremely costly to the building contractor in charge of the project.

(E) The established technologies of one country's building industry can be very different from those of another's.

16. Although the human population around the forestland in Middlesex County has increased, the amount of forestland has not been reduced. Therefore, the decrease in the county's songbird population cannot be attributed to the growth in the county's human population.

Which of the following, if true, most seriously weakens the conclusion above?

(A) As the human population of Middlesex County has grown, there has been an increase in the number of shopping malls built.

(B) The presence of more garbage cans resulting from the increase in the county's human population ensures the survival of more raccoons, which prey on songbird eggs whenever available.

(C) There has recently been a decrease in the amount of rain-forest land in Central and South America, where songbirds spend the winter months.

(D) Although several species of songbirds are disappearing from Middlesex County, these species are far from being endangered.

(E) The disappearance of songbirds, which eat insects, often results in increased destruction of trees by insects.

17. Researchers studying sets of identical twins who were raised apart in dissimilar environments found that in each case the twins were similar in character, medical history,

定技术可以做到这一点。不幸的是，这意味着建筑行业中永远不会有任何明显的技术创新。

下面哪个，如果正确，对上述结论提出最严重质疑？

(A) 监管新建筑的规则制定者中有以前的房屋承建商。

(B) 监管新建筑规则的规则制定者受到压力，必须设立严格的规则条款。

(C) 现在被视为确立下来的技术曾经是非常革新的，以至于那时实行的规则的制定者无法预见到这些技术。

(D) 不遵守关于新建筑的规则对负责工程的承建商来说可能是代价极大的。

(E) 一国建筑工业的确定的技术可能与他国有很大区别。

虽然在Middlesex县森林地区附近的人口增加了，但森林的数量并未减少。因此，该县鸣禽的数量减少不能被看作是该县人口增加的结果。

下面哪个，如果正确，最严重地削弱了上述结论？

(A) 随着Middlesex县人口的增长，商店的数量有所增加。

(B) 该县人口增多带来的垃圾桶的增加保证了更多浣熊的生存，一有鸣禽蛋这些浣熊就对之进行捕食。

(C) 最近中美和南美的雨林有所减少，而鸣禽在那里过冬。

(D) 虽然几种鸣禽正从Middlesex县消失，但这几种鸣禽远未到生存受威胁的地步。

(E) 食害虫的鸣禽的消失经常会导致害虫对树木毁坏的增加。

研究在不同环境下分别养大的同卵双胞胎的研究者发现，每一对这种双胞胎在性格上、医疗记录和生活经历上都相似。

and life experiences. The researchers saw these results as confirmation of the hypothesis that heredity is more important than environment in determining human personalities and life histories.

The existence of which of the following would tend to weaken the support for the hypothesis above most seriously?

(A) A set of identical twins raised together who are shown by appropriate tests to have very similar value systems.

(B) A pair or identical twins raised apart who differ markedly with respect to aggressiveness and other personality traits.

(C) A younger brother and older sister raised together who have similar personalities and life experiences.

(D) A mother and daughter who have the same profession even though they have very different temperaments.

(E) A pair of twins raised together who have similar personality traits but different value systems.

18. During his three years in office, the governor of a state has frequently been accused of having sexist attitudes toward women. Yet he has filled five of the nineteen vacant high-level positions in his administration with women appointees, all of whom are still serving. This shows that the governor is not sexist.

Which of the following statements, if true, would most seriously weaken the conclusion above?

(A) One of the women appointed by the governor to a high-level position is planning to resign her post.

(B) The platform of the governor's political party required him to appoint at least five women to high-level positions.

(C) Forty-seven percent of the women who voted in the state gubernatorial election three years ago voted for the governor.

(D) A governor of a neighboring state recently appointed seven women to high-level positions.

(E) The governor appointed two Black Americans, two Hispanic Americans, and one Asian American to high-level positions in his administration.

19. The large amounts of carbon dioxide now being released into the atmosphere by the burning of fossil fuels will not, in fact, result in a greenhouse effectan increase in average global temperatures. Since plants use carbon dioxide in larger

这些研究者认为这些结果证实了这种假设：遗传在决定人的性格和生活经历时比环境起更大的作用。

下面哪一项内容的存在将会最严重地削弱上述假设？

(A) 一对在一起抚养的同卵双胞胎，经适当的测试显示出非常接近的价值观。

(B) 一对不在一起抚养的同卵双胞胎，他们在攻击性和其他个人特征上明显不同。

(C) 一对在一起抚养的姐弟，他们有相似的性格和生活经历。

(D) 一对母女，虽然性情不同，但从事着同样的职业。

(E) 一对在一起抚养的双胞胎，有着相似的个性特征但有不同的价值观。

在其3年任职期间，某州长经常被指控对女性有性别歧视。但在其政府19个高层职位空缺中，他任命了5名女性，这5人目前仍然在职。这说明该州长并非性别歧视者。

下面哪个说法，如果正确，将最严重的削弱上述结论？

(A) 该州长任命的一位就职高层的女性打算辞职。

(B) 该州长所在政党的党纲要求他在高层职位中至少任命5名女性。

(C) 在3年前的州长选举中投票了的妇女中有47%的人投票选了该州长。

(D) 邻州的州长最近在高层职位中任命了7名女性。

(E) 该州长在其政府中，任命了2名黑人，2名西班牙裔美国人和1名亚裔美国人。

现在燃烧化石燃料释放到大气中的大量二氧化碳实际上不会导致温室效应——即全球平均温度的上升。因为如果二氧化碳的供应量上升，植物就会更大量地消耗

quantities if the supply is increased, they are able to grow larger and multiply more vigorously, and atmospheric carbon dioxide concentrations will eventually become stable.

Which of the following, if true, would most seriously weaken the conclusion that a greenhouse effect will not result from the current release of large amounts of carbon dioxide into the atmosphere?

(A) The expected rise in average global temperatures has not yet been observed.

(B) Ocean waters absorb carbon dioxide at a greater rate when the atmospheric concentration of carbon dioxide is higher.

(C) Since the beginning of the Industrial Revolution, increased atmospheric concentrations of carbon dioxide have resulted in improved agricultural productivity.

(D) When plants decay, they produce methane, another gas that can have a marked greenhouse effect.

(E) The fact that carbon dioxide levels have risen and fallen many times in the Earth's history suggests that there is some biological process that can reverse the greenhouse effect.

20. The number of people 85 or older in the United States started increasing dramatically during the last ten years. The good health care that these people enjoyed in the United States during their vulnerable childhood years is primarily responsible for this trend.

Which of the following, if true, most seriously weakens the explanation above?

(A) Seventy-five percent of the people in the United States who are 85 or older are the children of people who themselves lived less than 65 years.

(B) The people in the United States who are now 85 represent an age group that was smaller in numbers at birth than the immediately preceding and succeeding age groups.

(C) Thirty-five percent of the people in the United States who are 85 or older require some form of twenty-four-hour nursing care.

(D) Many of the people in the United States who are 85 or older immigrated to the United States when they were 20 years old or older.

(E) Because of decreased federal funding for medical care for pregnant mothers and for children, the life expectancy of United States citizens is likely to decrease.

该气体，所以它们会长得更大，繁殖得更茂盛，那么大气中二氧化碳的浓度终将保持稳定。

下面哪个，如果正确，将最严重地削弱这一结论，即目前释放到大气中的大量二氧化碳不会引起温室效应？

(A) 预计的全球平均温度的上升还没有被观察到。

(B) 当大气中二氧化碳的浓度上升时，海水就会更多地吸收二氧化碳。

(C) 从工业革命开始时起，大气中二氧化碳浓度的上升引起了农业生产率的提高。

(D) 植物腐烂时会产生甲烷，这是另一种能显著地产生温室效应的气体。

(E) 二氧化碳含量在地球的历史中多次上升和下降的事实说明有一些能逆转温室效应的生物作用。

在过去的十年中，美国年龄在85岁或以上的人口数开始大量增长。出现这一趋势的主要原因是这些人在脆弱的孩提时期受到了良好的健康医疗照顾。

下面哪个，如果正确，最严重地削弱了上面的解释？

(A) 在美国，年龄85岁或85岁以上的人中，有75%的人其父母的寿命小于65岁。

(B) 在美国，现在85岁的人们代表的年龄组的出生人数少于比这一年龄组大一点和小一点的年龄组。

(C) 在美国，年龄在85岁以上的人中，有35%需要24小时护理。

(D) 美国很多85岁以上的人是在20岁或20岁以后才移民到美国的。

(E) 由于联邦政府用于怀孕妇女和儿童的医疗护理的资金减少，美国公民的寿命有可能会缩短。

21. A steady decline in annual movie-ticket sales is about to begin. More than half of the tickets sold last year were sold to the age group under twenty-five years of age, representing twenty-seven percent of the population. However, the number of individuals under twenty-five will steadily decline during the next decade.

Which of the following, if true, casts most doubt on the prediction above regarding future movie-ticket sales?

(A) Medical advances have lowered the mortality rates for those who are forty to sixty years of age.

(B) Many people gradually lose interest in going to the movies after they reach twenty-five years of age.

(C) The number of movie theaters has been increasing, and this trend is expected to continue during the next ten years.

(D) Movie-ticket sales tend to increase as the size of the work force increases, and the size of the work force will increase annually during the next decade.

(E) Experts agree that people under twenty-five years of age will continue to account for more than half of the total number of tickets sold in each of the next ten years.

22. In a recent study on the connection between brain abnormalities and violent behavior, the researcher examined more than three hundred people who had engaged in unusually violent behavior toward friends and family members. In most of the people studied, the researcher found clues of brain abnormalities, including evidence of past brain injury and physical abnormality. The researcher concluded that evidence of brain abnormalities could be used to predict violent behavior.

Which of the following, if true, would most seriously weaken the researcher's conclusion?

(A) The incidence of brain abnormalities in the general population is as high as that in the group examined.

(B) The brain abnormalities discovered in those studied are of two distinct kinds.

(C) A wide variety of violent actions were exhibited by those studied.

(D) Those studied in the experiment acted violently toward strangers as well as toward people they knew.

(E) The study drew its subjects from a large geographical area.

电影的年票房收入将开始下降。去年售出的电影票中有一半以上卖给了占人口总数27%的25岁以下的年龄组，然而，在今后10年中，25岁以下的人口数将持续下降。

下面哪个，如果正确，对上述关于未来的电影票房收入的预测提出最大质疑？

(A) 医学进步降低了40岁到60岁的人的死亡率。

(B) 很多人在25岁以后渐渐失去了去电影院看电影的兴趣。

(C) 电影院的数目正在增多，预计这一趋势在将来的10年会继续。

(D) 电影票房趋向于随着劳动力的增加而增加，而在今后的10年里劳动力人数将逐年增加。

(E) 专家认为在今后10年的每一年中，卖出的电影票总数中有一多半是卖给25岁以下的人。

在最近关于大脑反常和暴力行为相关性的研究中，研究者对三百多个对自己朋友和家人有过度暴力行为的人进行研究。结果发现大部分研究对象有大脑反常的痕迹，包括过去脑损伤和身体不正常的迹象。研究者得出结论说大脑反常的迹象可以用于预测暴力行为。

下面哪一项，如果正确，将最严重地削弱研究者的结论？

(A) 在一般人口中大脑反常的发病率和这一组被研究人群的发病率一样高。

(B) 被研究的人所患大脑反常有区别明显的两种类型。

(C) 被研究的人显示出了多种暴力行为。

(D) 实验中被研究人对陌生人和他们认识的人都有暴力行为。

(E) 该研究的实验对象来自较大的地域范围。

23. Why can human beings outlast many faster four legged animals when running long distances? Perhaps because early humans evolved as hunters on the hot African savannas. Humans developed the ability to release heat by sweating, but most mammals must pant, a function hard to regulate while running. Also, four-legged animals must adopt a pace that lets them breathe once in mid-stride; otherwise, the impact of the front legs hitting the ground will prevent deep inhalation. Humans can vary the number of breaths per stride, set a pace unsuited to the prey, and so eventually exhaust it.

The author's explanation of why human beings have evolved as superior distance runners would be most weakened if it were shown that

(A) early humans typically hunted animals that were less well adapted than humans for long-distance running.

(B) early humans were only one of a number of species that hunted prey on the African savannas.

(C) early humans hunted mainly in groups by sneaking up on prey and trapping it within a circle.

(D) hunting was just as essential for later humans in colder climates as it was for early humans on the African savannas.

(E) human beings of today have retained the ability to run long distances but no longer hunt by chasing prey.

24. The teacher of yoga said that he knows how good the yoga exercises feel and how beneficial they are to his mental and spiritual health. After all, he said, there must be something sound to any human practice that endures more than three thousand years of history.

Which of the following, if true, is the strongest relevant objection to the argument the teacher makes on the basis of the time yoga has endured?

(A) The teacher benefits by the teaching of yoga and so, as a beneficiary, is not a disinterested witness.

(B) The practice of yoga has changed somewhat over three thousand years.

(C) The teacher cites the experience of only one person, whose well-being might be due to other causes.

(D) War, which cannot on balance be called sound, has lasted the length of human history.

(E) Three thousand years is an underestimate of the time period.

为什么人类在长距离跑方面要比跑得更快的四足动物更有耐力?也许这是因为早期人类是炎热的非洲热带草原上的猎人。人类发展出了通过出汗散热的能力,而大多哺乳动物只能靠喘气,这一功能在跑的时候很难调节。而且,四足动物必须采取一种速度能让它们在一步中间呼吸一次,否则,它的前足落地的撞击力将会阻碍深呼吸。人类可以改变每一步呼吸的次数,确定一种其猎物无法适应的速度,最终使之力竭。

该作者对人类为何会发展为更好的长跑者的解释将受到最严重地削弱,如果表明

(A) 早期人类一般猎捕那些没有人类擅长长跑的动物。

(B) 早期人类只是在非洲热带草原上进行狩猎的物种之一。

(C) 早期人类狩猎主要是通过偷偷靠近并围成圈捕捉猎物来结伙狩猎。

(D) 狩猎对于后来处在较寒冷气候中的人类与对早期非洲热带草原上的人类一样重要。

(E) 今天的人类保持了长跑的能力,但不再通过追赶猎物来狩猎了。

瑜珈功的教师说他知道做瑜珈功感觉多好并知道这种运动对他的心灵和精神健康多么有利。他说,不管怎么说,有着长达3000年历史的东西一定会对人类行为有其合理之处。

下面哪个,如果正确,是对瑜珈功教师基于瑜珈历经的时间的论断最强的相关性反驳?

(A) 该教师受益于教授瑜珈功,因此,他作为一名受益者不是一个公正的验证人。

(B) 瑜珈功的练习在3000年中有一些变化。

(C) 该教师只以一个人的经历来论证,他的健康可能是有其他原因。

(D) 战争贯穿整个人类历史,总的来说它不能被称为好的。

(E) 3000年是对这一时间段的过少估计。

25. People often recall having felt chilled before the onset of a cold. This supports the hypothesis that colds are, at least sometimes, caused by becoming chilled; it is the chill that allows a rhino virus, if present, to infect a person.

Which of the following, if true, most seriously weakens the force of the evidence cited above?

(A) Being chilled is a form of stress, and stress lowers the defenses of a person's immune system, which guards against infection.

(B) After a rhino virus has incubated in a person for several days, the first symptom it causes is a feeling of chilliness.

(C) People who are tired and then become chilled are more likely to catch severe colds than are people who are chilled without being tired.

(D) Some people who catch colds are not sure what it was that allowed them to catch cold.

(E) Rhino viruses are not always present in the environment, and so a person could become chilled without catching a cold.

人们经常能回忆起在感冒前有冷的感觉。这就支持了这样一种假设，即感冒是，至少有时候是由着凉引起的，是寒冷使rhino病毒，如果存在的话，感染人体。

下面哪个，如果正确，最严重地削弱上述论据的说服力？

(A) 着凉是一种压力，而压力会削弱防止人体染病的人体免疫系统的抵御能力。

(B) rhino病毒存在于人体内数日后，引起的第一个症状就是冷的感觉。

(C) 先受累然后着凉的人比不受累只受凉的人更容易患重感冒。

(D) 有些患感冒的人并不知道是什么引起了他们感冒。

(E) rhino病毒并不总是存在于环境中，因此一个人有可能只着凉而不得感冒。

26. It is impossible to believe scientific predictions that a long "nuclear winter" would envelop the Earth as a result of nuclear war. Atmospheric scientists and weather experts cannot reliably and accurately predict tomorrow's weather. Yet the effect of nuclear explosions on local and worldwide atmospheric conditions must follow the same laws that control everyday weather changes. If the weather cannot be predicted with present knowledge, neither can a nuclear-winter scenario.

Which of the following, if true, would most seriously weaken the argument made above that if scientists cannot reliably predict the daily weather, their predictions of a "nuclear winter" cannot be believed?

(A) The scientific theory of a nuclear winter uses data that is available to those who forecast the daily weather.

(B) Scientists' predictions about a nuclear winter are necessarily speculative, since they cannot be verified by harmless experimentation.

(C) Weather forecasters usually do not insist that their predictions are infallible.

(D) Scientific predictions of catastrophic natural events such as volcanic eruptions and earthquakes usually have less reliability than everyday weather predictions.

核战争将导致漫长的"核冬季"包围地球这种科学预测是不可相信的。大气科学家和天气专家无法可靠而准确地预测明天的天气。而核爆炸对本地和世界范围大气情况的影响一定遵循那些控制着日常天气变化的规律。如果天气无法用目前知识预测，那么核冬季这一假设用目前的知识也不能预测。

下面哪个，如果正确，将最严重地削弱上述论断：如果科学家无法准确地预测日常天气，他们对"核冬季"的预测也不可信？

(A) 核冬季的科学理论使用的是那些预报日常天气的人可得到的数据。

(B) 科学家对核冬季的预测只能是凭空构想的，因为这些预测无法通过不造成伤害的实验加以证实。

(C) 气象预报人员通常不坚持说他们的预测不会出错。

(D) 对灾难性自然事件，如火山爆发、地震所作的科学预测比日常天气预测的可信度要低。

(E) The scientific theory of a nuclear winter is concerned with drastic climatic changes rather than day-to-day fluctuations in the weather.

27. John: I have tried several different types of psychotherapy at various times in my life: three kinds of "talk" therapy (Freudian, Rogerian, and cognitive) and also behavior therapy. Since the periods when I was in therapy were the least happy times of my life, I have concluded that psychotherapy cannot work for me.

Which of the following statements, if true, would most weaken John's conclusion?

(A) Behavior therapy is designed to address different problems from those addressed by "talk" therapies.

(B) The techniques used in behavior therapy are quite different from those used in "talk" therapies.

(C) People who try several different types of psychotherapy tend to be happier than people who try only one type of psychotherapy.

(D) People who try several different types of psychotherapy are more likely to find one that works for them than are people who try only one type of psychotherapy.

(E) People undergoing psychotherapy that ultimately works are often unhappy while they are in therapy.

28. Grammarians have for years condemned as ungrammatical the English phrase "between you and I," insisting that the correct phrasing is "between you and me," with the objective case after a preposition. Such condemnations, however, are obviously unfounded, because Shakespeare himself, in The Merchant of Venice, wrote, "All debts are cleared between you and I."

Which of the following, if true, most seriously weakens the argument above?

(A) In his plays, Shakespeare intentionally had some of his characters use phrases he considered ungrammatical.

(B) The phrase "between you and I" appears infrequently in Shakespeare's writings.

(C) The more modern an English word or phrase, the less likely that modern grammarians will consider it acceptable for formal usage.

(D) Many modern speakers of English sometimes say "between you and I" and sometimes say "between you and me."

约翰：我在一生的各个时期中尝试了几种不同的心理治疗：三种"交谈"疗法（弗洛伊德式，荣格式和认知式）也尝试了行为疗法。我接受治疗期间是我一生中最不快乐的时间，因此我得出结论，心理治疗对我不起作用。

下面的哪一个陈述，如果正确，最能削弱John的结论？

(A) 行为疗法在设计时所针对的问题与"交谈"法所针对的问题不同。

(B) 行为疗法中所用的方法与"交谈"疗法中使用的方法大不相同。

(C) 尝试几种不同心理疗法的人要比只用一种疗法的人快乐。

(D) 尝试几种不同心理疗法的人要比只用一种疗法的人更容易找到对他们起作用的一种疗法。

(E) 接受最终有效的心理治疗的人在接受治疗时经常不快乐。

语法学家多年来一直在指责英语短语"between you and I"的用法是不合乎语法的，他们坚持认为正确的用法是"between you and me"，即在介词后接宾格。然而，这样的批评显然是没有根据的，因为莎士比亚自己在《威尼斯商人》中写到："All debts are cleared between you and I"。

下面哪个，如果正确，最严重地削弱了以上论述？

(A) 在莎士比亚的戏剧中，他有意让一些角色使用他认为不合语法的短语。

(B) "between you and I"这样的短语很少出现在莎士比亚的作品中。

(C) 越是现代的英语词语或短语，现代的语言学家越认为它们不适合在正式场合使用。

(D) 现代说英语的人有时说"between you and I"，有时说"between you and me"。

(E) Most native speakers of English who choose to say "between you and I" do so because they know that Shakespeare used that phrase.

29. Senator: Jones is highly qualified for appointment as a judge, as evidenced by Jones's receiving a unanimous vote of "qualified" on the formal rating scale used by the Lawyers' Committee. That committee advises the Senate on judicial appointments.

Which of the following, if true, is the best reason for dismissing the senator's claim that Jones is highly qualified?

(A) Several members of the Lawyers' Committee are not themselves qualified for judicial appointments.

(B) The Lawyers' Committee does not advise the Senate on all judicial appointments.

(C) The Lawyers' Committee gives a unanimous vote of "qualified" only to those candidates for judicial appointments who meet the committee's stringent standards for appropriate prior experience and ethical conduct.

(D) The Lawyers' Committee gives a unanimous vote of either "highly qualified" or "very highly qualified" to 95 percent of all candidates for judicial appointments.

(E) Jones, like most lawyers, is a member of the professional organization that originally suggested the establishment of the Lawyers' Committee.

30. Partha has withdrawn its troops from Baltia after five years of occupation. Earlier this year the country of Cardena began shipping mules to Baltia's resistance fighters to facilitate transport of weapons across Baltia's mountains to the battle areas. Cardena's diplomats now claim that without Cardena's aid to Baltia's resistance fighters, Partha would not have withdrawn.

Which of the following, if true, casts the most serious doubt on the accuracy of the assertion of Cardena's diplomats?

(A) No precise figures are available concerning the number of mules shipped to Baltia.

(B) During the past year, Cardena shipped weapons and food, as well as mules, to resistance fighters in Baltia.

(C) Last year a new government took power in Partha and decided that national interests were not served by the occupation of Baltia.

(D) Two years ago Partha had no plans to reduce its forces in

（E）许多把英语作为母语的人选择说"between you and I"是因为他们知道莎士比亚也用这个短语。

参议员：琼斯被任命为法官是符合标准的。她在律师委员会的正式评选中获得一致的"合格"票可以证明这一点。那个委员会给参议院的法官任命评议会提出建议。

下面哪个，如果正确，是对议员认为琼斯非常合格的说法的最好的反驳理由？

（A）律师委员会中的一些成员本身就不称职，没有资格任命执行者。

（B）律师委员会并不是对所有的执法者的任命都是要提出建议。

（C）律师委员会一致给予合格的条件必须是法官的候选人，在经历合适、行为符合道德标准方面达到了严格的标准。

（D）对于法官的候选人中的95%，律师委员会要么会一致给予"合格"的选票，要么会一致给予"非常合格"的选票。

（E）和大部分的律师一样，琼斯也是整个职业团体的一员，最初，就是这个团体提出建立了律师委员会。

占领了五年之后，Partha 从Baltia撤出了它的部队。今年年初，Cardena国开始给Baltia的抵抗军运送骡子，以帮助他们翻过Baltia的山脉把武器运送到战场。Cardena的外交官们目前声称，如果没有它对Baltia抵抗军的援助，Partha还不会撤军。

下面哪一个，如果正确，对Cardena外交官们的言论提出最严重的质疑？

（A）没有关于运送到Baltia的骡子的数量的准确数字。

（B）去年，Cardena也运送武器、食品和骡子来援助Baltia的抵抗军。

（C）去年，Partha的新政府上台了，它们认为占领Baltia不利于国家利益。

（D）两年前，Partha没有打算减少Baltia的驻军。

Baltia.

(E) Resistance fighters in Baltia fought for five years against Partha's occupying troops.

(E) Baltia的抵抗军和Partha的入侵军队战斗了五年。

31. A worldwide ban on the production of certain ozone-destroying chemicals would provide only an illusion of protection. Quantities of such chemicals, already produced, exist as coolants in millions of refrigerators. When they reach the ozone layer in the atmosphere, their action cannot be halted. So there is no way to prevent these chemicals from damaging the ozone layer further.

Which of the following, if true, most seriously weakens the argument above?

(A) It is impossible to measure with accuracy the quantity of ozone-destroying chemicals that exist as coolants in refrigerators.

(B) In modern societies, refrigeration of food is necessary to prevent unhealthy and potentially life-threatening conditions.

(C) Replacement chemicals that will not destroy ozone have not yet been developed and would be more expensive than the chemicals now used as coolants in refrigerators.

(D) Even if people should give up the use of refrigeration, the coolants already in existing refrigerators are a threat to atmospheric ozone.

(E) The coolants in refrigerators can be fully recovered at the end of the useful life of the refrigerators and reused.

一个世界范围的对生产某些破坏臭氧层的化学物质的禁令只能提供一种受到保护的幻觉。已经生产出的大量的这种化学物质已经作为制冷剂存在于数百万台冰箱中。一旦它们到达大气中的臭氧层时，它们引起的反应无法被停止。因此没有办法来阻止这些化学物质进一步破坏臭氧层。

下面哪个，如果正确，严重地削弱了以上的论述？

(A) 无法准确测出作为冰箱制冷剂存在的破坏臭氧层的化学物质的数量。

(B) 在现代社会，为避免不健康甚至对生命构成潜在威胁的状况，冷藏食物是必要的。

(C) 这些化学物质的替代品还没有被研制成功，并且这种替代品比现在使用的冰箱制冷剂要昂贵得多。

(D) 即使人们放弃使用冰箱，早已存在于冰箱中的制冷剂还是会威胁大气中的臭氧。

(E) 冰箱中的制冷剂可以在冰箱完成它的使命后被完全开发并重新使用。

32. Government department head: We already have a code of ethics that companies doing business with the department are urged to abide by. The fact that virtually all of the companies have agreed to abide by it indicates that it is successful. Therefore, neither stronger ethics regulations nor enforcement mechanisms are necessary to ensure ethical behavior by companies doing business with the department.

Which of the following, if true, casts most doubt on the department head's conclusion?

(A) The code of ethics applies only to companies that do business with the department.

(B) The code of ethics was instituted only after it was discovered that several companies had committed serious violations of ethics in their business with the department.

(C) A government investigation found that most of the companies that agreed to abide by the department's code

政府部门领导：我们已经有了一条应促使与政府部门有商业往来的公司遵循的道德规范。几乎所有公司都同意遵守它的事实说明它是成功的。因此，没有必要以更强的道德规范或强制机制来保证与政府部门有商业往来的公司做出符合道德的行为。

下面哪个，如果正确，对政府首脑的结论提出了最严重的质疑？

(A) 这些道德规范只要求和政府部门有商业往来的公司遵守。

(B) 只是在发现几家公司和政府部门进行商业往来时严重违反了道德规范以后，才制定了这些道德规范。

(C) 一项政府调查发现，大部分同意遵守这一规范的公司目前都没有实际执行。

of ethics are not complying with it.

(D) A survey of major companies found that several companies stopped doing business with the department because they did not want to agree to abide by the code of ethics.

(E) A study of codes of ethics for companies found that the codes are most effective when the top executives of companies that agree to abide by them are fully committed to following them.

33. The 1988 drought in North America was probably caused by shifts in the temperature patterns of large equatorial stretches of the Pacific Ocean. The drought, therefore, is not evidence for the hypothesis that a long-term global warming trend, allegedly caused by atmospheric pollutants such as carbon dioxide, is occurring.

Which of the following, if true, constitutes the best criticism of the argument above?

(A) Most pre-1988 droughts for which we have records were preceded by shifts in temperature patterns in the Pacific Ocean.

(B) There has been no warming trend in the United States over the last 100 years.

(C) The consequences of global warming occur long after the actual emission of pollutants into the atmosphere.

(D) Emissions of carbon dioxide gas into the atmosphere increased in 1988.

(E) A global warming trend could cause increases in the frequency and severity of shifts in temperature patterns in the Pacific Ocean.

34. The price of maple syrup has jumped from 22 dollars a gallon three years ago to 40 dollars a gallon today. It can be concluded that maple-syrup harvesters have been artificially inflating prices and that governmental price regulations are necessary to control rising prices.

Which of the following, if true, casts the most doubt on the conclusion drawn above?

(A) The government already requires maple-syrup harvesters to submit their facilities to licensing by the health department.

(B) Insect infestation and drought have stunted the growth of syrup-producing maple trees and caused less-abundant syrup harvests.

(D) 对大多数公司的调查发现，几家公司已经停止和政府部门进行商业往来，因为它们不想遵守这些道德规范。

(E) 通过对制约公司的这些道德规范的调查，发现同意遵守它们的这些公司的最高管理人员完全执行时，这些规范的效果才最好。

1988年北美的干旱可能是由太平洋赤道附近温度状况的大面积范围改变引起的。因此，这场干旱不能证明长期而言全球发生变暖趋势的假说，该趋势据称是由大气污染物如二氧化碳造成的。

下面哪个，如果正确，构成了对以上论述的最好的批判？

(A) 我们有所录的1988年以前的大部分干旱的前身是太平洋的天气形势的变化。

(B) 美国在过去的100年没有转暖的趋势。

(C) 从排放污染物到它所引起的全球转暖的发生之间的时间很长。

(D) 1988年排放到大气中的二氧化碳气体有所增加。

(E) 全球转暖的趋势会增加太平洋气温形势转变的频率及其严重性。

枫树糖浆的价格由三年前的每加仑22美元升到了现在的每加仑40美元。可以推断枫树糖浆的采集者人为地抬高了物价，政府有必要进行价格管制来控制不断上升的价格。

下面哪个，如果正确，对以上得出的结论提出最严重的质疑？

(A) 政府已经要求枫树糖浆的采集者向卫生部上交他们的设备，并由该部发放许可。

(B) 虫害和干旱阻碍了产糖浆的枫树的生长并导致了枫树糖浆的短缺。

(C) Maple syrup is produced in rural areas that suffer from high unemployment.

(D) Technological improvements in maple-syrup harvesting have reduced production costs.

(E) Maple-syrup prices have risen many times in the past, though never before at the rate recently observed.

(C) 枫树糖浆产于正面临着高失业率的农村地区。

(D) 枫树糖浆采集工艺的改善降低了生产成本。

(E) 过去枫树糖浆的价格上涨过多次，虽然从来不像最近这次幅度这么大。

35. Scientists now believe that artificial-hip implants, previously thought to be safe, may actually increase the risk of cancer in recipients after about 45 years of use. Though these implants do improve the quality of recipients' lives, the increased risk of cancer is an unacceptable price to pay for these improvements. Therefore, they should be banned.

Which of the following, if true, is the strongest counterargument to the argument above?

(A) Artificial-hip implant surgery can cause severe complications, such as infection, chronic fever, and bone degeneration, and these complications can themselves be crippling or even fatal.

(B) Almost all artificial-hip implant recipients receive their implants at an age when they are unlikely to live more than an additional 30 years.

(C) Although artificial-hip implants increase the risk of cancer after about 45 years of use, a few of the cancers they induce are not fatal.

(D) Since artificial-hip implants are not very common, banning them would cause little hardship.

(E) Although the benefits of artificial-hip implant surgery have remained substantially the same over the past decade, the price of the surgery has risen considerably.

科学家目前确信以往都认为，人工髋关节移植是安全的，然而它实际上却会在使用约45年之后提高接受移植者的患癌症的危险。虽然这种移植的确能改善接受植者的生活质量，患癌症危险的提高却是这种改进无法接受的代价。因此，它们应被禁止。

下面哪个，如果正确，是对以上陈述最好的反驳？

(A) 人工髋关节移植手术可能造成诸如感染、慢性发烧和骨骼退化等严重问题。这些问题本身有可能致残，甚至危及生命。

(B) 几乎所有接受人工髋关节移植手术的人在他们做手术时，已经不算年轻，最多也就能再活30年。

(C) 尽管使用45年后这种移植的人工髋关节会产生癌变，但它引起的癌症不会致命。

(D) 因为人工髋关节移植手术还不很普遍，所以禁止起来也不难。

(E) 虽然人工髋关节移植手术没有增加，但手术费却涨了许多。

36. According to official government records, in Greenland the suicide rate (suicides per 1,000 people) was seventeen times greater in 1987 than in 1960. Because Greenland changed from a hunting and fishing society to an industrial society between 1960 and 1987, the dramatic increase in suicide must be a result of this societal change.

Which of the following, if true, casts the most serious doubt on the conclusion drawn above?

(A) The change from a hunting and fishing society to an industrial society sometimes causes a dramatic increase in a society's crime rate.

(B) Even in a hunting and fishing society, some proportion of the society's members will choose to commit suicide.

根据政府记录，格陵兰的1987年的自杀率（每1000人中自杀的人数）比1960年高出17倍，因为格陵兰从1960年的狩猎捕鱼的社会发展成1987年的工业社会，所以自杀率的激增一定是由这一社会变化引起的。

下面哪个，如果正确，对上述结论提出了最严重的质疑？

(A) 从狩猎捕鱼的社会转变成工业社会造成犯罪的激增。

(B) 即使在狩猎捕鱼的社会，也有一部分社会成员选择自杀。

(C) According to official government records, most of those who committed suicide in Greenland in 1987 were male.

(D) The life expectancy of Greenland's inhabitants was not much greater in 1987 than it was in 1960, before the societal change occurred.

(E) In 1987 most suicides that occurred in Greenland were reported as suicides to the appropriate government office, whereas in 1960 most were not.

37. Scientists have rediscovered certain food crops, once commonly cultivated in the New World, which contain more protein per pound than do current staple food crops such as rice and wheat. Scientists claim that cultivation of these crops could greatly benefit densely populated countries that have low per-person caloric intake and inadequate source of protein.

Which of the following, if true, casts the most serious doubt on the claim made above?

(A) The average yield per acre of the rediscovered crops is substantially less than that of the current staple food crops.

(B) Many important food crops, such as tomato, originated in the New World.

(C) Wheat yields more protein per pound than does rice.

(D) The rediscovered crops have more caloric per pound than do current, staple food crops.

(E) As few as 20 different food crops provide the bulk of the planet's food supply.

38. The theory that the impact of a giant meteorite caused the extinction of the dinosaurs is based on evidence that a cloud of dust from the impact blocked off sunlight around the globe for months, reducing temperatures and destroying the dinosaurs' food supply.

Which of the following, if true, casts the most serious doubt on the theory above?

(A) Dinosaurs are believed to have been cold-blooded and thus very sensitive to any temperature change.

(B) Some dinosaurs lived in regions where their food supply was not well adapted for long periods of cold and darkness.

(C) Many large animals that existed during the time of the dinosaurs and shared a common food supply with them continued to populate the Earth long after the extinction

(C) 根据正式的政府记录，1987年格陵兰的自杀的人中大部分是男性。

(D) 1987年，格陵兰居民的寿命比1960年没有发生社会变化以前人的寿命短。

(E) 1987年，格陵兰发生的自杀事件都上报给相应的政府部门，而在1960年大多数自杀事件没有。

科学家再次发现曾经在新大陆普遍种植过的一种谷物每磅的蛋白质含量高于现在种植的作为主食的水稻、小麦等谷物。科学家宣称，种植这种谷物对人口稠密、人均摄入热量低和蛋白质来源不足的国家大有好处。

下面哪个，如果正确，对上述结论提出了最严重的质疑？

(A) 新发现的农作物的每亩平均产量比目前的粮食作物产量低得多。

(B) 许多重要的粮食作物，如马铃薯最初都原产自新大陆。

(C) 每磅小麦的蛋白质的含量比大米的高。

(D) 新发现的农作物每磅产生的热量比目前的粮食作物要高。

(E) 全球的粮食供应只来自于20种粮食作物。

巨大陨石的冲击造成了恐龙绝种的理论，这一理论依据这样一个事实，即冲击造成的大片尘埃将地球周围的阳光遮住了几个月，使温度降低，并破坏了恐龙的食物供应。

下面哪一个，如果正确，对以上结论提出了最严重的质疑？

(A) 恐龙是冷血动物，所以对温度的变化非常敏感。

(B) 一些恐龙生活的地区的食物供给由于长期的寒冷和黑暗而一直不充足。

(C) 当时许多大动物和恐龙吃一样的食物，它们在恐龙灭绝之后，一直生活在地球上。

of the dinosaurs.

(D) A large volcanic explosion that strewed dust in the air and blocked out sunlight was the cause of death of animals within hundreds of miles of the eruption.

(E) Many of the largest dinosaurs were herbivorous relying exclusively on vegetation for their dietary needs.

39. Until recently experts believed that environment, not genetics, largely determines human personality. A new study, however, has shown that there is more similarity in personality between identical twins raised together than between nonidentical twins raised together. The study concluded that genetics, therefore, does play an important role in determining personality.

Which of the following, if found to be true, would cast the most doubt on the study's conclusion?

(A) Identical twins raised separately in different adoptive families are usually more similar in personality than are nonidentical twins raised separately in different adoptive families.

(B) No matter how twins behave, parents treat identical twins in ways that tend to elicit similar personality traits but do not treat nonidentical twins in such ways.

(C) Parents of both identical and nonidentical twins have long claimed that their children, from early infanthood, had definite and well-established personality traits.

(D) Birth parents and their identical twin children tend to become more similar to each other in personality over time, but adoptive parents and their identical twin children do not.

(E) Neither identical nor nonidentical twins are likely to display drastic changes in their individual personalities as they grow up.

40. The major goal of physical education programs in schools is to help all children become physically fit. But only a small proportion of children ever participate in team sports. Moreover, team sports usually do less to encourage fitness in participants than do physical education programs that focus directly on aerobic exercise.

The considerations above, if true, could be used most effectively to argue against

(A) the use of in-school physical education programs to encourage lifelong fitness habits in students.

(D) 一次严重的火山爆发把灰尘散发到空气中，遮住了阳光，造成了方圆几百里内许多动物的丧生。

(E) 许多大恐龙是草食性动物，只靠植被为生。

直到最近专家还相信是环境而非基因对人类个性的影响最大，但是，一项新的研究却表明一起成长起来的同卵双生子的个性的相似之处比一起成长起来的非同卵双生子多。因此这项研究得出结论认为，基因在决定个性方面确实起重要作用。

下面哪个，如果被证实，对该研究的结论提出了最大的质疑？

(A) 在不同家庭抚养的同卵双胞胎表现出性格的相同之处比同种情况下的非同卵双生的双胞胎表现出来的相同之处多。

(B) 不论双胞胎举止如何，父母对待同卵双胞胎的方式总是容易激发出相似的性格特征，而对待非同卵的双胞胎的方式却并非如此。

(C) 拥有同卵双胞胎和非同卵双胞胎的父母一直认为他们的孩子从婴儿时起性格就已固定了。

(D) 亲生父母和他们的同卵双胞胎之间会有许多相似的性格，而养父母和双胞胎之间的相似性格则没有多少。

(E) 无论同卵双胞胎还是非同卵双胞胎，在他们成长过程中，他们个人性格的变化都不会发生明显变化。

学校体育教育课程的主要目标是促使所有的孩子身体健康。但只有一小部分孩子曾经参与过集体体育运动。而且，通常集体体育运动对促进参与者健康的效果不如直接集中于有氧锻炼的体育教育课程的效果好。

以上考虑，如果正确，可最有效地被用于反驳：

(A) 学校的体育教育课程是为了帮助学生们养成学生保持身体健康的好习惯。

(B) the participation by young children in community sports teams.

(C) schools' relying heavily on aerobic exercise programs to help all children become physically fit.

(D) the use of a large part of a school's physical education curriculum for team sports.

(E) the use of team sports in schools as an occasional activity for talented athletes.

41. Do you think cream cheese is too rich and luxurious to use as an everyday spread? Think again! Measure for measure, cream cheese has half the calories of butter. Indulge yourself with a clear conscience.

The advertisement above is potentially misleading if which of the following is true?

(A) Even butter is expensive in comparison with spreads that are still less expensive, such as margarine.

(B) When using cream cheese as a spread, people tend to use several times as much as when using butter.

(C) Other brands of cream cheese are approximately equal in caloric content to the brand advertised.

(D) Even apart from caloric content, people generally think of cream cheese as luxurious because of its smooth taste.

(E) Butter and cream cheese each contain a nutrient that the other does not.

42. Extraordinarily few people have the ability to be successful commodity traders. So rather than limit the number of people they hire, trading firms aim to hire all those applicants who are able to be successful and to reject the rest. By this standard Quinsey-Leerheim's record is perfect. All of its entry-level hirees over the past decade have become successful commodity traders.

Which of the following, if true, would cast the most doubt on the assessment given above of Quinsey-Leerheim's hiring performance?

(A) Over the past decade, Quinsey-Leerheim's trading practices and policies have changed in a way that gives much more responsibility to individual traders.

(B) Since the pool of entry-level applicants is mostly the same for all commodity-trading firms, Quinsey-Leerheim often competes with other trading firms for the strongest applicants.

(B) 孩子们加入社区的运动队。

(C) 学校主要依靠有氧训练来提高孩子们的健康状况。

(D) 学校体育课程大部分都是用来做集体体育活动。

(E) 学校的集体体育活动应偶尔作为有资质的田径运动员的活动。

你是否认为奶酪太奢侈、铺张了，不应作为日常食品？再想一想：前后衡量，奶酪含有的热量是黄油的一半。搞明白以后就放心地吃吧！

如果下面哪一项正确，这则广告即是一个潜在的误导：

(A) 和其他涂抹品如人造黄油相比，黄油仍是很贵的。

(B) 抹奶油干酪时，人们使用的数量是涂黄油时的几倍。

(C) 其他奶油干酪和广告中的这种奶油干酪含的热量相同。

(D) 即使抛开所含热量的优势，人们通常还是认为奶油干酪很可口，因为它口感滑腻。

(E) 黄油和奶油干酪中含有的营养成分是其他没有的。

很少有人具有成为成功的商品贸易商的能力。因此，贸易公司宁愿雇佣所有能够成为成功的商品贸易商的申请者而拒绝其余部分，也不愿限定他们雇佣的人数。通过这个标准，Qeuinsey-Leerheim的记录非常好。在过去的几十年中该公司所有达到入门水平的雇员都成为了成功的商品贸易商。

下面哪个，如果正确，能对以上关于Qeuinsey-Leerheim的雇佣表现的评价提出最大质疑？

(A) 在过去的10年，Qeuinsey-Leerheim的贸易政策和做法发生了改变，下放给做贸易的个人更多的职权。

(B) 因为所有的贸易公司可选择的入门水平的应征者总数是相同的，所以Qeuinsey-Leerheim公司常常和其他公

(C) Quinsey-Leerheim rejects some entry-level applicants who go on to become extremely successful commodity traders with other trading firms.

(D) Commodity trading requires skills that are needed in very few other occupations, so that trading firms' hiring procedures typically differ significantly from those of other financial firms.

(E) Commodity trading is very stressful, and even successful commodity traders rarely work as traders for longer than ten years, although they often earn substantial sums in those years.

43. Middletown's police currently remove an apparently abandoned car from the streets about two months after it is reported. The police have been unfairly criticized for allowing such cars to be vandalized during this period. Because it is illegal for car owners to abandon cars on the street, police need not be concerned about protecting such cars.

Which of the following, if true, most seriously weakens the argument above?

(A) In the past, vehicles abandoned in Middletown were removed from the streets an average of four months after initial reports to police.

(B) In one recent year, more than 150 abandoned vehicles were vandalized in Middletown, but police made no arrests for those actions.

(C) Some cars initially classified by Middletown's police as abandoned were later reclassified as stolen vehicles.

(D) Middletown's understaffed police force must give the disposition of abandoned cars low priority because of the number of violent crimes now committed there.

(E) In the most recent year for which data are available, there were 28 percent fewer reports of abandoned vehicles than the yearly average for the previous ten years.

44. When college students were asked about their experiences in childhood, those who remembered their parents frequently being in pain were also those who experienced common pains, like headaches, most frequently as adults. This evidence argues that a person's childhood observations of adults in pain can make that person more susceptible to pain as an adult.

Which of the following, if true, most seriously weakens the argument above?

(A) Students who most frequently remembered that they were

司竞争以获得最有能力的应征者。

(C) Qeuinsey-Leerheim公司拒绝的许多入门水平的申请者，后来在其他公司也成为了非常成功的商品贸易商。

(D) 商业贸易所需的技能很少有其他职业也需要，所以贸易公司招聘的程序和其他盈利性公司大不相同。

(E) 商业贸易令人非常紧张。即使很成功的商品贸易商工作也很少超过10年以上，虽然在这10年中，他们已经赚了相当多的钱。

Middletown的警察在接到报告两个月之后，将一辆明显被遗弃的车从大街上拖走了，警察因为在这期间允许这种车受到随意破坏而受到了不公正的批评。由于将汽车抛弃在马路上是非法的，警察不需要注意保护这种车。

下面哪个，如果正确，最严重地削弱了以上论述？

(A) 过去，Middletown被丢弃的汽车从第一次上报后四个月才会被警察拖走。

(B) 在最近一年，有150辆被丢弃在街上的车受到损坏，而警察没有为此逮捕任何人。

(C) 一些最初被Middletown的警察归为丢弃的汽车后来又被重新划为是被盗的汽车。

(D) Middletown警察人数短缺，他们必须先处理暴力犯罪，然后才能处理这些车。

(E) 能得到的最近一年的数据和前十年平均数相比，该年丢弃汽车的报告减少了28%。

当大学生被问到他们童年时代的经历时，那些记得其父母经常经历病痛的正是那些成年后本人也经常经历一些疼痛如头痛的人。

这个证据说明，一个人在儿童时代对成人病痛的观察会使其本人在成年后容易感染病痛。

下面哪个，如果正确，最严重地削弱了以上论述？

in pain as children were no more likely than the average student to experience common pains very frequently.

(B) Parents who were frequently in pain when their children were growing up often experience just as much pain after their children have grown up.

(C) College students are in general less susceptible to common pains, like headaches, than are older adults.

(D) Adult memories of the circumstances of childhood pain are often vivid, but adults can rarely recall the subjective experience of being in pain as a child.

(E) A person's adult recollections of childhood are likely to emphasize those memories that reflect the person's adult experiences.

(A) 那些记得自己小时候常处于病痛的学生不比其他大多数学生更容易经历疼痛。

(B) 经常处于病痛状态的父母在孩子长大后仍然经常经历病痛。

(C) 大学生比其他成年人经历的头疼等常见病痛少。

(D) 成年人能清晰地记住儿童时期病痛时周围的情形，却很少能想起孩提时代自身病痛的感觉。

(E) 一个人成年时对童年的回忆，总是注意那些能够反映本人成年后经历的事情。

45. One way for people to cut back on oil use is to switch to other types of fuel. Because wood is a renewable resource and can always be kept in constant supply, the use of wood instead of oil for home heating would be one way to assure the availability of energy resources in the future.

The argument above would be most seriously weakened if which of the following were true?

(A) In every country that uses wood for heating, wood is used to provide only part, not all, of the heat for a home.

(B) Every country that has ever used wood for heating has depleted its forests before the forests were able to regenerate themselves.

(C) Every country that has used wood for home heating has done so only because it possessed a limited amount of other natural resources.

(D) Many countries that use wood primarily for heating have a high incidence of fires that are due to improperly installed wood stoves.

(E) In some countries the wood that would be used for home heating is owned by the government.

人们缩减石油用量的一个办法是改用其他类型的燃料。由于木材是可再生的资源且可保持持续供应，家庭取暖用木头代替石油将是一个能确保将来有足够能源供应的办法。

如果下列哪项正确，将最严重地削弱以上论述？

(A) 在每个使用木柴取暖的国家，木材对每个家庭来说只能提供一部分热量。

(B) 到目前为止，每个使用木柴取暖的国家在森林再生之前就耗竭了它的森林资源。

(C) 每个使用木柴取暖的国家之所以这么做，是因为他们缺乏其他自然资源。

(D) 许多以木柴作为主要取暖手段的国家，火灾的发生率都很高。这些火灾发生的原因是燃烧木柴的火炉安装不合适。

(E) 在一些国家，那些被用作家庭取暖的木材属于政府。

46. Radioactive radon gas emanating from rock such as granite puts inhabitants of houses built on such rock at greater risk of lung cancer the longer the inhabitants are exposed. Protective steps should be taken if radon measurements exceed 4 picocuries per liter; this recommendation is based on 70 years of occupancy by any one person.

If a 65-year-old homeowner concludes from the information above that radon testing for the new home she has purchased

从花岗岩之类的岩石中释放出的具有放射性的氡气体会使住在建造在这种岩石上面的房屋里的人住得越久越可能患上肺癌。如果氡的含量超过每公升四皮居里，就应该采取保护措施。这一建议是基于任何居住了70年的人而说的。

如果一个65岁的房主由以上说法得出结论，她新买的房子的氡的含量不用测

will not be necessary, then each of the following, if true, weakens the homeowner's argument EXCEPT:

(A) Houses in which the homeowner previously lived were in an area where elevated radon levels have been found.

(B) Houses near the homeowner's new home have radon levels much higher than the 4 picocuries per liter threshold, levels that require immediate action to reduce exposure to any occupants.

(C) The homeowner's granddaughter, who is eventually to inherit the new house, now lives there with her children.

(D) The homeowner smokes cigarettes, and smoking increases the radon-exposure risks over those given in the information.

(E) The strata underlying the homeowner's new home are known to be of rock different from the kinds from which radon emanates.

47. Here is a new idea in agricultural weed control. Rather than trying to formulate herbicides that kill specific weeds but are harmless to grain crops, use a broad-spectrum herbicide effective against all kinds of plants and use genetic engineering specifically to make the crops impervious to the herbicide.

Which of the following, if true, is the most serious obstacle to an implementation of the new idea outlined above?

(A) Certain herbicides that are effective against specific weeds can inhibit the growth of certain crops as much as two years after application.

(B) Research to date suggests that the nutritional properties of crop plants would not improve as a result of the genetic alterations being contemplated.

(C) Most herbicides that kill only a narrow range of targets contain active ingredients that are harmful to domestic animals and wildlife.

(D) Effective broad-spectrum herbicides are on the market, but their very effectiveness has so far rendered them unsuitable for agricultural weed control.

(E) Although genetic modification has made individual plants of grain species resistant to broad-spectrum herbicides, the seeds that such plants produce will not sprout.

48. According to a recent cross-cultural study, married people in general have longer life expectancies than do people who divorce and do not remarry. This fact indicates that the stress

试，那么，如果下面每个都正确，均能削弱房主的论述，除了

(A) 这位房主以前住的房子所在的地区，氡的浓度超过了标准。

(B) 这位房主新房附近的其他房子，氡的浓度超过了每升4皮居里。这一浓度要求户主立即采取措施减少和它的接触。

(C) 将要继承这幢新房子房主的孙女如今和她的子女住在那里。

(D) 这住户吸烟，吸烟会有比上文信息所提的更多接触氡的危险。

(E) 这位房主的新房子地下的地层所含的不是会释放氡的岩石。

这里有一个控制农业杂草的新办法，它不是试图合成那种能杀死特殊野草而对谷物无害的除草剂，而是使用对所有植物都有效的除草剂，同时运用特别的基因工程来使谷物对除草剂具有免疫力。

下面哪个，如果正确，是以上提出的新办法实施的最严重障碍？

(A) 对某些特定种类杂草有效的除草剂，施用后两年内会阻碍某些作物的生长。

(B) 最新研究表明，进行基因重组并非想象的那样可以使农作物中的营养成分有所提高。

(C) 大部分的只能除掉少数特定杂草的除草剂含有的有效成分对家禽、家畜及野生动物有害。

(D) 这种万能除草剂已经上市，但它的万能作用使得人们认为它不适合作为农业控制杂草的方法。

(E) 虽然基因重组已使单个的谷物植株免受万能除草剂的影响，但这些作物产出的种子却由于万能除草剂的影响而不发芽。

根据最近一项跨文化的研究，已婚人口通常比离婚且没有再婚的人寿命长。这一事实表明与离婚相关的压力对健康有不

associated with divorce adversely affects health.

Which of the following, if true, points to a weakness in the argument above?

(A) Overall life expectancies differ among countries, even among countries with similar cultures.

(B) People often show signs of stress when undergoing a divorce.

(C) Life expectancy varies with age-group, even among married people.

(D) Stress of many kinds has been shown to affect health adversely.

(E) Adults who have never married have shorter life expectancies than do married people of the same age.

49. Grazing livestock on public land in the western United States is not causing widespread environmental damage in the region, since if it were, the condition of that land would not be improving. However, only 14 percent of public land in the area today is considered to have inadequate vegetation cover and, therefore, to be in poor condition, while in the 1930's, 36 percent had inadequate vegetation cover.

Which of the following, if true, most seriously weakens the argument above?

(A) In the western United States, private land is typically more lush than public land, and cattle that graze on private land can be fattened more quickly.

(B) Since the 1930's, recreational users of public land in the western United States have caused more environmental damage than have the cattle grazing there.

(C) During the 1930's, an unusually destructive drought prevailed throughout the region where most public lands in the western United States are located.

(D) Ranchers who use public land in the western United States pay only a fraction of what is paid by those who lease comparable private land for grazing.

(E) The amount of land purchased by the United States government since the 1930's is relatively insignificant.

50. In several nineteenth-century paintings the marble buildings of the Acropolis in Athens are portrayed as being reddish, but the buildings do not now appear reddish. The marble's natural color cannot have changed since the nineteenth century, so the paintings must not be showing the color of the buildings as they actually appeared.

利影响。

下面哪个，如果正确，指出了以上论述的一处缺陷？

(A) 人的寿命因国家而异，即使文化相似的国家也是这样。

(B) 离婚时，人们总会表现出一种压力。

(C) 即使是已婚人，寿命也是随着年龄段的不同而不同。

(D) 许多压力都对健康有不利影响。

(E) 从未结过婚的成年人的寿命比同龄的已婚人的寿命短。

在美国西部的公有土地放牧没有引起这一地区广泛的环境危害，否则那片土地的条件就不会改进。然而，目前此地区的公有土地只有14%被认为没有被足够的植被覆盖，并因此环境恶劣。而在20世纪30年代，36%的土地没有被足够的覆盖。

下面哪个，如果正确，最严重地削弱了以上论述？

(A) 美国西部，私有土地比公有土地植被茂盛。在私人土地上放牧的牛群能迅速增肥。

(B) 20世纪30年代以后，美国西部公有土地上娱乐消遣对环境造成的破坏比在此放牧的牛群造成的破坏严重得多。

(C) 20世纪30年代，发生了一场少见的破坏性极强的干旱，波及的地区刚好是美国西部公有土地所在地。

(D) 利用公有土地放牧的牧场主所付的金额，只是在租种同等私人土地放牧所交金额的一小部分。

(E) 20世纪30年代以来，美国政府购买的土地相对较多。

在一些19世纪的绘画作品中，雅典卫城的大理石建筑被画为红色，但这些建筑现在不是红色。而大理石的天然色彩从19世纪以来不可能发生变化，因此这些画表现的色彩一定不是这些建筑实际的色彩。

下面哪一个，如果正确，最严重地削

Which of the following, if true, most seriously undermines the argument above?

(A) The Acropolis can be clearly seen from virtually any location within the city of Athens.

(B) Tiny plants called lichens living on marble can cause the marble to appear reddish.

(C) Many nineteenth-century artists strove for true-to-life accuracy in every detail of their paintings.

(D) Some types of marble are naturally reddish, whereas other types are greenish or white.

(E) Not all nineteenth-century paintings of the Acropolis show the marble buildings as being reddish.

51. One randomly selected group saw a speaker lecture on environmental ethics to a large, attentive audience, and a different randomly selected group saw the same speaker give the same lecture, with identical mannerisms, but to a smaller, less attentive audience. The first group called the speaker thoughtful and assured. The second group called the speaker vague and long-winded.

The information above can best serve as part of an argument against which of the following claims?

(A) The same social behavior can appear quite differently to different people when it is viewed in different social contexts.

(B) If the second group had seen the speaker lecture to a more attentive audience, its judgment of the speaker's personal qualities might well have been different.

(C) People's judgments of a speaker's personal qualities are based primarily on what the speaker says and the mannerisms with which the speaker says it.

(D) A listener's convictions about a speaker's claims can be influenced by other people's reactions to those claims.

(E) A randomly selected group can sometimes arrive at a consensus about the personal qualifications of a speaker in a particular social situation.

52. As a promotional experiment, Omega Company distributed four million catalogs. In one of the two versions of the catalog, the description of each item for sale mentioned a "Made by Hand" label. The number of purchases from consumers receiving that catalog was twenty percent greater than the number of purchases from consumers receiving a

弱上面的论述?

(A) 雅典卫城几乎可以在雅典的任何地点被清楚地看见。

(B) 生长在大理石上的一种叫lichens的小植物可能使大理石呈现红色。

(C) 19世纪许多画家在作画时极力在细节上忠实于真实生活。

(D) 有些大理石本来就是红色的，另一些本来则是绿的或白的。

(E) 不是所有的19世纪的关于雅典卫城的油画都把这座大理石建筑描绘成红色。

一组随机挑选出来的人看了一位演讲者给一群人数较多且注意力集中的听众做关于环境道德的讲座。另一组随机挑选出来的人看了同一位演讲者以同样方式给一群不太专心、人数较少的听众做相同的讲座。头一组人认为演讲者思考深入、自信，后一组人认为演讲者表达模糊、冗长。

以上信息最好地成为反驳以下哪种说法的论证的一部分?

(A) 同样的社会行为在不同的社会背景下，给不同人的感觉可能很不一样。

(B) 如果第二组人看到该演讲者的第一批观众认真听取报告，他们对演讲者个人素质的判断很可能大不相同。

(C) 人们对演讲者个人素质的判断主要取决于他的谈话内容和说话的方式。

(D) 一个听众对演讲者发言的评论可能受到其他人的态度的影响。

(E) 随机选出的一批人在特定的社会环境下，对演讲者个人素质的认识可能达成一致。

作为一个促销实验，Omega公司分发了400万份产品目录。该目录两个版本之一对所售的每种产品的描述都有一个"手工制造"的标签。收到这种目录的消费者的购买量比收到没提这种标签目录的消费者的购买量要多20%。因此，提及这个标

catalog that did not mention the label. Thus, the mention of the label stimulated sales.

Which of the following, if true, could best be used to challenge the conclusion drawn above?

(A) Consumers receiving the catalog mentioning the label had previously purchased items from Omega Company by mail but consumers receiving the other catalog had not.

(B) Surveys showed that consumers returned purchased items to Omega Company during the promotional campaign at the same rate regardless of which catalog they received.

(C) The number of purchases from Omega Company declined substantially after the promotional campaign was completed.

(D) Omega Company mailed three times as many catalogs that did not mention the "Made by Hand" label as catalogs that did mention the label.

(E) Omega Company sold twenty percent fewer items during the year of the promotional campaign than it had during the previous year.

53. In the workplace, influenza is typically spread by infected individuals to others with whom they work in close quarters. A new medication that suppresses the symptoms of influenza therefore will actually increase the number of influenza cases, because this medication will allow people who would otherwise be home in bed to return to work while infected.

Which of the following, if true, most seriously challenges the prediction?

(A) Coughing, a symptom of influenza that the new medication suppresses, is a primary mechanism in the spread of this illness.

(B) Some medications that are used to suppress symptoms of influenza are also used by many people to treat symptoms that are caused not by influenza but by other illnesses.

(C) Many workers who now remain at home when infected with influenza do so because the symptoms of influenza prevent them from performing their jobs effectively.

(D) Most adults who are immunized against influenza in order to avoid being infected are over 65 years old and retired and thus do not work outside the home.

(E) Symptoms of an illness are often the body's means of curing itself of the illness, and therefore suppression of symptoms can prolong the illness that causes them.

签起到了促销的作用。

下列哪个，如果正确，能最有力地用来反驳以上结论？

(A) 得到有特殊说明的目录的消费者以前通过邮购购买过Omega公司的产品；而得到另一种目录的，以前没有这么做过。

(B) 调查表明在促销活动期间，不论消费者得到的是哪种目录，他们购买和退货的速度相等。

(C) 促销结束后，Omega公司的销售额大量减少了。

(D) Omega公司寄出的目录中，提到"手工制造"标签的目录是没有提到"手工制造"标签的目录的三倍。

(E) 在促销的这一年，Omega公司卖出的产品比前一年少20%。

在工作场所，流感通常由受感染的个人传染给其他在他附近工作的人，因此一种新型的抑制流感症状的药实际上增加了流感的受感染人数，因为这种药使本应在家中卧床休息的人在受感染时返回到工作场所。

下面哪个，如果正确，最严重地质疑了这一预测？

(A) 咳嗽——这种新药抑制的流感症状是流感传染的主要渠道。

(B) 一些用于抑制感冒症状的药也被人用来治由于其他病引起的症状。

(C) 许多染上流感的工人得呆在家中，因为流感症状妨碍他们有效地工作。

(D) 许多注射过流感疫苗的人是65岁以上的退休工人，因此不会外出工作。

(E) 一种疾病症状是身体本身治疗疾病的一种方法，因此压制症状会延长感冒的时间。

54. Although spinach is rich in calcium, it also contains large amounts of oxalic acid, a substance that greatly impedes calcium absorption by the body. Therefore, other calcium-containing foods must be eaten either instead of or in addition to spinach if a person is to be sure of getting enough calcium.

Which of the following, if true, most seriously weakens the argument above?

(A) Rice, which does not contain calcium, counteracts the effects of oxalic acid on calcium absorption.

(B) Dairy products, which contain even more calcium than spinach does, are often eaten by people who eat spinach on a regular basis.

(C) Neither the calcium nor the oxalic acid in spinach is destroyed when spinach is cooked.

(D) Many leafy green vegetables other than spinach that are rich in calcium also contain high concentrations of oxalic acid.

(E) Oxalic acid has little effect on the body's ability to absorb nutrients other than calcium.

尽管菠菜富含钙质，它同时也含有大量果酸，后者是一种能大大阻止人体对钙质的吸收的物质，因此，如果想摄入足够的钙质，我们必须改吃其他含钙食物，或者在菠菜之外吃一定量的含钙食物。

下面哪个，如果正确，最严重地削弱上述论证？

(A) 不含钙质的大米会抵消果酸对钙质吸收的影响。

(B) 经常吃菠菜的人也经常吃一些比菠菜含钙量更高的奶制品。

(C) 做菠菜的时候，其所含钙质与果酸都不会受损。

(D) 除菠菜外的其他多叶绿色蔬菜含钙的同时也含有高浓度的果酸。

(E) 除钙元素外，果酸对人体吸收养分的能力没有影响。

55. Conservationists have believed that by concentrating their preservation efforts on habitats rich in an easily surveyed group of species, such as birds, they would thereby be preserving areas rich in overall species diversity. This belief rests on a view that a geographical area rich in one group of species will also be rich in the other group's characteristic of the entire regional climate zone.

Which of the following findings about widely scattered tracts 10 kilometers by 10 kilometers in a temperate climate zone would most seriously challenge the conservationists' assumptions?

(A) The tracts show little damage from human intrusion and from pollution by human activities.

(B) Where a certain group of species, such as birds, is abundant, there is also an abundance of the species, such as insects, on which that group of species feeds, or in the case of plants, of the land and water resources it requires.

(C) The area of one of the tracts is generally large enough to contain a representative sample of the organisms in the region.

(D) There is little overlap between the list of tracts that are rich in species of butterflies and the list of those that are rich in species of birds.

自然资源保护论者相信通过集中进行其对某一易于观察的物种，如鸟的聚居地的保护，他们可以保护整个拥有各种生物的地区。这种意见基于下面的观点，即如果某一地区富有某一种生物，那么该地区也会富有其他同气候区的物种。

下列哪项关于一处广泛分散的十公里方圆的温带区的发现最严重地质疑了上述假设？

(A) 该地区由于人类活动而造成的破坏及污染很小。

(B) 一类生物，比如鸟，在某地数量多的话，就会有数量丰富的食物，如昆虫的存在；若是植物，则有其所需的丰富的土地及水资源。

(C) 该地区的面积足够大，可以让本地区的代表生物在其间生存下去。

(D) 在蝴蝶种类多的地区与鸟类种类多的地方没有什么重合之处。

(E) The highest concentration of individuals of rare species is found where the general diversity of species is greatest.

56. A certain type of shrimp habitually hovers around superheated deep-sea geysers, near which the bacteria that form the shrimps diet can be found. Because the geysers emit a faint light, scientists have concluded that the shrimps' light sensitive dorsal patches were developed to locate the geysers and thereby find food.

Which of the following, if true, casts the most doubt on the scientists' conclusion?

(A) The light to which the shrimps are sensitive is not the sort of light that the geysers emit.

(B) The light given off by the geysers too faint to be detected by the human eye.

(C) The heat inside a geyser's stream is sufficient to kill instantly any bacteria that move into it.

(D) Most other types of shrimp use eyes located at the end of eyestalks in order to see.

(E) In other types of shrimp a heat-sensing organ has developed that could serve the same geyser-detecting purposes as the light sensitive patches are said to serve.

57. Companies considering new cost-cutting manufacturing processes often compare the projected results of making the investment against the alternative of not making the investment with costs, selling prices, and share of market remaining constant.

Which of the following, assuming that each is a realistic possibility, constitutes the most serious disadvantage for companies of using the method above for evaluating the financial benefit of new manufacturing processes?

(A) The costs of materials required by the new process might not be known with certainty.

(B) In several years interest rates might go down, reducing the interest costs of borrowing money to pay for the investment.

(C) Some cost-cutting processes might require such expensive investments that there would be no net gain for many years, until the investment was paid for by savings in the manufacturing process.

(D) Competitors that do invest in a new process might reduce their selling prices and thus take market share away from companies that do not.

(E) 在物种总种类最多的地方，稀有物种越集中。

有一种虾总是习惯性地徘徊于非常热的深海喷泉周围，在这些喷泉附近生存着某种细菌，它们是这种虾的食物。因为喷泉能发出微光，所以科学家们得出结论，认为这种虾具有感光性的背部条纹的形成是为了发现喷泉，从而找到食物。

下列哪项，如果正确，最能反对科学家的结论？

(A) 这种虾能感知的光并不是喷泉所发出的那种光。

(B) 喷泉发出的光太微弱了，人们的肉眼无法察觉。

(C) 温泉流内的热量足以立即杀死任何进入温泉流内的细菌。

(D) 大部分其他种类的虾都用位于眼柄终端的眼睛来观察。

(E) 其他种类的虾形成了一种感热的器官，这种器官可以像感光斑纹一样起到寻找喷泉的作用。

考虑新的成本削减制造程序的公司经常把进行投资的预计结果与不进行投资的另一种选择进行比较（成本、售价、市场份额保持不变）。

假定每种选择都具有现实可能性，下面哪个构成了对采用以上方法评价新制造程序的财务利益的公司最严重的不利之处？

(A) 新程序需要的原料的成本可能不能确知。

(B) 几年内利率会下降，从而减少了借钱支付投资的利息成本。

(C) 一些成本削减程序可能需要一些昂贵的投资以至于很多年内不会有净收益，直到这些投资被制造程序中的积累赢利所偿付。

(D) 对新程序进行投资的竞争者们可能降低它们的出售价格从而从没有那么做的公司那里夺取市场份额。

(E) The period of year chosen for averaging out the cost of the investment might be somewhat longer or shorter, thus affecting the result.

58. Neighboring landholders: Air pollution from the giant aluminum refinery that has been built next to our land is killing our plants.

Company spokesperson: The refinery is not to blame, since our study shows that the damage is due to insects and fungi.

Which of the following, if true, most seriously weakens the conclusion drawn by the company spokesperson?

(A) The study did not measure the quantity of pollutants emitted into the surrounding air by the aluminum refinery.

(B) The neighboring landholders have made no change in the way they take care of their plants.

(C) Air pollution from the refinery has changed the chemical balance in the plants' environment, allowing the harmful insects and fungi to thrive.

(D) Pollutants that are invisible and odorless are emitted into the surrounding air by the refinery.

(E) The various species of insects and fungi mentioned in the study have been occasionally found in the locality during the past hundred years.

59. The average age of chief executive officers (CEOs) in a large sample of companies is 57. The average age of CEOs in those same companies 20 years ago was approximately eight years younger. On the basis of those data, it can be concluded that CEOs in general tend to be older now.

Which of the following casts the most doubt on the conclusion drawn above?

(A) The dates when the CEOs assumed their current positions have not been specified.

(B) No information is given concerning the average number of years that CEOs remain in office.

(C) The information is based only on companies that have been operating for at least 20 years.

(D) Only approximate information is given concerning the average age of the CEOs 20 years ago.

(E) Information concerning the exact number of companies in the sample has not been given.

（E）均摊完投资成本所选择的年份期间可能略长或略短，从而影响到最终的结果。

邻近的地主：建在我们土地旁边的庞大的炼铝厂造成的空气污染正在杀死我们的作物。

公司发言人，不应该怪罪炼铝厂，因为我们的研究表明，损害是由于昆虫和细菌造成的。

下面哪个，如果正确，最严重地削弱了公司发言人得出的结论？

（A）该研究并未测量炼铝厂排放到周围空气中的污染物数量。

（B）邻近的地主在他们照料作物的方法上没有任何变化。

（C）炼铝厂造成的空气污染改变了作物所处环境的化学平衡，使得有害的昆虫和细菌得以存活。

（D）炼铝厂排放出了看不见的、无味的污染物。

（E）该研究中涉及的不同类型的昆虫和细菌过去100年来在当地偶尔被发现。

一组抽样公司的首席执行官（CEOs）的平均年龄是57岁。20年前相同公司中CEO的平均年龄大约要年轻8岁。根据这些数据，可以得出结论认为CEO现在总体上年龄更大了。

下面哪个对以上的结论提出了最多的质疑？

（A）CEO取得他们现在的职位的时间没有被明确说明。

（B）没有提供关于CEO平均在位的年数的信息。

（C）信息仅仅依据于已经运营至少20年的公司。

（D）仅仅提供了关于20年前CEO的平均年龄的大概信息。

（E）关于抽样公司的确定数目的信息尚未被提供。

60. Tocqueville, a nineteenth-century writer known for his study of democracy in the United States, believed that a government that centralizes power in one individual or institution is dangerous to its citizens. Biographers claim that Tocqueville disliked-centralized government because he blamed Napoleon's rule for the poverty of his childhood in Normandy.

Which of the following, if true, would cast the most serious doubt on the biographers' claim?

(A) Although Napoleon was popularly blamed at the time for the terrible living conditions in Normandy, historians now know that bad harvests were really to blame for the poor economic conditions.

(B) Napoleon was notorious for refusing to share power with any of his political associates.

(C) Tocqueville said he knew that if his father had not suffered ill health, his family would have had a steady income and a comfortable standard of living.

(D) Although Tocqueville asserted that United States political life was democratic, the United States of the nineteenth century allowed political power to be concentrated in a few institutions.

(E) Tocqueville once wrote in a letter that, although his childhood was terribly impoverished, it was not different from the experience of his friends and neighbors in Normandy.

Tocqueville，一位19世纪的因对美国民主的研究而出名的作家，认为一个把权力集中在一个人或一个组织的政府对其公民而言是危险的。传记作者认为Tocqueville不喜欢集权政府，因为他把幼时在诺曼底的贫困归咎于拿破仑的统治。

下面哪个，如果正确，会对传记作者的看法提出最严重的质疑？

(A) 虽然拿破仑在当时因为诺曼底可怕的生活水平而遭受了普遍的谴责，历史学家们现在知道，贫困的经济状况真正来讲应归咎于收成不好。

(B) 拿破仑因拒绝把权力与他的政治盟友分享而臭名昭著。

(C) Tocqueville说，他知道如果不是父亲健康不佳，他的家庭会有一份稳定的收入和舒适的生活水准。

(D) 虽然Tocqueville肯定地认为美国的政治生活是民主的，19世纪的美国允许政治权力集中于某些机构。

(E) Tocqueville曾经在一封信中写道，尽管他的幼年生活极度贫困，他在诺曼底的朋友和邻居们的经历与他的经历没有什么不同。

61. Seven countries signed a treaty binding each of them to perform specified actions on a certain fixed date, with the actions of each conditional on simultaneous action taken by the other countries. Each country was also to notify the six other countries when it had completed its action.

The simultaneous-action provision of the treaty leaves open the possibility that

(A) the compliance date was subject to postponement, according to the terms of the treaty.

(B) one of the countries might not be required to make any changes or take any steps in order to comply with the treaty, whereas all the other countries are so required.

(C) each country might have a well-founded excuse, based on the provision, for its own lack of compliance.

(D) the treaty specified that the signal for one of the countries to initiate action was notification by the other countries that they had completed action.

七个国家签订了一项协议，规定每个国家在确定的具体日期采取指定的行动，每个国家的行动以其他国家同时采取的行动为条件。在完成行动之后，每个国家将通知其他六个国家。

该协议的同时行动条款忽视了这样的可能性：

(A) 根据协议条件，遵从协议的日期可能有所推迟。

(B) 某个国家不会被要求进行任何变化或采取任何步骤来遵守协议，尽管其他所有的国家被如此要求。

(C) 每个国家都可能有一个基于协议条款的有根据的未能遵守协议的借口。

(D) 协议规定某个国家开始行动标志是其他国家通知该国他们已完成行动。

(E) there was ambiguity with respect to the date after which all actions contemplated in the treaty are to be complete.

62. A greater number of newspapers are sold in Town S than in Town T. Therefore, the citizens of Town S are better informed about major world events than are the citizens of Town T.

Each of the following, if true, weakens the conclusion above EXCEPT:

(A) Town S has a larger population than Town T.

(B) Most citizens of Town T work in Town S and buy their newspapers there.

(C) The average citizen of Town S spends less time reading newspapers than does the average citizen of Town T.

(D) A weekly newspaper restricted to the coverage of local events is published in Town S.

(E) The average newsstand price of newspapers sold in Town S is lower than the average price of newspapers sold in Town T.

63. An overly centralized economy, not the changes in the climate, is responsible for the poor agricultural production in Country X since its new government came to power. Neighboring Country Y has experienced the same climatic conditions, but while agricultural production has been falling in Country X, it has been rising in Country Y.

Which of the following, if true, would most weaken the argument above?

(A) Industrial production also is declining in Country X.

(B) Whereas Country Y is landlocked, Country X has a major seaport.

(C) Both Country X and Country Y have been experiencing drought conditions.

(D) The crops that have always been grown in Country X are different from those that have always been grown in Country Y.

(E) Country X's new government instituted a centralized economy with the intention of ensuring an equitable distribution of goods.

64. Country Y uses its scarce foreign-exchange reserves to buy scrap iron for recycling into steel. Although the steel thus produced earns more foreign exchange than it costs, that policy is foolish. Country Y's own territory has vast deposits

(E) 在某一日期后协议中考虑的所有行动都要完成，对这一日期可做多种解释。

S城比T城售出的报纸多，因此S城的市民比T城的市民更好地掌握关于世界大事的信息。

以下每一项，如果是正确的，都将削弱以上结论，除了

(A) S城比T城人口多。

(B) T城大多数市民在S城工作，并在那里买他们需要的报纸。

(C) S城平均每个市民在读报上花费的时间比T城少。

(D) S城出版发行一种只涉及本地事务的周报。

(E) S城售报亭出售的报纸平均价格低于T城出售的报纸平均价格。

从X国新政府上台起来，过度集中的经济而非气候的变化成为X国农业产量贫乏的根源。邻近的Y国经历了相同的气候状况，但当X国的农业产量下降时，Y国的农业产量却在上升。

下面哪个，如果正确，最能削弱以上的论证？

(A) X国的工业产量同样也在不断下降。

(B) Y国为陆地所包围，而X国却有一个重要的海港。

(C) X国和Y国都遭受了干旱。

(D) 一直在X国种植的作物与一直在Y国种植的作物是不同的。

(E) X国的新政府建立了一个集中的经济目的，是要保证财物的平等分配。

Y国利用其稀少的外汇储备来购买废铁以将其再循环为钢。虽然这样生产出来的钢赚回了比购买成本更多的外汇，这一政策是愚蠢的。Y国自己的领土内有大量

of iron ore, which can be mined with minimal expenditure of foreign exchange.

Which of the following, if true, provides the strongest support for Country Y's policy of buying scrap iron abroad?

(A) The price of scrap iron international markets rose significantly in 1987.

(B) Country Y's foreign-exchange reserves dropped significantly in 1987.

(C) There is virtually no difference in quality between steel produced from scrap iron and that produced from iron ore.

(D) Scrap iron is now used in the production of roughly half the steel used in the world today, and experts predict that scrap iron will be used even more extensively in the future.

(E) Furnaces that process scrap iron can be built and operated in Country Y with substantially less foreign exchange than can furnaces that process iron ore.

65. In the United States in 1986, the average rate of violent crime in states with strict gun-control laws was 645 crimes per 100,000 persons—about 50 percent higher than the average rate in the eleven states where strict gun-control laws have never been passed. Thus one way to reduce violent crime is to repeal strict gun control laws.

Which of the following, if true, would most weaken the argument above?

(A) The annual rate of violent crime in states with strict gun-control laws has decreased since the passage of those laws.

(B) In states with strict gun-control laws, few individuals are prosecuted for violating such laws.

(C) In states without strict gun-control laws, many individuals have had no formal training in the use of firearms.

(D) The annual rate of nonviolent crime is lower in states with strict gun-control laws than in states without such laws.

(E) Less than half of the individuals who reside in states without strict gun-control laws own a gun.

66. The proposal to hire ten new police officers in Middletown is quite foolish. There is sufficient funding to pay the salaries of the new officers, but not the salaries of additional court and

的铁矿储备，这些铁矿可以用最少的外汇支出来进行冶炼。

下面哪个，如果正确，为Y国的从海外购买废铁的政策提供了最强有力的支持？

(A) 1987年以来国际市场的废铁价格显著上升了。

(B) Y国的外汇储备在1987年显著下降了。

(C) 事实上，采用废铁生产的钢和采用铁矿生产的钢在质量上没有区别。

(D) 目前，世界上使用的钢中约有一半以上在生产中使用了废铁，并且专家们预测，将来废铁会被更广泛地使用。

(E) 在Y国，建造和运营加工废铁的熔铁炉比建造和运营加工铁矿的熔铁炉需要少得多的外汇。

在美国，在有严格的枪支控制法律的州中，1986年平均犯罪率是100,000人中有645起犯罪——比11个从来没有通过严格的枪支控制法律的州的平均犯罪率高出约50%。所以，减少暴力犯罪的一个方法是废止严格的枪支控制法律。

下面哪个，如果正确，最能削弱以上的论证？

(A) 有严格的枪支控制法律的州中，每年的暴力犯罪率自从通过这些法律以来已经降低了。

(B) 在有严格的枪支控制法律的州中，违反了这些法律的人很少不受控告。

(C) 在没有严格的枪支控制法律的州中，许多人从来没有受过使用枪支的正规训练。

(D) 有严格的枪支控制法律的州中的非暴力犯罪率比没有严格的枪支控制法律的州中低。

(E) 在没有严格的枪支控制法律的州中居住的个人不到一半拥有一支枪。

在Middletown雇佣10名新警官的建议是非常愚蠢的。有足够的资金来支付新警官的薪水，但新警官经常带来待处理逮捕

prison employees to process the increased caseload of arrests and convictions that new officers usually generate.

Which of the following, if true, will most seriously weaken the conclusion drawn above?

(A) Studies have shown that an increase in a city's police force does not necessarily reduce crime.

(B) When one major city increased its police force by 19 percent last year, there were 40 percent more arrests and 13 percent more convictions.

(C) If funding for the new police officers' salaries is approved, support for other city services will have to be reduced during the next fiscal year.

(D) In most United States cities, not all arrests result in convictions, and not all convictions result in prison terms.

(E) Middletown's ratio of police officers to citizens has reached a level at which an increase in the number of officers will have a deterrent effect on crime.

67. A study comparing a group of chronically depressed individuals with an otherwise matched group of individuals free from depression found significantly more disorders of the immune system among the depressed group. According to the researchers, these results strongly support the hypothesis that mental states influence the body's vulnerability to infection.

Which of the following, if true, casts the most serious doubt on the researchers' interpretation of their findings?

(A) The researchers' view does little more than echo a familiar theme in folklore and literature.

(B) Chronically depressed individuals are no less careful than others to avoid exposure to infections.

(C) Disorders of the immune system cause many of those individuals who have them to become chronically depressed.

(D) Individuals who have previously been free from depression can become depressed quite suddenly.

(E) A high frequency of infections can stem from an unusually high level of exposure rater than from any disorder of the immune system.

68. In the United States, injuries to passengers involved in automobile accidents are typically more severe than in Europe, where laws require a different kind of safety belt. It

和判罪数量的增加，没有足够的资金来支付处理这些案件需要增加的法院和监狱雇员的薪水。

下面哪个，如果正确，会最严重地削弱以上得出的结论？

(A) 研究已经表明，城市中警察力量的增加并不必然会减少犯罪。

(B) 当一座大城市去年把其警力增加了19%以后，逮捕增加了40%，判罪增加了13%。

(C) 如果为新警官的薪水提供资金被批准了，对其他的城市服务的支持在下个财政年度就不得不被削减。

(D) 在大多数美国的城市里，并非所有的逮捕之后都有判罪，也并非所有的判罪后都会有刑期。

(E) Middletown的警官对市民比率已经达到了一个水平，在这个水平上警官数量的上升会对犯罪有一个抑制作用。

一项研究把一群有慢性抑郁症的人与另一群在其他方面一致、但没有抑郁症的人进行了对比，发现抑郁群体中明显有更多的免疫系统失调。根据研究人员的说法，这些结果强有力地支持了精神状况会影响身体对传染病的抵抗能力的观点。

下面哪个，如果正确，向研究人员对他们的发现的解释提出了最严重的质疑？

(A) 这些研究人员的观点并不比回应民间故事和文学中的一个熟悉的主题创作文学多做了什么事情。

(B) 有慢性抑郁症的人在防止接触传染病方面绝不比其他人粗心。

(C) 免疫系统失调导致许多有这种问题的人患上慢性抑郁症。

(D) 以前没有抑郁症的人可能非常迅速地变得抑郁。

(E) 很频繁的发生传染病可能来源于过多的接触而非由于免疫系统的失调。

在美国，卷入汽车事故的乘客所受的伤害通常比在欧洲严重，在那里法律要求使用一种不同种类的安全带。很明显，美

is clear from this that the United States needs to adopt more stringent standards for safety belt design to protect automobile passengers better.

Each of the following, if true, weakens the argument above EXCEPT:

(A) Europeans are more likely to wear safety belts than are people in the United States.

(B) Unlike United States drivers, European drivers receive training in how best to react in the event of an accident to minimize injuries to themselves and to their passengers.

(C) Cars built for the European market tend to have more sturdy construction than do cars built for the United States market.

(D) Automobile passengers in the United States have a greater statistical chance of being involved in an accident than do passengers in Europe.

(E) States that have recently begun requiring the European safety belt have experienced no reduction in the average severity of injuries suffered by passengers in automobile accidents.

69. F: We ought not to test the safety of new drugs on sentient animals, such as dogs and rabbits. Our benefit means their pain, and they are equal to us in the capacity to feel pain.

G: We must carry out such tests; otherwise, we would irresponsibly sacrifice the human lives that could have been saved by the drugs.

Which of the following, if true, is the best objection that could be made from F's point of view to counter G's point?

(A) Even though it is not necessary for people to use cosmetics, cosmetics are also being tested on sentient animals.

(B) Medical science already has at its disposal a great number of drugs and other treatments for serious illnesses.

(C) It is not possible to obtain scientifically adequate results by testing drugs in the test tube, without making tests on living tissue.

(D) Some of the drugs to be tested would save human beings from great pain.

(E) Many tests now performed on sentient animals can be performed equally well on fertilized chicken eggs that are at a very early stage of development.

国需要采用更严厉的安全带设计标准来更好地保护汽车司机。

下面每个，如果正确，都削弱了该论证，除了

(A) 欧洲人比美国的人更可能系安全带。

(B) 和美国司机不同，欧洲司机接受培训学习如何在发生事故时最好地做出反应以使对自己和乘客的伤害最小。

(C) 针对欧洲市场建造的汽车比针对美国市场建造的汽车倾向于有更健全的结构。

(D) 美国的汽车乘客比欧洲的乘客在统计上有更高的可能性卷入事故。

(E) 最近已经开始要求采用欧洲安全带的州中，乘客遭受汽车事故而受伤害的平均严重的程度没有减少。

　　F：我们不应该在有知觉的动物——例如狗和兔子——身上测试新药品的安全性。我们的利益意味着它们的痛苦，并且它们在感受痛苦的能力上与我们相同。

　　G：我们必须进行这些试验；否则，我们就会不负责任地牺牲本来可通过药物来挽救的人的生命。

　　下面哪个，如果正确，是可以从F的观点中得出的对G的观点最好的反对？

(A) 尽管对人们来讲，化妆品不是必须使用的，但化妆品也被在有知觉的动物身上进行试验。

(B) 医药科学已经放弃了许多治疗重病的药品和其他治疗手段。

(C) 不可能光靠在试管中试验药品但不在活的组织上进行试验而想取得科学上充分的结果。

(D) 一些将被试验的药品可能会保护人们免受巨大痛苦。

(E) 许多现在在有知觉的动物身上进行的试验可以同样好地在处于发育早期状态的受精鸡蛋上进行。

70. It is widely assumed that a museum is helped financially when a generous patron donates a potential exhibit. In truth, however, donated objects require storage space, which is not free, and routine conservation, which is rather expensive. Therefore, such gifts exacerbate rather than lighten the demands made on a museum's financial resources.

Which of the following, if true, most seriously weakens the argument above?

(A) To keep patrons well disposed, a museum will find it advisable to put at least some donated objects on exhibit rather than merely in storage.

(B) The people who are most likely to donate valuable objects to a museum are also the people who are most likely to make cash gifts to it.

(C) A museum cannot save money by resorting to cheap storage under less than adequate conditions, because so doing would drive up the cost of conservation.

(D) Patrons expect a museum to keep donated objects in its possession rather than to raise cash by selling them.

(E) Objects donated by a patron to a museum are often of such importance that the museum would be obliged to add them to its collection through purchase if necessary.

较普遍的假设认为，当一位慷慨的赞助人捐赠了有潜力的展品时，博物馆得到了财政上的支持。但是在事实上，捐赠物品需要贮藏空间，那不会是免费的，还需要非常昂贵的日常维护。所以，这些赠品加剧而非减轻了对博物馆财政资源的需求。

下面哪个，如果正确，最严重地削弱了以上的论证？

(A) 为了妥善地安排赠品，博物馆明智的做法是至少把一些捐赠品进行展览而不是仅仅贮存起来。

(B) 最可能向博物馆捐赠值钱的物品的人也是最可能向博物馆捐赠现金的人。

(C) 博物馆不能通过诉诸于低于充分条件的便宜的贮藏来达到，因为这么做会提高维护费用。

(D) 赞助人希望博物馆能把捐赠物保持在其财产中而不是出售它们来筹集现金。

(E) 赞助人给博物馆捐赠的物品常常如此重要以至于博物馆被迫在必要时通过购买来把其加入到收藏中。

注：exhibit 展览品，陈列品，证据
　　patron 资助人，赞助人；主顾，顾客

71. The geese that gather at the pond of a large corporation create a hazard for executives who use the corporate helicopter, whose landing site is 40 feet away from the pond. To solve the problem, the corporation plans to import a large number of herding dogs to keep the geese away from the helicopter.

Which of the following, if a realistic possibility, would cast the most serious doubt on the prospects for success of the corporation's plan?

(A) The dogs will form an uncontrollable pack.

(B) The dogs will require training to learn to herd the geese.

(C) The dogs will frighten away foxes that prey on old and sick geese.

(D) It will be necessary to keep the dogs in quarantine for 30 days after importing them.

(E) Some of the geese will move to the pond of another corporation in order to avoid being herded by the dogs.

聚集在一家大公司附近的鹅群对使用公司直升机——着陆点距池塘40英尺远——的行政人员们造成了威胁。为了解决这个问题，公司计划进口一大群猎狗来把鹅群赶离直升机。

下面哪个，如果具有现实可能性，对公司计划成功的前途提出了质疑？

(A) 狗会形成一个难以控制的狗群。

(B) 狗需要经过培训来学习赶鹅。

(C) 狗会吓跑捕食老鹅和病鹅的狐狸。

(D) 有必要在进口后对狗进行30天的检疫。

(E) 为了避免被狗赶，一些鹅会迁往另一家公司的池塘。

72. Houses built during the last ten years have been found to contain indoor air pollution at levels that are, on average, much higher than the levels found in older houses. The reason air-pollution levels are higher in the newer houses is that many such houses are built near the sites of old waste dumps or where automobile emissions are heavy.

Which of the following, if true, calls into question the explanation above?

(A) Many new houses are built with air-filtration systems that remove from the house pollutants that are generated indoors.

(B) The easing of standards for smokestack emissions has led to an increase in air-pollution levels in homes.

(C) New houses built in secluded rural areas are relatively free of air pollutants.

(D) Warm-weather conditions tend to slow down the movement of air, thus keeping pollution trapped near its source.

(E) Pressboard, an inexpensive new plywood substitute now often used in the construction of houses, emits the pollutant formaldehyde into the house.

73. In a study of the effect of color on productivity, 50 of 100 factory workers were moved from their drab workroom to a brightly colored workroom. Both these workers and the 50 who remained in the drab workroom increased their productivity, probably as a result of the interest taken by researchers in the work of both groups during the study.

Which of the following, if true, would cast most doubt upon the author's interpretation of the study results given above?

(A) The 50 workers moved to the brightly colored room performed precisely the same manufacturing task as the workers who remained in the drab workroom.

(B) The drab workroom was designed to provide adequate space for at most 65 workers.

(C) The 50 workers who moved to the brightly colored workroom were matched as closely as possible in age and level of training to the 50 workers who remained in the drab workroom.

(D) Nearly all the workers in both groups had volunteered to move to the brightly colored workroom.

(E) Many of the workers who moved to the brightly colored workroom reported that they liked the drab workroom

在过去的10年中建造的住房被发现含有比老房子中平均来讲程度高得多的室内空气污染。新房子中空气污染程度较高的原因在于，这些房子被建在旧垃圾场或汽车排放物严重的地区附近。

下面哪个，如果正确，对以上的解释提出了质疑？

(A) 许多新房子建造时带有空气过滤系统，可以把室内产生的房屋污染物去掉。

(B) 对烟囱排放物的标准的放松导致了家中空气污染水平的上升。

(C) 建造在僻静的乡村地区的新房子受空气污染物影响相对较少。

(D) 温暖的气候环境会减慢空气流动，从而使污染聚集在其源头。

(E) 压制板——一种新的现在常用于建造房子的便宜的胶合板替代物——把污染性的甲醛放射到屋子里。

在一项颜色对生产率作用的研究中，让100位工厂工人中的50位从其土褐色的工作间移到一间颜色明亮的工作间。这些工人和剩下在土褐色工作间的工人都增进了其生产率，可能是因为研究人员们在研究中同时对两个群体的工作都很感兴趣。

下面哪个，如果正确，会对上面提供的对研究结果的解释提出最多的质疑？

(A) 50位移到颜色明亮的工作间的工人和留在土褐色工作间的工人执行的是完全一样的制造任务。

(B) 土褐色的工作间被设计用来最多为65名工人提供足够的空间。

(C) 50位移到颜色明亮的工作间的工人与50位留在土褐色工作间的工人在年龄和培训水平上被尽量接近地进行匹配。

(D) 两个群体中几乎所有的工人都志愿移到颜色明亮的工作间。

(E) 许多移到颜色明亮的工作间里的工人报道说，他们比喜欢颜色明亮的工作间同样或更多地喜欢土褐色的工作间。

as well as or better than they liked the brightly colored workroom.

74. Low-income families are often unable to afford as much child care as they need. One government program would award low-income families a refund on the income taxes they pay of as much as $1,000 for each child under age four. This program would make it possible for all low-income families with children under age four to obtain more child care than they otherwise would have been able to afford.

Which of the following, if true, most seriously calls into question the claim that the program would make it possible for all low-income families to obtain more child care?

(A) The average family with children under age four spends more than $1,000 a year on child care.

(B) Some low-income families in which one of the parents is usually available to care for children under age four may not want to spend their income tax refund on child care.

(C) The reduction in government revenues stemming from the income tax refund will necessitate cuts in other government programs, such as grants for higher education.

(D) Many low-income families with children under age four do not pay any income taxes because their total income is too low to be subject to such taxes.

(E) Income taxes have increased substantially over the past twenty years, reducing the money that low-income families have available to spend on child care.

低收入家庭通常无力提供所需的儿童抚养费用。一项政府计划想给低收入家庭退还他们所支付的收入税，每个低于4岁的儿童1000美元。这一计划使所有的有4岁以下儿童的低收入家庭能获得比本来可支付的更多的儿童资助。

下面哪个，如果正确，最严重地对该计划可使所有低收入家庭获得更多的儿童资助的说法提出了质疑？

(A) 有4岁以下儿童的普通家庭每年花费1000美元以上用于抚养儿童。

(B) 一些父母一方有空照顾4岁以下儿童的低收入家庭也许不愿意把他们的收入税的退还款用于抚养儿童。

(C) 退还收入税导致的政府收入的降低使得其他政府计划的削减——如对高等教育的补助——成为必要。

(D) 许多有4岁以下孩子的低收入家庭不支付收入税，因为他们总的收入很低，尚未达到应税标准。

(E) 过去20年来收入税显著增加了，减少了低收入家庭可用于抚养儿童的资金。

75. Hotco oil burners, designed to be used in asphalt plants, are so efficient that Hotco will sell one to the Clifton Asphalt plant for no payment other than the cost savings between the total amount the asphalt plant actually paid for oil using its former burner during the last two years and the total amount it will pay for oil using the Hotco burner during the next two years. On installation, the plant will make an estimated payment, which will be adjusted after two years to equal the actual cost savings.

Which of the following, if it occurred, would constitute a disadvantage for Hotco of the plan described above?

(A) Another manufacturer's introduction to the market of a similarly efficient burner.

Hotco石油燃烧器——在沥青工厂中使用——是如此有效率，以至于Hotco将向Clifton沥青工厂出售一台这种燃烧器，价格是过去两年该沥青工厂使用以前的石油燃烧器而实际支付的总数与将来两年该沥青工厂使用Hotco的石油燃烧器将支付的总数之间的成本费用差额。在安装时，工厂会进行一次估计支付，两年以后再将其调整为与实际的成本差额相等。

下面哪个，如果它发生的话，会对上面描述的计划中的Hotco造成不利？

(A) 另一个制造商把有相似效率的燃烧器引入市场。

(B) The Clifton Asphalt plant's need for more than one new burner.

(C) Very poor efficiency in the Clifton Asphalt plant's old burner.

(D) A decrease in the demand for asphalt.

(E) A steady increase in the price of oil beginning soon after the new burner is installed.

(B) Clifton沥青工厂对不止一台新燃烧器的需要。

(C) Clifton沥青工厂的旧燃烧器非常差的效率。

(D) 对沥青的需求的下降。

(E) 新燃烧器安装后不久，石油价格的持续上涨。

76. A researcher studying drug addicts found that, on average, they tend to manipulate other people a great deal more than nonaddicts do. The researcher concluded that people who frequently manipulate other people are likely to become addicts.

Which of the following, if true, most seriously weakens the researcher's conclusion?

(A) After becoming addicted to drugs, drug addicts learn to manipulate other people as a way of obtaining drugs.

(B) When they are imprisoned, drug addicts often use their ability to manipulate other people to obtain better living conditions.

(C) Some nonaddicts manipulate other people more than some addicts do.

(D) People who are likely to become addicts exhibit unusual behavior patterns other than frequent manipulation of other people.

(E) The addicts that the researcher studied were often unsuccessful in obtaining what they wanted when they manipulated other people.

一位研究嗜毒者的研究人员发现，平均而言嗜毒者倾向于操纵其他人的程度比不嗜毒者高出很多。该研究人员得出结论认为，经常操纵别人的人容易吸毒上瘾。

下面哪个，如果正确，最严重地削弱了这位研究人员的结论?

(A) 在对吸毒上瘾之后，嗜毒者学会以操纵别人作为取得毒品的一种方法。

(B) 当被关入监狱时，嗜毒者经常运用他们操纵别人的能力来获得更好的生活条件。

(C) 一些不嗜毒者比一些嗜毒者更多地操纵别人。

(D) 可能成为嗜毒者的人除了经常操纵别人外，还表现出不正常的行为模式。

(E) 研究人员研究的嗜毒者在操纵别人时通常不能成功地获得他们所想要的。

77. A study of marital relationships in which one partner's sleeping and waking cycles differ from those of the other partner reveals that such couples share fewer activities with each other and have more violent arguments than do couples in a relationship in which both partners follow the same sleeping and waking patterns. Thus, mismatched sleeping and waking cycles can seriously jeopardize a marriage.

Which of the following, if true, most seriously weakens the argument above?

(A) Married couples in which both spouses follow the same sleeping and waking patterns also occasionally have arguments than can jeopardize the couple's marriage.

(B) The sleeping and waking cycles of individuals tend to vary from season to season.

一项对夫妻一方的睡眠和清醒周期与另一方不一样时夫妻间婚姻关系的研究表明，这些夫妻与那些婚姻关系中双方有相同的睡眠和清醒方式的夫妻相比起来，相互参与的活动要少，并且有更多的暴力争吵。所以，夫妻间不相配的睡眠和清醒周期会严重威胁到婚姻。

下面哪个，如果正确，最严重地削弱了以上的论证?

(A) 夫妻双方具有相同的睡眠和清醒方式的已婚夫妻偶尔也会产生可威胁到婚姻的争吵。

(B) 人们的睡眠和清醒周期倾向于随季节而变化。

(C) The individuals who have sleeping and waking cycles that differ significantly from those of their spouses tend to argue little with colleagues at work.

(D) People in unhappy marriages have been found to express hostility by adopting a different sleeping and waking cycle from that of their spouses.

(E) According to a recent study, most people's sleeping and waking cycles can be controlled and modified easily.

78. A company is considering changing its policy concerning daily working hours. Currently, this company requires all employees to arrive at work at 8 a.m. The proposed policy would permit each employee to decide when to arrive—from as early as 6 a.m. to as late as 11 a.m.

The adoption of this policy would be most likely to decrease employees' productivity if the employees' job functions required them to

(A) work without interruption from other employees.

(B) consult at least once a day with employees from other companies.

(C) submit their work for a supervisor's eventual approval.

(D) interact frequently with each other throughout the entire workday.

(E) undertake projects that take several days to complete.

79. Some anthropologists study modern-day societies of foragers in an effort to learn about our ancient ancestors who were also foragers. A flaw in this strategy is that forager societies are extremely varied. Indeed, any forager society with which anthropologists are familiar has had considerable contact with modern nonforager societies.

Which of the following, if true, would most weaken the criticism made above of the anthropologists' strategy?

(A) All forager societies throughout history have had a number of important features in common that are absent from other types of societies.

(B) Most ancient forager societies either dissolved or made a transition to another way of life.

(C) All anthropologists study one kind or another of modern-day society.

(D) Many anthropologists who study modern-day forager societies do not draw inferences about ancient societies on the basis of their studies.

(C) 睡眠和清醒周期与其配偶差别明显的人很少会在工作中与同事争吵。

(D) 生活在不快乐的婚姻中的人已被发现采用与其配偶不同的睡眠和清醒周期来表达敌意。

(E) 根据一项最新的调查，大多数人的睡眠和清醒周期可以被轻易地控制和调节。

一家公司正在考虑改变其关于日常工作时间的规定。目前，该公司要求所有的员工早上8：00到达并开始工作。提议中的规定会允许员工决定什么时候到——最早从早上6：00，最晚到早上11：00。

该规定的采用最可能降低员工的生产率，如果员工的工作职责要求他们

(A) 工作时不受其他员工的妨碍。

(B) 每天至少一次和其他公司的员工进行磋商。

(C) 把他们的工作提交给一位管理人员最后批准。

(D) 整个工作日中经常互相联系。

(E) 承担需要数日来完成的项目。

一些人类学家对现代的游牧社会进行了研究，目的是要弄明白曾经也是游牧者的我们的祖先。这种研究策略的缺陷在于游牧社会的变化很大。事实上，人类学家们所熟悉的任何游牧社会都已和现代非游牧社会进行了相当多的接触。

下面哪个，如果正确，会最多地削弱以上的对人类学家们的策略的批评？

(A) 所有历史上的游牧社会都有很多其他类型的社会所缺乏的重要的共同特征。

(B) 大多数古代的游牧社会或者消失了，或者转向了另一种生活方式。

(C) 所有的人类学家都研究一种或另一种现代社会。

(D) 许多研究现代游牧社会的人类学家没有根据其研究对古代社会做出推论。

(E) Even those modern-day forager societies that have not had significant contact with modern societies are importantly different from ancient forager societies.

(E) 即使那些与现代社会没有显著联系的现代游牧社会也和古代游牧社会有很大不同。

80. Advertisement:

For sinus pain, three out of four hospitals give their patients Novex. So when you want the most effective painkiller for sinus pain, Novex is the one to choose.

Which of the following, if true, most seriously undermines the advertisement's argument?

(A) Some competing brands of painkillers are intended to reduce other kinds of pain in addition to sinus pain.

(B) Many hospitals that do not usually use Novex will do so for those patients who cannot tolerate the drug the hospitals usually use.

(C) Many drug manufacturers increase sales of their products to hospitals by selling these products to the hospitals at the lowest price the manufacturers can afford.

(D) Unlike some competing brands of painkillers, Novex is available from pharmacies without a doctor's prescription.

(E) In clinical trials Novex has been found more effective than competing brands of painkillers that have been on the market longer than Novex.

广告：

对于窦炎痛，四家医院中三家会给他们的病人吃Novex，所以当你希望得到最有效的窦炎镇痛剂时，Novex就是所选。

下面哪个，如果正确，最严重地削弱了该广告的论证：

(A) 一些竞争的镇痛剂品牌能减少窦炎痛以外的其他类型的疼痛。

(B) 许多不经常使用Novex的医院会对那些不能忍受医院正常使用的药品的病人使用Novex。

(C) 通过以制造商所能负担的最低价格向医院出售他们的产品，许多药品制造商增加了其产品的销售量。

(D) 和一些竞争的镇痛剂品牌不同，Novex不需医生的处方就可以从药房买到。

(E) 临床试验发现Novex比进入市场时间长于Novex的竞争性镇痛剂品牌更加有效。

81. A new law gives ownership of patents—documents providing exclusive right to make and sell an invention—to universities, not the government, when those patents result from government-sponsored university research. Administrators at Logos University plan to sell any patents they acquire to corporations in order to fund programs to improve undergraduate teaching.

Which of the following, if true, would cast most doubt on the viability of the college administrators' plan described above?

(A) Profit-making corporations interested in developing products based on patents held by universities are likely to try to serve as exclusive sponsors of ongoing university research projects.

(B) Corporate sponsors of research in university facilities are entitled to tax credits under new federal tax-code guidelines.

(C) Research scientists at Logos University have few or no teaching responsibilities and participate little if at all in the undergraduate programs in their field.

一项新的法律把专利的所有权——提供制造和出售一项发明的专有权利的文件——给予了大学，而不是政府，当这些专利是从政府资助的大学研究中产生时。Logos大学的行政人员计划把他们取得的所有专利出售给公司以资助改善本科生教学的计划。

下面哪个，如果正确，会对上述的大学行政人员的计划的可行性提出最多的质疑？

(A) 对开发以大学特有的专利为基础的产品感兴趣的盈利性公司可能企图成为正在进行的大学研究计划的唯一赞助人。

(B) 大学研究设备的赞助人在新的联邦税则指标下可以获得税收优惠。

(C) Logos大学从事研究的科学家们有很少的或没有教学任务，并且如果有也很少参与他们领域中的本科生计划。

(D) Government-sponsored research conducted at Logos University for the most part duplicates research already completed by several profit-making corporations.

(E) Logos University is unlikely to attract corporate sponsorship of its scientific research.

(D) 在Logos大学进行的政府资助的研究很大程度上重复了已经被一些盈利性公司完成的研究。

(E) Logos大学不可能吸引资助它的科学研究的公司。

82. The function of government is to satisfy the genuine wants of the masses, and government cannot satisfy those wants unless it is informed about what those wants are. Freedom of speech ensures that such information will reach the ears of government officials. Therefore, freedom of speech is indispensable for a healthy state.

Which one of the following, if true, would NOT undermine the conclusion of the argument?

(A) People most often do not know what they genuinely want.

(B) Freedom of speech tends ultimately to undermine social order, and social order is a prerequisite for satisfying the wants of the masses.

(C) The proper function of government is not to satisfy wants, but to provide equality of opportunity.

(D) Freedom of speech is not sufficient for satisfying the wants of the masses: social order is necessary as well.

(E) Rulers already know what the people want.

政府的功能是满足群众的真正需要，除非政府知道那些需要是什么，否则政府就无法满足那些需要。言论自由能确保政府官员听到这样的需求信息。因此，对一个健康的国家来说，言论自由是必不可少的。

下面哪一条，如果正确，不能削弱上述论述的结论？

(A) 人民在多数情况下并不知道他们真正需要什么。

(B) 言论自由最终倾向于破坏社会秩序，而良好的社会秩序是满足群众需要的先决条件。

(C) 政府的正当功能不是去满足人民的需要，而是给人民提供平等的机会。

(D) 言论自由对满足群众的需要是不充分的，良好的社会秩序也是必不可少的。

(E) 统治者已经知道人民需要什么。

83. These days, everyone talks about being too busy. But all this busyness does not seem to result in things getting done. Just as many tasks are still left uncompleted, phone calls unreturned, and appointments missed as there were in the days before this outbreak of busyness. Therefore, people must not be as busy as they claim.

Which one of the following, if true, would most seriously weaken the conclusion in the passage?

(A) These days, looking busy is a status symbol.

(B) People have to do much more these days than before the so-called outbreak of busyness.

(C) People waste so much time talking about being busy that they fail to get things done.

(D) Just as many things are getting done now as before the so-called outbreak of busyness.

(E) People have more leisure time these days than before the so-called outbreak of busyness.

如今，每个人都说自己太忙了，但是，这些繁忙好像并不能促使事情的完成。现在，没有完成的工作，没有回的电话以及错过的约会的数量与这些繁忙发生之前一样的多。因此，人们一定没有他们声称的那样忙。

下面哪一条，如果正确，最能严重地削弱上述短文中的结论？

(A) 如今，看起来忙忙碌碌是一种地位的象征。

(B) 如今，人们不得不比所谓的繁忙发生之前做多得多的工作。

(C) 人们浪费如此多的时间来谈论繁忙以致于他们不能完成工作。

(D) 如今，人们做的事情与所谓的繁忙发生之前做的事情一样的多。

(E) 如今，人们比所谓的繁忙发生之前有更多的闲暇时间。

84. Fares on the city-run public buses in Greenville are subsidized by city tax revenues, but among the beneficiaries of the low fares are many people who commute from outside the city to jobs in Greenville. Some city councilors argue that city taxes should be used primarily to benefit the people who pay them, and therefore that bus fares should be raised enough to cover the cost of the service.

Each of the following, if true, would weaken the argument advanced by the city councillors EXCEPT:

(A) Many businesses whose presence in the city is beneficial to the city's taxpayers would relocate outside the city if public-transit fares were more expensive.

(B) By providing commuters with economic incentives to drive to work, higher transit fares would worsen air pollution in Greenville and increase the cost of maintaining the city's streets.

(C) Increasing transit fares would disadvantage those residents of the city whose low incomes make them exempt from city taxes, and all city councillors agree that these residents should be able to take advantage of city-run services.

(D) Voters in the city, many of whom benefit from the low transit fares, are strongly opposed to increasing local taxes.

(E) People who work in Greenville and earn wages above the nationally mandated minimum all pay the city wage tax of 5 percent.

85. A physician who is too thorough in conducting a medical checkup is likely to subject the patient to the discomfort and expense of unnecessary tests. One who is not thorough enough is likely to miss some serious problem and therefore give the patient a false sense of security. It is difficult for physicians to judge exactly how thorough they should be. Therefore, it is generally unwise for patients to have medical checkups when they do not feel ill.

Which one of the following, if true, would most seriously weaken the argument in the passage?

(A) Some serious diseases in their early stages have symptoms that physicians can readily detect, although patients are not aware of any problem.

(B) Under the pressure of reduced reimbursements, physicians have been reducing the average amount of time they spend on each medical checkup.

Greeville市政府管理的公共汽车的车费由本市的税收补贴，但是那些低车费的受益者中的许多人都是来自Greeville之外的到市区去上班的人。有些本市的议员争论说市政府的税收应该主要用来让那些交税的人受益。因此公共汽车的票价应该上升，直至足够支付这项服务的成本为止。

下面每一项，如果正确，除了哪一项之外都能削弱本市议员提出的论述？

(A) 如果本市的公共交通费用比较昂贵，那么许多位于本市的对该市的纳税人有益的商业就会迁到这个城市的外面。

(B) 较高的交通费用给上下班者提供了经济上的刺激，促使他们开车去上班，这将会加速Greeville的空气污染，并且还会增加本市街道的维护费用。

(C) 增加的交通费用对本市的那些因收入较低而被免税的居民不利，并且本市所有的议员都认为这些居民应该能利用市政府管理的服务项目。

(D) 许多本市的选民都是低交通费用的受益者，他们强烈地反对增加本地的税收。

(E) 所有在Greeville工作，并且工资收入在国家规定的最低限以上的人都给市政府上缴5%的工资税。

一个医生在进行健康检查时，如果检查进行得太彻底就会使病人感到不适，并且产生一些不必要的检查费用。如果检查进行得不够彻底又有可能错过一些严重的问题，因而给病人一种虚假的安全感。对医生来说要确切地判定检查应该进行的彻底程度是困难的。因此，一般对病人来说，当他们没有感觉到生病时去接受医疗检查的做法是不明智的。

下面哪一项，如果正确，能最严重地削弱上述段落中的论述？

(A) 有些严重的疾病在它们的早期阶段就具有很容易被医生察觉的症状，尽管病人们并没有意识到任何问题。

(B) 在减少费用的压力之下，医生们减少了他们在每项医疗检查上所花的时间。

(C) Patients not medically trained are unable to judge for themselves what degree of thoroughness is appropriate for physicians in conducting medical checkups.

(D) Many people are financially unable to afford regular medical checkups.

(E) Some physicians sometimes exercise exactly the right degree of thoroughness in performing a medical checkup.

(C) 没有在医疗上受过培训的病人在接受医生对他们进行的医疗检查时不能判断什么样的彻底程度对他们来说是合适的。

(D) 许多人在财政上付不起经常的医疗检查费用。

(E) 有些医生有时在进行医疗检查时，检查的彻底程度是恰如其分的。

86. Government-subsidized insurance available to homeowners makes it feasible for anyone to build a house on a section of coastline regularly struck by hurricanes. Each major storm causes billions of dollars worth of damage in such coastal areas, after which owners who have insurance are able to collect an amount of money sufficient to recoup a high percentage of their losses.

The passage provides the most support for an argument against a government bill proposing

(A) that power companies be required to bury power lines in areas of the coastline regularly struck by hurricanes.

(B) an increase in funding of weather service programs that provide a hurricane watch and warning system for coastal areas.

(C) renewal of federal funding for emergency life-support programs in hurricane-stricken areas.

(D) establishment of an agency committed to managing coastal lands in ecologically responsible ways.

(E) establishment of a contingency fund protecting owners of uninsured houses in the coastal areas from catastrophic losses due to the hurricane damage.

户主们可投保的政府补贴的保险项目使得任何人要在海边的一个经常被飓风袭击的区域建房变得可行。在这样的沿海地区，每次大风暴都能造成数亿美元的损失，大风暴过后，那些投了保险的户主能够领取到一定数量的钱，这些钱足以用来补偿他们的很大一部分的损失。

该段落为以下哪一项政府议案的反对意见提供了最有力的支持？

(A) 要求电力公司在经常受飓风袭击的沿海地区把电线埋在地下。

(B) 增加在天气服务项目上的投资，为沿海地区提供一个飓风观测站和报警系统。

(C) 在飓风袭击的区域，更新联邦政府对紧急生命维持项目的资助。

(D) 建立一个机构，以在生态上负责的方式管理沿海的土地。

(E) 建立一个意外资金，来保护那些沿海地区的没有投保的房子的所有者免受由于飓风破坏而给他们造成的灾难性的损失。

87. "This company will not be training any more pilots in the foreseeable future, since we have 400 trained pilots on our waiting list who are seeking employment. The other five major companies each have roughly the same number of trained pilots on their waiting lists, and since the projected requirement of each company is for not many more than 100 additional pilots, there will be no shortage of personnel despite the current upswing in the aviation industry."

Which one of the following, if true, casts the most doubt on the accuracy of the above conclusion?

因为我们公司有400个接受过培训的待业飞行员，所以在可以预见的未来，我们不会再培训新飞行员。其他的5个大公司中，每个都有差不多数目的接受过培训的飞行员在待业。既然每个公司对额外飞行员的规划需求量都不会超过100名，那么尽管目前航空工业在飞速发展，也不会出现飞行人员短缺的情况。

下面哪一项，如果正确，最能质疑上述结论的准确性？

(A) Most of the trained pilots who are on a waiting list for a job are on the waiting lists of all the major companies.

(B) In the long run, pilot training will become necessary to compensate for ordinary attrition.

(C) If no new pilots are trained, there will be an age imbalance in the pilot work force.

(D) The quoted personnel projections take account of the current upswing in the aviation industry.

(E) Some of the other major companies are still training pilots but with no presumption of subsequent employment.

(A) 大多数在一个大公司的待业名单上且接受过培训的飞行员也在其他所有大公司的待业名单上。

(B) 从长远的观点看，对飞行员进行培训用以补偿正常的人员损耗将变得非常必要。

(C) 如果没有新的飞行员被培训，那么在飞行员的劳动大军中将出现一个年龄失调现象。

(D) 被引用的职工规划已考虑了目前航空工业飞速增长的因素。

(E) 有些其他的大公司仍在培训飞行员，但并不承诺随后就雇佣他们。

88. Prominent business executives often play active roles in United States presidential campaigns as fundraisers or backroom strategists, but few actually seek to become president themselves. Throughout history the great majority of those who have sought to become president have been lawyers, military leaders, or full-time politicians. This is understandable, for the personality and skills that make for success in business do not make for success in politics. Business is largely hierarchical, whereas politics is coordinative. As a result, business executives tend to be uncomfortable with compromises and power-sharing, which are inherent in politics.

Which one of the following, if true, most seriously weakens the proposed explanation of why business executives do not run for president?

(A) Many of the most active presidential fundraisers and backroom strategists are themselves politicians.

(B) Military leaders are generally no more comfortable with compromises and power-sharing than are business executives.

(C) Some of the skills needed to become a successful lawyer are different from some of those needed to become a successful military leader.

(D) Some former presidents have engaged in business ventures after leaving office.

(E) Some hierarchically structured companies have been major financial supporters of candidates for president.

杰出的商业总裁在美国的总统竞选活动中通常扮演活跃的角色，他们往往充当竞选经费的筹募者或幕后的策划者，但是实际上他们中几乎没有人真正尝试过自己去做总统，整个历史上，绝大多数寻求成为总统的人都是律师、军方领导或全职的政客，这可以理解，因为在商业上取得成功的个性与技巧并不能在政治上取得成功。因为商业大体上都是等级体制，而政治上的体制却是互相协调的。因此，商业总裁在妥协以及分享权力时会感到非常的不自在，而这些都是政治家活动中所固有的。

下面哪一个，如果正确，能最严重地削弱上面文中对商业总裁为什么不竞选总统的解释？

(A) 许多最活跃的总统竞选经费的筹募者和幕后策划者本身就是政客。

(B) 军方领导在做出妥协或分权的时候，与商业总裁们一样的感到不自在。

(C) 成为一个成功的律师所需的某些技巧与成为一个成功的军方领导所需的某些技巧是不一样的。

(D) 有些前总统在离职后，从事风险商业投资。

(E) 有些等级体制的公司是总统候选人的财政支持者。

89. Sedimentary rock hardens within the earth's crust as layers of matter accumulate and the pressure of the layers above converts the layers below into rock. One particular layer of sedimentary rock that contains an unusual amount of the element iridium has been presented as support for a theory that a meteorite collided with the earth some sixty million years ago. Meteorites are rich in iridium compared to the earth's crust, and geologists theorize that a meteorite's collision with the earth raised a huge cloud of iridium-laden dust. The dust, they say, eventually settled to earth where it combined with other matter, and as new layers accumulated above it, it formed a layer of iridium-rich rock.

Which one of the following, if true, would counter the claim that the iridium-rich layer described in the passage is evidence for the meteorite collision theory?

(A) The huge dust cloud described in the passage would have blocked the transmission of sunlight and lowered the earth's temperature.

(B) A layer of sedimentary rock takes millions of years to harden.

(C) Layers of sedimentary rock are used to determine the dates of prehistoric events whether or not they contain iridium.

(D) Sixty million years ago there was a surge in volcanic activity in which the matter spewed from the volcanoes formed huge iridium-rich dust clouds.

(E) The iridium deposit occurred at about the same time that many animal species became extinct and some scientists have theorized that mass dinosaur extinctions were caused by a meteorite collision.

90. It is repeatedly claimed that the dumping of nuclear waste poses no threat to people living nearby.If this claim could be made with certainty, there would be no reason for not locating sites in areas of dense population. But the policy of dumping nuclear waste only in the more sparsely populated regions indicates, at the very least, some misgiving about safety on the part of those responsible for policy.

Which one of the following, if true, would most seriously weaken the argument?

(A) Evacuation plans in the event of an accident could not be guaranteed to work perfectly except where the population is small.

(B) In the event of an accident, it is certain that fewer people

---

地壳中的沉积岩随着层状物质的聚集以及上层的物质的压力使下层的物质变为岩石而硬化。某一特定沉积岩层中含有异常数量的钇元素被认为是6000万年前一陨石撞击地球的理论的有力证据。与地壳相比，陨石中富含钇元素。地质学家创立的理论认为，当陨石与地球相撞时，会升起巨大的富钇灰尘云。他们认为那些灰尘将最终落到地球上，并与其他的物质相混，当新层在上面沉积时，就形成了富含钇的岩石层。

下述哪一点，如果正确的话，能反对短文中所声称的富含钇的岩石层是陨石撞击地球的证据？

(A) 短文中所描述的巨大的尘迹云将会阻碍太阳光的传播，从而使地球的温度降低。

(B) 一层沉积岩的硬化要花上几千万年的时间。

(C) 不管沉积岩层中是否含有钇元素，它们都被用来确定史前时代事件发生的日期。

(D) 6000万年前，地球上发生了非常剧烈的火山爆发，这些火山喷发物形成了巨大的钇尘迹云。

(E) 大约在钇沉积的同时，许多种类的动物灭绝了。所以一些科学家提出了庞大恐龙的灭绝起因于陨石与地击相撞的理论。

有人再三声称倾倒核废物不会对附近的居民造成威胁。如果这种说法正确，那么不能把核垃圾场设在人口密集的地区就显得毫无道理。但是要把核废物倒在人口稀少的地区的方针表明，这项政策的负责者们至少在安全方法还是有些担忧的。

下面哪一点，如果正确，最能严重的削弱上述论述？

(A) 如果发生事故，除了在人口稀少的地区外，疏散方案不可能得以顺利实施。

(B) 如果发生事故，人口稀少地区的受害人数肯定比人口稠密地区的少。

would be harmed in a sparsely populated than in a densely populated area.

(C) Dumping of nuclear waste poses fewer economic and bureaucratic problems in sparsely populated than in densely populated areas.

(D) There are dangers associated with chemical waste, and it, too, is dumped away from areas of dense population.

(E) Until there is no shred of doubt that nuclear dumps are safe, it makes sense to situate them where they pose the least threat to the public.

(C) 在人口稀少的地区倾倒核废物所带来的经济和政治问题要比人口稠密地区的少。

(D) 化学废物也有危险，所以应把它倒在远离人口稠密的地区。

(E) 如果人们不能确保核废物是安全无疑的，那么就应当把它们放置在对公众造成最小威胁的地方。

91. Behind the hope that computers can replace teachers is the idea that the student's understanding of the subject being taught consists in knowing facts and rules, the job of a teacher being to make the facts and rules explicit and convey them to the student, either by practice drills or by coaching. If that were indeed the way the mind works, the teacher could transfer facts and rules to the computer, which would replace the teacher as drillmaster and coach. But since understanding does not consist merely of knowing facts and rules, but of the grasp of the general concepts underlying them, the hope that the computer will eventually replace the teacher is fundamentally misguided.

Which one of the following, if true, would most seriously undermine the author's conclusion that computers will not eventually be able to replace teachers?

(A) Computers are as good as teachers at drilling students on facts and rules.

(B) The job of a teacher is to make students understand the general concepts underlying specific facts and rules.

(C) It is possible to program computers so that they can teach the understanding of general concepts that underlie specific facts and rules.

(D) Because they are not subject to human error, computers are better than teachers at conveying facts and rules.

(E) It is not possible for students to develop an understanding of the concepts underlying facts and rules through practice drills and coaching.

计算机有望代替老师的想法是：学生们对所教的科目的理解在于他们知道事实和规则，老师的工作就是使事实和规则明确化，并通过做练习或者教授的方法把它们传授给学生，如果大脑确实是那样运行的话，教师可以把事实和规则输进计算机，计算机就可以作为教练和教官代替教师。但是既然理解并不仅在于知道事实和规则，而且在于对事实和规则所内含的整体概念的掌握。所以计算机有望最终代替老师的想法是从根本上说方向是错误的。

下面哪一点，如果正确的话，最能削弱作者关于计算机不能最终代替老师的结论？

(A) 计算机在事实和规则方面对学生的训练与教师是一样的。

(B) 教师的工作就是使学生们理解具体事实与规则所内含的全面概念。

(C) 计算机编程有可能使计算机教授学生如何理解具体事实与规则所内含的整体概念。

(D) 因为它们不会犯人类的错误，所以计算机在传递事实与规则方面比教师强。

(E) 学生们通过做练习和训练不可能理解事实与规则所内含的概念。

92. The high cost of production is severely limiting which operas are available to the public. These costs necessitate reliance on large corporate sponsors, who in return demand that only the most famous operas be produced. Determining which operas will be produced should rest only with ticket

高昂的制作成本严重地限制着观众可以看到哪些歌剧。这些费用必须依赖于大的团体赞助者，作为回报，这些赞助者又会要求仅制作最有名的歌剧。决定制作哪些歌剧只应当取决于票房的剧票购买者，

purchasers at the box office, not with large corporate sponsors. If we reduce production budgets so that operas can be supported exclusively by box-office receipts and donations from individuals, then the public will be able to see less famous operas.

Which one of the following, if true, would weaken the argument?

(A) A few opera ticket purchasers go to the opera for the sake of going to the opera, not to see specific operatic productions.

(B) The reduction of opera production budgets would not reduce the desire of large corporate sponsors to support operas.

(C) Without the support of large corporate sponsors, opera companies could not afford to produce any but the most famous of operas.

(D) Large corporate sponsors will stop supporting opera productions if they are denied control over which operas will be produced.

(E) The combination of individual donations and box-office receipts cannot match the amounts of money obtained through sponsorship by large corporations.

93. Samples from the floor of a rock shelter in Pennsylvania were dated by analyzing the carbon they contained. The dates assigned to samples associated with human activities formed a consistent series, beginning with the present and going back in time, a series that was correlated with the depth from which the samples came. The oldest and deepest sample was dated at 19,650 years before the present, plus or minus 2,400 years. Skeptics, viewing that date as too early and inconsistent with the accepted date of human migration into North America, suggested that the samples could have been contaminated by dissolved "old carbon" carried by percolating groundwater from nearby coal deposits.

Which one of the following considerations, if true, argues most strongly against the suggestion of the skeptics?

(A) No likely mechanism of contamination involving percolating groundwater would have affected the deeper samples from the site without affecting the uppermost sample.

(B) Not every application of the carbon-dating procedure has led to results that have been generally acceptable to scientists.

而不是大的团体赞助者，如果我们削减制作预算使得歌剧可以仅被票房收入和个人捐赠所支持，那么公众将会看到不太出名的歌剧。

下面哪一点，如果正确，最能削弱上述论断？

(A) 一些剧票购买者会为了看歌剧而去看歌剧，而不是看某些歌剧制作。

(B) 削减制作预算不会降低大团体赞助者的赞助欲望。

(C) 没有大团体赞助者的支持，歌剧公司只能制作最有名的歌剧。

(D) 如果大团体赞助者不能控制制作哪些歌剧，他们就会停止对歌剧作品的支持。

(E) 个人捐赠加上票房收入所得的钱抵不上大团体的赞助。

通过分析样品所含的碳元素，取自宾夕法尼亚州一个岩洞地面上的样品的日期得以确定。样品所标定的日期与人类的活动相联系，在时间上形成了一个从现在到过去的一个连续的系列，该系列与样品取自地面的深度相关联。最古老和最深处的样品被标定为是19650年前的遗物，误差在上下2400年之间。怀疑者认为该日期太早，与公认的人类移居南美洲的时间不符，提议该样品可能会被附近煤沉积层中渗出的地下水中溶解的碳所污染。

下面哪一个理由，如果正确，最能强有力地驳斥怀疑者的意见？

(A) 不可能会有渗出的地下水所造成的污染仅影响到那个地方较深处的样品而没影响到最上层样品的形成。

(B) 并不是每一种碳元素标定日期的方法都会被科学家们普遍接受。

(C) 没有迹象表明，人们在最深层可能沉积下的时候在使用煤做燃料。

(C) There is no evidence that people were using coal for fuel at any time when the deepest layer might have been laid down.

(D) No sample in the series, when retested by the carbon-dating procedure, was assigned an earlier date than that assigned to a sample from a layer above it.

(E) No North American site besides the one in Pennsylvania has ever yielded a sample to which the carbon-dating procedure assigned a date that was comparably ancient.

94. Before the printing press, books could be purchased only in expensive manuscript copies. The printing press produced books that were significantly less expensive than the manuscript editions. The public's demand for printed books in the first years after the invention of the printing press was many times greater than demand had been for manuscript copies. This increase demonstrates that there was a dramatic jump in the number of people who learned how to read in the years after publishers first started producing books on the printing press.

Which one of the following statements, if true, casts doubt on the argument?

(A) During the first years after the invention of the printing press, letter writing by people who wrote without the assistance of scribes or clerks exhibited a dramatic increase.

(B) Books produced on the printing press are often found with written comments in the margins in the handwriting of the people who owned the books.

(C) In the first years after the printing press was invented, printed books were purchased primarily by people who had always bought and read expensive manuscripts but could afford a greater number of printed books for the same money.

(D) Books that were printed on the printing press in the first years after its invention often circulated among friends in informal reading clubs or libraries.

(E) The first printed books published after the invention of the printing press would have been useless to illiterate people, since the books had virtually no illustrations.

95. Most disposable plastic containers are now labeled with a code number (from 1 to 9) indicating the type or quality of the plastic. Plastics with the lowest code numbers are the easiest

(D) 该系列中没有样品，当用碳元素标定日期法对这些样品的日期进行再次检测时，没有样品标定的日期会比它上面一层中样品得早。

(E) 在北美没有其他地方所产生的样品，通过碳元素日期标定法所确定的日期的古老程度能与宾夕法尼亚州的相比拟。

在印刷术出现之前，只能以昂贵手抄本的形式购买书。用印刷术制作的书比手抄本便宜得多。在印刷术出现后的第一年，公众对印刷版的书的需求量比对手抄书的大许多倍。这种增加表明，在出版商第一次使用印刷术的方法来制作书的那一年，学会读书的人的数量急剧增加。

下面哪一陈述，如果正确，对上述论述提出了质疑？

(A) 印刷术出现后的第一年里，人们在没有作家或职员帮助下写的信的数量在急剧增加。

(B) 印刷术制作的书的拥有者们常常在书的空白处写上一些评论的话。

(C) 印刷术出现后的第一年，印刷版图书的购买者主要是那些以前经常买昂贵手抄本的人，但是用同样多的钱，他们可以买许多印刷版的书。

(D) 印刷术出现后的第一年，印刷版的书主要是在非正式的读书俱乐部或图书馆里的朋友们之间相互传阅。

(E) 印刷术发明后的第一年，印刷发行的书对不识字的人来说是无用的，因为那些书中几乎没有插图。

现在，大多数用后即可废弃的塑料罐上都贴上了用以说明塑料的类型或质量的号码（从1到9）。具有最低编号的塑料品

for recycling plants to recycle and are thus the most likely to be recycled after use rather than dumped in landfills. Plastics labeled with the highest numbers are only rarely recycled. Consumers can make a significant long-term reduction in the amount of waste that goes unrecycled, therefore, by refusing to purchase those products packaged in plastic containers labeled with the highest code numbers.

Which one of the following, if true, most seriously undermines the conclusion above?

(A) The cost of collecting, sorting, and recycling discarded plastics is currently higher than the cost of manufacturing new plastics from virgin materials.

(B) Many consumers are unaware of the codes that are stamped on the plastic containers.

(C) A plastic container almost always has a higher code number after it is recycled than it had before recycling because the recycling process cause a degradation of the quality of the plastic.

(D) Products packaged in plastics with the lowest code numbers are often more expensive than those packaged in the higher-numbered plastics.

(E) Communities that collect all discarded plastic containers for potential recycling later dump in landfills plastics with higher-numbered codes only when it is clear that no recycler will take them.

96. Nuclear fusion is a process whereby the nuclei of atoms are joined, or "fused," and in which energy is released. One of the by-products of fusion is helium-4 gas. A recent fusion experiment was conducted using "heavy" water contained in a sealed flask. The flask was, in turn, contained in an air-filled chamber designed to eliminate extraneous vibration. After the experiment, a measurable amount of helium-4 gas was found in the air of the chamber. The experimenters cited this evidence in support of their conclusion that fusion had been achieved.

Which one of the following, if true, would cast doubt on the experimenters' conclusion?

(A) Helium 4 was not the only gas found in the experiment chamber.

(B) When fusion is achieved, it normally produces several by-products, including tritium and gamma rays.

(C) The amount of helium 4 found in the chamber's air did not exceed the amount of helium 4 that is found in

最容易被回收工厂回收，因此用后被回收而不是被倾倒到垃圾堆里的可能性最大。具有最高编号的塑料很少被回收。因此，消费者可以通过拒绝购买那些包装在最高编号的塑料制品内的产品，使不能回收的废物长期来看显著减少。

下面哪一点，如果正确，最能严重地削弱上面的结论？

(A) 目前，收集、分类和回收被抛弃的塑料废品的费用要比用原材料制造的新的塑料产品的高。

(B) 许多消费者没有注意到印在塑料容器上的号码。

(C) 塑料容器经回收后，编码几乎总是在增加，因为回收处理会使塑料产品的质量下降。

(D) 包装在最低编号的塑料制品内的产品通常要比那些包装在较高塑料制品内的产品贵。

(E) 那些将所有废弃的塑料容器收集起来以备将来回收的社区，只有在明显没有回收商来回收它们的情况下，才将有较高编码的塑料倾倒进垃圾堆里。

核聚变是这样一个过程——原子核聚合或被"熔化"，并且在这个过程中释放出能量，聚变的副产品之一是氦气。最近使用含在一密封烧瓶里的"重"水进行了一聚变试验，烧瓶放在一个充满空气的单间里，以消除外来振动。在试验之后，在单间的空气里有可测量到的氦-4气体，试验者以此证据支持他们的结论：核聚变已经完成。

下面哪一个，如果正确，将对试验的结论提出强有力的质疑？

(A) 氦-4不是试验的单间里发现的唯一气体。

(B) 当聚变完成时，通常产生几种包括氚和 γ 射线的副产品。

(C) 发现在单间里的氦-4的量没有超过普通空气里的氦气量。

ordinary air.

(D) Helium 4 gas rapidly breaks down, forming ordinary helium gas after a few hours.

(E) Nuclear fusion reactions are characterized by the release of large amounts of heat.

(D) 氦-4气体很快分解，在几个小时以后形成了普通的氦气。

(E) 核聚变反应的特征是释放大量的热。

97. A government agency publishes ratings of airlines, ranking highest the airlines that have the smallest proportion of late flights. The agency's purpose is to establish an objective measure of the relative efficiency of different airlines' personnel in meeting published flight schedules.

Which one of the following, if true, would tend to invalidate use of the ratings for the agency's purpose?

(A) Travelers sometimes have no choice of airlines for a given trip at a given time.

(B) Flights are often made late by bad weather conditions that affect some airlines more than others.

(C) The flight schedules of all airlines allow extra time for flights that go into or out of very busy airports.

(D) Airline personnel are aware that the government agency is monitoring all airline flights for lateness.

(E) Flights are defined as "late" only if they arrive more than fifteen minutes past their scheduled arrival time, and a record is made of how much later than fifteen minutes they are.

一政府机构出版了航空公司的信用等级，把晚点航班比例最小的航空公司列入最高信誉等级，这家机构的目的是要建立一个客观的方法来衡量不同航空公司在遵守出版的航空时刻表方面的相对有效性。

下面哪一个，如果正确，将使得这家机构信用等级的使用无效？

(A) 旅行者有时候对某一给定时间的确定旅程的航空公司别无选择。

(B) 班机经常由于糟糕的天气条件而晚点，而某些航空公司受坏天气影响要多于其他航空公司。

(C) 所有航空公司的班机时刻表允许班机有额外的时间进入或离开繁忙的机场。

(D) 航空公司的职员意识到这家政府机构正在监管所有晚点的航空公司班机。

(E) 当且仅当班机比预定到达时间晚到15分钟以上时，才定义为班机晚点，并且记录他们晚点超过15分钟的时间。

参考答案：

1. B	2. B	3. D	4. D	5. E
6. E	7. D	8. E	9. C	10. D
11. E	12. D	13. B	14. A	15. C
16. B	17. B	18. B	19. D	20. D
21. D	22. A	23. C	24. D	25. B
26. E	27. E	28. A	29. D	30. C
31. E	32. C	33. E	34. B	35. B
36. E	37. A	38. C	39. B	40. D
41. B	42. C	43. C	44. E	45. B
46. E	47. E	48. E	49. C	50. B
51. C	52. A	53. A	54. A	55. D
56. A	57. D	58. C	59. C	60. C
61. C	62. E	63. D	64. E	65. A
66. E	67. C	68. D	69. E	70. E
71. A	72. E	73. B	74. D	75. E
76. A	77. D	78. D	79. A	80. D

81. D	82. D	83. B	84. D	85. A
86. E	87. A	88. B	89. D	90. C
91. C	92. C	93. A	94. C	95. C
96. C	97. B			

2. **解析：**本题由一个evidence而得出一个解释性结论，属于典型的"B，A"模式，反对思路多针对段落推理的隐含假设，鉴于问题目的是要反对the traditional view，所以段落后半部分可以不读。(B)指出了另外一个因素可能影响B，所以(B)正确。(E)易误选，但一场流行病的流行并不能保证每一个人都染上这个病，所以(E)的"some"不能起到反对。(D)仅仅指出别的中东国家可能有alkaptonuria，但与我们讨论的"埃及有无alkaptonuria"无关，所以为无关答案。本题的另外一种思路是用问题目的中的核心关键词"alkaptonuria"来定位选项，发现(B)、(D)中有这个词，然后再把(D)排除掉，就可得到正确答案(B)。

3. **解析：**首先要明晰问题目的，注意到"LEAST damage"，所以答案方向应为无关答案或支持答案。段落推理为"因为母亲分娩持续的时间与孩子在出生第一个月哭泣的时间成正比关系，所以儿童的心理失调是由出生过程的压力造成的"。(D)只表明母亲分娩时间的计算依据于产科医师的估计，但不同的产科医师对婴儿何时出生的估计可能大相径庭，与上面段落推理无关，因此不能起到破坏作用，所以(D)正确。(A)否定了儿童哭泣时间与心理失调的关系；(B)否定了心理失调与儿童出生后第一个月里哭泣的时间之间的关系；(C)指出压力与分娩时间的反比关系，否定了分娩时间与孩子出生后第一个月里哭泣时间的正比关系；(E)表明了分娩的压力与哭泣的反相关系，否定了原因，从而驳斥了结论。所以(A)、(B)、(C)、(E)都从某一方面对段落推理起到了反对作用。

4. **解析：**本题推理为：从一个发现："洞穴中有人的骨骼，也有许多别的动物的骨骼"而得出一个解释性的结论："人把别的动物带回洞穴当肉吃"。当一个事实或发现中有件事情存在，如本题中的A_1(人的骨骼)、A_2(别的动物骨骼)，就说是A_1导致A_2时，反对思路必为A_2导致A_1。所以(D)通过指出人完全有可能是被当时庞大的猫科动物带回洞穴当肉吃而起到了反对作用，因此(D)正确。(A)、(B)、(C)、(E)均与段落推理无关。

5. **解析：**本题是由一个现象"离婚率升高"，而推导出结论说"生活在单亲家庭中的儿童比例必定上升"，这个推理暗含的假设为"只有离婚导致生活在单亲家庭的儿童比例上升"，反对应反对这个假设。(E)指出"由于父母中一位去世而由另一位家长抚养的儿童比例减小了"，因此反对了暗含的假设，所以(E)正确。(A)、(B)均与"儿童比例的变化"没有关联；(C)、(D)入选必定犯递进推理的错误，所以(C)、(D)也不正确。

6. **解析：**本题推理为：由一个事实"犯罪率下降52%"，得出一个解释性的结论"革新警察计划有效"，属于典型的"B，A"类型，反对的思路一般多用"除了A以外还有其他原因导致B"。如果最易犯罪的年龄组的人数有所减少，正如(E)所说，那么就从另外一个角度解释了B，所以对上面推理起到了反对作用，所以(E)正确。(A)探讨的是其他城市，与我们讨论的某城市无关；(B)说的是共同点，起到了支持的作用；(C)中的"suburban areas"实际上包括在city里面，并且如(C)所言，对段落推理起到的是支持作用。(D)是无关比较，必然不对。

7. **解析：**段落第一句话是个结论，而后面的几句话是对结论的进一步论证，因此读题重点在第一句话。如果"词汇可以缺乏准确但不至于无意义"，如(D)所说，那么将与段落第一句话"词汇是无意义的并且无法与其反义词区分开来"相违背。因此(D)为正确答案。(A)、(B)、(C)、(E)对推理不能起到任何作用，没有一个像正确答案但又绝对不是正确答案的选项。其实ETS命题人员也经常陷入这样一种尴尬的局面，有时设计出了一个正确答案，但怎么也设计不出一个迷惑答案。

10. **解析：**本题根据3岁以前的独生子与第一胎的孩子的对比得出了是否是独生子与其社会能力发展无关的结论。要对该结论进行削弱，就要削弱支持该结论的那一组对比，凡是认为这组对比不具代表性或不具可比性的选项都能削弱本题的结论。(D)指出一般情况下,第一胎的孩子在接近3岁时,他们的父母才要第二个孩子,就充分说明了得出本题结论的那个调查中的两个对照组的特征基本一致,没有可对比性,因此(D)对本题的结论构成了反对,所以(D)正确。(A)不是主要问题;(B)引入了新的比较,必然不对。(C)和(E)都不能从本题的段落中推出,且都是无关选项。

12. **解析**:本题推理比较简单,由一个事实而得出一个解释性结论:坐牢能使白领不愿再次犯罪。反对思路多为"有他因"。(D)指出白领犯罪之后被从监狱释放出来难以再次得到能使他们重新犯罪的机会,对上面的事实就做出了另外一个解释,所以起到了反对作用,因此(D)正确。(A)起到了部分支持作用;(B)做的无关比较与段落推理无关;(C)也不能解释上面事实;(E)也为无关选项。

13. **解析**:本题是由一个survey而外推,其段落推理成立所隐含的假设是A与B的探讨对象之间无本质差异。就这个推理而言,其隐含假设是16岁的美国公民的文盲比例不变。因此反对应找变化点,而(B)刚好指出了这种变化,所以(B)为正确答案。

18. **解析**:本题推理也是由一个事实"某州长在19个高层职位空缺中用了5名女性",得出一个解释性结论"州长不是性别歧视者"。反对思路比较固定。如果党纲要求州长至少任命5名女性,如(B)所说,就从另外一个角度对上述事实提出解释,从而起到了反对作用,所以(B)正确。(A)中的"一就职高层的女性打算辞职"与"州长是否性别歧视"无直接关系,这名女性要辞职可以有许多原因;(C)讨论的"三年前"与推理毫无关系;(D)中的"邻州的州长"与我们探讨的"某州州长"无关;(E)支持了州长不是一个racialist,但与本题探讨的"是否性别歧视"无关。

20. **解析**:要反对本题的结论,就要反对结论所依赖的前提,本题的段落中把人们年龄的增加归结为人们在孩提时代受到了良好的健康医疗照顾。因此凡是能对人们在孩提时代受到了良好的健康医疗照顾构成反对的选项都是正确答案。(D)指出美国很多85岁以上的人是在20岁或20岁以后才移居美国的,也就是说这些人在孩提时代是不可能接受良好的健康医疗照顾的,因此(D)正确。(A)、(C)都与本题的结论无关;(B)引入了新的比较,所以(B)也是不对的。

28. **解析**:本题读题重点应放在最后一句话上。若because-clause放在一个句子的后半部分时,反对大多要反对原因。若莎士比亚有意使用他认为不合语法的短语,如(A)所说,那么也就质疑了上面段落里的because-clause的有效性,所以(A)是正确答案。(B)的"infrequently"不能削弱原因,(C)、(D)、(E)均与推理无关。

31. **解析**:本题读题重点应放在最后两句话上。推理前提为"When they reach...",结论为:"So there is no way to..."。反对重点反对前提。若冰箱中的制冷剂可以在冰箱完成使命后被完全开发并重新使用,正如(E)所说,那么这些制冷剂就不可能到达臭氧层,所以(E)反对了前提,因此(E)为正确答案。(A)中的"the quantity",(B)中的"refrigeration of food"均与推理无关;(C)、(D)均起到部分支持作用。

34. **解析**:本题是由一个事实"枫糖价格上涨",而得出了一个解释性的结论:枫糖的采集者人为地抬高了价格,属于"B,A"题型,这个推理的成立所隐含的假设为:除了A以外无其他因素影响B。但这道题目是反对。如果由于虫害和干旱阻碍了枫树生长并造成枫糖短缺,那么段落推理所隐含的假设就不成立,所以推理结论必不正确,因此(B)为正确答案。(E)易误选,但(E)只表明过去枫糖价格上涨多次,但是不是采集者所为我们并不知道,所以(E)为无关选项。请大家注意:"that government price regulations are necessary to control rising prices"是上面推理的一个Suggestion。

35. **解析**:本题推理为:"因为该手术会提高接受者在使用45年之后得癌症的危险,所以该手术应被禁止"。反对可以反对原因。若几乎所有做该手术的人在接受手术时不大可能再活30年,如(B)所说,那么就使得接受者在45年之后得癌症的危险变得无意义,因此(B)正确。(A)是一个支持选项。(C)、(D)、(E)均与推理无直接关系。

36. **解析**:本题的推理是由一个事实:"自杀率上升",而得出一个解释性的结论:"社会变化是原因",属于"B,A"题型,推理所依赖的假设是"除了A以外没有别的因素导致B"。若1987年自杀事件上报到了有关部门但1960年大多数自杀没有上报，如(E)所说，就表明完全有可能是因为上报率高而导致自杀率高了，反对了上面推理的隐含假设，也就反对了段落推理，所以(E)正确。(A)中的"Sometimes"说明不了任何问题；(B)中的"Some"也对推理起不到任何作用；(C)、(D)均为无关选项。

37. **解析：** 本题根据每磅这种谷物的蛋白质含量高于其他主要农作物而做出这种谷物对人口稠密、人均摄入量低和蛋白质来源不足的国家有好处的结论。很显然本题的结论是以这种谷物的产量比其他主要农作物高或至少不能比其他农作物的明显地低为前提。(A)指出"新发现的农作物的每亩平均产量比目前粮食作物产量低得多，从而严重地削弱了结论所依赖的一个前提条件，因此(A)正确。(B)和(E)为无关选项；(C)和(D)引入新的比较，所以也都为错误选项。

40. **解析：** 读明白问题目的永远是最重要的，本题问题目的要求我们在段落论述正确的前提下，用段落信息去反对下面的一个选项，实质上是让我们找一个与段落推理完全违背的答案。本题可归入"归纳"题型，但在考试现场主要是靠一种正确、快速解题的感觉。可参阅本书239页27题。

47. **解析：** 要解答本题，就是要找一个选项说明新的除草剂不可行。(E)选项指出，虽然通过基因工程能使农作物不受除草剂的伤害，但是农作物的种子会因为万能除草剂的作用而不会发芽。种子不会发芽，该作物物种就要灭绝。(E)选项从而否定了新的除草剂的可行性，所以(E)正确。(D)容易被误选，选(D)的人会认为人们不信任这种新的万能除草剂肯定就是新的除草剂被实施的障碍，但是应注意的是人们只是在这种万能除草剂刚上市时，对它有这种不信任的态度，但是随着时间的推移，当万能除草剂的独特性能表现出来时，人们肯定就会争相购买，而选项(E)则指出了万能除草剂内在的致命缺陷，因此(E)是正确答案。

51. **解析：** 本题是要找一个选项对本题中的"不同的观众对同一个演讲者相同的演讲评价不一"的论述进行反驳，(C)指出人们对演讲者个人素质的判断主要取决于他的谈话内容和说话方式，根据这个选项，两组听众对这个演讲者的反应应该相同，与本题段落中的"相同的人作相同的演讲，而听众反应不一"相矛盾，所以(C)正确。(A)为无关选项；(B)、(D)和(E)都支持了文中的观点。

53. **解析：** 流行性感冒具有传染性，它主要通过传染的方法使其他的人感染，因此对本题最后的预测构成反对，就要找一选项说明新药能抑制感冒的传染性。(A)选项说明新药抑制了感冒传染的主要渠道——咳嗽，从而反对了卧床病人返回工作后会使患感冒的人数增加的推测。(B)和(D)都是无关选项；至于(C)，本题并不是要解释为什么工人们在患流感后会呆在家中，所以(C)不对；本文推理中并未涉及suppression of symptom，因此(E)也是不对的。

54. **解析：** 本题根据Spinach中的Oxalic acid 能阻碍人体对钙的吸收，做出了其他含钙的物质应该被食用的结论。要对本题的结论构成反对，就要从Oxalic acid入手。既然Oxalic acid能阻碍人体对钙的吸收，那么有没有其他的物质能抑制Oxalic acid的这种对人体吸收钙的不良影响？(A)选项指出大米可以与Oxalic acid中和，对结论成立的前提进行了削弱，从而对结论进行了削弱。因此(A)为正确答案。(B)、(C)、(D)、(E)都不能对本题结论成立的前提构成反对。

55. **解析：** 本题是要找一个选项对Conservationists assumption进行反对，即找一个选项说明富有一个物种的地区可能不会富有其他同气候区的物种。(D)选项指出在蝴蝶种类较多的地方，鸟类的种类不一定多，从而指出了Conservationists assumption的错误，所以(D)为正确答案。

58. **解析：** 本题虽属于"二人对话"型，但其问题目的是让我们反驳第二个人即公司发言人的观点，我们可以看到公司发言人的推理属于"A′, not A→B"（A=昆虫与细菌；A′=炼铝厂空气污染；B=杀死作物）反对思路要么为就是A导致B，要么为A导致A′。(C)指出A导致A′，从而起到了反对作用，所以(C)正确。

60. **解析：** 本题读题重点是段落最后一句话，且最后一句话中because放在后半部分，表示强调原因A，并暗示A是一个唯一原因。反对思路多为"有他因"。若Tocqueville认为他父亲身体不好导致了他家庭的贫困，正如(C)所说，那么就反对了拿破仑的统治使他的家庭贫困的说法，所以(C)正确。(A)易误选，一般地，有although的句子重点在后半部分，但后半部分仅仅说贫困的经济状况应归因于收成不好，但完全有可能Tocqueville的家庭贫困不是由于收成不好，而是由于拿破仑的统治，因此(A)不对。(E)中涉及的"not different from the experience..."与上面推理无关，因此为无关答案。

61. 解析：本题也可归入"逻辑应用与技法"题型，但我们在本书第一篇第二章已指出：在对待问题目的类型上，要明白"运用之妙，存乎一心"的重要性。

conditional on upon sth. 依赖某事物的，含有条件的

well-founded 基础牢固的，有根据的

62. 解析：要看清问题目的为"Weaken、Except"，所以其答案应为无关选项或支持选项。该结论是建立在比较S城和T城的报纸销量上的。有四个选项说明了为什么S城更大的报纸销量不一定意味着S城市民更好地掌握关于世界大事的信息。选项(B)指出S城出售的许多报纸使T城的市民掌握了信息，而不是S城。选项(A)和(C)都表明即使平均每个市民对新闻没有更多的了解的情况下，通过什么方式可以出现更大的报纸销量。最后，选项(D)指出S城市民阅读的很多报纸不是关于世界大事的信息来源。(E)中提到的价格差异有助于解释销量的差异，但不能削弱建立在销量差异基础上的该结论，因此，E是正确答案。

67. 解析：典型的"因果倒置"类型的反对。

68. 解析："Weaken Except"题型的答案方向必为支持或无关。(D)对结论起到了支持作用；(C)易误选，但(C)通过指出车不一样而间接斥了上面推理结论。

70. 解析：本题让我们反驳以上论点。论点是：这些赠品加剧而非减轻了对博物馆财政资源的需求。(E)说明这些赠品使博物馆省了钱从而带来了额外的利益，因此是减轻而非加剧了对博物馆财政资源的需求，与上面论点刚好相反，所以(E)正确。(A)没有直接说出收益，所以不对；(B)并未在现金大小与费用大小之间作出比较，因此对论点什么作用也起不到；(C)起到了支持作用。

71. 解析：典型的"就目的提方法"的思路，可以很容易看出(A)正确，本题关键是(C)为什么不对。(C)只告诉我们狗会吓跑捕食老鹅与病鹅的狐狸，并未告诉我们别的鹅怎么样，所以选(C)是属于违反"无递推"的错误。

73. 解析：本题为一典型的"B，A"类型，段落里面比较的两组对象说的均为相同点，因此反对重在寻找不同点。(B)指出土褐色的工作间被设计用来最多为65名工人提供足够空间，而移出50人则只剩下50人，所以完全有可能是因为空间大而导致剩下在土褐色工作间的工人增进了生产率，所以(B)正确。(A)中的"the same...as"、(C)中的"matched as"、(E)中的"as well as"都是与support答案有关的关键词；(D)易误选，但只解释了两组中的一组——自愿移到颜色明亮的工作间的人的效率提高，至于留下的50人的效率为什么提高并未涉及，所以(D)不正确。请警惕(D)的错误及其迷惑性。

75. 解析：警惕(A)、(D)的错误原因。(A)只表明竞争存在，但与"payment"无关；(D)与"payment"也无直接关系。选(A)、(D)的考生均违反了"无递推"的原则。

76. 解析：典型的"因果倒置"类思维的题目。

77. 解析：典型的"因果倒置"类思维的题目。

78. 解析：如果员工的工作职责要求他们在整个工作日中经常互相联系，正如(D)所说，那么提议中的规定将可能使得经常互相联系受到干扰，从而降低雇员生产率，所以(D)正确。(A)易误选，但选择(A)违反了无递推原则，因为(A)只表明员工工作时不受其他员工的妨碍，而"员工自己决定何时到达"与"是否会打扰别的员工"我们并不知道，因此(A)为无关选项。

79. 解析：段落推理为"一些人类学家想从对现代游牧社会的研究中去了解古代的游牧社会是有缺陷的，因为游牧社会是extremely varied"。反对上述推理，主要反对原因。(A)选项中的"in common"与"varied = different"相对应，很好地起到了反对作用。(E)易误选，但我们在明晰了问题目的之后，发现(E)中的"importantly different from"与段落推理中的"extremely varied"完全吻合，所以起到了支持作用。

80. **解析**：本题难度相对较大，是一个典型的"由一个事实得出一个解释性的结论"的"B，A"型，反对多用有其他原因。为什么对于窦头痛，四家医院中有三家会给病人用Novex呢？可能会有许多原因，如Novex有效；Novex很容易购买到；Novex的广告力度相当大以致于使许多病人要求医生开Novex药等等，但上述推理暗含：仅仅因为有效，所以四家医院中有三家给病人用Novex。(D)指出Novex不需医生处方就可得到指出了有效以外的其他原因，因此对上述推理起到了反对作用，所以(D)正确。(A)讨论的只是竞争者，与Novex无关；(B)中的"for those patients who..."说的是对于某类特殊病的处理情况，用局部来代替全部病人往往需要作出一个假设，所以(B)起不到任何作用；(C)中的"products"可能包含Novex，也可能不包含Novex，因此什么作用也起不到；(E)只表明了Novex比某类药有效的情况，但并未表明Novex是否比同类药都有效，所以也起不到任何作用，请大家注意(B)中的定语从句。

81. **解析**：本题让我们质疑计划可行性，主要把反对的重点放在实施计划的方法——sell any patents they acquire to corporations上，若该大学进行的政府资助的研究在很大程度上重复了盈利性公司的研究，如(D)所说，那么其出售给一些已有这些研究成果的公司将不大可能，所以起到了质疑的作用，所以(D)正确。

82. **解析**：读题时注意问题目的中的"NOT"。本题的结论为，言论自由是一个国家健康发展的一个必要条件。(D)说明言论自由不是一个国家健康发展的充分条件，因此从某种程度上对本题的结论构成了支持，因此(D)为正确答案。本题的逻辑关系为，在言论自由的条件下，人民能自由表达他们的需求，政府官员从而能了解到人民的需求，然后政府就可以根据人民的需求来履行它的功能。由此可以推出，如果人民不知道它们真正需要什么，那么给予他们言论自由对一个国家的健康发展来说是没用的；如果政府已经知道了人民的真正需求，那么在没有言论自由的条件下，政府照样可以正确履行它的功能。因此(A)、(E)均对本题的结论构成了反对，为错误选项。选项(B)、(C)通过找他因对本题的结论构成了反对，因此也是错误选项。

83. **解析**：本题的考点在过去与现在的整体与部分之间的数量概念上的差异。本题由现在没有完成的工作，没有回的电话以及错过的约会的数量与所谓的繁忙发生之前一样的多，推出人们一定没有他们声称的那样忙。由部分推出整体是以前后整体的大小一致为前提。因此本题结论成立的一个前提条件是过去和现在要做的事情一样多。(B)对本题结论成立的前提条件进行了否定，因此(B)为正确答案。(D)很明显就是本题结论成立的前提；(E)从另一个方面对本题的结论构成了支持；因为看起来忙忙碌碌是一种地位的象征，因此人们为提高其地位都会声称他们很忙，而实际上并没有他们声称的那样忙，所以(A)对本题的结论构成了支持；(C)为无关选项。

84. **解析**：注意问题目的中的"EXCEPT"。本市议员的论述的前提是本市的税收应该主要让那些交税的人受益，其结论是公共汽车票价该上升。(D)表明许多本市的从低交通费中受益的选民反对增加本地的税收，也就是说他们不愿市政府通过增加他们的税收的办法来补偿交通费用的不足，由此推出在不增加税收和维持较低的交通费用两者之间，他们选择了前者。因此选项(D)对本市议员的论述起支持作用，为正确答案。(A)、(B)和(C)都通过找它因的方法削弱了本市议员的公共汽车票价应该上涨的结论；选项(E)削弱了本市议员论述的前提。

85. **解析**：本题论证的重点是病人应该怎样地对待医疗健康检查，因此要削弱本题的论述，就应该从病人入手，而不是应该从医生的方面入手。根据这条原则，很容易发现(B)和(E)都是错误选项；(C)和(D)很显然与论述的内容无关；在(A)表明的条件下，若病人不去接受医疗检查，他们就会错过及早发现严重疾病的机会。因此在这种情况下，无不良感觉时不去接受医疗检查的做法很显然是不明智的，所以(A)是正确答案。

86. **解析**：政府补贴的保险项目是为了保护海边地区的户主们的意外灾难性损失，因此要反对政府补贴的保险项目，就要找出另一个可替换的能保护沿海地区户主们利益的办法，在5个选项中，只有选项(E)是针对户主们的利益而提出的，所以(E)是正确答案。

87. 解析：本题的结论是不培训飞行员不会出现飞行员短缺的情况，本题结论的前提是待业飞行员处于供过于求的状态。因此要使本题的结论的准确性陷入疑问，就要对结论的前提进行质疑。设想大多数接受过培训且在本公司待业的飞行员也在其他五个大公司的待业名单上，那么就有可能出现待业飞行员的供给小于需求的局面，也就是说，在航空工业内出现飞行人员短缺的局面，因此(A)是正确答案。(B)、(C)、(D)和(E)均是无关选项。

88. 解析：本题的论述根据商业总裁在妥协及分权时不如政治家们自在来解释他们不去竞选总统。要削弱这种解释，就要对该结论的前提进行削弱。若政治家们在妥协或分权时也如商业总裁们一样的感到不自在时，显然就不能用不自在来解释商业总裁们为什么不去竞选总统。由此分析可知(B)是正确答案显而易见。(A)、(C)、(D)和(E)均是无关选项。

89. 解析：选项(D)通过找他因的方法对段落中声称的富含铱的岩石层是陨石撞击地球的证据构成了反对，因此(D)为正确选项。(A)、(B)、(C)、(E)四选项都是无关选项。

90. 解析：选项(C)通过找他因的办法，排除了把核废物倒在人口稀少的地区的方针是出于安全上考虑的可能，从而严重地削弱了本题的论述，因此(C)正确。(A)、(B)和(E)三选项都对本题题干中的论证构成了支持，(D)为无关选项。

91. 解析：本题的论述根据计算机不能教授学生理解和掌握事实与规则所内含的整体概念，作出了计算机不能最终代替老师的结论，因此要削弱该结论，就要削弱该结论所依赖的前提。若计算机编程能使计算机具有教授学生如何理解具体事实和规则所内含的整体概念的能力，该结论显然将不能成立，因此(C)是正确答案。

92. 解析：当削减预算，没有大团体赞助时，歌剧公司就不得不制作一些有名的能吸引大众且增加票房收入的歌剧作品，以抵付高昂的制作费用。也就是说歌剧公司只能制作起有名的歌剧，公众也就只能看到最有名的歌剧，这与段落的最后一句话相冲突，由此分析可知(C)是正确答案。(A)、(B)、(D)和(E)均不能从短文中合理地推出。

93. 解析：怀疑者仅对取自最深处的样品的日期产生怀疑，但是若取自最深处的样品与取自其他地方的样品的形成机制是一样时，怀疑者的怀疑以及支持他们的怀疑的提议就不能站住脚，因此(A)是正确答案。(E)对怀疑者的建议构成了支持，(B)、(C)和(D)均为无关选项。

94. 解析：本题的结论显然是以印刷术出现后印刷版的书的销售增加量与学会读书的人数成比例为前提。(C)表明印刷版图书销售量的增加主要是由那些以前经常买昂贵手抄本的人现在买了许多印刷版的书所引起的，所以完全有可能是人数没变，而平均每人买了更多的书，因此(C)正确。(A)、(B)、(D)和(E)四个选项均为无关选项。

95. 解析：消费者们只购买那些装在较低编号的塑料包装内的产品，可以使塑料废物量减少，但是如果这些具有较低编号的塑料外包装，在回收再处理时，质量一直在下降，那么就不能使不可回收的废弃塑料长期显著地减少，因此(C)是正确答案。选项(A)、(B)和(D)似乎也能削弱本题的结论，但是应该注意的是本题只是在讨论消费者们可以拒绝购买那些包装在最高编号的塑料包装内的产品，也即本题是在讨论一种可能性，而非必要性，因此(A)、(B)和(D)都是错误的；(E)是无关选项。

96. 解析：本题为Weaken结论，而本题是由一个实验的结果而得出了一个结论，我们可以Weaken前提。(C)选项表明氦-4的量并没有超过普通空气里的氦气量，从而Weaken了上面暗含的前提。(A)、(B)均与段落中"one of the by-product of fusion is helium gas"吻合，不可能为反对，而(D)、(E)均为无关选项。

97. 解析：上面段落推理为了评价不同航空公司职员的相对有效，可以使用晚点的多少来客观衡量。就目的提方法时，一般用"有他因"来反对。(B)指出"某些班机受天气条件影响要大于其他班机"的其他原因的存在导致晚点，起到了很好的反对作用。(A)、(C)和(D)均为无关选项，(E)给出了晚点的定义，但与"客观公正与否"无关。

第 四 章

评 价

评价考题主要考查我们评价论点的能力，这类题往往用以下方式：

Which of the following would be most important to know in evaluating the accuracy of the argument above?

Knowledge of which of the following would be LEAST useful in evaluating the claims made in the passage above?

一、 评价题型的答案方向

这类题的答案方向大多也是针对段落推理的隐含假设，当选项为一般疑问句时，对这个问句有两方面的回答——Yes和No。若对这个问句回答yes是对段落推理起到了支持作用，那么对这个问句回答no，就对段落推理起到了驳斥作用；若对这个问句回答yes对段落推理起到了反对作用，那么对这个问句回答no，就对段落推理起到了支持作用。于是，这个问题就对段落推理有评价作用（注意一定是对这个问句的yes与no的回答都起作用，如果仅仅对一方面回答起作用，则不是评价）。当选项为特殊疑问句或陈述句时，如果对这些选项的回答的精确信息，可以使上面的推理成立或不成立（即对这个精确的信息，加入not之后，对段落推理成立方向刚好与原来相反），那么这个选项就为评价。

由于评价在很多情况下是针对段落推理成立的隐含假设起作用，所以读题时要注意体会段落推理的隐含假设，然后去寻找一个能对段落推理起到正反两方面作用的选项。

1. In the aftermath of a worldwide stock-market crash, Country T claimed that the severity of the stock-market crash it experienced resulted from the accelerated process of denationalization many of its industries underwent shortly before the crash.

Which of the following, if it could be carried out, would be most useful in an evaluation of Country T's assessment of the causes of the severity of its stock-market crash?

(A) Calculating the average loss experienced by individual traders in Country T during the crash.

(B) Using economic theory to predict the most likely date of the next crash in Country T.

(C) Comparing the total number of shares sold during the worst days of the crash in Country T to the total number of shares sold in Country T just prior to the crash.

(D) Comparing the severity of the crash in Country T to the severity of the crash in countries otherwise economically similar to Country T that have not experienced recent denationalization.

译文： 在一次世界范围内的股市剧跌之后的余波中，T国宣称该国经历的相当严重的股市下跌是由于在下跌之前不久，该国许多行业经历了过快的非国有化过程。

以下哪一项，如果能被执行，将最有助于对T国股票市场严重下跌原因的评估？

(A) 计算在下跌期间T国个人交易商的平均损失。

(B) 利用经济学理论预测T国下一次下跌最有可能的时间。

(C) 把T国下跌过程中最糟糕的那段时间抛出的股票总数同刚刚下跌前T国抛出的股票总数相比。

(D) 把T国下跌的严重程度同那些其他经济条件与T国相似，但没有经历最近的非国有化过程的国家下跌的严重程度相比。

(E) Comparing the long-term effects of the crash on the purchasing power of the currency of Country T to the immediate, more severe short-term effects of the crash on the purchasing power of the currency of Country T.

(E) 把这次下跌对T国货币购买力的长期影响与下跌对T国货币购买力的即时的、更严重的短期影响相比。

解析：(D)中提出的比较将有助于评价T国对该国股市下跌严重程度的解释。如果那些除了最近的非国有化，其他经济条件与T国类似的国家下跌的严重程度至少是一样大，那么就削弱了T国的解释。然而如果这些国家下跌的严重程度比T国小，就支持了该解释。因此，(D)是正确答案。选项(A)、(C)和(E)是好的选择，因为每项只关心衡量T国下跌的严重程度，没有对下跌原因的假想提出评估。T国下一次下跌的时间与评论这样的假想无关，因此，(B)不合适。

2. Guitar strings often go "dead"—become less responsive and bright in tone—after a few weeks of intense use. A researcher whose son is a classical guitarist hypothesized that dirt and oil, rather than changes in the material properties of the string, were responsible.

Which of the following investigations is most likely to yield significant information that would help to evaluate the researcher's hypothesis?

(A) Determining if a metal alloy is used to make the strings used by classical guitarists.

(B) Determining whether classical guitarists make their strings go dead faster than do folk guitarists.

(C) Determining whether identical lengths of string, of the same gauge, go dead at different rates when strung on various brands of guitars.

(D) Determining whether a dead string and a new string produce different qualities of sound.

(E) Determining whether smearing various substances on new guitar strings causes them to go dead.

译文：在频繁地使用几个星期之后吉他琴弦经常会"死掉"——反应更加迟钝，音调不那么响亮。一个其子为古典吉他演奏家的研究人员提出一个假想，认为这是由脏东西和油，而不是琴弦材料性质的改变而导致的结果。

以下哪一项调查最有可能得出有助于评价该研究人员假想的信息？

(A) 确定是否使用了一种金属合金来制作古典吉他演奏家使用的琴弦。

(B) 确定古典吉他演奏家使他们的琴弦死掉的速度是否比通俗吉他演奏家快。

(C) 确定把相同的标准长度相等的琴弦，安在不同品牌的吉他上，是否以不同的速度死掉。

(D) 确定一根死掉的弦和一根新弦是否会产生不同音质的声音。

(E) 确定在新吉他弦上抹上不同的物质是否能使它们死掉。

解析：该假想有两部分：第一，频繁地使用不会产生使琴弦死掉的材料变化；第二，是脏东西和油造成的这种现象，选项(E)建议的实验通过将那些已知具有它们原来材料性质的琴弦弄脏对这个假想进行直接测试，因此，(E)是正确答案；因为同演奏风格［选项(B)］和吉他品牌［选项(C)］相关的因素可能会影响到琴弦是如何变脏的，(B)和(C)中提出的调查得到的结果不会对该假想有清楚的评估；关于琴弦材料的信息［选项(A)］在明确同该假想的关系前需要相当多的补充信息；短文已经给出了(D)中调查所能得出的信息。

3. Although custom prosthetic bone replacements produced through a new computer-aided design process will cost more than twice as much as ordinary replacements, custom replacements should still be cost-effective. Not only will surgery and recovery time be reduced, but custom

译文：尽管通过一种新的计算机辅助设计过程生产出来的定制的修复用的骨替代物的价格是普通替代物的两倍多，定制的替代物仍然是节约成本的。定制的替代物不仅可以减少手术和术后恢复的时

replacements should last longer, thereby reducing the need for further hospital stays.

Which of the following must be studied in order to evaluate the argument presented above?

(A) The amount of time a patient spends in surgery versus the amount of time spent recovering from surgery.

(B) The amount by which the cost of producing custom replacements has declined with the introduction of the new technique for producing them.

(C) The degree to which the use of custom replacements is likely to reduce the need for repeat surgery when compared with the use of ordinary replacements.

(D) The degree to which custom replacements produced with the new technique are more carefully manufactured than are ordinary replacements.

(E) The amount by which custom replacements produced with the new technique will drop in cost as the production procedures become standardized and applicable on a larger scale.

间，而且它更耐用，因而减少再次住院的需要。

为评论以上提出的论述，必须研究以下哪一项？

(A) 一个病人花在手术中的时间同花在术后恢复的时间的比较。

(B) 随着生产定制替代物的新技术的出现，生产定制替代物减少的成本数量。

(C) 同使用普通替代物相比较，使用定制的替代物可以在多大程度上减少再次手术的需要。

(D) 用新技术生产的替代物比普通替代物生产得更仔细的程度。

(E) 当生产程度逐渐标准化，并可运用到更大规模上时，用新技术生产的定制替代物的成本将下降的数量。

解析：尽管生产成本更昂贵，由于其他开支的节省可以使定制的骨替代物成为节省成本的选择。为评论该论述，必须决定这些节省能否抵消增加的成本，因此需要研究期望的再次住院需要减少的情况，选项(C)是正确答案；该论述并不要求研究手术与恢复时间的比率，因此(A)不合适；过去和将来的成本变化与评论一项建立在目前计划的成本基础上的论述无关，因此选项(B)和(E)不合适；最后，由于研究生产定制替代物的仔细程度自身不能提供关于成本的信息，选项(D)也不正确。

4. Hardin argued that grazing land held in common (that is, open to any user) would always be used less carefully than private grazing land. Each rancher would be tempted to overuse common land because the benefits would accrue to the individual, while the costs of reduced land quality that results from overuse would be spread among all users. But a study comparing 217 million acres of common grazing land with 433 million acres of private grazing land showed that the common land was in better condition.

The answer to which of the following questions would be most useful in evaluating the significance, in relation to Hardin's claim, of the study described above?

(A) Did any of the ranchers whose land was studied use both common and private land?

(B) Did the ranchers whose land was studied tend to prefer using common land over using private land for grazing?

(C) Was the private land that was studied of comparable quality to the common land before either was used for

译文：Hardin争论说，人们使用起共同拥有的（即对任何使用者开放的）牧场比使用起私人的牧场更不注意。每个放牧者都有过度使用公地的冲动，因为从中获得的利益将归于个人，而由于过度使用土地而引起的土地质量下降的成本由所有使用者分摊。但一项研究比较了2.17亿英亩的公用牧场和4.33亿英亩的私人牧场，表明公用牧场的条件更好。

与Hardin的宣称做比较，评价以上描述的这项研究的意义时，以下哪一个问题的答案将最有用？

(A) 有没有一些放牧者，他们的土地属于被研究之列，既使用公用又使用私人土地？

(B) 那些自己的土地属于被研究之列的放牧者是否倾向于更愿意使用公地而不使用私人土地来放牧？

grazing?

(D) Were the users of the common land that was studied at least as prosperous as the users of the private land?

(E) Were there any owners of herds who used only common land, and no private land, for grazing?

(C) 在用来放牧之前该研究中的私人土地是否有与公地的质量相当？

(D) 该研究中的公地使用者是否至少与私人土地的使用者一样有钱？

(E) 是否有任何牧群的所有者只在公地，不在私人土地上放牧？

解析：Hardin的宣称是因为过度使用，公用牧地比私人牧地条件恶化得更快。研究表明，公用牧地现在的状况更好，但如果在放牧前，公用牧地的条件远远好于私人牧地，该研究中指出的现象就不会削弱Hardin的宣称。因此，选项(C)是正确答案；选项(A)和(E)不合适，因为不管某些放牧者使用两种土地还是只使用公地，该项研究都可以削弱Hardin的宣称；类似地，不管放牧者是否更喜欢使用公地，如(B)所说，该研究都可以削弱Hardin的宣称；最后，(D)不合适是因为如果公地的使用者更加富有，或更不富有，都不会使该研究的说服力减小。

二、 试题精练及解析

1. The cost of the average computer logic device is falling at the rate of 25 percent per year, and the cost of the average computer memory device at the rate of 40 percent per year. It can be concluded that if these rates of cost decline remain constant for a period of three years, at the end of that time the cost of the average computer memory device will have declined by a greater amount than the cost of the average computer logic device.

Accurate information about which of the following would be most useful in evaluating the correctness of the conclusion above?

(A) The number of logic devices and memory devices projected to be purchased during the next three years.

(B) The actual prices charged for the average computer logic device and the average computer memory device.

(C) The compatibility of different manufacturers' logic devices and memory devices.

(D) The relative durability of logic devices and memory devices.

(E) The average number of logic devices and memory devices needed for an average computer system.

一般计算机的逻辑器件成本正以每年25%的比例下降，一般的计算机存贮器件则以每年40%的比例下跌。如果成本下跌的比例在三年内不变，在三年后一般的计算机存贮器件的成本下降的数量要比一般逻辑器件成本下降的数量更大。

关于以下哪一项的准确信息在评价以上结论的正确性方面最有用？

(A) 今后三年内计划被购买的逻辑器件和存贮器件的数量。

(B) 一般的逻辑器件和存贮器件实际收取的价格。

(C) 不同厂家的逻辑器件和存贮器件的兼容性。

(D) 逻辑器件和存贮器件的相对耐用性。

(E) 一般计算机系统所需逻辑器件和存贮器件的平均数量。

2. The results of a recent poll in the United States indicate that the public, by 80 percent to 17 percent, opposes relaxation of existing regulation of air pollution. Furthermore, not a single major segment of the public wants environmental laws made less strict. The results of this poll reveal that legislators, by voting for renewal of the Clean Air Act, will be responsive to the will of the public without alienating any significant

美国最近一次的民意测验结果表明公众以80%对17%反对放松现存的空气污染的法规。而且，没有一个主要公众阶层想放宽环境法。这次投票的结果显示出立法者将通过投票支持更新空气洁净法，可以在不疏远任何有影响力的特殊利益集团的同时对公众意愿做出回应。

special-interest groups.

Which of the following pieces of information would be most useful in evaluating the logic of the argument presented above?

(A) The groups in the population that were defined as major segments of the public and the groups defined as special-interest groups.

(B) The length of time that current federal environmental laws have been in effect and the length of time that states have regulated air pollution.

(C) The probable economic effect of renewal of the Clean Air Act on those opposed to and those in favor of relaxing environmental laws.

(D) The people whom the author hopes to influence by citing the results of the poll.

(E) The percentage of those surveyed who chose not to respond to the questions asked of them.

3. According to a recent survey, marriage is fattening. Cited as evidence is the survey's finding that the average woman gains 23 pounds and the average man gains 18 pounds during 13 years of marriage.

The answer to which of the following questions would be most relevant in evaluating the reasoning presented in the survey?

(A) Why was the period of time studied in the survey 13 years, rather than 12 or 14?

(B) Did some of the men surveyed gain less than 18 pounds during the time they were married?

(C) How much weight is gained or lost in 13 years by single people of comparable age to those surveyed?

(D) Were the women surveyed as active as the men surveyed, at the time the survey was made?

(E) Will the reported gains be maintained over the lifetimes of the persons surveyed?

4. The facts show that the fear of flying in airplanes is not rational. In 1986 alone, there were 46,000 fatalities in highway accidents, but from 1980 to the present an average of only 77 per year in accidents on major domestic airlines. The rate for regional airlines was only slightly higher.

If the evidence cited above is accurate, which of the following would be most important to know in order to evaluate the force of that evidence?

下面哪条信息对评价上面陈述的逻辑性最有用？

(A) 被定义为主要阶层的群体和被定义为有特殊利益集团的群体。

(B) 现行的联邦环境法的有效期限和州规定的空气污染法的期限。

(C) 更新空气洁净法对反对和支持放宽环境法规的人可能带来的经济影响。

(D) 作者希望通过引用民意测验的结果来施加影响的人是哪些人。

(E) 在调查中对调查的问题选择不做回答的人数的百分比。

最近一项调查表明，婚姻能使人变胖。研究人员的发现可以证实这一点：在婚后的13年里，妇女们平均增长了23磅，男人平均增长18磅。

下面哪个问题的答案与评价该调查的推理最有关系？

(A) 为什么调查的时间取13年，而不是12年或14年？

(B) 被调查的男人中在婚后的时间里，有没有增重不到18磅的？

(C) 与被调查的这些人年纪相仿的独身者，在这13年里他们的体重又增减多少呢？

(D) 在做这项调查时，被调查的妇女与男人一样积极运动吗？

(E) 在被调查的这些人中，他们增加的体重会继续保持下去吗？

事实表明对坐飞机感到恐惧是没有道理的。仅在1986年一年，高速公路事故使得4.6万人死亡，而从1980年至今，大的国内航空公司平均年死亡率仅达77人。地方航空公司的事故死亡率也只略高一点。

如果上述论据是准确的，知道下面的哪一项对于评价该论据的说服力最重要？

(A) Whether repeated airplane travel allays fear of flying in airplanes.

(B) Whether regional and domestic airlines spend the same average amount of time per aircraft on maintenance.

(C) How many people reported a fear of flying in airplanes that was strong enough to prevent them from traveling by air.

(D) How many people per year have traveled by highway and how many by air since 1980.

(E) How much higher the accident rate has been for regional airlines than for major domestic airlines since 1980.

(A) 多次的乘飞机旅行经验是否会减轻对坐飞机的恐惧。

(B) 地方航空公司与国家航空公司在每架飞机的维护上是否花费相同的时间。

(C) 有多少人报告说对坐飞机的恐惧如此强烈以致他们无法乘坐飞机。

(D) 自1980年以来通过高速公路旅行的人次和乘坐飞机旅行的人次。

(E) 自1980年以来地方航空公司事故率比大的国内航空公司的事故率高出多少。

5. Since minors should not smoke, the proposed law prohibiting cigarette sales to minors is reasonable. However, the proposed ban on cigarette vending machines is like installing a roadblock to apprehend the one person in a hundred who drives without a license. A roadblock stops everyone, not just those who break the law.

The answer to which of the following questions would be most important in evaluating the objection above to a ban on cigarette vending machines?

(A) Do cigarette vending machines malfunction more frequently than do food vending machines?

(B) Are there current laws that prohibit the sale to minors of materials intended only for adults?

(C) Would an increase in taxes on cigarette sales help deter minors from purchasing cigarettes?

(D) Would a ban on cigarette vending machines inconvenience a significant number of cigarette-buying adults?

(E) Are items more expensive when sold from a vending machine than when sold in retail stores?

因为未成年人不应该吸烟，因此拟议中的禁止向未成年人销售香烟的法律是合理的。然而，拟议中的对售烟机的禁令就如同为捉拿100个中才有一个的没有驾照开车的人而设置路障一样。路障阻止了每个人，而不仅是那些违法的人。

对下列哪个问题的回答对评价上述对于售烟机的禁令的反对意见最重要？

(A) 自动售烟机比自动售食品机出现功能失灵的情况更频繁吗？

(B) 目前是否有法律禁止把成年人专用的东西出售给未成年人？

(C) 提高香烟销售税能阻止未成年人购买香烟吗？

(D) 禁止设置自动售烟机是否给许多购买香烟的成年人带来不便？

(E) 自动售烟机出售的商品比零售店出售的更贵吗？

6. The Planning Committee has decided in favor of redeveloping the city's western district and has issued a report that argues for the feasibility of such redevelopment. Lesley Johnston serves as a member of the Planning Committee and has done so from the committee's inception. Therefore it cannot be true that Johnston opposes redeveloping the western district.

The answer to which of the following questions would most help in evaluating the argument above?

(A) Did the feasibility report include information compiled by independent consultants rather than by members of

计划委员会已经决定同意再开发该市西区，并且发表了一个论证再开发可行性的报告。Lesley Johnston是计划委员会的一名成员而且从委员会一成立就已经是了。所以说Johnston不可能反对再开发西区。

对以下哪个问题的回答将最有助于评价以上论述？

(A) 这篇可行性报告是由独立的顾问团还是由委员会成员撰写的？

the committee?

(B) Do the committee's decisions require the unanimous support of its members?

(C) Has Johnston served on other municipal committees that are not concerned with issues of planning and development?

(D) Does the committee issue reports at regular intervals or only when a question on development is decided?

(E) Have other members of the committee served on the committee as long as Johnston has?

7. Sleep deprivation is a known cause of workplace error, and many physicians frequently go without sleep for periods of 24 hours or more. However, few of these physicians have, in the course of a routine examination by a peer, been diagnosed with sleep deprivation. So there is little cause for concern that habitual sleep deprivation will cause widespread physician error.

The answer to which of the following questions would be most helpful in evaluating the argument?

(A) Do physicians who have been diagnosed with sleep disorders also show signs of other ills not related to sleep deprivation?

(B) Is the ability to recognize the symptoms of sleep deprivation in others significantly impaired by habitual sleep deprivation?

(C) Do factors other than habitual sleep deprivation ever lead to errors in the workplace on the part of physicians?

(D) Of people who have recently been treated by physicians, what percentage believe that many physicians have occasionally suffered from sleep deprivation?

(E) Is the incidence of sleep deprivation higher among physicians than it is among other health care workers?

8. The United States is not usually thought of as a nation of parakeet lovers. Yet in a census of parakeet owners in selected comparable countries, the United States ranked second, with eleven parakeet owners per hundred people. The conclusion can be drawn from this that people in the United States are more likely to own parakeets than are people in most other countries.

Knowledge of which of the following would be most useful in judging the accuracy of the conclusion?

(A) The number of parakeets in the United States.

(B) 委员会的决定是否需要它的成员们一致同意？

(C) Johnston是否也在其他就某个不涉及规划、开发等问题的市政委员会中任职？

(D) 委员会是定期的还是就某个开发问题做出决定时发布报告？

(E) 其他委员会成员，作为该委员会成员的历史，有Johnston长吗？

睡眠不足是引起工作事故的众所周知的原因。许多医生经常连续24小时或更长时间不睡觉，然而在同事之间做的常规检查中，这些医生很少有被诊断为睡眠不足。因此没有理由担心习惯性睡眠不足会导致广泛的医疗事故。

对下列哪个问题的回答最有助于评价上面的论述？

(A) 诊断为睡眠不足的医生是否同时也表现出其他与睡眠无关的疾病征兆？

(B) 医生习惯性睡眠不足是否会严重减弱他判断他人睡眠不足征兆的能力？

(C) 是否除了习惯性睡眠不足之外还有其他的医生本身的因素而导致工作失误？

(D) 在最近接受治疗的人当中，相信医生有时受睡眠不足之苦的人占多大比例？

(E) 在医生中睡眠不足的发病率是否比在其他医疗工作人员中更高？

通常人们不认为美国是一个有很多长尾鹦鹉爱好者的国家，然而在对一批挑选出来进行比较的国家中养长尾鹦鹉的人做的一项人口调查中，美国以每百人中11人养长尾鹦鹉而排名第二。由此可得出结论，美国人比大多数其他国家的人更喜欢养长尾鹦鹉。

知道下列哪一项将最有助于判断以上结论的正确性？

(A) 美国拥有的长尾鹦鹉的数量。

(B) The number of parakeet owners in the United States.

(C) The number of parakeet owners per hundred people in the country that ranked first in the census.

(D) The number of parakeet owners in the United States compared to the numbers of owners of other pet birds in the United States.

(E) The numbers of parakeet owners per hundred people in the countries not included in the census.

(B) 美国养长尾鹦鹉的人的数量。

(C) 在普查中排名第一的国家里每100个人中养长尾鹦鹉的人的数量。

(D) 美国养长尾鹦鹉的人数和美国养有其他鸟类作为宠物的人数的比较。

(E) 该普查中未包括的国家每百人中养有长尾鹦鹉的人的数量。

9. College librarian: Until three years ago, nonstudents used the library without charge. Then, because of our decreased budget, they were asked to pay $100 per year. Nevertheless, about 150 nonstudents still use the library without paying. We will therefore gain financially if we hire a guard to identify nonstudents and ensure that they have paid the fee.

Which of the following would it be most important to know in order to evaluate the librarian's conclusion?

(A) The number of students who use the library annually.

(B) The library's budget this year.

(C) Whether the library has installed an expensive computerized cataloging system.

(D) How much the library's budget was decreased three years ago.

(E) The annual cost to the library of hiring a guard.

大学图书管理员：三年以前，非学生读者使用本图书馆是免费的。后来，因为我们的预算减少了，所以我们要求他们每年支付100美元的费用。然而，仍然约有150名非学生读者使用了图书馆而没有缴费。因此，如果我们雇用一名警卫来辨认非学生读者并令其缴费，那么我们就可以获得经济收益。

下列哪一项对于评价图书管理员的结论是最为重要的？

(A) 每年使用图书馆的学生人数。

(B) 今年图书馆的预算。

(C) 图书馆是否安装了昂贵的计算机分类系统。

(D) 三年前图书馆的预算降低了多少。

(E) 图书馆雇用一名警卫每年的成本是多少。

10. During the last hunting season, twice as many people were hit by cars while walking on public sidewalks as were hurt in hunting accidents in the woods. Therefore, during the last hunting season, people were safer in the woods than they were while walking on public sidewalks.

In evaluating the argument above, it would be most important to know

(A) the likelihood that during the next hunting season fewer people will be hurt in hunting accidents in the woods than were hurt during the last hunting season.

(B) the ratio during last hunting season of people who walked on public sidewalks to people who were in the woods.

(C) how many of the people hurt in hunting accidents during the last hunting season had been hurt in similar accidents in the past.

(D) how many of the accidents could have been avoided if the drivers of the cars or the hunters who fired the guns

在上个打猎季节，在人行道上行走时被汽车撞伤的人数是在树林中的打猎事故中受伤的人数的2倍。因此，在上个打猎季节，人们在树林里比在人行道上行走时安全。

为了评价上段陈述，最重要的是要知道：

(A) 下个打猎季节，在树林中打猎受伤的人数较上个季节减少的可能性。

(B) 上个打猎季节，马路上的行人和树林中人数的比例。

(C) 在上个打猎季节中，打猎事故中受伤的人中有多少在过去类似的事故中也受过伤。

(D) 如果汽车司机和开枪的猎手都小心点儿，有多少事故可以免于发生。

had been more careful.

(E) how many people, on average, are hurt in hunting accidents in the woods when it is not hunting season.

11. Science Academy study: It has been demonstrated that with natural methods, some well-managed farms are able to reduce the amounts of synthetic fertilizer and pesticide and also of antibiotics they use without necessarily decreasing yields; in some cases yields can be increased.

Critics: Not so. The farms the academy selected to study were the ones that seemed most likely to be successful in using natural methods. What about the farmers who have tried such methods and failed?

Which one of the following is the most adequate evaluation of the logical force of the critics' response?

(A) Success and failure in farming are rarely due only to luck, because farming is the management of chance occurrences.

(B) The critics show that the result of the study would have been different if twice as many farms had been studied.

(C) The critics assume without justification that the failures were not due to soil quality.

(D) The critics demonstrate that natural methods are not suitable for the majority of farmers.

(E) The issue is only to show that something is possible, so it is not relevant whether the instances studied were representative.

(E) 平均来讲，在非狩猎季节，有多少人在打猎事故中受伤。

科学院研究：已经证明使用自然方法可以使一些管理经营良好的农场在不明显降低产量，甚至某些情况下可以在提高产量的基础上，减少合成肥料，杀虫剂以及抗生素的使用量。

批评家：不是这样的，科学院选择用以研究的农场似乎是使用自然方法最有可能取得成功的农场。那些尝试了这样的自然方法且失败了的农场又会怎么样呢？

下面哪一项是对批评家应答的逻辑力量的最充分的评价？

(A) 农业上的成功和失败很少仅仅因为幸运与否，因为农业就是对或然事件的管理。

(B) 那些批评家表明如果被研究的农场的数量加倍，那么研究的结果将会不同。

(C) 那些批评家毫无理由地假设那些失败不是由土壤质量引起的。

(D) 那些批评家表明自然方法对大多数的农场主都不适合。

(E) 被讨论的问题仅仅是为了展示某些事情是可能的，所以与被研究的例子是否具有代表性并无关系。

参考答案：

1. B	2. A	3. C	4. D	5. D
6. B	7. B	8. E	9. E	10. B
11. E				

1. **解析**：本题由一个比例数据而得出一个外推与"数量"有关的结论，那么推理成立所隐含的假设是"logic device 与memory device的最初成本基本相似"。而评价大多针对隐含假设。(B)针对隐含假设，指出logic device和memory device 两者的actual prices是多少。若二者原来成本基本相同，那么就支持了上面推理；若memory device的actual price要远远小于logic device的actual price，则反对了段落推理，所以(B)是一个评价；(A)与(E)中的"number"与成本没有直接关系；(C)中的"compatibility"与(D)中的"durability"均与"成本"没有直接关系，因此(A)、(C)、(D)、(E)都不对。

3. **解析**：段落推理为由一个"evidence"而得出一个解释性的结论："marriage is fattening"。评价应寻求一个选项，对其"yes"与"no"两方面的回答起到不同的作用。若我们知道可比较年龄组的独身者在13年内体重增加的量，如(C)所说，那么若这些独身者体重增加大于上面统计数字，就反对了

221

上面的推理，因为这些独身者也变胖了，则可能并非婚姻使人变胖，完全有可能是人长大而体重自然增加了；若他们体重增加小于上面统计数据，则支持了上面的推理。所以(C)是一个很好的评价，因此(C)正确；(B)易误选，但(B)中的"some"并不能反对上面推理中的"average"。

5. **解析**：本题读题重点在于段落后半部分，其推理为：因为拟议中的对售烟机的禁令就如同为捉拿100个人中的一个没有驾照而开车的人一样，所以该禁令不合适。我们用问题中间的关键词"a ban on cigarette vending machine"来定位选项，发现(D)中涉及关键词，且与段落推理的原因所做的类比相关。如果对(D)的答案为"yes"，则禁令使大多数购买香烟的成年人感到不方便，所以支持了"该禁令不合适"的结论，如果对(D)的回答为"no"，即禁令没有给大多数购买香烟的成年人造成不便，则反了"该禁令不合适"的结论，所以(D)做了最好的评价，因此(D)正确；(A)在"cigarette vending machine"与"food vending machine"之间做了一个无关比较，所以(A)不对。

7. **解析**：本题通过睡眠不足的医生的同事对这些睡眠不足的医生的检查，得出了习惯性的睡眠不足不会引起工作出错的结论，因此本题结论暗含的一个假设是判断别的医生是否睡眠不足的能力会不会受自己本身就睡眠不足的影响。若受自身的影响时，则那些常规检查的结果就是不可靠的，因为缺乏睡眠的医生没有判断别人是否睡眠不足的能力；若不受自身的影响，则(B)就会支持段落中关于睡眠不足确实不是医疗事故的原因。由以上分析可知，(B)为正确答案。

8. **解析**：本题结论的前提是美国每百人拥有长尾鹦鹉的人数在"selected comparable countries"中位居第二，本题的结论是美国人比大多数其他国家的人更喜欢养长尾鹦鹉。考生应当注意的是前提的比较范围与结论的比较范围是不一样的，结论中的比较范围不但包括"selected comparable countries"，而且还包括其他未包括在该调查报告中的国家，因此要判断结论的正确性，还必须要知道未包括在该调查报告中的其他国家的每百人中拥有长尾鹦鹉的人数，也即(E)为正确答案；(A)不能说明本题的结论；不同国家的人数差异较大，因此知道美国的养长尾鹦鹉的人数也对本题的结论毫无帮助，所以(B)是错误的。本题结论比较的对象是most other countries，因此与排名第一的国家每百人中拥有长尾鹦鹉的人数无关；(D)引入了本题论述未提及的新比较，与结论无关，所以也是错误选项。

10. **解析**：本题推理为"在人行道上行走时被汽车撞伤的人数是在森林中打猎事故中受伤人数的2倍，因此在树林里行走比在人行道上行走安全"。一般地，当由数据得出结论时，结论是对上面数据的解释，评价一般从比例或单位方面的角度来进行。若我们知道，马路上的行人与树林中的人数的比例，那么我们就可以对上面推理作出评价。若该比例大于2，则反了段落推理；若该比例小于2，则支持了段落推理。因此(B)起到了很好的评价作用，所以(B)正确；(A)中的"the next hunting season"与上面推理无关；(C)、(D)、(E)也均与推理无关。

11. **解析**：通过认真读题，我们发现批评家答非所问，科学院的研究只是为了证明使用自然方法可以不明显降低甚至增加管理经营良好的农场的产量可能性，而批评家则指责科学院的研究结果不具代表性。因此(E)为正确答案。(A)、(B)、(C)和(D)四个选项都不能从段落中合理地推出。

第 五 章

归 纳

归纳（Generalization）在本书中泛指"自上而下"的考题，即假定我们所面临的段落的推理成立，让我们从段落推理中得出一些东西。它与我们前四章所讲的假设、支持、反对、评价题型的最大差异是：归纳所面临的段落推理是肯定成立的推理，因此归纳是从上面段落中必然能得到什么，我们不能怀疑段落推理的合理性；而假设、支持、反对、评价考题所面临的段落是有待评价的推理，因此这四类考题是让我们从五个选项中选择一个选项放到段落中对段落推理起到一定作用。从这个意义上讲，在做逻辑推理题时，明晰问题目的永远是很重要的。让我们来看一个简单的推理：Only birds can fly, so XYZ can fly。如问题目的属于归纳题型，则这一推理必定成立，且我们可知其隐含假设为"XYZ is a bird"；若问题目的属于假设、支持、反对或评价题型，那么这一推理不一定成立（即有待评价的推理）。因此我们只能根据问题目的不同，选择答案对该推理的成立与否起到相应的作用。

由于归纳题型的段落推理是肯定成立的推理，因此，我们不能够对段落的内容是否正确、结论是否荒谬、推理是否合理做出评价，我们的目标应锁定在怎么样才能找到能从段落推理中得出一个选项。

一、 归纳题的五种题型

归纳题常见的典型问题目的如下：

1. It can be inferred from the passage above that the author believes that...

2. Which of the following is implied by the passage above?

3. From the information above, which of the following can be most reasonably inferred about...

4. If the statements above are true, which of the following conclusions can be properly drawn?

5. Which of the following would provide the most logical conclusion for the preceding paragraph?

6. The statements in the passage, if true, best support which of the following conclusions?

7. The statement cited above conveys which of the following propositions?

8. The passage above emphasizes which of the following points?

9. The author in the passage above argues that...

10. Which of the following expresses the point the author of the passage above makes?

11. Choose the most logical completion for the following paragraph.

从上面常见的典型问题目的可以看出，归纳题的题型主要有以下5种：

（一）推断（Inference）：典型的问题目的如上面的1、2、3。

（二）结论（Conclusion）：典型的问题目的如上面的4、5。

（三）支持（Support）：典型的问题目的如上面的6（注意：绝对不同于本篇第二章我们所讲的支持，这里的支持方向是"从上到下"）。

（四）中心思想：典型的问题目的如上面的7、8、9、10。

（五）完成段落：典型的问题目的如上面的11。（注意：完成段落中有一类是要求我们挑选一个对段落推理起到解释作用的选项，与我们这里所讲的不一样）

下面通过6道例题来体会归纳题五种题型的基本解题思路：

1. Increases in the level of high-density lipoprotein (HDL) in the human bloodstream lower bloodstream-cholesterol levels by increasing the body's capacity to rid itself of excess cholesterol. Levels of HDL in the bloodstream of some individuals are significantly increased by a program of regular exercise and weight reduction.

Which of the following can be correctly inferred from the statements above?

(A) Individuals who are underweight do not run any risk of developing high levels of cholesterol in the bloodstream.

(B) Individuals who do not exercise regularly have a high risk of developing high levels of cholesterol in the bloodstream late in life.

(C) Exercise and weight reduction are the most effective methods of lowering bloodstream cholesterol levels in humans.

(D) A program of regular exercise and weight reduction lowers cholesterol levels in the bloodstream of some individuals.

(E) Only regular exercise is necessary to decrease cholesterol levels in the bloodstream of individuals of average weight.

译文：人体血液中高浓度脂蛋白含量的提高可以增加人体排除胆固醇的能力，从而使血液中的胆固醇含量降低。某些人通过一个经常锻炼和减轻体重的计划使血液中的高浓度脂蛋白含量显著提高。

以下哪一项能够从以上论述中正确地推导出来？

(A) 那些体重不足的人不会有血液中出现高含量胆固醇的风险。

(B) 那些不经常锻炼的人在人生晚期在血液中出现高含量胆固醇的风险较高。

(C) 锻炼和减轻体重是降低人体血液胆固醇含量的最有效办法。

(D) 一个经常锻炼和减轻体重的项目降低了某些人血液中的胆固醇含量。

(E) 要降低体重正常的人血液中的胆固醇含量，只有经常锻炼是必要的。

解析：如果高浓度脂蛋白的含量提高造成胆固醇含量降低，并且如果一个特定的项目增加了某些人的高浓度脂蛋白的含量，也就是说一些从事这个项目的人会使胆固醇含量降低，因此可以正确地推导出来选项(D)，因此(D)是正确答案；不能正确地推导出选项(A)，因为论述中没有提出任何关于体重不足与胆固醇含量之间的联系；选项(B)和(E)都无法被推导出来，因为没有说明锻炼本身对于增加高浓度脂蛋白含量或降低胆固醇含量是必要条件还是充分条件；选项(C)不合适，因为并没有提到关于降低胆固醇含量的其他办法。

2. Meteorite explosions in the Earth's atmosphere as large as the one that destroyed forests in Siberia, with approximately the force of a twelve-megaton nuclear blast, occur about once a century.

The response of highly automated systems controlled by complex computer programs to unexpected circumstances is unpredictable.

Which of the following conclusions can most properly be drawn, if the statements above are true, about a highly automated nuclear-missile defense system controlled by a complex computer program?

(A) Within a century after its construction, the system would react inappropriately and might accidentally start a nuclear war.

(B) The system would be destroyed if an explosion of a large meteorite occurred in the Earth's atmosphere.

译文：规模相当于摧毁西伯利亚森林的那一次在地球大气层中的陨石爆炸，威力大概相当于1200万吨级的核爆炸，一个世纪大概出现一次。

由复杂的计算机程序控制的高度自动化的系统对于未预料到的情况的反应是无法预测的。

如果以上关于由一个复杂的计算机程序控制的高度自动化的核导弹防御系统的陈述是正确的，可以最适当地得出以下哪一个结论？

(A) 在它建成后的一个世纪内，该系统会做出不适当的反应并且可能由于偶然性而引发一场核战争。

(B) 如果在地球大气层内发生一次大陨石爆炸，该系统将被摧毁。

(C) It would be impossible for the system to distinguish the explosion of a large meteorite from the explosion of a nuclear weapon.

(D) Whether the system would respond inappropriately to the explosion of a large meteorite would depend on the location of the blast.

(E) It is not certain what the system's response to the explosion of a large meteorite would be, if its designers did not plan for such a contingency.

(C) 对于该系统来说，不可能将一次大陨石爆炸和一件核武器的爆炸区分开来。

(D) 该系统是否对一次大陨石爆炸做出不适当的反应取决于爆炸发生的位置。

(E) 如果该系统的设计者没有考虑到陨石爆炸这种偶然性，那么该系统对一次大陨石爆炸将要做出的反应是不确定的。

解析： 归纳题应着重把握层次结构。如果该防御系统的设计者没有考虑到大陨石爆炸这种偶然性，这种爆炸，从该系统来看，是一种未预料的情况，该系统对这种爆炸的反应相应是无法预测的，选项(E)表述了这种推理，因而是正确答案；无法推出选项(A)和(C)，因为一个世纪内没有陨石爆炸发生和一个经过合理设计的核防御系统能够区分核爆炸和陨石爆炸同所提供的信息不矛盾；无法推出选项(B)和(D)，因为既没有信息表明大气层中的陨石爆炸会摧毁该系统，也没有信息表明爆炸发生的位置将决定该防御系统的反应是否适当。

3. The cost of producing radios in Country Q is ten percent less than the cost of producing radios in Country Y. Even after transportation fees and tariff charges are added, it is still cheaper for a company to import radios from Country Q to Country Y than to produce radios in Country Y.

The statements above, if true, best support which of the following assertions?

(A) Labor costs in Country Q are ten percent below those in Country Y.

(B) Importing radios from Country Q to Country Y will eliminate ten percent of the manufacturing jobs in Country Y.

(C) The tariff on a radio imported from Country Q to Country Y is less than ten percent of the cost of manufacturing the radio in Country Y.

(D) The fee for transporting a radio from Country Q to Country Y is more than ten percent of the cost of manufacturing the radio in Country Q.

(E) It takes ten percent less time to manufacture a radio in Country Q than it does in Country Y.

译文： 在Q国生产收音机的成本比在Y国生产收音机的成本少10%。即使把运输费用和关税加上，一个公司将收音机从Q进口到Y国仍比在Y国生产的收音机便宜。

以上所述，如果是正确的，最有力地支持以下哪一个论断？

(A) Q国的劳动力成本比Y国低10%。

(B) 从Q国进口收音机到Y国将减少Y国10%的制造业就业机会。

(C) 对从Q国进口到Y国的收音机征收的关税少于在Y国制造该收音机的成本的10%。

(D) 将收音机从Q国运到Y国的运费大于在Q国制造该收音机的成本的10%。

(E) 在Q国生产一台收音机的时间比在Y国的时间少10%。

解析： 如果对从Q国进口到Y国征收的关税等于或高于在Y国生产收音机的成本的10%，那么，同短文中所说的相反，从Q国进口收音机到Y国的成本将等于或高于在Y国生产收音机的成本。因此，关税不能有那么高，因此，(C)是正确答案；选项(A)和(E)给出了成本差异的可能的部分解释，但它们都没有得到短文的支持，因为Q国的成本优势可能归因于其他因素；选项(B)和(D)同文中提供的信息不矛盾，但是短文没有提供证据来支持它们。

4. Which of the following best completes the passage below? At a recent conference on environmental threats to the North Sea, most participating countries favored uniform controls on the quality of effluents, whether or not specific environmental damage could be attributed to a particular source of effluent. What must, of course, be shown, in order to avoid excessively restrictive controls, is that _____.

(A) any uniform controls that are adopted are likely to be implemented without delay

(B) any substance to be made subject to controls can actually cause environmental damage

(C) the countries favoring uniform controls are those generating the largest quantities of effluents

(D) all of any given pollutant that is to be controlled actually reaches the North Sea at present

(E) environmental damage already inflicted on the North Sea is reversible

译文：以下哪一项能最好地完成以下短文？

在最近一次关于对北海的环境威胁的会议上，大多数与会国同意一致控制排水质量，不管某些环境损害是否归因于某一特别的废水源。为避免过多的限制性控制，当然必须表明

(A) 采取的任何一致控制措施有可能立即执行。

(B) 控制辖内的任何物质实际都能造成环境损害。

(C) 那些赞成一致控制的国家是那些排出废水数量最大的国家。

(D) 所有的任何将被控制的确定的污染物现在实际上都排向北海。

(E) 已经使北海深受其害的环境损害是可以恢复的。

解析：如果不能造成环境损害的物质也在控制范围内，那些控制将是超过必要范围的限制性控制。因此选项(B)是正确答案；如(A)所述，确保立即实施控制措施，不是避免过多限制性控制的必要部分。尽管如果一些产生最多废水的国家赞成一致控制，它可能有助于避免过多的限制，但没必要所有的这些国家都这样做，如选项(C)所述；不是所有的确定的污染物都需要排向北海，如选项(D)所述，因为至多只有一些需要这样；即使这种已经困扰着人们的损害是可以恢复的，由于该控制可能会产生过多的限制，选项(E)不正确。

注：pollutant *n.* 污染物质（废气等）
  effluent *n.* (discharge of) liquid waste matter, sewage, etc. e.g. from a factory into a river 废液（污水）等的排放（如从工厂排到河流）

5. As soon as any part of a person's conduct affects prejudicially the interests of others, society has jurisdiction over it, and the question of whether the general welfare will or will not be promoted by interfering with it becomes open to discussion. If a person's conduct does not affect prejudicially the interests of others, it should not come under the jurisdiction of society in the first place.

The author in the passage above argues that

(A) society is independent of the actions of individuals.

(B) the general welfare of a society is promoted when a person's conduct benefits others.

(C) conduct that does not infringe on the interests of others should not be under the jurisdiction of society.

(D) interference with the actions of individuals does not enhance the general welfare.

(E) in general, the interests of persons are mutually exclusive.

译文：一旦一个人行为的任何部分有损害地影响他人利益，社会就对其有审判权，对这种行为的干涉是否能提高总体福利成为一个公开讨论的问题。假如一个人的行为没有损害他人利益，那么就不应该对其进行社会审判。

作者在上文中主张

(A) 社会是不依赖于个人行为的。

(B) 当一个人的行为对他人有利时，一个社会的总体福利被提高。

(C) 没有损害他人福利的行为不应当受到社会审判。

(D) 对个人行为的干涉没有提高总体福利。

(E) 总体上讲，人们的利益是相互排斥的。

解析： 本题的问题目的等于让我们寻求段落的中心思想，因此应在着重把握段落层次结构的基础上，体会作者的写作用意。段落第一句话前半部分表达的观点在第一句话后半部分中被表示为"open to discussion"，而第二句中的主句"should"表明了作者的观点。(C)选项与段落第二句话完全一致，所以为正确选项；(A)中的"independent"是段落中未出现的新观点；(B)和(D)均与段落第一个句子后半部分不吻合（段落推理明确表示对这种行为的干涉是否能提高总体福利尚未形成一致的观点）；(E)中的"exclusive"从上面段落中推不出来。

6. Which of the following best completes the passage below?
The more worried investors are about losing their money, the more they will demand a high potential return on their investment; great risks must be offset by the chance of great rewards. This principle is the fundamental one in determining interest rates, and it is illustrated by the fact that _____.

(A) successful investors are distinguished by an ability to make very risky investments without worrying about their money

(B) lender receive higher interest rates on unsecured loans than on loans backed by collateral

(C) in times of high inflation, the interest paid to depositors by banks can actually be below the rate of inflation

(D) at any one time, a commercial bank will have a single rate of interest that it will expect all of its individual borrowers to pay

(E) the potential return on investment in a new company is typically lower than the potential return on investment in a well-established company

译文： 以下哪一项能最好地完成以下短文？

投资者越担心他们的钱遭受损失，他们就越要求他们的投资有较高的潜在收益。大的风险必须要被高回报的机会所抵销，这项原则是决定利率时的基本原则，并且它可以从以下事实得到说明，即_____。

(A) 进行非常有风险的投资而不用担心他们的钱遭受损失，这种能力将成功的投资者与其他人区分开来。

(B) 贷款人对无担保贷款收取比抵押品担保的贷款更高的利率。

(C) 在高通货膨胀期间，银行向存款人支付的利息实际上可能低于通货膨胀率。

(D) 任何时候，一个商业银行有一个期望它的所有个人借款人支付的单一利率。

(E) 对新公司的投资的潜在回报率通常低于对地位稳固公司的投资。

解析： 由于无担保贷款从贷款人的角度来看，比有抵押品担保的贷款风险更大，贷款人对无担保贷款收取更高的利率这一事实是贯穿该短文的原则的具体说明，因此，选项(B)是正确答案。其他选项没有给出一个例子说明风险增加由潜在收益的提高来弥补。选项(A)根本没有关注投资的回报；选项(C)是一个与风险无关的低回报的例子；选项(D)中，与该原则相反，尽管风险可能发生变化，收益率保持不变；如果对地位稳固的公司投资风险较小的话，选项(E)也违背了该原则。

二、归纳题的思维切入点

（一）充分条件

我们可用题目推理中的充分条件来定位选项，这类题目一般有if, whenever等条件句。

7. Dormitories range from two to six stories in height. If a dormitory room is above the second floor, it has a fire escape. If the statements above are true, which of the following must also be true?

译文： 宿舍楼的高度为二层到六层不等，如果宿舍在二楼以上，它就有安全通道。如果上面陈述属实，则下面哪项也是正确的?

(A) Second-floor dormitory rooms do not have fire escapes.

(B) Third-floor dormitory rooms do not have fire escapes.

(C) Only dormitory rooms above the second floor have fire escapes.

(D) Fourth-floor dormitory rooms have fire escapes.

(E) Some two-story dormitories do not have fire escapes.

(A) 位于第二层的宿舍没有安全通道。

(B) 位于第三层的宿舍没有安全通道。

(C) 只有位于第二层以上的宿舍有安全通道。

(D) 位于第四层的宿舍有安全通道。

(E) 有些两层楼的宿舍楼没有安全通道。

解析：归纳题要关注条件句。用A表示三层或三层以上的宿舍，用B表示有安全通道，那么段落推理为A→B。(A)为否命题；(B)为A→B̄；(C)中的绝对化语言"only"在上文中没有出现；(E)中的关于二层宿舍楼的信息在上文中没有出现，因此也不对；(D)正好符合命题A→B，所以(D)为正确答案。

（二）必要条件

在很多情况下，归纳的推断题型答案为段落推理的一个隐含假设，可以把它转化为假设去思维。

8. Large national budget deficits do not cause large trade deficits. If they did, countries with the largest budget deficits would also have the largest trade deficits. In fact, when deficit figures are adjusted so that different countries are reliably comparable to each other, there is no such correlation.

If the statements above are all true, which of the following can properly be inferred on the basis of them?

(A) Countries with large national budget deficits tend to restrict foreign trade.

(B) Reliable comparisons of the deficit figures of one country with those of another are impossible.

(C) Reducing a country's national budget deficit will not necessarily result in a lowering of any trade deficit that country may have.

(D) When countries are ordered from largest to smallest in terms of population, the smallest countries generally have the smallest budget and trade deficits.

(E) Countries with the largest trade deficits never have similarly large national budget deficits.

译文：巨额国家预算赤字不会造成巨额贸易赤字。如果能造成，预算赤字最大的国家也会有最大的贸易赤字。实际上，当赤字的数字可以调节以致不同国家彼此确实相当时，没有这种联系。

如果以上陈述都是正确的，能在它们的基础上正确地推出以下哪一项？

(A) 有巨额国家预算赤字的国家倾向于限制对外贸易。

(B) 不可能把一国赤字的数字与其他国家的数字进行可靠的比较。

(C) 减少一国国家预算赤字不一定导致该国应该有的贸易赤字的降低。

(D) 按人口多少将所有国家从大到小排列，那些最小的国家通常有最小的预算和贸易赤字。

(E) 贸易赤字最大的国家从来没有类似的国家巨额预算赤字。

解析：该短文宣称巨额预算赤字不会造成贸易赤字。如果确实这样，一个有巨额预算和贸易赤字的国家可以减少它的预算赤字而仍然维持一个巨额的贸易赤字，因此选项(C)是正确答案；无法推出其他选项，该短文没有说任何关于国家是如何对巨额预算赤字做出反应的〔选项(A)〕；该短文指出不同国家的赤字数字的比较可以是比较可靠的〔同选项(B)相反〕；赤字规模和人口规模之间的联系〔选项(D)〕在该短文中没有讨论；最后，贸易赤字最大的国家有时有类似的巨额预算赤字〔选项(E)〕与该短文没有矛盾。

（三）逆否命题

由于归纳题的答案应是从段落中必然得到的，所以段落中的原命题的逆否命题往往是正确答案。

9. A person who agrees to serve as mediator between two warring factions at the request of both abandons by so agreeing the right later to take sides. To take sides at a later point would be to suggest that the earlier presumptive impartiality was a sham.

The passage above emphasizes which of the following points about mediators?

(A) They should try to form no opinions of their own about any issue that is related to the dispute.

(B) They should not agree to serve unless they are committed to maintaining a stance of impartiality.

(C) They should not agree to serve unless they are equally acceptable to all parties to a dispute.

(D) They should feel free to take sides in the dispute right from the start, provided that they make their biases publicly known.

(E) They should reserve the right to abandon their impartiality so as not to be open to the charge of having been deceitful.

译文：在应敌对双方一致要求之下同意做调解的人也就放弃了在以后袒护一方的权利。因为在以后任何一点上袒护一方就意味着原先假定的公正只是一场骗局。

上面一段强调了以下调解人的哪一方面？

(A) 他们不应对与争论有关的问题形成自己的观点。

(B) 除非他们答应保持公正的立场，否则他们就不应充当调解人。

(C) 除非争议双方都接受他为调解人，否则他不应该同意充当调解人。

(D) 如果他们把自己的偏见公布了，从一开始他们就可以在争论中偏向某一方。

(E) 他们应保留放弃公正态度的权利，以便免于被指责为带有欺骗性。

解析：笔者让一位美国考生练习本题，他很快就选出(B)，因为他觉得(B)与段落第一句话完全吻合，只不过是变了一种说法。本题难度主要在于阅读，当阅读较难时，一般通过抓主、谓、宾来把握句子架构。第一个句子的主语是"A person"，谓语是"abandon"，宾语是"the right"。若用A表示"一个人同意做调解人"，用B表示"放弃偏袒一方的权利"，那么第一句话可以表示为A→B。而(B)的not A unless B也为"A→B"，"maintain a stance of impartiality"为第一句中的"abandon the right"的同义重现，所以(B)正确；(A)易误选，但一个人有自己的观点与是否偏袒是两码事，所以(A)不正确。

10. If it is true that the streets and the sidewalks are wet whenever it is raining, which of the following must also be true?

I. If the streets and sidewalks are wet, it is raining.

II. If the streets are wet but the sidewalks are not wet, it is not raining.

III. If it is not raining, the streets and sidewalks are not wet.

(A) I only.

(B) II only.

(C) III only.

(D) I and II only.

(E) II and III only.

译文：每逢下雨，街道和人行道就变湿，如果这是正确的，则下面哪个也一定是正确的？

Ⅰ. 如果街道和人行道都是湿的，那么正在下雨。

Ⅱ. 如果街道湿了，但人行道没湿，那么没下雨。

Ⅲ. 如果没下雨，那么街道和人行道都不会湿。

(A) 只有Ⅰ

(B) 只有Ⅱ

(C) 只有Ⅲ

(D) 只有Ⅰ和Ⅱ

(E) 只有Ⅱ和Ⅲ

解析：归纳题读题要关注if, as long as, only if, whenever等条件句。若用A代表下雨，B_1代表街道湿，B_2代表人行道湿，那么段落推理为：$A \rightarrow B_1B_2$，其递否命题为：$\overline{B_1}+\overline{B_2} \rightarrow \overline{A}$。这种推理模式在85%以上情况下就是考查递否命题。段落中的 I 是递逆题，与原命题不等价，所以不对；III 是否命题，因此也不对；II 完全符合上面的递否命题，所以(B)正确。

（四）数学相关

数字在逻辑推理题中扮演着非常重要的角色，段落中出现的数字应引起我们的高度警觉。命题人员一般不考绝对的数值，而喜欢在相对的数字上故弄玄虚。一般来讲，数量与比例相结合才能说明问题，而仅仅有比例或数量大多不能说明问题，尽管比例要比数字重要。对于这一类题目，可转化为数学去思维（比例与数量作为"题眼"也在反对或支持题型中大量出现）。

11. The 38 corporations that filed United States income tax returns showing a net income of more than $100 million accounted for 53 percent of the total taxable income from foreign sources reported on all tax returns. Sixty percent of the total taxable income from foreign sources came from the 200 returns reporting income from 10 or more countries.

If the statements above are true, which of the following must also be true?

(A) Most of the total taxable income earned by corporations with net income above $100 million was earned from foreign sources.

(B) Wealthy individuals with large personal incomes reported 47 percent of the total taxable income from foreign sources.

(C) Income from foreign sources amounted to between 53 and 60 percent of all reported taxable income.

(D) Some of the corporations with net income above $100 million reported income from 10 or more countries.

(E) Most of the tax returns showing income from 10 or more countries reported net income of more than $100 million.

译文：在美国备案申报纳税的公司中有38家公司纯收入超过1亿美元，在所有税收报表上报道的国外来源总的应征税收入中，它们占了53%。在国外来源总的应征税收入中，有60%是来自10多个国家的200份纳税申报。

如上面陈述为真，则下面哪个也一定正确？

(A) 净收入超过1亿的公司赚取的大部分应征税收入都来自国外。

(B) 有大量个人收入的人有47%的应征税收入来自国外。

(C) 来自国外的收入相当于上报应征税收入的53%～60%。

(D) 一些净收入超过1亿美元的公司报告其收入来自10多个国家。

(E) 绝大部分收入来自10多个国家的公司净收入超过1亿美元。

解析：本题是与数学相关的题目，可转化为数学去思维。我们用A_1表示这38家公司，用B表示来自于外国的总的应征税收入，用A_2表示来自于10多个国家的200份纳税报表，那么由于A_1占B的53%，A_2占B的60%，所以$A_1+A_2=113\%$，因此A_1与A_2的交集最小为13%，最大为53%，所以A_1与A_2有共同的连接点，所以(D)正确。

12. A ten-year comparison between the United States and the Soviet Union in terms of crop yields per acre revealed that when only planted acreage is compared, Soviet yields are equal to 68 percent of United States yields. When total agricultural acreage (planted acreage plus fallow acreage) is compared, however, Soviet yield is 114 percent of United States yield.

译文：美国和前苏联的每英亩粮食产量进行的一次为期10年的对比分析结果表明，当仅以种植面积比较时，前苏联的产量是美国的68%。但当对农业总面积（包括种植面积和休耕面积）进行比较时，前苏联的产量是美国的114%。

From the information above, which of the following can be most reliably inferred about United States and Soviet agriculture during the ten-year period?

(A) A higher percentage of total agricultural acreage was fallow in the United States than in the Soviet Union.

(B) The United States had more fallow acreage than planted acreage.

(C) Fewer total acres of available agricultural land were fallow in the Soviet Union than in the United States.

(D) The Soviet Union had more planted acreage than fallow acreage.

(E) The Soviet Union produced a greater volume of crops than the United States produced.

根据以上信息，关于美国与前苏联在这10年期间的农业情况，下面哪个能最可靠地推断出来？

(A) 美国农业总面积中休耕地的比例要大于前苏联。

(B) 美国休耕地面积多于耕地面积。

(C) 前苏联闲置的可用农业面积要比美国少。

(D) 前苏联的耕种面积多于休耕地面积。

(E) 前苏联出产的粮食要比美国多。

解析：要注意读懂题目，题目所做比较对象是苏联与美国的Crop yields per acre。若用X表示苏联粮食总产量，a表示苏联planted acreage，a′表示苏联fallow acreage，用y表示美国粮食总产量，b表示美国planted acreage，b′表示美国fallow acreage，那么，$\frac{X}{a}=0.68\frac{y}{b}$，而$\frac{X}{a+a'}=1.14\frac{y}{b+b'}$。当一个分数的分子不变时，那么分母所增加的比例越小，其值就越大。因此我们由$\frac{X}{a+a'}>\frac{y}{b+b'}$就可以得出a′在(a+a′)中占的比重一定比b′在(b+b′)中占的比重小，所以(A)正确；(C)、(D)易误选，但仅仅一个数量一般不能说明问题。试体会(C)的一个反例：$\frac{1000}{100+100}>\frac{500}{25+90}$，其中X=1000，y=500，a′=100，b′=90。

（五）对比推理

当段落推理涉及两者比较，且结论重点涉及比较一方，这时考虑比较对象且重点思考隐含比较的另一方往往是有效的。当段落没有明显的两者比较，如段落仅涉及大企业，则多考虑小企业；如段落推理涉及结婚，对比推理多考虑没有结婚的。

13. Superficially, college graduates in 1982 resemble college graduates of 1964; they are fairly conservative, well dressed, and interested in tradition; they respect their parents. But there is a deep-seated difference: a majority of the members of the class of 1982 who were surveyed in their freshman year stated that making a good income was an important reason for their decision to go to college.

The statements in the passage above, if true, best support which of the following conclusions?

(A) The concerns of college graduates of 1964 were superficial compared to the financial worries of college graduates of 1982.

(B) Fewer than half the students of the class of 1964 declared as freshmen that they entered college in order to increase their earning potential.

译文：表面上看，1982年的大学毕业生很像1964年的大学毕业生。他们相当保守，衣着讲究，对传统感兴趣，尊敬父母。但他们却有一种根深蒂固的差异：大部分1982年的学生在大一学年被调查中都认为有一份好收入是他们决定上大学的一个重要原因。

上面的陈述，如果正确，最好地支持了下面哪个结论？

(A) 1964年的大学毕业生对财政问题的关心要比1982年的学生肤浅。

(B) 1964年的入学大学生中不到一半人在刚入学时宣称上大学是为了增加他们赚钱的潜力。

(C) Educational background did not play as significant a part in determining income in 1964 as it does in 1982.

(D) A majority of the members of the class of 1964 revised their reasons for attending college between their freshman year and college graduation.

(E) College graduates of 1964 were actually less conservative than college graduates of 1982.

(C) 教育背景对收入的决定在1964年没有在1982年时那么明显。

(D) 大多数1964年的学生在入学头一年和接受大学教育期间改变了他们上大学的理由。

(E) 1964年的毕业生实际上没有1982年的毕业生保守。

解析：本题读题重点为"but"后面的内容，并问从"but"后的那一句话能得到下面哪一个结论。一般地，当段落推理涉及两者比较的时候，考虑比较对象并且重点思考隐含比较的另一方往往是有效的。注意到段落中的"majority"，(B)中的"fewer than half"与之相对，并且指出隐含比较的另一方即1964年的大学生与1982年的大学生之间的差异，所以(B)正确；(A)中的"financial worries"是一个更加广泛的概念，且从上面段落也得不出这样一个比较，从某种程度上讲，(A)支持了上面的推理，但本题是"自上而下"的归纳，所以(A)不对；(C)是一个新的比较，(C)虽可以部分解释上面的推理，但从上面推不出来，所以(C)为无关答案；(D)与段落推理不沾边；而(E)直接与上面段落信息相违背，因此(D)、(E)都不对。

14. Experienced pilots often have more trouble than novice pilots in learning to fly the newly developed ultralight airplanes. Being accustomed to heavier aircraft, experienced pilots, when flying ultralight craft, seem not to respect the wind as much as they should.

The passage implies that the heavier aircraft mentioned above are

(A) harder to land than ultralight aircraft.

(B) not as popular with pilots as ultralight aircraft.

(C) not as safe as ultralight aircraft.

(D) more fuel-efficient than ultralight aircraft.

(E) easier to handle in wind than ultralight aircraft.

译文：有经验的飞行员在学习驾驶新研制的超轻型飞机时遇到的问题经常比新手还多。因为他们已经习惯了重型飞机，所以在驾驶超轻型飞机时，似乎对风没有引起应有的注意。

文中暗示上面提到的重型飞机：

(A) 比超轻型飞机更难着陆。

(B) 不像超轻型飞机那样在飞行员中受欢迎。

(C) 不如超轻型飞机安全。

(D) 比超轻型飞机节省燃料。

(E) 在风中比轻型飞机更易驾驶。

解析：本题为对比推理。段落推理两类飞行员在驾驶超轻型飞机时遇到的问题的差异主要在于对"wind"的注意。(E)中涉及"wind"，并且指出重型飞机在风中比轻型飞机更易驾驶，正好可以从上面段落中推出来，所以(E)正确；(A)、(B)、(C)、(D)均与上面推理无关或从上面推不出来。

15. The state with the greatest fraction of its population in urban areas, if the urban areas are considered to include the suburbs, is California. The West is highly urbanized, but California is exceptional even in that region: 91 percent of its population lives in urban areas. Geographically, however, California is rural: 96 percent of its land is outside urban areas.

If all of the statements above are true, which of the following must also be true?

(A) No state has a smaller fraction of its population in rural areas than California has.

译文：如果考虑城市地区时把郊区也包括在内的话，那么加利福尼亚州就是城市人口比例最大的州，美国西部已经高度城市化了，但加利福尼亚即使在那个地区也很特殊：91%的人口住在城市地区。然而，就地理分布而言，加利福尼亚属农村：96%的土地在城区外。

如果上面的叙述都是真的，那么下面哪个也一定是真的?

(A) 没有哪个州的农村人口比例比加州的低。

(B) The current rate of population growth in California's urban areas exceeds the current rate of population growth in California's rural areas.

(C) In California 96 percent of the population lives on 9 percent of the land.

(D) No state has a smaller area devoted to urban settlement than California has.

(E) California's population density is among the highest of all states in the United States.

(B) 加利福尼亚州现在的城市人口增长率超过了农村人口增长率。

(C) 在加利福尼亚州96%的人口住在9%的土地上。

(D) 没有哪个州比加利福尼亚州用于城市住房的面积更小。

(E) 加利福尼亚州的人口密度是美国所有州中最高的。

解析：本题为标准的归纳题型，一般而言，**段落推理中用到only、most、last、first或最高级时，应成为我们的读题重点**。这道题的读题重点为一句话"The state with the greatest fraction of its population in urban area, ..., is California,"并且由对比推理可知(A)的正确性，因为讨论加州的人口，提及的是urban population，由对比推理可想到rural population，且(A)正好符合题意；(B)中的"population growth"为新概念，必然不对；若把(C)换为91%的人住在4%的土地上，就是正确答案；(D)中的"area"绝对推不出来，因为段落探讨的是人口密度，而非"area"；(E)中的"California's population density"怎么样，我们也不能从上面推理中得到，因为段落探讨的仅仅是都市与农村的人口比例，所以得不出："California's population density"，因此(E)不对。

（六）语义相关

有一些较难的归纳题的答案必须细心品味其推理的语义才能得到。

16. Veteran screenwriters, aiming at creating a 120-page screenplay for a film, usually turn in a 135-page first draft. As one screenwriter put it, "That gives those in charge of the movie a chance to be creative when they get the script: at the very least, they can cut 15 pages."

The screenwriter's statement cited above conveys which of the following propositions?

(A) Screenwriters for a film are generally not involved in any aspects of filmmaking besides providing the script.

(B) Seasoned screenwriters are resigned to, and make allowance for, draft scripts being altered by those evaluating them.

(C) Truly creative screenwriters are too temperamental to adhere to page limits set for their work.

(D) It takes a special kind of creativity to recognize what is best left out of a film script.

(E) Even experienced screenwriters cannot be expected to write scripts of consistently high quality throughout.

译文：有经验的电影剧本作者在创作120页的电影剧本时，通常会交上135页的初稿。正如一位电影剧本作者说的，"这样使那些负责电影的人在接到剧本后有一个机会进行创造，他们至少可以删掉15页"。

以上引用的这位电影剧本作者的论述表达了下面哪个观点？

(A) 除了提供剧本外，通常电影剧本作者并不涉及电影制作的任何方面。

(B) 熟练的作者容忍和允许由审核人修改剧本草稿。

(C) 真正富有创意的电影剧本作者极易冲动因而不能固守规定的页数。

(D) 要想认识到剧本哪部分最适合保留下来，需要特殊的创造力。

(E) 即使最有经验的作者也不能写出自始至终质量都是上乘的剧本。

解析：本题的问题目的是让我们说明the screen writer's statement所表达的观点，因此读题重点在最后一句话。通过读最后一句话"That gives..."可以从语义上知道(B)正确，且(B)中的seasoned为段落中veteran的同义重现；(A)中的"any"，(C)中的"temperamental"，(D)中的"special"都是上文所没有出现的新的限制词，因此都不正确。

17. If an investment has produced no profit, tax relief predicated on having made the investment is no help; any corporate manager who fears that a new asset will not make money is scarcely comforted by promises of reductions in taxes the corporation will not owe.

Which of the following is the most reliable inference to draw from the passage above?

(A) An effective way to discourage unprofitable corporate investment is to predicate tax relief on the making of profitable investments.

(B) Corporate managers are likely to ignore tax considerations in deciding to invest in assets they believe will be profitable.

(C) The promise of tax benefits for making new investments will not in and of itself stimulate new investment.

(D) The less importance a corporate manager attaches to tax considerations, the more likely it is that the manager will accurately predict the profitability of an investment.

(E) The critical factor in a corporate investment decision is likely to be a corporate manager's emotional response to perceived business conditions.

译文：如果一项投资不能产生利润，那么以投资为基础的减轻赋税就是毫无用处的。任何一位担心新资产不会赚钱的公司经理都不会因减轻公司本来就不欠的税款的允诺而得到安慰。

下面哪项是从上文得出的最可靠的推论？

(A) 阻止效益不佳的投资的最有效的方法是对可以产生利润的投资减轻税赋。

(B) 公司经理在决定他们认为可以盈利的投资时，可能会不考虑税款问题。

(C) 对新投资减轻税款的承诺本身不会刺激新投资。

(D) 公司经理把税款问题的重要性看得越小，他就越可能正确地预测投资的有利性。

(E) 公司投资决策的一个关键因素可能是公司经理对感知到的商业状况的心理反应。

解析：归纳题要关注条件句，因此明白段落第一个句子的意思非常重要。若用A表示一项不能产生利润的投资，用B表示以投资为基础的减轻赋税没有用处，那么段落推理为A→B，其逆否命题$\overline{B}$→$\overline{A}$成立，即以投资为基础的减轻赋税若起作用，那么其必要条件是能产生利润。换而言之，对新投资减轻税款的承诺本身并不会刺激投资，如(C)所说，所以(C)正确；(A)中的"discourage"在段落中没有出现；(B)中的ignore也不能从上面得出；(E)中的"emotional"为新概念；(D)为新比较，因此必然不对。

三、如何理解归纳推理中的必要条件

自然界和社会中的各个现象都是与其他现象互相联系、互相制约的。如果某一个现象的存在必然引起另一个现象的发生，那么这两个现象之间就具有因果联系。其中，引起某一现象产生的现象叫做原因，被另一现象引起的现象叫做结果。因果现象是相对的，一个现象对于某现象来说是结果，而对于另一现象来说可能又是原因。例如，爆炸既是火药达到一定温度的结果，又是造成人员伤亡的原因。因果联系的一个重要特点是在时间上具有先后相继的顺序，即对一对因果事件来说，总是原因在前，结果在后，概莫例外。因果联系的另一个重要特点是确定的原因总是产生确定的结果，而确定的结果总是由确定的原因产生的，两者的关系是确定的。既无无因之果，也无无果之因。但任何确定事物的发生都依赖于许多条件或许多原因，现实生活中，我们很难找到某一确定发生的所有条件或原因，因此当问题目的让我们去寻求一个支持或反对段落推理的答案时，我们的目标是去寻求一个（仅仅是许多条件或许多原因中的一个）使结论成立的可能性增大或减小的答案，而绝非一定要去寻求一个使结论必然成立或必然错误的答案。

但是，在归纳题型中，我们所面临的段落推理是完成成立的推理，所以推理之中的隐含假设（而这个隐含假设是段落推理成立的必要条件，而且许多推断题的答案本质上就是隐含假设）必定成立。在归纳中，有时段落推理可能仅仅只列举了使推理成立的一些必要条件，但段落推理的成立可能依赖于许多条件，只有所有的必要条件都找到了，才可以构成充分条件推导出推理的结论。诚然，有原因才能有确定的结果，但只有找到了所有影响某一确定结果的原因，我们才能得出这个确定的结果。但如果我们知道了某一确定结果，必定可以推断它的一些原因（必要条件）存在。同样，有条件才能有确定的结论，但只有找到了所有影响某一确定结论的条件，我们才能得出这个确定的结论，但是如果我们知道了某一确定的结论，必定可以推出它的必要条件存在，而只由某一确定结论的一个或几个必要条件一般不能推出它的结论必然成立。下面我们看一个例子，尽管其问题目的属于反对题型，但可以很好地帮助我们说明什么是结论成立的必要条件。

18. In mammals it is the secondary palate that permits breathing while eating. Clearly, breathing while eating is necessary to maintain the high rate of metabolism of mammals.

The author's assertions would be most weakened by the discovery of a mammalian species that had a _____.

(A) high rate of metabolism and the ability to breathe while eating

(B) low rate of metabolism and the ability to breathe while eating

(C) low rate of metabolism and no ability to breathe while eating

(D) high rate of metabolism and no secondary palate

(E) low rate of metabolism and a secondary palate

译文： 哺乳动物的上颚使其在进食时能够呼吸。很明显，在进食时呼吸对保持哺乳动物的高速新陈代谢是必要的。

如发现了以下哪种哺乳动物，则作者的断言将得到最大的削弱？

(A) 新陈代谢快，能够在进食的时候呼吸。

(B) 新陈代谢慢，能够在进食的时候呼吸。

(C) 新陈代谢快，不能够在进食的时候呼吸。

(D) 新陈代谢快，没有上颚。

(E) 新陈代谢慢，没有上颚。

解析： 我们不妨用A表示"上颚"，B表示"进食时呼吸"，C表示"维持高频率的新陈代谢"。本题段落的第一句话只表明上颚使哺乳动物进食时呼吸，但确定结论"哺乳动物进食时呼吸"的成立需要依赖于很多条件，而上颚仅仅是使这个确定结论成立的一个必要条件，所以由A绝对推不出B；但是B既然存在，就必然可以得出A这个必要条件是存在的，因为没有A就没有B，所以第一句话的推理可以表示为B→A。段落的第二句话中的"is necessary to"表示B为C的一个必要条件，可表示为C→B。所以整个段落的推理可表示为C→B→A。这种推理的答案大多考察C→A。(D)指出C与$\overline{A}$同时存在，与C→A相反，所以起到了反对作用，所以(D)正确；(B)、(C)、(E)中的"low rate of metabolism"是$\overline{C}$，作为否命题与原命题无关；(A)与C→A完全吻合，所以不可能起到反对作用。

下面我们再来看两个例子：

19. Mass transit authorities in large cities are struggling with deficits. Riders complain about delays and breakdowns, cuts in service, and fares higher than they are accustomed to paying. For all these reasons and because the price of gasoline is still not prohibitive, the number of passengers using public transportation has fallen, adding to the deficits.

Which of the following statements about the relationship between the number of riders using public transportation and the price of gasoline is best supported by the passage above?

(A) As the price of gasoline rises, the number of riders using public transportation rises.

译文： 大城市的公共交通部门正在赤字中挣扎。乘客总抱怨汽车晚点和运输工具出毛病，服务种类的减少，以及票价高于他们过去习惯于支付的水平。由于上述所有原因，以及汽油的价格并未高至令人不敢问津的水平，所以公共交通车的乘客有所减少，更进一步增加了赤字。

下面哪一项关于公交乘客数量与汽油价格的关系的陈述最为上面文字所支持？

(A) 随着汽油价格的上升，公交乘客数也上升。

(B) Even if the price of gasoline rises, the number of riders using public transportation will continue to decline.

(C) If the price of gasoline rises to a prohibitive level, the number of riders using public transportation will rise.

(D) The majority of riders using public transportation do not use gasoline; hence, fluctuations in gasoline prices are unlikely to affect the number of riders using public transportation.

(E) The price of gasoline is always low enough to make private transportation cheaper than public transportation; hence, fluctuations in gasoline prices are unlikely to affect the number of riders using public transportation.

(B) 即使汽油价格上升，公交乘客数仍继续下降。

(C) 如果汽油价格升至令人不敢问津的水平，公交乘客数将上升。

(D) 大多数公交乘客不用汽油，因此，汽油价格波动不太可能影响公交乘客。

(E) 汽油的价格总是足够低，这使得私人交通比公共交通便宜，因此，汽油价格的波动不太可能影响公交乘客数。

解析：若用A_1表示"delays and breakdowns"，A_2表示"cuts in service"，A_3表示"fares higher..."，A_4表示"the price of gasoline is still not prohibitive"，用B表示"the number of passengers has fallen"，那么由"For all these reasons and because price of gasoline is still not prohibitive..."，我们知道，有A_1，A_2，A_3，A_4这几个因素，B必然成立，但是仅仅知道A_1、A_2、A_3或A_4中的一个因素，我们并不能得到B必然成立，但若知道B成立，那么其中的一个因素必然成立，换句话说，A_1，A_2，A_3，A_4是B成立的必要条件。因此我们可以推出B→A_4，其逆否命题$\overline{A_4}$→$\overline{B}$成立，而(C)刚好与之吻合，所以(C)正确。

20. A package is never accepted for delivery by the delivery service unless it is within the established size limits. All packages accepted for delivery by the delivery service have a return address.

If the statements above are true, which of the following must also be true?

(A) The delivery service charges more for heavier packages than for lighter packages.

(B) The delivery service will always accept for delivery a package that is within the established size limits.

(C) If a package is within the established size limits and has a return address, it will be accepted for delivery by the delivery service no matter how heavy the package is.

(D) A package that is not within the established size limits but has a return address is never accepted for delivery by the delivery service.

(E) The delivery service does not charge for packages that must be returned to the sender.

译文：一个包裹，除非其大小在规定的尺寸之内，否则投递服务公司不会接受。所有被接受投递的包裹都有退回地址。

如果上面陈述是正确的，下面哪一项也一定是正确的？

(A) 投递服务对重包裹的收费高于对轻包裹的收费。

(B) 投递服务总是接受大小在规定限度内的包裹的投递。

(C) 如果一个包裹大小在规定的限度之内，并有回邮地址，则无论它多重，都会被接受投递。

(D) 一个大小不在规定限度之内但是却有回邮地址的包裹，决不会被投递服务接受投递的。

(E) 投递服务对必须返回寄件人的包裹不收取费用。

解析：若用B表示包裹被接受投递，A_1表示在规定的尺寸之内，A_2表示有退回地址，那么段落推理模式为B→A_1A_2，其逆否命题为$\overline{A_1}$+$\overline{A_2}$→$\overline{B}$，其含义为$\overline{A_1}$或$\overline{A_2}$或$\overline{A_1A_2}$都能导致$\overline{B}$，所以(D)正确；(C)易误选，但(C)明显是把必要条件混为充分条件，所以(C)不对；(A)、(D)中的"charge"在上面段落中没有出现；(B)中的always为段落中没有出现的绝对化语言，因此也不对。

四、归纳题的读题与答案选择

归纳题的阅读难度一般要大于假设、支持、反对、评价这四类题，并且由于归纳题的段落中每一句话都可以作为出题方向，所以读题要求比较高，读题时需要注意的是：

1. 关注如if, as long as, only when之类的条件句。

2. 关注绝对化语言，如范围绝对化（most, almost, all, none等）与语气绝对化（only, must, cannot, impossible）。

3. 关注数字、比例、总量等，有时可化为数学进行思维。

4. 关注对比、变化点，注重从逻辑层次结构上去把握段落推理关系。

由于归纳题的段落推理是必定成立的推理，而且其答案是从上面段落中推出来的，因此，选项应为段落所涉及的内容。判断某一选项是否为答案的几个原则是：

1. 答案中不能出现段落中没有出现的本质不同的新概念（包括新的动词、形容词、名词等，并且这些新概念的内涵与段落中的概念的内涵有本质不同），但段落中关键词的同义词出现在很多情况下是必需的。

2. 若段落在某一信息点上没有绝对化概念，那么答案中也不应在这一信息点上有绝对化概念。

3. 不能出现上面段落中所没有的新的比较。

4. 切忌进行段落之外信息的进一步推理。

在把握逻辑层次结构的基础上，有几个算不上技巧的方法如下：

1. 与段落重合度越高的选项越可能为正确答案（not, except题型除外），若段落中出现关键的专有名词，那么答案中多出现该专有名词。

2. 出现if, unless, whenever等条件连词的选项成为正确答案的可能性要远远大于其他选项。

3. 在GRE考题中，NOT，EXCEPT考题的选项(E)为正确选项的概率为85%左右；(D)、(E)为正确答案的概率各为5%左右；(A)、(B)为正确答案的概率共5%。不过在LSAT考题中这种规律不太明显。

最后我们再来看几个归纳题，细心体会归纳题型的解题思路：

21. If there is an oil-supply disruption resulting in higher international oil prices, domestic oil prices in open-market countries such as the United States will rise as well, whether such countries import all or none of their oil.

Which of the following conclusions is best supported by the statement above?

(A) Domestic producers of oil in open-market countries are excluded from the international oil market when there is a disruption in the international oil supply.

(B) International oil-supply disruptions have little, if any, effect on the price of domestic oil as long as an open-market country has domestic supplies capable of meeting domestic demand.

(C) The oil market in an open-market country is actually part of the international oil market, even if most of that country's domestic oil is usually sold to consumers within its borders.

(D) Open-market countries that export little or none of their oil can maintain stable domestic oil prices even when international oil prices rise sharply.

译文： 如果石油供应出现波动导致国际油价上涨，在开放市场国家，如美国，国内油价也会上升，不管这些国家的石油是全部进口还是完全不进口。

以上论述最能支持以下哪一个结论？

(A) 当国际石油供应发生波动时，开放市场国家的国内石油生产商被排除在国际石油市场之外。

(B) 只要一个开放市场国家的国内石油供应能满足国内需求，国际石油供应的波动对国内石油价格即使有影响，也是很小的。

(C) 开放市场国家里的石油市场实际上是国际石油市场的一部分，即使该国国内生产的石油绝大部分卖给了国界之内的消费者。

(D) 很少出口或不出口石油的开放市场国家可以维持稳定的国内石油价格，即使在国际石油价格急剧上升的情况下。

(E) If international oil prices rise, domestic distributors of oil in open-market countries will begin to import more oil than they export.

(E) 如果国际石油价格上升，开放市场国家的国内石油分销商会开始进口比出口更多的石油。

解析： 如果开放市场国家的石油市场是独立的，国际石油价格的波动就不会影响国内石油价格。然而，如果关于石油供应波动的论述是正确的，那么，国内石油价格显然是依赖于国际市场的，因此国内石油市场是国际石油市场的一部分，所以，(C)是正确答案；选项(B)和(D)没有得到支持，因为每一项都与国际石油供应的波动导致开放市场国家油价的上升相矛盾；(A)和(E)也没有得到支持，因为该论述仅提供了关于波动对石油价格的影响的信息，而没有国内生产商或分销商的信息。

22. Rural households have more purchasing power than do urban or suburban households at the same income level, since some of the income urban and suburban households use for food and shelter can be used by rural households for other needs.

Which of the following inferences is best supported by the statement made above?

(A) The average rural household includes more people than does the average urban or suburban household.

(B) Rural households have lower food and housing costs than do either urban or suburban households.

(C) Suburban households generally have more purchasing power than do either rural or urban households.

(D) The median income of urban and suburban households is generally higher than that of rural households.

(E) All three types of households spend more of their income on food and housing than on all other purchases combined.

译文： 在相同的收入水平上，乡村家庭比城市或城市郊区的家庭有更大的购买力，因为城市或城市郊区家庭中用在食物或住所的一部分收入可以被乡村家庭用在其他的需要上。

以上论述最支持以下哪一个推断？

(A) 平均来说乡村家庭比城市或城市郊区的家庭包含有更多的人数。

(B) 乡村家庭在食物和住房上的开支比城市或城市郊区家庭的开支少。

(C) 城市郊区家庭通常比乡村或城市家庭有更大的购买力。

(D) 城市和城市郊区家庭的中等收入通常比乡村家庭的中等收入高。

(E) 所有三种类型的家庭在饮食和住房上花费的收入比在其他所有商品上的花费多。

解析： 如果由于乡村家庭在满足基本需要后剩下更多的钱从而有更大的购买力，也就是说，如(B)所说，那些费用对于乡村家庭比对于有相同收入水平的城市郊区或城市家庭来说要低，因此，(B)是正确答案；选项(A)是一个没有得到支持的推论，因为没有信息表明更大的家庭不可能有更大的购买力或更低的食物和住房支出；选项(C)和(D)也没有得到支持，因为该短文只比较有相同收入水平的家庭；因为没有指出各种家庭中花费在不同支出上的相对数量，(E)没有得到支持。

23. Neither a rising standard of living nor balanced trade, by itself, establishes a country's ability to compete in the international marketplace. Both are required simultaneously since standards of living can rise because of growing trade deficits and trade can be balanced by means of a decline in a country's standard of living.

If the facts stated in the passage above are true, a proper test of a country's ability to be competitive is its ability to

译文： 生活水平的提高或平衡贸易，仅凭它们自身，都不能形成一个国家在国际市场上的竞争能力。需要二者同时具备才行。因为生活水平可以通过日益增长的贸易赤字来提高，贸易可以通过一个国家生活水平的降低来平衡。

如果上述短文中陈述的事实是正确的，对于一个国家的竞争力的一种适当的测试应是它的哪一方面的能力？

(A) balance its trade while its standard of living rises.

(B) balance its trade while its standard of living falls.

(C) increase trade deficits while its standard of living rises.

(D) decrease trade deficits while its standard of living falls.

(E) keep its standard of living constant while trade deficits rise.

(A) 当它的生活水平提高时平衡它的贸易

(B) 当它的生活水平下降时平衡它的贸易

(C) 当它的生活水平提高时增加贸易赤字

(D) 当它的生活水平下降时减少贸易赤字

(E) 当贸易赤字上升时保持生活水平不变

解析：该短文指出一个在国际市场上有竞争力的国家必须能在生活水平上升时平衡贸易。利用这一信息，对于一个国家在国际市场上竞争能力的一个适当的测试应是两个条件同时满足，因为选项(B)，选项(C)，选项(D)或选项(E)都不能描述将两个标准融合起来的测试，这些回答都不合适；选项(A)描述了一个满足条件的测试，是正确答案。

24. High levels of fertilizer and pesticides, needed when farmers try to produce high yield of the same crop year after year, pollute water supplies. Experts therefore urge farmers to diversify their crops and to rotate their plantings yearly.

To receive governmental price-support benefits for a crop, farmers must have produced that same crop for the past several years.

The statements above, if true, best support which of the following conclusions?

(A) The rules for governmental support of farm prices work against efforts to reduce water pollution.

(B) The only solution to the problem of water pollution form fertilizers and pesticides is to take farmland out of production.

(C) Farmers can continue to make a profit by rotating diverse crops, thus reducing costs for chemicals, but not by planting the same crop each year.

(D) New farming techniques will be developed to make it possible for farmers to reduce the application of fertilizers and pesticides.

(E) Governmental price supports for farm products are set at levels that are not high enough to allow farmers to get out of debt.

译文：当农场主们希望年复一年种植的同样的农作物得到较高的产量时，就需要使用大量的化肥和杀虫剂，这些会污染水的供给。因此，专家们督促农场主们将他们的农作物分散化，每年轮流种植。

为获得政府对于一种作物的价格支持补贴，农场主必须种植与过去若干年相同的作物。

以上陈述，如果是正确的，最支持以下哪一个结论？

(A) 政府关于支持农产品价格的规定起到了阻碍人们减少水污染的努力的作用。

(B) 解决由化肥和杀虫剂引起的水污染问题的唯一办法是将农场退出生产。

(C) 农场主可以通过轮流种植不同的作物，从而减少了购买化工产品的费用来继续赢利，但不能通过每年种植相同的作物来赢利。

(D) 将发展新的耕作技术使农场主们减少化肥和杀虫剂的使用成为可能。

(E) 政府对农产品的价格补贴订立在不足以使农场主摆脱负债的水平上。

解析：农场主只有在他们年复一年地生产同一种作物时才能获得政府的价格补贴。那些希望获得这些价格补贴的农场主不可能减少对水的污染，因为他们不会听从专家们关于分散化和轮流种植的建议，因此，(A)是正确答案；由于专家们的建议显然是他们赞成的解决办法，而提出唯一的解决办法是别的什么〔选项(B)〕没有得到支持；该陈述既没有提到农场主的成本和收益，也没有提到耕作技术的发展（新概念），因此不支持关于赢利前景〔选项(C)〕或将来耕作技术〔选项(D)〕的结论；因为没有给出关于价格补贴数量或农场主的债务的信息，选项(E)也没有得到支持。

25. Which of the following best completes the passage below? Established companies concentrate on defending what they already have. Consequently, they tend not to be innovative themselves and tend to underestimate the effects of the innovations of others. The clearest example of this defensive strategy is the fact that

(A) ballpoint pens and soft-tip markers have eliminated the traditional market for fountain pens, clearing the way for the marketing of fountain pens as luxury of prestige items.

(B) a highly successful automobile was introduced by the same company that had earlier introduced a model that had been a dismal failure.

(C) a once-successful manufacturer of slide rules reacted to the introduction of electronic calculators by trying to make better slide rules.

(D) one of the first models of modern accounting machines, designed for use in the banking industry, was purchased by a public library as well as by banks.

(E) the inventor of a commonly used anesthetic did not intend the product to be used by dentists, who currently account for almost the entire market for that drug.

译文：以下哪一项能最好地完成下面的短文？

地位牢固的公司总是集中全力保卫他们已经拥有的东西。结果，他们不是倾向于努力改进自身而是倾向于低估其他人的改进的影响。这种防卫性的策略的一个更加清楚的例子是这样一个事实——

(A) 圆珠笔和软头笔生产商将吸水笔从传统市场中清除出去，同时为将吸水笔作为奢侈品和地位的象征来规划市场扫清了道路。

(B) 早些时候引入了一种导致灾难性失败的车型的公司，又引入了一款相当成功的车型。

(C) 一个曾经辉煌过的计算尺生产商对于电子计算器的出现的反应是努力生产更好的计算尺。

(D) 第一批为银行业设计的现代计账机中的一种型号，被一个公共图书馆以及银行购走。

(E) 一种普遍使用的麻醉剂的发明者并没有打算让牙医来使用这项产品，但牙医目前几乎包揽了这种药物的全部市场。

解析：选项(C)是一个防御性的，非创新的，并低估他人创新效果的策略的清楚例子，计算尺生产商的行为好像是只要改进旧的、更熟悉的产品就可以抵销一种竞争产品——电子计算器的更新式的完全不同的技术提供的优势，选项(C)因此是正确答案；其他选项都不是作者所说的防御性策略的例子。选项(D)和(E)是原来没有预料到的使用者，使用新的产品，而不是对其他人创新的反应；(B)也没有描述这种反应；选项(A)描述了一种情况，在这种情况下，新产品在传统市场上取代了旧产品，但同时也为旧产品提供了一个新的营销策略。

26. One analyst predicts that Hong Kong can retain its capitalist ways after it becomes part of mainland China in 1997 as long as a capitalist Hong Kong is useful to China; that a capitalist Hong Kong will be useful to China as long as Hong Kong is prosperous; and that Hong Kong will remain prosperous as long as it retains its capitalist ways.

If the predictions above are correct, which of the following further predictions can logically be derived from them?

(A) If Hong Kong fails to stay prosperous, it will no longer remain part of mainland China.

(B) If Hong Kong retains its capitalist ways until 1997, it will be allowed to do so afterward.

译文：一个分析家预测在1997年香港成为中国大陆一部分之后，只要一个资本主义的香港对中国有用，香港就能维持它的资本主义道路；只要香港经济繁荣，一个资本主义的香港对中国就有用；只要香港维持它的资本主义道路，香港就会保持繁荣。

如果以上预测都是正确的，由它们出发可以从逻辑上推出以下哪一项更进一步的预测？

(A) 如果香港不能保持繁荣，它就不再会是中国大陆的一部分。

(C) If there is a world economic crisis after 1997, it will not adversely affect the economy of Hong Kong.

(D) Hong Kong will be prosperous after 1997.

(E) The citizens of Hong Kong will have no restrictions placed on them by the government of mainland China.

(B) 如果香港维持资本主义道路直到1997年，它以后也会被允许维持资本主义道路。

(C) 如果在1997年后出现一次世界经济危机，它不会对香港经济产生负面影响。

(D) 香港在1997年后将繁荣兴旺。

(E) 香港市民将不会受到中国大陆政府施加的限制。

解析：回忆我们在前面所强调的得出结论题型要把握的三点：(1) 要把握段落层次结构；(2) 一般不能有新概念；(3) 不能与段落信息相违背；(4) 不能有新的绝对化语言。

如果香港维持资本主义道路直到1997年，根据预测，直到那时它将继续保持繁荣，那时它对中国有用，因此得到允许维持它的资本主义道路。同样的论述表明香港将得到允许从那以后维持它的资本主义道路，因此，选项(B)可以从该结论中推导出来，是正确答案；那些预测只说在一定条件下会发生什么，由于选项(A)和(C)都预先假设了其他条件，因此两个选项都不能被推导出来；相似地，由于那些预测没有说会无条件地发生什么，选项(D)是无条件的，不能被推导出来；因为没有做出关于加在市民身上的管制的预测，选项(E)也不能被推导出来。

27. Correctly measuring the productivity of service workers is complex. Consider, for example, postal workers: they are often said to be more productive if more letters are delivered per postal worker. But is this really true? What if more letters are lost or delayed per worker at the same time that more are delivered?

The objection implied above to the productivity measure described is based on doubts about the truth of which of the following statements?

(A) Postal workers are representative of service workers in general.

(B) The delivery of letters is the primary activity of the postal service.

(C) Productivity should be ascribed to categories of workers, not to individuals.

(D) The quality of services rendered can appropriately be ignored in computing productivity.

(E) The number of letters delivered is relevant to measuring he productivity of postal workers.

译文：正确地度量服务部门工人的生产率很复杂。例如，考虑邮政工人的情况：如果每个邮政工人平均投递更多的信件，就称他们有更高的生产率，但这真的正确吗？如果投递更多信件的同时每个工人平均丢失或延迟更多的信件会是什么情况呢？

以上对量度生产率的方法暗含的反对意见是基于对以下哪一项论述的怀疑？

(A) 邮政工人是总的服务部门工人的代表。

(B) 投递信件是邮政服务的主要活动。

(C) 生产率应归于工人所在的部门，而不是单个人。

(D) 在计算生产率时可以适当地忽略提供的服务的质量。

(E) 投递的信件的数量同度量邮政工人的生产率有关。

解析：读明白问题永远是最重要的。本题问题目的等同于：(1) 上面段落驳斥下面哪一个？(2) 若上面陈述正确，那么下面哪一个can be true except...?（答案不能为无关选项，因为无关也可以正确，基本思路是寻找与段落里的main idea直接取非。）(3) 下面哪一个信息直接和段落推理相违背？

对于建议的完全量化的生产率的度量方法的批评提出了服务质量的问题，暗示服务质量也是潜在的需要考虑的相关方面，因此，选项(D)是正确答案；该反对意见假设邮政工人是总的服务部门工人的适当的代表，因此，选项(A)不合适，由建议的从信件投递来度量生产率推论出，该论述认为投递信件是邮政工人的主要活动，因此选项(B)不合适；因为该短文清楚地将生产率归于工人所在的整个部门，选项(C)不合适；选项(E)不合适，因为该反对者没有质疑投递信件数量的相关性，而是暗示一些其他的因素也应该是相关的。请参考本书175页40题。

五、 试题精练及解析

1. That social institutions influence the formation of character has become a generally accepted proposition. This doctrine views individuals as but compliant recipients of social influence: personalities are entirely the products of society, and at any point in life an individual's personality can be changed by management of the social world. Crime is said to exist only because society has in some ways failed in its responsibility to give every person the resources to lead a productive life. However, whereas it is true that extreme poverty forces some people to steal, it is obvious that some persons will commit crimes no matter how well society treats them.

Which of the following is implied by the "doctrine" (line 2) described in the passage above?

(A) Social institutions may reflect personality as much as they shape it.

(B) Social influence on personality is most strongly felt by the affluent.

(C) The concentration of wealth in the hands of a privileged few accounts for the existence of crime.

(D) Bringing about social reform is the most likely means of curtailing crime.

(E) Less severe punishment of crime would be likely to result in more crime.

社会习俗影响人性格的形成这一主张已经被普遍接受了。这种说法只把个人当成社会影响的顺从的接受者，个性完全是社会的产物，在生活中任何一个方面个人的性格都会被社会的管理所改变。而犯罪之所以存在据说是因为社会在某些方面没能尽到使每人都过上富足的生活这一责任。然而，尽管极端贫穷会迫使人去偷盗是事实，但很明显，有些人不管社会如何善待他们，他们仍会去犯罪。

上文描述的 "doctrine" 所隐含的意思是下面哪一句？

(A) 社会习俗对性格的反映与对性格的影响不相上下。

(B) 富人最能强烈地感觉到社会对其性格的影响。

(C) 社会财富积聚到少数有特权的人中是犯罪存在的原因。

(D) 进行社会改革是最可能减少犯罪的办法。

(E) 犯罪惩罚力度的降低很可能导致更多的犯罪行为。

2. Nineteenth-century art critics judged art by the realism of its method of representation. It was assumed that the realistic method developed from primitive beginnings to the perfection of formal realism. It is one of the permanent gains of the aesthetic revolution of the twentieth century that we are rid of this type of aesthetics.

It can be inferred from the passage above that the artistic revolution of the twentieth century had which of the following effects?

(A) It deemphasized realistic representation as an evaluative consideration for judging works of art.

(B) It permitted modern critics to appreciate the simplicity of primitive art.

19世纪的艺术评论家根据表现手法中的现实主义来评价艺术作品。他们认为这种现实主义手法已从初始阶段发展到了正规的现实主义的完美阶段。而20世纪美学革命的永久性成果之一便是摆脱了这种审美类型。

从上文可以推断出20世纪的美学革命产生了下面哪个效果？

(A) 它降低了现实主义表现手法作为评价艺术作品的考虑因素的地位。

(B) 它允许现代评论家欣赏原始艺术的单纯性。

(C) It repudiated the realistic representation found in the art of the past.

(D) It reinforced traditional ways of looking at and judging great art.

(E) It allowed art critics to understand the evolution and nature of art.

(C) 它驳斥了在过去艺术作品中发现的现实主义的表现手法。

(D) 它增强了欣赏和评价伟大艺术的传统方式。

(E) 它允许评论家理解艺术的演变和本质。

3. Anyone who has owned a car knows that saving money in the short run by skimping on relatively minor repairs and routine maintenance will prove very costly in the long run. However, this basic truth is often forgotten by those who call for reduced government spending on social programs.

Which of the following is NOT implied by the analogy above as a point of comparison?

(A) Money that is spent on repairs and maintenance helps to ensure the continued functioning of a car.

(B) Owners can take chances on not maintaining or repairing their cars.

(C) In order to keep operating, cars will normally need some work.

(D) The problems with a car will become worse if they are not attended to.

(E) A car will last for only a limited period of time and then must be replaced.

有车的人都知道，从短期看在小型维修和日常保养上缩减开支可能省一笔钱，但从长远角度看，这样做成本很大。然而，这样一个基本的道理却经常被那些呼吁政府减少社会项目开销的人所忘记。

下面哪个不是上面对比所暗含的意思？

(A) 花在维修和保养上的费用能保证车辆持续地发挥功用。

(B) 车主们可以带着侥幸的心理不去进行车辆的维修和保养。

(C) 为了让车能一直正常行驶，通常需要对车进行维修。

(D) 如果车出了毛病而不及时处理，情况会变得更糟。

(E) 一辆车只能使用有限的时间，然后必须淘汰掉。

4. The Census Bureau reported that the median family income, after adjustment for inflation, increased 1.6 percent in 1983. Poverty normally declines when family income goes up, but the national poverty rate remained at its highest level in eighteen years in 1983. The Census Bureau offered two possible explanations: the lingering effects of the deep and lengthy 1981-1982 recession, and increases in the number of people living in families headed by women and in the number of adults not living with any relatives. Both groups are likely to be poorer than the population as a whole.

Which of the following conclusions can be properly drawn from this report?

(A) The national poverty rate has increased steadily over the last eighteen years.

(B) The national poverty rate will increase when there are lingering effects of an earlier recession.

(C) The median family income can increase even though the family income of some subgroups within the population declines or fails to increase.

据人口普查司报告说，扣除通货膨胀因素后，1983年中等家庭收入增加了1.6%。通常情况下，随着家庭收入上升，贫困人数就会减少，然而1983年全国贫困率是18年来的最高水平。人口普查司提供了两种可能的原因：影响深、持续时间长的1981～1982年经济衰退的持续影响；由妇女赡养的家庭人口数量和不与亲戚们同住的成年人数量的增多。这两种人都比整体人口更加贫困。

这个报告能得出以下哪个结论？

(A) 全国贫困率在最近18年里一直稳步增长。

(B) 如果早期的经济衰退仍带来持续的影响，那么全国贫困率会升高。

(C) 即使人口中有些家庭收入下降或未增加，中等家庭收入依然可能增加。

(D) The category of adults not living with any relatives is the most critical group in the determination of whether the economy has improved.

(E) The median family income is affected more by changes in family patterns than by the extent of expansion or recession of the national economy.

5. The nuclear polyhedrosis virus helps control gypsy moth populations by killing the moth's larvae. The virus is always present in the larvae, but only every sixth or seventh year does the virus seriously decimate the number of larvae, thereby drastically setting back the gypsy moth population. Scientists believe that the virus, ordinarily latent, is triggered only when the larvae experience biological stress.

If the scientists mentioned above are correct, it can be inferred that the decimation of gypsy moth larvae populations by the nuclear polyhedrosis virus would be most likely to be triggered by which of the following conditions?

(A) A shift from drought conditions to normal precipitation in areas infested by gypsy moths.

(B) The escalating stress of defoliation sustained by trees attacked by gypsy moths for the second consecutive year.

(C) Predation on larvae of all kinds by parasitic wasps and flies.

(D) Starvation of the gypsy moth larvae as a result of overpopulation.

(E) Spraying of areas infested by gypsy moths with laboratory-raised nuclear polyhedrosis virus.

6. Konstantin Stanislavski's justly praised method for training actors arose from Stanislavski's own awkwardness and susceptibility to theatrical clichés as a young actor. The "method" must be understood in terms of Stanislavski's personal search for release from the temptations of stock gestures, well-tried vocal intonations, and standard emotional formulas. Despite the pretensions of certain of his disciples in the United States, the Russian director never intended to formulate a textbook of rigid solutions to acting problems.

It can be inferred that the author of the preceding statements about Stanislavski's method holds which of the following opinions about acting?

(A) Acting is essentially spontaneous emotional expression, with which systematic training usually interferes.

(B) The Stanislavski method has lost some of its flexibility

P(polyhedrosis)核病毒可以通过杀死吉普赛蛾的幼虫从而有助于控制该蛾的数目。这种病毒一直存活于幼虫身上，但每隔六七年才能杀死大部分幼虫，从而大大降低吉普赛蛾的数目。科学家们认为，这种通常处于潜伏状态的病毒，只有当幼虫受到生理上的压抑时才会被激活。

如果上文中科学家所说是正确的，下面哪种情况最有可能把这种病毒激活？

(A) 在吉普赛蛾泛滥成灾的地区，天气由干旱转变为正常降雨。

(B) 连续两年被吉普赛蛾侵袭的树木，树叶脱落的情况日愈加剧。

(C) 寄生的黄蜂和苍蝇对各类幼虫的捕食。

(D) 由于吉普赛蛾的数量过多而导致的食物严重短缺。

(E) 在吉普赛蛾肆疟的地区喷洒实验室里培制的P(polyhedrosis)核病毒。

Konstantin Stanislavski那种受到公正赞扬的训练演员的方法，来自于他本人作为一名年轻演员时的笨拙表现和受到的戏剧中的陈词滥调的伤害。必须从Stanislavski个人为从陈腐的姿势、反复尝试的嗓音语调和标准的感情模式的诱惑中解脱出来进行的研究中去理解该方法。尽管他在美国的追随者有过要求，但这位俄国导演从未打算写一本对表演问题提出严格的解决方法的教科书。

从以上作者关于Stanislavski方法的陈述可以推出以下关于表演的哪一观点？

(A) 表演是自发的情感表达，系统化的训练通常会破坏它。

(B) 他的一些在美国的追随者在使用该方法时，使其丧失了灵活和富于探索的

and exploratory qualities as it has been used by some followers of Stanislavski in the United States.

(C) The Stanislavski method has misled those actors in the United States who have adopted it.

(D) Virtually the only advice young actors need be given is that they must systematically suppress theatrical clichés in their performances.

(E) The Stanislavski method is useful primarily for young actors who must overcome artificiality and immaturity in their performances.

7. Forty-five percent of all blood donated in the United States is type O. Type O blood is essential for emergencies where there is no time for determining the blood type of victims because type O blood can be used for everyone. Type O blood is unique in that it is compatible with blood of all types: any recipient, regardless of blood type, can be given it. But precisely because of this special usefulness, type O blood is chronically in short supply.

If the statements in the passage above are true, which of the following must also be true?

(A) The special usefulness of type O blood lies in the fact that it matches the blood type of most people.

(B) Supplies of type O blood are continuously so low that type O blood is unavailable for emergencies, where its usefulness would be greatest.

(C) Forty-five percent of the total population of the United State has type O blood, which makes type O the most common blood type.

(D) Any decision to give blood of any type other than O needs to be based on knowledge of the recipient's blood type.

(E) Type O blood is the only blood that cannot be typed as fast as needed in emergencies.

8. Dense snow cover can cause unusually harsh weather patterns to persist. If a severe winter storm blankets the Great Plains, the snow cover reflects the sun's radiation back into space and thus keeps the temperature of the ground low. Consequently, cold air moving down from Canada remains cold enough to cause more snowstorms.

Which of the following is a conclusion that can be properly drawn from the information above?

(A) Winter weather on the Great Plains is the product of unusual movements of air masses.

品质。

(C) 在美国Stanislavski方法误导了一些采纳这种方法的演员。

(D) 实际上，年轻演员唯一需要的一条建议是他们必须系统地克服表演戏剧中的陈词滥调。

(E) Stanislavski方法主要对那些需要克服表演中的造作和不成熟的年轻演员有用。

在美国所有捐献的血液中有45%是O型的。由于O型血适用于任何人，所以当在没有时间测定患者是何种血型的危急时刻，O型血是不可缺少的。O型血是唯一可与其他任何血型相融的血型，所以它可以输给任何受血者。然而正是由于这一特殊用途，O型血长期处于短缺状态。

如果上文陈述是正确的，那么下面哪一项也一定是正确的？

(A) O型血的特殊用途基于这样一个事实：它与大部分人的血型都相融。

(B) O型血的供应一直很少，以至于在最能体现它有用性的危急时刻，它往往是不够用的。

(C) 美国45%的人是O型血，这使得O型血成为最普遍的血型。

(D) 要决定输送任何非O型血时都必须以知道受血者的血型为基础。

(E) 只有O型血不能按照危急时刻的需要被快速地测定出来。

厚厚的积雪可以使非同寻常的恶劣天气持续下去。如果一场严重的冬季暴风雪覆盖了大平原地区，那么积雪将太阳光的辐射反射回空中从而保持地面低温。由此，从加拿大南下的冷空气可以保持足够冷的温度从而引发更多的暴风雪。

从上述信息中能适当地得出下列哪一结论？

(A) 大平原地区的冬天气候是气团不正常运动的结果。

(B) The Great Plains are more likely than other areas to suffer unusually harsh weather patterns.

(C) If the Great Plains get more snow than usual early in the winter and the snow remains until the spring thaw, the winter is likely to be colder than usual.

(D) Even if the temperatures on the Great Plains are not extremely cold but are just below freezing, a moderate snowstorm will probably turn into a blizzard.

(E) The temperature of the ground depends primarily on the thickness of the snow cover.

9. Consider three fish swimming together in a school. The space within which each fish can be seen by predator Y is defined by a sphere centered on the fish and having a radius that is the maximum distance Y can see. The school is vulnerable to attack when Y is within one of the three spheres. The spheres overlap to a great extent, since the fish are in a compact group.

Which of the following is a reliable inference to be drawn from the passage above?

(A) The vulnerability to attack of the school as a whole is not much greater than the vulnerability to attack of any one fish in the school.

(B) There is less chance that predator Y will attack a school of four fish than that it will attack a school of three fish.

(C) Fish who swim in schools are less likely to be devoured by predators than are fish who do not swim in schools.

(D) The maximum distance at which an individual fish is visible depends less on the size of the fish than on whether the fish is swimming in a school.

(E) The maximum distance at which predator Y can see its prey is increased if Y is itself swimming in a school of Y's.

10. Masterpieces of literature are "intertextual," that is, they tend to be written in response not to reality but to other works of literature. To the extent that a writing is intertextual, it becomes clouded as a mirror of social reality.

The statements above provide the most support for which of the following conclusions?

(A) To the extent that a writing fails to mirror social reality, the writing is intertextual.

(B) The author who wishes to write a masterpiece should avoid being influenced by other works of literature.

(B) 大平原比其他地区更易遭受非常恶劣的天气情况。

(C) 如果在大平原地区的初冬有比正常情况下更多的降雪，并且雪一直保留到春天才融化时，则该冬季很可能比通常的冬季更冷。

(D) 即使大平原的气温只是低于冰点而不是非常低，一场不大的降雪也可能会转变为大暴风雪。

(E) 地面温度主要取决于积雪的厚度。

设想一下三条鱼成群而游。一条鱼可能被捕食者Y看到的空间是以该鱼为圆心，Y能看见的最远距离为半径的圆。当Y在这三个圆之中的一个时，该鱼群可能受到攻击。由于三条鱼的鱼群之间距离很近，这三个圆在很大程度上重叠在一起。

下面的哪一项是从上面一段中得出的可靠推断？

(A) 整个鱼群的易受攻击性比鱼群中的每一条鱼的易受攻击性大不了很多。

(B) 捕食者Y攻击四条鱼的鱼群的可能性比攻击三条鱼的鱼群的可能性小。

(C) 成群而游的鱼比单独的鱼更不易被捕食者吞食。

(D) 一条鱼能被看见的最大距离不怎么取决于鱼的大小，而更多地取决于该鱼是否成群地游动。

(E) 如果捕食者Y本身游在一群Y之中，则Y能看到其猎物的最大距离有所增加。

文学杰作是"文学上相互关联的"，也就是说，它们不应是为反映现实而作，而应是为反映其他文学作品而作。就一部作品在文学上相关的程度而言，它作为一面反映社会现实的镜子变得不那么清晰了。

上面陈述最能支持下面哪一结论？

(A) 就一部作品未能反映社会现实的程度而言，这部作品是与文学相关的。

(B) 想创作出一篇杰作的作家应避免被其他文学作品所影响。

(C) A writing that is not intertextual can have no significant relationship to any other writings.

(D) Literary masterpieces of the past are suspect as sources of information about the social reality of the past.

(E) A work of literature is not intertextual if it is written in response to a writing that accurately mirrors social reality.

11. To many environmentalists, the extinction of plants—accompanied by the increasing genetic uniformity of species of food crops—is the single most serious environmental problem. Something must be done to prevent the loss of wild food plants or no-longer-cultivated food plants. Otherwise, the lack of genetic diversity could allow a significant portion of a major crop to be destroyed overnight. In 1970, for example, southern leaf blight destroyed approximately 20 percent of the United States corn crop, leaving very few varieties of corn unaffected in the areas over which the disease had spread.

Which of the following can be inferred from the passage above?

(A) Susceptibility to certain plant diseases is genetically determined.

(B) Eighty percent of the corn grown in the United States is resistant to southern leaf blight.

(C) The extinction of wild food plants can in almost every case be traced to destructive plant diseases.

(D) Plant breeders focus on developing plants that are resistant to plant disease.

(E) Corn is the only food crop threatened by southern leaf blight.

12. A placebo is a chemically inert substance prescribed more for the mental relief of a patient than for its effect on the patient's physical disorder. It is prescribed in the hope of instilling in the patient a positive attitude toward prospects for his or her recovery. In some cases, the placebo actually produces improvement in the patient's condition. In discussing the use and effect of placebos, a well-known medical researcher recently paid physicians the somewhat offbeat compliment of saying that physicians were the ultimate placebo.

By comparing a physician to a placebo, the researcher sought to imply that

(A) physicians should always maintain and communicate an optimistic attitude toward their patients, regardless of the

(C) 不具文学关联性的作品与其他作品之间不会有明显关系。

(D) 过去的文学杰作被怀疑是关于过去社会现实的信息来源。

(E) 一部文学作品如果是对一部准确反映社会现实的作品的反应，它就不是文学上相互关联的。

对许多环境学家来说，植物的灭绝（随之而来的是各种农作物种类不断增加的基因一致性）是环境问题中最严重的一个问题。必须采取行动来阻止野生可食植物及不再耕种的可食植物的减少。否则，基因多样性的缺乏可能引起主要农作物的一大部分在一夜之间被毁掉。例如，在1970年，南方的叶菌病毁坏了大约20%的美国玉米作物，在该疾病所到之处只剩下很少的几种玉米未受影响。

从上段可推知下面哪一选项？

(A) 某种植物疾病的易感染性是由基因决定的。

(B) 美国种植的80%的玉米对南方叶菌病有抵抗力。

(C) 野生可食植物的灭绝几乎总是可以追溯到毁灭性的植物疾病（这一原因）。

(D) 植物培养者致力于研究可抵抗植物疾病的植物。

(E) 玉米是唯一受到南方叶菌病威胁的粮食作物。

安慰药是一种化学性质为惰性的物质，更多地用来给予病人精神上的安慰而非治疗病人身体的紊乱。给病人用这种药是期望给病人灌输对其康复前景的积极态度。在某些情况下，安慰药确实起到了改善病人病情的效果。一位著名医药研究专家在最近讨论安慰药的应用及效果时，给了内科医生一些不寻常的赞扬，说内科医生就是最终的安慰药。

该研究学家通过将内科医生比作安慰药试图暗示：

(A) 不管诊断结果如何，内科医生应该总是保持乐观并将乐观的态度传达给他的病人。

prognosis.

(B) the health of some patients can improve simply form their knowledge that they are under a physician's care.

(C) many patients actually suffer from imagined illnesses that are best treated by placebos.

(D) physicians could prescribe less medication and achieve the same effect.

(E) it is difficult to determine what, if any, effect a physician's behavior has on a patient's condition.

13. In a study of more than 8,000 people using ten beaches on two of the Great Lakes, ecologists from the University of Toronto determined that the rate of respiratory and gastrointestinal illness among people who had been swimming was 69.6 per 1,000, whereas the respiratory and gastrointestinal illness rate among those who had not been swimming was only 29.5 per 1,000.

Which of the following conclusions can be most properly drawn from the data above?

(A) People tend to underestimate the risks of swimming in these lakes.

(B) Respiratory and gastrointestinal illnesses occur at a higher rate as a result of swimming in either of these lakes than they do as a result of swimming in any other lake.

(C) Illnesses of kinds other than respiratory and gastrointestinal are not likely to be associated with swimming in either of these lakes.

(D) The association between swimming in these lakes and respiratory and gastrointestinal illness is some evidence for a causal relationship between them.

(E) A large percentage of the people who swim in these lakes are immune to the diseases that swimming may cause.

14. In a recent year California produced an orange crop equal to only seventy-six percent of Florida's orange crop. However, when citrus crops as a group, including oranges, were compared, the California crop was twenty-three percent greater than Florida's crop for the same year.

If the information above is true, which of the following can properly be concluded about the Florida and California citrus crops in the year mentioned?

(A) Florida's climate was suited only to growing oranges.

(B) Florida produced larger oranges than California did.

(C) California produced more oranges than it did non-orange

(B) 有些病人的健康仅仅由于他们知道医生在给他们治疗而有所好转。

(C) 很多病人实际上患的是想象病，这些病最好的医治是安慰药。

(D) 医生可以少开一些药物而取得同样的疗效。

(E) 很难确定如果医生的行为对病人的状况有效果的话，是有什么样的效果。

在对使用五大湖中两个湖的10处沙滩的8000多人的调查研究中，多伦多大学的生态学家们发现游泳的人中呼吸道疾病和胃肠疾病的患病率达69.6‰，而没有游泳的人这两类病的患病率为29.5‰。

从上述数据能最恰当地得出如下哪一结论？

(A) 人们容易低估在这些湖中的游泳的危害。

(B) 在这两个湖中任意一个湖中游泳，患上呼吸道和胃肠疾病的患病率比在其他湖中游泳的患病率高。

(C) 除呼吸道、胃肠疾病之外的疾病不太可能与在这两个湖中的一个湖中游泳有关。

(D) 在这些湖中游泳与呼吸道、胃肠疾病之间的联系为这二者之间的因果关系提供了证据。

(E) 在这些湖中游泳的一大部分人对游泳可能引起的疾病有免疫力。

最近一年，加利福尼亚生产的桔子产量只是佛罗里达桔子产量的76%，然而，把柑橘类作物（包括桔子）的产量进行比较，则同年加利福尼亚的产量比佛罗里达的产量高出23%。

如果上面信息是正确的，可以正确地得出下面哪一项关于上述佛罗里达和加州的柑橘类作物在提到的这一年年产量的结论？

(A) 佛罗里达的气候只适于种植桔子。

(B) 佛罗里达生产的桔子比加利福尼亚生产的桔子个大。

citrus.

(D) California's proportion of non-orange citrus crops was higher than Florida's.

(E) California had more acreage that could be devoted to agriculture than did Florida.

(C) 加利福尼亚的桔子产量大于其他柑橘类产量。

(D) 加利福尼亚非桔子的柑橘类作物占柑橘类作物的比例高于佛罗里达的该比例。

(E) 加利福尼亚比佛罗里达有更多的土地可以用于农业。

15. As part of a delicately balanced system, the human heart secretes a hormone, a substance that controls the amount of salt in the blood and the volume of blood circulating within the body. Only very small quantities of the hormone are required. This hormone is extremely important in regulating blood pressure and is found in large amounts in the blood of those suffering a heart attack.

If the statements above are true, then it must also be true that

(A) if there is a deficiency in the amount of heart hormone secreted, low blood pressure will result.

(B) it is large quantities of the heart hormone that cause heart attacks to occur.

(C) the effects of a small amount of the heart hormone will be long-lasting in the body.

(D) if a device that is only a mechanical pump is used as an artificial heart, it will not perform all the functions of the human heart.

(E) any drug that regulates blood pressure will have its effect by influencing the amount of the heart hormone secreted.

作为一个微妙的平衡系统的一部分，人体的心脏能分泌一种激素，这种物质控制着血液中盐的含量以及人体中循环的血液量。人体只需很少量的这种荷尔蒙，它对调节血压极其重要。在患有心脏病的人的血液中发现有大量的这种物质。

如果上面的陈述正确，则下面哪一项也是正确的？

(A) 如果心脏分泌的这种荷尔蒙不足，则会导致低血压。

(B) 是大量的心脏荷尔蒙引起的心脏病发作。

(C) 少量的心脏荷尔蒙在人体内产生的效果是持久的。

(D) 如果一种装置仅仅是一个机械泵，它被用作人工心脏，那将无法执行人的心脏的所有功能。

(E) 任何调节血压的药都通过影响心脏分泌的荷尔蒙量而起到效果。

16. Ironically, people who use aspartame as a sweetener to reduce their caloric intake could wind up defeating their purpose, since studies show that high levels of aspartame may trigger a craving for carbohydrates by depleting the brain of a chemical that registers carbohydrate satiety.

Which of the following conclusions can most properly be drawn if the statements above are true?

(A) Aspartame can be more hazardous than carbohydrates to people's health.

(B) People who do not use aspartame are not likely to develop a craving for carbohydrates.

(C) The caloric content of foods that are high in carbohydrates is significant.

(D) People tend to prefer sweet foods to those high in carbohydrates.

具有讽刺意味的是，用aspartame作为发甜剂来减少摄入热量的人们可能最终无法达到目的，因为研究显示，高浓度的aspartame可能通过耗尽大脑中那些显示对糖类的满足的化学物质来引起人们对糖的强烈需求。

从上述陈述中能最适当地得出下面哪一个结论？

(A) aspartame可能比糖对人体的健康更为有害。

(B) 不使用aspartame的人不可能产生对糖的强烈需求。

(C) 含糖量高的食品含的热量很多。

(D) 人们趋向于更喜欢甜食，而不是那些含有较多碳水化合物的食品。

(E) Food products that contain aspartame are typically low in carbohydrates.

17. To be mentally healthy, people must have self-respect. People can maintain self-respect only by continually earning the respect of others they esteem. They can earn this respect only by treating these others morally.

Which of the following conclusions can be properly drawn from the statements above?

(A) People who are mentally healthy will be treated morally by others.

(B) People who are mentally healthy will have treated morally those they esteem.

(C) People who are mentally healthy must have self-respect in order to be treated morally by others.

(D) People can expect to be treated morally by others only if they esteem these others.

(E) People who have self-respect seldom treat morally those they esteem.

18. Figures issued by the government of a certain country show that in 1980 the public sector and the private sector each employed the same number of people. Between 1980 and 1984, according to the government, total employment decreased in the public sector more than it increased in the private sector.

If, according to governmental figures, the unemployment rate in this country was the same in both 1980 and 1984, which of the following statements must be true about this country?

(A) Fewer people were in the labor force, as counted by the government, in 1984 than in 1980.

(B) The competition for the available work increased between 1980 and 1984.

(C) The government's figures for total employment increased between 1980 and 1984.

(D) The number of people counted by the government as unemployed was the same in 1980 and 1984.

(E) In 1984 more people sought work in the private sector than in the public sector.

19. When released into the atmosphere, the refrigerant Freon damages the Earth's ozone layer. A new kind of refrigerant does not have this effect. The manufacturer claims that replacing Freon with the new refrigerant in both new and

（E）含aspartame的食品通常含有较少的碳水化合物。

人们必须拥有自尊才能保持精神健康。人们只有一直受到他们所尊敬的人的尊重，才能保持自尊。而这种尊重只有靠善待他人来获得。

从上述陈述能得出下面哪一个结论？

（A）精神健康的人会受到他人的善待。

（B）精神健康的人一定会善待他们所尊敬的人。

（C）精神健康的人一定有自尊，以受到他人的善待。

（D）只有尊敬他人，人们才能指望得到他人的善待。

（E）有自尊的人很少善待那些他们尊敬的人。

某国政府公布的数字显示在1980年公共部门和私人部门雇用了相同数量的人员。根据政府的数据，在1980年到1984年之间，公共部门减少的就业总数多于私人部门增加的就业总量。

根据政府数据，如果在1980年和1984年该国的失业率相同，下面哪一项关于该国的陈述一定是正确的？

（A）按照政府统计，1984年的劳动力数量少于1980年。

（B）从1980年到1984年间，对已有的工作的竞争增强了。

（C）政府统计的总就业数量，从1980年到1984年有所增加。

（D）在1980年和1984年被政府统计为失业的人数相等。

（E）在1984年，在私人部门求职的人比在公共部门求职的人多。

当被释放到大气中时，制冷剂氟利昂会破坏地球的臭氧层。一种新型制冷剂没有这种影响。制造商宣称，用这种新的制冷剂代替新生产出来的和已有的冰箱中的

existing refrigerators will prevent any further Freon damage to the ozone layer apart from that being done by the Freon already in the atmosphere.

Which of the following must be true if the manufacturer's prediction is to prove accurate?

(A) Freon can be replaced with the new refrigerant without releasing any Freon into the atmosphere.

(B) The damage already done to the ozone layer is not of environmentally significant proportions.

(C) The atmosphere can reverse the damage to the ozone layer caused by the past use of Freon.

(D) The new refrigerant can counteract the damaging effects of Freon on the Earth's atmosphere.

(E) The new refrigerant causes no environmental damage of any kind when it is released into the atmosphere.

20. Students can learn mathematics only by exploring it on their own, with generous room for trial and error. For what matters in the long run is not acquiring particular computational skills (since without constant use skills rapidly fade), but knowing how to find and use suitable mathematical tools whenever they become necessary.

If the position expressed above is correct, then each of the following can be true EXCEPT:

(A) Mathematics teachers are often afraid that someone will ask a question that they cannot answer, and this insecurity frequently leads to authoritarianism in the classroom.

(B) Prospective teachers should themselves learn mathematics as a process of constructing and interpreting patterns, of devising strategies for solving problems, and of discovering the beauties and applications of mathematics.

(C) Political leaders must accept responsibility for coordinating a nationwide plan for all levels of instruction if mathematics education is to improve.

(D) The most effective method for teaching students mathematics is for teachers to state the definitive rule for solving exercises of a given type and then to insist on rote practice in its proper application.

(E) Most current teaching presents mathematics as established doctrine, stressing the production of right answers rather than the ability to communicate reasons.

氟利昂可以防止已存在于大气中的氟利昂对臭氧层的破坏进一步恶化。

如果制造者的预言被证实，下列哪一项一定是正确的？

(A) 用新制冷剂代替氟利昂时，不会有任何氟利昂被释放到大气中。

(B) 对臭氧层已经造成的破坏从环境意义上讲还没有到很严重的程度。

(C) 大气可以扭转以前氟利昂对臭氧层造成的破坏。

(D) 新的制冷剂可以抵消氟利昂对地球大气的破坏作用。

(E) 新的制冷剂释放到大气中时不会引起任何环境破坏。

学生们只有通过自己的探索才能学好数学，这样能够有充分的自由进行尝试，因为从长期来看，重要的不是具备特别的计算技巧（因为不经常使用技巧就会很快变得生疏），而是懂得在必要的时候如何找到和运用适当的数学工具。

如果以上表达的立场正确，则以下除哪项外都可能是正确的？

(A) 数学老师通常担心某个学生会提出他们无法回答的问题，这种不安全感常常导致数学课上的一言堂局面。

(B) 未来的老师应该把数学作为建造模型和解释模型的过程，作为设计解决问题的策略的过程，作为发现数学的美和适用性的过程来学习。

(C) 如果要使数学教育有所改善，政治领导人必须负责对一个全国范围内的各级教育的计划进行协调。

(D) 向学生们教授数学的最有效办法是给出解决一类问题的确定规则，然后要求反复练习对其正确运用。

(E) 目前大部分的数学老师教授数学时把它作为一种教条，强调的是得出正确的结果，而不重视培养推理的能力。

21. False rumors of fiscal improprieties damage the reputation of a bank. If management does not attempt to refute these rumors, they will circulate and eventually destroy customer confidence. But if management makes an effort to refute them, the refutation will raise more suspicions than it allays.

If all of the statements above are true, which of the following must on the basis of them be true?

(A) The reputation of a bank cannot be influenced by heavy advertising campaigns.

(B) True rumors of fiscal improprieties do not do as much damage to customer confidence in a bank as false rumors do.

(C) The best strategy for bank managers to adopt in the face of false rumors of fiscal improprieties is to address them directly.

(D) Management cannot prevent already existing false rumors of fiscal improprieties from threatening a bank's reputation.

(E) A bank's reputation for fiscal responsibility can be enhanced by favorable word of mouth.

22. Economist: Any country that is economically efficient will generate wealth. Such a country will remain politically stable only if that wealth is distributed equitably. The equitable distribution of wealth puts an end to risk taking, the indispensable precondition of economic efficiency.

Which of the following conclusions can be properly drawn on the basis of the statements above?

(A) No country can indefinitely remain both economically efficient and politically stable.

(B) No country can indefinitely remain both politically unstable and wealthy.

(C) Economic efficiency is the indispensable precondition for the generation of wealth in a country.

(D) Any country in which wealth is distributed equitably will indefinitely remain politically stable.

(E) Growing economic efficiency encourages risk taking, which in turn leads to further growth in economic efficiency.

23. In "quick-response" manufacturing, the manufacturer receives electronic feedback directly from retailers about which models, patterns, or styles are selling, and in what quantities. This feedback triggers the manufacture of further

关于财务混乱的错误谣言损害了一家银行的声誉，如果管理人员不试图反驳这些谣言，它们就会传播开来并最终摧毁顾客的信心。但如果管理人员努力驳斥这种谣言，这种驳斥使怀疑增加的程度比使它减少的程度更大。

如果以上陈述都是正确的，根据这些陈述，下列哪一项一定是正确的?

(A) 银行的声誉不会受到猛烈的广告宣传活动的影响。

(B) 关于财政混乱的正确的传言，对银行储户对该银行的信心的影响没有错误的流言大。

(C) 面对错误的谣言，银行经理的最佳对策是直接说出财务的真实情况。

(D) 管理人员无法阻止已经出现的谣言，威胁银行的声誉。

(E) 有利的口碑可以提高银行在财务能力方面的声誉。

经济学家：任何有经济效率的国家都能创造财富。这种国家只有在财富平均分配时才能保持政治稳定。财富平均分配又会使冒险活动消失，而这些冒险活动正是经济有效运转必不可少的前提条件。

基于以上陈述，可适当推出下列哪一结论?

(A) 没有国家既能无限期地保持经济上的高效率，又能保证政治上的稳定。

(B) 没有国家能无限期地在政治不稳定的同时，经济上变得富裕。

(C) 经济效率是一个国家创造财富的不可缺少的前提。

(D) 任何国家只要财富平等分配，就能保证政治稳定。

(E) 经济效率增长促进了冒险，冒险又导致经济效率的进一步增长。

在"快速反应"生产中，制造商直接从零售商那里收到关于正在销售的有哪些型号、样式、种类的商品及销量有多少等电子反馈信息，这种反馈促使制造商进一

batches to replenish stocks of articles that have been sold. The advantage for retailers is that they are freshly stocked with just those articles that are most likely to sell.

For quick-response manufacturing to work to the retailer's advantage in the respect mentioned above, which of the following must be true?

(A) The cost per piece of manufacturing various articles in small batches exceeds the cost per piece of manufacturing large quantities of those articles.

(B) The equipment necessary to provide the direct feedback is different from the equipment that supports conventional inventory control.

(C) Consumers do not patronize a store that does not stock the model, pattern, or style that they prefer.

(D) Consumers can distinguish retailers that rely on quick-response manufacturing from retailers that do not.

(E) Consumers do not suddenly stop buying models patterns, or styles that have just become popular.

24. No ambitious politician will challenge an elected public official running for reelection unless that official appears vulnerable. Nonetheless, elected public officials who do not appear vulnerable as they attempt to win reelection rarely run unopposed.

If the statements above are true, which of the following conclusions can be properly drawn from them?

(A) If an elected official running for reelection appears vulnerable, that official's challengers will all be ambitious politicians.

(B) Some elected officials running for reelection are challenged by people who are not ambitious politicians.

(C) Elected officials running for reelection who do not appear vulnerable are themselves ambitious politicians.

(D) A person who is not an ambitious politician cannot win an election contested by the current officeholder.

(E) A politician's career will be seriously set back if the politician wages an unsuccessful campaign for elective office.

25. The toxin produced by certain marine snails contains various proteins, one of which, when injected into mice, made mice aged two weeks or younger fall asleep and made older

步生产以补充被售出的存货。对零售商的好处是他们新增加的存货正是那些最好卖的商品。

要使快速反应生产产生以上提到的对零售商的好处，下列哪项一定是正确的？

(A) 小批生产各种产品的单件成本比大量生产时的单件成本高。

(B) 提供直接反馈信息的商品所必需的设备和适用传统的存货控制方法的设备不同。

(C) 消费者不会光顾那些不储存他们喜欢的型号、图案和式样的产品的商店。

(D) 消费者能够区分依靠快速反馈生产的零售商和不使用该方法的零售商。

(E) 消费者不会突然停止购买那些型号、图案和花色刚开始流行的产品。

一个有野心的政治家不会向一位准备竞选连任的现任政府官员挑战，除非这个官员表现得很无能。然而，表现并不是很无能的政府官员在试图重新当选时，只在很少的情况下没有受到反对。

如果以上陈述正确，可以适当地得出下列哪一结论？

(A) 如果一个竞选连任的官员表现得很无能，他的竞争对手都将是些有野心的政治家。

(B) 一些竞选连任的现任官员，会受到一些没有野心的政治家的挑战。

(C) 竞选连任的现任官员，如果不是表现得很无能，那么这些官员本人就是有野心的政治家。

(D) 如果一个人不是有野心的政治家，他就不能在竞争对手是当前该职位拥有者的选举中获胜。

(E) 如果一个政治家发动了一场竞选活动却没有成功，他的职业生涯就会遭受挫折。

一种海洋蜗牛产生的毒素含有多种蛋白，将其中一种注入老鼠体内后，可以使只有两星期大的或更小的老鼠进入睡眠状态，

mice run for hiding places.

When mice are suddenly seriously threatened, very young ones react by staying perfectly still, whereas older ones run away.

The facts stated above provide the strongest support for which of the following working hypotheses?

(A) The reaction of mice to sudden, serious threats is triggered by a chemical produced by the body, and this chemical is similar to the protein that was injected into the mice.

(B) The protein contained in snail toxin that was injected into the mice ordinarily has the primary function of protecting snails by inducing in those snails complete immobility.

(C) The protein that was injected into the mice would have made the mature mice fall asleep, too, if they had been injected with larger doses.

(D) Very young mice are as likely to be exposed to sudden serious threats as are older mice.

(E) Very young mice are not developed enough to deal appropriately with even the stimuli that they are most likely to encounter.

26. Essentially all polar ice forms from precipitation that falls as snow. Extremely cold air cannot hold much moisture and consequently cannot produce much snowfall. In recent years, air masses in both polar regions have been, without exception, extremely cold.

The information above most strongly supports which of the following conclusions?

(A) If polar ice is currently growing and expanding at all, it is doing so only slowly.

(B) If air temperatures in the polar regions were considerably warmer, much polar ice would melt off.

(C) In the last few years, snowfall in the polar regions has been virtually continuous.

(D) The thicker the polar ice is, the colder the air masses that are in contact with it.

(E) For snow to turn into ice in the polar regions, the air has to be extremely cold.

27. In household electric ovens, the heating element has only two settings—on and off. A thermostat connected to the oven's temperature knob is the only control on temperature, automatically switching the element off when the indicated

而使大一点的老鼠到处寻找藏身之处。

当老鼠受到突然的严重威胁时，非常小的那些老鼠的反应是完全静止不动，而大一些的会逃跑。

以上陈述的事实最有力地支持下列哪一项假设？

(A) 老鼠对突然出现的严重威胁做出反应，是由于受到体内产生的一种化学物质的刺激，这种化学物质和注射入老鼠体内的蛋白质相似。

(B) 蜗牛毒素中含有的注入老鼠体内的那种蛋白质的常见主要功能是通过促使蜗牛完全不动来保护它。

(C) 注入老鼠体内的蛋白质，如果向成年的老鼠体内注射更大的剂量，也能使成年老鼠进入睡眠状态。

(D) 幼鼠遇到突发性的严重威胁情况的可能性和大老鼠差不多。

(E) 幼鼠还没有发育成熟以致不能正确处理他们最常见的刺激。

实质上，所有的极地冰都是由降雪形成的。特别冷的空气不能保持很多的水蒸汽，因此无法产生大量降雪。近年来，两极地区的空气无一例外地都特别冷。

以上信息最有力地支持了下列哪一结论？

(A) 如果极地冰目前确实有所增加、扩大，速度也是非常之慢。

(B) 如果极地的空气温度大幅度变暖，许多极地冰将融化。

(C) 在过去的几年，极地的降雪一直在继续。

(D) 极地冰越厚，和它接触的大气越寒冷。

(E) 在极地，要使雪变成冰，空气必须非常寒冷。

家用电烤箱的加热部件只有两个设置——开和关。一个与烤箱温度旋钮相连的恒温器是对温度的唯一控制，当达到指定温度时它会自动关闭加热部件，这在现

temperature is reached, which happens quickly in modern ovens, and subsequently on or off as needed to maintain temperature.

Which of the following statements is most strongly supported by the information above?

(A) Because in each case the heating element alternates between on and off, a modern household electric oven uses little more power at its maximum temperature setting than it does at its lowest temperature setting.

(B) Once the indicated temperature has been reached and is being maintained by the thermostat, the heating element will be switched off for a greater proportion of the time than it is switched on.

(C) The accuracy with which household electric ovens maintain their temperature could not be improved on by ovens whose heating elements have more than two settings.

(D) In a correctly functioning modern household electric oven, the thermostat will generally not switch the heating element off when the oven's temperature is more than a few degrees above the indicated temperature.

(E) If the thermostat of a modern household electric oven is disabled so that the heating element remains switched on, the oven's temperature can eventually become higher than the maximum temperature setting on its temperature knob.

28. Playing eighteenth-century music on the instruments of that period provides valuable information about how the music originally sounded. Eighteenth-century instruments cannot be played without being restored, however, and restoring such an instrument destroys all of the information that researchers could obtain from it about eighteenth-century instrument-making techniques.

If the statements above are true, which of the following must be true on the basis of them?

(A) Eighteenth-century instruments cannot be used to provide information about the original techniques used in playing such instruments if they have been restored.

(B) Eighteenth-century instruments that have been restored can provide information only about how eighteenth-century music originally sounded.

(C) Eighteenth-century instruments are the only source of information about the instrument-making techniques of that period.

代烤箱中可很快发生，然后根据保持温度的需要开或关。

以上信息最有力地支持了下列哪一陈述？

(A) 因为在各种情况下，加热部件只有两种设置——开和关。所以一个现代的家用电烤箱，在最高设定温度时的用电并不比在最低设定温度时耗电。

(B) 一旦达到了指定温度，并由恒温器保持温度，加热部件就会被自动关闭，而且关闭的时间比打开的时间要长。

(C) 加热部件多于两种设置的电烤箱也无法再提高其维持温度的准确性。

(D) 工作正常的家用电烤箱，当烤箱温度稍微超过目标温度时，恒温器一般不会关闭加热部件。

(E) 如果一个现代的家用电烤箱恒温器失灵，使得加热部件一直保持打开状态，那么烤箱温度最后将超过温度旋钮所示的最高设置温度。

在18世纪的乐器上演奏18世纪的乐曲能提供这些乐曲最初听起来怎么样的有用信息。18世纪的乐器如果不修复就无法弹奏，然而，修复这种乐器却破坏了研究者们可以从中获得18世纪乐器制造技术方面的所有信息。

如果上面的陈述是正确的，那么基于这些陈述的下面哪一项也一定是正确的？

(A) 如果18世纪的乐器被修复，它们就不能被用来提供最初使用的演奏技巧方面的信息。

(B) 被修复过的18世纪的乐器只能提供18世纪的乐器最初听起来怎么样的信息。

(C) 18世纪的乐器是获得那个时期乐器制作技术方面的信息的唯一来源。

(D) An eighteenth-century instrument that has not been restored can provide more information than can one that has been restored.

(E) An eighteenth-century instrument cannot serve as a source of new information about eighteenth-century instrument-making techniques once it can be played.

(D) 一件未经修复的18世纪的乐器比一件修复过的18世纪的乐器提供的信息多。

(E) 一旦18世纪的乐器可以被用来演奏乐曲，那么它就不能作为获得18世纪乐器制作技术的一个新的信息来源。

29. Car telephones have become increasingly popular because they permit people to make or receive business calls while driving. As an additional benefit, motorists can quickly call for help in the event of an accident or breakdown. Nevertheless, car telephones should be prohibited because their use causes hazardous driving.

It can be concluded from the statements above that the author is committed to the truth of which of the following statements?

(A) The increasing popularity of car telephones is due primarily to the fact that they permit motorists to call for help in the event of an accident.

(B) The reason that the use of car telephones causes hazardous driving is that while dialing calls drivers cannot keep both hands on the wheel.

(C) The advantages afforded by car telephones do not outweigh the risks of hazardous driving created by them.

(D) In order to dial or receive telephone calls, drivers must momentarily take their eyes off the road, and this practice is hazardous.

(E) The ability to use car telephones to call for help is a more important advantage than the ability to use these phones to engage in business calls.

车载电话越来越受欢迎，因为有了它，人们就能在开车的时候拨出或接收电话了。它的另一个好处是，如果有事故发生或汽车抛锚，司机就可以立即打电话求助。不过，车载电话还是应该被禁用，因为使用它会造成危险驾车。

根据上段所述，可推出作者支持下列哪一说法？

(A) 车载电话之所以受欢迎，主要是因为它能够在事故发生时使司机能够呼救。

(B) 使用车载电话会造成危险驾车，是因为司机在拨号时无法双手握住方向盘。

(C) 车载电话带来的好处不能抵消它给危险驾车带来的风险。

(D) 为了拨出或接收电话，司机必须暂时不看道路，这种做法是很危险的。

(E) 车载电话用于电话求救的作用比其用于商业电话的作用更加重要。

30. A recent survey of all auto accident victims in Dole County found that, of the severely injured drivers and front-seat passengers, 80 percent were not wearing seat belts at the time of their accidents. This indicates that, by wearing seat belts, drivers and front-seat passengers can greatly reduce their risk of being severely injured if they are in an auto accident.

The conclusion above is not properly drawn unless which of the following is true?

(A) Of all the drivers and front-seat passengers in the survey, more than 20 percent were wearing seat belts at the time of their accidents.

(B) Considerably more than 20 percent of drivers and front-

最近的一项对都乐县所有的汽车事故受害者的调查发现，在严重受伤的司机和前排乘客中，80%的人在事故发生时没有系安全带。这表明，通过系保险带，司机和前排乘客们可以在汽车事故发生时大幅降低他们严重受伤的风险。

上面结论的得出是不恰当的，除非下面哪个是正确的？

(A) 在所有调查中的司机和前排乘客中，超过20%的人在事故发生时系了安全带。

(B) 都乐县中远远超过20%的司机和前排乘客在驾车旅行时常系安全带。

seat passengers in Dole County always wear seat belts when traveling by car.

(C) More drivers and front-seat passengers in the survey than rear-seat passengers were very severely injured.

(D) More than half of the drivers and front-seat passengers in the survey were not wearing seat belts at the time of their accidents.

(E) Most of the auto accidents reported to police in Dole County do not involve any serious injury.

(C) 在这次调查中，受重伤的司机和前排乘客比后排乘客多。

(D) 调查中有超过一半的司机和前排乘客在事故发生时没有系安全带。

(E) 大多数向都乐县警方报告的汽车事故不涉及任何重伤。

31. The fewer restrictions there are on the advertising of legal services, the more lawyers there are who advertise their services, and the lawyers who advertise a specific service usually charge less for that service than lawyers who do not advertise. Therefore, if the state removes any of its current restrictions, such as the one against advertisements that do not specify fee arrangements, overall consumer legal costs will be lower than if the state retains its current restrictions.

If the statements above are true, which of the following must be true?

(A) Some lawyers who now advertise will charge more for specific services if they do not have to specify fee arrangements in the advertisements.

(B) More consumers will use legal services if there are fewer restrictions on the advertising of legal services.

(C) If the restriction against advertisements that do not specify fee arrangements is removed, more lawyers will advertise their services.

(D) If more lawyers advertise lower prices for specific services, some lawyers who do not advertise will also charge less than they currently charge for those services.

(E) It the only restriction on the advertising of legal services were those that apply to every type of advertising, most lawyers would advertise their services.

对法律服务进行广告宣传的限制越少，为他们的服务进行广告宣传的律师就越多，并且为某项服务进行广告宣传的律师对该项服务的收费比没有进行广告宣传的律师低。因此，如果这个州取消这些限制中的任何一项，例如针对那些没有标明收费标准的广告的限制，那么总的消费者在法律事务中的花费将低于该州保留目前的限制下的情况。

如果以上所述是正确的，下面哪一项肯定是正确的?

(A) 一些现在进行广告宣传的律师，如果他们不需在广告中标明收费标准，他们可能会对进行了广告宣传的服务项目收取更高的费用。

(B) 如果关于对法律服务进行广告宣传的限制越少，更多的消费者就会使用法律服务。

(C) 如果禁止那些没有标明收费标准的广告的限制被取消，更多的律师会为他们的服务进行广告宣传。

(D) 如果更多的律师在广告宣传中为某些服务标明较低的价格，一些没有进行广告宣传的律师也会对这些服务收取比现在低的费用。

(E) 如果关于对法律服务进行广告宣传的限制仅仅是那些对所有类型广告都适用的限制，那么大多数律师会对他们的服务进行广告宣传。

32. Radio interferometry is a technique for studying details of celestial objects that combines signals intercepted by widely spaced radio telescopes. This technique requires ultraprecise timing, exact knowledge of the locations of the telescopes,

无线电干扰仪是一项研究天体的详情的技术，它把由广泛分布的无线电望远镜中途截获的信号进行结合。这种技术需要极其精确的计时、望远镜定位的确切知识

and sophisticated computer programs. The successful interferometric linking of an Earth-based radio telescope with a radio telescope on an orbiting satellite was therefore a significant technological accomplishment.

Which of the following can be correctly inferred from the statements above?

(A) Special care was taken in the launching of the satellite so the calculations of its orbit would be facilitated.

(B) The signals received on the satellite are stronger than those received by a terrestrial telescope.

(C) The resolution of detail achieved by the satellite-Earth interferometer system is inferior to that achieved by exclusively terrestrial systems.

(D) The computer programs required for making use of the signals received by the satellite required a long time for development.

(E) The location of an orbiting satellite relative to locations on Earth can be well enough known for interferometric purposes.

33. Recent estimates predict that between 1982 and 1995 the greatest increase in the number of people employed will be in the category of low-paying service occupations. This category, however, will not increase its share of total employment, whereas the category of high-paying service occupations will increase its share.

If the estimates above are accurate, which of the following conclusions can be drawn?

(A) In 1982 more people were working in low-paying service occupations than were working in high-paying service occupations.

(B) In 1995 more people will be working in high-paying service occupations than will be working in low-paying service occupations.

(C) Nonservice occupations will account for the same share of total employment in 1995 as in 1982.

(D) Many of the people who were working in low-paying service occupations in 1982 will be working in high-paying service occupations by 1995.

(E) The rate of growth for low-paying service occupations will be greater than the overall rate of employment growth between 1982 and 1995.

和先进的计算机程序。所以，地面上的无线电望远镜与绕轨道运行的卫星上的无线电望远镜之间成功的干扰连接是一项重大的技术成就。

下面哪个能正确地被以上的叙述推断出来？

(A) 卫星发射时要加以特别小心以使其轨道的计算容易一些。

(B) 卫星接收到的信号比地球上的望远镜接收到的信号强。

(C) 卫星－地面干扰仪系统所达到的细节分辨率不如单独的地面系统所达到的高。

(D) 利用卫星接收到的信号所要求的计算机程序需要长时间来发展。

(E) 相对于地面位置的绕轨道运行卫星的定位可以被足够了解以应付干扰的目标。

最近的估计预测，1982～1995年间被雇用人数中上升最多的却是在低报酬的服务性工作部门，但是，这一部门不会增加其在总雇用人数中的份额。而高报酬的服务职位会提高其份额。

如果以上的估计准确，可以得出下面哪个结论？

(A) 1982年在低报酬的服务性职位上工作的人多于在高报酬的服务性职位上工作的人。

(B) 1995年在高报酬的服务性职位上工作的人多于在低报酬的服务性职位上工作的人。

(C) 1995年服务性职位占到的在总雇用人数中的比重与1982年相同。

(D) 1982年在低报酬的服务性职位上工作的人，1995年会在高报酬的服务性职位上工作。

(E) 1982～1995年间，低报酬的服务性职位的增长率会高于雇用人数增长的总比率。

34. For a local government to outlaw all strikes by its workers is a costly mistake, because all its labor disputes must then be settled by binding arbitration, without any negotiated public-sector labor settlements guiding the arbitrators. Strikes should be outlawed only for categories of public-sector workers for whose services no acceptable substitute exists.

The statements above best support which of the following conclusions?

(A) Where public-service workers are permitted to strike, contract negotiations with those workers are typically settled without a strike.

(B) Where strikes by all categories of pubic-sector workers are outlawed, no acceptable substitutes for the services provided by any of those workers are available.

(C) Binding arbitration tends to be more advantageous for public-service workers where it is the only available means of settling labor disputes with such workers.

(D) Most categories of public-sector workers have no counterparts in the private sector.

(E) A strike by workers in a local government is unlikely to be settled without help from and arbitrator.

一个地方政府宣布本地工人所有的罢工为非法是一个代价高昂的错误，因为此后当地所有的劳动争端都必须依靠有束缚力的仲裁来解决，但却没有磋商出来的公共部门劳动协议来指导仲裁者。罢工只有在公共部门的工人中才要被禁止，因为他们的服务不存在可接受的替代品。

以上的论述最好地支持了下面哪个结论?

(A) 在允许公共部门工人罢工的地方，与工人们的合同争端通常无需罢工来解决。

(B) 在所有行业的公共部门工人的罢工被禁止的地方，不能获得那些工人提供的服务的替代品。

(C) 当有束缚力的仲裁是解决公共部门的工人劳动争端的唯一可选方法时，有束缚力的仲裁计划会对公共部门的工人更为有利。

(D) 大多数种类的公共部门的工人在私人部门中没有对应物。

(E) 地方政府中的工人罢工不可能没有仲裁者协助就被解决。

35. Corporate officers and directors commonly buy and sell, for their own portfolios, stock in their own corporations. Generally, when the ratio of such inside sales to inside purchases falls below 2 to 1 for a given stock, a rise in stock prices is imminent. In recent days, while the price of MEGA Corporation stock has been falling, the corporation's officers and directors have bought up to nine times as much of it as they have sold.

The facts above best support which of the following predictions?

(A) The imbalance between inside purchases and inside sales of MEGA stock will grow even further.

(B) Inside purchases of MEGA stock are about to cease abruptly.

(C) The price of MEGA stock will soon begin to go up.

(D) The price of MEGA stock will continue to drop, but less rapidly.

(E) The majority of MEGA stock will soon be owned by MEGA's own officers and directors.

公司经理和董事通常为他们的投资组合而购买或出售自己公司的股票。一般来讲，当某种股票的这些内部出售与内部购买的比例降到2比1以下时，股票价格即将上升。最近，当MEGA公司的股票不断下跌时，公司经理和董事们已经购买的股票数量是已经出售的股票数量的9倍。

以上的事实最好地支持了下面哪个预测?

(A) MEGA股票的内部购买和内部出售之间的不均衡会更进一步增长。

(B) MEGA股票的内部购买将要突然停止。

(C) MEGA股票的价格不久就会开始上升。

(D) MEGA股票的价格会继续下降，但不那么快了。

(E) 大部分MEGA股票不久就会被MEGA自己的经理和董事所拥有。

36. In 1987 sinusitis was the most common chronic medical condition in the United States, followed by arthritis and high blood pressure, in that order. The incidence rates for both arthritis and high blood pressure increase with age, but the incidence rate for sinusitis is the same for people of all ages.

The average age of the United States population will increase between 1987 and 2000.

Which of the following conclusions can be most properly drawn about chronic medical conditions in the United States from the information given above?

(A) Sinusitis will be more common than either arthritis or high blood pressure in 2000.

(B) Arthritis will be the most common chronic medical condition in 2000.

(C) The average age of people suffering from sinusitis will increase between 1987 and 2000.

(D) Fewer people will suffer from sinusitis in 2000 than suffered from it in 1987'

(E) A majority of the population will suffer from at least one of the medical conditions mentioned above by the year 2000.

1987年美国最常见的慢性医学病况是窦炎，随后按顺序是关节炎和高血压。关节炎和高血压二者的发病率都随年龄而增长，但是窦炎的发病率对所有年龄的人都是相同的。

1987～2000年间美国人口的平均年龄会增加。

下面哪个关于美国慢性医学病况的结论能最适当地从以上信息中得出来？

(A) 2000年时窦炎要比关节炎和高血压都普遍。

(B) 关节炎在2000年会成为最常见的慢性医学病况。

(C) 1987～2000年间患窦炎的人口的平均年龄会增加。

(D) 2000年患窦炎的人比1987年患窦炎的人多。

(E) 到2000年，大多数人会患至少一种以上提到的医学病况。

37. Parasitic wasps lay their eggs directly into the eggs of various host insects in exactly the right numbers for any suitable size of host egg. If they laid too many eggs in a host egg, the developing wasp larvae would compete with each other to the death for nutrients and space. If too few eggs were laid, portions of the host egg would decay, killing the wasp larvae.

Which of the following conclusions can properly be drawn from the information above?

(A) The size of the smallest host egg that a wasp could theoretically parasitize can be determined from the wasp's egg-laying behavior.

(B) Host insects lack any effective defenses against the form of predation practiced by parasitic wasps.

(C) Parasitic wasps learn from experience how many eggs to lay into the eggs of different host species.

(D) Failure to lay enough eggs would lead to the death of the developing wasp larvae more quickly than would laying too many eggs.

(E) Parasitic wasps use visual clues to calculate the size of a host egg.

寄生黄蜂直接把它们的卵产到各种宿主的卵中，数量正好与宿主卵适合的多少相符。如果它们在一个宿主卵中产卵太多，不断成长的黄蜂幼虫会因为相互竞争营养和空间而死掉。如果产卵太少，宿主卵的一部分会腐坏并杀死黄蜂幼虫。

下面哪个结论可以适当地从以上的信息得出来？

(A) 黄蜂理论上能寄生的最小的宿主卵的多少可以由黄蜂的产卵行为来确定。

(B) 宿主缺乏有效的保护来防止寄生黄蜂的掠夺形式。

(C) 寄生黄蜂从实践中知道可以产多少卵在不同宿主的卵中。

(D) 不能产足够的卵与产过多的卵会更快地导致成长的黄蜂幼虫的死亡。

(E) 寄生黄蜂利用视觉线索来计算宿主卵的大小。

38. There are fundamentally two possible changes in an economy that will each cause inflation unless other compensating changes also occur. There changes are either reductions in the supply of goods and services or increases in demand. In a prebanking economy the quantity of money available, and hence the level of demand, is equivalent to the quantity of gold available.

If the statements above are true, then it is also true that in a prebanking economy

(A) any inflation is the result of reductions in the supply of goods and services.

(B) if other factors in the economy are unchanged, increasing the quantity of gold available will lead to inflation.

(C) if there is a reduction in the quantity of gold available, then, other things being equal, inflation must result.

(D) the quantity of goods and services purchasable by a given amount of gold is constant.

(E) whatever changes in demand occur, there will be compensating changes in the supply of goods and services.

39. George Bernard Shaw wrote: "That any sane nation, having observed that you could provide for the supply of bread by giving bakers a pecuniary interest in baking for you, should go on to give a surgeon a pecuniary interest in cutting off your leg is enough to make one despair of political humanity."

Shaw's statement would best serve as an illustration in an argument criticizing which of the following?

(A) Dentists who perform unnecessary dental work in order to earn a profit.

(B) Doctors who increase their profits by specializing only in diseases that affect a large percentage of the population.

(C) Grocers who raise the price of food in order to increase their profit margins.

(D) Oil companies that decrease the price of their oil in order to increase their market share.

(E) Bakers and surgeons who earn a profit by supplying other peoples' basic needs.

40. After graduating form high school, people rarely multiply fractions or discuss ancient Rome, but they are confronted daily with decisions relating to home economics. Yet whereas

经济中两种可能的基本变动每个都会导致通货膨胀，除非还发生了其他的抵消性变动。这两种变动或者是产品和服务供给的减少，或者是需求的增加。在银行信用产生前的经济中，可利用的货币数量以及随后的需求水平等于可利用的黄金数量。

如果以上的叙述正确，那么这一点也同样正确，即在银行信用产生前的经济中

(A) 任何的通货膨胀都是产品和服务供给减少的结果。

(B) 如果经济中的其他因素不变，可利用的黄金数量的增加会导致通货膨胀。

(C) 其他情况不变时，如果可利用的黄金数量减少了，会发生通货膨胀。

(D) 一定数量的黄金可以购买的产品和服务数量是一定的。

(E) 不管需求上发生什么变动，产品和服务在供给上都会有抵消性的变动。

乔治·肖伯纳写道："注意到通过给面包师一定的金钱利益让他为一个人烤制面包从而这个人可以提供面包的供应时，任何一个理智的国家或许会继续论证说可以通过给外科医生一定的金钱利益让他割掉一个人的腿，这足以使得人们对政治的人性感到绝望了。"

肖伯纳的叙述最好作为批评下面哪个论证中使用的例证？

(A) 为赚钱而进行不必要的牙科诊治的牙医。

(B) 为增加盈利而仅专门医治影响很大比例人口的疾病的医生。

(C) 为增加利润而提高食品价格的杂货商。

(D) 为增加市场份额而降低其石油价格的石油公司。

(E) 通过满足其他人的基本需要而盈利的面包师和外科医生。

从高中毕业以后，人们很少计算乘除法或讨论古代罗马，但他们每天都要面临与家庭经济学有关的决策。然而，当数学

mathematics and history are required courses in the high school curriculum, home economics is only an elective, and few students choose to take it.

Which of the following positions would be best supported by the considerations above?

(A) If mathematics and history were not required courses, few students would choose to take them.

(B) Whereas home economics would be the most useful subject for people facing the decisions they must make in daily life, often mathematics and history can also help them face these decisions.

(C) If it is important to teach high school students subjects that relate to decisions that will confront them in their daily lives, then home economics should be made an important part of the high school curriculum.

(D) Mathematics, history, and other courses that are not directly relevant to a person's daily life should not be a required part of the high school curriculum.

(E) Unless high schools put more emphasis on nonacademic subjects like home economics, people graduation from high school will never feel comfortable about making the decisions that will confront them in their daily lives.

41. The most important aspect of moviemaking is conveying a scene's rhythm. Conveying rhythm depends less on the artistic quality of the individual photographic images than on how the shots go together and the order in which they highlight different aspects of the action-taking place in front of the camera.

If the statements above are true, which of the following must be true on the basis of them?

(A) The artistic quality of the individual photographic image is unimportant in movie photography.

(B) Photographers known for the superb artistic quality of their photographs are seldom effective as moviemakers.

(C) Having the ability to produce photographs of superb artistic quality does not in itself guarantee having the ability to be a good moviemaker.

(D) Movie photographers who are good at their jobs rarely give serious thought to the artistic quality of the photographs they take.

(E) To convey a scene's rhythm effectively, a moviemaker must highlight many different aspects of the action-taking place.

和历史是高中课程中的必修课时，家庭经济学仅仅是一门选修课，并且很少有学生选这门课。

下面哪个观点能最好地被以上的论述所支持？

(A) 如果数学和历史不是必修课，很少有学生会学它们。

(B) 虽然家庭经济学对于面临日常生活中必须做出决策的人们是最有用的学科，但通常数学和历史也能帮助人们面临这些决策。

(C) 如果教给高中学生与他们以后在日常生活中会面临的决策相关的学科是重要的，那么家庭经济学就应该成为高中课程表中重要的一部分。

(D) 数学、历史和其他不是直接与一个人的日常生活有关的学科不应该成为高中课程表中的必修部分。

(E) 除非高中把更多的重心放到像家庭经济学这样的非专业学科上，从高中毕业的人们永远不会轻松地做出日常生活中面临的决策。

电影制片中最重要的方面在于传送一幅场景的节奏。传送节奏较少依赖于单个摄影形象的艺术质量，而是更多地依赖于不同画面是如何归在一起以及这些画面突出摄像机前发生活动的不同方面的顺序。

如果以上的论述是正确的，以其为基础，下面哪个一定是正确的？

(A) 在电影摄影中，单个摄影形象的艺术质量是不重要的。

(B) 凭他们的照片艺术质量高超而成名的摄影师很少能成功地作为电影制片人。

(C) 有能力照出具有高超艺术质量的照片本身并不保证可以成为一名优秀的电影制片人。

(D) 工作优秀的电影制片人很少看重他们所照照片的艺术质量。

(E) 为了有效地传送一幅场景的节奏，电影制片人必须突出正在发生的活动的许多不同方面。

42. For a trade embargo against a particular country to succeed, a high degree of both international accord and ability to prevent goods from entering or leaving that country must be sustained. A total blockade of Patria's ports is necessary to an embargo, but such an action would be likely to cause international discord over the embargo.

The claims above, if true, most strongly support which of the following conclusions?

(A) The balance of opinion is likely to favor Patria in the event of a blockade.

(B) As long as international opinion is unanimously against Patria, a trade embargo is likely to succeed.

(C) A naval blockade of Patria's ports would ensure that no goods enter or leave Patria.

(D) Any trade embargo against Patria would be likely to fail at some time.

(E) For a blockade of Patria's ports to be successful, international opinion must be unanimous.

要想使某项针对一个特定国家的贸易禁运成功，必须维持高水平的国际协调和阻止货物进入或离开该国的能力。若要施行禁运，对Patria的港口实行完全的封锁是有必要的，但这样的行动可能导致国际上对禁运的不协调。

以上的观点，如果正确，最有力地支持了下面哪个结论？

(A) 在封锁事件中意见的不一致可能有利于Patria。

(B) 只要国际意见一致反对Patria，贸易禁运就可能成功。

(C) 对Patria港口实行海上封锁可以保证没有货物进入或离开Patria。

(D) 任何针对Patria的贸易禁运都可能在某个时候失败。

(E) 为使对Patria港口的封锁成功，国际上的意见必须一致。

43. Although aspirin has been proven to eliminate moderate fever associated with some illnesses, many doctors no longer routinely recommend its use for this purpose.

A moderate fever stimulates the activity of the body's disease-fighting white blood cells and also inhibits the growth of many strains of disease-causing bacteria.

If the statements above are true, which of the following conclusions is most strongly supported by them?

(A) Aspirin, an effective painkiller, alleviates the pain and discomfort of many illnesses.

(B) Aspirin can prolong a patient's illness by eliminating moderate fever helpful in fighting some diseases.

(C) Aspirin inhibits the growth of white blood cells, which are necessary for fighting some illnesses.

(D) The more white blood cells a patient's body produces, the less severe the patient's illness will be.

(E) The focus of modern medicine is on inhibiting the growth of disease-causing bacteria within the body.

虽然阿斯匹林已经被证明可以消除中度的与某些疾病相联的发烧，许多医生不再惯例性地推荐使用它来消除发烧。中度发热刺激了体内抵抗疾病的白细胞的活动，还抑制了许多种疾病得以产生的细菌的生长。

如果以上的论述是正确的，下面哪个结论被它们最强有力地支持？

(A) 阿斯匹林———一种有效的镇痛剂———缓解了许多疾病的疼痛和不适。

(B) 通过消除对抵抗某些疾病方面的中度发烧，阿斯匹林可能延长病人患病的时间。

(C) 阿斯匹林抑制了白细胞的生长，后者对抵抗某些疾病来讲是必要的。

(D) 病人体内产生的白细胞越多，病人的疾病越不严重。

(E) 现代医学的焦点是抑制体内疾病得以产生的细菌的生长。

44. Biometric access-control systems—those using fingerprints, voiceprints, etc., to regulate admittance to restricted areas—work by degrees of similarity, not by identity. After all, even the same finger will rarely leave exactly identical prints. Such systems can be adjusted to

生命仪进入控制系统———运用指纹、声模等来管理对限制区域的进入———根据相似程度而非身份吻合来工作。毕竟，即使同一个手指也很少会留下完全相同的指纹。这些系统能被调节到对合法的寻求进

minimize refusals of access to legitimate access-seekers. Such adjustments, however, increase the likelihood of admitting impostors.

Which of the following conclusions is most strongly supported by the information above?

(A) If a biometric access-control system were made to work by identity, it would not produce any correct admittance decisions.

(B) If a biometric access-control system reliably prevents impostors from being admitted, it will sometimes turn away legitimate access-seekers.

(C) Biometric access-control systems are appropriate only in situations in which admittance of impostors is less of a problem than is mistaken refusal of access.

(D) Nonbiometric access-control systems—based, for example, on numerical codes—are less likely than biometric ones to admit impostors.

(E) Anyone choosing an access-control system should base the choice solely on the ratio of false refusals to false admittances.

入者的拒绝最小化的程度。但是，这些调节增加了允许冒名顶替者进入的可能性。

下面哪个结论被以上的信息最有力地支持？

(A) 如果一个生命仪进入控制系统被设计成根据是否身份吻合来工作，它不会形成任何正确的准入决策。

(B) 如果一个生命仪的控制进入系统可靠地防止冒名顶替者进入，它有时会拒绝合法的寻求进入者。

(C) 仅仅在冒名顶替者被允许进入的情况不如错误地拒绝进入情况严重时，生命仪进入控制系统才是恰当的。

(D) 非生命仪进入控制系统——例如根据的是数字代码——比生命仪进入控制系统更少可能允许冒名顶替者进入。

(E) 每个选择进入控制系统的人都应该只把其选择依托于错误拒绝与错误准入的比率。

注：identity = exact likeness = exact sameness

45. Most discussions of the factors contributing to improvements in public health greatly underestimate the influence of the values held by individuals. This influence is indicated by the fact that the astonishing decline mortality from infectious disease during the past century was primarily due to an improvement in living conditions. To a substantial degree, these improvements depended on the emphasis by an increasing share of the population on cleanliness, prudence, and moderation.

The main point of the passage is made primarily by

(A) analyzing existing data on medical practices and health outcomes.

(B) presenting a set of related cause-and-effect assertions.

(C) applying several general principles to a specific case.

(D) presenting a general observation and supporting it with several specific examples.

(E) refuting in detail a commonly accepted argument.

大多数关于有助于提高公众健康的因素的讨论都过低地估计了个人所拥有的价值观的影响，这种影响被这样的事实所揭示：在过去的一个世纪中，传染病死亡率的急剧下降主要是因为生活条件的改善。在很大程度上，这种改善依赖于越来越多的人对干净，谨慎和节制的重视。

段落的主要论点的提出主要通过

(A) 分析现存的医疗业务和健康结果的数据。

(B) 提出了一套相关的因果见解。

(C) 把几个普遍的原则应用于一具体的情况。

(D) 提出一个总的意见，然后用几个具体的例子来证实它。

(E) 详细地驳斥了一个普遍接受的论断。

46. One method of dating the emergence of species is to compare the genetic material of related species. Scientists theorize that the more genetically similar two species are to each other, the more recently they diverged from a common

确定物种出现的日期的一种方法是比较有亲戚关系的物种的遗传物质。科学家们建立理论认为，两种物种在遗传上越相似，两物种从同一祖先分出的日期距今就

ancestor. After comparing genetic material from giant pandas, red pandas, raccoons, coatis, and all seven bear species, scientists concluded that bears and raccoons diverged 30 to 50 million years ago. They further concluded that red pandas separated from the ancestor of today's raccoons and coatis a few million years later, some 10 million years before giant pandas diverged from the other bears.

Which one of the following can be properly inferred from the passage?

(A) Giant pandas and red pandas are more closely related than scientists originally thought they were.

(B) Scientists now count the giant panda as the eighth species of bear.

(C) It is possible to determine, within a margin of just a few years, the timing of divergence of various species.

(D) Scientists have found that giant pandas are more similar genetically to bears than to raccoons.

(E) There is substantial consensus among scientists that giant pandas and red pandas are equally related to raccoons.

越接近。通过比较大熊猫、红熊猫、浣熊、长鼻浣熊和所有七种熊的遗传物质后，科学家们推论出熊和浣熊分开于3000万年到5000万年前之间。他们进一步推论出红熊猫是在此几百万年之后，在大熊猫从其他的熊中分出大约1000万年之前从今天的浣熊和长鼻浣熊的祖先中分离出来的。

下面哪一条能从短文中合理地推出？

(A) 大熊猫和红熊猫的亲戚关系比科学家们起初认为的近得多。

(B) 今天，科学家们把大熊猫看作是第八种熊。

(C) 在几年的误差范围内，确定不同物种分离的时间是可能的。

(D) 科学家们已经发现大熊猫与熊和浣熊相比，在遗传上与熊更为相似。

(E) 科学家们一致认为大熊猫和红熊猫与浣熊的亲戚关系是一样。

47. There is little point in looking to artists for insights into political issues. Most of them hold political views that are less insightful than those of any reasonably well-educated person who is not an artist. Indeed, when taken as a whole, the statements made by artists, including those considered to be great, indicate that artistic talent and political insight are rarely found together.

Which one of the following can be inferred from the passage?

(A) There are no artists who have insights into political issues.

(B) A thorough education in art makes a person reasonably well educated.

(C) Every reasonably well-educated person who is not an artist has more insight into political issues than any artist.

(D) Politicians rarely have any artistic talent.

(E) Some artists are no less politically insightful than some reasonable well-educated persons who are not artists.

指望艺术家对政治问题具有洞察力是毫无意义的。大多数艺术家所持有的政治见解比那些受过相当良好的教育但不是艺术家的人中的任何人都缺乏洞察力。实际上，从整体上看，艺术家们，包括那些大家认为很伟大的艺术家们所作的陈述表明艺术天赋和政治洞察力很少能在一个人身上同时体现。

下面哪一项可从上述短文中推出？

(A) 没有哪位艺术家对政治问题具有洞察力。

(B) 完善的艺术教育使一个人受到了相当良好的教育。

(C) 每一个受过相当良好的教育，但不是艺术家的人在政治问题上都比艺术家们更具洞察力。

(D) 政治家们很少具有艺术天赋。

(E) 某些艺术家在政治问题上的洞察力比某些受过相当良好的教育，但不是艺术家的人强。

48. Some cleaning fluids, synthetic carpets, wall paneling, and other products release toxins, such as formaldehyde and benzene, into the household air supply. This is not a problem

有些清洁剂，合成地毯，墙镶板和其他产品会释放（如甲醛和苯的）毒素到家里的空气供给中。在通风良好的房子里，

in well-ventilated houses, but it is a problem in houses that are so well insulated that they trap toxins as well as heat. Recent tests, however, demonstrate that houseplants remove some household toxins from the air and thereby eliminate their danger. In one test, 20 large plants eliminated formaldehyde from a small, well-insulated house.

Assume that a person who lives in a small, well-insulated house that contains toxin-releasing products places houseplants, such as those tested, in the house.

Which one of the following can be expected as a result?

(A) There will no longer be any need to ventilate the house.

(B) The concentration of toxins in the household air supply will remain the same.

(C) The house will be warm and have a safe air supply.

(D) If there is formaldehyde in the household air supply, its level will decrease.

(E) If formaldehyde and benzene are being released into the household air supply, the quantities released of each will decrease.

49. Efficiency and redundancy are contradictory characteristics of linguistic systems; however, they can be used together to achieve usefulness and reliability in communication. If a spoken language is completely efficient, then every possible permutation of its basic language sounds can be an understandable word. However, if the human auditory system is an imperfect receptor of sounds, then it is not true that every possible permutation of a spoken language's basic language sounds can be an understandable word.

If all of the statements above are true, which one of the following must also be true?

(A) Efficiency causes a spoken language to be useful and redundancy causes it to be reliable.

(B) Neither efficiency nor redundancy can be completely achieved in spoken language.

(C) If a spoken language were completely redundant, then it could not be useful.

(D) If the human auditory system were a perfect receptor of sounds, then every permutation of language sounds would be an understandable word.

这不是一个问题。但是，如果房间的密闭性好得让热量和毒素都不能散发出去时，就会产生问题。然而，最近的测试表明室内盆栽植物可吸收空气中的毒素，从而能消除它们的危害。在某一测试中，20株较大的植物消除了一个较小的，密闭性良好的房间内的空气中的甲醛。

假设一个人居住在一个较小的，密闭性良好的房间里，这个房间里放有会释放毒素的产品，同时也放有如文中在小房间内进行测试所用的室内盆栽植物。

下面哪一项可以作为上述假设的结果？

(A) 不再需要对那个房间进行通风处理。

(B) 房间内的空气供给中的毒素浓度将会保持不变。

(C) 那个房间将有一个暖和的、安全的空气供给。

(D) 如果房间的空气供给中含有甲醛，那么它的水平将会下降。

(E) 如果甲醛和苯都被释放到房间的空气供给中，那么每种毒素物质的释放量均会下降。

有效和冗长是语言体系的一个自相矛盾的特性，然而，当它们一块使用时，却能增加交流的有效性和可信赖性。如果某一种口语非常地有效，那么它的每一个基本音素的所有可能排列都能组成一个可被理解的单词。但是，如果人类的听觉系统不是一个完善的声音接受器，那么一种口语的基本音素的每一个可能的排列都能构成一个可被理解的单词的想法就是不正确的。

如果上面所有的陈述都是正确的，那么下面哪一项也一定是正确的？

(A) 有效使一种口语有用，冗长使一种口语可信。

(B) 在口语中，有效和冗长不可能被完全达到。

(C) 如果一种口语非常的冗长，那么它就不可能有用。

(D) 如果人类的听觉系统是一个完善的声音接受器，那么语言音素的每一个排列都可产生一个能被理解的单词。

(E) If the human auditory system is an imperfect receptor of sounds, then a spoken language cannot be completely efficient.

50. The efficiency of microwave ovens in destroying the harmful bacteria frequently found in common foods is diminished by the presence of salt in the food being cooked. When heated in a microwave oven, the interior of unsalted food reaches temperatures high enough to kill bacteria that cause food poisoning, but the interior of salted food does not. Scientists theorize that salt effectively blocks the microwaves from heating the interior.

Which one of the following conclusions is most supported by the information above?

(A) The kinds of bacteria that cause food poisoning are more likely to be found on the exterior of food than in the interior of food.

(B) The incidence of serious food poisoning would be significantly reduced if microwave ovens were not used by consumers to cook or reheat food.

(C) The addition of salt to food that has been cooked or reheated in a microwave oven can increase the danger of food poisoning.

(D) The danger of food poisoning can be lessened if salt is not used to prepare foods that are to be cooked in a microwave oven.

(E) Salt is the primary cause of food poisoning resulting from food that is heated in microwave ovens.

51. Zelda: Dr. Ladlow, a research psychologist, has convincingly demonstrated that his theory about the determinants of rat behavior generates consistently accurate predictions about how rats will perform in a maze. On the basis of this evidence, Dr. Ladlow has claimed that his theory is irrefutably correct.

Anson: Then Dr. Ladlow is not a responsible psychologist. Dr. Ladlow's evidence does not conclusively prove that his theory is correct. Responsible psychologists always accept the possibility that new evidence will show that their theories are incorrect.

Which one of the following can be properly inferred from Anson's argument?

(E) 如果人类的听觉系统不是一个完善的声音接受器，那么口语就不可能非常地有效。

当烹调的食物中含有盐时，微波炉能杀死常见食物中经常发现的有害细菌的功效就会消失。当在微波炉中加热时，不含食盐的食物内部达到了很高的、足以把引起食物中毒的细菌杀死的温度，但是含有食盐的食物内部就达不到这样高的温度。于是科学家们就得出这样的结论，食盐可以有效地阻止微波加热食物的内部。

下面哪一个结论最能被上面的论述支持？

(A) 在食物的外部比在食物的内部更有可能发现那些引起食物中毒的细菌。

(B) 如果消费者们不使用微波炉来烹调或重新加热食物，那么严重食物中毒的发生率就会大大地降低。

(C) 给在微波炉内烹调过的或重新加热过的食物中加入食盐会加大食物中毒的危险性。

(D) 如果不向将要在微波炉内加热的食物中加盐，食物中毒的危险性就会降低。

(E) 食盐是导致微波炉内加热的食物中毒的主要原因。

Zelda：Ladlow博士，一个心理学研究专家，非常有说服力地证明了他的关于决定老鼠行为的因素的理论，该理论可对老鼠在迷宫中如何表现进行一致准确地预测。基于这些证据，Ladlow博士声称他的理论无懈可击。

Anson：那么Ladlow博士不是一个负责任的心理学家。Ladlow博士的证据并不能最终证明他的理论是正确的。负责任的心理学家通常都承认新证据的出现有可能会揭示他们的理论是不正确的。

下面哪一项能从Ansons的论述中合理地推出？

(A) Dr. Ladlow's evidence that his theory generates consistently accurate predictions about how rats will perform in a maze is inaccurate.

(B) Psychologists who can derive consistently accurate predictions about how rats will perform in a maze from their theories cannot responsibly conclude that those theories cannot be disproved.

(C) No matter how responsible psychologists are, they can never develop correct theoretical explanations.

(D) Responsible psychologists do not make predictions about how rats will perform in a maze.

(E) Psychologists who accept the possibility that new evidence will show that their theories are incorrect are responsible psychologists.

52. Nursing schools cannot attract a greater number of able applicants than they currently do unless the problems of low wages and high-stress working conditions in the nursing profession are solved. If the pool of able applicants to nursing school does not increase beyond the current level, either the profession will have to lower its entrance standards, or there will soon be an acute shortage of nurses. It is not certain, however, that lowering entrance standards will avert a shortage. It is clear that with either a shortage of nurses or lowered entrance standards for the profession, the current high quality of health care cannot be maintained.

Which one of the following can be properly inferred from the passage?

(A) If the nursing profession solves the problems of low wages and high-stress working conditions, it will attract able applicants in greater numbers than it currently does.

(B) The nursing profession will have to lower its entrance standards if the pool of able applicants to nursing school does not increase beyond the current level.

(C) If the nursing profession solves the problems of low wages and high-stress working conditions, high quality health care will be maintained.

(D) If the nursing profession fails to solve the problems of low wages and high-stress working conditions, there will soon be an acute shortage of nurses.

(E) The current high quality of health care will not be maintained if the problems of low wages and high-stress working conditions in the nursing profession are not solved.

(A) Ladlow博士的关于他的理论可对老鼠在迷宫中会如何表现进行一致准确地预测的证据是不准确的。

(B) 那些根据他们的理论，可对老鼠在迷宫会如何表现进行一致准确的预测的心理学家不能负责任地推出他们的理论是正确无疑的。

(C) 不管心理学家是怎样地认真负责，他们从来都不能提出正确的理论上的解释。

(D) 负责任的心理学家不做老鼠在迷宫中会如何表现的预测。

(E) 那些承认新证据有可能会证明他们的理论是不正确的心理学家是负责任的心理学家。

除非护士职业内的低工资和高度紧张的工作条件问题得到解决，否则护士学校就不能吸引到比目前数量更多的有才干的申请者。如果护士学校的有才干的申请者的数量不能超过目前的水平，那么，要么这种职业必须降低它的进入标准，要么很快就会出现护士亟缺的局面。然而，降低进入标准并不一定能解决护士的不足。很明显，不管是护士不足还是降低这个职业的进入标准，目前高质量的健康护理都不能维持下去。

下面哪一项可以从上述短文中合理地推出？

(A) 如果护士职业解决了低工资和高度紧张的工作条件问题，那么它吸引到的有才干的申请者的数量就比目前多。

(B) 如果有才干的护士学校的申请者的数量不能超过目前的水平，那么护士职业就不得不降低它的进入标准。

(C) 如果护士职业解决了低工资和高度紧张的工作条件问题，那么高质量的健康护理就可以维持下去。

(D) 如果护士职业不解决低工资和高度紧张的工作条件问题，那么很快就会出现护士紧缺的局面。

(E) 如果护士职业不解决低工资和高度紧张的工作条件问题，那么目前的高质量的健康护理就不能维持下去。

53. There are about 75 brands of microwave popcorn on the market; altogether, they account for a little over half of the money from sales of microwave food products. It takes three minutes to pop corn in the microwave, compared to seven minutes to pop corn conventionally. Yet by weight, microwave popcorn typically costs over five times as much as conventional popcorn. Judging by the popularity of microwave popcorn, many people are willing to pay a high price for just a little additional convenience.

If the statements in the passage are true, which one of the following must also be true?

(A) No single brand of microwave popcorn accounts for a large share of microwave food product sales.

(B) There are more brands of microwave popcorn on the market than there are of any other microwave food product.

(C) By volume, more microwave popcorn is sold than is conventional popcorn.

(D) More money is spent on microwave food products that take three minutes or less to cook than on microwave food products that take longer to cook.

(E) Of the total number of microwave food products on the market, most are microwave popcorn products.

54. Public reports by national commissions, governors' conferences, and leadership groups have stressed the great need for better understanding of international affairs by the citizenry. If the country is to remain a leading nation in an era of international competitiveness, the need is undeniable. If there is such a need for the citizenry to have a better understanding of international affairs, then all of our new teachers must be prepared to teach their subject matter with an international orientation.

If all of the statements in the passage are true, which one of the following must also be true?

(A) If the country is to remain a leading nation in an era of international competitiveness, then new teachers must be prepared to teach their subject matter with an international orientation.

(B) If new teachers are prepared to teach their subject matter with an international orientation, then the country will remain a leading nation in an era of international competitiveness.

市场上有75个品牌的微波爆米花，它们总共占微波食品销售额的一半还多一点。与传统爆米花要花七分钟相比，在微波炉内爆米花只需三分钟。然而，微波爆米花的价钱一般是相同重量的传统爆米花价钱的5倍还多。鉴于微波爆米花受欢迎的程度，很多人愿意为了一点点附加的方便而付高价。

如果上述短文中的陈述是正确的，那么下面哪一条也一定是正确的？

(A) 没有一个单一的微波爆米花品牌的销售额在微波食品销售额中占较大的份额。

(B) 在市场上，微波爆米花的品牌数目比其他任何的微波食品的品牌数目多。

(C) 按体积计算，微波爆米花的销售量比传统爆米花的销售量大。

(D) 花费在用三分钟或更少的时间来烹调的微波食品上的钱要比花费在用较长的时间来烹调的微波食品上面的钱多。

(E) 市场上的微波食品的总数量中，绝大多数是微波爆米花食品。

国家委员会、州长会议和领导机构所做的公众报告都强调了公民更好地理解国际事务的极大必要性。如果一个国家要在国际竞争时代保持主导地位，这种必要性就是无可辩驳的。如果需要公民对国际事务更好地理解，那么我们所有的新教师都必须按国际方向来准备和教授他们的课程。

如果段落中所有的陈述都是正确的，下面哪一条也一定是正确的？

(A) 如果一个国家要在国际竞争时代里保持主导地位，那么新教师必须按国际方向来准备和教授他们的课程。

(B) 如果新老师按国际方向来准备和教授他们的课程，那么这个国家在国际竞争时代就能保持主导地位。

(C) If there is better understanding of international affairs by the citizenry, then the country will remain a leading nation in an era of international competitiveness.

(D) If the country is to remain a leading nation in an era of international competitiveness, then there is no need for the citizenry to have a better understanding of international affairs.

(E) Public reports from various groups and commissions have stressed the need for a more international orientation in the education of teachers.

(C) 如果公民能更好地理解国际事务，那么这个国家在国际竞争时代就能保持主导地位。

(D) 如果一个国家要在国际竞争的时代里保持主导地位，那么就不需要公民们对国际事务有较好的理解。

(E) 不同机构和委员会所做的公众报告都强调在培训教师的过程中加强国际方向性的必要。

55. Anthropologists assert that cultures advance only when independence replaces dependence—that is, only when imposition by outsiders is replaced by initiative from within. In other words, the natives of a culture are the only ones who can move that culture forward. Non-natives may provide valuable advice, but any imposition of their views threatens independence and thus progress. If one looks at individual schools as separate cultures, therefore, the key to educational progress is obvious that .

Which one of the following best completes the passage?

(A) individual schools must be independent of outside imposition

(B) some schools require more independence than others, depending on the initiative of their staffs and students

(C) school system officials must tailor their initiatives for change to each individual school in the system

(D) outsiders must be prevented from participation in schools' efforts to advance

(E) the more independent a school is, the more educational progress it will make

人类学家宣称仅当独立性代替依赖性——也即仅当局外人的强行介入被局内人的首创精神取代时，文化才能进步。换句话说，只有本族文化的人才能推动本族文化的进步。非本族文化的人可以提供一些有价值的建议，但是他们的见解的任何强行介入都会对这个文化的独立性和进步造成威胁。如果一个人把单个的学校看作是独立的文化，那么教育进步的关键很明显就是。

下面哪一项能最好地完成上述短文？

(A) 单个学校必须不依赖于外部的强行介入。

(B) 根据学校职工和学生的首创性，有些学校需要比其他学校有更大的独立性。

(C) 教育系统的官员必须改变他们的首创精神以适应本系统的单个学校的需要。

(D) 必须防止局外人参加学校为进步而进行的尝试。

(E) 一个学校的独立性越强，它在教育上取得的进步就越大。

56. The mind and the immune system have been shown to be intimately linked, and scientists are consistently finding that doing good deeds benefits one's immune system. The bone marrow and spleen, which produce the white blood cells needed to fight infection, are both connected by neural pathways to the brain. Recent research has shown that the activity of these white blood cells is stimulated by beneficial chemicals produced by the brain as a result of magnanimous behavior.

精神与免疫系统已被证明是密切相联的，科学家们一致发现做好事有益于一个人的免疫系统。能产生抵抗感染所需的白血球的骨髓和脾脏与大脑之间都被神经束连接起来。最近的研究表明这些血白细胞的活性可被有益的化学物质所激励，这些有益化学物质是由于高尚行为而被大脑生产的。

The statements above, if true, support the view that

(A) good deeds must be based on unselfish motives.
(B) lack of magnanimity is the cause of most serious illnesses.
(C) magnanimous behavior can be regulated by the presence or absence of certain chemicals in the brain.
(D) magnanimity is beneficial to one's own interests.
(E) the number of white blood cells will increase radically if behavior is consistently magnanimous.

57. The United States Food and Drug Administration (FDA) regulates the introduction of new therapeutic agents into the marketplace. Consequently, it plays a critical role in improving health care in the United States. While it is those in the academic and government research communities who engage in the long process of initial discovery and clinical testing of new therapeutic agents, it is the FDA's role and responsibility to facilitate the transfer of new discoveries from the laboratory to the marketplace. Only after the transfer can important new therapies help patients.

Which one of the following statements can be inferred from the passage?

(A) The FDA is responsible for ensuring that any therapeutic agent that is marketed is then regulated.
(B) Before new therapeutic agents reach the marketplace they do not help patients.
(C) The research community is responsible for the excessively long testing period for new drugs, not the FDA.
(D) The FDA should work more closely with researchers to ensure that the quality of therapeutic agents is maintained.
(E) If a new medical discovery has been transferred from the laboratory to the marketplace, it will help patients.

58. High-technology medicine is driving up the nation's health care costs. Recent advances in cataract surgery illustrate why this is occurring. Cataracts are a major cause of blindness, especially in elderly people. Ten years ago, cataract surgery was painful and not always effective. Thanks to the new technology used in cataract surgery, the operation now restores vision dramatically and is less expensive. These

上面的陈述，如果正确，支持下面哪个观点？

(A) 做好事必须出自无私的动机。
(B) 缺乏高尚情操是许多严重疾病的起因。
(C) 高尚行为可以被大脑中出现或缺乏某种化学物质所控制。
(D) 高尚情操有益于个人利益。
(E) 如果一个人的行为一直很高尚，那么他的白血球的数量就会急剧地增加。

美国食品和药物管理局管理在市场中引入的新治疗药剂，因此它在提高美国人的健康保健方面起了非常关键的作用。那些在学院里和政府研究团体内的人的职责是从事长期的研究，以图首先发现新的治疗药剂，并对它们进行临床验证，而使实验室里的新发现比较容易地转移到市场上是FDA（食品和药物管理局）的作用和职责。新的重要的治疗方法只有在转移之后才能有助于病人。

下面哪一个陈述可从上述段落中推出？

(A) FDA有责任确保任何销售到市场上的治疗药剂在当时都处于受控状态。
(B) 在新的治疗药剂到达市场之前，它们不能帮助病人。
(C) 研究团体有职责对新药进行特别长期的测试，而FDA却没有这样的责任。
(D) FDA应该更紧密地与研究者合作以确保治疗药剂的质量不会下降。
(E) 如果一种新的医药发现已从实验室转移到了市场上，那么它将有助于病人。

高技术药品使国家的保健费用升高。最近在白内障手术上取得的进步说明了为什么会出现这种现象，特别是在老年人中，白内障是导致失明的主要原因。10年以前，白内障手术不但痛苦，而且不总是见效。现在由于在白内障手术中使用了新术，所以手术可以使视力得到极大的

two factors have caused the number of cataract operations performed to increase greatly, which has, in turn, driven up the total amount spent on cataract surgery.

Which one of the following can be inferred from the passage?

(A) Ten years ago, few people had successful cataract surgery.

(B) In the long run, the advantages of advanced medical technology are likely to be outweighed by the disadvantages.

(C) The total amount spent on cataract surgery has increased because the increased number of people electing to have the surgery more than offsets the decrease in cost per operation.

(D) Huge increases in the nation's health care costs are due primarily to increased demand for surgery for older people.

(E) Ten years ago, cataract surgery was affordable for more people than it was last year.

59. Book Review: When I read a novel set in a city I know well, I must see that the writer knows the city at least as well as I do if I am to take that writer seriously. If the writer is faking, I know immediately and do not trust that writer. When a novelist demonstrates the required knowledge, I trust the storyteller, so I trust the tale. This trust increases my enjoyment of a good novel. Peter Lee's second novel is set in San Francisco. In this novel, as in his first, Lee passes my test with flying colors.

Which one of the following can be properly inferred from the passage?

(A) The book reviewer enjoys virtually any novel written by a novelist whom she trusts.

(B) If the book reviewer trusts the novelist as a storyteller, the novel in question must be set in a city the book reviewer knows well.

 Lee's first novel was set in San Francisco.

 ook reviewer does not trust any novel set in a city
 es not know well.

 viewer does not believe that she knows San
 than Peter Lee does.

并且更便宜。这两个因素使医生做白内障手术的次数急剧增加，结果在白内障手术上所花的总的费用升高了。

下面哪一点可以从上述段落中推出？

(A) 10年以前，很少人的白内障手术是成功的。

(B) 从长期的观点看，医学技术进步的优点将有可能超过它的缺点。

(C) 在白内障手术上的总的花费增加了，这是因为参加手术治疗的人的数量的增加过多地抵消了每起手术费用的降低。

(D) 国家的保健费的巨大增加主要是由于老年人对手术需求量的增加。

(E) 10年以前，能付得起白内障手术费的人数比去年的多。

图书评论：当我阅读一本以我熟知的某一城市为背景的小说时，如果我要认真对待这个作家，我一定要使作家对这个城市的了解至少得和我一样的清楚。如果作家在捏造事实，那么我立即就能意识到，并且我不再信任那个作家。当一个小说家表现出了必要的知识后，我就相信这个小说家，因此我也相信这个故事。这种信任增加了我读一本好小说的兴趣。Peter Lee 的第二部小说以旧金山为背景。他的这部小说和他的第一部小说一样顺利地通过了我的检验。

下面哪一条可以从段落中合理地推出？

(A) 这个图书评论者实际上喜欢任何一本由她信任的作家所写的小说。

(B) 如果这个图书评论者相信某个小说家是个讲故事的人，那么正在被谈论的小说一定以这个图书评论者所熟知的某一城市为背景。

(C) Peter Lee的第一本小说以旧金山为背景。

(D) 这个图书评论者不信任任何一本以她不熟知的某一城市为背景的小说。

(E) 这个图书评论者认为她对旧金山的了解不比Peter Lee对旧金山的了解更清楚。

60. Comets do not give off their own light but reflect light from other sources, such as the Sun. Scientists estimate the mass of comets by their brightness: the greater a comet's mass, the more light that comet will reflect. A satellite probe, however, has revealed that the material of which Halley's comet is composed reflects 60 times less light per unit of mass than had been previously thought.

The statements above, if true, give the most support to which one of the following?

(A) Some comets are composed of material that reflects 60 times more light per unit of mass than the material of which Halley's comet is composed.

(B) Previous estimates of the mass of Halley's comet which were based on its brightness were too low.

(C) The total amount of light reflected from Halley's comet is less than scientists had previously thought.

(D) The reflective properties of the material of which comets are composed vary considerably from comet to comet.

(E) Scientists need more information before they can make a good estimate of the mass of Halley's comet.

61. Until recently, anthropologists generally agreed that higher primates originated about 30 million years ago in the Al Fayyum region of Egypt. However, a 40-million-year-old fossilized fragment of a lower jawbone discovered in Burma (now called Myanmar) in 1978 was used to support the theory that the earliest higher primates originated in Burma. However, the claim is premature for _____.

Which one of the following, if true, is the most logical completion of the paragraph above?

(A) there are no more primate species in Burma than there are in Egypt

(B) several anthropologists using different dating methods, independently confirmed the estimated age of the jawbone fragment

(C) higher primates cannot be identified solely by their lower jawbones

(D) several prominent anthropologists do not believe that higher primates could have originated in either Egypt or Burma

(E) other archaeological expeditions in Burma have unearthed higher-primate fossilized bone fragments that are clearly older than 40 million years

彗星自身并不发光，但它们可以反射来自其他光源，如太阳的光。科学家们通过彗星的亮度来估计它们的质量：一个彗星的质量越大，这个彗星反射的光就越多。然而一卫星探测器揭示构成哈雷彗星的物质每单位质量反射的光的强度比以前认为的低60倍。

上面的陈述如果正确，最能支持下面哪一项？

(A) 有些彗星的构成物质，每单位质量反射的光的强度比构成哈雷彗星的物质高出60倍。

(B) 以前基于亮度对哈雷彗星的质量的估计太低。

(C) 哈雷彗星反射的光的总量比起以前科学家们认为的要少。

(D) 构成彗星的物质的光反射性能在不同的彗星之间变化很大。

(E) 在对哈雷彗星的质量做一个精确的估计以前，科学家们需要更多的信息。

直到最近，人类学家才普遍认为高级灵长类动物起源于3000万年前的埃及的Al Fayyum地区。然而，1978年在缅甸（现在叫做Myanmar）发现的4000万年前的下颚骨化石碎片被用来证明最早的灵长类动物起源于缅甸的理论。无论如何，这个声明还为时过早，因为_____。

下面哪一项，如果正确，是上述段落最合乎逻辑的结尾。

(A) 缅甸的灵长类生物种类并不比埃及的多。

(B) 有几个人类学家使用不同的日期确定法各自独立地证实了颚骨碎片的估计年龄。

(C) 不能仅仅通过它的下颚骨来鉴定高级灵长类动物。

(D) 有几个著名的人类学家不相信高级灵长类动物会起源于埃及或缅甸。

(E) 其他考古学考察队在缅甸发掘的高级灵长类动物的骨头化石碎片很明显早于4000万年前。

62. Advertisements: In today's world, you make a statement about the person you are by the car you own. The message of the SKX Mach-5 is unambiguous: Its owner is Dynamic, Aggressive, and Successful. Shouldn't you own an SKX Mach-5?

If the claims made in the advertisement are true, which one of the following must also be true on the basis of them?

(A) Anyone who is dynamic and aggressive is also successful.

(B) Anyone who is not both dynamic and successful would misrepresent himself or herself by being the owner of an SKX Mach-5.

(C) People who buy the SKX Mach-5 are usually more aggressive than people who buy other cars.

(D) No car other than the SKX Mach-5 announces that its owner is successful.

(E) Almost no one would fail to recognize the kind of person who would choose to own an SKX Mach-5.

广告：在当今的世界上，你所拥有的汽车体现了你是怎么样的一个人。SKX Match-5的信息很明确：它的拥有者是一个充满活力，具有攻击性和富有成就的人。你难道不应该拥有一辆SKX Mach-5?

如果广告中所做的声明是正确的，那么根据那些声明下面哪一项也一定是正确的?

(A) 任何一个充满活力，具有攻击性的人也一定富有成就。

(B) 任何一个既无活力又无成就的人会因为拥有一辆SKX Mach-5汽车而错误地体现他或她自己。

(C) 那些购买SKX Mach-5的人通常比那些购买其他汽车的人更具攻击性。

(D) 除了SKX Mach-5之外，没有汽车能表明它的主人是成功的。

(E) 几乎没有人不能认出那些选择拥有一辆SKX Mach-5的人的类型。

63. The fire that destroyed the Municipal Building started before dawn this morning, and the last fire fighters did not leave until late this afternoon. No one could have been anywhere in the vicinity of a fire like that one and fail to notice it. Thomas must have seen it, whatever he now says to the contrary. He admits that, as usual, he went from his apartment to the library this morning, and there is no way for him to get from his apartment to the library without going past the Municipal Building.

The main conclusion of the argument is that

(A) Thomas was in the vicinity of the fire this morning.

(B) Thomas claimed not to have seem the fire.

(C) Thomas saw the fire this morning.

(D) Thomas went directly from his apartment to the library this morning.

(E) Thomas went by the Municipal Building this morning.

摧毁了市政大楼的那场火灾爆发于今晨黎明前，最后一个消防员直到今天下午晚些时候才离开。没有人会在那样一场大火的附近而又没注意到火灾的发生。Thomas一定看到了那场大火，不管他现在怎样地否认。他承认，他今天早上像通常一样从他的公寓去了图书馆。若不经过市政大楼，从他的公寓到图书馆之间就无路可走。

上述论述的主要结论是。

(A) Thomas今天早晨在那场火灾的附近。

(B) Thomas声称没有看到那场火灾。

(C) Thomas今天早晨看到了那场火灾。

(D) Thomas今天早晨从他的公寓直接到了图书馆。

(E) Thomas今天早晨从市政大楼前经过。

64. People cannot be morally responsible for things over which they have no control. Therefore, they should not be held morally responsible for any inevitable consequences of such things, either. Determining whether adults have any control over the treatment they are receiving can be difficult. Hence in some cases it can be difficult to know whether

从道义上讲，人们不能对他们无法控制的事情负责。因此他们也不应该在道义上对这类事情的不可避免的后果负责。要确定成年人能否控制它们接受的治疗是困难的，因此在某些情况下要想知道成年人是否对他们被治疗的方式承担某些道义上

adults bear any moral responsibility for the way they are treated. Everyone, however sometimes acts in ways that are an inevitable consequence of treatment received as an infant, and infants clearly cannot control, and so are not morally responsible for, the treatment they receive.

Anyone making the claims above would be logically committed to which one of the following further claims?

(A) An infant should never be held morally responsible for an action that infant has performed.

(B) There are certain commonly performed actions for which no one performing those actions should ever be held morally responsible.

(C) Adults who claim that they have no control over the treatment they are receiving should often be held at least partially responsible for being so treated.

(D) If a given action is within a certain person's control that person should be held morally responsible for the consequences of that action.

(E) No adult should be held morally responsible for every action he or she performs.

65. The body of anyone infected by virus X will, after a week, produce antibodies to fight the virus; the antibodies will increase in number for the next year or so. There is now a test that reliably indicates how many antibodies are present in a person's body. If positive, this test can be used during the first year of infection to estimate to within a month how long that person has had the virus.

Which one of the following conclusions is best supported by the statements above?

(A) Antibodies increase in number only until they have defeated the virus.

(B) Without the test for antibodies, there is no way of establishing whether a person has virus X.

(C) Antibodies are produced only for viral infections that cannot be fought by any other body defenses.

(D) If a person remains infected by virus X indefinitely, there is no limit to the number of antibodies that can be present in the person's body.

(E) Anyone infected by virus X will for a time fail to exhibit infection if tested by the antibody test.

的责任也是困难的。然而，每个人有时的行为方式就如同婴儿接受治疗的一种不可避免的方式一样。婴儿很明显是不能控制这些行为的，所以他们从道义上不对他们接受的治疗负责。

任何一个做出以上声明的人在逻辑上会进一步做出下面哪项声明？

(A) 婴儿在道义上从来不应该对他们的行为负责。

(B) 存在一些常见的行为，不管谁表现了这些行为，都不应负道义上的责任。

(C) 那些声称他们不能控制他们接受的治疗的成年人通常应该对他们如此被治疗至少负部分的责任。

(D) 如果某个行为在某个人的控制之中，那么这个人就应当对这个行为的后果负道义的责任。

(E) 没有一个成年人应该对他的或她的每一个行为都负道义上的责任。

任何一个人的身体感染了X病毒，一周以后就会产生抵抗这种病毒的抗体。这些抗体的数量在接下来的大约一年左右的时间内都会增加。现在，有一测试可靠地指出了一个人的身体内存在有多少个抗体。如果确实的话，这个测试可在一个人感染上某种病毒的第一年内被用来估计那个人已经感染上这种病毒多长时间了，估计误差在一个月之内。

下面哪一个结论能被上面的论述最有力地支持？

(A) 抗体的数量一直增加到它们击败病毒为止。

(B) 离开了对抗体的测试，就没有办法确定一个人是否感染上了X病毒。

(C) 抗体仅为那些不能被其他任何身体防御系统所抵抗的病毒感染产生。

(D) 如果一个人无限期地被X病毒感染，那么这个人的身体内可以出现的抗体的数量就是无限的。

(E) 任何一个感染了X病毒的人，如果用抗体测试法对他进行测试，将在一段时间内发现不了他有被感染的迹象。

66. When the rate of inflation exceeds the rate of return on the most profitable investment available, the difference between those two rates will be the percentage by which, at a minimum, the value of any investment will decline. If in such a circumstance the value of a particular investment declines by more than that percentage, it must be true that _____.

Which one of the following logically completes the argument?

(A) the rate of inflation has risen

(B) the investment in question is becoming less profitable

(C) the investment in question is less profitable than the most profitable investment available

(D) the rate of return on the most profitable investment available has declined

(E) there has been a chance in which particular investment happens to be the most profitable available

当通货膨胀的比率超过现有的盈利最大的投资收益率时，这两个比率的差值就是任何一个投资的价值下降的最小百分比。如果在这种情况下，某一个特定投资价值的下降超过了那个百分比，那么_____一定是正确的。

下面哪一项能合乎逻辑地完成上面的论述？

(A) 通货膨胀的比率已经上升。

(B) 正被谈论的那个投资的利润率在下降。

(C) 正被谈论的那个投资的利润率没有现有的盈利最大的投资利润率高。

(D) 现有的最有利可图的投资的利润率在下降。

(E) 存在这么一个可能性，那就是特定的投资恰巧是最有利润的投资。

67. All actors are exuberant people and all exuberant people are extroverts, but nevertheless it is true that some shy people are actors.

If the statements above are true, each of the following must also be true EXCEPT:

(A) Some shy people are extroverts.

(B) Some shy extroverts are not actors.

(C) Some exuberant people who are actors are shy.

(D) All people who are not extroverts are not actors.

(E) Some extroverts are shy.

所有的男演员都是精力充沛的人，所有精力充沛的人都是性格外向的人，但是仍然有一些害羞的人是男演员。

如果上面的陈述是正确的，下面除了哪一项之外也都是正确的。

(A) 有些害羞的人是性格外向的人。

(B) 有些害羞的性格外向者不是男演员。

(C) 有些精力充沛的男演员是害羞的人。

(D) 并非所有性格不外向的人都是男演员。

(E) 有些性格外向的人是害羞的人。

68. Unless negotiations begin soon, the cease-fire will be violated by one of the two sides to the dispute. Negotiations will be held only if other countries have pressured the two sides to negotiate; an agreement will emerge only if other countries continue such pressure throughout the negotiations. But no negotiations will be held until international troops enforcing the cease-fire have demonstrated their ability to counter any aggression from either side, thus suppressing a major incentive for the two sides to resume fighting.

If the statements above are true, and if negotiations between the two sides do begin soon, at the time those negotiations begin each of the following must also be true EXCEPT:

除非谈判马上开始，否则有争议的双方中将有一方会违犯停火协议，当且仅当别的国家迫使双方进行谈判时，才会举行谈判。当且仅当别的国家在谈判进行的整个过程中给双方都施加压力时，它们才能达成一个协议。但是直到强行执行停火的国际部队表明他们具有反击来自任一方进攻的能力，从而能压制住双方重新交战的一个主要诱因时，双方才会举行谈判。

如果上面的陈述是正确的，并且双方之间的谈判确实不久就要开始，在这些谈判开始时，下面除了哪一项之外也都一定

(A) The cease-fire has not been violated by either of the two sides.

(B) International troops enforcing the cease-fire have demonstrated that they can counter aggression from either of the two sides.

(C) A major incentive for the two sides to resume hostilities has been suppressed.

(D) Other countries have exerted pressure on the two sides to the dispute.

(E) The negotiations' reaching an agreement depends in part on the actions of other countries.

69. The town of Greenfield recently instituted a substantial supplementary tax on all households, whereby each household is taxed in proportion to the volume of the trash that it puts out for trash collectors to pick up, as measured by the number of standard-sized garbage bags put out. In order to reduce the volume of the trash on which their tax bill is based, Greenfield households can deliver their recyclable trash to a conveniently located local commercial recycling center, where such trash is accepted free of charge.

The supplementary tax provides some financial incentive to Greenfield households to do each of the following EXCEPT

(A) sort out recyclable trash thoroughly from their other trash.

(B) dump nonrecyclable trash illegally at parks and roadsides.

(C) compress and nest items of nonrecyclable trash before putting them out for pickup.

(D) deliver recyclable materials to the recycling center instead of passing them on to neighbors who want to reuse them.

(E) buy products without packaging or with recyclable rather than nonrecyclable packaging.

70. Politician: Unless our nation redistributes wealth, we will be unable to alleviate economic injustice and our current system will lead inevitably to intolerable economic inequities. If the inequities become intolerable, those who suffer from the injustice will resort to violence to coerce social reform. It is our nation's responsibility to do whatever is necessary to alleviate conditions that would otherwise give rise to violent

是正确的？

(A) 双方中的任何一方都没有违返停火。

(B) 强行执行停火的国际部队表明他们可以反击来自双方中任一方的侵略。

(C) 使双方恢复战争行动的主要诱因已被压制。

(D) 其他国家对有争议的双方施加了压力。

(E) 会谈达成的协议部分依赖于其他国家的行动。

Greenfield镇最近对所有的家庭征收了一项高额的附加税，依此税法，每个家庭应交的税与他们扔弃的让清洁工收集的垃圾的体积成比例，垃圾的体积根据他们扔弃的标准尺寸垃圾袋的数量来计算。为了减少他们的税单所依据的垃圾的体积，Greenfield的家庭可以把他们的可回收垃圾就近送到位于本地的商业回收中心，在这里垃圾是被免费接收的。

附加税给Greenfield的家庭提供了财政上的刺激，这使得他们做下面除了哪一项之外的每一项。

(A) 从他们的其他垃圾中详尽地挑选出可回收的垃圾。

(B) 把不可回收的垃圾非法地倾倒在停车场或道路旁。

(C) 在他们把拉圾扔弃供收集前，对它们进行压缩和嵌套处理。

(D) 把可回收的材料送往回收中心，而不是把它们送给想重新使用它们的邻居。

(E) 购买那些没有包装的或包装可以回收的产品，而不购买那些包装不可回收的产品。

政治家：除非我们国家重新分配财富，否则我们将不能减轻经济上的不公平，而我们现有的体制将不可避免地导致无法容忍的经济不公。如果这种不公平变得无法容忍，那么那些遭受不公平待遇的人就会诉诸暴力迫使社会改革。我们国家的职责是做任何必要的事情来缓和这种形

attempts at social reform.

The statements above logically commit the politician to which one of the following conclusions?

(A) The need for political reform never justifies a resort to violent remedies.

(B) It is our nation's responsibility to redistribute wealth.

(C) Politicians must base decisions on political expediency rather than on abstract moral principles.

(D) Economic injustice need not be remedied unless it leads to intolerable social conditions.

(E) All that is required to create conditions of economic justice is the redistribution of wealth.

71. Shanna: Owners of any work of art, simply by virtue of ownership, ethically have the right to destroy that artwork if they find it morally or aesthetically distasteful, or if caring for it becomes inconvenient.

Jorge: Ownership of unique artworks, unlike ownership of other kinds of objects carries the moral right to possess but not to destroy. A unique work of art with aesthetic or historical value belongs to posterity and so must be preserved, whatever the personal wishes of its legal owner.

On the basis of their statements, Shanna and Jorge are committed to disagreeing about the truth of which one of the following statements?

(A) Anyone who owns a portrait presenting his or her father in an unflattering light would for that reason alone be ethically justified in destroying it.

(B) People who own aesthetically valuable works of art have no moral obligation to make them available for public viewing.

(C) Valuable paintings by well-known artists are seldom intentionally damaged or destroyed by their owners.

(D) If a piece of sculpture is not unique, its owner has no ethical obligation to preserve it if doing so proves burdensome.

(E) It is legally permissible for a unique and historically valuable mural to be destroyed by its owner if he or she tires of it.

势，这种形势若不能得到缓和，就会引起企图产生社会改革的暴力事件。

上面的陈述从逻辑上能使政治家得出下面哪一个结论？

(A) 社会变革的需要从来不能使诉诸武力的补偿办法合理化。

(B) 我们国家的责任是重新分配财富。

(C) 政治家必须基于政治上的方便，而不是基于抽象的道德原理来做出他们的决定。

(D) 除非经济上的不公导致了不能容忍的社会状况，否则就不需要纠正它。

(E) 创建经济公正的环境所需要的所有条件就是要重新分配财富。

Shanna：任何艺术作品的拥有者，如果发现它在道德上或审美方面不合口味，或者如果照看它会引起不便，那么从伦理上讲，仅仅凭借他们拥有的所有权，他们就有破坏它的权利。

Jorge：珍奇的艺术品的所有权与其他类型的艺术品的所有权不同。拥有珍奇艺术品的人在道义上具有占有它的权利，但是却没有破坏它的权利。一件具有美学或历史价值的艺术珍品属于后代，不管他的合法拥有者想怎样地处理它，这件艺术品都必须被保存下来。

在上面陈述的基础上，Shanna和Jorge会在下面哪一项陈述的真实情况上发生分歧？

(A) 任何一个拥有一幅以贬低的色调来描绘他或她的父亲的肖像画的人，单单由于肖像画具有的贬低特性，就产生毁坏它的行为在道德上是合理的。

(B) 那些具有美学价值的艺术作品的拥有者并没有义务给公众提供观赏这幅画的机会。

(C) 出名的艺术家所画的有价值绘画很少被它们的拥有者故意地损坏或摧毁掉。

(D) 如果一件雕塑品不是珍品，并且保存它被证明是一种累赘时，它的拥有者就没有道德上的责任来保存它。

(E) 如果某一珍奇的具有历史价值的壁画的拥有者对此画感到厌倦，他或她破坏掉这幅画的行为在法律上是允许的。

72. No senator spoke at the convention unless he or she was a Democrat. No Democrat both spoke at the convention and was a senator.

Which one of the following conclusions can be correctly drawn from the statements above?

(A) No one but senators spoke at the convention.
(B) No Democrat spoke at the convention.
(C) Only Democrats spoke at the convention.
(D) No senator spoke at the convention.
(E) Some Democrat senators spoke at the convention.

参议员要在大会上演讲，那么他或她必定是一个民主党员。一个民主党员不能够同时在大会上演讲且是一个参议员。

下面哪一个结论能从上面陈述中正确地得出来？

(A) 除参议员们之外没有人在会议上演讲。
(B) 没有民主党员在会议上演讲。
(C) 只有民主党在会议上演讲。
(D) 没有参议员在会议上演讲。
(E) 一些民主党参议员在会议上演讲。

73. Some of the world's most beautiful cats are Persian cats. However, it must be acknowledged that all Persian cats are pompous, and pompous cats are invariably irritating.

If the statements above are true, each of the following must also be true on the basis of them EXCEPT:

(A) Some of the world's most beautiful cats are irritating.
(B) Some irritating cats are among the world's most beautiful cats.
(C) Any cat that is not irritating is not a Persian cat.
(D) Some pompous cats are among the world's most beautiful cats.
(E) Some irritating and beautiful cats are not Persian cats.

世界上最漂亮的猫中有一些是波斯猫，然而，人们必须承认，所有的波斯猫都是自负的，并且所有的自负的波斯猫总是让人生气。

如此上面的陈述正确，下面的每一个基于上述陈述也必然是正确的，除了：

(A) 世界上最漂亮的猫中有一些是让人生气的。
(B) 一些让人生气的波斯猫是世界上最漂亮的猫。
(C) 任何不让人生气的猫不是波斯猫。
(D) 一些自负的猫属于世界上最漂亮的猫。
(E) 一些让人生气且漂亮的猫不是波斯猫。

74. Most parents who are generous are good parents, but some self-centered parents are also good parents. Yet all good parents share one characteristic: they are good listeners.

If all of the statements in the passage are true, which one of the following must also be true?

(A) All parents who are good listeners are good parents.
(B) Some parents who are good listeners are not good parents.
(C) Most parents who are good listeners are generous.
(D) Some parents who are good listeners are self-centered.
(E) Fewer self-centered parents than generous parents are good listeners.

绝大多数慷慨的父母是好父母，但是一些自私自利的父母也是好父母。然而，所有好父母都有一个特征：他们都是好的听众。

如果上面段落里的所有陈述是正确的，下面哪一个也必然正确？

(A) 所有是好的听众的父母是好父母。
(B) 一些是好的听众的父母不是好父母。
(C) 绝大多数是好的听众的父母是慷慨大方的。
(D) 一些是好的听众的父母是自私自利的。
(E) 自私自利的父母中是好的听众的人数比慷慨的父母中的少。

1. 解析：本题让我们指出"the doctrine"中隐含什么，因此读题重点应放在however前的三句话。第一句话说明了"the doctrine"的观点，第二句与第三句进一步表达了这个观点的内容。注意第二句里面的"entirely"、"at any point"与第三句里面的"only because"。根据第三句话"crime is said to exist only because society..."与第二句话"at any point in life an individual's personality can be changed by the management of the social world"，又结合common sense"犯罪是一种personality"，所以(D)正确。(A)中的"reflect"属于新动词，且做了一个无关比较；(B)中的"the affluent"的内容从上文中得不到；(C) 易误选，选(C)的考生大多受段落第四句的影响，但读题重点和思考重点应放在前三句话，并且第四句话的意思与(C)有点相违背，所以(C)不对；(E)中的less severe punishment是一个新概念并且与段落推理没有任何关系。

3. 解析：首先要看清楚问题中的"...NOT implied by the analogy"。段落推理把"汽车维护"与"政府在社会项目上的开销"进行类比，通过说明短期内在汽车维护上省钱而最终必然代价更大，进而论证政府在社会项目上减少开销必将会造成更大的问题。(E)中的"only"与"must be replaced"在上面段落中无涉及，且也没有类比之处，所以(E)is Not implied，(E)正确；若花在维修上的开销能使车辆持续发挥作用，如(A)所说，那么其类比就是："花在社会项目上的开销有好作用"；(B)中的类比推理为：减少在社会项目上的钱是在碰运气；(C)、(D)均有比较点、类比点，所以(C)、(D)are all implied。

5. 解析：本题重点有两个：(1)明晰问题目的，当问题目的较长时尤应如此；(2)读题重点应放在段落最后一句话"only when the larvae experience biological stress"。(D)中的"overpopulation"与"biological stress"相吻合，所以(D)正确；(A)起到了驳斥作用；(B)中的"trees"为新概念；(C)中的"all kinds"把范围扩大化了；(E)也与段落推理无关。

6. 解析：本题难度主要在于阅读以及明晰问题目的。本题让我们从作者的陈述中推出一个观点。读题重点应放在第三个句子"Despite the pretension of..."上，并且只有这句话是作者想要表达的观点。根据第三句话，Stanislavski在美国的追随者要求他写本关于表演的书，正好说明这些追随者没有理解其表演方法的精髓：essentially spontaneous emotional expression，所以(B)正确；(A)易误选，但(A)明显表达的是Stanislavski的观点，而非段落作者的观点，所以(A)不正确；(C)中的"misled"与段落推理相违背；(D)、(E)中均有上面推理所没有涉及的新概念，所以都不对。

13. **解析**：本题通过对曾在湖中游泳和未曾在湖中游泳的人的调查，发现前者呼吸道疾病和肠胃疾病的发病率高于后者。根据调查的结果我们很容易得出(D)选项的结论，即在这些湖中游泳与呼吸道、胃肠疾病之间的联系为这两者之间的因果关系提供了证据，因此(D)正确。(A)、(B)、(C)和(E)四个选项所述及的内容都与本题段落中的内容无关。

15. **解析**：如果一个机械泵的装置被用作人工心脏，如(D)所说，那么它将不能分泌一种激素，因此就无法执行人体心脏的所有功能，所以(D)为正确答案；段落推理并未说明荷尔蒙少时会导致什么样的后果，因此(A)不对；段落最后一句只表明在患有心脏病的人的血液中有大量的荷尔蒙，但并没有说是由于荷尔蒙导致心脏病，所以(B)不对；(C)中的"long-lasting"是一个新概念，上文根本没有涉及，因此也不对。(E)中出现了上文中所没有出现的绝对化语言"any"，所以(E)也不对。另外，在归纳题中可首先看if、unless选项，这样我们可以将答案定位在选项(A)、(D)，再结合推理排除(A)，就可得出(D)为正确答案。

17. **解析**：本题重点在于明白must be及only所体现的必要条件的推理的特点。若用①表示"mentally healthy"，用②表示"self-respect"，③表示"earning respect of other"，④表示"treating these others morally"，那么段落的推理为：①→②→③→④，而(B)表明①→④，与上面推理完全吻合，所以(B)正确；(A)从上面推不出来；(C)为逆命题，一般和原命题不等价；(D)从上面推不出来；(E)中的"seldom"所表示的涵义与上面段落刚好相反。

20. **解析**：本题段落中的论述强调了学生在学习数学时要发挥自己的主观能动性，而(D)则指出教师给出规则，学生死记硬背的学习方法，完全否定了段落中有关学生可以自学的灵活性的特点，因此(D)正确；(A)、(B)、(C)和(E)四个选项虽都不能从本题的段落中推出，但它们不与段落中的内容相抵触，同时也存在一定的可能性，所以(A)、(B)、(C)和(E)都是错误选项。

28. **解析**：根据本题的论述可知获得18世纪的音乐听起来怎么样这方面的信息与获得18世纪的乐器制作技术方面的信息具有不兼容性。因此，能指出这两方面不兼容性的选项是正确答案的可能性较大。(E)选项的推理为既然要演奏就必然要先修复，一旦修复就不能成为新的信息来源，由此可知(E)选项的推理指出了这种不兼容性，所以(E)是正确答案；(C)易被误选，许多考生由destroy all of the information认为(C)中的only source成立，但他们忽略了from it，所以(C)选项因"only"一词而不能成立；(A)、(B)和(D)都不能从本题的论述中合理地推出。

30. **解析**：属于"数学相关"类的归纳，请转化为数学去思维。

31. **解析**：(C)中的假设谈到将对法律服务进行的广告宣传的限制减少一项，任何这种减少，如果短文中陈述的相关性存在的话，都将伴随着为他们的服务进行广告宣传的律师数量的增加，正如(C)预测的那样。因此，(C)是正确答案；选项(A)、(B)、(C)和(E)都没有遵从文中提到的信息，因为没有律师提高他们的收费［同(A)相反］，使用法律服务的消费者数量没有增加［同(B)相反］，没有进行广告宣传的律师都没有决定降低他们的收费［同(D)相反］和很少的律师为他们的法律服务进行广告宣传［同(E)相反］，这些情况都仍是有可能出现的。

32. **解析**：celestial   *a.* 天体的
   resolution   *n.* 分辨率

33. **解析**：属于"数学相关"类的归纳，请转化为数学去思维。

34. **解析**：arbitration   *n.*（由争执双方挑选的人所作的）仲裁，公诉
   outlaw   *v.* 宣布…非法；逃犯

35. **解析**：属于"数学相关"类的归纳，请转化为数学去思维。

37. **解析**：这是一道比较难的题目，在读题时要关注段落中的exactly与any，且读题重点为第一句话，由第一句话的"...in exactly the right numbers for any suitable size of host egg,"我们可以知道，(A)中的"the size of the smallest host egg"属于"any suitable size"的一种，因此把"The size of the smallest

host egg" 换为 "the size of the largest host egg" 也对，也可以取非验证；(B)中的 "effective defenses against"，(C)中的 "from experience"，(E)中的 "visual clues" 均为新概念，不能从上面段落中推出来；(D)为新比较，必然不对。

42. **解析**：如果用B表示贸易禁运成功，A_1 表示高水平的国际协调，A_2 表示阻止货物进出的能力，那么上面整个段落第一句话推理可表达为 $B \rightarrow A_1 A_2$，第二句话推理可表示为 $A_2 \rightarrow \overline{A_1}$。综合这两句话，可知 $\overline{A_1}\,\overline{A_2} \rightarrow \overline{B}$，所以(D)正确；(A)、(B)、(E)的错误均在于偷换概念，把accord换为了opinion。

44. **解析**：归纳题型首先看带有if, unless的选项，这样我们发现(A)，(B)有if或unless，(B)可以作为一个很好的归纳答案；(A)中的any、(C)中的only、(E)中的solely 都属于绝对化语言，必然不对；(D)中的 "nonbiometrics" 为新概念，也必然不对。

45. **解析**：本题首先提出论点，个人所具有的价值观对提高公众健康的影响被低估，然后举例证明导致公众健康状况提高的传染病死亡率的下降依赖于生活条件的改善，而生活条件的改善又依赖于人民的价值观的改变。由此本题通过一个因果相关的例子证明了它提出的论点，所以(B)为正确答案；(D)为迷惑选项，但(D)错在用几个具体的例子来证实它，很显然题中只有一个具体的例子，如果把答案(D)的后半句改为"然后用一个具体的例子来证实它，那么答案(D)也是可以接受的正确选项，但相比之下，(B)更贴切一些；(A)、(C)和(E)所描述的逻辑结构与题意明显不符，因此均为错误选项。

46. **解析**：本题首先提出一普遍性的理论，然后把这一理论应用于一具体的例子。由例子中所描述的几种熊从它们的祖先中分离开的时间可知，大熊猫从熊中分离开的时间比熊和浣熊从同一种祖先中分开时间晚一千零几百万年。因此，根据本题开始提出的两个物种在遗传上越相似，两个物种从同一祖先中分出的日期距今就越接近的理论，可知大熊猫与熊和浣熊相比，在遗传上与熊更为相似，也即(D)为正确答案；(A)、(B)都不能从题干中得出；(C)、(E)是很明显的错误选项。

47. **解析**：我们应当注意在逻辑论证中，如果一个命题正确，那么这个命题的逆否命题也正确。本题的结论为大多数的艺术家都比那些受过相当良好的教育但不是艺术家的人中的任何人缺乏政治洞察力。该结论的逆否命题为不是每一个受过良好教育但不是艺术家的人都比所有的艺术家具有更深刻的政治洞察力，也就是说有些艺术家在政治问题上的洞察力比某些受过相当良好的教育但不是艺术家的人强，所以(E)为正确答案；(A)、(C)是明显错误的；(D)不能从短文中合理地推出；从文中不能得出完善的艺术教育与相当良好的教育之间的必然性，所以(B)也是错误的。

48. **解析**：本题的结论为室内盆栽植物可以吸收空气中的毒素。因此若一个密闭性良好的房间内有释放毒素的产品时，放入较多的室内盆栽植物后，室内的空气中的毒素肯定会下降，所以(D)为正确答案；(B)为明显错误的选项；(E)具有迷惑性，但(E)错在每种毒素物质的释放量均会下降上，我们知道室内盆栽植物只能吸收毒素，而不能抑制毒素的排放；(A)和(C)都不能从本题的论述中合理地推出。

49. **解析**：本题为"逆否命题"类型的归纳题。如果某一种口语非常地有效，那么它的每一个基本音素的所有可能排列都能组成一个可被理解的单词的逆否命题为：如果某一种口语的每一个基本音素的所有可能排列不可能都能构成一个可被理解的单词，那么它就不可能非常地有效。根据此逆否命题，再根据本题论述中的最后一句话就可推出如果人类的听觉系统不是一个完善的听觉接受器，那么口语就不可能非常地有效，也即(E)为正确答案；(D)是迷惑选项，但是应当注意到(D)是本题论证中最后一句话的否命题，我们知道原命题正确，否命题不一定正确，所以(D)不是最佳答案；(A)、(B)和(C)都不能从本题的论证中合理地推出。

50. **解析**：本题的结论是食盐可以有效地阻止微波加热食物的内部。如果不向将要在微波炉内加热的食物中加盐，那么微波就可以有效地加热食物的内部，使食物的内部达到足够高的可以杀死细菌的湿度，从而食物中毒的危险性会降低，所以(D)为正确选项；(E)为迷惑选项，在这里应当注意的是食盐不能引起食物中毒，它只是不能使微波有效地加热食物的内部，因此(E)是错误选项；(A)、(B)、(C)都不能从上述论述中合理地推出。

51. **解析：** 本题的结论是负责任的心理学家通常都承认新证据的出现有可能揭示他们理论的不正确性，因此那些认为他们的理论是正确无疑的心理学家都不是负责任的心理学家，由此可知(B)为正确答案；本题的(E)为迷惑选项，该选项把一个结论成立的必要条件当作了该结论成立的一个充分条件，承认新的证据的出现会证明他们的理论不正确只是成为一个负责任的心理学家的一个必要条件；选项(A)、(C)都不能从题中的论述中合理地推出；选项(D)与本题的论述无关。

52. **解析：** 本题的逻辑关系是，由①护士职业内的低工资和高度紧张的工作条件问题得不到解决→②护士学校就不能吸引到比目前数量更多的有才干的申请者→③护士职业降低它的进入标准或者出现护士紧缺的局面→④目前高质量的健康护理不能维持下去。根据这个逻辑关系的第一句话和最后一句话即可得知(E)为正确答案；(A)和(C)分别是①→②与①→④的否命题，原命题正确，否命题不一定正确，所以(A)和(C)都不能从短文中合理地推出；(B)错在后半句，因为根据②→③可知，护士学校可以不降低它的入学标准，只不过是出现护士紧缺的局面罢了；(D)也错在后半句，由(D)的前半句可推出③，而由③却不能合理地推出(D)选项的后半句，因为短文中说得很明白，降低进入标准只是不一定能解决护士的不足，但仍存在能解决护士不足的可能性。

53. **解析：** 本题为归纳题型，结合段落的第一句话与第二句话，可以很容易知道花费在用三分钟或更少的时间来烹调的微波食品上的钱多于其他方面所花费的钱，所以本题的(D)是很明显的正确答案；短文中只是说75个品牌的微波爆米花的销售额占总微波食品销售额的一半多一点，但这并不能推出微波爆米花食品的数量较多，因为若微波爆米花的价钱较其他食品贵时，它也可在较少的销售数量的基础上占有较大的销售额，所以选项(E)是不一定正确的；同理可以推出选项(A)、(B)和(C)均有不正确的可能性。

54. **解析：** 本题的逻辑关系是：①一个国家要在国际竞争时代保持主导地位→②该国的公民必须对国际事务有较好的理解→③新教师必须按国际方向来准备和教授他们的课程。由上述可得到①→③成立，即(A)为正确答案；(B)和(C)分别是①→③和①→②的逆命题，所以都不是正确的选项；(D)是对短文中①→②的否定，因此也是不正确的；(E)错在不同机构和委员会所做的公众报告并没有强调在培训教师过程中加强国际方向性的必要，它们只是暗示了这种必要性。

55. **解析：** 只有当独立性代替依赖性时，文化才能进步，因此若把单个学校看作是独立的文化，那么独立文化发展所需的必要条件也是单个学校发展所需的必要条件。所以学校发展即教育进步的必要条件是不依赖于外部的力量，由此可知选项(A)为正确答案；(B)做了一个不相关的新比较，在逻辑单题中，与上文未提到的新概念的比较必然不对；(C)答非所问，教育系统的官员改变他们的首创精神固然能促使教育的进步，但是这个进步并不是单个学校所做出的努力；(D)太绝对化，一个学校要发展，只是要它不依赖于外部力量，而不是不可以借鉴或引入外部力量，他山之石，可以攻玉，局外人参加学校为进步而进行的尝试未尝不可，只是不要凡事都依赖他们就是了；(E)具有一定的迷惑性，但(E)太绝对化，过分地强调了独立性的作用。在逻辑论证中，太绝对化的命题往往都是不正确的。

56. **解析：** 一个人若具有高尚的情操，他就会不断地做好事。而根据本题的论述，做好事能使大脑产生beneficial chemicals，这些beneficial chemicals能激活人体内抗感染的白血球的activity，白血球的activity是免疫系统功能正常发挥的决定性因素。从而我们可以得出结论magnanimity有益于一个人的免疫系统，也就是说magnanimity有益于个人利益，因此(D)就是正确答案；因为段落中只是谈到了做好事，并没有说明做好事应该出于怎样的动机，所以(A)是错误的；因为(B)是本题结论——做好事有益于一个人的免疫系统的否命题，原命题正确推不出否命题也正确；选项(C)搞错了逻辑关系，应该是高尚行为控制着大脑中有益化学物质的产生；选项(E)有点偏激，高尚行为能使体内的白血球增加，但是从文中我们并不能发现高尚行为的增加与白血球的增加之间呈线性关系，所以(E)选项是错误的。

57. 解析: 本题最后的结论是,只有在新药转移到市场上之后,它们才能有助于病人,也就是在新药转移到市场上是它们有助于病人的必要条件。离开了必要条件,结论肯定就不能成立。所以新药在转移到市场上之前,它们无法帮助病人,也即(B)为正确选项;(E)是比较容易误选的答案,它的主要错误是混淆了充分条件与必要条件,新的医药发现转移到市场只是它们有助于病人的必要条件,因此它们究竟是否有助于病人还要受其他条件的制约。(A)、(C)和(D)均不能从短文的论述中合理地推出,所以都是错误选项。

58. 解析: 本题以白内障手术为例,证明了高技术药品使国家的保健费用升高,新的技术使白内障手术的成功率提高,并且使手术费用下降,因此新技术吸引了更多的白内障患者,其结果使总的医疗费用升高。通过比较,不难发现总的医疗费用升高一定是由于增加的人数所花的医疗费超过了所有手术费下降所节省的医疗费,因此(C)是正确答案;(A)、(B)、(D)、(E)都很明显不能从短文中合理地推出。

59. 解析: 这个图书评论者认为,一本以她熟知的某一城市为背景的小说要想通过她的检查,它的作者对这个城市的了解至少得和她一样深刻,也就是说只有在图书评论者认为她对这个城市的了解不如作家对这个城市的了解清楚时,她才肯相信这个作家。(A)和(D)都过于绝对化,都错误在any novel上,在逻辑论证中,绝对化的选项往往都是不正确的;(B)和(C)很显然都不能从上述短文中推出;既然Peter Lee的第二本以旧金山为背景的小说胜利地通过这个图书评论者的检验,那么这个图书评论者肯定认为她对旧金山的了解不会比Peter Lee对旧金山的了解更清楚,所以(E)为正确答案。

注:flying colors 胜利,大获全胜

60. 解析: 由题中的论述可知彗星的质量与它们反射的光的多少成比例,当发现单位质量的哈雷彗星的材料实际反射光的强度比以前认为的值低60倍时,在亮度不变的条件下,就可推出目前根据光的强度估算的哈雷彗星的质量就比以前估算的高得多,也就是说以前基于亮度对哈雷彗星的质量的估计太低,所以(B)为正确答案;选项(C)是明显错误的,因为哈雷彗星反射的光的总量是可以被科学家们实际测到的,它是科学家们对彗星质量进行估计的出发点,因此它的值几乎是不变的。(A)、(D)和(E)三选项都不能从段落中合理地推出。

61. 解析: 本题若仅从问题目的的角度看,应属于"解释"题型,但细心的读者会发现:若把段落最后一句话变为问题目的,则本题变为"反对"题型;若把段落最后一句话改为"However, it's believed that higher primates cannot be identified solely by their lower jawbones, so_____",则本题变为"归纳"题型。笔者特把该题放入本章,请读者对比相关题目仔细体会本题推理特点。要质疑一个论证的结论,首先就要质疑支持这个结论成立的证据。段落中支持最早的灵长类动物起源于缅甸的证据是1978年在缅甸发现了下颚骨化石碎片。但该证据并没证明这些下颚骨化石碎片就是高级灵长类动物的下颚骨碎片,换句话说高级灵长类动物不能仅仅通过它们的下颚骨来鉴定它们。由此可知(C)是正确答案;(A)是毫无根据的胡说八道;(B)只是加强了颚骨碎片源于3000万年的事实;(D)是在诉诸权威,而不是在诉诸证据;选项(E)引入了新的比较。因此,(A)、(B)、(D)和(E)选项都是错误的。

62. 解析: 本题的结论是SKX Mach-5的拥有者是一个充满活力、具有攻击性和富有成就的人。一个既无活力又无成就的人不会因为拥有一辆SKX Mach-5汽车而变得具有活力和富有成就,因此这样的人拥有一辆SKX Mach-5将会被错误地体现,也即(B)是正确答案;从文中不能发现充满活力、具有进攻性和富有成就三者之间有任何必然的联系,所以(A)是错误的;(C)和(D)引入了新的比较;(E)过于绝对化。

63. 解析: 读明白问题永远最重要,本题让寻找可以作为论述的main conclusion的选项,所以(C)正确。Thomas今天早晨从他的公寓出发去了图书馆,而市政大楼是Thomas从公寓到图书馆的必经之路,因此我们可以推出,Thomas今天早晨从市政大楼前经过,但它只是论述前提的一个推论,所以(E)不可能为正确选项;因为黎明前是一个很笼统的时间概念,单从此我们很难判定Thomas是在火灾发生

前还是在火灾发生后经过了市政大楼，因此(A)、(B)二选项都是不一定正确的结论，(D)不能从段落中合理地推出，因此为错误选项。

64. **解析**：本题的结论是：从道义上讲，人们不能对他们无法控制的事情负责。文中又提及，每一个成年人都有无法控制他们行为的时候。由以上两点我们很容易进一步推出没有哪位成年人应该对他的或她的每一个行为都负道义上的责任，也即(E)为正确答案；(D)是段落中的结论的逆命题，因此不一定正确；(A)选项过于绝对化；(B)和(C)都提及了短文中未涉及的新内容，因此都是错误选项。

65. **解析**：由本题的第一句话可知，任何一个感染了X病毒的人，在一周后身体内才会产生抵抗这种病毒的抗体。因此基于对抗体测试的方法将至少在一个人感染上X病毒后的一周内检查不出他已感染了这种病毒，所以(E)是正确的；从段落中可知抗体的数量只是在感染后的第一年内会增加，因此(A)和(D)都是错误的；(B)过于绝对化，因为抗体测试只是确定一个人是否感染了X病毒的一种方法，而不是仅有的方法；(C)引入了新的比较，因此也是不对的。

66. **解析**：根据本题的论述可知，当某一特定投资的价值下降的百分比超过盈利最大的投资价值下降的百分比时，这个投资的收益率一定没有盈利最大的投资的收益率高，也即这个投资的利润率没有现有的利润最高的投资的利润率高。根据上述分析可知(C)是正确的，而(E)是错误的；(A)、(B)和(D)均不能从上述段落中合理地推出。

67. **解析**：设男演员为①，精力充沛的人为②，性格外向的人为③，害羞的人为④，那么本题的逻辑关系就可表达为，所有的①→②，所有的②→③，有一些④→①。由所有的①→②，所有的②→③，我们很容易得出所有的①→③，即所有的男演员都是性格外向的人，所以(A)和(D)可以从段前推理中得到；同理可以推出(C)和(E)与上面段落吻合；从上述的逻辑关系式中我们只能推出有一些害羞的男演员是性格外向的人，而推不出有一些害羞的性格外向者不是男演员，因此(B)是错误的，即(B)为正确答案。

68. **解析**：注意：①此为"must be...EXCEPT"题型，其答案方向要么为无关选项，要么为违背选项。②not...unless；only if；not...until表示必要条件的表示方法。如果用A_1表示"停火协议不会被违反"，用A_2表示"谈判马上举行"，A_3表示"别国施加压力"，A_4表示"国际部分展示能力"，那么段落推理可表示为：$A_1→A_2→A_3A_4$。很明显，(B)、(C)、(D)、(E)与段落推理吻合，而(A)选项结合问题目的的信息，等于是"$A_2→A_1$"，为"$A_1→A_2$"的逆命题而逆命题与原命题不一定等价，所以(A)为无关选项，因此(A)为正确答案。

69. **解析**：(D)是本题明显该选的答案，因为不管是把回收的材料送给回收中心，还是把它们送给想重新使用它们的邻居，这些家庭都得不到经济上的利益。所以他们不会选择前者而舍弃后者，相反他们把可回收的材料送给他们的想重新使用这些材料的邻居的可能性更大一些。(A)、(B)、(C)和(E)都可以减少这些家庭的基于垃圾数量的税单，因此都不是正确答案。

70. **解析**：由本题的论述可知重新分配财富是能减轻经济上的不公平的必要条件，经济上的公平又是人们不会诉诸暴力迫使社会改革的必要条件。因此重新分配财富是人们不会诉诸暴力迫使社会改革的必要条件。该命题的逆否命题是：要使人们不诉诸暴力迫使社会改革的事件发生，国家就必须重新分配财富。所以(B)是正确答案，其他四个选项都不能从本题的论述中合理地推出。

71. **解析**：根据本题题干中的描述，我们知道Shanna对选项(A)的内容是赞成的，而Jorge可能就会认为毁坏这幅画在道德上是不合理的，因为这幅画虽然不符合它的拥有者的口味，但是它有可能是一幅珍奇的艺术大作，因此(A)是正确答案；(B)、(C)和(E)都不能从Shanna与Jorge的论述中推出；Shanna与Jorge都认同选项(D)的内容，因此(B)、(C)、(D)和(E)都是错误选项。

72. **解析**：本题推理为：Senator演讲→必为Democrat→不能二者兼得。作为归纳，(D)与上面的推理完全吻合。

73. **解析**：注意此为"must be...EXCEPT"题型，其答案方向要么是无关选项，要么为违背选项。(A)、(B)、(C)和(D)均可以从上面推理中得出，而选项(E)是一个无关选项，可以很好地作为答案（注意，从段落我们确实可以知道"Some irritating and beautiful cats are Persian cats"成立，但其否命题即(E)选项不一定成立，所以(E)为无关选项。请警惕(E)选项的迷惑之外）。请对此思考本书276页68题。

74. **解析**：(A)指出"所有是好的听众的父母是好父母"，是"所有的好父母都是好的听众"的逆命题，逆命题与原命题不等价；(B)里的some推不出来；(C)"most"也推不出来；(E)为一新的比较，作为归纳必然不对，因此(D)是正确答案。

第 六 章

解　释

解释题型的特征是，给出一段关于某些事实或现象的客观描述（有时为一个图表），要求你对这些事实、现象或图表做出合理的解释。在本书中泛指解释结果、解释现象、解释差异、解释矛盾、解释图表以及完成段落题中以since、because作结尾的试题。我们可以根据解释的侧重点把上面的这几类考题分为解释结论或现象、解释差异或缓解矛盾。

一、解释结论或现象

本类考题是指给出一段关于某些事实或现象的客观描述，让我们从5个选项中寻求一个选项来解释事实或现象发生的原因，找到一个能直接说明结论能够成立或现象为什么发生的选项即可。因此在解题时，应抓住要解释的对象，并用之来定位选项。完成段落考题中以 since、because作结尾的试题也属于这类考题，其读题重点是所要完成段落的最后一句话。

1. A program instituted in a particular state allows parents to prepay their children's future college tuition at current rates. The program then pays the tuition annually for the child at any of the state's public colleges in which the child enrolls. Parents should participate in the program as a means of decreasing the cost for their children's college education.

Which of the following, if true, is the most appropriate reason for parents not to participate in the program?

(A) The parents are unsure about which pubic college in the state the child will attend.

(B) The amount of money accunulated by putting the prepayment funds in an interest-bearing account today will be greater than the total cost of tuition for any of the public colleges when the child enrolls.

(C) The annual cost of tuition at the state's public colleges is expected to increase at a faster rate than the annual increase in the cost of living.

(D) Some of the state's public colleges are contemplating large increases in tuition next year.

(E) The prepayment plan would not cover the cost of room and boardtany of the state's public colleges.

译文： 某州设立了一个计划，允许父母亲们可以按当前的费率预付他们的孩子们未来的大学学费。然后该计划每年为被该州任一公立大学录取的（参加该项目的）孩子支付学费。父母亲们应该参加这个计划，把它作为一种减少他们的孩子大学教育费用的手段。

以下哪一个选项，如果是正确的，是父母亲们不参加这个计划的最合适的理由？

(A) 父母亲们不清楚孩子将会上哪一所公立大学。

(B) 将预付资金放到一个计息账户中，到孩子上大学时，所积累的金额将比任何一所公立大学所有的学费开支都要多。

(C) 该州公立大学的年学费开支预计将以比生活费用年增长更快的速度增加。

(D) 该州一些公立大学正在考虑下一年大幅增加学费。

(E) 预付学费计划不包括在该州任何公立大学中的食宿费用。

解析： 该短文建议父母亲们应该参加学费预付计划，把它作为一种减少他们的孩子们将来大学教育费用的手段，如果(B)是对的，将资金放到一个计息账户将比参加这个预付学费计划有更大的成本效益，因此(B)是一个不参加的理由，并且是正确答案；(A)和(E)同决定是否参加都不是明确相关。因为该计划应用于孩子选择上的任何公立大学，该计划已经考虑到了(A)中的偶然性；不管父母亲是否参与，(E)中提到的费用都没有包括在学费开支中；选项(C)和(D)通过指出学费要增加，为参加该计划提供了支持。

2. Defense Department analysts worry that the ability of the United States to wage a prolonged war would be seriously endangered if the machine-tool manufacturing base shrinks further. Before the Defense Department publicly connected this security issue with the import quota issue, however, the machine-tool industry raised the national security issue in its petition for import quotas.

Which of the following, if true, contributes most to an explanation of the machine-tool industry's raising the issue above regarding national security?

(A) When the aircraft industries retooled, they provided a large amount of work for tool builders.

(B) The Defense Department is only marginally concerned with the effects of foreign competition on the machine-tool industry.

(C) The machine-tool industry encountered difficulty in obtaining governmental protection against imports on grounds other than defense.

(D) A few weapons important for defense consist of parts that do not require extensive machining.

(E) Several federal governments programs have been designed which will enable domestic machine-tool manufacturing firms to compete successfully with foreign toolmakers.

译文： 国防部的分析家担心，如果机械用具制造工业进一步萎缩，会严重地威胁到美国进行一场长时期战争的能力。然而在国防部公开地把这个安全问题同进口配额问题联系起来之前，机械用具工业在为进口配额的请愿活动中已提出了国家安全问题。

以下哪一项，如果是正确的，能最有力地解释机械用具制造工业将该问题提高到有关国家安全的高度？

(A) 当飞机制造业重新装备机械用具时，为机械用具制造者提供了大量的工作机会。

(B) 国防部只是轻微地关注国外竞争对机械用具工业的影响。

(C) 机械用具工业在以除国防之外的其他理由来获得政府保护防止进口冲击的过程中遭到了困难。

(D) 一些对国防来说比较重要的武器是由那些不需要深机械加工的零件组成的。

(E) 已经设立了一些能使国内机械用具制造公司成功地同国外制造商竞争的联邦政府计划。

解析： 由于机械用具制造业的规模可假定为对除国家安全之外的领域有影响，在请愿中该行业提出关于国家安全问题让人吃惊。因此(C)是正确答案，解释说该行业提出这个问题是因为在取得政府保护的努力中其他办法都没有效果；另一方面，选项(A)和(B)仅解释了为什么该行业不应提出安全问题。选项(A)指出该行业应提出就业问题；选项(B)指出这个关心国家安全的政府部门对该行业的进口问题没有给予足够的重视而采取行动；(D)和(E)都与该行业争取进口配额的策略选择无关。

注： wage a war 开始（进行）一场战争

3. Fact 1: Television advertising is becoming less effective: the proportion of brand names promoted on television that viewers of the advertising can recall is slowly decreasing.

Fact 2: Television viewers recall commercials aired first or last in a cluster of consecutive commercials far better than they recall commercials aired somewhere in the middle.

Fact 2 would be most likely to contribute to an explanation of Fact 1 if which of the following were also true?

译文： 事实1：电视广告变得越来越没有效：广告观众能回忆起来的在电视上做促销的品牌名字的比例在慢慢降低。

事实2：电视观众回忆起在一组连续的商业广告中播放的第一个或最后一个广告的情况要比他们回忆起中间某一个地方播放的广告的情况好得多。

如果以下哪一项也是正确的，事实2

(A) The average television viewer currently recalls fewer than half the brand names promoted in commercials he or she saw.

(B) The total time allotted to the average cluster of consecutive television commercials is decreasing.

(C) The average number of hours per day that people spend watching television is decreasing.

(D) The average number of clusters of consecutive commercials per hour of television is increasing.

(E) The average number of television commercials in a cluster of consecutive commercials is increasing.

将很可能为事实1做出一个解释？

(A) 目前一般的电视观众只能回忆起他或她看到的在电视上做促销的不到一半的品牌。

(B) 分配给每一组连续电视广告的总时间逐渐减少。

(C) 人们每天花在看电视上的平均小时数逐渐减小。

(D) 每小时电视播放连续广告的组数逐渐增加。

(E) 一组连续广告中电视广告的平均数量逐渐增加。

解析：因为(E)指出在一组中广告的数量逐渐增加，(E)表明从比例上说，越来越多的广告是在中间位置播放的。因此，(E)通过表明越来越多的广告是在观众难以回忆起来的位置播放的，来帮助事实2来解释事实1，(E)是正确答案；选项(A)证明电视广告的无效，但不能帮助事实2来解释事实1；选项(B)指出事实2同事实1矛盾，而不是去解释事实1，因为它指出每一组中广告的数量是减少的；选项(C)和(D)帮助解释事实1，(C)通过描述观看习惯的一种变化，而(D)通过描述节目的一种变化，但都没有将事实2与事实1联系起来。

4. In 1985 state border colleges in Texas lost the enrollment of more than half, on average, of the Mexican nationals they had previously served each year. Teaching faculties have alleged that this extreme drop resulted from a rise in tuition for international and out-of-state students from $40 to $120 per credit hour.

Which of the following, if feasible, offers the best prospects for alleviating the problem of the drop in enrollment of Mexican nationals as the teaching faculties assessed it?

(A) Providing grants-in-aid to Mexican nationals to study in Mexican universities.

(B) Allowing Mexican nationals to study in Texas border colleges and to pay in-state tuition rates, which are the same as the previous international rate.

(C) Reemphasizing the goals and mission of the Texas state border colleges as serving both in-state students and Mexican nationals.

(D) Increasing the financial resources of Texas colleges by raising the tuition for in-state students attending state institutions.

(E) Offering career counseling for those Mexican nationals who graduate from state border colleges and intend to return to Mexico.

译文：1985年得克萨斯州边境附近的大学，平均说来，流失了一大半以前每年可以招收到的墨西哥生源。教职员工宣称这种急剧下降是由于对国际和该州以外的学生的学费从每学时40美元上涨到120美元。

如果正如教职员工评论的那样，以下哪一项，如果是可行的，为缓解招收的墨西哥学生下降问题提供了最好的前景？

(A) 向墨西哥人提供助学金，使他们到墨西哥的大学去学习。

(B) 允许墨西哥人在得克萨斯州边境附近的大学学习，按州内学生的学费标准付费，该标准同以前的国际学生费率相同。

(C) 重新强调得克萨斯州边境附近的大学的目标和使命是不仅为州内学生，也要为墨西哥人服务。

(D) 通过提高在州立学院上学的州内学生的学费来增加得克萨斯的大学的财政来源。

(E) 对那些从州边境附近的大学毕业并准备回墨西哥的墨西哥人提供职业咨询。

解析：教职员工把招收的墨西哥人的下降归因于学费的增加，如果教职员工是对的，降低这些费用就会使招收人数停止下降，选项(B)为减少这些成本提供了一个计划，因此是正确答案；(C)、(D)和(E)都没有提出计划来降低被认为应对招生人数下降负责的学费；(A)也没有提出这样一个计划：因为要讨论的问题是得克萨斯州边境附近的大学招收的墨西哥人数下降的问题，而向墨西哥人提供经济上的激励，使他们去墨西哥的大学上学，如(A)所说，对于缓解该问题没有任何帮助。

5. Which of the following best completes the passage below?
In a survey of job applicants, two-fifths admitted to being at least a little dishonest. However, the survey may underestimate the proportion of job applicants who are dishonest, because _____.

(A) some dishonest people taking the survey might have claimed on the survey to be honest

(B) some generally honest people taking the survey might have claimed on the survey to be dishonest

(C) some people who claimed on the survey to be at least a little dishonest may be very dishonest

(D) some people who claimed on the survey to be dishonest may have been answering honestly

(E) some people who are not job applicants are probably at least a little dishonest

译文：以下哪一选项能最好地完成下面的短文？

在一项关于求职人员的调查中，2/5的人承认至少有一些不诚实。然而，这项调查可能低估了有不诚实行为的求职人员的比例，因为_____。

(A) 一些接受调查的不诚实的人可能在调查中宣称自己是诚实的。

(B) 一些接受调查的，在一般情况下诚实的人可能在调查中宣称自己是不诚实的。

(C) 一些在调查中宣称自己至少有一些不诚实的人可能非常不诚实。

(D) 一些在调查中宣称自己不诚实的人可能诚实地回答了调查中的问题。

(E) 一些非求职人员可能至少有一些不诚实。

解析：本题要解释为什么这项调查可能低估了有不诚实行为的求职人员的比例。如果实际上不诚实的申请人宣称自己是诚实的，调查结果就会显示出比实际存在的不诚实的申请人比例小的比例。因此，选项(A)是正确答案；选项(B)不合适，因为在一般情况下诚实的人在调查中宣称自己不诚实会有助于高估，而不是低估不诚实的申请人的比例；选项(D)不合适，因为承认自己不诚实的申请人不会造成对不诚实的申请人的比例的低估；选项(C)和(E)不合适，因为该论述既与不诚实的程度无关，也与非申请人的诚实与否无关，即(C)、(E)为无关选项。

6. The tobacco industry is still profitable and projections are that it will remain so. In the United States this year, the total amount of tobacco sold by tobacco-farmers has increased, even though the number of adults who smoke has decreased.
Each of the following, if true, could explain the simultaneous increase in tobacco sales and decrease in the number of adults who smoke EXCEPT:

(A) During this year, the number of women who have begun to smoke is greater than the number of men who have quit smoking.

(B) The number of teen-age children who have begun to smoke this year is greater than the number of adults who have quit smoking during the same period.

译文：烟草行业仍然赢利，并且预测它将继续盈利。今年在美国，烟草种植者销售的总的烟草量继续上升，尽管吸烟的成年人人数继续下降。

以下每一项，如果是正确的，可以解释烟草销量的增长和吸烟的成年人数的下降同时出现，除了：

(A) 今年，开始吸烟的成年女性数量比戒烟的成年男性数量多。

(B) 今年开始吸烟的青少年人数比同期戒烟的成年人人数多。

(C) During this year, the number of nonsmokers who have begun to use chewing tobacco or snuff is greater than the number of people who have quit smoking.

(D) The people who have continued to smoke consume more tobacco per person than they did in the past.

(E) More of the cigarettes made in the United States this year were exported to other countries than was the case last year.

(C) 今年，开始使用咀嚼烟或鼻烟的非吸烟者人数比戒烟的人数多。

(D) 继续吸烟的人每人消耗的烟草比他们以前消耗的多。

(E) 今年有比去年更多的在美国制造的卷烟出口到其他国家。

解析：如果今年开始吸烟的成年女性数量比戒烟的成年男性的数量多，选项(A)将导致吸烟的成年人数的增加而不是减少。因此，(A)不能解释引述的事实，是正确答案；给定的吸烟的成年人数下降，烟草销售量增加的情况，可以被吸烟的非成年人或使用烟草的非吸烟者的更大比例的增加所解释。吸烟者使用的总的烟草量或者国外销售的美国烟草量的增加都可以解释引述的事实。因为(B)、(C)、(D)和(E)能解释引述的事实，它们都不能作最佳答案。

二、解释差异或缓解矛盾

本类考题在段落中描述了双方表面上的矛盾或差异，而本质上段落中比较双方的矛盾根本就不存在。表面上的矛盾，要么比较双方强调的是同一事物的两个方面，或者双方探讨的是截然不同的两个对象。因此在解这类题时，应着重抓住差异点、矛盾点、变化点，并结合矛盾或差异双方的关键词去定位选项。GRE考试中出现的图表题也属于解释差异或矛盾题型，看图或表的重点也应着重抓住图或表的对比变化点，并用这个对比变化点来定位选项，具体请参考本章练习题21、22与25题。

7. A milepost on the towpath read "21" on the side facing the hiker as she approached it and "23" on its back. She reasoned that the next milepost forward on the path would indicate that she was halfway between one end of the path and the other. However, the milepost one mile further on read "20" facing her and "24" behind.

Which of the following, if true, would explain the discrepancy described above?

(A) The numbers on the next milepost had been reversed.

(B) The numbers the mileposts indicate kilometers, not miles.

(C) The facing numbers indicate miles to the end of the path, not miles from the beginning.

(D) A milepost was missing between the two the hiker encountered.

(E) The mileposts had originally been put in place for the use of mountain bikers, not for hikers.

译文：纤路上有一个里程牌，当一个徒步旅行者走近它的时候，面对她的这一面写着"21"，而背面写着"23"。她推测如果沿着这条路继续向前走，下一个里程牌会显示她已经走到了这条路的一半的位置。然而她向前走了一英里后，里程牌面向她的一面是"20"，背面是"24"。

以下哪一项，如果是正确的，将解释以上描述的矛盾？

(A) 下一个里程牌上的数字放颠倒了。

(B) 里程牌上的数字指的是公里数，不是英里数。

(C) 面向她这面的数字指的是抵达路的终点的英里数，不是指到起点的英里数。

(D) 该旅行者遇到的两块里程牌之间丢失了一块里程牌。

(E) 设置里程牌最初是为了越野骑自行车的人使用，而不是为徒步旅行者。

解析：该旅行者的推理做了一个假设，即面向她的数字表示到这条路起点的距离，第二块里程牌上的数字显示这个假设是错误的。相反，它们是在正面表示到路的终点的距离而反面表示到起点的距离情况下得出的数字，因此，(C)解释了这种矛盾，是正确答案；下一个里程牌放颠倒了〔选项(A)〕不能作为解释，因为如果该旅行者的推理是准确的，那么该里程牌两面的数字都应为22；计量单位〔选项(B)〕不能影响该数字变小或变大；丢失一块里程牌〔选项(D)〕也不影响变化的方向；交通工具的形式〔选项(E)〕与距离无关。

8. Some communities in Florida are populated almost exclusively by retired people and contain few, if any, families with small children. Yet these communities are home to thriving businesses specializing in the rental of furniture for infants and small children.

Which of the following, if true, best reconciles the seeming discrepancy described above?

(A) The businesses specializing in the rental of children's furniture buy their furniture from distributors outside of Florida.

(B) The few children who do reside in these communities all know each other and often make overnight visits to one another's houses.

(C) Many residents of these communities who move frequently prefer renting their furniture to buying it outright.

(D) Many residents of these communities must provide for the needs of visiting grandchildren several weeks a year.

(E) Children's furniture available for rental is of the same quality as that available for sale in the stores.

译文：Florida的一些社区几乎全部是退休人员居住，如果有，也只有很少的带小孩的家庭居住。然而这些社区聚集了很多欣欣向荣的专门出租婴儿和小孩使用的家具的企业。

以下哪一项，如果是正确的，能最好地调和以上描述的表面矛盾？

(A) 专门出租小孩用的家具的企业是从Florida外的批发商那里买来的家具。

(B) 居住在这些社区的为数不多的孩子都相互认识，并经常到其他人的房子里过夜。

(C) 这些社区的许多居民经常搬家，更愿意租用他们的家具而不愿意去买。

(D) 这些社区的许多居民必须为一年来访几个星期的孙子或孙女们提供必要的用品。

(E) 出租的孩子用的家具与商店里拿来卖的家具质量相同。

解析：如果这些社区许多居民一年中有几个星期要接待来访的他们的孙子或孙女，如(D)所述，仅凭此就能产生对出租的小孩用的家具的足够需求来支持这些企业繁荣兴旺，因此，(D)有助于调和这个明显的矛盾，是正确答案；选项(B)中提到的少数家庭不可能产生使出租企业繁荣兴旺的足够的需求；相似地，选项(A)和(E)，尽管它们提供了关于在这些社区出租的家具的信息，但没有解释为什么有这种对小孩家具的需求这一首要问题；选项(C)有助于解释为什么这些社区对出租家具的需求非同寻常地高，但没有解释为什么这种需求是对孩子用的家具的需求。

三、试题精练及解析

1. In the 1980 United States census, marital status was described under one of five categories: single, now married (but not separated), separated, divorced, widowed. In the category "separated," including both those who were legally separated and those who were estranged and living apart from their spouses, one million more women than men were counted.

在美国1980年的人口普查中，婚姻状况被5种范畴所描述：单身、已婚（但是没有分居）、分居、离婚和守寡，分居这一范畴既包括那些合法分居者又包括那些与他们的配偶疏远的分居者，在该范畴中的女性比男性多100万人。

Which of the following, if true, provide(s) or contribute(s) to an explanation for this result?

Ⅰ. There are more women of marriageable age than men of marriageable age in the United States.

Ⅱ. More of the separated men than separated women in the United States could not be found by the census takers during the census.

Ⅲ. Many more separated men than separated women left the United States for residence in another country.

(A) Ⅰ only.

(B) Ⅱ only.

(C) Ⅲ only.

(D) Ⅰ and Ⅱ only.

(E) Ⅱ and Ⅲ only.

2. Japanese factory workers are guaranteed lifetime jobs, bonuses paid on the basis of productivity and corporate profits, and a wage rate that is not attached to a particular job. Paradoxically, these guarantees do not discourage factory owners from introducing labor-saving machinery. Such innovations are to the factory owners' advantage despite the fact that the owners must protect the wages of their workers.

Which of the following, if true, logically explains why the introduction of labor-saving machinery is advantageous to factory owners?

(A) Before a Japanese factory worker is hired, he or she must present a record of his or her previous productivity.

(B) Labor-saving machinery increases productivity, thus yielding profits that more than cover the cost of retraining workers for other jobs.

(C) The purchase and maintenance of new machinery adds significantly to the final cost of the goods produced.

(D) Factory workers demand a change of procedure in the routine tasks they perform.

(E) Limited competition exists among Japanese factories for consumer markets.

3. The population of elephant seals, reduced by hunting to perhaps a few dozen animals early in this century, has soared under federal protection during the last few decades. However, because the species repopulated itself through extensive inbreeding, it now exhibits a genetic uniformity that is almost unparalleled in other species of mammals, and thus it is in far greater danger of becoming extinct than are most

下面哪些，如果正确，能提供或有助于解释这个人口普查的结果？

Ⅰ 在美国达到结婚年龄的女性比男性多。

Ⅱ 在美国，不能被调查人员所发现的独身男性比不能被他们所发现的独身女性多。

Ⅲ 离开美国移居他国的单身男性比单身女性多。

(A) 只有Ⅰ

(B) 只有Ⅱ

(C) 只有Ⅲ

(D) 只有Ⅰ和Ⅱ

(E) 只有Ⅱ和Ⅲ

日本工厂的工人有终身工作的保证，有在生产率和共同利润的基础上发给的奖金，并且工资金额并不与具体工作相联。与此相矛盾的是，这些保证并没有抑制工厂主引进劳动节约型的机器设备。这样的革新对工厂主是有利的，尽管事实上工厂主必须保护工人的工资。

下面哪一项，如果是正确的，合理地解释了引进劳动节约型的机器对工厂主有利的原因？

(A) 在一个日本人被雇用之前，他或她必须提交一份以往工作效率的报告。

(B) 劳动节约型的机器提高了生产率，因此带来的利润要高于重新培训工人做其他工作的费用。

(C) 购买和维护新机器大大增加了制造出来的商品的最终成本。

(D) 工厂的工人要求改变他们日常工作的程序。

(E) 日本工厂之间为争夺消费者市场的竞争很小。

本世纪初海豹的数量由于捕猎已降到了几十只。在最近几十年，由于联邦政府的保护，其数量又迅速增加了。然而由于它们通过广泛的近交进行自我繁殖，所以现在显示出了基因的单一性，这是其他哺乳动物所没有的。因此它们面临灭绝的危险性要比其他种类大得多。

other species.

Given the information in the passage above, which of the following is most likely the reason that other species of mammals are less likely than elephant seals to become extinct?

(A) Other species of mammals have large populations, so the loss of a few members of the species is not significant.

(B) Other species of mammals have increased their knowledge of dangers through the experience of generation after generation of animals.

(C) In other species of mammals, hunters can readily distinguish between males and females or between young animals and adults.

(D) In other species of mammals, some members of the species are genetically better equipped to withstand a disease or event that destroys other members of the species.

(E) Other species of mammals have retained habits of caution and alertness because they have not been protected as endangered species.

4. The garment industry is labor-intensive; the production of garments requires the employment of a relatively large number of people. The auto industry is capital-intensive; a large amount of money is invested in elaborate equipment run by a relatively small number of people. If fringe benefits are not considered, a typical United States garment worker in 1979 earned 46 percent of a typical auto worker's wages.

Which of the following, if true, is likely to be among the factors that account for the disparity between auto workers' and garment workers' wages?

(A) There is generally less variation among the wages of garment industry workers than among those of auto industry workers.

(B) Wage increases in the auto industry have a smaller effect on manufacturers' total costs than do wage increases in the garment industry.

(C) The fringe benefits that auto makers provide for their employees are more comprehensive than are those provided for garment workers.

(D) The auto industry faces more competition from companies outside the United States paying low wages than does the garment industry.

(E) The auto industry employs a larger total number of workers than does the garment industry.

已知上文的信息的情况下，下面哪一项最可能是其他哺乳动物比海豹灭绝的危险要小的原因？

(A) 其他种类的哺乳动物数目多，因此该种类数量减少一些并不明显。

(B) 其他种类的哺乳动物经过一代代的经验，已经增加了对危险的了解。

(C) 猎人很容易辨认出其他种类的哺乳动物的雌雄或老少。

(D) 其他种类的哺乳动物中，一些成员因基因方面的原因能更好地抵抗毁灭了该种类中其他成员的疾病或灾害。

(E) 因为其他种类的哺乳动物没有被当作濒临灭绝的动物而加以保护，所以保留了谨慎和警惕的习惯。

服装业是劳动密集型产业，生产服装需要雇用一大批人。汽车业是资金密集型产业，大量资本投入到由相对少的人操纵的复杂设备上，如果不考虑附加收入的话，一个普通的美国服装工人在1979年的工资是一个普通的汽车工人的46%。

下面哪一项，如果是正确的，可能是造成汽车工人和服装业工人工资差异的因素之一？

(A) 通常，服装工人的工资比汽车工人的工资变化小。

(B) 汽车工人工资的增加对制造商总成本的影响比服装工人工资的增加所产生的影响小。

(C) 汽车制造者给雇员提供的附加收入比服装工人得到的更丰富。

(D) 汽车业面临的来自美国以外支付较低工资的公司的竞争要比服装业大。

(E) 汽车业比服装业雇用的工人总人数要多。

5. Currently, the number of first-time admissions of individuals diagnosed as manic-depressives to hospitals in Great Britain exceeds by nine times the number of admissions of such patients to public and private hospitals in the United States, even though the population size of the United States is many times that of Great Britain.

Which of the following, if true, would be most useful to an attempt to explain the situation described above?

(A) The term manic-depressive refers to a wider range of mentally ill patients in Great Britain than it does in the United States.

(B) The admission rate in the United States includes those individuals who visit clinics for the first time as well as those who are admitted directly to hospitals.

(C) A small percentage of patients diagnosed as manic-depressive in Great Britain are admitted to private nursing homes rather than hospitals.

(D) The variety of training institutions in psychology in the United States is greater than in Great Britain, reflecting the variety of schools of psychology that have developed in the United States.

(E) Seeking professional assistance for mental health problems no longer carries a social stigma in the United States, as it once did.

6. Despite the fact that the health-inspection procedures for catering establishments are more stringent than those for ordinary restaurants, more of the cases of food poisoning reported to the city health department were brought on by banquets served by catering services than were brought on by restaurant meals.

Which of the following, if true, helps explain the apparent paradox in the statement above?

(A) A significantly larger number of people eat in restaurants than attend catered banquets in any given time period.

(B) Catering establishments know how many people they expect to serve, and therefore are less likely than restaurants to have, and serve, leftover food, a major source of food poisoning.

(C) Many restaurants provide catering services for banquets in addition to serving individual meals.

(D) The number of reported food-poisoning cases at catered banquets is unrelated to whether the meal is served on the caterer's or the client's premises.

现在，在英国被诊断为疯狂压抑症而首次收容住院的人比美国因此病而收容住进公共和私人医院的人多9倍，尽管美国人口是英国的很多倍。

下面哪一项，如果正确，能解释上述情况？

(A) 在英国，疯狂压抑症一词所指的患精神疾病的病人要比在美国所指的范围广。

(B) 美国收容住院的人既包括首次去诊所的人也包括直接收容住进医院的人。

(C) 在英国诊断为患疯狂压抑症的病人被收容住进私人护理院的人的比例比收容住进医院的比例小。

(D) 美国心理训练协会的种类要比英国多，这反映了美国心理学流派的多样性。

(E) 寻求专职人员的帮助解决精神健康问题在美国曾被视为一种社会耻辱，而今再也不是这样了。

尽管对包办酒席的机构的卫生检查程序比对普通餐馆的检查更严格是一个事实，但是上报到市卫生部门的食物中毒案例更多的是由包办酒席服务的服务部门引起的，而不是由餐馆的饭菜引起的。

下面哪一项，如果是正确的，有助于解释上面陈述中的明显的矛盾？

(A) 在任何给出的时间段里，在餐馆吃饭的人比参加包办宴会酒席的人多很多。

(B) 包办酒席的企业知道他们将招待的人数，因此比餐馆提供剩饭的可能性小，而剩饭是食物中毒的一个主要来源。

(C) 很多餐馆除了提供个人饭菜之外，也提供包办酒席的服务。

(D) 报道出来的在宴会上的食物中毒案例与食品是否是包办酒席无关。

(E) People are unlikely to make a connection between a meal they have eaten and a subsequent illness unless the illness strikes a group who are in communication with one another.

(E) 人们不太可能将其所吃过的一顿饭与之后的疾病联系起来，除非一群互相有联系的人都得了这种病。

7. In October 1987 the United States stock market suffered a major drop in prices. During the weeks after the drop, the volume of stocks traded also dropped sharply to well below what had been the weekly average for the preceding year. However, the volume for the entire year was not appreciably different from the preceding year's volume.

Which of the following, if true, resolves the apparent contradiction presented in the passage above?

(A) Foreign investors usually buy United States stocks only when prices are low.

(B) The number of stock buyers in 1987 remained about the same as it had been the preceding year.

(C) For some portion of 1987, the volume of stocks traded was higher than the average for that year.

(D) The greater the volume of stocks traded in a given year, the lower the average price per share on the United States stock market for that year.

(E) The volume of stocks traded rises and falls in predictable cycles.

1987年10月，美国股票市场遭受了一次大的价格下跌。在下跌后的几周里，股票的交易量也剧烈下降，大大低于前一年平均周交易量。但是，这一整年的交易量与前一年的交易量并没有明显差异。

下面哪一项，如果正确，能解释上面短文中提出的明显矛盾？

(A) 外国投资者通常只有在价格低的时候才购买美国股票。

(B) 1987年的股票购买者人数与前一年人数大致相同。

(C) 1987年的某一段时间，股票交易量高于那一年平均交易量。

(D) 某一年股票的交易量越大，则美国股票市场该年每股的平均价格就越低。

(E) 股票交易量以可预测的周期形式涨落。

8. Because the process of freezing food consumes energy, many people keep their electric freezers half-empty, using them only to store commercially frozen foods. Yet freezers that are half-empty often consume more energy than they would if they were kept fully stocked.

Which of the following, if true, contributes most to an explanation of the apparent discrepancy described above?

(A) A given volume of air in a freezer requires much more energy to be maintained at a temperature below freezing than does an identical volume of frozen food.

(B) The more often a freezer's door is opened, the more energy is required to maintain that freezer's normal temperature.

(C) When unfrozen foods are placed in a freezer, the average temperature of a given volume of air inside that freezer rises temporarily.

(D) A person who normally maintains a half-empty freezer can cut energy costs considerably by using a freezer that is 50 percent smaller.

由于冷冻食品的过程消耗能量，因此很多人使他们的电冰箱保持半空状态，只用它们贮存购买的冷冻食品。但是半空的电冰箱经常比装满的电冰箱消耗的能量更多。

下面的哪一项，如果是正确的，最能解释上面描述的明显的矛盾？

(A) 冰箱中使一定体积的空气保持在低于冰点的某一温度比使相同体积的冷冻食品保持该温度需要更多的能量。

(B) 冰箱的门打开的次数越多，保持冰箱的正常温度所需的能量越多。

(C) 当将未冷冻的食品放入冰箱中时，冰箱内的一定体积空气的平均温度会暂时升高。

(D) 通常保持冰箱半空的人可以使用比该冰箱体积小一半的冰箱从而很大程度地削减能耗。

(E) An electric freezer can operate efficiently only if chilled air is free to circulate within the freezing compartment.

9. Although compact cars make up only 38 percent of the vehicles in traffic, 48 percent of the cars that are followed too closely ("tailgated") are compact. On the other hand, fewer than 27 percent of the cars tailgated are middle-sized, even though middle-sized cars make up 31 percent of the vehicles in traffic.

Which of the following, if true, most contributes to an explanation for the phenomenon described above?

(A) The shape of compact cars makes it easy for a tailgater to see far enough ahead around such cars to minimize the chances of a rear-end collision.

(B) Middle-sized cars, owned by families with children and pets, are likely to have bumper stickers that are so interesting to read that tailgaters stay behind such cars longer.

(C) Compact cars sometimes have superior engines that allow them to pass middle-sized cars on the highway easily.

(D) The percentage of cars on the highway that are middle-sized has been steadily decreasing over the last decade.

(E) Compact cars are often driven by fast drivers.

10. Two suits of battle armor worn by King Henry VIII were discovered, one from the beginning of his reign in 1510 and the other from 1540. Although both suits of armor were made for Henry VIII, the 1540 suit of armor was 40 pounds heavier than the 1510 suit of armor.

Which of the following, if true, contributes LEAST to an explanation of the discrepancy described above?

(A) Henry, although slim at the beginning of his reign, developed a bulky figure because of massive weight gain.

(B) During his reign Henry increased his arsenal of weapons because, despite his popularity in 1510, by 1540 the English populace was becoming disenchanted with his rule.

(C) Although the style of armor was plain and severe in the beginning of Henry's reign, he started the fashion of decorating armor with heavy and elaborate metal pieces because of his love for ornamentation.

(D) Henry ascended the throne while still an adolescent and grew three inches during his first five years as king.

(E) 只有当冷空气能够在冰箱的冷冻室里自由循环时，电冰箱才能有效地运行。

虽然小型车只占交通车辆的38%，但48%被追随得太近（"追尾"）的车是小型车。另一方面，不到27%的被追尾的车是中型车，而中型车占交通车辆的31%。

以下哪一项，如果是正确的，最能解释上述现象？

(A) 小型车的车型使其车主在紧跟其他车行驶时，能从其周围看到前面足够远从而减小与别的车的尾部相撞的可能性。

(B) 有孩子和宠物的家庭拥有的中型车，可能在保险杠上贴着一些有趣的话，追随其后的车跟在这种车后的距离会更远。

(C) 有些小型车上装有性能优良的发动机，使它们能够轻易地在高速公路上超过中型车。

(D) 在过去的10年中，高速公路上行驶的中型车的比例一直在下降。

(E) 小型车的司机通常开得很快。

人们发现了两件亨利八世穿过的盔甲，一件来自于他统治初期的1510年，另一件来自于1540年，虽然这两件盔甲都是为亨利八世制作的，但1540年的盔甲比1510年的重40磅。

以下哪项如果正确，最不可能成为对以上描述的差异的解释？

(A) 亨利八世尽管在刚执政时比较瘦，后来由于体重增加，逐渐发展成为一个体格强壮的人。

(B) 在他执政期间，亨利八世增加了他的武器贮备，因为虽然他刚执政时比较受欢迎，但到了1540年，人们已经开始对他的统治表示不满。

(C) 虽然在亨利八世执政初期铠甲的风格比较朴素，但由于他对装饰品的喜爱，他开始用重的装饰金属片装饰铠甲，开创了一种新的风格。

(D) 亨利在登基时还是一个少年，在他执

(E) Because of the improved design of battle weaponry during the 1530's, armor was given a multilayered design so that the sharper and stronger weapons could not pierce it.

11. Which of the following, if true, provides the most logical completion of the passage below?

Cars fueled by methanol have a much lower level of emissions of pollutants such as carbon monoxide and environmentally harmful hydrocarbons than gasoline-fueled cars do. Methanol fuel does produce somewhat higher formaldehyde emissions than gasoline does. Nevertheless, a methanol-powered car actually produces less atmospheric formaldehyde pollution than a comparable gasoline-powered car, because _____.

(A) compared to carbon monoxide and some hydrocarbons produced by gasoline-powered cars, formaldehyde pollution is not a serious threat to the environment

(B) the technical difficulties involved in mass producing methanol-powered cars will prevent them from seriously competing with gasoline-powered cars for several years

(C) gasoline-powered cars are required by United States law to be equipped with catalytic converters that reduce emissions of many pollutants

(D) measuring a car's emissions is generally an accurate method of assessing that car's contribution to atmospheric pollution

(E) most formaldehyde pollution generated by gasoline-powered cars results from the photochemical conversion of hydrocarbon emissions into formaldehyde in the atmosphere

12. Fewer than half of the jobs in the United States conform even loosely to the standard forty-hour, nine-to-five weekday schedule, according to demographic experts. This is largely due to the rapid increase in the number of service firms and in the proportion of the United States labor force these firms employ, the experts say.

Which of the following, if true, best helps to explain how the growth of the service sector has had the effect noted above?

(A) In order to supplement their incomes, a small percentage of workers in other sectors of the economy take service-sector jobs as sell.

(B) New service-sector firms have arisen to fill the need for day care for children, a need that was created by the increasing number of families in which both parents are

---

政的头5年内，他长高了3英寸。

(E) 在16世纪30年代，因为武器设计得到了改善，所以铠甲有多层设计，这样更锐利和更坚硬的武器就不能刺穿它。

以下哪项，如果正确，能最合逻辑地完成下文？

以甲醇为燃料的汽车释放的污染物如一氧化碳和对环境有害的碳氢化合物比以汽车油为燃料的汽车少得多。而甲醇燃料释放的甲醛却比汽油多。然而，一辆燃烧甲醇的汽车实际上比与之相当的燃烧汽油的汽车产生更少的大气甲醛污染。因为_____。

(A) 同燃烧汽油的汽车产生的一氧化碳和碳氢化合物相比，甲醛所造成的污染对环境来说算不上严重的威胁。

(B) 由于大量生产燃烧甲醇的汽车在技术上有困难，使得几年来，这种汽车一直也没有真正和燃烧汽油的汽车进行竞争。

(C) 燃烧汽油的汽车，按美国法律规定，必须安装上催化转化器从而减少许多污染性气体的排放。

(D) 测量汽车的尾气，通常是估算汽车造成的大气污染程度的一个准确方法。

(E) 燃烧汽油的汽车所造成的甲醛污染，大部分是由于它释放的碳氢化合物在大气中经过光化学反应转变成为甲醛而造成的。

据人口统计专家说，在美国只有不到一半的工作遵守标准的40小时，即朝九晚五一星期5个工作日的工作时间表。专家说这主要是由于服务性企业数量的迅速增加，以及美国劳动力中被这种公司雇用的劳动力的比例升高造成的。

下列哪项如果正确，最有助于解释服务性行业的增长是如何产生了上面提到的影响？

(A) 为了补贴收入，一小部分其他经济部门的工人也从事了一些服务行业的工作。

(B) 许多新服务性公司的出现是为了满足白天看护小孩的需要，这种需求是由于父母双方都工作的家庭日益增多而

employed.

(C) More part-time than full-time jobs have been created through the application of new technologies to traditional occupations.

(D) Manufacturing enterprises and other nonservice firms often operate twenty-four hours a day, seven days a week.

(E) The largest and fastest-growing segment of the service sector caters to leisure activities pursued outside the standard nine-to-five weekday schedule.

13. The Business Permit Office in Plains County claims that it has reduced processing time by one week by replacing the old application forms, which applicants filled out on the day of their interview, with mail-in, computer-readable forms and by letting the computer schedule the interviews. Businesspeople counter that getting a permit now averages a week longer.

Which of the following, if true, most helps to resolve the apparent discrepancy described above?

(A) County businesses can operate only with a permit, and during each day of processing they lose any income they might have generated.

(B) The permit office considers that processing begins after the interview, whereas the applicants consider that processing begins when they have submitted an application.

(C) There are fewer applicants for permits in the county since the permit office instituted the changes.

(D) Computer-readable forms have reduced the time necessary for the permit office to verity the statements made on applications and have thus reduced the amount of time an interview takes.

(E) The format of the application has not changed since the permit office began recording applications on the computer.

14. Stone Age potters crafted complicated and often delicate ceramic pots, tools, and jewelry. They also crafted crude pottery figurines. Many of the delicate ceramic pots, tools, and jewelry have been found intact or nearly so, whereas the figurines, crafted at roughly the same time as the ceramics, have largely been found in tiny fragments.

Which of the following, if true, best explains why few of the pottery figurines, but many of the delicate ceramics, have been found intact?

引起的。

(C) 由于传统职业中新技术的应用，创造出了比全日工作更多的兼职工作。

(D) 制造性企业和其他非服务性行业通常实行每周7天工作制，每天工作24小时。

(E) 最大且发展最快的服务性行业在朝九晚五的五天工作制之外给人们提供他们希望从事的休闲活动。

Plains郡商业许可办公室声称，他们通过把申请人在面谈那天填制旧式的申请表改为先邮寄过来计算机可读的表格并让计算机安排面谈，这样可以将手续时间减少一星期。而商人们反驳说得到一个许可现在平均要多花一个星期的时间。

下面哪一项，如果正确，能最有助于解释上面所提出的明显的差异？

(A) 该郡的企业只有获得许可之后才能营业，在审批期间，它们会损失很多它们应该得到的收入。

(B) 许可办公室认为这一过程是从面谈后开始的，但申请人认为这一审批过程从他们提交申请表就开始了。

(C) 自从许可办公室改变了程序，该郡申请许可证的申请人就减少了。

(D) 采用计算机可识别的表格，缩短了许可办公室验证申请表格上的陈述所必要的时间，所以缩短了面谈的时间。

(E) 自从许可办公室开始在计算机上记录申请时，申请的格式没有改变。

石器时代的陶工制作了复杂并且常常是精致的陶瓷水罐、工具和珠宝。他们也制作了粗糙的陶人。有许多这种精致的陶瓷水罐、工具和珠宝被发现时是完整的或几乎完整，然而大致与这些陶器在同时期制作的陶人却大多以小碎片的形式被发现。

如果正确，以下哪一项最佳地解释了为什么很少有陶人被发现是完整的而许多精致的陶器却如此？

(A) When a pottery piece from any batch was broken during finishing, Stone Age people sometimes deliberately smashed the rest of that batch, perhaps to avert bad luck.

(B) The composition of clay, which affects the durability of any pottery made from it, varies greatly from one area of the world to another.

(C) Pottery was invented in the Stone Age, and techniques for making pottery were mastered well before those required for delicate ceramic work.

(D) Stone Age potters crafted pottery figurines as frequently as they did ceramic pieces.

(E) Many Stone Age rituals involved the destruction of a pottery figurine, perhaps as a sacrifice to the gods.

(A) 最后修整期间，如果一组陶器中有一个碎了，石器时代的人有时会故意打碎整组东西，也许是为了避邪。

(B) 世界各地陶土的成分差别很大，而这种成分又相应地会影响陶器的持久性。

(C) 陶艺是石器时代发明的。人们早在掌握制作精致陶器技术以前就已经精通了制陶技术。

(D) 石器时代的陶工制作陶人和制作陶瓷制品的时候一样多。

(E) 许多石器时代的仪式需要打碎陶人，可能是作为对神的祭祀。

15. A new ordinance passed by the Gorenton Council a year ago banned the sale of all nonrecyclable plastic packaging for food being sold in Gorenton. A substantial percentage of Gorenton's plastic waste, however, is still composed of nonrecyclable plastic food packaging.

Which of the following, if true, best contributes to reconciling the apparent discrepancy above?

(A) Fewer food products are packaged in nonrecyclable plasticstoday than were so packaged a year ago.

(B) The new ordinance affects only plastic food packaging and not other products packaged in plastic, many of which are sold in Gorenton.

(C) Grocery and other stores in nearby suburban areas patronized by many Gorenton residents are unaffected by the new ordinance.

(D) Many food products formerly packaged in nonrecyclable plastics are now specially packaged in recyclable plastic before being shipped so that they can be sold in Gorenton.

(E) The total amount of both Gorenton's trash and its plastic waste grew considerably over the past year.

一个一年前由Gorenton市议会通过的新法令禁止了在Gorenton销售的食品使用所有不可回收的塑料包装。然而，仍有相当大比例Gorenton的塑料垃圾来自不可回收的塑料食品包装。

如果正确，下列哪项最有助于调和以上明显的分歧？

(A) 和一年前相比，现在使用这种无法回收的塑料包装的食品减少了。

(B) 这一新法令只涉及食品的塑料包装，而没有考虑到在Gorenton大量出售的其他产品的塑料包装。

(C) 新法令并没有影响到郊区附近的杂货店和其他商店，Gorenton 的许多居民都经常光顾那里。

(D) 许多以前由无法回收的塑料包装的食品现在在发运到Gorenton之前，都改用能回收的特殊塑料包装，这样才能在 Gorenton出售。

(E) 今年Gorenton的废物和塑料垃圾总量比去年明显增加。

16. In the past ten years, there have been several improvements in mountain-climbing equipment. These improvements have made the sport both safer and more enjoyable for experienced climbers. Despite these improvements, however, the rate of mountain-climbing injuries has doubled in the past ten years.

If all of the statements above are true, which of the following, if true, best reconciles their apparent discrepancy?

在过去的10年中，登山设备有了几项改进，这些改进使该运动对于经验丰富的登山者来说更加安全更加惬意了。然而虽然有了这些改进，过去10年中登山事故发生率仍旧翻了一番。

如果以上的陈述完全正确，下列哪一项如果正确，最好地调和了它们之间明显的分歧？

(A) Many climbers, lulled into a false sense of security, use the new equipment to attempt climbing feats of which they are not capable.

(B) Some mountain-climbing injuries are caused by unforeseeable weather conditions.

(C) Mountain climbing, although a dangerous sport, does not normally result in injury to the experienced climber.

(D) In the past ten years there have been improvements in mountain-climbing techniques as well as in mountain-climbing equipment.

(E) Although the rate of mountain-climbing injuries has increased, the rate of mountain-climbing deaths has not changed.

(A) 许多登山者误以为使用这些设备会很安全，试图使用新设备去创造他们能力所不及的登山业绩。

(B) 一些登山事故的发生是由无法预测的天气情况所引起的。

(C) 登山尽管是一种危险运动，但对于有经验的登山者，通常不会造成伤害。

(D) 在过去的10年，不仅登山技术有了改善。登山设备也有了提高。

(E) 尽管在登山活动中受伤的比例增加了，但在登山活动中死亡的比例没有变。

17. Regional and local telephone companies around the nation are beginning to offer customers an electronic operator system that allows customers to choose to make some operator-assisted calls through an electronic operator. Nevertheless, the number of human operators on staff will not be reduced in the foreseeable future.

Each of the following statements, if true, helps explain why the number of human operators is not being reduced EXCEPT:

(A) Demand for operator-assisted calls is increasing dramatically.

(B) The new electronic operator system, though it has been tested, is expected to require significant adjustments before it can become fully operational.

(C) The operators union would be quick to strike the companies involved if operators were dismissed during the current contract period.

(D) In one regional trial of the electronic system, virtually all consumers, given a choice, preferred a human operator to an electronic one.

(E) The new electronic operator system will complete operator-assisted calls twice as fast as human operator can.

全国各地区及本地的电话公司都开始向顾客提供一个电子接线系统，使顾客可以选择使用电子系统来拨打需要接线员帮助才能拨通的电话。然而，在可预见的未来，人工接线员的在职人数不会减少。

以下陈述，如果正确，除哪项外都可以解释人工接线员人数不会下降的原因？

(A) 拨打需要接线员帮助才能拨通的电话的数量急剧增长。

(B) 新的电子接线系统，虽然通过了测试，但在全面使用之前还需要做大量的调整工作。

(C) 如果接线员所在的公司在目前的合同期未满时把他们辞退，其工会就会迅速抨击该公司。

(D) 在一个地区，对该电子系统进行试运行，如果让消费者自己选择，几乎所有的消费者都选择人工接线员来接通电话。

(E) 新的电子接线系统完成一次接线电话的速度比人工接线快一倍。

18. A significant reduction in caloric intake, if accompanied by vitamin supplements, will double the life span of laboratory mice. Mice fed 40 percent of the standard food allowance had twice the life expectancy of mice in a group that was fed the standard allowance.

If the information above is accurate, each of the following

大量减少热量的摄入，如果同时伴随维生素的补充，可使实验室老鼠的寿命延长一倍。喂食40%标准食物量的老鼠的预期寿命是喂食标准食物量的老鼠的两倍。

如果以上信息正确，下列陈述如果正确，除哪项外都将有助于解释喂食比标准

statements, if true, would help explain why the laboratory mice on the reduced allowance lived twice as long as the mice fed on the standard allowance EXCEPT:

(A) The lack of food reduces a mouse's metabolic rate, thereby limiting wear and tear on the mouse's body.

(B) A lower-calorie diet delays the aging of the immune system and thus protects the mouse from some diseases that usually cause death.

(C) A drastic reduction in caloric intake signals the hormonal system to delay the aging process.

(D) Mice that are fed less than the standard allowance have cells that have life spans that are longer than average.

(E) The vitamin supplements that accompanied the reduced-calorie diet did not contribute calories to that diet.

食物量少的实验室老鼠活的时间是喂食标准食物量的老鼠的两倍。

(A) 由于吃得少，降低了老鼠的新陈代谢速度，也就减少了老鼠自身的消耗。

(B) 低热量的进食延缓了老鼠免疫系统的老化，从而保护老鼠免受一些常会致命的疾病的侵扰。

(C) 大量减少热量的摄入促使荷尔蒙系统延缓衰老进程。

(D) 比标准允许量吃得少的老鼠细胞的寿命比正常进食的老鼠的细胞寿命长。

(E) 伴随着减少了热量的饮食所做的对维生素的补充并没增加饮食中的热量。

19. Studies have shown that people who rarely take antibiotics, which are antibacterial drugs, have stronger immune systems than do people who take antibiotics frequently. Yet there is no evidence that taking antibiotics weakens the immune system.
Which of the following, if true, best reconciles the apparent discrepancy in the information above?

(A) People who have strong immune systems seldom get the kinds of infections for which people normally take antibiotics.

(B) People who have strong immune systems are seldom aware that their immune systems are unusually strong.

(C) People who have weak immune systems have great difficulty recovering from bacterial infections if they do not take antibiotics.

(D) Some people take antibiotics even though the antibiotics cause a variety of side effects.

(E) Some people take antibiotics frequently because their doctors prescribe antibiotics for viral infections as well as for bacterial infections.

研究表明，很少服用抗生素，即抗菌药的人比经常服用抗生素的人有更强的免疫系统。然而并无证据表明服用抗生素会削弱免疫系统。

如果正确，以下哪项最好地调和了以上信息中明显的分歧？

(A) 免疫力强的人很少被传染上人们通常用抗生素治疗的疾病。

(B) 免疫力很强的人很少意识到他们的免疫力很强这一事实。

(C) 免疫力很差的人，如果不吃抗生素类药，很难从细菌传染病下恢复过来。

(D) 尽管抗生素会产生许多副作用，有些人依然使用这类药。

(E) 有些人常吃抗生素类药，因为他们的医生无论是对病毒传染还是对细菌感染都开抗生素类药物。

20. A person's intake of refined sugar and of foods that break down into sugars during digestion is the dietary source of virtually all of the glucose (a type of sugar) that reaches that person's bloodstream. Coffee, however, which itself does not break down into sugars during digestion, sometimes causes a person's blood-glucose level to rise dramatically, even if the coffee is consumed without cream or any sweeteners.
Which of the following, if true, best helps to explain coffee's effect on blood-glucose levels as it is described above?

一个人摄取的精炼糖和在消化过程中由食物分解成的糖就是进入人体血液的几乎所有葡萄糖（一种糖）的饮食来源。虽然咖啡在消化时自身不能分解成糖，但有时却能使人的血糖水平急剧上升，即使咖啡没有和奶油或任何甜食一起饮用。

以下哪项，如果正确，最有助于解释上文提到的咖啡对血糖水平的影响？

(A) People often drink coffee after a meal consisting of several types of foods that themselves rapidly break down into sugars during digestion.

(B) Drinking more than two cups of coffee in an hour increases a person's level of stress, and the body reacts to stress by releasing stored glucose into the blood.

(C) People who eat very few foods that contain refined sugar often have higher blood-glucose levels than people who eat many such foods.

(D) For many people, the consumption of one piece of chocolate cake has the same stimulating effect as one cup of plain coffee.

(E) People with sedentary office jobs are more likely to drink large amounts of coffee and to have higher blood-glucose levels than are people with jobs requiring constant physical activity.

21. RESULTS OF TWO SURVEYS OF OPINIONS REGARDING THE EFFECTS OF SCIENCE ON HUMAN SOCIETY

Responses	August 1991	August 1992
Mostly beneficial	25%	81%
Equally harmful and beneficial	37%	9%
Mostly harmful	20%	7%
No opinion	18%	3%

Which of the following, if true, contributes most to explaining the shift in opinions about the effects of science on human society?

(A) The surveys questioned people who regularly watch prime-time television, and an innovative weekly prime-time television series called "Wonders of Science" had been steadily winning viewers since its widely seen premiere in January 1992.

(B) The surveys questioned college-educated adults, and a report called "The State of the Nation's Schools." published in June 1992, noted an increase in students' interest in science courses since 1982.

(C) The surveys were conducted in a suburban shopping area near a company that ceased operation in April 1992 as a result of lawsuits arising from unexpected toxic effects of the company's products.

(D) Both survey forms were mailed to equally large samples

(A) 人们饮用咖啡经常是在饭后，每餐饭中含有的几种食物本身在消化过程中迅速分解成糖类。

(B) 一小时内饮用两杯咖啡以上会增加人体的紧张程度，人体对此做出的反应就是把储存的葡萄糖释放到血液中。

(C) 很少吃含有精炼糖食物的人的血糖含量比大量食用这种食物的人的血糖含量高。

(D) 对许多人来说，吃一块巧克力蛋糕和喝一杯纯咖啡会同样使人兴奋。

(E) 和由于工作需要经常进行身体运动的人相比，久坐办公室的人会饮更多的咖啡，会有更高的血糖含量。

两个关于科学对人类社会影响的评价的调查结果

回答	1991.8	1992.8
益处多	25%	81%
利弊均衡	37%	9%
害处多	20%	7%
无意见	18%	3%

下面哪一项，如果正确最有助于解释人们对科学对人类社会影响的看法的变化？

(A) 这两个调查报告的调查对象是那些定期收看黄金时间电视节目的人，一个每周一次的，在黄金时间播出的片名为"科学的奇迹"的创新电视连续剧在1992年1月首次广泛公演后逐渐赢得了观众。

(B) 这两个调查报告的调查对象是接受过大学教育的成年人。一篇发表于1992年7月的名叫"国家的学校状况"的报告说明学生们对科学课程的兴趣自1982年以来呈上升趋势。

(C) 这两个调查报告是在一个郊区的购物区进行的，这个购物区与一个在1992年停止生产的公司相邻。该公司是因产品具有未预料到的有害影响受到控告而被迫停止经营的。

(D) 两个调查表被寄给了两个大小一样的

of the population, after returning the 1991 survey forms, respondents were sent discount coupons for food products, and after returning the 1992 survey forms, respondents were sent a pamphlet on recycling.

(E) The surveys questioned first-year college students across the country, and the people who did the questioning were all research scientists.

22. Which of the following most logically completes the argument below?

Alone among living species, human beings experience adolescence, a period of accelerated physical growth prior to full maturity. Whether other hominid species, which are now all extinct and are known only through the fossil record, went through adolescence cannot be known, since _____.

(A) the minimum acceleration in physical growth that would indicate adolescence might differ according to species

(B) the fossil record, though steadily expanding, will always remain incomplete

(C) detecting the adolescent growth spurt requires measurements on the same individual at different ages

(D) complete skeletons of extinct hominids are extremely rare

(E) human beings might be the first species to benefit from the survival advantages, if any, conferred by adolescence

23.

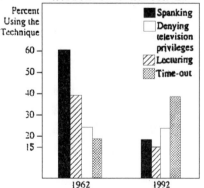

DISCIPLINARY TECHNIQUES USED BY NORTH AMERICAN PARENTS OF CHILDREN UNDER TWELVE 1962 SURVEY VS. 1992 SURVEY

The time-out technique involves removing the child from an undesirable situation in order to let the child think things over. Over the last two decades, family doctors have been advocating this technique as preferable to spanking, which is now known to be potentially injurious and no more effective.

抽样人口，寄回1991年调查表的应答者被赠送了一张食品打折券，寄回1992年调查表的应答者被赠送了一本环保小册子。

(E) 这两个调查报告的调查对象是这个国家的大学一年级的学生，那些进行这两个调查的人都是做研究的科学家。

以下哪一项能最合乎逻辑地完成下段论述？

在所有生物中只有人类要经历青春期，即在完全成熟前的一段身体加速发育的时间，其他现已灭绝的只能从化石中研究的灵长目动物是否也有青春期就不得而知了，因为：

(A) 身体发育的最低速度表明青春期可能因物种不同而不同。

(B) 化石记录虽然仍在不断增加，但总会是不完整的。

(C) 检测青春期迅速发育需要对同一个人的不同年龄段进行测量。

(D) 已绝迹的灵长目动物的完整骨架极端稀有。

(E) 人类可能是第一种（如果有的话）在适者生存的环境中得益于青春期的生物。

北美家长教育12岁以下孩子方法之比较：1962与1992年调查

■体罚
□剥夺看电视的权利
▨说教
▩反省

反省方法是让孩子离开不合意的环境，让他仔细思考一下。在过去20年中，家庭医生已经在倡导这种方法优于体罚，现在众所周知，体罚有潜在的危害且无效。

Which of the following can properly be concluded from the data presented in the graph?

(A) The 1962 survey was based on a larger sample than the 1992 survey was.

(B) In the period between the surveys, denying television privileges was never the disciplinary technique most popular with parents.

(C) The four disciplinary techniques featured in the graph were the only disciplinary techniques named by parents in either survey.

(D) The 1962 survey allowed parents to name more than one disciplinary technique, but the 1992 survey may not have allowed this.

(E) In the period between the surveys, there were no significant changes in the popularity of lecturing children as a disciplinary method.

24. Which of the following most logically completes the argument below?

In recent years, the proportion of car buyers who buy new cars rather than used cars has declined. Some consumers have attributed this change to an increase in new-car prices. As evidence of the price increase, they cite figures that show that, even adjusting for inflation, the price that the buyer of a new car pays, on average, is far higher now than a few years ago. This evidence is unpersuasive, however, because _____.

(A) the value of a car that is bought new declines much more rapidly than does the value of a car that is bought used

(B) after someone has bought a car, it might be several years before that person next buys a car

(C) a decline in the proportion of car buyers who buy new cars must necessarily mean that the proportion who buy used cars has increased

(D) the relative increase in used-car sales might be explained by the decisions of only a small proportion of all car buyers

(E) the change in the average price paid for a new car could result solely from more people's rejecting inexpensive new cars in favor of used cars

由图中数据可合理推断出下列哪一项?

(A) 1962年的调查基于的样本数量比1992年的调查大。

(B) 在两次调查之间的这段时间剥夺看电视的权利绝不会是父母亲们最常用的惩戒手段。

(C) 图中所示的四种惩戒手段是在两次调查中父母亲们提出的所有的惩戒手段。

(D) 1962年的调查允许父母提出多种教育方法,而1992年的调查可能不允许这样。

(E) 在两次调查之间的这段时间,把对孩子进行说教作为一种惩戒手段而经常加以使用的偏好程度没有显著的变化。

下列哪一项能最合逻辑地完成以下论述?

近年来,购车者中买新车而不买二手车的人的比例下降了。一些消费者将该变化归因于新车价格的上升。作为价格上升的证据,他们引用了一些数字来表明,即使经过对通货膨胀因素的调整之后,现在消费者购买新车的平均价格也比几年前高得多,然而,这一证据并没有说服力,因为:

(A) 新车的价值比二手车的价值要贬值得更快。

(B) 某人买了一辆车以后,可能要过好几年才再买一辆。

(C) 买新车的人的比例减少必然意味着买二手车的人的比例增加了。

(D) 二手车销量的相对增加,可能仅由所有买车者中的一小部分人的决定来解释。

(E) 每辆新车平均价格的变化可能仅仅归因于有更多的人因喜欢二手车而拒绝便宜的新车。

25.

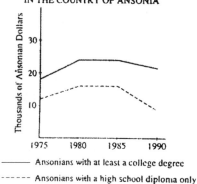

AVERAGE PER CAPITA YEARLY EARNINGS
FOR TWO POPULATION GROUPS
IN THE COUNTRY OF ANSONIA

——— Ansonians with at least a college degree

- - - - - Ansonians with a high school diploma only

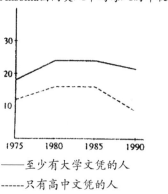

Ansonia国两类人平均每人的年收入

———至少有大学文凭的人

------只有高中文凭的人

Which of the following, if true, gives the best explanation for the growing disparity in the earning levels of the two groups in the graph presented above?

(A) Since 1985 there has been a decline in the total number of Ansonians who have only a high school diploma.

(B) Since 1985 the percentage of Ansonians without a college degree who are unemployed has remained relatively constant.

(C) Government financial support for educational research in Ansonia has declined since 1985.

(D) The enactment of generous social security legislation by the Ansonian parliament has allowed many Ansonians with only a high school diploma to retire at full salary at age 63.

(E) The shift in Ansonia from an industrial to a service economy has resulted in a net loss of high-paying jobs traditionally available Ansonians with only a high school diploma.

如果正确, 下列哪项是上图所示两组人的收入水平差距日益增大的最好解释?

(A) 自1985年以来, 只有高中文凭的Ansonia总人数减少了。

(B) 自1985年以来, 没有大学文凭没有工作的Ansonia人的比例一直保持不变。

(C) 自1985年以来, 政府对于Ansonia教育研究的经济资助减少了。

(D) 慷慨的社会保障法的实施使得许多只有高中文凭的Ansonia人在63岁退休后还能拿到全额薪水。

(E) Ansonia由工业经济向服务业经济的转变导致了一些高收入就业机会的净损失, 而这些工作传统上只需有高中文凭的人便可获得。

26. Which of the following best completes the passage below?
People buy prestige when they buy a premium product. They want to be associated with something special. Mass-marketing techniques and price-reduction strategies should not be used because _____.

(A) affluent purchasers currently represent a shrinking portion of the population of all purchasers

(B) continued sales depend directly on the maintenance of an aura of exclusivity

(C) purchasers of premium products are concerned with the quality as well as with the price of the products

以下哪一项能最好地完成以下短文?
人们购买一种溢价产品时是购买一种声誉, 他们想与一些与众不同的东西联系在一起。不应使用大规模营销技术和降价策略是因为_____。

(A) 富有的购买者目前在所有购买者人数中的比例日益减少。

(B) 持续的销售直接依赖于保持一种具有独特性的声誉。

(C) 溢价产品的购买者关心产品的价格, 也同样关心产品的质量。

(D) expansion of the market niche to include a broader spectrum of consumers will increase profits

(E) manufacturing a premium brand is not necessarily more costly than manufacturing a standard brand of the same product

(D) 扩大营销范围，将更大范围的消费者包括进来，将提高利润。

(E) 生产一种溢价品牌的产品不一定比生产标准品牌的同种产品耗费更多的成本。

注：aura = distinctive atmosphere that seems to surround and be caused by a person or thing（发自某人或某物而环绕其周围的）特殊气氛、氛围

27. In Asia, where palm trees are non-native, the trees' flowers have traditionally been pollinated by hand, which has kept palm fruit productivity unnaturally low. When weevils known to be efficient pollinators of palm flowers were introduced into Asia in 1980, palm fruit productivity increased—by up to fifty percent in some areas—but then decreased sharply in 1984.

Which of the following statements, if true, would best explain the 1984 decrease in productivity?

(A) Prices for palm fruit fell between 1980 and 1984 following the rise in production and a concurrent fall in demand.

(B) Imported trees are often more productive than native trees because the imported ones have left behind their pests and diseases in their native lands.

(C) Rapid increases in productivity tend to deplete trees of nutrients needed for the development of the fruit-producing female flowers.

(D) The weevil population in Asia remained at approximately the same level between 1980 and 1984.

(E) Prior to 1980 another species of insect pollinated the Asian palm trees, but not as efficiently as the species of weevil that was introduced in 1980.

亚洲并非棕榈树的原产地，在这儿传统上用手工为棕榈树的花授粉，这种办法使棕榈果实产量非常低。当1980年将作为棕榈花的有效授粉者而被熟知的象鼻虫引进亚洲后，棕榈果实产量上升——在某些地区上升了50%——但在1984年急剧下降。

以下哪一项，如果是正确的，将对1984年产量的下降提出最好的解释？

(A) 随着产量的上升同时需求下降，1980年到1984年之间，棕榈果实的价格持续下降。

(B) 进口树经常比本地树产量更大，因为进口树将它们的害虫与疾病留在它们本国的土地上。

(C) 产量的迅速提高耗尽了培育果实的雌花生长需要的营养物质。

(D) 在1980年到1984年之间，亚洲象鼻虫的数量保持在相同的水平上。

(E) 在1980年以前由其他种类的昆虫为亚洲棕榈授粉，但不如1980年引入的象鼻虫有效。

28. In January there was a large drop in the number of new houses sold, because interest rates for mortgages were falling and many consumers were waiting to see how low the rates would go. This large sales drop was accompanied by a sharp rise in the average price of new houses sold.

Which of the following, if true, best explains the sharp rise in the average price of new houses?

(A) Sales of higher-priced houses were unaffected by the sales drop because their purchasers have fewer constraints limiting the total amount they pay.

一月份出售的新房子数量大幅下降了，因为按揭贷款的利率正在降低，许多消费者在等待着看利率会低到什么程度，销售的大幅下降伴随着所售新房子平均价格的激增。

下面哪个，如果正确，最好地解释了新房子平均价格的激增？

(A) 价格较高的房子的销售没有受销量下降的影响，因为它们的买主较少有制约他们支付的总额的限制。

(B) Labor agreements of builders with construction unions are not due to expire until the next January.

(C) The prices of new houses have been rising slowly over the past three years because there is an increasing shortage of housing.

(D) There was a greater amount of moderate-priced housing available for resale by owners during January than in the preceding three months.

(E) Interest rates for home mortgages are expected to rise sharply later in the year if predictions of increased business activity in general prove to be accurate.

(B) 建筑商和建筑工会的劳动协议到明年一月才到期。

(C) 过去三年中，新房子的价格一直在缓慢上涨，因为住房不足的严重程度增加了。

(D) 一月份比先前的三个月中有更多的房屋所有者再次出售他们的中等价位的房子。

(E) 如果总体商业活动增加的预测被证明是准确的，今年晚些时候的房屋按揭贷款利率预计会大幅上升。

29. Extinction is a process that can depend on a variety of ecological, geographical, and physiological variables. These variables affect different species of organisms in different ways, and should, therefore, yield a random pattern of extinction. However, the fossil record shows that extinction occurs in a surprisingly definite pattern, with many species vanishing at the same time.

Which of the following, if true, forms the best basis for at lest a partial explanation of the patterned extinction revealed by the fossil record?

(A) Major episodes of extinction can result from widespread environmental disturbances that affect numerous different species.

(B) Certain extinction episodes selectively affect organisms with particular sets of characteristics unique to their species.

(C) Some species become extinct because of accumulated gradual changes in their local environments.

(D) In geologically recent times, for which there is no fossil record, human intervention has changed the pattern of extinction.

(E) Species that are widely dispersed are the least likely to become extinct.

生物种类的灭绝是一个依赖于生态、地理和生理变量的过程。这些变量以不同的方式影响不同种类的有机体，因而灭绝的方式应该是杂乱无章的。然而，化石记录显示生物以一种令人惊奇的确定的方式灭绝，很多种群同时消失。

以下哪一项，如果正确，为对于化石记录所显示的灭绝方式提供至少一个部分的解释形成了最好的基础？

(A) 主要的灭绝发生期是由于影响很多不同种群的范围很广的环境变化引起的。

(B) 某些灭绝发生期有选择性地影响那些拥有它们种群独一无二特征的有机体。

(C) 一些种群灭绝了是因为它们的当地环境逐渐累积的变化。

(D) 在地理上最近一段时间，没有什么化石记录，人类的干预已经改变了灭绝的方式。

(E) 那些广泛分布的种群最不可能灭绝。

30. Many institutions of higher education suffer declining enrollments during periods of economic slowdown. At two-year community colleges, however, enrollment figures boom during these periods when many people have less money and there is more competition for jobs.

Each of the following, if true, helps to explain the enrollment increases in two-year community colleges described above EXCEPT:

许多高等教育机构在经济增长放缓时期面临招收学生人数下降的问题，但是在两年制社区大学里，这段时期当许多人收入减少并且为获得工作的竞争更加激烈时，招收学生的人数大量增加。

以下每一项，如果是正确的，都有助于解释以上描述的两年制社区大学招生人数增加的情况，除了：

(A) During periods of economic slowdown, two-year community colleges are more likely than four-year colleges to prepare their students for the jobs that are still available.

(B) During periods of economic prosperity, graduates of two-year community colleges often continue their studies at four-year colleges.

(C) Tuition at most two-year community colleges is a fraction of that at four-year colleges.

(D) Two-year community colleges devote more resources than do other colleges to attracting those students especially affected by economic slowdowns.

(E) Students at two-year community colleges, but not those at most four-year colleges, can control the cost of their studies by choosing the number of courses they take each term.

31. Hardin argued that grazing land held in common (that is, open to any user) would always be used less carefully than private grazing land. Each rancher would be tempted to overuse common land because the benefits would accrue to the individual, while the costs of reduced land quality that results from overuse would be spread among all users. But a study comparing 217 million acres of common grazing land with 433 million acres of private grazing land showed that the common land was in better condition.

Which of the following, if true and known by the ranchers, would best help explain the results of the study?

(A) With private grazing land, both the costs and the benefits of overuse fall to the individual user.

(B) The cost in reduced land quality that is attributable to any individual user is less easily measured with common land than it is with private land.

(C) An individual who overuses common grazing land might be able to achieve higher returns than other users can, with the result that he or she would obtain a competitive advantage.

(D) If one user of common land overuses it even slightly, the other users are likely to do so even more, with the consequence that the costs to each user outweigh the benefits.

(E) There are more acres of grazing land held privately than there are held in common.

(A) 在经济增长放慢时期，两年制社区大学比四年制大学能更好地使学生们为仍能找到的工作做准备。

(B) 在经济繁荣时期，两年制社区大学的毕业生经常到四年制大学里继续学习。

(C) 大多数两年制社区大学的学费是四年制大学的一小部分。

(D) 两年制社区大学比其他大学投入更多的资源来吸引那些受经济增长放慢影响很大的学生。

(E) 两年制社区大学的学生可以通过选择每学期上的课程的数量来控制他们的学习费用，但大多数四年制大学的学生不能这样做。

Hardin争论说，人们使用共同拥有的（即对任何使用者开放的）牧场比使用私人的牧场更不注意。每个放牧者都有过度使用公地的冲动，因为从中获得的利益将归于个人，而由于过度使用土地引起的土地质量下降的成本由所有使用者分摊。但一项研究比较了2.17亿英亩的公用牧场和4.33亿英亩的私人牧场，结果表明公用牧场的条件更好。

以下哪一项，如果是正确的并为放牧者所知，将最有助于解释该项研究的结果？

(A) 对于私人牧地来说，过度使用的成本和收益都落在使用者个人身上。

(B) 归于每个个人使用者的土地质量下降的成本，对于公地比对于私人土地来说更不容易度量。

(C) 一个过度使用公用牧地的个人可能比其他使用者取得更高的收益，因此他或她会获得一种竞争优势。

(D) 如果公地的一个使用者即使只是稍微地过度使用，其他的使用者就会变本加厉地这样做，结果是每个使用者的成本超过了收益。

(E) 私人拥有的牧地比共同拥有的牧地多。

32. The fossil record shows that the climate of North America warmed and dried at the end of the Pleistocene period. Most of the species of large mammals then living on the continent became extinct, but the smaller mammalian species survived. Which of the following, if true, provides the best basis for an explanation of the contrast described above between species of large mammals and species of small mammals?

(A) Individual large mammals can, in general, travel further than small mammals and so are more able to migrate in search of a hospitable environment.

(B) The same pattern of comparative success in smaller, as opposed to larger, species that is observed in mammals is also found in bird species of the same period.

(C) The fossil record from the end of Pleistocene period is as clear for small mammals as it is for large mammals.

(D) Larger mammals have greater food and space requirements than smaller mammals and are thus less able to withstand environmental change.

(E) Many more of the species of larger mammals than of the species of smaller mammals living in North America in that period had originated in climates that were warmer than was that of North America before the end of the Pleistocene period.

33. For the safety-conscious Swedish market, a United States manufacturer of desktop computers developed a special display screen that produces a much weaker electromagnetic field surrounding the user than do ordinary screens. Despite an advantage in this respect over its competitors, the manufacturer is introducing the screen into the United States market without advertising it as a safety improvement.

Which of the following, if true, provides a rationale for the manufacturer's approach to advertising the screen in the United States?

(A) Many more desktop computers are sold each year in the United States market than are sold in the Swedish market.

(B) The manufacturer does not want its competitors to become aware of the means by which the company has achieved this advance in technology.

(C) Most business and scientific purchasers of desktop computers expect to replace such equipment eventually as better technology becomes available on the market.

(D) An emphasis on the comparative safety of the new screen would call into question the safety of the many screens

化石记录显示，北美的气候在更新世时期结束时变暖变干燥了。当时在该大陆生活的大多数种类的大型哺乳动物灭绝了，但较小的哺乳类动物存活了下来。

下面哪个，如果正确，为以上描述的大型和小型哺乳动物种类之间的对比的解释提供了最好的基础？

(A) 一般来讲，单个大型哺乳动物能比小型哺乳动物运动得更远，所以更能迁移去寻找一个合适的环境。

(B) 同样的在哺乳动物中观察到的小型动物相对于大型动物的成功模式也可以在同一时期的鸟类中发现。

(C) 更新世结束时的化石记录对小型哺乳动物和大型哺乳动物来讲都很清楚。

(D) 较大的哺乳动物比较小的哺乳动物有更多的食物和空间要求，所以承受环境变化的能力更小。

(E) 那个时期生活在北美的哺乳动物中，起源于比北美在更新世纪结束之前的气候更温暖的气候中的大型哺乳动物的种类要比小型哺乳动物的种类多得多。

针对很重视安全性的瑞典市场，美国的一家台式计算机制造商开发出了一种特别的显示屏，这种显示屏产生的环绕使用者的电磁场比正常的屏幕产生的电磁场弱很多。尽管比其竞争者具有这方面的优势，该制造商在把这种显示屏引入美国市场时并未在广告中宣扬其是一种改进了安全性的产品。

下面哪个，如果正确，为该制造商在美国做这种显示屏广告的手段提供了根本理由？

(A) 每年在美国市场上销售的台式计算机比在瑞典市场上销售的台式计算机多得多。

(B) 该制造商并不想让其竞争对手知道本公司是如何实现在技术上的进步的。

(C) 当市场上更好的技术成为可行时，台式计算机的大多数商业和学术购买者预期最终会更换这些机器。

(D) 对新屏幕相对安全性能的强调会对该

the manufacturer has already sold in the United States.

(E) Concern has been expressed in the United States over the health effects of the large electromagnetic fields surrounding electric power lines.

34. In the 1970's there was an oversupply of college graduates. The oversupply caused the average annual income of college graduates to fall to a level only 18 percent greater than that of workers with only high school diplomas. By the late 1980's the average annual income of college graduates was 43 percent higher than that of workers with only high school diplomas, even though between the 1970's and the late 1980's the supply of college graduates did not decrease.

Which of the following, if true in the late 1980's, best reconciles the apparent discrepancy described above?

(A) The economy slowed, thus creating a decreased demand for college graduates.

(B) The quality of high school education improved.

(C) Compared to the 1970's, a greater number of high schools offered vocational guidance programs for their students.

(D) The proportion of the population with at least a college-level education increased.

(E) There was for the first time in 20 years an oversupply of job seekers with only high school diplomas.

35. Which of the following, if true, best completes the argument below?

Comparisons of the average standards of living of the citizens of two countries should reflect the citizens' comparative access to goods and services. Reliable figures in a country's own currency for the average income of its citizens are easily obtained. But it is difficult to get an accurate comparison of average standards of living from these figures, because _____.

(A) there are usually no figures comparing how much of two different currencies must be spent in order to purchase a given quantity of goods and services

(B) wage levels for the same job vary greatly from country to country, depending on cultural as well as on purely economic factors

(C) these figures must be calculated by dividing the gross national product of a country by the size of its population

(D) comparative access to goods and services is only one of several factors relevant in determining quality of life

制造商已经在美国销售的屏幕的安全性提出质疑。

(E) 在美国已经有人开始关注环绕高压电线的巨大电磁场对健康的影响。

20世纪70年代出现了大学毕业生的过度供给，过度的供给使大学毕业生的平均年收入降到了比只持有高中文凭的工人仅高18%的水平。到了20世纪80年代，大学毕业生的平均年收入比只持有高中文凭的工人高43%，尽管20世纪70年代到80年代后期大学毕业生的供给量没有下降。

下面哪个，如果在20世纪80年代后期是正确的，最好地调解了上述明显的分歧？

(A) 经济放慢了，从而使对大学毕业生的需求减少了。

(B) 高中教育的质量提高了。

(C) 与20世纪70年代相比，更多的高中为它们的学生提供了职业指导计划。

(D) 至少受过一种大学水平教育的人所占的比例上升了。

(E) 20年来第一次出现了仅有高中文凭的求职者的过度供给。

下面哪个，如果正确，最好地完成了以下的论证：

对两个国家的居民平均生活水平的比较可以反映居民获取产品和服务的相对情况。以一国货币表示的其居民的平均收入的可靠数字可以轻易得到。但从这些数字中很难得到平均生活水平的准确比较。因为

(A) 通常没有数字来比较为购买一定数量的产品和服务需要花费多少两种不同货币。

(B) 同样工作的工资水平，因依赖于文化和纯粹的经济因素而在各国之间相差很大。

(C) 这些数字必须用一国的国民总收入除以其人口来计算。

(D) 获取产品和服务的相对情况只是决定生活质量的若干相关因素中的一个。

(E) the wealth, and hence the standard of living, of a country's citizens is very closely related to their income

36. Since 1975 there has been in the United States a dramatic decline in the incidence of traditional childhood diseases such as measles. This decline has been accompanied by an increased incidence of Peterson's disease, a hitherto rare viral infection, among children. Few adults, however, have been affected by the disease.

Which of the following, if true, would best help to explain the increased incidence of Peterson's disease among children?

(A) Hereditary factors determine in part the degree to which a person is susceptible to the virus that causes Peterson's disease.

(B) The decrease in traditional childhood diseases and the accompanying increase in Peterson's disease have not been found in any other country.

(C) Children who contract measles develop an immunity to the virus that causes Peterson's disease.

(D) Persons who did not contract measles in childhood might contract measles in adulthood, in which case the consequences of the disease would generally be more severe.

(E) Those who have contracted Peterson's disease are at increased risk of contracting chicken pox.

37. The number of musicians employed to play accompaniment for radio and television commercials has sharply decreased over the past ten years. This has occurred even though the number of commercials produced each year has not significantly changed for the last ten years.

Which of the following, if it occurred during the past ten years, would contribute LEAST to an explanation of the facts above?

(A) The type of music most popular for use in commercials has changed from a type that requires a large number of instruments to a type that requires very few instruments.

(B) There has been an increase in the number of commercials that use only the spoken word and sound effects, rather than musical accompaniment.

(C) There has been an increase in the number of commercials that use a synthesizer, an instrument on which one musician can reproduce the sound of many musicians playing together.

(E) 一国居民的财富以及生活水平与他们的收入紧密联系着。

1975年以来，美国的麻疹等传统儿童疾病的发病率已经有了显著的下降。这一下降的同时伴随着儿童中间Peterson病———一种迄今为止罕见的病毒感染——发病率的上升。但是，很少有成年人被这种疾病侵袭。

下面哪个，如果正确，最能帮助解释儿童中间Peterson病发病率的上升？

(A) 遗传因素部分决定了一个人易受导致Peterson病的病毒感染的程度。

(B) 传统儿童疾病的减少和与之相随的Peterson病的增加没有在其他任何国家发现。

(C) 得过麻疹的儿童形成了对导致Peterson病的病毒的免疫力。

(D) 儿童时期没有得麻疹的人到成年时可能得麻疹，在这种情况下疾病的后果一般会更加严重。

(E) 那些得了Peterson病的人得水痘的危险增加了。

过去10年来受雇为广播和电视中穿插的广告配乐的音乐家数量急剧减少了。尽管过去10年中每年制造的广告数量并没有显著变化，这种情况还是发生了。

下面哪个，如果它在过去的10年中发生了，最不能解释上述事实？

(A) 在广告中使用最流行的音乐类型已经从需要很多乐器的类型变成了需要非常少的乐器的类型。

(B) 只使用口语词汇和声音效果而不是音乐配乐的广告数量增加了。

(C) 使用合成乐器———一种一位音乐家可在上面复制许多音乐家一起演奏的声音的乐器———的广告数量增加了。

(D) There has been an increase in the number of commercials that use prerecorded music as their only source of music.

(E) There has been an increase in the number of commercials that use musicians just starting in the music industry rather than musicians experienced in accompanying commercials.

38. Financing for a large construction project was provided by a group of banks. When the money was gone before the project was completed, the banks approved additional loans. Now, with funds used up again and completion still not at hand, the banks refuse to extend further loans, although without those loans, the project is doomed.

Which of the following, if true, best explains why the bank's current reaction is different from their reaction in the previous instance of depletion of funds?

(A) The banks have reassessed the income potential of the completed project and have concluded that total income general would be less than total interest due on the old plus the needed new loans.

(B) The banks have identified several other projects that offer faster repayment of the principal if loans are approved now to get those projects started.

(C) The banks had agreed with the borrowers that the construction loans would be secured by the completed project.

(D) The cost overruns were largely due to unforeseeable problems that arose in the most difficult phase of the construction work.

(E) The project stimulated the development and refinement of several new construction techniques, which will make it easier and cheaper to carry out similar projects in the future.

39. An experiment was done in which human subjects recognize a pattern within a matrix of abstract designs and then select another design that completes that pattern. The results of the experiment were surprising. The lowest expenditure of energy in neurons in the brain was found in those subjects who performed most successfully in the experiments.

Which of the following hypotheses best accounts for the findings of the experiment?

(D) 使用先录好音的音乐作为唯一音乐来源的广告数量增加了。

(E) 使用刚进入音乐行业而不使用在为广告配乐方面有经验的音乐家的广告的数量增加了。

为一个大型建筑项目进行的融资是由一群银行提供的。当资金在项目完成前用完时，银行批准了进一步的贷款。现在，随着资金再度用完而项目仍未完成，银行拒绝增加进一步的贷款，虽然没有这些贷款该项目就泡汤了。

下面哪个，如果正确，最好地解释了为什么银行现在的反应和它们先前在资金用完的情况下的反应不同？

(A) 银行重新评估了完成后的项目的潜在收入，并且得出结论认为可产生的总收入会低于旧贷款加上需要的新贷款的总利息。

(B) 银行发现了几个其他的项目，如果现在批准对它们的贷款让这些项目启动，这些项目能促使本金更快地回收。

(C) 银行和借款方一致同意，建筑贷款以完成的项目作为担保。

(D) 成本超支主要是因为建筑工程最困难的阶段出现了没有预见的问题。

(E) 该项目促进了几个新建筑技术的发展和改进，这些技术的发展和改进会使将来相同项目的执行更加容易和便宜。

有人做了一个实验，在实验中，受试人从一个抽象设计的模型中识别出一个式样，然后选择另一个设计来完善这个式样，实验的结果是令人吃惊的。在实验中表现最成功的受试人被发现其大脑神经细胞消耗的能量是最低的。

下面哪个假设最好地解释了这个实验的发现？

(A) The neurons of the brain react less when a subject is trying to recognize patterns than when the subject is doing other kinds of reasoning.

(B) Those who performed best in the experiment experienced more satisfaction when working with abstract patterns than did those who performed less well.

(C) People who are better at abstract pattern recognition have more energy-efficient neural connections.

(D) The energy expenditure of the subjects brains increases when a design that completes the initially recognized pattern is determined.

(E) The task of completing a given design is more capable performed by athletes, whose energy expenditure is lower when they are at rest than is that of the general population.

(A) 当受试人试图识别式样时，大脑神经细胞要比当受试人做其他推理时反应得少。

(B) 在实验中表现最好的人在处理抽象式样时比表现差一点的人更加满意。

(C) 更善于识别抽象式样的人有更多的能量上有效的神经联系。

(D) 当完善最初被识别的式样的设计被确定时，被实验人大脑消耗的能量增加了。

(E) 运动员更适合完善某个既定设计的任务，他们休息时的能量消耗低于一般人的能量消耗。

40. One way to judge the performance of a company is to compare it with other companies. This technique, commonly called "benchmarking," permits the manager of a company to discover better industrial practices and can provide a justification for the adoption of good practices.

Any of the following, if true, is a valid reason for benchmarking the performance of a company against companies with which it is not in competition rather than against competitors EXCEPT:

(A) Comparisons with competitors are most likely to focus on practices that the manager making the comparisons already employs.

(B) Getting "inside" information about the unique practices of competitors is particularly difficult.

(C) Since companies that compete with each other are likely to have comparable levels of efficiency, only benchmarking against noncompetitors is likely to reveal practices that would aid in beating competitors.

(D) Managers are generally more receptive to new ideas that they find outside their own industry.

(E) Much of the success of good companies is due to their adoption of practices that take advantage of the special circumstances of their products of markets.

评判一家公司业绩的一种方法是将其与其他公司进行对比。这种技术，通常称为"对照基准点"，它使公司经理可以发现更好的行业行动并且能为采取好的行动提供正当的理由。

下面每个，如果正确，都是把一家公司的业绩和不与之形成竞争的公司而非竞争者进行基准点对照的正当理由，除了

(A) 和竞争者的对比最可能集中在进行对比的经理已经采取的行动上。

(B) 得到关于竞争者的独特行为的信息是相当困难的。

(C) 因为互相竞争的公司可能有可与之相比的效率水平，只有与非竞争者进行基准点对照才可能发现有助于击败竞争者的行动。

(D) 经理们一般对从本行业以外发现的想法更易接受。

(E) 许多优秀公司的成功应归因于它们采取了可利用它们的产品所在市场的特别环境的行动。

41. Sixty adults were asked to keep a diary of their meals, including what they consumed, when, and in the company of how many people. It was found that at meals with which they drank alcoholic beverages, they consumed about 175 calories

要求60个成年人对他们的饮食记日记，日记的内容包括他们吃些什么，在什么时候以及和多少人一块吃。结果发现，在含有酒精饮料的饮食中，他们从非酒精

more from nonalcoholic sources than they did at meals with which they did not drink alcoholic beverages.

Each of the following, if true, contributes to an explanation of the difference in caloric intake EXCEPT:

(A) Diners spent a much longer time at meals served with alcohol than they did at those served without alcohol.

(B) The meals eaten later in the day tended to be larger than those eaten earlier in the day, and later meals were more likely to include alcohol.

(C) People eat more when there are more people present at the meal, and more people tended to be present at meals served with alcohol than at meals served without alcohol.

(D) The meals that were most carefully prepared and most attractively served tended to be those at which alcoholic beverages were consumed.

(E) At meals that included alcohol, relatively more of the total calories consumed came from carbohydrates and relatively fewer of them came from fats and proteins.

42. A tree's age can be determined by counting the annual growth rings in its trunk. Each ring represents one year, and the ring's thickness reveals the relative amount of rainfall that year. Archaeologists successfully used annual rings to determine the relative ages of ancient tombs at Pazyryk. Each tomb was constructed from freshly cut logs, and the tombs' builders were constrained by tradition to use only logs from trees growing in the sacred Pazyryk Valley.

Which one of the following, if true, contributes most to an explanation of the archaeologists' success in using annual rings to establish the relative ages of the tombs at the Pazyryk site?

(A) The Pazyryk tombs were all robbed during ancient times, but breakage of the tombs' seals allowed the seepage of water, which soon froze permanently, thereby preserving the tombs' remaining artifacts.

(B) The Pazyryk Valley, surrounded by extremely high mountains, has a distinctive yearly pattern of rainfall, and so trees growing in the Pazyryk Valley have annual rings that are quite distinct from trees growing in nearby valleys.

(C) Each log in the Pazyryk tombs has among its rings a distinctive sequence of twelve annual rings representing six drought years followed by three rainy years and three more drought years.

类食物来源中摄入的热量比他们在不含酒精饮料的饮食中摄入的热量多175卡。

下面每一项，如果正确，除了哪一项之外都有助于解释摄入的热量的不同？

(A) 就餐者在有酒时吃饭用的时间比没酒时用的时间长。

(B) 一天中，吃得较晚的饭倾向于比吃得较早的饭丰盛，且吃得较晚的饭包含有酒的可能性大。

(C) 在一餐饭中，吃饭的人越多，人们吃得就越多，而且趋向于桌上有酒，吃饭的人就多；桌上没酒，吃饭的人就少。

(D) 那些精心制作且最具吸引力的饭菜倾向于给就餐者提供含有酒精的饮料。

(E) 在有酒的饭菜中，总的热量摄入中有相对较多的热量来自碳氢化合物，相对较少的热量来自脂肪和蛋白质。

树的年龄可以通过数树干中的年轮来确定。每一年轮代表一年，且每个年轮的厚度可反映那一年降雨量的多少。考古学家们利用年轮已成功地确定了Pazyryk地区的古墓的相对年龄。每个墓都是用新砍下的木材建成的，且受传统约束，古墓的建设者们仅使用生长在神圣的Pazyryk山谷中的树木上的木料。

下面哪一条，如果正确，最有助于解释考古学家们在使用年轮来确定Pazyryk地区的古墓的相对年龄时取得的成功？

(A) 在古代时，Pazyryk地区的墓全部被抢劫，但是这些墓封口的破坏使得水渗入其中，这些水很快就永远地冻结下来，因此这些墓中遗留的人工制品都被保存了下来。

(B) Pazyryk山谷被非常高的山所环绕，具有与众不同的年降雨方式，因此生长在Pazyryk山谷中的树所具有的年轮与生长在附近山谷的树的年轮截然不同。

(C) Pazyryk地区的墓中的每一块木料的年轮中都有一个富有特色的12年轮序列，这12个年轮序列代表了6年的干旱，接着是3年多雨和3年的干旱。

(D) The archaeologists determined that the youngest tree used in any of the tombs was 90 years old and that the oldest tree was 450 years old.

(E) All of the Pazyryk tombs contained cultural artifacts that can be dated to roughly 2300 years ago.

43. In essence, all rent-control policies involve specifying a maximum rent that a landlord may charge for a dwelling. The rationale for controlling rents is to protect tenants in situations where limited supply will cause rents to rise sharply in the face of increased demand. However, although rent control may help some tenants in the short run, it affects the rental-housing market adversely in the long run because landlords become reluctant to maintain the quality of their existing properties and even more reluctant to have additional rental-housing units built.

Which one of the following, if true, best explains the landlords' reluctance described above?

(A) Tenants prefer low-quality accommodations with rent control to high-quality accommodations without it.

(B) Rent control makes it very difficult for landlords to achieve reasonable returns on any investments in maintenance or in new construction.

(C) Rent control is a common practice even though it does nothing to alleviate shortages in rental housing.

(D) Rent control is generally introduced for political reasons and it takes political action to have it lifted again.

(E) Tenants prefer rent control to the alternative of receiving direct government subsidies toward rents they cannot afford.

44. The trustees of the Avonbridge summer drama workshop have decided to offer scholarships to the top 10 percent of local applicants and the top 10 percent of nonlocal applicants as judged on the basis of a qualifying audition. They are doing this to ensure that only the applicants with the most highly evaluated auditions are offered scholarships to the program.

Which one of the following points out why the trustees' plan might not be effective in achieving its goal?

(A) The best actors can also apply for admission to another program and then not enroll in the Avonbridge program.

实质上，所有租金管理政策都包含规定一个房东可向房客索要的最高租金。租金管理的基本原理是在对房子的需求增加而房子的供给有限致使租金急剧增加的情况下，来保护房客的利益。然而，尽管租金管理从短期来看能帮助某些房客，但是从长期来看它会对出租房屋市场造成负面影响，这是因为房东将会不情愿维持他们现有房地产的质量，甚至更不愿意额外再建一些供出租的房子。

下面哪一点，如果正确，能最好地解释上面描述的房东的不情愿行为？

(A) 房客喜欢租金管理下的低质量住宿设施，而不喜欢没有租金管理下的高质量的住宿设施。

(B) 租金管理使房东很难从维护或建筑新房的任何投资中取得公正合理的收益。

(C) 租金管理是一种常见的习惯做法，尽管它对缓和租房紧张毫无作用。

(D) 租金管理一般是由于政治原因而被引进的，因此它需要政治行为来解除它。

(E) 房客们喜欢租金管理，而不喜欢直接从政府那里接受津贴来补偿他们付不起的租金。

Avonbrige夏季戏剧研讨班的评委们决定根据申请者试演的好坏，给10%的最优秀的当地申请者和10%的最优秀的外地申请者提供奖学金。他们这样做是为了确保只向试演中得到最高评价的申请者提供这个项目的奖学金。

下面哪一点指出了为什么评委们的计划不可能有效地达到它的目的？

(A) 最好的演员也可申请加入另一项目，于是就不能加入Avonbrige项目。

(B) Audition materials that produce good results for one actor may disadvantage another, resulting in inaccurate assessment.

(C) The top 10 percent of local and nonlocal applicants might not need scholarships to the Avonbridge program.

(D) Some of the applicants who are offered scholarships should have less highly evaluated auditions than some of the applicants who are not offered scholarships.

(E) Dividing applicants into local and nonlocal groups is unfair because it favors nonsocial applicants.

45. Rumored declines in automobile-industry revenues are exaggerated. It is true that automobile manufacturers' share of the industry's revenues fell from 65 percent two years ago to 50 percent today, but over the same period suppliers of automobile parts had their share increase from 15 percent to 20 percent and service companies (for example, distributors, dealers, and repairers) had their share increase from 20 percent to 30 percent.

Which one of the following best indicates why the statistics given above provide by themselves no evidence for the conclusion they are intended to support?

(A) The possibility is left open that the statistics for manufacturer's share of revenues come from a different source than the other statistics.

(B) No matter what changes the automobile industry's overall revenues undergo, the total of all shares of these revenues must be 100 percent.

(C) No explanation is given for why the revenue shares of different sectors of the industry changed.

(D) Manufacturers and parts companies depend for their revenue on dealers' success in selling cars.

(E) Revenues are an important factor but are not the only factor in determining profits.

46. Police statistics have shown that automobile antitheft devices reduce the risk of car theft, but a statistical study of automobile theft by the automobile insurance industry claims that cars equipped with antitheft devices are, paradoxically, more likely to be stolen than cars that are not so equipped:

Which one of the following, if true, does the most to resolve the apparent paradox?

（B）对一个演员会产生良好效果的试演材料可能对另一个演员来说是不利的，从而导致了评价的不准确性。

（C）10%的最优秀的当地和外地申请者可能不需要Avonbrige项目的奖学金。

（D）有些获得奖学金的申请者的试演得到的评价可能没有某些没获得奖学金的申请者得到的评价高。

（E）把申请者分成当地组和外地组是不公平的，因为它偏袒了外地申请者。

传闻中的汽车工业收入的下降是言过其实的，汽车制造商在整个行业收入中的份额实际已从两年前的65%降到了今天的50%，但是在同一段时间内汽车零部件供应商的收入份额却从15%增加到20%，服务公司（例如，分配商，销售商和修理工）的收入份额也从20%上升到30%。

下面哪一条能最好地揭示为什么上面给出的统计数字自身不能提供它们要支持的结论的证据？

（A）这样的可能性是显而易见的，即制造商的收入份额与其他统计数字具有不同的出处。

（B）不管汽车工业总的收入经历什么样的变化，所有这些收入份额的总和必须是100%。

（C）没有给出解释为什么这个行业不同部门的收入份额会发生改变。

（D）制造商和零部件公司的收入依赖于销售商成功地销售汽车。

（E）收入是决定利润的重要因素，但并不是唯一的因素。

警察局的统计数字显示汽车防盗装置降低了汽车被盗的危险性，但是汽车保险业对被盗汽车的统计研究则声称装备了防盗装置的汽车相反比那些没装防盗装置的汽车更有可能被偷。

下面哪一条，如果正确，最能解决上述的明显矛盾？

(A) Owners of stolen cars almost invariably report the theft immediately to the police but tend to delay notifying their insurance company, in the hope that the vehicle will be recovered.

(B) Most cars that are stolen are not equipped with antitheft devices, and most cars that are equipped with antitheft devices are not stolen.

(C) The most common automobile antitheft devices are audible alarms, which typically produce ten false alarms for every actual attempted theft.

(D) Automobile owners who have particularly theft-prone cars and live in areas of greatest incidence of car theft are those who are most likely to have antitheft devices installed.

(E) Most automobile thefts are the work of professional thieves against whose efforts antitheft devices offer scant protection.

(A) 被盗汽车的失主几乎总是在案发以后立即向警察局报告失窃事件，但是却倾向于延缓通知他们的保险公司，他们希望他们丢失的车能被找回来。

(B) 大多数被盗的汽车都没装备汽车防盗装置，而大多数装备了汽车防盗装置的汽车都没被盗。

(C) 最常见的汽车防盗装置是可听得见的报警器，这些报警器对每一起实际的试图偷车事件通常发出10个虚假的警报。

(D) 那些最有可能给他们的汽车装备防盗系统的人都是汽车特别容易被盗的人，且都居住在汽车被盗事件发生率最高的地方。

(E) 大多数的汽车被盗事件都是职业窃贼所为，对他们的能力来说，防盗装置所提供的保护是不够的。

47. Much of the best scientific research of today shows that many of the results of earlier scientific work that was regarded in its time as good are in fact mistaken. Yet despite the fact that scientists are above all concerned to discover the truth, it is valuable for today's scientists to study firsthand accounts of earlier scientific work.

Which one of the following, if true, would best reconcile the two statements above?

(A) Many firsthand accounts of earlier, flawed scientific work are not generally known to be mistaken.

(B) Lessons in scientific methodology can be learned by seeing how earlier scientific work was carried out, sometimes especially when the results of that work are known to be incorrect.

(C) Scientists can make valuable contributions to the scientific work of their time even if the results of their work will later be shown to be mistaken.

(D) There are many scientists today who are not thoroughly familiar with earlier scientific research.

(E) Some of the better scientific research of today does not directly address earlier scientific work.

今天，许多最好的科学研究工作都揭示早些时候的科研工作的结果在那时被认为是正确的，实际上都是错误的。然而，尽管科学家们首要关心的事情是发现真理，但是对今天的科学家来说，研究早期科研工作的第一手报道仍是非常有价值的。

下面哪一项，如果正确，能最好地使上面的两个陈述相一致？

(A) 许多早些时候的第一手有缺陷的科研工作报道并不被普遍知道是错误的。

(B) 科学方法中的教训可以通过参考早些时候的科研工作是怎样进行的而学得，特别是在有时已经知道那个工作的结果是不正确的情况下。

(C) 科学家们可以对他们那个时代的科学研究做出有益的贡献，即使他们的工作结果后来被证明是错误的。

(D) 今天，有许多科学家对早些时候的科学研究并不完全了解。

(E) 今天的一些较好的科研工作不直接提及早些时候的研究工作。

48. Once consumers recognize that a period of inflation has begun, there is generally an increase in consumer spending. This increase can be readily explained by consumers' desire not to postpone purchases that will surely increase in price. But during protracted periods of inflation, consumers eventually begin to put off making even routine purchases, despite the fact that consumers continue to expect prices to rise and despite the fact that salaries also rise during inflationary periods.

Which one of the following, if true, most helps to explain the apparent inconsistency in consumer behavior described above?

(A) During times of inflation consumers save more money than they do in noninflationary periods.

(B) There is usually a lag between the leading economic indicators' first signaling the onset of an inflationary period and consumers' recognition of its onset.

(C) No generalization that describes human behavior will be true of every type of human behavior.

(D) If significant numbers of consumers are unable to make purchases, prices will eventually fall but salaries will not be directly affected.

(E) Consumers' purchasing power decreases during periods of protracted inflation since salaries do not keep pace with prices.

一旦消费者们认识到一个时期的通货膨胀已经开始。他们普遍都会增加消费。这种增加很容易被消费者们渴望不再推迟购买那些肯定会涨价的商品的现象所解释。尽管存在这样的事实，即消费者们预料到价格在持续上涨，在通货膨胀期间工资也在上涨，但是在长期通货膨胀期间，消费者们最终开始推迟那些甚至是日常生活品的购买。

下面哪一项，如果正确，最能有助于解释上面描述的消费者行为的明显不一致？

(A) 消费者在通货膨胀期间存的钱比非通货膨胀期间存的钱多。

(B) 通常先导经济指示器首先发出一个时期的通货膨胀已经开始的信号和消费者们意识到这种通货膨胀已经开始之间有一个滞后。

(C) 没有一种对人类行为的概括适用于每一种类型的人的行为。

(D) 如果很大数量的消费者不能购买商品，那么价格最终会降下来，但是工资不会受到影响。

(E) 因为工资的增长跟不上物价的上涨，所以消费者的购买力在长期的通货膨胀阶段有所下降。

49. A group of scientists studying calcium metabolism in laboratory rats discovered that removing the rats' parathyroid glands resulted in the rats' having substantially lower than normal levels of calcium in their blood. This discovery led the scientists to hypothesize that the function of the parathyroid gland is to regulate the level of calcium in the blood by raising that level when if falls below the normal range. In a further experiment, the scientists removed not only the parathyroid gland but also the adrenal gland from rats. They made the surprising discovery that the level of calcium in the rats' blood decreased much less sharply than when the parathyroid gland alone was removed.

Which one of the following, if true, explains the surprising discovery in a way most consistent with the scientists' hypothesis?

(A) The adrenal gland acts to lower the level of calcium in the blood.

一群在实验室里研究老鼠体内的钙新陈代谢的科学家发现去除老鼠的甲状旁腺可以导致老鼠血液中的钙的水平比正常水平低得多，这个发现使科学家们假设甲状旁腺的功能是调节血液中的钙的水平。当钙的水平降到正常范围之下，它就升高钙的水平。在进一步的实验中，科学家们不但去除了老鼠的甲状旁腺，而且去除了它们的肾上腺，他们出人意料地发现老鼠血液内钙的水平的下降比单是去除甲状旁腺时慢得多。

下面哪一项，如果正确，能与科学家的假设相一致地解释那个出人意料的发现？

(A) 肾上腺的作用是降低血液中的钙的水平。

(B) 肾上腺与甲状旁腺在调节血液内的钙的水平时的作用是一样的。

(B) The adrenal gland and the parathyroid gland play the same role in regulating calcium blood levels.

(C) The absence of a parathyroid gland causes the adrenal gland to increase the level of calcium in the blood.

(D) If the adrenal gland, and no other gland, of a rat were removed, the rat's calcium level would remain stable.

(E) The only function of the parathyroid gland is to regulate the level of calcium in the blood.

(C) 甲状旁腺的缺乏能促使肾上腺增加血液中的钙水平。

(D) 如果只是把老鼠的肾上腺，而没有把其他的腺移去，这只老鼠的血液内的钙的水平将会维持不变。

(E) 甲状旁腺的仅有功能是调节血液中的钙的水平。

50. A long-term health study that followed a group of people who were age 35 in 1950 found that those whose weight increased by approximately half a kilogram or one pound per year after the age of 35 tended, on the whole, to live longer than those who maintained the weight they had at age 35. This finding seems at variance with other studies that have associated weight gain with a host of health problems that tend to lower life expectancy.

Which one of the following, if true, most helps to resolve the apparently conflicting findings?

(A) As people age, muscle and bone tissue tends to make up a smaller and smaller proportion of total body weight.

(B) Individuals who reduce their cholesterol levels by losing weight can thereby also reduce their risk of dying from heart attacks or strokes.

(C) Smokers, who tend to be leaner than nonsmokers, tend to have shorter life spans than nonsmokers.

(D) The normal deterioration of the human immune system with age can be slowed down by a reduction in the number of calories consumed.

(E) Diets that tend to lead to weight gain often contain not only excess fat but also unhealthful concentrations of sugar and sodium.

对一群在1950年35岁的人的长期健康跟踪研究表明，从整体上讲，那些过了35岁以后平均每年体重增加半公斤或一磅的人倾向于比那些过了35岁以后体重保持不变的人活得长。这个结果好像与其他研究相矛盾，其他研究把体重增加与一大堆的健康问题联系起来，并且体重增加倾向于使一个人的平均寿命降低。

下面哪一项，如果正确，最有助于解决上面短文中明显的相互冲突的结果？

(A) 随着人们年龄的增加，肌肉和骨骼组织占人体总重的比例倾向于越来越小。

(B) 那些通过减轻体重来降低他们的胆固醇水平的人同时也降低了他们遭受心脏病或中风袭击的危险性。

(C) 抽烟者，倾向于比不抽烟者瘦，活的时间也倾向于比不抽烟者短。

(D) 人类免疫系统随着年龄增加的正常退化可以通过减少热量的消耗来抑制。

(E) 那些倾向于使人的体重增加的饮食通常不但含有过多的脂肪而且含有对健康有害的糖和钠的浓缩物。

51. Of the five bill collectors at Apex Collection Agency, Mr. Young has the highest rate of unsuccessful collections. Yet Mr. Young is the best bill collector on the agency's staff.

Which one of the following, if true, most helps to resolve the apparent discrepancy?

(A) Mr. Young is assigned the majority of the most difficult cases at the agency.

(B) The other four bill collectors at the agency all consider Mr. Young to be a very capable bill collector.

(C) Mr. Young's rate of collections per year has remained fairly steady in the last few years.

在Apex收款局的5个账单收款员中，Young先生收款的不成功率最高。然而Young先生是这个局的职员中最好的账单收款员。

下面哪一项，如果正确，最有助于解决上述短文中的明显分歧？

(A) 这个收款局的大多数最困难的事情都是派Young先生去做的。

(B) 收款局中的其他四个收款员都认为Young先生是一个非常能干的账单收款员。

(D) Before joining the agency, Mr.Young was affiliated with the credit department of a large department store.

(E) None of the bill collectors at the agency has been on the agency's staff longer than Mr.Young has.

(C) Young先生在过去的几年内，每年收款成功的比率都保持相当地稳定。

(D) 在加入收款局之前，Young先生是一个大百货公司的信贷部的一名职员。

(E) 收款局中收款员在那儿工作的时间都没有Young先生的长。

参考答案：

1. E	2. B	3. D	4. B	5. A
6. E	7. C	8. A	9. A	10. B
11. E	12. E	13. B	14. E	15. C
16. A	17. E	18. E	19. A	20. B
21. A	22. C	23. D	24. E	25. E
26. B	27. C	28. A	29. A	30. B
31. D	32. D	33. D	34. E	35. A
36. C	37. E	38. A	39. C	40. E
41. E	42. C	43. B	44. D	45. B
46. D	47. B	48. E	49. A	50. C
51. A				

1. **解析：** 本题就是要找一个能解释调查报告中所显示的单身男女人数的显著差异的选项。Ⅰ中所说的适合结婚的女性比适合结婚的男性多与独身的女性比独身的男性多之间无任何必然关系，所以Ⅰ是错误的；Ⅱ和Ⅲ都通过找他因的办法说明了调查报告的结果并不是对所有美国人的婚姻状况的调查结果，有一部分独身者是未被统计进去的，而未被统计的独身男性又比未被统计的独身女性多，因此调查报告的结果会显示出独身女性比独身男性多出100万。由以上分析可知，在给出的三项中，只有Ⅱ和Ⅲ正确，也即(E)为正确答案。

2. **解析：** 本题目的清晰，让我们寻求一个选项解释为什么引进劳动力节约型的机器对工厂主是有利的。(B)明显指出了劳动力节约型的机器所带来的利润要高于重新培训工人做其他工作的费用，说明了这样做的优点，因此起到了解释作用，所以(B)正确；(A)、(D)、(E)均为无关选择；(C)易误选，但(C)是一个削弱上面事实的选项，所以(C)不正确。

6. **解析：** 本题目的让我们解释the apparent paradox：包办酒席的机构卫生检查严格，但上报的更多的食物中毒是由包办酒席的机构引起的。人们一般不太可能把一顿饭与其后的疾病联系起来，因为人们并不能确认是否是这顿饭引起的病，但是若在banquets中的人们很多都是吃过酒席之后病了，那么这些相互认识的人就会建立起这种联系，并且集体上诉至市卫生部门，所以(E)正确；(A)、(B)起到部分反对的作用，与问题目的不符，所以不正确；我们并不知道报道的精确性，并且报道的内容也与推理无关，所以(D)不对；本题没做对的考生有80%选择(C)，但(C)只表明很多餐馆在提供个人饭菜之外，也提供包办酒席的服务，但并没有说明包办酒席服务所占比例以及中毒情况，所以不能够起到解释作用。**注意：GMAT的逻辑推理题的推理大多只在一个层面上进行，且不能进行段落之外信息的进一步推导。**

7. **解析：** 根据整体的一部分变小，而包含这部分的整体大小未变，我们很容易推出这个整体中的另一部分一定变大，以此来补偿变小的这一部分，因此1987年股票的交易量未变一定是由于1987年某一段时间股票的交易量较高补偿了交易量较低的那几周减少的交易量。由此分析可知(C)为正确答案。

8. **解析**：本题让我们解释the apparent discrepancy：半空的电冰箱比装满的电冰箱耗能更多，并且要解释双方的矛盾点或差异点是"energy"。因此，我们用关键词"energy"来定位选项，排除了(C)、(E)；若一定体积的空气维持某一温度比相同体积的食物耗能更多，如(A)所述，那么就解释了上面的"discrepancy"，因此(A)正确；(B)不能说明"半空状态为什么耗能更多"；(D)只能说明电冰箱如何才能有效运行，不能解释"半空状态为什么耗能更多"，所以(D)不正确。

9. **解析**：本题属于数学相关的题目，段落中出现了四个数字（表示为百分比）并涉及compact cars，middle-sized cars, tailgated cars和vehicles in traffic这四类车。数字38%与31%都比较于vehicles in traffic, 48%与27%都比较于tailgated cars，所以都可以进行比较。但很明显后者之间的差值较前者更大，因此应着重寻求能解释这种差异的选项。若compact cars的车型使得tailgater有更多的优势从而减少了撞车的可能，如(A)所说，那么它在tailgated cars中占了更大比例，所以(A)为正确答案。

10. **解析**：本题的(A)、(C)、(D)和(E)选项都通过找他因的方法，对亨利八世盔甲的重量的增加做出了解释。选项(B)把两件盔甲重量的差异归结为亨利八世在统治期间增加了武器贮备就显得牵强附会，因为武器贮备的增加只可能说明它的盔甲比较多，但不能解释他的盔甲变重的现象。因此(B)正确。

11. **解析**：本题是要找一个选项对以甲醇为燃料的汽车排放出的甲醛比燃烧汽油的汽车排放的甲醛多而污染却少做出合理的解释。(E)指出虽然燃烧汽油本身放出的甲醛不多，但是燃烧汽油所释放的其他碳氢化合物在大气中发生光化学反应而生成甲醛，因此，燃烧汽油的汽车的实际甲醛排放量应为直接排放量加上间接排放量，这两部分之和有可能大于燃烧甲醇的汽车排放的甲醛。由以上分析可知(E)正确。

16. **解析**：本题目的让我们解释"为什么登山设备改进但登山事故发生率反而增加"，可以用关键词"equipment"去定位选项，且选项应与"事故发生率增加"有关。(A)指出许多登山者误以为使用登山设备会很安全，就使用了他们能力所不及的登山设备，从而导致了事故发生率的增加，解释了登山设备改进但事故发生率增加的事实，所以(A)正确；(D)中虽也涉及equipment这个概念，但(D)与"事故增加"无关；(B)易误选，但无法预测的天气情况在过去和现在都存在，所以对推理起不到任何作用。

18. **解析**：(E)选项是本题结论成立的前提的重述，因此(E)选项不能被用来解释老鼠饮食的改变所导致的寿命的延长，所以(E)是本题的正确答案；(A)、(B)、(C)和(D)都通过找他因的办法，从不同的侧面对老鼠饮食的改变所带来的寿命的延长做了解释。

19. **解析**：本题的分歧之处在于没有证据表明吃抗生素会降低人体免疫功能，然而不吃抗生素的人的免疫系统比吃抗生素的人的免疫系统的功能更强。要解决这个分歧，就要找一个选项要么能说明抗生素确实能降低人体的免疫力，要么能说明不吃抗生素的人的免疫系统的功能较强是由他因所致。(A)选项指出免疫力强的人很少感染上人们通常用抗生素治疗的疾病，因而免疫力强的人，不吃抗生素；而免疫力差的人，感染上疾病，就需要吃抗生素，所以(A)解释了本题段落中的分歧，为正确答案。

21. **解析**：根据这两个调查报告的结果可以看出，1992年8月比1991年8月认为科学对人类的影响是"mostly beneficial"的人的比例大幅度地增加，而其他各项的比例则相应的大幅度降低，本题的要求就是要找一个能解释这种变化的原因的选项。(A)选项说明了人们态度的改变源于一个在黄金时间播出的新的关于科学的电视节目，因此(A)是正确答案。

22. **解析**：本题是要找一个能够用来解释为什么无法知道其他已灭绝的只能从化石中研究的灵长目动物是否具有青春期的选项。(C)指出检查青春期迅速发育需要对同一个人的不同年龄阶段进行测量，而生物的化石只能提供不同生物在同一阶段或不同阶段的发育情况，所以(C)是正确答案；(A)易被误选，许多考生会根据各种生物经历青春期的最低的生长速度不同，推出无法知道它们是否经历青春期的结论。这种推理是错误的，因为虽然生物的种类不同，可以区别对待，但是还是可以验证几种生物是否经历青春期的；生物的化石不完全并不一定就无法知道其是否具有青春期，所以(B)也无法合理完成本文；(D)和(E)也都无法完成本题段落中的论述。

23. **解析**：根据本题给出的图表可以清楚地看出，1962年惩罚12岁以下的孩子看电视的各项比例总和显著高于1992年的各项比例总和，因此能合理解释这种差异的选项是本题的正确答案，D选项的内容很好地解释了这种差异，在1962年接受调查的父母因为可以有多种选择，所以最后各项的总和能显著超过100%，而在1992年接受调查的父母因只有一种选择，各项比例之和约为100%，所以(D)为正确答案；(A)选项中指出的"1962年比1992年调查的样本大"不能被用来解释差异原因，因为本题图表中的统计结果是"percent using technique"。另一方面图表中所表明的调查仅仅是1962年和1992年的，所以所有关于："in the period between the surveys"的答案都无法从图表中得出，于是(B)和(E)不对；从1962年的各项比例分配中，无法看出"the four disciplinary were the only disciplinary techniques named by parents"，因此(C)也是不对的。

24. **解析**：本题是要寻找一个选项能用来解释新汽车实际价格的上升不是购买新车比率下降的真正原因。(E)说明新汽车价格升高的原因是因为人们喜欢二手车而放弃了对廉价新车的购买，也就是说，在所卖出的新车中，廉价新车所占比重下降，而豪华昂贵的新车所占比重上升，所以所卖新车的平均价格必定上升。由此分析可知，(E)选项既说明了新车购买比例下降的原因又说明了新车平均价格上涨的原因，所以(E)为正确答案；(A)选项仅为购买新车的比例下降提供了另一个原因，而本题的要求是找一个能解释价格升高不是新汽车购买比例下降的原因的答案，所以(A)选项答非所问，为错误选项；(B)、(C)和(D)都是无关选项。

25. **解析**：从本题的图表中可以看出拥有大学学位以上的人比只有高中文凭的人收入高，并且这两类人的收入在1975年到1990年期间的变化趋势基本相同：都是在前5年中保持增长，在中间5年中保持稳定而在后5年中保持下降。本图表另一个显著的特征是在1985年到1990年这5年期间仅拥有高中文凭的人的收入下降较拥有大学学位以上的人的收入下降要快得多。而解释这个明显的差异正是本题的目的所在。(E)中指出经济体制的变化，使只有高中文凭的人丧失了一些高收入的工作，从而合理地解释了1985年至1990年这5年中只有高中文凭的人年收入急剧下降的原因，所以(E)为正确答案；(A)、(B)和(C)三选项虽然都涉及了"since 1985"，但均不能说明图中所示的1985年到1990年这5年期间的大学毕业生和高中毕业生收入的变化；(D)中指出的社会保障法使只有高中文凭的Ansonian人63岁退休时可拿到全薪，导致的结果与上面图表相反。

26. **解析**：未完成的短文要求解释为什么对于溢价产品不应采取降价和大规模营销的办法。选项(B)，指出销售这些产品需要使这些产品看起来与众不同，提供了这样一种解释。因此，(B)是正确答案。并没有其他选项提供了一种合理的解释：选项(C)指出溢价商品的购买者会发现降低的价格很有吸引力，但并没有说明该办法影响质量或对质量的感知；(A)中引述的富有的购买者比例的减少论证了应采用降价的办法去吸引收入更低的购买者；而(D)论证了而不是反驳了应使用大规模营销；选项(E)不合适，因为没有迹象显示生产成本与主题有关。

27. **解析**：如果(C)是正确的，1980年后亚洲棕榈树产量的迅速提高耗尽了培育果实的雌花生长需要的营养物质，因此(C)解释了为什么棕榈的产量随后下降，即(C)为正确答案；选项(A)将棕榈果实价格的下降与产量的增加和需求的下降联系起来，但没有解释随后该树产量的下降；选项(B)没有给出这些引入亚洲的树产量下降的原因；(D)也没有，因为(D)中描述的象鼻虫数量的稳定应支持在1980年到1984年之间棕榈树果实产量的稳定，而不是下降；因为(E)描述了1980年以前该树的授粉情况，它没有解释发生在1984年的变化。

28. **解析**：决定所售新房子平均价格的因素主要看所售高价新房与所售低价新房之间的相对比例或权重。所售新房数目既定，而其中高价新房权重大的所售新房平均价格绝对大于高价新房权重比较小的所售新房平均价格。因此(A)指出高价房销量不变而低价房销量下降时，所售新房中高价房权重增大，所以所售新房价格激增。(A)解释了新房子平均价格的激增，因此(A)正确。

29. **解析**：选项(A)，正确答案，指出一些环境变化可以分布非常广，以致造成很多种群的灭绝。这个事实帮助解释了为什么化石记录经常显示许多种群同时灭绝，尽管能造成一个种群灭绝的因素有很

323

多。其他选项中没有一项能解释过去很多种群的灭绝是怎样同时发生的。选项(B)解释了为什么有时只有一些非常有限的种群灭绝了；选项(C)解释了一些个别的种群是如何灭绝的；选项(D)解释了为什么现代时期与化石记录时期不同；选项(E)指出哪些种群最不可能灭绝。

30. **解析**：四个选项就在经济增长放慢时期为什么许多人选择上两年制大学这个问题，提出了理由。选项(A)指出当经济状况不景气时，两年制的大学教育可以提供一个找到工作的更好机会；选项(C)和(E)指出为什么收入减少的人们更愿意上两年制大学；最后，选项(D)指出两年制大学比四年制大学花了更多精力来吸引那些生活受到经济增长放慢影响的人。选项(B)是正确答案，可能解释了经济增长放慢时期四年制大学招收学生人数为什么下降，但因为它仅与两年制大学的毕业生有关，它不能解释为什么这些大学招收学生的人数会增加，另外，(B)为段落推理的否命题，而否命题与原命题不等价。

31. **解析**：该研究指出，公地比私人土地条件更好，正确答案(D)，指出与Hardin的宣称相反，不去过度使用公地是符合每个放牧者的自身利益的，这样来解释为什么公地有相对较好的条件；选项(A)和(C)只能解释为什么私人土地比公地条件更好，而不是相反；将公地条件恶化的成本分摊给每个使用者更加困难这一事实〔选项(B)〕和公地与私人土地相对量的不同这一事实〔选项(E)〕都没有给出一个理由来解释农场主们为什么尽可能地不在公地上牧养他们的牧群。

33. **解析**：本题属于"解释"题型，答案要满足"直接、无推导"原则。(D)说明强调优势会对其已在美国销售的屏幕安全性提出质疑，解释了该制造商并未宣扬其优势的原因；(B)易误选，但段落里面并未告诉我们广告中一旦说出这种优点竞争者就知道，因此不能对结论提供一个很好的解释，所以(B)不对。

35. **解析**：完成句子考题要么从上面得出结论，要么解释前半部分，且必须与前半部分有关。因此很容易看出(A)正确；(D)易误选，但仔细分析，会发现它与段落第一句话 "...should reflect..." 相违背，所以(D)不正确。

36. **解析**：正确答案应能解释麻疹发病率的下降和Peterson病发病率的上升。(C)指出得过麻疹的儿童形成了Peterson的免疫力，既然麻疹发病率少了，那么更少的儿童有对Peterson的免疫力，因此，随着前者的下降而后者上升，所以(C)正确；(A)指出遗传因素的作用，但并不能解释为什么Peterson发病率上升；(B)中的"其他任何国家"，与"美国"无关；(D)、(E)均不能起到解释作用。

38. **解析**：解释主要应抓住对比点或变化点，(A)指出重新评估发现此项目潜在收入小于总成本，因此该项目必为亏损、资不抵债项目，再增加投入只能亏得更多，所以(A)解释了银行现在的反应；(B)易误选，但(B)只指有其他项目能提供更快的本金回收，但银行主要的目标是在收回本金之外追逐更高的利润，而这几个项目利润怎么样不知道；同时段落中并没有讲哪个人的项目本金回报快，就给他贷款，所以(B)不正确。

39. **解析**：本题主要考察我们空间想象能力与快速辨别差异性的能力，读题重点应该是让我们解释段落的最后一句话，即"在实验中表现最成功的受试人被发现其大脑神经细胞有the lowest expenditure of energy。结论中应涉及"those subjects who performed successfully"与"expenditure of energy"。(C)与两关键词有关，且能起到解释作用，所以(C)正确；(A)做的是无关比较，且与"成功"无关；(B)与"expenditure of energy"无关；(D)有反对作用；(E)中的两个引导词"athletes"与"at rest"说明(E)不正确。

40. **解析**：本题主要是读懂问题目的。benchmark 基准点（测量人员在岩石、混凝土等上面刻下的标记用以测量相对高度）；（供比较之用的）样板或参照点。

41. **解析**：要解释人们在吃有酒的饭菜时从非酒精类食物中摄入的热量较多，就要从有利于人们在这些饭菜中吃较多的非酒精类食物的因素着手。我们知道有酒的饭菜与无酒的饭菜相比一般制作精心，也较丰盛，出席的人也较多，因此人们倾向于吃得时间长且吃得多。所以(A)、(B)、(C)和(D)都能有助于解释文中所提及的热量的摄入量的不同；(E)说明了在有酒的饭菜中人们倾向于喝更多的酒而不是吃更多的其他食物，所以不能解释人们在有酒的饭菜中从非酒精类食物中摄入的热量较多，因此(E)为正确答案。

42. **解析**：本题的结论是考古学家们利用年轮已成功地确定了Pazyryk地区的古墓的相对年龄。要使用年轮来确定古墓的相对年龄，首先就要考虑具有这些年轮的木料之间有无相关性，即它们之间有无一致的地方。在5个选项中，只有(C)指出了这种相关性，即Pazyryk地区的墓中的每一块木料的年轮中都有一个有特色的12年龄序列，这也就是说Pazyryk地区的古墓修建时用的木料在生长过程中都经历了6年的干旱，接着是3年的多雨和3年的干旱，在用年轮来确定墓的相对年龄时，只要看一下这12个有特色序列的年轮在整个木料的年轮中的位置即可。若古墓用的木料中，这12个年轮位于树干的靠中间的位置，则此墓建得较晚；若这12个年轮位于树干的靠周边的位置，则此墓建得较早。根据这12个年轮在古墓的木料中出现的位置的差异，就可确定出古墓之间的相对年龄。本题的(A)、(B)、(D)和(E)选项都是与本题的结论无关的选项。

43. **解析**：要解释房东的不情愿行为，就要从房东的自身利益出发。设想在租金管理的政策下，若房东能从维持现有的房地产质量或额外建房中取得公正合理的收益，他们肯定不会在这两方面有不情愿行为。他们之所以有不情愿行为，那肯定是因为租金管理政策使他们很难取得公正合理的收益。不赚钱的事没有人愿干，因此(B)为正确答案。(A)、(C)、(D)和(E)即不能从文中合理地推出，也不能用来解释本题的结论。

44. **解析**：要解答此题，只要紧扣住评委们的目的就可以了。评委们的目的是让试演最优秀的申请者取得奖学金，因此申请者是否还申请了别的项目，是否需要这部分奖学金，都是申请者个人的事，与评委们的目的无任何关系。只有当获得奖学金的申请者的试演并不是最优秀的，或者说没有其他没获得奖学金的申请者的好时，评委们的目的才得到了限制。由此分析可知，选项(D)是正确选项；而(A)和(C)均为错误选项；(B)提到了上文中未提及的新比较，所以必然是不对的；(E)选项是评委们发放奖学金的一个出发点，因此不会对他们的目的有不良的影响。

45. **解析**：段落中为证明汽车工业收入的下降是言过其实的论点，列举了一大堆的统计数字，这些数字有些上升，有些下降让人看后有点丈二和尚摸不着头脑的感觉，因此这些数字也很难给它要支持的论点提供有力的证据。对这些数字进行简单的分析即可得出，尽管两年前与今天相比，汽车工业的收入在三个部门中有所变化，但是两年前这三个部门的收入份额总和(65%+15%+20%=100%)与今天的收入份额总和(50%+20%+30%=100%)仍是一样的，由此即可推出，不管汽车工业的收入经历了什么样的变化，所有这些收入的份额的总和必须是100%，所以(B)是正确答案。(A)是容易误选的选项，若制造商的收入份额与其他统计数字具有不同的出处，这些统计数字确实不利于被用来支持论点，但是具有不同的出处只是一种可能性，另一方面即使这些数字具有不同的出处，它们仍有相一致的可能性，由前面的分析可知这些统计数字确实是相一致的，所以选项(A)是错误的；选项(C)、(D)和(E)均为无关选项。

46. **解析**：警察局和汽车保险业在防盗装置能否降低汽车被盗的危险性上发生了分歧，要解决它们的分歧就要分析它们的结论成立所依赖的事实。通过简单的分析，我们很容易发现一个人所拥有的汽车越容易被盗，他就越有可能给他的汽车装防盗装置，他把他的汽车投保的可能性也越大。在汽车被盗案发生率较高的地方，人们也倾向于给他们的汽车装防盗装置，这部分人把他们的汽车投保的可能性也大。这也就是说保险公司的统计研究结果具有一定的片面性，5个选项中只有答案(D)指出了这种片面性，因此(D)为正确选项。

47. **解析**：对可能有误的甚至已经知道有误的科研报道的研究，可以发现为什么以前的研究工作中会出现那样的错误，通过借鉴这些错误，吸收前人成功的经验和失败的教训，一个人将在以后发现真理的探索中少走很多弯路，因此参考早些时候的科研工作仍是一件非常有意义的事情，由此可知(B)是正确的，其余四个选项很明显都不能解释段落中的明显分歧。

48. 解析： 根据消费者们在通货膨胀开始阶段对物价上涨所做的反应，我们可以推知只有在工资上涨跟不上物价的上涨，从而迫使消费者们的购买力下降的前提下，消费者们才不得不在长期的通货膨胀阶段推迟甚至是日常生活品的购买，因此(E)是正确答案；(A)、(B)、(C)和(D)都为无关选项。

49. 解析： 本题的两个结论是：(1)去除甲状旁腺时老鼠血液中的钙的水平比正常水平低得多；(2) 同时去除甲状旁腺和肾上腺时，老鼠血液内钙的水平的下降比单是去除甲状旁腺时慢得多。对这两个结论进行比较，我们不难发现肾上腺一定具有促使老鼠的血液中钙的水平降低的作用。因此(A)，肾上腺的作用是降低血液中的钙的水平是正确的；而(B)、(C)和(D)都是不正确的；从短文中我们只能推出调节血液中的钙的水平只是甲状旁腺的一个功能，因此(E)也是不正确的。

50. 解析： 本题没有逻辑上严密的答案，通过对5个选项的分析我们发现(A)与本题的论述无关；(B)、(D)和(E)都倾向于解释其他的研究结果；相比之下，只有(C)选项能较好地解决本题中的两种研究结果的分歧。从抽烟者倾向于比不抽烟者瘦，即可推出35岁以后体重不断增长的人大都是不抽烟的人，因此尽管他们的体重增加会给他们带来一大堆的健康问题，但是他们的寿命还是比那些较瘦的，体重保持不变的人长，所以(C)有助于解决本题段落中的相互冲突的研究结果。

51. 解析： 要使Yong先生收款的成功率不高的事实能够支持Yong先生是最好的账单收款员的结论，就要找致使Yong先生收款的成功率不高的原因。在本题的5个选项中，只有(A)指出了Yong先生收款成功率不高是因为收款局的大多数最困难的事情都是派Yong先生去做的，这样不但本题中证据与结论之间的明显分歧得到了解决，而且证据还更有力地支持了结论。

第 七 章

逻辑应用与技法

逻辑应用与技法这类考题主要考查我们在体会段落推理之后是否具备以下能力：把握推理方法或特点的能力；将一个论点的指导性原则用于另一论点的能力；识别论点的结构方法或技法的能力；论点构建中某句话对结论或前提是否起作用或起到什么作用的能力。常见的典型的问题目的如下：

Which of the following parallels the method of argumentation above?

The argument above is most like which of the following?

Which of the following suffers from a flaw that, in its logical aspects, is most like the difficulty described above?

Which of the following identifies a flaw in the speaker's reasoning?

The author's point is made primarily by...

The labor negotiator minimizes his differences with management by...

The passage above criticizes the authorities by...

一、指出推理缺陷(flaw)

1. The average normal infant born in the United States weighs between twelve and fourteen pounds at the age of three months. Therefore, if a three-month-old child weighs only ten pounds, its weight gain has been below the United States average.

Which of the following indicates a flaw in the reasoning above?

(A) Weight is only one measure of normal infant development.

(B) Some three-month-old children weigh as much as seventeen pounds.

(C) It is possible for a normal child to weigh ten pounds at birth.

(D) The phrase "below average" does not necessarily mean insufficient.

(E) Average weight gain is not the same as average weight.

译文：在美国出生的正常的婴儿在3个月大时平均体重在12～14磅之间。因此，如果一个3个月大的小孩体重只有10磅，那么他的体重增长低于美国平均水平。

以下哪一项指出了上面推理中的一处缺陷？

(A) 体重只是正常婴儿成长的一项指标。

(B) 一些3个月大的小孩体重有17磅。

(C) 一个正常的小孩出生时体重达到10磅是有可能的。

(D) 短语"低于平均水平"并不一定意味着不够。

(E) 平均体重增长同平均体重并不相同。

解析：该结论基于的论据仅考虑了平均体重，但该结论考虑的是平均体重增长。因为在一个绝对的量度—如体重—和一个增加率—如体重增长这两者之间没有必然的联系，该论述是有缺陷的。有关的推理错误如(E)所述，该项是正确答案；(A)和(D)都没有指出短文中的推理错误。因为短文既没有宣称体重是总的婴儿成长的唯一相关指标［选项(A)］，也没有提到是否足够［选项(D)］；(B)和(C)同短文中的论述并不矛盾，但没有指出论述中的缺陷，故不能为答案。

2. On the basis of a decrease in the college-age population, many colleges now anticipate increasingly smaller freshman classes each year. Surprised by a 40 percent increase in qualified applicants over the previous year, however, administrators at Nice College now plan to hire more faculty for courses taken by all freshmen.

Which of the following statements about Nice College's current qualified applicants, if true, would strongly suggest that the administrators' plan is flawed?

(A) A substantially higher percentage than usual plan to study for advanced degrees after graduation from college.

(B) According to their applications, their level of participation in extracurricular activities and varsity sports is unusually high.

(C) According to their applications, none of them lives in a foreign country.

(D) A substantially lower percentage than usual rate Nice College as their first choice among the colleges to which they are applying.

(E) A substantially lower percentage than usual list mathematics as their intended major.

译文：基于具有大学入学年龄的人数量日益减少，很多大学现在预测每年新生班级人数越来越少，然而Nice大学的管理者们对今年比前一年增加了40%的合格的申请者感到惊讶，因此现在为所有新生开设的课程雇用了更多的教职员工。

以下哪一项关于Nice大学目前合格的申请者的论述，如果是正确的，将最有力的指出那些管理者们的计划是有缺陷的？

(A) 比通常的计划比例高得多的人从大学毕业后攻读更高的学位。

(B) 根据他们的申请，他们参与课外活动和大学生代表团运动项目的水平非常高。

(C) 根据他们的申请，没有一个人居住在外国。

(D) 在他们申请的大学中把Nice大学作为第一选择的比例比通常比例低得多。

(E) 比通常低得多的比例的学生将数学列为他们期望的专业。

解析：如果像(D)所述，有很大比例的合格的申请者没有将Nice大学列为他们的第一选择，那么，如果许多这样的申请者被他们作为第一选择的大学接受并录取，申请Nice大学人数的增加并不会导致新生班级规模的扩大，因此(D)是正确答案；从(A)、(B)、(C)或(E)中不能得出任何关于新生班级规模的结论，因此这些选项同Nice大学是否应为教授所有新生开设的课程而雇用更多的教职员工无关。因此，这些选项都不合适。

3. Some People have questioned the judge's objectivity in cases of sex discrimination against women. But the record shows that in sixty percent of such cases, the judge has decided in favor of the women. This record demonstrates that the judge has not discriminated against women in cases of sex discrimination against women.

The argument above is flawed in that it ignores the possibility that_____

(A) a large number of the judge's cases arose out of allegations of sex discrimination against women.

(B) many judges find it difficult to be objective in cases of sex discrimination against women.

(C) the judge is biased against women defendants or plaintiffs in cases that do not involve sex discrimination.

(D) the majority of the cases of sex discrimination against

译文：一些人对某法官在针对妇女的性别歧视的案件中的客观性表示质疑。但是记录显示，这种案件中有60%的情况下该法官做出了有利于妇女的判决。这项记录证明在针对妇女的性别歧视的案件中，该法官并没有歧视妇女。

上述论述是有缺陷的，因为它忽略了一种可能性，即_____。

(A) 由该法官审理的大量案件是由对妇女的性别歧视的指控引起的。

(B) 许多法官发现在对妇女性别歧视的案件中很难做到客观公正。

(C) 在不牵涉性别歧视的案件中该法官对女被告或原告有偏见。

(D) 送到该法官的法庭的针对妇女的性别

women that have reached the judge's court have been appealed from a lower court.

(E) the evidence shows that the women should have won in more than sixty percent of the judge's cases involving sex discrimination against women.

歧视案件多数是从一个低级法院上诉来的。

(E) 有证据显示该法官关于针对妇女的性别歧视案件中，妇女应该赢得超过60%的案件。

解析： 论述中的缺陷是它错误地假设在性别歧视案件中做出有利于妇女的判决占这类案件的一大半就能证明做出这些判决的法官不存在对妇女的歧视行为，选项(E)通过指出该法官很可能在证据显示妇女应该赢的案件里却没有做出有利于妇女的判决，揭示了这个缺陷，因此，(E)是正确答案；选项(B)和(C)考虑了一些与论述推理无关的情况。因为论述只涉及一个特定的法官，(B)不合适；因为只涉及一些特定类型的案件，(C)不合适；选项(A)和(D)也同论述没有关系，因为这些案件的来源与论述讨论的问题无关。

二、有疑问的技法

4. "Fast cycle time" is a strategy of designing a manufacturing organization to eliminate bottlenecks and delays in production. Not only does it speed up production, but it also assures quality. The reason is that the bottlenecks and delays cannot be eliminated unless all work is done right the first time.

The claim about quality made above rests on a questionable presupposition that

(A) any flaw in work on a product would cause a bottleneck or delay and so would be prevented from occurring on a "fast cycle" production line.

(B) the strategy of "fast cycle time" would require fundamental rethinking of product design.

(C) the primary goal of the organization is to produce a product of unexcelled quality, rather than to generate profits for stockholders.

(D) "Fast cycle time" could be achieved by shaving time off each of the component processes in production cycle.

(E) "fast cycle time" is a concept in business strategy that has not yet been put into practice in a factory.

译文： "快速周转时间"是一项策略，通过对生产组织的设计来消除生产中的瓶颈和延迟。它不仅加速生产，而且确保质量，理由是除非所有的工作第一次就被全部正确地完成，否则瓶颈和延迟不能被消除。

以上作出的关于质量的宣称是建立在一个值得怀疑的假设的基础上，即

(A) 生产一项产品过程中的任何缺陷都会造成瓶颈或延迟，而在"快速周转"生产线中可以阻止这种情况发生。

(B) "快速周转时间"的策略要求从根本上重新思考产品的设计。

(C) 该组织的首要目标是生产一种质量无与伦比的产品，而不是为股东创造利润。

(D) 通过节省生产周期中每一个组成过程的时间可以成功地实施"快速周转时间"。

(E) "快速周转时间"是一个迄今尚未在任何一个工厂实施过的商业战略。

解析： 该论述预先假设，如果瓶颈和延迟被消除，生产工作一定会以更少的缺陷完成，这个预先假设是值得怀疑的，因为仍然会有并不阻碍生产过程的缺陷存在，因此正确答案是选项(A)；该段落推理没有预先假设其他选项。该论述与重新设计制造过程一致，但不是重新设计产品〔选项(B)〕；首要目标应是利润，质量仅仅是实现这个目标的手段〔选项(C)〕；该论述并不依赖于任何一种实施"快速周转时间"的手段的可行性〔选项(D)〕；最后，"快速周转时间"的策略可能已经开始在实际操作中实施了〔选项(E)〕。

三、逻辑描述

5. Each of two particular inspection systems that are based on different principles would detect all product flaws but would also erroneously reject three percent of flawless products. Assuming there is no overlap between the products erroneously rejected by the two systems and also no interference between the systems if both operate, using both systems and rejecting only those products found flawed by both would be a way of avoiding all erroneous rejections.

Which of the following most precisely characterizes the reasoning in the argument?

(A) The reasoning is conclusive; that is, the conclusion cannot be false if the statements offered in its support are true.

(B) The reasoning is strong but not conclusive; if the statements offered in support of the conclusion are true, they provide good grounds for that conclusion, though it is possible that additional information might weaken the argument.

(C) The reasoning is weak; the statements offered in support of the conclusion, though relevant to it, by themselves provide at best inadequate grounds for the conclusion.

(D) The reasoning is flawed in that the conclusion is no more than a paraphrase of one of the pieces of evidence offered in its support.

(E) The reasoning is flawed in that the argument treats evidence that a factor is necessary to bring about an event as if it were evidence that the factor is sufficient to bring about that event.

译文：两个基于不同原理的检测系统，每一个都能测出所有有瑕疵的产品，但也会错误地抛弃3%的无瑕疵的产品。假设两个系统错误抛弃的产品没有重叠，且如果同时运行也不会相互干扰，则使用两个系统并仅抛弃那些两个系统都认为有瑕疵的产品可以避免所有的错误抛弃。

下列哪一项最精确地描述了上面论述中的推理过程？

(A) 该推理是结论性的。如果支持结论的陈述正确，那么结论就不可能错。

(B) 该推理很强，但不是结论性的，如果支持结论的陈述正确，那么就为结论提供了很好的根据，尽管附加的信息可能会削弱该论述。

(C) 该推理很弱，支持结论的陈述，尽管与结论有关，但陈述本身最多只为该结论提供了不充分的根据。

(D) 该推理有缺陷，因为该结论也只是对支持该结论的一项证据的重新阐释而已。

(E) 该推理有缺陷，因为该论述把一个因素是某一事件发生的必要条件的证据当作了该事件发生的充分条件的证据。

解析： 本题为GRE国内1991年2月考题（见本书44页21题）。本题的五个选项所描述的逻辑关系都比较抽象，阅读这些选项具有一定的难度，但只要考生思路清晰，要解答对这道题并不难。根据题中所给的条件可以看出本题的结论依赖的条件很充分，如果本题中有关两套检查系统的陈述是正确的，那么我们根据这些条件很容易得到本题的结论。也就是说本题的结论无可质疑，因此本题的推理是结论性的。由以上分析可知(A)是正确答案。**请注意本题的五个选项的翻译，并请读者自己试译这五个句子。**

四、类比论证

6. It is true that it is against international law to sell plutonium to countries that do not yet have nuclear weapons. But if United States companies do not do so, companies in other countries will.

Which of the following is most like the argument above in its logical structure?

译文：毫无疑问，向尚没有核武器的国家出售钚是违反国际法的，但如果美国不这样做，其他国家的公司会这样做。

以下哪一项同以上论述在逻辑结构方面最为相似？

(A) It is true that it is against the police department's policy to negotiate with kidnappers. But if the police want to prevent loss of life, they must negotiate in some cases.

(B) It is true that it is illegal to refuse to register for military service. But there is a long tradition in the United States of conscientious objection to serving in the armed forces.

(C) It is true that it is illegal for a government official to participate in a transaction in which there is an apparent conflict of interest. But if the facts are examined carefully, it will clearly be seen that there was no actual conflict of interest in the defendant's case.

(D) It is true that it is against the law to burglarize People's homes. But someone else certainly would have burglarized that house if the defendant had not done so first.

(E) It is true that company policy forbids supervisors to fire employees without two written warnings. But there have been many supervisors who have disobeyed this policy.

(A) 毫无疑问，同绑架者谈判是违反警察部门的政策的。但如果警察想阻止生命损失，他们在某些情况下必须同绑架者谈判。

(B) 毫无疑问，拒绝登记服兵役是违法的。但在美国有一项历史很久、可以做到尽责地拒绝在军队服役的传统。

(C) 毫无疑问，一个政府官员参与一项有明显利益冲突的交易是违法的。但如果将事实调查得更清楚一些，很清楚地看到实际上在被告方面没有利益冲突。

(D) 毫无疑问，夜间潜入别人的住宅是违法的。但如果被告不先这样做，总会有别的某个人做夜盗潜入该房子。

(E) 毫无疑问，该公司的政策禁止管理者在没有两次书面警告的情况下将雇员解雇。但有很多不遵守这项政策的管理者。

解析：短文中的论述承认某一行为违反了法律，但它通过预先假设总会有人违反这项法律为该行为提供了一个借口，只有选项(D)具有相同的特征，因此是正确答案；在选项(A)中，为违反一项政策提出了一个借口，但是，同短文和选项(D)不同，没有预先假定该政策总会被违反；相似地，选项(B)和(E)都在没有预先假定违法活动总会发生的情况下，指出发生了违法行为。选项(C)描述了一个案例，在该案例中提到的法律是不适用的。

下面我们再看一个中文例子：

7. 某商场失窃，职员涉嫌被询问。公安局的办案人员的第一个问题是："你以后还敢不敢再偷？"
上述提问方式，和下列哪项最为类似？

(A) 张三考试粗心，数学只得了90分。爸爸问他："你以后还粗心吗？"

(B) 李四花了大笔钱游玩某地，结果大失所望，阿五幸灾乐祸，问李四："你以后还去吗？"

(C) 赵六酒后驾车，结果翻车住院，还被罚了款，赵六的爱人又气又急，问："你以后还敢再酒后驾车吗？"

(D) 某歌舞厅因提供色情服务被查封，半年后复业，执法人员问老板："你以后还敢不敢再犯了？"

(E) "文化大革命"中，在一次批斗会上，造反派质问被批斗的老干部："你以后还敢不敢再走资本主义道路了？"

解析：段落中的公安局办案人员的问题典型特征是预先假设了一个被提问者无法接受的前提，五个选取项中只有(E)中造反派的问题具有这个特征，他预先假设一个被提问者无法接受的前提：被提问者是走资本主义道路的。

五、对同一词语有多种定义

8. Simon: We still do not know whether machines might be able to think. Computers are able to perform very

译文：Simon：我们仍不知道机器是否能够思考。计算机能够执行非常复杂的

331

sophisticated tasks but lack the flexibility characteristic of human intelligence.

Roberta: We do not need more sophisticated computers to know whether machines could think; we humans are machines, and we think.

Roberta's response to Simon's based on a reinterpretation of the term

(A) "computer".

(B) "know".

(C) "machine".

(D) "sophisticated".

(E) "think".

任务但是却缺乏人类智慧的灵活特性。

Roberta：我们不需要更复杂的计算机来弄清机器是否能够思考，我们人类就是机器，而我们可以思考。

Roberta对Simon的回应基于对哪个词的重新解释？

(A) 计算机

(B) 知道

(C) 机器

(D) 复杂的

(E) 思考

解析： 从上面对话可知Simon认为的机器是包括计算机在内的机器，而Roberta认为的机器是包括人类在内的机器，(C)指出了这一点，即"机器"一词在两人的对话中有不同的解释。所以(C)为正确答案。

六、二人对话

9. X: When a rare but serious industrial accident occurs, people respond by believing that such accidents are becoming more frequent. This belief is irrational. After all, being dealt four aces in a hand of poker, a rare event, hardly increases one's chances of being dealt four aces in a future hand.

Y: To the contrary, the belief is rational because it results in people's sensing a danger to themselves not previously sensed and taking precautionary actions to prevent similar accidents in the future.

Y's attempt to counter X's claim is best described by which of the following?

(A) It questions the aptness of the analogy drawn by X.

(B) It makes apparent X's failure to consider how people vary in their responses to a serious accident.

(C) It shifts the basis for judging rationality to considerations of utility.

(D) It offers an alternative explanation of why people form incorrect beliefs.

(E) It challenges X's assumption that the occurrence of a single event is sufficient to change a belief.

译文： X：当一种很少发生但却很严重的工业事故发生时，人们的反应是认为这种事故越来越频繁了。这种想法是没有道理的。毕竟，在某一把扑克中起到4张A这一稀有的事并不增加将来某把牌起到4张A的机会。

Y：正相反，该看法是合理的，因为它使人们感觉到他们以前没感受到的危险，并采取预防措施来防止类似事故在未来发生。

Y反驳X观点的企图，在下面哪一项中得到最好的描述？

(A) 它对X所进行的类比的恰当性提出质疑。

(B) 它使X未能考虑人们对严重事故的反应是多么不同这一点变得很明显。

(C) 它将判断合理性的基础转变为对实用性的考虑。

(D) 它对人们为什么形成错误观点提出一种替代性的解释。

(E) 它对X的假设：一件事的发生足以改变人的信仰，提出了挑战。

解析： 本题为"二人对话"类型，描述Y对X的观点的驳斥。读题重点应是第一个人的最后一句话与第二个人的第一句话。很显然，X得出"irrational"的观点基于的考虑与Y得出截然相反的"rational"的观点所基于的考虑是不一样的。(C)指出Y将判断合理性的基础转变为对实用性的考虑，正好表明Y从另一个角度去评估合理性，所以(C)很好地指出了二人的推理关系，因此(C)正确；若Y对扑克牌起4张A

的概率与工业事故的发生之间的类比提出质疑，(A)才正确；(B)与上面推理明显不符；Y并没有认为人们的观点错误，所以(D)不对；X并未基于如(E)所说的假设，所以(E)也不正确。

10. <u>Keith</u>: Compliance with new government regulations requiring the installation of smoke alarms and sprinkler systems in all theaters and arenas will cost the entertainment industry $25 billion annually. Consequently, jobs will be lost and profits diminished. Therefore, these regulations will harm the country's economy.

<u>Laura</u>: The $25 billion spent by some businesses will be revenue for others. Jobs and profits will be gained as well as lost. Laura responds to Keith by _____.

(A) demonstrating that Keith's conclusion is based on evidence that is not relevant to the issue at hand

(B) challenging the plausibility of the evidence that serves as the basis for Keith's argument

(C) suggesting that Keith's argument overlooks a mitigating consequence

(D) reinforcing Keith's conclusion by supplying a complementary interpretation of the evidence Keith cites

(E) agreeing with the main conclusion of Keith's argument but construing that conclusion as grounds for optimism rather than for pessimism

译文：<u>Keith</u>：政府颁布的新法规要求所有的剧院和比赛场所都安装烟感装置并配备洒水系统，娱乐业若遵守该法规每年要花费250亿美元。因此，失业率将会增加，并会出现利润率下降的问题。所以这些法规会损害该国的经济。

<u>Laura</u>：某些产业业花费250亿美元将会给其他的产业带来收益，工作和利润减少的同时，也会有所增加。

Laura通过_____来回应Keith。

(A) 证明Keith的结论是建立在与当前论题无关的证据之上

(B) 质疑支持Keith论断的证据的合理性

(C) 指出Keith的论断忽视了一个可以使（该法规不良）后果有所改善的因素

(D) 通过给Keith的结论所引用的证据提供补充性的解释来加强Keith的结论

(E) 同意Keith的主要论断，但是提出该结论是基于乐观主义，而不是悲观主义

解析：Keith认为新法规的实施将会导致失业和利润下滑，从而损害国家的经济。Laura指出当一个产业受损失时，其他提供实施该法规所需要货物和服务的产业将会受益。我们要思考的是：Laura在反驳时使用了什么策略？很明显，Laura使用了相同的证据，遵守新法规得耗资250亿美元，但得出了完全不同的结论。Keith注重某一个产业的损失，而Laura则看到了其他产业的收益。通过指出Keith没有提及的一个因素，她比较正面地评价了该法规所产生的后果。(C)为正确答案，因为Laura指出Keith没有考虑到在这种情况下，一个产业的损失意味着其他个产业将会由此而受益，正确地表明了Laura在驳斥时所使用的策略。（A）不正确，因为Laura接受了Keith的证据，并且她自己也使用该证据，并指出某些产业花费的250亿美元会使其他的相关产业受益。(B)不正确，因为Laura没有质疑Keith的证据，她使用相同的证据来支持自己的论断。(D)不正确，因为Laura否认Keith的观点，而不是支持他的结论。当Keith指出失业和利润下滑损害经济时，Laura指出工作和利润减少的同时也会有所增加。(E)不正确，因为Laura并没有同意Keith的新法规会损害经济的观点，相反她辩论说其他产业的收益将会补偿该产业的损失。

七、黑体部分的作用

这类考题主要考查论点构建中的某一句话或某两句话对结论或前提是否起作用或起什么作用的能力。

黑体部分作用题是把论证段落中的一个或两个句子变成黑体，然后问黑体部分在段落推理中的作用。这种题型实质上相当于把假设、支持或反对题型的答案放入段落推理中，然后把这个答案划线，问其对段落推理的作用。从某种程度上讲，黑体部分作用题的难度较小。下面是几个GMAT机考的黑体部分作用的试题：

11. Although measuring the productivity of outside consultants is a complex endeavor, **Company K, which relies heavily on consultants for long-term projects, must find ways to assess the performance of these workers**. The risks to a company that does not review the productivity of its human resources are simply too great. **Last year, Company L was forced into receivership after its productivity declined for the third straight quarter**.

The bolded phrases play which of the following roles in the argument above?

(A) The first phrase states the author's conclusion, and the second phrase refutes that conclusion.

(B) The first phrase states an assumption of the argument, and the second phrase provides evidence to undermine that position.

(C) The first phrase states one of the author's premises, and the second phrase provides the argument's conclusion.

(D) The first phrase states a position, and the second phrase refutes that position.

(E) The first phrase states the conclusion, and the second phrase supports the conclusion with an analogy.

译文：尽管衡量外部咨询者的效率复杂费力，**但K公司的长期项目严重依赖咨询者，所以，就必须找到评估这些咨询者的绩效的方法**。如果一家公司没有评估其人力资源的效率，那么其风险就会非常之大。**去年，L公司在其效率在第三个季度下降后，被迫进入破产管理阶段**。

在上述论证中，黑体部分起到的作用是下面哪一个？

(A) 第一部分陈述了作者的结论，第二部分驳斥了作者的结论。

(B) 第一部分陈述了论证的假设，第二部分提供了削弱论点的论据。

(C) 第一部分陈述了作者的一个前提，第二部分提供了论断的结论。

(D) 第一部分陈述了一个论点，第二部分驳斥了这个论点。

(E) 第一部分陈述了论证的结论，第二部分运用类比支持了论证的结论。

解析：本题中，我们重点关注的是黑体部分在整个论证中所起的作用，而此类题目的关键是找到整个论证的结论。很明显，第一个句子的后半部分（即黑体第一部分）为整个论证的结论，也就是说，论证的结论是："K公司必须找到评估这些咨询者的绩效的方法"。第二句话仅仅重述了第一句话，而第三句话通过一个类似情景（K公司的情形与L公司的情形的比较）支持了论证的结论。所以，（E）为正确答案。

12. Consumer advocate: It is generally true, at least in this state, that lawyers who advertise a specific service charge less for that service than lawyers who do not advertise. It is also true that **each time restrictions on the advertising of legal services have been eliminated, the number of lawyers advertising their services has increased and legal costs to consumers have declined in consequence**. However, eliminating the state requirement that legal advertisements must specify fees for specific services would almost certainly increase rather than further reduce consumers' legal costs. Lawyers would no longer have an incentive to lower their fees when they begin advertising and **if no longer required to specify fee arrangements, many lawyers who now advertise would increase their fees**.

In the consumer advocate's argument, the two portions in boldface play which of the following roles?

(A) The first is a generalization that the consumer advocate

译文：消费者拥护者：整体而论，为一项具体服务登广告的律师的收费要少于没有这样做的律师的收费，至少在这个州的情况是这样。另外，**每当诉讼服务刊登广告的限制被取消，为服务刊登广告的律师的数量就会增加，并且消费者的诉讼成本随之下降**。然而，取消该州要求诉讼广告必须明晰具体服务的费用的做法不会减少消费者的诉讼成本，反而会几乎肯定地增加了消费者的诉讼成本。在律师们开始刊登广告时，他们将不再有动机来降低他们的收费，而且，**如果明晰收费标准的要求不再存在，那么许多现在刊登广告的律师将会增加他们的收费**。

在消费者拥护者的论证中，两处黑体部分起到的作用是下面哪一个？

(A) 第一部分是消费者拥护者认为真实的

accepts as true; the second is presented as a consequence that follows from the truth of that generalization.

(B) The first is a pattern of cause and effect that the consumer advocate argues will be repeated in the case at issue; the second acknowledges a circumstance in which that pattern would not hold.

(C) The first is a pattern of cause and effect that the consumer advocate predicts will not hold in the case at issue; the second offers a consideration in support of that prediction.

(D) The first is evidence that, the consumer advocate offers in support of a certain prediction; the second is that prediction.

(E) The first acknowledges a consideration that weighs against the main position that the consumer advocate defends; the second is that position.

归纳，第二部分是由该归纳的真实而得出的一个结果。

(B) 第一部分是一个消费者拥护者认为会在争论的情形中重复出现的一种因果模型，第二部分说明了该因果模型将不能成立的一种情形。

(C) 第一部分是消费者拥护者推测会在争论的情形中不能成立的一种因果模型，第二部分提供了支持这个推测的因素。

(D) 第一部分是消费者拥护者支持某预测的证据，第二部分是这个预测。

(E) 第一部分说明了一个反对消费者拥护者所辩护的主要观点的因素，第二部分就是这个观点。

解析：在上述论证中，我们重点关注的是黑体部分在整个论证中所起的作用，而此类题目的关键是找到整个论证的结论。这里，论证中的第三个句子中的"*However*"告知读者该消费者拥护者所要论证的观点："取消该州要求诉讼广告必须明晰具体服务的费用的做法肯定不会减少消费者的诉讼成本，反而会几乎肯定增加了消费者的诉讼成本"。很明显，在该观点之前的第一个句子与第二个句子表达了两种让步的情形，说明了一个消费者拥护者认同的论断：消费者的诉讼成本随着刊登广告的开放而下降。在该消费者拥护者所要论证的观点之后的第四个句子是消费者拥护者坚持该观点的原因。因此，我们发现，第一个黑体部分确实表达了一种因果模型，同时，消费者拥护者推测该因果模型在此时会有差异；第二个黑体部分是消费者拥护者用来支持这个推测的一个因素。所以，(C)为正确答案。尽管第一个黑体部分确实是消费者拥护者认为真实的归纳，但该归纳实际上与第二个黑体部分中所做的推测相冲突，所以(A)不正确。尽管第一个黑体部分确实说明了一种因果模型，但消费者拥护者的推测在该情形下这一模型并站不住脚，所以(B)不正确。由于消费者拥护者并没有用第一个黑体部分支持任何推测，反而它与消费者拥护者自身的推测相冲突，所以(D)不正确。尽管(E)中第一个黑体部分的作用的描述到位正确，但由于消费者拥护者捍卫的观点并不是第二个黑体部分，而是"取消该州要求诉讼广告必须明晰具体服务的费用的做法肯定不会减少消费者的诉讼成本，反而会几乎肯定增加了消费者的诉讼成本"，所以(E)不正确。

13. 美国某杂志减少了国际时事文章的比例。编辑的理由是："**国际时事比例高，杂志的销量就下降，这表明读者不喜欢读国际时事文章**。"而批评家们认为编辑的理由站不住脚，他们认为："**编辑应当引**
①
导读者的兴趣，而不是迎合读者的喜好。"
②

本题问的是黑体部分①、②在段落推理中起的作用。很明显，①是编辑减少国际时事文章的比例的原因（或evidence），而②是批评家的论据以支持批评家的论点。GMAT机考此题的正确答案为(A)：①支持一个批评家反对的结论，②是批评家用来反对the editor's reasoning。

14. The curator argues that **some critics must be wrong in saying that the dating of a self-portrait by X is not**
①

right. These critics' reason is that X cannot paint a picture of a young man with dark hair at that time when he was 63. The curator maintains there is no reason to think that X will not paint a picture of himself. After all, **X could paint a picture that he was at 30 at the age of 60**.
②

本题问的是黑体部分①、②在段落推理中的作用。GMAT机考题的答案是：①serves as the curator's assessment of the status of the critics statement and ②is evidence supporting the statement that the critics opposed.

15. 由于人们过量捕捉X鱼，所以X鱼的数量急剧减少。**但渔业部门认为不需要采取防止该鱼灭绝的保护**

①

措施。他的基本理由是当鱼减少到一定程度，就会很难捕捉以致经济上不再合算，因此，捕鱼人也就不会再捕捉该鱼。但有人反驳说，**该鱼越少越珍贵，捕捉该鱼的人也就越多；而且该鱼少到捕捉已经不合**

②

算的地步时该鱼的灭绝就无可挽救了。

本题问的是黑体部分①和②在段落推理中起到什么作用。GMAT机考的答案是：①是渔业部门的观点，②从另一角度驳斥了①。

八、常见的逻辑错误

逻辑描述题描述段落推理关系，并且这类题的关键在于其选项是用逻辑的语言进行描述，所以笔者在下面将常见的逻辑错误总结于下：

常见的逻辑错误有偷换概念（或混淆概念）、偷换论题（或转移论题）、以偏概全（或轻率概括）、自相矛盾、模棱两可（或模棱两不可）、无理类比、倒置因果、循环定义、概念不当并列、同语反复、循环论证、推不出等等，这里我们重点看以下几种：

1. 类比推理

类比推理是根据两个对象在一系列属性上是相同的，而且知道其中的一个对象还具有另一种属性，由此推出另一个对象也具有这一属性的推理。类比推理的客观依据是：现实中的事物的各个属性并不是孤立存在的，而是互相联系互相制约。如两个对象在一系列属性上是相似的，那它们完全可能在另外的属性上也是相似的。类比推理的结论是或然的，即尽管其前提是真实的，也不能保证结论的真实性。这是因为，A和B毕竟是两个对象，它们尽管在一系列属性上是相同的，但仍存在着差异性，这种差异性有时就表现为A对象具有某属性，而B对象不具有某属性。在类比推理中，如果仅仅根据某些非本质的属性或者与所要推出的属性不相关的属性来作为前提，就会犯"无理类比"的逻辑错误。

2. 假性因果和混淆充分条件与必要条件

自然界和社会中的各个现象都是与其他现象互相联系、互相制约的。如果某一个现象的存在必然引起另一个现象的发生，那么这两个现象之间就具有因果联系。其中，引起某一现象产生的现象叫做原因，被另一现象引起的现象叫做结果。因果现象是相对的，一个现象对于某现象来说是结果，而对于另一现象来说又是原因。例如，爆炸既是火药达到一定温度的结果，又是造成人员伤亡的原因。因果联系的一个重要特点是在时间上具有先后相继的顺序，即对一对因果事件来说，总是原因在前，结果在后，概莫例外。因果联系的另一个重要特点是一定的原因总是产生一定的结果，而一定的结果总是由一定的原因产生的，两者的关系是确定的。既无无因之果，也无无果之因。

有关因果关系的逻辑错误还有假性因果和混淆充分条件与必要条件。假性因果是将两种无因果关系的事件看作是一件事情引起另一件事情的发生。混淆充分条件与必要条件，如本篇第五章归纳部分的例题一，"下雨"是"街道与人行道湿"的充分条件，即下雨必然引起街道与人行道湿，而非必要条件，即街道与人行道湿不一定是下雨引起的。将充分条件等同于必要条件便可荒谬地得出"若街道与人行道都湿，那么下雨了"。

3. 倒置因果

因果关系是事物之间的普遍联系的一种方式。因果关系一方面具有相对性，即一个现象对于某现象来说是结果，但对于另一现象来说又是原因。例如，房屋倒塌是地震的结果，又是导致人员伤亡的原因。因果关系的相对性，使事物之间可以形成一个没有起点和终点的因果链条。因果关系另一方面又具有绝对性，对因果链条上的每个环节来说，原因就是原因，结果就是结果，既不可倒"因"为"果"，也不可倒"果"为"因"。例如，对于地震和房屋倒塌来说，地震就是原因，房屋倒塌就是结果，决不可以颠倒过来。

4. 循环论证 (Circular reasoning)

所谓论证，就是用若干真实命题确定另一命题真实性的思维过程。

论证由论题、论据和论证方式三部分组成。所谓论题，是通过论证要确定其真实性的命题；所谓论据，是被用来确定论题真实性的命题，它可以是一个命题，也可以是几个命题；论证方式则是把论题和论据联系起来的形式，它体现的是一个逻辑推理的过程。一个论证，就是从论据出发，依据一定的论证方式，合乎逻辑地推出论题，从而使人们确信论题的真实性。

作为论证的一条重要规则，论据的真实性不应依赖论题的真实性。道理很简单，既然论题的真实性是以论据的真实性作为依据的，如果论据的真实性反转过来又依赖论题的真实性来论证，那就等于什么也没有论证。违反这一规则所犯的逻辑错误，称为"循环论证"。

5. 循环定义

所谓定义，是明确概念内涵的逻辑方法。给一个概念下定义，就是用精炼的语句将这个概念的内涵揭示出来，也就是揭示这个概念所反映的对象的本质属性。

定义是由被定义项、定义项和定义联项三个部分组成的。被定义项就是通过定义来揭示其内涵的概念；定义项就是用来揭示被定义项内涵的概念；联接被定义项和定义项组成定义的是定义联项。例如：

生命是有机体的新陈代谢。

在这个定义中，定义项包含了"有机体"这个概念，而什么是"有机体"又必须用被定义项"生命"来说明，因此，这个定义实际上等于什么也没有说明，看了这个定义并不能使人们了解生命的本质属性。

6. 同语反复

同语反复也是属于违反定义规则的逻辑错误。和循环定义一样，它也违反了定义的一条规则：定义项中不得直接或间接地包含被定义项。所不同的是，循环定义是间接地包含了被定义项而同语反复则是直接地包含了被定义项。例如：

生命就是有生命的物体的重量现象。

在这个定义中，定义项中直接地包含了被定义项"生命"这一概念，或者说，定义项仅仅把被定义项"生命"这一词语重复一次而已。显然，这样的定义对于帮助人们了解生命的本质毫无意义。

7. 推不出

论证的另一条重要的规则是要求论据和论题之间要有必然的联系，即从论据出发，能合乎逻辑地推出论题。违反这一条规则，就会犯"推不出"的逻辑错误。

犯"推不出"的逻辑错误，一般有两种情况：一种是"论据和论题不相干"，另一种是"论据不足"。

"论据和论题不相干"是指论据的真实性和论题的真实性毫无关系，二者风马牛不相及。这样，从论据的真实性当然推不出论题的真实性。例如：

"论据不足"是指论据对于论证论题的真实性来说虽是必要的，但不是充分的，即仅仅依靠这些论据，还是不足于说明论题的真实性，还需要补充新的论据。

8. 语言谬误

当一个字、短语的表达方式具有两种以上的含义时，特别是其意义容易混淆时就会出现语言谬误。当不知道某种意义应用在某种场合时也会出现此问题。如"democracy"，"teamwork"，"the American way"，和"pay off"等字对不同的人有不同的含义并可用于不同的上下文中。例如，美国政府和印尼政府在"democracy"的含义上具有相同的理解吗？"teamwork"对日本工人和美国工人的意义相同吗？避免意义不清的唯一方法是通过上下文仔细确认字的含义。字义不清可被用来进行欺骗或混淆视听。

九、试题精练及解析

1. Why save endangered species? For the general public, endangered species appear to be little more than biological oddities. A very different perception is gained from considering the issue of extinction in a wider context. The important point is that many major social advances have been made on the basis of life forms whose worth would never have been perceived in advance. Consider the impact of rubber-producing plants on contemporary life and industry: approximately two-thirds of the world's rubber supply comes from rubber-producing plants and is made into objects as diverse as rubber washers and rubber boots.

The author's point is made chiefly by

(A) acknowledging the validity of two opposing points of view.

(B) appealing to the emotions of the audience rather than to their intellects.

(C) suggesting a useful perspective for viewing the question raised at the beginning of the passage.

(D) trying to discredit the view of an opponent without presenting an alternative hypothesis.

(E) generalizing from similar to dissimilar cases.

为什么要挽救濒临灭绝的物种呢？对公众来说，濒危动物与生物学上的奇异行为差不多。从更广的范围内考虑物种灭绝的问题，便得出了另一个不同的观点，其要点为：很多重要的社会进步都是以生命形式为基础的，而这些形式的价值不可能预先被感知，看看产橡胶的植物对当代生活和工业的影响吧：世界上大约有2/3的橡胶供应来自产橡胶的植物，这些橡胶被制成橡胶垫和橡胶靴等种类繁多的产品。

作者主要通过下面哪一项来表达观点的?

(A) 承认两种相反观点的有效性。

(B) 打动读者的感情而不是理性。

(C) 从一个实用的角度来看待文章开始提出的问题。

(D) 试图否定对方的观点而没有提出替代性的假说。

(E) 用相似和相异的例子概括出结论。

2. Roberta was born in 1967, and so in 1976 she was nine years old. It is clear from this example that the last two digits of a person's birth year will be the same as the last two digits of the year of that person's ninth birthday, except that the position of the digits will be reversed.

Which of the following is the best criticism of the assertions made above?

(A) The generalization is valid only for those birth years that do not end in two zeroes.

(B) The example does not exhibit the same principle as is expressed in the generalization based on it.

(C) The generalization is valid only for those birth years in which the last digit is one greater than the second-to-last digit.

(D) The example cannot be shown to be correct unless the truth of the generalization is already presupposed.

(E) The generalization is valid only for those birth years in which the last digit is greater than five.

罗伯塔出生于1967年，因此，1976年她9岁。从这个例子可以清楚地看到一个人出生年的最后两位数字与其9岁那年的后两位数相同，只是数字的位置颠倒了。

以下哪一项是对上述推论的最佳反驳?

(A) 这种归纳只对结尾数字不是两个零的年份有效。

(B) 例子显示的规律与建立在它的基础上的归纳中的规律并不一致。

(C) 这种归纳只是在末尾数字比倒数第二位大1的出生年份里才有效。

(D) 除非已经预先假定了这种归纳的正确性，否则不能表明给出的例子是正确的。

(E) 这种归纳只对末尾数字大于5的年份适用。

3. Spiritualism, the doctrine that it is possible to communicate with the spirits of the deceased through specially talented persons called mediums, is fraudulent. As long ago as the

招魂术认为可以通过有特殊才能的人——灵媒——与死人的灵魂交往，这种学说是骗人的。早在19世纪70年代，

1870's, Professor Edwin Lankester showed that the purported "spirit writing" of the famed medium Henry Slade was present on a slate before the "spirits" were supposed to have begun writing on it. This example demonstrates that the doctrine of spiritualism is worthless.

If the example above is correctly reported, which of the following is the best argument against the conclusion drawn above?

(A) There cannot be proof that the spirits of the deceased do not exist.

(B) The conclusion depends on a historical report, and such reports of past events do not recount all of the circumstances.

(C) The cited evidence presupposes what is to be proved.

(D) A single instance of fraud cannot show that the doctrine is false in general.

(E) The correctness of the report depends on the veracity of antispiritualists, who may be expected to be biased.

Edwin Lankester 教授便指出所谓的著名灵媒Henry Slade的"灵书"是在"灵魂"书写之前便在石板上有了的，这个例子说明招魂术毫无价值。

如果以上的报道是正确的，下面哪个最能反驳上面的结论？

(A) 没证据表明死人的灵魂并不存在。

(B) 这个结论依赖于一个历史报导，这些对以往事件的报导没详述所有的细节。

(C) 引用的证据预先假定所要证实的。

(D) 仅仅一例欺骗不能表明整个学说都是错误的。

(E) 报导的正确性取决于反招魂术者的诚实，因为他们可能有偏见。

注：medium person: who claims to be able to communicate with the spirits of the dead 通灵的人；灵媒；关亡人

4. In respectable periodicals, books are given reviewing space in inverse proportion to the likely size of their sales. Airport and supermarket bookstalls stock only books that are expected to sell in large numbers. Consequently, those who buy books at such bookstalls have to do so without any guidance whatever from the book reviewers whose work is published in respectable periodicals.

Which of the following is a valid criticism of the argument above?

(A) Bookstalls like those found at airports and in supermarkets are designed to induce people to buy books on impulse.

(B) The assortment of books available at airport bookstalls is different from the assortment of books available at supermarket bookstalls.

(C) The fact that a book is expected to sell well does not guarantee that actual sales will be large.

(D) Many who later come to be respected as book reviewers start their careers by writing for trashy magazines.

(E) The conclusion that respectable periodicals never publish reviews of projected bestsellers is unwarranted.

在品位高雅的期刊中，书评的版面与其销售量成反比。机场和超市的书摊只出售预计能大量销售的书。因此，在这些书摊上购书的人不得不在没有得到在高品位的期刊上发表文章的书评家的指导下买这些书了。

下面的哪一项是对上述论述的有效批评？

(A) 像机场和超市中的书摊是为引诱人们一时冲动地买书而设计的。

(B) 机场书摊上可以买到的书的类型与超市书摊上可以买到的图书的类型不同。

(C) 一本书预计会卖得好的事实并不能保证其实际销售量大。

(D) 很多后来被尊为书评家的人是以为垃圾杂志撰稿开始他们的职业生涯的。

(E) 高品位的期刊从不发表对预测出的畅销书的评论这一结论是无根据的。

5. Dear Editor: Jones's new book has the potential to destroy reputations of persons who have held high governmental responsibility during national crises. However, readers should dismiss Jones's criticisms. Jones's antigovernment attitude is

亲爱的编辑：琼斯的新书有可能会毁掉在国内危机期间担任高级政府职位的人的名誉。然而，读者们应该不考虑琼斯的批评。琼斯的反政府态度是众所周知的，

well known, and his criticisms will convince only those like himself, persons who have never had real responsibility and never will, and hence are not qualified to judge.

The argument above includes which of the following questionable techniques?

(A) It employs the term "responsibility" in more than one sense.

(B) It assumes that attacking the source of a claim is sufficient to disprove the claim.

(C) It assumes that the majority of people share Jones's attitude of opposition to government policies.

(D) It appeals to a person of unreliable authority as a supporter of its position.

(E) It confuses cause and effect.

他的批评只能说服和他一样的人，即那些从未有过，以后也不会有真正的责任感的人，因此他们没有资格作出评判。

上述论述用了下面的哪一种有质疑的技巧？

(A) 它用的"责任"这一词来表达了不同的意思。

(B) 它假设攻击某一宣称的来源就足以否定这一宣称。

(C) 它假定大多数人与琼斯持相同的反政府政策的态度。

(D) 它呼吁一个不可靠的权威人士作为它的立场的支持者。

(E) 它将因果混淆。

6. Many pregnant women suffer from vitamin deficiency, but this is frequently not due to vitamin deficiency in their diets; most often it is because they have higher requirements for vitamins than do the rest of the population.

The best criticism of the reasoning in the statement above is that it

(A) fails to specify the percentage of pregnant women who suffer from vitamin deficiency.

(B) gives insufficient information about why pregnant women have higher vitamin requirements than do other groups.

(C) fails to employ the same reference group for both uses of the term "vitamin deficiency."

(D) provides insufficient information about the incidence of vitamin deficiency in other groups with high vitamin requirements.

(E) uses "higher requirements" in an ambiguous manner.

很多怀孕的妇女患有缺乏维生素症状，但这常常不是由于她们饮食中缺乏维生素，更多见的是因为她们比其他人需要更多的维生素。

对上面陈述的推理最好的批评是：

(A) 它未能具体给出患维生素缺乏症的孕妇的比例。

(B) 它对为什么孕妇比其他人需要更多的维生素未能给出足够信息。

(C) 它在两次用到"缺乏维生素"一词时使用的参照群体是不同的。

(D) 它对其他种维生素需求量大的人的缺乏维生素现象未能给出足够信息。

(E) 它以模糊不清的方式使用"需求量大"一词。

7. Any United States flag manufactured outside the United States should be banned from importation, since some foreign manufacturers superimpose images on the United States flag and sell such products with relative impunity. United States manufacturers, on the other hand, would face penalties for such violations of the United States flag code.

Which of the following is the best criticism of the argument above?

(A) The argument reiterates its conclusion instead of providing a reason for it.

(B) The argument makes an irrelevant distinction between foreign and United States manufacturers.

应禁止在美国以外制造的任何美国国旗的进口。因为一些外国制造商在美国国旗上附加了一些图案并能相对不受惩罚地销售这种产品。另一方面，美国制造商却会因这种违反美国国旗法的行为受到惩罚。

以下哪一项是对上面论述最好的批驳？

(A) 该论述只是重申了它的结论，却没有提出支持它的理由。

(B) 该论述在外国和美国制造商之间作出了毫不相关的区分。

(C) The reason given for the ban undermines rather than supports the conclusion.

(D) The reason given for the ban does not explain why images superimposed on the United States flag are offensive.

(E) The reason given for the ban applies only to a part of the group of manufacturers whose flags are included in the ban, not necessarily to all.

8. New employees of Ace Industries are complaining about discomfort caused by excessive noise inside Ace's factory. Experienced Ace factory employees, however, do not suffer any such discomfort. Although Ace accepts responsibility for the health of its employees, it has decided not to issue earplugs to new employees. Ace reasoned that the new employees would also become accustomed to the noise without using earplugs.

Which of the following, if true, indicates a flaw in Ace's decision not to issue earplugs to new employees?

(A) Because the noise in Ace's factory is absorbed by soundproof walls, it cannot be heard by Ace executives in their offices.

(B) Many of the new employees interviewed said they would not wear earplugs on the job.

(C) Issuing earplugs to all new employees would be a less effective method of reducing employees' exposure to noise than altering the machinery to be less noisy would be.

(D) The experienced employees' lack of discomfort is attributable to hearing loss caused by the factory noise.

(E) The machines in Ace's factory have not become any noisier since the experienced workers were originally hired.

9. The nations biggest retailers reported strong sales during the last six months. During this period of strong sales, profits were weaker than usual. This state of affairs is unusual since or ordinary when sales increase, profits also increase.

Which of the following, if true during the last six months, most helps to account for the unusual state of affairs described above?

(A) A decrease in interest rates allowed many retailers to increase their inventories without having to pay high interest that cut into profits.

(B) Sales of women's and children clothing were up by more than 20 percent while sales of men's clothing were up by an insignificant amount.

（C）给出禁令的原因削弱了，而不是支持了该结论。

（D）给出禁令的理由没有解释为什么加图案于美国国旗是违法的。

（E）给出禁令的理由只适用于那些制造的国旗属于禁止之列的制造商，并不一定适用于所有的制造商。

Ace工业集团的新雇员抱怨由Ace工厂内噪音过大而引起的不适。然而有经验的Ace老雇员却没有任何这种不适，虽然Ace要对其雇员的健康负责，它还是决定不向新员工发耳塞。Ace的理由是不使用耳塞，新员工也会逐渐习惯这种噪音。

以下哪项如果正确，指出Ace决定不发耳塞给新员工的错误？

（A）因为Ace工厂的噪音被隔音墙吸收，公司行政人员在办公室里听不见噪音。

（B）许多接受采访的新雇员说他们不愿上班时戴耳塞。

（C）向所有的新雇员分发耳塞减小噪声对员工的影响的效果不如改换使用噪音较小的机器的效果好。

（D）老雇员之所以没有不舒适的感觉是因为工厂噪音已经导致他们的听力有所下降。

（E）Ace厂现在的机器发出的噪音自从老员工受雇以来没有任何增加。

全国最大的零售商报告了在过去的6个月中巨大的销售量。在这段销售旺盛的时间里，利润比平时少，这种情况不太寻常，因为当销量增加时利润一般情况下也会增加。

如果下列关于过去6个月的说法正确，哪一项最有助于解释以上不寻常的事情？

（A）由于利率下降，使得许多零售商可以增加存货，又不必支付较高的利息而减少利润。

（B）女士和儿童的服装的销售额增加了20%，而男士服装的销售额只有少量增加。

(C) Two of the largest independent retailers managed to buy their merchandise at lower prices.

(D) The nation's largest retailers attracted more customers by dramatically advertising the amount of money spent on advertising.

(E) Many retailers raised prices in order to take advantage of the recent growth in consumer spending.

(C) 两个最大的独立的零售商想要以更低的价格购进商品。

(D) 全国最大的零售商们通过对花在广告中的钱的数量大作广告来吸引更多的消费者。

(E) 许多零售商为了利用近来消费者扩大消费的时机，提高了价格。

10. John: It is permissible and even advisable to execute criminals convicted of brutal murders. After all, a publicized execution can serve to deter heinous crimes and thus minimize suffering in the long run. Capital punishment is a kind of societal self-defense.

Mary: You are ignoring the prior issue of whether a state or society has the right to take anyone's life. If there is no such right, then, the issue of whether capital punishment deters crime is irrelevant.

If it were determined dial capital punishment does not serve to deter crime, John's and Mary's positions would be affected in which of the following ways?

(A) Neither John's nor Mary's position would be affected.

(B) Both John's and Mary's positions would be weakened.

(C) Mary's position would be strengthened but John's position would not be affected.

(D) John's position would be weakened but Mary's position would not be affected.

(E) John's position would be weakened and Mary's position would be strengthened.

John：处死残忍的杀人犯是容许的甚至是明智的。毕竟公开处决可以起到遏制残酷的犯罪并减少长期遭受的痛苦。死刑是一种社会的自我防范。

Mary：你忽视了一个应该优先考虑的问题，即一个国家或社会是否有权力剥夺任何一个人的生命。如果没有这样的权力，那么死刑是否能遏制犯罪这一问题就不那么重要。

如果可以确定死刑不能遏制犯罪，则John和Mary的立场以下列哪种方式受到影响？

(A) John和Mary 的立场都不会受到影响。

(B) John和Mary的立场会受到削弱。

(C) Mary的立场得到了加强，而John的立场没有受到影响。

(D) John的立场受到削弱，Mary的立场不受影响。

(E) John的立场受到削弱，Mary的立场得到了加强。

11. Calvin: Fire insurance policies are disadvantageous to policyholders. The typical policyholder always pays more in premiums than he or she collects in payments on policies.

Lorraine: Yes, but policyholders are still right in thinking that it is to their advantage to hold an insurance policy. The peace of mind that comes from having an insurance policy is the main advantage to the policyholder.

Lorraine addresses Calvin's argument by

(A) questioning the source of Calvin's factual information.

(B) introducing a consideration neglected by Calvin's argument.

(C) showing that Calvin's argument assumes what it sets out to prove.

(D) challenging the truth of the evidence advanced in

Calvin：火灾保险单对投保人是不利的。典型的投保人支付的保险费通常比他或她通过保险单收到的偿付款要高。

Lorraine：是的，但是投保人认为持有一张保险单对他们有好处还是有道理的。通过持有一张保险单而得到的心境平和是投保人得到的主要好处。

Lorraine通过什么来回应Calvin的论述？

(A) 对Calvine真实信息的来源提出质疑。

(B) 引入Calvine的论述所忽略的一种想法。

(C) 指出Calvine的论述以它将要证明的东西作为假设前提。

(D) 对Calvine的论述中提出的证据的真实性表示怀疑。

Calvin's argument.

(E) showing the irrelevance of Calvin's evidence to the conclusion he draws.

12. No one can be licensed as an electrician in Parker County without first completing a certain course in electrical safety procedures. All students majoring in computer technology at Parker County Technical College must complete that course before graduating. Therefore, any of the college's graduates in computer technology can be licensed as an electrician in Parker County.

The reasoning in the argument above is open to question because the argument has not established that

(A) everyone who has completed the course in electrical safety procedures is equally knowledgeable about such procedures.

(B) all students majoring in computer technology who complete the course in electrical safety procedures at Parker County Technical College eventually graduate.

(C) completion of a course in electrical safety procedures is all that is necessary for a person to be licensed as an electrician in Parker County.

(D) the only way for a person to become knowledgeable about electrical safety procedures is to take a course in those procedures.

(E) the only students at Parker County Technical College who are eligible to take the course in electrical safety procedures are students majoring in computer technology.

13. Lumber Merchant: Because logging companies have long been replanting trees after logging, almost half of the tropical hardwood now sold is harvested from sustainable sources.

Environmentalist: On the contrary, barely one percent of the tropical hardwood sold is harvested from sustainable sources, since nearly all logging involves destruction of animal habitats that cannot be restored by replanting trees.

The environmentalist's response to the lumber merchant is based on a reinterpretation of

(A) "sustainable sources".

(B) "tropical".

(C) "replanting trees".

(D) "hardwood sold".

(E) "harvested".

(E) 指出Calvine的证据和他推出的结论无关。

不首先完成某一门用电安全程序课程，在Parker郡就不会获准成为电工。在Parker郡技术学院读计算机技术专业的所有学生毕业前都要完成这门课。因此该校任何计算机技术专业的毕业生在Parker郡都能被获准成为电工。

以上论述的推理会受到质疑，因为该论述没有指出：

(A) 所有修完"用电安全程序"这门课的人，对这一程序的知识了解程度是一样的。

(B) Parker郡技术学院计算机技术专业所有修完这门用电安全程序的课程的学生最终都毕业了。

(C) 修完"用电安全程序"这门课是被Parker郡批准成为电工所必要的所有条件。

(D) 一个人了解安全用电的知识的唯一途径是修一门关于那些程序的课程。

(E) Parker 郡的技术学院的大学生中，只有计算机技术专业的学生有资格修"用电安全程序"这门课。

木材商：由于伐木公司长期以来在伐木之后都会重新种上树，现在销售的热带硬木几乎一半都来自这些可再生资源。

环境保护主义者：相反，所销售的热带硬木只有1%是从可再生资源中得到的，因为几乎所有的砍伐活动都会对动物栖息地造成破坏，而这是不能由重新种树所恢复的。

环境保护主义者对木材商的反应是基于对下列哪一个词的重新解释?

(A) 可再生资源

(B) 热带的

(C) 重新植树

(D) 出售的硬木

(E) 开采

14. When six out of ten people who had eaten the egg salad at an office party became ill shortly afterward, the leftover egg salad was tested. Testing failed to confirm the presence of any harmful bacteria in the egg salad. It follows that the egg salad was not responsible for the illness of any of the people who ate it.

Which of the following is an error in the reasoning of the argument above?

(A) Treating the cause of a sequence of events as if it were the result of that sequence of events.

(B) Rejecting a possible explanation without suggesting an alternative explanation.

(C) Failing to consider the possibility that those who did not become ill shortly after eating the egg salad became ill later.

(D) Treating a lack of proof that something is the case as constituting sufficient proof that it is not the case.

(E) Overlooking the possibility that some people are more susceptible to harmful bacteria than are other people.

15. Kyle: The rate of highway fatalities per 100 million miles driven was about a third lower last year than ten years ago. The decrease is mainly attributable to greater use of seat belts and to less drinking of alcohol by drivers, but last year's sluggish economy also contributed, by curtailing driving.

Lisa: The economy could not have been a factor, because even if fewer fatalities occur when fewer miles are driven, the number "per 100 million miles driven" is what you were discussing, and that figure would not fall merely because fewer miles were driven.

Lisa's objection is based on

(A) indicating that a confusion between cause and effect has taken place.

(B) distinguishing between total number of instances and rate of occurrence.

(C) proposing an alternative way of interpreting the data presented.

(D) pointing out that statistics can be misleading if selected to prove a point.

(E) showing that lack of precision has caused a relevant ambiguity.

十个在办公室聚会上吃了鸡蛋沙拉的人中有六个过后很快就生了病。将剩下的鸡蛋沙拉拿去检验，检验没能证实鸡蛋沙拉中存在任何有害细菌。也就是说鸡蛋沙拉不对任何因吃了它而得了病的人负责任。

以下哪项是以上论述推理过程中的一个错误？

(A) 把一系列事件的起因当作一串事件的结果来对待。

(B) 抛弃一种可能的解释，又没有提出一种替代性的解释。

(C) 没有考虑到，吃过鸡蛋沙拉没有马上发病的人可能后来会发病。

(D) 本来缺少证明某事是某种情况的证据，但却把这种欠缺作为证明某事不是那种情况的充分证据。

(E) 忽略了一些人比其他人对有害细菌更敏感的可能性。

Kyle：去年每行驶一亿英里，在高速公路上发生的死亡率大概比十年前降低了三分之一。这一下降主要归功于司机更多地使用安全带和少喝酒，但去年的经济衰退也有影响，它减少了行驶的里程。

Lisa：经济状况不会是一个因素，因为即使当行驶里程降低后死亡人数也有降低，但你所讨论的数字是"每行驶一亿英里"，这个数字是不会仅由于行驶里程降低而下降的。

Lisa的反驳基于：

(A) 指出Kyle混淆了起因和结果。

(B) 把事故发生的总数和事故发生率区分来看。

(C) 提出用一种替代性的方式来解释提供的数据。

(D) 指出如果挑选一些数据来证明一个观点，那么统计数据可能会有误导的效果。

(E) 指出缺乏准确性造成了相关的模糊性。

16. Soft Drink Manufacturer: Our new children's soft drink, RipeCal, is fortified with calcium. Since calcium is essential for developing healthy bones, drinking RipeCal regularly will help make children healthy.

Consumer Advocate: But RipeCal also contains large amounts of sugar, and regularly consuming large amounts of sugar is unhealthful, especially for children.

In responding to the soft drink manufacturer, the consumer advocate does which of the following?

(A) Challenges the manufacturer's claim about the nutritional value of calcium in children's diets.

(B) Argues that the evidence cited by the manufacturer, when properly considered, leads to a conclusion opposite to that reached by the manufacturer.

(C) Implies that the manufacturer of a product is typically unconcerned with the nutritional value of that product.

(D) Questions whether a substance that is healthful when eaten in moderation can be unhealthful when eaten in excessive amounts.

(E) Presents additional facts that call into question the conclusion drawn by the manufacturer.

软饮料制造商：我们的新型儿童软饮料RipleCal增加了钙的含量。由于钙对形成健康的骨骼非常重要，所以经常饮用RipeCal会使孩子更加健康。

消费者代表：但RipeCal中同时含有大量的糖份，经常食用大量的糖是不利于健康的，尤其是对孩子。

在对软饮料制造商的回应中，消费者代表做了下列哪一项？

(A) 对制造商宣称的钙元素在儿童饮食中的营养价值提出质疑。

(B) 争论说如果对制造商引用的证据加以正确地考虑，会得出完全相反的结论。

(C) 暗示产品制造商通常对该产品的营养价值毫不关心。

(D) 怀疑某种物质是否在适度食用时有利于健康，而过度食用时则对健康有害。

(E) 举出其他事实以向制造商所做的结论提出质疑。

17. The organizers of tomorrow's outdoor concert announced that it will go on tomorrow on schedule unless bad weather is forecast or too few advance tickets are sold. If the concert is canceled, refunds will be made to ticket holders. Since some ticket holders have already been issued refunds even though more than enough advance tickets were sold, it must be the case that bad weather is forecast.

Which of the following is an error of reasoning contained in the argument?

(A) It proceeds as if a condition, which by itself is enough to guarantee a certain result, is the only condition under which that result would occur.

(B) It bases a conclusion that is known to require two conditions on evidence that bears on only one of those conditions.

(C) It explains one event as being caused by another event, even though both events must actually have been caused by some third, unidentified event.

(D) It treats evidence for the absence of one condition under which a circumstance would occur as conclusive evidence that that circumstance will not occur.

室外音乐会的组织者宣布，明天的音乐会将如期举行，除非预报了坏天气或预售票卖得太少了。如果音乐会被取消，将给已买了票的人退款。尽管预售票已卖得足够多，但仍有一些已买了票的人已经得到了退款，这一定是因为预报了坏天气的缘故。

下列哪一项是该论述中含有的推理错误？

(A) 该推理认为如果一个原因自身足以导致其一结果，那么导致这个结果的原因只能是它。

(B) 该推理将已知需要两个前提条件才能成立的结论建立在仅与这两个条件中的一个有关系的论据基础之上。

(C) 该推理仍解释说其中一事件是由另一事件引起的，即使这两件事都是由第三件未知的事件引起的。

(D) 该推理把缺少某一事件会发生的一项条件的证据当作了该事件不会发生的结论性证据。

18. Surveys show that every year only 10 percent of cigarette smokers switch brands. Yet the manufacturers have been spending an amount equal to 10 percent of their gross receipts on cigarette promotion in magazines. It follows from these figures that inducing cigarette smokers to switch brands did not pay, and that cigarette companies would have been no worse off economically if they had dropped their advertising.

Of the following, the best criticism of the conclusion that inducing cigarette smokers to switch brands did not pay is that the conclusion is based on

(A) computing advertising costs as a percentage of gross receipts, not of overall costs.

(B) past patterns of smoking and may not carry over to the future.

(C) the assumption that each smoker is loyal to a single brand of cigarettes at any one time.

(D) the assumption that each manufacturer produces only one brand of cigarettes.

(E) figures for the cigarette industry as a whole and may not hold for a particular company.

19. Certain messenger molecules fight damage to the lungs from noxious air by telling the muscle cells encircling the lungs' airways to contract. This partially seals off the lungs. An asthma attack occurs when the messenger molecules are activated unnecessarily, in response to harmless things like pollen or household dust.

Which of the following, if true, point to the most serious flaw of a plan to develop a medication that would prevent asthma attacks by blocking receipt of any messages sent by the messenger molecules referred to above?

(A) Researchers do not yet know how the body produces the messenger molecules that trigger asthma attacks.

(B) Researchers do not yet know what makes one person's messenger molecules more easily activated than another's.

(C) Such a medication would not become available for several years, because of long lead times in both development and manufacture.

(D) Such a medication would be unable to distinguish between messages triggered by pollen and household dust and messages triggered by noxious air.

调查显示，每年仅有10%的抽烟者换抽别的品牌。但是，烟草制造商每年用于在杂志上进行香烟促销的资金数额是其总收入的10%。由这些数字可知，诱使抽烟者换抽别的品牌不能奏效，如果烟草公司撤出他们的广告，在经济上不会变得更糟。

下面几种说法中，对"诱使抽烟者换抽别的品牌不能奏效"的结论提出的最好批评是，该结论基于：

(A) 计算广告费用占总收入的比重而非占总成本的比重。

(B) 以往的抽烟习惯，且这种习惯可能不会延续到将来。

(C) 假定每个抽烟者每次都会忠实于一种品牌。

(D) 假定每家烟草制造商只生产一种品牌的香烟。

(E) 把香烟行业作为一个整体得到的数字对特定的某家公司可能是无效的。

某些媒分子通过使环绕肺气管的肌肉细胞收缩来抵御有毒气体对肺部的损害。这使得肺部部分封闭起来。当这些媒分子被不必要的激活时，对某些无害的事物像花粉或家庭粉尘作出反应，就出现了哮喘病。

有一项计划是开发一种药物通过阻碍接收由上文所说的媒分子发出的信息来防止哮喘病的发生。以下哪一项，如果是正确的，将指出这项计划的最严重的缺陷？

(A) 研究人员仍不知身体是如何产生这种引发哮喘病的媒分子的。

(B) 研究人员仍不知是什么使一个人的媒分子比某他人的更易激活。

(C) 很多年内无法获得这样的药物，因为开发和生产这种药物都需要很长的时间。

(D) 这样的药物无法区分由花粉和家庭粉尘引发的信息与由有毒气体引发的信息。

(E) Such a medication would be a preventative only and would be unable to alleviate an asthma attack once it had started.

20. A certain mayor has proposed a fee of five dollars per day on private vehicles entering the city, claiming that the fee will alleviate the city's traffic congestion. The mayor reasons that, since the fee will exceed the cost of round-trip bus fare from many nearby points, many People will switch from using their cars to using the bus.

Which of the following statements, if true, provides the best evidence that the mayor's reasoning is flawed?

(A) Projected increases in the price of gasoline will increase the cost of taking a private vehicle into the city.

(B) The cost of parking fees already makes it considerably more expensive for most People to take a private vehicle into the city than to take a bus.

(C) Most of the people currently riding the bus do not own private vehicles.

(D) Many commuters opposing the mayor's plan have indicated that they would rather endure traffic congestion than pay a five-dollar-per day fee.

(E) During the average workday, private vehicles owned and operated by people living within the city account for twenty percent of the city's traffic congestion.

21. Many plant varieties used in industrially developed nations to improve cultivated crops come from less-developed nations. No compensation is paid on the grounds that the plants used are "the common heritage of humanity." Such reasoning is, however, flawed. After all, no one suggests that coal,oil, and ores should be extracted without payment.

Which of the following best describes an aspect of the method used by the author in the argument above?

(A) The author proceeds from a number of specific observations to a tentative generalization.

(B) The author applies to the case under discussion facts about phenomena assumed to be similar in some relevant respect.

(C) A position is strengthened by showing that the opposite of that position would have logically absurd consequences.

(D) A line of reasoning is called into question on the grounds that it confuses cause and effect in a causal relation.

（E）这样的药物只能是预防性的，一旦得上哮喘，它无法减轻哮喘的程度。

某一市长曾建议向进城的私人车辆每天收取五美元的费用，宣称这种费用的征收将缓解该城市的交通拥挤状况。该市长解释说，由于该费用比许多附近站点乘坐环线公共汽车的费用要高，许多人会由自己驾驶汽车转为乘坐公共汽车。

以下哪一项陈述，如果是正确的，为证明该市长的推理是有缺陷的提供了最好的证据？

（A）汽油价格的预期上升将提高进城的私人车辆的成本。

（B）停车费用已经使大多数开私人车辆进城的人觉得比乘坐公共汽车昂贵很多了。

（C）目前乘坐公共汽车的人多数没有自己的私家车。

（D）许多反对该市长计划的通勤者指出他们宁愿忍受交通拥挤，也不愿付每天五美元的费用。

（E）在一般的工作日，居住在城区里的人拥有和驾驶的私人车辆占到了该城整个交通流量的20%。

工业发达国家用来改善其载培作物的许多植物种类来自于欠发达国家。发达国家并未支付任何补偿，理由是这些植物是被作为"人类的共同遗产"而使用的。但是，这种逻辑是有缺陷的，不管怎么说，没有人提出煤、石油和矿石可以不付费地进行开采。

下面哪个最好地描述了作者在以上的论证中使用的方法的一个方面？

（A）作者从很多具体观察前进到一个假定的概括。

（B）作者把假定在相关方面类似的现象事实应用到正在讨论的情况中。

（C）通过表明一种立场的对立面会有逻辑上可笑的结果，来加强这种立场的说服力。

（D）以某一推理过程混淆了因果关系中的

(E) An argument is analyzed by separating statements of fact from individual value judgments.

22. Recent audits revealed that BanqueCard, a credit service, has erred in calculating the interest it charges its clients. But BanqueCard's chief accountant reasoned that the profits that the company shows would remain unaffected by a revision of its clients', credit statements to correct its previous billing errors, since just as many clients had been overcharged as undercharged.

Which of the following is a reasoning error that the accountant makes in concluding that correcting its clients' statements would leave BanqueCard's profits unaffected?

(A) Relying on the reputation of BanqueCard as a trustworthy credit service to maintain the company's clientele after the error becomes widely known.

(B) Failing to establish that BanqueCard charges the same rates of interest for all of its clients.

(C) Overlooking the possibility that the amount by which BanqueCard's clients had been overcharged might be greater than the amount by which they had been undercharged.

(D) Assuming that the clients who had been overcharged by BanqueCard had not noticed the error in their credit bills.

(E) Presupposing that each one of BanqueCard's clients had either been overcharged or else had been undercharged by the billing error.

23. The government should enact a bill that would prohibit the sale and consumption of alcohol on commuter trains. Recently, the state, exercising its legitimate authority, passed a law to protect the health of commuters by prohibiting smoking on the commuter line. When intoxicated riders get off the train, get in their cars, and drive, the public is exposed to at least as much danger as are nonsmoking rail passengers who are forced to inhale cigarette smoke.

In arguing that alcohol consumption on commuter trains should be banned, the author relies on

(A) the fact that drinking alcohol is dangerous to one's health.

(B) the principle that people need to be protected from their own actions.

原因和结果为理由，可以对这一推理过程提出质疑。

(E) 一个论点可以通过个人价值判断形成的分散的表述来进行分析。

最近的稽核显示出Banquecard——一种贷款服务——在计算向其客户收取利息时出现了错误。但是Banquecard的总会计师解释说，在修改了其客户的贷款账户以改正原先的账务错误以后，公司列示的利润会保持不受影响，因为被索价过高的客户和被索价过低的客户一样多。

该会计师在得出结论认为客户账户的改正不会影响Banquecard的利润的过程中，犯了下面哪个推理错误？

(A) 相信在这次错误广为人知以后，Banquecard作为值得信赖的贷款服务的名声可以维持住公司的客户。

(B) 未能确定Banquecard向所有客户收取了相同的利率。

(C) 忽视了Banquecard客户被索价过高的数额可能高于被索价过低的数额。

(D) 假定被Banquecard索价过高的客户没有注意到他们贷款账单中出现的错误。

(E) 预先假定账务错误使每个Banquecard的客户要么被索价过高，要么被索价过低。

政府应该实施一条法案来禁止在通勤火车上销售和饮用酒精饮料。最近，政府运用它的法律权力，通过了一条禁止在通勤火车上抽烟，来保护上下班人的健康的法律。当喝醉了的乘客下了火车，钻进他们的汽车后开车时，公众面临的危险与火车上不抽烟的乘客被迫呼吸香烟的烟尘所面临的危险至少是一样大。

在证明在通勤火车上喝含有酒精的饮料应该被禁止时作者依赖于_____。

(A) 喝含有酒精的饮料有害个人健康的事实。

(B) 人们需要保护以免受他们的行为对自

(C) the use of emotionally charged descriptions of smoking and drinking alcohol.

(D) the reader's sympathy for the problems of commuters.

(E) a comparison between the effects of smoking and the effects of drinking alcohol.

24. The usefulness of lie detectors cannot be overestimated. Although there is no employee screening procedure that is 100 percent accurate, the lie detector is a valuable tool for employers and employees alike. The lie detector's usefulness is amply demonstrated in a recent survey conducted by a prestigious university. In the survey, those employees of a large company who were applying for a newly created position within the company were asked if they had ever worked on Project X. More than one-third of the applicants studied lied and said they had worked on the project—a project that never existed.

Which one of the following best identifies a flaw in the author's argument about the usefulness of lie detectors?

(A) The argument depends on the assumption that whatever is good for the employer is good for the employee.

(B) Since lie detectors are known to be less than 100 percent accurate, the test will tend to help only those with something to hide.

(C) By referring to a prestigious university, the author is appealing to authority—rather than to evidence.

(D) The study shows only that certain individuals will lie, not that the lie detector can detect them.

(E) The author fails to address the issue that the use of lie detectors may fail to prevent embezzlement.

25. A large group of hyperactive children whose regular diets included food containing large amounts of additives was observed by researchers trained to assess the presence or absence of behavior problems. The children were then placed on a low-additive diet for several weeks, after which they were observed again. Originally nearly 60 percent of the children exhibited behavior problems; after the change in diet, only 30 percent did so. On the basis of these data, it can be concluded that food additives can contribute to behavior problems in hyperactive children.

已造成伤害的原则。

(C) 对抽烟和喝酒精饮料作了一个充满感情的指责性描述。

(D) 读者对通勤者所遭遇的问题的同情。

(E) 在抽烟的影响与喝含有酒精的饮料的影响两者之间作了一个比较。

对测谎仪的有用性无论怎样地过高估计都不为过。尽管没有100%准确的雇员审查程序，但是测谎仪对雇主和雇员来说都是一个非常有用的工具。最近，测谎仪的有用性被一名牌大学进行的一次调查报告充分地证实。在这个调查报告中，申请某一大公司内新设立的一个职位的职员被问及他们是否曾在X项目上工作过。被调查的申请者中，有超过三分之一的人撒了谎，他们说他们曾在那个项目上工作过，而这个项目是根本不存在的。

下面哪一项能最好地指出作者关于测谎仪的有用性的论述中的一个错误？

(A) 上述的论述依赖于这样的假设，对雇主有益的事情对雇员也有益。

(B) 因为众所周知，测谎仪的准确率不到100%，所以测试将倾向于仅帮助那些有一些东西要隐瞒的人。

(C) 通过提及一名牌大学，作者是在诉诸权威而不是在诉诸证据。

(D) 那个研究仅表明有些人会撒谎，而没说明测谎仪能探测到他们在撒谎。

(E) 作者没有提及这个问题，即使用测谎仪可能不能防止贪污。

一大群行为亢进的，且日常饮食中包括大量含有添加剂的食物的儿童被研究者观测用以评价他们是否存在行为问题。然后让这些儿童吃几个星期的含较少添加剂的食物，接下来再对他们进行观测。起初有接近60%的儿童有行为问题；改变了他们的饮食后，仅有30%的儿童有行为问题。基于这些数据，我们可以推出食物添加剂有助于引起行为亢进的儿童的行为问题。

The evidence cited fails to establish the conclusion because

(A) there is no evidence that the reduction in behavior problems was proportionate to the reduction in food-additive intake.

(B) there is no way to know what changes would have occurred without the change of diet, since only children who changed to a low-additive diet were studied.

(C) exactly how many children exhibited behavior problems after the change in diet cannot be determined, since the size of the group studied is not precisely given.

(D) there is no evidence that the behavior of some of the children was unaffected by additives.

(E) the evidence is consistent with the claim that some children exhibit more frequent behavior problems after being on the low-additive diet than they had exhibited when first observed.

26. The proper way to plan a scientific project is first to decide its goal and then to plan the best way to accomplish that goal. The United States space station project does not conform to this ideal. When the Cold War ended, the project lost its original purpose, so another purpose was quickly grafted onto the project, that of conducting limited-gravity experiments even though such experiments can be done in an alternative way. It is, therefore, abundantly clear the space station should not be built.

The reasoning in the argument is flawed because the argument

(A) attacks the proponents of a claim rather than arguing against the claim itself.

(B) presupposes what it sets out to prove.

(C) fruits planners for not foreseeing a certain event, when in fact that event was not foreseeable.

(D) contains statements that lead to a self-contradiction.

(E) concludes that a shortcoming is fatal, having produced evidence only of the existence of that shortcoming.

27. Philosopher: The eighteenth-century thesis that motion is absolute asserts that the change in an object's position over time could be measured without reference to the position of any other object. A well-respected physicist, however, claims that this thesis is incoherent. Since a thesis that is incoherent

上面引用的证据不能证明上面的结论, 因为_____。

(A) 没有证据显示行为问题的减少与食物添加剂摄入量的减小成比例。

(B) 因为仅对那些改变食用含较少添加剂食物的儿童进行了研究, 所以我们无法知道若不改变饮食会出现什么样的变化。

(C) 因为被研究的群体的大小没有精确地给出, 所以改变饮食后, 我们无法确定究竟有多少个儿童有行为问题。

(D) 没有出示有些儿童的行为不受添加剂影响的证据。

(E) 文中的证据与有些儿童在食用含较少添加剂的饮食后比他们起初表现出更加频繁的行为问题的声明相一致。

设计一个科学项目的正确方法是先确定它的目标, 然后计划完成这个目标的最佳方案。美国空间站项目不遵守这个模式。当冷战结束时, 这个项目就失去了它最初的目标。因此另一个目标, 即进行一些有限重力试验很快就被移植到这个项目中, 尽管也可选择其他的方法来做这样的实验。因此, 这就很充分地表明不应该建设那个空间站。

上面论述中的推理是有缺陷的, 因为上述论述。

(A) 只是抨击了那个主张的建议者, 而不是驳斥了那个主张。

(B) 预先假定了它要开始证明的内容。

(C) 指责那些设计者们没有预测到某一事件的发生, 即使事实上那个事件是不可预测的。

(D) 包含有能导致自相矛盾的陈述。

(E) 仅列举了一个缺点存在的证据, 就做出这个缺点是致命的结论。

哲学家: 18世纪的关于运动是绝对的论文断言一个物体在一段时间内的位置的变化可以不参考其他任何的物体的位置而测得。然而, 一位颇受尊敬的物理学家声称这篇论文是不连贯的。既然一篇不连贯

cannot be accepted as a description of reality, motion cannot be absolute.

The argument uses which one of the following argumentative techniques?

(A) Attempting to persuade by the mere use of technical terminology.

(B) Using experimental results to justify a change in definition.

(C) Relying on the authority of an expert to support a premise.

(D) Inferring from what has been observed to be the case under experimental conditions to what is in principle true.

(E) Generalizing from what is true in one region of space to what must be true in all regions of space.

28. Why should the government, rather than industry or universities, provide the money to put a network of supercomputers in place? Because there is a range of problems that can be attacked only with the massive data-managing capacity of a supercomputer network. No business or university has the resources to purchase by itself enough machines for a whole network, and no business or university wants to invest in a part of a network if no mechanism exists for coordinating establishment of the network as a whole.

Which one of the following indicates a weakness in the argument?

(A) It does not furnish a way in which the dilemma concerning the establishment of the network can be resolved.

(B) It does not establish the impossibility of creating a supercomputer network as an international network.

(C) It fails to address the question of who would maintain the network if the governments, rather than industry or universities provides the money for establishing it.

(D) It takes for granted and without justification that it would enhance national preeminence in science for the government to provide the network.

(E) It overlooks the possibility that businesses or universities, or both, could cooperate to build the network.

29. The proposal to extend clinical trials, which are routinely used as systematic tests of pharmaceutical innovations, to new surgical procedures should not be implemented. The point is that surgical procedures differ in one important respect from

的论文不能被认为是对现实的描述，那么运动也不可能是绝对的。

上述论证使用了下面哪一个论证技巧？

(A) 企图仅使用技术术语来说服别人。

(B) 使用实验结果来证明定义上的变化是合理的。

(C) 依赖于某个专家的权威来支持一个前提。

(D) 从实验条件下观察到某物是某种情况，推出该物在原则上也是这种情况。

(E) 从某个东西在空间中的一个区域内是正确的总结出这个东西在空间中所有的区域都正确。

为什么是政府，而不是企业或大学为超级计算机网络的实现出资？这是因为仅仅对超级计算机网络庞大的数据管理能力来说，就有一系列被抨击的问题。没有任何一个企业或大学自身具有购买整个网络的机器的足够财力，并且没有企业或大学会在不存在配套建设整个网络的机制下为网络的某一部分投资。

下面哪一项揭示了上面论述的一个缺点？

(A) 它没有提供一个能解决建设网络所遇的困境的方法。

(B) 它没有证明创建一个超级计算机网络作为一个国际网络是不可能的。

(C) 它没有说明如果是政府，而不是企业或大学提供建设网络的费用时，谁将来维护该网络。

(D) 它毫无理由地认为如果政府提供网络，将会增加这个国家在科学上的杰出贡献。

(E) 它忽视了企业或大学或它们两者可以合作建设网络的可能性。

临床验证通常被用来对医药上的创新进行系统测试，把临床验证延伸到新外科手术方法中去的建议，是不应该被执行的。问题在于外科手术方法在一个很重要

medicinal drugs: a correctly prescribed drug depends for its effectiveness only on the drug's composition, whereas the effectiveness of even the most appropriate surgical procedure is transparently related to the skills of the surgeon who uses it. The reasoning in the argument is flawed because the argument

(A) does not consider that new surgical procedures might be found to be intrinsically more harmful than the best treatment previously available.

(B) ignores the possibility that the challenged proposal is deliberately crude in a way designed to elicit criticism to be used in refining the proposal.

(C) assumes that a surgeon's skills remain unchanged throughout the surgeon's professional life.

(D) describes a dissimilarity without citing any scientific evidence for the existence of that dissimilarity.

(E) rejects a proposal presumably advanced in good faith without acknowledging any such good faith.

30. Mainstream economic theory holds that manufacturers, in deciding what kinds of products to manufacture and what form those products should have, simply respond to the needs and desires of consumers. However, most major manufacturers manipulate and even create consumer demand, as anyone who watches television knows. Since even mainstream economic theorists watch television, their motive in advancing this theory must be something other than disinterested concern for scientific truth.

The claim that manufacturers manipulate and create consumer demand plays which one of the following roles in the argument?

(A) It is one of the claims on which the conclusion is based.

(B) It is the conclusion of the argument.

(C) It states the position argued against.

(D) It states a possible objection to the argument's conclusion.

(E) It provides supplementary background information.

31. Jane: According to an article in this newsmagazine, children hand-eye coordination suffers when they spend a great amount of time watching television. Therefore, we must restrict the amount of time Jacqueline and Mildred are allowed to watch television.

的方面与医药不同，对症开的药的疗效仅依赖于药的成份，而外科手术方法，甚至是最适宜的外科手术方法的疗效很明显与使用这样方法的外科医生的技术相联系。

上述论述的推理是有缺陷的，因为该论述_____。

(A) 没有考虑到新的外科手术方法可能被发现内在上比以前最好的治疗方法更有害。

(B) 忽视了这种可能性，即被质疑的建议被蓄意地设计成粗糙的形式，目的是为了诱出能用于改进该建议的批评。

(C) 假设一个外科医生的技术在他的整个职业生涯中都是保持不变的。

(D) 对某一个存在的异点，在没有引用任何科学证据的情况下，对它进行了描述。

(E) 在不承认某一建议具有的较高的可信度的前提下，否认了这个武断地提出的具有较高可信度的建议。

主流经济理论认为，制造商仅仅根据消费者的需要和愿望来决定生产的产品的种类以及这些产品的形式。然而，每个看电视的人都知道，大多数的大生产商都能操纵甚至创造消费者的需求。既然连主流经济学家也要看电视，那么他们在提出这个理论时的动机一定不是在追求科学真理时应有的公正无私的动机。

制造商操纵和创造消费者需求的声明在上面论证中所起的作用是下面哪一项？

(A) 它是结论所依赖的一个声明之一。

(B) 它是上述论证的结论。

(C) 它陈述了驳斥的立场。

(D) 它陈述了一个可能反对上述论证的结论的理由。

(E) 它提供了补充的背景信息。

Jane: 根据这本新闻杂志中的一篇文章，当孩子们花大量的时间看电视时，他们的手和眼的协调性就会变差。因此，我们必须限制Jacqueline和Mildred可以看电视的时间。

Alan: Rubbish! The article says that only children under three are affected in that way. Jacqueline is ten and Mildred is eight. Therefore, we need not restrict their television viewing.

Alan's argument against Jane's conclusion makes which one of the following errors in reasoning?

(A) It relies on the same source that Jane cited in support of her conclusion.

(B) It confuses undermining an argument in support of a given conclusion with showing that the conclusion itself is false.

(C) It does not address the main point of Jane's argument and focuses instead on a side issue.

(D) It makes an irrelevant appeal to an authority.

(E) It fails to distinguish the consequences of a certain practice from the causes of the practice.

32. The problem that environmental economics aims to remedy is the following: people making economic decisions cannot readily compare environmental factors, such as clean air and the survival of endangered species, with other costs and benefits. As environmental economists recognize, solving this problem requires assigning monetary values to environmental factors. But monetary values result from people comparing costs and benefits in order to arrive at economic decisions. Thus, environmental economics is stymied by what motivates it.

If the considerations advanced in its support are true, the passage's conclusion is supported

(A) strongly, on the assumption that monetary values for environmental factors cannot be assigned unless people make economic decisions about these factors.

(B) strongly, unless economic decision-making has not yet had any effect on the things categorized as environmental factors.

(C) at best weakly, because the passage fails to establish that economic decision-makers do not by and large take adequate account of environmental factors.

(D) at best weakly, because the argument assumes that pollution and other effects on environmental factors rarely result from economic decision-making.

(E) not at all, since the argument is circular, taking that conclusion as one of its premises.

Alan：废话！那篇文章说只有那些三岁以下的孩子才会受到那样地影响，Jacqueline十岁，Mildred八岁，因此，我们不需要限制他们看电视。

Alan反对Jane的结论的论述在推理上犯了下面哪项错误?

(A) 它依赖的根据与Jane引用的用来支持她的结论的根据是一样的。

(B) 它把削弱支持某个结论的论述与证明那个结论的本身是谬误的相混淆。

(C) 它没有提及Jane论述的主要论点，相反它把注意力集中在一个次论点上。

(D) 它诉诸了一个不相关的权威。

(E) 它没有把某个实践的结果与这个实践的原因区别开来。

环境经济学要解决的问题如下：人们作出经济上的决定时不会爽快地把环境因素，例如清洁的空气，濒临灭绝的生物的生存与其他的成本和收益做比较。就像环境经济学家认识到的那样，解决这个问题需要赋予环境因素一定的金钱价值。但是金钱的价值源自人们为做出经济上的决定而对成本和收益的比较，因此，环境经济学被激发它的东西所阻碍。

如果短文中提出的支持结论的理由是正确的，那么对该段落的结论的支持是

(A) 强烈地，假设认为赋予环境因素金钱价值是不可能的，除非人们在做出经济上的决定时考虑这些因素。

(B) 强烈地，除非经济上的决策对被归类为环境因素的事情无任何影响。

(C) 充其量是微弱地，因为上述段落没有证明经济决策者大体上都不会考虑环境因素。

(D) 充其量是微弱地，因为上述论述假设污染和其他对环境因素的影响很少源自经济决策。

(E) 根本没有，因为上述论证是循环的，把结论当作它的一个前提。

33. A certain airport security scanner designed to detect explosives in luggage will alert the scanner's operator whenever the piece of luggage passing under the scanner contains an explosive. The scanner will erroneously alert the operator for only one percent of the pieces of luggage that contain no explosives. Thus in ninety-nine out of a hundred alerts explosives will actually be present.

The reasoning in the argument is flawed because the argument

(A) ignores the possibility of the scanner's failing to signal an alert when the luggage does contain an explosive.

(B) draws a general conclusion about reliability on the basis of a sample that is likely to be biased.

(C) ignores the possibility of human error on the part of the scanner's operator once the scanner has alerted him or her.

(D) fails to acknowledge the possibility that the scanner will not be equally sensitive to all kinds of explosives.

(E) substitutes one group for a different group in the statement of a percentage.

34. Pamela: Business has an interest in enabling employees to care for children, because those children will be the customers, employees, and managers of the future. Therefore, businesses should adopt policies, such as day-care benefits, that facilitate parenting.

Lee: No individual company, though, will be patronized, staffed, and managed only by its own employees' children, so it would not be to a company's advantage to provide such benefits to employees when other companies do not.

In which one of the following pairs consisting of argument and objection does the objection function most similarly to the way Lee's objection functions in relation to Pamela's argument?

(A) New roads will not serve to relieve this area's traffic congestion, because new roads would encourage new construction and generate additional traffic.

Objection: Failure to build new roads would mean that traffic congestion would strangle the area even earlier.

(B) Humanity needs clean air to breathe, so each person should make an effort to avoid polluting the air.

一种机场安全扫描器被设计用来探测行李中的爆炸性物质，每当通过扫描器的行李中包含有爆炸性物质时，扫描器就会提醒它的操作者。当100件不含有爆炸性物质的行李通过扫描器时，扫描器会错误地提醒它的操作者一次。因此，在100次有爆炸性物质的警报中，有99次实际上都存在有爆炸性物质。

上面论述中的推理是错误的，因为该论述

(A) 忽视了当一行李确实含有爆炸性物质时，扫描器有不发出警告信号的可能性。

(B) 基于那些可能有偏见的样品，做了一个关于可靠性的结论。

(C) 忽视了一旦扫描器给它的操作员发出警告，他或她有人为错误的可能性。

(D) 没有承认扫描器对各种不同的爆炸性物质的敏感程度是不一样的可能性。

(E) 在陈述说明百分比时，用一组代替另一个不同的组。

帕米拉：公司若能使雇员照顾好孩子，公司将有利可图。因为这些孩子将会成为公司未来的顾客、雇员甚至经理。因此公司应当采取诸如发放白天托儿津贴之类的措施来方便父母亲们。

李：但是，没有任何一个公司将会仅被它自己成员的孩子们所惠顾，仅雇用它自己雇员的孩子，仅被它自己雇员的孩子所经营。因此，只是一家公司向它的雇员们提供此类津贴，而其他的公司都不这样做，这样的措施对这家公司来说是无利可言的。

下面哪一对论述中的反对项的功能与李反对帕米拉的功能相类似？

(A) 新的公路不会起到缓解这个地区的交通阻塞的作用，因为新路促使更新的工程，新的工程会造成交通流量的增加。

反对：不建设新的道路就意味着交通阻塞将会使这个地区的交通更早地陷入瘫痪状态。

Objection: The air one person breathes is affected mainly by pollution caused by others, so it makes no sense to act alone to curb air pollution.

(C) Advertised discounts on products draw customers' attention to the products, so advertised discounts benefit sales.

Objection: Customers already planning to purchase a product accelerate buying to take advantage of advertised discounts, and thus subsequent sales suffer.

(D) If people always told lies, then no one would know what the truth was, so people should always tell the truth.

Objection: If people always told lies, then everyone would know that the truth was the opposite of what was said.

(E) Human social institutions have always change so even if we do not know what those changes will be, we do know that the social institutions of the future will differ from those of the past.

Objection: The existence of change in the past does not ensure that there will always be change in the future.

35. If a society encourages freedom of thought and expression, then, during the time when it does so, creativity will flourish in that society. In the United States creativity flourished during the eighteenth century. It is clear, therefore, that freedom of thought was encouraged in the United States during the eighteenth century.

An error of reasoning of the same kind as one contained in the passage is present in each of the following arguments EXCEPT:

(A) According to the airline industry, airfares have to rise if air travel is to be made safer; since airfares were just raised, we can rest assured that air travel will therefore become safer.

(B) We can conclude that the Hillside police department has improved its efficiency, because crime rates are down in Hillside, and it is an established fact that crime rates go down when police departments increase their efficiency.

(B) 人类需要呼吸清洁的空气，所以每个人都应当尽力避免污染空气。

反对：一个人呼吸的空气主要受其他人对空气的污染的影响，因此用单个人的行动来抑制空气污染是毫无意义的。

(C) 给产品登打折广告将吸引顾客对该产品的注意力，所以登广告打折有利于产品的销售。

反对：已经打算购买某一产品的顾客会利用打折广告的机会，加快对该产品的购买，从而使该产品随后的销售难以为继。

(D) 如果人们总是说谎，那么将没有人知道真理是什么。所以人们应当总是说真话。

反对：如果人们总是说谎，那么每个人都会知道真理就是人们所说的反面情况。

(E) 人类的社会制度总是处在变化之中，所以，即使我们不知道它将会发生怎样的变化，我们也确实知道，未来的社会制度将不同于过去的社会制度。

反对：过去社会制度所存在的变化并不能确保将来的社会制度也在不断地变化。

如果一个社会能够促进思想和言论的自由，那么在这一段能自由表达思想的时间内，这个社会的创造性将会得到激发，美国在18世纪时创造性得到了极大的激发。因此，很明显美国在18世纪时思想自由得到了极大的激励。

下面的论述除了哪一个之外，都犯了与文中论述同样的推理错误?

(A) 对航空业的来说，要使航空旅行更安全，机票价格就必须上涨，既然机票刚涨过价，因此我们可以非常确信地认为航空旅行比以前变得更安全了。

(B) 我们可以推断出Hillside警察局已提高了它的工作效率。因为Hillside的犯罪率有所下降，众所周知，当警察局的工作效率提高时，犯罪率就会下降。

(C) People who are really interested in the preservation of wildlife obviously do not go hunting for big game; since Gerda has never gone hunting for big game and intends never to do so, it is clear that she is really interested in the preservation of wildlife.

(D) If the contents of a bottle are safe to drink, the bottle will not be marked "poison," so, since the bottle is not marked "poison," its contents will be safe to drink.

(E) None of the so-called Western democracies is really democratic, because, for a country to be democratic, the opinion of each of its citizens must have a meaningful effect on government and in none of these countries does each citizen's opinion have such an effect.

36. Experienced gardeners advise against planting snap peas after late April because peas do not develop properly in warm weather. This year, however, the weather was unusually cool into late June, and therefore the fact that these snap peas were planted in mid-May is unlikely to result in crop failure despite the experts' warnings.

The pattern of reasoning displayed above is most closely paralleled in which one of the following?

(A) According to many gardening authorities, tomatoes should not be planted near dill because doing so is likely to affect their taste adversely; however, since these tomatoes were grown near dill and taste fine, there is clearly no reason to pay much attention to the so-called experts' advice.

(B) Since African violets do not thrive in direct sunlight, it is said that in this region these plants should be placed in windows facing north rather than south; however, since these south-facing windows are well shaded by evergreen trees, the African violets placed in them are likely to grow satisfactorily.

(C) Where flowers are to be planted under shade trees, gardening expertsoften advise using impatiens since impatiens does well in conditions of shade; however, it is unlikely to do well under maple tree since maple tree roots are so near the surface that they absorb all available moisture.

（C）真正对保护野生动植物感兴趣的人很明显是不会猎取大猎物的；既然Gerda从未猎取过大猎物，并从未打算去猎取它们，因此很明显，她是个真正关心，保护野生动植物的人。

（D）如果一个瓶内的东西可以被安全的喝下，那么这个瓶子就不会被标为"毒品"，所以，既然一个瓶子没被标为"毒品"，那么它里面的东西就可以被安全地喝下。

（E）没有一个所谓的西方民主是真正的民主，因为，如果一个国家是个民主国家的话，每个公民的见解就一定会对政府产生有意义的影响，而这些国家中没有一个国家中每一个公民的意见会有这样的效果。

富有经验的花匠不主张在四月的末期种植豌豆，因为豌豆在暖和的气候下不可能很好的生长。然而，今年直到六月的末期，天气仍异常的凉快，因此，尽管专家们已做出警告，今年五月中旬种植的豌豆也不可能会收成不好。

上面的推理模式与下面的哪一个最为接近？

（A）根据许多园艺专家的建议，西红柿不应该与蒔萝挨着种植，因为这样做会使它们的味道变差，然而，既然这些与蒔萝相邻种植的西红柿味道良好，那么对那些所谓的专家建议给予太多的关注很显然是毫无道理的。

（B）因为非洲紫罗兰在直射的阳光下不能茂盛的生长，所以人们都认为这个地区的这种植物应种在靠北的窗台上，而不是种在靠南的窗台上，然而，既然这些靠南的窗台都被常青树很好的笼罩，所以种在它们里面的非洲紫罗兰会很好的生长。

（C）当计划在树阴下种花时，园艺家总是推荐种风仙花，因为风仙花在有树阴的条件下能很好的生长。然而，在枫树下，它是不可能生长良好的，因为枫树的根离地面很近，这些根吸收了

(D) Most seeds tend to germinate at much higher rates when planted in warm soil than when planted in cold soil; spinach seeds, however are unlikely to germinate properly if the soil is too warm, and therefore experts advise that spinach should be planted earlier than most vegetables.

(E) House plants generally grow best in pots slightly larger than their existing root systems, so the usual advice is to repot when roots first reach the sides of the pot; this rule should not be followed with amaryllis plants, however, because they are likely to do best with tightly compressed roots.

37. Proposals for extending the United States school year to bring it more in line with its European and Japanese counterparts are often met with the objection that curtailing the schools' three-month summer vacation would violate an established United States tradition dating from the nineteenth century. However, this object misses its mark. True, in the nineteenth century the majority of schools closed for three months every summer, but only because they were in rural areas where successful harvests depended on children's labor. If any policy could be justified by those appeals to tradition, it would be the policy of determining the length of the school year according to the needs of the economy.

The argument counters the objection by

(A) providing evidence to show that the objection relies on a misunderstanding about the amount of time each year United States schools traditionally have been closed.

(B) calling into question the relevance of information about historical practices to current disputes about proposed social change.

(C) arguing for an alternative understanding of the nature of the United States tradition regarding the length of the school year.

(D) showing that those who oppose extending the school year have no genuine concern for tradition.

(E) demonstrating that tradition justifies bringing the United States school year in line with that of the rest of the industrialized world.

土壤中所有可以利用的水分。

(D) 大多数种植在温暖土壤中的种子比种植在较冷土壤中的种子有高得多的发芽率，然而，当土壤温度过高时，种子也不可能会很好的发芽，因此，专家建议菠菜应比大多数的蔬菜种植得早一些。

(E) 室内盆栽植物通常在比它们现有根系稍大的花盆中生长的最好，因此当植物的根一到达盆子的边缘时，一般就建议给它们移盆，然而，富人草却很例外，因为富人草在具有压缩得很紧的根时才有可能生长得最好。

延长美国的学年，使它与欧洲和日本的相一致的建议经常会遭到这样的反对：削减学校的三个月的暑假将会违反已确立的可追溯到19世纪的美国传统。然而，这种反对却不得要领。确实，在19世纪，大多数的学校在夏季时都放假三个月，但这仅仅是因为在农村地区，成功的收割离不开孩子们的劳作。如果任何政策只有迎合传统才是合理的，就应该根据经济的需要来确定学年长度。

上述论述通过_____来驳斥异议。

(A) 提供证据显示异议依赖于对美国学校传统上每年放假时间的误解。

(B) 使历史习惯作法的信息与现在提出的关于社会改变的争论的相关性陷入疑问。

(C) 主张从另一方面来理解美国在传统上关于学年长度的实质。

(D) 揭示了那些反对延长学年长度的人并不真正关心传统。

(E) 说明了传统使美国的学年与其他工业化国家的相一致的作法合理化。

38. The director of a secondary school where many students were having severe academic problems impaneled a committee to study the matter. The committee reported that these students were having academic problems because they spent large amounts of time on school sports and too little time studying. The director then prohibited all students who were having academic problems from taking part in sports in which they were active. He stated that this would ensure that such students would do well academically.

The reasoning on which the director bases his statement is not sound because he fails to establish that

(A) some students who spend time on sports do not have academic problems.

(B) all students who do well academically do so because of time saved by not participating in sports.

(C) at least some of the time the students will save by not participating in sports will be spent on solving their academic problems.

(D) no students who do well academically spend time on sports.

(E) the quality of the school's sports program would not suffer as a result of the ban.

39. College professor: College students do not write nearly as well as they used to. Almost all of the papers that my students have done for me this year have been poorly written and ungrammatical.

Which one of the following is the most serious weakness in the argument made by the professor?

(A) It requires confirmation that the change in the professor's students is representative of a change among college students in general.

(B) It offers no proof to the effect that the professor is an accurate judge of writing ability.

(C) It does not take into account the possibility that the professor is a poor teacher.

(D) It fails to present contrary evidence.

(E) It fails to define its terms sufficiently.

40. Any announcement authorized by the head of the department is important. However, announcements are sometimes issued, without authorization, by people other

某一中学有许多学生都有非常严重的学业问题，该校的教导主任组建了一委员会来研究这个问题。委员会的报告显示，那些在学业上有问题的学生，是因为他们在学校的运动项目上花了大量的时间，而在学习上花的时间太少。于是教导主任就禁止那些所有在学习上有问题的学生从事他们以前积极参与的运动项目。他说这样就可以使那些在学习上有问题的学生取得好成绩。

基于教学主任陈述的推理并不合理，这是因他没有证实_____。

(A) 有些参加运动项目的学生并没有学业问题。

(B) 所有在学习上表现出色的学生，都是因为他们不参加运动项目从而节省下时间好好学习。

(C) 学生们至少可以利用一些不参与运动项目而省下的时间时来解决他们的学业问题。

(D) 参与运动项目的学生的学习成绩都不好。

(E) 这个学校的运动项目的质量不会因为该禁令而受损。

大学教授：大学生并没有他们过去那样写得好，今年我的学生为我所做的几乎所有的论文写得都很差，并且不合语法。

下面哪一个将最严重地削弱上面教授所作的论述？

(A) 它需要证实那个教授的学生的变化是大学生作为一个整体的变化的代表。

(B) 它没有提供教授是一个写作能力的准确评判者的证据。

(C) 它没有考虑教授是一个糟糕老师的可能性。

(D) 它没有提供反面的证据。

(E) 它没有充分定义它的术语。

任何经部门的领导授权的通告都是重要的。然而，通告有时未经部门领导授权而由其他人发出，因此一些通告将必然被

than the head of the department, so some announcements will inevitably turn out not to be important.

The reasoning is flawed because the argument

(A) does not specify exactly which communications are to be classified as announcements.

(B) overlooks the possibility that people other than the head of the department have the authority to authorize announcements.

(C) leaves open the possibility that the head of the department never, in fact, authorizes any announcements.

(D) assumes without warrant that just because satisfying a given condition is enough to ensure an announcement's importance, satisfying that condition is necessary for its importance.

(E) fails to distinguish between the importance of the position someone holds and the importance of what that person may actually be announcing on a particular occasion.

41. Emperor: The enemy empire across the sea has harassed us for centuries. I want to conquer it and stop it once and for all. What advice can you give me?

Admiral: If you cross the sea a mighty empire will fall.

Emperor: In that case, prepare the troops. We set sail tonight.

Of the following, the strongest criticism of the Emperor's decision to invade would be that it

(A) is certain to lead to the emperor's defeat.

(B) is based on opinion rather than objective facts about troop strength.

(C) contradicts the Admiral's statement.

(D) falls to consider fully the possible meanings or the Admiral's advice.

(E) is a futile strategy for solving the problem at hand.

42. Brushing your teeth regularly no matter which toothpaste you use,will reduce your chances of tooth decay. Scientists have concluded that when you brush, you reduce tooth decay by removing the film of plaque that forms on teeth and gums. So, you can forget about fluorides: brush your teeth carefully and say goodbye to cavities.

Which one of the following is a criticism of the reasoning in the argument?

证明是不重要的。

上面的推理是有缺陷的，因为论述

(A) 没有确切指明哪些公文会被归为通告。

(B) 忽略了除了部门领导以外的人有权力授权发通告的可能性。

(C) 忽略了事实上部门领导从来没有授权发任何通告的可能性。

(D) 没有根据地做了假设：仅仅因为满足一给定条件足以保证一个通告的重要性，那么满足这个条件对这个通告的重要性是必要的。

(E) 没有区分某人所持观点的重要性与那个人在某一特定场合可能真正通告的内容的重要性。

注释：communications *n.* 散播的书信、公文或电讯等。

皇帝：大海另一边的敌国几个世纪以来一直骚扰我们，我想征服它并且一劳永逸地消除这种骚扰。你能给我什么建议？

海军上将：如果你穿过大海，一个强大的帝国将会衰落。

皇帝：那样的话，准备部队。今天晚上我们就出海。

在下面选项中，对皇帝决定入侵的最强有力的批评是它

(A) 必定导致那个皇帝的失败。

(B) 基于不是关于军队强弱的客观事实的观点。

(C) 与海军上将的陈述相冲突。

(D) 没有充分考虑海军上将的建议的可能的意义。

(E) 对解决即将发生的问题来说是一个无效的策略。

不管你使用哪种牙膏，经常刷牙将降低你牙齿腐烂的可能性，科学家得出结论：当刷牙时，你通过去除牙齿与牙龈上所形成的牙菌斑薄片减少牙齿腐烂。因此你可以不用加氟牙膏，只要认真刷牙就能告别蛀牙。

下面哪一个是对上面论述推理的一个批评？

(A) Brushing with fluoride toothpaste has been shown to reduce tooth decay.

(B) The fact that brushing will reduce tooth decay does not show that fluorides are of no value.

(C) Few people adequately remove plaque by brushing.

(D) People have plaque on their teeth most of the time.

(E) Scientists have been wrong about fluorides.

(A) 用加氟牙膏刷牙表明可以降低牙齿腐烂。

(B) 刷牙将减少牙齿腐烂的事实并没有表明氟无价值。

(C) 几乎没有人通过刷牙可以充分地消除牙菌斑。

(D) 在绝大多数的时间内，人们的牙齿上都有牙菌斑。

(E) 科学家关于氟的说法是错误的。

43. So-called environmentalists have argued that the proposed Golden Lake Development would interfere with bird-migration patterns. However the fact that these same people have raised environmental objections to virtually every development proposal brought before the council in recent years indicates that their expressed concern for bird-migration patterns is nothing but a mask for their antidevelopment antiprogress agenda. Their claim therefore should be dismissed without further consideration.

Which one of the following questionable argumentative techniques is employed in the passage?

(A) taking the failure of a given argument to establish its conclusion as the basis for claiming that the view expressed by that conclusion is false.

(B) rejecting the conclusion of an argument on the basis of a claim about the motives of those advancing the argument.

(C) using a few exceptional cases as the basis for a claim about what is true in general.

(D) misrepresenting evidence that supports the position the argument is intended to refute.

(E) assuming that what is true of a group as a whole is necessarily true of each member of that group.

所谓的环境保护论者争辩说，提议中的Golden湖发展计划将会干扰鸟的迁徙模式，然而同样的这些人近年来对议会提出的几乎每一个发展建议都提出环境上的反对这一事实表明，他们对鸟类迁徙模式所表达的关注只不过是他们反对发展阻碍进步的一个借口。因此，应该不用进一步考虑而应忽略他们的宣称。

上面段落使用了下面哪一个可疑的论证技术？

(A) 把不能够得出它的结论的某一论述作为那个结论所表达的观点是错误的宣称的基础。

(B) 基于提出论述的那些人的动机的宣称而反驳一个论点的结论。

(C) 使用一些例外案例作为一宣称总体上是正确的基础。

(D) 误用了支持那些该论述要去驳斥的立场的证据。

(E) 假设作为一个整体正确是整体里面每一个成员都正确的必要条件。

44. Anthony: It has been established that over 80 percent of those who use heroin have a history of having used marijuana. Such evidence would seem to prove that smoking marijuana definitely leads to heroin use.

Judith: Maybe smoking marijuana does lead to heroin use, but it is absurd to think that citing those statistics proves that it does. After all, 100 percent of the people who take up heroin had a previous history of drinking water. Judith's reply to Anthony's argument relies on which one of the following argumentative strategies?

(A) Offering evidence suggesting that the statistics Anthony

Anthony：据确认，服用海洛因的人当中超过80%都有吸大麻的历史，这样的证据好像可以证实，吸大麻毫无疑问导致服用海洛因。

Judith：或许吸大麻确实导致吸海洛因，但考虑引用这些统计数字去证实确实如此是荒谬的。毕竟，服用海洛因的人100%地都有喝过水的历史。

Judith对Anthony的论述的回答依赖于下面哪一个论证技巧？

(A) 提供证据表明Anthony所引用的支持

cites in support of his conclusion are inaccurate.

(B) Undermining the credibility of his conclusion by showing that it is a statement from which absurd consequences can be derived.

(C) Providing an example to show that not everything that promotes heroin use is unsafe.

(D) Demonstrating that Anthony's line of reasoning is flawed by showing that such reasoning can lead to clearly false conclusions.

(E) Calling into question the possibility of ever establishing causal connections solely on the basis of statistical evidence.

他的结论的统计数据是不准确的。

(B) 通过表明它是一个可以推导出荒唐后果的陈述来削弱他的结论的可信度。

(C) 提供一个例子表明，并非诱使服用海洛因的任何东西都是不安全的。

(D) 通过表明这样的推理将导致一个明显的错误结论而表明Anthony的推理是有缺陷的。

(E) 对仅仅基于统计证据而确立因果联系的可能性提出质疑。

45. The senator has long held to the general printable that no true work of art is obscene and thus that there is no conflict between the need to encourage free artistic expression and the need to protect the sensibilities of the public from obscenity. When well-known works generally viewed as obscene are cited as possible counterexamples, the senator justifies accepting the principle by saying that if these works really are obscene then they cannot be works of art.

The senator's reasoning contains which one of the following errors?

(A) It seeks to persuade by emotional rather than intellectual means.

(B) It contains an implicit contradiction.

(C) It relies on an assertion of the senator authority.

(D) It assumes what it seeks to establish.

(E) It attempts to justify a position by appeal to an irrelevant consideration.

参议员很长时间以来都对全体报界持有这样一种观点：没有真正的艺术品是淫秽的，因此，在需要鼓励自由的艺术表达与需要保护公众免受淫秽作品的侵染之间并不存在冲突。当人们举出一般被视作淫秽的名作作为可能的反例时，这位参议员认为如果这些作品的确是淫秽的，那么他们不可能是艺术品。以此来认定如上原则是正确的。

这位参议员的推理包含了下面哪一个错误？

(A) 它企图去用情感而不是用理智方法去说服。

(B) 它蕴含了一个暗含的矛盾。

(C) 它依赖于一个参议员的权威的宣称。

(D) 它假设了它要去证实的。

(E) 它企图通过反对一个不相关的理由来认定一个观点的正确。

46. Mayor Smith, one of our few government officials with a record of outspoken, informed, and consistent opposition to nuclear power plant construction projects, has now declared herself in favor of building the nuclear power plant at Littletown. If someone with her past antinuclear record now favors building this power plant, then there is good reason to believe that it will be safe and therefore should be built.

The argument is vulnerable to criticism on which one of the following grounds?

(A) It overlooks the possibility that not all those who fail to speak out on issues of nuclear power are necessarily opposed to it.

Smith市长曾是我们的少数几个坦率地，有见识地和一致地反对核电站建设项目的政府官员之一。现在她宣布她将赞成在Littletown兴建核电站。如果某人曾经拥有她过去的反对核电站的记录，现在热衷于兴建这个核电站，那么我们就有充分的理由相信这个核电站将是安全的，因此应该兴建这个核电站。

上面的论证最易受到下面哪个理由的批评？

(A) 它忽视了这样的可能性，即不是所有的没有直言不讳地谈论核电站问题的

(B) It assumes without warrant that the qualities enabling a person to be elected to public office confer on that person a grasp of the scientific principles on which technical decisions are based.

(C) It fails to establish that a consistent and outspoken opposition is necessarily an informed opposition.

(D) It leads to the further but unacceptable conclusion that any project favored by Mayor Smith should be sanctioned simply on the basis of her having spoken out in favor of it.

(E) It gives no indication of either the basis of Mayor Smith's former opposition to nuclear power plant construction or the reasons for her support for the Littletown project.

人都一定反对它。

(B) 它毫无根据地假设能让一个人被选举为公务员的品质赋予了那个人对科学原则有所了解的才能，在这种才能的基础上才能做出技术上的决定。

(C) 它没有证明一致的、坦率的反对意见必定是一个有见识的反对意见。

(D) 它导致得出进一步的、但不可接受的结论，即任何Smith市长热衷的项目都应被批准，仅仅是因为她曾明确地赞成过这个项目。

(E) 它既没有给出Smith市长先前反对建设核电站的出发点也没有给出她支持Littletown项目的原因。

47. Monroe, despite his generally poor appetite, thoroughly enjoyed the three meals he ate at the Tip-Top Restaurant, but, unfortunately, after each meal he became ill. The first time he ate an extra-large sausage pizza with a side order of hot peppers; the second time he took full advantage of the all-you-can-eat fried shrimp and hot peppers special; and the third time he had two of Tip-Top's gaint meatball sandwiches with hot peppers. Since the only food all three meals had in common was the hot peppers, Monroe concludes that it is solely due to Tip-Top's hot peppers that he became ill.

Monroe's reasoning is most vulnerable to which one of the following criticisms?

(A) He draws his conclusion on the basis of too few meals that were consumed at Tip-Top and that included hot peppers.

(B) He posits a causal relationship without ascertaining that the presumed cause preceded the presumed effect.

(C) He allows his desire to continue dining at Tip-Top to bias his conclusion.

(D) He fails to establish that everyone who ate Tip-Top's hot peppers became ill.

(E) He overlooks the fact that at all three meals he consumed what was, for him, an unusually large quantity of food.

尽管Monroe一贯胃口不好，但是他却非常喜欢他在Tip-Top饭店吃的三顿饭。然而不幸的是他每次饭后都得了病。第一次他吃了一块巨大的香肠比萨饼外加一道辣椒；第二次他尽其所能吃了"吃你所能吃炸虾"和辣椒特价菜；第三次他就着辣椒吃了两个Tip-Top的大肉团三明治。因为这三顿饭中每次都有的菜，只有辣椒，所以Monroe推论出他生病就是因为Tip-Top的辣椒。

Monroe的推理最易受到下面哪一项的批评？

(A) 作为得出他的结论的基础，在Tip-Top饭店食用的包括辣椒的饭的次数太少了。

(B) 他在没有确定假设的原因是否先于假设的结果的情况下，假定了一个因果关系。

(C) 他让自己继续在Tip-Top进餐的愿望使他的结论带上了偏见。

(D) 他没有证明每个在Tip-Top吃过辣椒的人都生了病。

(E) 他忽视了这样的事实，即对他来说所有这三餐饭他都吃得太多了。

48. If Blankenship Enterprises has to switch suppliers in the middle of a large production run, the company will not show a profit for the year. Therefore, if Blankenship Enterprises in

如果Blankenship企业不得不在产品大畅销期间改变的它的供货商，这个公司这一年就不会有利润。因此，如果

fact turns out to show no profit for the year, it will also turn out to be true that the company had to switch suppliers during a large production run.

The reasoning in the argument is most vulnerable to criticism on which one of the following grounds?

(A) The argument is a circular argument made up of an opening claim followed by a conclusion that merely paraphrases that claim.

(B) The argument fails to establish that a condition under which a phenomenon is said to occur is the only condition under which that phenomenon occurs.

(C) The argument involves an equivocation, in that the word "profit" is allowed to shift its meaning during the course of the argument.

(D) The argument erroneously uses an exceptional, isolated case to support a universal conclusion.

(E) The argument explains one event as being caused by another event, even though both events must actually have been caused by some third, unidentified event.

Blankenship企业这一年实际上是没有利润的，那么就可以确定该公司在产品大畅销期间改变了供货商。

上述论证的推理最易受到下面哪一项原因的批评？

(A) 上述论证是循环论证，它由开始的声明和随后的仅对那个声明作了意译的结论构成。

(B) 上述论证没有证明使某一个现象出现的某一个条件是这个现象出现的仅有的条件。

(C) 上述论证中涉及一个模棱两可的词语，因为"profit"一词在论述的过程中可以改变它的意思。

(D) 上述论述错误地使用了一个罕见的、孤立的情况来支持一个普遍性的结论。

(E) 上述论述解释一个事件是由另一事件引起，尽管这两个事件实际上一定都是由第三个没有认识到的事件引起的。

参考答案：

1. C	2. C	3. D	4. E	5. B
6. C	7. E	8. D	9. D	10. D
11. B	12. C	13. A	14. D	15. B
16. E	17. A	18. E	19. D	20. B
21. B	22. C	23. E	24. D	25. B
26. E	27. C	28. E	29. A	30. A
31. B	32. A	33. E	34. B	35. E
36. B	37. C	38. C	39. A	40. D
41. D	42. B	43. B	44. D	45. D
46. E	47. E	48. B		

3. **解析**：本题推理犯了典型的以偏概全的逻辑错误。问题目的是让我们去驳斥段落的观点：招魂术是骗人的，毫无价值的，而段落中仅引用了一个案例去作为证据，犯了以偏概全的逻辑错误。(D)指出了这一点，驳斥了文中结论，所以(D)是正确答案。

5. **解析**：本题段落推理的结论是："However, readers should dismiss Jone's criticisms"，其依赖的证据是琼斯这个人不好。换句话说，推理要否定的是"琼斯的新书可能会毁掉某些人的名誉"，而采用的论证方法是否定琼斯这个人，所以其隐含假设是攻击某一宣称的来源(琼斯这个人本身)，就是否定这一宣称（琼斯的新书可能会毁掉某些人的名誉），所以(B)正确。"responsibility"在段落推理中只有一个"责任"的意义，所以(A)不对；(C)与上面推理相违背；段落推理并未提到："a person of unreliable authority"，所以(D)不正确；段落推理的因果并未例置，所以(E)不正确。

6. 解析：本题的段落中有两个地方提及维生素缺乏：第一是怀孕妇女的维生素缺乏，指的是怀孕妇女身体内的维生素缺乏；第二是食物中维生素的缺乏，指的是食物中维生素的含量少。这两处的参照物很明显是不同的。(C)指出了这一点，因此(C)正确，其他的四个选项都不能对本题段落的推理构成批评。

9. 解析：本题在GRE机考中重考，只不过把(D)放入段落并划线，然后问(D)的作用。要解释"国家最大的零售商的销售量增加，但是利润下降"的事实，就要找产生这个差异的原因，该事实是由"the nations biggest retailers"提出，因此，找差异原因时应紧紧围绕这个关键词进行寻找，本题的五个选项中只有(D)涉及了这个关键词，(D)指出"销售量增加利润"，而"下降起因于广告费的增加"，因此，(D)是正确答案。(A)、(B)、(C)和(E)都与国家最大的零售商无关，所以都是错误选项。

12. 解析：本题的推理显然犯了把一个结论成立的必要条件与充分条件相混淆的错误，"complete the course in electrical safety procedure"只是"licensed as an electrician"的一个必要条件，而本题中的推理却把它当作一充分条件来使用。由此分析可知要使本题的结论成立，本题在辩论中还必须指出"修完《用电安全程序》这门课是被Parker郡批准成为电工的所必要的所有条件。"因此，(C)是正确答案。(A)、(B)、(D)和(E)都不能使充分条件成立，所以均为错误选项。

13. 解析：本题两人论述中的"可再生资源"具有不同的范畴，木材商的可再生资源仅是指树木的再生，而环境保护主义者的再生资源则指的是包括动物在内的整个生态环境的再生，所以(A)正确。

14. 解析：在逻辑论证中，要使结论正确，一定要时刻注意推理的严密性。本题在论证中没有指出鸡蛋沙拉中的有害细菌是引起人生病的唯一原因，因此把检查未发现有害细菌作为生病不是起因于沙拉的证据就显得无力，也就是说本题结论所依赖的证据不足以证明结论正确。另外，由对"剩余的鸡蛋沙拉"的检查结果类推至"吃过的鸡蛋沙拉"，犯了类比推理的错误："吃过的鸡蛋色拉"是生病的原因，但缺乏证据，而段落推理却把缺乏证据作为"吃过的鸡蛋色拉"不是原因的充分条件。(D)很好地描述了段落推理特点，所以，(D)为正确答案。(B)是容易误选的答案，本题在推理中确实"抛弃了一种可能的解释，却没有提出一种替代性的解释"，但这并不属于逻辑错误，在辩论中可以将别人提供的解释推翻来反驳其观点，而自己并不一定要提出更好的解释。(A)、(C)、(E)都是明显错误的选项。

16. 解析：根据本题的论述，我们很容易看出消费者代表在反对软饮料商的论述中，并非提及软饮料制造商所提出的他们的饮料因增加了钙的含量而更有益于孩子们健康的声明，而是指出了软饮料制造商的产品的一个内在缺点来表明他们的产品能给孩子们的健康造成一定的危害，也就是说消费者代表通过找出其他原因的方法削弱了软饮料制造商的饮料有益于孩子们健康的声明。由以上分析可知，(E)为正确答案，而(A)、(B)、(C)和(D)都是明显错误的选项。

17. 解析：根据本题的陈述，我们很容易推出：在预售票卖得很多的情况下，如果天气不好，那么音乐会将被取消，买了票的人会得到退款。而本题的结论则是在预售票卖得很多的情况下，根据一些买了票的人得到了退款推出音乐会一定是由于预报了不好的天气而被取消。若用A_1表示"bad weather"，用A_2表示"票卖得少"，用B表示"cancel音乐会"，用C表示"refund"，那么段落的推理关系可表示为：①$B \rightarrow A_1 + A_2$；②$B \rightarrow C$；③$C\overline{A_2} \rightarrow A_1$。诚然，$B\overline{A_2} \rightarrow A_1$成立，但$C\overline{A_2} \rightarrow A_1$要想成立，那么B必须是C成立的充分必要条件。因此，很明显，B是C成立的充分条件，即cancel足以导致refund，但推理却把cancel作为refund的唯一必要条件，即$B \leftrightarrow C$。(A)很好地描述了这一推理特点。由以上分析可知，本题推理犯的错误就是把某一结论成立的必要条件当作这一结论成立的充分条件，因此(A)是正确的。(B)、(C)、(D)和(E)都是错误选项。本题的类似推理在GRE1999年4月被重考。

19. 解析：要开发的药物是打算通过抑制肺部某些分子的自然行为来预防哮喘，选项(D)指出这种抑制不仅会在该分子的行为是多余时发生，也会在它是必要时发生，这将是这种药物的严重的缺陷。因此(D)是正确答案。

选项(A)和(B)提到缺乏关于媒分子是如何产生的或如何激活的知识，但没有提到它们在肺部是如何起作用的。选项(C)描述了开发药物会花多长时间，但没有排除成功的可能性。选项(E)仅指出该药物不能做一些没有打算让它做的事。

20. **解析**：该市长的推理建立在假设如果开车进城比乘坐公共汽车更贵，人们会选择乘坐公共汽车而不是自己开车上班，选项(B)提出一个这种假设是错误的证据，因此是正确答案。

选项(A)没有削弱该市长的观点即五美元将刺激人们换乘公共汽车。选项(C)使得如果吸引了新的乘客之后，公共汽车系统不太可能失去目前的乘客。选项(D)不合适，因为许多自己开车的人不转为乘从公共汽车与许多自己开车的人转为乘坐公共汽车完全没有矛盾。选项(E)通过指出进入市区的车辆占该城车流量的大部分来支持该市长的建议。

21. **解析**：作者在以上论证时把"没有人提出煤、石油和矿石可以不付费地进行开采"，应用到"工业发达国家用来改善其栽培作物的植物种类却未支付补偿"这种情况中，且假定两者类似。(B)很好地描述了上面推理过程。所以(B)正确。(C)讨论到"对立面"，但对立面的讨论对象应为全集，但植物+煤、油、矿石≠全集，所以(C)不正确；只有在段落推理过程中说了两件事情，且告知这两件事情发生的先后顺序，但后面运用时又把这两件事情谁前谁后搞反时，(D)才能为正确答案。

22. **解析**：audit *v.* 稽核，查账，清算

clients' statements 客户结单；客户账户

23. **解析**：本题首先提出论点，在通勤火车上销售和饮用酒精饮料的行为应当被法律禁止，接着举了一个法律上已禁止在通勤火车上抽烟的例子，然后说明两者对公众造成的危害或带来的危险具有相似性，由此得出结论，当一种行为—smoking被禁时，另一种行为—sale and consumption of alcohol也应当被禁止。因此本题是通过抽烟对他人的影响与喝酒精饮料对他人的影响的比较来证明它的论点的，所以选项(E)是正确答案；(A)、(B)、(C)和(D)都不能从题义中得出，所以均为错误选项。

24. **解析**：本题的论述所犯的一个较大的错误是论据与论点无相关性，即论据不能支持论点。本题的论点是测谎仪非常地有用，论据是在一调查报告中有1/3的接受调查的人撒了谎。但是本题中并没有指出是测谎仪发现这1/3的人在撒谎，而另外2/3的人都讲了实话，因此调查报告只说明了有些人会撒谎，而没有证实测谎仪探测到了他们在撒谎，所以(D)是正确选项。如果测谎仪有用，那么对每个人来说都是有用的，所以论述中认为测谎仪对雇主和雇员都有益的说法是正确的，即(A)不是论述中的错误；既便测谎仪的准确率达不到100%，它仍有很大的可能性发现那些有东西隐瞒的人在撒谎，所以测谎仪对他们来说有害无益，因此(B)也不能对本题的论点构成反对；本题虽然提及了一名牌大学，但从题义中并没发现有任何诉诸权威的嫌疑，因此(C)也是错误的；(E)选项很明显与本题的论点和论据无任何关系。

25. **解析**：当我们想通过比较来研究某一因素对某件事情的影响时，要在保证其他条件不变的情况下，仅改变这一因素来研究它，只有这样我们得到的数据才有可能是可信的。段落中的论据却没有这样做，根据段落中提供的证据，我们不难推出，它是以饮食中包含有较多添加剂的儿童在不改变饮食的情况下，过了几周以后，有行为问题的儿童的比率不变为前提的，也就是说该证据没有用发展的眼光来看待儿童的行为问题。因此当我们用发展的眼光来看待儿童的行为问题时，我们将无法知道若不改变饮食，那些儿童的行为是否也会发生变化。由此分析我们可以得知(B)是正确选项。(A)、(C)和(D)都不是这个证据应该解决的问题；(E)引入了新的比较，因此也是错误的。

26. **解析**：本题的论证只是指出了其他方法的存在，就认为在空间站上进行有限重力实验缺乏目的性，从而做出不应该建设那个空间站的结论。由此分析可知(E)为正确答案。

27. **解析**：本题的短文仅根据某一个颇受尊敬的物理学家认为这篇论文是不连贯的，就否定了该论文的结论，很显然作者支持他的结论的证据是在诉诸权威，而不是在诉诸事实，因此(C)是正确答案；(A)、(B)、(D)和(E)很明显都不是本题所用的论证技巧。

28. **解析**：本题段落论述所犯的一个致命的逻辑错误就是认为对某个个体适用的原则，对包含这个个体的整体或整体的一部分也适用。单个企业或学校不具有购买整个网络的机器的财力，但是多个企业，多个学校或多个企业与多个学校联合就有可能具备购买整个网络的财力。因此上述论述忽视了企业或大学或它们两者可以合作建设网络的可能性，也即选项(E)为正确答案。(A)、(B)、(C)和(D)都与本题的论述无关。

29. **解析**：如果一种新的外科手术内在上有一系列的缺陷，但该手术又不经临床上的验证，因此即使技术最高超的医生来做该手术，病人受到的伤害程度或该手术的副作用可能比以前最好的治疗方法的大，因此即使是与医生的技术紧密相连的外科手术在推广之前也应对它们进行临床验证。所以(A)指出了本题论述的推理错误，是正确选项。(D)和(E)所描述的逻辑错误与上述分析的不一致，所以为错误选项；(B)和(C)与本题的论述无关。

30. **解析**：本题的论述通过主流经济学家也看大生产商家能操纵甚至是创造消费者需求的广告的事实，而做出作为消费者的主流经济学家在提出他们的理论时动机不纯的结论。由此我们可以看出制造商操纵和创造消费者需求的声明是段落的论证所依赖的一个前提，因此(A)是正确的。

31. **解析**：Jane的结论的前提是当孩子们花大量的时间看电视时，他们的手和眼的协调性会变差，而Alan则认为只有三岁以下的孩子才会受到那样的影响，于是他就否定了Jane的结论。本题读题重点是第二个人的第一句话"Rubbish"。注意：某人论据不真，但结论不一定不真。Alan反对的Jane的论据，只能weaken Jane的结论，而不能必然证明Jane结论为错误的，所以(B)选项是正确的。(A)、(C)、(D)和(E)都不是Alan所犯的推理错误。

32. **解析**：本题的读题重点在第三和第四句话，第三句话为前提，第四句话为结论，结合段落的前两句话，第四句话等价于环境经济学不可能解决要解决的问题。因为第三句话表明"金钱的价值源自人们为做出经济上的决定而对成本和收益的比较"，而人们做出经济上的决定时，一般不会对其成本和收益进行比较（如第一句话所说）。若如(A)所说，"赋予环境因素金钱价值的必要条件是人们在做出经济上的决定时会考虑这些环境因素"，由于人们做出经济上的决定时，一般不会对其成本和收益进行比较，那么就不可能赋予环境因素一定的金钱价值，所以选项(A)通过做了一个假设支持了该段落的结论。

33. **解析**：本题依据扫描器检查无爆炸性物质的行李的准确率为99%，而作出了扫描器检查含有爆炸性物质的行李的成功率也是99%的结论，因此本题的论述很显然犯了(E)所陈述的推理错误。

34. **解析**：Lee通过指出Pamela的论述中所用的证据的片面性，反对了Pamela的结论。在五个选项中只有(B)的反对项指出了它要反对的论述所用的证据的片面性，因此(B)是正确答案。(A)和(C)两选项通过指出某一活动可以预测的不良后果，来反对它要反对的论述；(D)选项通过反证法来进行反对；(E)选项通过指出社会制度变革的不可演绎性来反对未来的社会制度将不同于过去的社会制度的论述。

35. **解析**：我们知道一个命题的原命题正确，推不出它的逆命题也是正确的，但是可以推出它的逆否命题是一定正确的。本题论述中的(A)、(B)、(C)和(D)四个选项都犯了由原命题成立推出逆命题成立的逻辑错误，而(E)的论述则是由原命题成立推出逆否命题也成立。因此(E)是本题的正确选项。

36. **解析**：本题段落中的论证是通过分析一件事情在不同条件下具有不同的结果的差异原因，然而把差异原因消除，从而得到了一件事情在不同的条件下仍有可能达到一致的结果。(B)通过消除南部窗台上的阳光，从而得出了不能在阳光下茂盛生长的非洲紫罗兰在南部窗台上也能很好地生长的结论，该结论的推理模式显然与题干中的推理模式相一致。因此(B)为正确选项。(A)、(C)、(D)和(E)四个论证中都没有用到消除差异原因的方法，因此均为错误选项。

37. **解析**：作者在驳斥异议时，对异议的论据进行了驳斥，指出在19世纪时，学校放三个月的暑假是因为孩子们要参加收割庄稼，很显然19世纪时学校放长假是出于经济上的需要。而今天美国已成了一个工业化国家，经济上不再有让孩子们帮助收割庄稼的需要。因此作者是从另一方面来理解美国在传统上学年长度的实质，并通过釜底抽薪的办法来驳斥异议，所以(C)是正确答案。(A)、(B)、(D)和(E)都不能从短文中合理地推出。

38. 解析：即使学习上有困难的学生不参加运动项目，如果他们没把省下来的时间用于学习，他们也会和以前一样不能取得好成绩。因此教导主任的推理错在他没有证实学生们至少可以利用一些不参与运动项目而省下的时间来解决他们的学业问题，所以(C)是正确答案。(B)对教导主任的推理构成了支持，(A)、(D)和(E)三选项均不能从段落中合理地推出。

39. 解析：对比"工程系的学生懒了是因为丹尼斯女士的学生不做工作"一题的思维。

40. 解析：本题重点在于读懂选项，一旦选项读懂了，那么正确答案便跃然纸上，请自己试着译这五个选项。

41. 解析：海军上将所提到的"a mighty empire"可能是自己的国家，(D)很好地指出了这一点。

42. 解析：段落推理可以简化为刷牙带来好处，因此忽视加氟牙膏。(B)却指出刷牙带来好处并不表明氟无价值，暗含两者并不一定无联系，因此起到了批评作用；(A)易误选，但没说明氟的作用；(C)、(D)和(E)均为无关选项。

43. 解析：有疑问的论证方法，相当于指出逻辑错误，属于"逻辑应用与技法"类题目。段落里根据"环境保护论者总是提出反对意见"，就得出结论"他们的宣称应该被忽略"。推理犯了什么错误或使用了哪种可疑的论证方法呢？很明显，(B)是正确的。

44. 解析：本题可作为GRE、GMAT作文的绝好范文。(D)选项正确争议不大，思考(B)为什么错至关重要。如果把Judith论述的第一句话去掉，那么(B)就可以正确了，但加上了"Maybe smoking marijuana does lead to heroin use"，正确答案就只能为(D)了。

45. 解析：本题重在思考(D)选项为什么正确以及体会此类题目选项所使用的语言。

46. 解析：从本题段落所给的证据，我们只知道Smith市长以前反对兴建核电站，但我们无从知道她为什么反对兴建核电站。Smith市长现在又突然热衷于兴建Littletown核电站，仅仅因为她以前反对兴建核电站，段落中就下结论认为该核电站是安全的。因此本文犯了诉诸权威的错误，也就是说它在既没给出Smith市长先前反对核电站的出发点，也没给出她支持Littletown项目的原因的情况下得出了它的结论，由此可知(E)是正确的。(D)是比较容易误选的选项，但(D)选项"any project"一词过于绝对化，在逻辑论证中过于绝对化的选项往往都有误；(A)、(B)和(C)三选项都与本题的结论无太大的关系。

47. 解析：根据本题对Monre在Tip-Top吃的三餐饭的描述，我们发现了他的这三餐饭的特点除了每餐都包含有辣椒之外，他每餐饭还都吃得特别多，而本题一开头就事先声明了Monre一贯胃口不好，因此每餐饭吃得太多的事实也有可能是胃口一向不好的他每餐饭后都有病的一个原因。由此分析可知(E)是正确答案。(D)是较易误选的选项。若Monre证明了每一个在Tip-Top进餐时吃了辣椒的人都生了病，将有助于支持他的结论。但是(D)选项中引入了新的内容，这些内容即每一个在Tip-Top进餐时吃了辣椒的人是否有病并不是本题中Monre的结论所依赖的事实，因此(D)不是最佳选项；(A)、(B)和(C)都是明显错误的选项。

48. 解析：改变供货商，只是Blankenship企业这一年不会有利润的的一个条件，因此论述中把该条件当作不会有利润的唯一条件是不合适。要使它的结论成立，它就必须证明改变供货商是这一年不会有利润的充要条件。由此分析可知选项(B)是正确答案，其余四个选项都不合适。

第 三 篇

GMAT考前逻辑推理冲刺训练试题与解析

一、GMAT考前逻辑推理冲刺训练试题及解析（一）

1. The ancient Greek playwright Euripides followed the established conventions of verse composition less rigorously at the end of his career than at the beginning. Since the lines from a recently discovered Euripidean play adhere to those conventions as rigorously as do lines from Euripides' early plays, the recently discovered play must have been composed early in Euripides' career.

Which of the following is an assumption made in the argument?

(A) All of Euripides' plays were written in verse.

(B) Euripides did not write any plays late in his career in which he imitated the style of his early plays.

(C) Euripides grew increasingly unaware of the established conventions of verse composition as his career progressed.

(D) Late in his career, Euripides was the only playwright of his day who consciously broke with the established conventions of verse composition.

(E) Ancient playwrights tended to be less willing to violate certain conventions early in their careers than they were later in their careers.

古希腊剧作家Euripides在其晚期的作品中没有像其早期那样严格遵守诗体结构的成规。由于最近发现的一部Euripides的剧本中的诗句像他早期的剧本一样严格地遵守了那些成规，因此该剧本一定创作于Euripides的早期。

下面哪一个是上面论述所做的假设？

(A) 所有Euripides的剧本都写成诗体。

(B) Euripides在其创作生涯的晚期没有写过任何模仿其早期作品风格的剧本。

(C) 随着创作的发展，Euripides日益意识不到其诗体结构的成规。

(D) 在其职业生涯晚期，Euripides是其时代唯一的有意打破诗体成规的剧作家。

(E) 古代的剧作家在其创作晚期比早期更倾向于不再愿意打破某种陈规。

2. In the United States, average fuel efficiency of newly manufactured domestic cars, although remaining worse than that of newly manufactured imported cars, substantially improved between 1983 and 1988. Average fuel efficiency of new domestic cars has not improved since, but the difference in average fuel efficiencies of new domestic cars and new imported cars has steadily decreased.

If the statements above are true, which of the following must also be true on the basis of them?

(A) Average fuel efficiency of domestic cars manufactured after 1988 was better than that of imported cars manufactured before 1988.

(B) Average fuel efficiency of newly manufactured domestic cars has steadily worsened since 1988.

在美国，尽管新制造的国产汽车的平均油效仍低于新制造的进口汽车，但它在1983年到1988年间却显著地增加了。自那以后，新制造的国产汽车的平均油效没再提高，但新制造的国产汽车与进口汽车在平均油效上的差距却逐渐缩小。

如以上论述正确，那么基于此的下面哪一项也一定正确？

(A) 1988年后制造的国产汽车的平均油效高于1988年制造的进口汽车的平均油效。

(B) 新制造的国产汽车的平均油效从1988年后逐渐趋向缩小。

368

(C) Average fuel efficiency of newly manufactured imported cars has steadily worsened since 1988.

(D) Average fuel efficiency of newly manufactured imported cars has steadily improved since 1983.

(E) Average fuel efficiency of imported cars manufactured in 1983 was better than that of imported cars manufactured in 1988.

(C) 新制造的进口汽车的平均油效从1988年以后趋向缩小。

(D) 新制造的进口汽车的平均油效在1983年后趋向增加。

(E) 1983年制造的进口汽车的平均油效高于1988年制造的进口汽车的平均油效。

3. Between 1970 and 1980, energy consumption by United States industry peaked and then declined, so that by 1980 total industrial use of energy was below the 1970 level even though total industrial output had grown substantially in the same period. Industry must have instituted highly effective energy conservation measures in those years to have achieved such impressive results.

Which of the following, if true, most seriously weakens the conclusion of the argument?

(A) Many industries switched to the greatest extent possible from high-priced oil to lower-priced alternatives throughout the 1970's.

(B) Total residential energy consumption was higher in the United States in 1980 than it had been in 1970.

(C) Many industrial users of energy had paid little attention to energy conservation prior to 1970.

(D) Industrial output grew less rapidly from 1970 to 1980 than it had from 1960 to 1970.

(E) The industries whose production dropped sharply during the 1970's included a disproportionately large number of energy-intensive industries.

在1970年到1980年之间，美国工业的能源消耗量在达到顶峰后又下降，这导致1980年虽然工业总产出量有显著提高，但工业的能源总耗用量却低于1970年的水平。在那些年里，工业部门一定采取了高效节能措施才取得如此惊人的成果。

下列哪一个，假如正确，最反对上面推理的结论？

(A) 在20世纪70年代，许多行业尽最大可能地从使用高价石油转向使用低价的替代物。

(B) 1980年美国总的居民能量消耗高于1970年。

(C) 在1970年前，许多工业能源的使用者很少注意保存能量。

(D) 工业总量的增长在1970年到1980年间没有在1960至1970年间增长得快。

(E) 20世纪70年代产量急剧下降的工业部门中包括相当一大批能源密集型工业部门。

4. Many people acquire software programs for their home computers by illegally copying those programs rather than purchasing them. People who own home computers must be making, on average, fewer illegal copies of software programs than before, however, since the average number of software programs that people purchase to use on their home computers has increased substantially over the past five years.

Which of the following, if true, most strengthens the argument?

(A) The number of home computers in use has increased substantially over the past five years.

(B) Five years ago, about half of the software programs used on home computers had been illegally copied rather than purchased.

许多人通过非法拷贝而不是购买为家中的计算机获得软件。但在过去的5年中，因为人们为家用计算机购买软件的平均数量显著增加，所以人们购买且用于家用计算机的平均非法拷贝软件的数量一定比以前少了。

下列哪一项，如果正确，最能支持以上论述？

(A) 家用计算机的使用数量在过去5年显著增加了。

(B) 5年前，大约一半用于家用计算机的软件是非法拷贝而不是购买的。

(C) Most people who have home computers use their computers more frequently the longer they have them.

(D) Few people who prefer to copy computer software programs illegally cannot copy the software programs they want because they have no acquaintances who have those software programs.

(E) On average, people with home computers have the same number of software programs today as people with home computers did five years ago.

5. From a newspaper editorial:

Many people who are addicted to heroin will eventually attempt to overcome their addiction, principally for two reasons: the expense of maintaining a heroin addiction and the fear of arrest. If heroin were legalized and made available cheaply, as some people advocate, neither of these reasons would apply.

The considerations above can best serve as part of an argument that

(A) legalizing the sale of heroin would cause the price of this drug to go down.

(B) making it easier for heroin addicts to obtain treatment for their addiction would encourage many heroin addicts to attempt to overcome their addiction.

(C) legalizing the sale of heroin would increase the number of crimes committed by heroin addicts to support their addiction.

(D) making heroin available legally and cheaply would make it less likely that heroin addicts will attempt to overcome their addiction.

(E) decreasing the severity of penalties for individuals who use heroin would not increase the number of new heroin addicts.

6. Stem borers are insect pests that often ruin North American corn crops. On some other continents, crop damage by stem borers is controlled by a certain species of wasp. Since these wasps eat nothing but stem borers, importing them into North America will keep crop damage from stem borers under control without endangering other North American insect species.

Which of the following is an assumption on which the argument depends?

(C) 大多数拥有家用计算机的人们使用他们的计算机越频繁，他们拥有计算机的时间就越长。

(D) 很少有偏好非法拷贝计算机软件的人因为他们没有熟人拥有这些软件而不能拷贝它们。

(E) 平均来说，如今拥有家用计算机的人与5年前相比基本上拥有相同数量的软件。

引自一篇报纸社论：

许多有海洛因瘾的人最终都会试图戒毒，这主要基于两个原因：维持吸毒的开支和害怕被捕。如果海洛因被合法化且可以廉价取得，正像一些人所鼓吹的，那么这两个原因都不适用了。

以上考虑可最好地用于下列哪一论述？

(A) 使海洛因销售合法化可能导致其价格下降。

(B) 使有海洛因瘾的人容易获得戒毒治疗可能鼓励许多有海洛因瘾的人努力戒毒。

(C) 使海洛因销售合法化可能增加有海洛因瘾的人为买毒品而造成的犯罪。

(D) 使海洛因能够合法且廉价地获得，将使那些对海洛因上瘾的人不大可能试图戒掉他们的毒瘾。

(E) 降低对吸海洛因的个人惩罚的力度，不会增加新的染海洛因瘾的人数。

Stem borers是一种经常毁坏北美谷类庄稼的有害昆虫。在其他一些大陆上，stem borers对庄稼的毁坏可以被某种蜂所控制。因为这种蜂只以stem borers为食，将其引进北美可使庄稼免遭stem borers的毁坏且不危害其他北美的昆虫。

下面哪一个是上面论述所基于的假设？

(A) Corn is the principal food of stem borers that live on continents other than North America.

(B) The wasps are capable of surviving in North America long enough to eat significant numbers of stem borers.

(C) No wasp in North America is closely related to the species of wasp that eats stem borers.

(D) On continents other than North America, the wasps control stem borers more effectively than does any other pest control measure.

(E) Corn crops on continents other than North America are not damaged by any insect pests other than stem borers.

(A) 谷物是生长在北美以外大陆的stem borers的主要食物。

(B) 这种蜂能够在北美长期存活以吃掉大量的stem borers。

(C) 在北美没有与吃stem borers的蜂相似的蜂。

(D) 在北美以外的大陆，这种蜂能比其他昆虫控制方法更有效地控制stem borers。

(E) 北美大陆以外的谷物庄稼不会被任何stem borers以外的昆虫毁坏。

7. In the country of Laurelia, legal restrictions on the sale of lock-picking equipment were relaxed ten years ago, and since then Laurelia's burglary rate has risen dramatically. Hence, since legally purchased lock-picking equipment was used in most burglaries, reintroducing strict limits on the sale of this equipment would help to reduce Laurelia's burglary rate.

Which of the following, if true, gives the strongest support to the argument?

(A) Laurelia's overall crime rate has risen dramatically over the last ten years.

(B) There is wide popular support in Laurelia for the reintroduction of strict limits on the sale of lock-picking equipment.

(C) The reintroduction of strict limits on the sale of lock-picking equipment in Laurelia would not prevent legitimate use of this equipment by police and other public safety officials.

(D) Most lock-picking equipment used in Laurelia is fragile and usually breaks irreparably within a few years of purchase.

(E) The introduction five years ago of harsher punishments for people convicted of burglary had little effect on Laurelia's burglary rate.

在Laurelia国，10年前放松了对销售拆锁设备的法律限制后，盗窃案发生率急剧上升。因为合法购置的拆锁设备被用于大多数盗窃案，所以重新引入对销售该设备的严格限制将有助于减少Laurelia国的盗窃发生率。

下面哪一项，如果正确，最有力地支持了以上论述？

(A) Laurelia的总体犯罪率在过去10年中急剧增加了。

(B) 对于重新引入对拆锁设备销售的严格限制，在Laurelia得到了广泛的支持。

(C) 在Laurelia重新引入对拆锁设备的严格限制不会阻碍警察和其他公共安全机构对这种设备的合法使用。

(D) 在Laurelia国使用的大多数拆锁设备是易坏的，并且通常会在购买几年后损坏而无法修好。

(E) 5年前引进的对被控盗窃的人更严厉的惩罚对Laurelia的盗窃率没有什么影响。

8. Salesperson: The picture tube is the central component of any television, and Picturesque televisions use the same high-quality picture tubes as those used in TruVue televisions. Since you pay a much lower price for a Picturesque, you pay a lower price for a television with the same picture quality when you buy a Picturesque instead of a TruVue.

售货员：显像管是任何一台电视的中心元件，Picturesque电视与TruVue电视使用相同质量的显像管。因为你为Picturesque付的价钱低，所以当你购买Picturesque而非TruVue时，付了更低的价钱却买了相同图像质量的电视。

Which of the following is an assumption that, if justified, would allow the conclusion of the salesperson's argument to be properly drawn?

(A) TruVue televisions are much more widely advertised than are Picturesque televisions.

(B) The picture quality of a television is determined solely by the quality of its picture tube.

(C) A salesperson earns much less on the sale of each Picturesque television than on the sale of each TruVue television.

(D) Many more Picturesque televisions are sold each year than TruVue televisions.

(E) Picturesque televisions are assembled in the same factory that assembles TruVue televisions.

下面哪种说法是一个假设，假如被认为正确，允许上面推销员做出正确的结论？

(A) TruVue电视比Picturesque电视被更广泛地做广告。

(B) 电视的图像质量仅仅由其显像管的质量决定。

(C) 售货员销售Picturesque电视赚的钱少于销售TruVue电视赚的钱。

(D) 每天Picturesque比TruVue销售得多。

(E) Picturesque电视是在组装TruVue电视的同一个工厂组装的。

Questions 9~10 are based on the following graph.

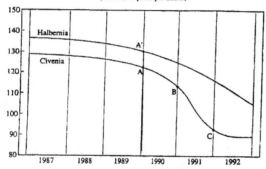

CIGARETTE SALES IN TWO NONADJACENT KIMMERLAND PROVINCES, 1987-1992
(millions of packs per month)

A: Civenia institutes 40% increase in cigarette tax.
A': Halbernia institutes 40% increase in cigarette tax.
B: Civenia begins intensive antismoking television advertising campaign.
C: Civenia concludes intensive antismoking television advertising campaign

Kimmerland两个不相邻的省自1987年至1992年香烟销售量（每月百万盒）

A：Civenia省香烟税增加40%。

A'：Halbernia省香烟税增加40%。

B：Civenia省开始广泛的反对吸烟电视广告活动。

C：Civenia省结束广泛的反对吸烟电视广告活动。

9. The claim that Civenia's antismoking television advertising campaign contributed significantly to the steep decline in cigarette purchases in that province during 1991 is best supported if which of the following has been true about the province of Halbernia from the beginning of 1991?

(A) It kept its cigarette tax at the 1990 level and instituted an antismoking television advertising campaign similar to Civenia's.

(B) It kept its cigarette tax at the 1990 level and did not institute an antismoking television advertising campaign.

(C) It rescinded the 1990 cigarette tax increase and did not institute an antismoking television advertising campaign.

下列哪一项关于Halbernia省自1991年初的说法，如果正确，将最有力地支持"Civenia省反对吸烟的电视广告活动对该省1991年香烟购买量骤减有极大作用"这一宣称？

(A) 它保持香烟税处于1990年的水平，并且开始类似于Civenia的反烟电视广告活动。

(B) 它保持了1990年的香烟税率水平且没有开展反对吸烟的电视广告活动。

(C) 它撤销了增加1990年香烟税，且没有开始反烟电视广告活动。

(D) It eliminated all cigarette taxes and did not institute an antismoking television advertising campaign.

(E) It increased its cigarette tax by an additional 40 percent over the 1990 level and instituted an antismoking television advertising campaign similar to Civenia's.

10. Which of the following, if true, most helps to explain why cigarette purchases in Civenia declined more slowly after the completion of the television antismoking advertising campaign than they did before the campaign began?

(A) Laws restricting smoking in public places in Civenia went into effect at the beginning of 1992.

(B) Most of those smokers in Civenia who were likely to quit or cut down on smoking had done so by the beginning of 1992.

(C) At the beginning of 1992, health insurance companies in Civenia offered lower rates to nonsmoking residents than to those who smoked.

(D) Cigarette companies increased their prices to Civenia distributors at the beginning of 1992 to offset the decrease in the number of packs sold.

(E) Some cigarette companies withdrew their advertisements from Civenia newspapers and magazines at the beginning of 1992.

11. In a recent film set in seventeenth-century Europe, the hero is seen doing the crawl, a swimming stroke not known in Europe before the 1920's. However, since moviegoers obviously are not experts in the history of swimming strokes, for most of the film's audience this blunder clearly cannot have interfered with whatever sense of historical authenticity the film otherwise achieved.

Which of the following, if true, most seriously weakens the argument given?

(A) The film was widely praised for being historically plausible, even though it portrayed many events that were not historically attested.

(B) The scene that shows the film's hero doing the crawl is a rescue scene pivotal to the film's action, and parts of it are even shown a second time, in a flashback.

(C) Makers of historical films, even of those set as recently as the nineteenth century, routinely strike compromises between historical authenticity and the need to keep their material accessible to a modern audience, as in the

(D) 它消除了所有香烟税，且没有开始反烟电视广告活动。

(E) 相比较于1990年的水平，它另外增加了40%的香烟税，且开始了类似于Civenia的反烟电视广告活动。

下列哪种说法，如果正确，最有助于解释为什么C省在结束了反对吸烟的电视广告活动后，香烟购买量的下降速度比开展活动前慢？

(A) 在Civenia公共场合限制吸烟的法律在1992年初开始生效。

(B) Civenia省大多数可能戒烟或减少吸烟的人在1992年初已经这样做了。

(C) 在1992年初，Civenia的健康保险公司对非吸烟者提供的保险费低于吸烟者的保险费。

(D) 在1992年初，香烟公司对Civenia分销商提高了香烟的价格以抵消香烟销售量的下降。

(E) 在1992年初，一些香烟公司撤回了他们在Civenia报纸和杂志上所做的广告。

在最近的一部以17世纪的欧洲为背景的电影中，有男主角自由泳的镜头，而自由泳在20世纪20年代以前的欧洲尚未出现。然而因为看电影的人明显对游泳动作史并不在行，因此对于大多数电影观众来说，这一错误显然不会影响该电影在其他方面所揭示的任何历史真实性。

下面哪一个，假如正确，最削弱已提出的论述？

(A) 尽管电影描述了许多未经历史证实的事件，但它因为描述历史事件合乎情理而受到了赞扬。

(B) 表现男主角做自由泳的电影场景是对于该电影情节至关重要的营救场景，并且部分场景在倒叙中被第二次放映。

(C) 历史电影的制作者，甚至包括那些19世纪的场景的电影制作者，通常在历史的真实性和保持素材让现代观众可接受的需要之间做妥协，就像演员们

actors' speech patterns.

(D) The crawl that European swimmers used in the 1920's was much less efficient and more awkward-looking than the crawl that is currently taught.

(E) A slightly earlier film featuring an eighteenth century sea battle in Europe was ridiculed in numerous popular reviews for the historical lapse of showing a sailor doing the crawl in swimming to safety.

的说话方式一样。

(D) 19世纪20年代的欧洲游泳者所使用的自由泳比现在所教的自由泳效率低且样子笨拙。

(E) 在这之前的一部描绘18世纪欧洲海战的影片展现了一个船员以自由泳逃生的场景，这一历史性错误被许多大众性的影评文章所嘲讽。

12. The government of Pontran claims that Tor City, one of the six major cities in that country, is alone among Pontran's cities in having sustained strong job growth this year. Clearly, however, any job growth there must be purely imaginary; in fact, in Tor City and only there, more people are unemployed this year than were last year.

The argument countering the government's claim depends on the assumption that

(A) unemployed workers in Pontran did not, in significant numbers, move to Tor City when the government claimed Tor City had strong job growth.

(B) the unemployment rate in Tor City is higher year than in any previous year.

(C) actions taken by the government of Pontran significantly affect the unemployment rate in Tor City.

(D) the unemployment rate in Tor City, though increased, is still the lowest of any city in Pontran.

(E) there is no significant seasonal variation in the unemployment rate for Pontran as a whole.

Pontran的政府宣称：六大城市之一的Tor城是今年Pontran的所有城市中唯一保持了强劲就业增长势头的城市。然而很明显，那里的任何就业增长纯粹是虚构的，实际上，仅Tor城，今年的失业人数就多于去年。

反对政府的宣称的论述取决于下列哪一个假设：

(A) Pontran的失业工人没有在政府宣称Tor城就业增长势头强劲后大量涌入Tor城。

(B) 今年Tor城的失业率高于以前任何一年。

(C) Pontran政府所采取的行动对Tor城的失业率影响巨大。

(D) Tor城的失业率尽管增加了，但在Pontran的任何城市中仍然是最低的。

(E) 作为一个整体而言，Pontran的失业率并没有显著的季节性变化。

13. As people age, the number of calories they need each day decreases while their daily requirement of vitamin B_6 increases. Clearly, unless older people take B_6 supplements or eat a diet that contains more B_6 than did the diet they ate when they were young adults, there is little likelihood that they will get B_6 in needed amounts.

Which of the following would be most helpful to know to evaluate the argument?

(A) Whether the relative decrease in the daily requirement of calories is greater than the relative increase in the daily requirement of vitamin B6.

(B) Whether the form of vitamin B6 found in dietary supplements is more readily absorbed and utilized by the body than is the from of this vitamin that is found in

随着年龄的增长，人们每天对卡路里的需求量日趋减少，而对维生素B_6的需求量却增加。明显地，除非老年人摄入维生素B_6作为补充或吃些比他们年轻时吃的含维生素B_6更多的食物，否则他们不太可能获得所需的维生素B_6。

下列哪项最有助于评价以上论述？

(A) 每天需要的卡路里量的相对减少是否比每天需要增加的维生素B_6的量要大。

(B) 饮食补充品中的维生素B_6的形式是否比饮食中维生素B_6的形式更容易被身体吸收和利用。

food.

(C) Whether the consequences of not getting vitamin B_6 in required daily amounts are more serious for older people than for young adults.

(D) Whether the diets of most people, when they are young adults, include vitamin B_6 in amounts far in excess of their daily needs.

(E) Whether the diets of older people are more likely than those of young adults to include one or more meals a day that are devoid of foods containing vitamin B_6.

(C) 未获得足够的每天所需的维生素B_6的量的后果对于老年人是否比青年人更严重。

(D) 大多数人在年轻时的饮食中是否包含了远远超出他们每天所需的维生素B_6的含量。

(E) 老年人的饮食是否比年轻人更可能在一天不止一顿的饮食中食用缺乏维生素B_6的食品。

参考答案：

1. B	2. C	3. E	4. E	5. D
6. B	7. D	8. B	9. B	10. B
11. E	12. A	13. D		

1. **解析：** 本题由一个discovery得出结论，属于"B，A"型，此类假设大多为"除了A以外没有别的原因"，可以用否定概念定位找到(B)，发现(B)确实为上述推理成立的必要条件。因为若Euripides在其晚期的作品模仿过早期的风格，则上述推理必不成立，因此此(B)正确。

2. **解析：** 本题属于数学相关类的归纳题，可以用简单的数学思维去判断。通过读题，发现重点为"新的国产汽车自1988年后平均油效未提高，而与进口汽车的平均油效的差距却减小了"，因此可以得出结论，进口汽车在1988年后的平均油效减小了。所以(C)正确。

3. **解析：** 本题属于"B，A"类型的反对，由事实"1970年至1980年间能源消耗达到顶峰后又下降，而工业产量急剧上升"，得出结论"工业部门采取了高效节能的措施"。显然解题思路为"除了A以外有其他原因"。(E)指出20世纪70年代中energy intensive industries产量大幅下降，能量使用也随之下降，解释了事实，因此(E)正确；(A)中的high-price，low-price 为无关概念；(B)属于新比较不对；(C)没有说明1970年的情况；(D)新比较也必然不对。

4. **解析：** 数学相关类的支持题，可由简单的数学思维来完成。假定一个集合有两个子集，若其中一个子集增大，则另外一个子集变小，但集合的总量不变。(E)通过指出现在和过去拥有的计算机软件数目相同，结合前提中购买软件的平均数量增加，从而支持了为什么非法拷贝软件数量的减少，所以(E)正确；(A)为反对；(B)无法说明现在的情况；(C)与软件无关；(D)只指出几乎没有人因无熟人而得不到非法软件，与本题推理无关。

5. **解析：** 本题问法特别，貌似新题型，实际上是近年来对完成段落即解释题型的一种变型，即以上考虑可用于以下哪一个论述，重点找一个在逻辑上与段落推理相连贯的一项，而(D)所表达的刚好与上述推理吻合，所以(D)正确；(A)、(B)、(C)、(E)都不符合连贯的目的。

6. **解析：** 注意本书48页29题的推理为："对蕨类植物的控制可以引入一种蛾子"，这是标准的对目的提问法，解题思路为A可行或A有意义，答案为"释放的蛾子可以充分繁殖以生殖足够多的蛾子来减少蕨类植物且阻碍它的增长"。很明显，本题为这一问题的重考考题，虽没有原样照搬，但其问题目的、段落内容与答案方向完全相同，我们通过比较这两道题，应当认识到熟做真题的重要作用。本题答案方向也为A可行或有意义，所以(B)正确。

7. **解析：** 支持题型要寻求一个选项，使得结论成立的可能性增大，因此在很多情况下用结论关键词定位答案。本题结论为"重新引入对销售该设备的严格限制将有助于减少Laurelia国的盗窃发生率"，关键词为"equipment"。(D)指出这种设备易坏，说明重新引入此设备的限制确实能够起到减少犯罪的作用，即使那些拥有此设备的盗窃犯不久以后也不会再拥有该设备，支持了本题的结论；(A)无关；(B)、(C)虽有此关键词，但起不到支持作用；(E)易误选，但除了限制以外的方法不起作用并不能支持此方法能够起作用。

8. **解析**：本题前提与结论之间有明显的跳跃，前提为"Same high-quality picture tubes"，而结论为"Same picture quality"，所以结论要想成立，必定要做一假设，把A与B联起来，即差异概念的桥梁。(B)将两个质量连了起来，因此(B)正确。

9. **解析**：由图上看出，1991年以前两省香烟销售量下降速度基本保持一致，Civenia省开展广告活动的1991年，其香烟销售量骤减，而1992年终止活动时，销售量基本上不再下降，而Halbernia省香烟销售量下降幅度与往年基本持平，(B)通过指出Halbernia省在1991年初没有进行广告活动，所以没有出现象Civenia那样的急剧下降，而起到了最好的支持作用。

10. **解析**：1992年香烟销售下降慢于1990年，为什么?(B)指出可能戒烟或减少吸烟的人付诸行动，所以，1992年香烟销售下降了，所以(B)正确；(A)只说明香烟销售下降快的原因；(C)、(D)、(E)无法解释上面问题目的。

11. **解析**：本题推理的前提：因为看电影的人并非游泳动作史的行家；结论：这个错误不会干扰电影在其他方面所提示的历史真实性，要求找弱化了这个论点的选项。(E)指出了与论据恰好相对立的一种现象，表明尽管大多数看电影的人不懂它是否与历史相左，但毕竟有内行人士，而他们可以指出这个错误，所以(E)正确；(A)无关；(B)第二次放映与知道错误是两个概念；(C)只是提到妥协，但却不能对上述论点产生任何影响；(D)无关比较，对上述论点推理不起作用。

注：crawl n. 自由式游泳 v. 爬行，使害怕，奉承

flashback n. 倒叙

12. **解析**：本题为假设题型，也是GRE逻辑推理题的重考题。本题推理为：Tor城失业人数多于去年，所以就业增长势头纯粹系虚构。因此，当我们读到(A)，感觉(A)对，就没有往下看的必要。因为(A)排除了失业人数的增加是来自于Tor城之外的可能性，排除了他因，从而可以作为一个很好的假设。

13. **解析**：本题让我们评价"老年人要想获得所需的B_6的量，一定要摄入B_6以做补充或吃比他们年轻时代吃的含B_6更多的食物。(D)选项可以作为一个很好的评价。因为我们回答了"yes"，那么老年人可能不需额外补充B_6；如果回答"no"，则老年人需吃B_6以做补充或吃年轻时吃的含B_6更多的食物，因此上述推理正确，所以(D)正确。

二、GMAT考前逻辑推理冲刺训练试题及解析（二）

1. The Environmental Protection Agency must respond to the hazard to children's health posed by exposure to asbestos fibers released in the air in school classrooms. Since it is impossible to close school buildings, the best plan would be to initiate programs that mandate the immediate removal of asbestos from all the school buildings that are found to contain asbestos, regardless of whether or not the buildings are in use.

Which of the following, if true, is the strongest reason for the Environmental Protection Agency not to follow the plan outlined above?

(A) The techniques available for removing asbestos often increase the level of airborne asbestos.

(B) Schools are places where asbestos is especially likely to

环保机构必须对接触教室空气中的石棉纤维给孩子健康带来的危害做出反应。因为不可能关闭学校的建筑。所以最好的方法就是着手实施强制性立即消除所有学校建筑中的石棉的计划，而不管这些建筑物是否在使用中。

下列哪一个，假如正确，是最强有力的原因来说明环境保护机构不应当实行上面所提出的计划?

(A) 可行的消除石棉的技术通常增加空中的石棉含量。

(B) 学校是居民活动最可能导致石棉释放到大气中的场所。

be released into the air by the action of the occupants.

(C) Children exposed to airborne asbestos run a greater risk of developing cancer than do adults exposed to airborne asbestos.

(D) The cost of removing asbestos varies from school to school, depending on accessibility and the quantity of asbestos to be removed.

(E) It is impossible to determine with any degree of certainty if and when construction materials that contain asbestos will break down and release asbestos fibers into the air.

2. *Aedes albopictus*, a variety of mosquito that has recently established itself in the southeastern United States, is less widespread than the indigenous swamp mosquito. Both the swamp mosquito and A.albopictus can carry viruses that are sometimes fatal to humans, but *A.albopictus* is a greater danger to public health.

Each of the following, if true, provides additional information that strengthens the judgment given about the danger to public health EXCEPT:

(A) Unlike the swamp mosquito, A.albopictus originated in Asia, and larvae of it were not observed in the United States before the mid-1980's.

(B) Unlike the swamp mosquito, *A.albopictus* tends to spend most of its adult life near human habitation.

(C) Unlike swamp mosquito larvae, A.albopictus larvae survive in flower pots, tin cans, and many small household objects that hold a little water.

(D) In comparison with the swamp mosquito, A.albopictus hosts a much wider variety of viruses known to cause serious diseases in humans.

(E) A.albopictus seeks out a much wider range of animal hosts than does the swamp mosquito, and it is more likely to bite humans.

3. A person's cholesterol level will decline significantly if that person increases the number of meals eaten per day, but only if there is no significant increase in the amount of food eaten. However, most people who increase the number of meals they eat each day will eat a lot more food as well.

If the statements above are true, which of the following is most strongly supported by them?

(A) For most people, cholesterol level is not significantly affected by the amount of food eaten per day.

(C) 接触空气中石棉的孩子比接触空中的石棉的成人得癌症的风险更大。

(D) 消除石棉的成本在各个学校中不同，它取决于被除去石棉的量及可接近的程度。

(E) 不可能确切判定含有石棉的建筑材料是否且什么时候将分解并且释放石棉纤维而进入空气。

*Aedes albopictus*是蚊子的一个变种，最近在美国东南部衍居，它没有当地的沼泽蚊子分布广。沼泽蚊子与A.都能携带有时能使人致命的病毒，但A.对公众健康危害更大。

下列选项除哪个外，如果正确，都能提供附加信息来支持以上所做出的对公共健康产生危害的判断。

(A) 与沼泽 蚊子不同，A.原产于亚洲，且20世纪80年代中期以前在美国还没有发现过A.的幼虫。

(B) 不同于沼泽蚊子，*A.albopictus*倾向于在人类居住地附近度过它们的大部分成熟期。

(C) 不同于沼泽蚊子的幼虫，*A.albopictus*幼虫生存于花盆、锡罐，和许多盛有少量水的家用物体中。

(D) 与沼泽蚊子相比较，*A.albopictus*是大量所知的能导致人类严重疾病的病毒的宿主。

(E) *A.albopictus*是比沼泽蚊子搜索更大范围的动物宿主，更可能叮咬人类。

一个人如果增加日进餐次数且不显著增加所摄入的食物总量，那么他的胆固醇水平会有显著下降。然而，大多数增加日进餐次数的人同时也摄入了更多的食物。

上面陈述如果正确，下列哪一个结论最能支持上面的陈述？

(A) 对于大多数人而言，胆固醇的水平不受每天吃的食物量的影响。

(B) For most people, the amount of food eaten per meal is most strongly affected by the time of day at which the meal is eaten.

(C) For most people, increasing the number of meals eaten per day will not result in a significantly lower cholesterol level.

(D) For most people, the total amount of food eaten per day is unaffected by the number of meals eaten per day.

(E) For most people, increasing the number of meals eaten per day will result in a significant change in the types of food eaten.

4. A certain type of dinnerware made in Ganandia contains lead. Lead can leach into acidic foods, and Ganandians tend to eat highly acidic foods. However, the extreme rarity of lead poisoning in Ganandia indicates that the dinnerware does not contain dangerous amounts of lead.

Which of the following, if true, most seriously weakens the argument above?

(A) The dinnerware is produced exclusively for sale outside Ganandia.

(B) Ganandian foods typically are much more acidic than foods anywhere else in the world.

(C) The only source of lead poisoning in Ganandia is lead that has leached into food.

(D) Most people who use the dinnerware are not aware that it contains lead.

(E) Acidic foods can leach lead from dinnerware even if that dinnerware has a protective coating.

5. Question 5 is based on the following graph.

EFFECTIVENESS OF DRUG X IN ERADICATING A BACTERIAL LUNG INFECTION IN ADULT PATIENTS

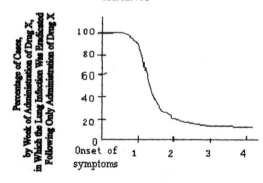

Point During the Course of the Infection at Which Drug X Was First Administered to Patients
(in weeks following the onset of symptoms)

(B) 对于大多数人而言，每顿饭吃的食物的量取决于吃饭的时间。

(C) 对于大多数人而言，增加每天吃饭的次数将不会导致胆固醇水平的显著下降。

(D) 对于大多数人而言，每天吃饭的总量不受每天吃饭的次数影响。

(E) 对于大多数人而言，增加每天吃饭的次数将导致吃的食物的种类的显著变化。

某种在Ganandia制造的晚用餐具中含有铅。铅会渗入酸性食物，且Ganandia人倾向于食用高酸性的食物。然而，在Ganandia铅中毒事件极少的事实说明那里的餐具不含达到危险水平的铅。

下面哪一项，如果正确，将最不能证实以上论述？

(A) 生产的晚餐用具全部在Ganandia以外销售。

(B) Ganandia 的食物通常比世界上其他地方的食物所含酸性更多。

(C) Ganandia铅中毒的唯一来源是渗入食物的铅。

(D) 大多数使用晚餐用具的人没有意识到它含有铅。

(E) 即使晚餐用具有一层保护性的涂层，酸性食物也能够把铅从晚餐用具中萃取出来。

本题基于下图
在成人患者中，X药消除细菌性肺部感染的有效性。

原点表示感染过程中患者首次服X药的那一点。
（症状发作后的各个星期）

Drug X, which kills on contact the bacteria that cause the infection, is administered to patients by means of an aerosol inhaler.

Which of the following, if true, contributes most to explaining the change in drug X's effectiveness during the course of the infection?

(A) Symptoms of the infection usually become evident during the first 48 hours following infection.

(B) Most patients with lung infections say they prefer aerosol inhalers to other means of administering antibacterial drugs.

(C) In most patients taking drug X, the dosage administered is increased slightly each week until symptoms disappear.

(D) In patients who have the infection, the ability to inhale becomes increasingly impaired beginning in the second week after the onset of symptoms.

(E) Drug X is not administered to any patient who shows signs of suffering from secondary infections.

6. Sergeant

Our police academy no longer requires its applicants to pass a physical examination before being admitted to the academy. As a result, several candidates with weak hearts and high blood pressure have been admitted. Hence, we can expect our future police force to have more health problems than our current police force.

Knowledge of each of the following would be relevant to determining the reliability of the sergeant's prediction EXCEPT whether

(A) police officer candidates are screened for high blood pressure before joining the police force.

(B) the police officer candidates who are not healthy now are likely to be unhealthy as police officers.

(C) graduates of the police academy are required to pass a physical examination.

(D) the health of the current police officer candidates is worse than was the health of police officer candidates in the past.

(E) a police officer's health is a reliable indicator of the officer's performance.

X药能消灭由接触而引起感染的细菌，它通过喷雾吸入器由病人服用。

下面哪一项如果正确，最有助于解释在感染过程中X药的效果变化？

(A) 在感染后的48个小时，感染的症状通常变得明显。

(B) 大多数有肺部感染的病人说他自己倾向于使用喷雾吸入器而不是其他形式的抗菌药。

(C) 在大多数服用X药的病人中，使用的剂量每周略微增加直至症状消失。

(D) 在受感染的病人中，在症状发生后的第二周开始吸入药的能力逐渐受到损害。

(E) X药没有被任何出现遭受第二次被感染症状的病人服用。

警官：

我们的警察学院不再要求申请者在被录取之前通过一项身体检查。这样，一些患有心脏病和高血压的候选人被录取了。因此，我们可以预测未来的警察队伍会比目前的警察队伍存在更多的健康问题。

下面每一个知识对决定警官预言的可靠性最为相关，除了是否

(A) 警官候选人在加入警官队伍前被测试有无高血压。

(B) 现在不健康的警官候选人作为警官后也可能不健康。

(C) 警官学院的毕业生要求通过身体检查。

(D) 目前警官候选人的健康比以前警官候选人的健康程度糟糕。

(E) 一个警官的健康是警官表现的一个可靠指示。

7. Because adult iguanas on Plazos Island are much smaller than adult iguanas of the same species on nearby islands, researchers assumed that environmental conditions on Plazos favor the survival of relatively smaller baby iguanas (hatchlings) in each yearly brood. They discovered instead that for each of the past three years, 10 percent of the smaller and 40 percent of the larger hatchlings survived, because larger hatchlings successfully evade their predators.

Which of the following, if true about Plazos but not about nearby islands, contributes most to an explanation of the long-standing tendency of iguanas on Plazos to be smaller than those of the same age on nearby islands?

(A) Periodic wind shifts cause extended dry spells on Plazos every year, putting the larger iguanas, whose bodies require relatively more water, at a great disadvantage.

(B) There are exactly three species of iguanas on Plazos but only two species of seagulls that feed on iguanas, and a relatively small percentage of each year's hatchlings are consumed by seagulls.

(C) Wild cats, which were introduced as pets by early settlers and which were formerly major predators of Plazos iguanas, were recently killed off by a disease specific to cats.

(D) The iguanas on Plazos are a relatively ancient part of the island's animal life.

(E) Both land and marine iguanas live on Plazos, and the land iguanas tend to be larger than marine iguanas of the same age.

因为Plazos岛上的成年蜥蜴比附近岛屿上相同种类的成年蜥蜴小很多，所以研究者假定Plazos岛上的环境条件有利于每年孵化的较小的小蜥蜴生存。但他们发现，过去三年中，因为较大的幼蜥蜴能够成功地躲避对它们的捕食。每年有10%的较小幼蜥蜴和40%的较大幼蜥蜴存活。

下面哪一项，如果关于Plazos而非邻近其他岛屿的叙述正确，最有助于解释Plazos岛上的成年蜥蜴比邻近岛屿上的小的长期趋势？

(A) 季风的移动使Plazos岛上每年发生长期干旱，这将置身体需要更多水分的大蜥蜴于不利地位。

(B) Plazos岛上有三种蜥蜴，但只有两种捕食蜥蜴的海鸥，以至于每天相对小的比例的幼虫被海鸥吃掉。

(C) 被早期的定居者引入，作为宠物并且以前是Plazos岛上蜥蜴的主要捕食者的野猫，最近在一场猫疫中死亡。

(D) Plazos岛上的蜥蜴是该岛相对古老的野生动物。

(E) 陆地蜥蜴和海洋蜥蜴居住在Plazos岛，并且陆地蜥蜴看来要大于相同年龄的海洋蜥蜴。

8. Every human being who has ever lived had two parents. Therefore, more people were alive three thousand years ago than are alive now.

The reasoning in the argument is flawed because it

(A) overlooks the number of people in each generation during the last three thousand years who left no descendants.

(B) disregards possible effects of disasters such as famines and plagues on human history.

(C) overestimates the mathematical effect of repeated doublings on population size.

(D) fails to take into account that people now alive have overlapping sets of ancestors.

(E) fails to consider that accurate estimation of the number of people alive three thousand years ago might be impossible.

每一个曾活着的人都有两个父母。因此，3000年前的人口多于现在活着的人口。

上面论点的推理是有缺陷的，因为它……

(A) 忽略过去3000年中的每一代中没有后代的人的数目。

(B) 忽视了诸如饥荒和瘟疫这样的灾难对人类历史造成的可能的影响。

(C) 过分估计人口的反复加倍的数学效果。

(D) 没有考虑现在生存的人有共同的祖先。

(E) 没有考虑到准确地估计3000年前人类的人数也许是不可能的。

9. Each of the academic journals *Thought* and *Ergo* has a review committee to prevent misattributed quotations from appearing in its published articles. Nevertheless, about ten percent of the quotations in *Thought's* published articles are misattributed, whereas *Ergo* contains no misattributions. *Ergo's* committee is more effective, therefore, than *Thought's* at finding misattributed quotations.

The argument above assumes that

(A) most of the articles submitted to *Thought* for publication contain misattributed quotations.

(B) there are at least some misattributed quotations in articles submitted to *Ergo* for publication.

(C) the members of *Ergo's* committee are, on the whole, more knowledgeable than are the members of *Thought's* committee.

(D) the number of misattributed quotations in a journal is an accurate measure of how carefully that journal is edited.

(E) the authors who submit articles to *Ergo* for publication are more thorough in attributing quotations than are the authors who submit articles to *Thought*.

10. Question 10 is based on the following table.

RESULTS OF A CONTROLLED STUDY OF THE EFFECTS OF CHEWING GUM ON TOOTH DECAY IN CHILDREN

Average total number of new cavities per child over the course of three years

Children who regularly chewed gum sweetened with X   4.0
Children who regularly chewed gum sweetened with Y   1.5
Children who did not chew gum   2.5

Which of the following, if true, most helps to explain the difference among the children who chewed gum sweetened with X, the children who chewed gum sweetened with Y, and the children who did not chew any gum?

(A) X, but not Y, consists of a substance that helps to protect teeth against harmful substances present in other foods.

(B) The children who did not chew any gum during the study ate fewer sweet foods than did either the children who chewed gum sweetened with X or the children who chewed gum sweetened with Y.

(C) The action of chewing gum stimulates the production of saliva, which contains a substance that helps fight tooth decay, but X, unlike Y, is a contributing factor to tooth decay.

学术期刊*Thought*和*Ergo*都有一个检查委员会负责防止错误的引语出现在其发表的文章中。然而，*Thought*发表的文章中10%的引语有误，而*Ergo*中却没有引语错误。因此，*Ergo*的检查委员会在发现错误引语上比*Thought*的检查委员会更有效。

上面的论述假设

(A) 大多数被提交到*Thought*发表的文章中包含错误引用的引语。

(B) 提交到*Ergo*发表的文章至少有一些错误引用的引语。

(C) 从总体上而言，*Ergo*委员会的成员比*Thought*委员会成员知识更渊博。

(D) 一个杂志上错误引语的数量是衡量该杂志编辑工作是否细致的一个精神标准。

(E) 提交文章到*Ergo*发表的作者比提交文章到*Thought*的作者在归类引语时更认真。

本题基于下表

一个关于孩子嚼口香糖对虫牙影响的控制性研究结果

每个孩子三年中平均共新生虫牙数
经常嚼用X致甜的口香糖的孩子 4.0
经常嚼用Y致甜的口香糖的孩子 1.5
不嚼口香糖的孩子   2.5

下列哪一项，如果正确，最有助于解释嚼用X致甜和用Y致甜的口香糖与不嚼口香糖的孩子的差异。

(A) X，而不是Y，含有一种保护牙齿抵抗其他食物中有害物质的成份。

(B) 在研究中，不嚼任何口香糖的孩子比嚼用X致甜的口香糖和用Y致甜的口香糖的孩子吃的甜食少。

(C) 嚼口香糖刺激唾液的产生，其中含有一种可预防牙齿腐坏的物质，而X可加速牙齿腐坏，Y却不会。

(D) Each group of children who chewed gum during the study brushed their teeth more often than did the children who did not chew gum during the study, but the children who chewed gum sweetened with Y brushed their teeth less often than did the children who chewed gum sweetened with X.

(E) The action of chewing gum improves the circulation of blood in the jaw and strengthens the roots of adult teeth, but is also causes baby teeth to fall out more quickly than they would otherwise.

11. In the last few decades, grassy wetlands, essential to the nesting and breeding of ducks, geese, swans, and most other species of waterfowl, have been extensively drained and cultivated in southern Canada and the northern United States, Duck populations in North American have plummeted during this time, but populations of swans and geese have been affected less dramatically.

Which of the following, if true, most helps to explain the difference mentioned above?

(A) Prohibition of hunting of waterfowl is easier to enforce in areas under cultivation than in wild lands.

(B) Most geese and swans nest and breed farther north than ducks do, in areas that still are not cultivated.

(C) Land that has been harvested rarely provides food suitable for waterfowl.

(D) Goose and swan populations decline in periods of drought, when breeding sites are fewer.

(E) Because they are larger than ducks, geese and swans have a harder time finding protected nesting sites in areas that are cultivated.

12. A researcher found that, in proportion to their body weights, children eat more carbohydrates than adults do. Children also exercise more than adults do. The researcher hypothesized that carbohydrate consumption varies in direct proportion to the calorie demands associated with different levels of exercise.

Which of the following, if true, most seriously undermines the researcher's hypothesis?

(A) More carbohydrates are eaten per capita in nations where the government spends more per capita on public exercise programs.

(D) 在研究中，嚼口香糖的每一组孩子与研究中不嚼口香糖的孩子刷牙更频繁，但是嚼用Y致甜的口香糖的孩子没有嚼用X致甜的口香糖的孩子刷牙频繁。

(E) 嚼口香糖的行为可提高腭部的血液循环并且加强成人牙齿的牙根，但它同时使幼儿牙齿比没有嚼口香糖的情况掉得快得多。

加拿大南部和美国北部多草的湿地在过去的几十年中被广泛地排水和开发，而这些地方对鸭子、鹅、天鹅及其他绝大多数水禽的筑巢和孵化是必不可少的。在此期间，北美的鸭类数量显著下降，而天鹅和鹅的数量却未受明显的影响。

下面哪一项，如果正确，最有助于解释上面提到的差异？

(A) 在被开发的地区对禁止捕猎水鸟的禁令比野生土地更容易被加强。

(B) 大多数鹅类、天鹅筑巢和孵化的地区是在比鸭类更靠北部的仍然未被开发的地区。

(C) 已经收获的土地很少提供适合于水鸟的食物。

(D) 鹅类和天鹅的数目在干旱期下降，那时孵化的地区越来越少。

(E) 因为鹅类和天鹅比鸭类更大，所以它们在被开发的土地上更难以发现受保护的筑巢点。

一位研究者发现，相对于体重而言，孩子吃的碳水化合物多于大人，孩子运动比大人也更多。研究者假设碳水化合物的消耗量与不同程度的运动相联系的卡路里的需求量成正比。

下列哪一个，假如正确，最削弱研究者的假说？

(A) 政府在公众运动项目中平均每人花费更多的国家里，人均食用碳水化合物更多。

(B) Children who do not participate in organized sports tend to eat fewer carbohydrates than children who participate in organized sports.

(C) Consumption of increased amounts of carbohydrates is a popular tactic of runners preparing for long-distance races.

(D) Periods of physical growth require a relatively higher level of carbohydrate consumption than otherwise.

(E) Though carbohydrates are necessary for the maintenance of good health, people who consume more carbohydrates are not necessarily healthier.

(B) 不参加有组织运动的孩子比参加有组织运动的孩子倾向于吃更少的碳水化合物。

(C) 增加碳水化合物消耗量是长跑运动员准备长距离奔跑的一个惯常的策略。

(D) 与其他情况相比，身体生长时期需要相对多的碳水化合物。

(E) 尽管碳水化合物是维持身体健康所必不可少的，但吃更多碳水化合物的人并不一定更健康。

13. Experts removed a layer of eighteenth-century red paint from a figure in a painting by a sixteenth-century Italian artist, revealing a layer of green paint underneath. Since the green paint dates from the sixteenth century, the figure must have been green, not red, when the painting was completed in 1563.

Which of the following, if true, most seriously weakens the argument?

(A) The experts had been commissioned to restore the painting to the colors it had when it was completed.

(B) X-rays reveal an additional layer of paint beneath the green paint on the figure.

(C) Chemical analyses were used to determine the ages of the red paint and the green paint.

(D) The red paint was added in the eighteenth century in an attempt to repair damage done in the late seventeenth century.

(E) Red paint on the robe of another figure in the painting dates from the sixteenth century.

专家从一幅16世纪意大利艺术家所作画中的人物上去除了一层18世纪加上的红颜料，发现下面有一层绿色。由于绿颜料来自16世纪，所以该人物像在1563年完成时应是绿色而非红色。

下列哪一个，如果正确，最削弱上面的论述？

(A) 专家们被委任去重新恢复该画被完成时的颜色。

(B) X射线揭示在人物的绿颜色下还有一层颜色。

(C) 化学分析被用于决定红颜色和绿颜色的年代。

(D) 在18世纪被加上的红色是修复17世纪晚期所导致的损害的一个补救。

(E) 画中另一个人物袍子上的红色可追溯到16世纪。

14. Although it is assumed that peacocks' magnificent tails function essentially to attract peahens, no one knows why it should be magnificent tails that give a competitive advantage in securing mates. One explanation is that peahens are more likely to mate with peacocks with magnificent tails than with peacocks that lack magnificent tails.

Which of the following is an error of reasoning exemplified by the explanation?

(A) Attributing to animals qualities that are characteristically human.

(B) Extending a conclusion that is true of only one species of a genus to all species of the genus.

尽管人们假定雄孔雀的漂亮尾羽主要是用于吸引雌孔雀的，但没人知道为什么漂亮的尾羽能在求偶中占优势。一种解释是雌孔雀更愿与拥有漂亮尾羽的雄孔雀为偶，而不是那些没有漂亮尾羽的雄孔雀。

下列哪一个是解释中举例论证的推理错误？

(A) 把人类的典型特征归属于动物。

(B) 把一个仅仅对一类中的一个物种正确的结论扩展到该类中所有物种。

(C) Offering as an explanation a hypothesis that in principle can be neither verified nor proved false.

(D) Offering the phenomenon that is to be explained as the explanation of that phenomenon.

(E) Assuming without warrant that peacocks with magnificent tails are likely to have other features strongly attractive to peahens.

(C) 提供一个原则上既没有被证真也没有被证伪的假说作为解释。

(D) 提供一个将要被解释的现象作为该现象的解释。

(E) 没有根据地假设有漂亮尾羽的雄孔雀可能有其他强烈吸引雌孔雀的特征。

15. Whenever a French novel is translated into English, the edition sold in Britain should be in British English. If the edition sold in Britain were in American English, its idioms and spellings would appear to British readers to be strikingly American and thus to conflict with the novel's setting.

The recommendation is based on which of the following assumptions?

(A) The authors of French novels are usually native speakers of French.

(B) A non-British reader of a novel written in British English will inevitably fail to understand the meanings of some of the words and idioms in the novel.

(C) No French novel that is to be sold in Britain in English translation is set in the United States.

(D) A British reader of a British novel will notice that the idioms and spellings used in the novel are British.

(E) Most French novels are not translated into both British English and American English.

当一部法国小说无论何时被译成英文后，在英国出售的版本都应是英国英语版。如果在英国出售的版本中是美国英语，那么它的习惯用语和拼写对英国读者而言都是明显的美国英语，这与小说的背景相冲突。

上面的建议基于下列哪一个假设？

(A) 法国小说的作者通常是以法语为母语的人。

(B) 非英国读者在读一部写成英国英语的小说时，将不可避免地无法理解小说中一些单词和习惯用法的意义。

(C) 在英国出售的翻译成英文的法国小说没有描述发生在美国的事。

(D) 英国小说的英国读者将注意到用于小说的习惯用法和拼写是英国式的。

(E) 绝大多数法国小说没有同时被翻译为英国英语和美国英语。

参考答案：

1. A	2. A	3. C	4. A	5. D
6. E	7. A	8. D	9. B	10. C
11. B	12. D	13. B	14. D	15. C

1. **解析**：本题实际上要找一个选项来支持不应着手实施强制性立即消除石棉的计划。(A)说明消除石棉的技术增加空气中的石棉含量，意味着消除石棉的效果反而更差，因此，支持了不应着手实施强制性立即消除石棉的计划；(B)与消除石棉的计划无关；(C)是一个新的比较；(D)涉及的成本不同，但只要利大于弊就应实施强制性立即消除石棉的计划；(E)与(B)一样，与消除石棉的计划较远。

2. **解析**：本题为strengthen EXCEPT题型，答案方向为无关选项或反对选项。上文的判断为A. albopictus is a greater danger to public health, (A)强调的是A.albopictus被发现的时间，与"是否对公众健康危害甚大无关，所以做为无关选项，必为正确答案；(B)、(C)、(E)说明A albopictus更可能与人类接触，所以起到支持作用；(D)是支持作用更为明显。

3. **解析**：本题为"自上而下"的support题型，即归纳类。注意把握此类推理的段落逻辑层次结构。仔细体会(C)作为正确答案的特点以及他们四个选项错在什么地方。

4. **解析**：本题推理重点在最后一句话，并且however也指引了读题重点，那么weaken应重点，weaken最后一句话。而最后一句话是用"Ganandia铅中毒事件极少"这一事实而得出结论"餐具不含有达到危险水平的铅"，属于推理的"B，A"型，思维重点应转向用"除了A之外有别的原因影响B"，而(A)指出生产的晚餐用具全部在Ganandia以外销售，指出了A之外的另外一个原因，所以(A)正确。

5. **解析**：本题为解释图表题，重在抓住图表的变化点。(D)指出受感染的病人在第二周吸入药的能力受到损害，解释了第二周以后图的变化，因此(D)正确；(A)解释不了图的变化；(B)中病人的愿望与药的疗效无关；(C)易误选，但每周使用剂量的增加并无法解释上图中第二周后，图线下降趋缓的事实，所以(C)不对；(E)无关。

6. **解析**：本题为EXCEPT题型，要找出一个不能评价警官预言可靠性的答案。(E)把健康与performance联了起来，但本题讨论的是健康与否，而不是表现如何，因此无关，所以(E)正确；(A)指出候选人在加入警官队伍之前要被测试有无高血压，则可以反驳警官的预言，所以(A)相关；(B)支持了警官的预言，也为相关选项；(C)起削弱作用的相关选项；(D)为支持警察预言的相关选项。

   注：screen sb/sth for sth 检查或测试某人（某事物）（有无疾病或缺陷）

7. **解析**：本题问题目的为解释两者差异，重点抓住差异点——本题中为"小"，并用之定位，在5个选项中涉及"大、小"概念的只有(A)与(E)两个选项。而(A)指出由于气候原因，Plazos岛上的大蜥蜴生存条件恶化，再加上问题目的中的"if true about plazos but not about nearby islands"，所以(A)正确，(E)只说明陆地蜥蜴比海洋蜥蜴大，却不能说明为什么比其他岛上的蜥蜴小。

8. **解析**：本题作为GRE国内考题罕见的简单题，阅读简单，思维推理也简单。本题推理中无考虑人们可能有兄弟姐妹，也即(D)中所说的人们有共同的祖先，使得"3000年前比现在人多"的成立性受到质疑，所以(D)正确。

9. **解析**：本题属于"B，A"类的假设，寻找假设应为"除了A以外没有其他原因来导致B"。而(B)恰恰说明提交到Ergo发表的文章至少有一些错误引用的术语，从而说明除了Ergo更有效以外，没有诸如提交到Ergo发表的文章压根就没有错误的因素导致B，所以(B)正确。本题(D)易误选，但它不是推理成立的必要条件，即使错误引语的数目不是杂志编辑工作是否认真的一个标准。上面推理仍可以成立，因为上面的错误是用"百分比"来计算的，而两个杂志每年的期数和每期上发表的文章数目可能相差较远，所以(D)必然不对。通过本题，仔细体会，数字与比例的思维与感觉。

10. **解析**：本题为"解释图表点"，抓住对比变化点，从上表中可以看出，嚼用X致甜的口香糖的孩子虫牙数为4；嚼用Y致甜的口香糖的孩子虫牙只有1.5个，而从不吃口香糖的孩子虫牙数却有2.5个。这个数字对比表明用Y致甜的口香糖能降低虫牙数目，而用X致甜的口香糖却增加虫牙数目。寻求一个能解释这一点的选项，仔细体味(C)的正确性。

11. **解析**：本题为解释差异，抓住差异点来定位答案，解释为什么许多水鸟筑巢和孵化的地区被开发，鸭类数目急剧下降，但鹅类与天鹅数目未受影响。显而易见，解释差异需寻求差异双方，duck geese和swan，定位选项发现只有(A)、(E)符合。(E)与上面差异刚好相反；(B)指出由于geese与swan比duck居住在更靠北部的仍未被开发的地区，所以解释了差异，因此(B)正确。

12. **解析**：本题属于一个典型的由一个discovery得到一个结论，属于"B，A"型，反对的思路多为"有其他原因来解释B"。(D)正确，因为它指出除了运动因素以外还有身体生长因素影响碳水化合物的服用量。

13. **解析**：本题推理关系为"去除了一层18世纪加上的红颜料后发现下面有一层绿色颜料，所以说人物像完成时为绿色。"属于"B，A"型的反对，思维切入点为"除了A以外还有别的原因导致B"，用B中关键词green paint定位，排除了(A)、(D)和(E)；而(C)说明不了任何问题；(B)指出绿色下面还有一层颜料，说明绿色可能是后来加上的，反对了结论，因此(B)正确。

14. **解析**：逻辑应用与技法类型题重点在于读懂题，明晰其中思维，并且要读懂选项。段落中假设雄孔雀绚丽的尾巴吸引雌孔雀，原因是雌孔雀更可能与有绚丽尾巴的雄孔雀交配。提供的原因仅仅重述了需要解释的现象。(D)指出了这个推理错误，因此正确；(A)错在本题推理与人类无关；(B)也为无关选项；(C)易误选，但本题症结在于重述了现象，而并不在于解释是否真假证明；(E)中other factors为本题中未涉及的新概念。

15. **解析**：本题为"A，B"类假设。(C)是一个典型的假设，因为如果将(C)中的"No"扔去，则结论 "conflict with the novel's setting"将不成立，所以(C)是上述推理成立的必要条件，所以(C)正确。

三、GMAT考前逻辑推理冲刺训练试题及解析（三）

1. Auditor from Acme Industries: Last week at Acme Bakery, about six percent of the pastries baked during the night shift were found to be imperfect, but no imperfect pastries were found among those baked during the day shift. Pastries are inspected during the same shift in which they are baked, so clearly the night-shift quality control inspectors were more alert, despite their nighttime work hours, than the dayshift quality control inspectors.

The argument depends on the assumption that

(A) at least some imperfect pastries were baked during the day shift at Acme Bakery last week.

(B) not all of the pastries that the night-shift quality control inspectors judged to be imperfect were in fact imperfect.

(C) the night-shift quality control inspectors received more training in quality control procedures than did the day-shift quality control inspectors.

(D) in a normal week, fewer than six percent of the pastries baked during the night shift at Acme Bakery are found to be imperfect.

(E) there are only two shifts per day at Acme Bakery, a day shift and a night shift.

Acme Industries的审计员：上星期在Acme的面包房，发现夜班制作的蛋糕中约有6%存在问题，但是在白班制作的蛋糕中却没有发现问题。检查是针对同一班上制作的蛋糕进行的，所以，很明显，尽管是在夜间工作，夜班上的质量控制检查人员也比白班上的质量控制检查人员更警觉。

以上论述基于下列哪种假设？

(A) 上星期在Acme面包房里，白班制作的糕点中至少有一些是存在质量问题的。

(B) 并不是所有的夜班质量控制检查员评判为有问题的点心实际上是有问题的。

(C) 夜班质量控制检查员在质量控制程序上比白班质量检查员接受了更多的训练。

(D) 在平常的日子，Acme面包厂夜班所烤制的不到6%的点心被发现有缺陷。

(E) Acme面包厂仅有两个班次：白班和夜班。

2. Spiders of many species change color to match the pigmentation of the flowers they sit on. The insects preyed on by those spiders, unlike human beings, possess color discrimination so acute that they can readily see the spiders despite the seeming camouflage. Clearly, then, it must be in evading their own predators that the spiders' color changes are useful to them.

Which of the following, if true, most strengthens the argument?

(A) Among the animals that feed on color-changing spiders are a few species of bat, which find their prey through sound echoes.

(B) Certain animals that feed on color-changing spiders do so only sparingly in order to keep from ingesting harmful amounts of spider venom.

许多种蜘蛛都会随着它们所附在花的颜色而改变颜色。不像人类,被那些蜘蛛捕食的昆虫拥有敏锐的颜色鉴别能力，可以辨别出这种伪装。那么，显然，蜘蛛颜色改变对它们本身的用处在于躲避自己的天敌。

下列哪一项，如果正确，最能支持以上论述？

(A) 捕食改变颜色的蜘蛛的动物是某些种类的蝙蝠，它们通过声波的回声捕食它们的猎物。

(B) 某些捕食改变颜色蜘蛛的动物所以谨慎地这样做仅仅是为了避免消化有毒的蜘蛛毒液。

(C) Color-changing spiders possess color discrimination that is more acute than that of spiders that lack the ability to change color.

(D) Color-changing spiders spin webs that are readily seen by the predators of those spiders.

(E) The color discrimination of certain birds that feed on color-changing spiders is no more acute than that of human beings.

3. Which of the following most logically completes the argument below?

Each year every employee of SAI Corporation must enroll in one of the two health insurance plans offered by SAI. One plan requires a sizable monetary contribution from employees; the other plan is paid for entirely by SAI. Many SAI employees enroll in the plan requiring employee contributions. This fact does not show that they feel that this plan's benefits are superior to those provided by the plan requiring no employee contribution since_____.

(A) the plan that requires an employee contribution costs and enrolled employee significantly less per year than do typical health insurance plans offered by corporations other than SAI

(B) only SAI employees who have worked for SAI for at least fifteen years are eligible to enroll in the plan paid for entirely by SAI

(C) the two health insurance plans currently offered by SAI are substantially the same plans SAI has offered for the past ten years

(D) most of the SAI employees enrolled in the plan paid for entirely by SAI are under 50 years old

(E) both plans offered by SAI provide benefits not only for employees of SAI but also for children and spouses of enrolled employees

4. V-shaped walled structures in central Asia were used by prehistoric hunters who drove hoofed animals into an enclosure at the point of the V. The central Asians who built these structures probably learned this hunting technique from invaders from southwest Asia, because the arrival of invaders from a region in southwest Asia where similar structures had long been used coincides roughly with the building of the earliest of such structures in central Asia.

(C) 改变颜色的蜘蛛拥有的辨色力比不能变色的蜘蛛更敏锐。

(D) 变色蜘蛛织的网易被那些蜘蛛的捕食者看到。

(E) 有些以变色蜘蛛为食的鸟类的辨色力不如人类敏锐。

下列哪一项能最合逻辑地完成以下论述?

每年SAI公司的每一个雇员都必须参加由SAI提供的两个健康保险计划中的一个。一个计划要求雇员自己支付一部分钱,另外一个计划则完全由SAI支付。许多SAI的雇员都参加要求自己支付一部分钱的计划。这个事实并不能表明他们觉得这个计划的好处比另一个不需要雇员付款的计划好处多,因为_____

(A) 要求雇员自己支付一部分钱的计划比SAI以外的公司所提供的一般健康保险计划使加入的雇员的花费显著地少。

(B) 只有那些已为SAI工作了至少15年的雇员才有资格参加完全由SAI付款的计划。

(C) 目前由SAI提供的两个健康保险计划实际是过去10年中SAI所提供的相同计划。

(D) 大多数参加完全由SAI付款的健康保险计划的雇员是小于50岁的。

(E) 由SAI所提供的两个计划不仅服务于SAI的雇员,还服务于参加计划的雇员的配偶和孩子。

中亚地区V形墙的结构被史前猎人用于将有蹄动物驱赶进入V形顶点的围墙内。建造这些结构的中亚人可能是从西南亚的入侵者那里学来的这种捕猎技术,因为长久使用相似结构的西南亚某地入侵者的入侵时间与中亚地区这种结构最早出现的时间几乎相同。

Which of the following, if true, most strengthens the argument?

(A) Excavations in the central Asian region do not indicate whether invaders from southwest Asia settled permanently in central Asia.

(B) The V-shaped structures in central Asia were roughly 70 meters long, whereas the similar structures in southwest Asia were usually over 300 meters long.

(C) The walls of the structures in central Asia were made from earth, whereas the walls of the structures in southwest Asia were made of rock.

(D) The earliest examples of V-shaped walled structures in central Asia were of an advanced design.

(E) Some of the walled structures used for hunting in southwest Asia were built well after the earliest such structures were built in central Asia.

5. Which of the following most logically completes the argument?

Virtually all respondents to a recent voter survey reported allegiance to one of the two major political parties. But over a third of the voters from each party reported being so disenchanted with the governing philosophies of both parties that they might join a third major party if one were formed. Even if this poll reflects general voter sentiment, however, there is no chance that a new party could attract a third of all voters, since_____.

(A) the current level of disenchantment with the governing philosophies of the two major parties is unprecedented

(B) the disenchanted members of the two major parties are attracted to very different governing philosophies

(C) most respondents overestimated the proportion of voters disenchanted with both parties, saving that the proportion was more than 50 percent

(D) nearly half of all respondents reported that they would be more likely to cease voting altogether than to switch their party affiliation

(E) any new party would be likely to inspire citizens who have not voted before to join and to become regular voters

6. When amphibians first appeared on Earth millions of years ago, the amount of ultraviolet radiation penetrating Earth's atmosphere was much greater than it is today. Therefore, current dramatic decreases in amphibian populations cannot

下列哪一个，假如正确，最支持以上论述？

(A) 在中亚地区的发掘没有指出来自西南亚洲的定居者是否永久定居于中亚。

(B) 中亚地区的V形结构约70米长，然而在西南亚相似结构超过300米长。

(C) 中亚地区的墙形结构由泥土造成，而西南亚地区的墙形结构则是由岩石造成。

(D) 中亚最早的V形墙结构的样本是一种改良设计。

(E) 一些西南亚地区用于狩猎的墙形结构正好在中亚最早的这类结构被建造之后建成。

以下哪项能最合逻辑地完成以下论述？

实际上，最近一次选民调查的所有应答者都表示效忠两个主要政党中的一个政党。但来自两个政党的选民中都有超过1/3的人表示不满意两党的统治哲学，如果有第三个主要政党存在，他们可能会加入。即使该民意测验反映了一般选民的情绪，然而成立一个新党，它也没有机会赢得1/3的投票者，因为：

(A) 目前对两个主要党派统治哲学的不满情绪的程度是史无前例的。

(B) 对两个主要政党不满的成员被完全不同的统治哲学所吸引。

(C) 大多数响应者除了那个比例高于50%以外，高估了对两党不满的投票者的比例。

(D) 将近一半的响应者报道他们更可能放弃投票而不是改变他们所效忠的党派。

(E) 任何新党派可能激励以前没有投票的公民参加并成为通常投票者。

当两栖动物在几百万年前首次出现在地球上时，穿透地球大气层的紫外线辐射量比现在大得多。因此，现在两栖动物数量剧减不会是最近穿透地球大气层的紫外

be the result of recent increases in ultraviolet radiation penetrating Earth's atmosphere.

Which of the following is an assumption on which the argument depends?

(A) The eggs of modern amphibians are not significantly more vulnerable to ultraviolet radiation than the eggs of the first amphibians were.

(B) Modern amphibians are not as likely as the first amphibians were to live in habitats that shield them from ultraviolet radiation.

(C) Populations of modern amphibians are not able to adapt to changing levels of radiation as readily as populations of early amphibians were.

(D) The skin of amphibians is generally more sensitive to ultraviolet radiation than the skin of other animals is.

(E) The skin of amphibians is less sensitive to ultraviolet radiation than to other types of radiation.

线辐射增加的结果。

以上论述基于下列哪项假设?

(A) 现代两栖动物的卵并不比最初两栖动物的卵显著地更易受紫外线辐射的伤害。

(B) 现代两栖动物不大可能像早期两栖动物居住的栖息地那样能够遮蔽紫外线。

(C) 现在两栖动物不能像早期两栖动物那样容易地适应辐射程度的改变。

(D) 两栖动物的皮肤通常比其他动物的皮肤对紫外线更敏感。

(E) 与其他形式辐射相比,两栖动物的皮肤对紫外线不那么敏感。

7. Chris: Hundreds of traffic accidents annually are attributable to the poor condition of our city's streets. The streets must therefore be repaired to save lives.

Leslie: For less than the cost of those repairs, the city could improve its mass transit system and thus dramatically reduce traffic congestion, which contributes significantly to those traffic accidents. The city cannot afford to do both, so it should improve mass transit, because reduced traffic congestion has additional advantages.

Which of the following best describes the point at issue between Chris and Leslie?

(A) Whether a certain problem in fact exists.

(B) How a certain problem came into being.

(C) Who is responsible for addressing a certain problem.

(D) Whether the city has sufficient financial resources to address a certain problem.

(E) How the city can best address a certain problem.

Chris:每年数以百计的交通事故都归因于我市街道条件太差,因此必须维修道路以挽救生命。

Leslie:城市可用少于维修街道的花费来改进其众多运输系统,从而大大减少交通拥挤,这对避免交通事故大有裨益。城市负担不起同时进行两项改善,因此它应该改进众多运输系统,因为减少交通拥挤还有其他好处。

下列哪一个最好地描述了Chris和Leslie争论的观点?

(A) 某一问题实际上是否存在。

(B) 某一问题怎样出现。

(C) 谁负责处理某一问题。

(D) 该城市是否有足够的财力来处理某一问题。

(E) 城市如何能够最佳地处理好某一问题。

8. According to ancient records, the first tax that the government of Selea imposed on a basic commodity was a tax of two centima coins on every jar of cooking oil sold in Selea. Tax records show that despite a stable population and strict enforcement of tax laws, revenues from the oil tax declined steeply over the first two years that the tax was in effect.

根据古代纪录,Selea政府对基本商品征收的第一种税是对在Selea出售的每一罐食用油征税两个生丁。税务纪录显示,尽管人口数量保持稳定且税法执行有力,食用油的税收额在税法生效的头两年中还是显著下降了。

Which of the following, if true, most helps to explain the decline in Selean oil-tax revenues?

(A) During the decade following the implementation of the tax, the average household income in Selea rose steadily.

(B) Two years after implementing the tax on cooking oil, the Selean government began to implement taxes on numerous other basic commodities.

(C) Jars of cooking oil were traditionally bought as wedding gifts in Selea at the time the tax went into effect, and gifts of cooking oil increased after the implementation of the tax.

(D) After the tax was imposed, Selean merchants began selling cooking oil in larger jars than before.

(E) Few Selean households began to produce their own cooking oil after the tax was imposed.

9. Housing construction materials give off distinctive sounds when exposed to high temperatures. Acoustic sensors accurately detect such sounds and fire alarms incorporating acoustic sensors can provide an early warning of house fires, allowing inhabitants to escape before being overcome by smoke. Since smoke inhalation is the most common cause of fatalities in house fires, mandating acoustic-sensor-based alarms instead of smoke detectors will eliminate house fire as a major cause of death.

Which of the following, if true, most weakens the argument given?

(A) The present high cost of acoustic-sensor-based alarm systems will decline if their use becomes widespread.

(B) When fully ignited, many materials used in housing construction give off sounds that are audible even from several hundred yards away.

(C) Many fires begin in cushions or in mattresses, producing large amounts of smoke without giving off any sounds.

(D) Two or more acoustic-sensor-based alarms would be needed to provide adequate protection in some larger houses.

(E) Smoke detectors have been responsible for saving many lives since their use became widespread.

10. In December 1992 Tideville Shopping Mall repaired and improved the lighting in the mall's parking lots, and in 1993 car thefts and attempted car thefts from those lots decreased

下列哪一项，如果正确，最有助于解释在Selea油税收入的下降？

(A) 在税法实施后的10年，Selea的平均家庭收入稳定增加。

(B) 在食用油税实行后的两年，Selea政府开始在许多其他基本商品上征税。

(C) 在Selea，食用油罐传统上被用作结婚礼物，在税法实施后，食用油的礼物增多了。

(D) Selea的商人，在税法实施后开始用比以前更大的罐子售油。

(E) 很少Selea的家庭在加税后开始生产他们自己的食用油。

暴露于高温时，房屋建筑材料发出独特的声音。声音感应器能够精确探测这些声音，内装声音感应器的火灾报警器能够提供一个房屋起火的早期警报，使居住者能在被烟雾困住之前逃离。由于受烟熏是房屋火灾最通常的致命因素，要求安装声音感应报警器来替代烟雾探测器将使房屋火灾不再是导致死亡的主要原因。

下列哪一个，假始正确，最反对上面的论述？

(A) 假如基于声音感应器的报警系统广泛使用的话，其高昂成本将下降。

(B) 在完全燃烧时，许多用于房屋建筑的材料发出的声音在几百码之外也可以听得见。

(C) 许多火灾开始于座垫和床垫，产生大量烟雾却不发出声音。

(D) 在一些较大的房屋中，需要两个或两个以上的声音探测器为基本要求的报警器以达到足够的保护。

(E) 在它们普遍使用后，烟雾探测器拯救了许多生命。

1992年12月，Tideville购物中心维修并改善了其停车场的照明，1993年该停车场偷车案和企图偷车案比上一年下降了

by 76 percent from the previous year. Since potential car thieves are generally deterred by good lighting, the decrease can be attributed to these improvements.

Which of the following, if true, most hepls to strengthen the argument above?

(A) Both in 1992 and in 1993, most of the cars stolen from the mall's parking lots were relatively new and expensive luxury models.

(B) Most of the cars that were stolen from the mall in 1992 were stolen between 11 A. M. and 4 P. M.

(C) Tideville Shopping Mall is one of only three shopping malls in the Tideville area.

(D) In the town of Tideville, where the mall is located, the number of car thefts was about the same in 1993 as in 1992.

(E) In 1993 the number of security officers patrolling the mall's parking lots at night was doubled.

11. Legislator: We should not waste any more of the taxpayers' money on the government's job-creation program. The unemployment rate in this country has actually risen since the program was begun, so the program has clearly been a failure.

Which of the following is an assumption on which the legislator's argument depends?

(A) The budget of the job-creation program has typically increased every year.

(B) The unemployment rate would not have risen even more than it has if the job-creation program had not been in existence.

(C) The unemployment rate is higher now than at any time before the inception of the job-creation program.

(D) If the job-creation program had been run more efficiently, it could have better served its purpose.

(E) Other government programs are no more effective in reducing unemployment than is the job-creation program.

12. Which of the following most logically completes the argument?

Each year a consumer agency ranks all domestic airlines for on-time performance during the previous year, using as its sole criterion the percentage of each airline's flights that left no more than fifteen minutes late. The agency does not count delays due to mechanical reasons, but the fact that the

76%。因为潜在的小偷通常受较好照明条件的威慑，偷车案的下降可归功于这些方面的改善。

下列哪一项，如果正确，最能支持以上论述？

(A) 在1992年和1993年，大多数在购物中心停车场被偷的车都是相对较新和较昂贵的豪华型汽车。

(B) 大多数购物中心的盗车案发生在上午10点到下午4点之间。

(C) Tideville购物中心是Tideville地区仅有的三个购物中心之一。

(D) 在购物中心所在的Tideville镇，汽车盗窃案1993年和1992年一样多。

(E) 在1993年购物中心停车场巡逻的安全警卫的数目在夜间加倍了。

立法者：我们不应该再在政府的创造就业项目上浪费纳税者的钱了。实际上，此项目开始生效后，该国的失业率上升了，所以，显然该项目是失败的。

立法者的论述基于下列哪项假设？

(A) 创造就业项目的预算每年明显增多。

(B) 如果没有这个创造就业项目生效，失业率不会比现在攀升得更高。

(C) 失业率高于创造就业项目开始的任何时间。

(D) 如果创造就业项目更有效地运作，则可以更好地达到目的。

(E) 其他政府项目在减少失业方面不比创造就业项目更有效。

下列哪项能最合逻辑地完成以下论述？

每年，一个消费者机构将所有国内航空公司按照在过去一年里飞机起降准时的表现排名，它所使用的唯一标准是每个航空公司晚点不超过15分钟的航班的比率。该机构不将因机械故障造成的延误计算在内，但去年因机械故障造成延误的航班的

percentage of delayed flights hat were delayed for mechanical reasons was approximately the same for all domestic airlines last year means that_____.

(A) including delays for mechanical reasons in calculating the airline rankings for on-time performance would have had little, if any, effect on last year's rankings

(B) airlines would work harder to reduce delays if delays for mechanical reasons were included in the determination of on-time performance rankings

(C) the agency's rankings do not give consumers an accurate idea of how a given airline compares to other airlines with respect to the percentage of flights delayed last year

(D) those airlines with the best on-time performance record last year also had the greatest number of delays for mechanical reasons

(E) on-time performance was approximately the same for all domestic airlines last year

比率在所有国内航空公司中大致相同，这一事实说明_____

(A) 将因机械故障造成的延误包括在航空公司起降准时表现排名的计算之内，如果有影响的话，那么它对去年的排名只有极小的影响。

(B) 如果把机械故障造成的延误包括在准时表现的排名中，航空公司可能努力工作来减少延误。

(C) 该机构的排名没有给予消费者关于一个航空公司与另一家航空公司相比较关于其晚点的比率的准确信息。

(D) 去年有最好的准时表现记录的航空公司同时也有最大数目的机械原因造成的晚点。

(E) 去年准时表现对于所有国内航空公司大约相同。

13. No one can be licensed as an electrician in Parker County without first completing a certain course in electrical safety procedures. All students majoring in computer technology at Parker County Technical College must complete that course before graduating. Therefore, any of the college's graduates in computer technology can be licensed as an electrician in Parker County.

The answer to which of the following would be most helpful in evaluating the argument?

(A) Is a college degree a requirement for being licensed as an electrician in Parker County?

(B) Do all students majoring in computer technology who complete the course in electrical safety procedures at Parker County Technical College eventually graduate?

(C) Is completion of a course in electrical safety procedures the only way a person licensed as an electrician in Parker County can have learned those procedures?

(D) Is a period of practical apprenticeship a requirement for becoming a licensed electrician in Parker County but not for graduating from the college in computer technology?

(E) Do any of the students at Parker County Technical College who are not majoring in computer technology take the course in electrical safety procedures?

不首先完成一门用电安全程序课程，没人能在Parker郡获准成为电工。所有在Parker郡技术学院主修计算机技术的学生在毕业前都必须完成这门课程。因此，任何一个在Parker计算机技术专业的大学毕业生都能被获准成为电工。

对下列哪一个问题的回答对评价上面的论述最有用？

(A) 大学学位是在Parker郡被获准成为电工所必需的吗？

(B) 所有在Parker郡主修计算机技术且完成用电安全程序课程的学生最终都毕业了吗？

(C) 用电安全程序课程的完成是在Parker郡获准成为电工的人学习这些程序的唯一途径吗？

(D) 是否有这样一段学徒实习期，对成为Parker郡一名特许电工来说是必需的，而对要从学院计算机技术系取得毕业证书的人来说却不是必需的？

(E) 在Parker郡技术大学非主修计算机技术的任一学生选用电安全程序课程吗？

14. Pollutants in the atmosphere can cause acid rain (rain with high acidity levels). While acid rain in itself cannot significantly affect the acidity of bodies of water into which it falls, it can greatly increase the acidity of nearby lakes by increasing the amount of decaying matter on a forest floor. A recent increase in the acidity of the water in Forest Lake, therefore, surely indicates that the rain falling nearby has become more acid.

Which of the following, if true, most seriously weakens the argument?

(A) Even in areas without significant amounts of acid rain, most lakes in regions with vegetation similar to the vegetation around Forest Lake have acidity levels higher than those of other lakes.

(B) Recent air-quality tests in the region around Forest Lake have revealed a slight increase in the amount of pollutants in the air.

(C) Large-scale logging, which was recently begun in the forest surrounding Forest Lake, has increased the amount of decaying matter on the forest floor.

(D) There is some disagreement among scientists about exactly how pollutants in the atmosphere cause acid rain.

(E) Decaying matter exists on all forest floors and is an important factor in maintaining the healthy growth of the forests.

15. Most of Earth's surface is ocean. The ocean floor is inaccessible for extensive research without equipment of greater technological sophistication than is currently available. It must therefore be true that scientists know less about the ocean floor environment than about almost any other environment on Earth.

Which of the following, if true, provides the most support for the conclusion?

(A) Many mountain ranges lie entirely beneath the ocean surface, yet new underwater surveying equipment has produced three-dimensional charts of them that are as accurate as those available for mountain ranges on land.

(B) Strong water currents circulate on the ocean floor, but the general pattern of their movement is not so well understood as is the pattern of air currents that circulate over land.

(C) In contrast to most land environments, temperature conditions at the ocean floor are generally stable and

大气污染物会造成酸雨（高酸性的雨）。然而酸雨本身并不能显著影响其落入水体的酸性，它能够通过增加森林地表上腐蚀物质的量来大幅度增加邻近湖水的酸性。因此最近Forest Lake中的水的酸性增加，必定表明附近的降水变得更酸了。

下列哪一项，如果正确，最能反驳以上论述?

(A) 即使没有大量酸雨的地区，位于植被类似与Forest湖附近植被地区的大多数湖水的酸性高于其他湖中水的酸性。

(B) 最近Forest湖附近地区的空气质量的测试已经揭示了空气中污染物量的略微增加。

(C) 在Forest Lake周围的森林中最近开始的大规模砍伐，增加了森林地表上的腐蚀物数量。

(D) 在科学家中，关于大气中的污染物确切地怎样导致酸雨有一些争议。

(E) 森林植被上的腐烂物质是决定森林生长的一个重要因素。

地球表面大部分是海洋。只有用比目前可获得的设备技术程度更为精密的仪器才可能对海底进行广泛的研究。因此，科学家对海底环境的了解一定比对地球上任何其他环境的了解少。

下列哪一个，假如正确，最支持上面的结论?

(A) 许多山脉完全在海平面下，然而新的水下探测设备产生的三维图像像地面上的山脉的三维图像一样精确。

(B) 强大的水流在海底循环，但是它们运动的总体形态不像气流在陆地上循环的形态那样易于理解。

(C) 与大多数陆地环境相反，海平面的温度条件通常是稳定和一致的，因为太阳光不能穿透到极深的海平面下。

(D) 非常少的人看过详细的海底延伸区域图，即使这样的图在几乎所有的大图

uniform, since sunlight does not penetrate far below the ocean surface.

(D) Very few people have seen detailed maps of extended regions of the ocean floor, even though such maps are available in almost all large libraries.

(E) Animals living on the ocean floor must be able to withstand water pressure that is far greater than the atmospheric pressure with which land animals live.

(E) 居住在海底的动物一定能够忍受比陆地动物居住地的大气压要更大的水压。

书馆中可以得到。

参考答案：

1. A	2. E	3. B	4. D	5. B
6. A	7. E	8. D	9. C	10. D
11. B	12. A	13. D	14. C	15. B

1. **解析**：典型的"B，A"型假设，且与上个练习中的第9题思维完全一样。请体会(A)为什么正确以及这一类题的思维。

2. **解析**：本题逻辑推理难度并不大，难主要难在阅读上，尤其是许多考生不能精确理解最后一句话的含义。本句是强调句型，其正常语序应为，"The spiders' color changes are useful to them in evading their own predators"，即蜘蛛颜色改变对它们本身的用处在于躲避自己的天敌，所以(E)选项支持了上面的结论。因为本题段落中已指出人类颜色鉴别能力差，而鸟类比人类更为逊色，因此就最好地支持蜘蛛改变颜色确实是躲避自己的捕食者。

3. **解析**：本题为完成段落题型的带since、because的解释题，即解释since之前的那一句话"为什么自己支付一部分钱的计划并不好于完全由SAI付款的计划，但许多雇员仍参加前一计划"。(B)说明完全由SAI支付的计划只对为SAI工作了15年的雇员有效，并不是每一个人都可以参加的，解释了since之前的那一句话，因此(B)正确。

4. **解析**：本题目的在于寻求一个选项支持中亚地区的V-shape walled structure是从西南亚的入侵者那里学来的。(D)说明中亚地区最早的V形结构为advanced design，指出这种结构并非中亚土生土长的，最好地支持了上述论断，所以(D)正确。

5. **解析**：本题作为本套题中第二个完成句子题，体现出了1998年度的考题倾向，与GMAT、LSAT题目的融合度逐渐增加，思路同第3题。(B)说明两党不满成员所倾向的主张完全不同，所以任意成立一个第三党不可能获得两类完全不同的选票，所以第三党不可能获得1/3选票，所以(B)正确。

6. **解析**：本题的推理为"因为早期紫外线辐射比现在强，所以现在两栖动物的剧减不能归因于紫外线辐射的增加"。(A)说明现在两栖动物的卵并不比最初两栖动物的卵更显著地易受伤害，显然是上述推理成立的必要条件，所以(A)正确。

7. **解析**：本题为两人对话类的逻辑应用的技法型题目。很明显，Chris坚持事故应归因于街道条件，而Leslie认为是交通拥挤，所以Chris认为通过修理街道来解决一个问题，而Leslie则认为应提高大众运输系统来处理这一问题。所以两人争论的观点为(E)，即城市如何能够最好地处理某一问题。

8. **解析**：本题问题目的为解释为何Selea油税收入下降。(D)指出Selea的商人在税法实施后，开始用比以前更大的罐子售油，回答了问题。

centime *n.* 生丁（1法郎之1%）［*pl.*］centima

9. **解析**：本题为Weaken题型，抓住原因中的关键词"sound"来定位，发现(B)、(C)中有关键词"sound"。而(C)指出有些火灾发作但却无声音，断开了两者联接，做出最好的反对，所以(C)正确。

10. **解析**：本题作为支持类考题，已考过许多题目。本题推理为"盗车案下降，因为照明条件改善"。

(D)说明Tideville镇总体盗车案没有下降，属于GRE典型支持模式"A可行或A有意义"的无因就无果类。所以(D)正确。

11. **解析**：GRE典型assumption或support结构"A可行或有意义"的无因就无果类。(B)为正确答案。

12. **解析**：本题的完成句子是要从上面推理中得出什么，因此，属于归纳类。注意归纳类思维及(A)的正确原因。另外，本题为LSAT的一道逻辑推理题的重考题，但问题目的与选项有所变化，这也反映出美国三大考试之间的互相参考命题趋势。

13. **解析**：本题为1993年10月GRE国内考题的一道逻辑推理重考题，但问题目的与选项都有较大变化。这反映出国内考题重考的命题侧重点。本题推理为：完成用电安全程序课程是在Parker郡成为电工的一个必要条件，但段落最后一句话显然认为完成用电安全课程是成为电工的充分条件，而(D)提出实习期是否是成为电工的一个必要条件。若回答yes，则上面推理被削弱；若回答"no"，则对推理作出支持。所以(D)正确。

14. **解析**：本题作为GRE的No.5的"A′, not A→B"型的一道逻辑推理题的重考，背景内容完全一样，可参阅反对部分的讲解。

15. **解析**：本题让我们支持结论，结论的重点关键词为"Ocean floor"，选项(B)、(E)中有此关键词。(B)说明由海底的水流不易于被理解而支持了结论，"海底环境的了解一定比其他环境少"。所以(B)正确。(A)反对，(C)、(D)、(E)均为无关选项。

四、GMAT考前逻辑推理冲刺训练试题及解析（四）

1. At the Shadybrook dog kennel, all the adult animals were given a new medication designed to reduce a dog's risk of contracting a certain common infection. Several days after the medication was administered, most of the puppies of these dogs had elevated temperatures. Since raised body temperature is a side effect of this medication, the kennel owner hypothesized that the puppies elevated temperatures resulted from the medication's being passed to them through their mothers' milk.

Which of the following, if true, provides the most support for the kennel owner's hypothesis?

(A) Some puppies have been given the new medication directly but have not suffered elevated temperatures as a side effect.

(B) The new medication has been well received by dog breeders as a safe and effective way of preventing the spread of certain common canine infections.

(C) None of the four puppies in the kennel who had been bottle-fed with formula had elevated temperatures.

(D) An elevated temperature is a side effect of a number of medications for dogs other than the new medication administered at the kennel.

(E) Elevated temperatures such as those suffered by most of the puppies in the kennel rarely have serious long-term effects on a puppy's health.

在Shadybrook的养狗场，所有的成年动物都服用了一种新药，这种药物的目的是降低狗类被感染上某种一般性传染病的风险。在用药的几天后，这群狗中的大多数幼狗都体温上升。由于体温上升是这种药的一个副作用，因此该养狗场的场主得出假设，认为幼狗们的体温上升是由于这种药通过幼狗母亲的乳汁进入了幼狗体内。

下列哪一项，如果正确，对养狗场场主的假设提供了最有力的支持？

(A) 有些幼狗直接服用了这种新药，但却没有引起体温上升的副作用。

(B) 狗的饲养员们完全接受了这种新药，认为它可以安全有效地阻止某种一般性狗类传染病的流行。

(C) 养狗场中有四条幼狗是由奶瓶喂养的，它们都没有发生体温上升的现象。

(D) 体温上升是养狗场对狗使用的该新药之外的另一些药物的副作用。

(E) 像该养狗场大多数幼狗所产生的这种体温上升现象基本不会对幼狗的健康产生长期影响。

2. Which of the following most logically completes the argument?

Alivia's government has approved funds for an electricity-generation project based on the construction of a pipeline that will carry water from Lake Cylus, in the mountains, to the much smaller Lake Tifele, in a nearby valley. The amount of electricity generated will be insufficient by itself to justify the project's cost, even if the price of imported oil—Alivia's primary source of electricity—increases sharply. Nonetheless, the pipeline project is worth its cost, because_____.

(A) the price of oil, once subject to frequent sharp increases, has fallen significantly and is now fairly stable

(B) the project could restore Lake Tifele, which is currently at risk of drying up and thus of being lost as a source of recreation income for Alivia

(C) the government of Alivia is currently on excellent terms with the governments of most of the countries from which it purchases oil

(D) it would cost less to generate electricity by moving water from Lake Cylus to Lake Tifele than to do so by moving water from Lake Cylus to another valley lake

(E) Alivian officials do not expect that the amount of electricity used in Alivia will increase substantially within the next ten years

3. Amusement rides at permanent fairgrounds are dismantled once a year for safety inspections by independent consultants. Traveling fairs, which relocate each month, can slip past the net of safety inspections and escape independent inspection for several years. Therefore, the rides at traveling fairs are less safe than the rides at permanent fairs.

Which of the following, if true about traveling fairs, most seriously weakens the argument?

(A) Before each relocation, the operators dismantle their rides, observing and repairing potential sources of danger, such as worn ball bearings.

(B) Their managers have less capital to spend on the safety and upkeep of the rides than do managers of permanent fairs.

(C) Since they can travel to new customers, they rely less on keeping up a good reputation for safety.

(D) While they are traveling, the fairs do not receive notices of equipment recalls sent out by the manufacturers of their rides.

下列哪一项最能从逻辑上将下面论述补充完整?

Alivia的政府批准了一项基金，用于建设一项发电工程，这项工程要求铺设一条管线，将山上的Cylus湖的水引到附近山谷中名为Tifele的小湖中。该项目所发的电本身不能平衡项目的成本，即使是进口石油——Alivia的电力的主要来源——的价格大幅上升时也不行。然而，这条管线是物有所值的，这是因为_____。

(A) 石油的价格曾经历经频繁的大幅上升，现在已经大幅下降，并且相当地稳定。

(B) 该项目可重建Tifele湖，该湖目前正面临干涸的危险，从而使Alivia面临减少一项渡假收入的危险。

(C) Alivia政府目前与其进口石油的来源国的政府们都保持着良好的关系。

(D) 将Cylas湖的水引入Tifele湖来进行发电的成本低于将Cylus湖水引入其他山谷湖泊来发电的成本。

(E) Alivian的官员们不认为Alivia的用电量在未来10年内会大幅上升。

永久型赛马场的休闲用骑乘每年都要拆卸一次，供独立顾问们进行安全检查。流动型赛马场每个月迁移一次，所以可以在长达几年的时间里逃过安全检查网及独立检查，因此，在流动型赛马场骑马比在永久型赛马场骑马更加危险。

下列哪一项，如果对于流动型赛马场而言是正确的，最能削弱上面论述?

(A) 在每次迁移前，管理员们都拆卸其骑乘，检查并修复潜在的危险源，如磨损的滚珠轴承。

(B) 它们的经理们拥有的用于安全方面及维护骑乘的资金要少于永久型赛马场的经理们。

(C) 由于它们可用迁移以寻找新的顾客，建立安全方面的良好信誉对于他们而言不是特别重要。

(D) 在它们迁移时，赛马场无法接收到来自它们的骑乘生产商的设备回收通知。

(E) The operators of the rides often do not pay careful attention to the instructions for operating their rides.

4. When cut, the synthetic material fiberglass, like asbestos, releases microscopic fibers into the air. It is known that people who inhale asbestos fibers suffer impairment of lung function. A study of 300 factory workers who regularly cut fiberglass showed that their lung capacity is, on average, only 90 percent of that of a comparable group of people who do not cut fiberglass.

The statements above, if true, most strongly support which of the following hypotheses?

(A) People who work with fiberglass are likely also to work with asbestos.

(B) Fiberglass fibers impair lung function in people who inhale them.

(C) Fiberglass releases as many fibers into the air when cut as does asbestos.

(D) Coarse fibers do not impair lung function in people who inhale them.

(E) If uncut, fiberglass poses no health risk to people who work with it.

5. Politician: Pundits claim that by voting for candidates who promise to cut taxes, people show that they want the government to provide fewer services than it has been providing. By that reasoning, however, people who drink too much alcohol at a party in the evening want a headache the next morning.

Which of the following could replace the statement about people who drink too much without undermining the force of the politician's argument?

(A) People who spend more money than they can afford want the things they spend that money on.

(B) People who seek different jobs than they currently have do not want to work at all.

(C) People who buy new cars want to own cars that are under manufacturer's warranty.

(D) People who decide to stay in bed a few extra minutes on a workday morning want to have to rush to arrive at work on time.

(E) People who buy lottery tickets want the economic freedom that winning the lottery would bring.

(E) 骑乘的管理员们经常忽视骑乘管理的操作指南。

合成材料的玻璃纤维，如石棉，在切割时会向空气中释放微小的纤维。众所周知，人们如果吸入了石棉纤维，他们的肺功能就会遭受伤害。一项对300名经常切割玻璃纤维的工厂工人的调查显示，平均而言，他们的肺活量仅是另一组不切割玻璃纤维的人的90%，这两组是具有可比性的。

上面的论述如果正确，最能支持下列哪项假设？

(A) 工作中接触玻璃纤维的人很有可能也会接触石棉。

(B) 玻璃纤维的纤维会损伤吸入它们的人的肺功能。

(C) 玻璃纤维在切割时向空气中释放的纤维量与石棉在切割时向空气中释放的纤维量一样多。

(D) 粗纤维不会损伤吸入它们的人的肺功能。

(E) 如果不切割，玻璃纤维不会对工作中接触它的人产生健康危险。

政治家：权威们声称，人们投票给了那些许诺减税的候选人，这显示出他们希望政府提供比现在更少的服务。然而，按照这种推理，那些在晚间宴会中饮用过多酒精的人，就是希望在第二天早上头痛。

下列哪一项能够代替上面关于人们饮酒过量的典故，而却不削弱该政治家的论断。

(A) 那些入不敷出的人确实需要他们所买的那些东西。

(B) 那些寻找与目前不同的工作的人们根本就不想工作。

(C) 那些购买新东西的人们希望拥有在生产商保修范围内的东西。

(D) 那些打算在工作日的早晨在床上多呆几分钟的人们希望不得不匆匆忙忙以按时上班。

(E) 那些买彩票的人们希望获得赢取彩票可能带来的经济上的宽松。

6. Like most other coastal towns in Norway, the town of Stavanger was quiet and peaceful until the early 1960's, when it became Norway's center for offshore oil exploration. Between then and now, violent crime and vandalism in Stavanger have greatly increased. Stavanger's social problems probably resulted from the oil boom, since violent crime and vandalism have remained low in coastal towns in Norway that have had no oil boom.

Which of the following most accurately describes the method of reasoning employed in the argument?

(A) Arguing that a circumstance is not a precondition for a phenomenon on the grounds that the phenomenon sometimes occurs where the circumstance is not present.

(B) Arguing that a circumstance is a cause of a phenomenon on the grounds that the phenomenon has not occurred where the circumstance is not present.

(C) Arguing that a particular thing cannot have caused a phenomenon because that thing was not present before the phenomenon occurred.

(D) Attempting to establish a claim by arguing that the denial of the claim is inconsistent with the observed facts.

(E) Attempting to establish that certain circumstances that would have had to occur for a particular explanation to be correct could not have occurred.

7. Excavations at a Mayan site have uncovered jewelry workshops located some distance from the center of the site on roads radiating outward from the center. Since the nobility lived only in the area of the center, archaeologists conclude that these workshops made jewelry, not for the nobility, but for a middle class that must have been prosperous enough to afford it.

The archaeologists' argument assumes which of the following about the artisans who worked in the workshops?

(A) They were themselves prosperous members of a middle class.

(B) They lived near their workshops.

(C) Their products were not made from the same materials as was jewelry for the nobility.

(D) They worked full-time at making jewelry and did not engage in farming.

(E) They did not take the jewelry they had made in the workshops to clients who were members of the nobility.

与挪威的许多其他海岸城镇一样，Stavanger直至20世纪60年代初以前都是安静平和的，从那以后，它成为挪威的远洋石油开采中心。从那时至今，Stavanger的暴力犯罪和蓄意破坏现象大幅增加。Stavanger城的社会问题可能来自这场石油兴盛，这是因为挪威那些没有石油兴盛的海岸城镇仍然保持着很低的暴力犯罪和蓄意破坏现象。

下面哪一项最准确地描述了上段论述中所采用的推理方法？

(A) 鉴于有时环境不存在的条件下现象也会发生，所以认为环境不是现象的前提。

(B) 鉴于环境不存在的时候现象没有发生，所以认为环境是现象的一个原因。

(C) 由于某一特定事件在现象发生前没有出现，所以认为这一事件不可能引发现象。

(D) 通过论证反驳一项论断来试图建立这项论断，是与观察到的事实不相符的。

(E) 试图说明某种环境是不可能发生的，而某种解释正确就必须要求这种环境发生。

玛雅遗址挖掘出一些珠宝作坊，这些作坊位于从遗址中心向外辐射的马路的边上，且离中心有一定的距离。由于贵族仅居住在中心地区，考古学家因此得出结论，认为这些作坊制作的珠宝不是供给贵族的，而是供给一个中等阶级，他们一定已足够富有，可以购买珠宝。

对在这些作坊工作的手工艺人，考古学家的论断中做了下列哪项假设？

(A) 他们自己本身就是富有的中等阶级的成员。

(B) 他们住在作坊附近。

(C) 他们的产品原料与供贵族享用的珠宝所用的原料不同。

(D) 他们全天的工作都是制造珠宝，而不从事农业劳动。

(E) 他们不把他们在作坊中制造的珠宝送交给贵族顾客。

8. Over the last 40 years there has been a great increase not only in the number of agricultural pesticides in use but also in the care and sophistication with which they are used by farmers. Nevertheless, the proportion of agricultural crops lost to certain pests worldwide has increased over the same period, even when the pests concerned have not developed resistance to existing pesticides.

Which of the following, if true, best explains how improvements in pesticide use have been accompanied by greater losses to certain pests?

(A) Some dangerous but relatively ineffective pesticides common 40 years ago are no longer in widespread use.

(B) As pesticides have become increasingly pest-specific, controlling certain pests with pesticides has turned out to cost more in many cases than the value of crop losses caused by those pests.

(C) Because today's pesticides typically have more specific application conditions than did pesticides in use 40 years ago, today's farmers observe their fields more closely than did farmers 40 years ago.

(D) Certain pest-control methods that some farmers use today do not involve the use of chemical pesticides but are just as effective in eliminating insect pests as those that do.

(E) Forty years ago, much less was known about the effects of pesticides on humans and other mammalian species than is now known.

在过去的40年里，不仅农业用杀虫剂的数量大大增加，而且农民们使用杀虫剂时的精心和熟练程度也不断增加。然而，在同一时期内，某些害虫在世界范围内对农作物造成的损失的比例也上升了，即使在这些害虫还没有产生对现有杀虫剂的抵抗性时也是如此。

下列哪项，如果正确，最好地解释了为什么在杀虫剂使用上的提高伴随了某些害虫造成的损失更大？

(A) 在40年前通用的一些危险但却相对无效的杀虫剂已经不再在世界范围内使用了。

(B) 由于杀虫剂对害虫的单个针对性越来越强，因此，用杀虫剂来控制某种害虫的成本在许多情况下变得比那些害虫本身造成的农作物损失的价值更大。

(C) 由于现在的杀虫剂对特定使用条件的要求要多于40年前，所以现在的农民们对他们农田观察的仔细程度要高于40年前。

(D) 现在有些农民们使用的某些害虫控制方法中不使用化学杀虫剂，但却和那些使用化学杀虫剂的害虫控制方法在减少害虫方面同样有效。

(E) 40年前人们对杀虫剂给人类及其他哺乳动物造成的影响的了解要比现在少得多。

9. Authorities in California required drivers to use their headlights on a certain road during the daytime as well as at night and found that annual accident rates on the road fell 15 percent from the previous level. They concluded that applying the daytime rule statewide would lead to a similar reduction in accidents.

Which of the following, if true, most strengthens the authorities' argument?

(A) Because an alternate route became available, the volume of traffic on the test road decreased during the test period.

(B) Drivers were informed of the requirement to use their headlights on the test road by means of a series of three conspicuous signs in each direction of travel.

加利福尼亚当局要求司机在通过某特定路段时，在白天也要像晚上一样使用头灯，结果发现这条路上的年事故发生率比从前降低了15%。他们得出结论说，在全州范围内都推行该项日间规定会同样地降低事故发生率。

下列哪项，如果正确，最能支持作者的论断？

(A) 由于可以选择其他路线，因此所测试路段的交通量在测试期间减少了。

(B) 司机们对在该测试路段使用头灯的要求的了解来自于在每个行驶方向上的三个显著的标牌。

(C) Under certain conditions, among them fog and heavy rain, most drivers in California already use their headlights during the daytime.

(D) Full-scale application of the daytime rule would cause headlight bulbs to burn out sooner than they currently do and thus to require more frequent replacement.

(E) The test road was selected to include a great variety of the sorts of road conditions that drivers in California are likely to encounter.

10. Which of the following, if true, most logically completes the passage?

Every fusion reaction releases neutrinos. To test a hypothesis about the frequency of fusion reactions in the Sun, physicists calculated the number of neutrinos the Sun would produce annually if the hypothesis were correct. From this they estimated how many neutrinos should pass through a particular location on Earth. The fact that far fewer neutrinos were counted than were predicted to pass through the location would seem to prove that the hypothesis is wrong, except that_____.

(A) the physicists, using a different method for estimating how many neutrinos should reach the location, confirmed their original estimate

(B) there are several competing hypotheses about the frequency of solar fusion reactions

(C) there is not enough energy in the Sun to destroy a neutrino once it is released

(D) the method used to count neutrinos detects no more than approximately ten percent of the neutrinos that pass through

(E) neutrinos released in the fusion reactions of other stars also reach the Earth

11. An economist concluded that Kregg Company deliberately discriminated against people with a history of union affiliation in hiring workers for its new plant. The economist's evidence is that, of the 1,500 people hired to work at the new plant, only 100 had ever belonged to a labor union, whereas in Kregg Company's older plants, a much higher proportion of workers have a history of union affiliation.

Which of the following is an assumption on which the economist's argument depends?

下列哪一项，如果正确，最能从逻辑上将下段补充完整？

每次核聚变都会发射出中子。为了检验一项关于太阳内部核聚变频繁程度的假设，物理学家们计算了在该假设正确的条件下，每年可能产生的中子数。他们再从这一点出发，计算出在地球某一特定地点应该经过的中子数。事实上，点数到的经过该地点的中子数要比预计的少得多，看起来这一事实证明了该假设是错误的，除了_____。

(A) 物理学家们应用了另一种方法来估计可能到达该地点的中子数，结果验证了他们最初的估计。

(B) 关于太阳核聚变反应频率还存在着其他几种竞争性假设。

(C) 太阳内部没有足够的能量来破坏它释放出的中子。

(D) 用来点数中子的方法仅发现了约不足10%的通过该地区的中子。

(E) 其他星球核聚变反应所发出的中子也到达了地球。

某经济学家得出结论，认为Kregg公司在为其新工厂招工时故意歧视那些参加过工会联盟的人。该经济学家的证据是，在新工厂雇用的1500人中，仅有100人曾经参加过工会，而在Kregg公司的老工厂中，参加过工会联盟的工人的比例要高得多。

该经济学家的论证建立在下列哪项假设之上？

(A) None of the people with a history of union affiliation who were hired to work at the new plant were union organizers.

(B) Applicants for jobs at the new plant were not asked by Kregg's recruiters whether they had every belonged to a labor union.

(C) In the plants of some of Kregg's competitors, the workforce consists predominantly of union members.

(D) The company believes that the cost of running the new plant will be lower if labor unions are not represented in the workforce.

(E) The pool of potential candidates for jobs at the new plant included some people, in addition to those Kregg hired, with a history of union affiliation.

(A) 新工厂雇用的工人中参加过工会联盟的人没有一个是工会的组织者。

(B) Kregg的招工人员并没有询问来新工厂找工作的人他们是否参加过工会。

(C) 在Kregg的一些竞争者的工厂中，工人中大部分是工会成员。

(D) 该公司认为如果工人中没有工会组织，新工厂的运营成本会更低。

(E) 适合新工厂工作岗位的潜在候选人中，包括Kregg雇用的人中，有一些人参加过工会联盟。

12. Hastings' contracture is a disorder of the connective tissue in one or both hands, most commonly causing loss of mobility. A survey of thousands of medical-insurance claims found that over 30 percent of people who had one hand operated on for Hastings' contracture underwent surgery a second time for this disorder within three years. Clearly, therefore, a single surgical treatment of Hastings' contracture is often ineffective at providing long-term correction of the disorder.

Which of the following, if true, most seriously weakens the argument?

(A) The medical-insurance claims did not specify whether the surgery was on the patient's right or left hand.

(B) The surgical techniques used to treat Hastings' contracture are identical to those used successfully to treat certain work-related injuries to the hand.

(C) A separate survey found that 90 percent of patients operated on for Hastings' contracture report increased hand mobility within one month after the surgery.

(D) All of the patients in the survey were required by their insurance companies to seek a second opinion from a qualified surgeon before undergoing the operation.

(E) Many people who have Hastings' contracture choose to tolerate its effects rather than undergo the risks of surgery.

Hastings挛缩是一种一只手或两只手的连接组织的失调，这通常会导致行动能力的丧失。一项对几千份医疗保险索赔的调查表明，一只手进行过Hastings挛缩手术的人中有30%在三年内会对该种失调进行第二次手术。因此，显而易见，对Hastings挛缩进行一次性手术治疗通常对于长期矫正这种失调是无效的。

下列哪一项，如果正确，最能削弱上述论断？

(A) 医疗保险索赔并没有说明手术是针对患者的左手还是右手进行的。

(B) 针对Hastings挛缩采取的手术技术与那些成功地用于处理某种手部工伤的手术技术相同。

(C) 一项独立的调查发现，动过Hastings挛缩手术的患者中有90%在术后一个月内手部的活动能力上升了。

(D) 调查中，所有的患者都被其保险公司要求在动手术前向一位有资格的医生寻求不同意见。

(E) 许多患有Hastings挛缩的人选择忍受该失调的影响，而不去冒动手术的风险。

13. The most widely used therapy for a certain type of ulcer completely heals such ulcers in 44 percent of patients within six months. In a six-month trial of a new therapy for this type of ulcer, 80 percent of ulcers treated achieved significant healing and 61 percent were completely healed. Since the trial

针对某种溃疡最常用的一种疗法可在6个月内将44%的患者的溃疡完全治愈。针对这种溃疡的一种新疗法在6个月的试验中使治疗的80%的溃疡取得了明显改善，61%的溃疡得到了痊愈。由于该试验只治

treated only ulcers of this type that were worse than average, the new therapy clearly promotes healing more effectively than the most widely used therapy.

The answer to which of the following would be most useful in evaluating the argument given?

(A) What differences are there, if any, in the ways that the two therapies are administered?

(B) Is there any significant difference between the costs associated with the two therapies?

(C) What percentage of people with ulcers of this type who were treated with the most widely used therapy for six months experienced significant healing?

(D) How quickly do ulcers of this type, if left untreated, become significantly worse?

(E) What percentage of patients involved in the six-month trial of the new therapy were disappointed at the rate of healing that were experiencing?

14. A society can achieve a fair distribution of resources only under conditions of economic growth. There can be no economic growth unless the society guarantees equality of economic opportunity to all of its citizens. Equality of economic opportunity cannot be guaranteed unless a society's government actively works to bring it about.

If the statements given are true, it can be properly concluded from them that

(A) no government can achieve a fair distribution of resources under conditions of economic growth.

(B) all societies that guarantee equality of economic opportunity to all of their members are societies that distribute resources fairly.

(C) a society can achieve a fair distribution of resources only if its government actively works to bring about equality of economic opportunity.

(D) there can be no economic growth in a society unless that society guarantees a fair distribution of resources.

(E) some societies that experience economic growth fail to guarantee equality of opportunity to all of their citizens.

15. High Towers, a company that occupies several office buildings, is considering installing new energy-efficient lightbulbs in its buildings. The new bulbs require less than half the electricity consumed by the conventional bulbs

疗了那些病情比较严重的溃疡，因此这种新疗法显然在疗效方面比最常用的疗法更显著。

对下列哪一项的回答最能有效地对上文论述做出评价？

(A) 这两种疗法使用的方法有何不同？

(B) 这两种疗法的使用成本是否存在很大差别？

(C) 在6个月中以最常用疗法治疗的该种溃疡的患者中，有多大比例取得了明显康复？

(D) 这种溃疡如果不进行治疗的话，病情显著恶化的速度有多快？

(E) 在参加6个月的新疗法试验的患者中，有多大比例的人对康复的比例不满意？

一个社会只有在经济增长的条件下才能对资源进行公平的分配，要想取得经济增长，该社会必须保障其每个公民的经济机会是均等的，要保障经济机会的均等就必然要求社会的政府去积极地推动它。

如果上文正确，那么从中可适当地得出结论：

(A) 没有政府可在经济增长的条件下对资源进行公平分配。

(B) 所有能够保障其全部成员经济机会均等的社会都是那些公平分配资源的社会。

(C) 一个社会只有在其政府积极地推动经济机会均等的条件下才能对资源进行公平分配。

(D) 一个社会要取得经济增长就必须保障对资源进行公平分配。

(E) 一些取得经济增长的社会没能保障其全部公民的机会均等。

High Tower是一家占用几栋办公楼的公司，它正在考虑在它所有的建筑内都安装节能灯泡，这种新灯泡与目前正在使用的传统灯泡发出同样多的光，而所需的电

currently used to produce the same amount of light. The new bulbs also last considerably longer. It follows that by replacing old bulbs as they burn out with the new kind of bulb, High Towers would significantly reduce its overall lighting costs.

Which of the following, if true, most strengthens the argument given?

(A) If the new bulbs are widely adopted, as seems likely, they will be produced in large enough quantities to be offered at prices comparable to those of conventional bulbs.

(B) The utility that supplies High Towers with electricity offers discounted rates to its largest customers.

(C) High Towers has recently signed a contract to occupy an additional small office building.

(D) High Towers has begun a campaign to encourage its employees to turn off lights whenever they leave a room.

(E) The company that manufactures the new bulbs has been granted a patent on the innovative technology used in the bulbs and thus has exclusive rights to manufacture them.

量仅是传统灯泡的一半。这种新灯泡的寿命也大大加长，因此通过在旧灯泡坏掉的时候换上这种新灯泡，HighTower公司可以大大地降低其总体照明的成本。

下列哪一项，如果正确，最能支持上面论述？

(A) 如果广泛地采用这种新灯泡，这是非常可能的，那么新灯泡的产量就会大大增加，从而使其价格与那些传统灯泡相当。

(B) 向High Tower提供电力的公共事业公司向其最大的客户们提供折扣。

(C) High Tower最近签订了一份合同，要再占用一栋小的办公楼。

(D) High Tower发起了一项运动，鼓励其员工每次在离开房间时关灯。

(E) 生产这种新灯泡的公司对灯泡中使用的革新技术取得了专利，因此它享有生产新灯泡的独家权利。

参考答案：

1. C	2. B	3. A	4. B	5. D
6. B	7. E	8. B	9. E	10. D
11. E	12. A	13. C	14. C	15. A

1. **解析**：本题问题目的明确，让我们支持养狗场场主的假设，所以读题重点放在最后一句话上，即体温上升是由于这种药通过幼狗母亲的乳汁进入了幼狗体内。选项(C)指出当狗用奶瓶喂养时没有体温上升，属于典型的"无因就无果"类的支持，即没有通过幼狗母亲的乳汁喂养就没有体温上升这个结果。(A)中的some说明不了段落中的most of the puppies of these dogs的情况；(B)饲养员的看法与上述假设无关；(D)为明显反对；(E)为无关选项。

2. **解析**：本题为完成句子题型的解释题，解释since之前的"这条管线是物有所值的"。(B)说明这个项目可重建Tifele湖，从而消除使Alivia面临减少一项度假收入的危险，意味着这条管道是能带来其他的益处，因此起到了解释的目的；(A)选项实际上起反对作用，因为油价现已大幅度降价且趋向稳定，因此作为石油发电替代物的这条管线的成本显得更高，铺设这条管线明显不利。(A)、(E)为无关选项，(D)为新的比较，与要解释的无关。

3. **解析**：本题为反对题型，要找出一个选项来削弱结论"在流动型赛马场骑马比在永久型赛马场骑马更加危险"，因此选项应与"是否危险有关"。(A)说明流动型赛马场在每次迁徙前，管理员都检查潜在危险并加以修复，从而使危险降低，明显削弱了结论；(B)易误选，但选(B)肯定犯了递进推理错误，认为资金多危险就小；(C)、(D)与"是否危险"无关；(E)泛泛地指出骑乘的管理员易忽视什么，但并未指出"流动型赛马场与永久型赛场的区别"，因此也不能构成解释。

4. **解析**：注意本题为"从上而下"类的support，即归纳，注意把握逻辑层次结构。(B)的内容恰好与段落中的第二句话相吻合，因此(B)正确；(A)的"工作中接触玻璃纤维的人非常有可能也会接触石棉"，在段落中并没有涉及；(C)为新的比较，必然不对；(D)中的Coarse fibers为新概念；(E)中的if

uncut在段落中也未提及。注意体会(E)选项可以作为一个支持上面段落的推理的答案，但本题为归纳类。

5. **解析**：许多人本题出错的原因主要在于没有把问题目的的意思理解明白。本题让我们去寻求一个选项在不削弱政治家的论断的前提下替代人们过量饮酒的典故。(D)说明一个人在工作日的早晨在床上多呆几分钟，就是希望必然是不得不匆匆忙忙按时上班，这个推理荒谬之极，与上面段落中"在晚间宴会上饮用酒精过多的人就是希望第二天早上头痛"思路一样，因此(D)正确。

6. **解析**：本题为GRE1992年2月国内考题的重考题目，但这里是把原题的答案放入段落中，变成逻辑应用与技法来考查。请体会最新考题的命题动向，并请参阅假设类的讲解进行思维。建议大家把本题的5个选项译成中文，体会(B)正确的原因。

7. **解析**：本题属于典型的由一个discovery而得出一个结论的"B，A"型，假设多为除了A以外没有别的原因导致B，用否定概念来进行定位，发现(C)、(D)、(E)中否定词not，(E)说明手工艺人不把他们在作坊中制造的珠宝交给贵族顾客，也就说明了珠宝确实不是供给贵族的，因此(E)正确；(C)中出现的materials为新概念；(D)与"贵族或中产阶级"无关，必然不对。

8. **解析**：本题为解释题型，让我们寻求一个选项去解释为什么杀虫剂使用方面的改进伴随某些害虫的损失却更大。(B)说明由于单个针对性增强，导致用杀虫剂控制某种害虫的成本变得比那种害虫带来的损失的价值更大，与我们要解释的相吻合，起到了解释作用，因此(B)正确；(A)选项起到部分反对作用；(C)只是解释了农民为什么更仔细；(D)说的是共同点，无法解释上面的似乎不合常理的说法；(E)为新比较，且了解程度与损失等无关。

9. **解析**：本题是一个典型的由一个现存事实得出一个对将来应用的推测，支持一般需要把现存事实与对将来的推测联系起来。(E)说明该测试路段在选取时包括了可能遇到的多种路况，从而说明该测试路段具有代表性，因此支持了作者论断，所以(E)正确。

10. **解析**：本题为LSAT一道逻辑推理题的变形。作为完成段落考题，重点是读懂最后一句。实际上，本题是让找一个选项说明这一事实不能证明该假设为错误，也就是找一个选项说明为什么点数到的、经过该地点的中子数要比预计的少得多。(D)说明用点数中子的方法仅发现了约不足10%的通过该地区的中子，解释了为什么点数到的比预计的要少，所以(D)正确。

11. **解析**：本题为"B，A"型的假设。(E)说明适合新工厂工作岗位的潜在候选人中有一些参加过工会联盟，表明确实存在有工会联盟的人合格的情况，但Kregg就是没有录用。如果我们把(E)取非，变为压根就没有适合新工厂工作的有工会联盟历史的人，那么上面结论"Kregg故意歧视参加过工会联盟的人"必然不对。因此，(E)是一个很好的假设；(A)、(B)、(C)均为无关选项；而(D)为一典型的"有他因"的反对选项。

12. **解析**：本题属于典型的由一个survey而得出一个结论，即"B，A"型的削弱，思路多为"有其他原因导致B"。(A)说明医疗保险索赔并没有说明是针对患者的左手还是右手进行的，可能有一些人第一次手术时只针对左手进行，因三个月后右手连接组织失调，而进行第二次手术，所以削弱以上结论；(C)易误选，但(C)讨论的是一个自由的情况，与"长期矫正是否有效"无关。

13. **解析**：本题为评价题型。(C)问及在6个月中以最常用疗法治疗的该种溃疡的患者中有多大比例获得了明显康复。若为100%，那么就高于新疗法的80%，新疗法疗效更显著受到质疑；若低于80%则新疗法疗效更显著成立。因此(C)为很好的评价。(A)、(B)离结论较远，许多人易犯递进推理；(D)、(E)均为无关选项。

14. **解析**：本题为归纳题型。注意第一个句子中的only under，说明only后的部分为前一部分的必要条件。因此本段落层次结构推理为：a society can achieve a fair distribution of resources→economic growth→equality of economic opportunity→a society's government actively works to bring it about. 很明显，(C)表明a society can achieve a fair distribution of resources→a society's government actively works to bring it about，与上面推理吻合，所以(C)正确。

15. 解析：支持重点读两句话，在本题中为"换为新灯泡，那么总体照明的成本降低"。而(A)说明大规模使用新灯泡导致新灯泡价格与旧灯泡相当，再加上新灯泡别的优势，确实可以实现本公司总体照明成本降低，所以(A)正确；而(B)、(C)、(E)为无关选项；(D)指出了另外一种原因，不可能起到支持作用。

五、GMAT考前逻辑推理冲刺训练试题及解析（五）

1. The painter Peter Brandon never dated his works, and their chronology is only now beginning to take shape in the critical literature. A recent dating of a Brandon self-portrait to 1930 is surely wrong. Brandon was 63 years old in 1930, yet the painting shows a young, dark-haired man—obviously Brandon, but clearly not a man of 63.

Which of the following, if justifiably assumed, allows the conclusion to be properly drawn?

(A) There is no securely dated self-portrait of Brandon that he painted when he was significantly younger than 63.

(B) In refraining from dating his works, Brandon intended to steer critical discussion of them away from considerations of chronology.

(C) Until recently, there was very little critical literature on the works of Brandon.

(D) Brandon at age 63 would not have portrayed himself in a painting as he had looked when he was a young man.

(E) Brandon painted several self-portraits that showed him as a man past the age of 60.

画家Peter Brandon从来不在其作品上标注日期，其作品的时间顺序现在才开始在评论文献中形成轮廓。最近将Brandon的一幅自画像的时间定位为1930年一定是错误的，1930年时Brandon已经63岁了，然而画中的年轻、黑发的男子显然是Brandon本人，但却绝不是63岁的男子。

下列哪一项，如果假设合理，允许上面结论成立？

(A) 在Brandon远未到60岁以前，他没画过明确标注日期的自画像。

(B) 通过不给其作品标注日期，Brandon试图使针对其作品的批评讨论抛开时间因素。

(C) 最近以前，几乎没有什么针对Brandon的作品的批评文献。

(D) Brandon在63岁时，不可能在画中将自己画成年轻时的样子。

(E) Brandon画过几幅显示他60岁以后的样子的自画像。

2. Dance critic from Europe: The improved quality of ballet in the United States is the result of more Europeans' teaching ballet in the United States than ever before. I know the proportion of teachers who were born and trained in Europe has gone up among ballet teachers in the United States, because last year, on my trip to New York, more of the ballet teachers I met were from Europe—born and trained there—than ever before.

Which of the following identifies a questionable assumption made by the dance critic's reasoning?

(A) The argument overlooks the possibility that some ballet teachers in the United States could have been born in Europe but trained in the United States.

(B) The argument assumes that the ballet teachers whom the critic met last year on the critic's trip to New York were a generally typical group of such teachers.

(C) The argument assumes that the teaching of ballet in

欧洲的舞蹈批评家：美国芭蕾水平的提高是由于现在有更多的欧洲人在美国教授芭蕾。在美国的芭蕾教师中，在欧洲出生并接受训练的教师比例上升了，我知道这一点是因为在我去年去纽约时，我所遇见的欧洲来的芭蕾教师——在欧洲出生并接受训练——比从前要多。

下列哪一项指出了该舞蹈批评家在推理中所使用的一项有疑问的假设？

(A) 该论述忽视了一种可能，即美国的一些芭蕾教师可能出生在欧洲但却是在美国接受的训练。

(B) 该论述假设该批评家在其去年去纽约时遇见的教师群在这类教师中具有典型代表性。

(C) 该论述假设美国的芭蕾教学水平比欧

the United States is superior to the teaching of ballet in Europe.

(D) Other possible reasons for the improved mental attitudes of United States dancers are not examined.

(E) The argument assumes that dancers born and trained in Europe are typically more talented than dancers born and trained in the United States.

洲的要高。

(D) 没有考虑导致美国舞蹈家思想状态水平上升的其他可能原因。

(E) 该论述假设在欧洲出生并受训的舞蹈家一般比在美国出生并受训的舞蹈家天赋更高。

3. Mayor: Four years ago when we reorganized the city police department in order to save money, critics claimed that the reorganization would make the police less responsive to citizens and would thus lead to more crime. The police have compiled theft statistics from the years following the reorganization that show that the critics were wrong. There was an overall decrease in reports of thefts of all kinds, including small thefts.

Which of the following, if true, most seriously challenges the mayor's argument?

(A) When city police are perceived as unresponsive, victims of theft are less likely to report thefts to the police.

(B) The mayor's critics generally agree that police statistics concerning crime reports provide the most reliable available data on crime rates.

(C) In other cities where police departments have been similarly reorganized, the numbers of reported thefts have generally risen following reorganization.

(D) The mayor's reorganization of the police department failed to save as much money as it was intended to save.

(E) During the four years immediately preceding the reorganization, reports of all types of theft had been rising steadily in comparison to reports of other crimes.

市长：当我们4年前重组城市警察部门以节省开支时，批评者们声称重组会导致警察对市民责任心的减少，会导致犯罪的增长。警察局整理了重组那年以后的偷盗统计资料，结果表明批评者们是错误的，包括小偷小摸在内的各种偷盗报告普遍地减少了。

下列哪一项，如果正确，最能削弱市长的论述？

(A) 当城市警察局被认为不负责时，偷盗的受害者们不愿向警察报告偷盗事故。

(B) 市长的批评者们一般同意认为警察局关于犯罪报告的统计资料是关于犯罪率的最可靠的有效数据。

(C) 在警察部门进行过类似重组的其他城市里，报告的偷盗数目在重组后一般都上升了。

(D) 市长对警察系统的重组所节省的钱比预期目标要少。

(E) 在重组之前的4年中，与其他犯罪报告相比，各种偷盗报告的数目节节上升。

4. It takes a particular talent to be a successful business manager. Business courses can help people to solve management problems, but such courses can do so only for those people with managerial talent. Such people should take business courses to acquire ideas that they can subsequently use to good advantage if management problems happen to arise.

If the statements above are true, which of the following must also be true on the basis of them?

(A) People who are helped by business courses in solving management problems also have managerial talent.

(B) People who are already skilled at solving management problems are unlikely to benefit from business courses.

要成为一名成功的商业经理需具备一定的天赋，商业课程可以帮助人们解决管理问题，但这种课程仅能帮助那些具有管理天赋的人，这些人应该通过商业课程来获得一些方法，如果这些管理问题恰巧发生时，他们就可以很好地应用这些方法。

如果上文论述正确，从其出发，下列哪一项也一定正确？

(A) 那些在解决管理问题方面受益于商业课程的人也具有管理天赋。

(B) 那些在解决管理问题方面已经很有办法的人不可能从商业课程中受益。

(C) Most ideas that are used successfully in solving management problems are those acquired in business courses.

(D) People who lack managerial talent are more likely to take business courses than are people who have managerial talent.

(E) Those people who have never taken business courses are unable to solve management problems when such problems arise.

5. When a driver is suspected of having had too much to drink, testing the driver's ability to walk a straight line gives a more reliable indication of fitness to drive than does testing the driver's blood-alcohol level.

Which of the following, if true, best supports the claim made in the statement above?

(A) Not all observers will agree whether or not an individual has succeeded in walking a straight line.

(B) Because of genetic differences and variations in acquired tolerance to alcohol, some individuals suffer more serious motor impairment from a given high blood-alcohol level than do others.

(C) Tests designed to measure blood-alcohol levels are accurate, inexpensive, and easy to administer.

(D) More than half the drivers involved in fatal accidents have blood-alcohol levels that exceed the legal limit, whereas in less-serious accidents the proportion of legally intoxicated drivers is lower.

(E) Some individuals with high blood-alcohol levels are capable of walking a straight line but are not capable of driving safely.

6. That sales can be increased by the presence of sunlight within a store has been shown by the experience of the only Savefast department store with a large skylight. The skylight allows sunlight into half of the store, reducing the need for artificial light. The rest of the store uses only artificial light. Since the store opened two years ago, the departments on the sunlit side have had substantially higher sales than the other departments.

Which of the following, if true, most strengthens the argument?

(A) On particularly cloudy days, more artificial light is used to illuminate the part of the store under the skylight.

(B) When the store is open at night, the departments in the

(C) 大多数成功地解决了管理问题的方法是从商业课程中学到的。

(D) 缺乏管理天赋的人与那些具有管理天赋的人相比，更有可能去学习商业课程。

(E) 那些没有学过商业课程的人在管理问题发生时无法解决这些问题。

当一名司机被怀疑饮用了过多的酒精时，检验该司机走直线的能力与检验该司机血液中的酒精水平相比，是检验该司机是否适于驾车的一个更可靠的指标。

下列哪一项，如果正确，能最好地支持上文中的声明？

(A) 观察者们对一个人是否成功地走了直线不能全部达成一致。

(B) 由于基因的不同和对酒精的抵抗能力的差别，一些人在高的血液酒精含量水平时所受的运动肌肉损伤比另一些人要多。

(C) 用于检验血液酒精含量水平的测试是准确、低成本，并且易于实施的。

(D) 造成致命性事故的司机中，一半以上的人的血液酒精含量水平高于法定限制，而在较轻的事故中，法律意义的醉酒司机的比率要低得多。

(E) 一些人在血液酒精含量水平很高的时候，还可以走直线，但却不能完全驾车。

具有大型天窗的独一无二的Savefast百货商场的经验表明，商店内射入的阳光可增加销售额。Savefast的大天窗可使商店的一半地方都有阳光射入，这样可以降低人工照明需要，商店的另一半地方只有人工照明。从该店两年前开张开始，天窗一边的各部门的销售量要远高于其他各部门的销售量。

下列哪一项，如果正确，最能支持上面论述？

(A) 在某些阴天里，商场中天窗下面的部分需要更多的人工灯光来照明。

part of the store under the skylight have sales that are no higher than those of other departments.

(C) Many customers purchase items from departments in both parts of the store on a single shopping trip.

(D) Besides the skylight, there are several significant architectural differences between the two parts of the store.

(E) The departments in the part of the store under the skylight are the departments that generally have the highest sales in other stores in the Savefast chain.

(B) 在商场夜间开放的时间里，位于商场中天窗下面部分的各部门的销售额不比其他部门高。

(C) 许多顾客在一次购物过程中，在商场两边的部门都购买商品。

(D) 除了天窗，商场两部分的建筑之间还有一些明显的差别。

(E) 位于商场天窗下面部分的各部门，在Savefast的其他一些连锁店中也是销售额最高的部门。

7. To protect beachfront buildings from ocean storms, ocean resorts have built massive seawalls between beaches and the buildings. Not only do the seawalls block off some buildings' ocean view, but the beaches themselves become ever narrower, because sand can no longer creep inland as storms erode it at the water's edge.

If the information is correct, which of the following conclusions is most strongly supported on the basis of it?

(A) Since the ferocity of ocean storms is increasing, increasingly high seawalls must be built between beaches and beachfront property.

(B) Even when beaches are heavily used by people, they are necessary to the survival of the many wild species that use them.

(C) Seawalls constructed to protect beachfront buildings will not themselves eventually be damaged by storms and will not require, if they are to protect the buildings, expensive repair or replacement.

(D) The conservation of beaches for future generations should be the overriding goal of shore management at ocean coasts.

(E) Trying to protect beachfront buildings by constructing seawalls is counterproductive in the long run for an oceanfront community wishing to maintain itself as a beach resort.

为保护海边建筑免遭海洋风暴的袭击，海洋度假地在海滩和建筑之间建起了巨大的防海墙。这些防海墙不仅遮住了一些建筑物的海景，而且使海岸本身也变窄了。这是因为在风暴从水的一边对沙子进行侵蚀的时候，沙子不再向内陆扩展。

如果上述信息正确，那些从其出发，下列哪一项得到了最有力的支持？

(A) 由于海洋风暴的猛烈程度不断加深，必须在海洋和海边财产之间建立起更多的高大的防海墙。

(B) 即使是在海滩被人类滥用着的时候，它们对于许多使用它们的野生物种的生存来说依然是必不可少的。

(C) 用来保护海边建筑的防海墙如果要保护那些建筑，它们自己最终不会被风暴破坏，也不需要昂贵的维修和更新。

(D) 为以后的世代保留下海滩应该是海岸管理的首要目标。

(E) 对于一个想要维护自己海滩疗养地功能的海边社区来说，通过建筑防海墙来保护海边建筑的努力，从长远来看，其作用是适得其反的。

8. A study found that 70 percent of children surveyed in 1970 had at one time had cavities, whereas only 50 percent of those surveyed in 1985 had ever had cavities. The researchers concluded that the level of dental disease in children had declined between 1970 and 1985.

Which of the following, if true, would most seriously undermine the researchers' conclusion presented above?

(A) Cavities are the most common kind of dental disease to

一项研究发现，1970年调查的孩子中有70%曾经有过牙洞，而在1985年的调查中，仅有50%的孩子曾经有过牙洞。研究者们得出结论，在1970～1985年这段时间内，孩子们中的牙病比率降低了。

下列哪一项，如果为真，最能削减研究者们上面得出的结论？

(A) 牙洞是孩子们可能得的最普通的一种

which children are subject.

(B) The children surveyed came from a broad variety of income backgrounds.

(C) The children surveyed were selected from among students of teachers cooperating with the researchers.

(D) The accuracy of cavity detection techniques has improved dramatically since 1970.

(E) The children surveyed in 1985 were younger on average than those surveyed in 1970.

9. David: Since attempting to preserve every species that is currently endangered is prohibitively expensive, the endangered species whose value to humanity is the greatest should be accorded the highest priority for preservation.

Karen: Such a policy would be unsound because it is impossible to predict the future value of a species, nor is it always possible to assess the present value of species whose contributions to humanity, though significant, are indirect.

Which of the following is the main point of Karen's reply to David?

(A) Although it would be desirable to preserve all endangered species, doing so is not economically feasible.

(B) Even if the value to humanity of a given species is known, that value should not be a factor in any decision on whether to expend effort to preserve that species.

(C) Species whose contributions to humanity are direct should have a higher priority for preservation efforts than species whose contributions to humanity are only indirect.

(D) Since the methods for deciding which species have the most value to humanity are imperfect, informed decisions cannot be made on the basis of the assessment of such value.

(E) The preservation of endangered species whose value to humanity can be reliably predicted is more important than the preservation of species whose value for humanity is unpredictable.

10. Roger: Reading a lot as a child causes nearsightedness—difficulty seeing things at a distance.

Louise: I disagree. Any correlation between nearsightedness and reading results from the fact that children who have trouble seeing things at a distance are likeliest to prefer those activities, such as reading, that involve looking at things close up.

牙病。

(B) 被调查的孩子来自不同收入背景的家庭。

(C) 被调查的孩子是从那些与这些研究者们进行合作的老师的学生中选取的。

(D) 1970年以来，发现牙洞的技术水平得到了突飞猛进的提高。

(E) 平均来说，1985年调查的孩子要比1970年调查的孩子的年龄要小。

David：由于要想保护每个目前濒临灭绝的物种将极为昂贵，所以那些对人类价值最大的濒危物种应该享有最优先的被保护权利。

Karen：这个政策是不合适的，这是因为一个物种的未来价值是无法预测的，另外那些对人类贡献很大，但却是间接贡献的物种的目前价值也是无法估计的。

下面哪一项是Karen针对David的回答的要点？

(A) 尽管应该保护所有濒危的物种，但这样做，从经济上来说是不可能的。

(B) 即使某一物种对人类的价值是已知的，该价值也不应作为决定是否应该尽力保护该物种的一个因素。

(C) 那些对人类有直接贡献的物种应该比那些对人类仅有间接贡献的物种享有更优先的被保护权。

(D) 由于用于确定哪一物种对人类的价值最大的方法是不完善的，所以无法根据对这种价值的估计做出明智的决定。

(E) 保护那些对人类的价值能够可靠预测的濒危物种比保护那些对人类来说价值无法预测的物种更加重要。

Roger：儿时进行大量阅读会导致近视眼——难于看清远处景物。

Louise：我不同意，近视眼与阅读之间的关联都来自以下事实：观看远处景物有困难的孩子最有可能选择那些需要从近处观看物体的活动，如阅读。

Louise disputes Roger's claim by

(A) demonstrating that an absurd conclusion would follow if Roger's claim were accepted.

(B) arguing that what Roger claims to be a cause of a given phenomenon is actually its effect.

(C) using an analogy to expose a flaw in Roger's reasoning.

(D) pointing out that Roger's claim is self-contradictory.

(E) attempting to demonstrate that Roger uses the term "nearsightedness" in an ambiguous way.

Louise对Roger的反驳是通过

(A) 说明如果接受Roger的声明，会导致荒谬的结论。

(B) 论证Roger的声明中某一现象的原因实际上是该现象的结果。

(C) 运用类比来说明Roger推理中的错误。

(D) 指出Roger的声明是自相矛盾的。

(E) 试图说明Roger对"近视眼"这一术语的使用是模棱两可的。

11. Years ago, consumers in Finland began paying an energy tax in the form of two Finland pennies for each unit of energy consumed that came from nonrenewable sources. Following the introduction of this energy tax, there was a steady reduction in the total yearly consumption of energy from nonrenewable sources.

If the statements in the passage are true, then which of the following must on the basis of them be true?

(A) There was a steady decline in the yearly revenues generated by the energy tax in Finland.

(B) There was a steady decline in the total amount of energy consumed each year in Finland.

(C) There was a steady increase in the use of renewable energy sources in Finland.

(D) The revenues generated by the energy tax were used to promote the use of energy from renewable sources.

(E) The use of renewable energy sources in Finland greatly increased relative to the use of nonrenewable energy sources.

几年前，芬兰的消费者开始缴纳一种能源税，他们每消费一单位来自非再生资源的能源就要缴纳2芬兰便士的能源税。自从引入这项能源税后，每年对来自非再生资源的能源的消费稳步减少。

如果文中所述正确，那么从其出发，下列哪一项也一定正确？

(A) 在芬兰，由该项能源税所形成的年税收不断减少。

(B) 芬兰每年消费的能源总量不断减少。

(C) 芬兰对可再生能源资源的使用不断上升。

(D) 由该项能源税所带来的年税收是用来推动对来自可再生资源的能源的使用。

(E) 芬兰对可再生能源资源的使用相对于不可再生能源资源的使用大大增加了。

12. Despite a dramatic increase in the number of people riding bicycles for recreation in Parkville, a recent report by the Parkville Department of Transportation shows that the number of accidents involving bicycles has decreased for the third consecutive year.

Which of the following, if true during the last three years, best reconciles the apparent discrepancy in the facts above?

(A) The Parkville Department of Recreation confiscated abandoned bicycles and sold them at auction to any interested Parkville residents.

(B) Increased automobile and bus traffic in Parkville has been the leading cause of the most recent increase in automobile accidents.

在Parkville，尽管骑自行车进行娱乐的人数显著上升，但最近一份来自Parkville的交通部门的报告显示，涉及自行车的事故已经连续三年呈现下降趋势。

下列哪一项，如果在过去三年中是正确的，最好地解释了上面事实中的明显的矛盾。

(A) Parkvile的娱乐部门没收了被遗弃的自行车，并向任何感兴趣的Parkvile居民拍卖出售。

(B) Parkville不断增加的汽车和公共交通一直是近来不断增加的汽车事故的主要原因。

(C) Because of the local increase in the number of people bicycling for recreation, many out-of-town bicyclists ride in the Parkville area.

(D) The Parkville Police Department enforced traffic rules for bicycle riders much more vigorously and began requiring recreational riders to pass a bicycle safety course.

(E) The Parkville Department of Transportation canceled a program that required all bicycles to be inspected and registered each year.

(C) 由于骑自行车进行娱乐的当地人不断增加，许多外地的自行车爱好者也在Parkville地区骑自行车。

(D) Parkville的警察部门向骑自行车的人们颁布了更加严厉的交通法规，开始要求骑自行车进行娱乐的人，要通过一项自行车安全课程。

(E) Parkville的交通部门取消了一项规定，该规定要求所有的自行车每年都要进行检查和注册。

13. Do strong electric currents, by means of the electromagnetic fields that accompany them, cause cancer in people who live and work nearby? Telephone line workers, who work near such currents every day, can provide a test case. They show elevated levels of brain cancer; therefore, the hypothesis of electromagnetic causation is supported.

Which of the following, if true, most seriously weakens the argument?

(A) Burying power lines and other measures to protect the public from such electromagnetic fields would be prohibitively expensive.

(B) Telephone line workers are exposed to levels of chemical solvents high enough to cause brain cancer.

(C) High exposure to strong electromagnetic fields is correlated with a slightly higher-than-normal incidence of childhood leukemia, which is a form of cancer.

(D) Public health officials who found that a group of different illnesses in people living near a power substation could not reliably be attributed to its electromagnetic field were accused of covering up the facts.

(E) Telephone line workers, like most people have electrical appliances at home, and most electrical appliances, when turned on, are surrounded by an electromagnetic field of some measurable level.

很强的电流会通过伴随电流产生的电磁场而使在其附近生活和工作的人产生癌症吗？电话线工人每天都工作在这样的电流旁边，他们可以作为测试的例子。他们显示出偏高的脑癌水平，因此，电磁场引发癌症的假设是成立的。

下列哪一项，如果正确，最不能削弱上面的论述？

(A) 通过掩埋电线或其他方法来使公众远离电磁场的影响的做法将是成本高昂、无法负担的。

(B) 电话线工人接触了过量的化学溶液，这足以引发脑癌。

(C) 高度暴露于强电磁场内与略高于正常的幼年白血病发病率相关联，白血病是癌症的一种。

(D) 一些公众健康官员们发现，没有完全把握能把居住在变电所附近的人们所患的各种疾病归因于电磁场，这些官员们被指控为掩盖了事实真相。

(E) 与大多数人一样，电话线工人家中也有电器，而大多数电器在运转的时候其周围产生的电磁场都会达到某种可观的程度。

14. Neither the Sami nor the Kephrian delegations attended the international conference. Beforehand, the delegations of Daqua and Kephria, allies whose governments had grievances against Tessia, officially announced that one or both of the two would stay away if the Tessian delegation attended the conference. In response, the Sami delegation officially announced that it would definitely attend if both the Daquan and Kephrian delegations stayed away.

Sami和Kephrian的代表团都没有参加某国际会议。事前，Daque和Kephria的代表团公开宣布，如果Tesian的代表团参加了这个会议，这两国中的一个或两个都会不出席会议，Daque和Kephroa的政府是强烈反对Tessia的联盟。与此相应，Sami的代表团公开宣布，如果Daquan与Kephiria代表团都不出席的话，Sami代表团就一定

If the statements given are all true and all the delegations adhered to their official announcements, it must also be true that the

(A) Daquan delegation attended the conference.

(B) Daquan delegation did not attend the conference.

(C) Sami government had no grievance against Tessia.

(D) Tessian delegation did not attend the conference.

(E) Tessian delegation made no official announcement regarding its attendance at the conference.

15. On turning 65 years old, everyone living in the town of Malton becomes eligible to receive a card that guarantees discounts on most goods and services sold in the town. Census records for 1990 show that 2,450 inhabitants of Malton turned 64 in that year. Yet, in 1991 over 3,000 people applied for and properly received discount cards. So clearly some of Malton's population growth between 1990 and 1992 must be attributable to migration into the city by people in their mid-60's.

Which of the following is an assumption on which the argument depends?

(A) The town of Malton has no complete census records for 1991.

(B) The overall size of the population of Malton grew by over 500 during 1990.

(C) Fewer people applied for and received discount cards in 1991 than did so in 1992.

(D) Among the people 65 years old or older who moved into Malton in 1991, there was no one who did not apply for a discount card.

(E) In general, people who applied for and received discount cards in 1991 first became eligible to do so in that year.

出席会议。

如果上面陈述正确，且所有的代表团都信守其公开声明，下面也一定正确的是：

(A) Daquan代表团参加了会议。

(B) Daquan代表团没有参加会议。

(C) Sami政府没有强烈地敌对Tessia。

(D) Tessian代表团没有参加会议。

(E) Tessian代表团没有针对是否参加会议发表过公开声明。

所有居住在Malton城的人在到达65岁以后都有权得到一张卡，保障他们对城中所售的大多数商品和服务享有折扣。1990年的人口普查记录显示，Malton城有2450的居民那一年到达了64岁，然而在1991年的时候，有超过3000人申请并合理地得到了折扣卡。因此，显而易见，1990年至1992年间Malton的人口增长肯定部分来源于六十多岁的人向该城的移民。

上面论述是基于下列哪项假设？

(A) Aalton城1991年没有完全的人口普查记录。

(B) Malton的人口总规模在1990年期间增长了不止500人。

(C) 1991年申请并得到折扣卡的人比1992年少。

(D) 1991年移居Malton的65岁或以上的人中，没有人没有申请过折扣卡。

(E) 总的来说，1991年申请并得到折扣卡的人在那一年是第一次有权申请该卡。

参考答案：

1. D	2. B	3. A	4. A	5. B
6. B	7. E	8. E	9. D	10. B
11. A	12. D	13. B	14. A	15. E

1. **解析**：本题推理为"因为1930年Brandon已经63岁了，然而画中的年轻黑发男子显然是Brandon本人，所以将Brandon的这幅画像的时间定位在1930年必定错误"。(D)指出Brandon在63岁时，不可能在画中将自己画成年轻时的样子，表明上面推理的原因A确实可能且有意义，因此可以作为一个很好的假设。若将(D)取非，即Brandon在63岁时可能在画中将自己画成年轻时的样子，那么将Brandon的这幅自画像定位在1930年必定错误这一结论受到质疑。所以(D)正确。

2. **解析**：本题实际上属于逻辑应用与技法类题目，并且这类推理范式已考查过许多。一般地，当由局部（纽约遇见的芭蕾舞教师）推至一般（美国的芭蕾舞教师）时，结论的正确所必须依据的假设是局部不特殊或局部具有代表性。(B)指出该论述假设该批评家在其去年去纽约时遇见的教师群在这类教师中具有典型代表性，从而指出了该批评家在推理过程中所使用的一项有疑问的假设。(A)并不能作为一个假设；(C)是上面段落中未提到的新比较；(D)、(E)均不沾边。

3. **解析**：本题为反对题型，上面推理是：统计资料表明包括小偷小摸在内的各种偷盗报告普遍减少，因此4年前的重组有效，属于"B，A"型。反对多用"有他因"来反对。(A)指出当警察局被认为不负责时，偷盗的受害者不愿意向警察局报告偷盗事故，从而说明了偷盗报告减少是有其他原因的，所以(A)反对了结论；(B)为明显支持选项；(C)探讨的是其他城市情况，与我们讨论的城市无关；(D)与"重组有效与否"无关；(E)探讨的是"重组之前的4年"而非"4年之前的重组"，所以也为无关选项。

4. **解析**：本题作为归纳题型，重点要把握其逻辑层次结构及推理关系。注意"but such courses can do so only for those people with managerial talent"表示those people with managerial talent是such courses can do so 的必要条件。(A)与上面段落的推理结构相吻合，所以(A)正确。

5. **解析**：本题为支持题型，相对阅读难度较小，(B)说明由于基因的不同和对酒精的抵抗能力的差异，一些人在高血液酒精含量时所受的运动肌肉损伤要比另一些人多，而这些人在肌肉受损伤时走直路能力受到影响，所以支持了段落里的推理；(A)、(C)、(E)都起到反对作用，(D)无关。

6. **解析**：本题属于"B，A"类型的支持，基本推理是天窗允许阳光射入进而导致销量增加。(B)说明在商场夜间开放时，天窗下面的各部门无阳光射入，那么其销售额也并不比其他部门高，我们明显感觉出(B)符合"无因就无果"的支持思路。

7. **解析**：本题属于归纳题型，重在把握逻辑层次结构。段落第一句表明建立巨大防护墙可避免海边建筑免遭海洋风暴的袭击，第二句表明若这样，那么不仅遮住了一些海景，而且使海岸本身也变窄了。很明显，对于一个想要维护自己海滩疗养功能的海边社区来说，通过建筑防海墙来保护海边建筑的话，同时将使海岸本身变窄，所以(E)正确。

8. **解析**：本题属于"B，A"型，反对的思路是"有他因"。(E)指出1985年调查有牙洞的孩子减少是因为1985年调查的孩子要比1970年调查的孩子要小，因此使得段落推理结论"孩子中的牙病水平降低了"被削弱；(A)、(B)与"牙病水平的降低"无关；(C)没有区分1970年与1985年；(D)起到了支持作用。

9. **解析**：本题属于二人对话类的逻辑应用与技法题型，让我们寻求描述Karen针对David的回答要点的一个选项，因此读题重点应放在第二人Karen上。(D)选项很好地描述Karen的回答，所以(D)正确；(A)为David想表述的意思；(B)与"未来价值"无关；(C)、(E)都为新的比较，必然不对。

10. **解析**：本题属于"逻辑应用与技法"题型，寻找一个描述Louise反驳Roger的选项。第一个人Roger认为阅读导致近视眼，而第二个人Louise认为看远处景物有困难的孩子最有可能选择需要从近处观看物体的活动，如阅读，换而言之，近视导致阅读。(B)说明论证Roger的声明中某一现象的原因（近视）实际上是该现象的结果，很好地描述了这一特点，所以(B)正确。

11. **解析**：本题属于数学相关类的归纳题型。很明显，对每单位再生资源的能源的消费征收税额既定，而引入此税后，每年对此能源的消费减少，所以稍运用数学思维，即知(A)正确，即由该能源所征的税收不断减少；(B)探讨的是每年消费的能源总量，范围过大；(C)、(D)、(E)中均有新概念"renewable energy"，归纳中必然不对。

12. **解析**：本题要求寻求一个选项，解释为什么骑自行车娱乐的人多了，但涉及自行车的事故却少了。(D)表明Parkville的交通法规更为严厉，而且骑自行车进行娱乐的人要通过一项自行车安全课程，这两者都可以导致涉及自行车的事故减少，所以(D)正确。

13. **解析**：本题属于典型的"B，A"类型的反对。反对思路是"除了A之外有其他原因导致B"。(B)说明电话线工人接触了过量的化学溶液，而这足以导致脑癌，表明"过量的化学溶液导致脑癌"，很好地用"有他因"来反对上面的结论。(A)只是提供了一种不可行的解决方案，不能起到反对的作用；(C)谈的是另外一个对象"白血症"与"脑癌"无关；(D)什么也说明不了；(E)起到了支持作用。

14. **解析**：本题与1996年10月GRE北美试题Section 6的23题相类似，但本题段落推理关系更复杂。假定用S、K、D、T分别代表Sami, Kephrian, Daque, Tessian代表团参加会议，$\overline{S}$、$\overline{K}$、$\overline{D}$、$\overline{T}$分别代表这些代表团不参加会议，则本题推理为：T→$\overline{D}$+K；$\overline{D}$ $\overline{K}$→S，现在让我们推证的是$\overline{S}$ $\overline{K}$→?稍加分析不难发现，$\overline{S}$ $\overline{K}$→D，因此(A)正确，请注意此类题的思维。

15. **解析**：本题数字比较多，因此很多人在做题时产生了困惑。实际上，本题属于"B，A"型的假设，基本思路应为没有他因。(E)说明1991年没有那些以前有权申请该卡却没有申请的人，指出了段落结论成立的一个必要条件，若对(E)取非，那么就表明1991年相比较1990年出乎意外的500多人是由于那些早已有权利申请但却没有申请的Malton城的人，那么结论必将错误。因此(E)正确；(A)、(B)均为无关选项；(C)为新的比较；(D)易误选，但(D)只说明1991年移居的65岁或以上人中都申请了折扣卡，如果对(D)取非，那么就表明有人没有申请，但上面结论仍然可以成立，因此(D)最多可作为一个支持。

六、GMAT考前逻辑推理冲刺训练试题及解析（六）

1. The Chanterelle, a type of wild mushroom, grows beneath host trees such as the Douglas fir, which provide it with necessary sugars. The underground filaments of Chanterelles, which extract the sugars, in turn provide nutrients and water for their hosts. Because of this mutually beneficial relationship, harvesting the chanterelles growing beneath a Douglas fir seriously endangers the tree.

Which of the following, if true, casts the most doubt on the conclusion drawn above?

(A) The number of wild mushrooms harvested has increased in recent years.

(B) Chanterelles grow not only beneath Douglas firs but also beneath other host trees.

(C) Many types of wild mushrooms are found only in forests and cannot easily be grown elsewhere.

(D) The harvesting of wild mushrooms stimulates future growth of those mushrooms.

(E) Young Douglas fir seedlings die without the nutrients and water provided by Chanterelle filaments.

Chanterelie是一种野生的蘑菇，生长在能为它提供所需糖分的寄主树木——例如道格拉斯冷杉下面。反过来，chanterelle在地下的根茎细丝可以分解这些糖分并为其寄主提供养分和水分。正是因为这种互惠的关系，采割道格拉斯冷杉下面生长的Chanterelle会给这种树木造成严重的伤害。

下面哪一个，如果正确，对上面的结论提出了最强有力的质疑？

(A) 近年来，野生蘑菇的采割数量一直在增加。

(B) Chanterelle不仅生长在道格拉斯冷杉树下，也生长在其他寄主树木下面。

(C) 许多种野生蘑菇只能在森林里找到，它们不能轻易在别处被种植。

(D) 对野生蘑菇的采割激发了这些蘑菇将来的生长。

(E) 如果离开了Chanterelle根茎细丝所提供的养分和水分，幼小的道格拉斯冷杉树种就会死掉。

2. The reason much refrigerated food spoils is that it ends up out of sight at the back of the shelf. So why not have round shelves that rotate? Because such rotating shelves would have just the same sort of drawback, since things would fall off the shelves' edges into the rear corners.

Which of the following is presupposed in the argument

很多冷藏食品腐坏的原因是这些食品在搁板后面变坏却看不见。那么为何不使用能旋转的圆形搁板呢？因为搁板上的东西可能从搁板边上掉到后面的角落去，从而这些搁板会具有同样的缺陷。

在反对引入旋转搁板的论证中，下面

against introducing rotating shelves?

(A) Refrigerators would not be made so that their interior space is cylindrical.

(B) Refrigerators would not be made to have a window in front for easy viewing of their contents without opening the door.

(C) The problem of spoilage of refrigerated food is not amenable to any solution based on design changes.

(D) Refrigerators are so well designed that there are bound to be drawbacks to any design change.

(E) Rotating shelves would be designed to rotate only while the refrigerator door was open.

哪个是被预先假定的？

(A) 无法制造出使其内部空间呈圆柱形的冰箱。

(B) 无法制造出前端有窗户、不用开门就可以观测到内部情况的冰箱。

(C) 靠改变外形的任何方法都无法解决冷藏食品腐坏的问题。

(D) 冰箱已经被设计得足够完美，任何设计上的改变都不可避免地会有缺陷。

(E) 旋转搁板会被设计成只有冰箱门打开时才能旋转。

3. It would cost Rosetown one million dollars to repair all of its roads. In the year after completion of those repairs, however, Rosetown would thereby avoid incurring three million dollars worth of damages, since currently Rosetown pays that amount annually in compensation for damage done to cars each year by its unrepaired roads.

Which of the following, if true, gives the strongest support to the argument above?

(A) Communities bordering on Rosetown also pay compensation for damage done to cars by their unrepaired roads.

(B) After any Rosetown road had been repaired, several years will elapse before that road begins to damage cars.

(C) Rosetown would need to raise additional taxes if it were to spend one million dollars in one year on road repairs.

(D) The degree of damage caused to Rosetown's roads by harsh weather can vary widely from year to year.

(E) Trucks cause much of the wear on Rosetown's roads, but owners of cars file almost all of the claims for compensation for damage caused by unrepaired roads.

罗斯镇修缮其所有的道路需要花费100万美元。但是在这些道路修缮完成之后的1年内，罗斯镇可以因此避免承担300万美元的损失，因为这个数目是现在罗斯镇每年对没有修缮的道路造成的汽车损害的赔偿额。

下面哪个，如果正确，对以上的论证提供了最强有力的支持？

(A) 与罗斯镇毗邻的社区同样对它们的道路所造成的汽车损害给予赔偿。

(B) 罗斯镇所有的道路都得到修缮之后，几年内不会出现道路损害汽车的情况。

(C) 如果罗斯镇要在1年内花费100万美元用于道路修缮，它就需要提高附加税。

(D) 恶劣的气候给罗斯镇的道路带来的损害程度各年之间相差很大。

(E) 卡车给罗斯镇的道路造成了很大的损耗，但几乎所有的对未经修缮的道路造成的损害提出赔偿要求的都是汽车主。

4. Two experimental garden plots were each planted with the same number of tomato plants. Magnesium salts were added to the first plot but not to the second. The first plot produced 20 pounds of tomatoes and the second plot produced 10 pounds. Since nothing else but water was added to either plot, the higher yields in the first plot must have been due to the magnesium salts.

Which of the following, if true, most seriously weakens the argument above?

在两块试验菜圃里每块种上相同数量的西红柿苗。给第一块菜圃加入镁盐但不给第二块加。第一块菜圃产出了20磅西红柿，第二块菜圃产出了10磅。因为除了水以外没有向哪块菜圃加入其他任何东西，第一块菜圃较高的产量必然是由于镁盐。

下面哪个，如果正确，最严重地削弱了以上的论证？

(A) 少量的镁盐从第一块菜圃渗入了第二

(A) A small amount of the magnesium salts from the first plot leached into the second plot.

(B) Tomato plants in a third experimental plot, to which a high-nitrogen fertilizer was added, but no magnesium salts, produced 15 pounds of tomatoes.

(C) Four different types of tomatoes were grown in equal proportions in each of the plots.

(D) Some weeds that compete with tomatoes cannot tolerate high amounts of magnesium salts in the soil.

(E) The two experimental plots differed from each other with respect to soil texture and exposure to sunlight.

5. Archaeologists have found wheeled ceramic toys made by the Toltec, twelfth-century inhabitants of what is now Veracruz. Although there is no archaeological evidence that the Toltec used wheels for anything but toys, some anthropologists hypothesize that wheeled utility vehicles were used to carry materials needed for the monumental structures the Toltec produced.

Which of the following, if true, would most help the anthropologists explain the lack of evidence noted above?

(A) The Toltec sometimes incorporated into their toys representations of utensils or other devices that served some practical purpose.

(B) Any wheeled utility vehicles used by the Toltec could have been made entirely of wood, and unlike ceramic, wood decays rapidly in the humid climate of Veracruz.

(C) Carvings in monument walls suggest that the Toltec's wheeled ceramic toys sometimes had ritual uses in addition to being used by both children and adults as decorations and playthings.

(D) Wheeled utility vehicles were used during the twelfth century in many areas of the world, but during this time wheeled toys were not very common in areas outside Veracruz.

(E) Some of the wheeled ceramic toys were found near the remains of monumental structures.

6. Demographers doing research for an international economics newsletter claim that the average per capita income in the country of Kuptala is substantially lower than that in the country of Bahlton. They also claim, however, that whereas poverty is relatively rare in Kuptala, over half the

块菜圃。

(B) 第三块菜圃加入了一种高氮肥料，但没有加镁盐，产出了15磅西红柿。

(C) 在每块菜圃中以相同份额种植了四种不同的西红柿。

(D) 有些与西红柿竞争生长的野草不能忍受土壤里大量的镁盐。

(E) 这两块试验菜圃的土质和日照量不同。

考古学家们已经发现了Toltec人——12世纪居住在现在称为维拉克鲁斯的居民——所制造的有轮子的陶瓷玩具。虽然还没有考古证明Toltec人除了玩具使用过轮子外，一些考古学家估计有轮的货车曾经被用来运送Toltec人建造纪念建筑所需要的材料。

下面哪个，如果正确，最能帮助考古学家们解释上文提到的证据缺乏的原因？

(A) Toltec人有时把器皿或其他有实际用途的装置的代表物结合到他们的玩具中去。

(B) Toltec人使用的任何有轮货车可能都是用木头制造的，和陶瓷不同，在维拉克鲁斯那样潮湿的气候下，木头会很快腐坏。

(C) 纪念墙壁上的雕刻显示，Toltec人的有轮陶瓷玩具除了被儿童和成年人用来做装饰品和玩物外，有时也具有宗教用途。

(D) 在20世纪，世界上很多地区使用有轮货车，但这一时期在维拉克鲁斯以外的地区，有轮的玩具并不很常见。

(E) 纪念建筑遗址附近发现了一些有轮的陶瓷玩具。

为一份国际经济学时事通讯做调研的人口统计学家们宣称，Kuptala的人均收入远远低于Bahlton的人均收入，但他们同时宣称，Kuptala的贫困现象相对很少，而Bahlton却有过半的人口生活在极端的贫困

population of Bahlton lives in extreme poverty. At least one of the demographers' claims must, therefore, be wrong.

The argument above is most vulnerable to which of the following criticisms?

(A) It rejects an empirical claim about the average per capita incomes in the two countries without making any attempt to discredit that claim by offering additional economic evidence.

(B) It treats the vague term "poverty" as thought it had a precise and universally accepted meaning.

(C) It overlooks the possibility that the number of people in the two countries who live in poverty could be the same even though the percentages of the two populations that live in poverty differ markedly.

(D) It fails to show that wealth and poverty have the same social significance in Kuptala as in Bahlton.

(E) It does not consider the possibility that incomes in Kuptala, unlike those in Bahlton, might all be very close to the country's average per capita income.

7. Normally, increases in the price of a product decrease its sales except when the price increase accompanies an improvement in the product. Wine is unusual, however. Often increases in the price of a particular producer's wine will result in increased sales, even when the wine itself is unchanged.

Which of the following, if true, does most to explain the anomaly described above?

(A) The retail wine market is characterized by an extremely wide range of competing products.

(B) Many consumers make decisions about which wines to purchase on the basis of reviews of wine published in books and periodicals.

(C) Consumers selecting wine in a store often use the price charged as their main guide to the wine's quality.

(D) Wine retailers and producers can generally increase the sales of a particular wine temporarily by introducing a price discount.

(E) Consumers who purchase wine regularly generally have strong opinions about which wines they prefer.

8. The recent decline in land prices has hurt many institutions that had invested heavily in real estate. Last year, before

状态。所以，人口统计学家们的观点至少有一种是错误的。

以上的论证最易受到下面哪个批评意见的攻击？

(A) 它拒绝了关于两国人均收入的经验性观点，没有尝试提供更多的经济证据来否定那种观点。

(B) 它把"贫困"这一模糊概念处理成似乎其已经有了一种精确和公认的意思。

(C) 它忽视了一种可能性，也就是即使两个国家中生活在贫困状态中的人口比例不同，这两个国家中生活在贫困状态的人口数量也许是相同的。

(D) 它未能表明财富和贫困在Kuptala和Bahlton具有相同的社会意义。

(E) 它没有考虑到这种可能性，即和在Bahlton的收入不一样，在Kuptala所有人的收入也许非常接近该国的人均收入。

一般来讲，某种产品价格的上升会减少其销量，除非价格上升同时伴随着该种产品质量的改进。但是，葡萄酒是例外的。某个特定生产商的葡萄酒价格上升往往会导致其销量的增加，尽管葡萄酒本身没有变化。

下面哪个，如果正确，最能解释以上描述的反常现象？

(A) 葡萄酒零售市场竞争性产品的类型极其广泛。

(B) 许多消费者在决定购买那种葡萄酒时，根据的是书籍和期刊上的评价。

(C) 在店铺里选购葡萄酒的消费者利用标价来作为判断葡萄酒质量的指导。

(D) 葡萄酒零售商和生产者一般可以通过价格折扣来暂时增加某种葡萄酒的销量。

(E) 定期购买葡萄酒的消费者普遍对自己偏好哪种葡萄酒有固定的看法。

近期土地价格的下跌已经使许多在房地产上大量投资的机构受到了损害。去

the decline began, a local college added 2,000 acres to its holdings. The college, however, did not purchase the land but received it as a gift. Therefore the price decline will probably not affect the college.

Which of the following, if true, casts most doubt on the conclusion above?

(A) The 2,000 acres that the college was given last year are located within the same community as the college itself.

(B) The college usually receives more contributions of money than of real estate.

(C) Land prices in the region in which the college is located are currently higher than the national average.

(D) Last year, the amount that the college allocated to pay for renovations included money it expected to receive by selling some of its land this year.

(E) Last year, the college paid no property taxes on land occupied by college buildings but instead paid fees to compensate the local government for services provided.

9. Civil trials often involve great complexities that are beyond the capacities of jurors to understand. As a result, jurors' decisions in such trials are frequently incorrect. Justice would therefore be better served if the more complex trials were decided by judges rather than juries.

The argument above depends on which of the following assumptions?

(A) A majority of civil trials involve complexities that jurors are not capable of understanding.

(B) The judges who would decide complex civil trials would be better able to understand the complexities of those trials than jurors are.

(C) The judges who would preside over civil trials would disallow the most complex sorts of evidence from being introduced into those trials.

(D) Jurors' decisions are frequently incorrect even in those civil trials that do not involve great complexities.

(E) The sole reason in favor of having juries decide civil trials is the supposition that their decisions will almost always be correct.

10. Some species of dolphins find their prey by echolocation; they emit clicking sounds and listen for echoes returning from distant objects in the water. Marine biologists have speculated that those same clicking sounds might have a second function:

年，在这次价格下跌尚未开始的时候，一所地方大学为其资产增加了2000英亩的土地。当然，这所大学并未购买这块土地，而是作为馈赠接受下来的。所以价格下降并没有影响到该大学。

下面哪个，如果正确，对以上的结论提出了最严重的质疑？

(A) 去年给予这所大学的2000英亩土地与该所大学处于同一社区。

(B) 与房地产馈赠相比，这所大学经常接受更多的资金捐赠。

(C) 这所大学所处地区目前的土地价格要高于全国的平均水平。

(D) 去年，这所大学预算用来进行翻修的资金包括今年出售一些土地的预期收入。

(E) 去年，这所大学没有交纳学校建筑物所占土地的地产税，相反却付费补偿地方政府所提供的服务。

民事审判常常包括许多在陪审员理解能力之外的复杂细节。结果是，在这些审判中陪审员们的判决往往是不正确的。所以，比较复杂的审判如果由法官而非陪审团来判决，公平会得到更好的体现。

上面的论证依赖于下面哪个假设？

(A) 大多数民事审判包括了陪审员无法理解的复杂因素。

(B) 对复杂的民事审判进行判决的法官比陪审团更能理解这些审判中的复杂细节。

(C) 主持民事审判的法官不会允许在这些审判中提供最复杂的那类证据。

(D) 即使在那些不包括很多复杂细节的民事审判中，陪审员们的判决通常也是不正确的。

(E) 支持让陪审团对民事审判进行判决的唯一理由是这样一种假定，即它们的判决基本上总是正确的。

某些种类的海豚通过回声定位来寻找猎物；它们在水中发出咔哒声并且听从远处物体返回的回声。海洋生物学家们推测这些相同的咔哒声也许还具有第二种功

particularly loud clicks might be used by the dolphins to stun their prey at close range through sensory overload.

Which of the following, if discovered to be true, would cast the most serious doubt on the correctness of the speculation described above?

(A) Dolphins that use echolocation to locate distant prey also emit frequent clicks at intermediate distances as they close in on their prey.

(B) The usefulness of echolocation as a means of locating prey depends on the clicking sounds being of a type that the prey is incapable of perceiving, regardless of volume.

(C) If dolphins stun their prey, the effect is bound to be so temporary that stunning from far away, even if possible, would be ineffective.

(D) Echolocation appears to give dolphins that use it information about the richness of a source of food as well as about its direction.

(E) The more distant a dolphin's prey, the louder the echolocation clicks must be if they are to reveal the prey's presence to the hunting dolphin.

11. Advertisement:

The world's best coffee beans come from Colombia. The more Colombian beans in a blend of coffee, the better the blend, and no company purchases more Colombian beans than Kreemo Coffee. Inc. So it only stands to reason that if you buy a can of Kreemo's coffee, you're buying the best blended coffee available today.

The reasoning of the argument in the advertisement is flawed because it overlooks the possibility that

(A) the equipment used by Kreemo to blend and package its coffee is no different from that used by most other coffee producers.

(B) not all of Kreemo's competitors use Colombian coffee beans in the blends of coffee they sell.

(C) Kreemo sells more coffee than does any other company.

(D) Kreemo's coffee is the most expensive blended coffee available today.

(E) the best unblended coffee is better than the best blended coffee.

能：特别高的咔哒声可能被海豚们用来使它们在近距离的猎物由于感官的过度负荷而失去知觉。

下面哪个，如果发现是正确的，对以上描述的推测的正确性提出了最严重的质疑？

(A) 使用回声定位来确定远处猎物位置的海豚们在进攻猎物时，也会在中等距离时发出频繁的咔哒声。

(B) 回声定位作为确定猎物位置的方法，其有效性依赖于猎物是不能感受到这种声波的，而与音量无关。

(C) 如果海豚们攻击它们的猎物，(回声定位的)效果是暂时性的，所以即使可能，从远处进行攻击也会是无效的。

(D) 回声定位给使用这种方法的海豚们提供了食物源丰富程度和方向的信息。

(E) 海豚的猎物距离越远，捕猎的海豚要想发现猎物的存在，就必须发出越高的回声定位的咔哒声。

广告：

世界最好的咖啡豆来自哥伦比亚。一种混合咖啡中含有的哥伦比亚咖啡豆越多，这种混合咖啡就越棒，而没有哪家公司比Kreemo咖啡有限公司购买了更多的哥伦比亚咖啡豆。所以，毫无疑问，如果你购买了一罐Kreemo的咖啡，你就买了现在可以买到的最好的混合咖啡。

这则广告中的论证推理过程是有缺陷的，因为它忽视了这种可能性：

(A) Kreemo用来混合和包装其咖啡的设备与其他咖啡生产者所使用的设备毫无区别。

(B) 并非所有Kreemo的竞争对手在他们销售的混合咖啡中都使用哥伦比亚咖啡豆。

(C) Kreemo比其他公司销售更多的咖啡。

(D) Kreemo的咖啡是目前可以买到的最贵的混合咖啡。

(E) 最好的未经混合的咖啡要比最好的混合咖啡棒。

12. The only purpose for which a particular type of tape is needed is to hold certain surgical wounds closed for ten days—the maximum time such wounds need tape. Newtape is a new brand of this type of tape. Newtape's salespeople claim that Newtape will improve healing because Newtape adheres twice as long as the currently used tape does.

Which of the following statements, if true, would most seriously call into question the claim made by Newtape's salespeople?

(A) Most surgical wounds take about ten days to heal.

(B) Most surgical tape is purchased by hospitals and clinics rather than by individual surgeons.

(C) The currently used tape's adhesiveness is more than sufficient to hold wounds closed for ten days.

(D) Neither Newtape nor the currently used tape adheres well to skin that has not been cleaned.

(E) Newtape's adhesion to skin that has been coated with a special chemical preparation is only half as good as the currently used tape's adhesion to such coated skin.

13. A severe drought can actually lessen the total amount of government aid that United States farmers receive as a group. The government pays farmers the amount, if any, by which the market price at which crops are actually sold falls short of a preset target price per bushel for the crops. The drought of 1983, for example, caused farm-program payments to drop by $10 billion.

Given the information above, which of the following, if true, best explains why the drought of 1983 resulted in a reduction in farm-program payments?

(A) Prior to the drought of 1983, the government raised the target price for crops in order to aid farmers in reducing their debt loads.

(B) Due to the drought of 1983, United States farmers exported less food in 1983 than in the preceding year.

(C) Due to the drought of 1983, United States farmers had smaller harvests and thus received a higher market price for the 1983 crop than for the larger crop of the preceding year.

(D) Due to the drought of 1983, United States farmers planned to plant smaller crops in 1984 than they had in 1983.

需要一种特殊棉纱带的唯一目的是把某些外科伤口包扎10天——这些伤口需要包扎的最多天数。Newtape是这种棉纱带的一个新品牌。Newtape的销售人员声称Newtape会有助于伤口愈合，因为Newtape的粘附能力是现在使用的棉纱带的2倍。

下面哪种说法，如果正确，会对Newtape的销售人员的声明提出最严重的疑问？

(A) 大多数外科伤口大约需要10天愈合。

(B) 大多数外科棉纱带是由医院和诊所而非私人外科医生购买的。

(C) 现在使用的棉纱带的粘附能力远超过包扎伤口10天所需的足够的粘附能力。

(D) Newtape和现在使用的棉纱带都不能很好地粘附未经洁净的皮肤。

(E) Newtape对已涂上一种特别化学药剂的皮肤的粘附能力仅为现在使用的棉纱带对那种皮肤的粘附能力的一半好。

一场严重的旱灾事实上会减少美国农民作为整体所得到的政府补助总额。如果有的话，政府支付给农民的补助是每蒲式耳粮食实际出售时的市场价格与预定目标价格之差。例如1983年的旱灾，使农场计划的支付额减少了100亿美元。

给定以上的信息，下面哪个，如果正确，最好地解释了为什么1983年的干旱导致了农场计划支付额的减少？

(A) 在1983年以前，政府为了帮助农民减少他们的债务负担而提高了粮食的目标价格。

(B) 由于1983年的干旱，美国的农民出口的食品在1983年比以前的年份减少了。

(C) 由于1983年的干旱，美国农民的收成变少了，从而1983年的粮食比以往粮食较多的年份获得了更高的市场价格。

(D) 由于1983年的干旱，美国农民计划在1984年种植比1983年更少的粮食。

(E) 尽管出现了１９８３年的干旱，

(E) Despite the drought of 1983, retail prices for food did not increase significantly between 1982 and 1983.

14. In order to increase revenues, an airport plans to change the parking fees it charges at its hourly parking lots. Rather than charging $2.00 for the first two-hour period, or part thereof, and $1.00 for each hour thereafter, the airport will charge $4.00 for the first four-hour period, or part thereof, and $1.00 for each hour thereafter.

Which of the following is a consideration that, if true, suggests that the plan will be successful in increasing revenues?

(A) Very few people who park their cars at the hourly parking lot at the airport leave their cars for more than two hours at a time.

(B) Over the past several years, the cost to the airport of operating its hourly parking facilities has been greater than the revenues it has received from them.

(C) People who leave their cars at the airport while on a trip generally park their cars in lots that charge by the day rather than by the hour.

(D) A significant portion of the money spent to operate the airport parking lot is spent to maintain the facilities rather than to pay the salaries of the personnel who collect the parking fees.

(E) The hourly parking lots at the airport have recently been expanded and are therefore rarely filled to capacity.

15. In the course of her researches, a historian recently found two documents mentioning the same person, Erich Schnitzler. One, dated May 3, 1739, is a record of Schnitzler's arrest for peddling without a license. The second, undated, is a statement by Schnitzler asserting that he has been peddling off and on for 20 years.

The facts above best support which of the following conclusions?

(A) Schnitzler started peddling around 1719.

(B) Schnitzler was arrested repeatedly for peddling.

(C) The undated document was written before 1765.

(D) The arrest record was written after the undated document.

(E) The arrest record provides better evidence that Schnitzler peddled than does the undated document.

1982～1983年间的食品价格并未明显上涨。

为了增加收入，一家机场计划改变其计时停车区收取的停车费。机场会在第一个4小时或不到4小时期间收取4美元，而后每小时收取1美元；而不是在第一个2小时或不到2小时其间收取2美元，而后每小时收取1美元。

下面哪种考虑，如果正确，表明该计划可以成功地增加收入？

(A) 很少有人会在机场的计时停车区内一次停车超过2小时。

(B) 在过去的几年内，机场运营其计时停车设备的成本要高于从中获得的收入。

(C) 把车停在机场进行短途旅行的人通常把车停在按天计费而非按时计费的停车区内。

(D) 用来运营机场停车区的资金很大一部分被用来维护设备而不是支付收取停车费的职工工资。

(E) 机场的计时停车区最近被扩展了，所以很少能发挥全部容量。

最近，一位历史学家在研究的过程中，发现了两份提到同一个人——Erich Schnitzler's的资料，其中一份标明的日期是1739年5月3日，是一份Schnitzler由于未经允许沿街叫卖而被逮捕的记录。第二份未标明日期，是一份Schnitzler宣称他已经断断续续地沿街叫卖20年的声明。

以上的事实最好地支持了以下那个结论？

(A) Schnitzler在1719年前后开始沿街叫卖。

(B) Schnitzler 因为沿街叫卖而不断被捕。

(C) 未标明日期的那份记录书写时间是在1765年之前。

(D) 逮捕记录在未标明日期之后被书写。

(E) 逮捕记录比未标明日期的文件更好地证明了Schnitzler曾经沿街叫卖。

16. The recent upheaval in the office-equipment retail business, in which many small firms have gone out of business, has been attributed to the advent of office equipment "superstores" whose high sales volume keeps their prices low. This analysis is flawed, however, since even today the superstores control a very small share of the retail market.

Which of the following, if true, would most weaken the argument that the analysis is flawed?

(A) Most of the larger customers for office equipment purchase under contract directly from manufacturers and thus do not participate in the retail market.

(B) The superstores' heavy advertising of their low prices has forced prices down throughout the retail market for office supplies.

(C) Some of the superstores that only recently opened have themselves gone out of business.

(D) Most of the office equipment superstores are owned by large retailing chains that also own stores selling other types of goods.

(E) The growing importance of computers in most offices has changed the kind of office equipment retailers must stock.

办公设备零售业——其中许多小企业已经破产——最近的巨变被归因于办公设备"超级商店"的到来，这些商店的高销售规模保证了低价格。但是，这种分析是有缺陷的，因为即使在今天超级商店也只控制了零售市场中很小的份额。

下面哪个，如果正确，会最大程度地削弱认为这种分析具有缺陷的论证？

(A) 大多数较大的办公设备可通过合同直接从制造商那里购买，从而并不参与零售市场。

(B) 超级商店对它们的低价格进行的大规模广告已经促使整个办公用品零售市场的价格降低了。

(C) 最近刚刚开张的一些超级商店自己已经破产了。

(D) 大多数办公设备超级商店由大型零售连锁集团拥有，这些连锁集团也拥有销售其他种类商品的商店。

(E) 计算机在大多数办公室里的重要性的不断提升已经改变了办公设备零售商必须贮存的货物类型。

参考答案：

1. D	2. A	3. B	4. E	5. B
6. E	7. C	8. D	9. B	10. B
11. C	12. C	13. C	14. A	15. C
16. B				

1. **解析：** 本题问题目的是让我们反对结论，因此可用结论中的关键词"harvesting the Chanterelles"即"harvesting the wild mushroom"来定位选项，发现(A)、(D)有此关键词。如果对野生蘑菇的采割激发了这些蘑菇未来的生长，正如(D)所说，那么说明采割这些蘑菇并不会给那些树木造成伤害，因此起到了反对作用，所以(D)正确；而(A)只说明近年来蘑菇采割数量在增加，但没有说明采割以后怎么样，所以对结论不能起到任何作用。

2. **解析：** 本题为假设题型，presupposed = assumed，如果可以制造出使其内部呈圆柱形的冰箱，那么旋转的圆形搁板上的东西则不掉到邻近角落去，那么上面结论就不正确。所以(A)是一个很好的假设；(E)易误选，但(E)只表明旋转搁板设计为旋转所需的必要条件，但与"round rotating shelves"无关，所以(E)不正确。

3. **解析：** 如果罗斯镇的道路在修缮之后，几年之内不会出现道路损害汽车的情况，如(B)所说，那么罗斯镇可以避免承担对道路修缮之前对汽车损害的赔偿，所以(B)支持了段落论据，因此(B)正确，而(A)、(B)、(C)、(D)都是无关选项。

4. **解析：** 本题属于典型的"B，A"型，由一experiment得出结论，且结论用来解释experiment，寻求反对，多为"有其他原因"。(E)指出这两块试验菜圃的土质与日照量不同，从而用"有其他原因"解释了第一块菜圃较高产量的原因。所以(E)正确。

5. **解析**：读明白问题永远是解题时最重要的。本题让我们去寻求选项来帮助考古学家解释段落中所提到的证据的缺乏，实际上也就是寻求一个选项去驳斥某些考古学家的估计，(B)很好地实现了问题目的，因此(B)正确；(E)易误选，但(E)与问题目的不符，所以(E)不正确。

6. **解析**：本题读题重点在however后面，并且是由一个claim得出一个结论，且用这个结论来解释claim，反对一般用"有其他原因"。(E)指出在Kuptala所有人的收入也许接近该国的人均收入，即Kuptala的每个人之间的收入差距较小，从而解释了上述claim，所以(E)正确。

7. **解析**：本题为解释反常变化，要抓住反常变化的关键点——价格来定位选项，根据"直接"的原则，(C)能很好地起到实现问题目的的作用。(D)易误选，但(D)与段落的"价格上升"相违背，所以(D)不对。

8. **解析**：读题重点为后两句话，结论是"Therefore the price decline will probably not affect the college."如果去年该大学预算用来进行翻修的资金包括出售一些土地的预期收入，正如(D)所说，那么由于今年土地的价格下跌必将导致该大学出售更多的土地，从而影响到该大学。所以(D)正确；(A)、(C)、(E)均为无关选项；(B)讨论的是一般情况，但本题讨论的是"个案"——今年土地价格下降，所以(B)不正确。

9. **解析**：本题作为假设，重点读一句话"Justice would therefore be better served if the more complex trails were decided by judges rather than juries,"我们发现这句话前后有明显的跳跃的感觉，而(B)就把"the judges who would decide complex civil trials"与"the complexities of those trials"连了起来，就可以作为一个很好的假设。所以(B)正确。

10. **解析**：通过这道题我们要培养读清楚问题与把握读题重点的好习惯。本题让我们质疑the correctness of the speculation，发现读题重点是echolocation可被用来"stun their prey at close range through sensory overload." 如果回声定位作为确定猎物位置的方法，无论音量如何，猎物不能听到，如(B)所说，那么就断开了the speculation中的前提与结论，反对了上面the correctness of the speculation，所以(B)正确；而(C)与"at close range"无关，是无关选项；(A)、(D)为无关选项；(E)从某种程度上支持了the speculation。

11. **解析**：本题属于"逻辑应用与技法"题型。推论的大前提是"混合咖啡中含有的哥伦比亚咖啡豆越多，则此混合咖啡就越好。"如果Kreemo比其他公司销售更多的咖啡，如(C)所说，那么即使Kreemo买的哥伦比亚咖啡豆最多，一罐Kreemo的咖啡里面含原哥伦比亚咖啡豆的量可能并不是最多，因此其混合咖啡最好也就受到了质疑。所以(C)通过指出上面推理的这种可能性从而说明上面推理是有缺陷的，因此(C)正确；(A)的"no different from"说的是共同点，多出现在support类的答案中；(B)中的并非所有"Kreemo的竞争对手"什么也说明不了，所以为无关选项；(D)中的expensive并不等于"the best"，所以也为无关选项；(E)是一个典型的无关比较，因此也不对。

12. **解析**：本题让我们去质疑Newtape's salespeople的宣称，因此读题点应为段落最后一句话，尤其是"because Newtape adheres twice as long as the currently used tape does"。另外，还要注意第一句里面的only，表明某棉纱带的唯一作用除了10天的时间外没有任何目的。如果现在的棉纱带粘附能力足以保持需10天愈合的伤口，如(D)所说，那就表明现在的棉纱带正是最好了，粘附时间更长的Newtape毫无意义，所以Newtape能提高治愈效果受到了质疑，因此(C)正确。由于段落中并未告知现有胶带能用多少天，所以(A)无任何意义；棉纱带由谁购买与推理无关，所以(B)不对；(D)指出的共性，多出现在support答案中；(E)易误选，但上面的第一个句子里的the only purpose表明棉纱带除了时间长短外，没有任何别的用处，所以(E)不对。

13. **解析**：解释矛盾题重点要抓住解释对象的关键词与矛盾点，本题的关键词应为1983，矛盾点应与"价格或钱"有关，寻找一个能够直接解释的现象，不能有自己的推理。通过考虑总量与单位这两方面因素，可以发现(C)实现了问题目的，所以(C)正确。

14. 解析：本题为就目的提方法的"B，A"类型，支持主要思路是"A可行或有意义"。(A)考虑了很少有人会在机场的计时停车区内一次停车超过两个小时，那么这些车的收费由原来的2美元涨至4美元，因此可以增加收入，实现目的。所以(A)正确。

15. 解析：本题属于"自上而下"的support题型。由于1739年Schnitzler由于未经允许沿街叫卖而被抓，而未标明日期的第二份资料表明Schnitzler已经断断续续地沿街叫卖了20年，所以第二份资料的书写应在1759年之前，所以(C)正确；(B)易误选，但其中的"repeatedly"从上面段落中推不出来，因此不对。

16. 解析：本题让我们去削弱段落最后一句话，且读题重点放在如何去驳斥原因。"since even today the superstores control a very small share of the retail market."(B)直接驳斥了原因；(A)、(E)与superstore无关；(C)的some为个案，并不能反对一般；(D)虽涉及superstore，但与"市场份额"和"价格"均无关，所以必然不对。

七、GMAT考前逻辑推理冲刺训练试题及解析（七）

1. A report on acid rain concluded, "Most forests in Canada are not being damaged by acid rain." Critics of the report insist the conclusion be changed to, "Most forests in Canada do not show visible symptoms of damage by acid rain, such as abnormal loss of leaves, slower rates of growth, or higher mortality."

Which of the following, if true, provides the best logical justification for the critics' insistence that the report's conclusion be changed?

(A) Some forests in Canada are being damaged by acid rain.

(B) Acid rain could be causing damage for which symptoms have not yet become visible.

(C) The report does not compare acid rain damage to Canadian forests with acid rain damage to forests in other countries.

(D) All forests in Canada have received acid rain during the past fifteen years.

(E) The severity of damage by acid rain differs from forest to forest.

一份关于酸雨的报告总结道，"加拿大的大多数森林没有被酸雨损害。"这份报告的批评者坚持认为这一结论必须改变为，"加拿大的大多数森林没有显示出明显的被酸雨损害的症状，如不正常的落叶、生长速度的减慢或者更高的死亡率。"

下面哪个，如果正确，为批评者坚持要改变报告结论提供了逻辑上最强有力的正当理由？

(A) 加拿大的一些森林正在被酸雨损害。

(B) 酸雨可能正在造成症状尚未明显的损害。

(C) 报告没有把酸雨对加拿大森林的损害与酸雨对其他国家森林的损害进行比较。

(D) 过去的15年内，加拿大所有森林都下过酸雨。

(E) 酸雨造成的损害程度在不同森林之间具有差异。

2. In the past most airline companies minimized aircraft weight to minimize fuel costs. The safest airline seats were heavy, and airlines equipped their planes with few of these seats. This year the seat that has sold best to airlines has been the safest one—a clear indication that airlines are assigning a higher priority to safe seating than to minimizing fuel costs.

Which of the following, if true, most seriously weakens the argument above?

(A) Last year's best-selling airline seat was not the safest airline seat on the market.

在过去，大多数航空公司尽量减少货物重量来使航空燃料成本最小化，最安全的客机座位很重，于是航空公司在它们的客机上装备了很少的这种座位。今年，向航空公司销售最好的座位是最安全的那种——这明显表明航空公司把安全放在了比最小化燃料成本更高的优先位置上。

下面哪个，如果正确，最严重地削弱了以上的论证？

(A) 去年最好卖的客机座位不是市场上最

(B) No airline company has announced that it would be making safe seating a higher priority this year.

(C) The price of fuel was higher this year than it had been in most of the years when the safest airline seats sold poorly.

(D) Because of increases in the cost of materials, all airline seats were more expensive to manufacture this year than in any previous year.

(E) Because of technological innovations, the safest airline seat on the market this year weighed less than most other airline seats on the market.

3. A computer equipped with signature-recognition software, which restricts access to a computer to those people whose signatures are on file, identifies a person's signature by analyzing not only the form of the signature but also such characteristics as pen pressure and signing speed. Even the most adept forgers cannot duplicate all of the characteristics the program analyzes.

Which of the following can be logically concluded from the passage above?

(A) The time it takes to record and analyze a signature makes the software impractical for everyday use.

(B) Computers equipped with the software will soon be installed in most banks.

(C) Nobody can gain access to a computer equipped with the software solely by virtue of skill at forging signatures.

(D) Signature-recognition software has taken many years to develop and perfect.

(E) In many cases even authorized users are denied legitimate access to computers equipped with the software.

4. Division manager: I want to replace the Microton computers in my division with Vitech computers.

General manager: Why?

Division manager: It costs 28 percent less to train new staff on the Vitech.

General manager: But that is not a good enough reason. We can simply hire only people who already know how to use the Microton computer.

Which of the following, if true, most seriously undermines the general manager's objection to the replacement of Microton computers with Vitechs?

安全的客机座位。

(B) 今年没有一家航空公司宣布其会把安全乘坐放在更高的优先位置。

(C) 今年的燃料价格比以往大多数最安全的座位销售不畅的年份要高。

(D) 由于原料价格的上升，所有的今年制造的座位都要比往年贵。

(E) 由于技术上的创新，今年市场上最安全的客机座位比市场上其他客机座位要轻。

一台安装了签名识别软件的电脑——这种软件仅限于那些签名在文档中的人进入计算机——不仅通过分析签名的形状，而且通过分析诸如笔尖压力和签名速度等特征来识别某人的签名。即使是最机灵的伪造者也不能复制该程序分析的所有特征。

下面哪个结论在逻辑上可以从上文得到？

(A) 记录和分析某个签名需花费的时间使这种软件的日常使用变得不现实。

(B) 安装有这种软件的计算机很快就会被大多数银行装备。

(C) 没有人可以仅通过伪造签名的技巧而进入安装了这种软件的计算机。

(D) 签名识别软件花费了很多年来进行发展和加以完善。

(E) 很多情况下，即使已经被授权的用户也会被拒绝合法进入安装有这种软件的计算机。

部门经理：我想把部门里的Microton计算机换成Vitech计算机。

总经理：为什么？

部门经理：培训新员工操作Vitech的成本可以减少28%。

总经理：但那还不是一个足够好的理由。我们可以简单地只雇用那些已经知道如何使用Microton计算机的人。

下面哪个，如果正确，最严重地削弱了总经理反对以Vitech计算机代替Microton计算机的意见？

(A) Currently all employees in the company are required to attend workshops on how to use Microton computers in new applications.

(B) Once employees learn how to use a computer, they tend to change employers more readily than before.

(C) Experienced users of Microton computers command much higher salaries than do prospective employees who have no experience in the use of computers.

(D) The average productivity of employees in the general manager's company is below the average productivity of the employees of its competitors.

(E) The high costs of replacement parts make Vitech computers more expensive to maintain than Microton computers.

5. An airplane engine manufacturer developed a new engine model with safety features lacking in the earlier model, which was still being manufactured. During the first year that both were sold, the earlier model far outsold the new model; the manufacturer thus concluded that safety was not the customers' primary consideration.

Which of the following, if true, would most seriously weaken the manufacturer's conclusion?

(A) Both private plane owners and commercial airlines buy engines from this airplane engine manufacturer.

(B) Many customers consider earlier engine models better safety risks than new engine models, since more is usually known about the safety of the earlier models.

(C) Many customers of this airplane engine manufacturer also bought airplane engines from manufacturers who did not provide additional safety features in their newer models.

(D) The newer engine model can be used in all planes in which the earlier engine model can be used.

(E) There was no significant difference in price between the newer engine model and the earlier engine model.

6. Between 1975 and 1985, nursing-home occupancy rates averaged 87 percent of capacity, while admission rates remained constant, at an average of 95 admissions per 1,000 beds per year. Between 1985 and 1988, however, occupancy rates rose to an average of 92 percent of capacity, while admission rates declined to 81 per 1,000 beds per year.

(A) 目前公司所有的员工都被要求参加学习如何使用应用中的Microton计算机。

(B) 一旦员工学会了如何使用计算机，他们就比以前更容易倾向于跳槽。

(C) 熟练使用Microton计算机的员工会比预期的没有计算机使用经验的员工要求更高的收入。

(D) 该总经理所在的公司里面员工的平均劳动生产率低于其竞争者的员工的平均劳动生产率。

(E) 替换配件的高成本使Vitech计算机的维护成本比Microton计算机要高。

一家飞机发动机制造商开发出了一种新的发动机，其所具备的安全性能是早期型号的发动机所缺乏的，而早期模型仍然在生产。在这两种型号的发动机同时被销售的第一年，早期的型号的销量超过了新型号的销量；该制造商于是得出结论认为安全性并非客户的首要考虑。

下面哪个，如果正确，会最严重地削弱该制造商的结论？

(A) 私人飞机主和商业航空公司都从这家飞机发动机制造商那里购买发动机。

(B) 许多客户认为早期的型号在安全性风险方面比新型号更小，因为他们对老型号的安全性知道得更多。

(C) 这家飞机发动机制造商的许多客户也从另一些飞机发动机制造商那里购买发动机，那些制造商在其新型号发动机中没有提供额外的安全性能。

(D) 新型号的发动机可以被所有的使用旧型号发动机的飞机使用。

(E) 在新型发动机和旧型发动机间没有重大的价格差别。

在1975~1985年间，疗养院入住比率平均为容纳能力的87%，而接受比率保持不变，每年中每1000张床位平均接受95人。在1985~1988年间，入住比率上升到平均为容纳能力的92%，而接受比率却下降到了每年中每1000张床位接受81人。

If the statements above are true, which of the following conclusions can be most properly drawn?

(A) The average length of time nursing-home residents stayed in nursing homes increased between 1985 and 1988.

(B) The proportion of older people living in nursing homes was greater in 1988 than in 1975.

(C) Nursing home admission rates tend to decline whenever occupancy rates rise.

(D) Nursing homes built prior to 1985 generally had fewer beds than did nursing homes built between 1985 and 1988.

(E) The more beds a nursing home has, the higher its occupancy rate is likely to be.

7. Firms adopting "profit-related-pay"(PRP) contracts pay wages at levels that vary with the firm's profits. In the metalworking industry last year, firms with PRP contracts in place showed productivity per worker on average 13 percent higher than that of their competitors who used more traditional contracts.

If, on the basis of the evidence above, it is argued that PRP contracts increase worker productivity, which of the following, if true, would most seriously weaken that argument?

(A) Results similar to those cited for the metalworking industry have been found in other industries where PRP contracts are used.

(B) Under PRP contracts costs other than labor costs, such as plant, machinery, and energy, make up an increased proportion of the total cost of each unit of output.

(C) Because introducing PRP contracts greatly changes individual workers' relationships to the firm, negotiating the introduction of PRP contracts is complex and time consuming.

(D) Many firms in the metalworking industry have modernized production equipment in the last five years, and most of these introduced PRP contracts at the same time.

(E) In firms in the metalworking industry where PRP contracts are in place, the average take-home pay is 15 percent higher than it is in those firms where workers have more traditional contracts.

如果以上的说法正确，下面哪一个结论可以被最合适地得出来？

(A) 疗养院中住户呆在疗养院的平均时间在1985年和1988年间增加了。

(B) 1988年在疗养院生活的老人比率比1975年要大。

(C) 在入住比率上升的同时，疗养院的接受比率却趋于下降。

(D) 1985年前建造的疗养院的床位比1985~1988年间建造的疗养院的床位少。

(E) 一家疗养院拥有的床位越多，它的入住比率可能越高。

采用"利润相关报酬"（PRP）合同的企业支付的工资水平随企业利润而变动。去年，金属工艺行业中适当采用PRP的企业的每个工人的生产率比那些仍然使用较传统合同的竞争者平均高13个百分点。

根据以上的证据，如果有意见认为PRP合同提高了工人的劳动生产率；下面哪个，如果正确，最严重地削弱了这种意见？

(A) 与以上引用的金属工艺行业相似的结论可以在使用PRP合同的其他行业中被发现。

(B) 在PRP合同之下，除了劳动力成本以外的那些成本——例如建筑、机器和能源成本——在单位产量的总成本中所占比重上升了。

(C) 因为引入PRP合同极大地改变了单个工人同企业之间的关系，对引入PRP合同进行谈判是复杂和费时的。

(D) 金属工业行业中很多企业在过去的5年中已经将其生产设备现代化了，同时这些企业中大多数引入了PRP合同。

(E) 在金属工艺行业中适当采用PRP合同的企业中，平均的实领工资比那些工人拥有更多传统合同的企业高出15个百分点。

8. Crops can be traded on the futures market before they are harvested. If a poor corn harvest is predicted, prices of corn futures rise; if a bountiful corn harvest is predicted, prices of corn futures fall. This morning meteorologists are predicting much-needed rain for the corn-growing region starting tomorrow. Therefore, since adequate moisture is essential for the current crop's survival, prices of corn futures will fall sharply today.

Which of the following, if true, most weakens the argument above?

(A) Corn that does not receive adequate moisture during its critical pollination stage will not produce a bountiful harvest.

(B) Futures prices for corn have been fluctuating more dramatically this season than last season.

(C) The rain that meteorologists predicted for tomorrow is expected to extend well beyond the corn-growing region.

(D) Agriculture experts announced today that a disease that has devastated some of the corn crop will spread widely before the end of the growing season.

(E) Most people who trade in corn futures rarely take physical possession of the corn they trade.

9. A discount retailer of basic household necessities employs thousands of people and pays most of them at the minimum wage rate. Yet following a federally mandated increase of the minimum wage rate that increased the retailer's operating costs considerably, the retailer's profits increased markedly.

Which of the following, if true, most helps to resolve the apparent paradox?

(A) Over half of the retailer's operating costs consist of payroll expenditures; yet only a small percentage of those expenditures go to pay management salaries.

(B) The retailer's customer base is made up primarily of people who earn, or who depend on the earnings of others who earn the minimum wage.

(C) The retailer's operating costs, other than wages, increased substantially after the increase in the minimum wage rate went into effect.

(D) When the increase in the minimum wage rate went into effect, the retailer also raised the wage rate for employees who had been earning just above minimum wage.

粮食可以在收割前在期货市场进行交易。如果预测谷物产量不足，谷物期货价格就会上升；如果预测谷物丰收，谷物期货价格就会下降。今天早上，气象学家们预测从明天开始谷物产区里会有非常需要的降雨。因为充分的潮湿对目前谷物的存活非常重要，所以今天的谷物期货价格会大幅下降。

下面哪个，如果正确，最严重地削弱了以上的观点？

(A) 在关键的授粉阶段没有接受足够潮湿的谷物不会取得丰收。

(B) 本季度谷物期货价格的波动比上季度更加剧烈。

(C) 气象学家们预测明天的降雨估计很可能会延伸到谷物产区以外。

(D) 农业专家们今天宣布，一种已经毁坏一些谷物作物的病菌在生长季节结束前会更广泛地传播。

(E) 许多在谷物期货市场交易的人很少实际拥有他们所交易的谷物。

一位销售基本的家庭必备品的折扣零售商雇用了上千人，并且支付给他们大多数人最低的工资水平。但随着一项联邦法令提高了最低工资水平从而大大增加了该零售商的运营成本之后，但该零售商的利润却显著提高了。

下面哪个，如果正确，最有助于解决这个明显的悖论？

(A) 该零售商的运营成本中超过一半是工资支出；但这些工资支出中仅有一小部分用来支付管理人员的薪水。

(B) 该零售商的顾客基础主要由那些赚取最低工资水平的人或那些依靠其他赚取最低工资水平的人构成。

(C) 该零售商的运营成本而非工资在增加最低工资水平的法令正式实施后明显上升了。

(D) 当增加最低工资水平的法令正式实施时，该零售商同样增加了那些收入一

(E) The majority of the retailer's employees work as cashiers, and most cashiers are paid the minimum wage.

10. The cotton farms of Country Q became so productive that the market could not absorb all that they produced. Consequently, cotton prices fell. The government tried to boost cotton prices by offering farmers who took 25 percent of their cotton acreage out of production direct support payments up to a specified maximum per farm.

The government's program, if successful, will not be a net burden on the budget. Which of the following, if true, is the best basis for an explanation of how this could be so?

(A) Depressed cotton prices meant operating losses for cotton farms, and the government lost revenue from taxes on farm profits.

(B) Cotton production in several counties other than Q declined slightly the year that the support-payment program went into effect in Q.

(C) The first year that the support-payment program was in effect, cotton acreage in Q was 5% below its level in the base year for the program.

(D) The specified maximum per farm meant that for very large cotton farms the support payments were less per acre for those acres that were withdrawn from production than they were for smaller farms.

(E) Farmers who wished to qualify for support payments could not use the cotton acreage that was withdrawn from production to grow any other crop.

11. United States hospitals have traditionally relied primarily on revenues from paying patients to offset losses from unreimbursed care. Almost all paying patients now rely on governmental or private health insurance to pay hospital bills. Recently, insurers have been strictly limiting what they pay hospitals for the care of insured patients to amounts at or below actual costs.

Which of the following conclusions is best supported by the information above?

(A) Although the advance of technology has made expensive medical procedures available to the wealthy, such procedures are out of the reach of low-income patients.

直刚好在最低工资水平以上的雇员的工资。

(E) 该零售商的雇员中主要是收款员，而大多数收款员的工资水平是最低的。

Q国的棉花农场变得如此多产以至于市场不能需求它们生产的所有产品。于是，棉花价格下降了。政府试图抬高棉花价格，支付给将25%棉花田闲置不生产的农民直接的支持金，每个农场的支付额有一个确定的最高限额。

该政府的计划如果成功实施，不会给财政带来净负担。下面哪个，如果正确，是解释之所以这样的最佳依据？

(A) 不景气的棉花价格意味着棉花农场的经营损失，而政府会损失依靠向农场利润征税而取得的收入。

(B) 在Q国支持支付计划正式实施的当年，Q国以外的一些地区棉花产量有轻微下降。

(C) 支持支付计划实施的第一年，Q国的棉花田比该计划的基期年份水平低了5%。

(D) 对每个农场确定的最高支付额意味着对非常大的棉花农场来说，退出生产的那些田地每亩得到的支持支付额要小于较小的农场所得到的。

(E) 想符合支持支付的要求的农民不能利用退出生产的棉花田种植其他任何作物。

美国的医院以前主要依靠从付款的病人那里取得的收入来弥补未付款治疗的损失。几乎所有付款的病人现在都依靠政府或私人的医疗保险来支付医院账单。最近，保险公司一直把他们为投保病人的治疗所进行的支付限制在等于或低于真实费用的水平。

下面哪个结论是以上的信息最能支持的？

(A) 虽然技术的进步已经使富人能够享受昂贵的医疗程序，这些医疗程序却在低收入病人的支付能力以外。

(B) If hospitals do not find ways of raising additional income for unreimbursed care, they must either deny some of that care or suffer losses if they give it.

(C) Some patients have incomes too high for eligibility for governmental health insurance but are unable to afford private insurance for hospital care.

(D) If the hospitals reduce their costs in providing care, insurance companies will maintain the current level of reimbursement, thereby providing more funds for unreimbursed care.

(E) Even though philanthropic donations have traditionally provided some support for the hospitals, such donations are at present declining.

12. Generally scientists enter their field with the goal of doing important new research and accept as their colleagues those with similar motivation. Therefore, when any scientist wins renown as an expounder of science to general audiences, most other scientists conclude that this popularizer should no longer be regarded as a true colleague.

The explanation offered above for the low esteem in which scientific popularizers are held by research scientists assumes that

(A) serious scientific research is not a solitary activity, but relies on active cooperation among a group of colleagues.

(B) research scientists tend not to regard as colleagues those scientists whose renown they envy.

(C) a scientist can become a famous popularizer without having completed any important research.

(D) research scientists believe that those who are well known as popularizer of science are not motivated to do important new research.

(E) no important new research can be accessible to or accurately assessed by those who are not themselves scientists.

13. Mouth cancer is a danger for people who rarely brush their teeth. In order to achieve early detection of mouth cancer in these individuals, a town's public health officials sent a pamphlet to all town residents, describing how to perform weekly self-examinations of the mouth for lumps.

Which of the following, if true, is the best criticism of the pamphlet as a method of achieving the public health officials' goal?

(B) 如果医院不能找到方法增加额外收入以此来补偿未付款的治疗，他们就必须或者拒绝为某些人治疗，或者接受下来并蒙受损失。

(C) 一些病人收入高于一定水平而没有资格参加政府医疗保险，但他们的收入水平却负担不起医院治疗的私人保险。

(D) 如果医院降低其提供治疗的成本，保险公司会保持现有的偿款水平，从而为未付款治疗提供更多资金。

(E) 尽管以往慈善捐款为医院提供了一些支持，这些捐款现在却在减少。

一般而言，科学家怀着进行重要的新科研的目标进入他们的领域，并且被那些具有相似动机的同事所接受。所以，当某位科学家作为向普通听众解释科学的人而获得声誉时，大多数其他科学家会认为这位名人不能再被视为一位真正的同事。

以上提供的关于科学普及者不为从事研究的科学家们尊重的解释假定：

(A) 严肃的科学研究不是一项个人的活动，而是要依赖一群同事的积极协作。

(B) 从事研究的科学家们不把他们所嫉妒的有名的科学家们视为同事。

(C) 一位科学家可以在没有完成任何重要研究的情况下成为一位知名人士。

(D) 从事研究的科学家们认为那些因成为科学名人而为大众所知的人没有动力去从事重要的新研究。

(E) 那些自己不是科学家的人不能去进行并且也不能准确评价任何重要的新研究。

口腔癌对那些很少刷牙的人是危险的。为了能在早期发觉这些人的口腔癌，一座城镇的公共卫生官员向所有的该镇居民散发了一份小册子，上面描述了如何进行每周口腔的自我检查以发现口腔内的肿瘤。

(A) Many dental diseases produce symptoms that cannot be detected in a weekly self-examination.

(B) Once mouth cancer has been detected, the effectiveness of treatment can vary from person to person.

(C) The pamphlet was sent to all town residents, including those individuals who brush their teeth regularly.

(D) Mouth cancer is much more common in adults than in children.

(E) People who rarely brush their teeth are unlikely to perform a weekly examination of their mouth.

14. Technological improvements and reduced equipment costs have made converting solar energy directly into electricity far more cost-efficient in the last decade. However, the threshold of economic viability for solar power (that is, the price per barrel to which oil would have to rise in order for new solar power plants to be more economical than new oil-fired power plants) is unchanged at thirty-five dollars.

Which of the following, if true, does most to help explain why the increased cost-efficiency of solar power has not decreased its threshold of economic viability?

(A) The cost of oil has fallen dramatically.

(B) The reduction in the cost of solar-power equipment has occurred despite increased raw material costs for that equipment.

(C) Technological changes have increased the efficiency of oil-fired power plants.

(D) Most electricity is generated by coal-fired or nuclear, rather than oil-fired, power plants.

(E) When the price of oil increases, reserves of oil not previously worth exploiting become economically viable.

15. Start-up companies financed by venture capitalist have a much lower failure rate than companies financed by other means. Source of financing, therefore, must be a more important causative factor in the success of a start-up company than are such factors as the personal characteristics of the entrepreneur, the quality of strategic planning, or the management structure of the company.

Which of the following, if true, most seriously weakens the argument above?

(A) Venture capitalists tend to be more responsive than other

下面哪个，如果正确，最好地批评了把这份小册子作为一种达到公共卫生官员的目标的方法？

(A) 许多牙病产生了不能在每周自我检查中被发觉的症状。

(B) 一旦口腔癌被发现后，治疗的有效性因人而异。

(C) 这份小册子被散发到所有的该镇居民，包括那些经常刷牙的人。

(D) 口腔癌在成年人中比在儿童中更为普遍。

(E) 很少刷牙的人不大可能每周对他们的口腔进行检查。

在过去的10年里，技术的进步和设备成本的降低已经在费用上使太阳能直接转化为电力更为有效。但是，太阳能经济可行性的门槛（也就是要想使新的太阳能发电机比新的燃油发电机更为节约，每桶石油必须提高的价格）没有变，仍是35美元。

下面哪个，如果正确，最有助于解释为什么太阳能费用上更为有效未能降低其经济可行性的门槛？

(A) 石油成本大幅下降了。

(B) 尽管太阳能设备成本下降了，该设备的原料成本却增加了。

(C) 技术上的变化提高了燃油发动机的效率。

(D) 大多数电力都是燃煤发动机或核力发电机生产出来的，而不是燃油发电机生产的。

(E) 当石油价格上升时，以前不值得开采的石油储备在经济上变得可行。

由风险资本家融资的初创公司比通过其他渠道融资的公司失败率要低。所以，与诸如企业家个人素质、战略规划质量或公司管理结构等因素相比，融资渠道在初创公司的成功上是更为重要的原因。

下面哪个，如果正确，最严重地削弱了以上的结论？

(A) 风险资本家对初创公司财务需要的变化比其他融资渠道更为敏感。

sources of financing to changes in a start-up company's financial needs.

(B) The strategic planning of a start-up company is a less important factor in the long-term success of the company than are the personal characteristics of the entrepreneur.

(C) More than half of all new companies fall within five years.

(D) The management structures of start-up companies are generally less formal than the management structures of ongoing businesses.

(E) Venture capitalists base their decisions to fund start-up companies on such factors as the characteristics of the entrepreneur and quality of strategic planning of the company.

16. The proportion of women among students enrolled in higher education programs has increased over the past decades. This is partly shown by the fact that in 1959, only 11 percent of the women between twenty and twenty-one were enrolled in college, while in 1981, 30 percent of the women between twenty and twenty-one were enrolled in college.

To evaluate the argument above, it would be most useful to compare 1959 and 1981 with regard to which of the following characteristics?

(A) The percentage of women between twenty and twenty-one who were not enrolled in college.

(B) The percentage of women between twenty and twenty-five who graduated from college.

(C) The percentage of women who, after attending college, entered highly paid professions.

(D) The percentage of men between twenty and twenty-one who were enrolled in college.

(E) The percentage of men who graduated from high school.

(B) 在公司的长期成功方面，初创公司的战略规划比起企业家个人素质来说是一个相对不重要的因素。

(C) 所有的新公司中有超过一半在5年内倒闭了。

(D) 一般来讲，初创公司的管理结构不如发展中的公司正式。

(E) 风险资本家在决定为初创公司提供资金时依据以下因素，如企业家素质和公司的战略规划质量。

过去几十年来，高等教育计划招收的学生中女性所占的比例呈上升趋势，这一点部分可通过以下事实表明，即在1959年，20～21岁间的女性只有11%被招进大学，而在1981年，30%的20～21岁间的女性被招进了大学。

为了评价以上的论证，对1959和1981年的下面哪个特征进行比较最有用？

(A) 20~21岁间的未被大学招收的女性比例。

(B) 20~21岁间的从大学毕业的女性比例。

(C) 接受大学教育后进入高报酬职位的女性比例。

(D) 20~21岁间的被大学招收的男性比例。

(E) 从高中毕业的男性的比例。

参考答案：

1. B	2. E	3. C	4. C	5. B
6. A	7. D	8. D	9. B	10. A
11. B	12. D	13. E	14. C	15. E
16. D				

1. **解析**：上面的段落隐含的推理可以提炼成"由于没有明显症状，所以酸雨没有造成危害"，本题让我们去反对这种说法以支持批评者的观点。如果酸雨可能正在造成症状尚未明显的危害，如(B)所说，那么就把前提A与B断开，表明A与B无联系，因此也就实现了问题目的，所以(B)正确；(A)中的"some"作为个案，只能反对绝对，不能反对一般，若把some改为many，即可起到反对作用；(C)是一个无关比较；(D)只表明"receive"，但"receive"不一定"被破坏"；(E)同样也是无关选项。

2. **解析**：本题论点是"航空公司把安全放在了比最小化燃料成本更高的优先位置上"，而论据是"向航空公司销售最好的是最安全的"。上述论点的成立要依赖于一个假设："过去最安全的座位很重，现在最安全的座位也很重"。如果由于技术上的创新，今年市场上最安全的客机座位比市场上其他客机座位要轻，正如(E)所说，那么上述论点成立所依赖的假设必将错误，所以削弱了上述论断，所以(E)正确；(A)只表明去年最好卖的客机座位不是市场上最安全的客机座位，但是与今年无关，所以(A)不对；(B)、(C)为无关选项；(D)与论点无关，所以，(B)、(C)、(D)不正确。

3. **解析**：本题为归纳题型，很容易知(C)为正确答案。需要强调的是归纳题的选项出现新概念，一般不对。(A)中的the time，(B)中的in most banks均为新概念，所以不正确；(D)中的many years to develop and perfect从上面推不出来；(E)和段落信息明显违背，因此也不可能是正确答案。

4. **解析**："两人对话型"的反对，并且是让第一个人反对第二个人时，在很多情况下，重点在于反对第二个人的最后一句话，即"We can simply hire only people who already know how to use the Microton computer."(C)指出熟练使用Microton的员工会要求更高的收入，从而雇用他们会提高成本，所以反对了the general manager的观点，因此(C)正确。

5. **解析**：本题比较容易，可以很容易得出(B)正确。需要强调的是，反对题型，若选项中说的是相同点或无差异，多为支持选项，不可能起到反对作用；(A)、(E)说的是共同点，不可能起到反对作用；(C)、(D)均为无关选项。

6. **解析**：本题为归纳题型。为什么疗养院入住比率上升但接受比率却在下降?必定是因为疗养院中住户呆在疗养院里的平均时间增加了，所以(A)正确；(B)中的older people为新概念；(C)中的whenever为段落里未出现过的绝对化语言，因此(B)和(C)都不正确。

7. **解析**：本题应把问题目的与段落结合起来进行思维，且论点包含于问题目的中。论点是：PRP提高了工人的劳动生产率；论据是"金属行业采用PRP比其他行业工人生产率高13%。当由数据得出一个对数据的解释时，反对一般用"有其他原因"的思路。(D)指出金属工业行业生产设备现代化了，其效率提高完全有可能是由于设备现代化的原因，从而削弱了上面的论点，所以(D)正确；(E)易误选，但(E)只表明税后支付高，至于与生产率高有什么关系不知道，换句话说，它并没有说明究竟是高工资导致了高生产率，还是高生产率导致了高工资，因此(E)是无关答案。

   注：take-home pay 税后工资；实领工资

8. **解析**：本题的推理可以提炼为：有雨→收成好→价格下降。(D)指出存在一种破坏作物的病菌，所以收成会受到影响，削弱了上面的论断，所以(D)正确；(A)指出谷物若在关键的授粉阶段没有接受足够潮湿，则谷物不会取得丰收，但究竟明天开始的降雨是否在授粉季节我们并不知道；(C)起到部分支持作用；(E)描述的是真理，但与上面推理无关，所以(E)不正确。

9. **解析**：本题非常简单，由大学生必备的common sense知道，利润等于收入减去成本。虽然由于最低工资水平上升提高了成本，但由于该零售店的顾客主要是从最低工资水平上升中受益的人，因此其收入上升，最终导致利润上升。所以(B)正确。

10. **解析**：本题思路也比较简单，不过运用了两个common sense：①供求规律；②Profit=Revenue-Cost，并且由此可知(A)正确。(B)讨论的是Q国以外的一些地区的情况，与段落推理无关；(C)与"价格"无关，说明不了任何问题；(D)是无关比较，且推不出结论；(E)讨论的是农民不能利用退出生产的棉花田种植其他作物，与上面推理没有直接关联。请回忆类似思维。

11. **解析**：本题是"归纳"题型。上面段落推理是：医院依赖于付款的病人，而付款的病人依赖保险，但保险公司最近严格把支付限制等于或低于真实费用的水平。(B)可以很好地作为上面推理的结论。一般而言，归纳题应先看带有if的选项，这样我们发现(B)、(D)中有if，但(D)中讨论的方向与上面推理正好相反，所以只有(B)正确。

12. **解析**：本题思维相对简单，可用取非方法验证。

13. **解析**：本题为典型的就目的提方法的"B，A"，反对思路可用"A不可行或A无意义"。如果很少刷牙的人不大可能每周对他们的口腔进行检查，(即A不可行或无意义)，正如(E)所说，那么也就表明能在早期发现很少刷牙人的口腔癌这个目的不能实现，所以(E)正确；(A)选项并未告知有无mouth cancer；(B)讨论的是"治疗"，但段落推理讨论的是"检查"；(C)为无关选项；(D)做了无关比较。

14. **解析：** 本题思维比较简单，主要是阅读能力。①太阳能经济可行性的门槛=②太阳能发电机的成本—③新的燃油发电机=35美元。让我们解释为什么②降低了，但②—③仍然是35美元，思维只有一点，那就是③也降低了。所以在读懂题目的情况下，(C)为什么正确一目了然。(A)易误选，但(A)里讨论的"cost"并不等于推理里面的"price"。

15. **解析：** 本题属于典型的因果倒置类的反对题，请参考本书第一篇总论第一章里面的三道题目。

16. **解析：** 本题让我们评价以上论点，但段落论点得出依赖于一个证据，因此读题重点在"This is partly shown by the fact that..."。又由前面讲述知道，evaluation题型必须是yes, no分别起到两个不同作用。(D)考虑了相关参照组20～21岁被大学招收的男生比例，可以起到很好的评价作用。(A)讨论的是未被大学招收的女生比例，偏离了推理的关键对象；(B)、(C)、(E)讨论的都是毕业的情况，与上面推理无关。

八、GMAT考前逻辑推理冲刺训练试题及解析（八）

1. Since a rhinoceros that has no horn is worthless to poachers, the Wildlife Protection Committee plans to protect selected rhinoceroses from being killed by poachers by cutting off the rhinos' horns.

The Wildlife Protection Committee's plan assumes that

(A) poachers do not kill rhinos that are worthless to them.

(B) hornless rhinos pose less of a threat to humans, including poachers, than do rhinos that have horns.

(C) rhinos are the only animals poachers kill for their horns.

(D) hornless rhinos can successfully defend their young against nonhuman predators.

(E) imposing more stringent penalties on poachers will not decrease the number of rhinos killed by poachers.

既然一只无角的犀牛对偷猎者来讲是没有价值的，野生动物保护组织计划通过割掉犀牛角来保护一批选定的犀牛免遭偷猎者的杀害。

野生动物保护组织的计划假定：

(A) 偷猎者不会杀害对他们没有价值的犀牛。

(B) 无角犀牛比有角犀牛对人类，包括对偷猎者而言威胁要小。

(C) 犀牛不是偷猎者捕杀后取角的唯一动物。

(D) 无角犀牛可以保护它们的幼兽免受来自非人类的捕食者的攻击。

(E) 对偷猎者实施更为严厉的制裁不会降低被偷猎者杀害的犀牛数量。

2. Crimes are mainly committed by the young, and for this reason merely increasing the number of police officers or expenditures on police services has little effect on reducing the crime rate. In fact, the only factor associated with a crime-rate drop is a decrease in the number of people in the community aged fourteen to thirty.

The findings above can best serve as part of an argument against

(A) the likelihood that any law enforcement program will be effective in reducing the crime rate within a short time.

(B) increasing prison terms for young people found guilty of crimes.

(C) introducing compulsory military conscription for people

犯罪的人主要是年轻人，由于这个原因，仅仅增加警官的数量或者仅仅增加警察服务的开支对降低犯罪率效果很小。事实上，与犯罪率降低相关的唯一因素是社会上14～30岁的人的数量得以减少。

以上的发现能最好地作为那种观点的部分反对意见？

(A) 任何的法律执行方案在降低犯罪率方面可能在短期内收效。

(B) 被发现犯罪了的年轻人的坐牢时间日益增加。

(C) 把年龄在17～19岁的人强制征募到部

aged seventeen to nineteen.

(D) raising the age at which students are permitted to leave school.

(E) a community's plan to increase the number of recreational and educational activities in which young adults can participate.

(D) 提高学生被允许离开学校的年龄。

(E) 一项提高年轻人参加的休闲和教育活动数量的计划。

3. A 20 percent decline in lobster catches in Maine waters since 1980 can be justifiably blamed on legislation passed in 1972 to protect harbor seals. Maine's population of harbor seals is now double the level existing before protection was initiated, and these seals are known to eat both fish and lobsters.

Which of the following, if true, would most seriously weaken the argument above?

(A) Harbor seals usually eat more fish than lobsters, but the seals are natural predators of both.

(B) Although harbor seals are skillful predators of lobsters, they rarely finish eating their catch.

(C) Harbor seals attract tourists to Maine's coastal areas, thus revitalizing the local economy.

(D) Authors of the 1972 legislation protecting harbor seals were convinced that an increase in that animal's numbers would not have a measurably negative impact on the lobster catch.

(E) The record lobster harvests of the late 1970's removed large numbers of mature lobsters from the reproductive stock.

1980年以来，缅因州水域的龙虾捕获量下降了20%，这可合理地归咎于1972年通过的保护港湾海豹的法案。缅因州的港湾海豹数量现在是开始加以保护前的水平的2倍，而我们知道这些海豹是吃鱼和龙虾的。

下面哪个，如果正确，会最严重地削弱以上的结论？

(A) 港湾海豹通常更多地吃鱼而非龙虾，但海豹是鱼和龙虾的天然捕猎者。

(B) 虽然港湾海豹是有经验的龙虾捕猎者，它们很少把捕获物吃完。

(C) 港湾海豹吸引游客来缅因州的海湾地区，从而使当地经济重新充满活力。

(D) 1972年保护港湾海豹法案的作者相信这种动物数量的增加不会给龙虾捕获量造成明显的负面作用。

(E) 70年代晚期龙虾创记录的捕获减少了大量可繁衍的成年龙虾数量。

4. Politician: Fewer people are entering the labor market now than previously. If the economy grows, the demand for motivated and educated people will far outstrip the supply. Some companies have already started to respond to this labor-market situation by finding better ways to keep their current employees. Their concern is a sure indicator that the economy is growing.

Which of the following is the best criticism of the politician's reasoning?

(A) The fact that companies are making prudent preparations for a possible future development does not mean that this development is already taking place.

(B) The fact that some companies now try harder to keep their employees does not mean that they used to be indifferent to employee morale.

政治家：现在进入劳动力市场的人比以前少了。如果经济增长，对有活力的和受教育的人的需求就会大大超过其供给。一些公司已经开始对这种劳动力市场的状况做出了反应，它们在寻找留住现有雇员的方法。它们关注的是经济正在增长的明确指标。

下面哪个最有力地批评了该政治家的推理过程？

(A) 公司为可能的将来的发展进行谨慎的准备这样一个事实并不意味着这种发展已经发生了。

(B) 一些公司现在更努力地留住其雇员的事实并不意味着它们以前对员工士气毫不关心。

(C) The fact that demand will outstrip supply does not mean that there will be no supply at all.

(D) The fact that the number of new entrants into the labor market is declining does not mean that the number of new entrants is lower than it has ever been.

(E) The fact that current employees have become more valuable to some companies does not mean that those employees will do their jobs better than they used to.

5. Under current federal law, employers are allowed to offer their employees free parking spaces as a tax-free benefit, but they can offer employees only up to $180 per year as a tax-free benefit for using mass transit. The government could significantly increase mass transit ridership by raising the limit of this benefit to meet commuters' transportation costs.

The proposal above to increase mass transit ridership assumes that

(A) current mass transit systems are subject to unexpected route closings and delays.

(B) using mass transit creates less air pollution per person than using a private automobile.

(C) the parking spaces offered by employers as tax-free benefits can be worth as much as $2,500 per year.

(D) many employees are deterred by financial considerations from using mass transit to commute to their places of employment.

(E) because of traffic congestion on major commuter routes, it is often faster to travel to one's place of employment by means of mass transit than by private automobile.

6. Which of the following best completes the passage below?

"Government" does not exist as an independent entity defining policy. Instead there exists a group of democratically elected pragmatists sensitive to the electorate, who establish policies that will result in their own reelection. Therefore, if public policy is hostile to, say, environmental concerns, it is not because of governmental perversity but because elected officials believe that

(A) environmentalists would be extremely difficult to satisfy with any policy, however environmentally sound.

(B) environmental concerns are being accommodated as well as public funds permit.

(C) the public is overly anxious about environmental deterioration.

(C) 需求会超过供给的事实并不表明一点供给都没有了。

(D) 新进入劳动力市场的人员数量正在减少的事实并不表明新进入的人数低于以往任何时期。

(E) 对一些公司来讲，现有的雇员更具价值的事实并不表明这些雇员干的工作会比以前好。

在现在的联邦法律下，雇主被允许向其员工提供免费的停车区作为一种免税津贴，但他们每年只能为员工提供最多180美元的免税津贴用来乘坐公共交通工具。通过提高这种津贴的限额来弥补经常乘车者的交通费用，政府可以显著增加公共交通工具的乘客数量。

上面的增加公共交通工具乘客数量的建议假设：

(A) 现在的公共交通工具常常有意外的线路停开和延误。

(B) 乘坐公共交通工具比起私人汽车来讲，每人制造的空气污染减少了。

(C) 雇主提供的作为免税津贴的停车区每年可值2500美元。

(D) 许多员工出于费用考虑而没有乘坐公共交通工具上班。

(E) 因为主要上班线路的交通拥挤，乘坐公共交通工具去上班比开私人汽车去上班要快得多。

下面哪个最好地补充了下文？

"政府"并非是作为一个制定政策的独立实体而存在的。相反，有一群对选民意见十分敏感的民主选举产生的实用主义者，他们制定能导致自己再次当选的政策。所以，比如说，如果公共政策与环境方面的考虑相对立，那么并非因为政府刚愎自用，而是因为被选出来的官员相信：

(A) 不管在环境方面多么完善，任何政策都很难满足环境保护主义者的要求。

(B) 环境方面的考虑要适应财政允许提供的资金。

(C) 公众对环境恶化过分担忧了。

(D) 选民中的大多数人投票支持某些政治

(D) the majority of voters vote for certain politicians because of those politicians' idiosyncratic positions on policy issues.

(E) the majority of voters do not strongly wish for a different policy.

7. Fresh potatoes generally cost about $2 for a 10-pound bag, whereas dehydrated instant potatoes cost, on average, about $3 per pound. It can be concluded that some consumers will pay 15 times as much for convenience, since sales of this convenience food continue to rise.

Which of the following, if true, indicates that there is a major flaw in the argument above?

(A) Fresh potatoes bought in convenient 2-pound bags are about $1 a bag, or 2 1/2 times more expensive than fresh potatoes bought in 10-pound bags.

(B) Since fresh potatoes are 80 percent water, one pound of dehydrated potatoes is the equivalent of 5 pounds of fresh potatoes.

(C) Peeled potatoes in cans are also more expensive than the less convenient fresh potatoes.

(D) Retail prices of dehydrated potatoes have declined by 20 percent since 1960 to the current level of about $3 a pound.

(E) As consequence of labor and processing costs, all convenience foods cost more than the basic foods from which they are derived.

8. Consumers in California seeking personal loans have fewer banks to turn to than do consumers elsewhere in the United States. This shortage of competition among banks explains why interest rates on personal loans in California are higher than in any other region of the United States.

Which of the following, if true, most substantially weakens the conclusion above?

(A) Because of the comparatively high wages they must pay to attract qualified workers, California banks charge depositors more than banks elsewhere do for many of the services they offer.

(B) Personal loans are riskier than other types of loans, such as home mortgage loans, that banks make.

(C) Since bank deposits in California are covered by the same type of insurance that guarantees bank deposits in other parts of the United States, they are no less secure than deposits elsewhere.

家是因为这些政治家在政治事件中的特有的习惯立场。

(E) 大多数选民并不非常希望有不同的政策。

一袋10磅的新鲜土豆一般值2美元，而脱水的速食土豆平均每磅值3美元。可以得出结论，一些消费者为了方便愿意支付15倍的价格，因为这种方便食品的销量在持续增加。

下面哪个，如果正确，指出了上面的论证有较大的缺陷？

(A) 购买方便的2磅一包的新鲜土豆每袋1美元，或者讲比10磅一包的新鲜土豆贵2.5倍。

(B) 因为新鲜土豆有80%的水分，每磅脱水土豆相当于5磅新鲜土豆。

(C) 罐装的削了皮的土豆也比相对不方便的土豆贵。

(D) 1960年以来脱水土豆的零售价格已经下降了20%，达到了目前的每磅3美元的水平。

(E) 作为劳动力成本和加工成本的结果，所有的方便食品要比制取它们的基本食品值钱。

加利福利亚的消费者在寻求个人贷款时可借助的银行比美国其他州少，银行间缺乏竞争，这点解释了为什么加利福利亚的个人贷款利率高于美国其他地区。

下面哪个，如果正确，最显著地削弱了以上的结论？

(A) 因为要支付相对高的工资来吸引胜任的员工，加利福利亚的银行为它们提供的许多服务向储户收取的费用比其他地方银行高。

(B) 个人贷款比银行做的其他种类贷款如住房按揭贷款风险大。

(C) 因为加利福利亚的银行存款和美国其他地区银行存款都受相同的保险保障，它们的安全性并不比其他地区的银行存款差。

437

(D) The proportion of consumers who default on their personal loans is lower in California than in any other region of the United States.

(E) Interest rates paid by California banks to depositors are lower than those paid by banks in other parts of the United States because in California there is less competition to attract depositors.

9. Technically a given category of insurance policy is underpriced if, over time, claims against it plus expenses associated with it exceed total income from premiums. But premium income can be invested and will then yield returns of its own. Therefore, an underpriced policy does not represent a net loss in every case.

The argument above is based on which of the following assumptions?

(A) No insurance policies are deliberately underpriced in order to attract customers to the insurance company offering such policies.

(B) A policy that represents a net loss to the insurance company is not an underpriced people in every case.

(C) There are policies for which the level of claims per year can be predicted with great accuracy before premiums are set.

(D) The income earned by investing premium income is the most important determinant of an insurance company's profits.

(E) The claims against at least some underpriced policies do not require paying out all of the premium income from those policies as soon as it is earned.

10. Purebred cows native to Mongolia produce, on average, 400 liters of milk per year, if Mongolian cattle are crossbred with European breeds, the crossbred cows can produce, on average, 2,700 liters per year. An international agency plans to increase the profitability of Mongolia's dairy sector by encouraging widespread crossbreeding of native Mongolian cattle with European breeds.

Which of the following, if true, casts the most serious doubt on the viability of the agency's plan?

(A) Not all European breeds of cattle can be successfully bred with native Mongolian cattle.

(B) Many young Mongolians now regard cattle raising as

（D）加利福利亚的消费者不能归还私人贷款的比率比美国其他地区低。

（E）加利福利亚的银行向储户支付的利率比美国其他地区的银行低，因此在加利福利亚，吸收储户的竞争较少。

从技术上来讲，随着时间的推移，如果索赔加上相关的费用超出了总的保险费，某种特定的保险计划就定价过低了。但是，保险费收入可以进行投资并且获得自己的收入。所以，一种定价过低的保险计划并非在每种情况下都意味着净损失。

上面的论述依据下面哪个假设？

（A）对于提供保险计划的保险公司来说，没有一项保险计划是被故意定价过低以吸引客户的。

（B）并非在所有情况下，对保险公司而言意味着净损失的保险计划都是定价过低的计划。

（C）有些保险计划在确定保险费之前可以很精确地预测每年的索赔额。

（D）把保险费收入进行投资所赚取的收入是决定保险利润的最重要因素。

（E）至少有些定价过低的保险计划的索赔不需要支付完这些计划最初赚取的所有保险费。

产自蒙古的纯种奶牛每年平均出产400升牛奶；如果蒙古种的牛与欧洲种的牛进行杂交，杂交生出的牛每年平均可出产2700升牛奶。一家国际机构计划通过鼓励推广把蒙古的牛与欧洲种的牛进行杂交来提高蒙古奶牛行业的利润。

下面哪个，如果正确，对该机构的计划的可行性提出了最严重的质疑？

（A）并非所有的欧洲种的牛都可以成功地与蒙古本地牛配育。

（B）许多年轻的蒙古人现在认为饲养牛是低等的工作，因为养牛的利润比其他

a low-status occupation because it is less lucrative than other endeavors open to them.

(C) Mongolia's terrain is suitable for grazing native herds but not for growing the fodder needed to keep crossbred animals healthy.

(D) Cowhide and leather products, not milk, make up the bulk of Mongolia's animal product exports to Europe.

(E) Many European breeds of cattle attain average milk production levels exceeding 2,700 liters.

11. Any combination of overwork and stress inevitably leads of insomnia. Managers at HiCorp, Inc., all suffer from stress. A majority of the managers— despite their doctors' warnings—work well over 60 hours per week, whereas the other managers work no more than the normal 40 hours per week. HiCorp gives regular bonuses only to employees who work more than 40 hours per week.

Which of the following conclusions is most strongly supported by the statements above?

(A) Managers at HiCorp work under conditions that are more stressful than the conditions under which managers at most other companies work.

(B) Most of the employee bonuses given by HiCorp are given to managers.

(C) At HiCorp, insomnia is more widespread among managers than among any other group of employees.

(D) No manager at HiCorp who works only 40 hours per week suffers from overwork.

(E) Most of the managers at HiCorp who receive regular bonuses have insomnia.

12. Holiday receipts—the total sales recorded in the fourth quarter of the year—determine the economic success or failure of many retail businesses. Camco, a retailer selling just one camera model, is an excellent example. Camco's holiday receipts, on average, account for a third of its yearly total receipts and about half of its yearly profits.

If the statements above are true, which of the following must also be true about Camco on the basis of them?

(A) Its fixed expenses per camera sold are higher during the fourth quarter than for any of the other three quarters.

(B) It makes more profit during the first and third quarters combined than during the fourth quarter.

可选择的工作低。

(C) 蒙古的地形适宜放牧本地的牛群，但不适宜种植保持杂交动物健康所需的饲料。

(D) 牛皮和皮革制品——而非牛奶——是蒙古向欧洲出口的动物产品。

(E) 许多欧洲种的牛可以取得超过2700升的平均牛奶产量。

过度操劳和紧张加在一起不可避免地会导致失眠，Hicorp公司的管理人员都深受紧张之苦，这些管理人员大多数不顾医生的忠告，每周工作60小时以上，而其他的管理人员每周工作不会超过通常的40个小时。Hicorp 只给那些每周工作40个小时以上的员工奖金。

以下的哪个结论最能被以上的论述所支持？

(A) Hicorp的管理人员工作的环境比其他公司管理人员的工作环境更具压力。

(B) Hicorp公司给予员工的奖金大部分给了管理人员。

(C) 在Hicorp，失眠在管理人员中比在其他员工中普遍。

(D) Hicorp中，没有哪位每周仅工作40小时的管理人员遭受了过度操劳的痛苦。

(E) Hicorp中大多数经常领取奖金的管理人员有失眠症。

假期收入——一年中第四季度发生的总销售额——决定了许多零售行业经济上的成功或失败。Camco——一家仅销售一种款式相机的零售商，就是一个很好的例子。Camco的假期收入平均占到其每年总收入的1/3和其年利润的一半。

如果以上的叙述是正确的，依据这些叙述，下面哪种关于camco的说法也必定是正确的？

(A) 它在第四季度销售每台相机的固定成本高于其他三个季度中的任何一个季度。

(B) 它在第一季度和第三季度获得的利润

(C) Its per-camera retail price is lower, on average, during the fourth quarter than during any one of the first three quarters.

(D) It makes less profit, on average, for a given dollar amount of sales during the first three quarters combined than during the fourth quarter.

(E) The per-camera price it pays to wholesalers is higher, on average, during the fourth quarter than during any of the other three quarters.

13. Canadians now increasingly engage in "out-shopping," which is shopping across the national border, where prices are lower. Prices are lower outside of Canada in large part because the goods-and-services tax that pays for Canadian social services is not applied.

Which one of the following is best supported on the basis of the information above?

(A) If the upward trend in out-shopping continues at a significant level and the amounts paid by the government for Canadian social services are maintained, the Canadian goods-and-services tax will be assessed at a higher rate.

(B) If Canada imposes a substantial tariff on the goods bought across the border, a reciprocal tariff on cross-border shopping in the other direction will be imposed, thereby harming Canadian businesses.

(C) The amounts the Canadian government pays out to those who provide social services to Canadians are increasing.

(D) The same brands of goods are available to Canadian shoppers across the border as are available in Canada.

(E) Out-shopping purchases are subject to Canadian taxes when the purchaser crosses the border to bring them into Canada.

14. Surveys indicate that 52 percent of all women aged eighteen to sixty-five are in the labor force (employed outside the home) in any given month. On the basis of these surveys, a market researcher concluded that 48 percent of all women aged eighteen to sixty-five are full-time homemakers year-round.

Which of the following, if true, would most seriously weaken the researcher's conclusion?

加起来比第四季度获得的利润高。

(C) 平均而言，它在第四季度的每台相机零售价格比其他三个季度中任何一个季度都低。

(D) 对于一定金额的销售数量而言，它在第四季度平均获得的利润比前三个季度合起来要多。

(E) 平均而言，它在第四季度支付给批发商的每台相机价格比其他三个季度中任何一个季度都高。

加拿大人现在越来越多地加入"境外购物"，即越过国界到价格较低的地方购物。加拿大以外的价格要低很多，很大一部分原因是支付给加拿大社会服务体系的商品和服务税不再适用。

根据以上的信息，下面哪个说法最可以被支持？

(A) 如果境外购物的上升趋势继续保持在较高的水平，并且政府支付给加拿大社会服务体系的金额不变，估计加拿大的商品和服务税税率就会上升。

(B) 如果加拿大对从境外购买的商品征收较多的关税，另一个方向上别国也会相应地对从加拿大购买的商品征收关税，从而损害加拿大的商业。

(C) 加拿大政府支付给为加拿大人提供社会服务的人的资金数额一直在增加。

(D) 同样品牌的商品，加拿大顾客在境外和在国内都可以买到。

(E) 境外购物所购商品在购物者越过边界进入加拿大境内时，要交纳加拿大规定的税收。

调查显示，在既定月份，18～65岁的所有妇女有52%属于劳动力群体（在家庭以外被雇用）。根据这些调查，一位市场调研人员得出结论认为，18～65岁的所有妇女中48%的人一年到头都是全职的家务劳动者。

下面哪个，如果正确，会最严重地削弱这位调研人员的结论？

(A) More women are in the labor force today than during any other period since the Second World War.

(B) Many workers, both men and women, enter and exit the labor force frequently.

(C) Although only a small sample of the total population is surveyed each month, these samples have been found to be a reliable indicator of total monthly employment.

(D) Surveys show that more women than ever before consider having a rewarding job an important priority.

(E) Women who are in the labor force have more discretionary income available to them than do women who are not.

15. Left-handed persons suffer more frequently than do right-handed persons from certain immune disorders, such as allergies. Left-handers tend to have an advantage over the right-handed majority, however, on tasks controlled by the right hemisphere of the brain, and mathematical reasoning is strongly under the influence of the right hemisphere in most people.

If the information above is true, it best supports which of the following hypotheses?

(A) Most people who suffer from allergies or other such immune disorders are left-handed rather than right-handed.

(B) Most left-handed mathematicians suffer from some kind of allergy.

(C) There are proportionally more left-handers among people whose ability to reason mathematically is above average than there are among people with poor mathematical reasoning ability.

(D) If a left-handed person suffers from an allergy, that person will probably be good at mathematics.

(E) There are proportionally more people who suffer from immune disorders such as allergies than there are people who are left-handed or people whose mathematical reasoning ability is unusually good.

16. After observing the Earth's weather patterns and the 11-year sunspot cycle of the Sun for 36 years, scientists have found that high levels of sunspot activity precede shifts in wind patterns that affect the Earth's weather. One can conclude that meteorologists will be able to improve their weather forecasts based on this information.

(A) 目前处于劳动力群体的妇女比二战以来每个时期都要多。

(B) 许多人，男女都有，很频繁地进入和退出劳动力群体。

(C) 虽然每个月只有总人口中很少的样本被调查，这些样本已经被发现是月雇用总数的可信的指标。

(D) 调查显示，比以往任何时候都要多的妇女把有一份带薪工作视为重要的、需要优先考虑的事情。

(E) 处于劳动力群体中的女性比那些不处于劳动力群体的女性有更多的可自由支配的收入。

左撇子的人比右撇子的人更经常患有免疫功能失调症，比如过敏。但是左撇子往往在完成由大脑右半球控制的任务上比右撇子具有优势，并且大多数人的数学推理能力都受到大脑右半球的强烈影响。

如果以上的信息正确，它最能支持下面哪个假设？

(A) 大多数患有过敏或其他免疫功能失调症的人是左撇子而非右撇子。

(B) 大多数左撇子的数学家患有某种过敏症。

(C) 数学推理能力强于平均水平的人中，左撇子的人的比例，要高于数学推理能力弱于平均水平的人中的左撇子比例。

(D) 如果一位左撇子患有过敏症，他很可能擅长数学。

(E) 比起左撇子的人或者数学推理能力不寻常地好的人所占的比例来讲，患有过敏等免疫功能失调症的人的比例要高一些。

在观察地球的气候类型和周期为11年的太阳黑子的活动长达36年以后，科学家们发现，在影响地球气候的风的类型变换之前，太阳黑子活动非常频繁。有人得出结论认为气象学家可以利用这一信息来改善天气预报。

Which of the following, if true, most seriously weakens the argument above?

(A) Weather forecasts are more detailed today than they were 36 years ago.

(B) Scientists can establish that sunspot activity directly affects the Earth's weather.

(C) Evidence other than sunspot activity has previously enabled meteorologists to forecast the weather conditions that are predictable on the basis of sunspot activity.

(D) Scientists have not determined why the sunspot activity on the Sun follows an 11-year cycle.

(E) It has been established that predictable wind patterns yield predictable weather patterns.

以下哪个，如果正确，最严重地削弱了以上的论证？

(A) 现在的天气预报要比36年前详细得多。

(B) 科学家们可以确定，太阳黑子活动直接影响地球的气候。

(C) 气象学家们以前可以利用太阳黑子活动以外的其他证据来预测现在可根据太阳黑子活动来预测的气候状况。

(D) 科学家们尚未确定为什么太阳黑子活动会遵循11年的周期。

(E) 已经可以确定，可预测的风的类型产生了可预测的气候类型。

参考答案：

1. A	2. A	3. E	4. A	5. D
6. E	7. B	8. A	9. E	10. C
11. E	12. D	13. A	14. B	15. C
16. C				

1. **解析：** 本题实际上为通过一方法达到某个目的的题型，即通过把rhinos' horns割掉来达到保护一批选定的犀牛的目的。答案方向只可能有三种，即①角割掉与保护必然有联系；②角能够被割掉；③割掉角之后，再没有别的因素影响保护。(A)说明割掉角确实有益于保护，所以是一个很好的假设，因此(A)正确；(C)只表明rhinos并不是唯一的偷猎者捕杀后取角的动物，而推理主要关注的是rhinos割掉角后能不能被保护，而(C)与"被保护"一点关系都没有；(D)易误选，但(D)只是一个支持，因为即使无角犀牛不能保护幼兽免受来自nonhuman的攻击，但只要能免受偷猎者的攻击，结论便仍然正确。

   注：poacher 偷捕动物的人，在他人范围内活动的人；挖走人员或窃取思想的人
   rhino=rhinoceros 犀牛

2. **解析：** 本题问题目的是上述发现能够驳斥下面哪一个，一般是把段落中的main idea取非即为答案。上面段落里的"the only factor..."取非，即(A)表明任何方案都可能只在短期内有效，所以与上面推理相违背，因此(A)正确；(E)易误选，选(E)的人认为娱乐、教育增加可以减少犯罪，从而反对了上面的"the only factor..."，但这是递推出来的，实际上(E)与犯罪率减少一点关系也没有，因此(E)不正确。

3. **解析：** 本题推理为"就现象提出解释"，一般暗含这种解释是唯一的原因，反对思路是"有他因"。(E)很好地实现了问题目的，所以(E)正确；(D)易误选，但(D)中的"相信"与"事实"是两码事，因此(D)起不到任何作用。

4. **解析：** 本题属于"逻辑应用与技法"类型，而(A)的描述正好把段落推理的A与B断开，因此构成了对推理的一个批评。所以(A)正确；(B)、(D)选项与"经济增长"与否无关，所以为无关答案。

5. **解析：** 本题读题重点为段落最后一句话，且本题为"提出一方法来实现某个目的"，即通过提高津贴，可以增加公共交通的乘客数量。而选项(D)说明出于费用考虑（没有提高津贴），许多人没有使用公共交通工具上班符合"无因就无果"的思路，所以(D)正确；(C)与"ridership"无关；(E)是一个无关比较，所以也不正确。

6. **解析**：本题作为"完成段落"题型，重点要把握最后要补充的这一句话和段落前边的论述是什么关系——是解释前面所述，还是从前面得出结论，并且补充的这一句话要与段落前半部分有关，而段落前半部分告诉我们the democratically elected pragmatists are sensitive to the electorate,即当选官员受选民影响决定，那么补充的内容应与此吻合。(E)中的voters=electorate, strongly wish有perversity的意思，并且(E)指出是因为大多数选民并不希望有不同的政策而并非政府刚愎自用，所以(E)正确；(A)、(B)、(C)与"选民"无关，为无关答案；(D)只说明选民为什么选某些政治家，但我们讨论的是政策决定的问题，所以(D)起不了任何作用。

7. **解析**：如果新鲜土豆有80%的水分，每磅脱水土豆相当于5磅新鲜土豆，如(B)所说，那么段落推理结论的"15倍的价格"便不成立，所以(B)正确；(A)是在"2-pound bags"与"10-pound bags"之间做了无关比较；(C)是在"peeled potatoes"与"the less convenient fresh potatoes."之间做了无关比较；(D)是无关答案；(E)是一个真理，但与上面推理无关。牢记：逻辑推理题是让我们找一个与上面推理有关且能实现问题目的的答案，而不仅仅是让我们找一个可以作为真理的答案。

8. **解析**：本题读题重点也是段落最后一句话，其推理关系为缺乏竞争→贷款利率高，实际上，我们发现"缺乏竞争"是对"贷款利率高"的解释，暗含其是唯一原因。反对多用"有他因"的思路。(A)指出是由于加州的服务成本高而导致贷款利率高，所以(A)正确；(B)是在"personal loans"与"other types of loans"之间做了无关比较，且上面推理并未涉及"other types of loans"；(E)易误选，但(E)表明加州银行向储户支付的利率低，说明其成本低，但成本低应导致贷款利率低才对，这与"贷款利率高"的事实不符，而事实一般不能反对，所以(E)不对。

9. **解析**：假设是结论成立的必要条件，本题推理的结论是"an underpriced policy does not represent a net loss in every case."而(E)选项明显可以作为上述结论的假设，且"at least some underpriced policies"与"not...in every case"相对应，说明由于至少有一些索赔不需支付完所有收入，所以可以有一部分保险收入用以投资以取得收入，所以说明原因可行有意义，因此(E)正确；(B)与段落推理相违背；(D)有两个错误：①段落中若无绝对化语言，选项中也应无绝对化语言，(D)中的"the most"得不到。②(D)只说明了决定保险利润的因素，但究竟能否有保费收入进行投资我们并不知道，因此(D)不正确。

10. **解析**：作为削弱计划可行性的题目，一般大多是反对为实施计划而采用的方法。若蒙古的自然条件不能得到杂交动物所需的饲料，如(C)所说，那么杂交牛在蒙古便不能生存，自然也就不能实现所提计划。段落推理并未说到"all"，因此(A)不可能起到反对作用；(E)易误选，但段落里面并未说出杂交牛最好，而且本题是让我们质疑计划的可行性，所以(E)不正确。

11. **解析**：本题重点把握逻辑层次结构，由"any combination of overwork and stress inevitably leads to insomnia."与"Hicorp gives regular bonuses only to employees who work more than 40 hours per week"，我们可以看出(E)正确；(B)指出大部分雇员奖金给了管理人员，但上面段落只说明Hicorp给工作40个小时以上的员工发奖金，究竟这些人中管理人员占多大比例我们并不知道，因此(B)不对；(D)完全是一个新比较，因此也不正确。

12. **解析**：本题作为归纳题型，属于对比推理类型。假定Camco年销售收入为X元，利润为Y，那么就一定金额的销售数量而言，第四季度的利润率为$\frac{1}{2}Y/\frac{1}{3}X=\frac{3Y}{2X}$，而其他三个季度为$\frac{1}{2}Y/\frac{2}{3}X=\frac{3Y}{4X}$，而$\frac{3Y}{4X}<\frac{3Y}{2X}$，所以(D)正确；(A)为新比较，因为我们只知道第四季度与前三个季度之和怎么样，而并不知道前三个季度的每一个季度怎么样，所以(A)不正确；(B)得不出；(C)中的retail price为新概念；(E)中的price为新概念且为新比较，而归纳中出现新比较，新概念必然不对。

13. **解析**：本题属于简单的数学相关的题目，很易知(A)为正确答案。由于段落并未提到外国人到加拿大买东西，所以(B)不对；(C)中"the same brands of goods"为新概念；段落中也无"out-shopping purchases are subject to Canadian taxes"，因此(E)也不对。

14. 解析： 本题是由一个数据事实而外推出了一个结论，反对的一般思路多为找差异点。结论中关键词为"full time homemakers year-round"，而(B)中的"enter and exit...frequently"很好地指出了与上面结论的差异，所以(B)正确。

15. 解析： 本题读题重点在however后面的话。(C)很容易可以得出。(A)中的"most"从上文中得不出，应把"most"改为"more"就可作为一个答案；(B)中的"allergy"是个新概念，必然不对；(D)中的推理与上面段落推理无关；(E)做了一个无关比较，因此也不对。

16. 解析： 本题推理为"利用太阳黑子活动情况可改善天气预报"。(C)指出无因(太阳黑子活动情况)却有果（运行天气预报），也就是把A与B断开，因此(C)是一个很好的削弱；(B)易误选，但(B)是支持，要注意看清问题目的。

九、GMAT考前逻辑推理冲刺训练试题及解析（九）

1. A publisher is now providing university professors with the option of ordering custom textbooks for their courses. The professors can edit out those chapters of a book they are not interested in and add material of their own choosing.

The widespread use of the option mentioned above is LEAST likely to contribute to fulfilling which of the following educational objectives?

(A) Coverage of material relevant to a particular student body's specific needs.

(B) Offering advanced elective courses that pursue in-depth investigation of selected topics in a field.

(C) Ensuring that students nationwide engaged in a specific course of study are uniformly exposed to a basic set of readings.

(D) Making the textbooks used in university courses more satisfactory from the individual teacher's point of view.

(E) Keeping students' interest in a course by offering lively, well-written reading assignments.

一位出版商现在为大学教授提供了课程订阅定制课本的选择。这些教授可以删掉一本书中他们不感兴趣的章节，同时可加入他们自己选择的材料。

上面提及的选择权的广泛使用最不可能有助于实现下面哪个教育目标？

(A) 涵盖与某个学生的特别需要相关的材料。

(B) 提供高级选修课程来对某领域中选择的课题进行深入考察。

(C) 保证全国参加一门具体课程学习的学生可以统一地接受一套基本的阅读材料。

(D) 使大学课程使用的课本从个别老师的角度看令人满意。

(E) 通过提供生动的、写得好的阅读材料来保持学生对一门课的兴趣。

2. Mechanicorp's newest product costs so little to make that it appears doubtful the company will be able to sell it without increasing the markup the company usually allows for profit: potential clients would simply not believe that something so inexpensive would really work. Yet Mechanicorp's reputation is built on fair prices incorporating only modest profit margins.

The statements above, if true, most strongly support which of the following?

(A) Mechanicorp will encounter difficulties in trying to set a price for its newest product that will promote sales without threatening to compromise the company's reputation.

(B) Mechanicorp achieves large annual profits, despite small

Mechanicorp的最新产品成本是如此之低，以至于公司不大可能在出售产品时不增加公司通常允许赚取的成本加价：潜在的客户可能完全不能相信这么便宜的东西会真好使。但Mechanicorp的信誉是建立在仅包括合理的边际利润的公平价格基础上的。

以上的论述，如果正确，最强有力地支持了下面哪个？

(A) Mechanicorp在试图为其最新产品定价、使价格能在不损害公司信誉的前提下促进销售时会遇到困难。

(B) 尽管售出的每件产品利润很小，但通

profits per unit sold, by means of a high volume of sales.

(C) Mechanicorp made a significant computational error in calculating the production costs for its newest product.

(D) Mechanicorp's newest product is intended to perform tasks that can be performed by other devices costing less to manufacture.

(E) Mechanicorp's production processes are designed with the same ingenuity as are the products that the company makes.

过大规模的销售，Mechanicorp仍取得了巨大的年利润。

(C) Mechanicorp在为其最新产品计算生产成本时犯了计算错误。

(D) Mechanicorp的最新产品将要执行的任务是其他制造成本更低的设备也能胜任的。

(E) Mechanicorp的生产程序的设计和该公司制造的产品一样具有新颖之处。

3. Companies in the country of Kollontay can sell semiconductors in the country of Valdivia at a price that is below the cost to Valdivian companies of producing them. To help those Valdivian companies, the Valdivian legislature plans to set a minimum selling price in Valdivian for semiconductors manufactured in Kollontay that is ten percent greater than the average production costs for companies in Valdivian.

Which of the following, if true, most seriously threatens the success of the plan?

(A) The annual rate of inflation in Kollontay is expected to exceed ten percent within the next year.

(B) Valdivian is not the only country where companies in Kollontay currently sell semiconductors.

(C) Some Valdivian companies that sell semiconductors have announced that they plan to decrease their price for semiconductors.

(D) The government of Kollontay will also set a minimum price for selling semiconductors in that country.

(E) Emerging companies in countries other than Kollontay will still be able to sell semiconductors in Valdivia at a price below that cost to Valdivian companies to manufacture them.

Kollontay 的公司在Valdivia销售的半导体价格可能低于Valdivia生产半导体的公司的成本。为了帮助那些Valdivia的公司，Valdivia的立法机构计划对Kollontay 生产的在Valdivia销售的半导体确定一个最低售价，这个价格比Valdivia公司的平均生产成本高10%。

下面哪个，如果正确，最严重地威胁到计划的成功？

(A) Kollontay 的年通货膨胀率预计明年会上升10%。

(B) Valdivia不是唯一的Kollontay的公司目前在该国销售半导体的国家。

(C) 一些销售半导体的Valdivia公司已经宣布它们计划要降低半导体价格。

(D) Kollontay的政府也会确定一个在该国出售半导体的最低价格。

(E) Kollontay以外的国家的新兴公司仍然可以在Valdivia以低于Valdivia 的公司制造半导体成本的价格销售半导体。

4. An experimental microwave clothes dryer heats neither air nor cloth. Rather, it heats water on clothes, thereby saving electricity and protecting delicate fibers by operating at a lower temperature. Microwaves are waves that usually heat metal objects, but developers of a microwave dryer are perfecting a process that will prevent thin metal objects such as hairpins from heating up and burning clothes.

Which of the following, if true, most strongly indicates that the process, when perfected, will be insufficient to make the dryer readily marketable?

一台实验性的微波衣服干燥机既不烘烤空气也不烘烤布料。相反，它烘烤的是衣服里的水，所以可以在较低温度下运作从而能节省电力和保护易损纤维。微波通常是用来加热金属物品，但微波干燥机的研究人员正在完善一项程序，可以阻止大头针等细金属被加热并燃烧衣服。

下面哪个，如果正确，最强有力地表明当该程序被完善后不足以使该干燥机可以立刻进入市场？

(A) Metal snap fasteners on clothes that are commonly put into drying machines are about the same thickness as most hairpins.

(B) Many clothes that are currently placed into mechanical dryers are not placed there along with hairpins or other thin metal objects.

(C) The experimental microwave dryer uses more electricity than future, improved models would be expected to use.

(D) Drying clothes with the process would not cause more shrinkage than the currently used mechanical drying process causes.

(E) Many clothes that are frequently machine-dried by prospective customers incorporate thick metal parts such as decorative brass studs or buttons.

5. Airplane manufacturer: I object to your characterization of our X-387 jets as dangerous. No X-387 in commercial use has ever crashed or even had a serious malfunction.

Airline regulator: The problem with the X-387 is not that it, itself, malfunctions, but that it creates a turbulence in its wake that can create hazardous conditions for aircraft in its vicinity.

The airline regulator responds to the manufacturer by doing which of the following?

(A) Characterizing the manufacturer's assertion as stemming from subjective interest rather than from objective evaluation of the facts.

(B) Drawing attention to the fact that the manufacturer's interpretation of the word "dangerous" is too narrow.

(C) Invoking evidence that the manufacturer has explicitly dismissed as irrelevant to the point at issue.

(D) Citing statistical evidence that refutes the manufacturer's claim.

(E) Casting doubt on the extent of the manufacturer's knowledge of the number of recent airline disasters.

6. Damaged nerves in the spinal cord do not regenerate themselves naturally, nor even under the spur of nerve-growth stimulants. The reason, recently discovered, is the presence of nerve-growth inhibitors in the spinal cord. Antibodies that deactivate those inhibitors have now been developed. Clearly, then, nerve repair will be a standard medical procedure in the foreseeable future.

Which of the following, if true, casts the most serious doubt on the accuracy of the prediction above?

(A) 通常被放入干燥机的金属厚度与大多数大头针基本一样。

(B) 目前被放入机械干燥机中的许多衣服并没有和大头针及其他细金属放在一起。

(C) 该实验性的微波干燥机比未来预期要使用的改良模型消耗更多的电力。

(D) 利用该程序干燥衣服导致的缩水程度小于目前使用的机械干燥程序。

(E) 将来的消费者经常用机器干燥的许多衣服包括粗金属部件，如装饰性的黄铜饰钉或钮扣。

飞机制造商：我反对你把我们的X-387型喷气机描述为危险的。商业使用的X-387飞机从未坠毁，也未曾有过严重的功能失调。

航空调度员：X-387飞机的问题并不在于其自身，而在于发动起来时会引起空气湍流，给附近的飞行器造成危险的环境。

航空调度员通过下面哪一个对制造者做出了回答？

(A) 把制造商的论断特征描述为来自主观兴趣，而不是来自于对事实的客观评价。

(B) 把注意力集中于这个事实：制造商对"危险"的阐释太狭隘了。

(C) 引用一些制造商把它们当作与争论问题无关而明显忽略的证据。

(D) 引用统计证据以反驳制造商的断言。

(E) 向制造商对最近空难数量的了解程度提出质疑。

脊髓中受损伤的神经不能自然地再生，即使在神经生长刺激物的激发下也不能再生。人们最近发现其原因是脊髓中存在着神经生长抑制剂。现在已经开发出降低这种抑制剂活性的抗体。那么很清楚，在可以预见的将来，神经修复将会是一项标准的医疗程序。

以下哪个如果正确，能对以上预测的准确性产生质疑？

(A) Prevention of the regeneration of damaged nerves is merely a by-product of the main function in the human body of the substances inhibiting nerve growth.

(B) Certain nerve-growth stimulants have similar chemical structures to those of the antibodies against nerve-growth inhibitors.

(C) Nerves in the brain are similar to nerves in the spinal cord in their inability to regenerate themselves naturally.

(D) Researchers have been able to stimulate the growth of nerves not located in the spinal cord by using only nerve-growth stimulants.

(E) Deactivating the substances inhibiting nerve growth for an extended period would require a steady supply of antibodies.

(A) 防止受损神经的再生只不过是人体中抑制神经生长的物质的主要功能的一个副作用。

(B) 某种神经生长刺激剂与那些减少神经生长抑制剂活性的抗体具有相似的化学结构。

(C) 大脑中的神经在不能自然再生方面与脊髓中的神经相似。

(D) 通过仅仅使用神经生长刺激剂，研究人员已经能够激发不在脊髓内的神经生长。

(E) 在持续的时期内降低抑制神经生长的物质的活性，需要抗体的稳定供给。

7. The human body secretes more pain-blocking hormones late at night than during the day. Consequently, surgical patients operated on at night need less anesthesia. Since larger amounts of anesthesia pose greater risks for patients, the risks of surgery could be reduced if operations routinely took place at night.

Which of the following, if true, argues most strongly against the view that surgical risks could be reduced by scheduling operations at night?

(A) Energy costs in hospitals are generally lower at night than they are during the day.

(B) More babies are born between midnight and seven o'clock in the morning than at any other time.

(C) Over the course of a year, people's biological rhythms shift slightly in response to changes in the amounts of daylight to which the people are exposed.

(D) Nurses and medical technicians are generally paid more per hour when they work during the night than when they work during the day.

(E) Manual dexterity and mental alertness are lower in the late night than they are during the day, even in people accustomed to working at high.

人体在深夜里要比在白天分泌更多的抑制疼痛的荷尔蒙。因此，在夜间进行手术的外科病人需要较少的麻醉剂。因为大量的麻醉剂会对病人造成较大的危险，所以如果手术经常在夜间进行，就会减少外科手术的风险。

下面哪一个，如果正确，最能反对在夜间进行手术会减少外科手术风险这个观点？

(A) 医院里在夜里的能量消耗通常比在白天少。

(B) 生在午夜至早上7点之间的婴儿要比在其他时间的多。

(C) 在一年期间，人的生物钟对人们暴露于日光照射之下的数量的变化有所反应而发生轻微地转变。

(D) 在夜间工作的护士和医疗技师每小时的收入比白天的高。

(E) 尽管一些人已习惯于夜间工作，但其手的灵巧程度和精神警觉性在夜间比在白天差。

Questions 8~9

Walter: A copy of an artwork should be worth exactly what the original is worth if the two works are visually indistinguishable. After all, if the two works are visually indistinguishable, they have all the same qualities, and if they have all the same qualities, their prices should be equal.

Walter：如果一件艺术作品的复制品和其真品看起来没有差别，那么复制品应与其真品等值。毕竟，如果两件作品看起来没有差别，那么它们具有相同的质量；如果他们拥有相同的质量，价格应该相等。

Marissa: How little you understand art! Even if someone could make a perfect copy that is visually indistinguishable from the original, the copy would have a different history and hence not have all the same qualities as the original.

Marissa：你对艺术的理解真是井底之蛙！即使某个人可以复制视觉上不能与其真品区分开来的完美的复制品，但复制品有一个不同的历史，因此，就不会与真品有相同的质量。

8. Which of the following is a point at issue between Walter and Marissa?
(A) Whether a copy of an artwork could ever be visually indistinguishable from the original.
(B) Whether the reproduction of a work of art is ever worth more than the original is worth.
(C) Whether a copy of a work of art is ever mistaken for the original.
(D) Whether a copy of a work of art could have all the same qualities as the original.
(E) Whether originality is the only valuable attribute that a work of art can possess.

下面哪一个是Walter和Marissa争论的重点？
(A) 一件艺术作品的复制品是否视觉上与真品区分不开。
(B) 对一件艺术作品的再创造是否会比真品更值钱。
(C) 一件艺术作品的复制品是否会被误认为是真品。
(D) 一件艺术作品的复制品是否在质量上与真品的所有方面都一样。
(E) 独创性是否是艺术作品拥有的唯一有价值的属性。

9. Marissa uses which of the following techniques in attempting to refute Walter's argument?
(A) Attacking his assumption that the price of an artwork indicates its worth.
(B) Raising a point that would undermine one of the claims on which his conclusion is based.
(C) Questioning his claim that a perfect copy of a work of art would be visually indistinguishable from the original.
(D) Giving reason to believe that Walter is unable to judge the quality of a work of art because of his inadequate understanding of the history of art.
(E) Proposing alternative criteria for determining whether two works of art are visually indistinguishable.

Marissa使用以下哪种技巧来企图驳斥Walter的论点？
(A) 攻击他的艺术品的价格代表其价值的假设。
(B) 提出了将削弱他的结论所基于的一个宣称的要点。
(C) 向他的一件精美的艺术品的复制品与其真品在视觉上不能区分的主张提出质疑。
(D) 给出使人们相信的原因：因为Walter对艺术历史的理解不充分，所以Walter不能确定一件艺术品的质量。
(E) 提供决定两件艺术品是否在视觉上不可区分的可替代的标准。

10. Magnetic resonance imaging (MRI)—a noninvasive diagnostic procedure—can be used to identify blockages in the coronary arteries. In contrast to angiograms—the invasive procedure customarily used—MRI's pose no risk to patients. Thus, to guarantee patient safety in the attempt to diagnose arterial blockages, MRI's should replace angiograms in all attempts at diagnosing coronary blockages.
Which of the following, if true, would most support the recommendation above?
(A) Angiograms can be used to diagnose conditions other

一种非侵犯性诊断程序——磁共振造影（MRI），能被用来确认冠状动脉堵塞。与一种经常使用的侵犯性诊断程序angiograms相比，磁共振造影不会对病人产生危害。因此，为了在尝试诊断动脉堵塞时确保病人安全，磁共振造影应在所有尝试诊断冠状动脉堵塞时取代angiograms。
下面哪一个，如果正确，将最支持上述建议？

than blockages in arteries.

(B) MRI's were designed primarily in order to diagnose blockages in the coronary arteries.

(C) Angiograms reveal more information about the nature of a blockage than an MRI can.

(D) An MRI is just as likely as an angiogram to identify an arterial blockage.

(E) Some patients for whom an angiogram presents no risk are unwilling to undergo an MRI.

(A) Angiograms 能被用来诊断动脉堵塞之外的情况。

(B) 磁共振造影主要是用来诊断冠状动脉堵塞的。

(C) Angiograms能比MRI揭示更多的关于堵塞物本性的信息。

(D) MRI与angiogram一样能够确认动脉堵塞。

(E) 使用angiogram没有造成风险的一些病人不愿意使用MRI。

11. Naturally occurring chemicals cannot be newly patented once their structures have been published. Before a naturally occurring chemical compound can be used as a drug, however, it must be put through the same rigorous testing program as any synthetic compound, culminating in a published report detailing the chemical's structure and observed effects.

If the statements above are true, which of the following must also be true on the basis of them?

(A) Any naturally occurring chemical can be reproduced synthetically once its structure is known.

(B) Synthetically produced chemical compounds cannot be patented unless their chemical structures are made public.

(C) If proven no less effective, naturally occurring chemicals are to be preferred to synthetic compounds for use in drugs.

(D) Once a naturally occurring compound has been approved for use as a drug, it can no longer be newly patented.

(E) A naturally occurring chemical cannot be patented unless its effectiveness as a drug has been rigorously established.

天然产生的化学物质的结构一旦被公布，就不能取得这种化学物质的专利。但是在一种天然产生的化学物质合成物被当作药物之前，它必须通过与人工合成药品一样严格地测试，最终在一份出版的报告中详细说明药品的结构和观察到的效果。

如果以上陈述正确，基于以上陈述，以下哪种说法也正确？

(A) 一旦结构公布于众，任何天然产生的化学物质都可以人工合成出来。

(B) 若人工生产的化学物质合成物取得专利，那么其化学结构一定公布于众。

(C) 如果天然生成化学物质被证明效果并不差，人们偏好于使用天然生成的化学物质作为药用而不偏好人工生成的药品。

(D) 一旦天然生成的化合物被许可作为药物使用，它就不能取得新专利了。

(E) 天然生成的化学物质申请专利，那么它作为药物的有效性必定受到了严格的证实。

12. A public-service advertisement advises that people who have consumed alcohol should not drive until they can do so safely. In a hospital study, however, subjects questioned immediately after they consumed alcohol underestimated the time necessary to regain their driving ability. This result indicates that many people who drink before driving will have difficulty following the advertisement's advice.

Which of the following, if true, most strongly supports the argument above?

一则公益广告建议喝酒的人应该等到他们能够安全开车时再开车。然而在一次医院调查中，在喝完酒之后就立即被询问的人低估了他们恢复开车能力所必需的时间。这个结果表明，在开车之前喝酒的许多人在遵从广告的建议方面有困难。

下面哪一个，如果正确，最能支持上面论述？

(A) Many people, if they plan to drink alcohol, make arrangements beforehand for a nondrinker to drive them home.

(B) The subjects in the hospital study generally rated their abilities more conservatively than would people drinking alcohol outside a hospital setting.

(C) Some people refrain from drinking if they will have to drive to get home afterward.

(D) The subjects in the hospital study were also questioned about the time necessary to regain abilities that do not play an important role in driving safely.

(E) Awareness of the public-service advertisement is higher among the general population than it was among the subjects in the hospital study.

13. Investigator: XYZ Coins has misled its clients by promoting some coins as "extremely rare" when in fact those coins are relatively common and readily available.

XYZ agent: That is ridiculous. XYZ Coins is one of the largest coin dealers in the world. We authenticate the coins we sell through a nationally recognized firm and operate a licensed coin dealership.

The XYZ agent's reply is most vulnerable to the criticism that it

(A) exaggerates the investigator's claims in order to make them appear absurd.

(B) accuses the investigator of bias but presents no evidence to support that accusation.

(C) fails to establish that other coin dealers do not also authenticate the coins those dealers sell.

(D) lists strengths of XYZ Coins while failing to address the investigator's charge.

(E) provides no definition for the inherently vague phrase "extremely rare."

14. Both Writewell and Express provide round-the-clock telephone assistance to any customer who uses their word-processing software. Since customers only call the hot lines when they find the software difficult to use, and the Writewell hot line receives four times as many calls as the Express hot line, Writewell's word-processing software must be more difficult to use than Express's.

(A) 如果许多人打算喝酒，他们将事先安排一个不喝酒的人开车送他们回家。

(B) 在医院调查中的被调查者对自己的能力估计，相对于那些在医院环境之外喝酒的人来说，要更保守一些。

(C) 有些人如果在喝酒之后必须开车回家，那么他们将会忍住不喝酒。

(D) 医院调查中的被调查者也被问及恢复那些在安全驾驶中起作用不大的能力所必需的时间。

(E) 总人口里意识到这些公益广告的人要高于医院调查中的被调查者。

调查人员：XYZ硬币公司通过宣传一些硬币"非常稀少"误导了消费者，实际上那些硬币相对来讲是常见的并可以很快买到。

XYZ代理人：这是可笑的，XYZ硬币公司是世界上最大的硬币交易商之一。我们通过一家全国认可的公司来证明所出售的硬币的真实性，并有经许可的硬币经销权。

该XYZ代理人的回答最易受到这样的攻击：

(A) 夸大了调查人员的说法以使其显得荒谬。

(B) 指责调查人员有偏见，但未能提供证据来支持那种指责。

(C) 未能证实其他硬币交易商没有证明所出售的硬币的真实性。

(D) 在不能对调查人员的指控进一步论述的情况下，列举XYZ的硬币公司的实力。

(E) 没有对"非常稀少"这个本质上模糊的概念提供定义。

Writewell和Express都为它们的文字处理软件客户提供全天候的电话帮助，由于客户只有在发现软件难用的时候才会打热线电话，并且Writewell的热线收到的电话是Express的热线收到的电话的4倍，Writewell的文字处理软件一定比Express的文字处理软件使用起来更加困难。

Which of the following, if true, most strengthens the argument above?

(A) Calls to the Express hot line are almost twice as long, on average, as are calls to the Writewell hot line.

(B) Express had three times the number of word-processing software customers that Writewell has.

(C) Express receives twice as many letters of complaint about its word-processing software as Writewell receives about its word-processing software.

(D) The number of calls received by each of the two hot lines has been gradually increasing.

(E) The Writewell hot-line number is more widely publicized than the Express hot-line number.

15. Over the last century, paleontologists have used small differences between fossil specimens to classify Triceratops into sixteen species. This classification is unjustified, however, since the specimens used to distinguish eleven of the species come from animals that lived in the same area at the same time.

Which of the following, if true, would enable the conclusion of the argument to be properly drawn?

(A) Not every species that lived in a given area is preserved as a fossil.

(B) At least one individual of every true species of Triceratops has been discovered as a fossil specimen.

(C) No geographical area ever supports more than three similar species at the same time.

(D) In many species, individuals display quite marked variation.

(E) Differences between fossil specimens of Triceratops that came from the same area are no less distinctive than differences between specimens that came from different areas.

16. Many consumers are concerned about the ecological effects of wasteful packaging. This concern probably explains why stores have been quick to stock new cleaning products that have been produced in a concentrated form. The concentrated form is packaged in smaller containers that use less plastic and require less transportation space.

Which of the following, if true, most seriously undermines the explanation offered above?

下面哪个，如果正确，最能加强以上的论证？

(A) 给Express热线的电话时间平均来讲是给Writewell热线的电话时间的两倍。

(B) Express的文字处理软件客户数量是Writewell的三倍。

(C) Express收到的对其文字处理软件的投诉信数量是Writewell收到的投诉信的数量的两倍。

(D) 这两条热线收到的电话数量都一直在逐渐增加。

(E) Writewell热线号码比Express热线号码更广泛地为人所知。

在过去的世纪中，古生物学家用化石标本间的细微差别把triceratops分为16类。但是这种划分并不正确，因为用来区分的样本中，11类的标本都是来自生活在同一地区同一时代的动物。

下面哪一个，如果正确，能使以上论点的结论正确地得出？

(A) 并不是每一种生活在指定地区的动物都作为化石被保存下来。

(B) Triceratops的每个真正种类中，至少会有一个个体被发现作为化石标本。

(C) 没有一个地理区域在同一时代会有超过三种相似的种类居住。

(D) 许多种类里的个体之间显示了很大的变异。

(E) 来自不同地区的Triceratops化石标本之间的差别与来自相同地区Triceratops化石标本之间的差别同样明显。

许多消费者对废弃的包装对生态的影响表示关注。这种关注也许可以解释为什么商店快速购进以浓缩形式生产的新型清洁产品。这种浓缩形式产品包装于小的容器中，可以只用较少的塑料，并且只需要较少的运输空间。

下面哪一个，如果正确，最能削弱以上所提供的解释？

(A) Few consumers believe that containers of concentrated cleaning products are merely small packages of regular cleaning products.

(B) The containers in which concentrated cleaning products are packaged are no harder to recycle than those in which regular cleaning products are packaged.

(C) Those concentrated cleaning products that are intended to be used diluted have clear instructions for dilution printed on their labels.

(D) The smaller containers of concentrated cleaning products enable supermarkets and drugstores to increase their revenues from a given shelf space.

(E) Consumer pressure has led to the elimination of wasteful cardboard packaging that was used for compact discs.

(A) 几乎没有消费者相信浓缩清洁产品的容器仅仅是常规清洁产品的小包装。

(B) 浓缩清洁产品的包装容器并不比常规清洁产品的包装容器更难回收。

(C) 那些要稀释使用的浓缩清洁产品在标签上印制了清晰的稀释说明。

(D) 浓缩清洁产品的较小容器可以使得超市与药店增加他们来自于特定货架空间的收入。

(E) 消费者压力导致取消用于简易圆盘状的东西的废卡板包装。

参考答案：

1. C	2. A	3. E	4. E	5. B
6. A	7. E	8. D	9. B	10. D
11. D	12. B	13. D	14. B	15. C
16. D				

1. **解析：**读懂问题目的是关键。本题让我们去说明出版商现在为大学教授提供的选择权最不可能实现什么样的教育目标。如果教授可以有足够的自由来按照他们的意愿来删增材料时，那么每个大学教授的教科书都可能有差异。(C)指出教育目标要保证全国参加一门具体课程学习的学生可以统一地接受一套材料，明显与上面的段落推理相冲突，因此(C)是正确答案；而(A)、(B)、(C)、(D)都从某种程度上与上面段落相一致。

2. **解析：**本题为"自上而下"的归纳题型，思维重点放在对逻辑层次结构的把握上。Mechanicorp的最新产品成本很低，但Mechanicorp的信誉要想维护，其最新产品的销售价格只能在成本基础上加上合理的边际利润，因此其最新产品的价格依然很低。但同时潜在的顾客可能质疑价格低的新产品的有效性，于是产生了悖论：如果Mechanicorp在成本上大幅度加价，那么将损伤其reputation；但若其维护他的reputation，则潜在客户会对新产品产生怀疑。而(A)指出了这种情况，即Mechanicorp在维护其信誉的前提下的产品销售会受到质疑，因此(A)正确；(B)、(C)、(D)、(E)从上面段落中推不出来。

3. **解析：**本题属于"为达到一个目的而提出一个方法"类型的反对。段落推理为"为了帮助Valdivia公司，要求Kollontay生产的在Valdivia销售的半导体的价格提高"。反对一般反对所提出的方法。(E)指出Kollontay以外的国家的公司仍然可以低价销售，也就质疑了"要求提高Kollontay生产的半导体价格"的可行性。

4. **解析：**本题的推理为：微波干燥机具有很大优点，但其缺陷是微波通常加热金属物品，因此微波干燥机完善一项程序即阻止大头针等细金属被加热后就可以进入市场。若将来的消费者经常用机器干燥的衣服包括了粗金属部件，正如(E)所说，那么即使完善了上述程序，该干燥机也不能立刻进入市场，所以(E)正确。(A)说的是与上面所提程序的共同点，因此支持了该干燥机可以立即进入市场。(B)、(C)、(D)都在部分程度上支持了干燥机在完善该程序之后可以进入市场。

5. **解析：**这道两人对话题的问题目的设计与答案方向应引起我们的注意，它与我们在前面讲过的一道题目几乎完全一样：第一个人说：由于保险商所支付的钱大于其所得到的钱，因此保险对保险者是不利的。第二个人说：的确是这样，但由于保险商在得到保险后得到了平静的心态，因此保险对保险者有利。问题目的：第二个人如何响应第一个人所说？答案：第二个人指出第一个的理解太狭隘了。

6. **解析**：本题属于"反对"题型。段落推理是：神经修复将成为可能，因为人们已开发出降低神经生长抑制剂活性的抗体。反对重点反对原因。如果防止受损神经的再生只是抑制神经生长的物质的主要功能的一个副作用，正如(A)所说，那么开发出降低神经生长抑制剂活性的抗体将消除神经生长抑制剂的主要功能，从而带来不利影响，因此结论必然不成立，所以(A)正确；(B)、(C)为无关比较；(D)的"不在脊髓内"与推理无关；(E)对上面推理起不到任何作用。

7. **解析**：明晰问题目的永远是解题时最重要的，而这个问题目的是让我们找一个能反对在夜间进行手术能减少surgical risks的选项，因此选项应与surgical risks有关。(E)指出人们在夜间手术的灵巧性与精神警觉性更差，从而可能会提高surgical risks，所以(E)正确；而(A)、(B)、(C)、(D)均与surgical risks无关。

8. **解析**：Walter和Marissa两人都谈到了"all the same qualities"，但Walter认为的两件艺术品的"all the same qualities基于"visually indistinguishable"，而Marissa对Walter所基于的论据进行攻击，指出即使visually indistinguishable，但是两件艺术品有a different history，因此，得不出结论"他们具有all the same quality"。(D)很好地描述了这一逻辑过程，所以(D)正确。

9. **解析**：同第8题。

10. **解析**：本题推理为：因为MRI不会对病人产生危害，因此在诊断动脉堵塞时应用MRI代替angograms。如果MRI与angiogram一样能确认动脉堵塞，正如(D)所说，那么上面推理成立可能性就增加，所以(D)正确，支持了上面建议；(A)、(C)、(E)都从某程度上反对上述建议；(B)易误选，但(B)仅仅说明MRI主要是用来诊断冠状动脉堵塞的，并没有说明angiogram怎么样，有可能angiogram也可以被用来诊断冠状动脉堵塞的。所以(B)为无关选项，请认真体会(B)错的原因。

11. **解析**：本题为归纳题型，注意把握逻辑层次结构。本题的推理为：天然产生的化学物质合成物当药物→在出版的报告中详细说明药品的结构→不能取得专利。(D)与此推理完全吻合，所以(D)正确。

12. **解析**：本题典型的"B，A"型支持，由一个study而得出一个结论，那么支持最重要的是支持结论"在开车前喝酒的人很多在遵从广告的建议方面有困难。医院里的被调查者低估了他们恢复开车能力所必需的时间，如果这些人相对那些在医院环境之外喝酒的人来说更加保守，正如(B)所说，那么所有开车之前喝酒的人都会低估他们恢复开车能力所必需的时间，所以他们在遵从广告建议方面有困难。因此(B)正确。

13. **解析**：本题比较简单，请思考本题对话的特点及选项(D)正确的原因。
注：authenticate *v.* 证实（某物）真实，合理［prove (sth.) to be valid or genuine or true］
dealership *n.* 代理权，分销商
bias *n.* 某人提到一事物两方面，但偏袒于某一方面
contradiction *n.* 提到两方面，且两方面互斥
address *v.* 对……进一步论述

14. **解析**：Writewell热线收到电话是Express热线收到电话的4倍，如果Express的客户是Writewell的三倍，正如(B)所说，那么对于单位客户群而言，Writewell热线收到的电话将是Express热线收到电话的12倍，因此加强了结论：Writewell的文字处理软件一定比Express的文字处理软件使用起来更加困难。所以(B)正确。

15. **解析**：本题貌似归纳，实为支持。如果没有一个地域区域在同一时代会有超过三种相似的种类居住，正如(C)所说，关于Triceratops的11类标本都来自于同一地区同一时代，那么必定样本的区分有误，因此这种划分不正确。所以(C)正确。

16. **解析**：本题是对一种现象提出一种解释，商业购进浓缩形式生产的清洁产品是因为消费者的关注。如果浓缩清洁产品的较小容器可以使得超市与药店增加他们来自于特定货架空间的收入，正如(D)所

说，那么就从另外一个角度解释了商业为什么购进浓缩形式生产的清洁产品，也就weaken了上面提出的解释是因为消费者关注的原因，所以(D)正确。

十、GMAT考前逻辑推理冲刺训练试题及解析（十）

1. In the first half of this year, from January to June, about three million videocassette recorders were sold. This number is only 35 percent of the total number of videocassette recorders sold last year. Therefore, total sales of videocassette recorders will almost certainly be lower for this year than they were for last year.

Which of the following, if true, most seriously weakens the conclusion above?

(A) The total number of videocassette recorders sold last year was lower than the total number sold in the year before that.

(B) Most people who are interested in owning a videocassette recorder have already purchased one.

(C) Videocassette recorders are less expensive this year than they were last year.

(D) Of the videocassette recorders sold last year, almost 60 percent were sold in January.

(E) Typically, over 70 percent of the sales of videocassette recorders made in a year occur in the months of November and December.

2. Mud from a lake on an uninhabited wooded island in northern Lake Superior contains toxic chemicals, including toxaphene, a banned pesticide for cotton that previously was manufactured and used, not in nearby region of Canada or the northern United States, but in the southern United States. No dumping has occurred on the island. The island lake is sufficiently elevated that water from Lake Superior does not reach it.

The statements above, if true, most strongly support which of the following hypotheses?

(A) The waters of the island lake are more severely polluted than those of Lake Superior.

(B) The toxaphene was carried to the island in the atmosphere by winds.

(C) Banning chemicals such as toxaphene does not aid the natural environment.

(D) Toxaphene has adverse effects on human beings but not on other organisms.

在今年上半年，从1月到6月，大约销售了300万台的录像机，这个数字仅仅是去年销售的录像机总数的35%。所以，今年录像机的总销售量几乎肯定要低于去年。

下面哪个，如果正确，最严重地削弱了以上的结论？

(A) 去年销售的录像机总数比前年低。

(B) 大多数对拥有一台录像机感兴趣的人都已经购买了一台。

(C) 今年的录像机比去年的便宜。

(D) 在去年销售的录像机中，近60%是在1月销售的。

(E) 一般来讲，一年中录像机的销售中超过70%是在11月和12月进行的。

来自于北Superior湖的无人定居的森林岛屿上，一湖泊的泥土含有有毒的化学品，这种有毒的化学品包括toxaphene一种已经禁止的以前为棉花而制造与使用的毒药。但toxaphene的制造与使用并不在加拿大或美国北部的附近区域，而是在美国的南部。这个岛上没有出现排放物。这个岛屿的湖已被足够地提高以致来自于Superior湖的水不会进入它里面。

上面陈述，如果正确，最强有力地支持下面哪一个假设？

(A) 这个岛屿湖泊的水域比Superior湖水域的污染程度更深。

(B) Toxaphene被风带到了这个岛上。

(C) 对诸如toxaphene的化学品的禁止无助于自然环境的改善。

(D) Toxaphene对人体有负面影响，但对其他生物没有。

(E) Concentrations of toxaphene in the soil of cotton-growing regions are not sufficient to be measurable.

3. Last year in the United States, women who ran for state and national offices were about as likely to win as men. However, only about fifteen percent of the candidates for these offices were women. Therefore, the reason there are so few women who win elections for these offices is not that women have difficulty winning elections but that so few women want to run.

Which of the following, if true, most seriously undermines the conclusion given?

(A) Last year the proportion of women incumbents who won reelection was smaller than the proportion of men incumbents who won reelection.

(B) Few women who run for state and national offices run against other women.

(C) Most women who have no strong desire to be politicians never run for state and national offices.

(D) The proportion of people holding local offices who are women is smaller than the proportion of people holding state and national offices who are women.

(E) Many more women than men who want to run for state and national offices do not because they cannot get adequate funding for their campaigns.

4. Samples from a ceramic vase found at a tomb in Sicily prove that the vase was manufactured in Greece. Since the occupant of the tomb died during the reign of a Sicilian ruler who lived 2,700 years ago, the location of the vase indicates that there was trade between Sicily and Greece 2,700 years ago.

Which of the following is an assumption on which the argument depends?

(A) Sicilian potters who lived during the reign of the ruler did not produce work of the same level of quality as did Greek potters.

(B) Sicilian clay that was used in the manufacture of pottery during the ruler's reign bore little resemblance to Greek clay used to manufacture pottery at that time.

(C) At the time that the occupant of the tomb was alive, there were ships capable of transporting large quantities of manufactured goods between Sicily and Greece.

(D) The vase that was found at the Sicilian tomb was not

(E) 在棉花种植区的土壤里的toxaphene的浓度不足以测量出来。

去年，美国竞选州和联邦政府官员的女性与男性一样可能获得成功，但是这些官员的候选人中仅有约15%是妇女。因此，竞选这些职位获成功的妇女人数如此少的原因并不是因为妇女难于竞选成功，而是因为想竞选的妇女太少了。

下面哪一个如果正确，最能削弱以上结论？

(A) 去年正在任职的妇女再次竞选成功的比例比正在任职的男人再次竞选成功的比例要低。

(B) 几乎没有竞选州和联邦政府官员的妇女与其他妇女竞争。

(C) 大多数没有很强欲望想成为政治家的妇女从来不去竞选州和联邦政府官员。

(D) 担任地方官员的妇女的比例比担任州和联邦政府官员中妇女的比例要低。

(E) 与男士相比，有更多的想竞选州和联邦政府官员职位的妇女因为不能得到竞选所需的足够资金而没有参与竞选。
注：(E)为一省略句，全句完整应在because前加上do so。

在西西里岛的一个坟墓中发现的一个陶瓷花瓶的样本证明，这个花瓶是在希腊制造的。由于该坟墓的主人死于2700年前西西里人统治的年代，所以这个花瓶的所处位置表明，在2700年前，西西里岛与希腊之间已有贸易往来了。

下面哪一个是上述论断所基于的假设？

(A) 生活在西西里人统治时代的西西里陶瓷工没有制造出与希腊陶瓷工制造的具有相同水平的作品。

(B) 在西西里人统治的年代，陶器制造中所使用的西西里粘土与同时代陶器制造中所使用的希腊粘土相似之处甚少。

(C) 在坟墓的主人生活的年代，西西里岛与希腊之间有能够运输大量货物的轮船。

(D) 西西里坟墓里发现的花瓶不是坟墓的

placed there many generations later by descendants of the occupant of the tomb.

(E) The occupant of the tomb was not a member of the royal family to which the Sicilian ruler belonged.

主人的后代在很多年以后放进去的。

(E) 坟墓的主人不是西西里统治者所属的皇家成员。

5. In several cities, the government is going ahead with ambitious construction projects despite the high office-vacancy rates in those cities. The vacant offices, though available for leasing, unfortunately do not meet the requirements for the facilities needed, such as court houses and laboratories. The government, therefore, is not guilty of any fiscal wastefulness. Which of the following is an assumption on which the argument above depends?

(A) Adaptation of vacant office space to meet the government's requirements, if possible, would not make leasing such office space a more cost-effective alternative to new construction.

(B) The government prefers leasing facilities to owning them in cases where the two alternatives are equally cost-effective.

(C) If facilities available for leasing come very close to meeting the government's requirements for facilities the government needs, the government can relax its own requirements slightly and consider those facilities in compliance.

(D) The government's construction projects would not on being completed, add to the stock of facilities available for leasing in the cities concerned.

(E) Before embarking on any major construction project, the government is required by law to establish beyond any reasonable doubt that there are no alternatives that are more cost-effective.

在某些城市，政府不顾这些城市中很高的办公楼闲置率，还在继续进行雄心勃勃的建造计划。闲置的办公楼虽然可以租出去，但不幸的是，它们并未具备作为法院和实验室等所需设施的要求。所以，政府并不为财政浪费而内疚。

下面哪个是以上的论证所依据的假设？

(A) 如果可能，把这些闲置的办公楼改造成符合政府需要不会使出租这些办公楼比重新建造更节省成本。

(B) 当两种替代性选择都在成本上具有效率时，政府更青睐于租借设施而非拥有它们。

(C) 如果可以租到的设施与满足政府要求的设施所要的条件非常相近，政府可以稍微放松其条件来妥协地考虑一下那些设施。

(D) 考虑到相关城市中可供出租的设施的存货，政府的建造计划不会最终完成。

(E) 在开始任何大型建筑计划之前，法律要求政府毫无疑义地确定不存在最节省成本的替代性选择。

6. Potato cyst nematodes are a pest of potato crops. The nematodes can lie dormant for several years in their cysts, which are protective capsules, and do not emerge except in the presence of chemicals emitted by potato roots. A company that has identified the relevant chemicals is planning to market them to potato farmers to spread on their fields when no potatoes are planted; any nematodes that emerge will soon starve to death.

Which of the following, if true, best supports the claim that the company's plan will be successful?

(A) Nematodes that have emerged from their cysts can be killed by ordinary pesticides.

土豆线囊虫是土豆作物的一种害虫，这种线虫能在保护囊中休眠好几年，除了土豆根散发化学物质之外，它不会出来。一个已确认了相关化学物质的公司正计划把这种化学物质投放市场，让农民把它喷洒在没有种土豆的地里，这样所有出来的线虫不久就会饿死。

下面哪一个，如果正确，最能支持这个公司的计划将会成功？

(A) 从囊中出来的线虫能被普通杀虫剂杀死。

(B) The only part of a potato plant that a nematode eats is the roots.

(C) Some bacteria commonly present in the roots of potatoes digest the chemicals that cause the nematodes to emerge from their cysts.

(D) Trials have shown that spreading even minute quantities of the chemicals on potato fields caused nine-tenths of the nematodes present to emerge from their cysts.

(E) The chemicals that cause the nematodes to emerge from their cysts are not emitted all the time the potato plant is growing.

7. It is better for the environment if as much of all packaging as possible is made from materials that are biodegradable in landfills. Therefore, it is always a change for the worse to replace packaging made from paper or cardboard with packaging made from plastics that are not biodegradable in landfills.

Which of the following, if true, constitutes the strongest objection to the argument above?

(A) The paper and cardboard used in packaging are usually not biodegradable in landfills.

(B) Some plastic used in packaging is biodegradable in landfills.

(C) In many landfills, a significant proportion of space is taken up by materials other than discarded packaging materials.

(D) It is impossible to avoid entirely the use of packaging materials that are not biodegradable in landfills.

(E) Sometimes, in packaging an item, plastics that are not biodegradable in landfills are combined with cardboard.

8. Any serious policy discussion about acceptable levels of risk in connection with explosions is not well served if the participants fail to use the word "explosion" and use the phrase "energetic disassembly" instead. In fact, the word "explosion" elicits desirable reactions, such as a heightened level of attention, whereas the substitute phrase does not. Therefore, of the two terms, "explosion" is the one that should be used throughout discussions of this sort.

Which of the following is an assumption on which the argument above depends?

(A) In the kind of discussion at issue, the advantages of desirable reactions to the term "explosion" outweigh the

(B) 线虫只吃土豆的根。

(C) 一些通常存在于土豆根里的细菌能消化那些导致线虫从囊中出来的化学物质。

(D) 试验显示，在土豆田里喷洒小量的化学物质可以使存在的9/10的线虫从囊中出来。

(E) 能使线虫从囊中出来的化学物质并不是在土豆生长的所有时间都能被释放

如果尽可能多的包装都用垃圾场里可生物降解的材料来制造的话，这将对环境更加有益。因此，用在垃圾场不可生物降解的塑料制造的包装来取代用纸或纸板制造的包装，总是一个更糟的变化。

以下哪一个，如果正确，将构成对上面论述的最强烈的反对？

(A) 通常用于包装的纸和纸板在垃圾场里是不能生物降解的。

(B) 在包装中所使用的一些塑料在垃圾场是可生物降解的。

(C) 在许多垃圾场，相当大一部分空间都被可丢弃材料之外的材料占据。

(D) 完全避免使用垃圾场中不可生物降解的包装材料是不可能的。

(E) 有时候，在包装一件物品时，在垃圾场里不可生物降解的塑料是与纸板配用的。

如果与会者不使用"爆炸"这个词而使用"能量分解"这个短语的话，那么任何严肃的关于与爆炸相连的可接受风险水平的政策讨论都是不恰当的。实际上，"爆炸"这个词可以引出合意的反应，诸如提高注意度，而那个替代的短语并没有这种效果。因此，在这两个术语中，"爆炸"应该在这种讨论的全过程中被使用。

以下哪一个是上述论断所基于的假设？

(A) 在该问题的讨论中，对"爆炸"这个术语产生合意反应的优点要超过其缺点。如果有缺点的话，它是产生于对

drawbacks, if any, arising from undesirable reactions to that term.

(B) The phrase "energetic disassembly" has not so far been used as a substitute for the word "explosion" in the kind of discussion at issue.

(C) In any serious policy discussion, what is said by the participants is more important than how it is put into words.

(D) The only reason that people would have for using "energetic disassembly" in place of "explosion" is to render impossible any serious policy discussion concerning explosions.

(E) The phrase "energetic disassembly" is not necessarily out of place in describing a controlled rather than an accidental explosion.

那个术语的不合意的反应。

(B) 在该问题讨论中，"能量分解"这个词组目前还没有被当作"爆炸"这个词的替代词使用。

(C) 在任何严肃的政策讨论中，与会者所说的内容要比如何表达重要得多。

(D) 人们将用"能量分解"来"代替"爆炸的唯一原因是让任何关于爆炸的严肃政策讨论成为不可能。

(E) 在描述可控制的而不是意外的爆炸时，"能量分解"这个短语并不必然是不恰当的。

9. Mannis Corporation's archival records are stored in an obsolete format that is accessible only by its current computer system; thus they are inaccessible when that system is not functioning properly. In order to avoid the possibility of losing access to their archival records in the case of computer malfunction, Mannis plans to replace its current computer system with a new system that stores records in a format that is accessible to several different systems.

The answer to which of the following questions would be most helpful in evaluating the effectiveness of the plan as a means of retaining access to the archival records?

(A) Will the new computer system require fewer operators than the current system requires?

(B) Has Mannis Corporation always stored its archival records in a computerized format?

(C) Will the new computer system that Mannis plans ensure greater security for the records stored than does Mannis' current system?

(D) Will Mannis' current collection of archival records be readily transferable to the new computer system?

(E) Will the new computer system be able to perform many more tasks than the current system is able to perform?

Mannis公司的档案记录被保存成一种只有通过其现在的计算机系统才能进入的格式，这样当系统不能适当运行时，就得不到这些记录。为了防止因计算机失灵而不能取得它们的记录的可能性。Mannis计划用一个新系统取代现在的计算机系统，该新系统保存记录的格式可以进入几个不同的系统。

下面哪个问题的答案对评价该计划作为保证取得档案记录的方法是最有利的？

(A) 新的计算机系统是否比现在系统要求更少的操作人员？

(B) Mannis公司是否经常以计算机化的形式来保存其档案记录？

(C) Mannis计划的新计算机系统能否保证保存记录比现在的系统有更大的安全性？

(D) Mannis现在所有的档案记录能否立刻转送到新计算机系统？

(E) 新计算机系统是否能够比现在的系统执行更多的任务？

10. Last year the worldwide paper industry used over twice as much fresh pulp (pulp made directly from raw plant fibers) as recycled pulp (pulp made from wastepaper). A paper-industry analyst has projected that by 2010 the industry will use at least as much recycled pulp annually as it does fresh pulp, while

去年全球造纸行业使用了两倍于再循环纸浆（用废纸制造的纸浆）的新鲜纸浆（直接用天然植物纤维制造的纸浆）。一位造纸行业的分析人员预计，到2010年该行业每年使用的再循环纸浆至少和其使用

using a greater quantity of fresh pulp than it did last year.

If the information above is correct and the analyst's projections prove to be accurate, which of the following projections must also be accurate?

(A) In 2010 the paper industry will use at least twice as much recycled pulp as it did last years.

(B) In 2010 the paper industry will use at least twice as much total pulp as it did last year.

(C) In 2010 the paper industry will produce more paper from a given amount of pulp than it did last year.

(D) As compared with last year, in 2010 the paper industry will make more paper that contains only recycled pulp.

(E) As compared with last year, in 2010 the paper industry will make less paper that contains only fresh pulp.

11. In malaria-infested areas, many children tend to suffer several bouts of malaria before becoming immune to the disease. Clearly, what must be happening is that those children's immune systems are only weakly stimulated by any single exposure to the malaria parasite and need to be challenged several times to produce an effective immune response.

Which of the following, if true, most seriously undermines the explanatory hypothesis?

(A) Immediately after a child has suffered a bout of malaria, the child's caregivers tend to go to great lengths in taking precautions to prevent another infection, but this level of attention is not sustained.

(B) Malaria is spread from person to person by mosquitoes, and mosquitoes have become increasingly resistant to the pesticides used to control them.

(C) A certain gene, if inherited by children from only one of their parents, can render those children largely immune to infection with malaria.

(D) Antimalaria vaccines, of which several are in development, are all designed to work by stimulating the body's immune system.

(E) There are several distinct strains of malaria, and the body's immune response to any one of them does not protect it against the others.

12. An advertisement designed to convince readers of the great durability of automobiles manufactured by the Deluxe Motor Car Company cites as evidence the fact that over half

的新鲜纸浆一样多，但使用的新鲜纸浆数量要比去年多。

如果以上的信息是正确的并且该分析人员的预测证明是准确的，下面哪个预测一定也是准确的？

(A) 在2010年，造纸行业使用的再循环纸浆至少会两倍于去年所使用的。

(B) 在2010年，造纸行业使用的纸浆总量至少会两倍于去年所使用的。

(C) 在2010年，造纸行业用一定数量的纸浆生产出来的纸比去年多。

(D) 与去年相比，在2010年，造纸行业会生产更多的仅包括再循环纸浆的纸。

(E) 与去年相比，在2010年，造纸行业会生产更少的仅包括新鲜纸浆的纸。

在疟疾横行的地区，许多孩子在对疟疾产生免疫力之前都要患几次疟疾。很明显，必将发生的是，当第一次暴露于疟原虫时，孩子们的免疫系统仅仅被微弱地激发，因此需要与之进行几次抗争来产生有效的免疫反应。

以下哪一个，如果正确，最能削弱以上解释性的假说？

(A) 孩子得了一回疟疾之后，孩子的看护者马上会尽力预防再次被感染，但这种程度的注意力不会持续下去。

(B) 疟疾是通过蚊子在人和人之间传播的，蚊子对用来控制它们的杀虫剂的抵制力在增长。

(C) 如果孩子仅从他们的父母中的一个人那里遗传到某种基因，那么这种基因能使这些孩子在很大程度上对疟疾的传染产生免疫力。

(D) 几种开发中的抗疟疾疫苗全部都是打算通过激发人体的免疫系统来起作用。

(E) 有几种不同的疟疾种类，人体对其中一种的免疫反应并不能保护人体抵抗其他几种。

一则广告设计用来让读者相信Deiuxe汽车公司制造的汽车很耐用。广告引以为证的是如下事实：1970年以来由该公司制

of all automobiles built by the company since 1970 are still on the road today, compared to no more than a third for any other manufacturer.

Which of the following, if true, most strongly supports the advertisement's argument?

(A) After taking inflation into account, a new Deluxe automobile costs only slightly more than a new model did in 1970.

(B) The number of automobiles built by Deluxe each year has not increased sharply since 1970.

(C) Owners of Deluxe automobiles typically keep their cars well maintained.

(D) Since 1970, Deluxe has made fewer changes in the automobiles it manufactures than other car companies have made in their automobiles.

(E) Deluxe automobiles have been selling at relatively stable prices in recent years.

13. Many state legislatures are considering proposals to the effect that certain policies should be determined not by the legislature itself but by public referenda in which every voter can take part. Critics of the proposals argue that the outcomes of public referenda would be biased, since wealthy special-interest groups are able to influence voters' views by means of television advertisements.

Which of the following, if true, most strengthens the critics' argument?

(A) Many state legislators regard public referenda as a way of avoiding voting on issues on which their constituents are divided.

(B) During elections for members of the legislature, the number of people who vote is unaffected by whether the candidates run television advertisements or not.

(C) Proponents of policies that are opposed by wealthy special-interest groups are often unable to afford advertising time on local television stations.

(D) Different special-interest groups often take opposing positions on questions of which policies the state should adopt.

(E) Television stations are reluctant to become associated with any one political opinion, for fear of losing viewers who do not share that opinion.

造的汽车超过一半仍然跑在路上、相比之下，别的制造商的则不到1/3。

以下哪一个，如果正确，最能支持广告的论述？

(A) 在考虑了通货膨胀以后，一辆新Deluxe汽车的成本仅仅比1970年的新车多一点。

(B) 自1970年以来，由Deluxe所生产的汽车数量没有急剧上升。

(C) Deluxe汽车的主人通常把他们的车维修得很好。

(D) 自1970年以来，Deluxe公司对其所制造的汽车的改动要少于其他公司制造的汽车。

(E) Deluxe汽车近年来以相对稳定的价格销售。

许多州议会正在考虑建议，某些政策不应当由议会自身决定，而应由每个投票者都能参与的全民投票决定。对这些建议的批评者争辩说，公众全民投票的结果会是偏袒的，因为富人特殊利益集团能够通过电视广告影响投票者的观点。

以下哪一个，如果正确，最能支持批评者的论述？

(A) 许多州议员把公众全民投票看作是避免对那些能使他们的选民分裂的问题进行投票的一个办法。

(B) 在议会成员选举中，投票人的数量不受候选人是否进行电视广告的影响。

(C) 被富人特殊利益集团所反对的政策的拥护者经常不能支付起当地电视台广告时间的费用。

(D) 不同的特殊利益集团经常在本州应采取哪一个政策上持反对观点。

(E) 电视台不情愿与任何政治观点有联系，因为他们害怕失去与他们观点相左的观众。

14. Advertisement:

Of the many over-the-counter medications marketed for the relief of sinus headache, SineEase costs the least per dose. And SineEase is as effective per dose as the most effective of those other medications. So for relief from sinus headaches, SineEase is the best buy.

Which of the following, if true, most seriously weakens the argument above?

(A) Most of the over-the-counter medications marketed for the relief of sinus headache are equally effective per dose in providing such relief.

(B) Many of the over-the-counter medications marketed for the relief of sinus headache contain the same active ingredient as SineEase.

(C) People who suffer from frequent sinus headaches are strongly advised to consult a doctor before taking any over-the-counter medication.

(D) An over-the-counter medication that is marketed for the relief of symptoms of head cold is identical in composition to SineEase but costs less per dose.

(E) The per dose price for any given over-the-counter medication marketed for the relief of sinus headache is higher for smaller packages than it is for larger packages.

15. In the United States, vacationers account for more than half of all visitors to what are technically called "pure aquariums" but for fewer than one quarter of all visitors to zoos, which usually include a "zoo aquarium" of relatively modest scope.

Which of the following, if true, most helps to account for the difference described above between visitors to zoos and visitors to pure aquariums?

(A) In cities that have both a zoo and a pure aquarium, local residents are twice as likely to visit the aquarium as they are to visit the zoo.

(B) Virtually all large metropolitan areas have zoos, whereas only a few large metropolitan areas have pure aquariums.

(C) Over the last ten years, newly constructed pure aquariums have outnumbered newly established zoos by a factor of two to one.

(D) People who visit a zoo in a given year are two times more likely to visit a pure aquarium that year than are people who do not visit a zoo.

(E) The zoo aquariums of zoos that are in the same city as a

广告：在许多投放市场的用于缓解窦头痛的非处方药中，SineEase每剂成本最低，并且每剂SineEase与别的药物中最有效的药一样有效。因此，为了缓解窦头痛，SineEase是最好的选择。

以下哪一个，如果正确，最严重地削弱上述论点？

(A) 投放到市场中用于缓解窦头痛的非处方药中，绝大多数药的每剂药效是相同的。

(B) 投放到市场中用于缓解窦头痛的非处方药中，许多含有与SineEase相同的活性成份。

(C) 患有经常性窦头痛的人被强烈建议在买非处方药之前请教医生。

(D) 一种投放到市场中用于缓解感冒症状的非处方药的组成与SineEase完全一样，但每剂成本更低。

(E) 任何给定的投放到市场中以缓解窦头痛的非处方药的每剂价格，较小包装的比较大包装的贵。

在美国，休假者占了所有专业上称为"纯水族馆"的参观者的一半以上，但只占去动物园——通常包括一个范围相对小的"动物园水族馆"——的参观者的不到1/4。

下面哪个，如果正确，最有利于解释上述的去动物院的参观者与去纯水族馆的参观者之间的区别？

(A) 在既有动物园也有纯水族馆的城市，当地居民参观水族馆的可能性是其参观动物园的可能性的两倍。

(B) 差不多所有的大城市都有动物园，但仅有一些大城市有纯水族馆。

(C) 在过去10年中，新建的纯水族馆数量超过了新建的动物园数量，比率是2:1。

(D) 在某一年中参观了动物园的人这一年去参观纯水族馆的可能性是没有参观动物园的人的两倍。

(E) 在有纯水族馆的同一座城市的动物园

pure aquarium tend to be smaller than the aquariums of zoos that have no pure aquarium nearby.

水族馆要比附近没有纯水族馆的动物园水族馆小。

16. Which of the following, if true, is the most logical completion of the argument below?

The tax system of the Republic of Grootland encourages borrowing by granting its taxpayers tax relief for interest paid on loans. The system also discourages saving by taxing any interest earned on savings. Nevertheless, it is clear that Grootland's tax system does not consistently favor borrowing over saving, for if it did, there would be no.

(A) tax relief in Grootland for those portions of a taxpayer's income, if any, that are set aside to increase that taxpayer's total savings

(B) tax relief in Grootland for the processing fees that taxpayers pay to lending institutions when obtaining certain kinds of loans

(C) tax relief in Grootland for interest that taxpayers are charged on the unpaid balance in credit card accounts

(D) taxes due in Grootland on the cash value of gifts received by taxpayers from banks trying to encourage people to open savings accounts

(E) taxes due in Grootland on the amount that a taxpayer has invested in interest-bearing savings accounts

以下哪一个，如果正确，能合乎逻辑地完成下列论断？

Grootland共和国的税制通过减免纳税人应付贷款利息税来鼓励贷款。该税制还通过征收存款的利息税来打击储蓄。尽管如此，很明显，Grootland的税制并没有一致地有利于借款而不利于储蓄，因为如果那样的话就不会有。

(A) 如果纳税人的收入中有一部分被留出用以增加纳税人的总储蓄的话，那么Grootland会对这一部分收入进行税收减免。

(B) 在Grootland，对纳税人在获得某种贷款时所支付给借款机构的手续费的税收减免。

(C) 在Grootland，对纳税人在信用卡账户上未支付余额所支付的利息的税收减免。

(D) 在Grootland，对纳税人从设法鼓励人们开立储蓄账户的银行所收到的现金价值的礼物的税款。

(E) 在Grootland，纳税人投资于可得利息的储蓄账户上的金额的税款。

参考答案：

1. E	2. B	3. E	4. D	5. A
6. D	7. A	8. A	9. D	10. A
11. E	12. B	13. C	14. D	15. B
16. A				

1. **解析**：段落的推理为今年1月到6月录像机销售仅为去年销售总数的35%，所以，今年总销量要低于去年。我们读题明显发现前提中的"1月到6月"与结论中的"今年"有跳跃，如果一年中录像机销售超过70%是在11月和12月进行的，正如(E)所说，那么就断开了前提与结论的连接，也就Weaken了推理的结论。因此(E)正确。

2. **解析**：本题为"上面段落支持下面哪一个假设"，这种题型大多与归纳题思维一样，但毕竟不完全等于归纳，它比归纳范围要大，这类题有时可以转化为解释现象来考查，即下面哪一个可以解释上面现象的考题。本题指出某岛屿湖泊的泥土里含有Toxaphene，但其制造不在附近区域，也不是从dumping中来，也不是来自于superior湖的水，那么怎么在这个岛屿湖泊泥土里会有Toxaphene？如果Toxaphene是被风带到了这个岛上，正如(B)所说，可以很好地解释上述现象，所以(B)正确。

3. **解析**：本题属于典型的"B，A"型，反对的思路大多是有其他原因。如果与男士相比，许多妇女因为不能得到竞选所需的足够的资金而没有参与竞选，正如(E)所说，那么就指出了确实存在其他原因导致妇女人数很少。所以(E)正确。

4. **解析**：本题为GRE机考重考的题目，属于典型的"B，A"类型，假设思路大多为"除了A以外没有别的原因"，可用否定概念来定位选项，发现(A)、(D)、(E)中间有否定词。(D)排除了他因，即花瓶是坟墓的主人的后代在很多年以后放进去的，可用取非方法去验证，是一个很好的假设。(A)、(B)、(E)都是无关选项；(C)是最易误选的答案，但(C)是支持而非假设，若把(C)改为"在2700年前，西西里岛与希腊之间能够进行贸易往来"，那么就可以作为一个假设。

5. **解析**：本题属于"since A,B"题型。本题推理为：因为闲置的办公楼并未具备作为法院等需要的条件而未出租，所以政府正在重新建造。选项(A)指出A确实有意义，而作为一个假设，可以取非验证，所以(A)正确。

6. **解析**：本题思路很清晰，主要在于读懂段落。

7. **解析**：段落推理为：包装用可生物降解的材料来制造对环境有益，所以用不可生物降解的塑料制造的包装代替纸包装将是一个更糟的变化。上面推理成立依赖的假设是：纸包装是可生物降解的。如果纸包装在垃圾场不能生物降解，正如(A)所说，那么就反对了上面的假设。所以上面推理必不成立，因此(A)正确；(E)仅仅说明不可降解的塑料与纸板配用，但究竟纸板什么属性，并未说出，因此是无关选项。

8. **解析**：Therefore前后分别为原因与结论，最后一句话实际上与第一句话相对应。因为"explosion"引出desirable的反应，而"energetic disassembly"不行，所以应使用"explosion"。假设的答案方向有三种：①A与B之间有联系；②引出desirable的反应的原因有意义；③没有其他原因影响使用"explosion"。如果讨论中，对"explosion"的合意反应优点超过缺点且若有缺点也是由于不合意的反应，正如(A)所说，就确实表明引出desirable的反应的原因有意义，即A可行或有意义，所以(A)正确；(B)、(E)无关；(C)起到了Weaken的作用；而(D)中的only属段落中未出现的绝对化语言，所以必错。

9. **解析**：本题为典型的"B，A"型，就实现某个目的而提出一个解决方法，评价的思路要么为"A可行或有意义吗"，要么为"有其他原因影响B吗"。而(D)指出"Mannis现有档案记录能否立即转送到新计算机系统？相当于说"A可行吗"，因此(D)可以作为一个很好的评价；(C)易误选，但(C)讨论的是数据获取的安全性问题，与本题问题目的"评价该计划可行性"无关，因此(C)不正确。

10. **解析**：本题为考过多次的应把握逻辑层次结构的归纳，请自己认真体会(A)的正确原因。(D)易误选，但(D)中绝对化语言only的出现告诉我们(D)不可能作为一个正确答案。

11. **解析**：本题比较简单，我们重点是去反对段落里的解释性假说，即孩子们通过暴露于疟原虫下并与之抗争数次可产生有效免疫反应。如果疟疾种类不止一种，而人们对其中一种的免疫反应并不能保护人体抵抗其他几种，正如(E)所说，那么孩子对疟疾产生免疫力可能还要借助于其他途径，所以(E)Weaken了解释性假说，所以(E)正确；(C)易误选，但(C)讨论的仅仅是特定的一组孩子，而未说明一般的孩子，因此错误。

12. **解析**：本题段落推理是从一个数字比较中得出Deluxe汽车公司制造的汽车耐用。现在要支持它，那么也应从数字入手。(B)涉及数字，并且说明1970年以来，由Deluxe生产的汽车数量无急剧上升，从而说明近几年来其卖的车和别的公司差不多，但其汽车仍有超过一半跑在路上，所以其汽车耐用。所以(B)起到了支持作用，因此(B)正确；(A)、(E)谈的是价格，与数量无关；(C)说明是人的因素而非车的因素，起到了反对作用；而(D)离结论的距离比较远。

13. **解析**：本题把since-clause放在后面，一般表示强调。而支持重点支持段落所强调的"since wealthy special-interest groups are able to influence voters' views by means of television advertisements"，而选项(C)说明被富人特殊利益集团所反对的政策的拥护者无能力做广告，因此他们无法通过广告影响别人观点，所以富人这样做就有利得多。所以(C)正确。

注：to the effect that...大意为……

　　referenda *n.* ［*pl.*］全民投票

14. **解析**：本题难度较大。其逻辑推理为：缓解窦头痛的非处方药中，SineEase成本低，所以缓解窦头痛最好用SineEase。简化推理就变为"因为SineEase成本低，所以购买SineEase"，(A)中的"equally"与(B)中的"the same...as"揭示的是相同点，不可能Weaken上面推断；(C)中any绝对化语言必然不对；(E)为无关比较；而(D)说明某药组成与SineEase一样，但每剂成本更低，起到了反对作用。很多同学之所以不理解(D)为什么正确，主要是忽略了(D)中的"identical in composition"。试想若某药与SineEase组成完全一样，那么它必可被用来缓解窦头痛且达到同样的效果，但它成本更低，因此更好地选择应为这种药，值得注意的是(D)并未反对事实，段落中的事实是SineEase是缓解窦头痛的非处方药中最便宜的，而(D)中的某种药是缓解感冒症状的非处方药中最便宜的。

15. **解析**：本题为解释差异，要抓住双方关键词及差异点数字来定位选项。(B)中涉及双方关键词"zoos"与"pure aquariums"，且又有数字"all"与"only a few"，且也能起到解释作用，所以(B)正确；(A)中讨论的是local residents，而段落中讨论的是"Vacationers"，因此(A)为无关选项；(C)中的"over the last ten years"为特指，但段落中为泛指，所以也不正确；(D)、(E)的比较对象压根就不对。

16. **解析**：本题虽是最后一题，但其难度并不大，主要在于阅读。请自己思考(A)正确的原因。

    tax relief   税收减免

    tax due   应付税，税款

    unpaid balance   未支付余额

十一、GMAT考前逻辑推理冲刺训练试题及解析（十一）

1. When butterfat was considered nutritious and healthful, a law was enacted requiring that manufacturers use the term "imitation butter" to indicate butter whose butterfat content had been diminished through the addition of water. Today, it is known that the high cholesterol content of butterfat makes it harmful to human health. Since the public should be encouraged to eat foods with lower rather than higher butterfat content and since the term "imitation" with its connotations of falsity deters many people from purchasing products so designated, manufacturers who wish to give reduced-butterfat butter the more appealing name of "lite butter" should be allowed to do so.

Which one of the following, if true, most seriously undermines the argument?

(A) The manufacturers who prefer to use the word "lite" instead of "imitation" are motivated principally by the financial interest of their stockholders.

(B) The manufacturers who wish to call their product "lite butter" plan to change the composition of the product so that it contains more water than it now does.

(C) Some individuals who need to reduce their intake of cholesterol are not deterred from using the reduced-butterfat product by the negative connotations of the term "imitation."

当奶油中的脂肪被认为是有营养的和有益健康时，国家就颁布了一条法律，要求所有的生产商使用"仿制奶油"的术语来说明他们的被水稀释的奶油中的奶油脂肪含量。今天，众所周知，奶油脂肪中较高的胆固醇含量使其有害于人类健康。既然鼓励公众吃低奶油脂肪含量而不是高奶油脂肪含量的食物，既然"仿制"一词所具有的假的含义阻止了人们购买那些希望降低奶油脂肪含量的厂家生产的如此命名的产品，就应该使用更具吸引力的名字，"清淡奶油"。

如果正确的话，下面哪一点最能驳斥以上论述？

(A) 喜欢用"清淡"一词代替"仿制"的厂商主要是被他们的股东的财政上的利益所驱使。

(B) 希望用"清淡奶油"称呼他们的产品的厂商计划改变他们产品的成份，以使它比现在含有更多的水份。

(C) 一些需要减少他们的胆固醇摄入量的人，并不因为稀释奶油产品具有"仿制"一词的负面含义而阻止（其购买）。

(D) Cholesterol is only one of many factors that contribute to the types of health problems with which the consumption of excessive amounts of cholesterol is often associated.

(E) Most people deterred from eating "imitation butter" because of its name choose alternatives with a lower butterfat content than this product has.

2. A study of adults who suffer from migraine headaches revealed that a significant proportion of the study participants suffer from a complex syndrome characterized by a set of three symptoms.Those who suffer from the syndrome experienced excessive anxiety during early childhood. As adolescents, these people began experiencing migraine headaches. As these people approached the age of 20, they also began to experience recurring bouts of depression. Since this pattern is invariant, always with excessive anxiety at its beginning, it follows that excessive anxiety in childhood is one of the causes of migraine headaches and depression in later life.

The reasoning in the argument is vulnerable to criticism on which one of the following grounds?

(A) It does not specify the proportion of those in the general population who suffer from thesyndrome.

(B) It fails to rule out the possibility that all of the characteristic symptoms of the syndrome have a common cause.

(C) It makes a generalization that is inconsistent with the evidence.

(D) It fails to demonstrate that the people who participated in the study are representative of migraine sufferers.

(E) It does not establish why the study of migraine sufferers was restricted to adult participants.

3. Until recently it was thought that ink used before the sixteenth century did not contain titanium. However, a new type of analysis detected titanium in the ink of the famous Bible printed by Johannes Gutenberg and in that of another fifteenth-century Bible known as B-36, though not in the ink of any of numerous other fifteenth-century books analyzed. This finding is of great significance, since it not only strongly supports the hypothesis that B-36 was printed by Gutenberg but also shows that the presence of titanium in the ink of the purportedly fifteenth-century Vinland Map can no longer be regarded as a reason for doubting the map's authenticity.

The reasoning in the passage is vulnerable to criticism on the ground that

(D) 胆固醇仅是导致多种通常与过量消耗胆固醇相联系的健康问题的多种因素之一。

(E) 大多数因"仿制奶油"的名字而不敢吃"仿制奶油"的人选择使用的替代品中的奶油含量比"仿制奶油"低。

对患有偏头痛的成年人的研究揭示,被研究者中有很大比例的人患有非常复杂的综合症,这种综合症的特征是有三种症状。那些患有综合症的人早在他们的孩童时代,就经历了极度的焦虑症。当到了青少年时,这些人开始患有偏头痛。当这些人到20岁时,他们还开始忍受循环性发作的抑郁症。既然这种模式是一成不变的,开始时总是伴随着过度焦虑症,那么就可推出孩童时代的过度焦虑症是偏头痛和后来的抑郁症的起因之一。

上述辩论的推理最易受到下面哪条理由的批评?

(A) 它没有指明整个人口中患有偏头痛的人的比例。

(B) 它没有排除该综合症的所有症状特征具有共同的起因的可能性。

(C) 它的概括性论述与证据不一致。

(D) 它没有证明被研究者是偏头痛患者的代表。

(E) 它没有证实为什么对偏头痛患者的研究只局限于成年受试人员。

直到目前为止,人们认为16世纪以前使用的油墨中不含钛。然而,一种新型分析方法表明尽管在众多的其他15世纪的书的墨迹中并没有发现钛,但是在Johannes Gutenberg印刷的著名的圣经中以及另一本15世纪的以B-36而闻名的圣经的墨迹中发现了钛。这个发现具有非常重大的意义,因为它不但强有力地印证了B-36是被Gutenberg所印刷的假想,而且揭示了号称为15世纪在Vinland Map 中发现的钛元素不能再被作为怀疑该画的真实性的一个原因。

(A) the results of the analysis are interpreted as indicating that the use of titanium as an ingredient in fifteenth-century ink both was, and was not, extremely restricted.

(B) if the technology that makes it possible to detect titanium in printing ink has only recently become available, it is unlikely that printers or artists in the fifteenth century would know whether their ink contained titanium or not.

(C) it is unreasonable to suppose that determination of the date and location of a document's printing or drawing can be made solely on the basis of the presence or absence of a single element in the ink used in the document.

(D) both the B-36 Bible and the Vinland Map are objects that can be appreciated on their own merits whether or not the precise date of their creation or the identity of the person who made them is known.

(E) the discovery of titanium in the ink of the Vinland Map must have occurred before titanium was discovered in the ink of the Gutenberg Bible and the B-36 Bible.

短文中的推理最易被下面哪条理由批评?

(A) 分析的结果被解释为, 15世纪时使用钛作为油墨的一种成份既非常有限又非常普遍。

(B) 如果探测油墨中是否含有钛元素的技术只是在最近才出现, 那么15世纪的印刷者和艺术家是不会知道他们的油墨中是否含有钛的。

(C) 只通过测定文献资料以及绘画的墨迹中是否含有某单一元素就能确定它们的日期和地点的主张是不合理的。

(D) 不管B-36圣经和Vinland Map创造的日期是否精确或其创作者是否知道, 它们本身就具有被欣赏的价值。

(E) 发现Vinland Map的墨迹中含有钛的日期一定比发现Guteberg圣经以及B-36圣经的墨迹中含有钛的日期早。

4. In a survey of consumers in an Eastern European nation, respondents were asked two questions about each of 400 famous Western brands: whether or not they recognized the brand name and whether or not they thought the products bearing that name were of high quality. The results of the survey were a rating and corresponding rank order for each brand based on recognition, and a second rating-plus-ranking based on approval. The brands ranked in the top 27 for recognition were those actually available in the nation. The approval rankings of these 27 brands often differed sharply from their recognition rankings. By contrast, most of the other brands had ratings, and thus rankings, that were essentially the same for recognition as for approval.

Which one of the following, if each is a principle about consumer surveys, is violated by the survey described?

(A) Never ask all respondents a question if it cannot reasonably be answered by respondents who make a particular response to another question in the same survey.

(B) Never ask a question that is likely to generate a large variety of responses that are difficult to group into a manageable number of categories.

(C) Never ask all respondents a question that respondents cannot answer without giving up their anonymity.

(D) It is better to ask the same question about ten different

在东欧一个国家对消费者的调查报告中, 应答者就400个著名的西方商标中的每一个都被询问两个问题: 他们是否能认出那个商标的名称以及他们是否认为具有那个商标的产品质量较高。调查报告的结果就是根据认识以及认可程度而对每种商标所定的等级以及相应的排序。在认识上, 位居前27名的商标都是那些在这个国家可以实际接触到的商标。这27种商标的认识排序通常与认可排序大相径庭。相比之下, 其他大多数的商标在定级及排序后, 在认识与认可上的排序实际上是一样的。

下面每一项如果都是消费调查报告的原则的话, 上面所描述的调查报告违反了哪一项?

(A) 从不询问所有应答者一个问题, 如果这个问题不能被那些会对同一个调查报告中的另一问题做出特定反应的应答者做合理回答的话。

(B) 从不询问一个可能会产生多种答案, 并且很难把多种答案归成几个可处理的范畴的问题。

(C) 从不询问所有应答者若不放弃匿名权就无法回答的问题。

(D) 对10种不同的产品询问同一个问题要

products than to ask ten different questions about a single product.

(E) It is best to ask questions that a respondent can answer without fear of having gotten the answer wrong.

5. Computer operating system software has become increasingly standardized. But when a large business with multiple, linked computer systems uses identical operating system software on all of its computers, a computer vandal who gains access to one computer automatically has access to the data on all the computers. Using a program known as a "virus," the vandal can then destroy much of the data on all the computers. If such a business introduced minor variations into its operating system software, unauthorized access to all the computers at the same time could be virtually eliminated. Furthermore, variations in operating system software can be created without any loss of computer compatibility to the business. Therefore, it is advisable for businesses to implement such variations.

Which one of the following, if true, supports the conclusion in the passage?

(A) Standardization of computer operating system software has increased computer compatibility among different businesses.

(B) Correcting any damage resulting from an invasion by a computer virus program is more expensive than preventing the damage.

(C) It is not costly for a business to maintain incompatible computer operating systems.

(D) There are other kinds of destructive computer programs that do not depend on intercomputer links.

(E) Not all businesses need to share data among their internal computer systems.

6. An examination of corruption provides the basis for rejecting the view that an exact science of society can ever be constructed. As with all other social phenomena that involve deliberate secrecy, it is intrinsically impossible to measure corruption, and this is not merely due to the fact that social science has not yet reached its goal, achievable to be sure, of developing adequate quantifying techniques. If people were ready to answer questions about their embezzlements and bribes, it would mean that these practices had acquired the

比对单一产品询问10种不同的问题好。

(E) 最好问一些应答者可以回答，且不怕答错的问题。

计算机的操作系统软件日益标准化。但当一大公司处于多重连接系统的每一台计算机都使用同一种操作系统软件时，一个进入一台计算机的计算机破坏者，就会自动地访问所有的计算机。使用一种叫做"病毒"的程序，破坏者可以破坏掉所有计算机中的许多数据，如果这样的公司在它的操作系统软件中做一些微小的变化，实际上就可消除在同一时间无经授权就可访问所有计算机的现象。并且，在操作系统软件上所做的改变并不会使公司的计算机的兼容性受损。因此实施这样的改变对公司来说是可取的。

下面哪一点，如果正确的话，能支持文中的结论？

(A) 计算机操作系统软件的标准化已使不同公司之间的计算机的兼容性增加。

(B) 改正由于计算机病毒程序入侵而造成的破坏的费用要比预防它昂贵得多。

(C) 对一个公司来说，维持不兼容的计算机操作系统的代价不高。

(D) 有其他类型的不依赖于计算机相互连接的破坏性计算机程序。

(E) 并不是所有的公司都需要在他们内部的计算机之间共享数据。

一项对腐败的检查为可以构造一个严格的社会科学的观念提供了否决依据。就像所有其他蓄意含有秘密的社会现象一样，对腐败进行估量实质上是不可能的，并且这不仅仅是由于社会科学还没有达到它的一定可以达到的、开发出足够的定量技术的目标。如果人们乐意回答有关他们贪污受贿的问题，那就意味着这些做法具有合法化的征税活动的特征，他们就会停

character of legitimate, taxable activities and had ceased to be corrupt. In other words, corruption must disappear if it is to be measurable.

Which one of the following most accurately states a hidden assumption that the author must make in order to advance the argument above?

(A) Some people believe that an exact science of society can be constructed.

(B) The primary purpose of an exact science is to quantify and measure phenomena.

(C) An intrinsic characteristic of social phenomena that involve deliberate secrecy is that they cannot be measured.

(D) An exact science of social phenomena that involve deliberate secrecy cannot be constructed.

(E) An exact science can be constructed only when the phenomena it studies can be measured.

7. In a recent experiment, a high school English teacher interspersed real, commonly used proverbs with several nonsensical proverbial-sounding statements that he had made up. He then asked his students to evaluate all of the statements on the list. In general, the students found the bogus proverbs and the real proverbs to be equally full of wisdom and meaning. The teacher concluded that proverbs attain their status as proverbs more through frequent usage than through their inherent wisdom.

Which one of the following, if true, would most effectively challenge the teacher's conclusion?

(A) Some proverbs are used more frequently than others.

(B) There were more real proverbs than bogus proverbs in the list of statements.

(C) There are stylistic differences between proverbial and proverbial-sounding statements.

(D) Some students view a statement in one way and other students view the same statement in a very different way.

(E) The students selected as evaluators were too inexperienced to judge the wisdom of the statements.

8. It is commonly accepted that we should be concerned about our own physical health. The desire to take responsibility for all aspects of our physical condition, however, produces a

止贪污。换句话说，如果贪污可被估量的话，那它一定会消失。

下面哪一条最准确地陈述了一个作者为加强论述而必须做的一个暗含的假设？

(A) 有些人认为可以建造一个严格的社会科学。

(B) 一个严格科学的首要目的是要对现象进行测量及定量化。

(C) 包含有蓄意含有秘密的社会现象的一个本质特征是它们不能被度量。

(D) 不能建造一个蓄意含有秘密的严格的社会科学。

(E) 只有当一科学研究对象可以被估量时，才有可能建造一个严格的科学。

一高中英语教师在最近的一次试验中，把一些真正的，通常使用的格言散置于几个他自己编造的、无意义的听起来像格言的句子之中。接着他让学生们对所有列出的句子进行评价。学生们普遍都认为伪造的格言与真正的格言一样地具有哲理和含意。这个老师于是就推论出格言之所以得到了格言的地位，主要是因为他们经常被使用，而不是因为它们具有内在的哲理。

下面哪一点，如果正确的话，最能质疑那个老师的结论？

(A) 有些格言使用的频率比其他格言的高。

(B) 在所列出的句子中，真正的格言的数量比伪造的格言的多。

(C) 格言型的句子与听起来像格言的句子具有不同的风格。

(D) 一些学生以一种方式来考虑一句子，另一些学生会以另一种截然不同的方式来考虑它。

(E) 那些被选择作为评价者的学生，缺乏判断句子哲理性的经验。

众所周知，我们应当关心我们自身的身体健康。然而，对我们身体状况各方面都负责的欲望会产生一些负面的结果。仅

number of negative consequences. By focusing exclusively on our physical health, we tend to ignore our mental health. Therefore, although we can derive physical benefits from our preoccupation with physical health, we often do so at the expense of our mental health.

The author establishes her position in the passage by doing which one of the following?

(A) She defends her position and then extends it into a second area.

(B) She reveals a contradiction in a position commonly held to be correct.

(C) She supports a commonly held point of view by providing additional evidence.

(D) She first states her position and then qualifies it with a number of concessions.

(E) She argues that a popular position can lead to problems if taken to an extreme.

9. The recent dramatic increase in commuter airline crashes is caused in large part by pilot inexperience. As a major growth industry, the commuter airlines have recently had a great increase in the demand for experienced pilots. It is impossible to define and assess pilot experience, however. For example, someone with 1,000 hours of flight experience as an instructor in Arizona, where the weather is good, cannot be compared to someone with 1,000 hours' experience as a night cargo pilot in the stormy northeastern United States.

The author's conclusion that the dramatic increase in commuter airline crashes is caused by pilot inexperience is most weakened by the fact that the author has

(A) argued that it is impossible to measure "pilot experience."

(B) used an example that does not relate logically to the point being illustrated.

(C) provided only a partial explanation for the increase in commuter airline crashes.

(D) made an unfair comparison between experience as a flight instructor and experience as a night cargo pilot.

(E) not specified how much of the recent increase in commuter airline crashes is due to pilot inexperience.

10. In a recent advertisement, a major cereal company contended that the better educated people are, the more likely it is that as children they regularly ate oatmeal. As evidence,

仅关注我们的身体健康，我们会疏忽我们的精神健康。因此，尽管我们可以从我们对身体健康的过分关注中获得身体上的益处，但是我们这样做通常是以牺牲我们的精神健康为代价的。

作者通过下面哪一项来证实她在上述段落中的立场？

(A) 她先为自己的立场辩护，接着把它扩展到第二个领域。

(B) 她揭示了通常被认为是正确的立场的自相矛盾性。

(C) 通过提供新的论据，她证实了一个被普遍接受的观点。

(D) 她先提出自己的立场，接着用几个让步对自己的立场进行修正。

(E) 她证明了一流行的观点，若走向极端会出现问题。

最近，通勤客机坠落的事故急剧增加在很大程度上是由飞行员缺乏经验所致。作为一个主要增长的工业部门，通勤客机最近对有经验的飞机驾驶员的需求量剧增。然而对飞机驾驶员的经验进行确定及评估是不可能的。例如，一个在气候良好的亚利桑那州飞行1000小时的教官，是不能和一个在充满暴风雨的东北部飞行1000小时的夜班货机飞行员相比的。

作者关于通勤客机坠毁事故的增加是由飞行员缺乏经验所致的结论最能被作者的（哪项）事实所削弱？

(A) 认为不可能衡量飞行员的经验。

(B) 使用了一个与所阐明的观点在逻辑上不相关的例子。

(C) 对往返航空公司飞机坠毁事件的增加，只给出了片面的解释。

(D) 对飞行教官的经验与夜班货机的经验做了一个不公平的比较。

(E) 没有指明最近有多少往返航空公司的飞机的坠毁是由飞行员缺乏经验所致。

在最近的一则广告里，一家大型谷物食品公司争论到，受过教育越好的人，在他们还是孩子的时候，经常吃燕麦粥的可

the company cited a national random survey of college graduates in which four-fifths of all those surveyed reported having eaten oatmeal at least once a week when they were young.

Which one of the following is an additional piece of information that would support the cereal company's conclusion?

(A) Four-fifths of all current college graduates eat oatmeal regularly.

(B) Fewer than four-fifths of those without a college degree ate oatmeal regularly when they were children.

(C) Among people who have additional education beyond college, four-fifths ate oatmeal regularly when they were children.

(D) More than four-fifths of the population at large—college graduates and nongraduates combined—ate oatmeal regularly when they were children.

(E) Those college graduates who did not eat oatmeal regularly when they were children did eat oatmeal on an occasional basis.

11. Odysseus answered well when the priests showed him a picture of those who had honored the gods and then escaped shipwreck, and asked him whether he did not now acknowledge the power of the gods. "Yes," he asked, "but where are those pictured who were drowned after their prayers?" And such is the way of all superstitions; wherein humans, having a delight in such vanities, mark the events there they are fulfilled, but where they fail, though this happens much oftener, neglect and pass them by.

Which one of the following contains the error of reasoning described by the author in the passage?

(A) I have discovered that Friday the 13th really is a day of misfortune. Just this past Friday, the 13th, I locked myself out of the house.

(B) Although Napoleon and Alexander the Great were short, Abraham Lincoln and Charies de Gaulle were tall. So short people seek leadership in order to overcome feelings of inferiority.

(C) Every semester for the past 15 years, an average of 10 percent of Ms.Elliot's history students have dropped her course before the exam. So, it seems likely that we can expert 10 percent to drop out this year.

(D) No reliable observer has ever actually seen a yeti. The strongest evidence seems to be some suspicious tracks.

能性就越大。该公司引用了对全国大学毕业生的随机调查报告来作为例证。报告显示，在被调查的人中有4/5的人在他们年幼的时候每周至少吃一次燕麦粥。

下面哪一点是支持谷物食品公司的结论的附加信息？

(A) 现在的大学毕业生中有4/5的人经常吃燕麦粥。

(B) 没有取得大学学位的人在他们是孩子时经常吃燕麦粥的比例不到4/5。

(C) 在那些除了接受过大学教育、还接受过其他教育的人中，有4/5的人在他们是孩子时经常吃燕麦粥。

(D) 大学毕业生与非大学毕业生合在一起的整个人口中，有多于4/5的人在他们是孩子时经常吃燕麦粥。

(E) 那些在他们是孩子时即使不经常吃燕麦粥的大学生，也偶而会吃燕麦粥。

当牧师向奥德塞斯展示一幅关于那些尊敬上帝并都从沉船中逃生的人的图画时，问他现在是否仍不承认上帝的力量，他回答得很好，"是的"，他说，"但是画中那些祈祷后又被淹死的人在哪呢？"这就是所有迷信的方式，在迷信上，人们都喜欢这样的虚荣心，把他们成功的事情都记下来，而忽视并且忘记那些他们失败的，即使是那些更经常发生的事情。

下面哪一点含有作者文中所叙述的推理错误？

(A) 我发现5月13号确实是不吉利的一天，就是在上个星期五，13号，我被锁在了门外。

(B) 尽管伟人拿破仑和亚历山大个子矮，但是亚伯拉罕·林肯和查利斯·得高利个子高。因此，个子矮的人追求当领导是为了克服他们的低人一等的感觉。

(C) 在过去15年的每个学期中，平均都有10名学生在考前放弃了爱丽特的历史课。因此，我们可以期望今年也有10%的学生会放弃她的历史课。

(D) 没有可信赖的观察者曾经真地看到过

So I think this search for a yeti is probably a wild-goose chase.

(E) I cannot trust my lucky shirt any longer, I wore it to the game today and our team lost.

12. A well-known former quarterback is probably very adept at analyzing the relative strengths of football teams. However, efforts by television advertisers to suggest that the quarterback is an expert on pantyhose or popcorn poppers should arouse skepticism among viewers. The same response should result when a popular television actor, who is frequently cast in the role of a doctor, appears in a commercial to endorse a brand of decaffeinated coffee. His views on televisior acting would deserve attention since he has had considerable experience in that field, but viewers have every right to doubt his authority in coffee advertisements.

Which one of the following is a presupposition essential to the reasoning in the passage above?

(A) The strength of authoritative evidence as legitimate proof is closely related to the authority's degree of expertness in the area in question.

(B) Practical experience counts for more than academic training in assessing the competence of authorities.

(C) The only kind of evidence being used in many television commercials is appeal to authority.

(D) The viewing audience is not sufficiently capable of evaluating authoritative appeals in advertisements.

(E) Television viewers will somehow mentally transfer the credibility of celebrities in one area of expertise to another represented by the product being advertised.

13. The Volunteers for Literacy Program would benefit if Dolores takes Victor's place as director, since Dolores is far more skillful than Victor is at securing the kind of financial support the program needs and Dolores does not have Victor's propensity for alienating the program's most dedicated volunteers.

The pattern of reasoning in the argument above is most closely paralleled in which one of the following?

(A) It would be more convenient for Deminique to take a bus to school than to take the subway, since the bus stops closer to her house than does the subway and, unlike the

雪人，最有力的证据好像是一些可疑的踪迹。因此，我认为这次搜寻雪人是毫无希望的愚蠢之举。

(E) 我不能再相信我的幸运衬衫了，我今天穿上它去看比赛，结果我们的队输了。

一著名的前四分卫可能在分析足球队的相对强弱方面非常在行。然而，一电视广告商提出的该四分卫在女连裤袜或爆玉米花方面也很在行的建议就不得不引起观众的怀疑。当一个受欢迎的经常扮演医生的男演员出现在一个支持某一个不含咖啡因的咖啡品牌的广告中时会产生同样的反应。因为他在电视表演方面有相当多的经验，所以他在那方面的观点就值得重视，但是观众有各种权利来怀疑他在咖啡广告中的权威性。

下面哪一项是上面段落的推理必不可少的前提？

(A) 权威作为合理证据的力量与权威在那个有争议的领域的专业化程度紧密相联。

(B) 在评价权威的能力时，实际经验比学术上接受的训练更重要。

(C) 许多商业电视广告中仅有的一种证据就是诉诸权威。

(D) 许多观众不能充分地评价电视广告中的权威性的呼吁。

(E) 电视观众会莫名其妙地从心理上把名人在某一专业领域的可信度转移到另一个他们做广告的产品领域。

如果Dolores代替Victor的董事长的地位，识字计划的自愿者们将会受益，因为Dolores在获得这个计划所需的财政支持方面比Victor能干得多，并且Dolores没有Victor的喜欢疏远这个计划的最虔诚的自愿者的嗜好。

上面论述中的推论方式与下面哪一个最为接近？

(A) 对Dominque来说，乘公共汽车去学校要比坐地铁方便，因为汽车站比地铁离她的家近，并且不像地铁那样不能

subway, the bus goes directly to the school.

(B) Joshua's interest would be better served by taking the bus to get to his parent's house rather than by taking an airplane, since his primary concern is to travel as cheaply as possible and taking the bus is less expensive than going by airplane.

(C) Belinda will get to the concert more quickly by subway than by taxi, since the concert takes place on a Friday evening and on Friday evenings traffic near the concert hall is exceptionally heavy.

(D) Anite would benefit financially by taking the train to work rather than driving her car, since when she drives she has to pay parking fees and the daily fee for parking a car is higher than a round-trip train ticket.

(E) It would be to Fred's advantage to exchange his bus tickets for train tickets, since he needs to arrive at his meeting before any of the other participants and if he goes by bus at least one of the other participants will arrive first.

直达，公共汽车直接到达他们学校。

(B) Joshua乘公共汽车而不是坐飞机去他的父母家将更符合他的利益，因为他所关心的是旅行费越少越好，坐公共汽车要比乘飞机便宜得多。

(C) Belinda乘地铁去参加音乐会要比坐出租车快，因为音乐会在星期五的晚上举行，而星期五晚上音乐厅附近的交通特别拥挤。

(D) Anide若坐火车而不是开车去上班，在财政上就会受益，因为当他开车时，她就必须付停车费，每日的停车费要比往返旅程的火车票价贵。

(E) 把汽车票换成火车票对Fred有利，因为他需要在所有其他的参加会谈者之前到会，如果他坐汽车，将至少有一个参会者会比他先到达。

14. The similarity between ichthyosaurs and fish is an example of convergence, a process by which different classes of organisms adapt to the same environment by independently developing one or more similar external body features. Ichthyosaurs were marine reptiles and thus do not belong to the same class of organisms as fish. However, ichthyosaurs adapted to their marine environment by converging on external body features similar to those of fish. Most strikingly ichthyosaurs, like fish, had fins.

If the statements above are true, which one of the following is an inference that can be properly drawn on the basis of them?

(A) The members of a single class of organisms that inhabit the same environment must be identical in all their external body features.

(B) The members of a singly class of organisms must exhibit one or more similar external body features that differentiate that class from all other classes of organisms.

(C) It is only as a result of adaptation to similar environments that one class of organisms develops external body features similar to those of another class of organisms.

(D) An organism does not necessarily belong to a class simply because the organism has one or more external body features similar to those of members of that class.

鱼龙与鱼之间的相似性是趋同性的一个例子，趋同性就是不同种类的生物为适应同一环境而独自发育形成一个或多个相似的外部身体特征的过程。鱼龙是海生爬行动物，因此它与鱼不属于同一纲的生物。然而，鱼龙通过把它们的外部身体特征与那些鱼类的趋于一致来适应海洋环境。最引人注意的是鱼龙像鱼一样具有鳍。

如果上面的陈述是正确的，下面哪一点是基于上述陈述的合理推论？

(A) 栖居于同一环境的单一类生物体的成员的所有外部身体特征一定完全相同。

(B) 某一单类的生物体成员一定具有一个或多个使它们与其他种类的生物体相区分的外部身体特征。

(C) 一种生物发育成与其他种类的生物相似的外部身体特征完全是它们适应相似环境的结果。

(D) 不能仅仅因为一生物具有一个或多个与某类生物体的成员相似的身体外部特征，就把该生物与它们归为一类。

(E) Whenever two classes of organisms share the same environment, members of one class will differ from members of the other class in several external body features.

15. Further evidence bearing on Jamison's activities must have come to light. On the basis of previously available evidence alone, it would have been impossible to prove that Jamison was a party to the fraud, and Jamison's active involvement in the fraud has now been definitively established.

The pattern of reasoning exhibited in the argument above most closely parallels that exhibited in which one of the following?

(A) Smith must not have purchased his house within the last year. He is listed as the owner of that house on the old list of property owners, and anyone on the old list could not have purchased his or her property within the last year.

(B) Turner must not have taken her usual train to Nantes today. Had she done so, she could not have been in Nantes until this afternoon, but she was seen having coffee in Nantes at 11 o'clock this morning.

(C) Nofris must have lied when she said that she had not authorized the investigation. There is no doubt that she did authorize it, and authorizing an investigation is not something anyone is likely to have forgotten.

(D) Waugh must have known that last night's class was canceled. Waugh was in the library yesterday, and it would have been impossible for anyone in the library not to have seen the cancellation notices.

(E) LaFort must have deeply resented being passed over for promotion. He maintains otherwise, but only someone who felt badly treated would have made the kind of remark. LaFort made at yesterday's meeting.

16. Editorialist: Additional restrictions should be placed on driver's licenses of teenagers because teenagers lack basic driving skills. Even though drivers of age nineteen and younger make up only 7 percent of registered drivers, they are responsible for over 14 percent of traffic fatalities.

Each of the following, if true, weakens the argument that teenagers lack basic driving skills EXCEPT:

(A) Teenagers tend to drive older and less stable cars than other drivers.

(E) 当两种生物共享同一环境时，一种生物的成员与另一种生物体的成员在数个外部身体特征上有所不同。

有关Jamison活动的进一步的证据一定已真相大白。单靠以前掌握的证据，不可能证明Jamison是欺诈活动的参与者，现在，Jamison积极参与欺诈活动已被最后证实。

上面论证中所展示的推理模式与下面哪一个最为接近？

(A) Smith一定不是在去年购买了他的房子，作为那个房子的房主，他被列在一旧的房产所有者名单上，而任何在那张旧名单上的人，都不可能是在去年购买了他的或她的房子。

(B) Turner今天一定没有坐她通常乘坐的火车去Nantes。如果她乘那个火车，她不可能在今天下午还在Nantes，但是，今天早上，有人看见她在Nantes喝咖啡。

(C) 当Nofris说她没有批准那个调查研究时，她一定在撒谎。毫无疑问，她已经批准它了，批准一调查研究不是一件任何人都可能会忘记的事情。

(D) Waugh一定知道昨天晚上的课被取消了。Waugh昨天在图书馆，而在图书馆的人不可能没有看到那个取消的通知。

(E) LaFort一定为他没被提升而深感愤恨。他说无所谓，但是只有那些受到不公正待遇的人才会做出那样的评论，LaFort在昨天的会上做了那样的评论。

社会撰写人：因为青少年缺乏基本的开车技巧，所以应给予青少年的驾驶执照附加限制。尽管19岁和再小一点的司机只占注册司机的7%，但是他们却是超过14%的交通死亡事故的肇事者。

下面每一项，如果正确，都能削弱青少年缺乏基本的开车技巧的论述，除了：

(A) 与其他人开的车相比，青少年开的车较旧，且稳定性也差。

(B) Teenagers and their passengers are less likely to use seat belts and shoulder straps than others.

(C) Teenagers drive, on average, over twice as far each year as other drivers.

(D) Teenagers cause car accidents that are more serious than those caused by others.

(E) Teenagers are likely to drive with more passengers than the average driver.

(B) 青少年司机和他们的乘客使用座带和肩带的可能性不如其他人的大。

(C) 青少年司机平均每年开车的距离超过其他司机的两倍。

(D) 青少年引起的交通事故比其他人引起的交通事故严重。

(E) 青少年开车时的乘客人数很有可能比一般的司机多。

参考答案：

1. E	2. B	3. A	4. A	5. B
6. E	7. E	8. E	9. A	10. B
11. A	12. A	13. A	14. D	15. B
16. D				

1. 解析：本题的结论是人们因为"imitation butter"中"imitation"一词的"connotation of falsity"而不敢买具有较低的奶油脂肪含量的"imitation butter"。要削弱上面的论述，就要削弱人们不敢购买的原因。选项(E)通过找他因的办法，说明了人们因不敢吃"imitation butter"而选择使用的替代品的奶油含量比"仿制奶油"的实际含量更低，因此更有利于健康，从而驳斥了将"仿制奶油"改为"清淡奶油"有利于消费者的暗含结论，所以推理成立可能性减少，因此(E)是正确的。(C)易误选，但是(C)选项只是说一些需要减少他们的胆固醇摄入量的人不被"reduced butterfat"产品所具有的"negative connotation"所吓住，这并不能对大多数人不被"negative connotation of the term imitation"所吓住构成反对。

2. 解析：对本题推理模式的分析发现，该论述把先出现的事物当作后出现的事物的原因来做出它的结论的，它的结论成立的前提是先后出现的事物不可能具有共同的起因，而文中却没有给出这个前提，因此(B)选项是最佳的答案；(A)、(C)、(D)、(E)均为无关选项。

3. 解析：从本题的论证中可以看出在15世纪时使用钛元素作为油墨的一种成份非常有限；而另一方面，在15世纪时，只有当含有钛的油墨被广泛使用时，被号称为15世纪的Vinland地图的墨迹中含有碳元素才不能作为怀疑该画的真实性的一个原因。由以上分析可以得出本题辩论中的自相矛盾，即15世纪使用钛作为墨水的一种成份，即非常地有限，又非常地普遍，因此(A)是正确答案；(B)是无关选项；(C)、(D)和(E)三个选项都不能从短文中推出。

4. 解析：调查报告的结果显示，位于27名以后的商标的认识和认可的排序是一样的，由此我们可以推出应答者若不能对本调查报告中的一个问题合理地回答时，他往往也很难合理地回答另一个问题。因此很明显本题描述的调查报告违反了(A)选项所描述的原则；(B)、(C)、(D)和(E)四原则都是本题的调查报告所遵循的原则。

5. 解析：要使公司的某一项措施可行，不但要求该措施在技术上可行，更重要的是要求该措施在经济上可行。选项(B)所描述的内容正是这个公司在操作系统软件上做出改变的前提条件，因此(B)选项是正确答案；(A)、(C)、(D)和(E)都与本题的结论无关。

6. 解析：根据对腐败进行估量实质上是不可能是否决可以构造一个严格的社会科学的证据，可以推知对腐败进行估量是可以构造一个严格的社会科学的必要条件。因此可以进一步推出只有当一科学研究对象可被估量时，才有可能建设一个严格的科学，因此(E)选项是作者为加强论述必须做的一个暗含的假设。(A)是无关选项；(B)、(C)和(D)三选项均不能从短文的论述中合理地推出。

7. 解析：要对那个老师的结论进行质疑，首先就应该质疑他的试验的对象具不具有代表性，如果他试验的对象——他的学生自身都缺乏判断句子哲理性的经验，那么他的结论就是明显站不住脚的，因此(E)是正确答案；(A)、(B)、(C)和(D)都是无关选项。

8. **解析**：本题属逻辑应用及技法题。由题中论述可知，若我们过分关注我们的身体健康时就会致使我们的精神健康受损。由此可知(E)是正确答案；而(A)、(B)、(C)和(D)都是明显错误的选项。

9. **解析**：作者的论述具有自相矛盾性，一方面他把飞机坠毁归因于飞行员缺乏经验，另一方面他又说对飞行员的经验进行确定和评价是不可能的，由此可知(A)是正确答案。

10. **解析**：谷物公司用一个正面例子，即被调查的大学毕业生中有4/5的人在他们年幼的时候经常吃燕麦粥来证明它的结论。若谷物公司能从反面即没有取得大学学位的人在年幼时吃燕麦粥的比例不到4/5来证明它的结论，它的结论将更加完美。(B)给了这样的例证，因此(B)是正确答案；(D)选项对谷物公司的结论构成了反对；(A)、(C)和(E)都是无关选项。

11. **解析**：作者段落中描述的推理错误是根据不具备代表性的证据得出了错误的结论。(A)仅仅因为被锁在了门外这一片面的事实，就做出了5月13日是不吉利的错误结论显然与作者文中描述的推理错误一致，因此(A)为正确答案；本题的(E)是比较容易误选的选项，但是应注意的是我们的队今天输了得出幸运衬衫不幸运的结论是正确的，因为幸运衬衫本身就无幸运可言；(B)犯了证据和结论在逻辑上不具相关性的推理错误；(C)选项用的是归纳论证法；(D)选项用的是演绎论证法。

wild-goose chase *n.* 荒谬无益的追求

12. **解析**：由本题所列举的两个关于足球队员及男演员的例子可以看出权威人士只有在他们自身的专业领域内发表见解时才能得到听众的认可，由此可知(A)是本题的论证所依赖的前提；(B)、(C)、(D)和(E)都是无关选项。

quarterback *n.*（美式足球）四分卫，进攻时指挥本队的选手。

13. **解析**：本题题干中的论证和5个选项中的论证都用了比较选择论证法，因此在推论方式上几乎都是一样的，要正确解答此题，只能从细微处入手。选项(A)与本题的论证在支持它们选择一个而不是另一个时，都用了两个比较，所以本题的正确答案为(A)。

14. **解析**：本题根据鱼和鱼龙的相似性来解释趋同性，由趋同性的定义和本题给出的例子我们很容易推出(D)是正确选项。

15. **解析**：本题用的推理方法是根据一个命题的原命题成立推出该命题的逆否命题成立。即如果A→B成立，那么$\overline{B}$→$\overline{A}$也一定成立，经分析后可知(B)选项所用的推理方法与本题的一样，(A)、(C)、(D)和(E)四选项的推理方法都是演绎法。

16. **解析**：一个司机卷入交通事故的多少，不仅仅取决于他的开车技巧，因此凡是能说明青少年引起的交通事故不是由于他的车技太差的论述都能削弱本题的结论。很显明在本题的5个选项中除了(D)之外的4个选项都通过找他因的办法证明了青少年引起的交通死亡事故较多不是由他们的车技太差所致。

十二、GMAT考前逻辑推理冲刺训练试题及解析（十二）

1. Several years ago, as a measure to reduce the population of gypsy moths, which depend on oak leaves for food, entomologists introduced into many oak forests a species of fungus that is poisonous to gypsy moth caterpillars. Since then, the population of both caterpillars and adult moths have significantly declined in those areas. Entomologists have concluded that the decline is attributable to the presence of the poisonous fungus.

Which one of the following, if true, most strongly supports the conclusion drawn by the entomologists?

几年以前，作为一个减少以橡树叶子为食的吉卜赛蛾数量的方法，昆虫学家在橡树林中引进了一种对吉卜赛蛾有毒的真菌。从此那个地区的毛虫和成熟的蛾的数量都显著下降，昆虫学家推论出这些数量的下降归因于有毒真菌的出现。

下面哪一点，如果正确的话，最能支持昆虫学家做出的结论？

(A) A strain of gypsy moth whose caterpillars are unaffected by the fungus has increased its share of the total gypsy moth population.

(B) The fungus that was introduced to control the gypsy moth population is poisonous to few insect species other than the gypsy moth.

(C) An increase in numbers of both gypsy moth caterpillars and gypsy moth adults followed a drop in the number of some of the species that prey on the moths.

(D) In the past several years, air pollution and acid rain have been responsible for a substantial decline in oak tree populations.

(E) The current decline in the gypsy moth population in forests where the fungus was introduced is no greater than a decline that occurred concurrently in other forests.

2. It is commonly held among marketing experts that in a nonexpanding market a company's best strategy is to go after a bigger share of the market and that the best way to do this is to run comparative advertisements that emphasize weaknesses in the products of rivals. In the stagnant market for food oil, soybean-oil and palm-oil producers did wage a two-year battle with comparative advertisements about the deleterious effect on health of each other's products. These campaigns, however, had little effect on respective market shares; rather, they stopped many people from buying any edible oils at all.

The statements above most strongly support the conclusion that comparative advertisements

(A) increase a company's market share in all cases in which that company's products are clearly superior to the products of rivals.

(B) should not be used in a market that is expanding or likely to expand.

(C) should under no circumstances be used as a retaliatory measure.

(D) carry the risk of causing a contraction of the market at which they are aimed.

(E) yield no long-term gains unless consumers can easily verify the claims made.

3. Because dinosaurs were reptiles, scientists once assumed that, like all reptiles alive today, dinosaurs were cold-blooded. The recent discovery of dinosaur fossils in the northern arctic, however, has led a number of researchers to conclude that at

(A) 一种其毛虫不受有毒真菌影响的吉卜赛蛾的数量在整个吉卜塞蛾中的比例在增加。

(B) 为控制吉卜赛蛾而引进的毒菌除了对吉卜赛蛾有毒外还对其他少数的几种昆虫有毒。

(C) 吉卜赛毛虫与成虫数量的增加伴随着以它们为食的一些物种的数量的减少。

(D) 在过去的几年中，空气污染和酸雨是造成橡树数量大量减少的原因。

(E) 森林中引入真菌后，吉卜赛蛾数目的减少量并不比目前同一时间内其他地区的减少量大。

销售学专家普遍认为，在一个不再扩张的市场中，一个公司最佳的策略是追求较大的市场份额，要做到这一点的最佳方式是做一些能突出竞争对手的产品缺点的比较广告。在一个萧条的食物油市场内，大豆油和棕榈油的生产商进行了两年的比较广告之战，相互指责对方产品对健康的有害影响。然而，这些战役对各自的市场份额影响甚小，并且它们使很多人不再购买任何的食用油。

上面的陈述最强有力地支持结论：比较广告

(A) 在任何情况下都能增加一个公司的市场份额如果该公司的产品比它的竞争对手的产品明显好的话。

(B) 不应该在一个正在扩张或可能扩张的市场中使用。

(C) 在任何情况下，都不应该作为一个报复手段来使用。

(D) 冒着使它们的目标市场收缩的危险。

(E) 不会产生任何长期收益，除非消费者能容易地判断那些声明的正确性。

因为恐龙是爬行类动物，所以科学家曾经认为，像今天所有生活着的爬行类动物一样，恐龙是冷血动物。然而，最近在北极北部发现的恐龙化石使一些研究者认

least some dinosaurs might have been warm-blooded. These researchers point out that only warm-blooded animals could have withstood the frigid temperature that are characteristic of arctic winters, whereas cold-blooded animal would have frozen to death in the extreme cold.

Which one of the following, if true, weakens the researchers' argument?

(A) Today's reptiles are generally confined to regions of temperate or even tropical climates.

(B) The fossils show the arctic dinosaurs to have been substantially smaller than other known species of dinosaurs.

(C) The arctic dinosaur fossils were found alongside fossils of plants known for their ability to withstand extremely cold temperatures.

(D) The number of fossils found together indicates herds of dinosaurs so large that they would need to migrate to find a continual food supply.

(E) Experts on prehistoric climate conditions believe that winter temperatures in the prehistoric northern arctic were not significantly different from what they are today.

Questions 4~5 are based on the following:
Any person who drops out of high school will be unemployed unless he or she finds a low-paying job or has relatives with good business connections.

4. Which one of the following conclusions CANNOT be validly drawn from the statement above?

(A) Any person who drops out of high school, will be unemployed, have a low-paying job, or have relatives with good business connections.

(B) Any high school dropout who has neither a low-paying job nor relatives with good business connections will be unemployed.

(C) Any employed person who has neither a low-paying job nor relatives with good business connections is not a high school dropout.

(D) Any high school dropout who has a job that is not low-paying must have relatives with good business connections.

(E) Any person who has relatives with good business connections and who is not a high school dropout must be employed at a job that is not low-paying.

为至少有一些恐龙是温血动物。这些研究者指出只有温血型动物才能经受住北极冬季严寒的气候，而冷血动物在极冷的情况下会被冻死。

下面哪一点，如果正确的话，最能削弱研究者的论证？

(A) 今天的爬行动物一般都生活在温和的甚至是热带的气候范围内。

(B) 那些化石显示北极恐龙比其他已知种类的恐龙小得多。

(C) 北极恐龙的化石是在极其耐寒的植物化石旁边发现的。

(D) 发现在一起的恐龙化石的数量表明恐龙群是如此的庞大以至于它们需要迁移以找到一个可持续供给食物的地方。

(E) 史前气候环境专家认为史前北极北部冬季的气温与它们今天相比无明显差别。

任何一高中生辍学都会失业，除非他或她找到一份低薪水的工作或者有良好商业关系的亲戚。

不能有效地从上面陈述中得出下面哪个结论？

(A) 任何高中退学的人要么失业，要么拥有一份低薪水的工作或拥有良好商业关系的亲戚。

(B) 任何既没有低薪水的工作也没有良好商业关系的亲戚的高中退学者将会失业。

(C) 任何既没有低薪水的工作也没有良好商业联系的亲戚的就业的人不是一高中退学者。

(D) 任何拥有薪水不低的工作的高中退学者必定有良好商业关系的亲戚。

(E) 任何拥有良好商业关系的亲戚但不是一名高中退学者的人一定找到了一份薪水不低的工作。

5. Assume that Tom is employed and does not have a low-paying job. Which one of the following statements, when added to this assumption, contradicts the original statement made in the statement above?

(A) Tom is a high school dropout.

(B) Tom does not have relatives with good business connections.

(C) Tom is a high school dropout and does not have any relatives.

(D) Tom completed high school and has relatives with good business connections.

(E) Tom has relatives with good business connections.

假定Tom被雇用且拥有的工作薪水不低，下面哪一个陈述，如果附加上这个假设，会与上面陈述里的原论断冲突？

(A) Tom是一名高中退学者。

(B) Tom没有有良好商业关系的亲戚。

(C) Tom是一高中退学者并且没有任何亲戚。

(D) Tom完成了高中学习并且拥有有良好商业关系的亲戚。

(E) Tom拥有有良好商业关系的亲戚。

6. Reporting on a civil war, a journalist encountered evidence that refugees were starving because the government would not permit food shipments to a rebel-held area. Government censors deleted all mention of the government's role in the starvation from the journalist's report, which had not implicated either nature or the rebels in the starvation. The journalist concluded that it was ethically permissible to file the censored report, because the journalist's news agency would precede it with the notice "Cleared by government censors."
Which one of the following ethical criteria, if valid, would serve to support the journalist's conclusion while placing the least constraint on the flow of reported information?

(A) It is ethical in general to report known facts, but unethical to do so while omitting other known facts if the omitted facts would substantially alter an impression of a person or institution that would be congruent with the reported facts.

(B) In a situation of conflict, it is ethical to report known facts and unethical to fail to report known facts that would tend to exonerate one party to the conflict.

(C) In a situation of censorship, it is unethical to make any report if the government represented by the censor deletes from the report material unfavorable to that government.

(D) It is ethical in general to report known facts but unethical to make a report in a situation of censorship if relevant facts have been deleted by the censor, unless the recipient of the report is warned that censorship existed.

(E) Although it is ethical in general to report known facts, it is unethical to make a report from which a censor has deleted relevant facts, unless the recipient of the reports

一新闻记者在报道国内战争时，遇到了由于政府不许向叛兵占据区输运粮食而使难民挨饿的证据。政府检查员删除了所有记者有关政府在饥饿中所起作用的报道，所以记者的报道没有说明是老百姓还是叛兵处于饥饿之中。记者得出结论，发送检查过的稿子是合理可行的，因为记者所工作的通讯社要在报道的前面写上"通过政府检查"的告示。

下面哪一项道德标准，如果有效，既能支持新闻记者的结论，又能使报道的信息的传播受到最少的限制？

(A) 一般来说，报道已知的事实是合乎道理的，但是如果在报道已知事实时，忽略其他与报道事实一致的、且能极大地改变人们对一个或某种情况的印象的已知事实的做法就是不道德的。

(B) 在战争的情况下，报道已知事实是道德的，而不报道那些能证明一方在战争中是无罪的已知事实的做法是不道德的。

(C) 在检查制度的形势下，如果代表政府的检查员删除了报道中对政府不利的材料，再做这样的报道是不道德的。

(D) 一般来说，报道已知事实是道德的，但是在检查制度的情况下，如果相关事实已被检查员删除，再做这样的报道就是不道德的，除非接受报道的人被预先通知该报道是检查后的作品。

(E) 尽管一般来说，报道已知事实是道德

is warned that there was censorship and the reported facts do not by themselves give a misleading impression.

的，但是做那些被检查员删除相关事实的报道是不道德的，除非报道的接受者被预先通知该报道接受过检查，并且所报道的事实的自身不会使人产生误解。

7. Although Damon had ample time earlier in the month to complete the paper he is scheduled to present at a professional conference tomorrow morning, he repeatedly put off doing it. Damon could still get the paper ready in time, but only if he works on it all evening without interruption. However, his seven-year-old daughter's tap-dance recital takes place this evening, and Damon had promised both to attend and to take his daughter and her friends out for ice cream afterward. Thus, because of his procrastination, Damon will be forced to choose between his professional and his family responsibilities.

The argument proceeds by_____.

(A) providing evidence that one event will occur in order to establish that an alternative event cannot occur

(B) showing that two situations are similar in order to justify the claim that someone with certain responsibilities in the first situation has similar responsibilities in the second situation

(C) invoking sympathy for someone who finds himself in a dilemma in order to excuse that person's failure to meet all of his responsibilities

(D) making clear the extent to which someone's actions resulted in harm to others in order to support the claim that those actions were irresponsible

(E) demonstrating that two situations cannot both occur by showing that something necessary for one of those situations is incompatible with something necessary for the other situations

尽管Damon在这个月早些时候有足够的时间来完成他计划要在明天上午的专业会议上提交的论文，他再三地推迟做它。Damon仍可以及时完成他的论文，但是只有当他不受干扰地工作整个晚上。然而，今天晚上，他7岁的女儿要参加踢踏舞表演，Damon已答应出席演奏会并答应随后带他女儿和他女儿的朋友们出去吃冰淇淋。因此，由于Damon的拖延，他被迫在他的职业和他的家庭职责之间做出选择。

上面通过_____进行论证

(A) 提供某一件事情将会发生的证据来证明一件可替代的事情不会发生。

(B) 为了证明某人在第一种情况下有一定的责任，在第二种情况下也有相似的责任的声明，揭示两种情况的相似性。

(C) 为了原谅某人没能履行他的职责，要求人们同情他进退两难的困境。

(D) 为了支持某人的行动是不负责任的声明，而澄清此人的行动给别人造成的伤害的程度。

(E) 通过展示一种情况下必不可少的事情与另一种情况下必不可少的事情的不兼容性，证明了两种情况不能同时发生。

8. Ann will either take a leave of absence from Technocomp and return in a year or else she will quit her job there, but she would not do either one unless she were offered a one-year teaching fellowship at a prestigious university.Technocomp will allow her to take a leave of absence if it does not find out that she has been offered the fellowship, but not otherwise. Therefore, Ann will quit her job at Technocomp only if Technocomp finds out she has been offered the fellowship.

Ann要么向Technocomp请假并在一年以后回来，要么辞去她现在的工作，除非她收到了一名牌大学的为期一年的助教奖学金，否则她不会这样做。如果Technocomp没有发现她收到奖学金的话，那么将准许她请假，否则将不给予批准。因此，Ann将辞去在Technocomp的工作，那么Technocomp必定发现Ann收到了奖学金。

Which one of the following, if assumed, allows the conclusion above to be properly drawn?

(A) Technocomp will find out about Ann being offered the fellowship only if someone informs on her.

(B) The reason Ann wants the fellowship is so she can quit her job a Technocomp.

(C) Technocomp does not allow any of its employees to take a leave of absence in order to work for one of its competitors.

(D) Ann will take a leave of absence if Technocome allows her to take a leave of absence.

(E) Ann would be offered the fellowship only if she quit her job at Technocomp.

9. If a mechanical aerator is installed in a fish pool, the water in the pool can be properly aerated. So, since John's fish pool does not have a mechanical aerator, it must be that his pool is not properly aerated. Without properly aerated water, fish cannot thrive. Therefore, any fish in John's pool will not thrive.

Which one of the following arguments contains an error of reasoning that is also contained in the argument above?

(A) If alum is added to pickle brine, brine can replace the water in the pickles. Therefore, since Pauls does not add alum to her pickle brine, the water in the pickles cannot be replaced by brine. Unless their water is replaced with brine, pickles will not stay crisp. Thus, Paula's pickles will not stay crisp.

(B) If pectin is added to jam, the jam will gel. Without a setting agent such as pectin, jam will not gel. So in order to make his jam gel, Harry should add a setting agent such as pectin to the jam.

(C) If stored potatoes are not exposed to ethylene, the potatoes will not sprout. Beets do not release ethylene. Therefore, if Sara stores her potatoes together with beets, the potatoes will not sprout.

(D) If a carrot patch is covered with mulch in the fall, the carrots can be left in the ground until spring. Without a mulch cover, carrots stored in the ground can suffer frost damage. Thus, since Kevin covers his carrot patch with mulch in the fall, the carrots can safely be left in the ground.

(E) If tomatoes are not stored in a dark place, their seeds sometimes sprout. Sprouted seeds can make tomatoes

下面哪一个，如果被假设，将能够使上面结论正确地得出？

(A) Technocomp发现Ann接到了奖学金，那么必定是有人告发了她。

(B) Ann想要奖学金的原因使她辞去在Technocomp的工作。

(C) Technocomp不允许它的任何雇员请假，为它的一个竞争者工作。

(D) 如果Technocomp允许她请假，那么Ann将请假。

(E) Ann被给予奖学金，那么她必定辞去了她在Technocomp的工作。

如果一鱼塘安装了机械充气机，鱼塘中的水就能保持合适的含氧量。所以，既然John的鱼塘没有安装机械充气机，那么他的鱼塘的含氧量一定不合适。没有合适含氧量的水，鱼儿就不能生气勃勃地发育成长。所以，John鱼塘里的鱼不会蓬勃地生长。

下面哪个论证含有以上论证中的一个推理错误？

(A) 如果明矾被加进泡菜的盐水中，盐水就可以取代泡菜中的水分。因此，既然Pauls没有向她的泡菜的盐水中加明矾，那么泡菜中的水就不能被盐水所取代。除非它们的水分被盐水取代，否则泡菜就不会保持新鲜。于是，Paula的泡菜不会保持新鲜。

(B) 如果果胶被加入果酱，果酱就会凝成胶状。没有像果胶这样的凝固剂，果酱不会凝成胶状。所以为了使他的果酱胶化，Harry应当向他的果酱中加入像果胶这样的凝固剂。

(C) 如果储藏的土豆不暴露于乙烯中，土豆就不会发芽。甜菜不释放乙稀。因此，如果Sara把她的土豆和甜菜放在一块，土豆就不会发芽。

(D) 如果胡萝卜在秋季时被麦杆等覆盖，胡萝卜可一直在地下呆到春季。没有覆盖物，胡萝卜就要遭受霜击。因此，既然Kevin在秋季时用覆盖物把他的胡萝卜盖上了，那么他的胡萝卜

inedible. Therefore, since Maria does not store her tomatoes in a dark place, some of Maria's tomatoes could be inedible.

Questions 10~11 are based on the following:

Antinuclear activist: The closing of the nuclear power plant is a victory for the antinuclear cause. It also represents a belated acknowledgment by the power industry that they cannot operate such plants safely.

Nuclear power plant manager: It represents no such thing. The availability of cheap power from nonnuclear sources, together with the cost of mandated safety inspections and safety repairs, made continued operation uneconomic. Thus it was not safety considerations but economic considerations that dictated the plant's closing.

10. The reasoning in the manger's argument is flawed because the argument_____.
(A) fails to acknowledge that the power industry might now believe nuclear power plants to be unsafe even though this plant was not closed for safety reasons
(B) overlooks the possibility that the sources from which cheap power is available might themselves be subject to safety concerns
(C) mistakes the issue of what the closure of the plant represents to the public for the issue of what the managers' reasons for the closure were
(D) takes as one of its premises a view about the power industry's attitude toward nuclear safety that contradicts the activist's view
(E) counts as purely economic considerations some expenses that arise as a result of the need to take safety precautions

11. Which one of the following, if true, most strongly supports the activist's claim of victory?
(A) The plant had reached the age at which its operating license expired.
(B) The mandate for inspections and repairs mentioned by the manager was recently enacted as a result of pressure

就可以安全地留在地下。
(E) 如果西红柿不储藏在黑暗的地方，它们的种子有时就会发芽，发芽的种子使西红柿不宜食用。因此，既然Maria没有把她的西红柿存放在暗处，那么有些Maria的西红柿就不宜食用。

反核活动家：关闭这个核电站是反核的胜利，它同时也体现了核工业很迟才肯承认它们不能安全运作这样的发电站的事实。

核电站经理：它并不体现这样的事情。从非核资源可得到便宜的电力，加上强制性的安全检查和安全维修，使继续运作变得不经济。因此，不是出于安全方面的考虑，而是出于经济方面的考虑，才下令关闭了这个核电站。

经理的论证的推论是有缺陷的，因为该论证_____。
(A) 没有承认即使这家核电站不是出于安全方面的原因而被关闭，电力公司现在也可能会认为核电站是不安全的。
(B) 忽略了那些可以利用的便宜电力资源本身也可能存在安全问题的可能性。
(C) 把关闭这个核电站对公众来说体现了什么的问题错认为是经理的关闭理由是什么的问题。
(D) 把电力工业对待核安全的态度与反核活动家的观点相抵触的态度的观点作为它的一个前提。
(E) 把由于需要采取安全预防措施而引起的一些费用的上升看作是纯粹的经济上的因素。

下面哪一项，如果正确，能最强有力地支持反核活动家胜利的主张？
(A) 那个电厂的工作许可期已满。
(B) 经理所提及的检查与修理的命令是迫于反核小组的压力才于最近颁布的。

from antinuclear groups.

(C) The plant would not have closed if cheap power from nonnuclear sources had not been available.

(D) Per unit of electricity produced, the plant had the highest operating costs of any nuclear power plant.

(E) The plant that closed had been able to provide backup power to an electrical network then parts of the network became overloaded.

(C) 如果不能从非核资源获得便宜的电力，这个核电站就不会被关闭。

(D) 在所有的核电站中，这个核电站发一度电所用的费用最高。

(E) 当电网的某些部分过载时，关闭的这家核电站可向电网提供后备电力。

12. An editorial in the *Grandbury Daily Herald* claims that Grandburg's voters would generally welcome the defeat of the political party now in control of the Grandburg City Council. The editorial bases its claim on a recent survey that found that 59 percent of Granburg's registered voters think that the party will definitely be out of power after next year's city council elections.

Which one of the following is a principle that, if established, would provided the strongest justification for the editorial's conclusion?

(A) The way voters feel about a political party at a given time can reasonably be considered a reliable indicator of the way they will continue to feel about that party, barring unforeseeable political developments.

(B) The results of surveys that gauge current voter sentiment toward a given political party can legitimately be used as the basis for making claims about the likely future prospects of that political party.

(C) An increase in ill-feeling toward a political party that is in power can reasonably be expected to result in a corresponding increase in support for rival political parties.

(D) The proportion of voters who expect a given political possibility to be realized can legitimately be assumed to approximate the proportion of voters who are in favor of that possibility being realized.

(E) It can reasonably be assumed that registered voters who respond to a survey regarding the outcome of a future election will exercise their right to vote in that election.

Grandburg每日通报的一篇社论声称，Grandburg的投票者会普通欢迎某前控制市议会的政党下台。该社论基于最近的一次调查报告发表了这个声明，调查报告显示有59%的Grandburg在册选民认为该政党在后年的市议会选举中肯定会下台。

下面哪一条原则，如果正确，能最强有力地为这篇社论的结论辩护？

(A) 投票者在某一限定时间对某一政党的态度可被合理地认为是他们将继续对该政党保持这一态度的可信赖的指示器，除了发生不可预测的政治发展之外。

(B) 对投票者对某一政党的情绪的估计的调查报告结果可被合理地用作发表关于那个政党可能会有的前景的声明的基础。

(C) 对某一执政党不满情绪的增加可被合理地认为它会导致在野党的被支持率将相应地增加。

(D) 期望某一政治上可能发生的事情能够实现的投票者的比例可被合理地认为与赞成这个可能事情实现的投票者的比例相近。

(E) 可以合理地认为，那些接受有关将来选举结果的调查的人会在这场选举中行使他们的投票权。

13. Anatomical bilateral symmetry is a common trait. It follows, therefore, that it confers survival advantages on organisms. After all, if bilateral symmetry did not confer such advantages, it would not be common.

The pattern of reasoning in which one of the following arguments is most similar to that in the argument above?

结构上的双边对称是一种常见的特性。因此，也就是说它赋予了生物生存的有利条件。毕竟，如果双边对称不能赋予这样的有利条件，那么它就不会成为一种常见的特性。

下面哪一辩论的推理模式与上面的辩

(A) Since it is Sawyer who is negotiating for the city government, it must be true that the city takes the matter seriously. After all, if Sawyer had not been available, the city would have insisted that the negotiations be deferred.

(B) Clearly, no candidate is better qualified for the job than Trumbull. In fact, even to suggest that there might be a more highly qualified candidate seems absurd to those who have seen Trumbull at work.

(C) If Powell lacked superior negotiating skills, she would not have been appointed arbitrator in this case. As everyone knows, she is the appointed arbitrator, so her negotiating skills are detractors notwithstanding, bound to be superior.

(D) Since Varga was away on vacation at the time, it must have been Rivers who conducted the secret negotiations. Any other scenario makes little sense, for Rivers never does the negotiating unless Varga is unavailable.

(E) If Wong is appointed arbitrator, a decision will be reached promptly. Since it would be absurd to appoint anyone other than Wong as arbitrator, a prompt decision can reasonably be expected.

14. Electrical engineers have repeatedly demonstrated that the best solid-state amplifiers are indistinguishable from the best vacuum-tube amplifiers with respect to the characteristics commonly measured in evaluating the quality of an amplifier's musical reproduction. Therefore, those music lovers who insist that recorded music sounds better when played with the best vacuum-tube amplifier than when played with the best solid-state amplifier must be imagining the difference in quality that they claim to bear.

Which one of the following, if true, most seriously weakens the argument?

(A) Many people cannot tell from listening to it whether a recording is being played with a very good solid-state amplifier or a very good vacuum-tube amplifier.

(B) The range of variation with respect to the quality of musical reproduction is greater for vacuum-tube amplifiers than for solid-state amplifiers.

论最为相似?

(A) 既然是Sawyer在与市政府谈判，那么市政府一定会认真考虑那件事情。毕竟，如果Sawyer不出现，市政府就会坚持推迟谈判。

(B) 很明显，没有人比Trumbull更胜任那个工作。实际上，甚至对那些看见过Trumbull工作的人建议可能会有一个更合格的候选人会显得非常地荒谬。

(C) 如果Powell缺乏谈判的高级技巧，她就不可能被委任为这个案子的仲裁人。众所周知，她是指派的仲裁人，因此，尽管有些人贬低她，但是她的谈判技巧一定较高。

(D) 既然Varga在那时外出度假，那么一定是Rivers进行了那个秘密的谈判。任何其他的解释几乎都是毫无意义的，因为Rivers从来不参与谈判，除非Varga不在。

(E) 如果Wong 被委任为仲裁人，他就能很快做出判决。既然任命除了Wong之外的任何人作仲裁人都是荒谬的，那么期望会有迅速的判决就是合情合理的。

　　电学工程师已反复重申，最好的晶体管扩音机与最好的电子管扩音机在通常测量评价扩音机的音乐再现质量方面的性能是一样的。因此那些坚持认为录制的音乐在最好的电子管扩音机里播放时要比在最好的晶体管扩音机里播放时听起来好的音乐爱好者，一定是在想象他们声称的听到的质量上的差异。

　　下面哪一点，如果正确，最能严重削弱上述辩论?

(A) 许多人仅凭耳听不能区分正在播放的音乐是在好的晶体管扩音机里播放还是在好的电子管扩音机里播放。

(B) 电子管扩音机的音乐再现质量的变化范围要比晶体管扩音机的大。

(C) Some of the characteristics that are important in determining how music sounds to a listener cannot be measured.

(D) Solid-state amplifiers are more compact, use less power, and generate less heat than vacuum-tube amplifiers that produce a comparable volume of sound.

(E) Some vacuum-tube amplifiers are clearly superior to some solid-state amplifiers with respect to the characteristics commonly measured in the laboratory to evaluate the quality of an amplifier's musical reproduction.

(C) 有些重要的决定音乐听起来怎么样的特性不能被测量出来。

(D) 当放出相同的音量时，晶体管扩音机比电子管扩音机的体积小，用电少且产生的热量少。

(E) 在试验室里通常测定的用以评价扩音机的音乐再现质量的特性方面，有些电子管扩音机明显地比晶体管扩音机好。

15. At the company picnic, all of the employees who participated in more than four of the scheduled events, and only those employees, were eligible for the raffle held at the end of the day. Since only a small proportion of the employees were eligibly for the raffle, most of the employees must have participated in fewer than four of the scheduled events.

Which one of the following arguments exhibits a flawed pattern of reasoning most like that exhibited by the argument above?

(A) Only third-and fourth-year students are allowed to keep cars on campus. Since one quarter of the third-year students keep cars on campus and one half of the fourth-year students keep cars on campus, it must be that fewer third-year students than fourth-year students keep cars on campus.

(B) Only those violin students who attended extra rehearsal sessions were eligible for selection as soloists. Since two of the violin students were selected as soloists, those two must have been the only violin students who attended the extra sessions.

(C) The only students honored at a special banquet were the band members who made the dean's list last semester. Since most the band members were honored, most of the band members must have made the dean's list.

(D) All of the members of the service club who volunteered at the hospital last summer were biology majors. Since ten of the club members are biology majors, those ten members must have volunteered at the hospital last summer.

(E) All of the swim team members who had decreased their racing times during the season were given awards that no other members were given. Since fewer than half the team members were given such awards, the racing times

在一个公司的野餐活动中，所有参加了超过四个预定节目的雇员，并且只有这些雇员在那天结束的时候有资格参加抽彩售货。既然仅有很小比例的雇员有资格参加抽彩售货，那么大多数的雇员参加的预定节目的个数一定少于四个。

下面哪个论述展示了与本文中论述最为相似的推理缺陷模式？

(A) 只允许三年级和四年级的学生在校园内拥有汽车。既然有1/4的三年级学生和1/2的四年级学生在校园内拥有汽车，那么在校园内，三年级学生中拥有汽车的人数一定比四年级中拥有汽车的人数少。

(B) 只有那些参加了额外排练班的小提琴班的学生才有资格被选为独奏者。既然有两个小提琴班的学生被选为独奏者，那么这两个学生一定是小提琴班仅有的两个参加了额外训练班的学生。

(C) 在一个特殊的宴会上，只有那些上学期完成系主任的清单的乐队成员才受到了赞扬。既然所有的乐队成员都受到了赞扬，那么乐队的大多数成员一定完成了系主任的清单。

(D) 所有那些去年夏季志愿到医院工作的服务俱乐部的成员都来自生物专业。既然有10个俱乐部的成员来自生物专业，那么这10人去年夏季一定志愿到医院工作了。

(E) 在所有的游泳队员中，只有那些在这个赛季中减少了他们比赛时间的队员

of more than half the team members must have increased during the season.

得到了奖励。既然只有不到一半的队员得到了这样的奖励，那么超过一半的队员在这个赛季的比赛时间一定是增加了。

16. Environmental scientist: It is true that over the past ten years, there has been a sixfold increase in government funding for the preservation of wetlands, while the total area of wetlands needing such preservation has increased only twofold (although this area was already large ten years ago). Even when inflation is taken into account, the amount of funding now is at least three times what it was ten years ago. Nevertheless, the current amount of governmental funding for the preservation of wetlands is inadequate and should be augmented.

Which one of the following, if true, most helps to reconcile the environmental scientist's conclusion with the evidence cited above?

(A) The governmental agency responsible for administering wetland-preservation funds has been consistently mismanaged and run inefficiently over the past ten years.

(B) Over the past ten years, the salaries of scientists employed by the government to work on the preservation of wetlands have increased at a rate higher than the inflation rate.

(C) Research over the past ten years has enabled scientists today to identify wetlands in need of preservation well before the areas are at serious risk of destruction.

(D) More people today, scientists and nonscientists alike, are working to preserve all natural resources including wetlands.

(E) Unlike today, funding for the preservation of wetlands was almost nonexistent ten years ago.

环境科学家：在过去的10年中，政府对保护湿地的投资确实增加了6倍，而同时需要这样保护的土地面积只增加了两倍（尽管这些区域在10年前已经很大了）。即使把通货膨胀考虑进去，今天的资金数额也至少是10年前的3倍。虽然如此，目前政府对保护湿地的投资仍是不够的，政府的投资应该进一步增加。

下面哪一点，如果正确，最有助于使环境科学家的结论与引用的证据相一致？

(A) 负责管理湿地保护资金的政府机构在过去的10年中一直管理不当且运行效率较低。

(B) 在过去的10年中，那些被政府雇来保护湿地的科学家的薪水的增长比率高于通货膨胀的比率。

(C) 过去10年的研究使今天的科学家在潮湿土地遭受严重破坏的危险之前就把它们定为需要保护的对象。

(D) 今天，有更多的像科学家和非科学家的人在为保护包括湿地在内的自然资源而工作。

(E) 不像今天，10年以前对保护湿地的投资几乎是不存在的。

参考答案：

1. A	2. D	3. D	4. E	5. C
6. D	7. E	8. D	9. A	10. E
11. B	12. D	13. C	14. C	15. E
16. E				

1. **解析**：(A)能支持昆虫学家得出的结论。因为我们由一种其毛虫不受真菌影响的吉卜赛蛾在整个吉卜赛蛾中的比例增加可推出，受真菌影响的吉卜赛蛾的数量在下降。(E)对昆虫学家的结论构成了反对，(B)、(C)和(D)都是无关选项。

2. **解析**：本题属于典型的归纳类的"support"题型，读题重点应放在最后一句话上，且最后一句话指出了进行比较广告之战的后果，(D)很明显为正确答案；(C)易误选，但(C)中的"any"是段落中未出现的绝对化语言，且上面段落中讨论的只是当市场处于不再扩张时的情况，所以(C)不正确。

3. **解析**：读题以后不难发现本题的结论是以史前时代北极地区的气温与今天的相比无明显差别以及化石被科学家们在北极发现的恐龙生前就一直栖息在北极为前提。选项(D)通过找他因，削弱了本题结论的前提，因此(D)是正确答案；(E)对结论构成支持；(A)、(B)和(C)均为无关选项。

4. **解析**：本题推理为：高中退学者就业→"低薪水工作"+"有良好商业的关系"，请注意B→A₁+A₂类的思维。

5. **解析**：本题思维同上题。

6. **解析**：根据记者的结论很容易看出(D)是正确答案；(E)是较易误选的选项，但(E)错在了最后半句上，即报道的事实的自身不会使人产生误解这句话并不能从本题的论述中推出；(A)、(B)和(C)三选项也都不能从本题的论述中合理地推出。

7. **解析**：根据本题的论述可知Damon今天晚上要么写他的论文，要么去参加他女儿的表演，但是鱼与熊掌不可兼得，因此(E)选项很明显是正确答案。

8. **解析**：本题推理为"请假"+"辞职"→收到Fellowship；Technocomp没有发现其得到fellowship→允许请假。把这两个融合到一起，我们将发现(D)可以作为得到结论(段落的最后一句话)所基于的一个假设。

   注：inform on/against sb. 告发或检举某人。

9. **解析**：本题的论证把某一件事成立的一个条件当作了它的一个必要条件来推理，从而得出了不正确的结论。选项(A)中的明矾加入泡菜的盐水只是盐水可以取代泡菜中的水分的一个条件，而非必要条件；而作者在论证中却把它当必要条件来使，显然犯了与本题的题干中的论证相一致的推理错误。(B)、(C)、(D)和(E)四选项一开始提出的某一命题成立的条件都是该命题成立的必要条件，因此它们的推理方式都是正确的。

10. **解析**：经理把强制性的安全检查和安全维修当作经济上的因素将会严重削弱他的结论。因为如果核电站在安全检查和维修上花了大量的钱，那我们一定可以推出这个核心电站在安全预防方面要做大量的工作，也即这个核电站的安全可靠性不强，因此(E)是正确答案；(A)、(B)、(C)和(D)均是无关选项。

11. **解析**：反核活动家对核电站的主要看法是认为它不安全，因此在5个选项中只有体现安全问题的选项才有可能是相关选项。(B)就说明反核小组认为核电站不安全的想法被验证，因此(B)是正确答案，其他选项都是无关选项。

12. **解析**：调查报告只是显示有59%的人认为该政党肯定会下台，但这并不表明这59%的人都希望这个政党下台，只有在认为这个政党会下台的人与希望这个政党下台的人是一致时，本题的结论才能可靠地推出，由此分析可知(D)是正确答案。

13. **解析**：本题用的推理方法是由原命题成立推出它的逆否命题也成立，因此很明显(C)是正确答案。

14. **解析**：本题根据两种扩音机在音乐再现方面的性能一样，做出了音乐爱好者们认为的性能差异是经他们主观臆测而得出的结论。要削弱结论，只要削弱前提即可。选项(C)通过找他因的方法对本题的辩论的前提进行了削弱，因此(C)为正确答案。

15. **解析**：本题的推理犯了不严谨的毛病，不超过四个的补集是等于或少于四个，因此本题的结论应该是大多数雇员参加的预定节目的个数一定不超过四个。选项(E)很明显犯了与题干中的论述相一致的推理错误，它忽视了有一定数量的队员的比赛时间能保持不变的可能性。

16. **解析**：环境科学家的证据是要保护的土地的面积比10年前增加了两倍，投资实际增加了3倍，他们的结论是目前的投资不够，如果结论成立，那么根据这些证据我们可以推出，10年前对保护土地的投资与现在相比更是远远不够的。5个选项中，只有(E)指出了10年前对保护湿地的投资非常匮乏，因此(E)为正确答案。

十三、GMAT考前逻辑推理冲刺训练试题及解析（十三）

1. Ethicist: A society is just when and only when first, each person has an equal right to basic liberties and second, inequalities in the distribution of income and wealth are not tolerated unless these inequalities are to everyone's advantage and are attached to jobs open to everyone.

Which one of the following judgments most closely conforms to the principle described above?

(A) Society S guarantees everyone equal right to basic liberties, while allowing inequalities in the distribution of income and wealth that are to the advantage of everyone. Further, the jobs to which these inequalities are attached are open to most people' Thus, society S is just.

(B) Society S gives everyone an equal right to basic liberties, but at the expense of creating inequalities in the distribution of income and wealth. Thus, society S is not just.

(C) Society S allows inequalities in the distribution of income and wealth, although everyone benefits and these inequalities are attached to jobs that are open to everyone. Thus, society S is just.

(D) Society S distributes income and wealth to everyone equally, but at the expense of creating inequalities in the right to basic liberties. Thus, society S is not just.

(E) Society S gives everyone an equal right to basic liberties, and although there is an inequality in the distribution of income and wealth, the jobs to which these inequalities are attached are open to all. Thus, society S is just.

伦理学家：一个社会是公正的当且仅当：第一，每一个人都有获得基本自由的平等权利；第二，只有在收入和财富的分配不平等对所有人都是有利的并且与对所有的人都开放的工作都相联系时，这些不平等才可以容忍。

下面哪一个判断与上面所描述的原则相符合？

(A) S社会在承认收入和财富的分配对每一个人都有利的同时，确保每一个人具有基本自由的平等权利。而且，这些不平等所涉及的工作对绝大多数人是开放的，因此S社会是公正的。

(B) S社会给予每一个人基本自由的平等权利，但其代价是在收入和财富的分配方面造成了不平等。因此，S社会是不公正的。

(C) S社会允许收入和财富的分配上的不平等，尽管每个人都从中受益，并且这些不平等与对每一个人都开放的工作相联系。因此，S社会是不公正的。

(D) S社会把收入和财富平等地分配给每一个人，但其代价是造成了人们在基本自由的权利方面不平等，因此S社会是公正的。

(E) S社会给予每一个人基本自由的平等权利，尽管在收入和财富的分配方面存在不平等，但是与这些不平等相联系的工作对每一个人来说都是开放的。因此，S社会是公正的。

2. Economist: In order to decide what to do about protecting the ozone layer, we must determine the monetary amount of the economic resources that we would willingly expend to protect it. Such a determination amounts to a calculation of the monetary value of the ozone layer.

Environmentalists argue that the ozone layer does not have a calculable monetary value. However, we would not willingly expend an amount equal to all of the world's economic resources to protect the ozone layer, so the ozone layer is demonstrably worth less than that amount. Thus, the ozone layer has a calculable monetary value.

经济学家：为了决定如何保护臭氧层，我们必须决定我们愿意为保护它而花的经济资源。这样的决定等同于预测臭氧层的货币价值。环境学家认为臭氧层的货币价值是不可计量的。然而，我们不会愿意花掉等同于世界上所有经济资源的货币价值来保护臭氧层。因此，这可以表明臭氧层不值那么多钱，从而臭氧层具有一个可计算的货币价值。

经济学家的论述存在缺陷，是因为该论述……

The reasoning in the economist's argument is flawed in that the argument

(A) uses evidence that the monetary value of a particular natural resource is less than a certain amount in order to establish that the monetary value of any natural resource is less than that amount.

(B) presupposes that the ozone layer should not be protected and then argues to that claim as a conclusion.

(C) takes advantage of an ambiguity in the term "value" to deflect the environmentalists charge.

(D) gives no reason for thinking that merely establishing an upper limit on a certain monetary value would allow the calculation of that monetary value.

(E) does not directly address the argument of the environmentalists.

Questions 3~4 are based on the following:

Magazine editor: I know that some of our regular advertisers have been pressuring us to give favorable mention to their products in our articles, but they should realize that for us to yield to their wishes would actually be against their interests. To remain an effective advertising vehicle we must have loyal readership, and we would soon lose that readership if our readers suspect that our editorial integrity has been compromised by pandering to advertisers.

Advertising-sales director: You underestimate the sophistication of our readers. They recognize that the advertisements we carry are not articles, so their response to the advertisements has never depended on their opinion of the editorial integrity of the magazine as a whole.

3. Which one of the following is the most accurate assessment of the advertising-sales director's argument as a response to the magazine editor's argument?

(A) It succeeds because it shows that the editor's argument depends on an unwarranted assumption about factors affecting an advertisement's effectiveness.

(B) It succeeds because it exposes as mistaken the editor's estimation of the sophistication of the magazine's readers.

(C) It succeeds because it undermines the editor's claim about how the magazine's editorial integrity should be affected by allowing advertisers to influence articles.

(A) 用某一特殊自然资源的货币价值比一定的数目少的证据来证明所有自然资源的货币价值都比那个数目少。

(B) 预先假定臭氧层不应该被保护，接着就证明该声明为一结论。

(C) 使用模棱两可的术语"价值"来转移环境学家的告诫。

(D) 没有给出仅确定了某一个货币价值的上限，就可以计算那个货币价值是多少的想法的根据。

(E) 没有直接解释环境学家的辩论。

杂志编辑：我知道有些经常在我们杂志上登广告的人一直在迫使我们在文章中对他们的产品给予好评。但是他们应当意识到，对我们来说，迎合他们的愿望将实际上有损于他们的利益。要保持成为一个有效的广告媒体，我们就必须得有忠实的读者，如果我们的读者怀疑我们编辑的诚实性因为迎合登广告者而遭到了损害，我们很快就会失去这些读者。

广告销售商理事：你过低地估计了我们读者的世故，他们能认识到我们所做的广告并非文章，因此他们对广告的反应从来不会赖于他们对整个杂志编辑的诚实性的看法。

下面哪一个能最准确地评价广告销售理事的论述？

(A) 它是成功的，因为它揭示了编辑的论述依赖于关于影响一则广告的有效性因素的一个无根据的假设。

(B) 它是成功的，因为它揭示了编辑对杂志读者世故的评价是错误的。

(C) 它是成功的，因为它削弱了编辑关于杂志社论的诚实性会怎样地通过允许登广告者影响文章的内容而受影响的声明。

(D) It fails because the editor's argument does not depend on any assumption about readers' response to the advertisements they see in the magazine.

(E) It fails because it is based on a misunderstanding of the editor's view about how readers respond to advertisements they see in the magazine.

4. The magazine editor's argument assumes which one of the following?

(A) A magazine editor should never be influenced in the performance of his or her professional duties by the wishes of the companies that regularly advertise in the magazine.

(B) The magazine cannot give any favorable mention in its articles to its regular advertises without compromising its reputation for editorial integrity.

(C) Favorable mention of their products in the magazine's articles is of less value to the advertisers than is the continued effectiveness of the magazine as an advertising vehicle.

(D) Giving favorable mention to a product in a magazine article is a more effective form of advertising than is an explicit advertisement for the product in the same magazine.

(E) Carrying paid advertisements can never pose any thread to the magazine's reputation for editorial integrity nor to the loyalty of its readership.

5. On Saturday Melvin suggested that Jerome take the following week off from work and accompany him on a trip to the mountains. Jerome refused, claiming that he could not afford the cost of the trip added to the wages he would forfeit by taking off without notice. It is clear, however, that cost cannot be the real reason, for Jerome's unwillingness to go with Melvin to the mountains, since he makes the same excuse every time. Melvin asks him to take an unscheduled vacation regardless of where Melvin propose to go.

The reasoning is most vulnerable to which one of the following criticisms?

(A) It attempts to forestall an attack on Melvin's behavior by focusing attention on the behavior of Jerome.

(B) It fails to establish that Melvin could no more afford to take an unscheduled vacation trip to the mountains than could Jerome.

下面哪一点是杂志编辑辩论的假设？

(A) 一个杂志的编辑在履行他的职业责任时不应该受那些经常在该杂志上做广告的公司意愿的影响。

(B) 在不损害一个杂志的社论的诚实声誉的情况下，该杂志也不能在它的文章中给经常在它上面登广告者好评。

(C) 对登广告者来说，在杂志的文章中给他们的产品好评不如让他们登广告的杂志成为一个持续有效的广告媒体。

(D) 在一杂志的文章中给某一产品好评是比在该杂志以直率的语言来为该产品做广告更为有效的广告形式。

(E) 做一些收费的广告从来不会给杂志社论的诚实声誉造成威胁，也不会危及它的读者的忠诚。

在星期六，Melvin建议Jerome下周不工作陪他到某个山区旅游，Jerome拒绝了，自称他既支付不起旅行费用又得因为没请假而被扣工资。然而，费用很明显不是Jerome不愿陪Melvin到那个山区旅游的真正原因，因为每次Melvin邀请他参加一个没事先安排的旅行时，不管Melvin计划上哪儿，Jerome都给出同样的理由。

上面的推理最易受下面哪一项批评的攻击？

(A) 它企图通过把注意力集中在Jerome的行为上从而预防Melvin的行为受攻击。

(B) 它没有证实Melvin和Jerome一样的支付不起一个没事先安排的假期旅行的费用。

(C) It overlooks the possibility that Jerome, unlike Melvin, prefers vacations that have been planned far in advance.

(D) It assumes that if Jerome's professed reason is not his only reason, then it cannot be a real reason for Jerome at all.

(E) It does not examine the possibility that Jerome's behavior is adequately explained by the reason he gives for it.

(C) 它忽视了这种可能性，即不像Melvin那样，Jerome喜欢一个早就计划好的假期。

(D) 它假定如果Jerome所说的原因不是他的唯一的原因，那么这个原因对Jerome来说根本就不是真正的原因。

(E) 它没有调查Jerome的行为可以被他所给出的原因所充分地解释的可能性。

6. Arnold: I was recently denied a seat on an airline flight for which I had a confirmed reservation, because the airline had overbooked the flight. Since I was forced to fly on the next available flight, which did not depart until two hours later, I missed an important business meeting. Even though the flight on which I had a reservation was canceled at the last minute due to bad weather, the airline should still pay me compensation for denying me a seat on the flight.

Jamie: The airline is not morally obligated to pay you any compensation. Even of you had not been denied a seat on the earlier flight, you would have missed your business meeting anyway.

Which is the principle that, if established, justifies Jamie's response to Arnold is that an airline is morally obligated to compensate a passenger who has been denied a seat on a flight for which the passenger has confirmed reservations?

(A) If the only reason the passenger is forced to take a later flight is that the airline overbooked the original flight.

(B) Only if there is a reason the passenger is forced to take a later flight other than the original flight's being canceled due to bad weather.

(C) Only if the passenger would not have been forced to take a later flight and the airline not overbooked the original flight.

(D) Even if the only reason the passenger is forced to take a later flight were that the original flight is canceled due to bad weather.

(E) Even if the passenger would still have been forced to take a later flight and the airline not overbooked the original flight.

Arnold：最近，我被一家航空公司的某一航班拒绝了一个我已经确认过的预定座位，因为这家航空公司超额预定了那个航班。因此，我被迫乘下一班可乘的航班，该航班两个小时后才起飞，我错过了一个非常重要的商业会议。即使我预定的那个航班在最后一分钟因为天气原因而被取消，航空公司也应该因没能让我乘坐那个航班而给我赔偿。

Jamie：从道义上来说，航空公司没有给你赔偿的责任，即使你没被拒绝乘坐早一点的航班，无论如何你都会错过你的商业会议。

下面哪一条原则，如果正确，能证明Jamie对Arnold的反应，即从道义上讲航空公司有责任赔偿那些在某一航班上确认了预定座位而又被拒绝乘坐该航班的乘客是合理的？

(A) 如果迫使乘客坐晚一点航班的唯一原因是航空公司已超额预定了那次航班。

(B) 只有当乘客被迫乘坐晚一点的航班的原因不是因为天气恶劣而取消了该航班。

(C) 只有当航空公司没有超额预定最初的那次航班，乘客也没有被迫乘坐晚一点的航班。

(D) 即使乘客被迫乘坐晚一点的航班的唯一原因是航空公司因为天气不好而取消了最初的那次航班。

(E) 即使在航空公司没有超额预定最初的那次航班的情况下，乘客仍被迫乘坐晚一点的航班。

7. Ditrama is a federation made up of three autonomous regions: Korva, Mitro and Guadar. Under the federal revenue-sharing plan, each region receives a share of federal revenues equal to the share of the total population of Ditrama residing in that region as shown by a yearly population survey. Last year, the percentage of federal revenues Korva received for its share decreased somewhat even though the population survey on which the revenue-sharing was based showed that Korva's population had increased.

If the statements above are true, which one of the following must also have been shown by the population survey on which last year's revenue-sharing in Ditrama was based?

(A) Of the three regions, Korva had the smallest number of residents.

(B) The population of Korva grew by a smaller percentage than it did in previous years.

(C) The populations of Mitro and Guadar each increased by a percentage that exceeded the percentage by which the population of Korva increased.

(D) Of the three regions, Korva's numerical increase in population was the smallest.

(E) Korva's population grew by a smaller percentage than did the population of at least one of the other two autonomous regions.

Ditrama是一个由三个自治区，即Korva, Mitro和Guadar组成的联邦政府。在联邦的税收方案下，每个地区收到的联邦的税收分摊份额与每年的人口调查报告中显示的该地区居住的人口占Dirtrama总人口的份额相等。去年，即使基于税收分摊的人口调查报告显示Korva的人口在增加，Korva收到的税收份额占联邦税收的比例却有所下降。

如果上面的陈述是正确的，基于去年Ditrama的税收分摊的人口普查报告还能说明下面哪一点？

(A) 在三个地区中，Ditrama的居民最少。

(B) Korva人口增长的比例比前一年的小。

(C) Mitro和Guadar的人口增长的比例都超过了Kora的人口增长的比例。

(D) 在三个地区中，Korva的人口增长数是最小的。

(E) Korva的人口增长的比例至少比其他两个自治区中的某一个的小。

8. By examining fossilized beetles, a research team has produced the most detailed description yet of temperatures in Britain over the past 22,000 years. Fossils of species that still exist were selected and dated. When individuals of several species found in the same place were found to date to the same period, the known temperature tolerances of the existing beetle species were used to determine the maximum summer temperature that could have existed at that place and period.

The procedure of the researchers assumes which one of the following?

(A) Beetles can tolerate warm weather better than cold weather.

(B) Fossils of different species found in the same place belonged to different periods.

(C) The process of dating is more accurate for beetles than for other organisms.

(D) The highest actual summer temperature at a place and period equaled the average of the highest temperatures that could have been tolerated by each of the beetle

通过检查甲虫化石，一研究小组对英国在过去2.2万年内的气温提出了到目前为止最为详尽的描述。该研究小组对现存的生物化石进行挑选，并确定了它们的日期。当发现在同一地方发现的几种生物的个体属于同一时间段时，现存的甲虫类生物的已知忍受温度就可以被用来决定那个地方在那段时间内的夏季的最高温度。

研究者的论述过程依赖于下面哪一条假设？

(A) 甲虫忍耐温暖天气的能力比忍耐寒冷天气的能力强。

(B) 在同一地方发现的不同物种的化石属于不同的时期。

(C) 确定甲虫日期的方法比确定其他生物日期的方法准确。

(D) 一个地方某个时期的实际最高夏季气温与在那个地方那段时间发现的每种甲虫类生物的平均最高可忍受气温相等。

species found there and dated to that period.

(E) The temperature tolerance of the beetle species did not change significantly during the 22,000-year period.

(E) 在过去的2.2万年的时间内，甲虫类生物的可忍受气温没有明显变化。

9. Medieval Arabs had manuscripts of many ancient Greek texts, which were translated into Arabic when there was a demand for them. Medieval Arab philosophers were very interested in Aristotle's *Poetics*, an interest that evidently was not shared by medieval Arab poets, because a poet interested in the Poetics would certainly have wanted to read Homer, to whose epics Aristotle frequently refers. But Homer was not translated into Arabic until modern times.

Which one of the following, if true, most strongly supports the argument above?

(A) A number of medieval Arab translators possessed manuscripts of the Homeric epics in their original Greek.

(B) Medieval Arabic story cycles, such as the *Arabian Nights*, are in some ways similar to parts of the Homeric epics.

(C) In addition to translating from Greek, medieval Arab translators produced Arabic editions of many works originally written in Indian languages and in Persian.

(D) Aristotle's *Poetics* has frequently been cited and commented on by modern Arab poets.

(E) Aristotle's *Poetics* is largely concerned with drama, and dramatic works were written and performed by medieval Arabs.

中世纪的阿拉伯人有许多古希腊原文的手稿。当需要的时候，人们就把它译成阿拉伯语。中世纪的阿拉伯哲学家对亚里士多德的《诗论》非常感兴趣，这种兴趣很明显并不被中世纪的阿拉伯诗人所分享，因为一个对《诗论》感兴趣的诗人一定会想读荷马的诗，亚里士多德就经常参考荷马的诗。但是荷马的诗一直到现在才被译成阿拉伯语。

下面哪一点，如果正确，能最强有力地支持上述论证？

(A) 有一些中世纪的翻译家拥有希腊原文的荷马诗手稿。

(B) 中世纪阿拉伯的系列故事，如《阿拉伯人的夜晚》，在某些方式上与荷马史诗的部分相似。

(C) 除了翻译希腊文之外，中世纪的阿拉伯翻译家还把许多原版为印第安语和波斯语的著作译成了阿拉伯语。

(D) 亚里士多德的《诗论》经常被现代的阿拉伯诗人引用和评论。

(E) 亚里士多德的《诗论》的大部分内容都与戏剧有关，中世纪的阿拉伯人也写戏剧作品，并表演它们。

10. A museum director, in order to finance expensive new acquisitions, discreetly sold some paintings by major artists. All of them were paintings that the director privately considered inferior. Critics roundly condemned the sale, charging that the museum had lost first-rate pieces, thereby violating its duty as a trustee of art for future generations. A few months after being sold by the museum, those paintings were resold, in an otherwise stagnant art market, at two to three times the price paid to the museum. Clearly, these prices settle the issue, since they demonstrate the correctness of the critics' evaluation.

The reasoning in the argument is vulnerable to the criticism that the argument does which one of the following?

(A) It concludes that a certain opinion is correct on the grounds that it is held by more people than hold the

一博物馆理事，为了给昂贵的新进物品筹措资金，谨慎地卖掉了一些主要画家的油画。所有这些画都是这个理事私自认为是较次的作品。批评家严厉谴责这次销售，指控博物馆失去了第一流的作品，因此违反了它为后代托管艺术的职责。那些画在被这家博物馆卖掉后的几个月被再次出售，在一个要不然很萧条的艺术品市场上，以两到三倍于这家博物馆的价钱售出。很明显，这些售价解决了上述争端，因为它们证明了批评家评价的正确性。

上述论述的推理很容易受到批评，因为上述论述犯了下面哪一项错误？

(A) 从某一观点的支持者比它的反对者多，推论出该观点正确。

opposing view.

(B) It rejects the judgment of the experts in an area in which there is no better guide to the truth than expert judgment.

(C) It rejects a proven means of accomplishing an objective without offering any alternative means of accomplishing that objective.

(D) It bases a firm conclusion about a state of affairs in the present on somewhat speculative claims about a future state of affairs.

(E) It bases its conclusion on facts that could, in the given situation, have resulted from causes other than those presupposed by the argument.

(B) 它否决了某一领域的专家的判断，在该领域没有比专家的判断更好的接近真理的方向。

(C) 它否决了一个被证实的能完成某个目标的方法，却没有提供另一个可完成该目标的方法。

(D) 它把关于目前事态的严格结论基于关于将来事态的有点推测性的声明。

(E) 它的结论基于这样的事实，即在给定的情况下，这些事实不是来源于论述中预先假定的原因。

11. The United States ranks far behind countries such as Sweden and Canada when it comes to workplace safety. In all three countries, joint labor-management committees that oversee workplace safety conditions have been very successful in reducing occupational injuries. In the United States, such committees are found only in the few companies that have voluntarily established them. However, in Sweden and several Canadian provinces, joint safety committees are required by law and exist in all medium-sized and large workplaces.

Which one of the following is supported by the information above?

(A) The establishment of joint safety committees in all medium-sized and large workplaces in the United States would result in a reduction of occupational injuries.

(B) A joint safety committee that is required by law is more effective at reducing occupational injuries than is a joint safety committee that is voluntarily established.

(C) Workplace safety in Sweden and Canada was superior to that in the United States even prior to the passage of laws requiring joint safety committees in all medium-sized and large workplaces.

(D) Joint safety committees had been voluntarily established in most medium-sized and large workplaces in Sweden and several Canadian provinces prior to the passage of laws requiring such committees.

(E) The United States would surpass Sweden and Canada in workplace safety of joint safety committees were required in all medium-sized and large workplaces in the United States.

当谈到工地的安全性时，美国远远排在像瑞典和加拿大等国的后面。在所有这三个国家中，监视工地安全情况的联合劳动管理委员会非常成功地减少了由职业引起的伤害。在美国，只有少数的几家公司有这样的委员会，并且是通过自愿的方式成立的。然而，在瑞典和几个加拿大的省内，联合安全委员会是法律所要求的，且在所有中等和大型工地都有这样的委员会。

下面哪一项被上面的论述所支持?

(A) 在美国的所有中等和大型工地创立联合安全委员会能导致由职业引起的伤害的减少。

(B) 被法律要求的联合安全委员会在减少由职业引起的伤害上要比自愿成立的联合安全委员会有效得多。

(C) 即使法律上要求在所有的中等和大型工地创立联合安全劳动委员会之前，瑞典和加拿大的工地安全性就比美国的高。

(D) 在瑞典和加拿大，联合安全委员会在法律要求之前，就已在大多数的中等和大型工地上自愿成立了。

(E) 如果美国要求在所有的中型和大型工地上都创立联合安全委员会，美国在工地的安全性方面将会超过瑞典和加拿大。

12. There is strong evidence that the cause of migraines(severe recurrent headaches) is not psychological but instead is purely physiological. Yet several studies have found that people being professionally treated for migraines rate higher on a standard psychological scale of anxiety than do people not being professionally treated for migraines.

Which one of the following, if true, most helps to resolve the apparent discrepancy in the information above?

(A) People who have migraine headaches tend to have relatives who also have migraine headaches.

(B) People who have migraine headaches often suffer these headaches when under emotional stress.

(C) People who rate higher on the standard psychological scale of anxiety are more likely to seek professional treatment than are people who rate lower on the scale.

(D) Of the many studies done on the cause of migraine headaches, most of those that suggest that psychological factors such as anxiety cause migraines have been widely publicized.

(E) Most people who have migraines and who seek professional treatment remain in treatment until they stop having migraines, whether their doctors consider the cause to be physiological or psychological.

13. Dinosaur expert: Some paleontologists have claimed that birds are descendants of a group of dinosaurs called dromeosaurs. They appeal to the fossil record, which indicates that dromeosaurs have characteristics more similar to birds than do most dinosaurs. But there is a fatal flaw in their argument: the earliest bird fossils that have been discovered date back tens of millions of years farther than the oldest known dromeosaur fossils. Thus the paleontologists' claim is false.

The expert's argument depends on assuming which one of the following?

(A) Having similar characteristics is not a sign that types of animals are evolutionarily related.

(B) Dromeosaurs and birds could have common ancestors.

(C) Knowledge of dromeosaur fossils and the earliest bird fossils is complete.

(D) Known fossils is indicate the relative dates of origin of birds and dromeosaurs.

(E) Dromeosaurs are dissimilar to birds in many significant ways.

有确凿的证据显示，偏头痛（严重的周期性头痛）不是由于心理上的原因引起的，而是完全由生理上的原因所致。然而，数项研究结果表明那些因为偏头痛受到专业化治疗的人患有标准心理尺度的焦虑症的比率比那些没经专业治疗的偏头痛患者的高。

下面哪一点，如果正确，最能有助于解决上面论述中的明显矛盾？

(A) 那些患有偏头痛的人，倾向于有患偏头痛的亲戚。

(B) 那些患偏头痛的人，在情绪紧张时经常头痛。

(C) 那些患有标准心理尺度的焦虑症且发作率较高的人追求专业治疗的可能性要比那些在同样尺度上发作率较低的人大。

(D) 在许多有关偏头痛起因的研究中，大多数认为偏头痛是由像焦虑这样的心理因素引起的研究已被广泛宣传。

(E) 不管他们的医生认为偏头痛的起因是心理方面的，还是生理方面的，大多数患有偏头痛且追求专业治疗的人在他们停止患有偏头痛后仍坚持治疗。

恐龙专家：一些古生物学家声称鸟类是一群叫做dromeosaurs的恐龙的后裔。他们求助于化石记录，结果发现，与鸟类和大多数的恐龙相比，dromeosaurs具有的特征与鸟类更为相似。但是，他们的论述存在致命的缺点，已发现的最早的鸟类的化石比最古老的已知dromeosaurs的化石早几千万年。因此，古生物学家的声明是错误的。

专家的论述依赖于下面哪条假设？

(A) 具有相似的特征不是不同类型的生物在进化上相联系的标志。

(B) dromeosaurs和鸟类可能会有共同的祖先。

(C) dromeosaurs化石和早期鸟类化石的知识是完整的。

(D) 已知化石揭示了鸟类和dromeosaurs起源的相对日期。

(E) dromeosaurs和鸟类在许多重要方面都不一样。

14. A member of the British Parliament is reputed to have said, "The First purpose of good social reform is to increase the sum total of human happiness. So, any reform which makes somebody happy is achieving its purpose. Since the reform I propose would make my constituents happy, it is a good social reform."

Which one of the following, if true, most seriously weakens the argument attributed to the member of Parliament?

(A) Different things make different people happy.

(B) The proposed reform would make a few people happy, but would not increase the happiness of most other people.

(C) The proposed reform would affect only the member of Parliament's constituents and would make them happy.

(D) Increasing some people's happiness might not increase the sum total of human happiness if others are made unhappy.

(E) Good social reforms usually have widespread support.

15. Shortly after the Persian Gulf War, investigators reported that the area, which had been subjected to hundreds of smoky oil fires and deliberate oil spills when regular oil production slowed down during the war displayed less oil contamination than they had witnessed in prewar surveys of the same area. They also reported that the levels of polycyclic aromatic hydrocarbons (PAHs)—used as a marker of combustion products spewed from oil wells ignited during the war—were also relatively low, comparable to those recorded in the temperate oil-producing areas of the Baltic Sea.

Which one of the following, if true, does most to resolve the apparent discrepancy in the information above?

(A) Oil contaminants have greater environmental effects in temperate regions than in desert regions.

(B) Oil contamination and PAH pollution dissipate more rapidly in temperate regions than in desert regions.

(C) Oil contamination and PAH pollution dissipate more rapidly in desert regions than in temperate regions.

(D) Peacetime oil production and transport in the Persian Gulf result in high levels of PAHs and massive oil dumping.

(E) The Persian Gulf War ended before the oil fires and spills caused as much damage as originally expected.

一位英国下院议员因说过这样的话而著名，"有益的社会改革的首要目的是增加人类幸福的总量。因此，任何使一些人幸福的改革都达到了它的目的，因为我所提出的改革会使我的选民们幸福，所以它是一个有益的社会改革。

下面哪一条，如果正确，能最严重地削弱那个下院议员的论述？

(A) 不同的事情会使不同的人幸福。

(B) 提出的那个改革，会使少数人幸福，但不会增加其他大多数人的幸福。

(C) 提出的那个改革只会影响到那个下院议员所代表的选民，并且能使他们幸福。

(D) 如果增加一些人的幸福，却给其他的人带来不幸，那么人类幸福的总量就不会增加。

(E) 有益的社会改革通常会受到广泛的支持。

海湾战争之后不久，调查研究者对这个地区进行了报道。在战争期间，当正常的石油生产减慢时，这个地区遭受了成百上千的浓烟滚滚的石油大火和蓄意的石油横流。战后这个地区的石油污染比他们战前对这个地区的调查显示的结果要轻。他们又报道说，与波罗的海气候温和的石油生产地区记录中的多环芳香族碳氢化合物的水平相比，这个地区的相对较低。多环芳香族碳氢化合物，简写为PAHs，被用来生产可燃产品，在战争期间曾从油井中喷出燃烧。

下面哪一点，如果正确，最能解决上述信息中的明显分歧？

(A) 气候温和地区的石油污染对环境的影响要比沙漠地区的大。

(B) 石油污染和PAH污染在气候温和地区要比在沙漠地区消散得快。

(C) 石油污染和PAH污染在沙漠地区要比在气候温和的地区消散得快。

(D) 和平时期，海湾的石油生产和运输致使高水平的PAHs和大规模的石油倾销。

(E) 海湾战争在石油大火之前结束，石油溢出造成的损失与最初料想的一样多。

16. One of the great difficulties in establishing animal rights based merely on the fact that animals are living things concerns scope. If one construes the term "living things" broadly, one is bound to bestow rights on organisms that are not animals (e.g., plants). But if this term is construed narrowly, one is apt to refuse rights to organisms that at least biologically, are considered members of the animal kingdom.

If the statements above are true, which one of the following can be most reasonably inferred from them?

(A) Not all animals should be given nights.

(B) One cannot bestow rights on animals without also bestowing rights on at least some plants.

(C) The problem of delineating the boundary of the set of living things interferes with every attempt to establish animal rights.

(D) Successful attempts to establish rights for all animals are likely either to establish rights for some plants or not to depend solely on the observation that animals are living things.

(E) The fact that animals are living things is irrelevant to the question of whether animals should or should not be accorded rights, because plants are living things too.

仅仅基于动物是"活着的东西"来确定动物的权利时，遇到的最大的困难之一涉及范围问题。如果一个人广义地解释"活着的东西"这一词语，他肯定要赋予不是动物（也即植物）的生物权利。但是，如果狭义地来解释这个词语，他就会拒绝给那些至少在生物学上被认为是动物王国的成员的生物权利。

如果上面的陈述是正确的，下面哪一项能从上面的陈述中最合理地推出？

(A) 不是所有的动物都应给予权利。

(B) 不赋予植物，至少是某些植物权利，就不能赋予动物权利。

(C) 描述"活着的事物"的边界的问题妨碍着每一个企图确定动物权利的尝试。

(D) 企图成功地确定所有动物的权利是可能的：要么确定一些植物的权利，要么不仅仅依赖于对动物是活着的事物的观察。

(E) 动物是活着的事物的事实，与动物该不该给予权利的问题不相干，因为植物也是活着的事物。

参考答案：

1. D	2. D	3. D	4. C	5. E
6. C	7. E	8. E	9. A	10. E
11. A	12. C	13. D	14. D	15. D
16. D				

1. **解析**：请用心体会我们讲过多次的B→A₁A₂推理模式的思维方法。

2. **解析**：经济学家只证明了臭氧层的货币价值存在一个上限，就驳斥了环境学家认为臭氧层的货币价值是不可预测的理论。很显然经济学家在没有给出确定了某物的货币价值上限就可预测那个货币价值是多少的根据，因此(D)是正确答案。

3. **解析**：广告销售理事驳斥杂志编辑的论述根本就没有击中要害，因为广告销售理事所做的反应与支持编辑的结论的证据无关，因此(D)是正确答案。

4. **解析**：编辑的论述"迎合他们的意愿将实际上有损于他们的利益"的逆否命题是"要有益于他们的利益就不能迎合他们的愿望"。有益于他们的利益的前提是"杂志是一个持续有效的广告媒体"，不能迎合他们的愿望就是不能给他们的产品好评。由此可知杂志编辑论述的假设是"给他们的产品好评不如让杂志成为一个持续有效的广告媒体"，因此(C)是正确答案。

5. **解析**：文中的论述仅仅根据Jerome每次都给出同样的理由，就毫无根据地认为Jerome的理由不是真正的理由。因此(E)是正确答案。

6. **解析**：要证明Jamie对Arnold反应是合理的，就是要找航空公司有责任赔偿乘客的必要条件。根据Jamie对Arnold论述的驳斥，可知航空公司在超额预定某一航班时在道义上不具有赔偿责任，要对Arnold论述进行进一步的驳斥，还要对Arnold提及的天气原因进行反驳，即航空公司在由于天气或其他原因而迫使乘客乘坐晚一点的航班也不应当负道义上的责任。综上所述只有在顾客预定的那个航班既没有被超额预定，也没有因其他原因被取消或推迟的情况下，乘客仍被拒绝了座位时，航空公司在道义上就具有赔偿的责任，所以(C)是正确答案。

7. **解析**：根据Korva的人口增加，但税收份额下降很容易推出(E)是正确选项。

8. **解析**：研究小组在实验中很显然是用今天的甲虫类生物的忍受温度来替代2'2万年内的甲虫类的生物的忍受温度，因此(E)是明显正确的答案。

9. **解析**：本题的(B)、(C)、(D)和(E)都是很明显的无关选项；(A)中的一些中世纪的翻译家拥有希腊原文的荷马手稿表明，荷马的诗在中世纪的阿拉伯有一定的读者，翻译家们也曾打算过翻译荷马的诗，因此(A)为正确答案。

10. **解析**：本题根据那些油画再次出售时售价较高断定了批评家评价的正确性。但是它忽视了这样的事实，即这些油画再次出售时价钱较高可能并不是因为它们本身具有相应的价值，也有可能正是因为批评家对这些画价值的肯定才导致它们再次被出售时售价较高，因此(E)是正确答案。

11. **解析**：根据本题中对美国与瑞典及加拿大的工地安全性的对比可以推出在工地创立联合安全委员会能导致由职业引起的伤害减少，所以(A)为正确答案；(B)、(C)、(D)和(E)四选项都不能从短文的论述中合理地推出。

12. **解析**：要解决本题论述中的明显分歧，就要给出接受专业治疗的偏头痛患者同时患有标准心理尺度焦虑症的比率较高的原因。(C)通过对比给出了差异原因，因此(C)为正确答案。

13. **解析**：既然已发现最早的鸟类化石比已发现的最古老的dromeosaurs化石早几千万年，那么一定是最早的鸟类化石与最古老的dromeosaurs化石的相对日期已经确定，即已知化石揭示了鸟类和dromeosaurs起源的相对日期，因此(D)为正确答案。

14. **解析**：这个议员的论述只是说明他提出的改革使部分人幸福，而没有证明他提出的改革不会给其他人带来不幸。因此(D)是最佳选项。

15. **解析**：石油污染和PAHs水平由多种因素引起，一个地区不同时期的石油污染的起因可能不同，因此(D)选项所给出的差异原因能很好地解决调查报告中的明显分歧。(A)、(B)和(C)三选项都不能解释海湾地区战前战后石油污染程度的差异；(E)为无关选项。

16. **解析**：根据题中对"living things"广义上和狭义上的解释很容易推出(D)为正确答案，其余四个选项都不能从短文中推出。

十四、GMAT考前逻辑推理冲刺训练试题及解析（十四）

1. Sasha: Handwriting analysis should be banned in court as evidence of a person's character: handwriting analysis called as witnesses habitually exaggerate the reliability of their analyses.

Gregory: You are right that the current use of handwriting analysis as evidence is problematic. But this problem exists only because there is no licensing board to set professional standards and thus deter irresponsible analysts from making exaggerated claims. When such a board is established,

Sasha：在法庭上，应该禁止将笔迹分析作为一个人性格的证据，笔迹分析家所谓的证据习惯性地夸大他们分析结果的可靠性。

Gregory：你说得很对，目前使用笔迹分析作为证据确实存在问题。这个问题的存在仅仅是因为没有许可委员会来制订专业的标准，以此来阻止不负责任的分析家做出夸大其实的声明。然而，当这样的委

however, handwriting analysis by licensed practitioners will be a legitimate courtroom tool for character assessment.

Gregory does which one of the following in responding to Sasha's argument?

(A) He ignores evidence introduced as support for Sasha's recommendation.

(B) He defends a principle by restricting the class to which it is to be applied.

(C) He abstracts a general principle from specific evidence.

(D) He identifies as self-contradictory statement in Sash's argument.

(E) He shows that Sasha's argument itself manifests the undesirable characteristic that it condemns.

2. In recent years the climate has been generally cool in northern Asia. But during periods when the average daily temperature and humidity in northern Asia were slightly higher than their normal levels the yields of most crops grown there increased significantly. In the next century, the increased average daily temperature and humidity attained during those periods are expected to become the norm. Yet scientists predict that the yearly yields of most of the region's crops will decrease during the next century.

Which one of the following, if true, most helps to resolve the apparent paradox in the information above?

(A) Crop yields in southern Asia are expected to remain constant even after the average daily temperature and humidity there increase from recent levels.

(B) Any increases in temperature and humidity would be accompanied by higher levels of atmospheric carbon dioxide, which is vital to plant respiration.

(C) The climate in northern Asia has generally been too cool and dry in recent years for populations of many crop insect pests to become established.

(D) In many parts of Asia, the increased annual precipitation that would result from warmer and wetter climates would cause most edible plant species to flourish.

(E) The recent climate of northern Asia prevents many crops from being farmed there during the winter.

员会被创立以后，那些持许可证的开业者的手迹分析结果就可以作为合法的法庭工具来评价一个人的性格。

Gregory在应答Sasha的论述时，用了下面哪一项？

(A) 他忽视为支持Sasha的建议而引用的证据。

(B) 他通过限定某一原则适用的范畴来为该原则辩护。

(C) 他从具体的证据中提取出一普遍性的原则。

(D) 他在Sasha的论述中发现了一个自相矛盾的陈述。

(E) 他揭示出Sasha的论述自身表明了一个不受欢迎的，并且是他的论述所批评的特征。

最近几年，北亚的气候普遍比较凉。但是，在北亚的日平均气温和湿度比正常水平稍高的那段时间内，那儿生长的庄稼的产量却显著增加。在下个世纪，在那一段时间内获得的增加的日平均气温和湿度将有望成为下个世纪的正常状态。然而科学家预测，在下个世纪大多数地区的庄稼的年产量会下降。

下面哪一点，如果正确，最能有助于解决以上信息中的矛盾？

(A) 即使南亚地区的日平均气温和湿度都比现在有所增加后，那儿的庄稼产量也有望保持不变。

(B) 任何有关温度和湿度的增加，都伴随着大气中二氧化碳含量的升高，二氧化碳对农作物的呼吸是至关重要的。

(C) 北亚最近几年的气候普遍太冷太干燥使得许多庄稼害虫不能大规模地生长。

(D) 在亚洲的许多地方，气候变得温暖湿润致使每年的降雨量增加，从而使大多数的可食作物茂盛地生长。

(E) 北亚最近的气候，妨碍了许多农作物冬季在那个地方的种植。

3. Chronic back pain is usually caused by a herniated or degenerated spinal disk. In most cases the disk will have been damaged years before chronic pain develops, and in fact an estimated one in five people over the age of 30 has a herniated or degenerated disk that shows no chronic symptoms. If chronic pain later develops in such a case, it is generally brought about by a deterioration of the abdominal and spinal muscles caused by insufficient exercise.

The statements above, if true, most strongly support which one of the following?

(A) Four out of five people over the age of 30 can be sure they will never develop chronic back pain.

(B) People who exercise their abdominal and spinal muscles regularly are sure to be free from chronic back pain.

(C) Patients rarely suffer even mild and fleeting back pain at the time that a spinal disk first becomes herniated or degenerated.

(D) Doctors can accurately predict which people who do not have chronic back pain will develop it in the future.

(E) There is a strategy that can be effective in delaying or preventing the onset of pain from a currently asymptomatic herniated or degenerated spinal disk.

慢性背疼通常是由成疝的或退化的脊椎骨引起。在大多数的情况下，脊椎骨在慢性疼痛形成之前就已受损。实际上，30岁以上的人中有1/5的人的脊椎骨成疝或退化但并不显示任何慢性症状。在这种情况下，如果后来发生慢性疼痛，一般都是由于缺乏锻炼致使腹部和脊部的肌肉退化而引起。

上面的陈述，如果正确，最能强有力地支持下面哪一点？

(A) 30岁以上的人中，有4/5的人可以确信他们从来不会患慢性背疼痛。

(B) 经常锻炼腹部和脊部肌肉的人可以确信不会患慢性背疼痛。

(C) 病人们在他们的脊椎骨第一次成疝或退化时，很少会遭受到甚至是轻微的和短暂的背疼。

(D) 医生可以准确地预测哪些没有患慢性背疼的人将来会患慢性背疼。

(E) 存在一个能有效延缓或防止起源于目前无症状的成疝的或退化的疹椎骨的疼痛出现的策略。

4. Tom: Employers complain that people graduating from high school too often lack the vocational skills required for full-time employment. Therefore, since these skills are best acquired on the job, we should require high school students to work at part-time jobs so that they acquire the skills needed for today's job market.

Mary: There are already too few part-time jobs for students who want to work, and simply requiring students to work will not create jobs for them.

Which one of the following most accurately describes how Mary's response is related to Tom's argument?

(A) It analyzes an undesirable result of undertaking the course of action that Tom recommends.

(B) It argues that Tom has mistaken an unavoidable trend for an avoidable one.

(C) It provides information that is inconsistent with an explicitly stated premise in Tom's argument.

(D) It presents a consideration that undercuts an assumption on which Tom's argument depends.

(E) It defends an alternative solution to the problem that Tom describes.

Tom：雇主们报怨高中毕业生通常缺乏专职工作所需的职业技巧。因此，既然在工作中最易获得这些技巧，那么我们就应该要求高中学生干一些兼职工作，以便他们能获得当今的工作市场上需要的技巧。

Mary：对想工作的学生来说，现有的兼职工作太少，仅仅要求学生们工作并不会给他们创造工作。

下面哪一点最准确地描述了Mary的应答怎样与Tom的论述相联系？

(A) 它分析了采取Tom推荐的行动方针会产生一个不合需要的结果。

(B) 它论证了Tom把一个不可避免的趋势错认为是一个可以避免的趋势。

(C) 它提供了与Tom的论述中的一个明确陈述的前提不相一致的信息。

(D) 它提出了一个削弱Tom的论述所依赖的假设的理由。

(E) 它为Tom所描述的问题的另一个可替换的解决办法辩护。

5. Private industry is trying to attract skilled research scientists by offering them high salaries. As a result, most research scientists employed in private industry now earn 50 percent more than do comparably skilled research scientists employed by the government. So, unless government-employed research scientists are motivated more by a sense of public duty than by their own interests, the government is likely to lose its most skilled research scientists to private industry, since none of these scientists would have problems finding private-sector jobs.

Which one of the following is an assumption on which the argument depends?

(A) Government research scientists are less likely to receive acknowledgment for their research contributions than are research scientists in the private sector.

(B) None of the research scientists currently employed by government earns more than the highest-paid researches employed in the private sector.

(C) The government does not employ as many research scientists who are highly skilled as does any large company in the private sector which employs research scientists.

(D) The government does not provide its research scientists with unusually good working conditions or fringe benefits that more than compensate for the lower salaries they receive.

(E) Research scientists employed in the private sector generally work longer hours than do researchers employed by the government.

6. Using fossil energy more efficiently is in the interest of the nation and the global environment, but major improvements are unlikely unless proposed government standards are implemented to eliminate products or practices that are among the least efficient in their class.

Objection: Decisions on energy use are best left to the operation of the market.

Which one of the following, if true, most directly undermines the objection above?

(A) It would be unrealistic to expect society to make the changes necessary to achieve maximum energy efficiency all at once.

(B) There are products, such as automobiles, that consume energy at a sufficient rate that persons who purchase and use them will become conscious of any unusual energy

私营行业通过提供高薪，试图吸引有技能的研究型科学家。结果，大多数受雇于私营行业的研究科学家赚的钱比技能相仿的在政府部门工作的研究型科学家多出50%。所以，除非政府雇用的研究科学家更多地被对公众的职责感而不是被他们的个人利益所驱使，否则政府就有可能使它的最有技能的科学家流失到私营行业，因为这些科学家中没有人会在私营部门中找不到工作。

下面哪一点是上述论述依赖的假设？

(A) 政府部门的研究型科学家的科研贡献没有在私营部门工作的研究科学家的易于被承认。

(B) 目前，在政府部门工作的研究型科学家中，没有人赚的钱比受雇于私营部门的薪水最高的研究科学家赚的钱多。

(C) 政府部门雇用的卓越技能研究科学家的人数没有雇用研究型科学家的私营部门中的任何一个大公司雇用的多。

(D) 政府不给它的研究型科学家提供非常好的工作条件或超过他们由于较低的薪水而得的补偿的额外福利。

(E) 受雇于私营部门的研究型科学家工作的时间普遍比受雇于政府部门的研究科学家的长。

充分地利用矿物能源是一个国家乃至全球环境的利益所在。但是除非用以消除那些在它们的同类中效率最低的产品和方法的拟议中的政府标准所实施，否则不可能出现较大的改进。

反对：有关能源使用的决定最好留给市场交易来完成。

下面哪一点，如果正确，能最直接地削弱上面的反对意见？

(A) 期望社会能一下子就做出必要的改变来获得最大能量效率的想法是不现实的。

(B) 有些产品，例如汽车，利用能源的效率较高，那些购买和使用这些产品的人，通过和其他同类产品相比就会意

inefficiency in comparison with other products in the same class.

(C) Whenever a new mode of generating energy, such as a mew fuel, is introduced, a number of support systems, such as a fuel-distribution system, must be created or adapted.

(D) When energy prices rise, consumers of energy tend to look for new ways to increase energy efficiency, such as by adding insulation to their houses.

(E) Often the purchaser of a product, such as a landlord buying an appliance, chooses on the basis of purchase price because the purchaser is not the person who will pay for energy used by the product.

7. Smoking in bed has long been the main cause of home fires. Despite a significant decline in cigarette smoking in the last two decades, however, there has been no comparable decline in the number of people killed in home fires.

Each one of the following statements, if true over the last two decades, helps to resolve the apparent discrepancy above EXCEPT:

(A) Compared to other types of home fires, home fires caused by smoking in bed usually cause relatively little damage before they are extinguished.

(B) Home fires caused by smoking in bed often break out after the home's occupants have fallen asleep.

(C) Smokers who smoke in bed tend to be heavy smokers who are less likely to quit smokers than are smokers who do not smoking in bed.

(D) An increasing number of people have been killed in home fires that started in the kitchen.

(E) Population densities have increased, with the result that one home fire can cause more deaths than in previous decades.

8. Professor Robinson: A large meteorite impact crater in a certain region was thought to be the clue to explaining the mass extinction of plant and animal species that occurred at the end of the Mesozoic era. However, the crystalline structure of rocks recovered at the site indicates that the impact that formed this crater was not the culprit. When molten rocks crystallize, they display the polarity of Earth's magnetic field at that time. But the recrystallized rocks recovered at the site display normal magnetic polarity, even though Earth's magnetic field was reversed at the time of the mass extinction.

识到任何一个能量利用率异常低的地方。

(C) 每当一种新型的产生能量的方式，例如一种新的燃料被引进时，一些支持系统，例如燃料分配系统就必须被创建或被改建。

(D) 当能量的价格上升时，消费者会倾向于寻找新的提高能量利用率的方法，例如给他们的房子加上一绝热层。

(E) 一产品的购买者，例如房东购买器具时通常是基于产品的价格购买产品，因为产品的购买者不是要为产品消耗的能量付费的人。

长期以来床上抽烟是家庭火灾的主要原因。尽管在过去的20年中，抽烟的人数显著下降，但是死于家庭火灾的人数并没有相应的下降。

下面的每一条陈述，如果在过去的20年中正确，除了哪一条之外都有助于解决上面论述中的明显的分歧？

(A) 与其他类型的家庭火灾相比，床上抽烟引起的家庭火灾在它们被扑灭之前，通常造成的破坏相对较小。

(B) 由床上抽烟引起的火灾通常发生于房主入睡以后。

(C) 在床上抽烟的人倾向于是抽烟抽得多的人，他们与那些不在床上抽烟的人相比更不可能把烟戒掉。

(D) 死于厨房发生的家庭火灾的人数在增加。

(E) 人口密度在增加，结果一次家庭火灾所造成的死亡人数比前20年的多。

Robinson教授：在某一地区发现的巨大陨石碰撞坑被认为是解释发生在中生代末期的动植物大规模地灭绝的线索。然而在那个地点发现的岩石的晶体结构显示产生陨石坑的碰撞并不是罪魁祸首。当熔化的岩石结晶时，它们表现出当时地球磁场的极性。尽管在大灭绝的时候地球的磁场发生了反转，但是在那个地方发现的重结晶的岩石却具有正常的磁极。

Each of the following is an assumption on which Professor Robinson's argument depends EXCEPT:

(A) The crater indicates an impact of more than sufficient size to have caused the mass extinction.

(B) The recovered rocks recrystallized shortly after they melted.

(C) No other event caused the rocks to melt after the impact formed the crater.

(D) The recovered rocks melted as a result of the impact that formed the crater.

(E) The mass extinction would have occurred soon after the impact that supposedly caused it.

9. A study of the difference in earnings between men and women in the country of Naota found that the average annual earnings of women who are employed full time is 80 percent of the average annual earnings of men who are employed full time. However, other research consistently shows that, in Naota, the average annual earnings of all employed women is 65 percent of the average annual earnings of all employed men.

Which one of the following, if also established by research, most helps explain the apparent discrepancy between the research results described above?

(A) In Naota, the difference between the average annual earnings of all female workers and the average annual earnings of all male workers has been gradually increasing over the past 30 years.

(B) In Naota, the average annual earnings of women who work full time in exactly the same occupations and under exactly the same conditions as men is almost the same as the men's average annual earnings.

(C) In Naota, a growing proportion of female workers hold full-time managerial, supervisory, or professional positions, and such positions typically pay more than other types of positions pay.

(D) In Naota, a larger proportion of female workers than male workers are part-time workers,and part-time workers typically earn less than full-time workers earn.

(E) In ten other countries where the proportion of women in the work force is similar to that of Naota, the average annual earnings of women who work full time ranges

下面除了哪一点之外，都是Robinson教授的论述依赖的假设？

(A) 陨石坑预示了一个足以引起大灭绝的大规模的碰撞。

(B) 被发现的岩石在熔化后很快又再结晶。

(C) 在碰撞形成陨石坑后，没有其他引起岩石熔化的事情发生。

(D) 发现的岩石的熔化起因于碰撞形成的陨石坑。

(E) 在那个被认为是引起大灭绝的碰撞发生之后不久就出现了大灭绝。

一项对Naota国男女收入差异的研究结果表明，全职工作的妇女的收入是全职工作的男人的收入的80%。然而，其他调查结果却一致显示，在Naota所有受雇妇女的平均年收入只是所有受雇男性的平均年收入的65%。

下面哪一点，如果也被调查所证实，最有助于解释上面研究结果之间的明显分歧？

(A) 在Naota，所有女性雇员的平均年收入与所有男性雇员的平均年收入的差距在过去的30年中一直在逐渐增大。

(B) 在Naota，全职工作的妇女的平均年收入与完全相同的职业和工作条件下的全职工作的男性的平均年收入是一样的。

(C) 在Naota，女性工作者占据全职的、管理的、监督的、专业的职位的比例在增加，这些职位赚的钱通常比其他类型的职位赚的钱多。

(D) 在Naota，妇女干兼职工作的比例比男性高，并且兼职工作者赚的钱通常比全职工作者的少。

(E) 在其他妇女在劳动力中的比例与Naota相似的10个国家中，全职工作的妇女的平均年收入与全职工作的男性的平均年收入相比，其比例从较低的50%到较高的90%不等。

from a low of 50 percent to a high of 90 percent of the average annual earnings of men who work full time.

10. A recent survey showed that 50 percent of people polled believe that elected officials should resign if indicted for a crime, whereas 35 percent believe that elected officials should resign only if they are convicted of a crime. Therefore, more people believe that elected officials should resign if indicted than believe that they should resign if convicted.

The reasoning above is flawed because it

(A) draws a conclusion about the population in general based only on a sample of that population.

(B) confuses a sufficient condition with a required condition.

(C) is based on an ambiguity of one of its terms.

(D) draws a conclusion about a specific belief based on responses to queries about two different specific beliefs.

(E) contains premises that cannot all be true.

最近的一则调查报告显示，参加民意测验的人中，有50%的人认为选举产生的官员如被控告有罪时就应辞职，而有35%的人认为仅当选举产生的官员被宣判有罪时，他们才应当辞职。因此，认为选举产生的官员被控告时应该辞职的人比认为选举产生的官员被宣判有罪时应该辞职的人多。

上面的推理有缺陷，因为它_____。

(A) 基于人口的一个抽样，做了一个关于整个人口的结论。

(B) 把充分条件和必要条件相混淆。

(C) 基于它的一个模棱两可的术语。

(D) 基于对两个具体信仰询问的回答，做了一个关于某一具体信仰的结论。

(E) 包含有不可能全部正确的前提。

11. When soil is plowed in the spring, pigweed seeds that have been buried in the soil all winter are churned up to the surface and redeposited just under the surface. The brief exposure of the seeds to sunlight stimulates receptors, which have become highly sensitive to sunlight during the months the seeds were buried in the soil, and the stimulated receptors trigger germination. Without the prolonged darkness, followed by exposure to sunlight, the seeds do not germinate.

The statements above, if true, most strongly support which one of the following statements about a field that will be plowed in the spring and in which pigweed seeds have been buried in the soil all winter?

(A) Fewer pigweed plants will grow in the field if it is plowed only at night than if it is plowed during the day.

(B) Fewer pigweed plants will grow in the field if it is not plowed at all than if it is plowed only at night.

(C) Fewer pigweed plants will grow in the field if it is plowed just before sunrise than if it is plowed just after sunset.

(D) The pigweed seeds that are churned up to the surface of the soil during the plowing will not germinate unless they are redeposited under the surface of the soil.

(E) All of the pigweed seeds that are already on the surface of the soil before the field is plowed will germinate.

当土地在春季被犁时，整个冬季都埋在土壤里的藜的种子被翻到表面，然后重新沉积到表层的正下面，种子短暂的曝光刺激了感受器。感受器在种子埋在土壤里的那几个月期间已对太阳光变得高度敏感。受刺激后的感受器激发种子发芽。没有漫长的黑暗和随后的曝光，藜的种子就不会发芽。

上面的陈述，如果正确，能最强有力地支持下面哪一个关于一块将要在春季犁的土地，且有藜的种子整个冬季都被埋在它的土壤里的陈述？

(A) 这块土地在夜晚犁要比在白天犁生长的藜类植物少。

(B) 这块土地根本就不犁要比它仅在夜晚犁生长的藜类植物少。

(C) 刚好在日出前犁这块地要比刚好在日落后犁这块地生长的藜类植物少。

(D) 在犁地的过程中，被翻到土壤表层的藜的种子不会发芽，除非它们被重新沉积到土壤表层的下面。

(E) 在这块土地被犁之前，所有已经位于土壤表层的藜的种子都会发芽。

12. Essayist: The existence of a moral order in the universe—i.e., an order in which bad is always eventually punished and good rewarded—depends upon human souls being immortal. In some cultures this moral order is regarded as the result of a karma that controls how one is reincarnated, in others it results from the actions of a supreme being who metes out justice to people after their death. But however a moral order is represented, if human souls are immortal, then it follows that the bad will be punished.

Which one of the following most accurately describes a flaw in the essayist's reasoning?

(A) From the assertion that something is necessary to a moral order the argument concludes that that thing is sufficient for an element of the moral order to be realized.

(B) The argument takes mere beliefs to be established facts.

(C) From the claim that the immortality of human souls implies that there is a moral order in the universe, the argument concludes that there being a moral order in the universe implies that human souls are immortal.

(D) The argument treats two fundamentally different conceptions of a moral order as essentially the same.

(E) The argument's conclusion is presupposed in the definition it gives of a moral order.

评论家：现存宇宙中的道德秩序，也就是善恶终有报的秩序，依赖于人类灵魂的不朽。在有些文化中，这种道德秩序被认为是一种控制一个人如何再生的因果报应的结果，换句话说它起因于上帝的行动，上帝在人们死后赋予他们正义。但是，不管道德秩序被怎样地体现，如果人类的灵魂是不朽的，坏人就一定会受到惩罚。

下面哪一点最准确地叙述了评论家的推理缺陷？

(A) 文中论述从某物对道德秩序是必要的，推论出那件事物是道德秩序的某一要素得以实现的充分条件。

(B) 文中论述把纯粹的信仰当作确定的事实。

(C) 根据人类灵魂的不朽暗示着宇宙中存在着一种道德秩序的声明，文中论述推论出宇宙中道德秩序的存在暗示着人类灵魂的不朽。

(D) 文中论述把两种完全不同的道德秩序概念看成本质上是一样的道德秩序概念。

(E) 文中论述的推论在定义中就预先假定存在一个道德秩序。

13. The publisher of a best-selling self-help book had in some promotional material, claimed that it showed readers how to become exceptionally successful. Of course, everyone knows that no book can deliver to the many what, by definition, must remain limited to the few exceptional success. Thus, although it is clear that the publisher knowingly made a false claim, dong so should not be considered unethical in this case.

Which one of the following principles, if valid, most strongly supports the reasoning above?

(A) Knowingly making a false claim is unethical only if it is reasonable for people to accept the claim as true.

(B) Knowingly making a false claim is unethical if those making it derive a gain at the expense of those acting as if the claim were true.

(C) Knowingly making a false claim is unethical in only those cases in which those who accept the claim as true suffer a hardship greater than the gain they were anticipating.

一畅销自助书的出版商在一些促销材料中声称这本书将向读者展示如何成为一个卓越成功的人。当然，每个人都知道没有书能给很多人带来那些从定义上一定仅局限于少数人的卓越的成功。因此，尽管出版商很明显故意地做了一个虚假的声明，但是在这种情况下这种做法不应该被认为是不道德的。

下面哪一原则，如果正确，能最强有力支持上面的推理？

(A) 只要人们能合情合理地接受某一虚假的声明为真，那么故意做出这样的声明就是不道德的。

(B) 如果做出虚假声明的人在损害那些认为该虚假声明为真的人的情况下获益，那么故意做出这样的声明是不道德的。

(C) 当那些认为某一虚假声明为真的人遭

(D) Knowingly making a false claim is unethical only if there is a possibility that someone will act as if the claim might be true.

(E) Knowingly making a false claim is unethical in at least those cases in which for someone else to discover that the claim is false, that person must have acted as if the claim were true.

14. When the Pinecrest Animal Shelter, a charitable organization, was in danger of closing because it could not pay for important repairs, its directors appealed to the townspeople to donate money that would be earmarked to pay for those repairs. Since more funds were ultimately donated than were used for the repairs, the directors plan to donate the surplus funds to other animal shelters. But before doing so, the directors should obtain permission from those who made the donations.

Which one of the following principles, if valid, most Helps to justify the position advocated above and yet places the least restriction on the allocation of funds by directors of charitable organizations?

(A) The directors of charitable organizations cannot allocate publicly solicited funds to any purposes for which the directors had not specifically earmarked the funds in advance.

(B) People who solicit charitable donations from the public for a specific cause should spend the funds only on that cause or, if that becomes impossible, should dispose of the funds according to the express wishes of the donors.

(C) Directors of charitable organizations who solicit money from the public must return all the money received from an appeal if more money is received than can practicably be used for the purposes specified in the appeal.

(D) Donors of money to charitable organizations cannot delegate to the directors of those organizations the responsibility of allocating the funds received to various purposes consonant with the purposes of the organization as the directors of the organization see fit.

(E) People who contribute money to charitable organizations should be considered to be placing their trust in the directors of those organizations to use the money wisely according to whatever circumstance might arise.

受的困难比他们期望的收益大时，故意做出这样的虚假声明是不道德的。

(D) 只要可能有人会认为某一虚假声明是真的，那么故意做出这样的声明就是不正确的。

(E) 至少在其他某个人发现某个虚假声明是假的，且这个人一定一度认为该声明是真的情况下，故意做出这样的声明是不道德的。

当Pinecrest动物收容所，一个慈善机构因不能支付重要的维修费用而面临关闭的危险时，该所的董事呼吁城镇里的人们捐钱，并特别指定捐的钱只用来偿还那些维修费用。因为最后捐的钱要比维修用的多，所以董事长决定把多余的资金捐给其他动物所。但是董事长在这样做之前，他应当获得那些捐钱人的许可。

下面哪一条原则，如果正确，最有助于证明上面提倡的立场是正当的，同时又能使那个慈善组织的董事在分配资金时受到最少的限制？

(A) 慈善组织的董事不能把征集公众的资金用于其他没有事先指明用途的任何目的。

(B) 那些为一特定原因而向公众征集慈善捐款的人，应当只把钱花在那件事情上，或者当不可能这样做时，应当根据捐赠者的确切愿望来处理那部分资金。

(C) 如果收到的钱比实际上用于求助中指定目的的钱多时，那些从公众处征集资金的慈善机构的董事就应当归还所有他们从求助中收到的钱。

(D) 向慈善机构捐钱的捐赠者不能把这样的责任，即把收到的资金分配给这些机构的董事认为的与这个机构目的相一致的各种目的责任，委托给这些组织的董事。

(E) 可以认为，那些向慈善组织捐钱的人，相信无论什么情况发生，这些慈善机构的董事都会明智地花钱。

15. The amount of electricity consumed in Millville on any day in August is directly proportional to peak humidity on that day. Since the average peak humidity this August was three points higher than the average peak humidity last August, it follows that more energy was consumed in Millville this August than last August.

Which one of the following arguments has a pattern of reasoning most similar to the one in the argument above?

(A) The amount of art supplies used in any of the Aesthetic Institute's 25 classes is directly proportional to the number of students in that class. Since in these classes the institute enrolled 20 percent more students overall last year than in the previous year, more art supplies were used in the institute's classes last year than in the previous year.

(B) The number of courses in painting offered by the Aesthetic Institute in any term is directly proportional to the number of students enrolled in the institute in that term. But the institute offers the same number of courses in sculpture each term. Hence, the institute usually offers more courses in painting than in sculpture.

(C) The number of new students enrolled at the Aesthetic Institute in any given year is directly proportional to the amount of advertising the institute has done in the previous year. Hence, if the institute seeks to increase its student body, it must increase the amount it spends on advertising.

(D) The fees paid by a student at the Aesthetic Institute are directly proportional to the number of classes in which that student enrolls. Since the number of students at the Aesthetic Institute is increasing, it follows that the institute is collecting a greater amount in fees paid by students than it used to.

(E) The number of instructors employed by the Aesthetic Institute in any term is directly proportional to the number of classes offered in that term and also directly proportional to the number of students enrolled at the institute. Thus, the number of classes offered by the institute in any term is directly proportional to the number of students enrolled in that term.

16. Historians of North American architecture who have studied early nineteenth-century houses with wooden floors have observed that the boards used on the floors of bigger

在Millville，8月中每一天电的消耗量与这一天湿度的最大值成正比。既然今年8月的平均湿度峰值比去年8月的高3个百分点，那么就可推出Millville今年8月的耗电量一定比去年8月的多。

下面哪一个论述的推理模式与上面的论述最相似？

(A) 在美学院25个班级中，任何一个班艺术用品的数量都与这个班的学生个数成正比。既然学院的这些班级去年比前年总共多招了20％的学生，那么去年学院的班级使用的艺术用品的数量就比前年的多。

(B) 美学院在任何一个学期所开的绘画课的数量，都与该学院这个学期招收的学生的数量成正比。但是学院每年开的雕塑课的数量都是一样的。因此，通常学院开的绘画课的数量比雕塑课的多。

(C) 美学院每年招收的新生数量都与它前一年所做广告的数量成正比。因此，如果学院想增加它的学生人数，它就必须增加在广告上的开支。

(D) 学生在美学院所交的学费与招收他的班级的数目成正比，既然美学院学生的人数在增加，那么就可推出学院收的学费的数额比过去的大。

(E) 美学院每学期雇用的讲师数目与该学期所开的课程以及学院所招生的人数成正比。因此，学院在任何一个学期所开的课程数都与该学期的招生人数成正比。

北美建筑历史学家对19世纪早期铺有木地板的房子进行了研究，结果发现较大的房间使用的木板一般都比较小的房间使

houses were generally much narrower than those used on the floors of smaller houses. These historians have argued that, since the people for whom the bigger houses were built were generally richer than the people for whom the smaller houses were built, floors made out of narrow floorboards were probably once a status symbol, designed to proclaim the owner's wealth.

Which one of the following, if true, most helps to strengthen the historians' argument?

(A) More original floorboards have survived from big early nineteenth-century houses than from small early nineteenth-century houses.

(B) In the early nineteenth century, a piece of narrow floorboard was not significantly less expensive than a piece of wide floorboard of the same length.

(C) In the early nineteenth-century, smaller houses generally had fewer rooms than did bigger houses.

(D) Some early nineteenth century houses had wide floorboards near the walls of each room and narrower floorboards in the center, where the floors were usually carpeted.

(E) Many of the biggest early nineteenth-century houses but very few small houses from that period had some floors that were made of materials that were considerably more expensive than wood, such as marble.

用的木板窄得多。这些历史学家认为，既然拥有大房子的人一般都比拥有小房子的人富有，那么用窄木板铺地板可能一度是地位的象征，是为表明房屋主人的财富而设计的。

下面哪一点，如果正确，最有助于加强历史学家的论述？

(A) 从19世纪早期的大房子里残存下来的原始地板木料要比从19世纪早期小房子里残存下来的多。

(B) 在19世纪早期，一块窄的地板木料并不比相同长度的宽地板木料明显地便宜。

(C) 在19世纪早期，小房子一般比大房子的房间数少。

(D) 有些19世纪早期的房子，在靠近墙的地方铺有较宽的木板，而在房间中间常铺地毯的地方铺的木板较窄。

(E) 在19世纪早期，有许多最大的房子，但是很少小房子的地板所用的材料，例如大理石比木头贵得多。

参考答案：

1. B	2. C	3. E	4. D	5. D
6. E	7. B	8. A	9. D	10. B
11. A	12. A	13. A	14. B	15. A
16. B				

1. **解析：** 本题属逻辑应用与技巧题。Gregory在应答Shasha时首先承认笔迹分析存在的问题，然后指出问题起因，接下来提出了一个消除这些问题的办法，最后下结论认为笔迹分析在他提出的这一方法的作用下将会变得有效，由此分析可知(B)为正确答案。

2. **解析：** 要解释分歧，就要找差异原因，(C)通过找他因的办法解决了上述分歧，为正确答案。最近几年，在气温和湿度较高的那一段时间内，庄稼产量显著升高是因为这几年气候普遍比较干燥，庄稼害虫不能大规模生长；下个世纪，虽然气温和湿度普遍较高有利于庄稼生长，但同时也有利于庄稼害虫大规模生长，因此产量会下降。

3. **解析：** 由短文的最后一句话可知，缺乏锻炼是引起慢性疼痛的主要原因，也即经常锻炼就可以有效地防止慢性疼痛，因此(E)是正确答案；(B)过于绝对化，因为在某些特殊情况下，慢性疼痛可能不是由缺乏锻炼引起，所以经常锻炼不一定能消除慢性疼痛；(A)、(C)和(D)都不能从短文中合理地推出。

4. **解析：** Tom认为兼职工作可以使高中生获得职业技巧，而Mary则表明兼职工作太少，也即Mary的应答削弱了Tom的论证所依赖的假设，因此(D)为正确答案。

5. **解析：** 除了薪水之外，工作条件以及福利待遇也是决定研究科学家在哪里工作的主要因素，因此本题的选项(D)是本题的论证所依赖的假设。

6. **解析：** 要对反对意见进行削弱，只要说明市场交易不能使矿物能源的利用率提高。(E)通过举例说明了市场交易并不一定能有效地使矿物能源利用率提高，因此(E)为正确答案；(A)、(B)、(C)和(D)都为无关选项。

7. **解析：** 在房主入睡以后发生的火灾很容易引起人员死亡，因此(B)选项不能解决本题论述中的明显分歧；(A)选项表明床上抽烟一般不引起伤亡事件，因此抽烟人数显著减少，但是死于家庭火灾的人数并没有相应地减少；(C)选项表明抽烟人数减少是由于不在床上抽烟的人不再抽烟所致，而这部分人又一般不引起家庭火灾，所以抽烟人数明显减少，死于家庭火灾的人数并没有显著减少；(D)通过他因说明了死亡人数为什么没相应减少；(E)选项表明火灾发生的次数可能随抽烟者的减少而减少，但随人员密度的增加，每次死亡的人数却增加了，所以死亡人数没有随抽烟人数的显著下降而做相应的下降。

8. **解析：** Robinson论述的结论是陨石碰撞坑不是引起大灭绝的罪魁祸首。因此，(A)明显与Robinson的结论相抵触，其他几个选项仔细分析后可发现它们都是Robinson教授的论述依赖的假设。

9. **解析：** 对解决分歧型的题，就是要找产生分歧的差异原因。在所有受雇的妇女中，既包含有全职工作者，又包含有兼职工作者，当从事兼职工作的妇女比例较高，且兼职工作的工资较低时，就可以解释两组结果的差异，因此(D)为正确答案；(A)、(B)、(C)和(E)均为无关选项。

10. **解析：** 本题推理中假设那些认为仅当选举产生的官员被宣判有罪时就应辞职的人数与那些认为选举产生的官员被宣判有罪时就应辞职的人数是一样的，因此本题论证的推理把充分条件与必要条件相混淆，所以(B)是正确答案。

11. **解析：** 根据本题的论述可知，离开了太阳光的刺激，藜的种子就不会发芽，因此在夜晚犁的地要比在白天犁的地生长的藜类植物少，即(A)为正确答案；同时推出(C)是错误的；(B)、(D)和(E)都不能从短文中合理地推出。

12. **解析：** 人类灵魂的不朽只是宇宙中道德秩序存在的一个必要条件。由这个必要条件很显然推不出道德秩序的某一个特征会因此而被体现，也就是说人类灵魂的不朽不是坏人一定会受到惩罚的充分条件。由此分析可知(A)是正确答案。

    karma *n.* 羯磨，因果报应

13. **解析：** 本题读重点在段落的第二句与第三句话，且第二句话是第三句话成立的论据。但A与B之间明显有了跳跃，难道每个人都知道的事实就能得出这个结论吗？(A)把这个跳跃连了起来，支持了段落推理。因为段落中并无论述关于某人损害他人而获益的情况，所以(B)不正确；(C)也犯了和(B)同样的错误；(D)、(E)均不能对段落推理起到支持作用。

14. **解析：** 解答这类题目时，要认真把题读懂，然后根据题意与题目要求选择答案。(B)所陈述的原则，既体现了捐钱人的愿望又使董事们的权利得到了最大的保障，因此(B)为正确答案；(A)和(C)选项对董事的权利限制得较多；(D)和(E)选项都不能支持短文中提倡的立场。

15. **解析：** 本题用的推理方法是：根据某一事物与另一事物构成比例推出当两件事物中的一件增加时，另一件也增加。在5个选项中，只有(A)和(C)用了这种推理方法。但是应注意本题的短文以及(A)选项都是基于某种事物的增加，对已经发生了的另一件事物的推测，并且都是由后者增加推出前者增加，而(C)则是对将来事件的推测，且从前者增加推出后者也增加。另一方面选项(C)在论证中又把增加广告开支看成了新生数量增加的必要条件，因此相比之下(A)是正确选项；(B)做了一个毫无根据的假设，把不变量当作最小量；(D)把班级的个数与学生人数混为一谈；(E)的逻辑结构明显与本题段落中论述的不符。

16. **解析：** 要加强窄木板是一种富贵的象征，就要证明用窄木板铺地要比用宽木板铺相同面积的地用的钱多。根据(B)，一块窄的地板木料并不比相同长度的宽地板木料明显地便宜，很容易推出用窄木板铺的面积与宽地板的相同时，花的钱要比宽木板的多，因此(B)是正确答案；(A)、(C)、(D)和(E)均为无关选项。

十五、GMAT考前逻辑推理冲刺训练试题及解析（十五）

1. John: As I was driving to work this morning, I was stopped by a police officer and ticketed for speeding. Since there were many other cars around me that were going as fast as I was, the police officer clearly treated me unfairly.

Mary: You were not treated unfairly, since the police officer was obviously unable to stop all the drivers who were speeding. Everyone who was speeding at that time and place had an equal chance of being stopped.

Which one of the following principles, if established, would most help to justify Mary's position?

(A) If all of those who violate a traffic law on a particular occasion are equally likely to be penalized for violating it, then the law is fairly applied to whoever among them is then penalized.

(B) The penalties attached to traffic laws should be applied not as punishments for breaking the law, but rather as deterrents to unsafe driving.

(C) The penalties attached to traffic laws should be imposed on all people who violate those laws, and only those people.

(D) It is fairer not to enforce a traffic law at all than it is to enforce it in some, but not all of the cases to which it applies.

(E) Fairness in the application of a traffic law is ensured not by all violators' having an equal chance of being penalized for their violation of the law, but rather by penalizing all known violators to the same extent.

2. In 1988, a significant percentage of seals in the Baltic Sea died from viral diseases: off the coast of Scotland, however, the death rate due to viral diseases was approximately half what it was for the Baltic seals. The Baltic seals had significantly higher levels of pollutants in their blood than did the Scottish seals, Since pollutants are known to impair marine mammals' ability to fight off viral infection, it is likely that the higher death rate among the Baltic seals was due to the higher levels of pollutants in their blood.

Which one of the following, if true, provides the most

John：今天早上我开车去上班时，被一警察拦住，并给我开了超速处罚单。因为当时在我周围有许多其他的车开得和我的车一样地快，所以很明显那个警察不公平地对待我。

Mary：你没有被不公平地对待，因为很明显那个警察不能拦住所有超速的司机。在那个时间、那个地点所有超速的人被拦住的可能性都是一样的。

下面哪一条原则，如果正确，会最有助于证明Mary的立场是合理的?

(A) 如果在某一特定场合，所有那些违反同一交通法则的人因违反它而受到惩罚的可能性是一样的，那么这些人中不管是谁那时受到了惩罚，法律对他来说都是公平的。

(B) 隶属于交通法的处罚不受该作为对违法的惩罚，而应作为对危险驾车的威慑而存在。

(C) 隶属于交通法的处罚应仅对所有违反那些法律的人实施惩罚，并且仅对那些人实施。

(D) 根本不实施交通法要比仅在它适用的人中的一些人身上实施更公平一些。

(E) 在实施交通法时，公平不是靠所有的违法者都有相同的被惩罚机率来保证，而是靠以相同程度来处罚所有已知的违法者来担保。

在1988年，波罗的海有很大比例的海豹死于病毒性疾病；然而在苏格兰的沿海一带，海豹由于病毒性疾病而死亡的比率大约是波罗的海的一半。波罗的海海豹血液内的污染性物质水平比苏格兰海豹的高得多。因为人们知道污染性物质能削弱海洋生哺乳动物对病毒感染的抵抗力，所以波罗的海中海豹的死亡率较高很可能是由于它们的血液中污染性物质的含量较高所致。

下面哪一点，如果正确，能给上述论

additional support for the argument?

(A) The large majority of Scottish seals that died were either old or unhealthy animals.

(B) The strain of virus that killed Scottish seals overwhelms impaired immune systems must more quickly than it does healthy immune systems.

(C) There were slight fluctuations in the levels of pollutants found in the blood of Baltic seals.

(D) The kinds of pollutants found in the Baltic Sea are significantly different from those that have been detected in the waters off the coast of Scotland.

(E) Among marine mammals other than seals, the death rate due to viral diseases in 1988 was higher in the Baltic Sea than it was off the Scottish coast.

3. When a stone is trimmed by a mason and exposed to the elements, a coating of clay and other minerals, called rock varnish, gradually accumulates on the freshly trimmed surface. Organic matter trapped beneath the varnish on stones of an Andean monument was found to be over 1,000 years old. Since the organic matter must have grown on the stone shortly after it was trimmed, it follows that the monument was built long before the arrival of Europeans in the Americas in 1492.

Which one of the following, if true, most seriously weakens the argument?

(A) Rock varnish itself contains some organic matter.

(B) The reuse of ancient trimmed stones was common in the Andes both before and after 1492.

(C) The Andean monument bears a striking resemblance to monuments found in ancient sites in western Asia.

(D) The earliest written reference to the Andean monument dates from 1778.

(E) Rock varnish forms very slowly, if at all, on trimmed stones that are stored in a dry, sheltered place.

4. If this parking policy is unpopular with the faculty, then we should modify it. If it is unpopular among students, we should adopt a new policy. And, it is bound to be unpopular either with the faculty or among students.

If the statements above are true, which one of the following must also be true?

述提供最多的附加支持？

(A) 绝大多数死亡的苏格兰海豹都是老的或不健康的海豹。

(B) 杀死苏格兰海豹的那种病毒击垮受损害的免疫系统的速度要比击垮健康的免疫系统的速度快得多。

(C) 在波罗的海海豹的血液中发现的污染性物质的水平略有波动。

(D) 在波罗的海发现的污染性物质种类与在苏格兰沿海水域发现的大相径庭。

(E) 1988年，在波罗的海内的除了海豹之外的海洋生哺乳动物死于病毒性疾病的死亡率要比苏格兰海岸沿海水域的高得多。

一块石头被石匠修整后，曝露于自然环境中时，一层泥土和其他的矿物便逐渐地开始在刚修整过的石头的表面聚集。这层泥土和矿物被称作岩石覆盖层。在一安迪斯纪念碑的石头的覆盖层下面，发现了被埋藏一千多年的有机物质。因为那些有机物质肯定是在石头被修理后不久就生长到它上面的，也就是说，那个纪念碑是在1492年欧洲人到达美洲之前很早建造的。

下面哪一点，如果正确，能最严重地削弱上述论述？

(A) 岩石覆盖层自身就含有有机物质。

(B) 在安迪斯，1492年前后重新使用古人修理过的石头的现象非常普遍。

(C) 安迪斯纪念碑与在西亚古代遗址发现的纪念碑极为相似。

(D) 最早的关于安迪斯纪念碑的书面资料始于1778年。

(E) 贮存在干燥和封闭地方的修理过的石头表面，倘若能形成岩石覆盖层的话，形成的速度也会非常地慢。

如果这个停车政策不受教职工欢迎，那么我们就应该修改它。如果它不受学生们的欢迎，我们就应该采用一个新的政策。并且这个政策必定是，要么不受教职工欢迎，要么不受学生们欢迎。

如果上面的陈述正确，下面哪一项也

(A) We should attempt to popularize this parking policy among either the faculty or students.

(B) We should modify this parking policy only if this will not reduce its popularity among students.

(C) We should modify this parking policy if modification will not reduce its popularity with the faculty.

(D) If this parking policy is popular among students, then we should adopt a new policy.

(E) If this parking policy is popular with the faculty, then we should adopt a new policy.

5. Politician: Nobody can deny that homelessness is a problem yet there seems to be little agreement on how to solve it. One thing, however, is clear: ignoring the problem will not make it go away. Only if the government steps in and provides the homeless with housing will this problem disappear, and this necessitates increased taxation. For this reason, we should raise taxes.

Which one of the following principles, if valid, most supports the politician's argument?

(A) Only if a measure is required to solve a problem should it be adopted.

(B) Only if a measure is sufficient to solve a problem should it be adopted.

(C) If a measure is required to solve a problem, then it should be adopted.

(D) If a measure is sufficient to solve a problem, then it should be adopted.

(E) If a measure is sufficient to solve a problem, any steps necessitated by that measure should be adopted.

6. Jack's aunt gave him her will, asking him to make it public when she died; he promised to do so. After her death, Jack looked at the will: it stipulated that all her money go to her friend George. Jack knew that if he made the will public, George would squander the money, benefiting neither George nor anyone else. Jack also knew that if he did not make the will public, the money would go to his own mother, who would use it to benefit herself and others, harming no one. After reflection, he decided not to make the will public.

一定是正确的?

(A) 我们应当尽力推广这项停车政策，或者在教职工中推广，或者在学生中推广。

(B) 我们应当修改这项停车政策，当且仅当这样做不会降低该政策在学生们中的声望时。

(C) 如果修改这项政策不会降低它在教职工们中受欢迎的程度，我们就应该修改它。

(D) 如果这项停车政策受学生们欢迎，那么我们就应当采取一项新政策。

(E) 如果这项停车政策受教职工们的欢迎，那么我们就应当采用一项新政策。

政治家：没有人可以否认无家可归是一个问题，然而怎样解决它，好像并没共识。可是，有一件事情很明显：忽视这个问题并不会使这个问题远离我们。当且仅当政府插手，给无家可归者提供住房时，这个问题方会消失。而这样做又会迫使政府增加税收。因此，我们应当增加税收。

下面哪一原则，如果正确，最能支持政治家的论述？

(A) 当且仅当解决一个问题需要某一个措施时，才应该采用这个措施。

(B) 当且仅当某一措施能充分解决某一个问题时，才能采取该措施。

(C) 如果一项措施被要求用来解决某一问题，那么就应当采用这项措施。

(D) 如果一项措施能充分解决某一问题，那么就应当采用这项措施。

(E) 如果一项措施能充分解决某一问题，该措施必需的任何步骤都应被采用。

Jack 的姨母把她的遗嘱给了他，并要求他在她死后公开她的遗嘱，Jack答应了她。姨母死后，Jack看了遗嘱：遗嘱中规定她所有的钱都归属于她的朋友George。Jack明白如果他公开了这个遗嘱，George就会挥霍那些钱，既不有益于George也不有益于其他任何人。Jack同时也明白，如果他不公开这个遗嘱，那些钱就会归属于他自己的母亲，她将使用这些钱，既有益

Which one of the following principles, if valid, would require Jack to act as he did in the situation described?

(A) Duties to family members take priority over duties to people who are not family members.

(B) Violating a promise is impermissible whenever doing so would become known by others.

(C) One must choose an alternative that benefits some and harms no one over an alternative that harms some and benefits no one.

(D) When faced with alternatives it is obligatory to choose whichever one will benefit the greatest number of people.

(E) A promise becomes nonbinding when the person to whom the promise was made is no longer living.

于她自己又有益于其他人，且不会损害任何人。George沉思之后，决定不公开这个遗嘱。

下面哪一条原则，如果正确，将会要求Jack像上面描述的情况中做的那样去做？

(A) 对家庭成员的职责高于对其他非家庭成员的职责。

(B) 违反诺言是不允许的，无论什么时候违反诺言都会被他人知道。

(C) 在有益于一些人，无害他人，与有害于一些人，无益于任何人的两个方案之间，一个人必须选择前者。

(D) 当面临选择时，一个人有义务选择那个对最多数人有益的方案。

(E) 当被承诺的那个人死后，承诺就再不具有约束力。

7. If the ivory trade continues, experts believe, the elephant will soon become extinct in Africa, because poaching is rife in many areas. A total ban on ivory trading would probably prevent the extinction. However, the country of Zimbabwe—which has virtually eliminated poaching within its borders and which relies on income from carefully culling elephant herds that threaten to become too big—objects to such a ban. Zimbabwe holds that the problem lies not with the ivory trade but with the conservation policies of other countries.

Which one of the following principles forms a logical basis for Zimbabwe's objection to a ban?

(A) International measures to correct a problem should not adversely affect countries that are not responsible for the problem.

(B) Freedom of trade is not a right but a consequence of agreements among nations.

(C) Respecting a country's sovereignty is more important than preventing the extinction of a species.

(D) Prohibitions affecting several countries should be enforced by a supranational agency.

(E) Effective conservation cannot be achieved without eliminating poaching.

如果象牙贸易继续进行下去，专家们相信，非洲的大象很快就会灭绝，因为偷捕大象的活动在许多地区都很盛行。全部禁止象牙贸易将有可能防止大象灭绝。然而，津巴布韦这个国家却反对这个禁令。该国实际上已消除了本国境内的偷捕活动，它依赖于谨慎地杀掉那些有可能会变得太大的大象群中的大象所得的收入。津巴布韦认为，问题不在于象牙贸易，而在于其他国家的保护政策。

下面哪一项构成了津巴布韦反对禁令的逻辑基础？

(A) 解决这一问题的国际方案不应当对那些不对该问题负责的国家造成负面影响。

(B) 自由贸易不是一项权利，而是国家之间协议的结果。

(C) 尊重一个国家的主权比保护物种的灭绝更重要。

(D) 影响几个国家的禁令应当由一个超国家的机构来实施。

(E) 不消除偷捕活动，就不可能达到有效的保护。

8. Unlike other primroses, self-pollinating primroses do not need to rely on insects for pollination. In many years insect pollinators are scarce, and in those years a typical non-self-pollinating primrose produces fewer seeds than does a typical self-pollinating primrose. In other years, seed production is approximately equal. Thus, self-pollinating primroses have the advantage of higher average seed production. Aside from seed production, these self-pollinating primroses are indistinguishable from non-self-pollinating primroses. Nevertheless, self-pollinating primrose plants remain rare among primroses.

Which one of the following, if true, most helps to resolve the apparent discrepancy in the information above?

(A) Insects that collect pollen from primroses do not discriminate between self-pollinating primroses and non-pollinating primroses.

(B) When insect pollinators are scarce, non-self-pollinating primroses produce larger seeds that are more likely to germinate than are seeds from self-pollinating primroses.

(C) Self-pollinating primroses that are located in areas with few insects produce no fewer seeds than do self-pollinating primroses that are located in areas with many insects.

(D) Many primroses are located in areas in which the soil conditions that are optimal for seed germination are not present.

(E) Self-pollinating primroses can be assisted by insects during pollination but do not require the assistance of insects to be pollinated.

9. Only computer scientists understand the architecture of personal computers, and only those who understand the architecture of personal computers appreciate the advances in technology made in the last decade. It follows that only those who appreciate these advances are computer scientists.

Which one of the following most accurately describes a flaw in the reasoning in the argument?

(A) The argument contains no stated or implied relationship between computer scientists and those who appreciate the advances in technology in the last decade.

(B) The argument ignores the fact that some computer scientists may not appreciate the advances in technology made in the last decade.

(C) The argument ignores the fact that computer scientists

不像其他樱草，自花授粉的樱草无需依赖昆虫给它们传粉。在很多年里，昆虫传粉者很缺乏，并且在这些年里，典型的非自由传粉的樱草结的种子比典型的自花传粉的樱草的少。在其他年份里，两种樱草的种子产量几乎相等。因此，自花传粉的樱草具有平均种子产量高的优点。除了种子产量不同之外，这些自花传粉的樱草和非自花传粉的樱草没有什么差别。虽然如此，在樱草中自花传粉的樱草仍然比较罕见。

下面哪一点，如果正确，最有助于解决上面论述中的明显矛盾？

(A) 那些收集樱草花粉的昆虫并不区分一樱草是自花传粉樱草还是非自花传粉樱草。

(B) 当昆虫传粉者稀少时，非自花传粉的樱草会结出较大的种子，这些种子发芽的可能性比自花传粉的樱草结出种子的可能性大。

(C) 那些位于昆虫稀少地区的自花传粉樱草结出的种子不比那些位于昆虫多的地区的自花传粉的樱草结出的种子少。

(D) 许多樱草位于土壤状况不适宜它们的种子发芽的地区。

(E) 自花传粉的樱草在传粉期间可接受昆虫的帮助，但它们并不需要昆虫来帮助它们完成传粉。

只有计算机科学家才懂得个人电脑的结构，并且只有那些懂得个人电脑结构的人才赞赏在过去10年中取得的技术进步。也就是说只有那些赞赏这些进步的人才是计算机科学家。

下面哪一点，最准确地描述了上述论述中的推理错误？

(A) 上述论述没有包含计算机科学家与那些赞赏在过去10年中取得技术进步的人之间的明确的或含蓄的关系。

(B) 上述论述忽视了这样的事实：有一些计算机科学家可能并不赞赏在过去10年中取得的技术进步。

(C) 上述论述忽视了这样的事实：计算机

may appreciate other things besides the advances in technology made in the last decade.

(D) The premises of the argument are stated in such a way that they exclude any possibility of drawing any logical conclusion.

(E) The premises of the argument presuppose that everyone understands the architecture of personal computers.

10. Speakers of the Caronian language constitute a minority of the population in several large countries. An international body has recommended that the regions where Caronian-speakers live be granted autonomy as an independent nation in which Caronian-speakers would form a majority. But Caronian-speakers live in several widely scattered areas that cannot be united within a single continuous boundary while at the same time allowing Caronian-speakers to be the majority population. Hence, the recommendation cannot be satisfied.

The argument relies on which one of the following assumptions?

(A) A nation once existed in which Caronian-speakers formed the majority of the population.

(B) Caronian-speakers tend to perceive themselves as constituting a single community.

(C) The recommendation would not be satisfied by the creation of a nation formed of disconnected regions.

(D) The new Caronian nation will not include as citizens anyone who does not speak Caronian.

(E) In most nations several different languages are spoken.

11. Martha's friend, who is very knowledgeable about edible flowers, told Martha that there are no edible daisies, at least not any that are palatable. Martha, however, reasons that since there are daisies that are a kind of chrysanthemum and since there are edible chrysanthemums that are quite palatable, what her friend told her must be incorrect.

Which one of the following has a flawed pattern of reasoning most like that in Martha's reasoning?

(A) Jeanne is member of the city chorus, and the city chorus is renowned. So Jeanne is an excellent singer.

(B) Rolfe belongs to the library reading group, and all members of that group are avid readers. So Rolfe is an avid reader.

(C) Some of Noriko's sisters are on the debate team, and

科学家除了赞赏在过去10年中取得的技术进步之外，还会赞赏其他事情。

(D) 上述论述的前提以这样的方式来陈述，即它们排除了得出任何合乎逻辑的结论的可能性。

(E) 上述论述的前提假定每个人都懂得个人计算机的结构。

在几个大国中，讲Caronian语言的人占人口的少数。一国际团体建议以一个独立国家的方式给予讲Caronian话的人居住的地区自主权，在那里讲Caronian话的人可以占人口的大多数。但是，讲Caronian话的人居住在几个广为分散的地区，这些地区不能以单一连续的边界相连结，同时也就不允许讲Caronian话的人占人口的多数。因此，那个建议不能得到满足。

上述论述依赖于下面哪条假设？

(A) 曾经存在一个讲Caronian话的人占人口的多数国家。

(B) 讲Caronian话的人倾向于认为他们自己构成了一个单独的社区。

(C) 那个建议不能以创建一个由不相连接的地区构成的国家的方式得到满足。

(D) 新Caronian国的公民不包括任何不说Caronian话的人。

(E) 大多数国家都有几种不同的语言。

Martha的一个在可食花方面非常博学的朋友告诉她，所有的雏菊都不能吃，至少都是不可口的。然而，Martha这样推理，因为存在一种属于菊花的雏菊，又因为存在味美可食的菊花，所以她的朋友告诉她的话肯定不正确。

下面哪一个推理的模式具有与Martha的推理模式最为相似的缺陷？

(A) Jeanne是一个城市合唱队的成员，且那个城市合唱队非常有名，因此，Jeanne是一个优秀的歌手。

(B) Rolfe是图书馆读书小组的一员，而那个小组的所有成员都是读起书来废寝忘食的人。因此，Rolfe也是读起书来

some members of the debate team are poor students. So at least one of Noriko's sisters must be a poor student.

(D) Most of Leon's friends are good swimmers, and good swimmers are quite strong. So it is likely that at least some of Leon's friends are quite strong.

(E) Many of Teresa's colleagues have written books. Most of the books they have written are on good writing. So some of Teresa's colleagues are good writers.

12. In a certain municipality, a judge overturned a suspect's conviction for possession of an illegal weapon. The suspect had fled upon seeing police and subsequently discarded the illegal weapon after the police gave chase. The judge reasoned as follows: the only cause for the police giving chase was the suspect's flight: by itself, flight from the police does not create a reasonable suspicion of a criminal act; evidence collected during an illegal chase is inadmissible; therefore, the evidence in this case was inadmissible.

Which one of the following principles, if valid, most helps to justify the judge's decision that the evidence was inadmissible?

(A) Flight from the police could create a reasonable suspicion of a criminal act as long as other significant factors are involved.

(B) People can legally flee from the police only when those people are not involved in a criminal act at the time.

(C) Police can legally give chase to a person only when the person's actions have created a reasonable suspicion of a criminal act.

(D) Flight from the police should not itself be considered a criminal act.

(E) In all cases in which a person's actions have created a reasonable suspicion of a criminal act, police can legally give chase to that person.

13. Even though trading in ivory has been outlawed by international agreement, some piano makers still use ivory, often obtained illegally, to cover piano keys. Recently, experts have devised a synthetic ivory that, unlike earlier ivory substitutes, has found favor with concert pianists throughout

废寝忘食的人。

(C) Noriko的某些姐姐参加了那个论述小组，且那个论述小组的某些成员是差生。所以Moriko至少有一个姐姐一定是差生。

(D) Leon的大多数朋友都是游泳健将，且游泳健将都十分强壮，所以很有可能，至少有一些Leon的朋友十分强壮。

(E) 许多Teresa的同事都出了书，他们写的书大多数都写得很好。因此有一些Teresa的同事是优秀的作家。

在某一市政府，一法官推翻了一嫌疑犯拥有非法武器的罪名。一看到警察，那个嫌疑犯就开始逃跑，当警察追他时，他就随即扔掉了那件非法武器。那个法官的推理如下：警察追击的唯一原因是嫌疑犯逃跑；从警察旁边逃跑的自身并不能使人合情合理地怀疑他有犯罪行为；在一非法追击中收集的证据是不能接受的。因此，这个案例中的证据是不能接受的。

下面哪一条原则，如果正确，最有助于证明那个法官关于那些证据是不能被接受的判决是合理的？

(A) 只要涉及其他重要因素，从警察那儿逃跑就能使人产生一个合情合理的有关犯罪行为的怀疑。

(B) 人们可以合法地从警察那儿逃跑，仅当这些人在不卷入任何犯罪行为时。

(C) 仅当一个人的举动使人合情合理地怀疑他有犯罪行为时，警察才能合法地追击他。

(D) 从警察那儿逃跑的自身不应被认为是一个犯罪行为。

(E) 在一个人的举动使人合情合理地怀疑他有犯罪行为的情况下，警察都能合法地追击那个人。

尽管象牙交易已被国际协议宣布为非法行为，一些钢琴的制造者，仍使用象牙来覆盖钢琴键，这些象牙通常通过非法手段获得。最近，专家们发明出一种合成象牙，不像早期的象牙替代物，这种合成象

the world. But because piano makers have never been major consumers of ivory, the development of the synthetic ivory will therefore probably do little to help curb the killing of elephants, from whose tusks most natural ivory is obtained.

Which one of the following, if true, most helps to strengthen the argument?

(A) Most people who play the piano but are not concert pianists can nonetheless easily distinguish between the new synthetic ivory and inferior ivory substitutes.

(B) The new synthetic ivory can be manufactured to resemble in color and surface texture any of the various types of natural ivory that have commercial uses.

(C) Other natural products such as bone or tortoise shell have not proven to be acceptable substitutes for natural ivory in piano keys.

(D) The most common use for natural ivory is in ornamental carvings, which are prized not only for the quality of their workmanship but also for the authenticity of their materials.

(E) It costs significantly less to produce the new synthetic ivory than it does to produce any of the ivory substitutes that scientists had developed previously.

14. The Levant—the area that borders the eastern Mediterranean—was heavily populated in prehistoric times. The southern Levant was abandoned about 6,000 years ago, although the northern Levant, which shared the same climate, remained heavily populated. Recently archaeologists have hypothesized that the sudden depopulation in the southern Levant was due to an economic collapse resulting from deforestation.

If the statements above are true and the archaeologists' hypothesis is correct, which one of the following CANNOT be true?

(A) The sheep and goats herded by the peoples of the southern Levant until 6,000 years ago grazed extensively on the seedlings and saplings of indigenous tree species.

(B) Trees were used in the production of lime plaster, a building material used extensively throughout the southern Levant until 6,000 years ago.

(C) Organic remains from the northern Levant reliably indicate that tree species flourished there without interruption during the period when the southern Levant

牙受到了全世界范围内音乐会钢琴家的好评。但是因为钢琴制造者从来不是象牙的主要消费者，所以合成象牙的发展可能对抑制为获得最自然的象牙而捕杀大象的活动没什么帮助。

下面哪一项，如果正确，最有助于加强上述论述？

(A) 大多数弹钢琴，但不是音乐会钢琴家的人也可以轻易地区分新的合成象牙和较次的象牙替代物。

(B) 新型的合成象牙可被生产出来，这种象牙的颜色表面质地可以与任何一种具有商业用途的自然象牙的质地相似。

(C) 其他自然产物，如骨头和乌龟壳证明不是自然象牙在钢琴键上的替代物。

(D) 自然象牙最普遍的应用是在装饰性雕刻品方面，这些雕刻品不但因为它们的工艺质量，而且因为它们的材料的真实性而被珍藏。

(E) 生产新型象牙的费用要比生产科学家们以前开发的任何象牙替代品的低得多。

Levant地区与地中海的东部接界，在史前时代，这个地区的人口相当稠密。尽管具有相同气候的Levant北部地区的人口仍相当稠密，Levant南部的人们却在6000年前离弃了这个地方。最近，考古学家假定南部Levant人口的突然减少起因于开伐森林引起的经济崩溃。

如果上面的陈述是正确的，且考古学家的假定也是正确的，那么下面哪一条不可能正确？

(A) 直到6000年以前，南部Levant人放牧的绵羊和山羊大量地吃本地树种的秧苗和幼苗。

(B) 在生产石灰时要用到树，直到6000年以前整个南部Levant的人都广泛地使用石灰这种建筑材料。

(C) 从北部Levant发现的有机物遗物可靠地表明，在南部Levant被遗弃的那段时间内，北部Levant地区的树木繁茂，没有受到打扰。

was being abandoned.

(D) Carbon dating of organic remains from the southern Levant reliably demonstrates that there were no forests present in that area prior to 6,000 years ago.

(E) Since there are few traces of either quarried stone or of mud brick in buildings excavated in the southern Levant, it is likely that the buildings built there prior to 6,000 years ago were made almost entirely of timber.

15. A person's dietary consumption of cholesterol and fat is one of the most important factors determining the level of cholesterol in the person's blood(serum cholesterol). Serum cholesterol levels rise proportionally to increased cholesterol and fat consumption until that consumption reaches a threshold, but once consumption of these substances exceeds that threshold, serum cholesterol levels rise only gradually, even with dramatic increases in consumption. The threshold is one fourth the consumption level of cholesterol and fat in today's average North American diet.

The statements above, if true, most strongly support which one of the following?

(A) The threshold can be lowered by lowering the dietary consumption of cholesterol and fat.

(B) People who consume an average North American diet cannot increase their consumption of cholesterol and fat without dramatically increasing their serum cholesterol levels.

(C) People who consume half as much cholesterol and fat as in the average North American diet will not necessarily have half the average serum cholesterol level.

(D) Serum cholesterol levels cannot be affected by nondietary modifications in behavior, such as exercising more or smoking less.

(E) People who consume less cholesterol and fat than the threshold cannot reduce their serum cholesterol levels.

16. The role of the Uplandian supreme court is to protect all human rights against abuses of government power. Since the constitution of Uplandia is not explicit about all human rights, the supreme court must sometimes resort to principles outside the explicit provisions of the constitution in justifying its decisions. However, human rights will be subject to the whim of whoever holds judicial power unless the supreme court is bound to adhere to a singly objective standard, namely, the

---

(D) 碳元素确定的来自南部Levant地区的有机物遗物的日期可靠地表明，在6000年以前那个地区没有森林。

(E) 因为在南部Levant地区挖出的建筑物中很少有采集的石头或泥砖的遗迹，所以很有可能在6000年以前，那儿的建筑物几乎全都是用木材建的。

一个人饮食消耗的胆固醇和脂肪量是决定他的血液中胆固醇（血清胆固醇）水平的最重要因素之一。在胆固醇与脂肪的消耗量达到某个界限之前，血清胆固醇水平的升高与胆固醇和脂肪的消耗量的增加成比例。但是，一旦这些物质的消耗量超过阈限，即使消耗量急剧增加，血清胆固醇水平也只是逐渐地增加。那个界限是今天北美人饮食平均消耗的胆固醇和脂肪量的1/4。

上面论述，如果正确，最强有力地支持下面哪一项？

(A) 那个界限可以通过降低胆固醇和脂肪的饮食消耗量而得到降低。

(B) 那些食用北美人平均饮食的人，不能做到既增加他们对胆固醇和脂肪的消耗量，又不使他们的血清胆固醇水平显著提高。

(C) 那些消耗胆固醇和脂肪的量只有北美平均饮食的一半的人的血清胆固醇水平不一定是普遍北美人的一半。

(D) 血清胆固醇的水平不会受非饮食性行为的改变，如增加锻炼和减少抽烟的影响。

(E) 那些消耗胆固醇和脂肪比阈限低的人不能降低他们的血清胆固醇水平。

Uplandian最高法院的作用是保障所有人的权利不受政府滥用权力的侵犯。因为Uplandian宪法没有明确所有人的权利，所以最高法院有时就必须借助于明确的宪法条款之外的原则来使它的判决具有公正性。然而，除非最高法院坚持单一的客观标准，即宪法，否则人们的权利就会受那些具有审判权的人的兴致所摆布。因此，

constitution. Therefore, nothing but the explicit provisions of the constitution can be used to justify the court's decisions. Since these conclusions are inconsistent with each other, it cannot be true that the role of the Uplandian supreme court is to protect all human rights against abuses of government power.

The reasoning that leads to the conclusion that the first sentence in the passage is false is flawed because the argument

(A) ignores data that offer reasonable support for a general claim and focuses on a single example that argues against that claim.

(B) seeks to defend a view on the grounds that the view is widely held and that decisions based on that view are often accepted as correct.

(C) rejects a claim as false on the grounds that those who make that claim could profit if that claim is accepted by others.

(D) makes an unwarranted assumption that what is true of each member of a group taken separately is also true of a group as a whole.

(E) concludes that a particular premise is false when it is equally possible for that premise to be true and some other premise false.

只有明确的宪法条款才能使法院的判决公正合理。既然这些结论相互之间并不一致，那么Uplandian最高法院的作用是保障所有人的权利，不受政府滥用权力的侵犯的说法就是不正确的。

得出短文中第一句话是错误的，这个结论的推理是有缺陷的，因为该论述_____。

(A) 忽视了给总的声明提供合理支持的数据，而把着重点放在了驳斥那个声明的单一例子。

(B) 企图为某一观点辩护，因为该观点被广泛支持，并且基于那个观点的判决常常被认为是正确的。

(C) 否决一被认为是谬误的声明，因为如果该声明被人接受的话，那么做出该声明的人就会受益。

(D) 做了一个没根据的假设，认为对一群人中每一个单独成员都是正确的，则对那个作为整体的人群是正确的。

(E) 当某一特殊前提是正确的可能性与其他前提是谬误的可能性一样时就判定那个特殊前提是谬误的。

参考答案:

1. A	2. E	3. B	4. E	5. C
6. D	7. A	8. B	9. B	10. C
11. C	12. C	13. D	14. D	15. C
16. E				

1. **解析**：根据Mary 的论述很容易推出，如果所有超速的人在当时被拦住的可能性一样时，警察只拦住某一个人并对他进行处罚，警察对他是公平的。因此(A)就是很明显的正确选项。

2. **解析**：要对本题的论述构成支持有两种途径：第一是证明波罗的海的海豹死亡率较高不是由他因所致；第二是证明污染性物质确实能使海豹对病毒性疾病的抵抗力降低，(E)的论述表明了污染性物质能使海洋生哺乳动物死于病毒性疾病的死亡率上升，因此(E)通过演绎的论证方法对本题的论述构成了支持。

3. **解析**：本题论述的结论很显然是以用于建造安迪斯纪念碑的石头是在修建纪念碑时修整的为前提。(B)否定了该前提，因此(B)为正确答案；(A)、(C)、(D)和(E)均为无关选项。

4. **解析**：本题的(E)选项是正确答案，推理如下：如果这项政策受教职工们欢迎，那么它就不受学生们欢迎。如果这项政策不受学生们欢迎，那么我们就要采用一个新的政策，由A→B，B→C可得出A→C，即如果这项政策受教职工们的欢迎，那么我们就应当采用一项新政策。(D)的推理是错误的；(A)、(B)和(C)都不能从短文的论述中推出。

5. **解析**：政治家根据解决无家可归问题需要增加税收做出了应该增加税收的结论。显然(C)所陈述的推理模式与政治家的相一致，因此(C)选项最能支持政治家的论述；增加税收只是解决无家可归的一个必要条件，因此(A)、(B)、(D)和(E)都不能支持政治家的论述。

6. **解析**：Jorge没有遵循他姨母的遗嘱，而选择了一个有益于多数人的方案，因此很明显(D)选项所陈述的内容与Jorge选择的方案相一致。

7. **解析**：本题的逻辑结构是：禁止象牙贸易可以防止大象灭绝，但是这个禁令损害了津巴布韦的利益，而津巴布韦又不该对该禁令所禁止的内容负责，因此，禁巴布韦反对这个禁令。由此分析可知(A)是津巴布韦反对禁令的基础。

8. **解析**：一种植物数量的多少，与其种子的数量以及种子的发芽率有关，一种植物在种子的数量较多但发芽率很低的情况下，其数量就有可能不会太多，选项(B)给出了两种樱草种子发芽率的差异，从而解释了论述中的明显分歧。

9. **解析**："only"大多表示必要条件。若用A表示"computer scientists"，用B表示"understand the architecture of personal computers"，用C表示"appreciate the advances..."，那么段落推理可表示为C→B→A。而段落推理的结论却是A→C，即"成为一名计算机科学家的必要条件为赞赏这些进步"，明显与C→A不吻合。(B)指出了这一缺陷，因此(B)为正确答案。

10. **解析**：本题结论成立的前提条件是不能把讲Carronian语的人居住的地区用单一连续的边界连接起来，因此(C)是正确答案。

11. **解析**：某一整体的两个组成部分之间并不一定有交集，某种雏菊属于菊花，但并不是所有的菊花都味美可口，因此很难推出这种雏菊味美可口。同样，在不是论述小组的所有成员都是差生的情况下，很难推出隶属于这个有差生的小组的某个成员是差生，因此(C)的推理模式缺陷与Martha的最为接近，(A)、(B)、(D)和(E)四选项的推理方式都正确。

12. **解析**：警察在没有合情合理的理由的情况下，对嫌疑犯进行非法追击，结果得到的证据不能被使用。因此要想对嫌疑犯进行合法的追击，警察就必须得有合情合理的理由，因此(C)为正确答案。

13. **解析**：根据合成象牙对抑制捕杀大象的活动收效甚微可以推出，合成象牙可能在许多方面无法替代自然象牙，(D)给出了这种可能性，因此(D)为正确答案。

14. **解析**：(A)、(B)和(E)三项都通过找他因的办法说明了6000年前南部Levant地区森林减少的原因；(C)通过对比，指出了Levant南部人们在6000年前离弃那个地方的原因。因此(A)、(B)、(C)和(E)都与文中论述的内容相一致；(D)表明6000年前南部 Levant没有森林的结论就与短文中所述及的南部Levant地区的人离弃那里的原因是过度砍伐森林的说法相矛盾，因此(D)为正确选项。

15. **解析**：根据在阈限以上血清胆固醇水平随胆固醇与脂肪量的消耗的增加而变缓可以推出(C)为正确答案。(A)、(B)和(E)与本题短文中陈述的内容相矛盾；(D)不能从本题的段落中合理地推出。

16. **解析**：本题的解题关键在对两句话的理解：其一是Uplandian宪法没有明确人们的所有权利；其二是只有明确的宪法条款才能使最高法院的判决公正合理。根据第一句话可知，Uplandian宪法虽然没有明确所有人的权利，但是还是明确了人们的一部分权利；再由第二句话可推出Uplandian最高法院可根据这一部分明确的权利在某些情况下做出公正合理的判决。也就是说Uplandian最高法院既有可能做出公正合理的判决，也有可能做不出公正合理的判决，而本题段落的论述却得出了Uplandian宪法是保障所有人的权利的说法不正确。由此分析可知，本题段落中的推理很明显犯了(E)选项所描述的推理错误。